WASHINGTON

A HISTORY OF THE CAPITAL
1800-1950

WASHINGTON

A HISTORY OF THE CAPITAL 1800-1950

BY CONSTANCE MC LAUGHLIN GREEN

PRINCETON, NEW JERSEY
PRINCETON UNIVERSITY PRESS

Copyright © 1962 by Princeton University Press
ALL RIGHTS RESERVED
Published by Princeton University Press, Princeton, N.J.
In the United Kingdom: Princeton University Press, Guildford, Surrey
LCC 62-7402
ISBN 0-691-00585-0 (one-vol. paperback edn.)
ISBN 0-691-04572-0 (vol. 1, hardcover edn.)
ISBN 0-691-04573-9 (vol. 2, hardcover edn.)

First PRINCETON PAPERBACK Printing, 1976

Printed in the United States of America

To Mina Curtiss

PUBLISHER'S NOTE

For some time before her unfortunate death in 1975, Constance McLaughlin Green had hoped to prepare a one-volume abridgment of her history of our nation's capital. Illness prevented her from completing her task, but her work is so valuable and the demand for it so great that Princeton University Press has reissued the history in its entirety. The cloth edition consists of the two volumes as originally published: Volume 1, *Washington: Village and Capital, 1800-1878*; Volume 2, *Washington: Capital City, 1879-1950*. For the paperback edition, the two volumes have been bound together, without change, and the resultant single volume has been given the title *Washington: A History of the Capital, 1800-1950*.

FOREWORD

THE nineteenth century American capital was an anomaly in the western world. Other towns and cities in the United States, as in Europe, grew up on a commercial foundation; even the frontier settlements laid out in advance of the arrival of permanent householders usually had some assured prospects of trade. Many Latin American cities, conversely, arose by fiat of the Spanish crown in locations where royal emissaries could exercise political and economic control over the hinterland of ranches, farms, and mines for the benefit of the empire. Washington fell into neither category. The purposes she was designed to serve certainly did not encompass autocratic direction of the sovereign states of the Union, nor did the thinly peopled countryside in which she was placed provide an established base for independent commercial or industrial growth. George Washington, Thomas Jefferson, and other well-informed Americans, it is true, believed the site to be of potential commercial importance, but that was a secondary consideration in creating the city. Yet her eighteenth-century founders, statesmen familiar either by travel or by study with the great cities of Europe, envisaged the American capital as more than a meeting place for Congress and a seat of the executive branch of the federal government. The carefully prepared plan of the city in itself proclaimed their dream of embodying in the stones of her buildings, in her parks and fountains, and in the broad sweep of her avenues a dignity and beauty that would symbolize the ideals of the new republic.

How that dream faded and began to revive eighty years later, and in the interim how economic dependence upon the federal government affected the city's inhabitants form central themes of this book. From the beginning Washington shared many of the characteristics of contemporary, like-sized American communities. Her problems of municipal housekeeping paralleled those of other cities, albeit with differences. Wherein she differed and why, I believe, may throw light upon national history. Closely related to those questions is the nature of Washington's humanitarianism, a useful gauge, sociologists have suggested, of the quality of an urban civilization. If her search for methods of promoting public welfare and for a wise expression of private philanthropy was sometimes clumsy, it nevertheless closely resembled that occurring elsewhere, just as her reaching out for a rich intellectual and artistic life reflected national as well as local aspirations. As a border city between North and South, the capital was early caught up in the sectional struggle over slavery. And yet a self-conscious Negro community came into being here, possessing a degree of cultivation and sense of responsibility unequalled at the time in any other city where Negroes had congregated in numbers. Hence the evolution of race relations becomes another central topic. Furthermore, inasmuch as the focus of attention throughout this study is the local community rather than the national capital as such, a constantly recurring line of inquiry emerges: who was a Washingtonian, who merely a temporary resident? That question involves the shifts in the city's social structure from period to period.

None of the discussion in this volume could draw upon the kind of data available in community studies made after 1920. The volume to follow this, covering the years of Washington's growth into a big city, will benefit from the comparisons made possible through the work of twentieth-century urban sociologists. For the first three-fourths of the nineteenth century such generalizations as I have dared attempt about American urban life and Washington's deviations from or adherence to a recognizable norm have had to be based on census figures and a handful of separate city histories; and in these it is sometimes difficult or impossible to find materials to illuminate the development of what would today be called "subcommunities." Washington's history before 1880 thus is of necessity more largely narrative than analytical.

This book is not in any true sense a definitive history. Some problems I have ignored altogether and some examined only superficially. Church history, court dockets, land records, and the successive occupants of historic houses have received short shrift; architectural developments net attention only insofar as they marked a change in public interest in the capital. Several questions obviously call for further exploration; an analysis, for example, of the background of key members of the House and Senate District committees, or a monograph on the early Negro community based upon the family papers of colored Washingtonians would be invaluable in clarifying matters about which I have felt obliged merely to speculate. For my primary purpose has been to show the interrelatedness of the forces that shaped the life of the city, a task that precluded intensive investigation of elusive or widely scattered sources. At times my justifying documentation resides less in the exact words than between the lines of the materials cited. The result may be called an interpretive rather than a comprehensive, fool-proof history.

The decision to append footnotes grew out of personal experience in trying to pin down the truth. Apocryphal stories about Washington's past are probably more prolific than about any other city in America. The shelves of Washingtonia collections are already filled with volumes, readable and dull alike, which give no clue to what the authors drew upon in compiling their accounts. Since I hope to encourage other students to pursue inquiry particularly in areas upon which I touched only lightly or about questions I raised without furnishing answers, I have supplied every guide that I could, even at the expense of weighting this book with formidable-looking references to government documents and hieroglyphically numbered manuscripts in the National Archives. Lest the reader be put off by the dreary ponderosity of some of these footnotes, let me point out that the most deadly looking items frequently contain intensely interesting data.

This study, initially inspired by Dr. Ernst Posner of the

American University and made possible by a grant from the Humanities Division of the Rockefeller Foundation, owes much to scores of people. Although the original aim of the Foundation had been a book describing the past of a "typical" American community, that is, a city whose development followed the usual pattern of commercial and industrial expansion and its accompanying social problems, the sponsors let me pursue what is in some measure a bypath, in hopes that it might lead to fresh perspectives on the over-all goal, namely a better understanding of the nature of urban growth in the United States and its place in American history. The American University, the recipient of the grant, has managed all the administrative details of the project. An advisory committee of distinguished historians and scholars appointed by President Anderson of the University has given me counsel. Over the years while this volume has been in preparation, Drs. Waldo G. Leland, Ernst Posner, Caroline Ware, Oliver W. Holmes, Solon J. Buck, Arthur A. Ekirch, Jr., and, till his death in 1958, John Ihlder, authority on housing problems in Washington, have read the manuscript chapter by chapter, offering constructive suggestions. A grant from the Chapelbrook Foundation enabled me to revise the manuscript carefully. Dr. Louis C. Hunter has scrutinized every sentence of the condensed version. I am deeply indebted to the staffs of the Library of Congress, the National Archives, and the Southern Historical Collections at the University of North Carolina for their helpfulness and unvarying courtesy. Without the imaginative and patient help of the Library of Congress Prints and Photographs Division, I should have had great difficulty in assembling the illustrations. The Minnesota Historical Society, the Wisconsin Historical Society, the Harper Library of the University of Chicago, the Duke University Library, and the Bancroft Library of the University of California have in turn contributed from their collections. My gratitude to the men and women who have gone out of their way to assist me is not to be told in these few brief words.

I want to pay special tribute to Atlee Shidler, now a member of the staff of the Washington Center for Metropolitan Studies. For three years, in carrying on research for this book and the succeeding volume, he not only did much of the laborious grubbing through acres of print but brought to his task insights and a dedicated thoroughness that have saved me from many a faulty judgment. Similarly I want to thank Mrs. Barbara Plegge, who, while typing the manuscript with inimitable skill, offered suggestions on content and form that have greatly improved the end product. And finally my thanks go to Mina K. Curtiss, scholar and friend, for constant encouragement and for reminding me periodically that the mechanics of city life—paving and street-lighting, sewage, policing, and tax-paying—inescapable as they are, are still only the mechanics. The substance lies in the hopes and fears, the frustrations and the achievements of the human beings who people the past.

CONSTANCE MC LAUGHLIN GREEN

Washington, D.C.
May 1961

CONTENTS

ILLUSTRATIONS

Illustrations 1 through 19 following page 108

ment today occupies the entire building. It symbolized civic dignity to Washington. Photograph. Courtesy Library of Congress

22. The Smithsonian Institution. Photograph by Mathew Brady, ca. 1860. Courtesy National Archives
23. Ferdinand Rudolph Hassler, first head of the Coast Survey. Lithograph by Charles Fenderich, 1834. Courtesy Library of Congress
24. Alexander Dallas Bache, successor to Hassler. Photograph, ca. 1863. Courtesy Library of Congress
25. Joseph Henry, first secretary of the Smithsonian Institution, ca. 1850. Daguerreotype. Courtesy Chicago Historical Society.
26. Spencer Fullerton Baird, first head of the National Museum, 1850. From William Healey Dall, *Spencer Fullerton Baird, A Biography* (Phila., 1915)
27. Clark Mills' statue of General Jackson, with the White House in the background. Lithograph by Thomas Sinclair, 1858. Courtesy Library of Congress
28. Riot at the Northern Liberties polls, 1857. Wood engraving from *Leslie's Illustrated Newspaper*, June 20, 1857
29. "View of Georgetown" from Washington, ca. 1854. Lithograph by E. Sachse & Co. Courtesy Library of Congress
30. Shad fishermen on the Eastern Branch near the Navy Yard, 1860. The arched roofed building on the right is a covered ship slip designed by the versatile Benjamin Latrobe. Wood engraving in *Harper's Weekly*, April 20, 1861
31. The swearing-in of the first District volunteers, April 1861, in front of the War Department building west of the White House. Wood engraving in *Harper's Weekly*, April 27, 1861
32. Arrival of New York troops at the B & O depot, April 1861, showing the greatly admired square tower of the depot. It stood at New Jersey Avenue and C Street, where the bus tunnel today emerges from under the hill near the Senate Office Building. Wood engraving in *Frank Leslie's Illustrated Newspaper*, May 18, 1861
33. "Balloon View of the city," ca. July 1861. Beyond the train puffing into the B & O depot, the line of the Washington Canal is visible; the stub of the Washington Monument and, on the

WASHINGTON

VOLUME I

VILLAGE AND CAPITAL

1800-1878

CHAPTER I

THE FOUNDING OF THE NATIONAL CAPITAL

IN LATE May 1800, when the sloops carrying government records and the personal belongings of federal officials docked at Lear's wharf on the Potomac near the mouth of Rock Creek, the new national capital bore little resemblance to a city. A half-mile below the landing a sluggish little stream, Tiber or Goose Creek, worked its way to the river through tidal flats. Above the marshy estuary rose the painted sandstone Executive Mansion, flanked on one side by the brick building designed for the Treasury, on the other by the partly built headquarters for the State and War Departments. A mile farther east one wing of the white freestone Capitol occupied a commanding position on Jenkins Hill, blocking off from view the houses on the wooded plateau beyond. Nearby, dwellings ready to turn into boarding houses for congressmen dotted the ridge along New Jersey Avenue, while on North Capitol Street stood the two houses General Washington had put up to encourage other investors. Between the Capitol and the President's "Palace" stretched Pennsylvania Avenue, planned as the federal city's main thoroughfare, its course marked by a tangle of elder bushes, swamp grasses, and tree stumps.[1]

Downstream from the tidal swamps bluffs edged the river nearly to Greenleaf's Point, where the "Eastern Branch" flowed into the Potomac. About the point, today the site of Fort McNair and the National War College, were substantial brick

[1] Proceedings of the Board of Commissioners for the District of Columbia, 24 Sep 1798, IV, 215-16, Record Group 42, National Archives (hereafter cited as Comrs' Prcdgs); George Washington to Dr. William Thornton, 6 Oct 1799, *The Writings of George Washington*, ed. John C. Fitzpatrick, XXXVII, 388; "Washington in 1800," *The Correspondence and Miscellanies of the Hon. John Cotton Smith*, pp. 204-209; John Ball Osborne, "The Removal of the Government to Washington," Columbia Historical Society *Records*, III, 158 (hereafter cited as CHS *Rec*).

houses, some of them occupied, more of them awaiting tenants. The speculators who had attempted to exploit this river-front area had also erected two rows of houses west of the President's House on Pennsylvania Avenue, the "Six Buildings" begun by James Greenleaf at 22nd Street, and at 19th Street the better-known "Seven Buildings," financed by Robert Morris, which would serve for a time as offices for the Department of State.

Other houses conforming to the federal commissioners' exacting specifications lay scattered over the four-mile expanse from the site of the Navy Yard on the Eastern Branch to Washington City's northwestern boundary at Rock Creek. Here and there clustered small frame houses which the commissioners in charge of building had reluctantly permitted because "mechanics" obviously could not afford to build or occupy three-story brick edifices and the city would have to accommodate some of the "lower orders." All told, Washington contained only 109 habitable brick houses and 263 wooden. But in midsummer the beauty of the natural setting impressed newcomers. The "romantic" scenery of river banks shaded by "tall and umbrageous forest trees" compensated somewhat for the "unformed" streets, the roofless houses, the distance from one group of buildings to the next, and the clutter of stone, lumber, and debris about the unfinished government buildings. Not until the November winds stripped the trees bare would the rawness and untidiness of the new capital afflict men fresh from the elegance and comforts of Philadelphia.[2]

In 1790 tobacco and cornfields, orchards and woods had covered most of the area. A few houses had been built in Carrollsburgh on the Eastern Branch, where in 1770 Charles Carroll, Jr., of Duddington had attempted to found a trading

[2] Allen C. Clark, *Greenleaf and Law in the Federal City*, pp. 123-43; William B. Webb, *The Laws of the Corporation of the City of Washington*, pp. 55-62; "Diary of Mrs. William Thornton, 1800-1863," CHS *Rec*, x, 88-226 (transcript of the entries for 1800, hereafter cited as Thornton Diary); *American State Papers, Miscellaneous*, I, 254-56 (hereafter cited as *ASP, Misc*); Margaret Bayard Smith, *The First Forty Years of Washington Society*, ed. Gaillard Hunt, p. 10 (hereafter cited as M. B. Smith, *First Forty Years*).

village. Twenty years later the plantation of the Carrolls of Duddington still extended northward to include Jenkins Hill with its fine old trees which Daniel Carroll cut to sell for timber and fire wood. A few dwellings stood also in Hamburg, a tiny settlement located to the east of Rock Creek near the Potomac, where Jacob Funk of Frederick, Maryland, had similarly tried to develop a town. Along Goose Creek had stretched David Burnes' fields; his story-and-a-half farmhouse nestled against the slope near the stream's mouth. A man named Pope had owned that land in the seventeenth century and, having called his plantation "Rome," had christened the brook "Tiber," but later generations who hunted the wild geese and ducks along its estuary had rechristened it Goose Creek, and that name endured locally until after 1800. While the Executive Mansion was rising on the high land above his house, Burnes had continued to plant his corn in the fields bordering the stream until, in 1796, the commissioners had cut a swath through to form Pennsylvania Avenue. A cherry orchard occupied most of the present-day Lafayette Square.[3]

On the heights of the Potomac upstream from Washington stood the city of Georgetown. Laid out in 1751 and incorporated in 1789, the little river port had flourished for some years as a shipping center for Maryland and Virginia tobacco. After 1793 she had suffered reverses as the small crops grown on depleted soil, the uncertain markets of war-ridden Europe and, hearsay reported, the diversion of local capital to speculation in Washington real estate combined to cut her tobacco exports by three-fourths. At the opening of the nineteenth century she still served as an outlet for the produce of the Maryland farms in her immediate vicinity, and her population together with that of the adjoining countryside outside her limits exceeded by some 1,900 the 3,000 inhabitants of Washington. Fine-looking brick

[3] George Watterston, *A New Guide to Washington*, 1842, Preface; Commissioners to David Burnes, 19 Feb 1796, Letters sent by the Board of Commissioners for the District of Columbia, RG 42, NA (hereafter cited as Comrs' Ltrs Sent); *Daily Patriot*, 8 Dec 1870.

houses stood in pleasant gardens running from Bridge Street to the river or along four or five other wide streets; the humble dwellings of working people occupied the land about the wharves and the warehouses. Suter's Tavern and the newer Union Tavern offered visitors comfortable accommodation. A handsome Presbyterian church and Trinity Catholic Church contributed to the settled atmosphere of the community, while Georgetown Seminary, founded eleven years before by Bishop John Carroll to train men for the Roman Catholic priesthood, lent the village special distinction. Congressmen seeking agreeable living quarters would be tempted to choose Georgetown, despite the inconvenience of the three miles of travel over rutted roads to reach the Capitol.[4]

Alexandria, five miles down the Potomac at the southern tip of the "ten-mile square," was still more firmly established and sophisticated. Beautiful houses built before the Revolution for the Scottish tobacco factors and the wheat merchants who had developed this chief seaport on the Potomac had made her, in the judgment of that observant Frenchman, the Duc de la Rochefoucauld-Liancourt, "beyond all comparison the handsomest town in Virginia."[5] By building a network of roads into the lower Shenandoah Valley in the 1760's and 1770's, Alexandrians had captured the lion's share of the export trade in Virginia wheat and flour. Although she was accessible to the new capital only by sailing vessel or by coach and ferry over the river, her 5,000 residents, like citizens of Georgetown and Washington City, saw in the transfer of the federal government to the Potomac the dawning of a bright new future. Later events would lead them to ask themselves why they had so con-

[4] Benjamin Stoddert to John Templeman, n.d., Benjamin Stoddert Mss, Library of Congress (unless otherwise noted, all nonofficial manuscripts cited are in the Library of Congress Manuscript Division); Avery O. Craven, *Soil Exhaustion as a Factor in the Agricultural History of Virginia and Maryland, 1606-1860*, in *University of Illinois Studies in the Social Sciences*, XIII (Mar 1925), pp. 76-77.

[5] Craven, *Soil Exhaustion*, p. 77; Fairfax Harrison, *Land-Marks of Old Prince William*, II, 407-11; Francois-Alexandre-Frédéric La Rochefoucauld-Liancourt, *Voyage dans les Etats-Unis d'Amérique*, VI, 167-68.

fidently expected prosperity to follow immediately, but in 1800 they believed that a mighty commercial expansion would rapidly occur at "the permanent seat of empire."[6]

Indeed Americans generally had assumed that wherever Congress chose to locate the federal city, there a great commercial center would arise. That conviction explains more fully than any consideration of prestige or legislators' convenience why sectional controversy had run so strong during the congressional debates on the "residence" bill. Expectations of long-term economic benefits as well as the immediate revenues the presence of Congress would bring to a community—$100,000 annually, a well-informed New Yorker estimated[7]—had led a half-dozen towns and states, months before the debates opened, to offer Congress land for a permanent meeting place and jurisdictional rights over it. During the nearly seven years of intermittent discussion between October 1783 and July 1790, representatives had agreed on the overriding importance of a central location for the seat of government. But whereas some men defined *central* as geographically half-way between southern Georgia and northern New Hampshire, to others the term meant center of population, a point considerably north of Virginia, even were slaves counted. Apparently no speaker mentioned the drawbacks of a capital in slave-holding territory. Southerners were persuaded, Thomas Jefferson perhaps as completely as anyone, that a capital below the Mason-Dixon line would attract "foreigners, manufacturers and settlers" to Virginia and Maryland and thus shift southward the center of both population and power.[8] The Potomac River Valley, moreover,

6 House of Representatives Report 59, 11C, 2S, *Papers of the First Fourteen Congresses*; Isaac Weld, *Travels Through the States of North America . . . during the Years of 1795, 1796 and 1797*, I, 90; *Alexandria Advertiser*, 8 Dec 1800; *Second Census of the United States*, 1800.

7 *Annals of the Congress of the United States*, 4C, 1S, pp. 825-40 (hereafter cited as *Annals*); Ezra L. Hommedieu to Governor Clinton of New York, 15 Aug 1783, quoted in Wilhelmus B. Bryan, *History of the National Capital*, I, 4, 11 (hereafter cited as Bryan, *Capital*).

8 Jefferson to the Governor of Virginia, 11 Nov 1783, and Notes on the Permanent Seat of Congress, [13 Apr 1784], quoted in *Thomas Jefferson*

gave the South one natural advantage: a link between the eastern seaboard and the trans-Alleghany West by river and the shortest traversable route over the mountains. Aware that the Ohio country, if left without commercial ties with the East, might align itself with the Spanish or French settlements of the interior, George Washington and several associates in 1784 organized the Potomac Company to improve navigation of the river westward.[9]

In the end neither geography nor demography so much as political bargaining fixed the location of the capital. As the controversy dragged on into 1790, Jefferson, Secretary of State in Washington's first administration, and Alexander Hamilton, Secretary of the Treasury, arranged a compromise. Over Jefferson's supper table in New York, the two cabinet members and congressmen Richard Bland Lee and Alexander White of Virginia agreed that, in return for Hamilton's aligning northern support for a southern capital, the Virginians would vote for federal assumption of the state debts incurred during the Revolution. Congress, in accepting the plan, specified Philadelphia as the seat of government for ten years while the federal city was building. Thus supporters of a strong national fiscal policy gained a vital concession and the proponents of a capital on the Potomac at once won special recognition for their section and, as they believed, a significant boost for the South's flagging commerce.[10]

Throughout the long and frequently acrimonious disagreements over where to locate the capital, few men had challenged the principle of congressional control of a federal district. The

---

and the National Capital, ed. Saul K. Padover, pp. 1-4, 6-9 (hereafter cited as Padover, *Jefferson*); *The State Records of North Carolina*, ed. Walter Clark, XVI, 908-10.

[9] Weld, *Travels*, I, 71-80; Walter S. Sanderlin, *The Great National Project: A History of the Chesapeake and Ohio Canal*, in *The Johns Hopkins University Studies in Historical and Political Science*, LXIV, No. 1, pp. 18, 28-44 (hereafter cited as Sanderlin, *National Project*).

[10] Note on the Residence Bill [ca. May 1790], in Padover, *Jefferson*, pp. 11-12. For more detailed discussion, see John B. McMaster, *A History of the People of the United States*, I, 555-62, and Bryan, *Capital*, I, 1, 27-35.

consensus outside and in Congress had already settled that basic problem. From first to last, every gift of land tendered to Congress, whether from the town of Kingston, New York, Nottingham, New Jersey, or the state governments of New York, Maryland, New Jersey, Virginia, or Pennsylvania, had included offers of complete jurisdiction free from state interference.[11] In the light of the jealousies with which the sovereign states composing the Confederation had guarded their prerogatives, the willingness of each contender for the capital to relinquish authority over a piece of its own territory may seem strange at first glance. Cession of lands in the West was a different matter, for they were remote, part of an unsettled wilderness; the capital would be the very center of American political and commercial activity. But compelling reasons for state self-denial were several. The very jealousies between the states made each loath to see a rival in a position to dominate the general government. At the same time any method of strengthening the Union without injuring any of its thirteen members had obvious merit. A fixed meeting place for Congress should provide the stability that peripatetic sessions had denied it. "Muteability of place," a delegate to the Constitutional Convention observed in 1787, "had dishonored the Federal Government."[12] Yet to place a permanent capital within the jurisdiction of one state was to imperil the influence of every other. The surest way of avoiding that risk was to vest in Congress rights of "exclusive legislation" over the capital and a small area about it. The debates on the residence bill had proceeded upon that premise.[13]

While the competitive bids for the capital were rolling in, an

[11] Papers of the Continental Congress, Item 20, Reports of Committees on "State Papers," 4 Jun 1783, I, 389, and Item 46, Proposals to Congress relative to locating the seat of government, *passim*, and especially 7 Mar 1783, pp. 9-10, and 16 Jun 1783, p. 43, RG 11, NA (hereafter cited as Papers Cont Cong).

[12] Quoted in Bryan, *Capital*, I, 12.

[13] E.g., *Journals of the Continental Congress*, XXIV, 381-83, XXV, 647-60, 706-14; Papers Cont Cong, Item 23, Reports of committees relating particularly to Congress . . . , 13 Aug 1788, I, 101-102, and 6 Aug 1788, I, 339-41.

episode occurred in Philadelphia that underscored the weakness of Congress and the necessity of bolstering its prestige if the Union were to be more than a meaningless name. In June 1783, Pennsylvania veterans not yet discharged from the army had prepared to march to the State House, where Congress was in session, to demand the pay long overdue them for service during the Revolution. Earlier petitions had elicited no answer from Congress, doubtless for the very good reason that with an empty federal treasury a satisfactory reply was not possible. Congress upon learning of the soldiers' impending arrival asked the Pennsylvania state council for protection. The council took no action; Philadelphians reportedly sympathized with the soldiers, who were, after all, seeking redress of real grievances by use of procedures recognized in America—free assembly, free speech, and direct appeal to elected representatives. On June 21 some 250 "mutineers" gathered about Independence Hall, only to find the doors locked against them while Congress huddled inside. Their nearest approach to violence consisted of "offensive language" and occasionally a musket pointed at the tightly shut windows. In mid-afternoon when Congress adjourned, the soldiers returned to their barracks. Congressmen thereupon scuttled out of the city to reconvene in Princeton the following week.[14] The "affront" to the dignity of Congress added ammunition for the campaigners for a federally controlled capital, but the movement to establish it had gained momentum weeks before. Only later did Congress, perhaps secretly chagrined at its own timidity, cite the humiliations it suffered from Pennsylvania as justification for an "Exempt jurisdiction."[15] And in time, after the excesses of the French Revolution had frightened moderates everywhere, the story of the mutiny in Philadelphia came to find place in school text books as the

[14] *The Writings of James Madison*, ed. Gaillard Hunt, 19, 21 Jun 1783, I, 480, 482-84.

[15] Papers Cont Cong, Item 23, 18 Sep 1783, I, 149-50; *Annals*, 6C, 2S, p. 996, 7C, 2S, pp. 50-54.

reason for founding a new capital city out of reach of mobs and powerful local interests.

In accepting the principle eventually written into the Constitution, that Congress must be supreme in the federal district, no one had equated sacrifice of state power with cancellation of political rights of citizens of the future federal territory. On the contrary, Americans of the 1780's had taken for granted that permanent residents, like citizens of any state, would "enjoy the privilege of trial by jury and of being governed by laws made by representatives of their own election."[16] Madison, to be sure, had recognized the puzzling character of the problem in a country where all political machinery operated through state organizations and only citizenship in a state enabled a man to vote in national elections. In 1783 the Virginian had noted merely that "the power of Government within the sd district [should be] concerted between Congress and the inhabitants thereof." Four years later he had gone further. In one of the *Federalist* papers, that collection of able essays urging adoption of the Constitution, he had declared the political status of citizens of a federal district amply protected, "as they will have had their voice in the election of the government which is to exercise authority over them; [and] as a municipal legislature for local purposes, derived from their own suffrages, will of course be allowed them." If the phrase "they will have had their voice" implied they could not continue to have it, few contemporaries had observed the nuance.[17]

In fact before 1800 few contemporaries apparently had thought at all about the local problem in the making. In the 1780's men concerned about building a stronger union had so firmly believed a federally controlled capital a necessary part of the plan that they had incorporated the provision into the Con-

[16] Papers Cont Cong, Item 46, Mar, May, and Jun 1783, pp. 5-10, 15, 55-57, 93.

[17] Papers Cont Cong, Item 23, 27 Dec 1783, I, 161; *The Federalist*, No. 43, p. 280 (1938 ed.).

stitution. At the state conventions called to ratify the Constitution, only in Virginia and North Carolina had delegates so much as spoken of the hazards of creating a federal district beyond the reach of state laws; and these criticisms, though pointing to possible tyrannies such as abolition of trial by jury within the district and grants of commercial monopolies to its merchants, had been in essence part of the over-all attack upon any plan for a strong central government.[18] After ratification of the Constitution and passage of the residence bill eighteen months later, the question of governing the ten-mile square on the Potomac had resolved itself for a decade. The act of July 16, 1790, had not only empowered the President to choose the exact location and to engage commissioners to take charge of planning and building the new capital but had also decreed that until Congress took up residence there and should "otherwise by law provide," Maryland law should prevail in the territory ceded by Maryland, Virginia law in the area given to the United States by the Old Dominion.[19] With that decision, Americans had thankfully dismissed the matter. As late as November 1800 local citizens therefore continued to vote in state and national elections.

President Washington, although free by the terms of the residence act to select any locality between the mouths of the Eastern Branch and the Connocheague River forty miles up the Potomac, had probably never seriously considered a site above tidewater. In an era when travel was slow and hazardous at best, a capital accessible to coastal and ocean-going vessels was virtually imperative. Twentieth-century residents of the District of Columbia, nevertheless, have wondered now and again why a trained surveyor who knew the countryside well chose a spot where tidal swamplands yearly bred fevers and oppressive damp heat would blanket the city every summer. The answer, apart from the undeniable importance of a location

[18] *Debates and Other Proceedings of the Convention of Virginia . . . , June 1788*, III, 27-31; *Proceedings and Debates of the North Carolina Convention, . . . July 1788*, pp. 229-36, 246-47, 273-74.

[19] *Annals*, 1C, 2S, pp. 2234-35.

below the falls of the Potomac, is doubtless twofold. Eighteenth-century Americans looked upon the weather as an act of God and climate a capricious condition of nature which need not affect any man-made decision. In the second place, as long as trees covered the shores of rivers and streams, the area below the Little Falls of the Potomac enjoyed a kind of natural "air conditioning," and, before deforestation produced a downwash of soil and vegetation that silted up brooks and created marshes, the site of the capital was probably nearly as healthful as any farther upstream. Residents of the early nineteenth century, to be sure, suffered so regularly from "flux" during the winter and "ague" in spring and summer that they expected to run fevers while going about their daily business. But ill health pervaded most communities, and the letters and diaries of the period rarely attributed its prevalence here to Washington's climate or unwholesomeness of location.[20]

During the ten years of preparation for the transfer of the government to the banks of the Potomac, President Washington and then President Adams, the commissioners, the French engineer Pierre Charles L'Enfant, whom the President had chosen to lay out the city, Thomas Jefferson, as renowned for his architectural talents as for his knowledge of statecraft, local landowners, and an array of carpenters, bricklayers, stone cutters, and day laborers struggled with financial and physical difficulties and with each other. The President persuaded the chief property-owners to convey to the United States in trust all their land that was to be included in the city limits. According to the agreement, the government was to pay nothing for the area shown on L'Enfant's plan as set aside for public buildings, "reservations," and streets; of the land remaining, half the lots were to revert to the original proprietors, and for the other half the United States would pay £25 Maryland currency, about $67 an acre. Since the state of Maryland had already advanced $72,000 and Virginia $120,000, sale of the government lots

[20] M. B. Smith, *First Forty Years*, p. 23; Benjamin Henry Latrobe, *The Journal of Latrobe*, pp. 131-32.

supposedly would raise enough additional money to cover the costs of erecting the public buildings.

Troubles cropped up almost at once. In September 1791, after the commissioners announced that they had named the ten-mile square "District of Columbia" and the capital-to-be "City of Washington," they advertised a public auction of city lots. L'Enfant protested that it was premature, beneficial only to local speculators who would acquire choice lots at bargain prices and in the process interfere with his plan of encouraging the simultaneous development of a series of neighborhoods. In some degree events proved him right. Held in October, the sale disposed of only thirty-five lots and netted scarcely $2,000, far less than expected, since the value of the 10,000 lots of varying sizes into which L'Enfant proposed to divide the government's salable land was estimated at some $800,000. The President and the commissioners then realized that before holding a second auction they must have a plat of the city ready to enable potential purchasers to see what they were bidding for. But the gifted L'Enfant, dedicated to his vast plans and prone to revise them at frequent intervals, either could not or would not hurry the preparation of an engraved map. He was manifestly unable to comprehend the political risks of delay and the President's sense of urgency about getting money with which to start the public buildings.[21] In February 1792, when L'Enfant had still not produced the engraved map, the President assigned that task to the surveyor Andrew Ellicott of Baltimore, for, as Washington wrote from Philadelphia, "if inactivity and contractedness mark the steps of the commissioners, whilst the contrary on the part of this state [Pennsylvania] is displayed in providing commodious buildings for Congress, etc., the government will remain where it now is." Since L'Enfant indignantly refused to cooperate with Ellicott or the commissioners, the President regretfully dismissed the temperamental Frenchman.[22]

[21] Elizabeth S. Kite, *L'Enfant and Washington, 1791-1792*, pp. 51-58, 73-93.

[22] Ltrs to the Comrs, 18 Dec 1791, 17 Jan, 6 Mar 1792, to the Sec/State,

Despite wide distribution of copies of Ellicott's map, which was based upon L'Enfant's incomplete drawing, the second auction of lots, held in October 1792, again brought in very little. Consequently when efforts to obtain a loan for building the Capitol and the Executive Mansion failed, the commissioners with the President's approval accepted the proposal of James Greenleaf, a member of a prominent Massachusetts family, to buy 3,000 lots at a reduced price to be paid in seven annual installments; he was to build ten houses yearly for seven years and lend the commissioners $2,200 every month till the public buildings were finished. Robert Morris of Philadelphia, the richest man in the United States at that time, and a friend, James Nicholson, soon associated themselves with Greenleaf, and the terms of the original agreement were then broadened to permit the syndicate to acquire title to lots without paying cash for them. This transaction, together with the purchase of lots from individual proprietors, gave the syndicate control of more than a third of the land for sale in Washington and stimulated a flurry of speculation in real estate in the new capital. But the syndicate overreached itself and ended in bankruptcy in 1797, leaving behind a score of unfinished dwellings, fresh problems for the commissioners, and, worst of all, a bad name for the capital as a place of investment. That reputation would handicap the city for years to come.[23]

From the beginning, moreover, the commissioners found that competent workmen were hard to recruit, possibly because slave labor kept wage rates in the South lower than in northern cities; in 1798 ninety slaves made up most of the work force engaged in building the Capitol. Feuds developed between the architects and the superintendents of building. Since the surveyors' plats, L'Enfant's drawing, and the physical features of the

---

26 Feb, 4 Mar 1792, to Pierre Charles L'Enfant, 28 Feb 1792, and to David Stuart, 8 Mar 1792, *Writings of Washington*, XXXI, 445-48, 461-62, 486-89, 495, 497-98, 504-508; "L'Enfant's Reports to President Washington bearing dates of March 26, June 22, and August 19, 1791," CHS *Rec*, II, 45, 53.

[23] Ltr to Daniel Carroll, 7 Jan 1795, *Writings of Washington*, XXXIV, 79-81; Clark, *Greenleaf and Law*, pp. 151-77.

terrain were frequently not in agreement, long-drawn-out quarrels arose between public officials and landowners. The chief proprietors of the land near the "Congress house" charged the commissioners with bad faith in placing the executive offices adjacent to the "President's Palace" and thereby encouraging the westward growth of the city at the expense of the area about the Capitol. Later stories of uncertain origin accused Daniel Carroll and his neighbors of holding their lots for such exorbitant prices that the buying public was driven to purchase the cheaper land along the swampy stretch of Pennsylvania Avenue and near Georgetown. For the prospective householder the advantages of proximity to the well-established community of Georgetown were undeniable, and Carroll in an effort to counterbalance this factor made extremely generous price concessions for his lots. But unhappily for historical justice, the tale of the greedy proprietors hoist on their own petard has stuck and is still the popularly accepted explanation of why the city spread westward instead of developing on the Hill as L'Enfant had supposedly intended.

In actuality nothing indicates that L'Enfant envisaged the Hill as the principal residential section of the city. Just as the deep water running close inshore along the Eastern Branch made its banks the logical place for the Navy Yard and merchants' wharves and warehouses, so the executive department buildings would be most conveniently placed within easy reach of the Executive Mansion on the city's north-south axis well to the west of the Capitol. And departmental officers and clerks, as more permanent residents than members of Congress, would be a larger factor in determining where people would live. Certainly no record suggests that the commissioners betrayed the proprietors of the eastern section by arbitrarily introducing significant changes in L'Enfant's plan. The controversies and recriminations merely complicated a difficult task. In fact, the commissioners encountered obstacles to progress at every turn.[24]

[24] Kite, *L'Enfant*, pp. 53-57; Padover, *Jefferson*, pp. 63-126, 150, 163-64, 178-87, 200-201, 322-34; Comrs' Ltrs Sent, 22 Nov 1798, v, 177-78;

Yet in June 1800 the new national capital, however unfinished, was at last a reality.

The arrival of executive officers and the public archives that month occasioned little excitement; the great moment would not come until Congress convened in November. Residents nevertheless welcomed the first official newcomers. On June 3, Georgetown sent a delegation of citizens on horseback to greet President Adams at the District line and to escort him to the city's Union Tavern, where a company of marines fired a salute in his honor. The next day the President drove on into Washington to inspect the Executive Mansion and the Treasury and on June 5th to attend a reception arranged by citizens at the Capitol. Following a call upon the recently widowed Mrs. Washington at Mt. Vernon and then a large banquet in Alexandria, the President departed for Massachusetts after spending only ten days in the District of Columbia. By then departmental heads or responsible subordinates had opened their offices for business in new, if too frequently cramped, quarters. Though the advent of 131 federal employees failed to bring the long-awaited prosperity, their presence dispelled citizens' uneasiness lest Congress postpone its first session in Washington.[25]

Meanwhile the commissioners hurried on with their preparations. They had obtained another $50,000, loaned by Maryland, but as the sale of lots in the city had virtually stopped in 1797,

---

Annals, 7C, 2S, pp. 1304-26; B. Henry Latrobe to Chairman House Committee, 28 Feb 1804, quoted in *Documentary History of the Construction and Development of the U.S. Capitol Building and Grounds*, H Rpt 646, 58C, 2S, pp. 107-108, Ser 4585 (hereafter cited as *History of the Capitol*); J. Dudley Morgan, et al., "Why the City Went Westward," CHS *Rec*, VII, 107-45.

[25] Osborne, "Removal of the Government," and Hugh T. Taggart, "The Presidential Journey, in 1800, from the old to the new seat of government," CHS *Rec*, III, 147-51, 187-201; Thornton Diary, 7 Jan, 5-12 Jun 1800, CHS *Rec*, X, 92, 151-54; "Extracts from the Report of the Committee" [to investigate federal expenditures], 29 Apr 1802, CHS *Rec*, IX, 226-41; Oliver Wolcott to his wife, 4 Jul 1800, quoted in George Gibbs, *Memoirs of the Administrations of Washington and John Adams, edited from the Papers of Oliver Wolcott, Secretary of the Treasury*, II, 276-78 (hereafter cited as Gibbs, *Memoirs*).

they were still short of money. Consequently in August 1800 they cut the price of lots nearly in half, keeping only to the stipulation that purchasers must build on at least part of their property. That scheme worked. Dr. William Thornton, chief architect of the Capitol, prophesied a city of 160,000 in a very few years. During the summer communication improved. Stage coach lines increased the number of runs to the "Federal City," and by November a traveller from Philadelphia might make the journey in thirty-three hours, though it generally took more. The theatre that opened in August closed in September after performances Mrs. Thornton considered "intolerably stupid," but already there was talk of another season. To provide some of the other amenities such as existed in Philadelphia, the half-dozen members of the Marine Corps band inaugurated weekly outdoor concerts, and during the early autumn subscribers organized two dancing "assemblies," gathering at Stelle's Tavern at five in the afternoon and ending at nine.[26]

Still more important for the city, that fall the *National Intelligencer* and its weekly version, the *Universal Gazette*, began publication in Washington, while the *Washington Federalist*, the *Museum* and the *Cabinet* appeared in Georgetown, and, across the river, was the *Alexandria Advertiser*. The Georgetown papers were short-lived, but the *Alexandria Advertiser*, renamed the *Gazette*, has had a continuous existence to this day, and the *Intelligencer*, though published in a city that would soon earn the name "graveyard of newspapers," lasted till 1869.[27] The *Intelligencer* initially owed its vigor to its owner, printer, and editor, Samuel Harrison Smith, friend of Jefferson and formerly secretary of the American Philosophical Society. As vehicles of local advertising, purveyors of national news, and organs of political opinion, the papers contributed to

[26] Comrs' Ltrs Sent, 13 May 1800, 27 Aug 1800; Comrs' Prcdgs, 20 Aug, 14 Nov 1800; Thornton Diary, 13 Aug 1800, CHS *Rec*, x, 178; *Centinel of Liberty*, 6 May, 6 Jun, 11 Jul 1800; *National Intelligencer*, 26 Nov 1800; *Washington Federalist*, 21 Nov 1800, 28 Apr 1802; Gibbs, *Memoirs*, II, 378; *ASP*, *Misc*, I, 254-55.

[27] Clarence S. Brigham, *History and Bibliography of American Newspapers, 1690-1820*, I, 87-108.

Washington a more nearly urban air than the years of planning and building had contrived. And because Samuel Harrison Smith and his charming wife, Margaret Bayard, were delighted with the young city, the columns of the *Intelligencer* and the exchange of ideas in Mrs. Smith's hospitable drawing room helped temper harsh judgments upon the new capital. Within a year after saying of Washington "there is no industry, society or business," Oliver Wolcott, in July 1800 still Secretary of the Treasury, might have conceded that the city had something to offer besides empty space.[28]

Progress notwithstanding, Washington City in November 1800 was still a small, isolated community. Of the 501 "heads of households" enumerated in the census return, nineteen were the "original proprietors" who had signed the agreement with President Washington in June 1791, and a score or more were smaller landowners who had accepted similar terms somewhat later. Most of the rest were newcomers. Land speculation had attracted some of them. Thomas Law was probably the most notable of that group. Brother of a British peer and himself a wealthy man when he emigrated in 1795, he was one of the few large-scale investors in Washington real estate to make his home here after the failure of the Greenleaf and Morris syndicate had caused a sharp drop in local property values. His marriage to Mrs. Washington's granddaughter, Eliza Custis, doubtless strengthened his ties to the new capital. Although the sugar refinery he financed near Greenleaf's Point in 1797 closed down before 1801, Law ranked as Washington's pioneer manufacturer. Professional men formed a third category of the city's residents. William Cranch, a nephew of Abigail Adams, at first came as business agent for Robert Morris and James Nicholson but stayed on to serve as a federal commissioner and later as a judge of the circuit court. Several other lawyers, three or four physicians, and a half-dozen pastors lengthened the list of specially trained men. Opportunity to work on government building projects had brought still others—

[28] Gibbs, *Memoirs*, II, 377.

Dr. William Thornton, remembered for his design of the Capitol, the Octagon House and other architectural triumphs; his rivals, English-born George Hadfield, the Irishman James Hoban, designer of the Executive Mansion; and several less talented rivals.

While categories overlap, and a man like Daniel Carroll of Duddington was at once an original landed proprietor and owner of the busiest brick kilns in the city, the men intent upon exploiting the commercial possibilities of the new capital made up a rather distinct fourth group of citizens. Besides the suppliers of building materials—Robert Brent, for example, whose family owned the quarry at Acquia Creek which furnished stone for houses and federal buildings—there were merchants who hoped to establish import-export businesses. Colonel Tobias Lear, former secretary of General Washington, represented this kind of investor. Though the collapse of 1797 had injured the prospects of mercantile firms, some of the disappointed commercial adventurers remained in the city in the belief that the convening of Congress would mend their fortunes. Of all the men who anticipated a business future in the capital, the printers and the tavern and boardinghouse keepers were among the few to gauge correctly the chances of financial success. Officers attached to the Navy Yard and the Marine Corps unit, while subject to transfer, also rated as local citizens: Captain Thomas Tingey, Superintendent of the Navy Yard, in fact would be a fixture in Washington till his death in 1829. The other 300-400 householders were largely craftsmen and day laborers, some of them free Negroes.[29] "The people are poor," wrote Oliver Wolcott, adding rather disdainfully, "as far as I can judge, they live like fishes, by eating each other."[30]

In addition to the people who chose to live in the federal District in 1800, its 14,093 souls included some 3,200 chattel bondsmen, a higher proportion than any later decade would

[29] Enumerator's Return for the District of Columbia, Second Census of the U.S., 1800, pp. 117-50, Ms, N.A.; Comrs' Prcdgs, 29 Jun 1791.

[30] Osborne, "Removal of the Government," CHS *Rec*, III, 158; Gibbs, *Memoirs*, II, 377.

show. Some were field hands owned by farmers in the area outside the cities' limits. (See Table I.) Ownership of the 623 slaves in Washington City was scattered; only 7 people had as many as 10, and only the former planter Daniel Carroll of Duddington and Ann Burns had as many as 20. The local

TABLE I

POPULATION OF THE DISTRICT OF COLUMBIA[a]

	1800	*1810*	*1820*	*1830*	*1840*	*1850*	*1860*	*1870*
D.C. TOTAL	14,093	24,023	33,039	39,834	43,712	51,687	75,080	131,700
White	10,266	16,088	23,164	27,563	29,655	37,941	60,764	88,298
Free Negro	783	2,549	4,048	6,152	8,461	10,059	11,131	43,422
Slave	3,244	5,505	6,277	6,119	4,694	3,687	3,185	
WASHINGTON								
TOTAL	3,210	8,208	13,117	18,826	23,364	40,001	61,122	109,199
White	2,464	5,904	9,376	13,367	16,843	29,730	50,139	73,731
Free Negro	123	867	1,796	3,129	4,808	8,158	9,209	35,455
Black							5,831	
Mulatto							3,378	
Slave	623	1,437	1,945	2,330	1,713	2,113	1,774	
GEORGETOWN								
TOTAL	2,993	4,948	7,360	8,441	7,312	8,366	8,733	11,384
White	3,394[b]	3,235	5,099	6,122	5,124	6,080	6,798	8,113
Free Negro	277[b]	551	894	1,204	1,403	1,561	1,358	3,271
Black							562	
Mulatto							796	
Slave	1,449[b]	1,162	1,521	1,115	785	725	577	
WASHINGTON								
COUNTY[c] TOTAL	1,941	2,135	2,729	2,994	3,069	3,320	5,225	11,117
White			1,514	1,828	1,929	2,131	3,827	6,434
Free Negro			168	167	288	340	564	4,678
Black							238	
Mulatto							326	
Slave			1,047	999	812	849	834	
ALEXANDRIA								
CITY TOTAL	4,971	7,227	8,345	8,241	8,459			
White	3,727	4,903	5,742	5,609	5,758			
Free Negro	369	836	1,168	1,371	1,627			
Slave	875	1,488	1,435	1,261	1,064			

[a] Compiled from *U.S. Census*, Second Through Ninth, 1800-1870

[b] Georgetown and Washington County together

[c] Washington County encompassed all the area beyond the Eastern Branch, and all above Washington's present-day Florida Avenue and Georgetown's present-day R Street.

attitude toward slavery, a visitor later remarked, was much like that in the West Indies. No one had expressed dismay at Andrew Ellicott's employing Benjamin Banneker, a free Negro skilled in mathematics, as an assistant surveyor for the capital. But slaves, whether hired out by their masters for building operations or used as household servants, comprised the core of the labor force. The "peculiar institution" of the South was an accepted part of the social order of the new capital from its very beginning.[31]

In November 1800 this was the community which, as the "permanent seat of empire," Americans hoped would cement national unity forever.

[31] *Third Census of the United States*, 1810; David B. Warden, *A Chorographical and Statistical Description of the District of Columbia*, p. 64.

CHAPTER II

THE "SEAT OF EMPIRE," 1800-1812

EVERY free resident of the District of Columbia looked forward to November 17, 1800, the date set for the first meeting of the "Grand Council of the Nation" in the new capital. On November 11, voters from Washington journeyed to Bladensburg, Maryland, to cast their ballots in the national election; Georgetowners and Alexandrians voted in their own cities. The outcome of the struggle between Federalists and Republicans would not be known until later in the month, but meanwhile leading citizens in the ten-mile square cheerfully laid plans for a formal welcome to the 106 representatives and 32 senators of the Sixth Congress.[1]

Nothing went as intended. For lack of a quorum Congress had to postpone its opening till November 21. The much talked-of procession of citizens to the Capitol did not take place at all, partly because of quarrels over who should be master of ceremonies and partly because of a three-inch snowfall the day before. Mrs. Adams on her arrival found most of the Executive Mansion still unplastered, few furnishings in place, no bell pulls, and a scarcity of firewood; she hung the family washing in the ceremonial East Room. Presidential levees would have to wait; even paying calls was difficult during the inclement weather. Congressmen complained of their crowded lodgings and of the city's inconveniences and dreary appearance. Representative Griswold of Connecticut called it "both melancholy and ludicrous . . . a city in ruins."[2] Only President Adams' message on the state of the Union seemed to hold out encouragement and to endow Washington with dignity: "In this city

[1] *National Intelligencer*, 12 Nov 1800 (hereafter cited as *N.I.*); *Washington Federalist*, 16 Oct 1800; H Doc 49, 18C, 1S, Ser 94.

[2] *N.I.*, 21 Nov 1800; Osborne, "Removal of the Government," CHS *Rec*, III, 152-53; *Letters of Mrs. Adams, Wife of John Adams*, pp. 432-35; *The Correspondence and Miscellanies of the Hon. John Cotton Smith*, pp. 6, 147; Richard Griswold to Mrs. Fanny Griswold, 6 Dec 1800, Griswold Mss (Yale Univ); Allen C. Clark, *Life and Letters of Dolly Madison*, pp. 37-38.

may . . . self-government which adorned the great character whose name it bears be forever held in veneration. . . .

"It is with you, gentlemen, to consider whether the local powers over the District of Columbia vested by the Constitution in the Congress of the United States, shall be immediately exercised."[3]

Congress chose to act promptly. Delay would leave the decision in the hands of the recently victorious Republicans, opponents of a strong central government; Federalists in the lame duck session of 1800-1801 had no time to lose if they were to make the federal capital a bulwark against the power of the states. Yet the bill presented to the House in December came as a shock to Washingtonians: the powers of the corporations of Alexandria and Georgetown and of all other incorporated bodies in the District were to remain unimpaired, the President was to have authority to replace with his own appointees the incumbents of state executive and judicial offices within the District, but residents of Washington were to have no self-government. The laws in force in Virginia on December 1, 1800, were to constitute the legal code for the trans-Potomac part of the area, Maryland laws of that date, the code for the rest. Still worse from local citizens' point of view, the bill ignored their rights to vote in national elections and have representation in Congress.[4]

Protests sounded immediately. The most vigorous attack appeared in a series of articles published in the *National Intelligencer* over the signature "Epaminondas," the pen name of Augustus Woodward, a Virginia-born lawyer recently moved from Alexandria to Washington.[5] He denied that the intent of the constitutional provision giving Congress exclusive legislative authority over the District was to strip local citizens of all

[3] *Annals*, 6C, 2S, p. 723.

[4] *Ibid.*, 6C, 2S, pp. 824-25.

[5] *The Museum and Washington and George-town Advertiser*, 24 Dec 1800, 12 Jan 1801; *N.I.*, 24, 26, 29, 31 Dec 1800; *Alexandria Advertiser*, 6, 7, 9, 14 Jan 1801; Charles Moore, "Augustus Brevoort Woodward—Citizen of Two Cities," CHS *Rec*, IV, 114-17.

participation in their own government. Admitting a constitutional amendment necessary to permit them to vote for the President and Vice-President, elect a senator and, when the population had grown sufficiently, a representative, he urged prompt adoption of the amendment and meanwhile the creation of a "Territory of Columbia" with an elected legislature. "No policy can be worse than to mingle *great* and *small* concerns. The latter become absorbed in the former; are neglected and forgotten." For, Woodward added, "It will impair the dignity of the national legislative, executive, and judicial authorities to be occupied with all the local concerns of the Territory of Columbia." He pointed to the drawbacks of a dual legal system and, prophetic of the complaints to be repeated for the next seventy-five years, to the handicaps of fastening upon a new community unrevised eighteenth-century state laws. Finally, he derided the failure to specify what part of the District's expenses should be borne by the federal government and what part by local taxpayers. Did the committee members imagine that the question would answer itself, or did they intend the federal government to lavish its resources upon "this favorite child"? Congress must consider "that we are legislating for posterity as well as for ourselves; and that the interest of millions unborn is confided to our hands."[6]

In the House of Representatives opposition to the bill arose from several mutually conflicting objections: the unsuitability of perpetuating state laws in a jurisdiction where the Constitution decreed Congress must be supreme; conversely, the desirability of continuing the existing workable arrangement, which protected citizens' political rights and was entirely proper since the Constitution did not require Congress to exercise its full authority; and, third, the unrighteousness of reducing men "in the very heart of the United States" to the condition of subjects whose rulers would be "independent and entirely above the control of the people."[7] Further consideration of the problem

[6] *N.I.*, 29, 31 Dec 1800.
[7] *Annals*, 6C, 2S, pp. 868-74, 876.

failed to bring agreement either in Congress or among local residents. A redrafted bill proposed a territorial legislature to be elected by District property-owners but gave it no authority to tax. In Washington, Georgetown, and Alexandria public meetings revealed the cleavage of opinion between men who abhorred the very thought of such restricted political power and those who considered federal rule their strongest economic anchor to windward. By February 1801 uncertainty about the political fate of the District had so undermined confidence in its future that a Maryland congressman declared, "serious doubts exist with judicious men how far the grants and acceptances of lands, or their papers, afford them security for value received."[8]

Meanwhile the future of the Union itself appeared to be imperiled by the partisan conflict brought about by the tie in the electoral college between Thomas Jefferson and Aaron Burr for President and Vice-President. Every lesser question had to wait until the House of Representatives, upon which the tie thrust the decision, chose a President or permitted an interregnum to occur. The voting began on February 11 while a snowstorm raged outside. The contest was so bitter that one congressman, seriously ill though he was, insisted on being carried to the House in his bed in order to vote. Six days later, after one thirty-six-hour session followed by shorter ones, the thirty-fourth ballot elected Thomas Jefferson. Relief spread through the capital that constitutional procedures had prevailed. But residents had had dramatic proof that the mingling of "*great* and *small* concerns" would always mean neglect of local interest.

Time was too short in the fortnight remaining before the presidential inauguration to permit any settlement of District affairs. Only one inadequate measure was possible. In the very last days of the session Congress established a judiciary for the ten-mile square, dividing it into Washington County where

[8] *Ibid.*, pp. 991-1004; *N.I.*, 30 Jan, 6, 9 Feb 1801; *Alexandria Advertiser*, 2, 19, 24, 26 Feb, 2, 3, 4, 11 Mar 1801.

Maryland law should run and Alexandria County across the Potomac where Virginia law should apply. Outside the cities' limits in each county, presidentially appointed officials known as the levy court, in keeping with Maryland and Virginia custom, would assess taxes and administer routine local affairs. A circuit court consisting of a chief justice and two associates was to hold four sessions yearly in each county, and procedures in each were to conform to the state's. Justices of the peace and a marshal selected by the President completed the judicial system. Among the twenty-three "midnight judges" whom John Adams appointed as his last act in office was his wife's nephew, William Cranch; the simultaneous appointment of William Marbury as a justice of the peace would make that otherwise obscure Marylander's name famous because Chief Justice Marshall of the Supreme Court used the case *Marbury* vs. *Madison* to proclaim for the first time his doctrine of the sanctity of the Constitution. The able Judge Cranch would serve the District circuit court with distinction for fifty-four years. But so far from unifying the District of Columbia, the new congressional laws formalized and widened its split into two jurisdictions.[9]

Yet in the months following the March day when Thomas Jefferson walked from his New Jersey Avenue boardinghouse to the Capitol to be sworn in as the third President of the United States, Washington began to taste a little of the long-hoped-for prosperity. Anxiety lest Congress vote to move to another locality subsided as the federal Treasury poured money into the completion of the building for the State and War Departments, furnishing the Executive Mansion, adding to the Capitol the "Oven," an elliptical chamber for the temporary accommodation of the House of Representatives, constructing barracks for the Marine Corps, and readying the Navy Yard for outfitting ships. Sale of public lots, it is true, lagged. The commissioners,

[9] Irving Brant, *James Madison, Secretary of State, 1800-1809*, pp. 21-33; *Annals*, 6C, 2S, pp. 1552-55, 1563-65; Walter S. Cox, "Efforts to Obtain a Code of Laws for the District of Columbia," CHS *Rec*, III, 115-16.

obliged to raise money to meet payment due on the government's debt to Maryland, held two auctions during 1801 without netting for some of the land as much as the purchase price of 1791. But in spite of that sign that Americans elsewhere lacked faith in the city, and in spite of renewed controversy about what was public and what private property, business in Washington quickened. New dry goods, grocery, and jewelry shops opened. Additional boardinghouses began to compete with those on New Jersey Avenue and with Pontius S. Stelle's hotel on Capitol Square, Tunnicliffe's Tavern nearby, and the inns on Pennsylvania Avenue. New establishments also appeared in Georgetown. Andrew MacDonald's Mechanics' Hall offered men who did not "think themselves above a mechanic," several "genteel rooms, with fireplaces," and a ready supply of beer and porter. Before the end of the year Washington had 599 habitable houses, and rentals were bringing an annual 20 percent return on the investment. "No town in the Union," asserted the *Intelligencer*, "has advanced so rapidly."[10]

Moreover when the Potomac Company in 1802, after seventeen years of work, completed the locks and canal around the Great Falls above Georgetown, merchants in all three District cities anticipated an unparalleled growth of trade with the hinterland. Although Thomas Law had lost most of the fortune he had invested in Washington real estate in the 1790's, he and several associates seized upon what appeared to be a new opportunity. They obtained from Congress a charter to dig a canal from the Tiber to the Eastern Branch below the Navy Yard. L'Enfant's plan had included such a canal but, for want of money, the commissioners had abandoned the scheme in 1792. It promised to enable shippers to move upcountry grain and flour across the city from the mouth of Tiber Creek to ocean-going vessels docked on the Eastern Branch and thence to transport imports inland without risking the dangers of sailing

[10] *Annals*, 7C, 2S, pp. 1304-16; *N.I.*, 15, 26 Dec 1800, 7 Sep, 18, 21, 28 Dec 1801, 21 Jul, 6 Oct 1802; *American State Papers*, *Miscellaneous*, I, 219, 221, 254, 257, 260, 330-38 (hereafter cited as *ASP*, *Misc*); Comrs' Prcdgs, 27 May, 20 Jun 1801; Bryan, *Capital*, I, 518-19.

around Greenleaf's Point and beating upstream against the current. Promoters believed the Washington Canal Company would enable the city to compete commercially with Alexandria and Georgetown.[11]

Still businessmen knew their future must be precarious as long as the political relationship of community and federal government remained unsettled. Alexandria and Georgetown had retained their city governments, but they too were uneasy. Early in 1802, however, the revival in Congress of the proposal for a single territorial government with an appointed governor and an elected legislature again showed the lack of unanimity and fierce competitiveness among the three cities. Protests against "taxation without representation" rose in all three. Alexandrians opposed also any consolidation with the Maryland section of the District: "The inhabitants of the two divisions have been long under the influence of different systems of laws, paying allegiance to different authorities . . . and [are] competitors in commerce." So great was the diversity "that no subordinate legislature can be expected to give general satisfaction." In May Washingtonians petitioned for and obtained a charter creating a municipal corporation that put them on a nearly equal political footing with their rivals but did not resolve the larger problem of District voting in national elections and representation in Congress.[12]

Within seven months of electing a city council, Washington property-owners, joined by men in Washington County, asked for a territorial government. Again Alexandria objected. At that point a Massachusetts congressman suggested retroceding the two segments of the District back to Maryland and Virginia. That plan in one form or another occupied the attention of Congress at intervals over the next four years, for important principles as well as private interests were at stake. Supporters

[11] Sanderlin, *National Project*, p. 36; *Annals*, 7C, 1S, pp. 426, 1300, 1351-55; [Thomas Law], "Observations on the Intended Canal in Washington City," CHS *Rec*, VIII, 159-68; *ASP*, *Misc*, I, 258-59.

[12] *N.I.*, 22 Jan, 5, 16 Feb 3, 24 Mar, 30 Apr, 4 Jun 1802; *Annals*, 7C, 1S, p. 463.

argued that retrocession would restore to local citizens their rights as free men and save Congress the time and annoyance of handling purely local problems. The opposition pointed to the binding character of the constitutional provision, the advantages for the area of beneficent federal rule and some citizens' avowed preference for it. Behind the eloquent words of both attackers and defenders lay implicit the thought that retrocession was but a first step on a course that would end in moving the capital to a northern city.[13] By 1808 the debate had come to revolve solely upon the desirability of transferring the government to Philadelphia. Washington, congressmen declared, would never become a metropolis; living costs were excessive, inconveniences numberless, and the "debasement" of citizens willing to sacrifice their political freedom for pecuniary gain left them with no claim to consideration. Washingtonians breathed easier when the discussion ranged so far afield that the House dropped the subject altogether.[14]

Whether, in the interest of reclaiming full political rights, any Washingtonian had ever stood ready to risk loss of the capital is doubtful. Men had invested in property in the city because here was to be the seat of government. Stripped of that privilege, Washington would wither. Alexandria, in the years ahead, would repeatedly seek to cut her ties to the federal government, and Georgetown would unsuccessfully try to return to Maryland. Citizens of Washington, on the other hand, alarmed by the talk of removing the capital, after 1806 foreswore their campaign to get a voice in national affairs. At the great public dinner celebrating Captain Meriwether Lewis' safe return from his 4,000-mile journey up the Missouri and on to the western ocean, one of the twenty-seven toasts offered was "To the District of Columbia: unrepresented in the national councils, may she never experience the want of national patron-

[13] *N.I.*, 10 Jan, 23 May 1803, 27 Feb 1804; *Annals*, 7C, 2S, pp. 426-27, 493-507, 8C, 1S, pp. 1199-1200, 8C, 2S, pp. 874-981, 9C, 1S, pp. 457-58, 532.

[14] *N.I.*, 8 Jan 1808; *Alex. Advertiser*, 20 Jan 1808; *Annals*, 10C, 1S, pp. 1531-80, 1583-96.

age." For the time being, such subtle reminders had to suffice. Washington's qualified voters saw fit to make the most of the degree of local self-government they had won.[15]

The first act of incorporation granted Washington a two-year charter. The President, empowered to appoint the mayor, chose the dignified Robert Brent, a representative of the original landed proprietors of the area. The mayor had a veto over the acts of the city council, although a three-fourths majority of both chambers might override his negative. Free white male taxpayers with a year of residence elected from the city at large a common council which then chose five of its members to serve as an upper house. Amendments in 1804 made both chambers directly elective, and a new charter in 1812 vested the choice of mayor in the hands of a twenty-man council now composed of two aldermen and three councilmen elected by voters in each of the four wards into which the city was divided. The council was to provide for support of the poor, see to repair of the streets, build bridges, safeguard health and abate nuisances, regulate licenses, establish fire wards and night patrols, levy a real estate tax, and, after 1804, it might open public schools. Local property assessment fell to presidentially appointed justices of the peace, and a superintendent, also chosen by the President, replaced the commissioners who had had charge of the sale of public lots in the city. In 1811 an attempt to override the property qualification for suffrage brought male inmates of the poor house to the polls where candidates for office paid the 25-cent property tax for each prospective supporter, and each cast his vote. The entire election was thereupon declared void. To safeguard against such disruptions in the future, the charter of 1812 limited the voters' list to names entered on the assessors' books at least two months in advance.[16]

[15] *N.I.*, 24 Dec 1802, 23 May 1803, 16 Jan 1807; *Annals*, 8C, 2S, pp. 1686-90.

[16] *Annals*, 7C, 1S, pp. 1377-80, 8C, 1S, pp. 1258-59, 12C, 1S, pp. 2284-91; H Rpt 83, 19C, 1S, Ser 14; ptn, H12A-F4.7, 13 Dec 1811, RG 233, NA (Since all petitions to the House are in RG 233, and all to the Senate in RG 46, hereafter that detail will be omitted.)

If Oliver Wolcott correctly described Washingtonians of 1800 as living "by eating each other," in time able-bodied workmen obviously found other means of survival. By 1810 the city had 5,900 white and some 860 free colored inhabitants. But in spite of that growth, material progress was slow. Ups were followed by downs, affected in part by the insecurity born of congressional flirtations with moving the capital, in part by the cutthroat competition among the District's three cities, and in part by business fluctuations in the rest of the country.[17] Yet reverses notwithstanding, belief endured that, once investment capital flowed in, the natural resources of the Potomac region would make the District of Columbia a commercial and industrial center of the United States.

In a period before men understood the perils of navigating the upper Potomac or the full difficulty of developing manufactures, that faith appeared better founded than it would look later. The riches of the Ohio Valley seemingly could flow more easily over the mountains to the Potomac than over the longer routes to Philadelphia or by way of Lake Erie and the Hudson River to New York. Furs and farm produce brought down the Potomac to tidewater would move from Alexandria, Georgetown, and, upon completion of the Washington Canal, from wharves on the Eastern Branch to Europe, the West Indies, and American seaboard markets; in due course shops along the brooks and factories at the fall line of the river above Georgetown would turn out manufactures to ship upstream and over the mountains to the West. In 1802 the Shenandoah Valley of Virginia was already supplying Alexandria with flour for export; within a ten-week period some fifty sloops and brigs cleared the port. Five years later Alexandria and Georgetown merchants between them exported $800,000 of flour during the early summer, and the entire District, according to the local press, "experienced an almost incredible addition to its commercial ability. Besides an unusual supply of tobacco, corn,

[17] *Third Census of the United States*, 1810; Clark, *Greenleaf and Law*, p. 181.

bacon, butter [and] whiskey . . . above 80,000 barrels of flour have been brought down the Potomac this season, which is more than double the quantity ever received in one season before." Optimism thus seemed warranted. But just as a prolonged struggle to raise $80,000 delayed a start on the Washington Canal until 1810, so lack of capital, men were convinced, was the one great obstacle to rapid expansion of all District enterprises.[18]

Banks appeared to be the surest source of capital. The signatures of bank officials on notes that circulated as money seemed automatically to create wealth. And insofar as credit rested on faith, in a country of boundless natural resources credit wisely used could create wealth. Persuaded that the trade of the back country would go to Baltimore and Philadelphia unless a local bank could extend credit to farmers, the Virginia Assembly had chartered the Bank of Alexandria as early as 1792, and a year later Maryland chartered the Bank of Columbia in Georgetown, primarily for use of the commissioners in charge of building the federal city. In 1801 the Bank of the United States opened a branch in Washington. Three more banks founded before 1809 brought nominal banking capital in the District to more than $1,500,000. But the demand for credit to use in building roads and canals outran the supply.[19] Nor was it only local men who saw a great commercial future awaiting the District. In considering the petition of local banking houses for more liberal charters, in 1810 a committee of the House of Representatives declared: "that the founding and erection of so extensive a city as the permanent seat of empire for the United States, must obviously require the aid of vast resources,

[18] *Alex. Advertiser*, 26 Apr, 15 Jun, 4 Nov 1802, 13 Jun 1803, 17 Jul 1807; Padover, *Jefferson*, p. 321; *N.I.*, 18 May, 1 Jun, 17 Jul 1807, 4 May 1810; "Observations on the Intended Canal," CHS *Rec*, VIII, 164; Clark, *Greenleaf and Law*, pp. 256-57; *Annals*, 10C, 1S, p. 853, 12C, 1S, pp. 2291-92.

[19] Harry E. Miller, *Banking Theories in the United States before 1860*, pp. 11-12; *N.I.*, 11 Apr, 24 Sep 1806, 19 Sep 1812; "Petition of Merchants of Alexandria, 1792," *The William and Mary Quarterly*, 2nd Series, III, (Jul 1923), pp. 206-07; Bryan, *Capital*, I, 222-23; Davis R. Dewey, *State Banking before the Civil War*, pp. 53-54, 57.

and that that consideration offers additional inducements to give the most advantageous extension to the monied capital it may possess. . . . It can no longer be doubted that, the District of Columbia is destined to an enviable, and perhaps unrivalled enjoyment of commerce."[20]

Congress granted charters giving the banks virtual carte blanche to stretch their credit resources to the limit and beyond. Furthermore, when the Senate refused to renew the charter of the Bank of the United States, the Treasury deposited most of its funds with the Bank of Columbia in Georgetown and, for a time, small amounts with other District banks. Officials of the local institutions felt themselves permanent financial agents of the federal government. Although shareholders even in the long-established Bank of Columbia had paid only part of their subscriptions, dividends in some years ran as high as 10 percent on the authorized capital.[21]

The first concern both of bankers and borrowers was to improve communication and to widen markets and sources of supply. Each city fought for herself and had no compunction about ruining her neighbors. When the federal Embargo and the later Non-Intercourse Acts halted trade with Europe, duties on District imports dropped from $124,000 to $20,000 in a single year, but common troubles failed to make common cause among the three rivals.[22] While Washingtonians struggled to finance the Washington Canal, Georgetown merchants, who were threatened by the silting up of the river channel approaching their wharves, poured money into dredging along the river front. As spreading mud banks and shallows continued to interfere with navigation, the town obtained permission from Congress to build a dam downstream where the river divided at Mason's, or Analostan, Island: a causeway from the island to the Virginia shore might divert the river's main flow so that the full force of the current would scour out the mud blocking

[20] *ASP*, *Misc.* II, 45-47.

[21] *Annals*, 11C, 2S, pp. 1368-73, 11C, 3S, pp. 837-40, 1302-25; *N.I.*, 19 Sep 1812; *ASP*, *Finance*, II, 516-17; ptn, H 12A-F4.2, 15 Mar 1812.

[22] H Doc 22, 15C, 1S, Ser 6.

the approach to Georgetown. Inasmuch as boats sailing downriver for Alexandria had always used the western channel, the causeway built during 1810 handicapped Alexandria. Nor did it greatly benefit her competitor; obstructions in the main channel withstood every effort to clear them.[23] Alexandria meanwhile got congressional approval of bridging the Potomac from the low-lying promontory on the southwestern shore to the foot of Maryland Avenue in Washington. Although Georgetowners and Washingtonians who owned property near the mouth of the Tiber Creek argued that a bridge would impede river navigation, the bridge when completed in 1809 halved the distance by road from the capital to Alexandria. And roads were only less important than waterways in opening up trade. Alexandrians built several highways westward and a road to "Bridge Point," while across the Potomac companies undertook the construction of turnpikes northward toward Baltimore and Montgomery.[24]

Visions of turning the District into a manufacturing center, however, remained only visionary. Craftsmen turned out articles by hand for local purchasers—hats, boots, and shoes, some furniture and nails, a little tinware, rope for ships' rigging, a few firearms from an Alexandria gunsmithy, beer brewed in the building that Thomas Law had erected for a sugar refinery at Greenleaf's Point, and, after 1807, window panes made by Bohemian workmen in the "Glass House" near Easby's Point on the Potomac.[25] When Jefferson's Embargo Act gave impetus to making the United States "independent of the workshops of Europe," Samuel Harrison Smith declared that in pursuing an

[23] *Annals*, 8C, 2S, pp. 711-21, 792-807, 809-11, 1660; *Ordinances of the Corporation of Georgetown*, 16 Jun 10, pp. 244-45; *Alexandria Gazette*, 6 Jun 1811.

[24] *Annals*, 7C, 1S, pp. 349, 422, 424, 8C, 2S, pp. 1175-76, 10C, 1S, pp. 2819-26, 2854-57, 10C, 2S, pp. 1837-55, 11C, 2S, pp. 2530-40, 12C, 1S, pp. 2319-22; *N.I.*, 8 Feb 1808, 17 Feb, 23 May 1809; ptn, H11A-F3.3, 19 Dec 1809.

[25] Clark, *Greenleaf and Law*, p. 146; *N.I.*, 11 Mar 1801, 5 Dec 1803, 22 Jul 1807; David B. Warden, *Chorographical Description*, p. 78; *ASP*, *Finance*, II, 812; Robert H. Harkness, "The Old Glass House," CHS *Rec*, XVIII, 218-21.

object "at once local and national . . . few towns in the Union have greater natural advantages."[26] In June 1808 Mayor Brent called a public meeting to formulate plans for a company to manufacture "cotton, wool, hemp and flax." While Alexandrians, unwilling to join in Washington's venture, organized their own cotton companies, Samuel Harrison Smith, Judge Cranch, and Dr. Cornelius Coningham obtained 400 subscriptions to the Columbia Manufacturing Company. The shop opened on Pennsylvania Avenue between 14th and 15th Streets. But, like similar attempts at home manufactures in other parts of the country, the local companies went out of business before 1813.[27]

Although private industrial enterprise proved abortive, a variety of government undertakings spurred Washington's growth. Men who had originally come for business careers were frequently drawn into government service either by choice or necessity. So William Cranch became a federal judge; Tobias Lear, his mercantile venture ruined, accepted assignment in the consular service; and Samuel Harrison Smith, after illness obliged him to sell the *National Intelligencer* in 1810, kept his recently acquired presidency of the Bank of Washington but also became federal commissioner of revenue in 1813. The chief manufacturing establishment in the city was the Navy Yard. Until 1806 it was limited to equipping and repairing ships, but that year a commission to build fifty gunboats opened up jobs for 175 civilian workmen at pay that for some ran as high as $1.81 a day. Navy Yard orders kept two local rope-walks busy and benefited whiskey dealers, for workmen expected the equivalent of the modern coffee break, and Commandant Tingey, upon discovering how much time went into their morning visits to the grog shops, purchased 100-barrel lots of whiskey and issued "refreshments" on the job. When the Office of the Superintendent of the Indian Trade moved from Philadel-

[26] *N.I.*, 20 Jun 1808.

[27] *Ibid.*, 15, 22 Jun, 4, 13 Jul 1808, 23 Aug. 20, 24 Nov 1809, 13 Apr 1813; *Alexandria Gazette*, 20 Oct 1809.

phia to Georgetown in 1808, that government installation also created business for local suppliers. Shipments of kettles, blankets, and smaller articles went from the warehouse on Falls Street to government factors in the West, who were to trade them for furs without cheating the Indians. On Greenleaf's Point the building of ordnance storehouses and powder caches held out prospects for a manufacturing arsenal there.

Perhaps most reassuring of all to the city was the construction of the south wing of the Capitol and completion of the Senate wing. Under the direction of the talented architect Benjamin Latrobe, skilled workmen built the chamber for the House of Representatives. At the instigation of President Jefferson, Guiseppe Franzoni and Giovanni Andrei came from Carrara, Italy, to carve the decorative stone work of the building's interior, notably the slender fluted columns that Latrobe designed, using corn tassles instead of acanthus leaves for the motif of the capitals. "These capitals," Latrobe noted wryly, "obtained me more applause from members of Congress than all the works of magnitude or difficulty that surrounded them."[28]

As the community acquired some sense of permanence, churches began to rise. At first the chamber of the House of Representatives did duty. There, in an atmosphere more social than religious, chaplains of Congress or visiting ministers of every denomination preached from the Speaker's desk, and the Marine Band, resplendent in uniform, played "pieces of psalmody." People who preferred more formal services might journey to Georgetown or perhaps join the small group of Scottish Presbyterians who worshipped in a corridor of the Treasury. In 1806 St. Patrick's Roman Catholic Church on F Street was consecrated and by 1810 an organ installed. A converted tobacco warehouse on New Jersey Avenue bought from Daniel Carroll served Episcopalians of Washington parish

[28] Padover, *Jefferson*, pp. 355, 462; Anthony G. Dietz, "The Government Factory System and the Indian Trade," pp. 146-63 (M.A. Thesis, 1953, American Univ.); Henry B. Hibben, *Navy Yard, Washington, History from Organization, 1799, to Present Date*, pp. 33-39, 47; Bryan, *Capital*, I, 526-27; Warden, *Chorographical Description*, 45-46.

until Benjamin Latrobe in 1807 completed Christ Church on southeast G Street. Methodists then moved into the warehouse until they in turn erected a church near the Navy Yard. A Society of Friends built a meetinghouse on I Street in 1808, a Baptist church rose on F Street, a Presbyterian church nearby, and later a second south of the Capitol. Except for St. Patrick's and the exquisitely proportioned Christ Church, none of these buildings had architectural distinction. Indeed the congregations were generally poor, and several pastors, the rector of Christ Church included, ministered to their flocks on Sundays but kept the wolf from their own doors during the week by holding clerkships in the Treasury Department.[29]

While government jobs and government enterprises were Washington's mainstay, congressional refusal after 1801 to spend money on improving the federal city was a constant source of irritation of local taxpayers. Most of the streets were little more than paths. If a person lodging west of the President's House wished to call upon friends living near the Navy Yard, he must walk or ride over three or four miles of rough rutted roads deep in mud or thick with dust. At night the journey was hazardous; pot-holes and tree stumps threatened to overturn carriages; most of the thoroughfares lay in utter darkness and the feeble light of the occasional oil lamp near a government building intensified rather than lessened the blackness beyond. Like Americans, foreign visitors invariably complained bitterly about these discomforts and, unlike their hosts, tended to see in the very layout of the capital a sign of American delusions of grandeur.[30] The satirical verses of the Irish poet, Thomas

[29] Charles Jared Ingersoll, *Inchiquin, the Jesuit's Letters*, p. 53; *Annals*, 7C, 1S, p. 1096, 10C, 2S, pp. 856-57; Ethan Allen, Sketch of Washington Parish, 1794-1855, D.C. Miscellany; William P. and Julia P. Cutler, *Life, Journals, and Correspondence of Rev. Manasseh Cutler, L.L.D.*, II, 183; *N.I.*, 15, 25 May 1801, 4 Mar 1803, 28 May 1806, 5 Aug 1807; John Haskins, "Music in the District of Columbia, 1800-1814," p. 7 (M.A. Thesis, 1952, Catholic Univ.). For a more detailed account of the churches see Bryan, *Capital*, I, 84-88, 599-607.

[30] Padover, *Jefferson*, pp. 222-23, 230; Charles William Janson, *The Stranger in America*, 1792-1806, ed. Carl S. Driver, pp. 209-14; Augustus John Foster, *Jeffersonian America, Notes on the United States of America*,

Moore, who visited Washington in 1804, ridiculed the pretentiousness of the straggling untidy little city:

> Where tribunes rule, where dusky Davi bow,
> And what was Goose Creek once is Tiber now:
> This embryo capital, where Fancy sees
> Squares in morasses, obelisks in trees;
> Where second-sighted seers e'en now adorn
> With shrines unbuilt and heroes yet unborn
> Though now but woods—and Jefferson—they see
> Where streets should run and sages ought to be.[31]

Except for approving President Jefferson's request to plant Lombardy poplars along the avenue from the Treasury to the Capitol and in 1807 appropriating $3,000 for repairs to that thoroughfare, Congress left to local taxpayers the entire burden of grading and gravelling the streets. As L'Enfant's plan called for avenues 160 feet wide and streets not less than 80, the cost of paving was far too high for a city of perhaps 350 taxpayers. The most valuable real estate was federally owned and therefore tax-exempt.[32] Yet as long as proposals were recurring on the Hill to return the capital to Philadelphia, local property-owners saw the wisdom of making Washington as comfortable as possible for Congress. After the Embargo Act passed, moreover, talk of New England secession from the Union, while not wholly believed, caused enough uneasiness in Washington to suggest the folly of criticizing a harried Congress for neglect of the city. After a final temperate plea for federal funds Mayor Brent dropped the matter.[33]

The streets and avenues, by the terms of the proprietors' agreement with the President in 1791, were clearly federal

---

Collected in the Years 1805-6-7 and 11-12, ed. Richard Beale Davis, p. 86; Christian Hines, *Early Recollections of Washington City*, p. 20.

31 Quoted in Beckles Willson, *Friendly Relations, A Narrative of Britain's Ministers and Ambassadors to America* (*1791-1930*), p. 97.

32 M. B. Smith, *First Forty Years*, p. 394; *Annals*, 7C, 2S, pp. 1601-02, 8C, 2S, p. 1662, 9C, 1S, p. 1284, 9C, 2S, pp. 1272-73, 11C, 2S, pp. 2583-84.

33 Brant, *Madison, Secretary*, pp. 414, 415; and *James Madison, the President, 1809-1812*, pp. 475-78; Padover, *Jefferson*, p. 384.

property, but individual subscriptions paid for a sidewalk along part of F Street, municipal taxes paved one or two other stretches, and, all told, expenditures on highways and bridges represented in most years a sizable part of the city's annual budget—in 1805-1806, for example, nearly $4,300 out of $9,000 collected in taxes and license fees.[34] The fiscal powers vested in county officials further complicated Washington's finances. Inasmuch as Congress perpetuated the levy courts, originally an eighteenth-century Maryland and Virginia institution charged with collecting taxes, building roads, and keeping order in rural areas, presidentially appointed justices of the peace continued to assess city as well as county property-owners. Fortunately for Washingtonians clarification of the law in 1812 relieved them of all county charges except "general" expenses. The municipal tax rate was set at 25 cents on every $100 of assessed valuation until 1808, at 50 cents thereafter. License fees brought in nearly a third of the city's yearly income; the charges for retail stores and "ordinaries" netted the largest amount, "pleasurable" carriages and hackney coaches another several hundred dollars, and imposts on slaves and on "all animals of the dog kind" most of the rest. Still all sources together failed to produce adequate revenue. Within two years of her incorporation Washington had to borrow money. The theme of municipal poverty that would dominate most periods of the city's history for the next eighty years had taken form by 1804.[35]

Indeed the attitude of many members of Congress suggested that they expected Washington to embody all the graces and conveniences they had enjoyed in the wealthiest and second largest city in the country. Without financial assistance that expectation was patently unreasonable. A new city could not afford water works like Philadelphia's. The corporation dug

[34] *N.I.*, 1 Jun 1803, 2 Jun 1806; Comrs' Prcdgs, 23, 27 May 1800; Padover, *Jefferson*, pp. 229-30, 273-75; *Acts of the Corporation of the City of Washington*, 9 Sep 1805, 4 Nov 1807, (hereafter cited as *Wshg Acts*).

[35] *Wshg Acts*, 22 Jun 1804, 30 Apr 1805, 17 Apr 1806, 4 Nov 1807, 25 May, 28 Sep, 8 Nov 1808, 4 Aug 1809, 18 Aug 1810; *Annals*, 12C, 1S, pp. 2341-44.

wells in the public squares and engaged a "pump mender," but only householders on two blocks of lower Pennsylvania Avenue had piped water brought into their dwellings at their own expense from a spring in the neighborhood. The municipality had to protect as best it could both federal and private property. Although major crime was rare and ordinarily most of the occupants of the county jail were insolvent debtors and runaway slaves, Washington was overrun with petty thieves. More than one federal official followed President Jefferson's example of spending the summer months away from the capital, leaving untenanted houses prey to the burglar. A single officer strove to police the area from Rock Creek to the Navy Yard until Mayor Brent and the council doubled the force in 1811. Whether one man or two, the police had the further responsibility of inspecting the fire buckets of the volunteer fire companies and of enforcing the few sanitary regulations designed to prevent the spread of dysentery, yellow fever, small pox, and malaria in a city dotted with swampy stretches and pools of stagnant water.[36] Probably the community's most distressing burden, however, was relief of the poor, including the "transient paupers" for whom Congress made no provision.

Why a new city should contain a disproportionate number of needy people was a question no one could answer with certainty. Benjamin Latrobe, while supervising construction of the south wing of the Capitol, wrote indignantly of the troubles of workmen brought to the city to work on public buildings and then left high and dry when Congress failed to appropriate money to complete the work. The states, inheritors of the English legal system, accepted the principle embodied in the Elizabethan poor laws that cities and parishes need not support "transient paupers"; the care of those who could not be shipped home fell to the states. Because Congress recognized no similar obligation to the District of Columbia, transients stranded penniless in

[36] Allen C. Clark, "The Mayoralty of Robert Brent," CHS *Rec*, XXXIII-IV, 269; *N.I.*, 12 Jan, 8 Aug, 12, 28 Sep 1803, 2 Aug, 19 Oct 1805; *Wshg Acts*, 20 Aug 1803, 24 Jul 1804, 28 Sep, 6 Dec 1808, 1, 18, 31 May 1811; Foster, *Jeffersonian America*, pp. 8, 105; Brant, *Madison, Secretary*, p. 42.

Washington became a charge upon the thin municipal purse. In 1802 about 42 percent of the city's revenues went for poor relief, 28 percent the following year, and $1,700, plus $51 for "lunatics," out of the $10,000 budget of 1806. While Mayor Brent engaged a physician and appointed Trustees of the Poor to determine who should receive help, the city council authorized the trustees to issue clothing bought from public funds, to pay over to needy "resident families" a sum not to exceed $2 a week each, and to contract for room and board for single persons either in private households, at the Washington County almshouse, or after 1809 at the city poorhouse built at 6th and M Streets on the city's northern rim. To supplement these provisions, charitable citizens organized systematic canvasses for voluntary contributions, and during the particularly severe winter of 1810 the Washington Benevolent Society of Young Men established a regular fund "to alleviate the distresses" of the poor.[37]

In spite of the financial pressures upon the city, in 1804 leading citizens petitioned for the right to establish a tax-supported school system. They were doubtless influenced by hopes that Congress would found a national university in the capital and thus turn the city into a center of American cultural and intellectual life. Common schools would form the base of an educational pyramid with a college and a federally financed university at the top. President Washington had set aside nineteen acres of land in the city for a national university and had willed his shares in the Potomac Company for its support, but Congress delayed action until the stock was worthless and then, under pressure from extreme states' rights advocates, concluded that the Constitution forbade an appropriation for such a purpose.[38] No congressman, on the other hand, objected to the municipal-

[37] *N.I.*, 1 Nov 1802, 1 Jun 7, 12 Sep 1803, 30 May 1804, 21, 23 Jan 1805, 2 Jun 1806, 29 Nov 10, 25 Jun 1811; *Wshg Acts*, 31 Oct 1806, 30 May 1808, 23 May 1809, 9 Jan 1811, 11 Aug 1812; Latrobe, *Journal*, pp. 131-32.

[38] *ASP*, *Misc*, I, 153-54; *Annals*, 7C, 2S, p. 426, 11C, 3S, pp. 13-14, 976-77; Public Schools, Minutes of the Board of Trustees, 1805-1818, pp. 44-45 (hereafter cited as School Trustee Min).

ity's paying for public schools. When the city council discovered that it could not expect federal financial help, certainly none comparable to the grants of public land for schools in the territories, free education seemed for a time to be a luxury the city could not afford; one councilman argued that to settle a "large salary" on a "professor" was merely to encourage him to sloth. Most communities outside New England still considered the education of children a private, not a public, responsibility. Nevertheless in December 1804 the city enacted a measure turning over to elected trustees for public schools $1,500 annually from the license fees for hacks, peddlers, taverns, dogs, and slaves. Six months later when private subscriptions from 190 individuals had brought in an additional $4,000, Thomas Jefferson, Mayor Brent, Captain Thomas Tingey, Judge Cranch, Samuel Harrison Smith, and eight other distinguished citizens became trustees of the "Permanent Institution for the Education of Youth."[39]

The scope of the school system thus started soon proved far narrower than the board of trustees had intended. Because "most of the plans projected in the city have failed principally from undertaking them before the necessary means were acquired," the trustees chose initially to provide free schooling only for poor children; those whose parents could afford tuition were to pay. Negro children were excluded not by any rule but as a matter of course. Free pupils were to get instruction in the three R's and grammar; pay pupils were to have geography and Latin lessons as well. Every poor child must apply for admission, but the trustees hoped to impose secrecy upon the teachers about his charity status. This attempt to combine public and private education would end in fastening upon the institutions the label "pauper schools" to which self-respecting parents would not send their children. Yet in 1805 the arrangement was probably the only one feasible. Most of the fund raised by subscriptions was to go into two schoolhouses, one

[39] *N.I.*, 29 Jun, 17, 22 Aug 1804, 17 Jul, 7 Aug 1805; *Wshg Acts*, 5 Dec 1804.

near the Capitol, the other near the President's House. For teaching six to eight hours five days a week forty-seven weeks of the year, two principals were to receive annual salaries of $500, two assistants $250 to $300 each.

The western school opened in February 1806 in a rented building on Pennsylvania Avenue between 17th and 18th Streets, the eastern school in May in one of Daniel Carroll's row houses on 1st Street, where the Library of Congress stands today. President Jefferson later allowed the trustees to build on land belonging to the United States, but the cost, nearly $1,600, exceeded the funds subscribed and collected. The trustees then cancelled the fixed salaries and let the principals instead pocket all tuition fees and $20 for each "pauper." Still expenses ran so high that taxpayers complained of the wild extravagances that ate up 15 percent of the municipal budget. The council thereupon cut the city's contribution from $1,500 to $800. The trustees, unable to get the cut restored and consequently unable to support the "institution for the education of youth in anything like a state of respectability," reluctantly decided to resort to a Lancastrian school where one teacher could preside over a hundred or more children and the older pupils instruct the younger. Georgetown already had a successful Lancastrian school in operation. An experienced teacher brought over from England should be able to make the scheme work in Washington, releasing funds for two academies for more advanced scholars. With the help of money raised by a lottery, two Lancastrian schools opened in 1812, but their quality was disappointing. Private schools meanwhile were multiplying; interest in free public education was clearly on the wane. The trustees of the Permanent Institution for the Education of Youth declared their functions ended, killed by public indifference.[40]

Sophisticated Europeans dismayed at the physical incon-

[40] School Trustee Min, pp. 22-27, 54, 65-67, 75, 182-203; *N.I.*, 23 Aug, 29 Sep 1805, 16 May, 17 Dec 1806, 29 May 1807, 10 Nov 1809, 18 Jul 1811, 5 May, 23 Aug 1812; *Wshg Acts*, 29 Oct 1808; *Special Report of the Commissioner of Education*, 1870, H Ex Doc 315, 41C, 2S, pp. 51-52, Ser 1427.

veniences of the new capital were prone to be even more critical of the paucity of the city's social amenities. Diversions were few: shooting the wild geese, ducks, and snipe in the tidal swamps along Tiber Creek; during a week in autumn the Washington Jockey Club races; besides an occasional official ball, the dancing assemblies held once or twice a month at 5:30 in the afternoon; public dinners in honor of public heroes at which the amount of whiskey and rum consumed would have floored twentieth-century topers; the plays presented at the Washington Theatre by the Philadelphia Company on its annual two-month tour; and the "olios," or potpourri of recitations, musical numbers, and acrobatic acts given whenever an enterprising impresario assisted by itinerant "artists" felt he could secure an audience. Built by subscription on land given by John Van Ness, husband of David Burnes' daughter and heir Marcia, the theatre was ill-equipped—a "miserable little rope-walking theatre," a disdainful Englishman called it. The plays ranged from abbreviated versions of Shakespeare and Sheridan to liberal adaptations of popular English melodrama, and, once in 1810, an original local product, *Child of Feeling*, written by George Watterston, a future Librarian of Congress. Annually when John Tayloe, famed for his wealth, his beautiful residence, the Octagon House, and his blooded horses, entered his trotters at the Jockey Club meets, the halls of Congress emptied, no matter what important public business was pending. At the track laid out in a field north of the city "persons of all descriptions from the president and chief officers of state, down to their negro slaves, . . . collected together, driving full speed about the course, shouting, betting, drinking, quarrelling and fighting."[41]

Bookshops carried the latest novels, tomes like *Malthus on Population* and Parson Weems' *The Private Life of George*

[41] Wm. Plumer to Daniel Plumer, 15 Nov 1803, Plumer Mss; *N.I.*, 23 Apr, 24 Jun 1803, 9 Sep, 2 Dec 1805, 27 Oct 1806, Jan 1807, 3 Jul 1809; Foster, *Jeffersonian America*, pp. 37-38; Janson, *Stranger in America*, pp. 215-17; Haskins, "Music in the District," pp. 14-56; Ingersoll, *Jesuit's Letters*, p. 43; "Dr. Mitchill's Letters from Washington, 1801-1813," *Harpers New Monthly Magazine*, LVIII, Apr 1879, pp. 740-47.

Washington priced at 87½ cents. Local printers advertised for backing to publish Benjamin Franklin's writings and other informing works, while the Library of Congress, with an annual appropriation of $1,000 for book purchases, enlarged the city's literary resources. Neighbors in the Navy Yard section formed a book-buying club in 1805, and six years later 200 subscribers founded the Washington Library Company. On Saturday afternoons between May and November the Marine Band gave public outdoor concerts, usually in the grounds about the President's House, but even after the addition of two French horns, two clarinets, a bassoon, and a bass drum, the performances so offended President Jefferson's trained ear that he set negotiations afoot to enlist Italian musicians. In 1805 eighteen Italian players led by Gaetani Carusi arrived, only then to be ensnarled in military red tape until all but a half-dozen of the newcomers resigned. The quality of the concerts nevertheless improved. At intervals talented artists visited the new capital. Gilbert Stuart painted some of his finest portraits during his two-year sojourn here. J. D. Mollot, the miniaturist, Charles St. Memin, whose enchanting crayons have given immortality to people who would otherwise long ago have been forgotten, and David Boudon of Geneva, a specialist in "profiles in water color," also found appreciative patrons. Both St. Memin and Boudon painted some of the Indian chiefs in Washington during the winter of 1806. Travelled people, however, were very much aware of the contrasts between the new capital and Philadelphia, to say nothing of great European cities.[42]

The lack of official pomp in the Jeffersonian capital, furthermore, often shocked foreigners. When John Merry, His Britannic Majesty's minister to the United States, went in full dress to present his credentials, he was horrified to be received by the American chief of state attired in "an old brown coat, red waistcoat, old corduroy small clothes much soiled, woolen hose and

[42] *N.I.*, 6 Feb 1805, 28 Sep 1811 and advertisements, 1801-1812; Haskins, "Music in the District," pp. 7-9; *Annals*, 9C, 1S, p. 1227; Anne Hollingsworth Wharton, *Social Life in the Early Republic*, pp. 143-44.

slippers without heels." "Toujours Gai," as the French minister dubbed the pompous Merry, was further incensed at the President's escorting Mrs. James Madison to the seat of honor at a state dinner and at his later announcement that the order at all official functions thence-forward would be "pele-mele," in order to make clear that European court rules of precedence had no place in a republic.[43] Augustus Foster, Merry's aide, while recognizing Jefferson's behavior as partly political pose, was so irked by the brash manners, slovenly dress, and the addiction to chewing tobacco he observed among Americans that he declared "to judge from their Congress, one should suppose the nation to be the most blackguard society that was ever brought together." An official dispatch to London in 1807 commented that "the excess of the democratic ferment in this people is conspicuously evinced by the dregs having got up to the top."[44]

On the other hand, Americans who stayed more than a few days in the city generally found Washington delightful. Anyone and everyone felt free to approach the President. On New Year's day not only political leaders and the rich and well-born but also relatively humble citizens flocked to the Executive Mansion to pay their respects. As late as 1805 guests could still partake of the mammoth 1,600-pound cheese which Republicans of Cheshire, Massachusetts, had made from the milk of "Republican" cows and delivered by ox-drawn sledge to the President during his first winter in office.[45] President Jefferson, "appearing like a tall large-boned farmer," dispensed with the afternoon levees his predecessors had held in Philadelphia and reduced the number of state dinners, but his informal hospitality was gracious. His steward remarked, "it sometimes cost fifty dollars a day to provide for his many guests." They gathered around his dinner table at four in the afternoon and, after

[43] Willson, *Friendly Relations*, pp. 40-48.

[44] Quoted in Brant, *Madison, Secretary*, p. 405; Foster, *Jeffersonian America*, pp. 55-57.

[45] Wm Plumer to Samuel Plumer, 7 Dec 1802, and to Daniel Plumer, 9 Dec 1802, Plumer Mss; Cutler, *Life of Manasseh Cutler*, II, 54n; *N.I.*, 7 Jul 1802, 6 Jul 1803, 8 Jul 1805, 4 Jan 1808.

enjoying the fine wines and the choice dishes prepared by the President's French chef, they often stayed on and talked till night. Whether European savants, American men of letters, or well-informed politicians, the people privileged to share in the sparkling wide-ranging conversation around that board never deplored the lack of ceremony.[46]

Augustus Foster himself later confessed that of all the places he had visited in the United States, Washington was "the most agreeable town to reside in for any length of time." The drawing room of Secretary of State and Mrs. Madison early became a favorite social rendezvous. To their house on F Street two blocks from the Treasury came every distinguished newcomer and countless friends, drawn by their host's wisdom and fund of amusing anecdotes and by "Dolly's" warmth. When Madison became President, entertaining took on slightly greater formality at what, by 1809, was coming to be called the White House, but the first lady, "a woman . . . esteemed and admired by the rich and beloved by the poor," still put every guest at ease. "Being so low of stature," observed a contemporary, the President "was in imminent danger of being confounded with the plebeian crowd and [at White House levees] was pushed and jostled about like a common citizen—but not so her ladyship. The towering feathers and excessive throng distinctly pointed out her station wherever she moved." The timid, inexperienced daughter of a government clerk received from Mrs. Madison as cordial a welcome as the European dignitary or the Washington banker. And well-bred Washingtonians and Georgetowners without public posts were as much part of federal society as officeholders. The most eminent figures of the day gathered at the Samuel Harrison Smiths' to converse, engage in a game of whist or chess, and enjoy "Silky Milky's" excellent cellar. Congressmen, living as most of them did in boardinghouses, frequently dropped in for tea or for supper at the houses of friends. Conversation, though more likely to center on politics than the

[46] Anne Hollingsworth Wharton, *Salons Colonial and Republican*, pp. 188-90; "Dr. Mitchill's Letters," pp. 742-47.

arts or sciences, was stimulating, none the less so for extending occasionally to the scandalous behavior of Eliza Custis Law in deserting her elderly husband or to the future of Betsy Patterson Bonaparte, whose spouse, Jerome, at the order of his brother the Emperor abandoned her for a throne. Men always far outnumbered women, but some officials brought their families for the height of the "season," and their daughters and the local belles turned the capital, in Foster's phrase, into "one of the most marrying places of the whole continent."[47]

There were often curious sights in this outwardly primitive little capital. On the President's lawn, cages contained the grizzly bears that Meriwether Lewis, head of the famous exploring expedition to the far West, had brought back from the Rockies. Foreign diplomats were as fascinated as Washingtonians by the Osage and Sac chiefs and braves with partly shaven heads and gaudily painted faces and bodies who came, accompanied by their squaws, to negotiate with the white man's government. What the squaws should wear to the President's reception created an official quandary finally resolved by the wife of the Secretary of War: she selected flowered chintz skirts and wide petticoats; what besides, deponent sayeth not. The Tunisian envoy and "his splendid and numerous suite," wrote Margaret Bayard Smith, also delighted the public. "Their turbaned heads, their bearded faces, their Turkish costume, rich as silk, velvet, cashmere, gold and pearls could make it, attracted more general and marked attention than the more familiar appearance of the European ministers." Still the glitter of the gold lace and orders set in diamonds ornamenting the European *corps diplomatique* on state occasions was scarcely less breathtaking.[48]

[47] Foster, *Jeffersonian America*, pp. 84-85; Brant, *Madison, The President*, pp. 32-33, 288; Wharton, *Salons*, p. 203, and *Social Life*, pp. 145-47; *N.I.*, 8 Mar 1809, 6 Jul 1811; see also *Dictionary of American Biography* for S. H. Smith.

[48] Foster, *Jeffersonian America*, pp. 31-35, 288; M. B. Smith, *First Forty Years*, pp. 393-403, and for quotation, Common Place Book, n.d., M. B. Smith Mss; Wharton, *Salons*, pp. 194-95.

Above all, it was the charm and intelligence of the people in the capital of those early years that made Washington agreeable. It is easy to overromanticize the era. Unpleasantly self-assertive boors also collected here, some of them intelligent, some merely rude. Attention to dress and use of soap and water was frequently sketchy. Even the gentlemen whose snowy neckcloths and blue brass-buttoned coats look immaculate in Gilbert Stuart's portraits probably rarely wore spotless clothes, and, in a world where chewing tobacco was replacing snuff, waistcoats stained with tobacco juice must have been commonplace. Water brought by the bucket from wells in the public squares was not to be used lavishly in most households. Augustus Foster indeed wrinkled his patrician nose over several southern belles who substituted applications of powder for bathing; he took the precaution of supplying the ladies' room at the legation with a selection of white, pink, and lavendar powders.[49] Yet for all these disconcerting actualities of life, the "court circles of the Republic" in the first decade of the nineteenth century had a grace and a vitality no later generation has exceeded.

Although an acid Federalist contended that "information, riches and talents" would keep their possessor out of Congress,[50] no unbiased person belittled the attainments and the magnetism of Dr. Samuel Mitchill, member from New York, whom Jefferson nicknamed "the Congressional Dictionary," or despised the scholarship of Dr. Samuel Dana of Connecticut, or denied the perceptiveness of the affable young Henry Clay and the intellectual powers of the savage-tempered yet humane aristocrat John Randolph of Roanoke. Senators and representatives, to be sure, were rarely in Washington more than five or six months of the year, but the quality of the permanent residents in the community would have honored any city. Washington interested men as unusual as that able journalist, "Silky Milky"

49 Foster, *Jeffersonian America*, p. 85.

50 Brant, *Madison, Secretary*, p. 405.

Smith, the still little known young novelist and playwright George Watterston, and the stately, eccentric Thomas Law with his penchant for penning verse, sipping fine Madeira, and promoting the city's commerce. John Tayloe, Virginia planter and horse-breeder that he was, chose to spend part of his time in Washington, while Mayor Robert Brent and Daniel Carroll exercised a kind of courtly, albeit stiff, eighteenth-century hospitality. The man largely responsible for extending the reach of the Phi Beta Kappa Society of William and Mary College was another distinguished resident; in 1780 when British troops were overrunning Virginia, John James Beckley had carried out the plan of sending charters to Harvard and Yale "in the sure and certain hope that the Fraternity will one day rise to life everlasting and Glory immortal." From 1801 till his death in 1815 Beckley served as clerk of the House of Representatives and simultaneously as Librarian of Congress, sharing his wide knowledge of books and men with his fellow citizens. Dr. James Ewell, long Washington's foremost physician, contributed his cultivation and insights, Judge Cranch his learning, and big, bluff Thomas Tingey, Commandant of the Navy Yard for twenty-nine years, his engaging good humor. The less colorful, gentle Peter Hagner, who came in 1800 as a clerk in the War Department and would hold office till his death in 1847, added his dignified solidity and the high spirits of a houseful of children. If hostesses displayed at times a touch of the provincial, the beauty of the younger women invariably evoked the admiration of diplomats familiar with all the refinements of European courts.[51]

Gifted newcomers came, saw, and stayed. The tall impressive-looking John Van Ness of New York, after Congress refused to seat him in the House of Representatives because he

[51] Hagner Mss, Southern Historical Collection, University of North Carolina; J. Dudley Morgan, "Robert Brent, First Mayor of Washington City," CHS *Rec*, II, 236-51; "Dr. Mitchill's Letters," p. 740; Foster, *Jeffersonian America*, pp. 55-56, 85-86; Virginia Waller Davis, "Fifty Names on a Bronze Tablet, The Founders of Phi Beta Kappa," *The Key Reporter*, XXV (Summer 1960), p. 2.

had accepted a commission in the District militia, turned Washington banker and, with his beautiful young wife, made their home a center of society. Joseph Gales, Jr., energetic, British-born, and North Carolina-bred, arrived in 1807 to work on the *National Intelligencer*, bought the paper in 1810, and two years later brought his brother-in-law, William Seaton, to Washington. Gales was short in stature, round-faced, and, except for his eyes, generally unprepossessing in appearance, but his knowledge of men, his journalistic talents, and his warm-hearted interest in other people made him both respected and beloved. The debonair William Winston Seaton and his witty, intelligent wife quickly came to occupy a very special place in the society of the capital. Seaton, as tall and handsome as Gales was small and homely, had inherited from distinguished Virginia forebears an intellectual perception and graceful manners that won him friends everywhere and put him later in life into office as mayor of the city five times over.[52]

People born and bred in Maryland, Virginia, and farther south predominated in the new capital, but sectional differences over slavery had not yet arisen to strain the urbanity of social relations. Apparently neither southerners nor northerners saw any reason to discuss the matter; slavery was an inescapable, if somewhat unpleasant, fact of life in the District of Columbia. A good many southerners themselves disliked the "peculiar institution." Madison never justified or approved of it, and in 1814 Jefferson declared the republic's failure to eradicate it "a mortal reproach to us" and a source of "moral and political reprobation." Few like-minded Washingtonians felt as strongly as Edward Coles, President Madison's charming young secretary, for Coles not only freed the slaves he had inherited but moved them out of Virginia to land he gave them in Illinois, where they could live out their lives as free people. Yet manumission was not unknown in Washington, and, judging by the

[52] *ASP, Misc*, I, 336; Anne Royall, *Sketches of History, Life and Manners in the United States*, pp. 150-54; [Josephine Seaton], *William Winston Seaton of the "National Intelligencer."*

nearly sevenfold increase in the number of free Negro inhabitants between 1800 and 1810, free people of color considered the capital a friendlier, or at least a safer, place than cities farther south. The defeat of a resolution of 1805 which would have freed slaves in the District of Columbia when they reached maturity ended hopes of early congressional action, but antislavery sentiment, if indeed widespread, was not deep enough to lead the local community to vigorous protest. In fact, white householders, irrespective of conscience, found themselves largely dependent upon slave labor. Other than some of the free Negroes, virtually the only trained servants to be hired were slaves.[53]

Matter-of-fact acceptance of slavery as an institution did not, however, reconcile many a District citizen to the domestic slave trade. It forced upon residents and visitors "a scene of wretchedness and human degradation disgraceful to our characters as citizens of a free government." Coles reminded Madison of the effect upon foreign ministers of "such a revolting sight" on the streets of the nation's capital—"gangs of Negroes, some in chains, on their way to a southern market." From Alexandria, destined later to be one of the principal centers of the domestic slave trade, came a petition in 1802 vainly begging Congress to forbid "the practise of persons coming from distant parts of the United States into this district for the purpose of purchasing slaves."[54] Until 1808 when, by the terms of the Constitution, the importation of African slaves was outlawed, the volume of the trade in the District was small: an occasional sale of one or two slaves, perhaps twice a year an auction of as many as sixty, usually in Alexandria. But when cotton planters of the deep South could no longer get field hands from Africa and markets for the surplus of Virginia and Maryland planta-

[53] Ralph L. Ketcham, "The Dictates of Conscience: Edward Coles and Slavery," *Virginia Quarterly Review*, XXXVI (Winter 1960), pp. 46-62, especially p. 53 quoting ltr, Jefferson to Coles; *Annals*, 8C, 2S, pp. 995-96; Warden, *Chorographical Description*, pp. 45-46.

[54] Ketcham, "Dictates of Conscience," p. 52; *N.I.*, 22 Jan 1802.

tion owners expanded, the vested interests strengthened. Was not the right to sell one's property, human or otherwise, implicit in ownership? Gradually the trade in Washington swelled as owners of the exhausted soil of the surrounding countryside shipped their one profitable crop to dealers at the Potomac port.[55]

In 1808 mayor and council, several of whom were slaveowners, enacted Washington's first black code. By southern standards it was moderate. It imposed a $5 fine upon any colored person found on the streets or at a dance or meeting after 10 at night and decreed a whipping for a slave whose master refused to pay his fine. Uneasy over the growth of the free Negro population, an unwelcome element in most cities below the Mason-Dixon line, officials evidently concluded that irresponsible and undesirable freedmen from the rest of the South would swarm into the city if they enjoyed here privileges denied them in their native states. Yet immigration accounted for only part of the increase. Manumission added to it, and "hiring their own time," a not uncommon arrangement whereby masters allowed slaves to work independently and keep any earnings above a fixed sum, enabled ambitious, hard-working slaves over the years to buy their freedom and then that of their relatives. And unlike most of the slave states, Washington's city government permitted newly emancipated Negroes to stay on in the city. Again unlike the slave states, the municipality put no legal obstacle in the path of Negro education. In 1807 three illiterate colored men, two of them Navy Yard employees, erected a small frame schoolhouse and engaged a white man to teach Negro children. Within the next two or three years Henry Potter, an Englishman, started a second Negro school, while a colored woman taught a third on Capitol Hill, and an Englishwoman opened one in Georgetown.

In 1812 the city fathers with congressional approval authorized six-month jail sentences for free Negroes and mulattoes

[55] Walter C. Clephane, "The Local Aspects of Slavery in the District of Columbia," CHS *Rec*, III, 225; ptn, H12A-F4.7, 16 Mar 1808; *Annals*, 12C, 1S, p. 2325; *N.I.* and *Alex. Advertiser*, advertisements of sales, 1801-1812.

and forty lashes for slaves caught at "nightly and disorderly meetings." At the same time, to check over-zealous slave traders, the city council required every free Negro to register and carry with him a certificate of freedom. Without such proof he might be jailed as a runaway slave, and, by the terms of the eighteenth-century Maryland laws that Congress had fastened upon the community, unless some white man supplied evidence that the Negro was indeed free and then paid the costs of his keep while in prison, he could be sold by the federal marshal or his deputy to recoup the loss. The city ordinance offset part of the harshness of the law by affording free Negroes some protection from kidnapping. By and large, free colored families in Washington were better off than their fellows in the deep South.[56]

By 1812 Washingtonians dared believe that Congress would never move the capital from the banks of the Potomac. As that anxiety evaporated, fears that political impotence might hamstring the city's economic growth also dwindled. Population had nearly tripled since 1800. The United States Treasury was using the Bank of Columbia as its agent and thus supplying financial stability. Patience should overcome Washington's manifest drawbacks, and she would then become the chief city of the United States. True, American relations with France and England were uncertain, and war with either might be disastrous; but the United States had weathered the crises of 1807 and 1808 when Napoleon's highhandedness, the British Navy's search of American vessels on the high seas, and the attack on the *Chesapeake* in American coastal waters had made war seem unavoidable. The threat to peace in the early months of 1812 looked relatively small to people unaware of President Madison's convictions.[57] Residents of the capital watching developments in Congress felt no alarm about what the future would bring.

[56] *N.I.*, 17 Sep 1802, 9 May 1804, 8 Jun, 30 Sep 1808; *Spec Rpt Comr Educ*, 1870, pp. 195-99, Ser 1427; *Wshg Acts*, 6 Dec 1808, 16 Dec 1812; 2 *U.S. Statutes at Large*, pp. 721-27 (hereafter cited as 2 *Stat.*).

[57] See Brant, *Madison, the President*, pp. 425-51.

CHAPTER III

PHOENIX ON THE POTOMAC, 1812-1817

THE declaration of war in June 1812 came as a surprise to Washington. President Madison had long believed this course inevitable, but as month after month passed without congressional action, Washingtonians had inclined to believe with Augustus Foster, the British minister, that the United States would continue to seek peaceful redress from both France and Great Britain. On June 4 a secret ballot showed a belligerent spirit prevailing in the House of Representatives, but not until the 17th, as the deluded Foster described events, did the war party in the Senate round up a "drunken" member usually absent from important sessions and pass a resolution for war against Britain. The President signed the paper the next afternoon. When the news reached the New Jersey Avenue boardinghouses, thirty-year-old John Calhoun of South Carolina reportedly threw his arms around the neck of his friend Henry Clay, Speaker of the House, and joined by others of the congressional "mess" performed a Shawnee war dance about the table.[1]

Federalist merchants, particularly in Alexandria, decried the prying open of the "Pandora's Box" which loosed the "deadliest of evils: war with Great Britain," but much of the local public, led by "Joe" Gales of the *National Intelligencer*, apparently felt that the country had embarked upon a "National Jubilee." When war had looked imminent over the *Chesapeake* affair in 1807 and 1808, the District militia had offered fifteen companies for immediate action. Now, Federalist grumblings notwithstanding, military ardor again swept over Washington. By law, all able-bodied white male residents between the ages of 18 and 45, not excepting government clerks, were subject to service in the District militia, but Washingtonians too old for

[1] Foster, *Jeffersonian America*, pp. 96-103; Brant, *Madison the President*, pp. 421-83; Glenn Tucker, *Poltroons and Patriots, A Popular Account of the War of 1812*, I, 19.

militia duty showed their enthusiasm for the cause by forming a company of volunteers.[2]

Delight in the "National Jubilee" lasted through the autumn and winter. In spite of American reverses on the Canadian border, the surrender of Detroit, and the continuing hostility of Indian tribes aroused by Tecumseh, Canada and the West were too far away to affect daily pursuits in the capital on the Potomac. British naval raids on the Chesapeake had not yet begun, and, Secretary of War Armstrong insisted, if the enemy were eventually to set foot on American soil, the army would promptly engage him in the field. In October all Washington and Georgetown turned out in gala mood for the annual Jockey Club races. On New Year's day friends and acquaintances thronged to the White House as usual. "Mrs. Madison," wrote Mrs. William Seaton, "received in a robe of pink satin, trimmed elaborately with ermine, gold chains and clasps about her waist and wrists, and upon her head a white satin and velvet turban with a crescent in front and crowned with nodding ostrich plumes." If the President, still looking like "a schoolmaster dressed up for a funeral," felt anxieties, he hid them from his guests.[3] The diary of Michael Shiner, an ex-slave employed at the Navy Yard, described in some detail the new volunteer fire company and its dashing yellow-fringed uniforms but scarcely mentioned the war. Onlookers at the inaugural parade on March 4 remarked upon the "animating" appearance of the volunteers lining Pennsylvania Avenue in the brilliant sunshine as the District cavalry escorted the President to the Capitol; that night couples danced gaily at the ball held at Davis' Hotel.[4] A few weeks afterward light-heartedness gave way to alarm: a British fleet was blockading Chesapeake Bay.

[2] *Alex. Gazette*, 20 Jun, 18 Aug, 15 Oct, 24 Nov, 1 Dec 1812; *N.I.*, 15, 17, 20, 24 Jul 1807, 5 Dec 1808, 8, 28 Jul, 1, 6, 8, 18 Aug, 8, 10 Sep. 1812; Henry Adams, *History of the United States of America During the Administrations of Jefferson and Madison*, VI, 407-408; 2 *Stat.* 215-25; *Annals*, 7C, 2S, pp. 1575-88.

[3] *N.I.*, 3 Nov 1812; Wharton, *Salons*, p. 203, and *Life in the Early Republic*, pp. 131, 146-47.

[4] *N.I.*, 6 Mar, 2 Apr 1813; Diary of Michael Shiner, 1813-1865, entries through Mar 1813.

Early in May 1813 Rear Admiral Cockburn's tars and marines pillaged and burned Havre de Grace at the mouth of the Susquehanna, and the swaggering Cockburn sent Mrs. Madison word that "he would make his bow" at her drawing-room very soon. President Madison hastily sent troops to repair Fort Washington, twelve miles down the Potomac and the capital's chief defense against naval attack, and, in Henry Adams' scathing words, while "all the city and Georgetown (except the cabinet) . . . expected a visit from the enemy," units of the District militia encamped on the hill beyond the White House where the Naval Observatory would rise thirty years later. By July British ships were moving up the Potomac river and by the 15th were within sixty miles of Washington. The frigate and the gunboats at the Navy Yard sailed at once; army regulars accompanied by most of the District volunteer companies and several members of Congress marched for Fort Washington; and District householders packed up their effects preparatory to flight.[5] Meanwhile, more terrifying than the approach of Redcoats were the rumors of impending slave uprisings. Mrs. Samuel Harrison Smith writing from Sidney, the Smith farm on which Catholic University stands today, spoke of "our enemy at home" who would join with the British as the invaders drew near. Washington, stripped of troops, lay exposed not only to rebellious blacks but to lawless whites ready to loot the city. At this point Mayor James Blake appointed a night watch to patrol the streets after dark and, as standbys, several home defense units composed of elderly volunteers. Construction of earthworks to mount heavy guns began at Greenleaf's Point and at the Navy Yard, with a furnace at each location to supply red-hot cannon balls.

The immediate crisis passed. The British ships sailed back down the Potomac, and the militia came home. Slaves in and about Washington made no strike for freedom, although along

[5] *N.I.*, 11, 25 May, 1 Jun, 16 Jul 1813; Allen C. Clark, *Life and Letters of Dolly Madison*, p. 90; Adams, *History*, VII, 56-57.

the Chesapeake some offered their help to Admiral Cockburn only to discover too late that he was not above selling them to planters in Barbados. In the capital, as fear of the British Lion subsided, the 400-pound "Royal Tiger of Asia" on exhibit at the front of the Capitol engaged people's interest. Life resumed its normal course.[6]

Business, in fact, assumed abnormal proportions. The Secretary of the Treasury reported higher internal revenue duties paid in the District of Columbia than the sum of those in New Hampshire, Vermont, Delaware, Tennessee, and Louisiana. As military purchasing went forward and men seeking government contracts came and went, two new banks opened, the Bank of the Metropolis in Washington and the Farmers and Mechanics in Georgetown. Indeed, District bankers felt themselves in a position to offer the hard-pressed federal Treasury a loan. Disregarding the high costs of materials and workmen's demands for wage increases, hopeful investors organized new turnpike companies and a company to enlarge Georgetown's water supply. A daily evening newspaper appeared and a guide book to the capital, the first of an endless succession. Men had enough confidence in the city's future to hold a lottery with a $30,000 prize to raise a fund for building a monument to George Washington. Crews and marines from every vessel that docked spent money in the city. As ships damaged in encounters with the enemy put in for repairs, activity at the Navy Yard mounted steadily. For the first time the yard received a commission to build a frigate, a sloop of war, and a 5-gun schooner.

Although a British squadron still patrolled Chesapeake Bay, American naval successes at sea and on Lake Erie provided the occasion for public dinners in honor of Commodore William Bainbridge and Captain Oliver Hazard Perry. During the spring of 1814 when a peace mission sent to Europe reported the British terms unacceptable, apprehensions about an attack

[6] M. B. Smith, *First Forty Years*, pp. 89-91; *N.I.*, 13, 17, 19, 21, 22, 29 Jul, 17 Aug 1813; Tucker, *Poltroons*, I, 290 and 395n; *Diary of Elbridge Gerry, Jr.*, pp. 173-202.

upon the capital revived, but Secretary of War Armstrong insisted that no enemy having Baltimore within reach would invade the "sheep walk" on the Potomac.[7]

But time was running out. In June 1814 landing parties from Admiral Cockburn's ships came within twenty-two miles of Washington. The District militia took the field, only to be ordered home and mustered out after failing to locate the British. When news arrived that part of Wellington's victorious army under General Robert Ross was en route to America, the Secretary of War belatedly made half-hearted plans for the protection of the capital. Worried Washingtonians urged the President to take more vigorous measures. At the same time Alexandrians drew attention to the defenseless state of their port. The War Department undertook to align militia from neighboring states to strengthen the District forces, but, with the British harrying the Maryland and Virginia settlements on the Bay, the gesture was futile. Troops from the northern and western states had their hands full elsewhere. The ships under construction at the Navy Yard were not yet ready for launching. Sufficient arms, ammunition, tents, and food for the citizens' army were still wanting in mid-August when 4,500 British regulars landed at a town on the Patuxent River, thirty-five miles to the southeast. On Saturday, August 20, the District's ill-equipped, green militia, under the command of the easy-going Brigadier General William Winder of Baltimore, encamped near the bridge over the Eastern Branch. Mayor Blake appealed the next day for men remaining in Washington to assemble at the Capitol and march thence to dig earthworks at Bladensburg at the District line; he even begged free colored men to join the citizens' corps of workers.[8] Whites later had

[7] *N.I.*, 25 Nov 1813, 1, 26, 27 Jan, 26 Feb, 23 May, 24 Oct 1814; *Annals*, 13C, 1S, pp. 2682-99, 13C, 2S, pp. 2825-30; *A Register of Officers of the United States*, 1817, p. 89; Adams, *History*, VIII, 121; *ASP*, *Finance*, II, 847; Hibben, *Navy Yard*, pp. 49-53; Tucker, *Poltroons*, II, 525; *Alex. Gazette*, 18 Aug 1814.

[8] *N.I.*, 20, 29 Jun, 19, 25, 26, 28 Jul, 20, 23, Aug 1814; *ASP*, *Military Affairs*, I, 564; Adams, *History*, VIII, 140-42.

the grace to make grateful acknowledgment: "The free people of color of this city, acted as became patriots: there is scarcely an exception of any failing to be on the spot . . . manifesting by their exertions all the zeal of freemen. At the same time highly to their credit, conducting themselves with the utmost order and propriety."[9]

Events moved swiftly during the next days. Government clerks hurriedly packed up official papers and scoured the city for wagons to cart them to safety, householders loaded their valuables into such conveyances as they could find, and the exodus began. By Tuesday night few women and children remained in Washington. The public offices and every shop had closed that day, and while the President and Cabinet officials, after a special conference at sunrise, rode back and forth between General Winder's camp and the capital, Mrs. Madison and one or two Negro slaves at the White House filled trunks with Cabinet papers. In the blistering heat of the early afternoon of August 24 the British invaders reached the Eastern Branch at Bladensburg. "The Bladensburg Races," as angry humiliated citizens dubbed the rout of the American army, took scarcely half an hour. Mrs. Madison with Gilbert Stuart's portrait of Washington beside her in the presidential carriage drove out of the city in mid-afternoon shortly before the President's return from the battlefield; at the White House the table was already set for dinner. Winder's troops scattered over the countryside; some fled through Washington and northwestward before encamping above Tenleytown near the District line.

The Redcoats entered Washington at dusk. As they set fire to the Capitol and the President's House, Captain Tingey, Commandant of the Navy Yard, ordered the buildings, the naval stores and the newly built ships burned. A violent thunderstorm that night alone prevented a conflagration of the entire city. British troops continued the demolition the next day—the Potomac bridge, the War and Treasury buildings, and the arsenal

[9] *N.I.*, 24 Aug 1814.

at Greenleaf's Point, where an explosion of a powder cache caused virtually the only enemy casualties. Because Admiral Cockburn contended "dear Josey" Gales was a British traitor, the office of the *Intelligencer* was destroyed. Only the pleas of Dr. Thornton, Superintendent of Patents, saved the building housing the Patent Office and the Post Office; Thornton convinced the British Major that the patent models were private property and to destroy them would be a crime against civilization, like the Saracens' burning of the famous Alexandria library "for which the Turks have been ever since condemned by all enlightened nations." Later that day a tornado struck, whipping roofs off houses, toppling chimneys, and adding to the wreckage created by the British soldiers. When the invading troops withdrew that night and returned to their ships on the Patuxent, the American capital lay in ruins.[10]

The danger was by no means past. Four days later, while Washingtonians were dazedly beginning to tidy up the debris, caring for the wounded, and burying the dead, British ships sailed up the river to Alexandria; the commanding officer at Fort Washington had blown up the fortifications when he sighted the enemy squadron. The British demanded and immediately obtained the capitulation of defenseless Alexandria, and, after loading the vessels at her wharves with the flour, tobacco, cotton, sugar, and wines in her warehouses and with the goods of her citizens, dropped safely back down the Potomac with their booty. People who had remained in the District cities during the invasion now swelled the throngs of earlier refugees to the country. Sadly Margaret Bayard Smith observed: "I do not suppose the Government will ever return to Washington. All those whose property was invested in that place, will be reduced to poverty. . . . The consternation about us is general.

[10] *Annals*, 13C, 3S, pp. 305-308; M. B. Smith, *First Forty Years*, pp. 98, 109-12; Adams, *History*, VIII, 145-50; "Diary of Mrs. Thornton, Capture of Washington by the British," 20-31 Aug 1814, CHS *Rec*, XIX, 173-82; "Unwelcome Visitors to Early Washington," CHS *Rec*, I, 55-87 (a reprint of Dr. James Ewell's "Capture of Washington," in *Planters and Mariners Medical Companion*, 3rd ed); Tucker, *Poltroons*, II, 552-84; *N.I.*, 30, 31 Aug, 7, 10 Sep 1814; Hibben, *Navy Yard*, pp. 50-54.

The despondency still greater." Her only comfort was that the "negroes all hid and instead of a mutinous spirit, have never evinced so much attachment to the whites and such dread of the enemy." The British troops generally spared private property, but fear that they might overrun the entire countryside persisted for a fortnight. New Englanders who had opposed the war from the beginning and had carried on a contraband trade with Nova Scotia appeared to take an "I-told-you-so" attitude. Then a repulse of the invaders at Baltimore and in mid-September Commodore McDonough's naval victory on Lake Champlain ended the immediate anxiety, but not American humiliation.[11]

The President and the departmental officials returned to Washington within a few days of the British withdrawal. Since the Executive Mansion was a shell, the Madisons moved into the Octagon House on New York Avenue. Mrs. Smith's forebodings, nevertheless, appeared to be all too sound. That none of the foreign legations reopened heightened the trepidation of Washingtonians painfully aware of the discomforts in prospect when Congress convened in special session on September 19. Multiplying charges that the District militia had behaved with abominable cowardice mortified citizens who believed the incompetence and timidity of the Secretary of War and General Winder solely responsible for the disgraceful defeat at Bladensburg, but the accusations increased doubts that Congress would consent to stay on in so ill-protected a city. The *Intelligencer*, which with borrowed type resumed publication at the end of August, strove to forestall any plan for a temporary capital elsewhere, lest the arrangement become permanent; that move would constitute a "treacherous breach of faith" with citizens who had "laid out fortunes in the purchase of property in and about the city." The very thought filled Washingtonians with "abhorrence and astonishment." The *Intelligencer* also appealed to patriotic pride: removal of the capital from Washington

[11] *Alex. Gazette*, 15 Sep 1814; M. B. Smith, *First Forty Years*, pp. 101-15; *N.I.*, 31 Aug, 1, 4, 9 Sep 1814; Thornton Diary, CHS *Rec*, XIX, 177-81.

"would be kissing the rod an enemy has wielded." For the moment citizens could do little more than abet the work of preparing a hall where Congress could meet.[12]

The sight that greeted senators and representatives upon their return was grim. The blackened walls of the President's House, White House no longer, stood out starkly against the hill beyond, where a small force of army regulars was encamped. The Treasury and the War Department offices were almost as badly gutted as the Executive Mansion. The dome of the Capitol and the roofs of both wings lay in ashes over which towered smoke-stained walls pierced by gaping holes where windows had been. Some of the walls now bore angry inscriptions and pencil drawings: "The capital and the Union lost by cowardice"; "A______ [Armstrong, Secretary of War] sold the city for 5,000 dollars"; cartoons of the President running off without his hat or wig and of Admiral Cockburn burning hen roosts. Nothing remained of the books or papers that had formed the Library of Congress. The Navy Yard and the arsenal grounds at Greenleaf's Point were stretches of rubble. Except for the two houses George Washington had built and three or four others, private houses stood unharmed, but the only undamaged public building was the Post Office. There perforce Congress convened, the House meeting in a room so small that, although 19 of the 176 members were absent, "every spot up to the fireplace and windows" was occupied.[13]

The expected proposal to relocate the capital came almost at once. Philadelphia and Lancaster, Pennsylvania, promptly offered Congress comfortable accommodations, while the city council of Georgetown tendered the use of the seminary building and board at $10 a week instead of the $16 charged by Washington hotels. The impassioned debates in the House involved

[12] *N.I.*, 2, 4, 6, 9, 28, 30 Sep, 7, 8, 28 Oct 1814, 25 Feb 1815; Thornton Diary, CHS *Rec*, XIX, 182; M. B. Smith, *First Forty Years*, p. 115.

[13] Henry B. Fearon, *Sketches of America, A Narrative of a Journey of Five Thousand Miles through the Eastern and Western States of America*, 3rd ed., pp. 284-85; *N.I.*, 9, 16 Sep, 6 Oct 1814; *Annals*, 13C, 3S, pp. 354, 1100.

both partisan and sectional politics as well as purely patriotic considerations. Enemies of the administration were nothing loath to cause it embarrassment. Southern members could scarcely ignore the probability that a vote to move the seat of government would mean a northern capital. Reminding his listeners of the troubles that had attended the passage of the original residence act, Joseph Pearson of North Carolina warned against breaking asunder "this strongest link in the federal chain." From the first a good many representatives contended that dignity and patriotism forbade decamping from Washington even temporarily; one congressman declared he would prefer a seat under canvas in the established capital to accommodation in a palace beyond her limits. Washington bankers, furthermore, presented a telling argument: they volunteered a half-million-dollar loan to the government to enable it to rebuild the public buildings on their old sites. For three weeks the decision hung in the balance. Then, by a vote of 83 to 54, primarily sectional in character, the House rejected the bill for removal and accepted the bank loan.[14]

The Senate delayed concurrence for three and a half months. In November a young Virginian passing through the city wrote dejectedly: "The appearance of our public buildings is enough to make one cut his throat, if that were a remedy—The dissolution of the Union is the theme of almost every private conversation. . . . There is great contrariety of opinion concerning the probability of the event." In the meantime committees of Washingtonians and Alexandrians raised funds to restore Fort Washington and other District defenses and pushed the work forward rapidly. On February 3, 1815, the Senate passed the bill ordering the rebuilding of the federal offices on their former sites. News of General Andrew Jackson's victory at New Orleans reached Washington the next day. A fortnight later, in the exquisitely proportioned drawing room at the Octagon House,

[14] *Annals*, 13C, 3S, pp. 311-23, 341-42, 345-56, 357-76 (Pearson's speech), 387-98; *N.I.*, 28, 30 Sep, 1, 5, 7, 8, 10, 18 Oct 1814; D. Randall to Peter Hagner, 1 Oct 1814, Hagner Mss (SHC).

President Madison signed the peace treaty. The "most brilliant" reception Washington had ever known celebrated the occasion. As the radiant Mrs. Madison moved among her guests, Sir Charles Bagot, the British minister, declared she looked "every inch a queen." The presence of the robed justices of the Supreme Court headed by Chief Justice Marshall, Major Generals and their aides in dress uniform, and the entire diplomatic corps in full regalia, all showed, an eyewitness noted, that "the return of peace had restored the kindest feeling at home and abroad."[15] The war was over and Washington was still the national capital.

Yet some uneasiness lingered on in the city. Experience during the first decade of the century suggested that the political maneuverings which again and again had jeopardized local investments and stunted the city's growth might resume at any moment until reconstruction of the government buildings had gone too far to permit another change of plan. And perceptive residents sensed in many members of Congress the feeling which William Lowndes revealed to his wife about "this city to which so many are willing to come to and all so anxious to leave." Now and again letters to the newspapers expressed resentment at Washington's being the shuttlecock in the congressional game of battledore: so far from enjoying "that fostering patronage" which the government should have offered, the city was "the scapegoat of capricious malignity and ignorance." Another complaint declared that Congress had no concern for the District: "If a national bank is created, the head is fixed elsewhere. If a military school is to be founded, some other situation is sought. If a national university is proposed, the earnest recommendation of every successive president in its favour . . . is disregarded. . . . Every member takes care of the needs of his constituents, but we are the constituents of no one."[16]

[15] Francis Walker Gilmer to Peter Minor, Nov 1814, quoted in Richard Beale Davis, *The Abbé Correa in America, 1812-1820*, American Philosophical Society, *Transactions*, new series, XLV, Pt. 2, (1955), p. 101; *N.I.*, 2, 3, 9 Nov 1814, 7 Feb 1815; *Annals*, 13C, 1S, pp. 216-22; Wharton, *Salons*, pp. 206-207.

[16] *N.I.*, 17 Nov 1810, 29 Mar 1815, 6 Jan, 19 Mar 1816; Ggtn *Messenger*, 15 May 1816; William Lowndes to his wife, 8 Jan 1815, Lowndes Mss (SHC).

But the men with most at stake in the city chose a different tack. Convinced that congressional convenience would influence congressional attitudes toward the community, Thomas Law, Daniel Carroll, and a dozen other leading citizens in May 1815 set about erecting a substantial brick building in which Congress could meet in reasonable comfort until the Capitol was rebuilt. The brick hall, placed on the site of Tunnicliffe's Tavern where the Supreme Court stands today, was completed within six months. There the 14th Congress convened in December. Grateful contemporaries later asserted that the group who had built the "Brick Capitol" had kept the "seat of empire" in Washington. Improbable as that claim seems, certainly serious talk about moving the capital would not recur for the next half-century. Some citizens in fact came to label the British capture "a blessing in disguise." In 1817 a foreigner remarked that General Ross's visit had halted the progressive decay which had been undermining the city since 1802; she "seems to have risen, like the phoenix from the flames, and is once more partially increasing in prosperity."[17]

In actuality, once Congress had reached its decision, federal commissioners appointed in March 1815 acted with dispatch. Appropriations for replacing the public buildings were not ungenerous, and the work moved along steadily. Benjamin Latrobe returned to take charge of erecting the new Capitol, and Guiseppe Franzoni, reinforced by his brother Carlo and five or six other skilled Italians, again undertook its sculptural décor. The executive departments were able to move into their rebuilt offices within a year, the President and Mrs. James Monroe into a completely refurnished substantial new White House in September 1817. Well before then the arsenal buildings on Greenleaf's Point had been restored, and at the re-equipped Navy Yard a ship of the line was under construction. The Capitol would not be ready for occupancy until December 1819 and not finished until

[17] Thomas Law to President Madison, 7 May 1815, Madison Mss; Law, Carroll and Frederick May to Comrs, 7 May 1815, D.C. Miscellany; Clark, *Greenleaf and Law*, pp. 291-95; Fearon, *Sketches of America*, pp. 285-86; *N.I.*, 30 Mar, 3 Aug 1815, 16 Aug 1816, 17 Dec 1817.

1825, but satisfaction with the looks of the building as it rose offset disappointment.[18]

Nor was the physical reconstruction the only sign that a new Washington might be emerging. Congress lost no time in accepting Thomas Jefferson's offer to sell most of his books to replace the destroyed congressional library, and as the volumes began to arrive from Monticello President Madison appointed the Washington writer, George Watterston, to the newly created post of Librarian of Congress. By then Josiah Meigs, who had arrived in 1814 to head the General Land Office authorized just before the war, was exerting his very considerable prestige to make his organization more than a group of rule-of-thumb surveyors and a roomful of record keepers. A mathematician himself, a former preceptor at Yale College, and then President of the University of Georgia, Meigs strove to gather about him men trained or trainable in mathematics and able to make meteorological observations. About the same time the possibility of enlisting government support for scientific projects brightened when Rudolph Hassler, a Swiss-born geodesist, presented the details of his plan for an accurate coastal survey. As early as 1807 Jefferson had induced Congress to vote $50,000 for the undertaking, but the necessity of procuring instruments abroad and international complications had prevented launching the work until Hassler returned late in 1815 with specially made English equipment. Hassler spent little time in Washington either before or after approval of his plan, but the mere fact that he won endorsement for a proposal as scientific in character as it was expensive to execute encouraged faith that a new era lay ahead for the capital. John Quincy Adams would later privately label the scheme too costly to survive congressional attack, but few men of scientific bent in Washington during the last year of Madison's administration foresaw that by 1818 Congress would cut the project short. Madison's last

[18] *N.I.*, 3 Aug 1815, 16 Aug 1819; *Annals*, 14C, 2S, pp. 1280, 1300, 1336, 15C, 1S, pp. 2510, 2579-80, 15C, 2S, pp. 2526-27; H Doc 8, 18C, 2S, Ser 114.

message as President again urged the founding of a national university. That the plea met with no response in Congress failed to kill hope that a vigorous young nation whose material prosperity was growing daily would seek to make its capital a source of new intellectual and scientific achievement.[19]

In the autumn of 1816 a score of men of the stature of John Quincy Adams, Josiah Meigs, Benjamin Latrobe, and Dr. Edward Cutbush, a Navy surgeon, founded in Washington the Columbian Institute for "the promotion of arts and sciences." Amateurs like Thomas Law, Robert Brent, and Samuel Harrison Smith also were charter members of a body intended to be the Washington equivalent of the American Philosophical Society in Philadelphia. From the impetus supplied by the Institute sprang the Washington Botanical Society in 1817 and a catalogue of 296 species of flowering plants in the District. Perhaps the Abbé Correa, the newly appointed Portuguese minister, awakened special interest in botany, for he had lectured on the subject in Philadelphia and, according to Jefferson, was "without exception the most learned man I have met in any country." Congress was sufficiently impressed with the potentialities of the Columbian Institute to incorporate it in 1818 and shortly afterward to turn over to it six acres of land at the foot of Capitol Hill for a botanical garden. But botany was not the Institute's sole field. The findings of William Lambert, a clerk in the pension office, evoked considerable response, for he discussed the importance to the country of determining Washington's prime meridian in order to free American chart makers and navigators from dependence upon Greenwich, England. Years later the survey would occur, giving Meridian Hill its name. More immediately valuable to people living in the still desolate-looking city of 1816 was the intellectual stimulus the Institute offered.[20]

[19] Florian Cajori, *Early Mathematics in North and South America*, pp. 82-83, and *The Chequered Career of Ferdinand Rudolph Hassler*, pp. 45-49, 69-71, 76, 80; A. Hunter Dupree, *Science in the Federal Government, A History of Policies and Activities to 1940*, pp. 31-33.

[20] Columbian Institute, D.C. Miscellany; G. Brown Goode, "The Genesis

War had not only destroyed the public buildings but brought suffering to working men's families: for some unknown reason the number of destitute children in the city in 1815 had increased distressingly. The almshouse, the one public institution to which they might be sent, was unsuitable, if only because the city council had recently combined the poorhouse with the workhouse, where vagrants and petty law-breakers were confined. Public-spirited women in Washington concluded they must open a permanent home for orphans, where a resident matron could give them a Christian upbringing and a certain amount of schooling. The moving spirits behind the plan were Marcia Burnes Van Ness, wife of the well-to-do banker, John P. Van Ness, and Mrs. Obadiah Brown, wife of the pastor of the First Baptist Church. Mrs. Madison and Mrs. Samuel Harrison Smith also signed the notice placed in the *National Intelligencer* calling for a meeting of women ready to help. The group gathered in the scarcely finished chamber of the House of Representatives at the Brick Capitol. There they organized a society pledged to house, feed, clothe, and educate the children entrusted to its care and, when the children were old enough, to bind them out to service. As custom decreed that women should not manage money matters without male guidance, a board of male trustees was to take charge of finances; otherwise, women headed by a "first directress" and a "second directress" would take full responsibility for running the institution in the war-ravaged capital. Once projected, the Washington City Orphan Asylum rapidly took visible shape.

In late November 1815, the women originating the plan were able to announce that the new society had rented a house on northwest 10th Street near Pennsylvania Avenue and was ready to receive "destitute female orphans." That they were all to be

---

of the United States National Museum," pp. 276-79, in *Report of the U.S. National Museum*, 1891; *N.I.*, 15 Aug 1816; *Annals*, 15C, 1S, pp. 2594-95; Frederick V. Coville, "Early Botanical Activity in the District of Columbia," CHS *Rec*, v, 176, 94; Dupree, *Science in the Federal Government*, pp. 34-35; Davis, *The Abbé Correa*, p. 102.

white children was understood. The decision to take only "female orphans" arose from the society's meagre resources, although shortage of funds did not prevent acceptance of a few children of living, but desperately needy, parents. Thus the home, for years known as the Washington Female Orphan Asylum, opened its doors to a long succession of little girls. Mrs. Madison was "first directress" until her husband's retirement took her from Washington; Mrs. Van Ness then succeeded her. The "lady managers" took their responsibilities seriously; one member of the board visited the Asylum every week. They laid down careful rules about lessons and playtime, daily prayers, and daily cold water washing of every orphan's close-cropped hair. In belief that public humiliation was a more humane form of punishment than whipping, the then standard method of discipline, the managers decreed that a constantly disobedient child must wear a tag inscribed "BAD" on the day of the society's annual meeting, whereas the exemplary child was to be allowed to discard the usual green frock and beige shawl and to wear a pure white dress for the occasion. The institution quickly captured the imagination of the community. The city corporation voted a $200 appropriation, St. Patrick's Catholic Church gave $155, the Thespians, an amateur drama society, presented a benefit play, and individual subscriptions poured in. Georgetown women soon followed their neighbors' example by founding an orphange on Cherry Street.[21]

Although poverty and cases of destitution did not disappear, by 1816 much of Washington was enjoying a prosperity seemingly more firmly rooted than that of the war boom. During the first twenty months of peace more houses were built than in the preceding five years, and by the end of 1817 an estimate put the increase in Washington and Georgetown real estate sales

[21] *N.I.*, 13, 14 Oct, 28 Nov, 9 Dec 1815, 3, 30 Jan 1816; *Wshg Acts*, 6 Apr, 8 Dec 1815; Papers of the Lady Managers and Proceedings of the Washington Female Orphan Asylum, 1815-1851 (Archives of the Washington City Orphan Asylum at Hillcrest Children's Center); Jonathan Elliot, *Historical Sketches of the Ten Miles Square Forming the District of Columbia*, pp. 310-12; *Messenger*, Nov 1816.

since 1813 at 500 percent. The neighborhood about the President's Square had acquired so many residents by 1816 that Episcopalians forming a second parish engaged Benjamin Latrobe to build St. John's Church across the square from the new White House. Some six blocks away rose the Foundry Methodist Chapel erected by Henry Foxhall in thanks to God that the British had not destroyed his cannon foundry above Georgetown. Shops multiplied along Pennsylvania Avenue.[22] The flourishing condition of the printing trade inspired skilled workmen as early as 1815 to form the Columbia Typographical Union, one of the first workingmen's organizations in the United States. In most trades wages spiralled upward, although white men usually got over twice the pay equally skilled Negroes earned for the same work.[23] Bridges rebuilt across the Potomac and the Eastern Branch and steamboats plying regularly between the three cities eased travel within the District, while rapid communication with the South opened up when the steamboat *Washington* began runs every other day to Acquia Creek, Virginia, whence passengers could take the stage to Fredericksburg. In the course of the next year or two, stage coach lines scheduled more frequent trips to Baltimore and Philadelphia. The Washington Canal, which opened amid ceremonial fanfare in November 1815, eventually proved a secret disappointment, as tidal wash and silting up made it useless for heavily laden barges, but its promoters refused to consider it a failure.[24]

Washington, on the whole, grew faster than her neighbors. Alexandria's export trade rose enormously in the first months of peace but then lost momentum when Great Britain again closed her West Indian ports to American vessels. The value

[22] *N.I.*, 16, 31 Aug, 30 Nov 1816, 5 Mar, 18 May 1818; Madison Davis, "The Old Cannon Factory above Georgetown, D.C., and Its First Owner, Henry Foxall," CHS *Rec*, xi, 42-43.

[23] *History of the Capitol*, pp. 232-33, Ser 4585; Warden, *Chorographical View*, pp. 63-64.

[24] *N.I.*, 10 Jun, 20 May, 3 Aug, 23 Nov, 15 Dec 1815, 1 Jan, 23 Aug 1817; *Alex. Gazette*, 1 Jun 1815; Thomas Dornton, Notice of "The Steamboat Washington," 6 Jun 1815, 9 Jan 1816, and Comrs' Notices, 24 Mar 1815, 1 Apr 1816, D.C. Miscellany; *Wshg Acts*, 9 Jan, 28 Jun 1816.

of private property in Washington at the end of 1815 was higher than in the older city. Georgetown recovered more slowly than either of her rivals, chiefly because of the old problem of mud banks along her river front, which took a year of work and a $50,000 loan to remove. Although hopes for rapid industrial development rose when the Potomac Company expressed willingness to lease water power for factories below the Little Falls, the scheme largely fell apart when most prospective mill-owners rejected company terms; in 1817 a small woolen establishment and a flour mill were the sole result of negotiations. Henry Fearon, an Englishman touring the United States in the interest of compatriots who were considering emigrating, saw little to recommend any part of the District of Columbia, least of all the federal city. "Here is fine natural scenery, but no decidedly great natural advantages; little external commerce, a barren soil, a scanty population, enfeebled too by the deadly weight of absolute slavery and no direct means of communication with the western country."[25] As it happened, a half-dozen English families did settle in Georgetown. But meanwhile all three cities set themselves to open up communication with the West by resuming their campaign to induce the financially hard-pressed Potomac Company to improve river navigation above tidewater. Were that done, a sanguine writer prophesied in the *Intelligencer* "few years would elapse before the riches of the West would be unladen at our wharves."[26]

Want of credit facilities, "a defect now obvious to everyone," again seemed to be the one obstacle to tapping those riches, and again the House Committee on the District, as in 1810, agreed with the petitioners seeking new bank charters, larger capitalization, and greater freedom from regulation. "When we take into the estimate," reported the committee, "the extensive and rich country on the shores of the Potomac, and even of the

[25] *Alex. Gazette*, 31 Jul, 5 Sep 1815; Sanderlin, *National Project*, pp. 42-43; *Messenger*, 25 May, 28 Sep 1816, 12 Sep 1817; *N.I.*, 10, 16 Dec 1815, 3 Feb, 11 Mar, 13 May, 4 Jun 1817; *Ggtn Ordinances*, 18 Sep 1816; Fearon, *Sketches*, pp. xi-xv, 286-88.

[26] *Evening Star*, 14 Jul 1873; *N.I.*, 31 Jul 1817.

Shenandoah . . . whose prosperity is . . . dependent on the command of capital here, we may venture to doubt the accuracy of that opinion which pronounces the banking capital too large."[27] Some members of Congress objected: District banking practices were already too loose and the issues of paper excessive. In the autumn of 1814, according to one critic, "The Department of State was so bare of money as to be unable to pay its stationery bill; the government was subsisting on the drainage of unchartered banks in the District," and at the end of the war Washington and Georgetown banks were still loaning the government money in paper already 50 percent depreciated. During 1815, moreover, three new banks had opened. Any measure that would force the resumption of specie payments would be wiser than multiplying District institutions, chartered or unchartered. While the local question hung in abeyance, Congress created the Second Bank of the United States with is headquarters in Philadelphia. In the eyes of District promoters, that was no answer at all to their pleas, especially as it meant the end of Treasury deposits in Georgetown and Washington banks.[28] Furthermore a new stipulation that after February 1, 1817, all government dues must be paid in specie, Treasury notes, or convertible notes of state banks caused some initial consternation. But the resolution of the local problem in March 1817 satisfied the community. Congress renewed the old bank charters and granted new ones to the six unincorporated banks. They were to submit annual reports to the Secretary of the Treasury on their financial condition and to redeem notes in specie on demand, but otherwise bank officials could carry on their business much as they chose. In mid-February 1817, as the District institutions announced the resumption of specie payments and the government itself undertook to pay federal salaries in gold, confidence rose. With "the sound of dollars

[27] *ASP*, *Finance*, III, 114-15; *Messenger*, 15 May, 17 Jul 1816; *N.I.*, 1 Jan, 30 Mar 1816; ptns, H13A-G3.3, 7 Jun 1813 and H14A-F3.2, 13 Feb 1816.

[28] *Annals*, 14C, 1S, pp. 1115, 1264-68; *ASP*, *Finance*, III, pp. 113-15, 121-22; *Messenger*, 30 Oct, 6, 23 Nov 1816; *N.I.*, 16, 19 Nov 1816.

jingling on every counter" in District business houses, caution flew out the window. The selection of Washington for the location of a branch of the Bank of the United States merely heightened exuberance. But for all their commitment to specie payments, the local banks were soon issuing notes with little or no specie reserve to cover them, many of them in small, easily counterfeitable denominations. By the end of 1817 speculation was riding high.[29]

The corporation of Washington, in turn, abetted the flooding of the city with paper by continuing the issue of "due bills." These slips of paper signed by the mayor and bearing a face value of anything from a penny to a dollar had been designed to supply change for local transactions at a time when coppers and silver coins were scarce. An English traveller described the alternative procedure: in buying a fifty-cent pair of worsted gloves he offered a Washington shopkeeper a dollar bill, whereupon the man whipped out shears, cut the note in half, and returned one piece as change. When the municipality first adopted the due bill scheme in 1814 it was partly as defense "against the torrent of similar paper from Georgetown, Alexandria and fifty other towns." Unfortunately Washington's city council was soon seduced into authorizing additional issues until by August 1817 the total in circulation came to $25,000. A letter of protest signed "Love Gold" argued that due bills were no longer necessary; specie was again available and taxes no longer hard to collect. But city officials and much of the public found the local currency convenient. And as long as it did not have to be redeemed in coin, the paper money enlarged the sums available for public purposes.[30]

Besides voting a little money to the female orphanage and equipping the combined workhouse and almshouse, thence-

[29] *ASP*, *Finance*, III, 213, IV, 991; *Messenger*, 5, 21 Feb, 14 May 1817; *Annals*, 14C, 2S, pp. 1328-36; S Doc 121, 14C, 2S, *Papers of the First Fourteen Congresses;* Davis R. Dewey, *State Banking before the Civil War*, pp. 64, 67; H Doc 86, 16C, 1S, Ser 36; John J. Walsh, *Early Banks in the District of Columbia, 1792-1818.*

[30] *Wshg Acts*, 18 Oct, 1 Dec 1814, 26 Jul 1815, 13 Aug 1817; *N.I.*, 25 Sep 1817; Fearon, *Sketches of America*, pp. 287-88.

forward called the Washington Asylum, the city fathers spent tax funds much as they had before the war—for policing, lighting, and gravelling the streets, laying a few sidewalks, and keeping the bridges and three public market houses in repair. The one change in policy was a big increase in appropriations for schools and the creation of two school districts. The act decreed that the city council should appoint all the trustees except three who were to be elected by the subscribers to the nearly defunct Permanent Institution for the Education of Youth. That body, discouraged and indignant at the lack of community support, had virtually given up during the first summer of the war. The trustees had continued to meet, but the city had not paid over the annual $800, the eastern academy had had to close, the western had only a handful of free pupils enrolled, and both Lancastrian schools had shut down in 1814 and 1815, respectively. With the revival of prosperity in 1816, however, the city council voted $1,500 from taxes of the first and second wards for schools in the first district and $600 from third and fourth ward taxes for the poorer second district covering the Navy Yard section, Capitol Hill, and the thinly populated area to the northeast.

The meagre resources of the second district had predictable consequences; the eastern academy disappeared entirely and the Lancastrian school barely survived. In the first district, on the other hand, under the guidance of Josiah Meigs and the Scottish Presbyterian minister, James Laurie, the trustees drew up elaborate bylaws, outlined a curriculum, and established criteria for choosing textbooks: those "best calculated to facilitate the learning of the scholars and at the same time, such as are replete with moral lessons, correct style, National Sentiment and simplicity of arrangement." Still, memory of the financial troubles of the past led the board to require fees from children whose parents could afford to pay. With a single teacher in charge, assisted by the slightly advanced pupils, the Lancastrian school reopened, not as first planned in the President's stables at 14th and G Streets, but in a small rented house in southwest

Washington. Unhappily the trustees' avowed zeal for mass schooling had limitations: a ruling that the academy was to admit only children who could "read with facility, a plain paragraph in one of the School Books" left the free education of beginners to the ill-equipped Lancastrian schools.[31]

The inauguration of President James Monroe, held on the steps of the Brick Capitol in March 1817, introduced a period that came to be called the "era of good feeling." The phrase applied more aptly to the last year and a half of Madison's administration: that period saw a harmonious flowering of the spirit such as Washington was not to know again until long after civil war had freed Negro slaves in America. Greed, excessive ambition, and folly were certainly in evidence, and before the decade was out they would reap the whirlwind of business depression and want. But in 1816 and the early months of 1817 hope gilded every prospect and an untrammelled energy pushed men on toward their goals. If free Negroes had dared expect more palpable thanks than grateful words for their help in defending the city in 1814, they met with disappointment, just as conscientious objectors to the slave trade grieved at the failure of John Randolph's passionate plea in the House to forbid the nefarious traffic in the capital of a free nation. With the founding of the American Colonization Society headed by George Washington's nephew, Supreme Court Justice Bushrod Washington, white people, however, believed an answer to the future of free Negroes within sight: money supplied by the society would take them back to Africa to a land of their own, there to live happily ever after. That colored people in the city solemnly declared the plan unacceptable apparently made no impression upon members of the society. Meanwhile, unless the mayor grossly exaggerated, "acquisition of many wealthy citizens" augured well for Washington.[32]

[31] *Wshg Acts*, 15 Aug 1812, 28 Jun 1816; School Trustee Min, pp. 187-268; *Spec Rpt Comr Ed*, 1870, pp. 51-52, Ser 1427.

[32] *Annals*, 14C, 1S, pp. 1115-17; *N.I.*, 7 Jan 1817.

Whether wealthy in worldly goods or not, men of exceptional "colloquial parts" were drawn to the capital. Daniel Webster, if not yet a prominent figure in Washington drawing rooms, was making his eloquence and sharp intelligence count on the Hill. Physicians elected to the new Medical Society of the District of Columbia met to discuss practical professional problems and their tentative theories.[33] The intellectual oligarchy that had led a hesitant Congress to endorse a scientific coastal survey still imbued the capital with a respect for learning that lent reasonableness to the aspirations of the Columbian Institute; in an atmosphere of intellectual curiosity major obstacles to making Washington a wellspring of scientific research should be few. As long as James Madison held the reins of government, the temporary White House remained a center of more than political planning and social festivity.

The Madisons spent their last seventeen months in Washington in the largest of the Seven Buildings, the corner house on Pennsylvania Avenue at 19th Street. When magnificent evening receptions took place there, the candle-lit rooms and the torches held aloft by Negro slaves stationed along the walk and at the entrance created a myth that long afterward gave the temporary Executive Mansion the aprocryphal name "House of 1,000 Candles." In the gracious friendliness of such occasions, European diplomats could forget the discomforts of the raw little capital which the Abbé Correa tactfully called the "city of magnificent distances." Sure at last of her permanence as the seat of empire, residents could laugh with the witty Portuguese when he added: "Every man is born with a bag of follies which attends him through life. Washington was born with a small bag which he kept to himself, and never imparted any of it to the world until the metropolis of the nation was founded, when he emptied the whole of it in this city."[34] But

[33] Joseph M. Toner, *Anniversary Oration delivered before the Medical Society of the District of Columbia, September 26, 1866*, pp. 7-10; *N.I.*, 25 Sep 1817.

[34] Davis, *The Abbé Correa*, p. 107; interview with Irving Brant, 15 Aug 1960, who believes the name "House of 1,000 Candles" never used during Mrs. Madison's life-time.

while Correa preferred living in Philadelphia to rooming in a boardinghouse in the Seven Buildings, he and other ministers obviously found much that was congenial in Washington society. The President's devoted friends and admirers knew that after March 4, 1817, official and purely social gatherings would not retain the flavor the "little Virginian" and the ebullient Dolly had imparted to them. Nor would any future chief of state be so much at one with the city he had helped to found. As Secretary of State and then as President, Madison had been Washington's leading citizen for nearly sixteen years, almost as long as the city had been the seat of government. And in a community of fewer than 9,000 white people, some feeling of intimacy with one's neighbors was natural, irrespective of economic or political differences. Not improbably even the Irish day laborers who had come to dig the Washington Canal looked upon the reserved James Madison not only as President but also as a fellow citizen.

While regretting the Madisons' departure, Washingtonians apparently felt no anxiety lest the new administration effect unwanted changes. James Monroe was a personage only less well-known in the city than his predecessor. The elegant rather aloof Mrs. Monroe was not a Dolly Madison, but until the new President and his household moved into the White House six months after the inauguration, no one expected official entertaining to begin, and until Congress convened in December the formal season would not open. In the interval everything seemed to move along much as before. Something was missing, but new developments would surely fill the gap. Prosperity was still mounting, and, as the new President kept on three of Madison's five cabinet members, only the appointment of John Quincy Adams as Secretary of State caused qualms: Federalists considered him a turncoat. Reorganization of the army had already fixed headquarters for the services in Washington, and under Secretary of War John Calhoun, able officers with colorful careers were taking up long-term or permanent residence in the city. Government clerks who had arrived in 1800 or 1801 still filled departmental offices and were very much part of the local community.[35] Breaks with the policy of the past appeared highly unlikely, and the evaporation of factional feuds in Congress promised to perpetuate the era of good feeling so auspiciously begun. What was gone was not evident in the autumn of 1817. The missing element was the warmth and the intellectual's view of life which had distinguished the capital of Jefferson and Madison.

[35] Leonard D. White, *The Jeffersonians, A Study in Administrative History, 1801-1829*, pp. 238-39; Robert Smith to John Eppes, 21 Dec 1810, Domestic Letters of the Department of State, xv, 467-71 RG 59, NA; *A Register of Officers and Agents, Civil, Military, and Naval, in the Service of the United States*, 1817.

CHAPTER IV

DISILLUSIONMENT AND READJUSTMENTS, 1818-1828

Expectations that everything agreeable in Washington would continue unchanged underwent modification before the winter of 1817-1818 was gone. In late November President Monroe, perhaps hoping to conceal his own indecisiveness by holding diplomats at arms' length, determined to restore the formality that had obtained under President Washington: henceforward the President would receive foreign ministers only by appointment or at official dinners and levees. While that decision appeared defensible in light of the United States' growing international stature, dismay stirred in Washington when Mrs. Monroe let it be known that she would not pay calls upon anyone. That new arrangement seemed like a rebuff to a community long accustomed to a cordial give-and-take with the first lady. But when the President's older daughter, Mrs. George Hay, whose husband had no official position whatever, announced that she would make no first calls, resentment flared up. The Senate then resolved that its dignity would not permit its members to make first calls on anyone but the President. Thus for the first time since Jefferson entered the Executive Mansion, the question of precedence loomed large in society.

Secretary of State John Quincy Adams, upon whom fell the burden of working out logical rules of official etiquette, complained in his private journal about the undignified quarrels that ensued and the unmannerliness to be seen from time to time at the White House levees. The new rules did not bar anyone from the presidential "Drawing Rooms" held twice a month from December to March. There, wrote Henry Fearon, "conversation, tea, ice, music, chewing tobacco and excessive spitting afford employment for the evening." But beneath the bad manners lay a new stiffness. Heart-burnings over who outranked whom undercut political harmony among officials; and private citizens without federal office necessarily found themselves pushed toward the perimeter of a circle in the center of which they had only recently moved freely.[1]

White House dinners became dreary affairs. A congressman from New York described the new order in 1818. When he and three associates arrived at 5:30, the President's secretary led them "Indian file" into the East Room. At the far end Mrs. Monroe and several ladies were ensconced; the President, dressed in small clothes and white silk stockings, his upswept powdered hair cut short in back, sat alone near the center of the room while his male guests occupied chairs "in a row in solemn state" against one wall. After shaking hands with the President and being greeted by Mrs. Monroe, the new arrivals perforce joined the immobilized stag line. Minutes passed; "not a whisper broke upon the ear to interrupt the silence of the place, and everyone looked as if the next moment would be his last." When finally the President engaged the person nearest him in conversation, "directly the Secretary ushered in more victims, who submitted to the same ordeal we had experienced. This continued for fully half an hour when dinner was announced." Dinner was good and the table "most richly furnished," dominated by an eight-foot oval centerpiece of mirror and eight-inch-high gilt figures holding bouquets. But guests who had known the warm delight of dining with Jefferson or the Madisons were not vastly impressed by the chilly Parisian décor.[2] The intimacy of days when private citizens and important federal officers were equally welcome in the White House was gone forever.

Grievances over the new rigid etiquette dropped into the background, however, when more serious troubles set in. By the end of 1818 the nation-wide orgy of speculation, financed by

[1] *Memoirs of John Quincy Adams*, ed. Charles Francis Adams, IV, 22-23, 45-46, 486-94, 509; Fearon, *Sketches of America*, p. 291.

[2] Robert J. Hubbard, "Political and Social Life in Washington during the Administration of President Monroe," Oneida Historical Society *Transactions*, IX (1903), pp. 63-64.

what one historian has called "one of the most extraordinary emissions of dubious paper money in the history of the modern world," had run its course; early in 1819 the entire country faced the collapse of the inflated values. In the District of Columbia the volume of commerce dwindled steadily, commodity prices shrank, and real estate sold at fractions of its original cost. A wharf and storehouses purchased two or three years before for $17,000 brought $1,250. The federal government itself was unable to find buyers for lots in Washington, the sale of which was to have paid for completing the Capitol. Credit became unobtainable. Stock in the Washington Canal Company, which had operated at a loss during the boom, fell from $100 a share to $30. Specie evaporated as the Bank of the United States began calling in government balances in the local banks and sending hard money to Philadelphia. The Bank of Washington's funds plummeted from $26,500 to $4,700, the formerly powerful Bank of Columbia saw its specie reserve cut in half, and the Merchants Bank of Alexandria could produce only $1,400 in coin. When the Virginia Assembly enacted measures to stop circulation of District notes in the Old Dominion, the Washington branch of the Bank of the United States took a loss of some $71,000. Making bad matters worse, in October 1819 the corporation of Washington released $10,000 in new due bills.[3]

Threatened with bankruptcy, unscrupulous men tried various unsavory schemes, especially counterfeiting even nearly worthless paper. A Georgetown bank chalked up on the credit side of its ledger $33,000 in counterfeit bills in order to strike a balance with its debits. Inasmuch as most of the counterfeits

[3] *N.I.*, 15 Sep 17, 13 Mar 1818, 25 Jan, 3 Mar 1820, 19 Jul 1821; *Messenger*, 28 Jan, 10 Mar 1820, 19 Mar 1821; George Dangerfield, *Era of Good Feelings*, p. 179; *Alex. Gazette*, 7 Sep 1819; *Annals*, 17C, 1S, pp. 586-87; Charles S. Sydnor, *The Development of Southern Sectionalism*, p. 113; Ralph C H. Catterall, *The Second Bank of the United States*, pp. 51, 66; Dewey, *State Banking*, pp. 67-68; *Niles Register*, XIV, No. 24, p. 396, XVII, No. 8, p. 116; H Doc 165, 15C, 2S, Ser 22; S Doc 50, 16C, 2S, Ser 43; Andrew Rothwell, *Laws of the Corporation of the City of Washington*, 29 Oct 1819.

were small notes that usually fell into the hands of workingmen, the laboring classes suffered acutely. Already pinched by wage cuts and by the competition of Philadelphia and New York craftsmen brought in for jobs on government buildings, a group of mechanics begged Congress for a lien law to protect them from the "wiley, cunning and dishonest spirit which . . . so unfortunately abounds within [the] city."[4]

As the depression deepened, citizens in many walks of life accused the banks of being "the sole authors of the pecuniary distress." But worried men on Capitol Hill concluded that punitive action against banks that had overstepped their charter privileges would only cause failures and expose to sale "at a great sacrifice much of the real property in the District." In hopes that the crisis would pass within a few months, Congress renewed the charters for a year, and the Secretary of the Treasury bolstered up some of the banks by depositing government funds with them. But four banking houses failed during 1820. Persuaded that the remaining nine must be sound, in 1821 Congress granted them fifteen-year charters limited only by provisions for redemption of notes in specie on demand and a prohibition on issue of denominations of less than $5. Troubles were not over and the volume of investments dropped along with the price of bank stocks, but after 1822 the public ceased to regard bankers as the villains in the tragedies of the panic. For the next dozen years local banks and banking practices received scant congressional attention.[5]

Economic distress in Washington, while pronounced between 1819 and 1821, was less severe than in the country's big commercial centers, for government operations materially lessened business stagnation in the federal city. Other than occasionally

[4] *N.I.*, 17 May 1819, 31 Mar 1820; *ASP*, *Finance*, III, 796; William M. Gouge, *A Short History of Paper Money and Banking in the United States*, p. 47; Dewey, *State Banking*, p. 64; *History of the Capitol*, pp. 232-33, 247, Ser 4585; *Annals*, 17C, 1S, p. 73.

[5] *N.I.*, 16, 20 Oct 1819, 3, 7 Jan, 26 Aug, 20, 21 Jul 1821; *Messenger*, 1 May 1820; ptn, H16A-G5.1, 20 Dec 1819; *Annals*, 16C, 1S, pp. 646-48, 1043-45, 1825-32, 16C, 2S, pp. 1814-19, 17C, 2S, pp. 225, 305-06; Gouge, *Paper Money*, p. 61; *ASP*, *Finance*, III, 795-97; *Wshg Gazette*, 12 Feb 1823; S Doc 117, 16C, 1S, Ser 27.

depositing government funds in the District banks, officials took no steps to hasten recovery, but neither did Congress curtail routine expenditures. The mere existence of federal offices in Washington had a stabilizing effect. The roster of government clerks changed very little, the salary scale not at all. Furthermore, the expanding business of the General Land Office opened new opportunities to private citizens. Not only purchasers of federal land buying through branch offices in the West but men who accepted land warrants in payment for military service began to turn to agents in Washington and Georgetown to straighten out tangles of red tape, validate titles, and expedite the issue of the final patents. At the same time a new pension law of 1818, which increased the number of claimants, and official disapproval of government clerks' representing private clients gave rise to a body of semi-professional claim agents. They frequently combined selling real estate and a modicum of legal business or banking with handling claims. Work at the Navy Yard was another source of equilibrium to the community. When industrial enterprise in much of the United States was at low ebb, the Navy Yard was employing 380 civilians in addition to 67 officers and enlisted men. Although workmen had to accept wage cuts, new smithies and anchor shops helped maintain lengthy payrolls at the yard. Following the launching in 1819 of the *Columbus*, a ship of the line that cost $426,000, a schooner slid down the runway in 1820 and the frigate *Potomac* two years later.[6]

The government activities that kept Washington from feeling the full force of the country-wide depression had relatively little effect upon the rest of the District. During the darkest days of 1819 and 1820 Georgetown and Alexandria merchants benefited from dealings with the Office of Indian Trade, but in 1822 Congress, apparently yielding to pressure from Senator Benton of Missouri, abandoned the system of government-con-

[6] *Register of Officers of the United States*, 1818, 1820, 1822; Leonard D. White, *The Jeffersonians*, pp. 519-20; Hibben, *Navy Yard*, pp. 62-63; *ASP, Misc*, II, 495-97; G. R. Fitzgerald to Richard Wallack, 20 Sep 1818, D.C. Miscellany; H Doc 55, 16C, 1S, pp. 665-67, Ser 34.

trolled trade with the Indians and closed the local factory. Although the two older cities carried on virtually all the shipping for the area, Alexandria, the port the Duc de La Rochefoucauld had so greatly admired in the 1790's, had only 8,200 inhabitants in 1820, 25 percent of them Negro slaves; Georgetown had about 5,950 free residents and 1,400 slaves. Both towns attributed Washington's more rapid growth to congressional favors. At the peak of prosperity in 1817 the *Messenger* had pointed to the identity of interests of Georgetown and Washington and suggested their union, but not until hard times set in did the idea receive careful attention.[7]

In December 1818 President Monroe revived the plan of territorial status for the District. For the next eight years Congress at intervals debated the proposal in one form or another, while permanent residents argued fiercely among themselves. Some contended that although a territorial legislature might not reconcile conflicting interests, even limited representation in Congress would be useful. But counterproposals in Georgetown and Alexandria for retrocession to Maryland and Virginia, respectively, sounded louder. The depression strengthened the clamor for the return of state citizenship, for a number of men, although admitting that District tax rates were lower than Virginia's, believed Congress responsible for their economic plight.[8] The District's dual law system, moreover, worked against the proposed consolidation. Congress had instructed the judges of the circuit court in 1816 to prepare a single code for the District but had then rejected the version Judge Cranch submitted because it covered only statute law. Hence lawyers dreaded the legal confusions likely to arise under a territory in part of which eighteenth-century Maryland laws would run,

[7] *N.I.*, 6 Jan, 28 Dec 1821; Dietz, "The Government Factory System," p. 180; *Register of Debates*, 18C, 2S, 15 Feb 1825; *Fourth Census of the U.S.*, 1820; *Messenger*, 12 Sep 1817, 22 May, 8, 29 Jul 1818; *Alex. Gazette*, 19 Feb 1817.

[8] *Messenger*, 11, 16 Dec 1818, 8 Jan 1819, 17 Jan 1820; *Alex. Gazette*, 5, 7, 8 Jan, 14 Oct 1819; *N.I.*, 10 Nov 1810, 21 Oct, 18, 24 Nov, 12 Dec 1818; ptn, H17A-F4.1, 9 Mar 1822.

in the rest antiquated Virginia laws.[9] Opposition in Washington grew chiefly out of fear that she would lose her privileged position and that Congress, freed of responsibility for the city, would cease to take any interest in improvements and perhaps even renew talk of moving the capital. The corporation's delegation that waited upon the House District Committee in 1820 urged continuation of the *status quo*. Although a number of congressmen believed a territorial government would save them time and trouble and relieve the federal Treasury of onerous demands, the Senate shelved the bill. The answer to a representative's complaint that the District courts alone had cost the government over $350,000 in nineteen years was the enactment of a law placing upon local taxpayers the entire expense of building a federal court house, a measure later cancelled.[10]

But the territorial question did not stay buried. In 1822 Representative Kent of Maryland called for a convention of elected delegates to frame a plan of union. An "old inhabitant" promptly wrote that the notion had the support "mostly of persons who have little or no interest in property within the District"; the "largest proprietors" disapproved. Washington's city council declared a delegate in Congress useless and the District "more fully and ably represented than any other portion of our Country . . . by the whole assembled Congress."[11] Two years after the death of the Kent bill uneasiness about the District's commercial future reopened the discussion. Not only was taxation without representation an indignity, ran one argument, but also, as Richard Bland Lee, former Virginian and one-time federal commissioner of Washington, proved from his own experience, the denial to the District of legal status equal to that of a state meant in practice that no local citizen,

[9] Cox, "Efforts to Obtain a Code of Laws for the District of Columbia," CHS *Rec*, III, 115-20; *Annals*, 17C, 1S, p. 1487.

[10] *N.I.*, 28 Dec 1818, 6 Jan 1819; *Wshg Gazette*, 6 Jan 1820; *Wshg Laws*, 24 Dec 1818; Sen Doc 128, 16C, 1S, Ser 27; H Docs 43 and 91, 16C, 1S, Sers 33 and 36; *Annals*, 16C, 1S, pp. 551-53, 566-67, 794-800, 930-33, 937.

[11] *Annals*, 17C, 1S, pp. 1244, 1338; *Wshg Gazette*, 15 Mar, 10 Apr 1822.

however just his cause, could sue the citizen of a state successfully, since the case would be heard outside the District courts; enterprising men would naturally avoid permanent residence in an area where such discrimination obtained. But again shortsightedness, inertia, and a division of opinion over whether to seek unabridged political and legal rights through a territory or through retrocession to the parent states prevented a convincing appeal to congresses apparently ready to act on any unified local mandate. Thus the chance to seat a delegate in the House of Representatives was lost. Not until the troubled reconstruction era would a truncated District of Columbia attain for a few brief years a territorial government.[12]

Washingtonians, meantime, whatever their faith in the "fostering care of the national authorities," wanted some self-rule. As the city charter ran only till 1820, a memorial to Congress asked for continuation of existing corporate authority with greatly enlarged powers: the right to create a board of health which could enforce sanitary regulations, to impose a housebuilding code, open alleyways, lay special taxes for street improvements but also to exact reimbursement from the federal Commissioner of Public Buildings for half the costs of work done on any street adjoining or cutting through government property, and, doubtless a reflection of the hard times of 1819, power to bind out orphans and children of paupers and exclude from the city vagrants likely to become public charges. In addition, the corporation asked for authority to prohibit traders from transporting slaves through Washington or depositing them within the city preparatory to shipment south. There was no debate on the Hill. A new charter took effect on May 15, 1820, giving the municipality everything it had asked for except the right to bar vagrants and slave traders from the city. The franchise limited the electorate to white males who paid

[12] Richard Bland Lee, Statement, n.d., Gales and Seaton Mss, Feb-Apr 1824, D.C. Miscellany; ptns, H18A-F4.2, 26 Jan, 23 Mar, 26 Apr 1824; H Doc 49, 18C, 1S, Ser 94; H Doc 17, 18C, 2S, Ser 114; *Annals*, 18C, 1S, pp. 532, 1504-06; *N.I.*, 17 Mar, 20 Nov 1824, 9 Dec 1825, 2 Mar, 6 Nov 1826.

at least fifty cents in taxes and had resided in the city for a year, but voters gained the privilege of electing the mayor instead of having the council choose him.[13]

Among articulate citizens interest in local politics waned thereafter except for a brief flurry of excitement when propertyless men in two wards balloted in the city election of 1822, much as poorhouse inmates had cast their "25-cent votes" in 1811. Thomas Carbery, the poor man's successful candidate for mayor, found his election challenged, but as soon as a court decision seated him he enrolled on the assessment books the names of men who, according to outraged conservatives, owned no property but their clothes. Three years later the city fathers re-established the rigid property qualification, but for a brief interval the "common man" in Washington had a taste of political power.[14] It had no discernible ill effects. Eminently respectable citizens were elected to office, struggled, generally ineffectually, with familiar civic problems, and sooner or later gladly passed on their responsibilities to their elected successors.

The municipality's chief troubles still grew out of the disparity between resources and needs. Subtle pressures always bore upon the city to present to the world an aspect worthy of the capital of the nation. Yet in flush times wealthy property-owners were few, and during and after the panic, tax delinquence reduced the city's available funds by over 25 percent. In more than twenty years Congress had appropriated for the capital about $15,000 exclusively for work on Pennsylvania Avenue and roads about the President's house, whereas in 1821 alone the condition of the streets impelled the city to spend $43,000 on them. The law granting Washington a new charter, it is true, recognized the government's obligation to share the costs of improvements to federal property but specified that the money must come exclusively from the sale of public lots in the city. And the lots sold very slowly. At the ceremonies of laying

[13] *N.I.*, 1 Apr 1818; *Wshg Laws*, 17 Nov, 24 Dec 1818, 29 Nov 1819; *Annals*, 16C, 1S, pp. 2554, 2600-10.

[14] *N.I.*, 5, 6, 13, 16, 24 Jun 1822; *Wshg Gazette*, 12 Jun 1822, 22 May 1824; H Rpt 83, 19C, 1S, Ser 141.

the cornerstone of the new City Hall, Thomas Law's son John, the principal orator, contrasted the munificence of Constantine in building Byzantium and "the Autocrat of Russia" in creating St. Petersburg with the niggardliness of Congress toward the American capital. For a city whose public debt had jumped from $17,000 in 1816 to $46,000 five years later, the $40,000 by then spent on the City Hall seemed an extravagance, but a lottery which was to have met the cost failed when the manager absconded with the cash. By and large, mayors and council members watched every penny of tax money. To their gratification, Congress had a change of heart in 1823 and contributed $10,000 to the municipal building in return for the use of one wing for the circuit court and in 1826 voted $5,000 for repairs to the jail.[15]

When the city enlarged the Washington Asylum in 1815, it had appeared to be big enough to serve at once as poorhouse and workhouse for the "safeguarding of vagrants." But since the institution was the one place in which "migrant paupers" could receive medical or other care, by 1819, as impoverished veterans of the Revolution and War of 1812 thronged to the capital to press pension claims, the number who ended up at the Asylum strained its facilities badly. Although local citizens averred that Washington had her "full proportion of paupers of native growth" and should not have to support the indigent of other localities, pleas for federal aid were unheeded. Congress waited till the 1840's to give it.[16] Until the end of the 1820's the Asylum also housed petty lawbreakers, inasmuch as the Washington County jail was always overcrowded with debtors, runaway slaves, and men, women, and children convicted in

[15] *Wshg Acts*, 29 Feb, 10 May 1816; *Wshg Laws*, 19 Oct 1818, 29 Oct 1819; *Annals*, 17C, 1S, pp. 528, 1645, 1777, 1888, 2623-25; *N.I.*, 2 Jun 1819, 22 May, 27 Apr 1821; "Ceremonies and Oration at Laying the Cornerstone of the City Hall of the City of Washington," 22 Aug 1820, pp. 10-11, *Miscellaneous Pamphlets*, 227:4; *Reg Deb*, 19C, 1S, pp. 1475-91, xxvi-vii; 3 Stat 785; S Doc 97, 23C, 2S, Ser 268.

[16] *Wshg Laws*, 29 Oct 1819, 9 Jul, 27 Sep 1822; *Annals*, 15C, 1S, pp. 2523-24; *N.I.*, 10 Aug, 21 Oct 1818, 14 Feb, 2 May 1820, 8 Mar 1821; ptn, H16A-G5.5, 20 Dec 1819.

federal courts of violating federal statutes or for committing one of the many offenses listed in the criminal code inherited from eighteenth-century Maryland. Impassioned complaints about conditions in the jail at length persuaded the House to investigate and then to authorize the construction of a penitentiary on Arsenal Point. Unfortunately, if the completion of the federal prison in 1827 eased congestion in the jail and, indirectly, in the workhouse, inadequacies remained in the Asylum's care of the indigent aged and ill.[17]

Moreover, the character of public assistance extended to needy families depended in considerable part upon where they lived. For the method the city early adopted in distributing funds for poor relief, policing, and other public purposes penalized the poorer parts of the city. Each ward collected its own taxes, paid a small part into the city treasury and spent the rest within its own limits; each ward independently solicited contributions for relief of its own poverty-stricken inhabitants. The result was small separate financial kingdoms with unequal opportunity for growth. Under the circumstances it was as well that the philosophy of the day expected private charity to meet most of the wants of the helpless. After 1820 when a rearrangement made six wards out of the original four, the second and third wards were the wealthiest, and, because they could afford expensive improvements, the area above southwest E Street stretching from the Capitol to the Treasury rapidly drew to itself the most enterprising householders. The wards to the northeast and along the river front, where poor people lived and where want was greatest, lost progressively the capacity to attract the well-to-do.[18] (See Table II)

The effects of the ward system of taxing and spending were clearly seen in the provisions for public schools. Aldermen and councilmen obviously believed that the wards in the eastern

[17] Ptns, H18A-F4.2, 31 Jan 1825, H19A-G5.3, 6, 22 Jan 1827; *Reg Deb*, 19C, 1S, pp. 1475-91, xiv, xxvi-xxvii; H Rpt 52, 18C, 2S, Ser 122; *Wshg Laws*, pp. 443-46.

[18] *Wshg Acts*, 10 May 1816; *Wshg Laws*, 4 Apr, 22, 24 May, 1 Jun 1820; *N.I.*, 31 Jan 1816, 2 Jun 1819, 22 May 1821, 17 May 1822.

TABLE II[a]

DISTRIBUTION OF RESIDENTS AND PROPERTY IN WASHINGTON, 1832

Wards	Population	Voters	Assessment	Taxes	Dwellings
1st	3,678	380	$1,573,477	$ 8,793.55	609
2nd	4,058	421	1,617,133	8,683.46	676
3rd	5,750	577	2,438,610	13,498.18	970
TOTAL	13,486	1,378	$5,629,220	$30,975.19	2,255
4th	1,859	156	588,823	3,139.33	321
5th	1,357	108	533,871	3,028.08	232
6th	2,138	237	463,435	2,588.92	425
TOTAL	5,354	501	$1,586,129	$ 8,756.33	978
OVER-ALL TOTALS	18,840	1,879	$7,215,349	$39,731.52	3,233

[a] *National Intelligencer*, April 25, 1832.

part of the city comprising the second school district could not or should not raise more than $600 to $850 in taxes to spend educating their children. Consequently, in the section where few parents could afford the cost of private schools, the only free white institution was the rump of the Lancastrian school of 1816. The free school for Negro children opened in 1818 by the colored Resolute Beneficial Society did not count in white men's calculations and indeed got no municipal help. In the second district the situation looked so hopeless that the public school trustees ceased to keep records. The wealthier first school district also suffered, though less sharply, for in 1818 the city council reduced the amount of tax money the first and second wards might raise for schools to $1,000, "no part of which shall be expended, except in the instruction of Poor Children." The District's school board, upon which now only appointees of the council could serve, might select a few gifted pupils to send for advanced study in private schools, provided the cost not exceed $150 in any year or $40 for any one child; but at a good private school a year's tuition ran to about $200. As the city fathers discouraged private gifts, the Permanent Institution for the Education of Youth disappeared. In an attempt to supplement tax funds, during the early 1820's the trustees conducted lotteries which brought in about $40,000, but in 1826 a municipal ordinance decreed that the mayor invest the $40,000 in safe 6 percent bonds and use two-thirds of the annual income to maintain two "public pauper schools," one in each district. Thereafter "it shall not be lawful to suffer any child to be taught for pay." If the attitude reflected in the first guide book to Washington were representative, taxpayers were proud of having two free schools supported "entirely by lotteries etc., without costing the city anything."[19]

Somehow or other, one of the two academies started by the trustees for the Permanent Institution for the Education of Youth continued to function off and on for some years, but since it had to charge modest fees, it no longer ranked as a public school. Some of the excellent private schools, such as the new Catholic Seminary near St. Patrick's Church or the new Columbian preparatory school, might grant promising boys scholarships, and the canny John McLeod, head of the locally famous and financially successful Central Academy, offered free tuition to mechanics' daughters in return for free repairs to his building. Scholarships, however, were not for the rank and file, and as few parents, however impecunious, were willing to send their children to anything labelled "pauper school," education became largely the privilege of the well-to-do.[20]

Washingtonians voiced more concern about shortcomings in the city's sanitation than about public education, particularly after population in the 1820's began to creep up toward 15,000. With the exception of householders along the two-block stretch of Pennsylvania Avenue, who had arranged to pipe water to their dwellings, every family pumped water from its own cistern or carried it from wells in the public squares; every family disposed of its own garbage, not infrequently by dumping it

[19] School Trustee Min, pp. 271-72; *Wshg Laws*, 11 Jul 1818, 24 Oct 1820, 9 Jul 1821, 27 Jul 1826; *Spec Rpt Comr Educ*, 1870, pp. 50-52, 195-97, Ser 1427; Jonathan Elliot, *Historical Sketches of the Ten Miles Square*, p. 256.

[20] *N.I.*, 24 Jun 1817, 8 Apr, 9 Jun 1819, 1 Jun, 18 Aug 1820; James C. Welling, *Brief Chronicles of the Columbian College from 1821 to 1873*, p. 8.

into the street for roving pigs, and before 1820 every household had to engage a private scavenger to clean its privy. That year the city hired public scavengers to make regular rounds, but carelessness in getting rid of the night soil made the service of doubtful utility. One complainant spoke of "several immense excavations of brick yards always full of green stagnant water, with the large deposit on the surface of the ground made by the scavenger of the first ward and the numerous dead carcasses left to putrify." Dr. Henry Huntt, a rather bumptious young man defensively proud of Washington, became so distressed at the derogatory tales current about her unhealthfulness that he volunteered to act as health officer without salary and collect mortality data to prove her detractors wrong. His zeal obviously affected the validity of his monthly reports; although nearly 29 percent of the population was colored, he sometimes omitted all figures on Negro deaths. But accurate vital statistics would probably not have bettered the record of a city without a sewage system and with tidal swamps yearly spreading along her river front. When the corporation created a board of health composed of a physician and a layman from every ward, the new body continued to assemble reports, but it had little control over the abatement of nuisances and no way at all to enforce preventive measures. "Bilious fevers are universal," wrote Margaret Bayard Smith in 1822. They would worsen every summer for the next forty years.[21]

In preventing serious fires, the city did better, partly because houses were not crowded closely together. Between 1806 and 1816 no major fire loss occurred other than that caused by the British captors. Every householder kept leather buckets in readiness, and every ward had its volunteer fire company equipped with engine and hose. The company president and

[21] Dr. Henry Huntt to Mayor Benjamin Orr, 6 Jan 1818, Lewis Grant Davidson Mss; Notice, Mayor Samuel Smallwood, 19 Aug 1819, D.C. Miscellany; Joseph M. Toner, *Anniversary Oration delivered before the Medical Society*, pp. 33-34, 76; M. B. Smith, *First Forty Years*, pp. 158-59; *Wshg Laws*, 8 Jul 1820, 23 Mar 1822; *Wshg Gazette*, 17 Apr 1822; Sarah H. Porter, *The Life and Times of Anne Royall*, pp. 153-54.

vice-presidents, each distinguishable at a fire by a "white wand or staff, at least five feet in length and a good speaking trumpet," might fine any man present for refusing to help. When incorporation of the Franklin Fire Insurance Company in 1818 brought forth public demands for additional safeguards, the municipality empowered the mayor to build reservoirs to be filled by water piped from springs in each section of the city; each ward might also dig additional wells and install pumps in the public squares. Economy cancelled the expensive plan the next year, but fear for the safety of federal property then inspired Congress to appropriate $4,500 for the purchase of two engines and construction of one fire house near the Capitol and a second near the White House. Unhappily nothing saved the Washington Theatre from burning to the ground in 1821. Gaetani Carusi, one-time member of the Marine Band, and his son then bought the 11th and C Streets site and built there Assembly Rooms which soon became the city's chief public gathering place and the scene of inaugural balls.[22]

Congressional inaction on forbidding the slave trade in the District of Columbia or at least allowing the city government to exclude it from Washington naturally distressed some citizens more than others. Probably slave-owners among the aldermen and councilmen who begged for authority to halt the traffic were moved primarily by expediency: outlawing a trade which had few or no local benefits would redeem the city's reputation among northern and European visitors and, in the process, greatly reduce the chances of their stirring up unrest among local Negroes. Publication of Jesse Torrey's *A Portraiture of Domestic Slavery in the United States* may have sharpened the nearly universal eagerness of Washingtonians to stop the trade. For Torrey's eye-witness account of the human tragedies he had seen while visiting the city in 1815 was one of the first effective pieces of anti-slavery propaganda in Amer-

[22] *Wshg Acts*, 3 Mar 1815, 10, 24 May, 28 Jun 1816; *Wshg Laws*, 11 Jul 1818, 14 Aug, 29 Oct, 29 Nov 1819; *N.I.*, 9 Dec 1816, 8, 12 Apr, 2 Jun 1819, 22 May 1821, 17 May 1822; *Annals*, 15C, 1S, pp. 2527-30, 15C, 2S, p. 2536; John Haskins, "Music in the District of Columbia," p. 9.

ica. From the door of the Capitol he had watched a coffle of slaves shuffle by, "a procession of men, women and children, resembling that of a funeral . . . they were bound together in pairs, some with ropes, and some with *iron chains.*" Calling the jail a "store house" for slave merchants, he explained that "several hundred people, including not legal slaves only, but many kidnapped freemen . . . are annually collected at Washington (as if it were an emporium of slavery) for transportation to the slave regions."[23] At best a sordid business conducted by men whom most reputable citizens of the capital despised, the trade had expanded under the mounting demand of southern planters for field hands. Knowledgeable Washingtonians, "the constituents of no one," realized that they must enlist outside support to campaign successfully against the vested interests represented by an increasingly powerful pro-slavery bloc in Congress. And at a time when leading householders in the capital from the President down owned or hired slaves as servants, the question of how to attack the trade without advocating simultaneously the abolition of the peculiar institution itself presented difficulties. The problem endured after John Quincy Adams became President. Nevertheless anti-slavery sentiment in Washington deepened slowly through most of the 1820's.

A Maryland statute of 1796, one of several laws forming the legal basis of the trade in Washington, sanctioned the passage of slaves through the county but forbade importing them for sale. Hence most of the big auctions held in the city were patently illegal. A law of 1719, on the other hand, expressly authorized the jailing of any Negro unable to prove himself free and therefore presumed to be a runaway slave. Northerners were especially shocked to discover that it was the presidentially appointed Marshal of the District or his deputy who sold the Negro into slavery if, though he established his free status, he could not pay for his keep while in prison. The

[23] Jesse Torrey, *A Portraiture of Domestic Slavery in the United States*, pp. 33-34, 41.

first angry protest in Congress over this procedure arose in 1826 when a free Negro from New York, come to see the sights of the capital, was arrested and jailed as a runaway; only the intervention of the state governor saved him from being sold into slavery for life. A New York congressman demanded to know what law authorized such action. The House investigated. The remedy proposed was not the repeal of the statute but an arrangement whereby the city corporation of Washington or Georgetown should pay the jail fees for a free Negro arrested as a fugitive slave. The bill met with an indignant outcry from Georgetown. Congress dropped the plan.[24]

Two years later Congressman Charles Miner of Pennsylvania told the House that thirty years of neglect of the local slave laws had allowed "numerous and gross corruptions" to creep in; slave dealers exploiting their general "impunity" had made the District their headquarters; they used the federal jails freely to house their chattels in transit. He objected to allowing officers of the federal government to receive "emoluments" from the trade. If, he asked, a free Negro was sold for $300 in order to recoup $50 in jail fees, what happened to the remaining $250? It did not go into the public treasury but into the Marshal's pocket. Investigation showed, Miner asserted, that in five years' time the District jails had lodged 452 slaves and 290 Negroes taken as runaways; fifteen Negroes had later proved to be free men but five had been sold into life slavery. A hundred years later a study in the *Journal of Negro History* presented the thesis that kidnapping in the District of Columbia was relatively rare, that most of the Negroes taken into custody and sold had in fact been fugitive slaves. Late in 1828 the House called for a report but took no other action.[25]

For nearly seven years after Congress had denied the city

[24] *N.I.*, 11 Apr 1816; *Reg Deb*, 19C, 2S, pp. 555-57; H Doc 71, 19C, 2S, Ser 151; Clephane, "The Local Aspects of Slavery," CHS *Rec*, III, 225ff.

[25] *Reg Deb*, 20C, 2S, pp. 167-68, 175-87, 191-92; H Doc 215, 20C, 1S, Ser 173; H Rpt 60, 20C, 2S, Ser 190; William T. Laprade, "The Domestic Slave Trade in the District of Columbia," *Journal of Negro History*, XI (Jan 1926), 17-34.

government any control over the slave trade, few Washingtonians had seen any use in hammering away with fresh petitions touching upon any aspect of slavery. And indeed there was reason to hesitate about seeking to make the District of Columbia an island of freedom surrounded by slave territory. The anti-slavery movement was gaining ground in Virginia. When the Old Dominion enacted emancipation, then would be the moment to launch a vigorous campaign in the ten-mile square. Meanwhile many sensitive people undertook to abet the work of the American Colonization Society, which had helped a first group of Negroes to settle in Liberia in 1822.[26] No one suggested that local slave-owners abused their bondsmen. On the contrary, people familiar with conditions in the city admitted that slaves, mostly household servants, were generally well-treated and in some ways were better off than free Negroes. Still the recently organized Washington society for the abolition of slavery in the District of Columbia believed the time ripe in 1827 to issue a summary of slavery's "deleterious influence upon the welfare and prosperity of our city."

Captain Basil Hall, an English visitor in Washington, publicized this statement. Disclaiming any "squeamish sensibility" and passing over "the detrimental effects of slavery upon the morals of the community [as] too obvious to need illustration," the officers of the society declared "the first evil consequence . . . is the prostration of industry; an effect especially visible in the labouring classes of the community, but felt in its remote ramifications in every class of society." Although the city levied a large tax on the slaves of non-residents, the use of hired slaves on public works continued, leaving free laborers unemployed. As masters usually allowed their hired slaves only a pittance to live on and that little frequently went for intoxicants, "the burden of the support of many of these labourers falls upon society at large, while the proceeds of their labour go to fill the coffers of a distant master." Consequently "industrious and enterprising men, from various parts of our country" refused

[26] Ptn, H19A-G.42, 8 Jan, 5 Feb 1827; *Reg Deb*, 19C, 2S, pp. 1099-1101.

to settle in Washington. Because immediate wholesale emancipation might endanger the "tranquillity" of the South, the society urged a system of gradual emancipation in the District and, a far more radical idea, "enfranchisement of all that shall be born after such period as the wisdom of Congress may determine upon."[27]

Probably it was alarm at so revolutionary a proposal as enfranchisement and fear of its drawing a stream of Negroes to Washington that led the municipality in 1827 to place larger restrictions upon colored people—heavier fines for disturbing the peace, a stricter curfew, and, as guarantee for good behavior, for every free Negro family a $500 bond signed by two white men. When enforced, the curfew prevented Negroes from attending the theatre as they had once; the actor-manager Joseph Jefferson complained that the regulation cost his company $10 a night, since colored people, forced to leave early, no longer formed part of his audience. In 1828 Congress instructed the Commissioner of Public Buildings to bar Negroes from the Capitol except when there on "business," presumably to carry out some menial task. Still the new rulings failed to check Negro migration into the city or to weaken the abolitionist drive. Eleven hundred memorialists appeared to be in 1828 merely the vanguard of a growing local army determined to rid the District of slavery. If many conscientious people were troubled about how the community was to assimilate a large free colored population, the view of a Savannah, Georgia, newspaper that free Negroes were "the filth and offal of society" was rare in Washington. Education and then settlement of freedmen in Liberia seemed to be a solution.[28]

Free Negroes in the interim not only resisted every overture of the American Colonization Society but increased their efforts

[27] Basil Hall, *Travels in North America during the Years 1827 and 1828*, III, 34-39, 41-47; *Wshg Laws*, 5 Apr 1823; *N.I.*, 18 May, 2 Aug 1827.

[28] *Wshg Laws*, 31 May 1827; Jeannie Tree Rives, "Old Families and Houses, Greenleaf's Point," CHS *Rec*, v, 57, 59; *Washington Directory*, 1855; *Spec Rpt Comr Educ*, 1870, p. 197, Ser 1427; Leonidas Polk to Col. D. Polk, 21 Jan 1829, Leonidas Polk Mss (SHC).

to make themselves worthy and self-sufficient citizens independent of whites. About 1822, after the Resolute Beneficial Society had had to shut its school, Henry Smothers provided a classroom and taught his neighbors' children free of charge; he then built a schoolhouse at northwest 14th and H Streets, where as many as a hundred pupils attended. When he could no longer carry the expense, John Prout, another colored man, took over, charging every child 12½ cents a month tuition. White people, so far from objecting, frequently helped. Mrs. Mary Billings, the Englishwoman who had earlier opened a colored school in Georgetown, later moved it to Washington. Upon her death two fellow countrymen carried her school on, while Thomas Tabbs, a Maryland philanthropist, from time to time taught classes of Negro children outdoors under a tree when he could find no suitable indoor space. Two churches organized Sunday evening classes where adult Negroes might learn to read, and every denomination in Washington enrolled Negro children in Sunday school, at first in classes with white children, later, as the colored population increased, in separate units. In 1827 Father Vanlomen, priest of the Holy Trinity Church in Georgetown, founded the first seminary for colored girls and himself taught classes of Negro boys. Moreover, contrary to the assumption of later generations, during the 1820's colored children in Washington and Georgetown sometimes attended private white schools.

At the same time Negroes began to establish their own churches. In 1814 the liberality of Henry Foxhall, benefactor of the Washington Foundry Methodist Church, had enabled colored Methodists in Georgetown to build the Mt. Zion Negro church; but for many years that remained subject to the parent white congregation. Independence of white churches began in Washington in 1820 when a group of Negro parishioners withdrew from the Ebenezer Methodist Episcopal Church to form the African Methodist Episcopal Church. Within a few years they purchased the building erected by Presbyterians early in the century on South Capitol Street. Probably unrecognized by white people as momentous, this unobtrusive reminder that Negroes' souls might enter Heaven without white intervention would come to play a significant part in creating a self-conscious responsible Negro community within the city. The drawback of the separation lay in its tendency to cut off colored people from the material help white churches usually gave colored members.[29]

The churches as a rule watched over their needy parishioners; indeed, a sense of Christian obligation underlay most of Washington's philanthropy. But the poverty in the city of the 1820's created greater demands than the relief funds of separate denominations could supply. In 1822 a "town meeting" resolved to raise an endowment for that symbol of civic conscience, the Washington Female Orphan Asylum, and that winter citizens, irrespective of church affiliation, ran a soup kitchen on Capitol Hill. Two years later, as enlightened members of the community saw the weaknesses of palliatives, the Howard Society came into being, named for the great English humanitarian and prison reformer. Headed by Samuel Southard, then Secretary of the Navy, William Seaton of the *Intelligencer*, and William A. Bradley, later, like Seaton, a mayor of the city, the society set itself not only to relieve want but also to forestall it by providing work that would make otherwise helpless people self-supporting: in rented buildings on Eastern and Centre Market Squares teachers instructed "indigent females" in picking oakum, spinning yarn, and making clothes. Sale of the articles produced made some of the society's protégés independent within a few years and helped finance its distribution of the necessities of life to others. Nevertheless, scores of destitute white children still roamed the streets, although a second orphanage opened in 1825 under the direction of Sisters of Charity and Father Matthews of St. Patrick's Church. Apparently citizens of all faiths contributed. Before the end of the decade a new building went up

[29] *Spec Rpt Comr Educ*, 1870, pp. 197-215, Ser 1427; Richard Jackson, *Chronicles of Georgetown*, p. 214; *Centennial Sketch of Methodism in Georgetown*, cited in Bryan, *Capital*, II, 187; Wshg *Sun*, 12, 26 Feb, 9 Apr 1915.

on H Street near 9th on a site given by John and Marcia Van Ness for the older orphanage, now renamed the Washington City Orphan Asylum since thenceforward it would admit boys as well as girls. The lady managers raised the money by holding a great fair; a considerable part of the proceeds came from the sale of *What Is Gentility?*, a novel of Washington society by Margaret Bayard Smith, which she donated to the cause.[30]

While sectarian religion was thus a minor factor in Washington's charities, religious feeling expressed itself in fostering Christian education. A Catholic school for boys and somewhat later a Jesuit novitiate opened in a building on F Street adjoining the pasture where cows grazed on the hillside sloping down to Tiber Creek and the Centre Market. When Baptists decided to transfer their recently organized theological school from Philadelphia to the District of Columbia, Luther Rice, agent of the Baptist association for foreign missions, and the Reverend Obadiah Brown of Washington's First Baptist Church raised some $7,000 and purchased 46½ acres of land on the high ground touching the city's northwestern edge. There a building for the Columbian College rose during 1821. The congressional charter obtained that year expressly stipulated that the college must admit persons of all denominations and recognize no distinctions based upon "religious sentiments," but a distinctly devout atmosphere enveloped the campus as students began to enroll.[31]

In the early 1820's Washingtonians still dreamed of a federally endowed national university, but, while taking no action on that, Congress had granted a charter to Georgetown Seminary in 1815 sanctioning its awarding degrees; and Columbian College offered courses in secular as well as religious subjects.

[30] *N.I.*, 30 Oct, 31 Dec 1822, 16 Nov 1824, 14 Jan, 31 Dec 1825, 15 Oct, 24 Nov 1828; Elliot, *Historical Sketches*, pp. 212, 311-12; Prcdgs . . . Washington Female Orphan Asylum; M. B. Smith, *First Forty Years*, p. 210.

[31] Virginia King Frye, "St. Patricks, First Catholic Church of the Federal City," CHS *Rec*, XXIII, 39-40; Elliot, *Historical Sketches*, pp. 233-36, 245-50; *American Baptist Magazine*, IV, 137 and V, 157; *Annals*, 16C, 1S, pp. 780-81, 16C, 2S, pp. 1792-95; *N.I.*, 24 Jun 1817, 9 Jun 1819, 25 Sep 1827; Welling, *Brief Chronicles of the Columbian College*, p. 4.

Hence, for a time, prospects brightened that with the help of the Columbian Institute the capital still might turn into the center of learning and the arts its founders had envisaged. As the decade wore on, that hope dimmed. Georgetown College remained primarily a training school for the priesthood. Luther Rice's evangelical fervor coupled with his financial vagueness so involved Columbian College in a morass of debts that mere survival looked doubtful, a great university impossible. The Columbian Institute itself was withering away. Josiah Meigs, its president during the last years of his life, died in 1822. John Quincy Adams, whose masterly report to Congress on weights and measures had presented a compelling analysis of the place of science in a civilized nation, was no better able as President than as Secretary of State to elicit public support for an institution dedicated to widening the reach of human knowledge. His plea for a national observatory, a "lighthouse of the skies," received no serious consideration on Capitol Hill. Dr. Edward Cutbush, one of the Columbian Institute's leading spirits, left Washington in 1826 in disillusionment. The Abbé Correa, whose learning had promised to inspire younger men to research, had departed in 1820. Although the botanical garden at the foot of Capitol Hill still showed traces of the Columbian Institute's initial planting, lack of money and the encroachment of swamp land along the adjacent Washington Canal discouraged further efforts. John Calhoun, while he was Monroe's Secretary of War, had set the Army Corps of Engineers upon a series of explorations in the West that netted a certain amount of scientific data, and Surgeon General Joseph Lovell supported medical research at army outposts, but there was little likelihood that those beginnings could grow into scientific bureaus of the government. The Coast Survey, after 1818 in the hands of a Navy chaplain and officers wholly unqualified to carry out the tasks Rudolph Hassler had outlined, no longer held promise.[32]

[32] Obadiah Brown to Philip Richard Fendall, 26 Jan 1847, Fendall Mss, (Duke Univ); G. Brown Goode, "Genesis of the U.S. National Museum," p. 279; Dupree, *Science in the Federal Government*, pp. 32-42.

Cultivation of the arts had made correspondingly little progress. George Watterston, Librarian of Congress, had two popular novels to his credit, *L- - - - - Family in Washington* and *The Wanderer in Washington*, and Margaret Bayard Smith also had two. In 1824 an impoverished, courageous, dumpy, little widow, Anne Royall, began her *Sketches of History, Life and Manners in the United States*, a rambling but highly readable volume which disconcerted Washingtonians with such comments as that "ignorance, impudence and pride" characterized the bulk of them; when she was indicted as a common scold for airing some of her opinions, Judge Cranch had to stretch the law to substitute a fine for the ducking the criminal code demanded. While literary critics and genteel society denied Mrs. Royall recognition, people the country over read her controversial writings; for nearly thirty years her frilled mobcap topping her wispy gray locks would be a land mark in the capital. But most writers in the city were newspapermen concerned only with political reporting. The olios and the plays presented at the Washington Theatre after it was rebuilt were not local productions and were still performed by companies on tour. Soloists occasionally gave public concerts, and the Marine Band, perhaps better trained than in earlier days, played at the Capitol and on the White House grounds. Although President and Mrs. Adams introduced musical evenings at some of their levees and the pianofortes in other drawing rooms were an attraction, musical talent rarely evoked comment. If choral groups and singing societies such as flourished in rural New England existed at all in Washington, nobody spoke of them as a significant feature of the city's life.[33]

Giovanni Andrei and his fellow sculptors had completed most of the stone-carving for the Capitol before his death in 1824, but the murals and canvases Congress had commissioned for the building failed to create a permanent artistic colony in

[33] Mrs. Basil Hall, *Aristocratic Journey*, p. 83; Porter, *Life of Anne Royall;* Anne Royall, *Sketches of History, Life and Manners in the United States*, pp. 155-57; Elliot, *Historical Sketches*, pp. 165-66, 419-47.

Washington. Charles Bird King, it is true, kept his studio here, perhaps because of the Indian chiefs who came from time to time for treaty negotiations; his lengthening array of Indian portraits hanging in a corridor outside the War Department offices won him wide recognition. Otherwise, painters—Rembrandt Peale, Thomas Sully, John Trumball, Samuel Finley Breese Morse, and others—came and went without making Washington their headquarters. Although the gifted Bostonian, Charles Bulfinch, succeeded Benjamin Latrobe as architect of the Capitol after the older man left to complete the installation of water works in New Orleans, and although the talents of King and George Hadfield, who designed Arlington on the heights across the Potomac for George Washington Parke Custis, were still available to the city, architecture largely fell to local craftsmen-builders, some of them blessed with an eye for artistry, many of them without taste.[34]

The city L'Enfant had laid out on a scale to represent the genius of the new republic had in fact attained little aesthetic distinction. Partial execution of the plan left large areas untouched, which spoiled the effect. Bulfinch obtained appropriations to fence and landscape the twenty acres of grounds about the imposing new Capitol and an Irish gardener lovingly began the planting of shrubs and flower beds. President Adams himself devoted hours to developing a garden about the White House, which, unlike the gardens adjoining private houses, was not fenced off from the view of passers-by. The Executive Mansion, the Treasury, and the State and War Department buildings formed an architectually harmonious group, and some handsome private dwellings scattered from the Navy Yard to the section about the Octagon House and about the square named for Lafayette in 1825 were pleasing to the eye, perhaps above all the house Latrobe built for Captain Stephen Decatur and that of Army Surgeon General Joseph Lovell, today known as Blair House. A second Latrobe masterpiece, the John Van Ness

[34] *History of the Capitol*, pp. 74-75, Ser 4585; Charles Fairman, *Art and Artists of the Capitol*, pp. 29-48, 72-74.

house, stood on the present site of the Pan American Union building. In the open country beyond the city limits other beautiful private houses rose, notably the Linnean mansion in Rock Creek valley, converted a hundred-odd years later into the Natural History Museum of the zoo, and Eckington, the charming, still only partly finished, pillared house designed by Charles Bird King for Joseph Gales, Jr. But the beauties of the countryside underscored the unkempt appearance of the capital itself. The City Hall planned by George Hadfield was exquisitely proportioned, but the unfinished state of the building commandingly located on Judiciary Square looking out over the Mall turned a potential asset into a handicap. Most of the Mall was a wasteland of swamps dotted with clusters of sheds along the canal. Vacant lots occupied much of the city of magnificent distances, and the streets connecting one village with the others that together comprised the capital were still little more than rutted paths. Plan notwithstanding, the city exhibited to newcomers neither utility nor beauty—"immense" but "uncomfortable," in the words of a congressman from Maine. Her residents, he added, "live alltogether out of [the federal] Treasury and the Members and persons who are necessarily here at the sitting of Congress." Many another representative shared that opinion.[35]

While Washington's mayors and councils were pleased at appropriations for the City Hall and the jail, rapport between members of Congress and the local community deteriorated during the 1820's. Growth in numbers may have been partly responsible, as an expanding population and the admission of new states to the Union increased the size of Senate and House and accordingly made warm social intercourse with Washington families hard to maintain. The new rules of official etiquette

[35] Samuel Flagg Bemis, *John Quincy Adams and the Union*, pp. 122-23; Allen C. Clark, "Joseph Gales, Junior, Editor and Mayor," CHS *Rec*, XXIII, pp. 98-99; Katherine E. Crane, *Blair House, Past and Present*, pp. 5-7; John to Edward Anderson, 16 Apr 1826, quoted in Neal W. Allen, Jr., "John Anderson (1813) and the Parson Smith House," *Bowdoin Alumnus*, Jun 1957, p. 5.

did not help, differentiating as they did between town and, as it were, federal gown. Probably more important was the gradual shrinking in the caliber of men occupying seats in the House. The new rules of precedence relegated representatives to an inferior social position; and, as John Calhoun had foreseen in 1817, the defeat of a bill to raise congressional salaries to a figure equal to or above those of presidential appointees had the effect of lowering the prestige of the House until the most able men in the country were no longer eager to stand for election. Certainly after 1818 the House contained fewer distinguished men than once it had.[36]

Behavior during sessions through which members "lounged . . . whittling and spitting incessantly" testified to the lack of a sense of decorum, although for years past the manners John Randolph had affected were equally questionable: accompanied by his hunting dogs, he was not above striding into the chamber in riding boots, flicking his riding crop in menacing fashion; and, when delivering a speech, reportedly he frequently called for refills of the tankard on his desk. Such displays probably enlarged the crowd in the galleries when an important issue was under debate. During the last winter of sessions in the Brick Capitol, Henry Clay's speech on the Seminole War drew such a throng that ladies penned into the mobbed gallery were able to receive refreshments only because gentlemen on the floor tied oranges wrapped in their handkerchiefs to poles and passed the fruit up over the railing of the gallery. But cultivated Washingtonians felt no obligation to open their drawing rooms to congressmen of very modest political, and still less social, *savoir-faire*. And the Senate's arrogation to itself of a superior status was no guarantee to the brash and unpolished of a welcome in the city's most agreeable households.

Dozens of members of Congress consequently, when not engaged on official business, spent their time in sitting about their boardinghouses waiting impatiently for the end of the

[36] Charles E. Wiltse, *John C. Calhoun, Nationalist*, pp. 128-30.

session and the return home. Gambling became their foremost diversion. Few of them lived in Georgetown now that Washington had enough boardinghouses to allow every man a room to himself, but accommodations were dreary at best. The hotels were expensive and uninviting. The city's most noted hostelry, the miserably untidy "Indian Queen," charged as much as "the very first London hotel." Since only a man of independent means could afford to bring his wife to Washington even for the height of the season, the loneliness legislators were likely to encounter contributed to their lack of interest in the community. "Many," observed the *Intelligencer*, "come here with high-wrought hopes of office, emoluments and honors, and when disappointment comes, it is identified with the place."[37]

Furthermore, the collapse of the era of good feeling among political leaders cast a shadow over the city. Cracks had begun to show in 1818, and after the election of 1820 they widened into open breaches as rivals for the presidency in 1824 jockeyed for position. Former Governor Middleton of South Carolina, perhaps because he was not himself a candidate, saw fit to invite women as well as men to his dinner parties: "the ladies, dressed in white with deep flounces of some bright color, wore their bonnets at dinner and during the evening." But politics ordinarily entered at every door and dominated every occasion. With complete disregard of the hostess, at a private reception John Quincy Adams' friends gathered about him in one saloon, Andrew Jackson's about Old Hickory in another. Henry Clay gave dinners two or three times a week. In the beautiful house today known as Dumbarton Oaks, but in 1823 called Oakly by its new owner, John Calhoun held court, enthralling his guests with his brilliant conversation but winning few new supporters for his presidential aspirations. The victory of the reticent New Englander in 1824 did little to relieve tensions. Adams, watery-eyed, short, stocky, and unconcerned with the outer trappings

[37] Fearon, *Sketches of America*, p. 292; *N.I.*, 13 Jul 1822; diary of Louisa Kalisky, 1822-23, Lee Palfrey Mss; M. B. Smith, *First Forty Years*, pp. 145-47.

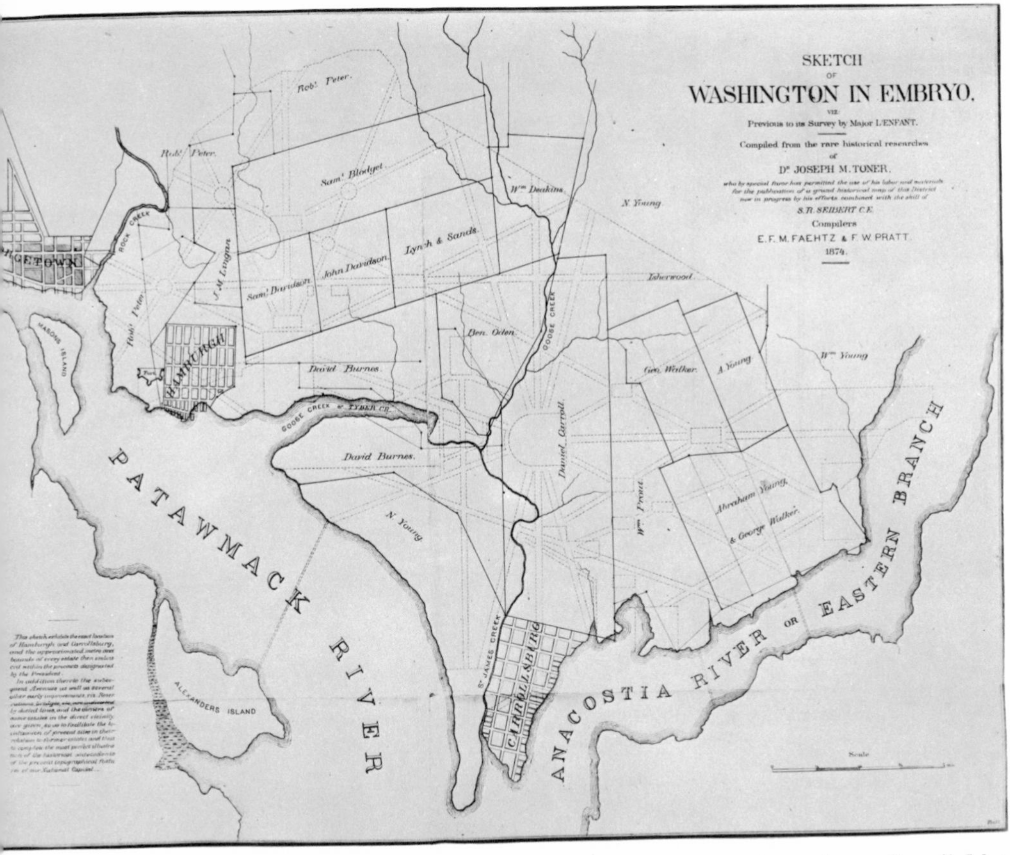

SKETCH
OF
WASHINGTON IN EMBRYO.
VIZ:
Previous to its Survey by Major L'ENFANT.
Compiled from the rare historical researches
of
Dr. JOSEPH M. TONER.
S. R. SEIBERT C.E.
Compilers
E. F. M. FAEHTZ & F. W. PRATT.
1874.

1. "Sketch of Washington in Embryo," 1791, showing the lands of the original proprietors. Compiled by E. F. M. Faelitz and F. W. Pratt, 1874, from materials assembled by Dr. J. Toner of Washington

2. Pierre L'Enfant, father of the city's planner

3. Surveyor, Benjamin Banneker

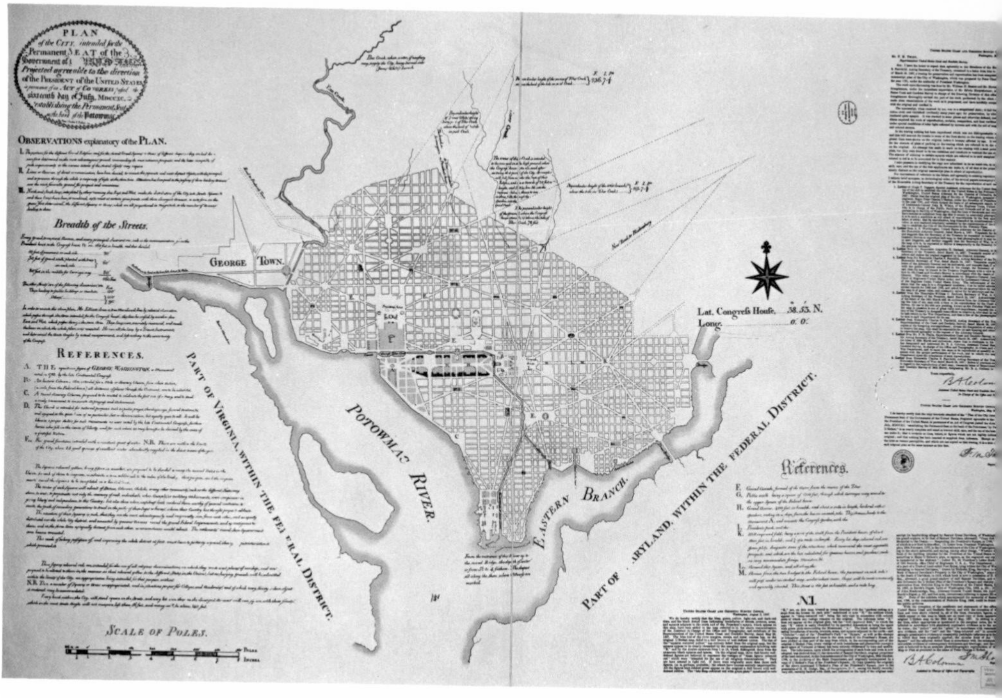

4. L'Enfant's plan of the city, 1791, reproduced from the original drawing by the Coast and Geodetic Survey, 1887

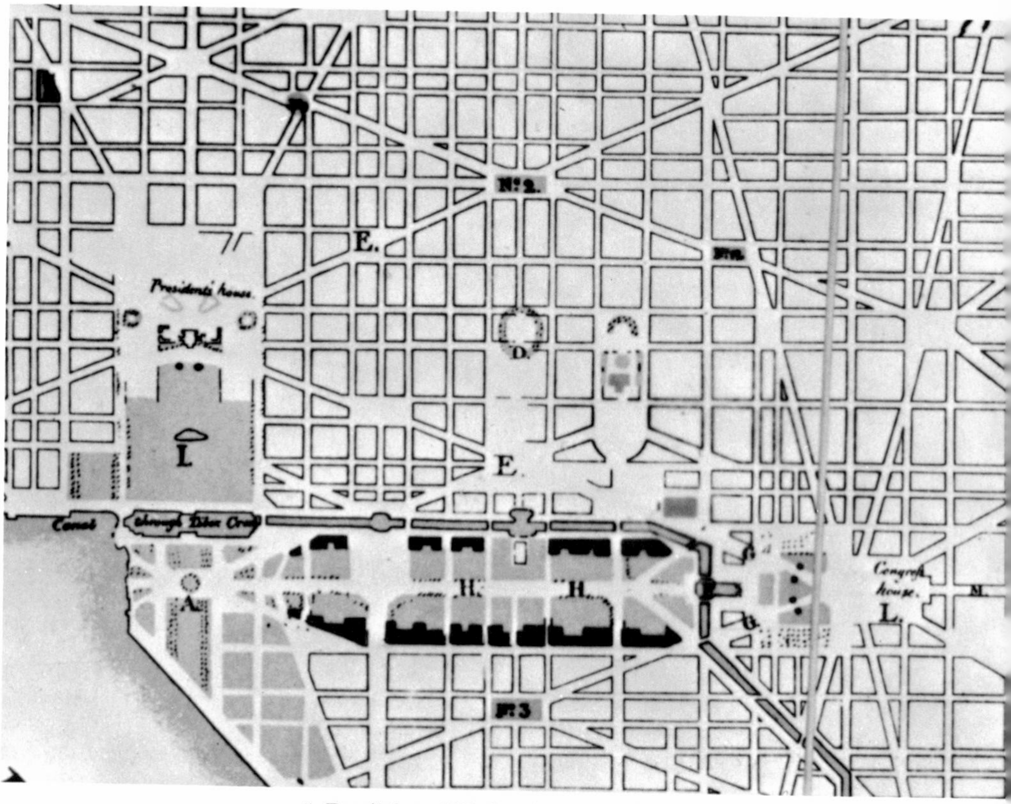

5. Detail from L'Enfant's plan of the city

6. North, or Senate, wing of the Capitol, 1800. Watercolor by William R. Birch

7. The Capitol from Pennsylvania Avenue as it looked in 1812. The passage way between the two wings was constructed of rough boards. In the foreground stand Jefferson's Lombardy poplars. Watercolor by Benjamin Latrobe, painted from memory ca. 1819

8. The President's House as shown in Charles Janson, *Stranger in America*, 1807

9. The Octagon House, residence of President and Mrs. Madison from October 1814 to August 1815, built by William Thornton for John Tayloe, 1798-1800

10. The "Seven Buildings" erected by James Greenleaf ca. 1796 at Pennsylvania Avenue and 19th Street, N.W. The corner house served the Madisons as Executive Mansion from August 1815 till March 1817 and long afterward won the apocryphal name "House of a Thousand Candles." The row was torn down in 1959 to make place for a modern office building. Pencil sketch by D. C. Heath

11. The White House, viewed from the south, after the British burned it; St. John's Church is in the background. Watercolor by Benjamin Latrobe, ca. 1816

12. Entrance hall of the Decatur house built by Latrobe, 1817-1819, for Commodore Stephen Decatur, who put into it the prize money he had won in the war with the Barbary pirates

13. The Blair House, originally a two-story structure, built by Surgeon-General Joseph Lovell in 1824, purchased by Francis Preston Blair in 1836, and by the U.S. government in 1943

14. The Capitol after the conflagration of August 24, 1814. Aquatint by W. Strickland after G. Munger

15. The Capitol as rebuilt by Latrobe and his successor Charles Bulfinch, showing the Bulfinch dome from Pennsylvania Avenue. Engraving by Alfred Jones, 1848

16. The new Treasury designed by Robert Mills, viewed from Fifteenth Street, ca. 1838. The State Department is at the right

17. The State Department adjoining the Treasury on the north, viewed from Pennsylvania Avenue. Photograph by Mathew Brady or an assistant ca. 1866

18. "President's Levee or all Creation going to the White House, Washington." A caricature of the Jackson era from an aquatint by Robert Cruikshank in the *Playfair Papers*, 1841

19. The Indian Queen on Pennsylvania Avenue, Washington's most famous hostelry of the 1830's and 1840's. Lithograph printed by Endicott & Swett, ca. 1832

of high office, was the first President to adopt pantaloons instead of knee breeches and silk hose; but the more democratic mode of dress proved no substitute for social and political finesse, and the President's intellectual arrogance, even though justified by his extraordinary intellectual powers, alienated followers. Adams' chief virtue in the opinion of many Washingtonians apparently was his refusal to dismiss on partisan grounds any of the approximately three hundred federal employees.[38]

That continuity contributed to the enduring southern atmosphere of Washington society, inasmuch as appointees from Maryland and Virginia alone still composed nearly half the civil and military list in the District of Columbia. Private householders were even more preponderantly southern in origin.[39] If that background endowed the community with certain social graces, the southerner's "code of honor" imposed upon the city customs that northerners found barbaric. Their half-hearted attempts to force a local anti-duelling law through Congress invariably met with defeat. Southerners themselves were sometimes shocked by the outcome of a duel. In March 1820 Commodore Stephen Decatur, hero of the war with Barbary pirates, and his beautiful wife gave a splendid ball in their chastely elegant new house in honor of the marriage of the President's younger daughter. The week after was to have been the gayest of the season. Tragedy intervened. When Commodore James Barron, obliged as a gentleman to defend his good name from slander, challenged his one-time protégé, Decatur's arrogant refusal to consider tendering an explanation, let alone an apology, led to the duelling ground in Bladensburg, Maryland. Twenty-four hours later Washington learned with horror that the dashing officer lay dead of wounds received on the "field of honor." The cry of "murderer" directed at Barron subsided in time as public opinion veered to the defense of a man deemed

[38] Hubbard, "Social and Political Life," p. 67; Kalisky Diary; Wiltse, *John C. Calhoun*, p. 269; Bemis, *John Quincy Adams*, pp. 134-36; M. B. Smith, *First Forty Years*, p. 162.

[39] *Washington Directory*, 1822; *Register of Officers*, 1828.

more sinned against than sinning.[40] Not till the end of the century would an uninformed brand of patriotism assign to the romantic Decatur the role of martyr, to Barron the part of coward and villain. But duelling over real and imagined affronts went on during the 1820's and through the 1830's. In 1826 a famous exchange of shots followed upon John Randolph's accusation that Adams and Clay had entered into a corrupt bargain, a "coalition of puritan and blackleg." One account implied that only Randolph's long white coat which Clay's second shot pierced "saved him [Randolph] from a sore bottom at least."[41]

For the completely detached or frivolous observer the prolonged struggle for power with its accompanying episodes of absurdity, pathos, jealousy, and nobility was never-endingly amusing. Gossip battened on it. During the season ladies, virtually by definition women who could afford servants, spent several afternoons a week driving about behind their "darky" coachmen to pay calls, and, while etiquette sanctioned merely leaving the cards with the servant at the door, the news to be gathered at the tea table of any fashionable hostess made calling in person not only a diverting pastime but, for the new arrival, practically an essential to social success. Where else would one learn so quickly of a fresh scandal brewing? A decade before Peggy Eaton upset the balance of political power under President Jackson, Washington's tea tables undertook to weight the scales in favor of one candidate or one faction or another. When the German woman whom Governor Middleton of South Carolina had brought to Washington as governess for his daughters married the Prussian minister, consternation reigned while society decided on the minimum civility feasible to ex-

[40] J. Q. Adams, *Memoirs*, IV, 246, V, 15, 31, 36; *Annals*, 15C, 2S, 8 Feb 1819, pp. 212-13, 16C, 1S, 23, 24 Mar 1820, pp. 1670, 1675; M. B. Smith, *First Forty Years*, p. 150; Seaton, *William Winston Seaton*, p. 148; Ronald W. May to the Editor, *Washington Post and Times Herald*, 23 Mar 1957; *Washingtonian*, 17 Dec 1836.

[41] Washington *Evening Star*, 4 May 1896; John Anderson to Edward Anderson, 16 Apr 1826, *Bowdoin Alumnus*, Jun 1957, p. 5.

tend to a former servant. As Sir Charles Bagot or his successors at the British legation drove from boardinghouse to boardinghouse to drop cards on the people to whom the rules of precedence now gave importance, the diplomats must have marvelled at the human vagaries in the capital of a nation ostensibly dedicated to equality. Much of the gossip was good-natured. Who could fail to enjoy the mental picture of the dignified John Quincy Adams caught during his usual early morning swim in the Potomac by an insistent woman, identified by rumor as Mrs. Anne Royall, who supposedly stood over his clothes on the bank until he granted her an interview?[42]

Nor were the troubled 1820's without their stirring occasions. Most memorable of all were General Lafayette's visits as guest of the municipality in the autumn of 1824 and the summer of 1825. William Seaton, who met him at the District line, reported that the elderly hero had breakfasted on "fine Bay perch, six of which he consumed, bread *à discretion*, all washed down with generous Bordeaux; the culmination of his enthusiasm, however, being reserved for the unsurpassed canvas-back duck and hominy." The city fêted him with a magnificent reception, dinners and balls at a cost of more money than the entire annual public school budget. Together with President Monroe and most of the Cabinet, he attended the first commencement at Columbian College. School children paraded for him. Although Samuel Morse's portrait shows a raddled old man obviously suffering from elephantiasis, decades later elderly ladies still cherished as their dearest childhood memory having touched the aged hero's hand. On the 4th of July 1826 the celebration of a half-century of American independence marked another great moment, observed by a huge parade and "an impressive and argumentative" oration at the Capitol.[43]

42 Kalisky Diary; Hubbard, "Political and Social Life," p. 68; Anne Royall, *Sketches of History, Life and Manners*, p. 130.

43 J. Q. Adams, *Memoirs*, VII, 39, 40; Seaton, *William Winston Seaton*, pp. 166-70; *N.I.*, 2 Oct 1824, 12 Aug, 9 Sep 1825, 6 Jul 1826; Rothwell, *Laws*, p. 300; Welling, *Brief Chronicles of the Columbian College*, p. 10;

Yet people with a permanent stake in the city had reason to feel that her status of capital was not enough. Unless she achieved a solid economic basis independent of Congress, their aspirations for her and for themselves were unlikely to flower. Congress showed no disposition to widen local political control over race relations and the slave trade. Without congressional cooperation neither external beautification of the city nor enduring enrichment of her cultural life could go far. Philanthropy in turn must suffer if the municipality and private citizens were impoverished. They agreed with the statement of a Rhode Island newspaper that the capital should "stand as a monument of wealth and power, as a rallying point for popular partialities which will exalt the pride of patriotism." But until the federal government accepted that point of view and acted, the one direction in which the community could move to help itself was toward commercial pre-eminence. By 1822 other American cities had not only recovered from the panic but were flourishing. In spite of federal payrolls, trade and private manufacturing in Washington were at a standstill. The Washington Canal held only a few inches of water and was unusable except at very high tide; the Potomac Company was manifestly moribund. But the river was still there. New York state had started the Erie Canal in 1817, and the "big ditch" had crept westward all through the depression years. The route to the West by way of the Potomac was sixty miles shorter. Surely in that fortuitous circumstance lay the best hope of economic salvation for the District of Columbia.[44]

Local businessmen realized they must make a fresh start on the long-talked-of project if they were to tap the trade of the Ohio Valley. In the summer of 1822 while western Pennsylva-

---

Eunice Tripler: Some Notes of Her Personal Recollections, ed. Louis A. Arthur, pp. 33-35.

[44] *N.I.*, 1 Sep 1820, quoting the *Rhode Island American*; William Crammond to Peter Hagner, 4 Nov 1822, Hagner Mss (SHC); H Rpt 800, 24C, 1S, p. 24, Ser 295; Thomas Law to Robert Gilmore, 1 Oct 1820, Wright Collection (George Washington Univ); Sanderlin, *National Project*, pp. 38-39, 315.

nians petitioned Congress for improvement of Potomac River navigation, representatives of the three District cities discussed the matter and, after a conference with men from Leesburg, Virginia, and Baltimore, called a convention to meet in Washington in November 1823. From that moment on, the prospective canal became the all-important theme of newspaper articles and conversation among men deeply concerned for the District's well-being.[45] Delegates to the convention came from Maryland, Virginia, Pennsylvania, and Ohio as well as the District, among them Albert Gallatin, Jefferson's Secretary of the Treasury, Henry Clay, Francis Scott Key, Judge Bushrod Washington, George Washington Parke Custis, and Thaddeus Stevens, who was at that time still a Pennsylvania iron-monger. Their fame lent importance to the proceedings. John Quincy Adams and other Cabinet members attended a dinner given for the delegates; newspapers publicized the convention speeches and resolutions. The results were gratifying. The President's State of the Union message recommended federal support, the Virginia Assembly incorporated a new canal company, and Congress, urged on by constituents, appropriated money for a survey of a feasible route and an estimate of cost.[46]

Opposition from Baltimore and Philadelphia delayed endorsement from their states, but the Maryland legislature approved early in 1825, and in March a favorable preliminary report from the Board of Army Engineers led Congress to confirm the Virginia and Maryland acts. Two months later the Potomac Company dissolved, relinquishing all its property rights to the new Chesapeake and Ohio Canal Company. Enthusiasts considered the battle now won: the new company need only raise four or five million dollars, dig a canal along the Potomac, install locks to carry the waterway over the 1900-foot elevation

[45] *Annals*, 17C, 1S, pp. 1864-67; *N.I.*, 6 Jan, 24 Apr 1821, 3 Aug 1822, 20 Aug 1823; ptns, HR17A-F4.1, 4 Mar 1820 and 18 Jan 1822; *Wshg Gazette*, 21, 23, 27 Oct 1823.

[46] *Wshg Gazette*, 10 Nov 1823; Sanderlin, *National Project*, pp. 51-53; *Annals*, 18C, 1S, pp. 534-69, 838-39.

to the Monongahela River, and Pittsburgh would then be only 341 miles distant by water from Washington. The Pennsylvania legislature, caught up in the general excitement, chartered the canal company in 1826.[47]

A shock awaited the promoters. The final report of the Army Board of Engineers put the cost of the project at $22,300,000, about four times the figure expected and far more than the most optimistic canal advocates knew they could raise. Persuaded that the Army had miscalculated, they induced President Adams to appoint civil engineers to re-examine the adverse findings. Most business in the District had continued to languish even when the canal had seemed a certainty. Washington's mayor wrung his hands over the city's "almost total absence" of commerce. The Bank of Columbia closed, and its directors gloomily reported "thirty-two years of bad management, neglect, and confusion" dimmed the chance of salvaging anything. While pressing for congressional approval of a new bridge across the Potomac below the Little Falls, Georgetown declared: "Our town, notwithstanding its local and natural advantages for trade, has been gradually declining; our population is deminished; our houses untenanted; and the people earnestly pleading that the avenues of commerce may be opened."[48]

To the relief of local merchants, in the spring of 1827 the civil engineers submitted a report estimating the cost of a canal to Cumberland, Maryland, at the foot of the mountains, at $4,500,000. Georgetown and Alexandria citizens requested their city councils each to subscribe $250,000 to stock, and Washingtonians recommended a corporate subscription of $1,000,000. A reassured Congress authorized the municipalities to borrow the money, levying taxes to pay the interest until

[47] *Reg Deb*, 18C, 2S, Appendix, p. 102; *N.I.*, 11 Aug 1824, 2 Feb, 20 May 1825, 10 Feb, 27 Nov 1826.

[48] Sanderlin, *National Project*, 53-57; *Report to Stockholders of the Bank of Columbia*, 20 March 1826, in *Miscellaneous Pamphlets* 750:2; S. Doc 86, 19C, 1S, Ser 128; H Doc 51, 20C, 1S, Ser 170.

dividends should cover the costs, and, better still in the community's view, sanctioned purchase by the United States Treasury of 10,000 shares of $100 par value. If some taxpayers questioned the wisdom of incurring such heavy municipal debts, their voices were drowned in the general chorus of approval. A congressman from New York warned that under the "influence of enthusiasm" the District might be succumbing to "false lures," but, apart from specifying that the United States would not be responsible for either interest or principal, Congress refused to curb local investment.[49]

Two features of developments during 1827, however, might well have given citizens pause. First was the paring down of the original plan to develop a commercially usable waterway between the tidewater cities on the Potomac and the Ohio Valley. The very name Chesapeake and Ohio Canal advertised the intended challenge to New York City and the Erie Canal. A canal to Cumberland would make the District cities distributing points for the coal and farm produce of the upper Potomac Valley but would not reach over the mountains into the fertile Ohio country. Perhaps District investors believed the link with the Monongahela would be easy to finance once the canal had reached the base of the mountains; perhaps they looked to a serviceable portage. Whatever their reasoning, they seemed satisfied with the reduced scope of the undertaking. The second factor in the situation as it unfolded during 1827 was the chartering of the Baltimore and Ohio Railroad.

Along the Potomac disbelief in the utility of a railroad was not unnatural, if only because the project originated in Baltimore, and Baltimore would logically grasp at straws to prevent diversion to rivals of her trade with the backcountry. The *Intelligencer* dubbed a railroad a costly experiment, certainly not a transport system that could compete with a canal. While Baltimore bankers and merchants organized the railroad com-

[49] *N.I.*, 20 Jun, 18 Jul, 2 Aug, 18 Sep, 8, 14 Nov 1827; *Reg Deb*, 20C, 1S, pp. 2695, xxvii-xxviii.

pany and sold stock to the Maryland legislature, the corporation of Baltimore, and private citizens, District businessmen watched with the detached interest of outsiders witnessing the admirable but futile struggle of a community to halt its inescapable decline. So far from seeking to share in an enterprise for which their neighbors had raised $3,000,000 in a few months, Washingtonians redoubled efforts to finance their own undertaking. For more than forty years American inland towns and cities had pinned their hopes of commercial progress upon improved river navigation and canals. Why should the District cities abandon that plan now in favor of a newfangled substitute of doubtful value? As the railroad age opened, they threw their energies into a project that would eat up their resources and sharply limit their economic expansion.[50]

On the 4th of July 1828 ceremonies inaugurating the two new ventures took place simultaneously. In Baltimore, Charles Carroll of Carrollton, the last surviving signer of the Declaration of Independence, turned the first spade of earth to start work on the Baltimore and Ohio Railroad, while on the Potomac above Georgetown President John Quincy Adams broke ground for the Chesapeake and Ohio Canal. The superstitious might have seen an ill omen in the President's difficulties when his shovel struck a hickory tree root. Only after he had stripped off his coat and dug fiercely at the obstruction did he succeed in turning the earth. But John Quincy Adams profited from the setback: for the first time in a long distinguished career he won delighted cheers from the spectators who read into the episode symbolic proof of the triumphant progress of the canal.[51]

Unhappily altercation among the District cities posed a threat to the canal before it was well begun. Washington and Alexandria were determined to have it extend far enough downstream to enable the barges to unload in deep water at their

[50] Edward Hungerford, *The Story of the Baltimore and Ohio Railroad, 1827-1927*, I, 120-40; *N.I.*, 27 Oct, 8 Nov 1827, 30 Jan, 13 Apr 1830.

[51] Bemis, *John Quincy Adams*, p. 102; *N.I.*, 7 Jul 1828.

wharves. Georgetown, anxious to pre-empt the traffic, argued that the terminus should be at the head of tidewater at the Little Falls; to carry the canal down to a terminal basin on the Eastern Branch would be utmost extravagance. But Washington, holding four times as much stock as Georgetown, enlisted the support of Richard Rush, Secretary of the Treasury, who represented the million-dollar interest of the United States government. The upshot was a compromise largely in the favor of the capital: the waterway was to come through Georgetown into Rock Creek below the present K Street and continue thence on the Washington side to the mouth of the Tiber. From that point barges could pass to the Eastern Branch via the Washington Canal. Washington had already taken steps to force the impecunious Washington Canal Company to deepen and widen its channel, and when President Adams as one of his last acts in office approved construction of a canal boat basin at "the foot of the President's Square," citizens elatedly envisaged coal barges loaded in Cumberland discharging their cargoes direct on to ocean-going vessels docked on the Eastern Branch above and below the Navy Yard. Washingtonians and Georgetowners showed no concern for Alexandria. That she would have to build first an aqueduct to take heavily laden horse-drawn barges over the Potomac and then a seven-mile lateral canal into the city merely insured more trade for her competitors.[52] Their problem was to collect the subscriptions of individual investors and find an organization willing to lend the two corporations the $1,250,000 they had pledged to the enterprise.

As the autumn of 1828 wore on, valiant efforts to expedite the financing of the venture upon which scores of citizens believed their future hinged slowly gave way to profound discouragement. The election of Andrew Jackson that November was little short of alarming to men fearful of his known opposi-

[52] Sanderlin, *National Project*, pp. 65-66; H Doc 102, 18C, 2S, Ser 118; *N.I.*, 9 May 1826; Memorial, Mayor Joseph Gales to President J. Q. Adams, 2 Mar 1829, and map showing the proposed location of the basin, D.C. Misc; *Reg Deb*, 19C, 1S, pp. 754, xxvi.

tion to federally supported "internal improvements." If a Jacksonian Congress were to cancel the United States $1,000,000 subscription to canal stock, the great national project would collapse and with it, paradoxically, Washingtonians' hopes of attaining economic independence of the federal government.

CHAPTER V

THE JACKSONIAN "REVOLUTION" AND AFTER, 1829-1840

WHETHER Andrew Jackson's impending occupancy of the White House spelled the catastrophic end of a great era in the capital or the dawn of a brighter day depended upon the point of view of the individual citizen of the disenfranchised community. The Hero of New Orleans had devoted adherents in the District of Columbia among both the well-to-do and the working classes. John Van Ness, President of the Bank of the Metropolis, and Thomas Corcoran, dry goods merchant and former mayor of Georgetown, headed a committee that took charge of inaugural preparations. Democratic party organs like Duff Green's *United States Telegraph* in January 1829 began announcing triumphantly what the new order would mean: curtailment of "special privilege" in the interests of the common man and a clean sweep from the executive departments of all Adams supporters and all long-time incumbents. Warm as was Anne Royall's regard for John Quincy Adams, even she upheld his enemies in proclaiming "rotation of office" a sound method whereby the uninitiated could gain experience in running the government. No federal officeholder in Washington felt entirely safe, and those known to be anti-Jacksonians trembled in their boots. Mrs. Smith thought the affectation of gaiety at President Adams' drawing room oppressive. The defeated President and his wife "came out in a brilliant masquerade dress of social, gay, frank, cordial manners . . . a change from the silent, repulsive, haughty reserve by which they have hitherto been distinguished." But permanent residents of the city dreaded the imminent departure of old friends and more than half expected a bloodless but far-reaching social and economic revolution.[1]

[1] *United States Telegraph*, 3 Jan 1829; Wshg *National Journal*, 12 Jan 1829; Sarah H. Porter, *Life of Anne Royall*, pp. 167-68; M. B. Smith, *First Forty Years*, pp. 248, 281-82.

The weather during January and February was bitterly cold. Illness invaded almost every household, and the family that did not lose a child counted itself lucky. The suffering in the poorer parts of the city appalled Amos Kendall of Kentucky upon his arrival. Apparently unprepared to find desperate want everywhere, Kendall, who would soon be the chief power in Jackson's "kitchen cabinet," approved of the congressional vote to distribute fifty cords of firewood to families without fuel; only later would he learn that the wood had to be taken from supplies purchased to heat government buildings.[2] Amidst the general misery no one put into words apprehensions about the future of the Chesapeake and Ohio Canal.

The local Democratic committee proclaimed how different everything would be after the inauguration. A forerunner of the national committee that would soon substitute the party convention for the congressional caucus in nominating presidential candidates, the Washington committee ignored the District Marshal, Mayor Gales, and members of the city council, officials formerly responsible for inaugural celebrations. But the committee in turn faced embarrassments. Because Mrs. Jackson had died only a day or two before the General set out from Tennessee, he refused to permit a grand parade with Jackson Riflemen escorting him to the Capitol. No advance festivities of any kind were possible, as the grief-stricken widower declined every invitation. His vanquished opponents had nothing to celebrate.[3]

The brilliant sunshine that warmed the capital on March 4, 1829, lightened the gloom that had enveloped apprehensive Washingtonians. Like Thomas Jefferson twenty-eight years before, Andrew Jackson chose to walk from his lodgings to the Capitol, and, again like Jefferson, he went unattended by the retiring President. John Quincy Adams had left the White House the preceding night to take up residence in a rented

[2] *Ibid.*, pp. 257, 262, 269, 276-78, 283-84; *Autobiography of Amos Kendall*, ed. William Stickney, p. 285.

[3] *U.S. Telegraph*, 2 Jan, 10, 24 Feb, 2-4 Mar 1829; M. B. Smith, *First Forty Years*, pp. 272-73, 290.

house on Meridian Hill. On the grounds of the Capitol a huge crowd gathered quietly to await the white-haired old General. As he walked across the untidy stretch of Mall at the foot of the Hill, past the new iron fence, and through the west gate into the recently planted grounds, his simple dignity impressed the most critical onlookers. "Even from a distance," wrote Margaret Bayard Smith, "he could be discerned from those accompanying him, for he only was uncovered (the Servant in the presence of his Sovereign, the People)." The throng on the west terrace was so great that he was obliged to climb an area wall and make his way into the building through the subbasement. The swearing-in ceremony, "an imposing and majestic spectacle," for the first time took place outdoors on the east portico of the Capitol. When the inaugural address was over, delivered amid an almost "breathless silence," and Chief Justice Marshall had administered the oath, the President kissed the Bible reverently and "then bowed again to the people—yes, to the people in all their majesty."

Suddenly the majesty of the people vanished. The crowds rushed upon the President to shake his hand, trampled over the lawns and newly planted flowerbeds to reach him before he got to the gate and the horse awaiting him there, and then raced to the White House to ensure themselves a place at the reception and a chance at the refreshments. Uncouth-looking small-town politicians and farmers who admired Old Hickory or hoped to land appointments to office rubbed elbows with city bankers and blue-coated colonels and commodores. The press of people soon jammed the President against the wall until he escaped through the broken furniture and smashed china out the south door and returned to Gadsby's Hotel. The "rabble" stayed on, "a mob of boys, negroes, women, children, scrambling, fighting, romping." A story, doubtless apocryphal, tells of a small child, lost in the crowd, whose anxious parents at last found her delightedly jumping up and down on an old sofa in one of the President's private rooms; she cried out to her mother, "Just think, Mama! This sofa is a millionth part mine."[4] Later receptions at the White House were less boisterous, but the popular Jacksonian assumption that all government property belonged to all the American people, particularly to all friends of the party, endured.

Official society, furthermore, soon faced open conflict with the President over his insistence upon having Mrs. John Eaton accorded every courtesy. "Peggy" O'Neale Eaton, wife of the new Secretary of War and daughter of a Washington tavern keeper, was a beautiful, vivacious woman whose earlier life appeared to justify the charge that she was a "loose" female. The pastor of the Second Presbyterian Church indulged in frank criticism of her, only to find himself summoned to the White House to be rebuked by the President for maligning an innocent woman and to lose Andrew Jackson as a member of the congregation. Mrs. Calhoun, wife of the Vice-President, and most other gently bred ladies, believing all moral standards the issue, flatly refused to receive the notorious Peggy. In her autobiography written forty years later Mrs. Eaton exclaimed "God help the woman who must live in Washington." The result was a deep rift in Washington society healed only by time and by Eaton's eventual resignation from the Cabinet.[5]

The anticipated wholesale proscription of officeholders in Washington, on the other hand, did not occur. By 1831, of the 301 men who had held government posts under John Quincy Adams 205 were still on the rolls, and of those who were dropped several, certainly, had reached an age to warrant retirement. Dismissal, it was true, was a severe blow to competent men who found themselves turned out after years of faithful service to make way for party supporters. People not otherwise touched felt the shock when long-established members of the community had to seek a livelihood elsewhere. As the expense

[4] *N.I.*, 6 Mar 1829; M. B. Smith, *First Forty Years*, pp. 293-97; Professor A. C. McLaughlin of the University of Chicago told his students the story of the child and the sofa.

[5] M. B. Smith, *First Forty Years*, pp. 252, 285-89, 305-306, 310-11, 320-21; James Stuart, *Three Years in North America*, II, 75; *The Autobiography of Peggy Eaton*, p. 209.

of transport precluded families' taking their household effects with them, the melancholy sight of furnishings stacked up for auction was repeated again and again. Only an occasional ousted official, George Watterston for one, stayed on to find other work in Washington; Richard Rush, Adams' Secretary of the Treasury, accepted a commission from the District cities in the spring of 1829 to negotiate a loan in Europe to finance the corporations' purchase of Chesapeake and Ohio Canal stock. Yet dismissals were far fewer than either party friends or foes had prophesied, and an employee who survived the first year's "house-cleaning" could count with some certainty on holding his job till the next major political upset. In the early 1830's that moment was not imminent. Furthermore, however saddened by removal of old friends, people rooted in Washington could derive some consolation from the signs of an expansion of the federal establishment; fifteen new clerkships in the Post Office Department and the prospect of more to come.[6]

Nevertheless the social structure of the capital underwent a subtle change. The line drawn between official and resident society in Monroe's administration, if preparing the way, had affected very few people. The new division, initially not so evident as it would become later, had more significant and long-lasting consequences. Individual government employees in the 1830's and after, as in the past, would identify themselves with the community, but general acceptance of the principle of rotation in office, whether acted upon or not, tended to put all federal officeholders into the category of temporary residents. Those who manifested a wholehearted interest in the city and a readiness to share her civic burdens gradually slid over the invisible line to become Washingtonians, but at every social level a new differentiation developed between people who thought of the federal city as home and those ephemeral inhabitants to whom only her federal functions seemed important.

[6] Figures reached by a check of every name on the *Register of Officers of the U.S.*, 1828 and 1831; see also *ibid.*, 1833; M. B. Smith, *First Forty Years*, pp. 290, 297-99, 301; Leonidas Polk to Col. D. Polk, 18 Jan 1829, Leonidas Polk Mss (SHC); *Wshg Metropolis*, 19 Jan 1838, 25 Jun 1839.

In 1829, however, of more direct and immediate concern to District bankers and investors was the uncertainty about the monetary policies of the new administration. If the "enemy of privilege" in the White House were to ask for investigations of local banking houses, no one dared guess at the outcome. Certainly the President's known hostility to the Bank of the United States stood as a threat to the branch located since 1824 opposite the Treasury. Samuel Harrison Smith, who had become head of the branch in 1828, presumably in time lost his epithet of "Silky Milky," while the institution's president, that Philadelphia dandy, Nicholas Biddle, learned the truth of his own witticism: "The world is ruled by three boxes, the ballot box, the ammunition box and the band box." But in the absence of intensive congressional scrutiny, local bankers gradually ceased to worry. When the President, after ordering withdrawal of government deposits from the Bank of the United States in 1833, chose the Bank of the Metropolis for one of the federal depositories, the possibility that he might add other District houses to his list of "pet banks" seemed encouraging.[7]

Jackson's second term killed the bankers' lingering complacency, for the failure of the Bank of Maryland in 1834 caused three District banks to suspend payments. The President's political opponents blamed the disaster on his war on the Bank of the United States; his friends apparently held the "monster monopoly" guilty. A supporter of Peter Force, Whig candidate for mayor, declared that Jackson had "placed upon our city . . . the hand of Death. . . . To the truth of this picture, let the answer be given by our suspended banks, the closed doors, depreciated business and protested notes of merchants; by the suspended operations of our brickmakers, carpenters, lumber yards, cartmen, and laborers, and the Sabbath-day appearance of our streets." Whigs in Washington's wealthiest ward formally resolved: "At this important crisis in our na-

[7] *N.I.*, 14 Jan, 23 Mar, 1 May, 31 Aug 1829, 27 Jan, 12 Apr 1830, 4 Jul 1831; *Columbian Gazette*, 27 Mar, 6 Nov 1832; H Doc 84, 21C, 2S, Ser 208; H Ex Doc 83, 33C, 2S, Ser 234; S Doc 16, 23C, 1S, p. 6, Ser 238; Wharton, *Salons*, pp. 248-49.

tional affairs, when the greatest embarrassments exist in our city, . . . it is the duty of all patriots and freemen to oppose the authors of such a state of things."[8]

The majority in Congress, suspecting that local banking practices were largely responsible, ordered the municipalities to retire their due bills and instructed the House Committee on the District to investigate the condition of the District banks. The cities reluctantly complied. The committee did nothing until the local bank charters were about to expire. District banking capital, in the past perhaps larger than local needs justified, slowly shrank; it dropped to a sixth of New York's, less than a third of Boston's, and one-half of Baltimore's; bank stock sold below par; dividends hovered between a mere 4 and 7 percent; and local merchants still complained of the difficulty of obtaining loans. The House committee then produced some scandalous findings: bankers, "respectable citizens," had used the suspension of 1834 for their own profit; their "ruinous desolating" manipulations over the years had measurably retarded the growth of the cities, and bank failures since 1821 had cost the people of the District $1,700,000, money "taken from the profits of labor and . . . absorbed by adventurers and speculators."[9] Nevertheless, in the face of outraged denunciations from "Old Bullion" Benton and a few associates, Congress renewed the charters of the seven surviving banks until 1838 on condition that they not issue notes in excess of their capital. In 1838 they won another two-year reprieve.[10]

Skilled workmen who might have welcomed an investigation of working conditions were left, on the contrary, to fend for themselves. Trade associations had begun to appear in the 1820's, although, like the Columbia Typographical Society, at first they were rather mutual benefit societies than labor

[8] *N.I.*, 19 May 1834; *Reg Deb*, 23C, 1S, pp. 3749-52, Appendix, pp. 350-51; James Graham to Wm. A. Graham, 16 Apr 1834, William A. Graham Mss (SHC); S Doc 374, 23C, 1S, Ser 242.

[9] H Rpt 800, 24C, 1S, Ser 295.

[10] *Reg Deb*, 24C, 1S, pp. 1698-1720, 4437-40; *Congressional Globe*, 24C, 1S, pp. 60-62, 69, 426, Appendix, pp. 27-28; H Doc 181, 24C, 2S, Ser 304; 5 Stat. 309.

unions seeking wage increases and shorter hours. In 1830 the newly formed Association of Mechanics of the City of Washington announced that "it is the interest and bounden duty of every member of this community to promote that system of public policy, the tendency of which is to increase the numbers, diversify the pursuits and augment the happiness of our citizens who look to their own labor for support." That October working men celebrated "the freedom of the Press and the late Revolution in France" by holding a great parade in which "the different trades exhibited on platforms, the mysteries of their Arts." The President, the Cabinet, the Marines, and the entire French legation marched in the procession.[11] Printers and craftsmen founded a newspaper, *The American Mechanic*, and after that collapsed, the *Washingtonian* replaced it for a few months. Several trade groups banded together in 1833 to form a General Trades' Union dedicated to securing "the right of fixing the price of their own labor." Like similar organizations in other American cities, the union advocated free public education in place of the mockery of "pauper schools" and opposed the innovation introduced by prison reformers whereby convicts were taught trades and the prison-made articles sold to the public at reduced prices. When bitter conflict over wage rates and apprenticeships broke out between the Typographical Union and Duff Green, in 1835 publisher of the *Reformer*, the printers got no encouragement from the Jacksonians in Congress. Before the panic of 1837, country-wide inflation produced an upward spiral of prices unmatched by wage increases; within one three-month period the cost of flour in Georgetown rose from $4.50 to $6.00 a barrel. The craft organizations indeed failed in their every objective but one: the reduction in 1840 of hours on federal works to ten a day. And unlike workingmen in most of the states, in Washington only men with property could vote in municipal elections.[12]

[11] *Address of the Association of Mechanics . . . of Washington to the Operatives throughout the United States*, in *Miscellaneous Pamphlets*, 750:11; Minutes, Columbia Typographical Society, 28 Oct 1830; *N.I.*, 30 Oct 1830.

[12] *N.I.*, 9 Apr, 21 Aug 1830, 16, 22 Jun 1831, 23 Apr, 19 May, 4, 22

Unskilled day laborers, white or black, were too inarticulate to voice their wants even for full employment. In the spring of 1829 they could count on jobs on the C & O Canal, but that summer the company resorted to importation of European workmen under contract. Unless Congress authorized extensive public works and, unlikely event, forbade the practice of hiring slaves for building operations, help for common labor appeared remote. Federal building in Washington came to a halt in 1829 and did not resume until the mid-1830's. Men employed on maintenance and repair were chiefly craftsmen. When the city began widening and deepening of the Washington Canal in 1831, ditch diggers fared better, but not because of Jacksonian policies. The next year the $115,000 appropriated for macadamizing Pennsylvania Avenue and grading the President's square and the $23,000 spent for piping water into the Capitol, the departmental offices, and the White House provided work for the unskilled, but inasmuch as approximately a thousand newly arrived Irish immigrants seized upon those ill-paid jobs, native laborers were little better off than before.[13] In fact, during a period when much of the United States was enjoying a boom far exceeding that of the postwar years, the capital was facing an economic crisis.

Troubles over the C & O Canal precipitated that crisis. Late in 1829 Richard Rush obtained from Dutch bankers a $1,500,000 loan to the District cities to finance their purchase of canal stock, but in the interim the slowness of individual subscribers in making payments left the company too short of cash to purchase land and place contracts on favorable terms. More alarming, litigation with the Baltimore and Ohio Railroad Company over claims to the right of way in narrow stretches of the Potomac Valley endangered the entire enter-

Aug, 27 Oct, 1 Nov 1834, 8 Jun, 26 Nov 1835; A. F. Cunningham, *Oration delivered before the General Trades-union of the District of Columbia*, 1834; *Washingtonian*, 17 Dec 1836; H Doc 49, 22C, 2S, Ser 234; S Doc 174, 24C, 3S, Ser 340; *Protest of the Columbia Typographical Union against the Washington Institute*, 1834.

[13] *N.I.*, 14 Jan, 23 Sep 1829, 19 May 1834; H Doc 19, 23C, 1S, Ser 254; M. B. Smith, *First Forty Years*, pp. 225-36.

prise; the fight dragged on into 1832, costing the canal company precious time, money, and secret anxiety lest Congress cancel the Treasury's purchase of stock. The work, to be sure, went on. In September 1831 Georgetowners elatedly witnessed "the passage of the waters of the river Potomac through the canal into Rock Creek" and the "packet" *Charles Fenton Mercer* lowered through the locks. In the course of two days of the following May, 99 "boats and arks" carrying 11,322 barrels of flour, 277 barrels of whiskey, 400 tons of granite, as well as coal, wood, and farm produce, came down the canal into Georgetown. Nevertheless by 1833 financial ruin hung over Washington.

Delays in completing the "big ditch" as far as Harpers Ferry had deprived all three District cities of the revenues from which they had expected to pay the interest on the Dutch loan. For Washington alone that charge amounted to $55,000 annually. To meet it she had borrowed $250,000 before 1834, on top of increasing the tax rate from 56 cents to $1.10—a higher figure per $100, the assessors averred, than that of any other city in America. And since the C & O Canal would be of little commercial value to the capital unless the barges could move through the city to deep water on the Eastern Branch, the municipality had contracted a further debt to buy and deepen the Washington Canal. Losses from the lottery intended to pay for the City Hall had saddled her with another $197,000 of debt, bringing the total for a city of some 20,000 souls, nearly an eighth of them slaves, to $1,719,000. Annual deficits of about $25,000 pointed to bankruptcy unless federal funds were to bail the city out.[14]

To the relief of the community, Congress stepped into the breach. First came an appropriation that paid for the purchase and deepening of the Washington Canal; a second sum bought

[14] Sanderlin, *National Project*, pp. 82-88; Convention between Richard Rush and Daniel Crommelin & Sons, 1830, and Washington Canal Stock Papers, 1832, D.C. Miscellany; *Wshg Laws*, 3 Jan, 1 Aug 1831, 16, 26 Dec 1832; *Columbian Gazette*, 20 Sep 1831, 10 May 1832; *N.I.*, 25 Jan, 8 Dec 1830, 22, 25 Mar 1833, 24 Jan, 25, 31 Jul 1834.

out the Washington Bridge Company, built a solid causeway at the foot of 14th Street and constructed the toll-free "Long" bridge over the Potomac; far more important, upon learning that agents of the Dutch creditors had arrived in the city to collect their money by forced sale of property in the capital, Congress reluctantly voted $70,000 to fend off that disgrace and in 1835 granted a like amount annually for five years. But by January 1836 Washington had again fallen into arrears on her interest payments. Alexandria had not yet defaulted but foresaw having to do so shortly, and Georgetown officials had concluded that only sale of the town's C & O stock would keep her solvent. Manifestly the municipalities could no longer help themselves. National honor was involved; the United States was a stockholder in the canal company and, many people asserted, had encouraged the District cities to extravagant investment in the scheme. In any case, neither Democrats nor Whigs in Congress were willing to allow foreign bankers to control large amounts of real estate and other private property in the American capital. In May 1836 the United States government assumed the cities' $1,500,000 canal debts.[15] Freed of that albatross, Washington quickly recovered a measure of financial equilibrium.

Throughout these negotiations, some congressmen, particularly those unfamiliar with the city's past, attributed the trouble mainly to irresponsibility in City Hall. Certainly mayors and councilmen appeared to have acted foolhardily in letting the corporation plunge so deep. But even in the darkest hours the local public refused to look upon city officials as stupid, self-seeking politicians. In 1835 when the B & O railroad branch line reached the capital and the first steam cars deposited passengers at the city's outskirts to be carried thence by omnibus to the foot of the Hill, Joseph Gales may have thought back ruefully upon his scornful dismissal of a railroad as a sound

[15] *N.I.*, 25 Jan, 6, 10, 28 Aug 1835; S Doc 97, 23C, 2S, Ser 268; S Docs 31, 48, 53 and 111, 24C, 1S, Ser 280; S Doc 450, 26C, 1S, Ser 360; *Reg Deb*, 22C, 2S, pp. 1296-98, 1812-16, 23C, 1S, pp. 2078-79, 23C, 2S, pp. 616-19, 24C, 1S, pp. 3475-93; 5 Stat. 31-32.

investment.[16] But neither Gales, nor the banker John Van Ness, who succeeded him as mayor in 1830, nor the next mayor, the banker William Bradley, nor Peter Force, mayor from 1836 to 1840, could be fairly accused of anything worse than mistaken judgment. Intelligent men of every political stripe had believed the city must have a firmer economic basis than federal patronage alone could supply. Once committed to the C & O Canal as an answer, city officials had a bear by the tail: to let go would leave the community with a crippling debt and nothing to show for it, and to hang on might bankrupt the municipality and thereby hurt scores of business enterprises in the city. Members of Congress who had lived long enough in Washington to realize that her plight was not entirely of her own making undertook to analyze the problem of the fiscal relationship of city and federal government. Samuel Southard, Secretary of the Navy during most of the 1820's and then senator from New Jersey, took the lead.

The Southard report, submitted to the Senate in February 1835, offered a closely reasoned justification for federal spending within the federal District. The national capital, the report stated, was the concern of the entire nation. Alexandria and Georgetown, having suffered by their separation from their respective states and by the creation of a rival city in their vicinity, also deserved help. Washington's financial difficulties derived partly from the C & O Canal but more largely from her expenditures on the public streets. Congress should reimburse her for at least half that total. The United States had contributed $10,000 to the cost of building the City Hall, but the federal courts occupied half the space rent-free, a patent inequity. The government had paid a nominal $36,099 for land within the city, in actuality nothing, inasmuch as sales of lots offset the purchase price. In short, the United States acquired gratis property worth over two and a half million dollars; if taxed from the beginning, that would have brought the city twice the amount of her indebtedness. The indisputable figures

[16] *N.I.*, 27 Oct, 8 Nov 1827; Hungerford, *Baltimore and Ohio Railroad*, I, 169-71.

and dispassionate argument of the Southard report carried weight. For the next eighty years whenever Washington's financial problems came up for discussion in Congress, men quoted from that classic on the subject.[17]

Unfortunately neither Southard nor any like-minded associate offered a clear-cut plan for a permanent fiscal relationship between the federal government and the city. Members of Congress sufficiently convinced of the need to vote measures of immediate relief were unprepared to lay down principles for future action. The periodic turnover in House and Senate therefore meant that again and again experienced members would have to educate newcomers if Congress were to follow a consistent course of responsible legislation for the capital. At no time in national history was the moment for defining mutual obligations so propitious as 1836—no acute foreign entanglements, Texas' declaration of independence from Mexico notwithstanding, no critical split as yet between slave states and free, and, with the national debt wiped out, a surplus in the United States Treasury to be distributed to the states.

Yet between 1830 and 1836 Jacksonians in Congress, whatever their theoretical principles, displayed not only an understanding of the impasse over the C & O Canal debt but also a surprising awareness of other local difficulties. When the President asked for penal reform, a new criminal code became law: imprisonment replaced the death penalty for most of Washington County's fourteen capital crimes and Alexandria County's thirty; juries once unwilling to condemn a man to hang for a five-shilling burglary were now ready to bring in proper verdicts. Imprisonment for debt continued into the 1840's, the criminal provisions of common law still ran, and the eighteenth-century Maryland and Virginia civil codes remained untouched, but at least the most oppressive features of the old legal system were now gone. In the unusually cold winter of 1831 and again in 1835 Congress donated firewood to needy families, and in 1832 and 1833 turned over as an

[17] S Doc 97, 23C, 2S, Ser 268.

endowment to the debt-ridden Columbian College lots in Washington valued at $25,000, an equal amount to Georgetown College, and to each of the two orphan asylums land supposedly worth $10,000. And in 1835 the President, perhaps thankfully, agreed to let the lady managers of the older orphanage auction off for the benefit of both asylums the Numidian lion presented to him by the King of Morocco. Each orphanage got about $1,650; who got the lion is not known.[18]

But all these acts of generosity applied only to particular situations. The Democratic congresses, having rather unwillingly done so much for the federal capital, wanted to forget about it. Nor were its needs a party issue. When District problems were occupying the House, John Robertson, a Virginia Whig, made a point of visiting the Senate. In the midst of an acrimonious debate on the canal debt, one representative declared indignantly that he had never known the House to discuss any question concerning Washington without some members' attempting to curry favor at home by ridiculing the citizens of the capital. The chairman of the House District Committee spoke of the "unpleasantness" of his task because of "the temper and spirit with which the most ordinary appropriations for the benefit of this District are received in this House. Some gentlemen seem to regard the District of Columbia . . . as a rat under an exhausted receiver, where political empirics may display the quackery of legislation without any danger of being called to an account for their folly or their ignorance."[19] An unnamed senator's statement, if betraying an exaggerated indifference, still throws light on attitudes on the Hill. When asked by a German traveller about the desperate poverty in the capital, the solon replied: "I am glad the people here are poor, and unable to give splendid entertainments. . . . From these evils [the corruptions of wealth] we are happily

[18] *Reg Deb*, 21C, 2S, pp. 558-59, Appendix, pp. 20-23, 22C, 1S, p. xlviii, 22C, 2S, Appendix, p. 26; M. B. Smith, *First Forty Years*, pp. 367-68; John Robertson to Wyndham Robertson, 5 Jan 1835, Robertson Mss (Univ of Chicago).

[19] *Reg Deb*, 23C, 1S, pp. 4398-99, 24C, 1S, pp. 3496-97; *Washingtonian*, 9 Jun 1836; John to Wyndham Robertson, 5 Feb 1837, Robertson Mss.

exempted by the almost hopeless condition of the inhabitants of this place." Halfhearted congressional attempts to slough off upon a District territorial government the time-consuming and boring responsibilities for the community were again defeated by outcries about the incompatibility of interests of the three cities, while petitions from Alexandria and Georgetown for retrocession to the states met with no serious response.[20]

After federal assumption of the C & O Canal debt, however, Washingtonians knew they had much to be thankful for. While the city still carried a $450,000 municipal debt, in 1837 when panic and depression hit the rest of the United States and local banks suspended specie payment, Mayor Peter Force, himself a businessman with a printing establishment to maintain, declared in July that no business had failed: "The late pecuniary embarrassments of the country . . . have scarcely been felt here. We, so far, have suffered little more than a temporary inconvenience, arising from the sudden conversion of a specie into a paper currency." The government payrolls tided the city over.[21] Throughout the decade upkeep of the streets and poor relief were burdensome, but federal money had paid for macadamizing Pennsylvania Avenue, and private citizens, though frequently overwhelmed by the wretchedness in the city, still looked upon charity less as a public than as an individual obligation.

Under the leadership of John McLeod, the Irish schoolmaster, in 1830 a group founded the Washington Relief Society dedicated to helping "indigent and disabled emigrants" and other distressed people whom local ordinances barred from admission to the city almshouse. In one winter the organization boarded forty people in private homes or taverns, and in 1833

[20] *Aristocracy in America, from the Sketchbook of a German Nobleman*, ed. Francis J. Grund, II, 268; *Reg Deb*, 22C, 1S, p. 1449; H Rpt 337, 22C, 1S, Ser 226; John to Wyndham Robertson, 6 Feb 1836, Robertson Mss; *Cong Globe*, 25C, 2S, pp. 271, 296-97; ptns, S26A-G4, 10 Apr 1838, S28A-G5, 18 Jan 1839; Resolution, *Ordinances of the Corporation of Georgetown*, 26 Mar 1838.

[21] *Alex. Gazette*, 15, 23 May 1837; *N.I.*, 17, 23 May, 5 Jun, 8 Sep 1837; Ggtn *Metropolitan*, 24 May, 3 Jul 1837; *Potomac Advocate*, 7 Aug 1837.

it opened an infirmary for destitute foreigners. Five years later the Female Union Benevolent Society came into being with the avowed purpose of assisting the "necessitous poor" after the lady managers had made "careful observation and inquiry as to the needs." President Van Buren contributed to the work by donating for sale the remaining half of a 1,400-pound cheese presented to President Jackson toward the end of his term. Although lack of funds forced the Howard Society to curtail its workshops' activities, one of its earliest supporters, a government clerk by the name of Peter Gallaudet, awakened considerable interest in a plan for a manual labor school and orphanage for boys in which they could learn trades and agricultural skills and thus become self-supporting. The money raised by selling copies of *Monuments of Washington's Patriotism* was too little to open the school, but the $4,600 contributed would go in 1860 to an institution for the deaf and dumb headed by Gallaudet's grandson.[22] Belief that intemperance caused much of the misery in the city for a time encouraged efforts to eradicate poverty by preaching abstinence and campaigning against the sale of "ardent" spirits in Washington. But the new temperance societies won few converts among wage-earners, and the inroads of disease which incapacitated breadwinners and left their families destitute suggested that better medical care might be a sounder answer to public ills than prohibition.

Forty-odd years before Pasteur's discoveries began to revolutionize medical science, tuberculosis, then known as consumption, typhoid fever, malaria, diphtheria, measles, and a host of other communicable diseases scourged the country periodically. Probably doctors in the District were as alert and as well-informed about preventives and cures as physicians elsewhere, but faulty drainage and the muggy heat of summer made Washington peculiarly vulnerable. The swampy stretches

[22] M. B. Smith, *First Forty Years*, pp. 348-49; *N.I.*, 26 Aug 1830, 20 Apr, 21, 26 Dec 1831, 26, 30 Sep 1833, 23 Apr 1834, 7 Jan 1835, 22 Feb, 7 Jul 1837, 17 Dec 1838, 8 Jan 1839; Minutes of the Trustees of the Washington Manual Labor School and Male Orphanage, 1835-1860; *Proceedings of the Sixth Annual Meeting of the Female Union Benevolent Society of Washington City and Report of the Managers*, 1844.

along the Washington Canal had become such an obvious menace to health in the 1820's that the city fathers begged the federal government to let them use any money derived from sales of publicly owned lots to drain the area. Congress ignored the plea.

In the summer of 1832 an epidemic of Asiatic cholera took heavy toll, first among the workmen on the C & O Canal and the laborers engaged in laying the water mains for government buildings and then among the citizens generally. The board of health did what it could, forbidding the importation of fresh fruits and vegetables, "abolishing" hog sties within the city limits during the emergency, prohibiting public entertainments, and annulling licenses to sell liquor for ninety days. The only treatment physicians prescribed was bleeding, doses of calomel, and abstention from all stimulants. City funds and private subscriptions provided a staff of doctors and three temporary hospitals in rented houses, but for weeks the "dead carts" made the rounds every morning while the mournful sound of the drivers' horns and the call "Bring out the dead" echoed in the streets. Marcia Burnes Van Ness, wife of the mayor, nursed the afflicted until she too died of the disease. Its spread, according to the board of health, was chiefly due to the "large number of foreign emigrants [sic] . . . employed on the public works. Most of these were from Germany and Ireland, men who neither understood our language, nor were accustomed to our climate, habits and mode of living." Physicians noted that the cholera was also "extremely fatal to our colored population, and more especially to the free blacks." When small pox appeared a few months later, members of the Medical Society undertook to vaccinate poor people free of charge.[23]

Epidemics emphasized the need of a public hospital for transients as well as a proper city infirmary. But despite proof that in most years three out of every four patients cared for at

[23] Ptn, H25A-G4.1, 8 Jan 1838; *N.I.*, almost daily accounts of the epidemic from 8 Aug to 29 Sep 1832, and 7, 8 Jan, 10 Apr 1833; M. B. Smith, *First Forty Years*, pp. 335-38; *Sunday Star*, 22 Sep 1918.

the Washington Asylum were non-residents of the city, the bill to erect a federally financed hospital for them failed in Congress. By 1839 as overcrowding had made the Asylum unfit for use, city officials obtained President Van Buren's permission to use part of Marine Hospital Square bordering the Eastern Branch for a new Asylum which should include an infirmary along with an almshouse and a workhouse, but difficulty in raising the money postponed a start on the buildings until 1843.[24]

Destructive fires forced the federal government, on the other hand, into a building program in the mid-thirties. When an incendiary burned the Treasury to the ground in 1833, one story runs that sixty-six-year-old John Quincy Adams, by then a Massachusetts congressman, worked all night with the bucket brigade to save the building and its precious records. A three-year congressional debate over where to locate a new and necessarily larger Treasury opened at once and finally ended in a recommendation of the old site but left the final decision to the Executive. Two days later the President announced that he had chosen the old location and Robert Mills as architect. Mills' design called for a three-story structure stretched lengthwise along 15th Street. Perhaps anti-Jacksonians originated the tale current to this day that Old Hickory, at odds with Congress at the time, had stalked out of the White House, planted his cane firmly and decreed that the Treasury should stand there where it would block his view of the Capitol and its stiff-necked occupants. But as the walls began to rise above the foundations, members of Congress realized with dismay that so large a structure would indeed interrupt the sweep of Pennsylvania Avenue and thus obliterate a significant feature of L'Enfant's layout of the city. Agitation to redesign or relocate the building ensued, but Robert Mills stoutly defended his work by pointing to the impossibility otherwise of reconciling Treasury specifications for 114 rooms and the requirement of using the narrow

[24] *N.I.*, 6 Jan 1837; *Cong Globe*, 25C, 2S, pp. 70-71, 360; William B. Webb, *Laws of the Corporation of the City of Washington*, pp. 22-23.

original lot. And the expense of tearing down the partially constructed building eventually silenced his critics.[25]

When the Post Office, which still housed patent records and models, burned in December 1836, a new General Post Office had to be built. Again the site was the old one at E and 7th Streets. In the square to the north, work had already begun on a separate building for the Patent Office, since patent applications had trebled over the years. Both buildings lacked the spacious setting L'Enfant had assigned to every public edifice, but Thomas U. Walter's use of Corinthian pilasters on the Post Office and William P. Elliot's design for the Patent Office excited general admiration. The main portico of the Patent Office fronting on F Street was a replica of the Parthenon. The proportions of the building with its broad flight of steps leading up to the columned porch created an air of stateliness hard to imagine after twentieth-century changes sheared off the steps. While construction was still under way, the Commissioner of Patents laid plans for adding at the rear a greenhouse and a garden in which to propagate the plants and seeds collected by government-sponsored exploring parties. In the 1840's the garden would become one of Washington's show places.[26]

The future of science in the capital, however, commanded deeper interest than urban aesthetics. President Jackson possessed none of John Quincy Adams' passion for extending the boundaries of human knowledge and had little understanding of the scientific world, but Old Hickory and his followers who guffawed at Adams' "lighthouses of the sky" were not averse to endorsing programs that promised to meet immediate practical needs. Contrary to every expectation of 1829, the next several years saw the federal government revive or initiate scientific projects that differed very little from some of Adams' most derided proposals.

[25] *Cong Globe*, 25C, 2S, App. pp. 336-40, 371-72, 410-12, 418-21; H Doc 38, 25C, 2S, Ser 322; H Rpt 737, 25C, 2S, Ser 335.

[26] William Quereau Force, *Picture of the City of Washington and Its Vicinity for 1845*, pp. 43-46; Louise Hall, "The Design of the Old Patent Office Building," *Journal of the Society of Architectural Historians*, xv (Mar 1956), pp. 27-30.

When the discrepancies in the weights and measures used in American customhouses evoked complaints, Jackson turned to Rudolph Hassler. In 1830 the elderly Swiss had driven up to the White House door in his specially designed carriage equipped with heavy springs to prevent jolting of the delicate surveying instruments fitted into the trunk forming the seat; the President, impressed with his caller's talents, assigned him the task of checking the Treasury's weights and measures. When in 1832, constituents' pressures for reliable charts of American coastal waters led Congress to resurrect the Coast Survey by removing the restrictions on employing civilians, Hassler again took charge. His insistence on scientific methods and the care with which he trained the men assigned to him, largely Army and Navy officers, gave the government almost in spite of itself a true scientific agency with headquarters in Washington. Similarly the Navy's want of a central depository for expensive navigational equipment when it was not in use brought into being a Depot of Charts and Instruments. Lt. Charles Wilkes, head of the depot from 1833 to 1836, finding that astronomical observations were essential to rate Navy chronometers for accurate time, erected a sixteen-foot-square observatory on the Capitol grounds and mounted there one of the transits Hassler had brought back from England in 1815. Wilkes' successor, Lt. James M. Gilliss, carried matters further by undertaking observations of culminations of the moon and stars, eclipses and meteorological phenomena calculated to furnish needed data to a new exploring expedition authorized by Congress in 1836. That year a reorganization of the Patent Office, rejected when President Adams urged it, went into effect without a hitch.[27]

Just as public demand re-established a scientific Coast Survey and revamped the Patent Office, and just as navigational needs permitted the forerunner of a national observatory to rise under the very noses of congressmen, so what people came to call

[27] A. Hunter Dupree, *Science in the Federal Government*, pp. 43-44, 51-54, 56-65; Florian Cajori, *The Chequered Career of Ferdinand Rudolph Hassler*, pp. 82, 93, 170-72.

the "first National Expedition" grew out of practical Americans' desire for information about the geography of distant places. The expedition, with several qualified civilian scientists attached to it, sailed under Lieutenant Wilkes' command in 1838 to be gone four years. At the same time American eagerness for facts about the natural resources of the country inspired congressional appropriations for scientific explorations in the trans-Mississippi West, most of them under the aegis of Army topographical engineers.

For Washington, however, prospects of more immediate benefits suddenly arose in 1836 when word filtered through diplomatic channels of a bequest from a little known Englishman: James Smithson had left his entire fortune to "the United States of America to found at Washington, under the name of the Smithsonian Institution, an Establishment for the increase and diffusion of knowledge among men." Congress immediately entered upon a debate about the constitutionality and propriety of accepting. But the possibilities the gift opened up overcame scruples. The President dispatched Richard Rush to England to claim the legacy. Rush returned in 1838 with $500,000 in gold and James Smithson's library and collection of minerals. Discussion of how to use the windfall revolved around whether Smithson had intended it to establish a national university, a great museum or some kind of research foundation. Until final agreement could be reached, Congress voted to invest the money in state bonds. But the stipulation that the Smithsonian Institution should be located at Washington encouraged faith that at last the city might turn into the cultural and intellectual center Jefferson had envisioned and the Columbian Institute had struggled to create.[28]

The Columbian Institute itself was past reviving. Aware that its energies were spent, in 1840 Secretary of War Joel Poinsett, an amateur scientist in his own right, called together seven leading federal officials, organized the National Institute for the Promotion of Science, and invited members of the older

[28] Dupree, *Science in the Federal Government*, pp. 68-70.

Institute to join in making the new body a force in American life. At the same time the opportunities the Smithson money dangled before the eyes of every aspiring local organization produced numerous competing ideas. While the Commissioner of Patents laid plans to develop his office as a museum and a clearinghouse of agricultural information and the president of Columbian College dreamed of transforming the college into a national university, John Quincy Adams accused the municipal corporation of coveting the fund for the city's schools. They needed help. A survey taken in 1839 showed that of the 5,200 white children in the city 900 were enrolled in private schools, 293 in the two pauper schools, and the other 4,000 left to learn what they could pick up for themselves. Were that record not bettered, the chances were dim that Washington could emerge in the near future as an epitome of American educational aims and achievements.[29]

Meanwhile, at least among northerners, the city lost prestige in another realm, for such enlightened humanitarianism in race relations as she had once shown vanished. In 1829 white people zealous for the emancipation and removal of Negroes to Liberia organized the African Education Society to provide "persons of color destined to Africa" with schooling "in letters, Agriculture and Mechanic Arts." Petitions for the prohibition of the slave trade in the District of Columbia multiplied simultaneously. In 1830 no one objected publicly to William Lloyd Garrison's advertised plan of publishing a weekly abolitionist paper, the *Liberator*, in the capital or, when he chose Boston instead, to Benjamin Lundy's issuing the *Genius of Universal Emancipation* from Washington.[30] Antislavery sentiment was also gaining ground rapidly in Virginia. Unhappily a slave insurrection in southern Virginia in the sum-

[29] *Ibid.*, pp. 70-71; G. Brown Goode, "The Genesis of the National Museum," pp. 274-75, 287; *Spec Rpt Comr Educ*, 1870, p. 53, Ser 1427.

[30] *The Life, Travels and Opinions of Benjamin Lundy*, pp. 236, 238; *N.I.*, 20 Aug 1830, 9 Jun 1831; *Report of the Proceedings at the Formation of the African Education Society Instituted at Washington, December 28, 1829*, in *Misc Pamphlets*, 411:20; Leonidas Polk to Colonel D. Polk, 21 Jan 1829, Leonidas Polk Mss (SHC).

mer of 1831 caused a revulsion of feeling. Early in 1832 a bill for gradual emancipation failed in the Virginia Assembly by only one vote, but Nat Turner's rebellion frightened many southerners. In the eyes of otherwise sensible citizens of the District of Columbia abolitionists became dangerous agitators; slaves were creatures "unfit for freedom; ignorant, servile and depraved." For the first time in her history Georgetown enacted a black code, listing among punishable Negro offenses the possession or circulation of literature "calculated to excite insurrection or insubordination among the slaves or colored people . . . and particularly a newspaper called the *Liberator.*" Eight months after the Turner insurrection Benjamin Lundy observed that "opposition to everything like emancipation runs high." The local abolition society ceased to meet, and fear of "inflammatory" abolitionist literature gradually rose to hysteria. It was heightened by an avalanche of antislavery petitions pouring in upon Congress from northerners.[31]

Tension reached the bursting point in 1835 when one of Mrs. William Thornton's slaves attempted to murder her; hearsay had it that the man had been "inflamed" by abolitionist teachings. Inasmuch as a new arrival from the North, a botany teacher who had come to study and lecture in Washington, had brought with him specimens wrapped in abolitionist newspapers, a visitor to his lodgings, seeing the wrappings, denounced him as an agent sent to stir up local Negroes. His arrest started a week's witch hunt carried on, like many another race riot in America, chiefly by gangs of boys and irresponsible young men out of work. The mob's main objective was the intimidation of free Negroes and "the punishment of such as have circulated the incendiary pamphlets." Mayor Bradley, knowing that the half-dozen ward constables could not restrain several hundred angry men, called for military protection. Soldiers and clerks guarded government buildings while citizens enrolled as patrols under the command of the mayor and the

[31] *N.I.*, 12 Aug, 19 Sep, 6 Aug 1825; *Columbian*, 8 Nov 1831; H Rpt 691, 24C, 1S, p. 18, Ser 295; Kenneth Stampp, *The Peculiar Institution*, pp. 132-37; *Benjamin Lundy*, p. 277; Bemis, *John Quincy Adams*, p. 340.

head of the District militia. No Negro was injured bodily, but the mob demolished a Negro school and several Negro tenements, broke the windows of a colored church, burned a house of ill fame, and smashed the furnishings of a fashionable restaurant owned by a mulatto, Beverly Snow, who reportedly had made derogatory remarks about the wives of white mechanics. At the height of the riot a clerk in the Patent Office wrote: "The principal messenger of our office (who is a cold. man) decamped today; it seems there was some danger of the mob getting hold of him. He had been a great patron of the abolition journals, and used to get leave of absence every summer to attend the negro congress at Philadelphia as the Washington delegate." Most Negroes simply laid low, keeping their feelings to themselves. Upper-class whites attempted to explain that riots in Baltimore coupled with some weeks of layoffs at the Navy Yard had inspired the demonstrations. "Mechanics" deprecated the lawlessness and denied responsibility for it. Nevertheless the "Snow storm" severely damaged the spirit of the community.

White men's shame over the violence intensified rather than lessened their resentments at the mere presence of free blacks in Washington. "We have already too many free negroes and mulattoes in this city, and the policy of our corporate authorities should tend to the diminution of this insolent class," declared an anonymous letter-writer. "A motion is now before the Common Council for prohibiting shop-licenses henceforth to this class of people. If they wish to live here, let them become subordinates and laborers, as nature has designed." The city council passed the new ordinance. Thenceforward Negroes could drive carts and hackneys but could not run taverns or eating houses. Urged on by complaints that the black code had "resumed its old character of a dead letter," the municipality also increased the bond required of every Negro family to $1,000 and denied colored people without special permits the right to be on the streets after 10:00 at night for any purpose.[32]

[32] *N.I.*, 6, 11-15, 20, 28 Aug, 15 Sep 1835; Seaton, *William Winston*

Further evidence of change in the prevailing temper of the white community lay in the cessation of local petitions for prohibition of the slave trade. But the flood of appeals from the North reached such a volume and debates in Congress became so bitter that in 1836 the House voted to receive no petitions relating to slavery or the trade in the District. The "gag rule" which John Quincy Adams, "Old Man Eloquent," fought against for the next eight years was a denial of freedom of speech and petition. Yet even publishers like Joseph Gales, William Seaton, and Peter Force who disapproved of slavery but believed that local citizens should be allowed to settle their own domestic problems tacitly approved the gag. The labor paper, the *Washingtonian*, advocated hanging northerners who invaded the South to stir up slaves. Until 1837 most of the city tried to ignore the battles raging on the Hill. That year members of the Grand Jury of Washington County protested at what they labelled outside interference: they had maintained silence till then in hope "that time and due reflection" would cause critics of District institutions to stop "their iniquitous proceedings," but now Congress should intervene. Georgetown, long the most liberal of the three cities in race matters, added her objections to being "the political football of the nation," and in 1839 leading Washingtonians presented a formal memorial to Congress: "It is not that your memorialists are slaveholders . . . many of them do not own slaves, and some of them might be forbidden by conscience to hold any, but these, nevertheless, unite with others in this prayer . . . not only from the just respect due to the legal rights of those of their neighbors who do possess slaves, but from a deep conviction that the continual agitation of the subject by those who can have no right to interfere with it is calculated to have an injurious influence on the peace and tranquility of the community." The petitioners,

---

Seaton, pp. 217-19; James W. Sheahan, *Corporation Laws of the City of Washington*, pp. 248-50; William P. Hoyt, "Washington's Living History: The Post Office Fire and Other Matters, 1834-1839," CHS *Rec*, XLVI-XLVII, 63-65.

however, had no plan beyond a vague notion of discouraging free people of color from making their homes in the capital.[33]

The attempt to limit the colored population was futile. By 1840 the 3,100 free Negroes of 1830 had become 4,800, although the city had 600 fewer slaves than ten years before. Manumission and slaves' purchase of their freedom obviously accounted for part of the change, but migration of free Negroes into Washington from Maryland and Virginia or farther south appeared to be a larger factor. Freed slaves were forbidden by law to remain in the Old Dominion. Unless they were willing to venture into the alien-seeming northern states, free Negroes could not hope for less hostile treatment than they would find in the capital. Northerners in Congress, furthermore, probably represented to them safeguards against excesses. The "Snow storm" occurred when Congress was not in session. Here, once any given crisis passed, relaxation of the black code tended to occur; Washington, if no longer a sure haven, was as safe a place as any below the Mason-Dixon line.

While a large proportion of the 16,800 white residents of the city would doubtless have welcomed laws forbidding the ingress of more colored people, intelligent upper-class families differentiated between the undesirables and those with admirable qualities. Not every free Negro was law-abiding, but official statistics showing that half the inmates of the penitentiary and jail were Negroes charged with acts of violence or, more frequently, drunkenness and thieving, probably reflected the prejudices of the police and the courts quite as sharply as Negro criminal tendencies. Ex-slaves who had had the tenacity and ambition to spend years in purchasing their freedom and that of their relatives were unquestionably people of character. They were capable of showing true civic spirit. Hence although a seemingly unprejudiced outlander described Washington's freedmen as "ignorant, poor and vicious," Judge Cranch re-

[33] Bemis, *John Quincy Adams*, pp. 326-83; H Doc 140, 23C, 2S, Ser 274; ptns, S24A-G4, 17 Jan 1837, S25A-G5, 24 Jan 1838, S25A-G4, 7 Feb 1839; *Washingtonian*, 10 Dec 1836; Seaton, *William Winston Seaton*, pp. 265-66.

marked of the Methodists among them: "They are seldom or never brought before the criminal courts for misconduct." And some whites admitted that their free colored neighbors "constituted a very superior class of their race."[34]

That superiority was most evident among Negroes who had lived for some years in Washington. From them new arrivals learned how to conduct themselves as responsible free men and city-dwellers; those who failed to do so had no recognized place in the distinctive colored community taking form in the 1830's. The struggle for education and the new Negro churches knit that group closely together. John Prout's school for colored children rarely had fewer than 150 pupils. There during the 1820's John F. Cook got the training that he then put to use as a teacher. In 1835, as head of the largest Negro school in Washington and thus a leader among his fellows, Cook had to flee for his life during the "Snow storm," but he returned a year later, reopened the school, and taught until he was ordained as Washington's first colored Presbyterian minister in 1843. Five or six other schools were in operation in the meantime. One of some note was Louisa Parke Costin's school on Capitol Hill. Louisa's father provided the schoolhouse. For twenty-four years a trusted messenger at the Bank of Washington, William Costin was a remarkable man. His father was believed to be a member of a distinguished Virginia family and his mother, granddaughter of a Cherokee Indian chief, was reputedly the child of William Dandridge, father of Martha Dandridge Custis Washington. William Costin, by Virginia law born free because of his descent from an Indian chief, bought his wife's freedom from Eliza Custis Law. He imbued his daughters with a passion for service to their race. Upon Louisa's death her younger sister carried on her school until 1839. All told, several

[34] H Ex Doc 49, 22C, 2S, Ser 234; H Ex Doc 81, 24C, 1S, Ser 288; H Ex Doc 140, 25C, 2S, Ser 326; Ethan Allen Andrews, *Slavery and the Domestic Slave Trade in the United States*, pp. 119, 121-22, 127-28; *Columbian Gazette*, 20 Aug 1832; *Spec Rpt Comr Educ*, pp. 198-204, Ser 1427. Unless otherwise noted, all data in the following paragraphs dealing with Negro schools and churches derive from *Spec Rpt Comr Educ*, pp. 195-222.

hundred colored children yearly obtained some schooling during the thirties. In the interval Negroes organized a Baptist church and two additional Methodist churches, bringing the number of independent colored congregations to four.

Those churches at once became the center of Negro social as well as religious life. Colored people without church affiliation had little standing in the Negro community. Class distinctions within it developed early: they still marked it in mid-twentieth century. Lower-class Negroes looked up to superior colored persons as fully as the upper class looked down upon the inferior. Not improbably, well before 1840 all Negroes in Washington were employing the prefix Mr. or Mrs. in speaking of their most respected fellows, the ministers and teachers above all; the rest remained Tom and Sam or Mary and Sally. It was John Prout who presided at the "large and very respectable" gathering at the African Methodist Episcopal church in 1831 when Negroes, repeating their earlier rejection of the Colonization Society's program, formally declared that "the soil that gave us birth is our only true and veritable home."[35] Determination to prove their right to remain and be acknowledged as Americans contributed to the stress upper-class Negroes placed upon exemplary behavior.

Little by little free Negroes overcame the worst of the hostility under which they suffered between 1831 and 1836. They mingled with the crowds at public outdoor celebrations, although the congressional ruling of 1828 barred them from the terrace of the Capitol where the Marine band played on summer afternoons. They would not again attend an inaugural reception as they had in 1829, but like everybody else they enjoyed the sunshine of March 4, 1837, which made Martin Van Buren's inauguration festive, the more so because bitter weather and President Jackson's feeble health had prevented a parade four years before. Dislike of some of Van Buren's policies failed to interfere with the pleasure of Washingtonians, white or black, who cheered as the President-elect, accompanied

[35] *N.I.*, 4 May 1831.

by a resplendent military escort, rode to the Capitol in a phaeton built of wood from the frigate *Constitution.* Later that year when the famous and still fearsome Black Hawk, Chief Keokuk, and some thirty Sac and Fox braves got off the steam cars at the B & O railroad depot, a fascinated many-complexioned throng gathered and followed them up Pennsylvania Avenue to the beat of Indian drums and the wail of Sac musical instruments. Negroes as well as whites doubtless relished telling of the fierce Winnebagos who were persuaded to enter the "Rotundo" of the Capitol and, upon seeing the frieze of Daniel Boone slaying a savage, suddenly uttered a dreadful war whoop and fled from the building.[36]

Thoughtful citizens, even the observant and indefatigable letter-writer Margaret Bayard Smith, seldom examined the entire picture Washington presented in the thirties. Much of it was a painful contrast to what old residents had hoped to see. It was abundantly clear before the end of the decade that the city was never going to rival Baltimore or New York or Philadelphia commercially. After 1834, with the C & O Canal dug beyond Seneca, Maryland, barges brought limestone to new kilns built along Rock Creek at 27th and L Streets, and, after the deepened Washington Canal opened in 1837, boats moved through the Georgetown locks, past the gatehouse at the foot of the President's Square, and into the heart of the city or on to wharves on the Eastern Branch. But Georgetown, not Washington, reaped most of the modest profits of the canal trade. If few Washingtonians regarded the location of the new Treasury as an irretrievable error, still fewer saw any reason to expect rapid development of the beautiful city that L'Enfant's plan had portended. On the contrary, foreigners' criticisms of her appearance left no room for self-delusion. Tyrone Power, the Irish actor on tour in the United States, marvelled at "the utter indifference with which Americans looked upon the exceedingly unworthy condition of their capital."[37] The government's

[36] *Ibid.*, 6 Mar 1833, 25 Feb, 6 Mar, 2 Oct 1837, 11 Nov 1839; Force, *Picture of Washington*, pp. 18-19.

[37] *N.I.*, 13 Jun, 29 Jul 1834; H Doc 73, 26C, 1S, Ser 365; Wshg *Metrop-*

scientific activities and the Smithson legacy held hopes for the city's future, but the illiteracy and ignorance of a considerable segment of her population discouraged belief that Washington would soon emerge as a center of culture. It was impossible not to feel the sting of Harriet Martineau's comment that her five weeks in Washington were the most informing and least agreeable of her western travels. And irrespective of individual residents' feeling about slavery, the ill name it gave the American capital in much of the North and abroad was uncomfortable to think about.[38] Yet with all the community's failures, the city still had power to charm.

That charm, while failing to work upon many a lonely congressman and upon reformers like Miss Martineau, made itself felt among people appreciative of the capital's curious combination of sophistication and small-town simplicity. White House hospitality again took on an engaging cordiality once the Peggy Eaton feud had worn itself out. People who had been uneasy over Old Hickory's attitude about official etiquette were impressed at the elegance of his dinner parties. "Such a variety and profusion," wrote a knowledgeable North Carolina congressman, "and costly table furniture I have never seen." James Graham's later comment, moreover, indicated that the distinctions between official and non-official society had faded since 1818: "I rarely meet any of my colleagues at the parties. They appear to be afraid of the urbanity of City company." The fearful and gauche ones found their chief diversion at the gaming tables where stakes often ran so high that one congressman reported losing $3,500, over a year's salary, in a single night's play. The advent of Martin Van Buren changed the social scene

---

olis, 28 May, 18 Jul, 16 Nov 1839; George Watterston, *A New Guide to Washington*, p. 92; Tyrone Power, *Impressions of America*, I, 264-65; Adolphe Fourier de Bacourt, *Souvenirs of a Diplomat, Private Letters from America during the Administrations of Presidents Van Buren, Harrison and Tyler*, pp. 62-63; Captain Frederick Marryat, *Diary in America, The Complete Account of His Trials, Wrangles and Tribulations in the United States and Canada 1837-38*, ed. Jules Zanger, pp. 188-99.

[38] M. B. Smith, *First Forty Years*, pp. 362-67; Harriet Martineau, *Retrospect of Western Travels*, I, 143.

very little. A tactful and gracious host, the new President continued the traditional drawing rooms but refused invitations except to dine with department heads and foreign ministers. Fanny Elssler, the Viennese dancer who had captivated all Europe, remarked that "what surprised her most was to find the manners of Mr. Van Buren as distinguished as those of Metternich." Political enemies made use of skillfully colored tales of the oriental splendor in which the occupant of the "President's Palace" lived, eating *pate de fois gras* and *dinde désossé* from silver plates with forks of gold, but partisan feeling rarely spoiled the sociability of occasions like Mrs. Joseph Gales' "splendid" Friday evening parties at Eckington. Soon after Van Buren's inauguration, furthermore, the recently widowed Mrs. James Madison returned to live in Washington in the house built by her brother-in-law on Madison Place fronting on Lafayette Square. Thenceforward, till her death in 1849, her house was a focus of the city's social life; New Year's callers customarily went directly from the White House to pay their respects to her.[39]

Perhaps the marriage of the Czarist minister, the wealthy and worldly-wise Baron Bodisco, to the sixteen-year-old daughter of a minor government clerk completed the obliteration of any line between officialdom and "City company." Both elements of society witnessed the wedding of "April and October," carefully arranged by the fifty-six-year-old baron. The groom ordered from Paris the gowns for the bridesmaids, schoolgirl friends of the bride at Miss Lydia English's school in Georgetown, and the baron himself instructed them in how to walk and conduct themselves in fashion to match the dignity of the elderly diplomats and federal officers who attended the groom. Neither Senator Benton's fourteen-year-old daughter Jessie, one of the bridesmaids, nor older and more sedate Washingtonians

[39] James Graham to William Graham, 23 Feb 1834, 21 Jan 1838, Graham Mss (SHC); John to Wyndham Robertson, 16 Feb 1837, Robertson Mss; de Bacourt, *Souvenirs of a Diplomat*, p. 87; Adams, *Memoirs*, IX, 418, 462; Stefan Lorant, *The Presidency, A Pictorial History of Presidential Elections from Washington to Truman*, p. 160.

ever forgot that magnificent evening; and forty years later, long after the baron's death, they still marvelled at the enduring success of so unsuitable-seeming a marriage.[40]

By 1840 Washington bore the air of a city without driving ambition. Native sons might build careers in the Army or Navy and a few young men made their mark in other fields. William Wilson Corcoran, for example, son of a mayor of Georgetown, after failing in the dry goods business in the 1820's, had opened a successful commission house and, in partnership with George Riggs, in the 1840's would make a fortune marketing the bonds to finance the Mexican War. But as Washington's main business was national politics, the rank and file of disenfranchised citizens could not count on cutting a swathe. Recognizing their inability to hasten change or direct its course by struggle, they seemed willing to settle for what they had, accepting as a community a minor role in national life.

Except for hopelessly impoverished families, the Washington world was pleasant enough as it was. People of very modest means could enjoy it. Popular diversions were simple. The annual Jockey Club races petered out at the end of the thirties, but the fishing and the hunting of river fowl were still unexcelled. Musicians gave occasional concerts at Carusi's Assembly Rooms, while the olios yielded to full length plays at the theatre when companies on tour began to play during the winter months. Mrs. Trollope termed the building of 1830 "very small and most astonishingly dirty and void of decoration," but in 1834 Tyrone Power observed "it was filled nightly with a very delightful audience and nothing could be more pleasant than to witness the perfect *abandon* with which the gravest of the senate laughed over the diplomacy of the 'Irish Ambassador.' " Actors as famous as Charles and Fanny Kemble, Edwin Booth and Joseph Jefferson were not above playing in the "miserable-looking place." And when the National Theatre opened in 1835 on the site it still occupies, the audience watching Joseph Jefferson in *The Man of the World* could sit

[40] Jessie Benton Fremont, *Souvenir of My Time*, pp. 14-25.

in boxes "embellished with sketches in imitation bas relief and surrounded by correspondent ornaments, representing brilliant events . . . in maritime history and discovery."[41]

Washingtonians with social standing enjoyed also the season's round of balls and formal dinners. Paying calls, drinking tea, and joining the "squeeze" of evening receptions were part of the winter's daily routine. "Mustaches, whiskers, epaulettes, stars and ribbons," wrote a senator, "are badges of a Washington party. . . . The ladies sport a chain or braid around the head, with a jewel on the forehead. And all waltz like children's tops." But, he added, "it is a congregation in a great measure of strangers who never met before, and don't care (most of them) if they never meet again." Washingtonians preferred the late spring and summer after Congress had adjourned and the autumn "half season" before it reconvened; in those months they reclaimed the capital for their own. Tourists were few. Government offices closed at three o'clock and, as the customary dinner hour was four, the end of pleasant afternoons brought leisurely house-holders out to promenade along the "Avenue," exchange greetings with friends and acquaintances and then adjourn for tea at each others' houses. Twice a week young and old gathered on the west terrace of the Capitol to hear the Marine Band concerts. At such times, released from "the whirl of congressional excitement and strife," Washington appeared at her best.[42]

[41] Frances Trollope, *Domestic Manners of the Americans*, ed. Donald Smalley, p. 233; Power, *Impressions*, I, 210; *N.I.*, 23 Nov 1832, 19 Jan 1833, 12 Mar 1834, 20 Apr, 7 Dec 1835, 28 Jan 1836.

[42] William A. Graham to his wife, 8 Jan 1841, Graham Mss; Fremont, *Souvenir of My Time*, pp. 57-58; M. B. Smith, *First Forty Years*, pp. 369-70; Wshg *Metropolis*, 14 Nov 1839.

CHAPTER VI

QUIESCENT INTERLUDE, 1840-1848

IN MOST of the United States the 1840's were exciting years, as the country, having recovered from the panic of 1837, burst into a new era of expansion. While wagon trains moved westward into unoccupied trans-Mississippi lands and inventive and enterprising men launched new exploring and manufacturing ventures, Americans' intellectual horizons widened. War with Mexico foreshadowed sectional troubles to come, but settlement of the Oregon dispute with Great Britain, the annexation of Texas, and in 1848 the acquisition of the vast territory stretching to the Pacific gave vital meaning to the phrase "our Manifest Destiny to overspread the continent." Despite mounting anxieties over the slavery issue, from the end of the hard cider campaign of 1840 to the election of General Zachary Taylor eight years later, energy and optimism marched together across the continent: nothing seemed impossible for Americans to accomplish. In the capital, political maneuverings and partisan controversy swirled about the city's permanent residents without unduly disturbing them and, on the whole, without drawing them into the main current of national life. Most of them, so far from seeking new worlds to conquer, set themselves to consolidating the gains of the past.

Washington society was gay during this period of national euphoria. Although a good many citizens were staunch Democrats, the most elaborate parade the capital had ever staged celebrated the inauguration of "Tippecanoe and Tyler too." General Harrison rode to the Capitol on a white charger and sprinkled his inaugural address liberally with allusions to Roman proconsuls. A month later he was dead. John Tyler, quietly sworn in as President, was a far less popular figure, but the city was prosperous and the social atmosphere pleasantly relaxed during most of his administration. A brief flutter of excitement stirred when Senator Benton's seventeen-year-old daughter Jessie eloped with the dashing but little known young Lt. John C. Fremont upon his return from an exploring expedition in the West, but gossip could not live long on a successful marriage. Hostesses customarily invited three times as many guests as their houses could accommodate comfortably; while everyone complained about the "crush," everyone accepted the next invitation with alacrity. If fewer exceptionally cultivated Washingtonians graced these occasions than in earlier decades, in the eyes of the younger generation visiting notables filled any gap—royalty in the person of the Prince de Joinville, heir of the "Citizen" King of France, the lively, if hypercritical, Charles Dickens, and the stately Lord Ashburton, who spent months in the house next to St. John's Church on H Street in negotiating a northeast boundary treaty with Secretary of State Daniel Webster. Furthermore, President Tyler's personal affairs during his last year in the White House afforded the local public endless amusement, although the return of a more sedate, less colorful, social regime after James Polk became President was evidently easy enough for Washington to adjust to.

In 1844 tragedy was the prelude to comedy. In February when the Navy's first steam-powered cruiser, the *Princeton*, with President Tyler and other dignitaries aboard, made a trial run down the Potomac, the firing of a salute burst one of her big guns, killing several men in the party. Among them was the father of twenty-year-old Julia Gardiner whom the widowed President had been courting. "Miss Gardiner," Senator Jarnagin informed his wife in April, "who you recollect was said was going to marry him has kicked the old man." Had her father lived, "it is believed by many . . . he would have made his daughter marry old Tyler to get the Collectorship at New York for himself." In July the prophets were confounded: the fifty-six-year-old President brought his bride to the White House. There, seated in a large arm chair alone on a dais in the Blue Room, young Mrs. Tyler received. Outdoing the formality President Monroe had instituted and aping the ceremonial of

Windsor Castle, she had each guest announced first to her and then to that lesser personage, her husband. When she took the air, two spanking pairs of horses drew her carriage. Nevertheless, while the first lady caused a buzz of talk, Julia Tyler's little-girl delight in her brief reign of glory stripped her manners of offense.[1]

At James Polk's inauguration a downpour of cold rain somewhat dampened the morning's enthusiasm, but that night two rival inaugural balls took place, both with unexpected results. The National Theatre was the scene of the larger party; because the stage manager had to prepare for the opening of a play the next day, at midnight he had guests' wraps moved to the building next door, whence came "a chaos of cloaks and hats" which took a fortnight to untangle; the theatre burned to the ground on March 5. At the smaller ball, to which tickets cost $10, the managers at Carusi's Assembly Rooms discovered they had a $1,000 profit; they divided it between the city's two orphanages. The preoccupation of the new President, an avowed expansionist, with foreign relations and other public affairs and Mrs. Polk's puritanical disapproval of anything smacking of frivolity gave official entertaining a more sober air than when Julia Tyler had held sway. Time, moreover, in recasting the dramatis personae, altered the character of the drama played out in the drawing rooms of the capital. By the end of Polk's administration the nearly fifty years that had elapsed since Abigail Adams hung the family wash in the East Room had thinned the ranks of the charming group of first Washingtonians. Thomas Law, Margaret Bayard and Samuel Harrison Smith, John and Marcia Burnes Van Ness were dead. John Quincy Adams, who, if not technically a Washingtonian, had spent most of the last forty years of his life here and placed the imprint of his learning upon the city, died in 1847. Daniel Carroll died two years later. Mrs. Madison made her last public

[1] Stefan Lorant, *The Presidency*, p. 162; *N.I.*, 29 Feb, 27-29 May, 3 Jul 1844; Laurence A. Gobright, *Recollection of Men and Things at Washington during the Third of a Century*, p. 67; Spencer Jarnagin to his wife, 19 Apr 1844, Jarnagin Mss (SHC); Fremont, *Souvenir of My Time*, pp. 90-100.

appearance at a White House reception in February 1849; she died in July. With the exception of William Winston Seaton and his wife, most survivors among the distinguished early comers to the city were no longer active in social and civic affairs.

The increasing volume of public business and consequent lengthening of congressional sessions also affected the social structure of the city during the 1840's, for a growing number of congressmen, weary of the loneliness imposed by prolonged separation from their families, abandoned the congressional mess, rented suites of rooms, and brought wives and children to Washington. By 1845, some 19 of the 52 senators and 72 of the 221 representatives had at least part of their families established in the city during the winter months.[2] The larger seasonal influx tended to sharpen the contrast between the capital congressmen and outsiders knew and the city Washingtonians loved, but any secret regrets the community may have felt about this dual personality were purely sentimental. "Our city," wrote a young man in June 1848 to his bride-to-be, "has finally put on its white drillings and taken off winter pantaloons: 'Panama hats' are common and beaver scarce and quaint. Strangers are leaving. . . . Old residents are again renewing acquaintance with old friends and organizing into the summer social cliques. Ladies are gadding about in cob-web dresses 'shopping'—i.e. bleeding their unfortunate husbands, papas and brothers. . . . 'Sherry cobblers' and mint juleps are in extensive demand, although very successful efforts have been made to put them down."[3] Yet after all, residents well knew, Washington's primary reason for being was to serve as capital, and the more Americans to interest themselves in her the better.

Shopkeepers profited by the new arrangement. Stores multiplied, and scores of new houses went up, over 320 in 1844 alone. Trade, however, remained almost exclusively local. Farms

[2] *Globe*, 5 Mar 1845; *N.I.*, 20 Mar 1845; Jarnagin to his wife, 9 Mar, 4 Apr 1846; Force, *Picture of Washington*, Appendix.

[3] Benedict J. Semmes to Jorantha Jordan, 12 Jun 1848, Semmes Mss (SHC).

in the neighborhood supplied the four public markets with fruit, vegetables, dairy products, pork, and some beef; French wines, Parisian millinery, and fine English woollens imported via New York, cheap New England cottons, Kentucky bourbon, and Maryland rye brought in by rail or coastal vessels varied the stocks available to customers. But lack of outgoing shipments created imbalance.[4] In 1841 Charles Lyell, the famous English geologist, observed that "the estuary of the Potomac is so long and winding that to ascend from its mouth to Washington is said often to take as long as to cross from Liverpool to the mouth of the river." That circumstance, he suggested, would always limit the commerce of the Potomac cities. For Georgetown, moreover, the problem of the silting up of the channel above the Long Bridge became yearly more acute. Army Engineers pointed out that deforestation of the upper valley caused a steady downwash of soil that built up mud banks at the bend of the river below Georgetown; the only solution was constant expensive dredging. Washington merchants, on the other hand, knowing that the Eastern Branch was deep enough for ocean-going vessels, optimistically looked to the day when the steamship would replace the sailing ship. If memory of the illusions they had cherished about the C & O Canal in the late 1820's made them wary of taking further big risks, as the canal approached Cumberland, Maryland, in 1848, some of them began to envisage Washington as the principal outlet for Maryland coal.[5] Unhappily for that dream, Baltimore, with her easier accessibility for ships and the B & O Railroad, which had reached Cumberland in 1842 and could carry freight in winter as well as summer, was already firmly entrenched as the chief entrepot for the regional coal trade. Neither steam freighters nor sailing vessels could make the District cities busy com-

[4] *Saturday Evening News and District General Advertiser*, 6 Nov, 18 Dec 1847, 22 Apr 1848 (hereafter cited as *News*); "The Sessford Annals," CHS *Rec*, XI, 277-388; *Wshg Laws*, Mayor's Communication, 29 Jul 1844, 4 Aug 1845.

[5] Charles Lyell, *Travels in North America in the Years 1841-42*, I, 103; *Ggtn Ordinances*, 6 Mar, 6 Nov, 27 Dec 1847; H Doc 46, 29C, 2S, Ser 499; H Ex Doc 24, 30C, 1S, Ser 516.

mercial ports as long as a thinly settled, relatively infertile hinterland produced scanty surpluses and local manufacturing lagged.

In Georgetown industrial development made some headway in the mid-forties when several firms, having reached an agreement with the C & O directors, built flour mills along the canal and drew upon its surplus water for power. A more ambitious venture, started in 1846, was the 2,560-spindle, 84-loom factory of the Pioneer Cotton Company.[6] But Washington had nothing comparable to flour and cotton cloth to sell in markets outside the District; the output of her printing establishments and the production of political news was unlikely to give her a place among American manufacturing centers. To advertise her potentialities, in the spring of 1846 Washington businessmen organized a national fair. They persuaded promoters in other parts of the country who were anxious to set a pro-tariff argument before Congress to join in the undertaking. The American-made wares spread out in a large cloth-covered pavilion erected on Judiciary Square came from many states of the Union and reportedly attracted "thousands" of visitors. The grand finale was an Odd Fellows' parade, in which gay flower-decked floats filled with orphans dressed in white "imparted a loveliness and moral grandeur to the scene which no pen can adequately portray."[7] The moral grandeur produced no material results: hopes that the exhibition would attract outside investment capital and launch industry in the city proved abortive. But the declaration of war with Mexico widened other opportunities.

While the Secretary of War placed only small contracts with local shippers for Army supplies, the banking house of Corcoran and Riggs, founded in 1843, negotiated the government loan to finance the war. Rumor later placed the partners' profits from that transaction at $1,000,000. Whatever the exact figure, it put the firm into a specially favorable position to purchase

[6] *News*, 15 May 1847; Ggtn *Advocate*, 31 Mar, 4 Apr, 3 Oct 1846, 28 Aug 1848.

[7] *N.I.*, 22, 28 Apr, 7, 11, 14, 26-29 May, 4, 5 Jun 1846.

large tracts of the western lands which the General Land Office was opening for sale, or, as an equally lucrative alternative, to lend money to other buyers and handle the details of purchase for them. Before the peace treaty was signed in 1848, a dozen agents in Washington and Georgetown were advertising their ability to deal effectively with the Land Office; some of them boasted of making "40 to 60 percent" for their clients. Land scrip indeed became a form of currency, an ante-bellum equivalent of travellers' checks: congressmen journeying home to the West not infrequently set out supplied with land warrants purchased in Washington which tavern-keepers and stage-coach drivers gladly accepted in lieu of state bank notes. The status of District banks meanwhile had ceased to be a problem, for, after a series of congressional acts alternately authorizing and then withdrawing charter privileges, local bankers turned their corporations into partnerships and from 1846 to 1863 operated under the common law.[8] Washington's economic development, while less spectacular than that of Baltimore or Cincinnati or St. Louis or various other American cities, was gratifying. A 71-percent increase in population represented a bigger gain than in any decade since the first of the century. Businessmen accordingly saw no occasion to worry.

Workingmen, on the other hand, especially those with too little property to qualify as voters in city elections, were far from satisfied with their place in the scheme of things. For men with little or no education, chances to move up the economic ladder appeared fewer in this predominantly white-collar community than in commercial and industrial cities, and "the common man," if not entirely forgotten, had little voice in matters that concerned him closely. Here where thirteen newspapers were published, the printers had long been the aristocrats of labor; Gales' and Seaton's establishment alone had provided the training and experience for a dozen men who in

[8] Wshg *Directory*, 1843, 1846; *Alex. Gazette*, 9 Apr 1846; *N.I.*, 3 Mar 1847; *Cong Globe*, 26C, 1S, App, p. 631, 27C, 2S, pp. 564-65; 5 Stat. 449-51; H Rpt 182, 28C, 2S, Ser 468; Paul W. Gates, "Southern Investments in Northern Lands Before the Civil War," *Journal of Southern History*, V (May 1939), pp. 164-85.

time made their mark—Simon Cameron, President Lincoln's first Secretary of War, for one, for another, John Tower, in 1854 mayor of Washington. Yet by 1840 even skilled typesetters who lacked capital or credit were finding themselves, along with mechanics and men employed in the building trades, merely part of "the lower orders." In endeavor to obtain such remedy as political recognition might offer, six months before the city charter was due to expire in 1840 they listed their complaints in doggerel:

> Our charter, almost out of date
> Has only served to help the great. . . .
> We want a better one indeed—
> One that will give us what we need,
> A good *police*, and lamps by night, . . .
> A *District School*, to teach our sons,
> Who wander now like Goths or Huns. . . .
> And more than all we want the right
> To vote for those who rule in might.

Congress professed some interest in local white manhood suffrage until nearly a third of the existing electorate, some 550 men, opposed the plan. Congressional zeal thereupon cooled; inaction kept the old charter in force for another eight years.[9] In that interval, however, conscientious citizens became aroused over the city's disorderliness and the shocking inadequacy of the school system.

Lawlessness had been increasing for years. One source of trouble was the changed character of the volunteer fire companies. In the early 1830's irresponsible boys had begun to take the place of mature men who no longer wanted to be subject to call. After the destruction of the Treasury and the fire at the General Post Office, Congress had tried to induce public-

[9] Wshg *Metropolis*, 26 Oct 1839, and "Carrier's Address to the Patrons of the Washington City *Metropolis* on the Commencement of the Year, 1840"; S Docs, 518 and 609, 26C, 1S, Sers 360 and 361; *Wshg Laws*, 7 Jul 1840; ptns, H26A-G4.1, 17 Dec 1840, H26A-G5, 26 Jan 1841, H27A-G5.3, 24 Dec 1844; *Cong Globe*, 26C, 2S, pp. 45-46; H Doc 236, 28C, 1S, Ser 443.

spirited men to serve; the first bait was exemption from militia duty, the second the privilege of buying insurance at reduced rates. Neither scheme had worked. In the forties rowdies made up the fire companies, turning the six engine houses into headquarters for six competing quarrelsome gangs. New York City faced the same situation. Not infrequently on a Sunday evening one company or another sounded the fire alarm in the vicinity of a church for the sheer sport of watching the frightened congregation pour into the streets. Law-abiding citizens repeatedly accused the firemen of deliberately starting fires in order to enjoy the commotion of putting them out. "English Hill," east of City Hall, "Swampoodle" to the north, the "Northern Liberties" near the new market on G Street, the Navy Yard section, "Frogtown" south of the Capitol, and the "Island," cut off from the rest of the city by the Washington Canal, each had its gang, each more interested in fighting its rivals than in fighting fires.[10]

The skeleton police force was powerless to stop the firehouse gangs. Ward constables served only part-time and were rarely on duty at night. An unpleasant episode in the summer of 1841 emphasized the need of a night patrol: a drunken crowd, angered at President Tyler's veto of a bank bill, gathered one night at the portico of the White House to hiss and jeer at the chief executive. Robberies and incendiary fires became so frequent that Congress, fearful for the safety of government buildings, in 1842 established an "auxiliary guard" which for the first time provided some nighttime policing. The guards were federal officers, paid out of federal funds and charged with safeguarding federal property, but, lest they turn into a presidential "praetorian guard," the law specified that the mayor of Washington select the captain, and the captain his subordinates. The auxiliary guard and stricter enforcement of liquor licenses and Sunday closing ordinances reduced violence thereafter. Five years later Mayor Seaton wrote, "I believe

[10] H Doc 22, 23C, 2S, Ser 272; *The Diary of Philip Hone*, ed. Allan Nevins, p. 90; *N.I.*, 5 Dec 1836, 11, 25 Jul 1837, 22 May, 4 Sep 1840, 14 Feb 1842, 30 Sep 1844, 21 Apr 1845.

there is no place of equal population in which there is so little of riot, breach of the peace or serious crime as in this city; but I apprehend there is scarcely one which is more disturbed by idle, rowdy and disorderly boys."[11]

To the niggardly indifference of the bulk of taxpayers must be attributed the protracted penny-pinching neglect of public education. The income from the $40,000 which the school trustees had raised by lottery in the 1820's, and which the mayor had then invested in 6 percent municipal bonds, provided an $800 salary for a teacher and $100 for all other expenses at each of the two pauper schools. Before 1840 mayors and councils yearly had added the unexpended surplus to principal, against the moment when they had accumulated enough money to open a third school. At intervals, particularly when Congress voted gifts to the colleges and orphanages, city officials had asked for federal aid for common schools, but when those pleas failed, plans for other action had evaporated, leaving four-fifths of the white children in the city without schooling. Since influential people objected to "the immoral tendency of mingling a great number of the two sexes together," girls were excluded entirely from the eastern school and rarely accepted in the western. Yet in 1840, when ladies of the Presbyterian churches prevailed upon the city fathers to let them use the unspent surplus of the school fund to found "female charity schools," protests arose over sanctioning sectarian education.[12]

But a good many people were distressed at the prospect of a predominantly illiterate community. William Winston Seaton led the fight for a full-scale public school system. Shortly after he began his second term as mayor, he urged the city to follow the New England example and, by means of a special tax, make free schooling available to every white child in Washington. His proposal won supporters among all classes of people;

[11] Ptn, H27A-G5.2, 25 Aug 1841; *N.I.*, 20 Aug 1841, 3 Sep 1842; *Wshg Laws*, 21 Sep 1842, 1 Nov 1843, Mayor's Communications, 4 Aug 1845, 6 Aug 1849; *Cong Globe*, 27C, 2S, pp. 570-71; H Rpt 836, 27C, 2S, Ser 410.

[12] Ptns, H22A-G5.3, 6 Mar 1832, 9 Jan 1833, H26A-G5.3, 12 Mar 1838; *Wshg Laws*, 30 May 1840; *N.I.*, 3 Apr 1839, 29 Jul 1840; S Doc 59, 26C, 2S, Ser 376.

it also met unyielding opposition. Rather than abandon the plan altogether, he modified it: let the municipality build at least one new school from public funds, open all the city schools to all white children, rich and poor alike, and charge fifty cents a month tuition for any child whose parents could pay. In December 1844 the city council, perhaps influenced by Baltimore's recent moves to inaugurate a tax-supported school system, accepted the mayor's plan. Money squeezed out of the regular municipal budget and the lottery fund built one new schoolhouse near the City Hall on Judiciary Square and another on the "Island"; these, together with the two long used for the pauper schools, provided a building in each of four school districts. A single school board composed of three men appointed from each district mapped out the curriculum, engaged teachers, ordered supplies, and strongly recommended no more than fifty or sixty pupils to a teacher.[13] For the next four years part of the taxpaying community fought off the introduction of wholly tax-supported schools, but by 1848 the trustees' report revealed the weaknesses of the makeshift arrangement: daily attendance had dropped to about 420 pupils. The colored schools voluntarily maintained by the poorest element of the population had a relatively better record. Fortunately the new city charter that went into effect that May promised to supply an answer. A dollar poll tax earmarked for school support enabled the trustees to dispense with tuition. Within a year enrollment both in the male and female classes tripled.[14]

The new municipal charter and its workings interested most of the city far more than the effect of the poll tax upon the schools. Four years of ward meetings and city-wide "conventions" had gone into drafting the terms. Congress enacted them without change. A special referendum of white men had shown

[13] *N.I.*, 13, 20 Oct, 11, 14 Nov 1842; *Wshg Laws*, 25 Nov 1842, 18 May 1843, 1 Nov 1843, 6 Dec 1844, Mayor's Com, 24 Jul 1843, 27 Jul 1844, 4 Aug 1845 and Annual Report of the Trustees of the Public Schools, 18 Aug 1845.

[14] *N.I.*, 7 Aug 1848; *Wshg Laws*, 7 Aug 1848 and Mayor's Com, 6 Aug 1849.

an overwhelming majority in favor of removing the $100 property qualification for voting but keeping the year's residence requirement. Thus white manhood suffrage became law in Washington nearly a generation after the states one by one had adopted it and almost forty years after poorhouse inmates had first tried to cast their ballots in a local election. Every provision of the charter had been the subject of city-wide discussion and had won popular, if not unanimous, endorsement—the seventy-five-cent tax ceiling, the prohibition on municipal borrowing without the express approval of two-thirds of the electorate, and the grant of authority to the corporation to tax stocks and bonds in order to lighten the burden on real estate. In June some 2,800 men, more than twice as many as ever before, voted peaceably in the city election. Unhappily it would be the last for sixteen years not to be marred by disorderliness. With Seaton returned to the mayor's office for the fifth time and moderates elected to the board of aldermen and common council, in 1848 radicalism manifestly was not going to rule in the City Hall.[15]

Seaton's long service as mayor was a blessing to the city. The continuity of policy was in itself useful. He had known the community since 1812, and his insights enabled him to diagnose civic needs accurately. His tact frequently won adherents to his plans among council members who initially balked at any innovation. Yearly he submitted to the board of aldermen and common council a "communication" summarizing the achievements of the year past and succinctly spelling out weaknesses which municipal action could correct. While he failed to convince his associates of the wisdom of discarding the ward system of financing, his persuasiveness ultimately triumphed on the school question, and he obtained the new Asylum as well as a "pest house" for cases of contagious disease built on the city's south-eastern rim near the Eastern Branch. He commanded wide respect on the Hill. No mayor before or after him

[15] H Doc 236, 28C, 1S, Ser 443; *N.I.*, 23 Jan 1847, 17, 23 Feb 1848; *Wshg Laws*, 24 Feb 1848; *Cong Globe*, 30C, 1S, pp. 776-78; *News*, 6 Mar, 11 Dec 1847, 8, 28 Jan, 19, 23 Feb, 27 May, 5, 17 Jun 1848.

carried so much weight with Congress. His part-ownership of the *National Intelligencer* gave him political influence irrespective of whether Whigs or Democrats were in power, and his technique of thanking Congress for its "kind consideration" of the city was ingratiating. His position in Washington society was unassailable. His impressive good looks and his affable manners doubtless charmed congressional wives. During his years in the mayor's office, city and Congress arrived at a more satisfactory mutual relationship than they had achieved since 1816.

After 1840 the corporation undertook street improvements without carping at the lack of federal aid, and congressmen apparently accepted muddy unpaved avenues bordered here and there by rubbish-strewn vacant lots as one of the unavoidable discomforts of convening in Washington. Congress supplied a modicum of street illumination first by placing lamps along Pennsylvania Avenue and in 1847 by authorizing the inventor of a "solar gas" process to install a sixteen-foot lantern on a seventy-five-foot pole on top of the Capitol dome and later to put gas lamps into several government offices. Nobody on the Hill expected the city to contract with the newly organized Washington Gas Light Company for gas street lights. Seemingly everyone but an occasional foreigner took for granted the cows and geese and swine that roamed loose in the streets. When the French minister, the Chevalier de Bacourt, inquired why people put up with the nuisance, a senator assured him that most American cities looked upon pigs as the ideal refuse scavengers: "nothing was more convenient or conducive to health."[16]

More helpful to the community than that easy-going tolerance were the measures Congress undertook that reduced the burden upon the city of providing medical care for nonresident paupers, one of Washington's forty-year-old grievances. In 1841 an act instructed the Treasury to pay the costs of sending the

[16] 5 Stat. 498; *N.I.*, 3 Mar 1847; *News*, 21 Aug, 20 Nov 1847, 4 Mar, 6 May 1848; de Bacourt, *Souvenirs of a Diplomat*, pp. 62-63, 72, 157.

indigent insane to an asylum in Baltimore; formerly the municipality had had to house them at city expense in the county jail or at the workhouse at the Washington Asylum. The government still left to local taxpayers responsibility for transient paupers not adjudged insane, and, as in the past, over half the inmates of the almshouse and workhouse for many years continued to be people who had drifted into the capital from the states. But in 1843, upon completion of a new jail, a federal appropriation made possible the remodelling of the old building on Judiciary Square for use as the Washington Infirmary. Although the next year Congress failed to vote further sums, a law permitted the medical faculty of Columbian College to take charge and convert the institution into a teaching center under the name National Medical College. There, while medical students got professional experience, for modest fees poverty-stricken local people could receive care, and after 1845 federal appropriations paid for nonresident paupers admitted to the infirmary.[17]

The community still had troubles in helping the local poor. Destitution in the midst of plenty was a commonplace in all American cities. When the Howard Society disbanded in 1842, the Female Union Benevolent Society became the major philanthropic organization other than the orphanages. Less than $1,400 raised annually mostly by fairs and charity balls restricted largesse, but in 1844, for example, when curtailed operations threw men out of work at the Navy Yard, the society somehow managed to provide relief for three hundred families. James Laurie, the Presbyterian minister who presented the board of managers' report that year, declared almsgiving "but a part of our charity"; its higher aims were "to promote religious improvement . . . and to effect as far as possible a moral regeneration in the character and condition of the indigent classes of our population. But experience teaches,

[17] William B. Webb, *Laws*, p. 23; *Cong Globe*, 28C, 1S, pp. 251-52, 660; Wshg *Metropolis*, 3 Jul 1837; *Wshg Laws*, 10 May 1843, 26 May 1845, Mayor's Com, 4 Aug 1845, and p. 229 in *Laws* for 1844-45; *N.I.*, 12 Sep, 17 Oct 1842, 3 Apr 1843; *News*, 18 Jul, 19 Aug, 7, 21 Nov 1846.

that unless immediate relief is given to suffering, the words of counsel and consolation fall coldly on the ear; they will not suffice to clothe the naked nor satisfy the cravings of hunger; we can only hope to render the mind susceptible of advice . . . by relieving the body from its pressing wants." Pauperism, "that giant evil," Laurie concluded, could only be checked "by diminishing the causes that lead to it. Want of employment properly remunerated is a chief cause." In the 1840's those pronouncements betokened an unusual breadth of vision, a vision that unhappily would be largely lost in the next fifty years. While men on the Hill, presumably those especially whose wives were now part-time Washington residents, undoubtedly often contributed individually to the society's work, the general assumption was that local charity was a local affair. Mutual acceptance of that simple rule, always acknowledged in theory, probably went far toward preserving cordiality between city and Congress.[18]

As half the decade came and went without a congressional decision about the Smithsonian fund, many Americans grew restive; in fact, the losses incurred by the investment of the original $500,000 of gold in state bonds had become a minor national scandal. Progress on other government projects, however, somewhat mollified Washingtonians with strong scientific interests. Powerful members of Congress persisted in objecting to federal sponsorship of any program that the states could undertake, but House and Senate were willing to appropriate $5,000 for the preservation of the specimens sent back in 1841 by the naturalists accompanying the Wilkes expedition. To the gratification of the more than two hundred Washington members of the National Institution for the Promotion of Science, Congress entrusted the collections to them and incorporated the National Institute the next year. Here appeared to be the long-awaited opportunity to put the capital into the front ranks of scientific research under the aegis of a learned society

[18] *Proceedings of the Sixth Annual Meeting of the Female Union Benevolent Society*, 1844, pp. 4-5, 9-10.

assisted by federal money. The Patent Office provided space, and a clergyman whom the Institute chose as curator set to work unpacking the boxes. Unfortunately the energy of the Reverend Henry King outran his knowledge; he dried pickled specimens, ran them through with pins and removed the labels; proper cataloguing thus became impossible and the scientific value of most of the collections was destroyed. Upon the return of the Wilkes expedition itself in 1842 with more "objects of natural history," Congress voted $20,000 for their care and appointed a member of the expedition as curator. The next year Commissioner of Patents Ellsworth succeeded in getting the collections assigned to his official control. With some of the botanical specimens he was able to start in the Patent Office greenhouse and garden a semblance of a first government agricultural experiment station. A delighted sightseer in 1845 remarked upon the array of "curious Exotics mostly brought in by Lieutenant Wilkes . . . embracing a very great variety of flowers now in full blow and shrubs, also the coffee tree." Members of the National Institute continued for a time to send to the Patent Office mineral collections and zoological specimens, but Ellsworth considered the accumulation a nuisance, and most of it, the irreplaceable along with the junk, gradually disappeared. The society made its last effective gesture in 1844 by bringing together in Washington the first congress of American men of science. Thereafter, while government projects strengthened, the Institute faded into insignificance.[19]

Of far greater ultimate scientific value was the enlarged program initiated by Lt. James Gilliss. His presentation induced Congress to authorize a building in which the Depot of Charts and Instruments could conduct studies in hydrography, meteorology, and astronomy, which the Navy's practical needs required. In 1843 as the new building began to rise on the hilltop between the White House and the Potomac, the architecture must have startled some members of Congress, but

[19] Dupree, *Science in the Federal Government*, pp. 70-76; G. Brown Goode, "Genesis of the National Museum," pp. 278-79; Diary of John Houston Bill, 9 Jul 1845 (SHC).

John Quincy Adams was delighted that "an astronomical observatory . . . had been smuggled into the institutions of the country." The telescope in the twenty-two-foot revolving dome provided a very small "light-house of the sky," and Lt. Matthew Maury, Gilliss' successor, chose to stress hydrography and meteorology rather than astronomy, but the opening of the National Observatory in 1844 represented a milestone in Washington's history. As Georgetown College about the same time built a small observatory on its campus, astronomy bade fair to become an important field of research in the District.[20]

The Coast Survey also acquired fresh vitality after Rudolph Hassler's death in 1843, for the old Swiss with his irascible temper and his heavy foreign accent, unintelligible when he became excited, had never fully convinced Congress that his exacting methods were necessary. The new head, Alexander Dallas Bache, educated at West Point and in Europe, shared Hassler's dedication to high standards, but Bache possessed in addition to his scientific background the advantages of influential political connections, great suavity of manner, and, despite his short stature, a commanding presence. A descendant of Benjamin Franklin, a nephew of Polk's Vice-President, and a brother-in-law of Senator Robert Walker of Mississippi, Bache came to government service from a professorship in natural philosophy at the University of Pennsylvania. By drawing upon the talents of a new generation of professionally trained men, he was able to step up the pace of the survey without sacrificing the quality of the work. Whereas Hassler had always been harassed by fears lest funds be cut off, Bache persuaded the holders of the purse-strings that this must be a task of years. Thus the office of the Coast Survey became a semi-permanent scientific headquarters manned by qualified Army and Navy officers as well as by gifted civilians eager to work under Bache. And as the Oregon country and then the former Spanish territories of the Southwest called for mapping,

[20] Dupree, *Science*, pp. 62-63; *Alex. Gazette*, 8 Oct 1844; Force, *Picture of Washington*, pp. 47-49; Charles O. Paullin, "Early Movements for a National Observatory," CHS *Rec*, xxv, 50-51.

the Topographical Engineers in turn brought to Washington a succession of able young officers, many of them carefully schooled at West Point, occasionally a man like John Charles Fremont, who learned his skills in the field during an exploring expedition in the trans-Mississippi West.[21]

Probably much of the local public regarded these developments as less significant than the demonstration in 1844 of Samuel Finley Breese Morse's "magnetic telegraph." The officials and guests assembled in the Supreme Court chamber at the Capitol heard with their own ears the mysterious clickings of the instrument that transmitted over wires strung from Baltimore a message "What hath God wrought." Yet the invention was not destined to have any major effect upon the city. Newspaper correspondents for the next twenty-five years would send off their dispatches by mail, not by wire. As private interests took over the exploitation of the new scientific wonder, its importance to the community came to lie chiefly in heightening popular belief that Americans could do anything.[22]

In August 1846 when Congress at last acted to fulfill James Smithson's will, the enthusiasm that swept over Washington dwarfed interest in every other public event. After eight years of altercation and delay, a bill passed appointing regents and authorizing construction of a building for the Smithsonian Institution. Jubilantly Mayor Seaton declared that "since the legislation of the year 1814 and the rebuilding of the Capitol nothing has occurred calculated to exert such an influence on the fortunes of the city, even unto the most distant future, as the founding of this great and annually growing institution."[23] It affected everybody—day laborers, skilled artisans, merchants handling building supplies, people hoping for improvements in the city's appearance, and, above all, men eager to have the capital attain eminence in the American intellectual world. The

[21] Dupree, *Science*, pp. 50, 62-64, 79-80, 91, 100-105; M. M. Odgers, *Alexander Dallas Bache: Scientist and Educator*, p. 144.

[22] Dupree, *Science*, p. 48; *N.I.*, 3 Jul 1844; Oliver W. Larkin, *Samuel F. B. Morse and American Democratic Art*, pp. 147-58; Francis A. Richardson, "Recollections of a Newspaper Correspondent in Washington," CHS *Rec*, VI.

[23] *Cong Globe*, 29C, 1S, 10 Aug 1846, p. 1223; *N.I.*, 28 Aug 1846.

regents' choice of a secretary guaranteed the new institution distinction. Prompted by Alexander Bache, they selected Joseph Henry, in 1846 professor of natural philosophy at the College of New Jersey, forerunner of Princeton University. Henry had done the basic work in electric magnetic fields that had made the telegraph possible. A man dedicated to fundamental research, he would throw his weight into the scales to see that some part of the Smithsonian funds went into the "increase" of knowledge rather than entirely into the "diffusion of knowledge among men."[24]

While the regents argued the question of what the Institution's primary function should be, lesser controversy arose over the site and architecture for the building. The location agreed upon early in 1847 lay on the south side of the Mall midway between the Hill and the Potomac; there space was ample, and proximity to the Washington Canal would permit delivery of building materials by barge. The regents, undeterred by the classical style and white stone of other public buildings, selected James Renwick's design, a Norman castle of red sandstone. On May 1 the ceremony of laying the cornerstone took place in the presence of 6,000 people. Because John Quincy Adams, fearful lest the Smithsonian fund be frittered away, had succeeded in inserting into the act a stipulation that only the income of the bequest be spent, the building would take eight years to finish. But for the city it was the start that mattered. The dismay of some people over the Mall location rapidly yielded to pleasure in the "romantic" appearance of the red turrets slowly rising against the skyline. And as a newspaper correspondent observed in 1848, "If there be one question set at rest in this community, it is that public opinion has decided that the national metropolis shall be distinguished for the cultivation of the mind."[25]

Another civic and patriotic ambition seemed close to realization in 1848 when obstacles to the erection of a monument to

[24] Dupree, *Science*, pp. 79-85; Goode, "Genesis of the National Museum," pp. 278-79; *Union*, 15 Feb 1847.

[25] *N.I.*, 17, 19, 24 Feb, 1, 23 Mar, 3, 17 May 1847, 27 Nov 1848; *News*, 13 Feb, 20 Mar, 20 Nov, 18 Dec 1847.

George Washington suddenly vanished. Since the turn of the century Congress had talked of a memorial to the first President, but in 1833 George Watterston, a free lance writer and a city alderman after losing his post as Librarian of Congress, had concluded that only a direct public appeal would get results. He was the moving spirit that brought the Washington Monument Society into being. Under the presidency first of Chief Justice Marshall, then of James Madison, and thereafter of each President of the United States, the society at first had solicited one-dollar subscriptions from Americans everywhere. After 1836 when the trustees accepted Robert Mills' design for a seven-hundred-foot obelisk encircled by a colonnaded pantheon at its base, every contributor had received a print of the monument that his money would help build. Yet funds had come in slowly. Equally discouraging, Congress had shown a certain suspiciousness of the project along with an unwillingness to donate a site. Perhaps some members believed Congress had already paid ample tribute in commissioning Horatio Greenough in the 1830's to execute an imposing statue of the Father of his Country. But when Horatio Greenough's sculpture, lovingly completed at the cost of nine years of work, was emplaced on the east lawn of the Capitol in 1843, the twenty-ton marble had offended public taste. "The spectator," wrote one outraged citizen, "will always be shocked at the nudity of the figure," a lifeless seated colossus partly draped in a Roman toga. Apparently disappointment over that travesty spurred the Monument Society on to widen its fund-raising campaign. By the end of 1847 the trustees had some $87,000 on hand, and, since Congress still seemed loath to allow the use of a public reservation, they decided to purchase land and begin building at once. Unexpectedly Congress capitulated: the society might have any available public site President Polk and the trustees deemed suitable.

The Potomac end of the Mall below the President's Square was the most dramatic location. L'Enfant's plan had included an equestrian statue at the intersection of the city's east-west and north-south axes, but a hundred yards off center the elevation above the tidal estuary of Tiber Creek was slightly greater, and there, to the consternation of symmetry-conscious twentieth-century city landscapists, the foundations were dug. On the 4th of July the Masonic lodge of Washington took charge of laying the cornerstone. Matthew Emery, a skilled mason and twenty-two years later the city's last mayor, wielded the trowel. High-ranking state and federal officials, foreign ministers, Masons, Odd Fellows, members of local temperance and benevolent societies, Mrs. Madison, "bedaubed with Pearl powder and rouge," as one young man unkindly observed, Mrs. Alexander Hamilton and hundreds of obscure citizens marched in the mile-and-a-half-long procession. The ceremonies, in the opinion of the press, "surpassed in magnificence and moral grandeur anything of the kind ever witnessed in this metropolis, since the formation of the Republic."[26]

More than passing meaning attached to the event. Not only did it call attention to George Washington's fathering of the city, but the building of the monument promised to inspire a continuing program of beautifying the capital. For years past, one man noted ruefully, Washington had been "the butt for the small wits of our country," all of whom felt qualified to pass disparaging judgments upon the community. Those were more irritating to residents than the belittling comments of Europeans; foreigners' gibes were usually directed at all Americans. Mrs. Basil Hall in 1827 had dreaded "the purgatory of a winter in American society," but she implied it would be no worse in Washington than elsewhere. In 1842 Charles Dickens wrote of the "City of Magnificent Intentions" laid out with "broad avenues that begin in nothing and lead nowhere" and

[26] Frederick L. Harvey, *History of the Washington National Monument and the National Washington Monument Society*, pp. 25-55, S Doc 224, 57C, 2S, Ser 4436; Watterston, *New Guide*, pp. 113-114; Charles E. Fairman, *Art and Artists of the Capitol*, pp. 65, 99-104; *N.I.*, 14 Apr 1843; Benedict Semmes to Jorantha Jordan, 5 Jul 1848, Semmes Mss (SHC); *News*, 8 Jul 1848.

space wanting "only houses, roads and inhabitants." Yet he obviously thought the scene characteristic of empty American bragging, and in dubbing the city, "the headquarters of tobacco-tinctured saliva," he was clearly indicting the national rather than the local habit of chewing tobacco and spitting. Even the Chevalier de Bacourt's scathing description of "the so-called city of Washington, which is neither city nor village, . . . [and] has a miserable, desolate look" was largely a reflection of his distaste for a people in whom he found "nothing to sympathize with, nothing to inspire confidence, nothing to admire."[27] Washingtonians believed the obelisk when completed would notably improve the looks of the capital; and, knowing themselves to be the chief instrumentalities, they could be forgiven if they hoped the monument would convince other Americans of the community's taste and enterprise.

Meanwhile with astonishingly little discussion Congress took a step that would have serious consequences fifteen years later and would complicate the metropolitan problems of the mid-twentieth century. In 1846 an act reduced by nearly a third the size of the District of Columbia. The trans-Potomac segment had never netted much consideration on the Hill. In 1840 and 1841 Alexandrians had again begged for retrocession to Virginia, but not until they took the precaution of first obtaining the approval of the Virginia Assembly did their pleas get a hearing. "It is a fact which it is useless longer to attempt to conceal," declared the memorialists, "that we have long been and are yet in a very depressed state; that our business, in a measure, is paralyzed; that our mechanics are not kept employed; that many of them have been compelled to leave us; and that more must follow them unless we speedily obtain *Retrocession* and *Relief*." Why the Commonwealth was willing to reclaim a section in such economic straits might be hard to understand had Alexandria not been an important center for

[27] *N.I.*, 1 Apr 1835; Margaret Hall, *The Aristocratic Journey*, p. 184; Charles Dickens, *American Notes for General Circulation*, pp. 163, 168-69, 177 (1892 ed.); de Bacourt, *Souvenirs of a Diplomat*, pp. 2, 72.

the slave trade; two pro-slavery members added to the Virginia Assembly would certainly strengthen the position of tidewater planters in their intensifying political struggle with piedmont and mountain county farmers. A Republican Congress in 1861 would regret the act that relinquished federal control over the heights across the Potomac, but in May 1846 a single letter to the *National Intelligencer* called attention to what that action could mean. At the moment war with Mexico was a far more engrossing matter.[28]

Congressman R. M. T. Hunter of Virginia presented Alexandria's case effectively. Although his adroit advocacy failed to move sixty-five members of the House, nineteen of them southerners, ninety-six ayes carried the measure. Washington's city council took a stand against it: it might "prove the first step toward abrogating or destroying the compact by which the seat of government was permanently located in the District, and result in the removal of the capital to some other place." Private citizens, on the contrary, expressed little concern, and Georgetown remained officially silent. When the Senate acted on July 2, the bill passed quickly. It contained only one proviso, that a referendum of white men in Alexandria County, including the votes of those without property, must show a majority in favor of return to Virginia. Voting by voice at the court house in early September, 763 men declared for retrocession, 222 against. An angry protest from residents of the county contended that an unholy alliance between self-seeking men in Alexandria city and Richmond had railroaded the deal through, but the appeal for reconsideration proved futile. For the slave-owning South, Virginia's reacquisition of a third of the ten-mile square was a victory.[29]

[28] *Alex. Gazette*, 20, 24 Jan, 5 Feb 1846; ptns, S26A-G5, 18 Jul 1840, H27A-G5.3, 8 Jul 1841, H29A-D4.1, 20 Jan and 25 Feb 1846, H29A-G3.1, 27 Jan, 9 Feb, 8 Apr 1846, H29A-G3, S29A-G3, 21, 28 May, 4, 6, 14, 15 Jun 1846; *N.I.*, 11 May 1846; *Cong Globe*, 29C, 1S, p. 778.

[29] *Cong Globe*, 29C, 1S, pp. 778-81, 985-86, 1045-46, 1057, 1846, and App., pp. 894-98; *Wshg Laws*, 28 May 1846; *News* 5 Sep 1846; *Alex. Gazette*, 3 Sep 1846; Amos Casselman, "The Virginia Portion of the District of Columbia," CHS *Rec*, XII, 115-41.

Migration of free Negroes from the Old Dominion into Washington and Georgetown presumably accelerated in the next few years, if only because Virginia law forbade a freed slave's remaining in the state more than six months. The number of free colored people in Washington at the end of the decade had increased by almost 70 percent over the 1840 figure, until the proportion of free to slave was nearly four to one. (See Table I.) The solidity of the established Negro community here naturally attracted ambitious freed men. Where else could they hope to find schools for their children and independent colored churches, at one church a minister solemnly ordained by the regional Presbyterian synod? John F. Cook's ordination sermon in 1843 had impressed white as well as colored people. For the exceptionally able Negro, moreover, there was the extremely remote but nonetheless challenging possibility of a salaried government job in the capital, albeit only at the bottom of the roster and with only the slimmest chance of promotion. Yet just as a Negro had been chief messenger in the Patent Office in 1835, so Solomon J. Brown, thanks to the recommendation of his white mentor, got a departmental appointment in 1844.[30]

White people were still reluctant to see the city's free colored population expand, but economic and political expediency, if not moral conviction, militated to modify their point of view about slavery. When the House of Representatives discarded the gag rule in 1844 and Congress again accepted the thousands of petitions begging for the outlawing of the slave trade in the District, Washingtonians did not renew their complaints about outside interference. Nor did the city attempt to tighten the restrictions upon free Negroes. Northerners coming to live in the capital tended to develop ambivalent feelings. In 1846 a young woman born and bred in New York state wrote soon after her arrival: "No sane-minded man acquainted with the black population South could wish them liberated and allowed

[30] William J. Simmons, *Men of Mark, Eminent, Progressive and Rising*, p. 302; Washington *Sun*, 12, 26 Feb, 9 Apr 1915.

to remain in the States. If the black population could be expelled from the south the greatest advantage would accrue to the white population. Slave labor is the bane of all industry and enterprises, labour is looked upon as so degrading. I think that is the most despicable trait in the southern character . . . and that feeling is engendered by an inferior race of people performing all manual labour." Mary Bowen later changed her mind about emancipation as her husband became one of Washington's leading Free-Soilers, but even people who accepted the morality of slavery were beginning to doubt the utility of the peculiar institution in the capital; men spoke of the worthlessness of slaves constantly exposed to the corrupting influence of the city's free Negroes.[31]

The shift in public opinion was by no means universal. In 1848 shortly after Dr. Gamaliel Bailey of Boston began publication in Washington of an anti-slavery newspaper, the *National Era*, an episode threatened to end the life of the paper before it was well started. On a Sunday morning in April a number of Washington and Georgetown householders, including Mrs. Madison, awakened to find no breakfast in preparation and the family slaves absconded. Immediate pursuit of the schooner *Pearl* which had sailed before dawn discovered the seventy-six slaves aboard bound for the North under the protection of Captain Daniel Drayton. Drayton and his mate were immediately jailed, while an angry mob, sure that Dr. Bailey had abetted the abduction, gathered at his shop to demand that he leave the city. The courage of the captain of police and several private citizens prevented violence, the *National Era* continued publication, and eventually public wrath subsided. The owners of the runaways sold them to dealers who shipped them South, and Drayton and his mate after a prolonged and fiercely fought trial were finally sentenced to long prison terms as kidnappers. But slaveholders' indignation over the Drayton affair did not

[31] Mary Barker Bowen to Harriet Barker Underhill, 14 Nov 1846, Bowen Mss (in possession of Prof. C. A. Barker of Johns Hopkins University); ptn, H30A-G5.1, 24 Mar 1848; *N.I.*, 29 Dec 1848.

blind them to the economic disadvantages of slave-owning in the District of Columbia.[32] In December 1848 a conservative Georgetown paper, remarking upon local eagerness to be rid of the slave trade, concluded: "Or, if the public would make provision to purchase out the slaves now held in the District, compensating the owners of them therefore, we do not suppose that the slaveholders of the District would have any serious objection thereto. . . . From the increasing insecurity, and unsatisfactoriness of this kind of property, the pecuniary advantage of slave owners would probably be promoted by such a course."[33]

With the signing of the treaty of Guadalupe-Hidalgo in February 1848 and the consequent addition of a large piece of the continent to the United States, informed Americans realized that outspoken conflict in national councils over the extension of slavery into the new territories could not long be postponed. At the same time every knowledgeable Washingtonian knew that the congressional debates would almost certainly involve the fate of slavery and the slave trade in the District of Columbia. "The slavery question," wrote a businessman in July, "is here the all-absorbing topic of the day."[34] The Whig victory in November and Zachary Taylor's noncommittal stand on these matters failed to blot out uneasiness in the capital about the future of the Union. "The national metropolis," however dedicated to "cultivation of the mind," sensed that the era of calm was over.

[32] *National Era*, 4 Feb 1848, 4 Jan 1849; *News*, 22, 29 Apr, 1 Jul, 5, 12, 19, 26 Aug, 30 Sep, 7 Oct 1848; ptns, S30A-H2, 13 Jun 1848, H30A-G5.1, 22 Jan 1849; *N.I.*, 29 Dec 1848; *Cong Globe*, 30C, 1S, pp. 649-50 and App., pp. 500-10, 537-40, 30C, 2S, p. 31.

[33] *Ggtn Advocate*, 30 Dec 1848.

[34] B. J. Semmes to Jorantha Jordan, 24 Jul 1848, Semmes Mss (SHC).

CHAPTER VII

THE EYE OF THE HURRICANE, 1849-1860

THE twenty-one months preceding the Compromise of 1850 were anxious days in Washington. Thoughtful Americans everywhere felt the strain, as the sectional fight in Congress over the extension of slavery into the territories threatened to burst the bonds of the Union, but in other parts of the country men could occasionally forget the danger; here the sense of imminent catastrophe was ever-present. Feeling ran so high that some people were ready to believe in July 1850 that President Taylor had been hounded to his death by the insistent harassment of southern senators. As anticipated, the congressional debates early involved the question of slavery and the slave trade in the District of Columbia. An obscure Illinois congressman named Abraham Lincoln in January 1849 proposed abolition for the federal area, a measure which, he contended, the majority of its residents would endorse.[1] Only the larger issue, preservation of the Union, mattered greatly to the local community.

Seemingly fearful of precipitating disaster, Washingtonians kept very quiet about local slave-owning. Petitions and published letters dealing with the problem virtually ceased; a single memorial signed by about seventy men, two-thirds of them county farmers, merely requested Congress not to change the laws without first obtaining local approval by formal referendum. Prohibition of the slave trade was another matter. The Washington city council pronounced it "alike prejudicial to the interest of our city and offensive to public sentiment." Southerners in Congress, on the contrary, believed with Senator Pierre Soulé of Louisiana that to outlaw the trade here would be merely a first step on a path that would end in emancipation. They fought the proposal for months, and then probably only

[1] Ulrich Phillips, *The Life of Robert Toombs*, pp. 84-85; John Nicolay and John Hay, *Abraham Lincoln, A History*, I, 285-88; *Cong Globe*, 30C, 2S, pp. 212ff.

Henry Clay's insistence that it was an essential part of the great compromise persuaded them to yield. When the compromise acts became law in September 1850, with the exception of the five or six local dealers and their on-hangers who had been making small fortunes from the trade, Washingtonians felt intense relief. Most of them subscribed to Clay's view that the prohibition of the traffic in the District "should give peace and security to the maintenance of slavery within this District, until it exhausts itself by the process of time, as it would seem to be most rapidly doing." Faith in that ultimate outcome comforted people who had hoped for abolition.[2]

Within two years of accepting the compromise both sections of the country began to voice deep dissatisfaction. The South felt it had given more than it won when it agreed to the admission of California as a free state and the prohibition of the slave trade in the District of Columbia, while the North found the new Fugitive Slave Law increasingly hard to accept; and both were uncertain about the future of the territories. The struggle resumed in Congress in 1854 over the territorial organization of Kansas and Nebraska, sharpened in 1856 over the settlement of "Bleeding Kansas," reached a new peak of bitterness in the North with the Supreme Court decision in the Dred Scott case in 1857, and two years later produced the violence of John Brown's raid at Harpers Ferry. Through this succession of crises, public opinion north and south crystallized, swiftly deepening the gulf between the sections. But the fiercer and more outspoken the mutual hostilities in the rest of the United States, the more discreet citizens of the District of Columbia became.

Whatever opinions about southern states' rights Washingtonians voiced within the walls of their homes, they rarely aired their ideas unguardedly in public. Denunciation of the "impudence" of free Negroes in Washington seldom appeared in

[2] Ptns, H30A-G5.1, 7 Feb 1849, S30A-H, 23 Jan 1849; *Cong Globe*, 31C, 1S, pp. 944-48, 1179, 1743-44, 1794-95, 1810, 1829-30, 1837, 1858-61, 1954, and App., pp. 619-20, 784-85, 1620-74; Clay's remark is on p. 1647 of the Appendix; Frederic Bancroft, *Slave-Trading in the Old South*, ed. 1959, pp. 50-54.

the local press after the early 1850's. Citizens expressed gratification over new public works, argued about the function of the Smithsonian Institution, discussed plans for new railroads, talked of the spread of juvenile delinquency, and took strong positions on city politics, but they avoided the race question. An exhilarating material prosperity and signs that the city was acquiring new stature in the scientific and artistic world made it relatively easy to censor from consciousness ominous thoughts about new strife over slavery. No Washingtonian advocated restricting freedom of speech, and very occasionally a brief outburst occurred attacking or defending the position taken by North or South, but a tacit rule of conduct nevertheless emerged: abide by the law, but say nothing, do nothing, that might upset the precarious sectional balance. The fiercer the storm blew roundabout, the greater the quiet at the center. It was like the stillness at the eye of a hurricane. Not until the Republican victory in November 1860 threatened to change a repressible into an irrepressible conflict did Washingtonians acknowledge that the time for silent inaction might have passed.

In the autumn of 1850 Washingtonians, sensitive to northern opinion, were glad to be able to walk past the rear of the new Smithsonian building without suffering the discomfort of seeing across the street the slave pens long maintained there by two of the chief traders in the capital. Moreover, the steady decline in the number of locally owned slaves indicated that Senator Clay and Representative Lincoln had correctly gauged local sentiment about slave-holding. But the old quandary remained: how to prevent the District cities from becoming the catch-all for the freedmen of Maryland and Virginia. Both before and for a year or two after the passage of the compromise acts, whites in the capital talked uneasily about the rapid growth of Washington's colored community; none of them welcomed the prospect of its further expansion. Perhaps that uneasiness explained their outward acquiescence in the harsh new Fugitive Slave Law, for if runaways were unapprehended in the District, they would be absorbed into the free black population and increase it further. Probably a larger factor in the silence with which most of the city greeted the compromise measures was the conviction that nothing could be greater folly than to reopen by so much as a word a controversy that had nearly ended in national catastrophe. Stricter enforcement of the local black code, on the other hand, might keep the proportion of blacks to whites to its then 26 percent. Certainly the Colonization Society, while still in existence, held out no hope of a mass migration of Negroes to Liberia. Baltimore, protected by Maryland laws forbidding the ingress of free Negroes from other states, was only 20 percent colored, St. Louis in slave-owning Missouri 5.4 percent, and Cincinnati, adjacent to slave-holding Kentucky, 2.8 percent. Washington's colored intelligentsia itself probably realized that the smaller the relative number of Negroes, the better off they individually would be. In October 1850 the city council set itself to re-examine the local ordinances.[3]

The severe black code of 1836 had never been strictly enforced; part of it was patently unenforceable. The council consequently chose to try modifications. The amendments reduced the bond required of every free Negro over twelve years of age from $1,000 to $50 and demanded the surety of one white freeholder instead of five, but every colored person applying for residence must report within five days of his arrival or pay the penalty of a fine or a term in the workhouse, followed in either case by expulsion from the city. The mayor must give express permission for any public gathering of Negroes, and secret meetings were forbidden. The results satisfied the authorities. In 1854 only 8 of the 603 persons sent to the workhouse were committed for being "out after set hours" and only two for being "resident without bonds"; those two, however, were not forced to leave the city.[4] Gradually white fears of a black in-

[3] *News*, 5 Jun 1847, 2, 16, 23, 30 Nov, 7 Dec 1850, 31 May, 6 Dec 1851, 6 May 1852, 20 Apr 1853; *Sixth U.S. Census*, 1840; *Seventh U.S. Census*, 1850, pp. 221, 235-36, 662, 830.

[4] *Washington Laws*, 10 Dec 1850, 18 Jan, 20 Oct 1851, 28 Feb, 28 Apr, 3 Jun, 15 Dec 1853, 20 Jan, 3 Apr 1854, 14 Nov 1856, 4 Mar 1857; *News*, 19 Jan, 20 Apr, 19 Oct, 21 Dec 1853, 22 Apr 1854, 23 Jan 1858; *Eve-*

undation waned, for, contrary to alarmists' predictions, the 1850's saw an increase of only 1,050 free Negroes in Washington compared to 3,350 in the 1840's. While the white population rose in ten years by nearly 69 percent, the increase for slave and free Negro together was less than 7 percent. The colored population of Georgetown dropped at the same time from 27 to 22 percent of the whole; by 1860 the town had about four hundred fewer free Negroes and slaves than a decade before.[5] (See Tables I and III).

Yet in spite of rigid surveillance, considerable police brutality toward Negroes suspected of minor transgressions, and all too frequent attacks by white bullies, hard working Negro families who observed the law meticulously made astonishing material progress and won new respect from upper-class whites. White workingmen, particularly the Irish immigrants who depended upon common laborers' jobs, resented the competition of black men and seized every opportunity to proclaim their own superiority, but Negroes nevertheless established themselves firmly in certain occupations. Colored "washerwomen" and nurses, Negro oystermen, carpenter handy-men, and draymen were in demand. Dozens of Negroes accumulated enough money to buy horses and carriages and set up as hackmen, and before the end of the decade the city occasionally licensed colored shopkeepers. Alfred Jones, for example, possessor of some $16,000 in personal property, had a flourishing feed store, and James Wormley ran a successful restaurant. In various jobs tinged with menial service scores of Negroes acquired enviable skills. The cooks were the most notable example: slave boys, for years past sent by their owners to serve apprenticeships under the experienced French chefs in the households of foreign diplomats, learned the secrets of the art, and those like James Wormley

---

ning Star, 22 Aug 1859, 5 Apr 1860. The text of the black codes of 1827, 1836 and 1850 is given in Sheahan, *Corporation Laws*, pp. 245-54.

[5] *Seventh U.S. Census*, 1850, pp. 235-36, and *Eighth U.S. Census*, 1860, *Population*, pp. 616-23; Luther P. Jackson, *Free Negro Labor and Property Holding in Virginia, 1830-1860*, pp. 6-13, 25-26, 155.

TABLE III

Population of Washington[a]

	1800	1810	1820	1830	1840	1850	1860	1870
TOTALS	3,210	8,208	13,247	18,827	23,364	40,001	61,122	109,199
TOTAL WHITE	2,464	5,904	9,606	13,365	16,843	29,730	50,139	73,731
Native						24,817[b]	48,299[b]	59,974
Foreign-born						4,913[b]	12,465[b]	13,757
Germany and Austria							3,254[b]	4,159
United Kingdom							1,306[b]	1,557
Ireland							7,258[b]	6,948
TOTAL COLORED	746	2,304	3,641	5,448	6,521	10,271	10,983	35,392
Free	123	867	1,696	3,129	4,808	8,158	9,209	
Slave	623	1,437	1,945	2,319	1,713	2,113	1,774	
% Colored of total pop.	23.24	28.07	27.48	28.93	27.92	25.68	17.97	32.38
% Free Negro of total pop.	3.83	10.56	12.80	16.61	20.58	20.39	15.06	
% Free Negro of colored pop.	16.48	37.63	46.88	57.43	73.50	79.42	83.83	
% Foreign-born of total pop.						12.28	17.61	12.59
% Foreign-born of white pop.						16.19	21.49	22.93
% Increase in white pop. in ten years		139.65	62.70	28.86	25.89	76.14	68.98	40.60
% Increase in colored pop. in ten years		208.84	58.02	49.61	19.69	57.51	6.93	222.24
% Increase in Free Negro pop. in ten years		604.87	95.61	84.49	52.75	69.67	12.88	

[a] Compiled from *U.S. Census*, Second through Ninth.

[b] Figures for entire District, but since the growth of the white population between 1810 and 1850 was only 2,545 in Georgetown and 925 in the county, and during the next decade 718 and 1,696, respectively, the assumption seems reasonable that the bulk of European immigration was into Washington. The rapid increase in the white population of the county between 1850 and 1860, however, may have been the result of immigrants' choosing to live in the cheap quarters available across the Eastern Branch in and about Uniontown.

who then bought their freedom held the key to economic security. In the 1860's Wormley became the proprietor of a fashionable hotel patronized by the southern gentry.[6] Although circumspect behavior was no guarantee of freedom from persecution, hundreds of free colored people lived peacefully in the District of Columbia during these years when white men were endeavoring to drive them altogether out of the deep South.

In midcentury councilman Jesse E. Dow in campaigning for the office of mayor of Washington urged the city to establish colored public schools, but his defeat ended discussion of his plan. It was little more than a courageous gesture in a community where Negro taxes brought the city very little, colored men could not vote, and, after the Dred Scott decision in 1857, by Supreme Court decree people of African descent could not be American citizens. Colored schools, nevertheless, continued to expand, some of them charging a small tuition fee, a few of them free to the penniless, some of them taught by Negroes, others by white teachers. Arabella Jones' school was one of the best known in the 1850's. A free servant in John Quincy Adams' household when he was Secretary of State, the young Negress had later acquired an unusually fine education at St. Agnes' in Baltimore. In her school on the Island she held up to her pupils the ideal of serving their people at home as well as native tribesmen in Liberia. Of the schools taught by whites, the St. Vincent de Paul Free Catholic Colored School sponsored by the priest at St. Matthew's was important, if only because it stood as a rebuke to Protestant churches where the color line interfered with the founding of day schools for Negroes.

Most Negro schools comprised only the elementary grades, but the extraordinary success of Myrtilla Miner's "high school" for colored girls opened up a larger vista to colored people and awakened animosity in some whites. Miss Miner, after a pov-

[6] Washington *Directory*, 1860; Fremont, *Souvenir of My Time*, pp. 97-98; Carter Woodson, *A Century of Negro Migration*, pp. 36-40; *News*, 9 Jan 1854; *Star*, 19 Sep 1860; Jeffrey R. Brackett, *The Negro in Maryland*, p. 179; ptn, H32A-F5.6, 10 Mar 1852; enumerators' returns, Free Inhabitants, D of C, for Eighth U.S. Census, 1860, N.A.

erty-stricken childhood on her father's farm in New York state and a struggle to get her own education, came to Washington in 1851 to open a more advanced school for colored children than any then in operation. With the backing of the Society of Friends, the frail middle-aged white woman started with a handful of colored children in rented rooms on New York Avenue. The hostility of her neighbors twice forced her to move her charges, but through her voluminous correspondence with northerners she raised money enough in 1853 to buy a house on the outskirts of the city on New Hampshire Avenue between O and N Streets. Among her supporters were Johns Hopkins of Baltimore, Harriet Beecher Stowe, and Henry Ward Beecher. The reputation of the school rested at once upon the thoroughness of the teaching, the range of subjects, and the pervasive atmosphere of mutual affection and mannerliness between white staff and Negro pupils. Miss Miner's work made so wide an impression that in 1857 ex-Mayor Walter Lenox accused her of stirring up trouble by educating colored children beyond their station in life and giving them better schooling than white children could get. Above all he feared that her success would turn Washington into a Negro educational center. Her failing health and the outbreak of war closed the school in 1861.[7]

At the end of the fifties 1,100 children were attending colored schools in Washington and Georgetown. It was no longer, as in the early years of the century, "a common thing for colored and white children to associate in the same school," but whites generally approved of Negro elementary schools supported by Negroes. Like a good many children in the white public schools, most Negro pupils learned little beyond reading, simple ciphering, and how to write. Nearly 58 percent of colored adults were still illiterate, but the census showed a 3 percent drop in a decade, while white illiteracy had risen a little. The 15th

[7] *Spec Rpt Comr Educ*, 1870, p. 222, Ser 1427; *News*, 9 May 1857; *National Era*, 14 May 1857; Ellen M. O'Connor, *Myrtilla Miner, A Memoir*, pp. 59-79.

Street colored Presbyterian Church now had carpeting on the floor, handsome chandeliers, and the most famous choir in the city; the congregations of the newer 19th Street Baptist Church at I Street and the Asbury Methodist Church also had buildings of their own. This proven capacity to maintain schools and churches and the growing number of educated Negroes heightened colored people's faith in themselves and at the same time encouraged intelligent whites to believe Negroes need not always be the white man's burden.[8]

In the decade preceding the Civil War, northerners who read William Goodell's *Slavery and Anti-Slavery* might readily believe that District citizens were pledged to strengthening that peculiar institution, that kidnapping of free Negroes to sell into slavery was a common occurrence, and that the slave trade, although outlawed in 1850, still operated on an enormous scale in the national capital. The volume written in the 1830's was an abolitionist's presentation designed to paint a picture so starkly black that humanitarians could not rest until they had changed it. Deep-seated prejudices, it is true, still marked race relations in Washington. In proportion to the size of the colored population, Negro arrests were three times as frequent as white, the testimony of a colored person had no legal validity against that of a white man, and local magistrates now and again meted out excessively harsh sentences for trivial misdemeanors, particularly during the mid-1850's when a "Know-Nothing" city administration led men to see a conspiracy behind every bush. The episode Frederick Law Olmsted reported in his *Journey in the Seaboard Slave States*, a far more dispassionate account of conditions than Goodell's, leaves no doubt about the animus that pervaded the courts: of twenty-four "genteel colored men," as the police record described them, arrested for meeting privately to devise plans "to relieve the sick, and bury the dead" and to purchase the freedom of a young slave woman, four of

[8] *Spec Rpt Comr Educ*, pp. 213-22: illiteracy figures computed from *Seventh U.S. Census*, 1850, pp. 235-37, and *Eighth Census*, 1860, *Misc Statistics*, p. 508; Horace M. Bond, *The Education of the Negro in the American Social Order*, p. 178.

the free men were sent to the workhouse, the others were fined $111. Law, while forbidding the importation of slaves for auction, still sanctioned the sale of slaves owned in the District; newspapers still carried advertisements for fugitives, and the rewards offered for their apprehension corrupted unscrupulous white men into acting as slave-chasers.[9]

Yet except for the municipal black code, the laws affecting colored people in the District of Columbia were fixed by Congress; the District marshal, the judges, and the justices of the peace who carried those laws out were federal officials appointed by the President. And the slavocracy dominated the federal government. The *National Era*, abolitionist as it was, pointed out that Americans who chose to send "blackguards" to Congress should not blame the consequences upon Washingtonians. The most damning charge that humanitarians could justly bring against the local community was its ruthlessness in trying to keep the free Negro population to a minimum. Manumission consequently was rarer here than in Maryland or Delaware; yet occasional selling of local slaves steadily reduced the number of chattel bondsmen in the city. The advertisements for runaways were almost entirely for Virginia and Maryland slaves. Negroes with residence permits, while hating the indignity of the black code, gained from it some protection against illegal seizure, and more than a few civic-minded white Washingtonians strove to check abuses. Not only the *National Era* but more conservative and more widely read local newspapers like W. D. Wallach's *Evening Star* decried unprovoked attacks upon Negroes. The *National Intelligencer* generally avoided discussion of the local issue.[10]

[9] William Goodell, *Slavery and Anti-Slavery*, pp. 226, 243-246; *Wshg Laws*, Mayor's rpt, 9 Sep 1850; H Ex Doc 43, 31C, 1S, Ser 599; H Ex Doc 72, 33C, 1S, Ser 723; Frederick Law Olmsted, *A Journey in the Seaboard Slave States in the Years 1853-1854*, 1904 ed., I, 16-17; *News*, 15 Feb 1851, 14, 17 Sep 1853, 9 Jan 1854; *Ntl Era*, 2 Aug 1849, 6 Jan 1854, 19 Apr 1855, 23 Dec 1858.

[10] *Ntl Era*, 2 Dec 1852; *News*, 6 Sep 1851, 5 Aug 1854, 10 May 1856, 26 Sep 1857, 16 Jan 1858; *Star*, 12 Oct 1858, 28 Mar, 1 Apr, 12, 15, 19 Aug 1859, 9, 11 Feb, 3 Mar 1860. The evidence for my interpretation is inferen-

The new Free-Soil Republican party steadily gained local adherents after 1855. The change of heart B. B. French's personal letters reveal was certainly not unique in Washington's business and professional world, although severing life-long ties with the "democracy" was probably less painful for a man born and bred in New Hampshire than for a native southerner. Yet French, after nearly twenty years' residence in the capital, had come to identify himself with Washington. A claims agent and lawyer who had repeatedly served on the city council, "B. B." had written his brother early in 1851, "Why the people of the North should, after 60 years of unalloyed prosperity under our Constitution, set out, all at once to go out of their way to beat their own brains against a stone entirely out of their path, I do not see. What is slavery to them or they to slavery that they should overturn our Constitution to get rid of it—no *not* even to get *rid of it*!" In 1855, however, after two years as federal Commissioner of Public Buildings, a post to which his boyhood friend, President "Frank" Pierce, had appointed him, French resigned, convinced that the nation and hence the capital, so far from suffering under a Free-Soil administration, would be more secure than under Democrats dominated by the slave interests. According to the *National Era*, northern representatives in Congress showed no more anti-slavery zeal than native Washingtonians. When Congress convened in December 1856, anti-slavery households, for all their concern for peace, made a point of refusing to illuminate their windows to acclaim the unity of a nation in which pro-slavery men had just won a victory. Among Democrats only exercise of utmost restraint on the part of all factions enabled them to patch up matters enough to stage an inaugural ball for James Buchanan on March 4, 1857.[11]

---

tial and negative rather than positive. Whereas all local newspapers had formerly carried frequent articles or letters about race matters, the number dwindles so sharply after 1851 as to suggest a deliberate policy of avoiding the topic, lest the community and business interests suffer.

[11] B. B. French to H. F. French, 25 Apr 1851, 30 Jun, 9 Dec 1855, 29

So passionate an abolitionist as Dr. Gamaliel Bailey of the *National Era* believed Washington's record in handling race problems in the mid-1850's better than that of many northern cities. Whites in the capital, he remarked, were too often blind to the virtues of their Negro neighbors, to the "thrift and industry of the great mass of them," and to the "dignity, decorum and good taste they display," but speech was as free here as in the North and toleration rather greater. And, as the editor who first published *Uncle Tom's Cabin*, he had reason to know. In a city where race questions, however glossed over, were ever present, "a young clergyman has stood up in his place in a Washington pulpit, and preached on Slavery to his congregation, in a way that would have split many a conservative church at the North. But he has neither lost caste nor position—the majority of his church while dissenting from his views, recognize the independence of the pulpit."[12] Unhappily later, as tensions rose over "Bleeding Kansas," the young Unitarian was dismissed; over half his congregation considered his sermons inflammatory, and in the late fifties conservative Washingtonians, irrespective of their convictions about the evils of slavery, thought advocacy of political action too dangerous to the Union. Bailey himself continued to publish the *National Era* till his death in 1859, and, in spite of his unwavering advocacy of abolition, commanded a growing respect from fellow citizens.[13]

Nothing better illustrates the determination of Washingtonians who placed the Union above any race matter to set an example of rationality and propriety than the city's behavior during the anxious days following John Brown's raid at Harpers Ferry in October 1859. Apprehensive lest "hostile demonstrations from outside the city" develop, the mayor counter-

---

May, 15 July 1856, B. B. French Mss; Charles Billinghurst to his wife, 6 Dec 1856, Billinghurst Mss (Wisconsin Historical Society); *Ntl Era*, 1 Feb, 23 Aug 1855, 11 Dec 1856, 27 Jan 1857; *Star*, 7, 16 Jan, 4 Mar 1857, 19 May 1858, 20 Oct 1859.

12 *Ntl Era*, 2 Dec 1852, 9 Nov 1854, 27 Mar 1856; *News*, quoting *Ntl Era*, 10 May 1856.

13 *Ntl Era*, 11 Dec 1856, 30 Jun 1859; *Star*, 22 Jun 1859.

manded the permits he had granted colored people "to hold balls and festivals." For twenty-four hours crowds waiting for news gathered about the telegraph offices and the hotels, and for a time rumors ran that an attack was impending on the *National Era* office. No untoward incident occurred. The city quickly returned to an outwardly normal routine.[14] Far less than other American citizens could District residents, unrepresented in national councils, forestall disaster growing out of the slavery question. Their one contribution must lie in concealing their inner fears and maintaining an air of calm.

Individual members of the white churches in Washington and Georgetown may have helped secretly the Washington station of the underground railway smuggle slaves north to free soil, but, in spite of divided opinion in nearly every congregation, none of the churches officially endorsed abolitionist tactics. Even in Washington's new Congregational church, organized by New Englanders in 1851, the trustees objected to the label "anti-slavery church." Conservatism about political action predominated among Quakers as well as among Unitarians, the most radical group in matters of Christian doctrine. The laity of McKendree and Wesley chapels protested against the strong anti-slavery pronouncement of the General Conference of Northern Methodists in 1860, but except for St. Paul's, which affiliated with the southern wing, all the local Methodist churches refused to separate from the northern body. Similarly, the eight white Presbyterian congregations remained with the northern church, and outward unity prevailed in Washington's six Episcopal, four white Baptist, and three Lutheran churches. Racial segregation generally obtained in Protestant congregations, but while anti-foreign and religious bigotry had struck at Washington's six Catholic churches, the anti-Negro feeling of their new Irish and German parishioners failed to alter the nondiscriminatory policies of the hierarchy. Racial antagonisms touched Washington's Jews lightly, probably because the Hebrew congregation formed in 1856 was small. A congressional

[14] *Star*, 18-20 Oct 1859, 29 Mar 1860.

act extended to it all the privileges and immunities of other religious bodies. Although Jewish peddlers hawked ready-made clothing through Washington's streets, few people realized that a new minority had appeared in their midst.[15]

Whether or not business leaders deliberately evolved a careful plan of avoiding controversy, their eagerness to perpetuate the extraordinary prosperity they enjoyed in the late 1840's and 1850's nevertheless nurtured racial tolerance. Faith that this material well-being would sift down to lower strata of society, provided the slavery question were not allowed to interfere, apparently also affected people of rather modest means. District bankers and brokers representing "big money," to be sure, tended to ignore local investment; western lands and railroads offered a larger and seemingly more profitable field. Corcoran and Riggs, the most powerful firm in Washington, continued to purchase large tracts of land in Wisconsin and Kansas; when the partnership dissolved in 1854, each man singly or with other associates bought thousands of acres in Illinois, Mississippi, and Iowa. W. W. Corcoran also bought some Washington and Georgetown real estate, but otherwise he no longer concerned himself with local enterprises.[16] In the lower ranks of the city's business world, on the other hand, fresh interest appeared in expanding Washington's economy.

Relatively little money went into manufacturing in spite of the efforts of Joseph Henry of the Smithsonian Institution, Dallas Bache, B. B. French, and a dozen others to organize a Mechanics Institute for the promotion of industry. In 1850 John Rives' printing establishment, which published the *Congressional Globe*, and Ritchie & Co., were capitalized at $50,000

15 *Ibid.*, 19 Dec 1857, 12 Aug, 5 Dec 1859, 27 Jul, 3 Aug 1860; *N.I.*, 22 Nov 1851; *News*, 2 Nov 1850, 15 Jan 1853, 3 May 1854; *Cong Globe*, 34C, 1S, App., p. 6; B. J. Semmes to J. Jordan, 18 Apr 1849, Semmes Mss (SHC): Lorenzo D. Johnson, *The Churches and Pastors of Washington, D.C.*

16 Paul W. Gates, "Southern Investments in Northern Lands Before the Civil War," *Journal of Southern History*, v (May 1939), pp. 164-85, and "The Struggle for Land and the 'Irrepressible Conflict,'" *Political Science Quarterly*, LXVI (June 1951), pp. 248-71; H Rpt 648, 36C, 1S, pp. 511-12, Ser 1071; Corcoran Letter Press Book, XIX, 21 Feb 1861, and pp. 474-75.

and $35,000, respectively; Rives ran four, Ritchie six, steam-powered presses; William McDermott had $30,000 invested in his carriage shop; but about $5,000 was the capitalization of the average firm. The government arsenal and the Navy Yard were equipped with some machinery and together had several hundred men on their payrolls, but of the privately owned plants only ten—four printers', three foundries, a brewery, a lumber mill, and a small machine shop—used anything but manpower. Ritchie & Co. employed eighty hands, most concerns fifteen or fewer. As the local market expanded in the course of the decade, thirty-four concerns installed steam engines, using coal brought down the Chesapeake and Ohio Canal. The Washington Brewery in Foggy Bottom, the Baldwin Sash and Blind Factory, and John Rives' printing house had each an annual output valued at over $75,000. Twelve newspapers, five of them dailies, were published in Washington.

Several enterprises, however, dwindled in importance or disappeared during the 1850's. Transformation of the federal arsenal from a manufacturing armory into a storage depot was a blow to the city, the curtailment of shipbuilding at the Navy Yard another. "In view of the great inconvenience attending the building and equipping of ships at a point so distant from the sea," the Navy Department in 1860 limited production at the Washington yard to anchors, cables, and steam engines. In Georgetown and the county beyond along the canal where flour milling was a mainstay in mid-century, operations slowly shrank also: at the end of the fifties only two mills ground as much as $50,000 worth of flour annually. Furthermore, the Pioneer Cotton Factory in which the town had earlier taken special pride was clearly on its last legs. All told, whether because of insufficient capital, too small a skilled labor force, a limited market, or inadequate shipping facilities, the District could claim scant industrial progress in a decade during which factories were mushrooming throughout the North.[17]

[17] Enumerators' returns, Schedules for manufactures, Seventh and Eighth U.S. Censuses, 1850 and 1860, mcf, L.C.; *News*, 22 Feb, 22 Mar 1851, 26

Confidence in the region's commercial potential, however, survived repeated setbacks. In 1849 influential businessmen still viewed the C & O Canal as the key to a golden future, but over the years accumulating silt had nearly filled the canal boat basin on Rock Creek and much of the Washington Canal; thus extensive dredging of both would be necessary if the District cities were to benefit from completion of the "great national project." Unless they could transship direct to ocean-going vessels, the bulk of the trade in prospect would go to Alexandria via the aqueduct over the Potomac and the seven-mile-long lateral canal to her wharves in deep water. Unexpectedly Congress came to Washington's rescue by appropriating $20,000 to clear the city canal where it passed through the public grounds, on condition that the municipality dredge the rest of the three-mile stretch. The work began at once.[18]

Yet nothing was in readiness when the C & O Canal reached Cumberland in October 1850. A fortnight later when a first barge laden with eighty tons of coal docked at the Navy Yard, the Washington *News* noted that "owing to the bad condition of the so-called Basin at Georgetown, as well as that of our city canal (the progress on which has been unaccountably delayed) it was necessary to use a Steamer to tow the boat from the outlet of the canal to the Navy Yard." The basin was never fully restored and, in spite of the thousands of dollars spent on dredging, some stretches of the Washington Canal became impassable almost as soon as the first round of work ended in 1852. For the next two or three years boats drawing up to 3½ feet of water passed from 17th Street as far east as the Centre Market and from the Eastern Branch north to the Mall, but by 1856 the intervening section along the foot of Capitol Hill was unnavigable. Horse-drawn barges moved through the aqueduct canal over the Potomac and on to Alexandria or discharged

Jun, 18 Aug, 11 Sep 1852, 6 Aug, 14 Sep 1853; Olmsted, *Seaboard Slave States*, I, 14-15; *Ntl Era*, 9 Jan 1854; Rpt Sec/Int, 1850, p. 316, Ser 595; H Ex Doc 34, 36C, 1S, p. 75, Ser 1048.

18 Ptn, S30A-46, 25 May 1849; *Wshg Laws*, 2 Feb 1849; *N.I.*, 16 Nov 1849; H Doc 5, 38C, 2S, Ser 1223.

their cargoes in Georgetown, but the few boats that nosed their way along the Washington Canal to the coal and lumber yards on its banks west of the Centre Market represented civic disillusionment.[19]

The business community as a whole, having pinned its hopes on the C & O Canal for twenty-five years, was slow to consider alternatives to water transport. Virginia had chartered the Orange and Alexandria Railroad in 1848 to run to Manassas and thence west, and four years later incorporated another railroad to connect Alexandria with the main lines to the south; but Washington merchants delayed concerted efforts to pursue any comparable plan. The city council meanwhile was carrying on a losing fight with the B & O Railroad over fares to and from Baltimore, over putting up a depot, and over the company's refusal to pay Washington taxes. Not until 1852 did the city fathers permit locomotives to run into the city; for seventeen years the engines had had to stop outside the city limits, whence horses hitched to the "steam cars" had drawn passengers and freight to sheds at 2nd Street and Pennsylvania Avenue. When the company at last agreed to erect a depot on New Jersey Avenue at northwest C Street and in August 1852 opened the brownstone station, complete with a seventy-foot quadrangular tower, sky-lighted hall and "elegantly furnished dressing rooms, supplied with mirrors, sofas, water closets of peculiar construction, and numerous little comforts," only then did the discovery that the B & O had increased its local business "at least five-fold" within a year prod businessmen into taking steps to introduce a competing railroad that should reduce Washington's "alarming" vassalage to Baltimore.[20]

[19] *Wshg Laws*, 5 Dec 1850, 26 Apr 1851, and half a dozen entries every year thereafter through 1854, 14 Oct 1858, 12 Nov 1859, 12 May 1860, and mayors' rpts, 3 Apr, 30 Oct 1854, 3 Mar 1856; Sanderlin, *National Project*, pp. 178-82; ptns, S31A-H5, 24 Sep 1850, S32A-H4, 28 Jan 1852; *News*, 3 Nov 1849, 19 Oct, 2 Nov 1850, 26 Apr 1851, 20 Nov 1852, 2 Jul 1853, 11 Feb 1854, 20 Oct 1855; *Star*, 2 Apr, 26 Nov 1858, 28 Sep, 8 Oct 1860.

[20] *N.I.*, 19 Apr, 23 Jul 1847, 26 Nov 1849; *News*, 27 May, 3 Jun 1848, 15 Feb 1851, 21 Aug, 20 Nov 1852; *Wshg Laws*, 31 May 1850.

While Washington's council belatedly put out tentative feelers for connections with the Orange and Alexandria Railroad, in 1853 Georgetown enlisted congressional approval of a railroad to run westward to a junction with the B & O at Point of Rocks, Maryland, some ten miles from Harpers Ferry. Maryland chartered the western section under the name of the Metropolitan Railroad, while Congress chartered the District section as the Georgetown and Catoctin Railroad. Outlining plans to extend the road into Washington, the company attempted to get stock subscriptions in the larger city but met with little response. In the face of protests from small taxpayers the town thereupon chose to finance the undertaking by a special levy of ten cents on every $100 of assessed property. In 1856, however, when a few miles of grading were finished, Mayor Henry Addison, evidently concluding the project too big for so small a city to carry on unaided, refused to pay over further installments of money. Construction came to a halt. Nevertheless Georgetown's enterprise spurred on Washington. Because her neighbor had pre-empted the best route to the West, or because Baltimore's domination of Maryland markets left Virginia as a better outlet for District products, Washingtonians sought to develop a line to the South.[21]

To link the city by rail to a Virginia railroad posed the problem of crossing the Potomac. That question quickly involved Congress in acrimonious debates over the use of the Long Bridge and the city streets. In the summer of 1854, after the Virginia Assembly chartered the Alexandria & Washington Railroad, Congress grudgingly agreed to let the municipality determine a route into the city as long as the tracks did not run on Pennsylvania Avenue; but opinion in House and Senate divided over whether even temporarily to allow rails on the Long Bridge. Georgetowners fought the proposal; they wanted a

[21] *Wshg Laws*, 27 Nov, 31 Dec 1852; ptns, H32A-G5.3, 14, 17 Dec 1852, 3 Jan 1853, H33A-G5.4, 10 Jun 1853, 26 Jan 1854, H33A-G5.2, 1 Jan 1854, H33A-G5.9, 18 Apr 1854; *Cong Globe*, 32C, 2S, pp. 648-49, App., p. 359; *First Annual Report and Second Annual Report, Metropolitan Railroad*, 1854 and 1855; *N.I.*, 15 Nov 1852; *News*, 6 Jul 1853.

permanent railroad bridge built upstream from the Alexandria aqueduct and contended that once tracks were laid on the Long Bridge, there they would remain. Congress postponed a decision.[22] In the interim the speeches of senators who strongly advocated an unbroken rail connection between North and South gave Washington the courage to act with unaccustomed swiftness and singular indiscretion. The corporation underwrote $60,000 of the railroad company bonds and authorized tracks from the bridge along Maryland Avenue to the foot of Capitol Hill, thence over 1st Street and across Pennsylvania Avenue to the B & O depot.

When Congress convened in December 1855, astounded members beheld rails laid through the city and the line nearly complete except over the bridge. The outcry that arose on the Hill came largely from northerners. "Washington," declared Senator Stuart of Michigan, "was not intended to be a great business mart." Senator Pugh of Ohio accused the municipality and the company of counting on congressional acquiescence in an accomplished fact and hence of deliberately flouting the prohibition of tracks on Pennsylvania Avenue. Outraged congressmen pointed to the inconvenience of having horse-drawn cars traverse the Mall at the foot of the Hill and insisted that when the company began to run locomotives through the city the annoyance would become intolerable. More than a few Washingtonians agreed. James Mason of Virginia and Robert Toombs of Georgia defended the deed. Rails crossing were not rails along the Avenue, and cars on tracks would be no greater nuisance than the omnibuses that discharged passengers at the base of the Hill. Furthermore, the entire country would welcome the closing of the one break in rail connections between New England, New York, and the deep South; only on the stretch between Washington, Acquia Creek, and Fredericksburg,

[22] *N.I.*, 16 May 1854; *News*, 9, 24 Apr 1852, 8 Jun 1853; S Misc Doc 68, 33C, 1S, Ser 705; *Cong Globe*, 33C, 1S, pp. 1472-75, 1601, 1997-99, 2165, 2250; S Misc Docs 106 and 107, 32C, 1S, Ser 629; ptns H32A-G5.1, 29 Apr 1852, H32A-F5.1, 30 Dec 1853, H33A-G5.9, 14 Mar 1854; *Wshg Laws*, 6 Apr 1854.

Virginia, were travellers obliged to resort to steam ferry and stage coach.[23]

The Virginia section of the railroad from Alexandria to the southern end of the Long Bridge went into operation late in 1856, but congressional opposition to tracks over the Mall and the Avenue persisted: let the company bridge the Potomac upstream and route a line into the city from the northwest. Counterproposals to tunnel under Pennsylvania Avenue and the Mall and build a railroad bridge below the Long Bridge were too expensive to consider; that solution would have to wait till the twentieth century. Indeed by 1858 the protracted struggle over the right of way had virtually ruined the company financially. That year it defaulted on its bonds, forcing the city to shoulder the interest payments on the $60,000 the municipal council had underwritten. Although Congress authorized the Commissioner of Public Buildings to remove the rails along 1st Street past the western entrance to the Capitol grounds, lack of funds left them rusting there unused; when war came, the Army would thankfully put them to use for military transport. In the meantime, omnibuses carried passengers to the end of Maryland Avenue and over the bridge where they transferred to steam cars on the Virginia side. Washington investors watching the collapse of their plans were inclined to think the exercise of local initiative futile.[24]

In 1860 access to the two District cities was thus scarcely easier than in 1835. In response to pleas that free bridges would revive the tobacco trade with Maryland, in 1848 the government had bought the Benning's and Navy Yard bridges over the Eastern Branch, but the tobacco output of the region remained so small that the city-owned warehouses in Georgetown and southwest Washington continued to lie empty. Endeavors to tap the resources of the Virginia countryside were in turn fre-

[23] *Wshg Laws*, 8 Feb, 27 Jul 1855; *News*, 13, 20, 27 Oct 1855; *Cong Globe*, 34C, 1S, pp. 1025-27; S Rpt 136, 34C, 1S, Ser 836; "Sessford Annals," CHS *Rec*, XI, 360-73.

[24] *Cong Globe*, 34C, 3S, pp. 453-55, 36C, 1S, p. 3283; *N.I.*, 26 Jan 1857; ptns, H35A-G4.3, 17 Dec 1857, 2 Mar 1858, H36A-G4.1, 21 Feb, 30 May 1860; *Star*, 20 Mar 1858, 6 Jul 1859, 13 Jan 1860.

quently thwarted. In 1857, when a freshet washed away a span of the Long Bridge for the fourth time in a decade, Washington, unable to extract an appropriation for repairs, undertook the work with only a vague commitment of future reimbursement from Congress.[25] Shipments of upcountry produce also were still meagre; for, as a boatman noted in 1858, from Cumberland to Georgetown the C & O Canal ran "through an uninhabited solitude." Georgetowners resolutely looked for ways of promoting her growth, including an occasional proposal for a union with Washington and in 1856 a last attempt to obtain retrocession to Maryland, but her isolation had become so pronounced that 1860 found her with fewer inhabitants than the 9,400 of 1830—now only 6,798 whites, 1,358 free Negroes, and 577 slaves. Washington, on the contrary, grew astonishingly. While seemingly she shared most of Georgetown's handicaps, here expanding government activities overbalanced the failures of local merchants to make her the "great business mart" Senator Stuart believed she was never intended to be. Between 1840 and 1860 her population nearly trebled.[26]

New houses, big hotels, and new shops multiplied yearly. By 1854 building lots that had sold for four cents a square foot in 1843 commanded thirty cents, and real estate values as well as building costs continued to rise through the rest of the decade. Gas lighted the "Avenue," the government offices, the hotels, and a number of private houses. Omnibuses running with some frequency now simplified communication within the city, and men talked confidently of the improvements in prospect as soon as Congress chartered a street railway. Unlike government clerks whose salary scale rose in 1852, mechanics

[25] H Rpt 643, 30C, 1S, Ser 526; S Rpt 176, 32C, 1S, Ser 630; *Cong Globe*, 33C, 2S, p. 1150; *Star*, 26 Jan 1859, 17 Jan 1860; *News*, 30 Oct 1852, 14 Mar, 22 Apr, 23 May 1857; *Wshg Laws*, 18 Jan 1851, 11 Feb, 27 May 1857, 18 Nov 1858, 19 Aug 1859, 6 Apr 1860; H Rpt 410, 35C, 1S, Ser 966; Rpt Sec/Int, 1854, p. 600, Ser 777; *Ggtn Ordinances*, 25 May 1850.

[26] Anon., Canal Boat Journey, 1858; *Seventh U.S. Census*, 1850, pp. 236-37; *Eighth U.S. Census*, 1860, *Population*, pp. 620-23; *Ggtn Ordinances*, 23 Feb 1856, 2 Aug 1857; ptns, S35A-H2, 21, 31 Dec 1858, 5, 7, 14, 24 Jan 1859; *Cong Globe*, 34C, 1S, p. 1423, 34C, 3S, pp. 455-56; H Rpt 98, 35C, 1S, Ser 964; *Star*, 7 Feb 1860.

and common laborers suffered from rising prices without corresponding wage increases, but the consensus nevertheless was that Washington enjoyed an enviable security. The panic of 1857 which paralyzed other American cities, according to the *News*, "prevailed to a very limited extent" here, and eighteen months later the *Star* observed that "the general prostration of trade" had been so brief that most of Washington by early 1859 was "in a far better condition than before the blow came. There never was more hard cash in the hands of our fellow citizens than at this time." The increase in city revenues, despite cuts in the tax rate, bore out the accuracy of that estimate.[27] (See Table IV) That this economic stability derived not from local enterprise but almost solely from the presence of the federal government and from federal spending no longer troubled permanent residents greatly. Only dissolution of the Union stood as a threat to Washington's privileged position.

[27] Washington Gas Light Company, *Growing with Washington, The Story of Our First Hundred Years; Star*, 31 Jan, 19 Nov 1859; Geo. W. Mitchell to Alexander H. H. Stuart, 20 Jun 1854, Alexander Stuart Mss; *Ntl Era*, 9 Jan 1854; Mary Barker Bowen to Julia Barker, 6 Dec 1853, and Sayles J. Bowen to Julia Barker, 12 Jan 1855, 23 Jul 1857, Bowen Mss (in possession Prof. Charles A. Barker); Rpt Sec/Int, 1858, p. 701, Ser 974; H Ex Doc 29, 39C, 1S, Ser 1255; and almost weekly items in the *News* during the years 1849 to 1858.

CHAPTER VIII

THE CITY AND THE HILL, 1849-1860

IN THE midst of the debates on the great compromise, Congress made time to pass appropriations for large-scale public works in the District of Columbia. Northern and southern congressmen together, as if bent upon parrying every blow that might weaken the Union, set about enhancing the dignity of the national capital by pouring money into stone and mortar, the outer and visible signs of impregnable national strength. After voting funds in 1849 to ornament the public grounds, House and Senate passed bills to add a pillared central porch and stucco to the exterior of the long neglected City Hall, where the United States district courts sat, enlarge the Patent Office, and move the greenhouse and botanical garden to the foot of Capitol Hill. Then one after the other came appropriations to build two enormous wings and a massive new dome for the Capitol, adorn the eastern portico with two groups of statuary, establish a home for soldiers incapacitated in the Mexican War, place an equestrian bronze of General Washington in Washington Circle, construct a mighty aqueduct to supply water to protect government property from fire, open a government hospital for the insane, and erect on the Mall adjacent to the Smithsonian Institution an armory for the District militia. If as these projects began to take shape, the funereally romantic landscaping Andrew Jackson Downing laid out on the Smithsonian grounds inspired some fault-finding, and objections arose to various features of building designs, the effects of this unprecedented federal spending program were nonetheless stimulating to the city.[1]

The extension of the Capitol had psychological importance, attesting to faith in the permanence of the United States of America and its capital on the Potomac. Building operations, moreover, promised to give employment to several hundred

[1] Christopher Tunnard and Henry H. Reed, *American Skyline*, p. 105.

workmen; and when finished, the magnificent edifice with its towering dome should attract visitors from every state in the Union. The laying of the cornerstone on the 4th of July 1851 thus became a momentous occasion. Every federal dignitary from President Fillmore down attended, as well as the "venerable Custis, a distinguished surviving member of the Washington family, our worthy fellow citizen Z. Walker, who was present at the laying of the cornerstone of the Capitol in 1793, [and] B. B. French, Grand Master of the Masonic Fraternity of the District of Columbia, wearing the apron that Washington wore and bearing the gavel which Washington used in 1793." To save the cost of raising the level of the Hill on the south and the west, the President had approved Thomas Walter's plan, which put the new wings at right angles to the main axis of the Capitol and placed the dome off-center almost over the eastern portico. The imbalance that would offend some architects for the next hundred years elicited no criticism while the work was in progress. In December 1851 fire destroyed the Library of Congress in the main building, a disaster that delayed work on the wings but emphasized the necessity of solid construction. Five hundred men were employed on the job during 1852, but in 1858 when Congress moved into its new halls the pillars of the eastern porticos were not yet in place. For the next four years huge blocks of marble cluttered the grounds and the streets nearby. The dome would not be finished until 1863.[2]

The Soldiers' Home opened its doors to about forty invalid veterans in 1853. A drive out to the well-tended 240-acre farm two miles to the north of Washington made a pleasant summer outing, but city-dwellers knew little about the home until President Buchanan, and later President Lincoln, took up summer residence in a house on the grounds. The Government Hospital for the Insane, on the contrary, immediately interested citizens.

[2] S Rpt 273, 31C, 2S, Ser 593; H Ex Doc 2, 32C, 1S, p. 23, Ser 634; Rpt Sec/Int, 1852, pp. 583-85, Ser 658; *News*, 5 Jul, 27 Dec 1851, 29 Sep 1852; Rpt Sec/War, 1858, pp. 748-51, Ser 975; Glenn Brown, *History of the United States Capitol*, II, 119-42; *N.I.*, 2 Jan 1852.

It was the fruit of Dorothea Dix's long crusade for humane treatment of the mentally ill. It was she who induced Thomas Blagden to sell his farm on the rolling hills beyond the Eastern Branch, and it was her eloquence that persuaded Congress to put a qualified physician in charge of the hospital. The spacious, well-lighted building, its beams cut from the great trees and its brick kilned from the clay on the farm, received its first inmates in 1855. Here under the watchful care of the superintendent, Dr. Charles Nichols, mentally unbalanced soldiers and sailors and residents of the District, men and women, white and colored, underwent treatment; for most patients the household and farm chores were useful therapy, in sharpest contrast to the enforced idleness at the jail. Indeed, the establishment of the asylum was as epoch-making in its way as the founding of the Smithsonian Institution.[8]

Where the enlarged Capitol stood for national grandeur and the Government Hospital for the Insane for new humanitarian perception, the inauguration of a water system planned on a scale to supply a million people promised a sanitary revolution. Until the forties when a number of well-to-do families had had cisterns dug and pumps installed in their kitchens, spring water carried from the wells in the public squares had supplied most households; in mid-century every morning the slave woman with a pail of water in each hand and another balanced on her gaily bandana-wrapped head was still a familiar part of the Washington scene. In 1830 Robert Mills, after studying the water works of other municipalities, had prepared detailed recommendations for the city, but, as congressional approval and some federal funds were essential, the plan had lapsed; Congress had piped spring water only into the Capitol, the White House, and the departmental offices. The meagreness of the means of protecting government property from fire was self-evident; Congress sponsored surveys in 1851. That December the burning of the Library of Congress emphasized the

[8] Ptns, S31A-H5, 25 Jun, 9 Dec 1850; S Ex Doc 11, 32C, 2S, Ser 660; *Cong Globe*, 33C, 2S, p. 1138 and App., pp. 400-401; Rpt Sec/Int, 1855, pp. 629-38, Ser 840.

necessity for action. In 1853, the President chose the most comprehensive of several alternative plans, and although it entailed at least $2,000,000, Congress voted to build a water system at government expense.

The most costly feature of the system mapped out by Lt. Montgomery Meigs of the Army Engineer Corps was an enormous aqueduct running from the Great Falls ten miles northwest of Georgetown through rocky hillsides and over a deep ravine at "Cabin John" to empty into receiving and distributing reservoirs above Washington. The very magnitude of the engineering task excited widespread interest. While the District cities appointed water registrars and laid mains in the principal residential areas—work financed by a $150,000 loan in Washington and by a special tax in Georgetown—private householders looked forward to the moment when running water in every dwelling would make outhouses needless. The autumn of 1858 saw the first phase of the great work finished. On January 3, 1859, the surface water accumulated in the temporary receiving reservoir was turned into the mains, and for the first time Washingtonians beheld the now familiar sight of public fountains playing: "The jet of aqueduct water rose . . . from the basin west of the Capitol to the height of one hundred feet or more." Laying the eight-foot conduit from the Great Falls to a distributing reservoir to supply every house would take another five years, but in the meantime "Powder Mill Creek" water piped into a number of residences furnished owners with a novel luxury.[4]

The unveiling of the first equestrian statue in the capital, moreover, evoked civic pride. The Jackson Democratic Society had commissioned a bronze by Clark Mills, a sculptor who had gained renown in Charleston, South Carolina. In 1853 when his statue of Andrew Jackson mounted on a rearing horse went

[4] *Eunice Tripler, Some Notes of Her Personal Recollections*, p. 58; Rpt Sec/War, 1854, p. 167, Ser 778; Rpts Sec/Int, 1859, pp. 903-18, Ser 1023, and 1860, pp. 564-66, Ser 1078; *Cong Globe*, 32C, 2S, App., p. 348; *News*, 6 Jul, 21 Dec 1853, 4 Mar 1854; ptns, S31A-G2, 27 Dec 1850, S31A-H5, 30 Apr 1851, H33A-D3.2, 10 Jun 1854; *Star*, 3, 5 Jan, 28 Mar, 29 Jul 1859; *Wshg Laws*, 2 Jun 1859.

into place in Lafayette Square, patriotic sentiment acclaimed the work as proof of American artistic skill. Critics of Captain Meigs asserted that he "ostracized American artists, employing a host of French, German and Italian workmen" to decorate the Capitol, and they saw Mills' achievement as a confounding of that error. Proud of having a bronze cast in the United States and impressed at the sculptor's feat in balancing a horse weighing several tons on its hind legs, Congress overlooked the accusations by Mills' rivals that he had simply poured cannon ball into the tail; admiration for the result won him a $20,000 bonus and a congressional commission for an equestrian statue of George Washington. That commitment perhaps lessened the chagrin of the city at the stoppage of work on the Washington Monument when in 1855 lack of money and quarrels over control of the society's records brought the project to a halt with the shaft only 150 feet above ground. All the greater importance attached to the celebration held on February 22, 1860: every Washingtonian of consequence took part in the ceremonial dedication of Mills' bronze of the General placed in Washington Circle. That day marked the last great public nonpartisan demonstration in the ante-bellum capital.[5]

Contrary to hopeful assumptions, friendly feelings among members of Congress toward the local community diminished with every new improvement made in the federal city. In 1849 when an appropriation was passed for building a boat basin and deepening the Washington Canal, a senator who objected to the grant noted that it was "almost useless" to oppose District appropriations, "because the District, having nobody to represent it on this floor, has everybody."[6] After William Seaton left the mayor's office in 1850, however, representatives and senators expostulated with increasing frequency over the city's dependence upon the federal government. The generosity of Congress, declaimed members, gave Washingtonians a magnifi-

[5] *Star*, 10 Oct 1859; *N.I.*, 22 Dec 1848, 7 May 1849, 15 Aug 1853, 8 Jan 1860; *Ntl Era*, 27 May 1858; H Rpt 198, 35C, 2S, Ser 1018; S. H. Kauffmann, "Equestrian Statuary in Washington," CHS *Rec*, v, 116-22.

[6] *Cong Globe*, 30C, 2S, pp. 523-27.

cent Capitol, completed their City Hall, lighted and policed their streets at night, built them water works, provided an armory, hospitalized their insane, and, through funds for a school for the deaf, dumb, and blind, educated their handicapped children; federal public works offered laborers and mechanics well-paid employment, added to the population, and enriched tradesmen and real estate dealers; but despite the huge federal expenditures within the city, the municipality perpetually cried poverty, while keeping the tax rate at a ridiculously low level.

Some of these complaints revealed a ludicrous unwillingness to differentiate between national and purely local interests. In 1856, for example, Senator Brodhead of Pennsylvania opened a diatribe against repairing the government-owned Long Bridge with the statement, "I know very well that most people in the cities of Washington and Georgetown live from the drippings of the Treasury." Ignoring the fact that the safety of government property was the sole reason for spending from three to five million dollars to supply Washington with water, that national pride was the only reason for allotting $500,000 to $1,000,000 for a new dome on the Capitol, and the increase in federal business the compelling reason for enlarging the halls of Congress and the Patent Office and planning new buildings for the War and Navy Departments, the orator concluded: "These demands on the public Treasury—the people's money—for purposes of expenditure in the cities of Washington and Georgetown, are shameful; and the manner in which our money is poured out to these people is shameless." Two years later Senator Iverson of Georgia held forth in somewhat similar vein: "At the last session of Congress there were over four million dollars appropriated, to be expended within twelve months, in the District of Columbia . . . and then, when you come to consider the money spent here by members of Congress, by strangers who visit the city on public business, and by the clerks and other officers of the Government, you find that there is a vast amount of money expended here for the benefit of the resident inhabitants." But always, Iverson insisted, they asked for more, and before long "the Federal Treasury will have to feed and clothe the citizens." No one pointed out to him that congressmen's and visitors' money invested in consumer goods was not productive capital or that the seasonal character of building operations frequently forced upon the city the burden of caring for the families of government workmen during winter layoffs.[7]

Yet Washington was not without official defenders. Captain Meigs reminded her detractors that the aqueduct was a national necessity vital to the protection of irreplaceable government records and public buildings. "A large part of the population of Washington is composed of strangers who are brought here by the Congress," he added. "Are the citizens to build an aqueduct out of their miserable salaries to protect the United States?" As it happened, a good many District citizens advocated building the water system by private rather than government enterprise. A Mississippi senator with more earnestness than humor rebuked his associates for attributing the new Capitol dome to Washingtonians' greedy importunities; the Secretary of War justified building an armory for the District militia because national security required a place in which to store the arms needed to safeguard the capital from "illegal combinations." And in 1859 the Commissioner of Public Buildings, the man best acquainted with the municipality's difficulties, championed the community: "During the last ten years the corporation has raised by taxation the sum of $2,376,042.86, which has been expended for general purposes; and the city has, from first to last, opened and made more than fifty miles of avenues and streets, at a cost of about one million and a half dollars. It may safely be affirmed that no city, in proportion to its population and wealth, has done more for itself than Washington, notwithstanding nearly one half of the property within

[7] *Ibid.*, 32C, 2S, p. 899, 34C, 1S, p. 703, 35C, 1S, pp. 1463-64; *News*, 6 Dec 1854.

its limits belongs to the government, and is not subject to taxation."[8]

The barrage of criticism directed at the city was to have more serious consequences than its victims realized at the time. They had faced similar disparagement in the 1830's, and much of it now seemed to be intended largely for home consumption by congressional constituents. Unhappily the ill will that accumulated on the Hill during the fifties would feed the hostility of the wartime Congresses toward people whom northern members had attacked sharply and often unjustly during the preceding decade.

Meanwhile a disturbing new element entered into the city's relations with the federal government. Ever since Congress had agreed in the 1820's to use the proceeds of sales of land acquired from the original proprietors to reimburse the municipality for work undertaken on federal property, the corporation had anxiously watched the shrinkage of salable lots. By 1855 only valueless sites remained, "the refuse lots that have been in the market more than sixty years," and by 1856 no unsold lots whatsoever. Consequently when a Senate report declared a gift of western lands for local school support inexpedient and of "doubtful constitutionality," citizens saw that thenceforward they could not count on federal aid for any local project. In fact, Congress would haggle for years over paying the city for repairs to the government-owned Long Bridge. After 1857 the only concession the city corporation won was conditional title to the Pennsylvania Avenue site of the sixty-year-old Centre Market, a grant contingent upon the city's completing before mid-1862 a new market-house to replace the dilapidated, old, moss-covered frame building. That proviso, plus the congressional fiat to increase the municipal debt to pay for the building, robbed the gift of most of its value.[9]

[8] *News*, 7 Feb 1852, 18 Feb 1854; *Cong Globe*, 32C, 2S, p. 901, 34C, 1S, pp. 699-705, 903-12; H Ex Doc 33, 31C, 2S, Ser 599; ptns, H32A-G18.2, 23 Dec 1850, H32A-G5.2, 5 Feb 1852; S Rpt 479, 33C, 2S, Ser 775; S Ex Doc 88, 34C, 1S, Ser 823; Rpts Sec/Int, 1855, pp. 595-612, Ser 840, and 1859, p. 849, Ser 1023.

[9] *News*, 10, 24 Apr, 22 May, 23 Oct, 13 Nov 1852; H Misc Doc 20, 32C,

City officials, for their part, did little to earn congressional respect. They were on the whole a quarrelsome and undistinguished lot. Their task, it is true, was far more difficult than had been Seaton's and his associates' in the 1840's, for population rose by 50 percent during the fifties, and some 5,800 European immigrants, a number of them non-English-speaking, complicated problems in a city in which a year's residence opened the polls to every adult white male. Possibly the lesser calibre of councilmen grew out of the reluctance of voters long denied the franchise to elect men from the propertied class that had ruled "in might" for nearly half a century; representatives of the lower ranks of society may well have seemed safer, and American equalitarianism pronounced one man's opinion as good as another's. The turnover in office was constant. Attorney Walter Lenox, mayor from 1850 to 1852 and scion of an old Washington family, was a defender of slavery and an aristocrat to whose views the rank and file of the council soon took exception. His successor, the gentle John Maury, was beloved as a man but was a singularly inept politician, while John Towers, a printer elected by the Know Nothings in 1854, was the helpless creature of his party. Bluff Dr. William Magruder divided his energies between his medical practice and his mayoral duties, to the cost of both. Self-important ex-Postmaster James Berret, first elected mayor in 1858, won a second term in 1860, but, like his four predecessors, he was unable to conduct an effective administration. All five men tended to view Washington as a national monument for which Congress should bear a large part of the cost, an attitude that created resentment on the Hill and lowered civic morale.[10]

2S, Ser 685; Rpts Sec/Int, 1854, pp. 38-39, Ser 777, and 1856, pp. 853-54, Ser 893; S Misc Doc 22, 33C, 2S, Ser 772; *Cong Globe*, 31C, 1S, p. 1622, 32C, 2S, App., p. 22, 34C, 1S, p. 1025, 34C, 3S, p. 807, 35C, 1S, p. 62, 36C, 1S, pp. 847, 1715-16, 1959; S Rpt 88, 34C, 1S, Ser 836; S Rpt 112, 35C, 1S, Ser 938; S Rpt 8, 36C, 1S, Ser 1039; *Wshg Laws*, 18 Feb 1858, 3 Sep 1859, 4 Feb 1860.

[10] Allen C. Clark, "Walter Lenox, the Thirteenth Mayor of the City of Washington," CHS *Rec*, xx, 167-92; William A. Maury, "John Walker Maury, His Lineage and Life," CHS *Rec*, xix, 160-71; Robert H. Harkness,

As municipal revenues mounted to three times the figure for 1849, instead of using the money for the needs of the growing community, mayors and councils cut the tax rate, slice by slice, from 75 to 60 cents and in 1859 to 55 cents, half the rate of the mid-thirties. Georgetown, with far less wealth, during most of the decade imposed 25 percent higher taxes than her neighbor. Curtailment of the proportion of Washington's budget allotted to debt reduction more than balanced the increased expenditures for streets and water mains.[11] (See Table IV.) Indeed, the entire record of the 1850's indicates a community caught unprepared for expansion, a village formerly controlled by two or three hundred knowledgeable property-owners which found itself suddenly converted into a burgeoning city run by inexperienced men who did not know what they wanted or how to get it.

Improvement in the condition of the streets constituted the corporation's chief claim to efficiency, although, as grading and gravelling went forward, altercation attended every change until Congress in 1859 issued an official listing of grades. In 1853 the city installed gas lamps along the principal thoroughfares and employed a tender to light them on moonless nights. For the first time street signs then went up on the lamp posts, and an ordinance required every building to display its number. About the same time the council got congressional permission to lay sewers to drain surface water into the canal or the river. The consequent digging in the streets coupled with the excavating for new buildings created clouds of dust in dry weather and left the highways thick with mud after every rain. Representative Billinghurst, fresh from Juneau, Wisconsin, described the winds "lifting the sand and dust of the streets and filling the whole atmosphere, sometimes for hours making the streets al-

---

"Dr. William B. Magruder," CHS *Rec*, XVI, 150-87; *Wshg Laws*, mayors' rpts, 9 Sep 1850, 3 Apr 1854, 3 Mar 1856.

[11] *Wshg Laws*, 7 Jun 1854, 31 May 1855, 24 Jul 1856, 9 Jul 1857, 2 Dec 1858, 27 May 1859; W. B. Webb, *Laws*, p. 168; *N.I.*, 2 Jan 1854, 5 Jan 1857; *Ggtn Ordinances*, 20 May 1854, 9 Jun 1855, 16 May 1857, 6 Feb 1858.

TABLE IV

City Expenditures 1849-1860[a]

	1848-49	*1853-54*	*1857-58*	*1859-60*
Total	$122,140	$235,023	$299,125	$377,344
% of total for:				
ADMINISTRATION[b]	14.6	13.5	10.3	9.6
INTEREST & REDUCTION OF DEBT	48.0	26.4	25.1	22.5
POOR RELIEF (including Washington Asylum)	5.4	4.6	6.1	5.8
HEALTH (including abatement of nuisances and medical services to poor)	.6	3.7	4.5	2.1
SCHOOLS	7.1	6.6	6.4	7.6
LAW ENFORCEMENT	.4	6.7	6.1	12.3
PUBLIC WORKS	17.7	34.4	33.9	37.7
Street grading and lighting	12.3	24.4	19.8	14.8
Laying Sewers		1.8	3.4	.3
Maintenance of pumps and laying of water mains	4.0	3.0	2.8	19.2
Bridges and canals	.4	4.1	4.4	1.9
Markets and wharfs	1.0	1.1	3.0	1.5
AID TO PRIVATE FIRE COMPANIES	1.1	1.5	2.1	.7
MISCELLANEOUS	5.1	2.6	5.5	1.7

[a] Data compiled from *Wshg Laws.*

[b] Including salaries of ward commissioners and the pay of ward scavengers.

most impassible. Men . . . go with hankerchiefs or screens before their faces. I've been caught . . . two or three times and nearly suffocated and blinded." Impossible as it was to keep gravelled surfaces clean, Pennsylvania Avenue was little better. In the summer of 1856 Congress was driven to spend nearly $2,000 for watering the stretch between the Hill and the Treasury and in 1860 to order that mile laid with cobblestones.[12]

Householders still dumped garbage and slops into the alleys and roadways. The result, unpleasant when the city had contained only a few hundred families, was a menace to health when that number tripled. Pigs scavenged freely, dug hog wallows in the roads, and besmirched buildings and fences. Slaughter houses heightened the nauseous odors. Rats and cockroaches infested most dwellings, including the White House. In summer, flies swarmed from stables and the dung on the streets, and mosquitoes bred by millions in the stagnant ponds scattered through the city. Faulty drainage about some of the public pumps exposed whole neighborhoods to dysentery and typhoid fever. Fear of a cholera epidemic like that of 1832 inspired Mayor Seaton in 1849 to appoint ward "sanitary committees" to assist the board of health in seeing that lime was spread over the worst danger spots, but the mortality rate that year ran close to 35 per 1,000, nearly half among children under one year of age. Infant mortality was appalling. The board of health explained that "the larger proportion of these deaths are from among the children of negro, of foreign, and of destitute native parents, who usually reside in alleys and in the suburbs." Doctors had no remedy to offer. One mayor after another talked of enforcing the ordinances against throwing refuse into the streets, but all agreed that "the difficulty of ascertaining the violators of the law, and procuring the testi-

[12] *Wshg Laws*, 28 May 1853, 17 Mar, 18 May 1854, 4 Aug 1859 and scattered through every volume entries recording money voted for street work; *Cong Globe*, 34C, 1S, pp. 1101-02; ptns, H32A-G5.5, 11 Dec 1851, 28 Jan 1852; H Misc Doc 11, 33C, 1S, Ser 741; H Rpts 354 and 356, 35C, 1S, Ser 966; S Rpt 155, 36C, 1S, Ser 1039; Charles Billinghurst to his wife, 25 Dec 1855, Billinghurst Mss (Wis. His. Soc.). Comments on street improvements or lack thereof appear in every local newspaper at frequent intervals.

mony necessary to convict, has rendered it almost a nullity." The city councils decided to employ additional scavengers and let other action wait till the finished aqueduct furnished abundant water to street hydrants.[13]

While looking forward to the introduction of aqueduct water, officials made no preparations for a city-wide system of sanitary sewers. Certainly the scheme the federal government had introduced provided no useful model. The sewers from the Capitol emptied underground near the brow of the Hill and from there drained harmlessly down toward the Mall, but the sewage from the White House and the departmental offices nearby debouched in the low-lying ground between the Executive Mansion and the canal; what is today the Ellipse thus became a fetid marsh. The later extension of the pipes to discharge into the canal was a very minor improvement. From the Patent Office and Post Office the sewers fed into a branch of Tiber Creek that cut between 9th and 10th Streets and emptied into the canal. In that shallow waterway the sewage which had been carried out into the river at ebb tide was washed back in at high. Accumulated sediment at times stopped the flow altogether and turned the canal into a stagnating open cesspool. Yet the city fathers, after building several sewers for surface drainage, expressly forbade their use for sanitary purposes. Upon payment of a special tax householders might drain water from their cellars into a city main, but the sewage from the hotels and the few private houses equipped with water closets fed into nearby streams and vacant lots.[14]

Progress on developing a good public school system was also dishearteningly slight. By the mid-fifties 37 teachers in 24 school rooms were trying to instruct 2,200 children; in some classes the pupil-teacher ratio stood at 70 to 1, and the more

[13] *News*, 24 Aug 1850, 23 Aug, 6, 7, Sep 1851, 24 Nov 1855, 25 Jul 1857; *Star*, 14 May 1858, 11 Feb, 5 Aug 1859, 10 Mar 1860; *Wshg Laws*, 19, 26 Aug 1852, 17 Jan 1856, 26 Aug 1859, and mayors' rpts, 6 Aug 1849, 3 Mar 1856; Board of Health, *Nuisances*, Broadside, 1856.

[14] H Ex Doc 34, 30C, 2S, Ser 540; H Ex Doc 30, 31C, 1S, Ser 576; *N.I.*, 1 Dec 1849; *Star*, 25 Mar, 6 Apr 1857, 11 Jun 1859; Rpt Sec/Int, 1859, p. 848, Ser 1023.

advanced pupils had to teach the younger. Moreover, to the intense disappointment of people who had hoped to see all children in the city enrolled in schools under competent teachers, half the white population of school age was getting no schooling at all. Washington's quandary indeed epitomized the problems that public education in America would face for the next hundred years. The trustees anxiously discussed whether to open additional schools, regardless of quality, or whether to attempt to raise teachers' pitifully small salaries, multiply staff, build schoolhouses to replace overcrowded, ill-ventilated, badly lighted, rented rooms, and otherwise improve the existing schools. Either course would take money.

While a few people believed a two-dollar instead of a one-dollar poll tax would finance expansion, others, wary of the spectre of higher taxes, urged well-to-do parents to send their children to private schools and thus lighten the public burden. Although the salaries of low ranking government clerks averaged $1,200 a year, one councilman contended that teachers with $500 and $600 salaries were overpaid; he conceded that $200 might be too little. To some Washingtonians the obvious solution seemed to be an annual appropriation from Congress.

Georgetowners joined in making an appeal, while residents of the county where 4,000 people had only two "languishing" private schools added a petition of their own. Congress obliged the county to the extent of authorizing it to tax itself for the purpose, on condition that a referendum of taxpayers endorse the plan. The county overwhelmingly rejected it; the considerable area beyond the cities' limits was to remain practically schoolless for another nine years. Several senators believed the District entitled to the same kind of aid the states and territories obtained from the federal government, but local importuning irked many members. A bill nevertheless passed the Senate in 1858 which, while ignoring Georgetown, granted Washington $20,000 a year for five years, provided that the city raise yearly an equal amount by special tax. John Hale of New Hampshire proposed that Negro taxes be set aside for colored public schools, but, when Senator Toombs of Georgia objected, a compromise exempted all Negro property from the new tax. The House never so much as discussed the bill; it died on the vine.[15]

Left to draw on her own resources, Washington increased the school budget enough to allow a salary scale ranging from $300 for female assistant teachers to $900 for male principals and to cover the costs of three night classes for boys who worked in printers' shops during the day. The night classes never materialized, and the public school teachers, if conscientious, were rarely well trained. A Teachers' Institute formed in 1849 at the suggestion of Joseph Henry of the Smithsonian Institution awakened discouragingly little interest. By 1860 about twenty-nine hundred pupils, approximately 29 percent of the white children of school age, were enrolled in the public schools, in contrast to 78 percent in some northern cities. Illiteracy in the District had by then risen to nearly 11 percent of the white population.[16]

Private schools provided all education beyond the elementary in both Washington and Georgetown. Some thirty-three hundred boys and girls attended private institutions, either those for beginners or one of the forty-two academies and young ladies' seminaries. Sisters taught at the Catholic orphanages and at the Convent of the Visitation in Georgetown, where daughters of many well-to-do families, Protestant as well as Catholic, received an excellent education. At the Washington Seminary Jesuits prepared young men for admission to Georgetown College, and after 1858 the seminary, under the name of Gonzaga College, offered an enlarged curriculum. But, like Georgetown and

[15] *News*, 19 Jan, 24 Sep, 31 Dec 1853, 28 Jan 1854; S Misc Doc 22, 33C, 2S, Ser 772; ptns, H32A-G5.4, 28 May 1852, H34A-G4.4, 12 Mar 1856; *Cong Globe*, 34C, 1S, pp. 1426, 1920, and App., pp. 12-15, 35C, 1S, App., pp. 370-79.

[16] *Wshg Laws*, 2 Dec 1858 and Anl Rpt School Trustees, 1860-61, p. 24; *News*, 17 Nov 1849, 6 Mar 1852; ptn, H35A-G4.6, 30 Mar 1858; *Seventh U.S. Census*, 1850, p. 235; *Eighth U.S. Census*, 1860, *Population*, pp. 613-23, and *Statistics (Including Mortality, Property, etc)*, pp. 508-10.

Columbian Colleges, the academies and finishing schools did not touch the lives of most District residents.[17] People troubled at seeing the capital of the republic disregard the public obligation to educate its children were unable to overcome the parsimony or obliviousness of their fellow citizens.

Growing lawlessness was another source of humiliation to civic-minded Washingtonians. In the mid-forties they had believed in the city's essential orderliness, in spite of the firehouse gangs; after 1850 vandalism, arson, prostitution, thievery, robbery, and assault worsened every year. By 1858 a Senate committee reported: "Riot and bloodshed are of daily occurrence. Innocent and unoffending persons are shot, stabbed, and otherwise shamefully maltreated, and not unfrequently the offender is not even arrested." The increase in juvenile delinquency was especially distressing. Public opinion advocated special treatment of juvenile lawbreakers, but the District legal system provided neither the court machinery nor any place to keep them in custody except in the county jail along with hardened criminals. Several members of the House suggested that the presence of Congress attracted criminals like flies around a honey-pot; upon adjournment crime seemed to subside. Joseph Gales and William Seaton viewed the rise in violence more perceptively as a natural, albeit deplorable, accompaniment of rapid urban growth, and Senator Andrew Johnson of Tennessee, pointing to Baltimore, New York, Cincinnati, and New Orleans, reminded his associates: "Pockets are picked, men are garroted or robbed in those cities as well as here." That was thin comfort to conscientious local citizens. And the District marshal declared "troubles and disorders have increased much faster than the population."[18]

Some of these troubles were manifestly the fruit of extreme partisan feeling, particularly during the years when the Know

[17] *News*, 27 Oct 1849, 20 Jul 1850, 6 Feb 1858; *Sketch of Gonzaga College*.

[18] *Wshg Laws*, 16 Jul 1852; Rpt Sec/Int, 1858, p. 701, Ser 974; *Cong Globe*, 35C, 1S, pp. 1460, 1462, 1671-72; *N.I.*, 5 Jun 1855, 8 Jun 1858 and items in almost every issue of every other local newspaper, 1850-1860.

Nothing party was spreading its anti-foreign, anti-Catholic credo throughout the country. The "Pope stone episode" was an example: in 1854 a band of Know Nothings gathered at midnight at the Washington Monument, locked up the watchman, and then defaced and threw into the Potomac a block of marble from the Temple of Concord in Rome which the Pope had presented for the memorial shaft. The next year Know Nothings acting under a thin cloak of legality seized all the property of the Monument Society, thereby destroying its chances of raising money for the work. Political feuding took more serious form two years later when partisans, abetted by "Plug Uglies" from Baltimore, in a fight at the polls at the Northern Liberties Market, brought up a loaded cannon; the President, at Mayor Magruder's request, called out the Marines, but city officials then closed the polls because it was "inconsistent with the principles of free government to ask citizens to exercise the right of suffrage under the guns and bayonets of the regulars." The regulars nevertheless in dispersing the crowd fired into it and killed or wounded a score of spectators. Political warfare, only slightly less vicious in succeeding elections, created golden opportunities for the city's new underworld.[19]

Nor was crime confined to the lower ranks of society. Members of Congress addicted to gambling, duelling, and other vices set a sorry example. A congressman shot a waiter in a Washington hotel and went scot free. On the floor of the Senate an assailant threatened Thomas Benton of Missouri at the point of a pistol, Preston Brooks of South Carolina subjected Charles Sumner to a savage caning, and fist fights during sessions more than once ended in duels. In Lafayette Square on a Sunday afternoon in 1859 Congressman Daniel Sickles, after learning of his wife's infidelity, openly murdered her lover, Philip Barton Key, son of the author of the *Star Spangled Banner.* Sickles' acquittal and the cheers with which the court-room audience

[19] *History Wshg Monument*, pp. 52-64, Ser 4436; *N.I.*, 29, 30 May 1855, 1, 15, 30 Jun 1857; ptns, H34A-G4.7, 3 Mar 1856, H35A-F4.8, n.d.; *News*, 26 Apr 1856, 23 May, 6 Jun, 23 Jul 1857.

greeted the verdict convinced many Americans of "the unparalleled depravity of Washington society."[20]

The establishment of a salaried police department in 1851 at first seemed to improve matters, but even when the corporation added 10 constables to the staff of 17 daytime officers, put the men in uniform, and employed an emergency night watch of 40 men to supplement the 30-man federal auxiliary guard, the force was too small to patrol effectively so spread-out a city. Baltimore, considerably smaller in area than Washington, maintained a 400-man department, about one patrolman to every 850 residents, whereas the capital with valuable government property to protect had a permanent force of 57, a ratio of one officer for every 1,050 inhabitants. The Senate District Committee advocated a metropolitan police force under federal control, but angry disagreement in both houses over who should appoint the officers and who pay the bills shelved the proposal.[21]

Congress and city, however, saw eye to eye about the need of legal and judicial reform. Court sentences were at times severe—a prison term of fifteen months, for example, for stealing "a blue cloak." What a senator in mid-century dubbed "the present old and infirm system of laws" not only occasioned maddening and expensive delays in litigation but sometimes inflicted injustice. To get a divorce in the District of Columbia required a special act of Congress; to get a judgment in a criminal case might take months of waiting in jail pending trial. Old and young, guilty and innocent, including people held merely as material witnesses, were thrown together in the evil-smelling building on Judiciary Square under conditions more prone to breed than discourage crime. The rehabilitation of prisoners was equally unlikely at the federal penitentiary. There, inspectors noted, a shortage of uniforms forced convicts "to wear winter clothing for eight months of the year without

[20] Dr. Thomas Foster to Alexander Ramsey, 28 Sep 1850, and John H. Stevens to Ramsey 25 Feb 1851, Ramsey Mss (Minn. His. Soc.); *N.I.*, 19 Apr 1850; *Star*, 28 Feb, 11 Mar, 27 Apr 1859; *Ntl Era*, 17 Mar 1859.

[21] *Wshg Laws*, 11 Mar 1851, 1 Apr, 30 Jun, 24, 30 Dec 1858, 20 Jan 1860; S Rpt 149, 35C, 1S, Ser 938; ptn, H36A-G4.1, 9 Jun 1860; *Cong Globe*, 35C, 1S, pp. 1460-73, 1477-79, 1564-76, 1616-18, 1670-78, 1867.

change" even during a dysentery epidemic. Convinced that the machinery of law enforcement would run smoother under better laws, in 1855 Congress appointed commissioners to revise and codify District law, but the draft when submitted to a citizens' referendum in 1858 met with nearly universal criticism; only a small minority thought the proposed code better than none. The rejection meant that the District had to wait till 1863 for a reorganized judiciary and till 1901 for a codification of its laws.[22]

"Intemperance," Mayor Lenox asserted in 1851, "is the cause almost exclusively of all the disturbances and pauperism which afflict our community." Unlike the Reverend James Lowrie, who seven years earlier had identified unemployment and low wages as the chief source of dependency in the city, the mayor put his faith in "anti-tippling" ordinances and the exhortations of total abstinence societies.[23] Although Congress occasionally voted small sums for relief, by 1859 suffering had become so acute in the poorer wards of the city that Mayor Berret and the council created a central board which took over most of the functions of the former ward overseers of the poor. Nearly 6 percent of the municipal budget that year went for direct relief and for care of the poor at the Washington Asylum. Otherwise public assistance to the needy repeated the pattern established when the community was little more than a village. When the Asylum burned in 1857, a number of Washingtonians urged a geographical separation between the almshouse and the workhouse, but the corporation, presumably as a matter of economy, again put one alongside the other, thereby forcing "the unfortunate poor" into close association with convicted vagrants, prostitutes, and drunkards.[24]

[22] Ptns, S31A-H5, May, Jun, Jul 1850, S32A-H4, 29 Mar 52, S35A-H2, 29 Mar 1852, S35A-H2, 29 Apr 1858; Rpts Sec/Int, 1858, p. 701, Ser 974, and 1859, p. 861, Ser 1023; *News*, 21 Mar 1855, 24 Jan 1857, 23, 30 Jan, 6, 20 Feb 1858; *Cong Globe*, 33C, 2S, App., p. 401.

[23] *Wshg Laws*, 20 Jan, 9 Oct 1854, 18, 25 Nov 1857, and mayor's rpt, 25 Aug 1851; *News*, 8 Jun, 28 Oct 1854; ptn, H32A-F5.6, 2 Mar 1853.

[24] *Wshg Laws*, 12, 20 Jan, 9, 12 Oct 1854, 28 Jan, 16 Jul, 25 Nov 1857, and rpts of commissioners of the Asylum, Jul 1852 and Jun 1858; *News*, 1

The churches, charitable societies, and individuals were still the community's chief almoners. In Georgetown, where acute want ordinarily was less widespread than in Washington, a legacy from a private citizen built a poorhouse, and later a gift of $10,000 from W. W. Corcoran enabled the city to handle poor relief without appealing to Congress. The transient paupers who complicated Washington's problem rarely sought refuge in the smaller city. In the capital the orphanages enlisted more interest than any other philanthropy. Besides the Washington Orphan Asylum and St. Vincent's, two additional institutions opened, first, St. Joseph's Orphanage for boys under the aegis of Catholic laymen and, in 1860, through the efforts of a Catholic sister, St. Ann's home for foundlings. Of a dozen other new charities some were short-lived, some were the successors of disintegrating older societies. Thus the Guardian Society founded in 1853 took over much of the work of the Female Union Benevolent and Employment Society, though not before the aging ladies of that enlightened organization had vainly tried to introduce system into fund-raising by means of regular yearly subscriptions instead of haphazard contributions. The newer body, the three hundred "Guardians of the Poor," undertook to find jobs for the unemployed, open Sunday and weekday schools with the help of the Washington Bible Society, and established a widows' and orphans' home, which, with the cooperation of the courts, might serve as a "House of Refuge" for destitute children charged with delinquency.[25]

Only one significant philanthropic innovation came about. It originated with that extraordinary humanitarian, Amos Kendall, President Jackson's Postmaster General, chief figure in the "Kitchen cabinet," and later head of the telegraph company;

Sep 1852, 26 Jan 1856, 7 Mar 1857, 23 Jan 1858; ptn, H32A-F5.6, 2 Mar 1853; *Cong Globe*, 34C, 1S, pp. 355-57, 362-64, 385, 432.

[25] *Ggtn Ordinances*, 30 Dec 1854, 28 Apr 1855, 7 Feb 1857; *News*, 8 Feb 1851, 15 Sep, 17 Nov 1852, 21 Nov 1857; *Cong Globe*, 33C, 2S, pp. 169, 228, 34C, 1S, 388-89 and App., p. 6, 35C, 1S, p. 791; ptn, H36A-G4.1, 2 Apr 1860. See also "Historical Sketches of the Charities and Reformatory Institutions in the District of Columbia," pp. 2-5, 8-18, 102-03, 116, in S Rpt 781, 55C, 2S, Ser 3665.

the fear he had inspired in political enemies and his unwillingness to mingle in society had long concealed from his neighbors in his adopted city his tender-hearted concern for the weak and helpless. In 1856 he found a half-dozen deaf and dumb children living in squalor, virtually enslaved by a man who claimed them as apprentices. Kendall took them into his own house and began teaching them there while he and his friends pressed Congress to charter a school and appropriate money for its support. Congress moved quickly. The act of incorporation of February 1857 set up a board of trustees and provided for the payment from Treasury funds of $150 yearly for the tuition and keep of "each deaf, dumb or blind pupil properly belonging to the District of Columbia" whose parents could not afford to pay fees. Kendall deeded to the Columbia Institution for the Deaf, Dumb, and Blind his land and farmhouse at Kendall Green just north of Boundary Street, the city contributed a small sum of money, and individual donors gave more. The trustees put Dr. Edward Gallaudet in charge, an experienced teacher and the son of Thomas Gallaudet, who had first introduced into America the sign language method of teaching deaf mutes.

Dr. Gallaudet with three other teachers, two of them instructors for the blind, and with his mother as matron opened the school to fifteen children in August 1857. Enrollment increased rapidly; Congress soon included Army and Navy children among the beneficiaries, and the spreading fame of the school drew paying pupils from the District, Maryland, and other states. In 1860 the trustees fell heir to the $4,000 which Dr. Gallaudet's grandfather and his associates had raised twenty years before to found a manual labor and agricultural school for orphans. Manual training and work on the farm were important features of the school at Kendall Green from the first. Dr. Gallaudet's skillful, albeit highly sentimental, appeals in his annual reports to Congress elicited added appropriations year after year, but the institution remained quasi-public; private citizens directed its course and individual gifts supplemented federal and municipal money.[26]

While the fumbling of city officials reflected the uncertainty of much of the local public about civic aims, men who wanted above all to make Washington the intellectual and artistic as well as the political capital of the United States could see some progress during the 1850's. For the achievements of the Smithsonian Institution, the scientific work of the Coast Survey and the Naval Observatory, in 1857 the founding of the American Institute of Architects with headquarters in Washington, and W. W. Corcoran's decision to build an art gallery for his collection of paintings and sculpture opened up long vistas. Numerous comments, no one conclusive by itself, indicate that a growing body of Washingtonians had come to believe that the city's ultimate place in American life would depend not so much upon an outer mien of order and efficient municipal service as upon an inner distinction born of contributions to human knowledge and awareness of beauty.

In 1849 dissension about the proper interpretation of James Smithson's will was still dividing the board of regents of the Smithsonian Institution. For the time being, Joseph Henry, Dallas Bache, and others of the regents compromised with those who wanted to use the entire $30,000 annual income for a great national library or for a museum and art gallery; until 1854 half the total went into those semi-popular projects. Henry, however, won a valuable ally in 1850 when he engaged an outstanding young naturalist, Spencer Fullerton Baird of Carlyle, Pennsylvania, to take charge of the museum. Slight in stature and mild in manner, Baird possessed the true scientist's passion for research, a benign disposition, and an extraordinary capacity to convert other people to his point of

26 S Rpt 781, 55C, 2S, pp. 21-24, Ser 3665; Rpts Sec/Int, 1857, pp. 744-49, Ser 919, and 1859, pp. 894-97, Ser 1023; *Cong Globe*, 34C, 3S, pp. 560-61, 678; Edward M. Gallaudet, "A History of the Columbia Institution for the Deaf and Dumb," CHS *Rec*, xv, 1-22.

view.[27] Due to Baird's loyal, unobtrusive support and Bache's vigorous backing, Henry succeeded before the end of the fifties in setting the Smithsonian Institution upon the path he believed it should follow.

From the beginning Henry had advocated some support for applied research. Soon after he came to Washington he had arranged to have telegraph offices in every part of the country send in regular weather reports on the basis of which meteorologists could in time evolve a weather forecasting system. Yet, like government scientists a hundred years later, he felt the United States paid disproportionate attention to the diffusion of knowledge and too little to its increase, that is, to basic research. The function of the Smithsonian, he argued, was "to give an impulse to original thought, which, amidst the strife of politics, and the inordinate pursuit of wealth, is of all things most desirable." His report for 1853 noted: "A miscellaneous and general library, museum and gallery of art, though important in themselves, have from the first been considered . . . to be too restricted in their operations and too local in their influence, to meet the comprehensive intentions of the testator; and the hope has been cherished that . . . the whole income of the Smithsonian fund may be devoted to the more legitimate objects of the noble bequest." That plea killed the plan to make the Institution a library. In the meantime Baird's learning and skill were quietly converting into real research tools the specimens brought to Washington by government exploring parties. When Henry saw that the museum was in fact contributing to the advance of knowledge, he accepted for the Smithsonian custody of the remains of the "National Cabinet of Curiosities" long moldering in the Patent Office, on condition that Congress recognize federal responsibility for the national collections. The upshot was an annual appropriation from Congress of $4,000 for the "Museum of the Smithsonian Institution," leaving the bulk of the legacy for the publication of research findings in the

[27] Dupree, *Science*, pp. 79-82; *Annual Reports of the Board of Regents of the Smithsonian Institution*, 1849-1853.

Smithsonian *Contributions to Knowledge* and for badly needed support of strategically selected projects of inductive science. In unfurling the banner of original research, Joseph Henry performed his single greatest service. By 1859 Smithsonian funds were dedicated first and foremost to "the encouragement of the study of theoretical principles and the advancement of abstract knowledge."[28]

The museum under Baird's direction nevertheless constituted for much of the public the mainstay of the Institution. Visitors were fascinated and informed by the exhibits—a stuffed orangutan in a glass case, "all kinds of birds, fish, animals and many beautiful pictures." Two rooms of the museum housed an art gallery where gifts and paintings on loan lined the walls. Some two hundred canvases by John Mix Stanley hung in one room while he waited in vain for Congress to vote the money to buy them. Painted on the western plains and in the mountains when he was accompanying transcontinental exploring parties in the 1840's, Stanley's scenes of Indian life and portraits of Indian chiefs presented an authentic record of forty-three different tribes which was invaluable to ethnologists; his dramatic landscapes delighted the more casual viewer. Unfortunately fire would destroy the Stanley collection in 1865. Small as the gallery was in the fifties, its existence quickened interest in painting and sculpture. The succession of European portrait painters who once had set up studios in Washington had ceased long before mid-century, but a newly formed Washington Art Association held a first exhibit in 1857: "the pictures and statuary, all by native artists of the U.S.," wrote one enthusiast, "have excited the admiration of visitors from all quarters of the Union as well as foreigners resident in Washington." The Smithsonian opened its halls also for meetings of scientific societies and once or twice a year for artists' and music teachers' conventions. Washingtonians, moreover, had free access to the 32,000 volumes acquired for the Smithsonian library. Indeed,

[28] Dupree, *Science*, pp. 84-90; Misc Doc 73, 33C, 1S, pp. 24-25, Ser 705; H Rpt 141, 33C, 2S, Ser 808; *Anl Rpt . . . Smithsonian Institution*, 1859, p. 17.

although neither Henry nor Baird were concerned with popularizing, and occasional complaints sounded about the excessively erudite character of the public lectures held under their auspices, the Norman castle on the Mall by 1860 had become in a very real sense a community cultural center.[29]

Despite the resources of the federal government, a city of 40,000 inhabitants in mid-century, more than 10,000 of them colored and therefore without influence, could not supply the richness of artistic opportunity to be found in larger American cities. Yet music, some of it provided by Negro church choirs, commanded more receptive audiences than ever before. In December 1850 Jenny Lind sang at the National Theatre. If the Swedish nightingale evoked less rapture in the capital than in Cincinnati, for example, a young Washingtonian declared it was only because "we are too dignified, we are supposed to be too well acquainted with Talent and Genius, to exhibit any very great wonder. . . . But as for me I was perfectly entranced." To hear Jenny "cost us thirty dollars, fourteen dollars for two tickets, four for hack hire," and twelve for the clothes the occasion demanded, but Mary Bowen considered the reward well worth the inroads upon her husband's modest income. Chamber music was still a rarity in 1860, a full orchestra concert unknown, and grand opera companies never allotted the city more than seven or eight performances a year, but whereas in the 1840's Washington "managed to get along reasonably well with Ethiopian minstrels, peripatetic Italian vocalists, a brace of musical conventions, to say nothing of the slow and softly-subdued home productions of our own Marine Band," during the 1850's German residents organized a Maennerchor, and other choral societies were formed.[30]

[29] S Rpt 79, 25C, 1S, Ser 938; *News*, 18 Aug, 11 Sep 1852, 14 Sep 1853, 6 May 1854, 17 Mar 1855; Dupree, *Science*, pp. 85-86; *Star*, 16 Feb 1860; "Portraits of North American Indians with Sketches of Scenery etc. Painted by John Mix Stanley," *Smithsonian Miscellaneous Collections*, II, Article 3; Kate S. Carney, Diary, 24 Aug 1859 (SHC).

[30] Mary Bowen to Harriet Underhill, 12 Dec 1850, Bowen Mss; B. Semmes to J. Jordan, 10 Jun 1848, Semmes Mss (SHC); *News*, 14 Dec 1850, 12 Jan 1856; *Star*, 25, 26, 30 Apr, 2 May 1860.

Other than newspaper correspondents, writers were few. Thackeray enjoyed being lionized in the American capital during his lecture tour of 1853, but he was not impressed by any local literary lights at the parties given in his honor. George Watterston was no longer writing by that time, and he died in 1854. The verses and historical sketches of that dedicated Mason, B. B. French, were appearing at intervals in Masonic journals, and Thomas Benton spent two of the last years of his life in his pleasant house near Judiciary Square in writing *Thirty Years' View*. In 1852 Emma D. E. N. Southworth, a courageous young Georgetown widow, published the first of the fifty-odd novels by which she would keep the wolf from her door for the next forty years, while Abigail Dodge, using Gail Hamilton as her pen name, during visits in the Gamaliel Bailey household wrote some of the pieces for the *Congregationalist* and the *National Era* which early won her a considerable reputation. But Washingtonians, however "well acquainted with Talent and Genius," produced no literary masterpieces. In the winter of 1849-1850, however, Bulwer Lytton, then aide to his uncle, the British minister, composed the romantic poem which, when published in 1860, led countless readers to name their daughters *Lucile*. Not until later did Washington hostesses learn that "Owen Meredith" was one and the same as the attractive young Englishman who had secretly written poetry in the brownstone house looking out over Lafayette Square when he was not dining and dancing with the belles of the capital.[31]

Neither did society leaders realize that the amusing and penniless young government clerk who attended their parties with such gusto was destined to become one of the most famous American painters of the century. Years after he had been dismissed from the Coast Survey for his inattention to his job, James McNeill Whistler wrote: "I was apt to be late, I was so

[31] Eyre Crowe, *With Thackeray in America*, pp. 112-24; Paul Wilstach, "Literary Landmarks of the National Capital," *Bookman*, CLIII (Jul 1916), pp. 493-94; *Gail Hamilton's Life in Letters*, I, 161ff.

busy socially. I lived in a small room, but it was amazing how I was asked and went everywhere—to balls, to the legations, to all that was going on . . . and, when I had not a dress-suit, pinning up the tails of my black frock coat, and turning it into a dress coat for the occasion."[32]

Social functions, if lacking some of the *élan* of earlier years, went on much as before, albeit with little or no help from the Presidents' wives. Mrs. Zachary Taylor shut herself up on the second floor of the White House and received only a few intimate friends; Mrs. Fillmore, formerly an impecunious schoolteacher, possessed abundant good sense and good will but had scant social finesse, and Mrs. Pierce, shattered by the death of her only son shortly before her husband's election, gave herself over to her grief. Harriet Lane, however, President Buchanan's beautiful niece who acted as hostess for her bachelor uncle, showed a tact and poise in presiding over the White House which, rising political tensions notwithstanding, restored grace to official dinners and receptions. By and large, "society as usual" appeared to be the tacit motto. While the considerable group who enjoyed sociable evenings in the Gamaliel Bailey's hospitable parlor preferred to avoid the company of advocates of the slavocracy, good manners enabled political opposites to exchange civilities. Not many months after Chief Justice Taney read out the Supreme Court's momentous Dred Scott decision denying American citizenship to anyone of African descent, southerners and northerners together attended the magnificent masquerade given by Senator and Mrs. William Gwin of California in their I Street house, later the site of Doctors' Hospital. Rumor had it that that ball launched the fatal liaison between southern-bred Philip Barton Key and the wife of northern-born Daniel Sickels. Political differences failed to disrupt the charmed circle that Dallas Bache drew about him in his living quarters at the Coast Survey in the "old-fashioned barrack of a house on the edge of Capitol Hill overlooking Pennsylvania avenue." There Senator and Mrs. Jefferson Davis were always

[32] E. R. and J. Pennell, *The Life of James McNeill Whistler*, p. 29.

welcome. After the Civil War Mrs. Davis recalled the "real noctes ambrosianae" when the eminent scientist and his petite, witty wife swept their guests into a large sparsely furnished hall, warmed by bright wood fires, the walls lined with strange-looking instruments that showed dimly in the yellow candlelight; having dismissed the servants, host and hostess themselves served their friends, Bache with the connoisseur's enthusiasm decanting the choice wines he had learned to appreciate during his European sojourn.[33]

In the autumn of 1859, the *Star*, always eager to boost Washington's standing, painted a picture of the "Federal Metropolis" unshadowed by divisive controversy: "Persons of wealth and taste . . . are coming more and more to appreciate the advantages and pleasures of having a home among the public men of America while the latter are assembled together. Nowhere else in this country is equal intellectual and social society within the reach of any and all respectable persons as here, if anywhere else in the world. . . . In the northern cities what is termed fashionable society is intensely exclusive, the key to admission to it being a golden one. Here, the lock is off and the door stands wide open for any to enter who may be so intelligent, entertaining and well-behaved as to prove agreeable acquaintances."[34]

Royal visitors helped lighten the social atmosphere in 1860. In May two Japanese princes and some twelve nobles, accompanied by about sixty servants, engaged the attention of everyone in Washington. Come to negotiate a commercial treaty with the United States, the silk-kimonoed orientals were objects of wonder. "There we all stood," wrote B. B. French, "men, women and children, niggers, irish and dutch; catholics, protestants and Mohammedans; Members of Congress, Judges, Governors, Diplomats, Artizans, Mechanics, Laborers, upper servants and menials; all in one democratic conglomerate . . . with our eyes and mouths open, gazing and gaping at that row

[33] *Wshg Post and Times Herald*, 17 Jan 1961; *Gail Hamilton's Life*, I, 181-200; M. M. Odgers, *Alexander Dallas Bache*, pp. 203-204.

[34] *Star*, 3 Oct 1859.

of Japanware paraded upon the portico of the White House." Since even "Japanese Tommy," the chief interpreter, spoke no western language but Dutch, social intercourse was limited largely to bows, handshakes, and smiles, but the brief stay of the "celestials" formed a welcome diversion in a city uneasy over the recent choices of presidential nominating conventions. Also that autumn "Lord Renfrew" and a carefully chosen entourage captivated the upper brackets of Washington society. The fiction that the Prince of Wales was incognito enabled hostesses to entertain His Royal Highness without becoming hopelessly entangled in problems of etiquette. Inasmuch as "old Buck" considered a ball at the White House unsuitable, Miss Lane danced with Lord Renfrew at private houses, and in due course signed photographs of the royal family brought acknowledgment from Windsor Castle of these courtesies.[35]

No decade of Washington's history presents sharper contrasts than the 1850's. Poverty, squalor, prejudice, and violence were as abundantly evident as the "wealth and taste" to which the *Star* drew attention and as the tolerance and generosity that impressed Gamaliel Bailey. Few of the city's critics then or later attributed any of the "depravity" they deplored to her temporary population or recognized that similar conditions prevailed in other American cities of the time. By the 1890's Washingtonians themselves would tend to belittle the qualities and achievements of the ante-bellum capital. Later generations, assuming that dirty, ill-lighted streets, parsimonious municipal councils, and an ineffectual police represented an utterly backward and graceless city, would be persuaded that such minor attractions as she could claim had stemmed solely from the contributions of outsiders—leading members of Congress, the diplomatic corps, and the most eminent of the seventeen hundred federal employees in the executive departments. Her most famous or gifted residents, it is true, were natives of other

[35] B. B. French to H. F. French, 20 May 1860, B. B. French Mss; *Star*, 16 May 1860; Lida Mayo, "Japanese Fever," ms in possession of the author; James D. Horan, *Mathew Brady, Historian with a Camera*, p. 32; *Wshg Post*, 17 Jan 1961.

places, but whether scientists like Bache and Henry, soldiers like old "Fuss and Feathers" General Scott, or former government officials like Amos Kendall, scores of notables thought of Washington as home and had thus become in effect Washingtonians. Class distinctions were clear-cut, but a family's place in the social structure of the city rested less upon money than upon accomplishments and manners. The *News* pointed out that on Sundays workingmen and their families, "clean in their persons and decent in their dress," promenaded on the terrace of the Capitol with "the beauty and fashion of the Nation."[36] Whatever the community's vices, pretentiousness was not one.

In the 1850's Congress sniped at the municipality; mayors and councilmen frequently felt grievances against Congress. City and nation nevertheless were partners. President and Cabinet members repeatedly turned to voteless local citizens for help; they it was who served as hosts for the nation. Their carefully concealed fears for the safety of the Union betokened their identification with the United States. Behind the untidy outer shell lay a warm community spirit never exceeded in the grander city of later years.

[36] *News*, 5 Jul 1856.

CHAPTER IX

THE EVE OF WAR, NOVEMBER 1860-MAY 1861

NORTH AND SOUTH, Americans knew that the presidential election of 1860 would be critical for the United States. A decade of mounting passion over the slavery issue meant that only the utmost statesmanship could avert an open break between the slavocracy and the Free-Soil North. Upon the character of the man placed in the White House would rest the future of the nation. Washingtonians' knowledge that they could not vote in November in no way lessened the excitement in the capital. Although a rally reportedly attended by "not less than 10,000" supporters of John Breckenridge of Kentucky took place in July, a month earlier heavy voting in the municipal election had brought an independent candidate, Richard Wallach, within 24 ballots of defeating his Democratic opponent, Mayor James Berret, and put several avowed Republicans into the city council. In October a band of "Wide Awakes" led a parade of some five hundred members of the local Republican Association, a number that led the *Star* to suggest that men who "sniffed" a Republican victory were hurriedly climbing on to the band wagon. As a few Negroes followed the procession, shouts greeted it: "D - - n Niggers! They oughtn't to be allowed on the streets," until an Indiana congressman assured the crowd that Republicans wanted only to prevent the expansion of slavery into the territories. Yet hatred of abolitionists flared up anew; northerners as well as southerners in Washington thought them anarchists ready to tear the Union apart.[1]

On Wednesday the 8th of November, a North Carolinian wrote from Washington: "Abraham Lincoln, the Black Republican, is elected President of the United States, the greatest calamity that has ever befallen the United States. The sun that

[1] *Star*, 4 May, 5 Jun, 10 Jul, 1, 31 Aug, 13, 29 Oct, 7 Nov 1860; H Rpt 79, 36C, 2S, p. 90, Ser 1105; anonymous to Thomas M. Newson, n.d. except 1860, Thomas M. Newson Mss (Minn. His. Soc.).

rose on Tuesday morning cast its bright rays upon a powerful & noble Republic, in the evening it went down on a ruined tattered Union, for such I believe will be the result."

Washingtonians refused to believe in the inevitability of that judgment. Six weeks later when South Carolina announced her secession from the Union, businessmen and private householders ran up Union flags to underscore their disapproval, and the sight of anyone wearing the secessionist cockade evoked dismayed astonishment. Foreign-born residents of the capital were apparently as strongly opposed to disunion as were native Americans. Certainly Irish immigrants, though hostile to the remnants of anti-Catholic, anti-foreign Know-Nothingism in the Republican party, and though prone to despise Negroes, had little sympathy with the cause of southern planters.[2] A large part of the District's native American population, on the other hand, had close family ties with the South. Of the 75,000 inhabitants of 1860, 14 percent were Maryland-born, 10 percent Virginia-born, and undoubtedly more than half the 47 percent born in the District were members of families southern in origin. Those figures, to be sure, included 11,100 free Negroes whose opinions did not count.[3] But influential citizens, however anxious to have the Union endure, shrank from the idea of using coercion against the South. And a few men flatly announced that they would not tolerate such measures.[4]

Nevertheless, during those months of uncertainty between November 1860 and May 1861 more than sentiment affected men's behavior. Fear for the country's business rode high in the big northern cities. Boston cotton brokers and mill owners assured each other that North and South would inevitably reach some compromise rather than permit civil war, with its evil consequences for southern cotton growers and northern

[2] Andrew Harllee to John Harllee, 8 Nov 1860, William Curry Harllee Mss (SHC); *Star*, 11, 13, 18, 22, 26 Dec 1860; Frederick Douglass, *The Life and Times of Frederick Douglass*, p. 562; David Macrae, *The Americans at Home*, p. 59.

[3] *Eighth U.S. Census*, 1860, *Population*, pp. 616-19.

[4] H Rpt 79, 36C, 2S, p. 108, Ser 1105.

spinners alike. New York bankers prepared to exercise their power over the country's money market, while worried merchants and shippers in Cincinnati and St. Louis considered ways to bring to bear all the pressure of the mid-West's commercial interests to prevent war. Washingtonians and Georgetowners lacking a strong industrial and commercial position had no comparable weapon at their command. The Democratic defeat had undermined the position of W. W. Corcoran and other Washington bankers, leaving them without influence in national counsels.

For Washington dissolution of the Union would spell far more than economic reverses; it would mean virtual annihilation. Were the Union to split peacefully, Washington, near the northern border of a southern confederacy, could not expect to be its capital; nor, in the seemingly unlikely event of Maryland's aligning herself with the non-slaveholding states, could the city hope to be the capital of a northern union. If no longer a capital, she must sink into insignificance. The Smithsonian Institution could hardly forestall that consequence. Yet if the incoming Republican administration refused either to make concessions to the South or to "let the erring sisters go in peace," war must come, and in all probability Washington would become a beleaguered city and the entire District a battleground. Local business had already slumped. The price of slaves in Maryland and Virginia had been dropping for months. A week after the November election the Washington real estate market collapsed, and a few days later local banks suspended specie payments. In the eyes of permanent residents only a political compromise could save the Union. Without it, Washington was doomed. Optimists clung to faith that Congress would steer a way out of the dilemma, preferably by accepting Senator Crittenden's proposal to extend the line of the Missouri Compromise to the California border and to leave slavery untouched in the District of Columbia as long as it existed in Virginia and Maryland. Former congresses had dealt with the problem in

1820 and 1850. Surely the 36th and 37th Congress could act as wisely.[5]

Still doubts persisted. Before Congress convened in December, some 250 respected citizens formed a Washington unit of the National Volunteers, an organization that had sprung up in Baltimore and other cities where Democrats anticipated trouble from Republican Wide Awakes. Stories circulated about "Black Republican" fanaticism; attacks on private property and individual liberties might be in store for the city as soon as Lincoln arrived to inaugurate "the reign of terror." The sinister tales gained currency when in mid-January General Winfield Scott, the aged hero of the Mexican War and the commanding general of the Army, ordered 650 soldiers to the capital. Was President Buchanan about to proclaim martial law? Patently the President was seeking to protect federal property; the present 30-man auxiliary guard included southern political appointees, the city police force was small, and the local militia ill-organized. Any small incident could precipitate a crisis. Rumors filled the street-corners and barrooms that a "southern conspiracy" was afoot to seize the city for the southern states, "string up the Black Republicans" and prevent Lincoln's inauguration. The stories had a certain underlying logic: with the capital in secessionists' hands, foreign governments might recognize a new southern nation; possession of the American state papers, the Treasury, the arsenal, and the Washington Navy Yard would strengthen the South immeasurably. In fact, without naming his source of information, General Scott asserted: "The leaders say secession is dead without Washington city; and it is still their intention to get possession of Washington by the fourth of March next, if possible."[6] If residents collaborated the deed might be done quickly. Most substantial householders, however, refused to take stock in the tale of an organized Fifth Column composed of responsible Washingtonians; property-

[5] *New York Herald*, 13, 23 Nov 1860; *Star*, 15 Jan 1861; *N.I.*, 17 Jan, 28 Feb 1861.

[6] H Rpt 79, 36C, 2S, pp. 28, 74, 90, 105, Ser 1105; *N.I.*, 6 Mar 1861.

owners, regardless of their political affiliations, had too much at stake to risk an invitation to violence. And yet, remembering the local gangs and the Baltimore "Plug-uglies" who had terrorized voters at the city elections of 1857 and 1858, solid citizens were alarmed.[7]

In the tense atmosphere of the capital as the Buchanan administration neared its end, northern congressmen began to look with suspicion upon the National Volunteers. That group might be the nucleus in Washington of the much-talked-of southern conspiracy. In late January a committee of the House undertook to investigate. General Scott's testimony was not reassuring. While refusing to name his correspondents, he read to the committee three of the eighty-odd warning letters he had received. One described the impending seizure of Fort Sumter, and two gave detailed accounts of the plan to take possession of Washington. Men with arms hidden in their baggage would drift into the city by two's and three's, house themselves unobtrusively with friends, and at 3:30 in the morning of Sunday, March 3, quietly sally forth to take the principal government buildings; when the city awoke she would find herself in secessionists' hands. Less than half the local militia, General Scott declared, could be counted loyal. Other witnesses subpoenaed by the committee had little specific to offer. Most of them expressed belief that the rumors were groundless. The federal Commissioner of Buildings explained, "There are a great many idle people here about Washington, who have no particular pursuit, and who hunt up all manner of stories and circulate them, give them to the gentlemen of the press who are here, and they are not over particular in inquiring into the facts, but use them as they receive them." The mayor denied that anyone would attempt to interfere with Lincoln's inauguration, but committee members, knowing him to be an ardent Democrat and displeased at his easy-going assumption that the militia could handle any local disturbance, were less than cordial to him. Seven months later Mayor Berret would be under arrest

[7] *Star*, 2, 5, 10, 11, 15 Jan 1861.

as a secessionist. The investigation ended without establishing evidence of a plot within the city.

Arch southerners in and about Washington expressed their feelings plainly. A resident of Montgomery County, Maryland, who had been organizing a company of militia in order to protect slaveholders, announced that his own slaves were worth $10,000 less than a year before. Montgomery County men, he said, intended to safeguard their property, and their neighbors in Prince Georges County, where a number of individuals had each a half million dollars invested in slaves, were equally determined. Enoch Lowe, a former Governor of Maryland, though labelling the stories of a conspiracy to seize the capital "a premeditated and scandalous libel," declared: "I suppose the State of Maryland, in the event of her secession, as a matter of course, would claim the reversion of the District, which was granted the United States for specific purposes, which purposes would then have failed." More dramatic was the angry testimony of the head of the National Volunteers, Dr. Cornelius Boyle, an eminent Washington physician. He, also, repudiated as nonsense the tale of a "conspiracy," but he read to the committee the resolutions he had drafted for the National Volunteers. Its members would not take a position of hostility to southern interests. They would oppose the reign of terror about to be inaugurated and aid each other and "all good citizens" against insults and attacks on private property. If Virginia and Maryland seceded, the National Volunteers would protect themselves and those states "from the evils of a foreign and hostile government within and near their borders." The organization would put down any mob from the North or the South. "We are propertyholders. . . . Under all circumstances we cast our lot with Maryland. We are Marylanders; and when the case arises, then we will decide." Four-fifths of Washington, Dr. Boyle concluded, would go with Maryland.[8]

Later events proved Dr. Boyle's estimate correct, although not in the way he apparently anticipated: more than four-fifths

[8] H Rpt 79, 36C, 2S, pp. 26, 98, 105-106.

of the District's population would take Maryland's course and, whatever their inner disquiet, would remain loyal to the Union in deed and speech. Whether an equal number would have sworn allegiance to the Confederacy had Maryland chosen to secede is doubtful, for Dr. Boyle admittedly spoke for people of his own social stratum, tacitly dismissing as unimportant the thousands of residents who disliked slavery, owned little local property, or had northern antecedents. But his summary of attitudes among old established families was probably sound; most of them would accept Maryland's decision when the break came. Few leaders of ante-bellum Washington would move to the South bag and baggage as did former Mayor Lenox and Boyle himself, and after two years of war only forty-four property-owners in the entire District would face formal court charges of aiding and abetting the rebellion.[9] Yet within the closely-knit circle of families socially prominent in the fifties, feeling for the South would remain to harrow hearts during the war and to affect the city's destiny.

Meanwhile in January 1861 men observing the dreadful indecisiveness of President Buchanan and his Cabinet and shocked at the idea of armed action against the government were preparing to forestall trouble in Washington. Charles P. Stone, appointed Inspector-General of Volunteers on New Year's Day, sent out letters to "some forty well-known and esteemed gentlemen of the District" proposing that each organize a military company of volunteers. Stone, representative of that large group in Washington which had opposed Lincoln's election but believed in upholding the Constitution at all costs, assured General Scott that "two-thirds of the fighting stock of the District are ready to protect the Government." Although Stone received some refusals, the general response to his appeal was enthusiastic. Led by influential citizens, members of hose companies and German *Turnevereine*, carpenters and stone cutters, enrolled at once. Within a few weeks thirty-three newly organized companies of infantry and two troops of cavalry were drilling reg-

[9] District Court Docket, No 1, 21 Apr 1863, cited in Bryan, *Capital*, II, 516.

20. "Laying of the Cornerstone at the Capitol," July 1851. Wood engraving in *Gleason's Pictorial Drawing Room Companion*

21. The completed City Hall, ca. 1860. Designed by George Hadfield, architect of Arlington house across the Potomac, the building was begun in 1820, but left unfinished till the 1850's. The U.S. courts used the west wing, and the federal government today occupies the entire building. It symbolized civic dignity to Washington

22. The Smithsonian Institution. Photograph by Mathew Brady, ca. 1860

23. Ferdinand Rudolph Hassler, first head of the Coast Survey. Lithograph by Charles Fenderich, 1834

24. Alexander Dallas Bache, successor to Hassler. Photograph ca. 1863

25. Joseph Henry, first secretary of the Smithsonian Institution, ca. 1850. Daguerreotype

26. Spencer Fullerton Baird, first head of the National Museum, 1850. Daguerreotype

27. Clark Mills' statue of General Jackson, with the White House in the background. Lithograph by Thomas Sinclair, 1858

28. Riot at the Northern Liberties polls, 1857. Wood engraving from *Leslie's Illustrated Newspaper*

29. "View of Georgetown" from Washington, ca. 1854. Lithograph by E. Sachse & Co.

30. Shad fishermen on the Eastern Branch near the Navy Yard, 1860. The arched roofed building on the right is a covered ship slip designed by the versatile Benjamin Latrobe. Wood engraving in *Harper's Weekly*, 1861

31. The swearing-in of the first District volunteers, April 1861, in front of the War Department building west of the White House. Wood engraving in *Harper's Weekly*

32. Arrival of New York troops at the B & O depot, April 1861, showing the greatly admired square tower of the depot. It stood at New Jersey Avenue and C Street, where the bus tunnel today emerges from under the hill near the Senate Office Building. Wood engraving in *Frank Leslie's Illustrated Newspaper*

33. "Balloon View of the city," ca. July 1861. Beyond the train puffing ... stub of the Washington Monument and, on the right, the National

34. Review of troops on the plain east of the Capitol near the Eastern Branch, October 1861. Wood engraving in *Harper's Weekly*

35. Sentries on guard at the Long Bridge, 1865. The railroad trestle ran alongside

36. Cattle on the Monument grounds and, in the background, the fenced-in part of the President's Square which, because the fence was whitewashed, gave to the area the name "White Lot." Photograph by Mathew Brady, ca. 1863

37. Washington Canal and a muddy stretch of lower Pennsylvania Avenue, ca. 1863

ularly. On Washington's birthday the parade of more than a thousand of these men, uniformed and under arms, was a comforting sight to people who feared mob violence in the city. Years later, General Stone declared that these volunteers, the first sworn into federal service, saved the capital and the Union with it.[10]

Before the end of February, the air in Washington had cleared slightly. Not only did the parade on the 22nd indicate that the city was not utterly defenseless, but the resignation and departure of officials unwilling longer to serve the federal government lessened the tensions of earlier weeks when southern senators were making farewell speeches and representatives from the cotton states were hurrying home to share in the forming of the Confederacy. Furthermore, Lincoln upon his arrival brought the city unexpected reassurance. Here was no fire-eater. The newspapers remarked with gratification upon his friendly greeting to the mayors and councils of Washington and Georgetown when they called upon him at his lodgings. Men dared believe that so mild-spoken a man would after all act with moderation. Perhaps everything would blow over, and the seceded states, after sulking a while, would return to the Union without demanding more than the North would yield. At least the rump of the 36th Congress was still debating compromise measures, and until February 27 the "Conference Convention" remained in session at the Willard Hotel. There under the chairmanship of ex-President John Tyler delegates from twenty-one northern and border states led by Virginia struggled to devise a workable formula for peace and reunion.[11] At the same time, preparations for the inauguration and the building of a large frame ballroom adjoining the City Hall in which to hold the inaugural ball created some diversion. The hotels and boardinghouses were filling with new arrivals even as defeated congressmen were making ready to depart. The theatres were

[10] Charles P. Stone, "Washington on the Eve of War," *Century Magazine*, IV (Jul 1883), pp. 458-64; *Star*, 22, 23 Feb 1861.

[11] *N.I.*, 27 Feb 1861; *Cong Globe*, 36C, 2S, p. 1433; Roy F. Nichols, *The Disruption of American Democracy*, pp. 474-91.

crowded nightly. If in the eyes of old Washingtonians the motley throng of Republican office-seekers seemed crude and unmannerly, everyone knew that their money was as good as that of polished southerners who stayed at home. And Washington's "first families," if unwilling to consider attending the inaugural ball, could recall that the community had always survived the advent of the spoilsmen who had swept into the city every four years since 1829. Life had to go on.

Newcomers, when not too absorbed in the political future to look about them, saw little to admire. Some of the public buildings were impressive—the President's house set in wide lawns, the colonnaded Treasury adjoining the "unpretending" brick State Department building, the harmoniously proportioned Patent Office and the Post Office—but the clutter of stone cutters' equipment and blocks of marble on the Capitol grounds and the scaffolding about the unfinished dome marred the appearance of the Hill. Much of the Mall despite the loops of trees and shrubs with which A. J. Downing had adorned the Smithsonian grounds, was unkempt; lumber and coal yards trespassed upon its northern edge along the Washington Canal, and at the Potomac end the stub of the Washington Monument surrounded by debris rose dejectedly above the tidal marshes that stretched out in a wide arc of swamp grass, pools of water, and evil-smelling mud, obliterating the shore from which John Quincy Adams had taken his early morning swims thirty-odd years before. Strung out along lower Pennsylvania Avenue where today the National Archives proclaims "The Past is Prologue" stood the stalls of the Centre Market with the Fish Market at its rear. "To make a Washington street," wrote an Englishman, "take one marble temple or public office, a dozen good houses of brick, and a dozen of wood, and fill in with sheds and fields."[12] "Senators' Row" on C Street near Judiciary Square and other neighborhoods scattered from the Navy Yard

[12] Joseph T. Kelly, "Memories of a Life-Time in Washington," CHS *Rec*, XXXI-XXXII, 117-49; William Richstein, *The Stranger's Guide to Washington City*, pp. 22-34; Rpt Sec/Int, 1861, p. 854, Ser 1117; Henry Latham, *Black and White, a Journal of a Three Months' Tour in the United States*, p. 59.

to Washington Circle contained some handsome houses, but vacant lots rank with weeds or strewn with rubbish punctuated the sweep of every avenue. Less immediately visible to a casual inspection, alleyways destined shortly to become teeming slums inhabited by freedmen were already dotted with groggeries and ramshackle shanties.

Criticism of the city's appearance was an old story to permanent residents. Their concern was March 4 and its aftermath. Unwelcome as the incoming administration was to conservatives, once the inauguration was an accomplished fact they hoped to settle down to making the best of it. People watching the presidential carriage roll along Pennsylvania Avenue on that chilly gray day could not fail to observe the close formation of the cavalry escort riding on either side; the absence of the civic groups and political clubs, traditionally part of inaugural parades, was striking. Nothing looked truly gay. But at least the waiting was over. Lincoln's inaugural speech caused no furor; it contained no alarming pronouncements, even while it outlined no positive course of action.[13] With huge relief, citizens now prepared to go about their business.

A grateful calm settled upon Washington after March 4. As the new President began to wield the power of federal patronage, hopes rose that he might mend the breach in the Union. Mr. Lincoln appeared ready to let the South come gradually to its senses. In the state convention in Richmond, Virginia, the Union party seemed to be safely in control. Governor Hicks of Maryland was teetering back and forth, but his refusal to summon the legislature for a vote on secession encouraged Union supporters in the District.[14] The President's local appointments

[13] Stone, "Washington on the Eve of the War," *Century*, IV, 458-64; *N.I.*, 5 Mar 1861; *Star*, 4 Mar 1861; George W. Smith, "Critical Moment for Washington," CHS *Rec*, XXI, 87-113.

[14] Charles P. Stone, "Washington in March and April, 1861," *Magazine of American History*, XIV (July 1885), pp. 1-3; Harry J. Carman and Reinhard H. Luthin, *Lincoln and the Patronage*, pp. 186-227; Henry T. Shanks, *The Secession Movement in Virginia, 1847-1861*, pp. 191-208; George L. P. Radcliffe, *Governor Thomas H. Hicks of Maryland and the Civil War*, in *Johns Hopkins University Studies in Historical and Political Science*, Series XIX, Nov-Dec 1901, pp. 21-50.

seemed suitable—Virginia-born Ward Lamon as Marshal of the District, the trusted B. B. French as Commissioner of Public Buildings, Sayles J. Bowen as collector of revenue, and Lewis Clephane, former assistant to Gamaliel Bailey of the *National Era*, city postmaster. When Mrs. Lincoln resumed the customary Saturday afternoon receptions at the White House, Washingtonians dared feel that life in the capital was returning to normal. Although reports from Montgomery, Alabama, and Charleston revealed mounting ardor for the Confederacy throughout the deep South, Washington newspapers cautiously suggested that no warlike move was imminent. In Washington and Georgetown the companies of volunteers were insuring order and, when in early April a number were quietly sworn into the federal service and began unobtrusively to stand guard at night about the White House and the public buildings, residents of the city read no ominous meaning into the act.[15]

News of the firing on Fort Sumter on April 12 hit like a thunderbolt, despite every forewarning. Scarcely had Washington digested that fact than Lincoln's call for 75,000 volunteers proved all earlier estimates of the President's passivity wrong. On April 17 Governor Letcher of Virginia, long known for his pro-Union sentiment, informed the administration in Washington that the Old Dominion had passed a secession ordinance. High-ranking Army and Navy officers loyal to their native Virginia immediately resigned their commissions. While the War and Navy Departments sought replacements, fears lest troops assembling across the Potomac march into Washington added to the general alarm. Even southern sympathizers, perhaps envisaging street fighting in the city, showed no elation.[16] In this crisis the District volunteers faced a difficult decision. Most of them had offered their services for protection of the capital. Now asked to enlist without any strings tied, all but three companies declined until the War Department

[15] *Star*, 9 Mar, 8 Apr 1861; Stone, "Washington in March and April, 1861," *Magazine of American History*, XIV, 11-17.

[16] *Star*, 15-20 Apr 1861.

guaranteed not to send them out of the District. The volunteers' hesitation later lent color to charges of widespread disloyalty, although the Provost Marshal General reported "these troops, in whole or in part, did subsequently serve out of the District without opposition or protest."[17]

The swift movement of events in late April left people in the capital dazed. New recruits swelled the ranks of the District volunteers till they numbered nearly 3,500, but the transfer of Army regulars downstream to Fort Washington left only unseasoned men to defend the city. On April 19 when a Baltimore mob attacked a Massachusetts regiment en route to Washington, Maryland officials, ostensibly to avoid further hostile demonstrations, sanctioned the burning of the railroad bridges linking Baltimore and the North. The Massachusetts troops, their wounded on stretchers, reached Washington that night. For five days thereafter the District lay isolated. Agreement between the President and the Governor of Maryland that volunteers from the northern states should land at Annapolis and thence move to Washington seemed like a meaningless gesture to householders hourly expecting a Confederate army to seize the capital. Some of them attempted to flee, setting out for the country in carriages, carts, or on foot; in their eagerness to go supplied with hard money, they caused a run on the banks. Colonel Stone's foresight prevented a shortage of bread in the city, for the War Department, acting upon his warning that supplies were low, commandeered the flour stored in Georgetown mills and aboard ships docked at her wharves and about to sail; wagoners carted it off to the basement of the Capitol and Treasury.[18]

At the end of April as northern regiments transported via Annapolis began to arrive, panic subsided but confusion increased. Companies of high-spirited young men in strangely

[17] Final Rpt Provost Marshal General, H Ex Doc 1, 39C, 1S, p. 7, Ser 1251; *Star*, 11, 12 Apr 1861.

[18] See notes 15 and 16; Elizabeth Lindsay Lomax, *Leaves from an Old Washington Diary, 1854-1863*, pp. 149-51; Radcliffe, *Governor Thomas H. Hicks of Maryland*, pp. 40-42.

varied "uniforms" were soon overrunning the city. Quartered in the Capitol, the Treasury, and the Patent Office, in the buildings of the Georgetown Seminary, or in tents on Franklin Square and Meridian Hill, volunteers who had come to save the Union were shortly seeking to save themselves from boredom by swaggering about the streets, frequenting the barrooms, quarreling, gambling, and indulging in horseplay at citizens' expense. To supply bread to the troops, the government hastily opened a bakery in the basement of the Capitol. The army commissariat all but broke down; the officer in charge had held the post since 1818 and was now a helpless invalid. Distribution of equipment was equally inefficient; the Quartermaster General, Virginian Joseph E. Johnston, had resigned, and the Secretary of War had not as yet appointed a successor. Northerners hungry for contracts were beginning to swarm about the government offices, while local merchants did their best to meet the demand for supplies or hesitated over sharing in preparations for war.[19] Contributing to fratricide would be a high price to pay for improving trade.

It was at this point that hundreds of District citizens felt they must choose between deeply conflicting loyalties. Some had already made up their minds; others would wait till oaths of allegiance forced a choice; a few would silently evade the issue altogether. Maryland's decision to stay with the Union made the choice easier, but every day saw irreconcilables, government clerks among them, depart for the South. Parents faced the shock of finding that romantic fourteen- and fifteen-year-old sons were running away to join the Confederate Army. Most families felt helpless and fervently prayed that even now the nation might avoid bloodshed. And then one morning late in May, as companies of volunteers marched over the bridges to seize the Arlington heights above the Potomac, Colonel Elmer Ellsworth and his New York Zouaves, gay in their red caps and baggy "Turkish" trousers, landed in Alexandria to occupy

[19] Alexander Howard Meneely, *The War Department, 1861*, pp. 111-12, 117-18, 149-53.

the rebel city. Confederate troops had withdrawn days before, but the Zouaves determined to tear down the Confederate flag that flew from the Marshall House. Hours later grieving angry soldiers bore Colonel Ellsworth's body back to the Washington Navy Yard. Shot by an indignant hotel proprietor, Ellsworth was the first man to die in action for the Union. The fighting war had begun.

CHAPTER X

THE CIVIC AND ECONOMIC IMPACT OF WAR, 1861-1865

IN THE early summer of 1861 people in the capital talked hopefully of a short war.[1] While the War Department under Simon Cameron struggled to organize itself and the President and General Scott dealt with northern governors and their emissaries demanding immediate annihilation of the rebel army, District companies did guard duty, draymen hauled army supplies from the wharves and the railroad freight yards, and hotels, restaurants, and barrooms carried on a rushing business. Soldiers were everywhere. Reviews of troops and martial music lent an air of brittle gaiety. At the National Theatre, usually closed in summer, a stock company staged a week's run to welcome Congress back to the special session called for July 4. The houses vacated by southern families still stood empty, real estate transactions had ceased, and the price of foodstuffs, which had soared in April, remained high: flour formerly sold at $7.50 a barrel now cost $12. But belief that a single pitched battle would settle once and for all the quarrel between North and South inspired Washingtonians to patience. Troops assembled here could soon disband, Congress would presumably dispose of its business quickly and adjourn, and peace and order would return to the city.[2]

Nevertheless beneath the shiny surface of confidence, many people were troubled. Ordinary business, which had quickened at first, declined as May turned into June. Military preparations overshadowed all other activities. Although by late June, according to newspaper estimates, over 50,000 volunteers were stationed in and about the capital, neither Washington nor Georgetown profited greatly from this friendly invasion. The

[1] Alexander Howard Meneely, *The War Department, 1861*, pp. 182-83.
[2] *Star*, 22, 23 Apr, 14 May, 2 Jul 1861.

new Commissary and Quartermaster Generals placed their orders for supplies with big houses in New York, Philadelphia, and Baltimore, and, except for the Georgetown and county flour mills, local firms shared in none of this first war boom. Work on the Capitol extension had ceased when the War Department quartered troops in the building, and after their removal to encampments outside the city, Congress convened in halls daily filled with alcoholic fumes of the bread baking in the ovens below them. On the first of July when masons laid the last stones in the great arch of the Cabin John Bridge, work on the aqueduct also stopped.[3] Day laborers found jobs laying railroad tracks to the wharves or erecting Army warehouses and corrals for mules and horses, and any man who could drive a team could get work as an Army wagoner. Other men, unless political connections opened to them federal clerkships, faced hard times. Because the Army finance office was still disorganized, District volunteers had received no pay since they were sworn into federal service in April, and by mid-June their wives and children were in real, if temporary, distress. Only the contributions of private citizens, led by a group of Germans, and funds voted by the city council saved a number of families from want.[4]

Equally disturbing was the mounting distrust of District citizens that government officials displayed. Lincoln's suspension of the writ of habeas corpus for soldiers, arrests of reputable civilians on mere suspicion of disloyalty, and the growing feeling that malicious tale-bearing was enough to make trouble for innocent people cast heavy shadows over the city. Householders southern in origin but long settled in Washington and devoted to the Union cause were under particular pressure. Individuals who continued to write letters to friends in the South risked investigation, although, the *Intelligencer* observed, the newspapers told all that enemy agents wanted to know.

[3] *Ibid.*, 17 May, 26 Jun, 3 July 1861; Rpt Sec/Int, 1861, p. 849, Ser 1117; Rpt Sec/War, 1861, p. 72, Ser 1118.

[4] *N.I.*, 13, 18 Jun 1861; *Star*, 25 Jun 1861.

Reasons for surveillance did, of course, exist; spies swarmed about Washington as they did about Richmond. North and South, every town and city contained dissidents to their government's course. This was indeed civil war. Without a complete censorship of all mail leaving Washington, officials charged with the security of the capital had to act upon vague hints and gossip. More than one indiscreet lady of southern antecedents did herself and her friends harm by idle chatter critical of government procedures.[5] In this uncomfortable atmosphere everyone looked forward impatiently to a battle that would put an end to the war.

With astonishing light-heartedness on July 16, 1861, troops stationed in the District set off toward Manassas and the creek called Bull Run. If over-confident soldiers of the Thirteenth Brooklyn Regiment no longer looped their muskets with ropes with which to drag back Confederate prisoners, the omission was a mere gesture to discipline. Some of the men stopped to pick blackberries along the line of march. In Washington suspense filled the next few days. During the heat of Saturday and Sunday, the 20th and 21st, anxious listeners could hear the faint boom of the cannon thirty miles distant, until, toward evening of the 21st, wagons and carriages began to clatter over the Long Bridge bringing back panicky teamsters and frightened congressmen and their ladies who had driven out to picnic while they watched the Union triumph. At dawn of the day following, exhausted soldiers singly and in half-formed companies began straggling back into the city, while carts filled with wounded men jolted through the streets.[6]

"The men appear," wrote Walt Whitman, "at first sparsely and shame-faced enough, then thicker, . . . Sidewalks . . . crowded, jamm'd with citizens, darkies, clerks, everybody, lookers-on; swarms of dirt-cover'd return'd soldiers there (will

[5] *N.I.*, 7 Jun 1861; *Sunday Morning Chronicle*, 23, 30 Jun 1861; (hereafter cited as *Sun Chronicle*); Eugenia Phillips, A Southern Woman's Story of Her Imprisonment, 1861-62; *Frank Leslie's Illustrated Newspaper*, 31 Aug 1861.

[6] William Owner's Diary, 22, 24 Jul 1861; Meneely, *War Department*, p. 187.

they never end?) move by; but nothing said, no comments; (half our lookers-on secesh of the most venomous kind—they say nothing; but the devil snickers in their faces.) . . . Good people (but not over-many of them either,) hurry up something for their grub. They put wash-kettles on the fire, for soup, for coffee. They set tables on the side-walks—wagon-loads of bread are purchas'd, swiftly cut in stout chunks. . . . Amid the deep excitement, crowds and motion, and desperate eagerness, it seems strange to see many, very many, of the soldiers sleeping. . . . They drop down anywhere, on the steps of houses, up close by the basements or fences, on the sidewalk, aside on some vacant lot, and deeply sleep . . . and on them as they lay, sulkily drips the rain.

"As afternoon pass'd, and evening came, the streets, the bar-rooms, knots everywhere, listeners, questioners, terrible yarns." Perhaps those yarns formed the warp of Whitman's account, since there is doubt about his being here at the time. "Meantime," he added, "in Washington, among the great persons and their entourage, a mixture of awful consternation, uncertainty, rage, shame, helplessness, and stupefying disappointment."[7]

The humane did not linger to mourn or to gloat. The wounded needed help. While the newly organized Sanitary Commission rushed supplies to the hastily improvised hospitals and women volunteered as nurses, the Army surgeons set to the work of grisly amputations. Householders turned their dwellings into nursing homes, and when that added space did not suffice, the government commandeered buildings at the Georgetown Seminary and Columbian College, a schoolhouse, and the former residence of the British minister near Washington Circle. Later battles were to fill churches and half the federal office buildings with wounded.[8]

Throughout the North, as the meaning of the defeat was realized, grim determination replaced the easy optimism of early

[7] *The Complete Poetry and Prose of Walt Whitman*, ed. Malcolm Cowley, II, 17-18.

[8] *Star*, 31 Jul, 6, 14 Aug, 10 Sep 1861; Meneely, *War Department*, pp. 133-34.

summer. While the War and Navy Departments revised and expanded their plans, Congress, having legalized the measures that officials had already taken and having voted huge war appropriations, turned to consideration of bills designed to better safeguard the nation and the federal capital. In April the government had required civilian employees and men enlisting in military service to take, or to take again, the oath of allegiance to the Constitution as established by law in 1789 and administered to federal officials thereafter. By August Congress felt that was not enough. Lincoln himself later said that southern sympathizers "pervaded all departments of the government and nearly all communities of people." Secret hearings before a House committee on subversion among federal employees produced enough evidence to bring about the imposition of a new oath. It demanded a solemn affirmation from every person in government service to uphold the Constitution and the government of the United States both then and thereafter.[9] Some men refused the oath because they were at best lukewarm towards the Union, others because they were unwilling to pledge future support to an administration becoming increasingly partisan and increasingly high-handed. And several department heads, armed with secret and perhaps dubious testimony, dismissed employees who had unhesitatingly taken the oath. Between August and the end of the year at least a hundred civilians left government service in Washington, and more departed as the war went on. Of the 727 Army officers listed in January, 313 resigned during 1861.[10] Disrupting as was the turnover in government offices, for the local community the poison of constantly recurring suspicion was more deadly.

A second fateful act, passed on August 6, created a metropolitan police force under federal control. Coupled with the loyalty act, the new law touched off a brief explosion that had immediate and disastrous consequences for the city. The law

[9] *Abraham Lincoln, His Speeches and Writings*, ed. Roy P. Basler, p. 701; *Cong Globe*, 37C, 1S, App., p. 45.

[10] H Rpt 16, 37C, 1S, Ser 1144; Harold Hyman, *Era of the Oath, Northern Loyalty Tests during the Civil War and Reconstruction*, pp. 1-50; Meneely, *War Department*, p. 106.

specified that the mayors of Washington and Georgetown were to be ex-officio members of the police board; the other five members, appointed by the President, fell into the category of federal employees and therefore were subject to the loyalty oath.[11] At the formal swearing in of these new officials, Mayor Addison of Georgetown took the oath with the others, but Mayor Berret of Washington refused. Political rivals promptly called him a traitor, and even his friends thought him unduly impressed with the dignity of his office. Berret, evidently troubled at the prospect of federal encroachment upon the city's corporate rights, contended that a mayor legally elected by popular vote was exempt from the operation of the new loyalty act. His reasoning, however valid, sounded specious; it convinced few people in a city still smarting from the recent Union defeat. The United States Provost Marshal considered his attitude cause for action against him. Before dawn of a mid-August morning armed guards hurried him off to Fort Lafayette in New York harbor, where he remained imprisoned for a month until he resigned the mayoralty, took the loyalty oath, and thus obtained his release.[12] But Berret did the city great disservice by supplying ammunition to the assailants of her loyalty.

The board of aldermen, without waiting for Berret's resignation, pronounced the mayor's office vacant and elected the board president, Richard Wallach, to the post. Wallach, a lawyer by profession, had had considerable administrative experience as a former District Marshal. His contemporaries thought him "strikingly handsome." More important, his fellow citizens trusted him, and he had the full support of the *Evening Star*, which his brother owned and edited. Although not an outright Republican and less liberal than Mayor Addison of Georgetown, Dick Wallach could accept with fewer misgivings than could older Washingtonians the strictures war imposed upon the city. In view of the problems confronting the city which no local official could avert or control, less ambitious or less conscientious

[11] *Cong Globe*, 37C, 1S, App., pp. 43-44.

[12] *Star*, 16, 20, 24 Aug, 13 Sep, 15 Oct 1861; *N.I.*, 22, 26 Aug 1861; *National Republican*, 21 Aug 1861.

men may have wondered why he was willing to serve more than one term. Elected by popular vote in June 1862 amid scenes at the polls as disorderly as those of the 1850's, and twice re-elected, he presided over the corporation till 1868. Although his nonaggressiveness, bordering on a timorousness suggestive of descent from a long line of maiden aunts, prevented his exercising personal leadership, he represented the views dominant within his community during the war.[13]

If Washingtonians sensed that doubt of their loyalty was a factor in the decision of Congress to replace the municipal police with a body controlled and partly paid for by the federal government, they nevertheless welcomed the measure. Referring to a local petition begging Congress to act, a minor official noted: "There is ten Thousand siners for that bill." They had wanted it in the 1850's; in the war-ridden capital it was essential, for the expanding, shifting population required a constabulary whose authority extended beyond the city limits. In the summer of 1861 the Provost Marshal guards were fully occupied with searching out spies and deserters, most of the troops encamped in and about Washington were still undisciplined, and discharge of the "90-day" volunteers in late July turned loose in the city men no longer under military control and ready to spend their pay in the bars and brothels.[14]

Unhappily the Metropolitan Police Board, though armed with authority over the entire District, supplied with an annual appropriation of $92,000 of federal money, and empowered to employ 150 patrolmen, 10 sergeants, and a superintendent, soon found itself echoing the complaints of Washington's former police chiefs. "Confidence men," gamblers, prostitutes, thieves, the worst of the riff-raff of other cities gathered in the capital where money was "easy" and 230 miles of streets and 77 miles of alleys simplified law evasion. With Washington's civilian population having doubled since 1861, by the fall of

[13] *Ibid.*, 27 Aug 1861; Allen C. Clark, "Richard Wallach and the Times of His Mayoralty," CHS *Rec*, XXI, 200-45. For an account of the city elections, see Margaret Leech, *Reveille in Washington*, pp. 242-43.

[14] Ptn, S37A-H7, Aug 1861; *Star*, 15, 18, 27 Jul, 2, 7 Aug 1861.

1863 the 88 policemen assigned to patrol the city were virtually helpless. Morale suffered from a pay rate of $1.31 a day at a time when the 90-odd watchmen at government buildings were getting half again as much and "mechanics" were earning $3 and $3.50; in 1864 Congress felt obliged to double police pay, charging the added cost to local taxpayers.

Meanwhile the superintendent reported that without the several thousand soldiers on guard duty in Washington "this District would have been simply uninhabitable."[15] The 24,000 arrests of 1863 were three and a half times the number in Brooklyn, a city with more than twice the population of the District. The Provost Marshal tried ordering restaurant and hotel bars to close at 9:30 P.M.; but drunken brawls continued. The *Star*, abandoning its Victorian reticence, denied that 15,000 women were plying their ancient trade in Washington; a tally, made ward by ward, showed only about 2,300 white and 1,600 colored prostitutes, seven-eighths of them "colonized" since the war. While the city council vaguely considered licensing houses of ill fame in order to have some control over vice, General Hooker took steps to simplify surveillance by concentrating the "colony" in the triangle below Pennsylvania Avenue near the Treasury, a section that promptly came to be known as "Joe Hooker's Division." To clear the city of thieves, the authorities on one occasion hung red placards labelled "Pickpocket and Thief" upon culprits and paraded them through the streets. "A file of soldiers and a corps of drummers and fifers preceded them playing the Rogues March."[16]

Juvenile delinquency, that persistent evil of the fifties, also reached new heights. "The army," the police explained with characteristic oversimplification, "has following it an immense number of boys, attracted most of them by the species of fascination that the life of the soldier has for such young minds.

[15] Rpts Sec/Int, 1861, pp. 911-13, Ser 1117, 1862, p. 649, Ser 1157, 1863, pp. 719-24, Ser 1182, and 1864, p. 763, Ser 1220; *Star*, 11 Nov 1863.

[16] *Daily Morning Chronicle*, 14 Nov 1862, 25 Mar, 4, 11 Apr, 28 Sep 1863 (hereafter cited as *Chronicle*); *Star*, 6 Feb, 29 Jul 1862, 3, 7 Apr, 27 Oct, 12 Nov 1863; interview with Louis Brownlow, District Commissioner, 1915-1920, 6 Nov 1959.

These boys . . . find their way, after a very brief experience of the hardships of camp life, or perhaps by reason of some severe order from headquarters, into our city, and are soon denizens of our streets. In a very little while they become petty criminals, requiring the attentions of the police, and the question becomes a very important one. What is to be done with them?"[17] The House District Committee, after commenting upon the "severity and imperfections of the criminal code of the District," submitted a vigorous plea for a federal reformatory; $250,000 would suffice, less than one-twelfth the federal expenditures for a single day. In proposing that District taxpayers pay only $100,000 of the total, the committee reiterated the long-familiar theme that "it is for violating laws passed by Congress, administered by judges not chosen by the people, that these penitentiaries, jails and house of correction become necessary." The bill failed to pass. Children convicted of relatively trivial offenses were still cooped up in the county jail with hardened criminals, with the result that boys emerged showing "a degree of precocious villany hard to conceive of."[18]

Imprisonment in the county jail was itself a terrible punishment. Pleas to replace the old building on Judiciary Square had poured in upon Congress yearly since the mid-fifties. In the first summer of the war the Old Brick Capitol, which had housed a public school in 1860, was commandeered by the Provost Marshal for a military prison for spies and political suspects, but while that move lessened the congestion at the jail, the building, constructed in 1830 to accommodate eighty to one hundred prisoners, by mid 1862 contained 240 criminals, fugitive slaves, and people awaiting trial. At times ten men occupied a single cell eight feet by ten. The lack of water closets and the filthy yard half-filled with stagnant water turned the place into what the Secretary of the Interior described as "little better than the black hole of Calcutta." Conditions in the federal penitentiary were little better. A hundred court-martialed sol-

[17] Rpt Sec/Int, 1863, p. 731, Ser 1182.
[18] H Rpt 41, 38C, 1S, Ser 1206; Rpt Sec/Int, 1864, pp. 774-76, Ser 1220.

diers and some 230 convicts, white, black, men and women, were packed into the old building on the arsenal grounds when in September 1862 the Ordnance Department took it over for a munitions storehouse. The government then sent the convicts to the New York state penitentiary in Albany and court-martialed soldiers to buildings in charge of the Provost Marshal. Thereafter the Washington workhouse at the far end of East Capitol Street had to take the overflow from the jail, while the inmates of the Almshouse complained at finding themselves close neighbors to, and hence "indistinguishable from," the 1,500-odd criminal occupants of the workhouse. The mounting number of people arrested by the Provost Guard for seditious language or acts, or merely suspected of collaborating with the enemy, increased the problem. The Metropolitan Police Board declared no community in the entire United States "so inadequately supplied with prison accommodations, and none in which ample provisions are more needed."[19]

Nor did the reorganization of the courts help matters. The four judges of the new District Supreme Court, with jurisdiction over all cases formerly heard in the circuit, district, and criminal courts, were newcomers unfamiliar with the intricacies of the local legal system and were handicapped further by the lack of a police court to handle minor misdemeanors summarily. And an attempt to revise and codify District law again came to nothing.[20]

In the summer of 1862 Congress widened the duties of the Metropolitan Police to include sanitary inspections and abatement of nuisances. Small pox had struck during the winter. Mayor Wallach had ordered "the vaccine physician" to visit the public schools, but by 1863 scarcely a neighborhood was wholly free of "that most loathsome of all diseases"; President Lincoln

[19] *Journal of the 61st Council of the City of Washington*, p. 474; Rpts Sec/Int, 1856-1865, especially 1861, pp. 852-56, 1862, pp. 300, 661, and 1863, p. 729; S Ex Doc 55, 37C, 2S, Ser 1162; S. Rpt 60, 37C, 2S, p. 6, Ser 1125.

[20] *Cong Globe*, 37C, 3S, App., pp. 219-20; ptns, S37A-H7, 19, 20 Feb 1863; *Chronicle*, 24 Feb 1863, 30 Nov 1864; *Star*, 23 Mar 1863; Walter Cox, "Efforts to Obtain a Code of Laws," CHS *Rec*, III, 122-27.

himself had a light case. The need of a hospital at which victims, "strangers, discharged soldiers, contrabands and followers of the Army," could receive prompt care became so urgent that the government hospital established at Kalorama was set aside for small pox cases and other "eruptive" diseases, and eventually the Surgeon General of the Army contracted with the Sisters of Mercy at the Roman Catholic Providence Hospital to provide sixty beds for transient paupers. An ordinance of 1864 made vaccination of every child compulsory, but the ruling was enforceable only for children enrolled in the public schools. Throughout the war small pox stalked the city.[21] Despite the efforts of local physicians, the city board of health, and the ten police inspectors of the new Sanitary Corps, disease remained a greater threat to wartime Washington than the Confederate Army.

"What should you think," wrote a young army wife to her mother, "if all the slops from sleeping rooms were thrown either into the gutters or alley. Here there are no sewers, no cess pools or vaults for any purpose in the yards. . . . I was never in such a place for *smells*." To these the slaughter houses and the corrals for Army horses and mules contributed. Although Washington was a major supply depot for the Army of the Potomac and the location of fifteen to nineteen military hospitals, the War Department waited till 1863 to take any responsibility for sanitation in the city. Then, when a military commission reported "large deposits of night soil in the vicinity of various hospitals in open or shallow pits or scattered on the ground," and half-buried carcasses of horses and mules about the government corrals near a pond at the foot of 19th Street, orders assigned Negroes to the task of carting night soil and dead animals to fields beyond the city limits. The instructions forced the levy court to withdraw its prohibition of any dump-

[21] *Cong Globe*, 37C, 2S, App., p. 409; Rpt Sec/Int, 1862, pp. 651-52, Ser 1157; Georgetown Board of Aldermen, Minutes, 2 Dec 1861, 7 Feb 1862; *Star*, 11, 16 Jan, 8 Aug 1863; ptn, S37A-H7, 19 Jan 1863; *Journal 61st Council*, pp. 339-42, 349, and *62nd Council*, 10 Apr 1865, p. 7; Medical Society of the District of Columbia, *Report on the Sanitary Conditions of the Cities of Washington and Georgetown, March, 1864.*

ing of city refuse within the county but resulted in merely transferring to the suburbs the "hideous malaria of artificial swamps."[22] Municipal garbage carts began making regular rounds in the summer of 1863, thereby reducing the mounds of offal in streets and alleys; when an inventor demonstrated his new street sweeping machine on Pennsylvania Avenue, in one day with the help of a hundred Negro refugees and fifteen carts he removed "several thousand loads of dirt to the United States public grounds." But, in a city containing closer to 200,000 than the 61,000 people of 1860, sewage disposal needed some less primitive scheme. By the summer of 1864, 10,000,000 gallons of aqueduct water were available daily, but without a network of sewer mains Washington could not exploit the supply for sanitary purposes. The level of the Washington Canal, into which some seven sewers drained, dropped only six inches between 12th Street and the mouth at 17th; dredging and installation of tide gates proved futile: the dredging was not deep enough, and the gates at 12th Street were not strong enough to resist the tidal backwash. The "miasmatic swamp near the Presidential mansion" and "the shallow open sewer, of about one hundred fifty feet in width, (sometimes called a canal)" remained.[23]

The aqueduct, however, saved the military hospitals and the civilian community from untold misery in the last summer of the war. Until then, except for the wells in the public squares, the water supply depended upon surface drainage into the distributing reservoir; in dry weather that source ran dangerously low. Although work on the laying of the nine-mile conduit from the Great Falls to the receiving reservoir above Georgetown had resumed in the autumn of 1861, manpower shortages and threats of enemy raids slowed progress; then ten days after the engineer in charge turned the Potomac water into the reservoir

22 Harriet Cushman Balch to her mother, 10 Mar 1863, Balch Mss (Bancroft Lib, Univ of Calif); *Star*, 16, 28 May 1863; *Chronicle*, 3 Jun 1864.

23 *Journal 61st Council*, pp. 134-35; Rpts Sec/Int, 1863, pp. 687-88, Ser 1182 and 1864, pp. 686-87, Ser 1220; S Misc Doc 84, 38C, 1S, Ser 1177, which contains an excellent map of the canal topography.

in December 1863, leaks in the conduit necessitated shutting off the water. Before the repairs were finished, Washington and Georgetown with thousands of sick and wounded in the military hospitals faced a water famine. Fortunately when the system again went into operation in late July, in the midst of a three-month drought the water supply proved ample. Adequate pressure at street hydrants made fire fighting easier.[24]

Fire losses had run high in the preceding three years. Two severe fires occurred in August 1861 when all but one of the volunteer hose and ladder companies were on active military duty. In November the Washington Infirmary on Judiciary Square burned to the ground, and seven weeks later a conflagration of the pine board wagon sheds, stables, and fences around the Army corrals between 21st and 22nd Streets near the river sent frightened, stampeding horses bolting into the streets. The Quartermaster General thereupon purchased two steam engines to protect the Army repair shops six blocks beyond the White House and to safeguard the railroad "park" and warehouses in Swampoodle. After persuading the eight separate hose and hook and ladder companies to act under a single chief, in 1864 the city council set up a salaried fire department and bought it equipment. Yet in February 1865 fire destroyed most of the Indian paintings hanging at the Smithsonian Institution—all but a few of the portraits painted by Charles Bird King over a period of years when tribal chieftains were visiting the capital and John Mix Stanley's entire collection, which was still on loan to the government.[25]

While local taxpayers benefited from a federal police force, from the new water supply, and, less directly, from the Army fire engines, the damage done to the streets early caused the city acute annoyance and some financial anxiety. Heavily laden

[24] Rpt Sec/Int, 1864, pp. 697-99, Ser 1220; H Ex Doc 35, 38C, 2S, Ser 1223.

[25] *Star*, 2 Sep, 4 Nov 1861, 15 Apr, 9 Jun, 20 Sep 1862, 24 Jul 1863, 11 Feb 1864; ptn, S37A-H7, 27 Feb 1863; *Journal 61st Council*, pp. 212-14, 309-10, 418, and *62nd Council*, 15 Aug 1864, pp. 7-8; John C. Ewers, "Charles Bird King," *Rpt Smithsonian Institution*, 1953, pp. 463-73.

wagon trains jolting through the city and the hooves of thousands of horses, mules and cattle thudding by toward the Army corrals and slaughter houses cut the avenues and streets to ribbons; teamsters and cavalrymen riding on the sidewalks to avoid the muck in the roads demolished the footways too. Experience had shown that Congress was unlikely to appropriate money for repairs. A vote of 1864 approved sharing with the city the cost of work on streets adjacent to federal property, but no federal funds were forthcoming. Despairing property-owners along Pennsylvania Avenue hired sprinkling carts one summer to lay the dust and talked of engaging an engineer at their own expense to supervise paving, draining, cleaning, and watering the Avenue. Other than an amendment to Washington's charter authorizing the corporation to assess abutting property-owners for any street improvements, the only aid the government gave was in employing gangs of Negroes to patch the pot-holes on New York Avenue and an appropriation in 1863 for lighting the streets most essential to government transport. Because the Washington Gas Light Company rates were exorbitant, the city council requested congressional permission to organize and run municipal gas works; when that plea failed, the corporation abandoned attempts to light the streets properly as long as the war was going on.[26]

Shortages of materials together with high labor costs militated against undertaking any physical improvement during the war. Yet the war itself forced Washington to expand her white school system. In 1860 approximately 10,000 white children in the District of Columbia over six years of age had never attended a school; some 4,000 were enrolled in private schools and academies, about 2,800 in Washington's public schools, a few hundred in Georgetown's, none in the county. Consequently when Congress passed a law in 1862 requiring three months' schooling yearly for every child in the District between the

[26] Ptns, S37A-H7, 6 Jun 1862 and S38A-H6, 28 Nov 1863, 28 Mar, 30 Apr 1864, 3 Feb 1865; Rpt Sec/Int, 1864, pp. 685-86, Ser 1220; *Journal 61st Council*, pp. 136, 169-70, 348-49, 355, 366-67. The *Star* and the *Chronicle* carried almost weekly complaints about the condition of the streets.

ages of six and fourteen, whether white, black, or mixed, Washington's city council, while grumbling over lack of federal aid for so much as a high school, promptly increased the school tax and added a new levy for building schoolhouses. Georgetown and the county for the time being did nothing. Although the dollar capitation tax paid by men who actually voted at Washington's polls brought in less than $7,500 a year, the city school fund rose from $41,000 in 1862 to $64,000 in 1864.

In order to use to best advantage the $10,000 annual accrual from the new school building tax, Mayor Wallach appointed a special committee to map out a plan of action. The decision was to erect in each of the four school districts a building big enough to house several grades, an innovation that would simplify administration. Initially the money available limited the program to the purchase of one site and the construction of a ten-room schoolhouse on Pennsylvania Avenue southeast of the Capitol. When the new Wallach School opened on July 4, 1864, trustees, teachers, parents, and children quickly discovered the convenience of having ten separate classes under one roof. The building became a model for schools the country over. Although the Wallach School accommodated several hundred pupils, and the city tried to limit enrollment in any public school to children of "bona fide" residents of Washington, space was still lacking for three-quarters of the children of school age. The dearth of teachers was an even greater obstacle to expansion. Sixty-odd men and women, many of them only grammar school graduates, could not teach 10,000 children; with living costs rising steadily, the salary scale of $300 to $800 prevented recruitment of staff. During the war ditch diggers earned almost as much. Under these circumstances, compulsory school attendance was a fiction.[27]

[27] *Spec Rpt Comr Educ*, 1870, pp. 53-60, Ser 1427; *Star*, 25 Jan, 15 Apr, 4, 9 Jun, 8 Dec 1862, 11 Jul, 1 Dec 1863; *Chronicle*, 18 Nov 1862, 7 Jun 1864, 2 Mar 1865; *Journals 61st Council*, pp. 87-88, and *62nd Council*, 11 Jul 1864, p. 9; Samuel Yorke At Lee, *History of the Public Schools of Washington City, D.C., 1805-1875*, pp. 130-31.

Although demands upon the Washington Asylum and the Georgetown poorhouse increased as the war went on, and direct relief for the noninstitutionalized poor was a constant drain upon the cities' treasuries, federal funds allotted to the Washington Infirmary before it burned and paid over later to the sisters of the Providence Hospital continued to pay for the care of the bodily ill among transient paupers, and the Government Hospital for the Insane and the Kendall Green school for deaf, dumb, and blind children lightened municipal obligations. In 1862 Congress incorporated the Guardian Society to care for homeless children who had come under court supervision, while private philanthropists organized the Newsboys' Aid. Women volunteering their service to the hospitals did not think of that as charity; years afterward medical science would discover that in cleaning the maggots out of men's wounds these amateur nurses probably caused countless deaths. The Washington Young Men's Christian Association, nine years old when the war broke out, though a religious rather than a charitable society, helped newcomers to find decent places to live; and the YMCA reading rooms and library probably reduced the nightly population of Washington's barrooms. The most noticeable difference in charitable activities during the war as compared to the 1850's, however, lay in the energy expended on relieving the distress of freedmen, teaching the teachable to help themselves, and founding a home for destitute colored women and children. Through the persistence of Elizabeth Peabody of Boston, Secretary of War Stanton arranged to have the new colored home established in the house of Richard Coxe, a former mayor of Georgetown who had defected to the Confederacy.[28]

As municipal wants multiplied, so also did the cost of supplying them. But while prices of everything spiralled upward, new sources of city revenue remained few. In making the Washington & Georgetown Street Railroad Company a free gift of the

[28] *Cong Globe*, 37C, 2S, pp. 2825-26; *N.I.*, 11 Jun 1852, 12 Jun 1861; *Spec Rpt Comr Educ*, pp. 235-39; *Star*, 9 Dec 1861, 3 Mar, 21 Dec 1863; *Chronicle*, 17 Mar 1863.

right of way in 1862, Congress denied the cities the profits of selling a valuable franchise. On top of a federal income tax, local tax rates had increased by 1864 to $1.00 on every $100 of assessed valuation and even then brought Washington less than $420,000 annually, too little to maintain, let alone widen, community services and still pay out of current revenue over $100,000 in soldiers' bounties. Merely to extend the water mains into every section of the city would cost $1,000,000 at a time when water fees netted the corporation $14,000. To forestall still higher taxes, citizens raised money by private subscriptions for soldiers' bounties and the hire of substitutes. Still city revenues lagged so far behind needs that the council, at last shutting its eyes to the future, passed bill after bill for improvements without making provision to pay for them. In alarm Mayor Wallach asserted that the public works approved in the last year of the war would consume Washington's entire income for two years to come. Yet, he admitted, "We are wofully deficient in charitable and reformatory institutions." In view of the war boom then at its peak, federal officials showed little sympathy. On the contrary, the Secretary of the Interior declared that Washington had a lower tax rate and lighter obligations than any city he knew: no state government to support, few charities to maintain and virtually no courts to pay for; her dilatoriness about undertaking needed services, he argued, was a device for saddling the burden upon Congress.[29]

These municipal troubles were only pinpricks, however, as long as the Army of the Potomac, under McDowell and then McClellan, under Burnside, Meade, and then Grant, was fighting the Confederate Army in nearby Virginia and Maryland. Almost harder to bear were the periods of military inaction when, as one woman wrote, "our armies are doing nothing and our generals little else except quarreling among themselves. . . .

[29] *Journal 61st Council*, pp. 116, 347, 386, 398, and *62nd Council*, 1 Aug 1864, pp. 3-5, 31 Oct 1864, p. 12, and 20 Mar 1865, pp. 2-3; *Star*, 2 May, 21 Jun, 29 Jul 1862, 13 Nov, 3 Dec 1863; *Chronicle*, 5 Nov 1862, 23 Jul, 1, 3, 20, 22, 23 Sep, 14 Oct, 15 Nov 1864; Rpt Sec/Int, 1864, p. 13, Ser 1220.

Our future looks dark." From the secession of Virginia in April 1861 to General Early's raid in July 1864, fears for the safety of the capital rose and subsided and rose again at intervals. No one could forget that Washington was a main goal of the enemy, just as was Richmond for the Union. By 1862 forty-eight forts ringed the District; a clearing fifteen miles long and a mile and a half wide cut through the woodlands from the Eastern Branch above the Almshouse to the Potomac at the Chain Bridge formed a barricade of felled trees designed to prevent surprise attacks. But except for the wounded and ill, seasoned soldiers were few in the capital during much of the war; inexperienced militia and hastily organized companies of government clerks afforded thin protection. In the summer of 1864 when Jubal Early's men in gray marched through Silver Spring, Maryland, and advanced upon Fort Stevens, scarcely five miles above Boundary Street, only the arrival of the VI Army Corps rushed up from Petersburg seemingly kept Washington from capture.

Moreover, from the first battle of Bull Run to the end of the war and after, householders unable to perform more than minor services had to see thousands of soldiers no one knew how to save die of wounds and dysentery and typhoid fever. At times 50,000 men lay in the military hospitals within sight of the Capitol—"a population," Walt Whitman remarked, "more numerous in itself than the Washington of ten or fifteen years ago." Wounded men filled improvised wards in churches, in St. Elizabeths rooms at the Insane Asylum, in the halls of the Capitol, and at the Patent Office in passageways between ponderous glass cases crowded with miniature models of inventions. Carts carrying the dead nightly lumbered through the streets leading to the cemeteries, to Oak Hill, or Glenwood, or Mt. Olivet, or, after June 1864, to the newly dedicated Arlington National Cemetery across the Potomac on part of what had been General Robert E. Lee's plantation, where Confederate and Union dead shared the fields and wooded hillsides. In

Washington and Georgetown, as throughout the North, beneath anxiety for the Union and for the capital, beneath grief for the dead and the maimed, lay heavy fear for husbands and sweethearts, sons and brothers still fighting on the war's bloody battlefields.[30]

Yet amid the anguish of mind and spirit and the physical discomforts, the city enjoyed a wholly new material prosperity as the war went on. Commissary and Quartermaster supplies poured into the city month after month. The government put up new warehouses near the 7th Street wharves and built, bought, or leased accommodations for offices, hospitals, and workshops for repair of military equipment until, by mid-1862, real estate prices had become as inflated as they had been depressed in the first months of the war. Cattle pens and a slaughterhouse occupied the Monument grounds; Foggy Bottom was filled with wagon sheds and corrals for 30,000 horses and mules. Quartermaster General Montgomery C. Meigs commandeered for his headquarters the still unfinished Corcoran Gallery of Art next to the Blair House and established nearby the principal army clothing depot. From the cavalry depot at Giesboro Point, now part of Bolling Field of the Air Force, some 21,600 tons of forage were shipped monthly to the Army of the Potomac. The Baltimore and Ohio Railroad was choked with incoming freight, some of it supplies for the Bureau of Medicine and the twenty-five military hospitals in the area. To move matériel on promptly to the Army in northern Virginia, the government put to use the tracks on the Mall laid in the 1850's by the Alexandria and Washington Railroad, built a trestle just below the long Bridge to carry the rails across the river, and in 1863 permitted the company also to run its trains along the foot of the Hill into the Baltimore and Ohio

[30] Harriet Balch to her mother, 3 Mar 1863, Balch Mss (Bancroft Lib, U of Calif); *Star*, 14, 16, 20, 25 Jun, 1 Sep, 3 Nov, 7 Dec 1862; *Chronicle*, 14 May 1863; ptn, S37A-H7, 21 Feb 1863; Rpt QM Gen, p. 136, H Ex Doc 83, 38C, 2S, Ser 1230; Rpt Sec/War, 1862, p. 51, Ser 1159, and 1863, pp. 68-71, Ser 1184; *Prose of Walt Whitman*, II, 26, 42; Bruce Catton, *A Stillness at Appomattox*, pp. 263-66.

depot. In three and a half years more than 30,000 loaded cars passed over these tracks. The Navy Yard was employing 1,700 workmen by 1862 and built a new foundry the next year. Army contractors, men seeking special favors, and heavy-hearted men and women come to inquire for wounded relatives filled the hotels to overflowing; five hundred new arrivals a day came to be a commonplace.[31]

At first this sudden activity scarcely benefited local residents. Big firms in the North got most of the contracts for military supplies, and the rentals the government paid for buildings were not high initially. But as the war moved into its second year, northern businessmen began to buy Washington real estate at rapidly mounting prices, and new stores and hotels rose. When Philadelphians outbid local investors for a controlling interest in the newly chartered Washington & Georgetown Street Railroad and began running horsecars from the Navy Yard to Rock Creek and beyond, local men organized the Metropolitan Street Railway with tracks along F Street to the railroad station. The demand for food, lodging, household wares, and clothes sent prices skyrocketing. According to a newspaper correspondent, the landlords of the three largest hotels were clearing between $30,000 and $100,000 a year, and the war was enriching tailors, stationers, blacksmiths, saddlers, and local suppliers of mattresses and iron bedsteads. Harvey's "fish house" installed kettles for steaming oysters, and some 450 other restaurants and bars flourished. Liquor license fees ran to about $91,000 in 1863, whereas $10,000 had been normal before the war. "The inspiration of Northern ideas and industry," declared the *Chronicle*, was behind the boom; Washington's lackadaisical prewar leaders must not be allowed hereafter to blot out the effect of "Northern enterprise and thrift."[32]

[31] *Star*, 19 Aug, 5 Nov 1861, 6 Feb, 2 Mar 1862, 4 Apr, 14 Sep 1863; *Chronicle*, 5 Aug, 7 Sep 1863; S Ex Doc 17, 42C, 2S, Ser 1478; Rpts Sec/War, 1861, p. 72, Ser 1118, 1865, pp. 252-54, Ser 1249, and 1866, p. 5, Ser 1251; S Doc 220, 57C, 2S, Ser 4430.

[32] *Star*, 25 Nov 1863 quoting *New York Express; Chronicle*, 3 Nov 1862, 1 Jun 1863, 22 Feb 1864. See also city *Directories*, 1862-1865.

Expectations that much of this new business would vanish at the end of the war probably explain Mayor Wallach's reluctance to let municipal expenditures rise sharply. Yet the Metropolitan Police reported that population, apart from transients, had climbed to 140,000 before 1864, and Postmaster Lewis Clephane estimated that the 61,000 people he had to serve when Lincoln appointed him in 1861 had become in two years over a million if he counted the soldiers stationed in the immediate vicinity. Mayor Wallach himself boasted that, while manufacturing in most parts of the country had shrunk, "ours has increased in an almost inverse ratio." Clephane looked forward to seeing "the banks of the Potomac above Georgetown lined with manufactories worked by white labor." The hundred-foot drop in the water level between the Great Falls and Washington could furnish cheap power, and for the first time local banks might be ready to finance new industrial ventures. Riggs and Company had advanced a half million dollars to Army contractors in the first year of the war, Jay Cooke and Company had set up a banking house on 15th Street and, upon the passage of the National Banking Act of 1863, the First National Bank opened with $500,000 of capital and Henry D. Cooke, brother of the financial wizard, Jay, as its president; in 1864 the Merchants' National Bank got a charter, and in March 1865 the Bank of the Metropolis became the National Metropolitan Bank of Washington. Available capital, enormous power potential, and growing local demand all promised a future for manufacturing. Only skilled labor was scarce, and demobilization of the army eventually should meet that want.[33]

Not everybody profited. Skilled workmen commanded unheard-of wages, some of them as much as $3.50 a day, merchants with stock bought cheap could sell at huge markups, and people with real estate to dispose of made killings; but petty tradesmen without the credit to purchase goods at the right moment, common laborers, and people on salaries suffered. Families whose income had derived from the South or from

[33] *Star*, 5 Feb, 4, 9 Jun 1862, 2 Apr, 20 May, 30 Sep, 23 Dec 1863.

the hire of their slaves faced real want. When the government began to pay its employees in greenbacks instead of gold, until Treasury issues of one- and two-dollar bills appeared, tradesmen unable to make change were forced to accept the small notes issued by state banks, paper of depreciated or uncertain value. By the President's order, work on the Capitol had resumed in August 1861, an extension to the Treasury began in 1862, and over a two-year period the superintendent of the aqueduct needed day laborers, but seasonal layoffs, during which the cost of necessities rose ever higher, constituted a recurrent hazard for unskilled and semi-skilled workmen. Perhaps the pinch was still worse for gentle people who had never before had to earn their livings and for ministers, clerks, and teachers with fixed salaries and with appearances to maintain.

Military priorities and the loss of easy access to former sources of supply heightened inflation. Housing in Washington was at such a premium that in 1863 a number of "meritorious mechanics" moved their families across the Eastern Branch opposite the Navy Yard to build up Uniontown. Produce and coal, before the war shipped down the C & O Canal, across the aqueduct canal into Alexandria, and then back by barge to Washington, could no longer take that inexpensive route once the army had transformed the aqueduct canal into a military bridge; instead, cargoes had to be unloaded in Georgetown and carted thence into Washington, since Georgetown, in order to maintain her monopoly on canal traffic, had carefully built her bridges too low to give canal boats direct access to the river. Living costs drove citizens to try to form a Consumers' Protective Association for cooperative buying. Government employees at one point organized a Clerks' Emigration Society when investigation showed prices in Baltimore well below those in Washington; the difference between $940 a year for rent, food, and fuel in Baltimore and $1,333 in the capital pointed to the economy of commuting even at an annual cost of $125 for railroad fare. Reputable citizens fell behind on their taxes, and landlords had trouble in collecting their rents. In the summer of 1864 flour went up to $20 a barrel, potatoes to $5 a bushel, and butter to 70 cents a pound. Only the end of the war promised relief.[34]

Meanwhile fears lest the destructive forces of war blot out all concern for pure science troubled Joseph Henry. In 1861 he believed the Union doomed and the role of the Smithsonian imperilled. In fact the loss of money invested in southern securities sharply curtailed the endowment funds of the Institution. Desperately anxious to keep it free of "inauspicious connexions" with political entanglements, the secretary, after two or three unhappy experiences with abolitionist lecturers, refused to let any partisan group use the Smithsonian halls. In 1862, however, Henry grimly noted that "the art of destroying life, as well as that of preserving it, calls for the application of scientific principles and the institution of experiments on a scale of magnitude which would never be attempted in time of peace." The Smithsonian consequently, while endeavoring to carry on its normal activities, undertook some military research programs; the chemical laboratory developed a "disinfecting fluid" and Henry himself contributed his knowledge of gases, meteorology, and wind currents to assist the aeronauts of the short-lived Army observation balloon corps. Army doctors, in turn, quickly discovered the unequalled chances open to them to enrich medical science through observation of thousands of cases. From the records and statistics compiled by officers of the Medical Corps would come new research tools after the war, notably the Army Medical Library and Museum.

Unlike Henry, Dallas Bache saw immediately how to keep intact his scientific staff and use it for military purposes. Coast Survey teams accompanied troop units into the field and, with the collaboration of high-ranking Navy and Army officers, Bache prepared maps and data to ensure the success of coastal

[34] Ptns, S37A-H7, 17 Jan, 13 Feb, 27 Jun 1862; S Ex Doc 65, 37C, 2S, Ser 1122; *Star*, 1 Feb 1862, 12 Oct, 2, 3, 24, 25, 30 Nov 1863; *Sun Chronicle*, 29 Nov 1863; *Chronicle*, 5 Apr, 14 Jul, 31 Aug 1864, 7 Mar 1865.

blockades and amphibious operations in the South. Furthermore, upon the defection of Commander Matthew Maury to the Confederacy, the assignment of Commander Charles H. Davis to Washington opened up a new regime at the Naval Observatory. A trained mathematician who had had charge of work on the *Nautical Almanac* in Cambridge, Massachusetts, when the government launched that undertaking in 1849, Davis promptly reinstated Lt. James Gilliss as head of the observatory. Thenceforward astronomy rather than hydrography received first attention. Attracted by the challenge of the program, an obscure young man with a leonine head and an engaging manner came from Cambridge to join Gilliss' staff in 1861; the intellectual vitality Simon Newcomb brought to the task was destined to make the Naval Observatory in time one of the great scientific organizations of the country.

To Joseph Henry's astonishment, Bache and Davis enlisted the help of Senator Henry Wilson of Massachusetts and slid through a preoccupied Congress a bill creating a National Academy of Sciences in March 1863. That body of fifty eminent men seemed likely to enlarge the sphere of science in Washington. As it happened, the members met only once in the capital during the war and their services to the government were minor, but the Academy appeared to have large potentialities for peacetime. Although basic research made no headway, the preservation of scientific organizations and a certain amount of applied research accomplished as much as Washington's intellectual world dared expect.[35]

For most Washingtonians this bloodiest, bitterest war the United States ever fought changed every-day routines very little. Georgetown Seminary and Columbian College enrolled fewer students than formerly, but men not in the Army generally carried on their usual pursuits. On Sundays families attended church services, at times in makeshift quarters when the church buildings were in use as hospitals. On Saturdays mem-

[35] Dupree, *Science in the Federal Government*, pp. 127-48. For Henry's statement, see *Anl Rpt Smithsonian Institution for 1862*, pp. 13-14.

bers of the Washington Hebrew Congregation gathered in the synagogue opened in 1861. Children trudged to school, played noisily at home, roamed the streets, and when the circus appeared each summer crowded into the tents put up at the city limits. County farmers and their wives spread their chickens and garden truck out in the market stalls. Women ran their households and sewed for the men serving their country. Foreign ministers dined out and sent their governments dispatches estimating the Union's chances of survival. When the "Turkey Drivers" rode through the streets, each lancer carrying a twelve-foot black spear tipped by the small red pennant that gave the battalion its name, people cheered; but soldiers and even parades quickly came to be part of the familiar day-by-day scene. Sophisticated citizens snickered when "Professor" Scala led the Marine Band in playing the "Marseillaise" to welcome the imperial "Prince Napoleon" to Washington in 1861, but everyone missed the concerts when they ceased at Mrs. Lincoln's request after eleven-year-old Willie Lincoln died of typhoid fever. One of the stirring moments of those four long winters of war came on December 3, 1863, when, to the boom of cannon from every fort about Washington, Thomas Crawford's bronze "Freedom," hoisted by horses, ropes and pulleys, rose to her place on the crowning cupola of the new Capitol dome.[36]

Because anxiety and pain and death were omnipresent, people sought release in hectic gaiety. "Washington seems crazy," wrote a newcomer, "four and five parties in one evening seems the fashion. Last evening there was a 'Hop' at Willards . . . General Tom Thumb and wife were there. She is very beautiful, I understand only thirty inches tall, he thirty-two." Businessmen, visitors, soldiers on leave or convalescent, congressmen, departmental officials, occasionally the President himself, attended Ford's or Grover's or Nixon's or the National Theatre, where plays for every taste appeared—*Macbeth* and *Othello*, *Pocahontas*, the *French Spy*, *Napoleon's Old Guard*, or melo-

[36] *Star*, 5 Sep 1861, 2 Dec 1863; Ben: Perley Poore, *Reminiscences of Sixty Years in the National Metropolis*, II, 61.

drama like *Six Degrees of Crime* advertised as illustrating "with absorbing power, the progress towards ruin of INTEMPERANCE, LICENTIOUSNESS, GAMBLING, THEFT, MURDER, and the SCAFFOLD." The popular young John Wilkes Booth made his last formal stage appearance in Washington at Ford's theatre in *The Apostate*. Hotel barrooms, dance halls, and less reputable places, including doubtless some of the houses in Hooker's Division, catered nightly to a large clientele. The Burns' Club celebrated "Bobby's" birthday, and the Union Chess Club organized tournaments. Sporting men raced their horses along E Street near the old Congressional Cemetery and, when the police arrested them for reckless driving, opened a "trotting course" across the river adjacent to the Government Hospital for the Insane. Interest in baseball revived whenever Washington's star three-year-old team played on the old Potomac grounds. People flocked to the opera during its brief winter seasons and crowded into the Baptist church on 10th Street to hear Adeline Patti make her Washington debut.

"You'd be astonished to see what dresses ladies wear . . . light lavender silks, *tulle* bonnets looking as though a breath might blow them away," commented an Army wife. "One would hardly think we were at war, to see the crowds of well-dressed men and women flitting about."[37] Until grief over Willie's death led Mrs. Lincoln to withdraw from society as completely as possible, her elaborate gowns and jewels and extravagant mode of entertaining evoked endless gossip. At a White House reception in February 1862, Maillard of New York catered, decorating the tables with spun sugar helmets, American frigates, and goddesses of liberty. Rumor had it that the First Lady's dress cost $2,000. Indeed malicious talk and political intrigue marked most social occasions. Cabinet wives might recall the exchange between Mrs. Lincoln and the beautiful auburn-haired Kate Chase at the President's first dinner for his Cabinet; in response to her hostess's greeting, "I shall

[37] Harriet Balch to her mother, 10, 15 Feb 1863, Balch Mss. The newspapers were filled with notices about various sorts of entertainment.

be glad to see you anytime, Miss Chase," the ambitious twenty-year-old daughter of the ambitious Secretary of the Treasury replied: "Mrs. Lincoln, I shall be glad to have *you* call on *me* at anytime." Kate's marriage to millionaire Senator William Sprague of Rhode Island was a special event; the bride wore a "magnificent tiara on her head studded with diamonds." Her most envious detractors could not have foreseen that within a half dozen years her husband would have difficulty in wriggling out of charges of wartime treason or that she would end her days peddling chickens in the city where she had once held sway like a queen.[38] No one in a position of power was safe from oblique attack. People poked fun at the gullible head of the new Department of Agriculture who reportedly asked Congress for funds to buy two hydraulic rams because he had learned they were "the best sheep in Europe and we should by all means secure the breed." While critics of the President bristled with indignation or laughed in spite of themselves, Mr. Lincoln parried their thrusts with humorous home-spun stories. That Vinnie Ream, an unknown sixteen-year-old school girl, should obtain permission to model from life that bewhiskered, deeply lined face and massive head must have seemed to his enemies merely another wartime aberration.

Tales of international plots went the rounds, rarely impeded by exact information. When four vessels of the Imperial Russian fleet anchored in the Potomac above Alexandria rumors ran that these represented a threat or, conversely, Czarist help for the United States. Men angered by British dalliance with the Confederacy early in the war took pleasure in Lord Lyons' eventual recall, although it occurred three years after the British minister had brusquely demanded: "Passports or Mason and Slidell," a reference to the Confederate emissaries forcibly removed by an American naval vessel from a British ship on the high seas. In the absence of other excitement there was always speculation about how many peddlers of military secrets had escaped the vigilance of Colonel Baker and his secret service

[38] Thomas and Marva Belden, *So Fell the Angels*, pp. 3-4, 27-149, 241-350.

men or how many "petticoat spies" had successfully smuggled gold, drugs, or contraband whiskey across the lines under their ample skirts.[39]

With the fall of Petersburg and Richmond drawing near, March 1865 brought an easing of tensions. The lame duck session of the 38th Congress closed quietly, the 39th Congress would not convene before fall, and, while waiting for word that the Confederacy had collapsed, people in Washington let themselves relax. For the first time organizations of colored citizens took part in an inaugural parade. The inaugural ball held at the Patent Office turned into a lavish affair. The menu of sixty-five dishes included terrapin stew, "Filet de Beef," "Leg of Veal Fricandeau," grouse, pheasant, quail, "Patete of Duck en gelee," lobster salad, "Ornamental Pyramids: Nougate, Orange, Caramel with fancy cream candy," macaroons, almond sponge, "Tart a la Nelson," "Tarte a L'Orleans," "Bombe a la Vanilla," ice creams, ices, chocolate and coffee.[40] When early April at last brought news of the capture of Richmond, Washington embarked upon wild celebrations—illuminations, bonfires, speeches. And on the heels of that came Grant's communique telling of Lee's surrender at Appomattox Courthouse on Sunday, April 9. The end was at hand.

[39] *Star*, 6, 22 Feb, 11 Jul 1862, 13 Nov 1863; *Chronicle*, 29 Oct 1863; Poore, *Reminiscences*, II, 112, 138-41.

[40] *Chronicle*, 7 Mar 1865.

CHAPTER XI

CONTRABANDS, "SECESH," AND IMPENDING SOCIAL REVOLUTION, 1861-1865

ABRAHAM LINCOLN regarded preservation of the Union as the only reason for fighting a civil war; the extinction of slavery was not in itself an issue at all. In 1861 all shades of opinion were to be found among Washingtonians about the righteousness of a war to save the Union. An Alexander Bache, a B. B. French, a Richard Wallach less positively, and a host of less prominent men looked upon recourse to arms as an inescapable obligation. At the other extreme stood a Walter Lenox, who thought coercion of the southern states morally wrong, a form of tyranny that drove him before the year was out to leave his native city for Richmond. W. W. Corcoran, whose only daughter had married a Louisiana congressman, said nothing but, after shipping a million and a quarter dollars in gold to England in 1862, departed to Paris for the war's duration. Joseph Henry, though carefully avoiding any public statement, secretly believed the Union already doomed and bloodshed, therefore, worse than useless.[1] Consensus, on the other hand, during the first year of the war ran that the President's position was unassailable in declaring slavery and race questions not fundamental elements in the conflict. Yet, as time went on, few Washingtonians could fail to perceive that, whether or not they and the President wanted it so, the future of Negroes in America was inextricably intertwined with the more basic issue. Indeed by 1865 the status of colored people in the rebel states and in the District of Columbia seemingly had become as important to radicals in Congress as reuniting the nation.

In spite of Washingtonians' initial view, changes in the character of the city's population, brought about chiefly by the arrival of "contrabands," early interjected novel dimensions

[1] Thomas Coulson, *Joseph Henry: His Life and Work*, pp. 237-38.

into the community's racial picture. Weeks before the first battle of Bull Run, fugitive slaves from Maryland and Virginia in larger numbers than for years past were finding their way into the capital. Runaways from masters in Maryland, a state loyal to the Union, were still subject to arrest under the terms of the Fugitive Slave Law of 1850, but the most legalistically minded magistrate in the District of Columbia could see the impropriety of returning the property of rebels and the practical difficulties of sending fugitives back to Virginia. In June 1861 General Ben Butler, in command at Fortress Monroe, produced the formula for justifying the army's custody of runaways; they were "contraband."[2] Amused and relieved at so simple a legal evasion, the entire North adopted the term. But "contrabands" soon ceased to be a source of amusement to Washington. As the stream of black field hands, old men, women, and children trickled over the Long Bridge day after day and month after month, a series of new troubles confronted the federal government and private citizens. Slaves, accustomed to constant supervision, were rarely ready to fend for themselves. Someone had to attempt to find them employment, to house, feed, and clothe them until they could support themselves, to watch over their health lest they suffer needlessly or spread epidemics, and to prevent them from turning lawless.

Contrabands, termed by Secretary of State Seward "the property of the United States," were at first neither fugitive slaves nor free people. Protégés of the government though they were—"government pets" a southern sympathizer called them—until Congress passed a law in July 1862 expressly freeing them, they were not safe from arrest as runaways. If jailed on any pretext, a contraband was likely to be at the mercy of the new warden of the District jail, a notorious Negro-hater who reportedly sold more than one free colored man into slavery.[3]

[2] *N.I.*, 1 Jun 1861; S Misc Doc 2, 37C, 2S, Ser 1124; *Star*, 7 Apr, 19 May 1862.

[3] *Star*, 5 Dec 1861, quoting ltr, Sec/State Seward to General McClellan; *Star*, 4 Dec 1861, 16 Jan, 13 Feb, 22 May 1862; *Cong Globe*, 37C, 2S, pp. 412-13; H Rpt 11, 37C, 2S, Ser 1144; S Rpt 60, 37C, 2S, pp. 1-5, Ser 1125;

A Negro refugee from Virginia might have difficulty in proving that he was not a Maryland fugitive salable for jail fees when no master claimed him. Most Marylanders early in the war abandoned attempts to recapture their runaways in the District of Columbia, where mobs or Union soldiers undertook now and again to abduct slaves before the federal marshal could get them back to their lawful owners. Although that kind of disturbance largely ceased before the repeal of the Fugitive Slave Act in July 1864 and Maryland's adoption of a new state constitution outlawing slavery,[4] passions aroused over the place of colored people in the scheme of things contributed to the turmoil war imposed upon Washington.

If anyone was able to persuade himself that contrabands were merely a temporary phenomenon, certainly no Washingtonian questioned the permanence of the social change effected by a congressional act of April 1862 emancipating the 3,100 slaves owned by District citizens. The act ensured owners compensation and included a provision for colonizing freedmen outside the United States; nobody put faith in the colonization plan. While the bill was under debate, District householders, fearful of the timing, fought the main proposal with petitions and memorials, published letters and newspaper editorials. Mayor Wallach and the majority of Washington's councilmen besought Congress to delay legislation which at this "critical juncture in our national affairs" would convert the city, "located as it is between two slaveholding states, into an asylum for free negroes, a population undesirable in every American community, and which it has been deemed necessary to exclude altogether from some even of the non-slaveholding states."[5] The strongly pro-administration *National Republican* supported the bill on the grounds that Washington would benefit from "the free princi-

Diary of William Owner, 5 Apr 1862; *National Republican*, 14 Aug 1862; *Chronicle*, 15 Apr, 31 Jul, 1 Aug, 2 Sep 1863.

[4] *Republican*, 24, 28 Feb 1862; *Star*, 17, 22, 23 May 1862; *Chronicle*, 15 Apr, 13 May 1863.

[5] *Cong Globe*, 37C, 2S, App., pp. 347-48; *Star*, 19, 21, 25 Mar 1862; *Republican*, 20 Aug, 24 Sep 1862; ptn, S37A-H7, 2 Apr 1862.

ples and free industry which have built up the great cities of the North," but the *Star* and the *Intelligencer*, although favoring gradual emancipation, insisted it should be in conjunction with the border states, and both papers deplored the burden to be put upon local taxpayers to care for infirm and helpless ex-slaves. The *Star*, moreover, considered the compensation offered, $300 at most for each slave, wholly inadequate. Probably the *Intelligencer* summed up fairly the prevailing white point of view: no one would regret the end of slavery in the District were the act not plainly a first move toward congressional "regulation of society of the slave states."[6]

Emancipation in the District of Columbia marked the first break in sixty years in the protective wall about slavery. To the joy of the colored community, the repeal of the municipal black codes followed within a matter of weeks, thereby opening up new opportunities to enterprising Negroes. Colored men could now engage in any kind of business and several who had patrons on the Hill obtained government clerkships. Negroes, no longer impeded by a curfew, could occupy the "nigger heaven" at Grover's Theatre. Intelligent colored people, nevertheless, almost certainly foresaw that an inundation of black field hands from the South would create acute difficulties for all Washington residents.

Yet the pessimists of both races were not immediately proved right in anticipating serious trouble. Household slaves who had long lived in Washington and Georgetown in frequent association with free Negroes had learned something about the responsibilities of freedom; a few went North, some took service with army officers, and others apparently stayed on as paid servants to their former masters. The contrabands, on the other hand, were generally trained only to the hoe. Loath as they were to leave the District, where they felt sure of government protection, contrary to every expectation they were not at first a heavy financial burden upon the community. During 1862

[6] *Republican*, 15 Feb 1862; *Star*, 8, 17, 29 Mar, 4 Apr 1862; *N.I.*, 4, 12, 17 Apr 1862.

about four hundred lived in Duff Green's Row on East Capitol Street where seventy years later the Folger Shakespeare Library would stand. As the early comers moved out to live with other Negro families in Washington or found quarters of their own, new arrivals moved into the Row. Ignorant, penniless, ragged, dirty, and hungry on arrival, some of them never adjusted to the new mode of life, but until the number of contrabands ran into thousands, a good many of these ex-field hands, aided by the government and private philanthropy, got on astonishingly well.[7]

In March 1862, humane people in Washington and the North organized first a local and then a national Freedmen's Relief Association to furnish contrabands "clothing, temporary homes, and employment, and, as far as possible, to teach them to read and write, and bring them under moral influences."[8] Federal officials, moreover, saw that the government must undertake a systematic program for handling the multiplying throng. In June the Governor of the Military District of Washington appointed the Reverend D. B. Nichols, former head of the Chicago Reform School, to be superintendent of a "contraband department" with headquarters at an army barracks on the outskirts of the city at north 12th and O Streets. There contrabands registered and received passes to ensure them military protection. The government furnished them rations and employed the able-bodied men at 40 cents a day at the army corrals, at menial tasks in and about the military hospitals, or in repairing the avenues used for army transport. The Freedmen's Relief Association provided clothing and supplied food for the ill. When the military converted Duff Green's Row into a prison, the contraband department moved its charges to tents at "Camp Barker" adjacent to its own headquarters. Till the end of 1862 these arrangements sufficed, although the number of refugees grew from about 400 in April to some 4,200 in October. Nichols,

[7] H Ex Doc 42, 37C, 3S, p. 8, Ser 1189; *Republican*, 31 Oct 1862; *Star*, 30 May 1862.

[8] National Freedmen's Relief Association, *First Annual Report*, 1863 (hereafter cited as NFR Assn); *Star*, 22 Mar, 10 Apr 1862.

defending the work of his department, declared that all of his charges except a very few old and infirm had found work. Employers in the northern and western states were eager to hire these Negroes, but "not *one* in a *hundred* can in anywise be persuaded to go North."[9] He later added that they seldom saved their earnings, a few enjoyed idleness, and drunkenness was increasing, but they were generally "a docile people."[10]

By the spring of 1863, in addition to the 3,000 in Alexandria, 10,000 contrabands had gathered in Washington. And they continued to pour in: by 1865 some estimates put the four-year total of black newcomers at 40,000. In May 1863 the government opened a contraband village across the river in the bottomlands of Arlington west of the Alexandria Canal, where a thousand Negroes raised hay and vegetables for the army. A year later the contraband department persuaded about 3,000 more to move to the village from the northern sections of Washington. But most freedmen refused to budge from the District. Their ignorance of elementary hygiene coupled with the overcrowding in the government quarters or the housing they found for themselves rapidly converted whole areas of Washington into breeding spots for small pox and other disease.[11] Living conditions deteriorated steadily. Shanties sprang up in the alleyways, and, on the swampy land along the lower stretches of the Washington Canal, the clusters of huts pieced together from scrap lumber, tar paper, and odd bits of junk composed a slum that won the name "Murder Bay." "I have visited the freedmen in their cabins," wrote one man in the last year of the war, "their sufferings are most heart rending. The weather is cold; they have little or no wood. Snow covers the

[9] *Star*, 30 May, 24 Oct 1862; *Republican*, 21 Jul, 11 Aug, 31 Oct 1862; *Chronicle*, 3, 11 Nov, 1 Dec 1862.

[10] "Reports and Addresses," *Documents Relating to Freedmen*, 16 Dec 1862, pp. 9-11 (Howard Univ Library).

[11] NFR Assn, *1st Anl Rpt*, pp. 1-6; S Ex Doc 53, 38C, 1S, Ser 1176; *Chronicle*, 6, 7 Nov, 5, 9, 15 Dec 1862, 7 Jan, 19 Feb, 9 Apr, 14 Aug 1863, 31 May 1864, 2 Mar 1865; *Republican*, 3 Jul 1862; S Rpt 17, 38C, 1S, Ser 1178; Medical Society, D.C., *Report*, 1864; *Star*, 22 May, 31 Aug, 4 Dec 1863, 14 Jul 1864.

ground; and they have a scanty supply of rags called clothes. The hospital is crowded with the sick. . . . Government gives them a very, *Very* small allowance of soup. Ninety gallons was given yesterday; but what is that to feed thousands of families. . . . The feeling against them, among many in this place, is bitter malignant, devilish. . . . Many will die."[12] Many did die, exactly how many no record told.

While more than a few white Washingtonians were generous in their help, the kindness well-established colored families showed the newcomers was more remarkable, for the contraband invasion threatened the complete disruption of the well-ordered colored community. Throughout the South, a sociologist of mixed blood later wrote, "generations of distrust had built up a wall of enmity between the darker-skinned field hands and the favored mulatto house servants." That enmity had not appeared in ante-bellum Washington and Georgetown since virtually all slaves had been household servants except for the temporary gangs that "masters in distant places" hired out on construction jobs; and nearly half the free colored people of both cities had some white blood. Now alien blacks seemed about to engulf them all, as whites appeared increasingly prone to make no distinction between educated, responsible colored people and the mass of ignorant, often shiftless freedmen flooding in from the South. When Negro leaders from northern cities met in Washington to celebrate the eighteenth anniversary of the founding of the Grand United Order of Colored Odd Fellows, a military guard had to accompany the parade to "quell any outbreak."

The upper stratum of the Negro community struggled to preserve its position as best it could. In 1863 a group of colored men, some of them government clerks, organized the Lotus Club to which only leading Negroes might belong. White people and contrabands knew nothing about it, and yet its founding was a significant event in a city where, only twelve

[12] *The National Freedman*, I, 1 Mar 1865, p. 60.

months before, a curfew had interfered with all Negro social life. Insofar as the club's originators intended it to set a standard of civilized behavior, they fell short of their aim, for the very exclusiveness of the organization soon encouraged a form of unwholesome snobbery. The Freedmen's Relief Association congratulated colored Washingtonians for "contributing largely to [freedmen's] comfort from their slender stores," but the praise contained a note of condescension and failed to recognize the rapidly widening rift between upper and lower class Negroes.[13]

The predominant white attitude toward all colored people became increasingly hostile from mid-1862 onward. As the proportion of Negroes in the population rose, apprehensions grew about what Congress would next force upon Washington and Georgetown. The history of the preceding fifteen years and the report of the commissioners appointed by the President to handle the compensation of local slave-owners indicate clearly that citizens reluctant to have emancipation go into effect in wartime had nevertheless generally recognized the ultimate, if not the immediate, rightness of the law. But emancipation was only a beginning. After the repeal of the municipal black codes white people felt they had lost control of irresponsible blacks. Not infrequently the misdeeds of contrabands who used their new freedom to turn to thieving or worse were attributed to their law-abiding fellows; complaints against all Negroes multiplied. As early as July 1862 a congressional committee reported that with the disappearance of the legal barriers established by slavery, "the prejudice of caste becomes stronger and public opinion more intolerant to the negro." White supremacy, a phrase not as yet coined, had been a basic social premise too long to be discarded quickly and painlessly. Government protection could not guarantee black people toleration. Hoodlums attacked Negroes on the least provocation or none. The Wash-

[13] Pauli Murray, *Proud Shoes, The Story of an American Family*, p. 53; *Star*, 5 Jun 1862, 9 Oct 1863; *Chronicle*, 6 Jun 1864; NFR Assn, *1st Anl Rpt*; enumerators' returns, Free Inhabitants, D.C., Seventh U.S. Census, 1860, NA.

ington and Georgetown Street Railroad Company refused to permit them to ride inside its cars until Congress threatened to revoke its charter.[14] New colored school laws and the enlistment of colored troops crystallized the resentment of white people.

The law enacted in May 1862 that required Washington, Georgetown, and the county to open public schools for Negro children initially offended the community but then went down rather easily. As the 58 percent illiteracy among free colored adults before the war climbed to an undetermined figure after the freeing of slaves and the influx of contrabands, white people could admit the wisdom of helping Negro education, if only because an ignorant colored population, no longer restrained by the black code, might be a danger to society. By the terms of the law, 10 percent of the taxes on Negro property was to be set aside to finance colored schools under the supervision of a separate board of trustees to be appointed by the Secretary of the Interior. The colored schools were thus legally under federal control, although the money was to come from local taxes. Congress, apparently persuaded that Negro property in Washington and Georgetown was extensive, expected the arrangement to produce some $3,600 yearly, enough to start a primary school system. Neither city, however, kept separate records of white and colored taxes; officials merely allotted what they thought just to the trustees of the colored schools—Washington $265 in 1862 and $410 in 1863, Georgetown nothing in 1862, $70 the next year. No white taxpayer had to feel alarmed over those sums.[15]

The American Tract Society of New York had started a free school for contrabands in the spring of 1862. Soon afterward the National Freedmen's Relief Association had opened two evening schools and eighteen months later a day school on the

[14] *Star*, 22 May 1862; H Rpt 148, 37C, 2S, Ser 1145; Rpt Sec/Int, 1863, p. 726, Ser 1182.

[15] *Star*, 20 May, 9 Jun 1862; *Cong Globe*, 37C, 2S, p. 1854 and App., pp. 356-57; H Misc Doc 48, 38C, 1S, Ser 1200.

Island; by early 1864 association volunteers were teaching five Negro classes in church basements and halls. That March the trustees of the colored schools, having accumulated money enough to engage a teacher at $400 a year, opened the first colored public school in the Ebenezer Church, southeast of the Capitol. A hundred adults and children immediately tried to enroll, but one teacher and an inexperienced assistant, unable to handle so many, had to turn some away. Philanthropic groups then redoubled their efforts. Government employees offered to teach evening classes, and in the course of a few weeks nearly eight hundred colored adults and children were learning to read. By summer the newly formed Association of Volunteer Teachers of Colored Schools reported 32 persons sharing the teaching of 12 classes.[16] Privately sponsored schools, however, did not build the tax-supported system Congress had instructed the city corporations and the levy court of the county to establish.

The second colored school law, enacted in June 1864, put teeth into the first: each city was to pay over to the colored schools the same proportion of the total school funds as the number of Negro children between the ages of six and seventeen bore to the number of white children; to ease the financial strain, the federal courts of the District were to pay into the school fund all money accruing from fines and forfeitures, a quarter of it to the colored schools of the county, a quarter to the cities' colored schools, and a quarter each to Washington and Georgetown white schools.[17] If some enlightened residents admitted the necessity of prodding the corporations into action, many more taxpayers indignantly dubbed the act unwarranted coercion, an interference foreshadowing other forms of arbitrary social regulation of loyal Union supporters.

Their anger was not entirely groundless. From the Ordinance

[16] H Misc Doc 48, 38C, 1S, Ser 1200; NFR Assn, *2nd Anl Rpt*, 1864, p. 4; *Star*, 24 Dec 1863; *Chronicle*, 7 Jan, 6 Feb, 8 Jul 1864; *Spec Rpt Comr Educ*, 1870, pp. 223-29, Ser 1427.

[17] *Cong Globe*, 38C, 1S, App., pp. 196-98.

of 1787 onward, federal land grants had helped support public schools in the territories and states, but Congress had never contributed a penny to common schools in the District of Columbia. The trustees of the colored schools themselves observed in 1864 that the propertyless new freedmen increased educational needs without adding to the cities' revenues.[18] Colored people's taxes in Washington, according to judicious local estimates, amounted to 2 percent of whites', the colored school population to perhaps 50 percent of the white. Washington spent yearly a fifth of her revenues for public education, and still the 36 classrooms of 1862 could accommodate only a fraction of the city's children. Among those who attended, furthermore, were children of federal employees who paid no local taxes. The sums henceforward obtainable from fines promised to be a drop in the bucket that Washington and Georgetown taxpayers must fill. Citizens felt, and with reason, that senators and representatives were enacting legislation for an unrepresented area that they would not dare propose for their home states and leaving the local community to pay the costs of educating black people who were properly a federal charge.[19]

The city council consequently continued mere token payments to the Negro schools—in 1864-1865 only $628 out of a total school fund of $25,000. At the end of the war colored schools in the county still existed only on paper. Everywhere in the District indignation flared out at Congress and at hypercritical temporary residents without stakes in the community. And indeed, many a northerner who would later return home tended to display a self-righteousness coupled with a sentimentality about the virtuousness of all Negroes that infuriated Washingtonians who knew that it would eventually fall to them to construct a stable social order. Anger burned hottest of all at the intended beneficiaries of the congressional acts, for property owners believed that but for the contraband invasion

[18] H Misc Doc 48, 38C, 1S, Ser 1200.

[19] *Star*, 9 Jun 1862; *Chronicle*, 23 Jul 1863; *Journal 63rd Council*, p. 188; *Spec Rpt Comr Educ*, pp. 268-69.

the District would have escaped many problems that peace would not solve.[20]

The decision in the spring of 1863 to recruit Negro troops was a second, though short-lived, irritant in race relations. The plan grew out of the difficulties of meeting the local quota of volunteers in 1862. Washington's council had voted $50,000 for bounties, $50 for each man enlisting, but bounty jumping and "a stampede among the foreign element," had run the costs up; the price of substitutes in November 1862 rose as high as $1,000 a man. As the 1863 draft became imminent, official disapproval of enlisting Negroes therefore yielded to expediency. Whites who were not themselves responsible for raising the draft were horrified, evidently fearful lest colored troops inspire "uppityness" in all colored people. Although recruiting agents reported encountering "serious and sometimes violent opposition," before mid-1863 two companies of colored troops were mustered in and encamped on Analostan Island, once the home of James Mason, a former slave-owning United States Senator from Virginia and later Confederate emissary to Great Britain.[21] The island location protected the recruits from white hostility, but demonstrations against colored civilians occurred more than once. Hatred of colored people, the *Star* observed that summer, was growing. Only the lag in recruitment of the District's draft quota, 3,863 men to be drawn from 19,327 males between the ages of 20 and 45, wore down the objections of whites. By 1864 "substitute brokers" offering a bounty first of $30 and later of $150 a man were advertising for colored recruits and, according to later accounts, with official connivance were taking Negro prisoners from the county jail to fill the quotas.[22] All

[20] *Star*, 25 Jan, 22, 27, 28 May, 3 Jun 1862; *Journal 62nd Council*, 27 Mar 1865, p. 2.

[21] *Star*, 29 Jul, 7, 9 Aug 1862, 22 May 1863; *Journal 63rd Council*, p. 189; *Chronicle*, 5 Nov 1862, 8, 16 May 1863; Baltimore *Sun*, 16 May 1863; H Rpt 80, 38C, 1S, Ser 1206.

[22] *Star*, 16, 18 May, 10 Jun, 18 Jul 1863; Baltimore *Sun*, 23 May, 4, 5 Jun 1863; *Chronicle*, 30 Jul, 2 Oct, 12 Dec 1863, 25 Apr, 1, 9, 20 Sep, 14 Oct, 15 Nov 1864, 1, 3 Mar 1865; H Rpt 23, 38C, 2S, Ser 1235.

told, in the course of the war the District furnished to the Union forces 3,269 colored and 13,265 white men.[23]

The number of colored soldiers recruited supplied an argument for Negro enfranchisement. In the spring of 1864 a petition to Congress signed by 2,500 colored men quoted the Declaration of Independence and stated that "a large portion of the colored citizens of the District are property holders," which was unfortunately, as the colored school trustees' statement indicated, a palpable exaggeration. "The experience of the Past teaches that all reforms have their opponents; but" the petition concluded, "apprehensions of evils rising from reforms founded, in justice are scarcely, if ever realized."[24] Congress tabled the petition.

Not only the upper ranks of the Negro community but most white citizens suffered from the sudden changes brought in the wake of the contrabands of war. Certainly the shift in white attitudes from acceptance of Negroes as servants to dislike and undefined fear of them as future fellow citizens contributed to the worsening of relations with Congress. Although the Senate tabled the petition for Negro enfranchisement, among leaders of the Republican party the conviction was manifestly growing that suppression of the rebellion, because it meant eradication of the slave power, also meant new status for Negroes. Hence, little by little the idea gained ground that anyone devoted to the Union cause must endorse a program of rights for colored people in the capital. From this premise radicals apparently reached the conclusion that anyone prepared to uphold the doctrine of white supremacy in the District of Columbia was probably anti-Union. The evidence is inferential, to be read between the lines of public pronouncements and newspaper comment. To have voiced that opinion openly on the floor of House or Senate would have alienated moderates throughout the North and en-

[23] Rpt Sec/War, 1863, pp. 55, 134-36, Ser 1184; Rpt Board of Colored Troops, in Rpt Sec/War, 1865, p. 58, Ser 1249; Dyer's *Compendium*, p. 11; Final Rpt Provost Marshal Gen, in Rpt Sec/War, 1865, pp. 69, 78, Ser 1251.

[24] Ptn, S38A-H3, 15 Apr 1864; *Journal 63rd Council*, p. 380.

raged the border states, and in 1864 the war was not yet won. Yet nothing except honest belief or partisan pretense that local antagonism toward Negroes was an expression of secret secessionist sympathy seems to explain the mounting hostility in Congress toward the people of Washington and Georgetown. Late in December 1864 an overwhelming majority of the Senate voted an inquiry into the desirability of forcing every local resident to take the "iron clad" loyalty oath.[25]

Suspiciousness of Washingtonians had taken root in Congress before the Republican administration came into power. The accusations of greed and ineptitude brought by senators against the city in the late 1850's may have prepared the ground; beyond question the conspiracy tales told during January 1861 fostered doubts about the community's loyalty. After the firing on Sumter, those doubts were deepened by the hesitation of the District volunteers to enlist for unlimited service, and, after the secession of Virginia, by the early departure to the South of several eminent local property owners and by the stream of army and navy officers who left to join the Confederate forces. Walt Whitman's description of the scenes in Washington immediately after the first battle of Bull Run represents a not untypical northern interpretation of local attitudes. The furor over the new loyalty oath that August and Mayor Berret's pompous attempt to put the dignity of his office above the needs of national security as Congress saw them increased resentment on the Hill. Thereafter the lengthening list of resignations or dismissals from government service and the number of arrests in Washington for real or suspected sedition fastened the label "secesh" upon the city's residents.

The capital in fact was a "hotbed of secession," but intemperate members of Congress and constituents in distant places apparently let themselves hold local citizens responsible for the disloyalty of all people who had held office or lived here.[26] Yet

[25] *Cong Globe*, 38C, 2S, pp. 91-93.

[26] *Ibid.* The article on Whitman in the *Dictionary of American Biography* raises the question of his presence in Washington in the summer of 1861.

who was a local citizen? In addition to families who had lived in Washington for years but kept formal voting citizenship in one or another of the states, the capital of the Civil War era contained an indeterminate number of residents without strong local ties. The extension of the municipal franchise in mid-century to any white man who had lived in a ward of Washington or Georgetown for a year and then an 1863 amendment reducing the residence requirement from twelve months to three heightened the confusions. A District citizen might be anybody who had drifted into the area for evil purposes or good, stayed for a few months and decamped if trouble threatened him. The boasts of southern newspapers in 1861 that Confederate sympathizers lined the northern bank of the Potomac automatically blackened the cities' reputation in the North. Of the people arrested in Washington for seditious talk or deeds during the war only a very small percentage had been listed as residents in the 1860 *Directory*. Declarations of devotion to the Union sounded empty to prejudiced ears, and countless patriotic deeds were so quickly forgotten that even the partisan *National Republican* protested the belittling of the services of the District volunteers.[27] To northern communities, people *in* Washington, however temporarily, tended to become synonymous with the people *of* Washington, and thousands of Americans evidently came to associate every act of sedition in the capital, regardless of the perpetrator, with its "traitorous" citizens. Long after the assassination of Lincoln in 1865, Washington and Georgetown had to endure the anger of a nation that felt itself betrayed by its protégés.

That where there's smoke there must be fire was so generally accepted a maxim that succeeding generations would rarely question its application to Civil War Washington. The flaws in that form of logic would first become evident to many an American during the McCarthy era ninety years later. Wash-

[27] *Star*, 8 Aug 1861, quoting Richmond correspondent to the Memphis *Argus*; *Republican*, 31 Jul 1862; ptn, S37A-H7, 28 Mar 1862.

ingtonians, indignant at the disparagement of their patriotism, were particularly incensed at a law enacted in May 1862 requiring voters challenged at the polls in city elections to take the loyalty oath or lose their votes. The *Intelligencer*, which ordinarily eschewed comment on District affairs, wrathfully called the act unwarranted discrimination against citizens who had abundantly proven their loyalty and, in proportion to their numbers, supplied more soldiers to the Union army than had many of the states. While the city council ruled that public school teachers must take the oath, Mayor Wallach contented himself with stating that, all allegations to the contrary, "our city is true to the principles that made the capital of the greatest nation on earth." Having estimated that about 600 men from the District, among them several prominent in ante-bellum Washington, were serving in the Confederate army, in 1862 the *Star* upheld the propriety of special acts to protect the capital from "secessionist sympathizers and agents," but a year later the *Star* also was taking offense at the impugning of the loyalty of the city as a whole.[28] Not improbably the social position many of the defectors had once commanded accounted for the tarring of the entire community. By 1863 the bulk of the evidence indicates that most southern sympathizers were in jail or had departed to more congenial climes, leaving the District to Unionists, to professional spies from the South, to a few elderly householders clinging to the past, and to several gangs of contraband runners interested only in the money to be made in trade with the enemy. Yet at one point whispers ran that even Joseph Henry was guilty of treachery: the man who refused to permit abolitionist lectures at the Smithsonian was signalling the enemy from its turrets while pretending to be conducting meteorological experiments. General McClellan told a local mass meeting in May 1863: "I have never thought that sufficient justice has been done to the citizens of Washington in . . . regard to your

[28] *Cong Globe*, 37C, 2S, App., p. 355; *N.I.*, 2 Apr 1862, 21 Apr 1863; *Star*, 20, 22, 31 May, 3 Jun, 2 Aug 1862.

loyalty but history will do you justice as your own consciences do now."[29]

The *Daily Morning Chronicle*, owned by Clerk of the Senate John Forney, appointed itself the scourge of the community. The *Star* angrily rebuked the newer paper for accusing Washingtonians of professing pro-Unionism merely for the sake of feathering their nests. The Baltimore *Sun* in turn scoffed at the *Chronicle's* contention that Washington voters wanted only "secesh" in the City Hall; naturally they preferred to elect men long known in the city: new arrivals were too prone to be "pro-colored" to find favor. Forney, however, unflaggingly portrayed Washington as a city virtually captured from her rebel inhabitants and thus properly subject to all the punitive measures the Union army employed in the South; instead of refusing to accept newspapers as "witnesses and public rumor proof" of collaboration with the enemy, the United States Attorney General should waive legalities and immediately confiscate the "vast amount" of rebel property in Washington.[30] As Forney had obtained for his newspapers the advertising of government departments and published the only Sunday paper in the capital, he had a certain amount of official backing and large financial resources; just or otherwise, he had influence in high places. When Confederate troops under General Early swept up to Washington's outer defenses in the summer of 1864, the *Chronicle* declared the raid showed "a very considerable proportion of the population here and in Georgetown . . . cognizant of, longing for, and many of them facilitating, the coming of the rebels."[31] Such an accusation was not to be dismissed lightly, for if it truly reflected the view on the Hill, Congress might seek a terrible revenge. The Senate plan introduced in December 1864 to exact the "iron clad" loyalty oath of every District citizen might be a mere foretaste of greater indignities to come.

[29] *Star*, 16 May 1863.

[30] *Ibid.*, 11 May, 2 Jun 1863; Baltimore *Sun*, 2 May 1863; *Sun Chronicle*, 25 May 1862; *Chronicle*, 1, 18, 22 Dec 1862, 21 Jan, 30 Apr, 2 May, 1 Jun 1863; H Ex Doc 32, 37C, 3S, Ser 1161; Poore, *Reminiscences*, II, 127.

[31] *Chronicle*, 18 Jul 1864. See also n.25.

Whether Washingtonians who had thought Lincoln's election a national disaster in 1860 still looked upon him as their Nemesis in the early spring of 1865 is a matter of conjecture. Presumably many of them were able by then to put faith in the words of his second inaugural: "With malice toward none; with charity for all . . . let us strive on . . . to bind up the nation's wounds, . . . to do all which may achieve and cherish a just and lasting peace among ourselves, and with all nations." Hopes rose during the next few weeks that vindictiveness would not prevail. During the five days following the news of Lee's surrender at Appomattox, it was enough to know that the bloodshed would soon be over. On the night of Good Friday, April 14, the President, yielding to his wife's insistence, went to see *Our American Cousin* at Ford's Theatre. There John Wilkes Booth's murderous shot turned thankfulness into sorrow and new anxiety.

Washington had lived through threats of betrayal and seizure, through physical hardships and travail of spirit. Old residents had felt wrath over vilification by radical Republicans, dismay at the influx of freedmen, and alarm at the portents of the future. Yet probably no Washingtonian realized how completely the war had swept the old life away. Clouds of suspicion not quickly to be dissipated by peace enveloped families once honored as among the best of the South. Money made during the war gave prominence to men hitherto obscure. Alexander Shepherd, for example, in 1861 a gasfitter's assistant, would soon emerge as a power in the city, one of four proprietors of the *Evening Star*, possessor of a farm in the county valued at $65,000, and owner of considerable real estate in Washington. New Yorkers and Philadelphians, having gained control of the local banks and the principal street railway, now overshadowed native capitalists like W. W. Corcoran and his associates. A community formerly made of "Society," including a handful of scientists and amiable high-ranking army and navy officers, but otherwise chiefly composed of small tradesmen, clerks, artisans, white day laborers, free Negroes and slaves had become largely a city of rich men and poor, "niggers," "nigger-lovers," and "nigger-haters." Citizens resentful of the social revolution thrusting in upon them would fight further change, but the old Washington was gone forever.

That late April morning as the sixteen-foot, black-velvet-draped hearse drawn by six gray cavalry horses moved slowly down Pennsylvania Avenue toward the Capitol, where Abraham Lincoln's body would lie in state before beginning the journey through the cities of the North and on to Springfield, Illinois, men watching the procession and hearing the muffled roll of the drums sensed only dimly that they had come to the end of an era.

CHAPTER XII

RECONSTRUCTION AND RESISTANCE, 1865-1868

IN April 1865 knowledgeable Washingtonians felt sure that if radical Republicans like Ben Wade of Ohio, Charles Sumner of Massachusetts, and Thaddeus Stevens of Pennsylvania were in a position to dictate reconstruction policy, they would treat the District of Columbia like enemy territory. If that realization heightened distress at Lincoln's assassination, the horror in the city was none the less genuine. The day Lincoln died, the city council voted a $20,000 reward for the assassins' arrest—eloquent testimony to the strong emotion of the financially hard-pressed corporation. Shortly thereafter the council issued an angry warning to former citizens who had supported the rebellion not to attempt a return to the District, a statement modified a week later to express confidence in President Johnson and readiness to leave decisions on amnesty to him. Once the panic about a Confederacy-inspired, city-wide conspiracy had died down, evaporating under proof that the plot was the work of a half-dozen "outsiders," not even Secretary of War Stanton, who had taken command the night of the shooting of the President and the simultaneous attack on Secretary of State Seward, accused the city of negligence; the Provost Marshal's guard and the Metropolitan Police were federal employees outside municipal control. Yet the murder cast long shadows upon the community. Heavy-hearted residents set about raising a subscription for a memorial statue of Abraham Lincoln to stand in front of the City Hall, but meanwhile the killing of John Wilkes Booth and the hanging of three of the conspirators—as well as the almost certainly innocent, mousy little roominghouse-keeper, Mrs. Surratt—did little to dispel anxiety.[1]

Demobilization of the army provided distraction for a time.

[1] *Journal 62nd Council*, 15 Apr 1865, pp. 2, 3, 6, 8 May 1865, pp. 14-15, 18-24, and 15 May 1865, pp. 4-5.

In the forty days between late May and early July, nearly a quarter of a million soldiers passed through the capital. Hour after hour, through the brilliant sunshine of May 23, the Army of the Potomac, rank after rank, paraded up Pennsylvania Avenue to the reviewing stand in front of the White House. Thousands of school children stood on the slope below the north doors of the Capitol, each child wearing a red, white, and blue rosette and carrying a miniature flag, while school banners marked "Welcome Heroes of the Republic, Honor to the Brave," swung in the breeze. Years later Washingtonians who had been part of that throng of children remembered the breath-taking moment when the flower garland flung to Colonel George Custer startled his horse and sent it rearing and plunging down the slope until the gallant rider, his long yellow locks streaming out behind him, brought his mount under control. The next day came Sherman's veterans of the march through Georgia, followed by the notorious "Bummers" who had attached themselves to the Division of the Mississippi and by long strings of mules and horses laden with tents, knapsacks, clothing and an occasional pickaninny. Cheering crowds from every state in the North lined the Avenue. Perhaps few onlookers, observing the lean hardness of these soldiers, could recall the youthful gaiety of those who had set out for Bull Run less than four years before. The military hospitals, crowded during much of the summer, emptied slowly, until by late autumn only two, given over to stubborn and chronic cases, remained. In November came the execution of Captain Henry Wirz, one-time commanding officer at Andersonville prison and originator of the infamous "deadline"; the outcome of his trial had been a foregone conclusion, but the torchlight parade staged to celebrate the hanging in the Old Capitol prison yard revealed the savagery of the tempers that might rule in Washington.[2]

By December, when Congress convened and debates on reconstruction opened, the troubles of the District of Columbia

[2] Rpt Sec/War, 1865, p. 102, Ser 1249, and pp. 894-96, Ser 1250; H Ex Doc 23, 40C, 2S, Ser 1331; Poore, *Reminiscences*, II, 187-92; J. O. Wilson, "Eighty Years of the Public Schools of Washington," CHS *Rec*, I, 144-46.

were looming large. Three problems so closely related as to be virtually one confronted the community. The most basic was economic: how to halt and reverse the decline in business by developing new commercial and industrial interests. The second, the status of Negroes, affected not only the material well-being but the social and political structure of both cities. The third was how to supply Washington and Georgetown with the urban conveniences northern city-dwellers had come to demand—easy transportation, well-paved, well-lighted streets, adequate sanitation, good schools, and effective protection of persons and property—but all without raising taxes to levels that would discourage new investment. Yet to be dilatory about undertaking these improvements would be to invite a decision in Congress to make a fresh start by establishing the national capital in the West.

The shrinkage of business began at the very moment when men returning to civilian life most needed jobs. Hotel registrations no longer ran to hundreds daily. Employment at the Navy Yard and in the Quarter Master repair shops dropped precipitously. Local suppliers, who reportedly had all found war a bonanza, were now forced to curtail. In attempt to halt further losses a group of businessmen formed a Board of Trade, while old residents anxious to keep green the memories of the city of the past founded the Oldest Inhabitants Association. The federal Bureau of Refugees, Freedmen and Abandoned Lands, established in March 1865, was concentrating on finding work for freedmen, but the unemployed blacks thronging Washington's streets were constant reminders that further social changes might come.[3] Perhaps the best gauge of the business decline was the loss reported by the Washington and Georgetown Street Railroad Company for the second six months of 1865.

[3] Rpt Sec/Navy, 1865, pp. x, xxv-xxvii, Ser 1253; Rpt Sec/War, 1865, pp. 19, 88-89, 252-53, 622-27, Ser 1249; Ledgers, James Topham, 1860-72, Mss (CHS); *Chronicle*, 13, 25, 27 Oct 1865; Rpt Asst Comr Freedmen's Bureau, S Ex Doc 27, 39C, 1S, pp. 151-55, Ser 1238; S. N. Clark to Brig Gen C. H. Howard, 31 Mar 1866, D.C. file, RG 105, N.A. (All Freedmen's Bureau Reports and correspondence hereafter cited as F.B., and, unless otherwise noted, located in D.C. file, R.G. 105, N.A.).

Instead of the 9 percent profits of the two previous years, the company declared that, owing to the dwindling population, receipts between July and the end of December had fallen off 30 percent and, although equipment was up-to-date and the horsecars had carried over seven and a half million passengers during the year, the company was barely solvent. Deficits appeared in the next several years.[4] In 1866 the Merchants' National Bank failed. Spared the tribulations of Alexandria in trying to recover from four years of military occupation, the District cities had to consider the possibility of fresh confusion if Congress were to reannex the Virginia part of the original ten-mile square, as Lincoln had urged in 1861 and some Alexandrians were now requesting.[5]

Happily, fears of further business reverses proved groundless. The plan of reclaiming northern Virginia for the District lapsed, and, had Congress acted upon the proposal, it would probably have injured only Old Dominion pride. In Washington the rapid enlargement of the force at the Government Printing Office and the expanding functions of the Department of Agriculture, for which a new high-shouldered, mansard-roofed building would begin to rise on the Mall in 1867, helped offset the reduction in army and navy activities. During 1866, furthermore, war claims filed by both northerners and southerners again began to bring visitors to the capital. At the same time the President's temperate policies permitted the return of former citizens who had left in 1861 to serve the Confederacy. W. W. Corcoran, who for two and a half years had kept the ocean between him and his war-torn country, met with a surprisingly cordial reception upon his return. Walter Lenox had died in a federal prison; Richard Coxe whose Georgetown house had been turned into a home for destitute colored women and children was unable to reclaim his confiscated property until 1868; and a score or more of other leaders of the ante-bellum community who had sided with the South faced similar

[4] H Misc Doc 69, 39C, 1S, Ser 1271; H Misc Doc 158, 40C, 2S, Ser 1350.
[5] *N.I.*, 12 Jan 1863; *Cong Globe*, 37C, 1S, p. 420; S Ex Doc 1, 37C, 2S, p. 12, Ser 1117.

troubles. Yet the economic aftermath of the war proved far less damaging to most families than had at first seemed likely.

House-building gradually resumed; row houses sprang up in the section east of the Capitol, and several well-to-do senators bought or built residences in the more sophisticated northwest areas, along Massachusetts Avenue and K Street beyond 13th. Speculators began to purchase land on Meridian Hill north of the city, and a number of families of limited means built houses farther out in the Mt. Pleasant area. Since business was always briskest when Congress was in session, the protracted fights between the White House and the Hill during most of President Johnson's administration benefited tradesmen by keeping senators and representatives in Washington long months at a time.[6] Whether or not men accepted Mayor Wallach's thesis that natural developments, not "adventitious causes," were restoring prosperity, the building of a new YMCA and a Masonic Temple on 9th Street in 1867 marked a return of confidence in the city. That year showed a population of 106,052, a big drop from the estimated 140,000 of 1864, but still a 57.8 percent increase over 1860. Only 89,451 persons, including about 30,000 Negroes, listed themselves as permanent residents, but as long as Congress ignored the overtures of western cities to move the capital to the Mississippi Valley, Washington's prospects looked bright enough.[7]

Local enterprise, as in years past, had relatively little to do with the improvement. It derived primarily from the expansion of government business and from the steps Congress took to encourage better transport. Businessmen had recognized the importance of railroads since the mid-fifties, but the disasters that befell the Alexandria & Washington Railroad Company had instilled wariness in local investors: let Congress make the

[6] See n. 1; ptns, S39A-H3, 14 May, 11 Jun 1866; *Cong Globe*, 39C, 1S, 5 Jul 1866, pp. 3577-81, 40C, 2S, p. 4093; John Pickett to Charles T. Helm, 14 Apr 1866, Letterbook, 1861-67, Pickett Mss; Baltimore *Sun*, 25 Oct 1867; Henry Latham, *Black and White*, p. 94.

[7] *Spec Rpt Comr Educ*, 1870, pp. 28, 37, Ser 1427; *Journal 65th Council*, pp. 34-35; *Star*, 4 May 1867.

first move. Congress did. In 1865 it chartered the Metropolitan Branch of the B & O which would shorten by some forty miles the distance by rail from Washington to the Ohio Valley. The city council talked of buying $500,000 in bonds of the road to hasten construction; the proposal came to nothing for the very good reason that the municipality had neither cash nor credit to invest. Nevertheless, the work moved on rapidly; in 1869 a train would make the six-mile run to Silver Spring in eighteen minutes. Meanwhile, although the tracks laid during the war on a trestle below the Long Bridge still crossed into northern Virginia and the government kept control until 1867, a successor to the defunct Alexandria & Washington Railroad Company was obviously going to have to finance and operate the road. To Washingtonian's delight, in 1868 the Baltimore & Potomac Railroad, a newly formed affiliate of the powerful Pennsylvania, began building a line to enter the city by way of a bridge over the Eastern Branch. Not until 1870 would the new company obtain from Congress a formal grant to the right of way and the use of the tracks over the Potomac to connect with Virginia railroads, but in the interim the imminent termination of the B & O's 33-year rail monopoly in the District and the gradual elimination of tolls on wagon roads between the city and the county gratified the local public.[8]

For part of the white public, however, the new social order Congress sought to impose upon the community soured the sweets of prosperity. Citizens had long realized that the District of Columbia, where state laws and constituents' preferences could not interfere, was likely to serve the Republican party as a proving ground for legislation later to be applied to the country at large. Just as a federal act had wiped out slavery here nearly nine months before the Emancipation Proclamation had ended it in the rebel states, so a postwar constitutional

[8] *Sunday Chronicle*, 2 Nov 1863; *Star*, 14 Feb 1869; *Journal 62nd Council*, 13 Mar, 1865, p. 2; H. W. Schotter, *The Growth and Development of the Pennsylvania Railroad Company*, pp. 86-87; William B. Wilson, *History of the Pennsylvania Railroad Company*, I, 333-40; S Doc 220, 57C, 2S, Ser 4430.

amendment would forbid it throughout the United States, but whether the northern states would ratify amendments carrying political and social innovations further was problematical. Distasteful to many a white Washingtonian as was the prospect in 1865 of having to accept the Negro as a fellow citizen, the strong possibility of having federal law force racial equality exclusively upon the District of Columbia was far harder to swallow. Aware that thousands of contrabands were determined to stay permanently within the federal area, white taxpayers might have shouldered with a semblance of grace the economic burden of a greatly enlarged, ignorant black population, had they felt certain of keeping social and political control. For that they were prepared to fight as best they could.

Washington's city council knew in the autumn of 1865 that a bill proposing Negro suffrage in city elections would come before the 39th Congress as soon as it convened in December. In November a committee of the common council had drafted a statement of the city's official view:

"The white man, being the superior race, must . . . rule the black. . . . Why he is black and we white, or why we the superior and he the inferior race are matters past our comprehension. It, then, becomes a civil as well as a Christian duty to weigh his capacity for advancement in civil rights, and the only test by which his claim to the right of suffrage can best be ascertained will be by a comparison with the white race under like circumstances. . . .

"If it took the ancient Briton a thousand years to emerge from his only half-civilized condition . . . to reach the point to qualify him for the exercise of this right, how long would it reasonably take the black man, who but about two hundred years ago was brought from Africa. . . ." Observing that some colored men had increased in intelligence and might qualify for suffrage, the councilmen nevertheless declared "that not one grown-up Negro in a hundred can read or write" and that "more forcible means exist why ladies of a given age should be entitled to the privilege." The United States was a white man's country;

let the dissatisfied colored man go elsewhere. "Already does there exist among the laboring men in our midst, a deep-seated hostility because employment is made more scarce by their [Negroes'] great influx into this city since the rebellion began, and a trivial circumstance will be made a pretext for collision."[9]

The council discarded an alternative statement: "That we are not opposed to granting the right of suffrage to colored men *simply because they are colored men*, but that we believe the safety of our free institutions demands that the elective franchise should only be granted to men who can read or write" or to those who, "*without regard to color*," possess mental and moral qualifications acceptable to an enlightened public.[10]

A month later Benjamin Wade, a determined defender of the Negro, presented his franchise bill in the Senate. Some 2,500 Negroes headed by John F. Cook, son of the distinguished educator and Presbyterian minister, petitioned Congress to enact the bill; Mayor Wallach immediately checked the names on the list and reported only 573 taxpayers among the signers. The president of the board of aldermen, in answer to the frequently heard Negro argument that colored men who had served in the army had every right to vote, insisted that the District's first colored regiment had been recruited, not by voluntary enlistment, but by kidnapping carried on by Negro agents. "Of the Negroes residing here in 1861 and 1862, . . . not one hundred entered the service of the United States, but those who did go were refugees and contrabands who came here to seek bread and who were taken possession of by men of their own color, and sold into the service of the United States."[11] In mid-December Washington and Georgetown each conducted a referendum. In Washington the outcome was 6,591 against, 35 for, Negro suffrage, in Georgetown 465 against, no one in favor. The vote was small, and some citizens labelled it unrepresentative. Sayles J. Bowen, postmaster of Washington and later mayor, believed

[9] *Journal 63rd Council*, pp. 313-16.
[10] *Ibid.*, p. 318.
[11] *Ibid.*, p. 380, and *65th Council*, p. 9; *N.I.*, 18 Dec 1865.

the referendum invalid because the assessors registered only men they wished to see vote; "experience has proved that a fair election cannot be held in this city." And the *Star* fulminated: "The ballot box at the special election doubtless received many ballots from fingers that pulled rebel triggers."[12]

The House debate on the bill began in January 1866. A minority protested the proposal as a tyrannical imposition upon an unwilling people. Representative Thomas, pointing out that he himself had worked and voted for emancipation in Maryland, argued that congressmen from northern states where the proportion of Negroes was small should not pass upon a problem with which they had no first-hand experience.[13] But the abolitionist wing of the 39th Congress and men of more political acumen than scruples held the floor. A speech of George Julian of Indiana, an idealist, a proponent of woman suffrage, a land reformer, and usually a man of sound judgment, revealed the temper of the radicals. After asserting that District Negroes owned property worth "at least $1,225,000," supported twenty-one churches, twenty Sabbath schools, and thirty benevolent and civic organizations, had furnished three full regiments to the Union Army, and supplied 60 to 70 percent of the men for the drafts, Julian concluded:

"I have argued that the ballot should be given to the negroes as a matter of justice to them. It should likewise be done as a matter of retributive justice to the slaveholders and rebels. According to the best information I can obtain, a very large majority of the white people of this District have been rebels in heart during the war, and are rebels in heart still. That contempt for the negro and scorn of free industry which constituted the mainspring of the rebellion cropped out here during the war in every form. . . . Meaner rebels than many in this District could scarcely have been found in the whole land. . . . Congress in this District has the power to punish by ballot, and there will be a beautiful, poetic justice in the exercise of this power.

[12] *Star*, 23 Dec 1865; *Chronicle*, 16 Dec 1865.
[13] *Cong Globe*, 39C, 1S, pp. 261-63; H Rpt 2, 39C, 1S, Ser 1272.

. . . The rebels here will recoil from it with horror. . . . To be voted down by Yankee and negro ballots will seem to them an intolerable grievance, and this is among the excellent reasons why I am in favor of it. . . . Nor shall I stop to inquire very critically whether the negroes are *fit* to vote. As between themselves and white rebels, who deserve to be hung, they are eminently fit."[14]

In the Senate a counterproposal, fights over modifications to the original bill, and the excessive heat of that June of 1866 combined to delay action. Lot Morrill of Maine wished precedence for a bill revoking the two cities' charters, returning their powers to Congress, and thus eliminating all local suffrage, both white and black. When that plan was dropped, he and several supporters urged a literacy qualification for every male except taxpayers and returned soldiers; 19 nays to 15 yeas defeated the amendment. In order to prevent a pocket veto of the original bill, the Senate chose to let the final vote wait till the next session.

In December 1866, nineteen months before ratification of the 14th amendment, the bill for unrestricted manhood suffrage in the District went through quickly. President Johnson's message pronounced the measure premature and, in view of local sentiment, unjust; many of the men who voted for Negro enfranchisement here would not have advocated it at home. Connecticut, Minnesota, and Wisconsin had already refused to let colored men vote, and Kansas, Ohio, and Michigan would soon forbid it. A majority in Congress, however, looked upon Andrew Johnson as an intolerable obstructionist. House and Senate overrode the veto the day after it reached Capitol Hill. A by-product of the struggle was the shelving of the President's proposal to give the District representation in Congress.[15]

Omission of a literacy qualification from the suffrage act threatened the District cities with several thousand new voters who, if elated at the prospect of sharing white men's political

[14] *Cong Globe*, 39C, 1S, pp. 256-59.

[15] *Ibid.*, 39C, 1S, pp. 3191, 3432, 39C, 2S, pp. 303-14, and App., p. 9.

privileges, still were unfamiliar with the obligations of citizenship. At least two-thirds of the colored men in the District had been slaves only three or four years before, and as slaves had been denied education. Now as freedmen they were little better qualified for political responsibility than as slaves. Small wonder that intelligent white women at times marvelled at the vagaries of a Congress which enfranchised ignorant male contrabands and refused educated white women votes. Forebodings rose during the spring of 1867 when some 9,800 white and 8,200 colored men registered to vote in Washington's municipal election.[16] Yet contrary to gloomy expectations, colored voters under the guidance of Negro leaders displayed discretion; not until June 1868 did they elect Negroes to office.

Neither congressional law, nor the Freedmen's Bureau, nor public-spirited educated Negroes, however, could greatly lighten the immediate miseries of freedmen. Ill-prepared to earn a living in a competitive world, contrabands who had had jobs of sorts during the war found themselves out of work when the army demobilized, the corrals shut down, and the military hospitals closed. The Freedmen's Bureau during 1865 turned army barracks into tenements for about 350 families, issued weekly rations of food and fuel, and now and again found jobs for some of the able-bodied, but need constantly outran what that bureau could supply. Relief societies and individuals contributed food, clothing, medicines, and even rudimentary lessons in housekeeping. The Association for the Relief of Destitute Colored Women and Children found homes in the North for a few contraband orphans and, after the official pardon of the rebel whose Georgetown house had served as the orphanage during the war, moved its charges to a farm in the county near Kendall Green. In eleven months the recently opened Freedmen's Hospital treated 22,798 Negroes and reduced the death rate among patients to less than four per hundred.[17] Neverthe-

[16] See Table III; Bryan, *Capital*, II, 563, n. 3.

[17] Rpt F.B., H Ex Doc 11, 39C, 1S, pp. 16, 24, 36-39, Ser 1255; Rpt Asst Comr F.B., S Ex Doc 6, 39C, 2S, pp. 35-42, Ser 1276; ptn, S39A-H3, 24 Jan 1866; S Misc Doc 14, 39C, 2S, Ser 1278.

less, according to a Washington councilman, official records showed that "of these people who have migrated to this District between the first of January 1862 and the first of January 1866, more than a third are already in their graves." And in early 1867 an observant Englishman, writing of the country-wide situation, noted: "Mortality has been so great that some [white men] have predicted a solution of the difficulty in the disappearance of the whole colored race in the next fifty years."[18]

In Washington thousands of freedmen lived in utmost squalor. Some of them occupied hovels near the river below L Street on the Island; others crowded into "Adams shanties" east of the Capitol; in 1866 in "Fredericksburg" on Rhode Island Avenue 213 persons lived in a space 200 feet square. "Murder Bay," located on land where the buildings of the Departments of Commerce and Labor would later stand, was still more notorious. "Here," reported the Superintendent of the Metropolitan Police, "crime, filth and poverty seem to vie with each other in a career of degradation and death. Whole families . . . are crowded into mere apologies for shanties. . . . During storms of rain or snow their roofs afford but slight protection, while from beneath a few rough boards used for floors, the miasmatic effluvia from the most disgustingly filthy and stagnant water . . . renders the atmosphere within these hovels stifling and sickening in the extreme. . . . In a space about fifty yards square I found about one hundred families, composed of from three to ten persons each, . . . living in shanties one story high . . . and from five to eight dollars per month are paid for the rent of these shanties except . . . where a ground rent of three dollars per month is paid for a few square feet—there some of the more enterprising have erected cabins of their own. There are no proper privy accommodations. . . . Nor can the sanitary laws be properly enforced against delinquents, for they have no means wherewith to pay fines and a commitment to the workhouse is no punishment."[19] An officer of the Freedmen's Bureau

[18] *Journal 65th Council*, pp. 711-27; Latham, *Black and White*, p. 270.
[19] *Cong Globe*, 39C, 1S, pp. 1507-08.

spent four months and used 1,000 barrels of lime in whitewashing freedmen's quarters, but disinfectant, though forestalling city-wide epidemics of typhoid and dysentery, ended neither overcrowding nor unsanitary living conditions. The once half-empty, sprawling city of "magnificent distances" had suddenly acquired slums as horrifying as those of New York.[20]

Men in charge of the Freedmen's Bureau employment office tried in vain to persuade former field hands to take the jobs that farm labor shortages in other parts of the country opened to them; even a threat to strike from the relief rolls the names of those who balked at settling on farmland across the Eastern Branch failed to move them out of the capital. Indeed, so far from an exodus, during 1866 and 1867 a fresh influx of freedmen poured in. Hundreds of them qualified as voters in June 1867. Nor was misery confined to contrabands. A widely travelled Quaker woman declared "the suffering and the poverty of the poor of this city in excess of anything she had seen anywhere else on the face of the globe." Congress chartered the Freedmen's Savings and Trust Company in order to encourage thrift among colored people who might be able to get their heads above water, but the plight of the utterly helpless continued to receive greater attention on the Hill. Authority vested in the Freedmen's Bureau to convert additional government-owned buildings into low rental tenements for freedmen of "good character" promised at first to offer substantial relief, but "good character" meant to bureau officials people who would pay their rent promptly, keep their homes clean, and live by the moral code of whites. "No persons professing to be husband and wife," read one regulation, "will be permitted to occupy a tenement until they give satisfactory proof of lawful marriage."[21] Freedmen without jobs could not pay their rent, fami-

[20] See n. 17; H Ex Doc 142, 41C, 2S, pp. 29-30, Ser 1417; J. N. Vandenburgh to F.B., 20 Oct 1866, W. W. Rogers to Lt. Col. S. M. Beebe, 1 Apr 1867, and C. H. Howard to Miss Lowell, 4 Apr 1867, and to Sayles J. Bowen, 14 Jul 1868, F.B. files.

[21] J. W. Bushong to F.B., 10 Oct 1865, S. N. Clark to Rev. Roberts, 27 Mar 1866, circular ltr, 1 Oct 1866, and F.B. to Supt. O. S. B. Wall, 24 Jul 1868, F.B. files.

lies living in overcrowded quarters and ignorant of the elementary principles of hygiene soon turned their tenements into filthy shambles, and former slaves who understood cohabitation rarely understood the legal formalities of marriage. Patient teaching and opportunities to earn a living manifestly offered the only way out of the wilderness through which, Henry Ward Beecher declared, all must pass "who travel from the Egypt of ignorance to the promised land of civilization."[22]

An adequate colored school system would hasten that journey. At the end of the war Mayor Wallach announced Washington's readiness to remit to the trustees of the colored schools the entire amount Negroes paid yearly in taxes, but he stated flatly that the city could not do more and still support "the thousands of colored forced upon the city by the General Government." In the summer of 1866 Congress authorized the use of empty army barracks for Negro schoolrooms, appropriated $10,000 for building schoolhouses for colored children in the county, gave three lots for a similar purpose in Washington, and, without extending any help to the white schools, empowered the trustees of the colored schools to sue the cities for the principal and 10 percent interest on the money long overdue.[23] Still both city corporations procrastinated. Indeed so far from welcoming any federal contribution, however small, most council members came to resent congressional aid to Negro education as a form of discrimination against whites.

In the autumn of 1865 a polite but forceful letter from Mayor Wallach to the Secretary of the Interior reviewed the historical facts of what President Washington, with the full endorsement of Congress, had pledged in the 1790's to the city-to-be in return for title to more than half the land involved; the mayor's figures then indicated how far short of redeeming its promises the federal government had fallen since it sold the last of the federally owned lots in the city in the mid-1850's. The presenta-

[22] *Journal 65th Council*, pp. 711-27.

[23] *Journal 63rd Council*, pp. 182-89; *Spec Rpt Comr Educ*, pp. 259-60.

tion was convincing. While aldermen and councilmen repeated the theme, the Secretary of the Interior supported Wallach's plea for federal aid. Congress remained obdurate, refusing to admit the propriety of appropriations for sewers or street repair, for direct relief of impoverished whites or for grants to white as well as colored schools. City officials thereupon chose to defy the congressional mandates. The chain of reasoning apparently ran thus: since the District had no spokesman in Congress, only constant agitation would keep local problems before the national legislature; once the cities accepted the colored school laws the issue would die, inasmuch as newcomers in Congress, unfamiliar with the District's history and present troubles, were unlikely to bother with revisions of legislation of no national significance. Unfortunately anger warped Washingtonians' judgment. George Julian's speech on Negro enfranchisement pointed to the punitive character of recent laws for the District, laws seemingly inspired by belief in the wickedness of local people whose anti-Negro sentiment, rooted in the doctrine of white supremacy, proved them all rebels. At city council meetings the pleas for moderation urged by men who believed in Negro rights and in the wisdom of cooperating with Congress consequently fell on deaf ears; indignation got the upper hand.[24]

Unwise and ungenerous as this defiance was, the die-hards marshalled statistics to defend their position. Freedmen's Bureau records, a councilman averred, showed nearly a third of all District children to be colored, whereas the value of Negro property, but a seventieth of white, brought in "very little in excess of a sum sufficient to meet the burdens their presence imposes upon society here." Another man asserted that in contrast to the 8 percent of New York's annual municipal income spent for schools, Washington spent 20 percent, more than any other city in the United States; he characterized the authors of the local school laws as "locomotive philanthropists," wealthy

[24] Rpt Sec/Int, 1865, pp. xxiii, 855-69, Ser 1248; *Journal 63rd Council*, p. 146, and *65th Council*, p. 14.

TABLE V

SPECIAL CENSUS OF 1867[a]

	WASHINGTON	GEORGETOWN	COUNTY	TOTAL
Total population	106,052	11,793	9,145	126,990
White population	74,115	8,509	5,703	88,327
Colored population	31,937	3,284	3,442	38,663
White children ages 6 to 18	17,801	2,152	1,494	21,447
Colored children ages 6 to 18	8,401	894	951	10,246
% Negro children of all children	32.1	29.3	37.4	32.3
Av. attendance in white public schools	4,631	362	356	5,349
Av. attendance in colored public schools	2,415	333	323	3,071
Av. attendance white private schools	4,717	635	—	5,352
Av. attendance colored private schools	232	—	—	232
% white children in public school of total white children	26.	16.8	23.8	24.9
% Negro children in public school of total Negro children	28.7	37.24	33.9	29.9
Teachers, white pub. schools	89	8	8	105
Teachers, Negro pub. schools	49	8	7	64
% illiteracy among whites over 20 yrs				2.66
% illiteracy among Negroes over 20 yrs:				
unable to read				45.7
unable to write				51.9

[a] *Spec Rpt Comr Ed*, pp. 5-9, 15-76, Ser 1427. The figures on illiteracy are computed from the tables listing the number of inhabitants of every age between one and twenty-one, and from the total illiteracy figures given on pp. 30, 42, 76.

men seeking national prominence but indifferent to the welfare of the ignorant impoverished children in their own states.[25] Mayor Wallach, in 1867 throwing discretion and conciliation to the winds, observed sarcastically that Congress, "in its zeal for education" had given "to states and other territories, 78,130,-

[25] *Journal 63rd Council*, pp. 412-17, App., pp. 3-15, *64th Council*, pp. 376-78, 395, 432-33, 442-43, and *65th Council*, pp. 663-69.

000 acres of public land, which . . . would yield the enormous sum of $97,662,500, [but] to the District of Columbia, which is supposed to be under the fostering care of the general government . . . and whose people it now inordinately taxes to educate the thousands of contrabands allured to this 'paradise of freedmen' by the temptation to indolence offered by the gratuities of the Freedmen's Bureau, it has never given a foot of land or a dollar of money." And the school board reported that 34 percent of the pupils attending the white public schools were the children of government employees; in a city of 20,073 families 10,050 taxpayers were bearing the cost of educating the children of temporary non-taxpaying residents.[26]

Still the unequal fight with Congress could not last forever. Because the 1860 census data were clearly inapplicable to the postwar District, and more reliable figures on the relative numbers of white and colored children would be more useful than name-calling in determining a just division of school funds, in the fall of 1867 Mayor Wallach and Mayor Addison, Henry Barnard, the newly appointed federal Commissioner of Education, and Charles Nichols, head of the Government Hospital for the Insane and president of the county levy court, jointly requested a special census calculated to show "the wants of the local government." Congress approved, though it made no appropriation to cover the expenses. Directed with scrupulous care by Franklin B. Hough, the skilled statistician who had directed the New York State census of 1865 and who later took charge of the federal census of 1870, the District census of 1867 turned into far more than an enumeration of school children. The final report, running to more than 900 closely printed pages, included comparative data on public schools in Europe and in other American cities, a history of education in the District since its beginning, and a wealth of detailed information ranging from analyses of occupations to tables showing where residents voted—altogether a more elaborate compilation

[26] *Journal 65th Council*, pp. 28-30; School Trustees, *22nd Anl Rpt*, 1867, p. 28; *Spec Rpt Comr Educ*, pp. 40-44.

of facts and figures on social conditions than any decennial census had ever assembled. If the essay on the history of Negro education in Washington and Georgetown presented a somewhat uncritical eulogy of Negro achievements and the figures on Negro illiteracy in 1867 were too low, the findings nevertheless were sufficiently illuminating to serve the primary purpose of the survey. Georgetown immediately paid over the sums due the colored schools, and Washington agreed to remit $34,000 of the $51,000 the trustees claimed.[27]

Of the facts the special census brought to light perhaps none was more surprising than the evidence that a larger percentage of colored children than of white were attending the public schools. The federal figures collected three years later would show 75 percent of Negro adults unable to write, instead of the 52 percent claimed in 1867, but, even allowing for exaggeration in the local census, the record was astonishing, inasmuch as over three-fifths of the colored population had come from southern states after 1861. For the extraordinary progress of Negro schooling in the District of Columbia the Freedmen's Aid societies and the federal Freedmen's Bureau could claim most of the credit; they had supplied most of the teachers and kept interest in the school crusade alive in the North. In January 1866, some 100 men and women were teaching about 5,600 colored children in 54 day schools; 25 Sabbath schools had enrolled over 2,300 pupils; and another 500 children were attending the "eight or ten self-supporting schools taught by colored teachers." Six months later the Freedmen's Bureau reported 10,000 Negroes receiving some instruction. By 1868 northern philanthropists concluded the Negro education program so well established that it no longer needed their help; all but one group withdrew their aid.[28]

Congress, moreover, acting upon the request of General

[27] *Journal 66th Council*, pp. 543, 558-60, 629; S Ex Doc 20, 41C, 3S, pp. 4-5, Ser 1440; *4th Rpt F.B.*, 10 Oct 1868, p. 10, in *Documents Relating to Freedmen* (Howard Univ).

[28] S Ex Doc 56, 40C, 3S, Ser 1360; Williston Lofton, "The Development of Public Education for Negroes in Washington, D.C., a Study of Separate but Equal Accommodations," pp. 143-44 (Dissertation, American Univ., 1943).

O. O. Howard of the Freedmen's Bureau and some of his friends, chartered Howard University in 1867 and voted it an annual appropriation thereafter. Private gifts and student tuition fees of $3 a term supplied other funds. Although Baptist money had enabled Wayland Seminary to open in 1865 to train Negroes for the ministry, Howard University, the first university south of the Mason-Dixon line to be expressly dedicated to bi-racial education, seemed to its founders to mark the path to racial peace. Several of their sons enrolled in the first classes along with young Negroes.[29]

Richard Wallach and lesser city officials found little inspiration in those developments. Instead of setting themselves vigorously to the task of showing outsiders that Washingtonians could meet a challenge, the city fathers sulked. They concluded that without federal assistance they could not afford to increase the school budget, and $168,000 would not stretch to engage additional trained teachers, pay higher salaries, or build new schoolhouses. Much the same dreary story was repeated in other realms of municipal administration. In 1866 the city spent $75,000 on carting earth and muck dredged from the Washington Canal to fill some 3,000,000 square feet of the "White lot," the marshy land below the White House, but when Congress showed no readiness to share the costs of laying down a city-wide sewer system, further work came to a halt. Indeed as federal property abutted on the Mall side of the canal, any plan to use that waterway as a sewer main required congressional approval and some federal money. Here was an illustration of a difficulty about which Councilman Alexander Shepherd had protested during the war: the city charter vested in the corporation too limited powers to carry out "imperatively necessary" improvements.[30] His observations might have applied equally to the entire time span of the local municipal government. While army engineers and private citizens presented various

[29] Abstract of Circular Relative to Howard University, 1867, #20, Appendix F, F.B. files; *Cong Globe*, 39C, 2S, App., p. 1992.

[30] Rpt Sec/Int, 1865, pp. xix-xx, Ser 1248; *Journal 61st Council*, p. 25, and *64th Council*, pp. 9-11; *Cong Globe*, 39C, 1S, p. 4157; S Ex Doc 35, 39C, 1S, Ser 1238.

recommendations on how to proceed, Washington's sanitary condition worsened steadily. At the same time to pour gravel into the "fearful canals of mud" that constituted the streets was manifestly futile, but to hard-surface thoroughfares before laying sewers would be folly. Schools, sewers, and paving thus remained a trio of troubles which the city must somehow resolve unless she were to sink permanently into a state calculated to inspire Congress to move the capital elsewhere.

Yet recognition of the dilemma merely multiplied impolitic municipal complaints about congressional parsimony. Local officials forgot that federal money founded the Columbia Hospital for Women and Lying-in Asylum in 1865. Equipped with 50 free beds, 20 of them for wives, widows, and daughters of soldiers and sailors, the hospital opened in 1866; its modest charges—$10 a week at most—or none at all and its out-patient dispensary made better medical care possible for white women than even well-to-do families had had at their disposal in the past. Congressional appropriations for the school for the deaf and dumb and for the insane asylum, now coming to be known as St. Elizabeths, similarly appeared to drop out of the reckoning of people with chips on their shoulders. They took for granted the $30,000 voted to complete the Providence Hospital, where sisters under a contract with the Surgeon General would nurse the ill among transient paupers. Disappointment was natural that Congress contributed only sparingly to the expenses of the Guardian Society and to the House of Correction for Boys which private citizens opened in 1866 and maintained on a farm above Georgetown. And the women who started the Industrial Home School in 1867 had in turn some reason to think the federal government should take larger financial responsibility than it did for an undertaking designed to forestall juvenile delinquency by keeping boys off the streets and giving them some vocational training.[31] Although, as some Washingtonians must have remembered, in the days of amicable rela-

[31] H Rpt 34, 40C, 2S, Ser 1357; *Cong Globe*, 39C, 1S, p. 4117; ptns, S39A-E4, 5 Apr 1866, and S39A-H3, 25, 30 Jan 1867.

tions between city and Hill, local charities had been a matter for the local community, a majority of the city corporation in the early postwar years persisted in blaming Congress for the gaps in municipal services.

Congress, as a body an impersonal entity, was a convenient target. No local critic felt obliged to name names. In a city that had bristled with indignation at indiscriminate charges labelling all Washington unregenerate "secesh," mayor and councilmen now dubbed Congress as a whole guilty of attempting to turn the capital into a Negro paradise at the expense of the whites.

In actuality the 39th Congress, after passing the Negro suffrage act in early January 1867, paid little attention to the District of Columbia, and the 40th Congress was soon too engrossed in the impeachment of President Johnson to heed the buzzing of bluebottles in Washington's City Hall. As the trial opened in March 1868, the drama staged in the Senate chamber absorbed every politically minded person in the capital and, in fact, drew hordes of visitors hopeful of obtaining tickets to the galleries. Certainly no local measure would receive careful consideration until the President's fate was settled. In mid-April Washingtonians dedicated their memorial to Abraham Lincoln. President Johnson's acquittal came in late May. Meanwhile, as Washington's twenty-year city charter was about to expire, Congress hastily renewed it but only until the District committees of House and Senate could explore alternatives. In the eyes of the rest of the country the city's affairs were only a tempest in a teapot. Postwar Washington, ran the saying, was full of colonels, and the colonels were full of corn. The foreigners who came and went, anxious to describe the United States after the ordeal of war, rarely remarked upon the local community. A mellowed "Boz" had come on a second lecture tour, his twenty-five-year-old criticisms of the "city of magnificent intentions" apparently forgotten in the warmth of the welcome extended to him. But to Dickens, to David MacCrea, to Henry Latham, and indeed to the British minister, Washington in and of herself seemingly had no existence. For a year or more past a good many local citizens themselves, weary of municipal bickering, had ceased to concern themselves with its vagaries.[32]

Congressional temporizing about the future of the local government nevertheless jolted thoughtful Washingtonians. Public opinion had already begun to revolt at the do-nothing policies of Mayor Wallach and his supporters. Business prosperity had revived; the city's poverty no longer offered a valid excuse. Carping at the increased proportion of Negroes in the population and congressional favors to them was obviously nonconstructive. Furthermore, the sheer physical discomforts of living in Washington had become close to intolerable. Visitors, like congressmen, apparently shared Horace Greeley's view: "The rents are high, the food is bad, the dust is disgusting, the mud is deep and the morals are deplorable." Now that Congress implied doubts about the city's capacity to provide anything better, the local electorate saw the time for action had come. The autumn would bring a national election, the selection of a new President, and set the stage for the arrival in 1869 of a new Congress likely to have disturbing ideas about the District of Columbia, including notions about transferring the capital to the Midwest.

Postmaster Sayles J. Bowen, a staunch believer in equal rights for Negroes and one of the first trustees of the colored schools, led the campaign against the old guard in the City Hall. His slogan, "A vote for Bowen is a vote to keep the capital in Washington," was an effective lever.[33] With the backing of most of the Negro community, he swept into office in June 1868 ready not only to inaugurate essential physical improvements but also to collaborate with Congress and complete the scarcely begun social revolution. The election of John F. Cook to the board of aldermen and Carter Stewart, a colored barber, to the common council indicated that an era of rapid change had dawned.

[32] Helen Nicolay, *Sixty Years of the Literary Society*, p. 7; *Journal 65th Council*, p. 687; *Star*, 15 Apr 1868.

[33] *Ibid.*, 14 Dec 1867, 3 Jun 1868.

CHAPTER XIII

THE ADVANCE OF THE SOCIAL REVOLUTION, 1868-1871

"THE SOCIAL side of Washington was to be taken for granted as three-fourths of existence," Henry Adams wrote of the city in 1868. "Politics and reform became the detail, and waltzing the profession." While Charles Sumner and Ben Wade clung to the detail, gay young blades like John Hay, President Lincoln's personal secretary, and the never entirely young or wholly gay Adams pursued the profession, varied with horseback rides through the enchanting countryside surrounding the city and with elbowings through the crowded receptions where a competitive display of jewels and elaborate gowns was part of the evening's business. Tired of the bitter political fights that had followed upon the bloodshed of the war, most people in the upper stratum of Washington society dismissed them from mind once the impeachment trial was over and General Grant installed in the White House. Mrs. Grant, a wholesome, ample-bosomed woman lacking Mary Todd Lincoln's ambition to rule society and possessing only a modicum of the passion of Andrew Johnson's wife and daughters for spotless housekeeping was an agreeable unobtrusive hostess who successfully concealed her dismay at finding herself playing second fiddle to the beautiful, elegantly dressed Kate Chase Sprague whenever the domineering Kate was in Washington. Nor was there at first much eyebrow-raising over the vulgarity of newly rich people whose social ambitions brought them to the capital to try cutting a swathe. For a time they furnished old residents with as much amusement as irritation and supplied Mark Twain with some of the material for *The Gilded Age* and Henry Adams with the makings of his novel *Democracy*.[1]

[1] Henry Adams, *The Education of Henry Adams*, p. 256; Thomas and Marva Belden, *So Fell the Angels*, pp. 259-60, 337.

As leisure and affluence were waltzing partners, to the rank and file of the community who possessed neither, the dance floor was part of a world that could not concern them. Business leaders, on the contrary, sensed that the ballroom might encompass much of the city's future. Growing wealth and its corollary, assurance that the capital would remain on the Potomac, thus became factors in survival. While the former largely depended upon the latter, among a group of ambitious Washingtonians the old hope began to revive of developing a flourishing economy separate from, although enriched by, governmental business. In 1869 they conceived the plan of holding a world's fair in the capital. An international exposition patterned on the Crystal Palace exhibition of 1851 in London and the Paris fair of 1867 should bring a stream of visitors to Washington and give her stature as an enterprising commercial city. Enthusiastic citizens within a matter of months subscribed some $2,000,000 to finance the fair. It needed only the blessing of Congress. Congress refused: the scheme might involve government spending, and members of House and Senate believed the undertaking would prove a dismal failure. "The idea of inviting the world to see this town, with its want of railroads and its muddy streets," expostulated Senator Stewart of Nevada, "seems to me altogether out of the question."[2] He labelled the capital "the ugliest city in the whole country," the worst possible advertisement for the United States. Ruefully Washington watched Philadelphia selected for the first American exposition.

Industrial promotion, however, appeared to offer an alternative, requiring only investment capital. "Washington," announced a formal resolution of the city council, "possesses a good harbor, a fine, healthy climate, and has in and about it water power unsurpassed, which, with its geographical position (lying close to the grain and cotton growing districts of the South) should make it one of the leading commercial and manufacturing cities of the country." The *Star* carried the campaign further:

[2] *Cong Globe*, 41C, 2S, pp. 303-4, 1386, 1394-96; S Rpt 298, 41C, 3S, Ser 1443.

"That the water power of the Potomac, now running to waste at our doors, will be utilized before many years there can be no doubt. The manufacturers of the north are even now obliged to eke out their water supply by expensive purchases of lake lands, hundreds of miles away from their mills. . . .

"Instead of waiting for northern capitalists to take the thing in hand, let us develop our own Spragues, Browns, Hills and Bateses. Our citizens have shown the ability to subscribe a million or two of dollars for an international exposition. This same amount put into manufacturing enterprises would create a means of permanent prosperity for the District of Columbia, and we would suggest that if the exposition enterprises should be nipped in the bud through the failure of Congress to give a proper charter, the money subscribed for it, or an equivalent subscription be devoted to the noble work of starting a line of factories on the Potomac. Any dozen, or score, or fifty or hundred gentlemen who would undertake this work may count on an honorable immortality as the creators of a self-respecting independent existence for the people of Washington."[3]

The federal census of 1870 indicated larger capital resources in the community than people had supposed: personal property valued at more than $53,000,000 and real estate worth over $60,000,000. In view of that showing, W. W. Corcoran or Riggs and Company, which for years had accepted Washington municipal bonds as security for loans, might see fit to finance large-scale industrial enterprise. But lining factories along the Potomac from the Chain Bridge to Easby's Point, even if practicable or profitable for Georgetown, would not greatly benefit her neighbor. Quite apart from the complications of obtaining water rights without interfering with the prior claims of the C & O Canal and the United States-owned aqueduct, the cost of piping water so great a distance discouraged the most intrepid investor. Neither a dozen, nor a score, nor a hundred gentlemen came forward to put the plan into effect.[4]

[3] *Journal 67th Council*, pp. 219-20; *Star*, 21 Feb 1870.

[4] *Journal 62nd Council*, 20 Mar 1865, pp. 2-3; enumerators' returns, Social Statistics, D.C., Ninth U.S. Census, 1870 (Mcf).

Meanwhile the necessity of bettering living conditions in the city was self-evident. "The delightful climate, the beautiful suburban surroundings and the unequalled social attractions" which the *Star* had touted, were no longer sufficient inducement to "persons of means and culture residing elsewhere to invest in property here." At President Grant's inauguration, hackmen, realizing that no lady would risk soiling her gown in the filth on the avenues, charged $40 a day for a carriage, $10 merely for driving a couple to the inaugural ball.[5] The city was dirty and unsanitary, beggars besieged the residential areas and, since the public schools were inadequate and there were no truant officers, hundreds of children of school age roamed the streets. Senator Edmunds complained to Congress of "the infinite, abominable nuisance of cows, and horses, and sheep and goats, running through all the streets of this city, and whenever we appropriate money to set up a shade tree, there comes along a cow or a horse or a goat, and tears it down the next day, and then we appropriate again. There are not today two trees in a hundred in this city . . . which do not show the marks of ill-treatment by horned animals or by pigs or by some animals that are running at large." And, quoting a local wit, the Vermonter concluded, when the board of health abolished the nuisance, the city council abolished the board of health for interfering with voters. Foreign ministers disliked assignments to Washington not only because the United States was not a great power in European eyes and decisions reached on the Potomac seemed unimportant, but also because living in this overgrown village was uncomfortable. The muggy heat of summer was so oppressive that when Prevost Paradahl, Napoleon III's minister to the United States, shot himself in Georgetown at the outbreak of the Franco-Prussian War, naïve explanations ran that the excessive heat had unhinged his mind.[6]

While no one expected a city official to remake the summer

[5] *Star*, 30 Oct 1869.

[6] *Cong Globe*, 41C, 2S, p. 844, 41C, 3S, p. 687; S Rpt 453, 43C, 1S, pp. 502-03, Ser 1590.

climate, Sayles J. Bowen was elected mayor in 1868 in belief that a slightly left-wing Republican would be *personna grata* on the Hill and therefore able to extract federal appropriations for modernizing the city. Bowen's career contains elements of true tragedy. Tall and well-built, slow-moving and slow-spoken, he had come to Washington in 1844 as a penniless young man from upper New York State, and, after holding a clerkship in the Treasury Department and then setting up as a private claims agent, emerged into local prominence when Lincoln rewarded him for his devoted service to the Republican cause by appointing him first to the Metropolitan Police board and in 1863 to be postmaster of Washington.[7] Although his political enemies accused him of posing as a friend to the Negro for his own political advantage, his faith in the potentialities of colored people never wavered during periods when pro-Negro sympathies meant virtual political annihilation. Racial tolerance was not his only qualification for running the city during the second stage of reconstruction. As mayor at a critical point in Washington's history, he hit upon solutions to several practical problems for which other men later won acclaim. In a less troubled era he might have ended his days as one of the city's most eminent and honored public servants, instead of concluding as an object of scorn consigned to so complete an oblivion that within a generation few Washingtonians would even remember his name. His generous social philosophy and sound ideas unhappily outran his political finesse. Lacking a sense of humor, he also lacked a sense of proportion. Stubbornness led him to resort to injudicious partisan tactics that discredited his plans along with their author, and his lack of the assured position in Washington society which had bolstered up Richard Wallach left him without personal friends and supporters in high places.

Handicapped initially by a protracted fight within the board of aldermen over selection of a presiding officer, Bowen lost

[7] Madison Davis, "History of the City Post-Office," CHS *Rec*, VI, 194; Bowen's ideals and character emerge from the fragments of his private correspondence preserved in Bowen Mss in Charles A. Barker's possession.

popularity rapidly when his fellow citizens discovered that Congress was not going to vote appropriations for a large-scale program of public works in the city. His standing among white people suffered further when they concluded that he cared more about providing Negroes with work than about building a city-wide sewage system as cheaply and as quickly as possible. But Bowen, having watched the results of the Freedmen's Bureau methods, clung to his convictions that hiring the unemployed on jobs that needed doing was a wiser form of poor relief than doling out rations and firewood. The Freedmen's Bureau had succeeded in getting a number of Negro families to move across the Eastern Branch to settle on the Barry farm where by a special arrangement they could buy home lots on easy terms, but unemployment was still the great problem for freedmen. A Senate committee wanted to devise a scheme "that would send that population from this sink of poverty, wretchedness and vice, and colonize them all over the country, and enable them to get suitable labor."[8] Still, as their enforced removal from the District of Columbia was out of the question and a wholesale voluntary exodus highly unlikely, Bowen decided that if Congress would not act on his local make-work plan the city must.

During his two years in office men on the municipal payroll levelled the bluff along the river front below the Long Bridge, cut 9th Street through to the water and laid fifteen miles of sidewalks and four miles of sewers. He persuaded Congress to agree to his scheme of lowering paving costs by letting the city narrow the widest streets to a 35-foot carriage way flanked by 35-foot strips of parking and 10-foot sidewalks. When northwest K Street between 12th and 16th was thus narrowed and paved, the broad sweeps of parking planted with trees and grass won universal approval. But there Bowen's triumph ended. Large taxpayers, like their counterparts in the mid-1930's, fumed about the laziness of men who leaned on their shovels, and one accusation ran that Bowen put colored men to work

[8] *Cong Globe*, 40C, 3S, p. 776, 41C, 2S, pp. 841-48; S Misc Doc 153, 41C, 2S, Ser 1408.

with pen knives to dig out grass from between the cobblestones on Pennsylvania Avenue. In June 1870 some two hundred miles of streets were still unpaved and more lacked sewers.[9]

The mayor was no more successful in eliciting federal aid for schools than in inducing Congress to share paving expenses. The gift of a lot and an unused army mess hall at 22nd and I Streets for a white school was the only token of assistance. As the city council was unwilling to raise the school tax, white parents had to be content with the appointment of a superintendent of schools and the building of the Franklin schoolhouse modelled on the ten-room Wallach School.[10] In 1868 the Secretary of the Interior appointed a Negro to the board of trustees of the colored schools, and the trustees put a superintendent in charge, but after the withdrawal of help from northern aid societies the progress of Negro education slowed. Classes for adults stopped. In the public schools the trustees reported tardiness nearly universal, probably because most colored families had no way of telling time. Although by law three months' schooling a year was compulsory for every child, by 1870 few more than a third of the Negro children of school age in the city were attending any school. The colored private schools taught little beyond the ABC's. Washington, Georgetown, and the county together had only 66 classes for colored children. Superintendent Cook and the trustees had to contend with restricted budgets, inadequate equipment, the opposition of white people to having Negro schoolhouses built in their neighborhoods, and, still more discouraging, with numbers of uncooperative Negro parents, badly trained Negro teachers, and bored, undisciplined children.[11]

Early in 1869 Congress passed a bill merging the white and colored school boards; Negroes, fearful lest their own schools

[9] *Star*, 15 Dec 1869; *Journal 66th Council*, pp. 151, 165-67, and *68th Council*, p. 28; *Cong Globe*, 41C, 2S, p. 2332.

[10] S Misc Doc 24, 41C, 2S, Ser 1408; S Rpt 453, 43C, 1S, p. 545, Ser 1590; *Patriot*, 22 Nov 1870.

[11] S Ex Doc 20, 41C, 3S, pp. 1-18, Ser 1440.

suffer, persuaded President Johnson to veto the act.[12] Seven months later a group of white and Negro citizens of the fourth ward threw a bombshell: they requested a mixed school in their neighborhood. Living east of North Capitol Street in a thinly built up, poor section where the streets were unusually muddy in winter, the 57 white and 28 Negro petitioners stressed the economy and other benefits of having one school for the 120 to 130 children of both races. Several aldermen and school trustees approved. Negro voting, they reasoned, had caused no disturbance, colored men sat on the city council, and liberals saw no occasion now to forbid educating white and colored children together. Just what occurred in the school board is uncertain, beyond the fact that a storm of sufficient proportions had blown up to leave a gap in the records: a single report covering the years since 1866 provided an excuse for omitting any mention of the controversy. The city council took no formal action. Presumably during that winter colored and white children in Ward Four attended the same school.[13]

In the end the hopeful experiment failed because only a timid, ill-organized minority endorsed it. To citizens on the other side of the fence who looked upon all Negroes as intrinsically inferior, the mere existence of a racially mixed school was doubtless alarming; the idea might prove contagious. It did not. Three months after Bowen was voted out of office, Ward Four abandoned the plan. The *Patriot*, a local newspaper managed by former Mayor James Berret, asserted that the trial of nonsegregation had all but wrecked the school system. White people deploring racial segregation on principle or because of the extravagance of maintaining two separate systems were as impotent to win over the community at large as were the Negroes who protested the "depressing effect [of segregation] on the minds of colored children." Educated Negroes them-

[12] *Cong Globe*, 40C, 2S, p. 3928, 40C, 3S, pp. 935, 1164; S Ex Doc 47, 40C, 3S, Ser 1360.

[13] *Journal 67th Council*, pp. 463-69, 828-29; *Star*, 5 Jan, 3 Mar 1870; *Chronicle*, 5 Jan 1870; *Twenty-Third Rpt of the Trustees of Public Schools*, 1866-70.

selves were not solidly behind integration. A good many felt it would subject Negro children to competitive stresses they were not yet able to endure and would deny professional opportunities to qualified colored teachers; better to let the race prove its ability to handle an independent educational system. The trustees of colored schools did not accept that view. They appointed George F. Cook, brother of the city's first Negro alderman, to the post of superintendent of the colored schools, but they posed the unanswerable question: "If the fathers are fit to associate, why are not the children equally so?"[14] Twice Congress considered intervening, but neither bill forbidding distinctions "in the admission of pupils to any of the schools," came to a final vote.[15]

The social revolution that had begun with Negro suffrage nevertheless moved forward. In fighting racial discrimination Negro leaders, with the help of men like Bowen, won several victories. In March 1869 federal law struck out the word *white* from every passage where it occurred in Washington's and Georgetown's charters and laws. The city directories dropped the asterisk or a *c* to denote a colored resident. Clerical jobs in the government departments multiplied for educated Negroes who had sponsors in Congress, and colored men who set up in business found patrons among whites. A source of peculiar gratification to the Negro community was the launching of the *New Era*, later named *New National Era*, a readable, well-edited Negro newspaper.[16]

Still more dramatic proof of change in the climate of local opinion was the passage of two civil rights laws enacted by the Washington city council in June 1869 and March 1870. The first ordinance imposed a $10 to $20 fine upon the proprietor of any place of public entertainment who refused accommodations to well-behaved colored people. The second, introduced by

[14] S Misc Doc 130, 41C, 2S, Ser 1408; *Patriot*, 6, 9 Feb, 3 Apr 1871; *New National Era*, 5 Jun 1872, 31 Jul 1873, 6 Nov 1873; S Ex Doc, 41C, 3S, Ser 1440.

[15] *Cong Globe*, 41C, 3S, pp. 1053-54, 1365-67.

[16] *Ibid.*, 41C, 1S, App., p. 35; *New Era*, 20 Jan, 24 Mar, 14 Apr 1870.

a recently elected colored councilman, was wider in scope: it forbade discriminatory treatment of Negroes in restaurants, bars, hotels, and places of amusement, and named as penalty for noncompliance a $50 fine, half of it to go to the informer. Oddly enough, the only dissent came from two colored councilmen who argued that prejudice was fast disappearing, making a new ordinance needless. Both men yielded, perhaps moved by reminders that the powerful Typographical Union and the Medical Society of the District of Columbia still refused to admit Negroes to membership. Again rather oddly, the second law, like the first, occasioned little stir. The three principal dailies in Washington reported the voting but withheld comment. More surprising, the *New Era* omitted all mention of the new legislation, revolutionary though it was in a city where less than eight years earlier a municipal black code had severely restricted Negro activities. Yet the civil rights acts were not empty gestures; a test case taken to court the next winter won a verdict for the complainant which was sustained when appealed.[17]

The quality of the *New Era* astonished a good many white people, even those who recognized the distinction of its editors, the internationally famous ex-slave and abolitionist lecturer, Frederick Douglass, and the Reverend Sella Martin, a former pastor of the 15th Street colored Presbyterian Church and a man highly regarded in England. The paper veered between pride in the progress the race had made in a scant half-dozen years and anger at white people's imperceptiveness or deliberate snubs. An article discussing the growth of Negro self-reliance since Negro enfranchisement in Washington and Georgetown concluded: "Each feels that he is a part, and has an interest in, the welfare of the city, the District, and the nation." A particularly elegant Negro party might get brief coverage, but

[17] *Journal 66th Council*, p. 22, and *67th Council*, 7 Mar 1870, pp. 22-23; *Star*, 30 Nov 1869, 4 Jan, 1 Mar 1870; *Chronicle*, 4 Jan 1870; *Republican*, 1 Mar 1870; *New Era*, 12 Jul 1871; Phineas Indritz, "Post Civil War Ordinances Prohibiting Racial Discrimination in the District of Columbia," *Georgetown Law Journal*, XLII, 179-207.

when John Forney of the *Chronicle* invited several Negroes to a "gentlemen's" party which President Grant and Cabinet officers also attended, the *Era* called it a "noticeable matter; but we doubt not, that, in the newer and better life upon which we have now entered, the color of the skin will cease to be a bar to recognition of gentlemanly qualifications here in the United States." Not long afterward the paper remarked: "No man need be afraid now, since the Chief Magistrate of the nation receives all alike at his levees—since, in fact, the chief men of Washington society invite colored men to their receptions." At the same time editorials blasted the "skin aristocrats" of Washington who, displaying "the inherent prejudices of slaveholders, violate the whole spirit of our institutions and put us to shame before the world." The discriminatory attitudes of white workingmen received still sharper censure. Very occasionally the editors' criticisms extended also to colored merchants, physicians, and lawyers who catered more to white than to Negro patrons: "The worst form of infidelity in regard to negro capacity is to be found among negroes themselves."[18]

Although notables like Douglass and Martin, Dr. Alexander T. Augusta, a surgeon in the Union army during the war, Dr. Charles B. Purvis, professor at Howard and a surgeon at the Freedmen's Hospital, and a dozen other men rather recently settled in the capital were leaders in colored Washington, it was the members of old, established families who had grown up in freedom who formed the backbone of the enlightened colored community. They had little in common with contrabands and, in spite of the *Era's* optimistic statements about the progress of all Negroes, the intelligent could not blink the fact that the great mass of freedmen, concerned primarily with sheer survival, was still a fearful drag upon men who had fought their way up the social and economic ladder. As white people tended to lump all Negroes together, self-interest put pressure upon Negro aristocrats to do what they could to raise the level

[18] *New Era*, 20, 27 Jan, 24 Feb, 24 Mar, 14 Apr 1870; 2 Feb 1871.

of intelligence of their inferiors and to inspire in them a sense of responsibility as citizens. Some upper-class Negroes, overwhelmed by the magnitude of the task, evaded it; others accepted the challenge. But the class distinctions that had developed among Washington Negroes in the 1830's or earlier were sharpened during the reconstruction period.

Old families generally occupied a higher social position than newcomers. Education, professional status, and money were also important and, according to critics of the class structure of the next generation, sheer character—selflessness, honesty, and industriousness—still counted in the late 1860's. How much at that time degree of color affected a person's place in the Negro social hierarchy is uncertain. While a black skin manifestly did not constitute an insurmountable barrier to social recognition, light color, a sign of the admixture of white blood, was unquestionably an asset. It was not improbably a carryover from the days when household slaves, many of whom were mulattoes, felt themselves and, indeed often were, several cuts above the lowly black field hand. In the 1940's a Negro student of the post Civil War era in Washington meticulously noted the complexion of every Negro officeholder in the city government. The two men elected in 1868, Alderman John F. Cook, a clerk in the tax collector's office, and Councilman Carter Stewart, were both "light." Stewart was the only colored alderman during the last two years of the municipality. Of the seven Negro councilmen elected in 1869, three, a caterer, a preacher, and a brickmaker, were "black," four were "light," a government messenger, a cloak room attendant at the Capitol, and two laborers. The common council chosen in June 1870 included a black preacher, a black government clerk, and four light men, two of them government messengers, one a teacher, and one a day laborer.[19] The prestige attaching to a minister,

[19] *Ibid.*, 13 Nov 1873; Ada Piper, "Activities of Negroes in the Territorial Government of the District of Columbia, 1871-1874," p. 61 (M.A. thesis Howard Univ); see also Bryan, *Capital*, II, 559-60n. My interpretation of the class structure of the Negro community cannot be documented from con-

a government clerk, or a businessman apparently offset the handicap of blackness, while the light skin of a common laborer counterbalanced the humbleness of his occupation.

If color lines in local Negro society were already checking its fluidity and creating a rigidity that had no counterpart in white society, at the end of the sixties the most enterprising and adaptable freedmen still were able to narrow the gulf between themselves and upper-class Negroes. Ambitious ex-contrabands made use of their chances for education, moved out of the Negro slums as soon as they could afford anything better, and by the exercise of utmost frugality some of them succeeded in following the example of provident upper-class Negroes in salting away savings in the Freedmen's Savings and Trust Company. There in the handsome new building on Pennsylvania Avenue across from the Treasury, the affable Negro cashier and elegantly dressed Negro tellers gave depositors a sense of security.[20]

In the early months of 1870, however, the struggles and successes of the Negro community received less and less attention from white Washingtonians anxious about the city's future. Congress, still temporizing over a long-term renewal of the municipal charter, betrayed dismaying distrust of the municipal government. For example, an act appropriating $30,000 for the relief of the destitute vested in the Secretary of War the responsibility for distributing the benefits, lest the funds become an electioneering weapon in the hands of city officials and lest indigent whites get too large a share. The report of the army lieutenant put in charge showed, moreover, how far Mayor Bowen had fallen short of his goal of ending unemployment

---

temporaneous materials. I base my presentation upon nuances in Negro newspaper articles of the later 1870's and the 1880's, upon some of the sketches in William J. Simmons, *Men of Mark, Eminent, Progressive and Rising*, published in 1887, and upon the educated guesses of colored Washingtonians of the 1950's.

[20] *Journal 68th Council*, pp. 16-19; Investigation into the Freedmen's Bank, H Rpt 502, 44C, 1S, pp. 92-93, Ser 1710; *Star*, 29 May 1867, 15 Oct 1869; Baltimore *Sun*, 30 Sep, 16 Oct 1869.

and want: in a single month charity societies had recommended for relief 23,221 colored adults and 25,348 colored children, figures which, even allowing for duplication, indicated half the District's Negro population in need of help. Although Lt. Bridges feared "that relief has been denied to some who should have been aided," in one month he issued rations and coal to about 16,600 freedmen.[21]

Congress recognized that helpless blacks were not the city's only needy, but the measure passed in 1870 to ease Washington's over-all welfare problem introduced a curious arrangement. An act chartering the Washington Market Company granted the new corporation a 99-year lease of the site of the old Centre Market on Pennsylvania Avenue on condition that within the next two years the company build a new market house and pay the city an annual ground rent of $25,000 to be used for poor relief. Students of Washington's history believed the gift to a private company improper, inasmuch as Presidents Washington and Adams and in 1798 Congress itself had pledged the square to the use of a public market, but the futility of raising the legal question or of pointing out that only the war had prevented the city's erecting a new market house there and thereby acquiring permanent title to the land silenced objections. And city officials were pleased at controlling a relief fund of $25,000 yearly not all of which need go to Negroes.[22]

Perceptive Washingtonians still saw a lack of congressional confidence in local competence in a dozen realms. House and Senate had acknowledged the necessity of a federal reformatory for juvenile delinquents but had voted only $12,000 in four years to the school opened by private citizens. Congress agreed to pay $200,000 of the $300,000 needed for a new jail and sanctioned the creation of a police court to handle petty offenses, but, remembering the $3,300,000 spent on the aqueduct, it ordered Washington and Georgetown to pay nearly half a million dollars for a new 36-inch water main from the distribut-

[21] H Ex Doc 57, 41C, 3S, Ser 1453.
[22] S Rpt 449, 43C, 1S, Ser 1587.

ing reservoir to Capitol Hill. Without increasing the federal appropriation, Congress added 70 men to the Metropolitan Police and raised patrolmen's salaries, whittled down the city's bills for work done on "the public squares and reservations," and then forced the municipality to wait for reimbursement.[23] Men on the Hill, arguing that the federal government had created the city and displayed consistent benevolence toward her, remained unimpressed by a tabulation compiled from Treasury records showing that between 1790 and 1870 federal expenditures in the District for purposes that directly benefited the community came to less than $9,000,000 out of a total of $44,000,000; more than $35,000,000 had gone into government buildings and services for federal officials. Yet the value of the original proprietors' gift of land now stood at more than $100,-000,000.[24]

By the late spring of 1870 the local electorate had lost all faith in Mayor Bowen's program. The municipal funded debt had risen to $1,500,000, the floating debt to nearly $900,000, almost a third of those totals incurred during the preceding two years. And the useful visible results looked meagre to taxpayers. Whites generally blamed the mayor and his Negro associates on the city council. Negroes believed their vastly strengthened position in the community the fruit of their own and congressional action, not Mayor Bowen's; seemingly the social revolution had advanced too far to be reversed under a new administration in the City Hall. Charged with graft in the letting of city contracts and with other forms of corruption, Bowen went down in defeat in June, repudiated even by the colored people whom he had championed.[25]

The new mayor, Matthew Emery, a quiet, matter-of-fact man, best known as the stonemason who had placed the cornerstone of the Washington Monument, soon found himself buffeted

[23] H Ex Doc 56, 40C, 2S, Ser 1417; H Ex Doc 39, 41C, 3S, Ser 1453; H Rpt 39, 42C, 2S, Ser 1528; *Cong Globe*, 40C, 3S, App., p. 315; 41C, 1S, pp. 1096-97 and App., p. 666; *Patriot*, 10 Dec 1870, 16 Apr 1871.

[24] H Ex Doc 156, 41C, 2S, Ser 1418; *Cong Globe*, 41C, 2S, p. 842.

[25] *New Era*, 27 Jan, 19 May, 16 Jun 1870.

by crosscurrents that threatened to capsize the municipal ship. While denouncing his predecessors for extravagance, he considered larger expenditures essential. Shortly after taking office, he presented his ultimatum: the tax rate must rise to $1.80 per $100 in order to bring in over a million dollars of revenue; otherwise he would cancel all work on the streets and every other public project. In view of the complaints on the Hill about the city's physical condition, the second course was unthinkable. The tax increase went into effect, and that autumn, while work began on repaving Pennsylvania Avenue, Emery with congressional approval let a contract for deep dredging of the Washington Canal as a first step in constructing an adequate sanitary sewage system.[26] Dissatisfaction with the city government had bitten too deep to allow him to carry out his plans. Within six months he was to find his office abolished.

Fear lest Congress relocate the "Seat of Empire" was a factor in producing that change. The threat, to be sure, was as old as the city, but, after the rebuilding of the Capitol and the White House two generations before, no one took the recurrent proposals very seriously until reconstruction policies suddenly multiplied the number and urgency of petitions from the Midwest asking for transfer of the capital to the Mississippi Valley. Kansas begged Congress to spend no more money in the District of Columbia; the heart of the country now lay inland. Memorials from other state legislatures and from conventions held in Cincinnati and St. Louis carried insidious appeals to all northern prejudices: Indiana, Illinois, Iowa, and Missouri, while professing to cherish "no mean spirit of hostility to the District," urged abandoning the Potomac location in order to save the capital "from the bane of secession, from any taint of the spirit of treason, and to place it where no hostile power could ever threaten its safety."[27] The shadows of the Civil War

[26] *Journal 68th Council*, pp. 9, 11-14, 84-89, 251-59; H Misc Doc 36, 40C, 3S, Ser 1385; *Patriot*, 14, 22 Nov 1870.

[27] *Star*, 25 Mar 1862, 3 Jun 1868, 3 Aug, 9 Nov 1869; H Misc Docs 91 and 105, 41C, 3S, Ser 1463; H Rpt 52, 41C, 3S, pp. 1-12, Ser 1464.

still lay black over Washington, a blackness intensified by the recalcitrance of Richard Wallach and his colleagues during the first stages of reconstruction. Seemingly the one argument in the District of Columbia's favor was the fact that George Washington had selected the site. Common sense also pointed to the wisdom of General Sherman's prophecy that rival cities would cease bidding for the honor when they learned that residents of the national capital, wherever located, would have to sacrifice their state citizenship and their votes.[28] Common sense might not prevail.

For Washington the cost of an adverse decision was painfully obvious. Government payrolls were a mainstay of her economy, and, whenever Congress voted to erect new federal buildings, immediately masons, carpenters, and common laborers would benefit. During the season here, a Georgetown newspaper remarked, "every afternoon and evening the 'fashionables' are in a whirl of excitement and find it difficult, even with the aid of fine equipage and fast horses to make the round of calls between noon and midnight."[29] The triviality of most of the "fashionables" notwithstanding, their presence supplied a livelihood to many a family. Tradesmen, hotel keepers, claims agents, brokers who handled real estate along with insurance and investments profited directly from the influx of winter visitors. Newspaper correspondents left the imprint of their alertness and wit upon social gatherings; without the bait of national news few of those writers would stay—neither John James Piatt, poet as well as reporter, nor George Alfred Townsend, nor William Douglass O'Connor, the journalist and novelist who had defended the Good Gray Poet when the Secretary of the Interior dismissed the author of the "immoral" *Leaves of Grass*. The succession of foreign visitors also would cease, whether a Leslie Stephen and his wife, Thackeray's daughter, or diplomats like Sir Edward Thornton. James Smithson's will fixed the Smithsonian Institution in Washington, but were the federal govern-

[28] *Star*, 25 Nov 1869; *Patriot*, 17 Nov 1870.
[29] Georgetown *Courier*, 28 Jan 1871.

ment to move to the West, the National Museum might go too. The Library of Congress, for which the Librarian, Ainsworth Spofford, had recently purchased the pamphlets and other rare Americana collected over the years by the bibliophile Peter Force, would necessarily accompany Congress. Certainly the gifted men attached to the Coast Survey and to the new scientific bureaus emerging in several government departments would follow their chiefs; the Naval Observatory on the shore of the Potomac might well close. Probably only a handful of Washingtonians grasped the significance of the new government-sponsored research programs, but the group that still cherished the hope of seeing the city become the intellectual center of the nation appreciated their potentialities.

Although Congress had long talked of rapidly winding up the Coast Survey, at Dallas Bache's death in 1867 the appointment of the eminent mathematician, Benjamin Peirce of Harvard, as his successor gave this oldest of government scientific projects a new lease on life. Peirce, so far from curtailing, extended the work by undertaking the triangulation of a transcontinental arc along the 39th parallel to connect the Atlantic and Pacific surveys. His son, Charles S. Peirce, symbolic logician and mathematical genius, joined the staff in 1870. At the new Army Medical Museum housed in Ford's Theatre where Lincoln had been shot, compilation of the *Medical and Surgical History of the War of the Rebellion* was taking on the dimensions of an important scientific work, while Assistant Surgeon John Shaw Billings, using a windfall of $80,000 left over from the war, set about building up the Surgeon General's Library into a valuable research tool. Colonel Albert J. Myer, Chief Signal Officer of the Army, was taking the first steps in organizing a weather bureau, using meteorological information telegraphed in from army posts and stations along the Great Lakes. Under new officials, the Department of Agriculture, furthermore, had begun to add research in botany, chemistry, and entomology to the routine tasks of answering farmers' queries.

And the brilliant Simon Newcomb now in charge of the Naval Observatory was launching a program of fundamental research in astronomy that would have delighted John Quincy Adams. After acquiring a new German-built transit circle in 1866, Newcomb obtained an appropriation for a new 26-inch telescope to ensure longer range observations. If relatively few people understood the nature of his scientific work, his many-faceted intellectual interests, his personal magnetism, and his physical vitality made him a citizen any community would like to claim.[30] Were the capital to be established in St. Louis or Cincinnati, Washington would lose her most distinguished residents and with them a share in future scientific developments.

The city on the Potomac, nevertheless, believed she had several assets peculiarly her own. Eight months of the year her climate was mild, in spring and autumn delightful. While the campaign to bring in industry had failed thus far, the failure had left her free of the smoke of factory chimneys and prevented what nativists deemed an undesirable influx of foreign immigrants whose extreme poverty and strange tongues were thrusting special problems upon other American cities. In the decade since 1860 Washington had added fewer than 1,300 foreign-born to her population; altogether they represented a scant eighth of her 109,000 souls. She remained thus a community of native Americans, a third of them colored, it is true, but, because of their color, people whom whites might ignore. The noisome slums occupied by freedmen were generally tucked out of sight in alleyways and areas whites rarely frequented. Despite the overcrowding in her Negro sections, housing was ample: the average number of occupants per dwelling was 6.16, whereas the figure for Cincinnati was 8.81, for St. Louis 7.4, and for New York nearly 15.[31] Washington and Georgetown, moreover, laid claim to some intellectual and artistic distinction

[30] Dupree, *Science in the Federal Government*, pp. 152-53, 184-85, 195-97, 256-58.

[31] *Eighth U.S. Census*, 1860, *Population*, pp. 620-23; *Ninth Census*, 1870, *Population*, p. 110, and *Mortality and Misc Statistics*, p. 67.

independent of what the Smithsonian provided. The Corcoran Gallery of Art, at last reclaimed from the Quartermaster General who had occupied the building since 1861, would soon open its doors to the public. Georgetown University, Columbian College, Howard University, Wayland Seminary, and after 1869 a new small college hopefully named the National University gave the District a footing in the world of higher education. Georgetown, enriched by a gift from her native son George Peabody, was about to open a town library and consolidate all her Sunday school libraries. Seventy-three white and twenty colored religious bodies in Washington made the church-going community a power.

Urban aesthetics had received no attention since the outbreak of the war; the stump of the Washington Monument surrounded by blocks of stone and the debris left from Army cattle-pens and slaughter houses were eyesores, symbols of civic defeat. Still Washington's potentialities for beauty, unrealized but present, stood as a challenge to men of imagination. The elaborate plan of the city, the broad sweep of the avenues, the very spaciousness that led foreign visitors to poke fun at the emptiness, all held magnificent promise. Patience, high taxes, bond issues, and the good will of Congress, together could make a city so beautiful that talk of moving the government elsewhere would die.[32]

All the law and the prophets hung upon congressional favor. At the end of the 1860's ideas about how to regain and use that favor varied from the conviction that long-term renewal of Washington's charter with enlarged powers would suffice to the diametrically opposite belief that nothing short of local disenfranchisement and full congressional control would end criticisms of the community, elicit federal aid, and keep the capital on the Potomac. Between these extremes lay the plan considered and discarded at intervals over the past seventy years: consolidation of the entire county into a single jurisdiction with a con-

[32] Richard Jackson, *Chronicles of Georgetown*, pp. 231-33, 264; Georgetown *Courier*, 25 Feb 1871.

centration of authority that could carry through needed reforms. During the war Washington's city council had discussed the advantages of a union with Georgetown; her neighbor wanted none of it. Yet patently local administrative machinery had become needlessly complex—two city governments, two white schools boards, federally appointed trustees of the colored schools, a county levy court, and a federal metropolitan police force, all of them supported wholly or in part by local taxes.

In 1866 when Senator Lot Morrill had proposed congressional "resumption" of the government of the District, some Washingtonians, "willing," one congressman noted contemptuously, "to surrender their own rights rather than to respect the rights of others," had welcomed any substitute for a local government in which Negroes would have a voice. Other citizens had protested that the Morrill plan "takes away the fragments of self-government which from the creation of this District had been accorded to its people; it subjects us to the rule of men utter strangers to our habits, feelings and interests."[33] Strangers to the Washington of ante-bellum days, however, made up over 40 percent of her white postwar population; the Oldest Inhabitants Association founded in 1865 to preserve her traditions wielded little influence.[34] The Morrill bill had failed partly because some members of Congress objected to depriving free men of their rightful prerogatives and more largely because radical Republicans wanted to try out the politically important experiment of Negro suffrage.

Within three years citizens as conscientious as Lewis Clephane, Chief Justice David K. Cartter of the District Supreme Court, J. Ormond Wilson, superintendent of schools, and A. C. Richards, head of the Metropolitan Police, had swung over to think a measure like the Morrill bill the only way to halt paralyzing conflicts with Congress and ensure civic improvements.[35] Among the petitioners requesting rule by federal com-

[33] Ptn S39A-H3, 15 Jun 1866; *Journal 63rd Council*, pp. 438, 482.
[34] *Spec Rpt Comr Educ*, pp. 28-29, 37, Ser 1427.
[35] *Star*, 26 Feb, 5 Mar 1867; S Misc Doc 24, 41C, 1S, Ser 1399.

missioners were also men whose motives presumably were less altruistic. Washington's common council, stating that the proposal had no "parallel in the history of the country," accused proponents of wanting the District governed by "a moneyed aristocracy." The plan of disenfranchisement originated, the council contended, "in the selfish, aristocratical and bitter spirit of those who either sympathized with the rebellion, or who can see nothing good . . . in the liberty of all men, or in the minds of selfish speculators and their allies or political demagogues who for money, place, and power would barter the dearest interests and privileges of the happiest and freest Government on Earth."[36] Nevertheless a newspaper editorial observed in the autumn of 1869:

"The number who continue to hope against hope that anything can be done under the present form of municipal government, to set things to rights here is small, and growing smaller every day. . . . It may be said that . . . a board of commissioners may be both arbitrary and corrupt. But most of our citizens, we take it, will cheerfully stand the chances of the experiment. If it works badly it would be easy to return to a charter government. . . . The citizens of Washington would like a change."[37]

Still, the less drastic course of consolidation under an elected territorial government gradually gained support. Georgetown, in 1862 determined to keep her 111-year-old separate identity, now inclined slowly toward union with her rival as a lesser sacrifice than loss of all voice in the management of local affairs.[38] Senator Davis of Kentucky probably added to white taxpayers' uncertainties about entrusting their future solely to federally appointed officials. Never in all his years in Congress, he said, had any member of the District committees been a true friend of the District. "These committees . . . have been organized upon the principle of elevating the negro and, when there was a conflict, of subordinating the rights and interest and

[36] *Journal 65th Council*, pp. 476, 507, and *67th Council*, pp. 997, 1036-39, 1189-90.

[37] *Star*, 5 Oct 1869.

[38] *Ibid.*, 28 Jan 1862, 12 Oct 1869.

feelings of the white man to those of the negro." Early in 1870 a meeting of 150 influential citizens, urged on by Alderman Alexander Shepherd, tendered a request for a territorial government covering the entire District.[39] The *New Era* labelled the plan a step backward, but at least it appeared to be side-tracking talk of moving the capital.[40]

To the relief of sober-minded men, the bill that passed the Senate late in May 1870 was temperate, indeed generous. It incorporated the main features of the territorial government requested by the special citizens' group, namely a popularly elected governor and council to act as executive and legislature, and, like other territories, a nonvoting delegate in Congress; a clause forbade the annulment of the municipal charters without the express approval of a majority of the legal voters in each city. Better still, a provision implied that the United States would bear its proportionate share of the costs of running the new territory.[41] Anxiously the community awaited the action of the House.

In January 1871, when the House District Committee presented its recommendations, the bill had undergone significant changes. Who inspired them initially and why remains a mystery; rumor attributed them to the committee chairman, Burton Cook of Illinois. The first revision proposed presidential appointment of the governor and an eleven-man upper chamber, leaving only a lower house to be elected by popular vote. A second change dropped the provision for including federal property in valuations for tax purposes, an indication that private property alone might have to carry all the territorial expenses. Third, the House added a new section creating a presidentially appointed board of public works to take charge of public improvements and assess the costs as it saw fit. Opposition in Congress centered around only the first of these changes. Congressman Ela of New Hampshire, for example, objected strongly

[39] *Cong Globe*, 41C, 2S, p. 847; *Patriot*, 20 Aug 1872.
[40] *New Era*, 27 Jan, 10 Mar 1870; *Star*, 4 Jan 1870.
[41] *Cong Globe*, 41C, 2S, pp. 3912-14.

to an appointed upper chamber because it constituted a slur upon the local public "and I do not believe there is a body of men in equal numbers in any city upon the continent who are so well-behaved, and whose life and property are more secure, than in the District of Columbia." If the new territory were to be denied the right to elect its legislature as other United States territories did, Congress would do better to appoint commissioners clothed with arbitrary powers. Vainly George Julian urged provision for woman suffrage, and equally vainly Senator Sumner begged for a civil rights clause. No one spoke out against the power vested in an appointed board of public works. The District territorial act which became law on February 21, 1871, was in essentials the bill as rewritten in the House and rushed through, men later asserted angrily, before most people discovered that "plotters" had altered the Senate version in vitally important particulars.[42]

At the time the act seemed reasonably satisfactory. The provision that the governor and the members of his council must have lived in the District for at least a year appeared to forestall the possibility of the President's using his appointive powers to pay his political debts. In April 1871 voters qualifying by three months' residence in any one of the eleven precincts into which the District was to be divided were to elect two members from each for a one-year term in the House of Delegates. The territory's delegate to Congress would be a nonvoting member of the House District committee. The duties of the five men to be appointed to a board of health would include abatement of nuisances like the free-running pigs and goats about which Senator Edmunds had complained so graphically. The five-man board of public works, destined shortly to be the storm center of controversy in Washington, was empowered to plan and contract for all public improvements, assessing a third of the costs upon adjoining private property; the only limitation upon the board's authority was a requirement that the territorial

[42] *Ibid.*, 41C, 3S, pp. 639-47, 685-88; Franklin T. Howe, "The Board of Public Works," CHS *Rec*, III, 257-62; *Patriot*, 20 Aug 1872.

legislature must approve expenditures in advance by appropriating the money or sanctioning bond issues to cover costs not met by assessments. Public indebtedness must not exceed 5 percent of assessed property values unless a popular referendum expressly permitted. The tax ceiling was set at $2 on every $100. The city charters were to run until June 1, 1871, but neither corporation might impose new taxes in the interim.

Federal commitments, on the other hand, were disappointing. The United States would pay the salaries of appointed officials, but Congress reserved the right to annul any act of the District legislature, and federal property was to remain tax-exempt. An appraisal to be made by a federal official once every five years would determine the value of public lands other than parks and public squares and presumably thereby guide Congress in making appropriations for improvements; but the failure to assign to the federal treasury any definite financial responsibility for the new territory perpetuated the fiscal uncertainties which Senator Southard had tried to eliminate 35 years before.[43]

Most Washingtonians, however, felt the new scheme of government would work well. Certainly Congress, having used the District as a testing ground for reconstruction measures, was glad now to wash its hands of time-consuming problems. Citizens who had carped about Washington's "negro government" expected the curtailed power of the electorate to ensure white rule in the future. Negro leaders like Frederick Douglass apparently agreed regretfully, but after all the law still guaranteed colored men the same political rights as white men, and the civil rights ordinances still stood. In a sunny atmosphere of harmony between Congress and local community race relations should improve further. Men of property believed the new order, headed by persons prominent enough to attract the notice of the President, would safeguard vested interests. Above all, the act gave some assurance that the capital would remain in Washington. The city council, doomed soon to expire, called "a uniform system of government for the District of Columbia"

[43] 16 Stat. 419-29.

the means of "developing its great natural resources, giving increased vitality to commerce and manufactures, the building of new railroads, beautifying and improving its splendid streets and avenues, increasing its population, investment of capital from abroad, and opening a 'new era' in its history."[44]

On February 20, 1871, Washington inaugurated a three-day celebration of her "new era." Citizens had planned a carnival in honor of completing the last stretch of new wood pavement on Pennsylvania Avenue, and now passage of the territorial act and the opening of Mr. Corcoran's Gallery of Art tripled causes for rejoicing. Crowds in holiday mood watched the Mardi Gras parade and the races in which horsemen drove six-in-hands while boys raced goat-drawn carts over the smooth surface of the Avenue. At night, calcium lamps, gas jets, and Chinese lanterns illuminated the thoroughfare for admiring throngs and for carnival-costumed people en route to the masked balls. At the Corcoran Gallery at 17th Street and Pennsylvania Avenue, foreign diplomats and other distinguished guests danced in the picture-lined halls.[45] Might not the time be approaching when every class of society could waltz light-heartedly? Washington's birthday, in 1871 not yet a national holiday, seemed to citizens of the capital to mark Washington City's rebirth.

[44] F. C. Adams, *Our Little Monarchy, Who Runs It and What It Costs*, pp. 7, 9; *Journal 68th Council*, pp. 595-96.

[45] *Star*, 23 Feb 1871.

CHAPTER XIV

BOSS SHEPHERD AND THE BUILDING OF THE "NEW WASHINGTON," 1871-1874

THE SHORT LIFE of the Territory of the District of Columbia was tumultuous. Its creation was an outgrowth of the revolutionary social changes of the preceding decade, but the "Uncivil War"[1] that followed was initially a political contest closely tied to national party conflicts. For the working classes it became also a struggle to hold their economic gains of the past, and for Negroes a fight to keep and extend their recently won civil rights. People in the rest of the country took little or no interest in the new regime during its first two years. Its inception occurred at a time when Congress was debating the Ku Klux bill, the passage of which with its provision for the suspension of the writ of habeas corpus seemed to the British minister to pose a threat to free government everywhere.[2] Before 1873 Americans troubled over the accumulating evidence of corruption in Congress and improper behavior in high federal office dismissed the affair of the District of Columbia as a petty domestic squabble. Some of the quarrelling indeed was. Yet the bitter feuding notwithstanding, a "new" physically attractive Washington emerged.

During the spring of 1871 the golden hopes born in late winter endured. When uneasiness stirred, the signs of new business activity tended to quiet doubts. In March congressional authorization of a multi-million dollar building to house the State, War, and Navy Departments laid to rest the last fears of losing the capital to the Mississippi Valley. As soon as the architect's plans were ready and construction began, unemployment promised to ease. Private real estate transactions immediately picked up. Compared to the $4,927,000 spent dur-

1 James Whyte, *The Uncivil War.*

2 Sir Edward Thornton to the British Foreign Office, 10, 12, 17, 22 Apr 1871, Nos 119, 123, 126, 132, 135, photostats, Foreign Office Correspondence.

ing the entire preceding year, the sales of property transferred in the four months between March and July 1871 totalled over $2,500,000.[3] And real estate values in the 1870's, as in the twentieth century, were the best gauge of prosperity in Washington.

President Grant's appointment to posts in the territorial government, however, had already planted the seeds of fresh dissension. Individually the men he selected were inoffensive, but they were all Simon-pure Republicans. Henry D. Cooke, president of the First National Bank of Washington, brother of the Civil War financier Jay Cooke, won the coveted governorship. He had lived in Georgetown since 1863, had pleasant manners, and, rumor said, had the still greater appeal of a large bank account. Norton P. Chipman, a patent attorney with many friends in Congress and a fluent speaker who had capitalized on his opportunities as one of the prosecutors of Major Henry Wirz, was appointed secretary. The members of the governor's council were unremarkable except for Frederick Douglass, ex-slave, lecturer, and in 1871 editor of the *New National Era*. Two other of the eleven men were Negroes, but, while highly respected in the colored community, neither was well known to white people. The board of public works, besides Governor Cooke, consisted of a war-time contractor and a successful speculator in Washington real estate, the Architect of the Treasury and of the new State Department building, the United States collector of customs in Georgetown, and Alexander Shepherd, alderman under Mayor Emery and during 1869 and 1870 the most active promoter of the new form of government.

Alexander Shepherd, six feet tall, powerfully built, and handsome in a florid style, possessed an easy hail-fellow-well-met approachability. President Grant found him congenial. At thirty-seven he had a driving force that his fellow citizens admired, although he seemed to householders of the old school an unfortunate choice for the board of public works; for his recent large-scale building ventures which had lifted him from

[3] *Star*, 25 Mar 1872.

obscurity bespoke the reckless gambler. Unlike the others, he at least was a native Washingtonian. Most people tacitly admitted that Frederick Douglass' reputation as a spokesman for his people entitled him to a place on the council, but the Georgetown *Courier*, dubbing council members "the fit nominees of a pigmy on a pedestal," complained: "Not an old resident, nor a Democrat, nor a Catholic, nor an Irishman, and yet we have three darkies, Douglass, Gray and Hall, a German, two natives of Maine and one of Massachusetts." Among Democrats, who reportedly paid three quarters of all taxes in the District, dissatisfaction ran strong; they believed they had been promised a nonpartisan administration.[4] Curiously enough, no hostile comment greeted the appointment to the board of health of John Mercer Langston, a Negro lawyer recently come to Washington to head the Howard University Law School.

As the campaign opened for nomination of candidates for the House of Delegates and the seat in Congress, the least astute voter in the new territory could see that Republicans looked upon it as a handy tool with which to entrench the national party in power. "Upon the result of the election in this District," one speaker said, would depend Republican success in the presidential election in 1872, and Governor Cooke announced that insofar as he could control the territorial government it would "be administered in the interest of the Republican party and no one who was not a well-tried Republican should, with his consent, hold office thereunder." To men who believed that what was good for the Republican party was good for the United States and for the United States capital, those views were sound. They justified the registration of government clerks for local voting.[5] If federal employees disliked being corralled, women suffragists were more than ready to go to the polls. Petitions from several hundred women in 1866 had begged for the privilege granted to illiterate black men; later arguments

[4] *Patriot*, 12, 14 Apr 1871; Georgetown *Courier*, 15 Apr 1871; Franklin T. Howe, "The Board of Public Works," CHS *Rec*, III, 257-78.

[5] *Patriot*, 8 Mar, 15 Apr 1871; *Republican*, 19 Apr 1871.

that the 14th Amendment nowhere mentioned the word *male* and thus opened the voting booth to women netted the "petticoat politicians" only ridicule. During the convention of the National Woman's Suffrage Association in 1870, Emily Briggs, that novelty, a woman reporter, had described with more vivacity than sympathy the performance of a delegation appealing to the Senate and House District committees. But in 1871 stalwarts of the party, however anxious to enlist "safe" votes, wanted no dealings with unpredictable female suffragists, and the District Supreme Court soon afterward ruled the 14th Amendment inapplicable to women.[6]

Public interest centered on the election of the nonvoting representative in Congress, for his persuasiveness might affect the course of federal legislation for the territory. Norton Chipman, labelled "carpetbagger" by the *Patriot*, the only Democratic organ in Washington since the demise of the *National Intelligencer* in 1869, won easily. His adversaries ascribed his success to his appeal "to the cupidity of the blacks and the necessities of Government clerks," and to his supposed advocacy of mixed schools. Chipman called that charge ridiculous, as it undoubtedly was.[7] After having had six and seven colored men in Washington's city council, Negroes' capture of only two of the twenty-two seats in the House of Delegates was a surprise. It bore out the prophecy of the *New National Era* that a territorial government would mean lesser influence for the colored community. On April 21 the *Star* elatedly reported the election results as a victory "of the class of citizens who wish to see Washington take its proper rank among the attractive cities of the world." Wearied by a decade of bitter controversy, people stood ready "to give the new government a fair trial unbiased by party affiliation."[8]

At the induction ceremonies of the new officials on May 15

[6] S Misc Doc 47, 41C, 2S, Ser 1408; [Emily Edson Briggs], *The Olivia Letters*, pp. 130-63; *Patriot*, 12 May, 1 Nov, 9, 23 Dec 1871; *Courier*, 22 Apr 1871.

[7] *Patriot*, 4, 7, 15-17, 19, 21 Apr 1871.

[8] *Ibid.*, 8 Mar, 12 Apr 1871; *New Era*, 10 Feb 1870; *Star*, 21 Apr 1871.

Governor Cooke outlined the tasks that lay ahead and the methods of financing that he recommended, namely bond issues instead of higher taxes. He called attention to the shortcomings of the school system and suggested that the $70,000 Washington spent yearly on poor relief might be better administered by a board of charities and corrections. He sounded nonpartisan, his ideas sensible. That night a torch-light parade accompanied by Washington's fire engines wound up Pennsylvania Avenue and on to Governor Cooke's house in Georgetown, where the governor and several others again spoke. Norton Chipman chose the occasion to remind "all thoughtful citizens" of their duty "first as members of the great republican party of this country, and second, as citizens of this District."[9]

In the course of the next few weeks the legislature created some 400 public offices—all to be filled by appointment—to handle the duties formerly carried out by about 160 city and county officials. Many of these new-grown plums fell to constituents of influential senators and representatives, for, as *The Nation* later observed, "When the question of expensive improvements was under discussion, the people of Washington were told that they were like the citizens of other towns, and must pay the bills. But when any of the local offices were vacant, they were told that Washington was the seat of Government, and the politicians all over the country were equally entitled with its residents to share in its official plunder." In addition to tripling the size of the District payroll, the governor's council and the delegates promptly authorized the rental of four buildings for District offices—for the Governor and his staff the building on Pennsylvania Avenue across 17th Street from the Corcoran Gallery, for the board of public works and lesser functionaries two buildings on John Marshall Place below the City Hall, and for the legislature a building on Pennsylvania Avenue near 9th Street. Remodelling these rented quarters and furnishing them with "Brussels carpets, great mirrors with elaborately gilt frames, frescoed ceilings and black walnut

[9] *Star*, 15, 16 May 1871.

furniture, all carved," cost $100,000, a third again as much as the United States government offered for the purchase of the City Hall.[10]

Taxpayers' dismay at the workings of the spoils system and at the legislature's extravagance, however, quickly became secondary to their consternation over the plans the board of public works unfolded in late June 1871. To mid-twentieth century ears the proposals sound modest enough—$6,250,000 to be spent for laying sewers, grading and paving streets, planting trees, and removing unsightly nuisances, $4,000,000 of the cost to be met by a bond issue, the rest by assessments on private property. Yet however much small-minded parsimony affected men's thinking, other reasons for anxiety existed: first, the practically untrammelled power of a body of men responsible neither to the local public, nor, save indirectly, to Congress; second, the character of the individuals who composed the board, and third, a corollary, the extreme haste with which they acted. Events quickly showed that legislative review of plans as required by law was cursory and the advance authorization of spending a formality the board dispensed with. The explanation for the irresponsible behavior of the House of Delegates lay, according to the *Patriot*, in the fact that all its members together paid scarcely $2,500 in taxes.[11] The personality of Alexander Shepherd, who at once took command of the board of public works, overawed the delegates, moreover; they felt sure he knew what was best. He himself was equally sure. His postwar business career had heightened his self-confidence; operating on a financial shoestring, he had borrowed extensively, and built row after row of houses for sale, until his personal indebtedness reportedly ran into six figures. Here was a man who would not hesitate to plunge the District into debt

[10] Investigation into the Affairs of the District of Columbia, H Rpt 72, 42C, 2S, pp. 185, 229, 363-64, 493, 521-22, Ser 1542 (hereafter cited as Investigation, 1872); *The Nation*, xv, 329; Adams, *Our Little Monarchy*, p. 20.

[11] Investigation, 1872, pp. 229, 248-52, 267-73; S Misc Doc 84, 42C, 3S, Ser 1546; *Patriot*, 25 Nov 1871.

to achieve a goal he thought worthwhile. He cherished visions for Washington, and, in his determination to embody them quickly, he would ride roughshod over everybody and everything that stood in his way. After a first meeting, his associates on the board of public works entrusted all decisions to him. He immediately became "Boss Shepherd." Other officials of the new territory faded into virtual anonymity.[12]

Arbitrary power vested in a strong-willed but essentially honest man might have had few unhappy consequences had Shepherd had an engineer's training. A "show of activity and energy" in the management of District affairs, the *Nation* remarked, had to do duty for "technical knowledge and administrative experience." Ignorant of the technical problems involved, Boss Shepherd saw no reason to wait for advice or for accurate blueprints of the terrain before starting in upon execution of a "comprehensive plan of improvements" for the District of Columbia. Baron Haussmann took nearly twenty years to modernize Paris. Shepherd's readiness to improvise and his insistence upon trying to complete a vast program within the span of three years caused his downfall and brought bankruptcy upon the community he wanted to serve.[13]

The "comprehensive plan" called for altering street levels to make possible a drainage system capable of carrying off all surface water and sewage for the thickly settled areas of Washington and Georgetown. Otherwise, except for new bridges across Rock Creek, Georgetown was to undergo only minor changes. Better bridging of the Eastern Branch and grading of some of the roads to the north and east was to suffice for the county. In the heart of Washington's residential and business section, on the other hand, hilly stretches were to be levelled and hollows filled in order to give the avenues uniform gradients and to open the Capitol to view from every point in that part

[12] Investigation into the Affairs of the District of Columbia, S Rpt 453, 43C, 1S, I, x-xi, Ser 1590 (hereafter cited as Investigation, 1874); Howe, "Board of Public Works," CHS *Rec*, III, 267, 275-76.

[13] Investigation, 1874, II, 396, 425, Ser 1591; *Nation*, XVIII, 407; Howe, "Board of Public Works," p. 272.

of the city. There, since Shepherd was building for the future, streets still empty of buildings were to be improved with the rest. Within an area roughly encompassed between the Mall and P Street on the north, New Jersey Avenue on the east, and New Hampshire Avenue on the west all streets were to be paved, as well as all the main arteries extending to the city limits and the connecting county roads. Parking such as Mayor Bowen had introduced would narrow the streets, reduce costs, and leave space for shade trees. The Island below the Mall, the Navy Yard section, much of Capitol Hill, and most of northeast Washington netted relatively little attention.

City planning in the twentieth-century sense and as L'Enfant had conceived it in the 1790's was an unrecognized art in the America of the 1870's. Land use, architectural design, and the relationship of buildings to the space they would occupy and to the surrounding areas did not concern Shepherd. Neither the board of public works nor Congress observed that to permit the huge French Renaissance stone pile, designed for the State, Army, and Navy Departments, to rise where it would block off the sweep of New York Avenue from the river to the White House would do as much violence to L'Enfant's original layout as the Jacksonian Treasury had done. Nor did objections develop to having the Baltimore & Potomac Railroad Company lay its tracks across the Mall between the Smithsonian "park" and the Capitol grounds and erect a massive Gothic stone depot at 6th and north B Streets. Shepherd's comprehensive plan involved primarily engineering changes calculated to create a city with unrivalled sanitary facilities and clean, well-paved, well-lighted thoroughfares. Yet amid all the complaints that soon burst forth, none sounded at allowing a main sewer to empty into Rock Creek, a mere trickle of water in dry weather. The one feature of the proposed program aimed exclusively at beautification of the capital was the planting of trees, a task fortunately put into the hands of horticultural experts.

When the plan was first presented in June 1871, it was more comprehensive than specific; many of the particulars were vague. All that was abundantly clear was that its authors had been hurried and the expense of carrying it out would be heavy. In the face of private citizens' protests that five weeks was too short a time to produce an adequate engineering survey or a sound estimate of costs, the legislature approved the entire plan early in July and authorized the $4,000,000 bond issue the board of public works requested. The work of tearing up the streets began almost at once. Shepherd later justified his precipitousness by declaring that the board's function was to effect improvements "as rapidly as possible . . . in order that in this respect the capital of the nation might not remain a quarter of a century behind the times." Large taxpayers urged a pay-as-you-go method, raising $1,500,000 by a special tax and undertaking, to begin with, only part of the program, but Shepherd believed that piecemeal execution would imperil completion of the job.[14] In early 1871, despite some postwar building, every section of Washington contained unkempt vacant lots; open fields still ringed the area north of O Street and that east of the Capitol beyond the newly laid out Lincoln Park. On 7th Street horsecars ran to the city limits, but on 14th and 9th Streets the lines ended at S and M Streets, respectively. A single house, occupied by a fortuneteller, stood on Massachusetts Avenue west of 17th Street, while the debris left from the recent removal of Hopkins' brickyard cluttered the stretch beyond Dupont Circle. Shepherd, however, reasoned that once supplied with urban facilities the capital would grow, and the city must be ready. The upturn in real estate strengthened his convictions. In the spring of 1871 a syndicate of California mine operators, which included Curtis J. Hillyer and Senator William Stewart of Virginia City, Nevada, put some $600,000 into land near Dupont Circle. There on the square to the northwest "Stewart Castle," as imposing as its name implied, began to rise two years later, while Hillyer built an elaborate house on Massa-

[14] Investigation, 1872, pp. 45, 735, 739; *Patriot*, 27, 30 Jun, 1, 4, 15 Jul, 3 Aug 1871. Maps showing the areas of work on sewers and streets appear in *Report of Board of Public Works*, 1872, H Ex Doc 1, 42C, 3S, Ser 1562 (hereafter cited as Rpt BPW).

chusetts Avenue where the Cosmos Club stands today. If California miners saw fit to invest in Washington real estate, why should any one worry about the city's future financial resources?[15]

Conservative Washingtonians, nevertheless, did worry. Convinced of the dangers of attempting too much too fast, in August 1871 they obtained a court injunction against sale of the newly authorized bonds, on the grounds that the organic act creating the territory required voters' approval of any increase in the public debt above 5 percent of the assessed valuation of property. The legislature, subservient to Boss Shepherd's wishes, promptly got around the injunction by imposing a 5 percent income tax and permitting anticipation of $500,000 of current revenue in order to carry on the work until a special referendum on the loan could take place in November.[16] The board of public works, using the half million dollars at its disposal, made the most of its patronage. Where the corporation of Washington had had 10 salaried officials in the street department, Shepherd engaged 86. Undoubtedly he also counted on the thousands of men employed in digging up the streets to vote for the loan. At the polls in the autumn, ballots bearing the invidious label "Against Special Improvements" were so hard to find that most dissidents had to write out their own; and a great many men of property feeling this a hopeless contest with the have-nots, stayed at home. Approval of the loan went through by a 12 to 1 vote. In protesting to Congress about the coercion to which workingmen had been subjected, a colored preacher asserted that the voting was no more free than "was the pretended election of Napoleon to be Emperor of France."[17]

Boss Shepherd from first to last displayed myopic indifference to the cost of attaining his goals. He later admitted to assuming

[15] Investigation, 1874, II, 209, 220, Ser 1591; *Patriot*, 20 Aug 1872.

[16] Baltimore *Sun*, 25, 26 Jul 1871; *Patriot*, 24 Jul, 5, 20 Aug 1871, 15 Feb 1872; *Star*, 1, 5 Aug 1871; *Journal of the House of Delegates*, I, 685 (hereafter cited as *Delegates' Journal*); *Journal of the Council*, I, 139, 161 (hereafter cited as *Council Journal*).

[17] Investigation, 1872, pp. 9, 89, 170, 190, 442, 614, 698; Balt. *Sun*, 7 Aug, 18 Nov 1871; *Patriot*, 29 Oct, 25 Nov 1871; H Misc Doc 58, 42C, 2S, Ser 1525.

that, when finished, the job would so delight Congress that the United States Treasury would foot the bills. The bills immediately began to fall thick and fast. The board enlarged its staff to 203 salaried men, expanded its program, and specified for most of the streets asphalt or wood paving instead of the much cheaper macadam planned at first. To ensure against being stopped before it was too late, Shepherd ordered work to start in every section of the city at once. When Congress reconvened in December 1871, members beheld "miles of incomplete sewers, half-graded streets and half-paved sidewalks." Although cold weather halted digging, by the following March the board had spent over $2,000,000. During 1871, moreover, the legislature approved bond issues totalling $1,450,000, for purposes not originally included in the public works program—for the extension of water mains, for the Centre market-house, for an interest in a new railroad project, and $100,000 for relief of Chicagoans after fire razed that city in October 1871. Belated discretion stopped the issue of the railroad bonds and half the market-house bonds, but taxpayers discovered that in a half-year the territorial government had sanctioned an indebtedness larger than that of all but seven states of the Union, all told $9,450,000, nearly three times the total accumulated by Washington, Georgetown, and the county together in seventy years.

In January 1872 the House Committee on the District, in response to memorials signed by some 1,200 citizens, opened the first of two long investigations into the "Affairs of the District of Columbia." The charges against the territorial government and the board of public works ranged from carelessness and extravagance to outright corruption. At the end of the century one of Shepherd's staunch admirers noted that "but few of the small real estate owners were among those who became opponents to the march of improvements. Those who were the most active in opposition to the Board and its work were men of wealth who could well afford to pay the special taxes assessed against their property because of the increased value that the improvements gave it." Well-to-do men, it is true, led the fight, but inasmuch as a good many householders lost their homes through inability to pay the special assessments, taxes when due, or the 3 percent penalties for every month of delinquence, humble people as well as wealthy must have felt alarm.[18]

The altering of street grades "without discretion or fixed plan" about which the memorialist complained, left houses along F Street west of the White House, for example, perched upon embankments that barred access to stables and outbuildings in the rear. Workmen laying a sewer on 2nd Street found when digging reached the point of junction with a main sewer that because the engineer in charge had guessed at the levels, the lateral line was over ten feet too low. The petitioners protested at the "arbitrary" decision of the board of public works to fill in the Washington Canal instead of continuing the dredging that was to have opened it to navigation and permitted a one-way flow of water to wash sewage far out into the Eastern Branch. Furthermore, a payroll of $600,000 for salaried officials, contingent expenses for seven months amounting to a larger sum than the wealthiest state in the Union allowed for a year, the $100,000 spent on rented offices, and the $143,000 used for advertising, all pointed to a deplorable fiscal irresponsibility. One witness set the expenses of the District government at 300 to 400 percent higher than the city's had been. The District auditor testified that he knew nothing about the expenditures of the board of public works, since one of its members paid the bills without submitting vouchers of any kind. Two years later, in fact, the books would reveal that no one had kept track of what sums of money had gone for what.

The hearings lasted four months and ended with a majority report of the committee commending the achievements of the "high-minded," energetic men who made up the board of public works and urging "generous appropriations from Congress" to abet their program. Such mistakes as they had made were

[18] Investigation, 1872, pp. 1-2, 8-10, 158, 363-64, 404, 589-97; Balt. *Sun*, 5 Dec 1871; Howe, "Board of Public Works," CHS *Rec*, III, 267; *Patriot*, 30 Nov 1871; Marian Gouverneur, *As I Remember*, p. 353; *Cong Globe*, 42C, 2S, pp. 504-06.

honest errors, the public, while inconvenienced at times, had suffered no real injury and later would benefit, and, if excessive zeal for improvements had led those in charge to take shortcuts, their ultimate goal was so desirable that criticisms of their procedures were uncalled for. The $50,000 spent under Mayor Emery for dredging the canal was a regrettable loss, but the opinions of sanitary experts varied, and competent engineers upheld the decision to build a huge culvert along the bed of Tiber Creek for a sewer main and fill the land above. Congress, however, while accepting the majority report, set a debt limit of $10,000,000 for the territory which, in view of the debt already incurred, left less than a million dollars to complete "the comprehensive plan." Boss Shepherd assured Congress that when the United States Treasury paid over the $1,240,920 owed by the United States for improvements to federal property, the costs of winding up the program would not exceed his original estimate of $6,250,000.[19]

While the *Patriot* cried "whitewash," other local newspapers heralded the outcome of the investigation as the triumph of progress over petty fault-finding. Congress had not as yet appropriated any federal money, but local newspapermen, like numberless other citizens, apparently were persuaded that once improvements had gone far enough, the federal government would assume payment of the $4,000,000 loan. Shepherd always put his best foot forward in dealing with the press. After the *Patriot* expired, the board of public works remained all but sacrosanct to Washington newspapers till the day of its death in June 1874. The hearings of 1872 attracted little notice from outside journals; only months later did big city dailies begin to allude to Washington's "Tammany" and speak of analogies between the "Board of Public Works Ring" and the ring of the recently indicted Boss Tweed.[20]

[19] Investigation, 1872, pp. ii-xix and *passim; Cong Globe*, 42C, 2S, App., pp. 428-36, 42C, 3S, p. 23; S Misc Doc 14, 42C, 2S, Ser 1481; H Rpt 7, 42C, 3S, Ser 1576.

[20] *Patriot*, 3, 25 Jul, 20 Aug 1872; *Star*, 3 Mar 1873; Adams, *Our Little Monarchy*, p. 23.

Meanwhile Shepherd, armed with congressional blessings, hurried forward the work suspended during the investigation. Seemingly nothing now need slow progress—except the occasional necessity for redoing improperly planned or shoddily performed jobs, such as ripping up newly paved streets in order to lay sewer pipes somehow forgotten when paving began. Although serious delays occurred in the autumn when an epizootic disease killed or crippled hundreds of draft horses needed to cart the tons of earth removed from cuts and wanted for fills, Shepherd swept aside all man-made interference. Yet multiplying suits brought for over-assessments and, in September, sixteen pages of official advertisements in the *Star* listing property to be sold at auction for nonpayment of taxes suggested some truth in *The Nation*'s comment that "property originally valuable has been 'improved' and assessed out of existence." One resident later wrote, "It was a daily occurrence for citizens to leave their houses as usual in the morning, and when they returned at evening to find sidewalks and curbs, which not unfrequently had, but recently [been] laid anew, at their own expense, all torn up and carted away." In a fight between marketmen and the wrecking crew assigned to demolition of the Northern Liberties market-house, falling timbers killed one of the butchers. "Unfortunate accident," explained defenders of the board of public works. Its employees ripped up the rails laid by the Alexandria & Washington Railroad Company at the foot of the Hill even as the Baltimore & Potomac Railroad began laying its tracks across the Mall at 6th Street. "Obstructionists" of the "factious . . . malignant and mendacious opposition" published pamphlets bearing titles like *Our Little Monarchy* and *More about our Washington Tammany, Its Tool in Congress*, but the national election in November returned Grant to the White House and supporters of "this revolutionary Washington" to Congress and to the District legislature.[21]

[21] *Patriot*, 28 Aug, 9, 14, 19, 20 Sep, 8 Oct 1872; *Star*, 30 Sep 1872, 29 Jul, 15 Oct 1873; Balt. *Sun*, 4 Sep 1872; *Nation*, xv, 330; E. E. Barton, *Historical and Commercial Sketches of Washington and Environs*, pp. 29-30; Investigation, 1874, I, 6, 11, III, 1985, Sers 1590 and 1592.

The "obstructionists" were so absorbed in battling the board of public works that they took little notice of other weak spots in the territorial administration. Board proponents were equally oblivious. "There was never a time in Washington," wrote one observant resident, "when the wants of the laboring man and the poor were so little understood and so much neglected." The *Star* which for many years had carried sympathetic stories of needy families and charitable endeavors to help them now rarely gave space to any civic ills other than those due to opposing the public works program. The House of Delegates, composed though it was of rather humble men, evinced similar ostrich-like qualities. It considered bills introduced by Negro members to widen racial nondiscrimination and passed a civil rights act but tended to ignore other social problems. In 1872, while a handful of private citizens struggled to lessen the abject poverty in the city, the legislature entered into an extraordinary agreement with the Washington Market Company: in return for the company's relinquishing to the territorial government the space in which to build a hall along the Pennsylvania Avenue frontage of the still unfinished market-house, delegates and members of the governor's council reduced from $25,000 to $7,500 the company's annual ground rent which Congress had earmarked for relief of the poor. Such folly apparently grew out of the assumption that the board of public works was providing employment for every able-bodied person who wanted it, and out of belief that the federal government would continue generous support of the public hospitals and the cities' orphan asylums and contribute sums large enough to care for the aged destitute. The miscalculation was painfully obvious to its victims.[22]

Nevertheless by the spring of 1873 physical changes had created an outwardly "new Washington." Visitors' enthusiasm took much of the wind out of the sails of Boss Shepherd's critics. Where the old canal had stretched its smelly length from 7th Street to the Potomac below the White House "park," solid

[22] Adams, *Our Little Monarchy*, p. 15; *Council Journal*, III, 144, IV, 72, 211; H Ex Doc 16, 42C, 3S, Ser 1563; *Patriot*, 1 Jul 1872; *Congressional Record*, 43C, 1S, p. 3996.

ground extended, drained by a strongly constructed underground sewer. To the east another main emptied into the Eastern Branch, while the L Street line debouching into Rock Creek served a section of the city hitherto lacking any sewerage. The extension of water mains enabled several neighborhoods to abandon reliance on the wells in the public squares, while brick or cement sidewalks, miles of wooden pavement, and some concrete and some macadamized roadways ended the misery of dust in summer and heavy mire at other seasons. The expensive wood pavements seemed to contrast favorably with the tarred crushed stone surfaces in Paris, where "Imperial Hausmann [sic] humbugged the world for a short space of time into believing in macadam for city uses." Since streets and alleys occupied 54 percent of all the area within Washington's limits, compared to 35 percent in Vienna, 25 percent in Paris, 35 percent in New York and 29 percent in Philadelphia, the most resentful taxpayer could see that the job done was tremendous and that his money had served some useful purpose. Gone was the filth on Pennsylvania Avenue which had annoyed the Russian Grand Duke Alexis during his visit in 1871. And along the parkings, grass and sapling shade trees were beginning to give a touch of green beauty to the public ways.[23]

The visible progress of the territory's public works inspired other enterprise also. Long-postponed discussion of how to finance completion of the Washington Monument resumed. In 1873 when the Baltimore & Potomac Railroad depot opened on the site where the National Gallery of Art would rise in the 1930's, the location in the bed of the old Washington Canal enabled envious B & O officials to gibe at the "Sewer Route," but businessmen welcomed it, and the heavy square tower of the station gave the city a new landmark. Little by little householders felt stirred by an unfamiliar civic pride which, the *Star* proclaimed, "promises almost as much in behalf of the future

[23] Rpts, BPW, 1872, Ser 1562, and 1873, Ser 1603; *Star*, 4 Nov 1871, 20, 21 Nov 1872, and 14 Feb 1873 quoting *Lippincott's Magazine*.

growth of the city as the grand system of public works." Despite the special assessments and tax increases, a number of people began to look upon the "new Washington" as a sound place for real estate investment. Over 1,200 new buildings went up during 1872, and sales of real property during the next few months topped earlier records. Extension of street railways north, west, and eastward across the Eastern Branch opened up new residential areas. As the Connecticut Avenue line crept out toward Dupont Circle, Alexander Shepherd built an elaborate "mansion" at the corner of the avenue and L Street, and two blocks above, nearer Senator Stewart's "castle," the British government erected a house for Her Majesty's minister. Except for the building purchased by Prussia in 1866, this was the first foreign-owned legation in the American capital.[24]

The United States government itself caught the fever for improvement. Purchase of W. W. Corcoran's country estate, "Harewood," enlarged the grounds of the Soldiers' Home and provided a charming park on Washington's outskirts. The Commissioner of Public Buildings, eager to start a national zoological garden, put a caged American eagle into Franklin Square, two deer and later a pair of prairie dogs into Lafayette Square, and, having "purchased and liberated" a hundred pairs of English and German sparrows, reported proudly that these "valuable" birds were multiplying. After the board of public works removed the railway tracks at the edge of the Capitol grounds, Congress authorized the development of "Capitol Park" where Frederick Olmstead would again display the talent for landscape architecture that had made his layout of New York's Central Park famous. Even *The Nation*, in the past skeptical of Shepherd's competence, admitted that public and private improvements together "have attracted a respectable

[24] *Courier*, 18 May 1872; *Patriot*, 5 Sep 1872; H Rpt 48, 42C, 2S, Ser 1528; *Cong Globe*, 42C, 2S, pp. 2587-88, 3409; H. W. Schotter, *The Growth and Development of the Pennsylvania Railroad Company*, pp. 86-87; *Star*, 4, 11 Jan, 17 Jul, 19 Dec 1873, 24 Jan, 18 May 1874; Investigation, 1874, II, 261; Balt. *Sun*, 27 Feb, 4 Nov 1872.

class of winter residents who formerly held it [Washington] in great contempt."[25]

The arrival of new winter residents fanned hopes that Washington would not long remain "simply the seat of the General Government and . . . be without a single manufacturing establishment or a single wholesale business house." Coal shipments down the C & O Canal made fuel inexpensive. While the local newspapers drummed away at the advantages of the District for manufacturing, the House of Delegates talked of putting up a building equipped with steam power where mechanics could rent space. Why, asked one delegate, was the District not "the Lowell, the Lynn, or the Worcester, of the country?" Congress had consented to let the Orange, Alexandria and Manassas and the Washington and Point Lookout railroads run tracks into the District and authorized the territorial government's subscribing to stock in the projected Piedmont and Potomac Railroad. A federal appropriation of $50,000 for dredging the river and deepening Washington's and Georgetown's harbors promised to increase river shipping. If the price of land between Georgetown and the Great Falls were lowered, promoters argued, the power available there would attract northern capital and the skilled workers to man new factories; the 34-foot drop from canal to river could supply textile plants and at least one large rolling mill besides the ten flour and sawmills already drawing power from the canal. One enthusiast undertook to raise money in England to develop a mill village at the Great Falls. Compared to the 60 percent of the District's working population engaged in personal service and professional occupations, the 23 percent listed in "manufacturing and mechanical" jobs was small, but in early 1873 optimism prevailed among business leaders. New insurance companies formed, canal traffic was growing, a new national bank opened, and two of

[25] Rpt Sec/War, 1872, pp. 1110-30, Ser 1555, 1873, pp. 1151-69, Ser 1598, 1874, pp. 385-402, Ser 1637; Rpt Sec/Int, 1873, p. 768, Ser 1601, 1874, p. 734, Ser 1639; *Nation*, XVIII, 376; *Star*, 10 Dec 1872, 10 Sep, 17 Dec 1875.

Washington's four savings banks were paying 6 percent interest on deposits.[26]

Small tradesmen and workingmen unable to carry on by borrowing were less certain of their future. Shopowners lost money because streets torn up for months at a time made their places of business inaccessible. Although the board of public works had set a minimum wage of $1.50 a day for common labor, unskilled workmen employed by local contractors had to accept the wage rates paid men brought in by competing New York and Philadelphia contracting firms. Plasterers and carpenters made feeble attempts to organize unions, a Trade Union Central Committee formed, and the National Labor Council held two or three meetings. The results were negligible. And since unions as a matter of course excluded Negroes, that segment of the local work force was shorn of any possible benefit. Skilled artisans such as members of the typographical, bookbinders', and stone-cutters' unions and the thousand men employed at the Navy Yard were earning from $2.50 to $5.00 a day, but those who owned property in the District were subject to heavy taxation.[27] When the panic of 1873 struck in September, craftsmen suffered along with common laborers and capitalists.

Financial disaster had already overtaken the District of Columbia. Friends of the board of public works had long scoffed at hints that its books needed auditing, but by midsummer 1873 even a congressional appropriation of $3,500,000 to cover the costs of improvements to federal property was insufficient to stave off bankruptcy. An empty territorial treasury left school teachers, clerks, police, firemen, and day laborers without pay for months.[28] In September came the failure of the banking

[26] *Nation*, xv, 328-30; *Patriot*, 3, 21 Feb, 6 Mar, 27 Aug, 19 Sep, 2 Oct 1872; *Star*, 11 May 1871, 12 Apr, 5 Jun, 2 Jul 1872, 8 Jul 1873; *Delegates Journal*, i, 686; S Misc Docs 15, 68 and 88, 42C, 3S, Ser 1546; Rpt Sec/Int, 1872, p. 398, Ser 1560.

[27] City *Directory*, 1871; *Patriot*, 3 Jun 1871, 1 Oct 1872; *Star*, 12 Feb, 17 Jun 1872, 3, 8, 11, 25 Jul 1873, 23 Jan, 6 Apr 1874; *Chronicle*, 13 Apr 1874; *Nation*, xviii, 407.

[28] *Star*, 30 Apr, 9 Jun, 13 Jul 1873; *Patriot*, 29 Jun 1872; Investigation, 1874, i, 462, 469, ii, 12, 428; *Nation*, xvii, 86; 17 Stat. 406, 526.

house of Jay Cooke & Company and the beginning of a country-wide depression. Bank after bank suspended payment. When the First National Bank of Washington closed its doors, its president, Henry D. Cooke, resigned as governor of the District. President Grant appointed Alexander Shepherd to the post, but Shepherd, for all his assurance, could no longer obtain credit for the District. "The recent financial troubles," he reported in November, "prevented any realization from a sale of the sewer certificates," by means of which the board of public works had expected to pay its contractors. Property owners could not or would not pay the special assessments. Taxpayers angry during prosperous times grew panicky under the mounting financial pressures.[29] As the murmurs of wrath reached a roar, a second congressional investigation of the affairs of the District of Columbia opened in February 1874.

Unlike the first, the second investigation caught the attention of people throughout the country. Doubtless the panic and depression led them to suspect that cleaning up "the mess in Washington" would be directly helpful to them. In the capital the local newspapers attempted to belittle the attack on Boss Shepherd. Many of the ills of the District of Columbia long antedated the board of public works. Certainly that body was not responsible for the lack of school accommodations for 10,000 white and 5,800 Negro children. Shepherd's friends characterized his enemies as scalawags. One of them the *Chronicle* called "a red-hot Democrat and an original rebel," another reputedly "the owner of several houses on ______ alley, used for purposes which cannot be mentioned in a family newspaper"; and Sayles J. Bowen, once "fraudently" elected mayor, had earned "the just censure and anathema of every man." W. W. Corcoran, on the other hand, was too much revered as Washington's foremost philanthropist to be dismissed in that fashion; yet he had to publish his bill of particulars against the District government in a Baltimore newspaper because, he said, no local paper would

[29] Rpt BPW, 1873, p. 5, Ser 1603; *Star*, 18-20, 22, 24, 27 Sep 1873, 24 Jan 1874; Investigation, 1874, I, 467; *Cong Record*, 43C, 1S, p. 2183.

print it. Although impassioned defenders of the board of public works insisted that selfishness and petty vindictiveness motivated the appeal to Congress, the opposition now counted in its ranks citizens of every social and economic stratum. Mutual distrust reached a pitch as intense as that of the spring of 1861, born then of suspicions of disloyalty, in 1874 of belief that dishonesty and self-seeking were undermining the community.[30]

The published hearings cover 3,000 pages of fine print and contain some extraordinary testimony. Most District officials, ran the charges, were "negligent, careless, improvident, unjust, oppressive and illegal." A long list of specifics backed by a mass of detail laid the heaviest blame upon the presidential appointees, Alexander Shepherd above all. Some of the accusations needed no elaboration. Anyone traversing Washington's streets in 1874 could see, for example, that the wooden pavements laid at vast expense were already rotting; had the planners heeded the experience of other American cities that costly mistake could not have occurred. Shepherd had permitted favoritism to influence his selection of contractors. Jobbery had resulted. Adventurers from distant cities had pocketed as much as $97,000 as the fee for landing a contract of only about $700,000 for a firm that would undertake the work. The fact that skulduggery in letting municipal contracts was almost routine in other big American cities in no way lessened the offense in the eyes of the investigating committee. Here, however, the most "pernicious" error lay in imposing upon the community a hastily conceived project far too expensive to be met from local resources unless the work were spread over a number of years. The figures Governor Shepherd himself provided showed that, instead of $6,578,397, the board of public works had already spent $18,872,565, and approximately $2,000,000 more would have to go to pay for jobs under formal contract and still in process. Yet law set the debt limit at $10,000,000. By June 1874 the deficit for ordinary operating expenses would come to

[30] *Chronicle*, 28 Jan 1874; *Star*, 26 Feb 1874; Balt. *Sun*, 5 Feb 1874; *Nation*, XVIII, 18; Adams, *Our Little Monarchy*, pp. 4-9; Investigation, 1874, I, 6.

a minimum of $1,000,000. Shepherd's tacit admission that he expected Congress to foot half the bills did not endear him to the congressional committee.[31]

When the committee submitted its conclusions, most of the local press rejoiced that "not one word" of the report could "be fairly construed into censure" of District officials, least of all Shepherd, the "Bayard without fear and without reproach." Metropolitan journals, on the contrary, lashed out at the committee's mildness. The reason for it, the New York *Tribune* opined and the Washington *Chronicle* agreed, was plain: Grant had so closely identified himself with his appointees that a strong indictment of them would have amounted to censuring the President. The management of the national capital had at last become an issue of national significance. But satisfaction or anger over congressional forgivingness faded as the future of the District came up for discussion on the Hill. While the investigation was still in process, Congress had appropriated money to pay school teachers' salaries. In June, with the opening of debate on how to handle the District's other debts, Washingtonians still hoped for further assistance. Obviously the first necessity was to straighten out the financial tangle; the question of how the District was to be governed thereafter could wait.[32]

No one expected the territorial government to endure. Congress, pronouncing it a failure, voted without debate to abolish the governorship, the legislature, and the board of public works, and temporarily to place control in the hands of three commissioners to be appointed by the President. A 3 percent tax on Washington real estate, 2½ percent on Georgetown's, and 2 percent on the county's would meet current expenses. The First and Second Comptroller of the Treasury were to audit the

[31] Investigation, 1874, I, ii, vii-x, 464-69, II, 997-1011, 1013-14, 1124-26, 1209-17, III, 2115, 2143, 2146, 2356; ptn, S43A-E22, 10 Mar 1874; Report of the Commissioners of the District of Columbia, H Ex Doc 1, 43C, 2S, pp. 166, 170, Ser 1641.

[32] Investigation, 1874, I, x-xx; *Courier*, 11, 25 Apr, 30 May 1874; *Star*, 7, 24, 29 May 1874 and, quoting Cincinnati *Commercial*, 19 Jun 1874; *Chronicle* 6 Apr, 16 May, 10 Jun 1874; New York *Tribune*, 9, 19 Jun 1874; Chicago *Tribune*, 10 Jun 1874; *Nation*, XVIII, 375-76, 407-8.

accounts of the territory and of the board of works and examine property holders' claims to damages. Special commissioners were to handle funding of the District debt through 50-year bonds bearing 3.65 interest and guaranteed by the "faith" of the United States. The board of health and the school boards were to remain intact. Finally, two senators selected by the Vice-President and two representatives chosen by the Speaker of the House were to draft a bill for a permanent form of government and recommend what share of the cost should fall upon the United States, what upon the community.[33]

Most citizens drew a long breath of relief. The credit of the United States would prevent a financial collapse, wanton spending would cease, injured property owners could anticipate collecting damages, and Congress would eventually return control of their own affairs to District citizens if by then they wanted it. For the time being the new law disposed of what the Georgetown *Courier* labelled the "curse" of Negro suffrage. A preposterous incident silenced men who regretted the change. Several members of the House of Delegates, upon hearing of the territory's demise, rushed to the legislature's hall and pocketed inkwells and other small objects; one pilferer, caught walking out with a red feather duster protruding from his trouser leg, fastened the label "Feather Duster legislature" upon the entire assembly. Ridicule killed it more thoroughly than congressional law. Thereafter whites opposed to the return of any local suffrage that included colored voters spoke of "the Feather Dusters" and "the Murder Bay politicians"; by implication Negroes, in short, were responsible for every disaster of the territorial regime.[34] The high hopes its creation had aroused less than three and a half years before were buried deep.

The President immediately nominated Shepherd as one of the three commissioners; the Senate refused to confirm him. Senator Logan of Illinois declared that in the West "the people were feeling more strongly about the District investigation than

[33] *Cong Record*, 43C, 1S, pp. 5116-24, 5154-56; 18 Stat. 116-21.

[34] *Courier*, 20 Jun 1874; *Chronicle*, 21 Jun 1874; *Star*, 18 Jun 1874, 28 Jan, 25 Feb 1878.

about the currency itself." The post went to William Dennison, one-time Governor of Ohio and Postmaster General in Lincoln's second Cabinet, and to two former congressmen. Shepherd remarked "a sacrifice was needed" and he was selected for the role.[35] In 1876, his fortune gone and his hopes of new public office withered, he moved himself and his family to Mexico, leaving behind him a disenfranchised city still undergoing the physical renovations he had begun.

[35] *Nation*, XVIII, 403; *Star*, 3 Jul 1874, 22 Mar 1875; *Courier*, 18 Jul 1874.

CHAPTER XV

SOCIAL AND CULTURAL CROSSCURRENTS, 1871-1874

CIVIC PRIDE in 1874 as in 1870 had little to feed on in half a dozen areas of Washington. Poverty and crime still bestrode much of the city, the penal and legal systems still needed reform, and preoccupation with the public works controversy, with politics and frivolous social affairs, or with personal financial tribulations had lessened the flow of charity. The comprehensive plan of improvement had scarcely touched the Island; that area, long cut off from the rest of the city first by the canal and then by railroad tracks, had become one vast slum. Its shanties and crowded tenements bred half the crime in the District. The overloaded dockets of the District Supreme Court and the new police court, a police force limited to 238 officers, and the greed and ignorance of law displayed by some of the justices of the peace offered small hope of bettering law enforcement, let alone drying up the well springs of delinquency and felony. The appearance in 1874 of an official volume entitled *Revised Statutes of the District of Columbia*, incomplete and badly organized as it was, helped reduce the "hodge-podge of unreality" that had constituted local law since 1801, but the new compilation failed appreciably to check thieving and gambling, prostitution, assault, and murder.[1] The strongest deterrent to crime no doubt was still fear of even a brief sojourn in the old District jail: four to eight persons in 8- by 10-foot windowless cells without water closets and for an entire corridor only one tub of water daily for prisoners to wash in. Here, under conditions worse than during the Civil War, all sorts and kinds of people awaited trial or served their sentences.

[1] *Cong Record*, 43C, 1S, pp. 3916-17; Report of the Commissioners of the District of Columbia, 1874, pp. 20-25, H Ex Doc 1, 43C, 2S, Ser 1641 and 1875, pp. 40-41, H Ex Doc 1, 44C, 1S, Ser 1682 (hereafter cited as Comrs Rpts); Walter Cox, "Efforts to Obtain a Code of Laws," CHS *Rec*, III, 125-29; *Star*, 25 Apr 1873, 6 Apr 1874; H Misc Doc 25, 42C, 3S, Ser 1571.

The only other place for law-breakers was the workhouse or the Reform School for Boys.[2]

"There is in this [District]," wrote an official, "a large number of boys whose only home is the streets, whose dormitory is the market house, a stable, an out-house or sometimes the lee-side of a wall, or door-step; and others who have parents, but might better, perhaps, be orphans." By 1874 over a hundred children averaging in age about thirteen and a half years were penned up at the workhouse where they had to consort with "old and hardened characters." As the Reform School could accommodate only 65 boys, the trustees felt obliged periodically to release some prematurely to make room for others. Firmly believing in the school's "salutary" effect upon its inmates, the trustees again and again begged Congress for a larger building in a more healthful location than the malaria-ridden farm above Georgetown, and Congress, perhaps feeling guilty at having appropriated nothing for the federal institution since 1870, responded at last by voting $100,000 for a building capacious enough to take 300 boys. Located near the District line northeast of the Capitol, the building when opened in late 1874 housed 55 white and 58 colored boys in carefully segregated corridors.[3]

The fact that the preponderance of want, like the preponderance of crime, was to be found among Negroes undoubtedly affected the community's philanthropy, for, after the founding of the Freedmen's Bureau in 1865, white citizens had come to expect the federal agency to relieve them of the care of indigent blacks. When the demise of the bureau in 1871 returned the responsibility to local organizations, the adjustment was both painful and slow. Moreover, to a degree unknown in the Washington of earlier years, the "fashionables" drawn to the capital at the height of the gilded age successfully ignored most of the

[2] The official reports of the Metropolitan Police, the Warden of the Jail, and the Trustees of the Reform School are in the Rpts Sec/Int, 1870-74, Sers 1449, 1505, 1560, 1601 and 1639. *Patriot*, 7 Oct 1871; *Chronicle*, 28 Sep 1874; *Star*, 30, 31 Jul, 13 Aug 1873, 1 Jul 1874; *Nation*, xv, 329-30.

[3] H Rpt 39, 42C, 2S, Ser 1528; Comrs Rpt, 1874, pp. 109-11.

38. "The Grand Review of the Glorious Army of the Potomac," May 1865. From a painting by James E. Taylor

39. Lobby of the House of Representatives during debates on the Civil Rights Bill of 1866. Wood engraving in *Harper's Weekly*

40. The Impeachment Trial of Andrew Johnson, 1868. Wood engraving in *Harper's Weekly*

41. C & O Canal and the Aqueduct Bridge from Georgetown, ca. 1867

42. Richard Wallach, Mayor of Washington, 1861-1868. Photograph by Mathew Brady

43. Alexander Shepherd, head of Board of Publ Works, 1871-1874 and Governor of the Territor 1873-1874

44. Frederick Douglass, in 1871 editor of the *New Era*, Washington's first Negro newspaper

45. John Mercer Langston, counsel to the Board c Health, 1871-1874

46. The new Baltimore and Potomac Railroad Station located on the Mall on the present site of the National Gallery. The train sheds extended southward nearly half-way across the Mall

47. The Shepherd Mansion on L Street and Connecticut Avenue

48. A Reception at ex-Governor Shepherd's, 1876. Wood engraving in the New York *Daily Graphic*

49. The Reading Room of the Library of Congress, ca. 1878

50. "Image of the City," 1852. Aquatint by E. Sachse & Co.

51. The Actuality, 1876. Beyond the Smithsonian stands the mansard-roofed Department of Agriculture building set in its formal garden. The ponds near the base of the Monument were formed when the Washington Canal was filled in and B Street, the present-day Constitution Avenue, became a road of sorts

misery about them. The charity ball and the benefit whist party were not yet a fixed society routine. W. W. Corcoran built and endowed in memory of his wife the beautiful Louise Home for impoverished elderly gentlewomen to which, the saying went, three P's gave admission: personality, pedigree, and poverty. Several score of old residents of the city contributed time and money to the Industrial Home School, to the white orphan asylums, and, less generously, to the Home for Destitute Colored Women and Children. The 111 churches in the District helped selected "worthy" causes; a woman's club sought to rescue unwilling inmates of houses in "Joe Hooker's Division"; and volunteers composing a citizens' relief committee collaborated with the Army Depot Commissary in trying to dole out federal relief funds wisely. Yet charity during the years of the territorial regime was on the whole lean. Governor Cooke taught a Sunday School class and served on the board of the YMCA; other than members of the board of health, most officials apparently paid no more attention to the plight of the poor than did temporary residents intent upon entrenching themselves in high official society.[4]

Amid the widespread obliviousness to suffering in Washington and Georgetown, the services performed by the board of health stood out as a signal achievement. Of the local newspapers, only the *Patriot* recognized its value; the rest were generally unsympathetic to the health officers' programs. When Congress was abolishing the territorial government, the *Star* urged dispensing with a body whose five members got $2,000 apiece "earned by throwing night soil at each other." Fortunately their work spoke for itself. Their reports presented facts a reluctant public needed to know, and while doctors and sanitary inspectors were rarely in a position to eradicate the evils they described, they made an essential beginning by carrying on a campaign of education, underscoring the importance of accurate

[4] *Nation*, xviii, 186, 202; *Patriot*, 18, 19 Sep, 30 Nov 1871, 18 Jan 1872; Rpt Sec/Int, 1872, p. 398, Ser 1560; *Star*, 8, 9, 13 May 1873, 8 Feb 1920.

vital statistics and strict enforcement of a sound sanitary code. By exercising such authority to quarantine as the law allowed them, they gradually reduced the incidence of contagious disease. After an 18-month fight to make vaccination compulsory for "every man, woman and child" in the District, they halted a severe epidemic of small pox which was ravaging northern cities; that Washington was freed of it by midsummer 1873 was a tribute to the board of health.[5]

Its members were a dedicated group of men. Of the three physicians, Dr. William Bliss, his lean, swarthy-skinned face broadened by side-burns, was the best known in the profession; his reputation and his calm strength in the face of attack made him a formidable adversary. Dr. T. S. Verdi, a young homeopathic physician, did much of the leg work and wrote several of the board's most telling reports; to these he contributed not only detailed information about existing conditions but also the passion of his convictions that ignorance and selfishness must not be permitted to interfere with the safeguarding of public health. John Mercer Langston, legal counsel to the board, was a graduate of Oberlin and, before becoming the head of the Howard University Law School, had served as roving inspector for the Freedmen's Bureau; the touch of naïve braggadocio which his autobiography reveals was more endearing than irritating. Endowed with patrician features and lighter-skinned than his warm friend Dr. Bliss, Langston was impressive looking. When the two men were attending a conference with eminent physicians in Boston, one of the New Englanders, remarking that he had heard that one of the Washingtonians was a Negro, turned inquiringly to them. Langston mischievously pointed to his darker complexioned companion, whereupon, to the confusion of their hosts, both men burst into laughter. Dr. Bliss, like his fellows on the board, appreciated

[5] *Star*, 6 Feb, 13, 21 Mar, 12, 13, 17 Jun, 20 Aug, 16, 18 Oct 1872, 15 Feb, 8, 9, 13 May, 23, 26 Jul 1873, 15 Jun 1874; *Patriot*, 11 May, 16 Aug 1871, 25 Sep 1872; *Cong Globe*, 42C, 2S, pp. 2429, 2526; Rpt of Brd of Health in Comrs Rpt, 1874, pp. 281-82, 289.

Langston's ability, and their need of competent legal advice early became evident.[6]

Preventive measures were from the beginning one of the board's chief goals. The physicians urged reclamation along the river front of "the vast areas now partially submerged, and on receding tides giving out poisonous vegetable emanations, generating malaria." They fought for public baths and wash houses: "Personal filth . . . and the saturation of unwashed undergarments are among the prolific generators of plague and pestilence." They strove to organize efficient street-cleaning and garbage collecting services and, though the results were disappointing, at least the District cities were cleaner than in many years past. In an effort to end the nuisance of animals running loose in the streets, the board of health introduced a system of impounding. The first catch, to everyone's amusement, was three of President Grant's horses strayed from the White House stable; it cost the President $6 to redeem them. Because hundreds of privies still existed in Washington and Georgetown, disposal of night soil was a more serious problem. In 1874 a contract with the "Odorless Excavating Apparatus Company" introduced the use of suction pumps and air-tight containers instead of the buckets and open carts formerly employed, but wagons still carted the contents to the wharf at 17th Street below the White House and thence barges carried the load down the Potomac.[7]

Although the board of health congratulated "a community unaccustomed to sanitary restraints" for its general conformity to new regulations, the public balked at the proposal to eliminate alley-dwellings. Dr. Verdi put the case for wiping out that menace, a danger "on account of its permanency; existing at all hours, in every part of the city, behind the palatial mansion as well as in front of the poor man's hut." He spoke of "the hundred

[6] John Mercer Langston, *From Virginia Plantation to National Capitol, or the First and Only Negro Representative in Congress from the Old Dominion*, pp. 298, 318-34.

[7] Comrs Rpt, 1874, pp. 289, 292-95; *Patriot*, 10 Aug 1871; *Star*, 6 Jul, 25 Aug 1871, 9 Jul, 5 Aug 1873.

miles or more of alleys which run through our squares, and which receive the filth that flows from almost every house in our city. They are generally badly paved and undrained and yet are used as the repository of all the disgusting and foul refuse of our dwellings . . . these alleys should not exist, and if they are tolerated at all, they should serve only for the transportation of wood, coal, or such articles as require easy access to the back premises of the dwellings." Cobblestone paving was "worse than useless, for it allows . . . filth to be absorbed and retained between interstices." Every alley should be paved with concrete, be supplied with a sewer, and so graded that a nightly hosing from hydrants in each block could flush the alley clean. Execution of such a plan, however, meant inducing the board of public works to act, and the board of public works, more concerned with making a fine showing where it would be immediately visible than with cleaning up the cities' hidden recesses, confined itself to paving with "useless" cobblestone. The inhabited alleys remained. "Disposal of the squalid shanties that line them . . . and subjecting them to the same public regulations as the streets and avenues" seemed unimportant to the community and to men on the Hill.[8] Not until forty years later would Congress belatedly heed that plea.

In 1874, realizing that corrective legislation would be slow to materialize, the board of health took the unprecedented step of condemning 389 unsanitary buildings. The whitewashing that the Freedmen's Bureau had performed in Negro quarters had come to an end in 1870; the numerous small tenement houses in which large families each occupied a room scarcely ten feet square had become "dens of filth," and proceedings against the occupants rather than the landlords were manifestly futile. Washingtonians' fright over the small pox epidemic of 1872 probably explains their acquiescence in the revolutionary decree ordering the demolition of private property. At the same time health officers, determined to have reliable data on infant

[8] *Patriot*, 23 Jul 1873; Rpt BPW, 1873, p. 54, Ser 1603; Comrs Rpt, 1874, pp. 279, 287.

mortality as a weapon with which to fight, persuaded Congress to enact a law making registration of births obligatory. Board reports called attention to the airlessness and dirt in which thousands of families had to live as one of "the constantly operating causes which destroy our cherished offspring." Nor did the federal government escape censure; at the Treasury and recently finished Pension Office, the "rooms are crowded with clerks and employees much beyond their capacity. These, for an average of six hours per day, breathe an atmosphere saturated with carbonic acid." The top story of the Treasury was "a barbarous den for cattle" likely to inspire outraged protest from the Society for the Prevention of Cruelty to Animals.[9] The "new Washington" clearly was not entirely beautiful.

Although public education evoked wider interest than sanitation, the weaknesses in the school system were still a source of chagrin to thoughtful citizens. Nearly 29,000 illiterates in the District in 1871 was indeed alarming. Yet in a community where taxpayers felt pinched by the special public works assessments and where the schools were eating up 38 percent of total revenues, Superintendent of Schools J. Ormand Wilson and the school board hesitated to ask the House of Delegates to increase the levy. Well-to-do white parents tended to side-step the problem by sending their children to one or another of the numerous good private schools in the area; in 1873 only 44 percent of all white and about 53 percent of all colored children of school age in the District were enrolled in the public schools. By then the New England Friends Mission had closed the four schools it had maintained for Negroes. In Washington, continuation of the building program begun under Mayor Wallach had added the Seaton, Curtis, Jefferson, and Cranch schools for whites, and the Sumner and Capitol Hill schools for colored, and still accommodations were so cramped that class enrollment averaged 59 pupils. When Norman Chipman, District delegate in the House, appealed for help in providing for the nearly

[9] Rpt Sec/Int, 1870, p. 933, Ser 1449 and 1872, p. 914, Ser 1560; Comrs Rpt, 1874, pp. 282-84, 296.

16,000 children receiving no schooling, Congress responded by giving, not the 2,500,000 acres of public land Chipman asked for, but part of a square on Virginia Avenue in southeast Washington.

As school receipts dropped during 1873, white and colored trustees in desperation extended to most of the schools the half-day sessions already in effect in several elementary classes. The scheme of having half the pupils attend in the morning, the rest in the afternoon, doubled the load upon teachers at the very time a bankrupt District treasury was leaving them without pay. Inasmuch as voluntary attendance more than filled the classrooms, the truancy law passed in 1864 remained a dead letter, and the demand for additional elementary schools stifled hopes for a high school. Yet the need for more primary grade teachers led to the opening of a white normal school in 1873; the twenty candidates were selected for the year's training from the most promising of the grammar school graduates.[10]

The Negro intelligentsia was disappointed and angry at the barring of colored students from the new normal school. When discussing the authorizing bill the House of Delegates amended the original version so as to make the school biracial. At the instigation of the Negro who had taken Frederick Douglass' place on the governor's council, the upper chamber rejected the amendment. "The recreancy of our [Negro] representatives in the Council," a group of colored citizens observed bitterly, killed the best possibility of breaking the wall of prejudice that guarded the dual school system. Leading Negroes like John F. Cook, Adolphus Hall, John Langston, Dr. Charles Purvis of the Freedmen's Hospital, and the Douglasses, father and son, believed school integration essential to Negro progress and to building mutual understanding between the races. Proponents

[10] *Patriot*, 29 Jan 1872; *Star*, 29 Jun, 3, 14 Oct 1873, 9 Feb 1874; *Cong Globe*, 42C, 2S, pp. 2526-27, 4035; Investigation 1874, pp. 481-545. The illiteracy figures appear in the Report of the Commissioner of Education, in Rpt Sec/Int, 1871, pp. 64-65, Ser 1506; additional statistics on both the white and colored schools are to be found in the Reports Sec/Int, 1872, Ser 1561, 1873, Ser 1602, and 1874, Ser 1640. For a long list of private schools see *Star*, 11, 19, 27 Aug 1873.

of mixed schools may have gained adherents when the governor's council failed to endorse Frederick Douglass' proposal to guarantee the colored schools every benefit enjoyed by the white, but nearly ten years of separate systems had strengthened the vested interest of Negro teachers in keeping the Negro schools independent. Furthermore, minor Negro functionaries, in the view of the *New National Era*, upheld them in order to curry political favor with influential whites. And without the solid backing of the Negro community the change could not take place. If a fair division of funds were assured, a considerable number of colored people preferred the "separate but equal" arrangement. Throughout the seventies unhappily the phrase represented only a half-truth; the seven years of schooling available to the intelligent Negro child left him with a far sketchier education than the white child could get. The Miner Fund, established by philanthropists in memory of Myrtilla Miner, enabled Howard University to open an elementary teacher training unit, and with that the colored community had to be content.[11]

In other respects the campaign for equal rights made some headway. Although the House of Delegates never had more than five of its twenty-two seats occupied by Negroes, and the *New National Era* complained that few important appointive posts fell to Negroes, the governor's council nevertheless always had at least two colored members, and Langston on the board of health, a Negro as treasurer of the District, and other colored men in lesser appointive jobs represented political recognition. Congress failed to pass two bills presented by Senator Sumner in 1872, one barring racial discrimination in the selection of teachers and the admission of children to Washington's and Georgetown's public schools, the other, anticipating most of the national Civil Rights Act of 1875, forbidding segregation in public places of entertainment, churches, and, for ultimate thoroughness, in cemeteries; but on the second proposal the

[11] *Patriot*, 30 May 1871, 10 May 1872; *Star*, 30 Jun, 1 Jul 1873; *New National Era*, 22 Feb 1872, 5 Jun, 3, 10, 31 Jul, 9 Oct 1873, 22 Jan 1874.

territorial legislature stepped into the breach with a District civil rights law. It carried further the provisions of the municipal ordinances passed under Mayor Bowen, and the new law applied to Georgetown and the county as well as Washington. It imposed a $100 fine upon any hotel, restaurant, saloon, or barber shop that refused to serve "any respectable and well-behaved person regardless of color." The police and the courts set about enforcing the act in the face of various attempts at evasion, such as barber shop and restaurant notices announcing "Haircut, $30, shampoo, $40," or "steak, $2, ham and eggs, $3," with a line of small print offering "a liberal reduction . . . to our regular patrons." The famous Arlington Hotel near Lafayette Square faced a suit for denying a Negro a room.[12]

At President Grant's second inauguration colored congressmen's wives danced at the ball alongside West Point cadets. A few Negroes experienced business success; the Wormley House owned and run by one-time slave James Wormley was considered one of Washington's best. Only the Congregational church welcomed colored parishioners, but Negro churches had multiplied. In June 1874 the laying of the cornerstone of St. Augustine's on 15th Street above K marked the building of the city's first exclusively Negro Roman Catholic church. And colored men registered and voted in territorial elections with as much freedom as whites. Not only did equal protection under the laws seem reasonably secure, but here and there an ungrudging acceptance of colored people appeared to be taking root. In the autumn of 1873 the *Era*, attributing progress to the presence of Congress, concluded: "Probably to a greater extent than elsewhere in the country is the equality of citizens in the matter of public rights accorded in the District of Columbia.

[12] *Cong Globe*, 42C, 2S, pp. 2539-42, 3057, 3738-41; *Council Journal*, II, 29, III, 157, IV, 38, 211, 430, 550; *Patriot*, 25 Apr, 22-23 Jul, 9 Oct 1872; *Star*, 13, 27, 30 Aug, 3 Sep, 2 Nov, 5 Dec 1872; *New Ntl Era*, 13, 20, 27 Jun, 25 Jul, 7 Nov, 19 Dec 1872; Phineas Indritz, "Post Civil War Ordinances in the District of Columbia Prohibiting Racial Discrimination," *The Georgetown Law Journal*, XLII, 179-207, and "Racial Ramparts in the Nation's Capital," *ibid.*, XLI, 297-329.

. . . Our only drawback today is in the matter of schools."[13]

Belief that the somewhat stronger position of Negroes in the District derived from Congress rather than from the growth of racial tolerance within the local white community probably accounts for the apparent indifference of colored people to the extinction of the territory and the accompanying sacrifice of the local franchise. Insofar as the *New National Era* represented the thinking of enlightened Negroes, they already had come to look upon the territorial experiment as a substantial loss to the cause of self-government. In realms outside direct political control, racial prejudice in Washington and Georgetown had diminished with discouraging slowness since Washington's municipal council passed the first civil rights ordinance in 1869. The Medical Society of the District of Columbia and the Bar Association still refused to admit Negro doctors and lawyers to membership; the space allotted to Negroes at St. Elizabeths indicated that anything would do for "crazy niggers"; the three hundred patients at Freedmen's Hospital got inadequate care; the colored battalion of the District militia was still denied privileges accorded white units; street railway employees behaved rudely to colored passengers; and, worst of all for the rank and file of colored working people, white merchants never engaged colored salesmen, and trade unions refused to accept Negro apprentices or to work alongside skilled Negro craftsmen. White people, Frederick Douglass remarked, misinterpreted the Negro demand for equality as meaning a determined effort to mingle with them on every social occasion. They never dreamed that Negroes, given a choice, might find their own society more congenial.[14] Colored people wanted courteous treatment, but above all they wanted a fair chance to rise in the economic scale. Only then would racial barriers collapse. In 1874 that great desideratum looked quite as attainable under

[13] *Nation*, XVI, 173; *New Ntl Era*, 8 Feb, 10 May 1872, 9 Oct 1873; *Star*, 15 Jun 1874; Rev. Francis Grimke to G. Smith Wormley, 23 Aug 1934, Carter Woodson Mss.

[14] *Patriot*, 10 May 1872; *New Ntl Era*, 20 Jun, 15 Aug, 20 Feb, 20 May, 26 Jun, 11 Sep 1873.

the rule of federally appointed commissioners as under territorial officials.

It is worth noting that the *Era* put some of the blame for the slowing of the Negro advance upon the younger generation of colored Washingtonians. James Berret of the *Patriot* contended that the relationship of white and colored people had deteriorated because of the invasion of newcomers from the South. "The native and natural colored population of this District is excellent in character, intelligent, and has always been respected." Where there had been 14,000 Negroes in 1860, immigration had brought the number to 43,404 by 1870 and, Berret estimated, to 48,000 by September 1872; the shiftless new arrivals who "are eating us out of house and home," he argued, were the source of all the trouble. Not so the *Era*. "How many sons," asked the editors, "have inherited the undoubtedly good traits of their fathers?" The latter had always recognized the moral and social obligation of correcting a wrong when they had done one, but was it not true that now "a systematic depreciation of young colored men by each other has stripped them of whatever consideration their talents or their standing might entitle them to among the whites?" It was the "modesty, public spirit, and independence" of the older generation that had "helped to create the possibilities of the present day, and nothing but these traits of character in young colored men will save them from the failures begot by egotism, the guilt of selfishness, the disgrace of sycophancy, and the disgust which ever waits on bad manners."[15]

Much of white society set a dubious example. The fashion begun with President Grant's first inaugural "for everyone who entertains at all to think to outdo everyone in extravagance" became still more pronounced as time went on. Although a simplicity that included dining at five in the afternoon characterized the President's household, Governor Cooke entertained prodigally. "If refined taste did not prevail, the defect was

[15] *Patriot*, 26 Sep 1872; *New Ntl Era*, 13 Nov 1873.

covered by Oriental splendor," wrote Emily Briggs. "An official reception is given in mid-winter and $1500 is paid for the single item of roses alone." The *Olivia Letters* added, "In other cities of the Union the mansions of the opulent and hospitable are thrown open because the host and hostess desire to see their guests. In Washington this order of things is reversed." The society columns of metropolitan dailies fed "the passion for notoriety to be won by prodigal display." Important public figures flocked to the endless succession of elaborate formal receptions where "were to be seen a galaxy of diamonds, with Mrs. Fernando Wood attached to the back of them." In the early weeks of 1874 the *Star*, uneasy over the impending investigation of District affairs, proposed: "Let us have cheaper pleasures, and it cannot be doubted that we shall soon hear less of 'rings' and deficits from the public treasury." The new governor of "the Monumental city so celebrated for its lavish but tasteful hospitality," was loath to accept that counsel. At the crowded receptions, masquerade balls, and dances held in Governor Shepherd's Connecticut Avenue mansion the amiable host and his guests continued to exude as much satisfaction "as if no previous opportunity had been given to enjoy the hospitality of the Governor's residence." Only after Nellie Grant's wedding at the White House in 1874 did the growing severity of the national business depression and mounting criticisms of the Grant administration check the earlier flamboyance.[16]

Out of the growing distaste of old established Washington families for the "carpetbaggers" and newly rich people who indulged in most of the ostentatious display rose a phenomenon unknown in society of the capital since the battle over Peggy Eaton. The rift of the early 1870's was different in character, but the immediate result was the same: a division within the ranks of influential people. President Jackson, Secretary of War Eaton, and his wife had deeply resented the snubs to which

[16] Poore, *Reminiscences*, II, 194, 259; *Olivia Letters*, pp. 194, 257, 340-41; Balt. *Sun*, 5, 13 Feb 1872; *Star*, 2, 6, 16, 19, 24, 28 Jan, 11-12 Feb, 24 May 1874; *Chronicle*, 27 Feb 1874.

moralizing ladies of the capital had subjected her; forty years later the group disdained by Washington blue-bloods seemed scarcely aware of any lack of welcome. The "parvenus," on the contrary, felt themselves in command; only envy could dictate any aloofness on the part of those whom the book on etiquette prepared by Admiral Dahlgren's widow called "the very elite." There was no open feud. Mrs. Dahlgren's "old residential society" simply withdrew, becoming the antecedents of the twentieth-century "cave-dwellers." Although an aversion to northerners without distinguished backgrounds probably contributed to this split, sheer dislike of bad manners apparently was a greater factor; for the first generation of cave-dwellers was cordial to cultivated newcomers, the more so if they held government posts that promised to make them fixtures in the community. Thus the dividing line fell not between government employees and private citizens, or between temporary and permanent residents, or between affluent people and impoverished. Standards of behavior became the principal criterion of acceptability.

While "the political element," in Olivia's phrase, frequented the showy official receptions, old Washingtonians preferred evenings spent in Professor Henry's parlors at the Smithsonian where young scientists and scholars recently arrived in government service might also be found. Friends with a literary penchant made much of the "King's Reunions," gatherings at Horatio King's pleasant H Street house, where the host, a member of the Union Literary Society of the 1840's and Postmaster General in the last days of President Buchanan's administration, arranged soirees of poetry readings, original essays, and personal reminiscences. Pleasure in these meetings inspired the founding of the Washington Literary Society in 1874, its forty members chosen quite as much for their social as their literary qualifications. Certainly had Walt Whitman still lived in Washington, he would not have been one of "des élus des élus," as a diplomat's wife sardonically labelled the members. At the same time the generals, admirals, bankers, and other well-to-do old residents who organized the Metropolitan Club were in turn selective: neither moneybags nor political power guaranteed a candidate membership. While some Georgetowners joined the club, political union with Washington did little to restore the intimate social give-and-take that had obtained between the two cities seventy years before. Georgetown, on the contrary, gradually developed her own cave-dwellers with little interest in the neighboring elite.[17]

If the new social exclusiveness redeemed Washington in the eyes of conservative old residents, unquestionably the city's growing reputation as a center of learning was more instrumental in preserving her dignity in much of the country. For illogical as it seems, amid all the corruption and vulgarity of the capital of the period, a vigorous intellectual curiosity flowered. To the richness and variety of this interest and the distinction of the men who fostered it, the roster of members of the Washington Philosophical Society bore testimony. Founded in 1871 by men intent upon exploring "the positive facts and laws of the physical and moral universe," the society embraced virtually every field of knowledge and included not only government scientists, but several generals, jurists, economists, and private citizens whose contributions were independent of their professions. Joseph Henry presided over the biweekly meetings which brought together such eminent men as Simon Newcomb; Chief Justice of the Supreme Court Salmon P. Chase; the scholarly Ainsworth Spofford, Librarian of Congress; Francis A. Walker, who, in directing the federal census of 1880, would make it a compendium of American scientific knowledge; James Ormond Wilson, superintendent of Washington's public schools; the bibliophile Dr. Joseph Toner; and, perhaps most surprising of all, in view of his lowly place in the

[17] *Olivia Letters*, pp. 520-22; Marian Gouverneur, *As I Remember*, pp. 359-64; Horatio King, *Turning on the Light*, pp. 14-16; Francis P. B. Sands, *The Founders and Original Organizers of the Metropolitan Club*; Madeleine Vinton Dahlgren, *Etiquette of Social Life in Washington*, p. 33; Helen Nicolay, *Sixty Years of the Literary Society*, pp. 4-7; Thomas M. Spaulding, *The Literary Society in War and Peace*, pp. 4-9.

governmental hierarchy, Lester Frank Ward whose penetrating mind was already evolving a system for applying science, "the great iconoclast," to a planned human society. The meetings were anything but perfunctory, and the publications of the Philosophical Society spread its fame into communities that despised Washington's political life.[18]

The local universities played a minor role in these developments. Howard University was still little more than a preparatory school. The faculty of the new National University founded in 1869 was made up largely of practicing lawyers and physicians who taught part-time, usually in the evening, and who had no time or inclination to encourage students in independent research. Georgetown, though beginning to win recognition for its work in seismology, was still first of all a seminary for training men for the priesthood. Although a gift of $85,000 from W. W. Corcoran to Columbian College in 1872 enabled it to expand into Columbian University, in 1874 the broadened curriculum was just going into effect. Widespread opposition spearheaded by President Eliot of Harvard killed the proposals of 1872 and 1873 to revive the long-buried plan of a federally financed national university.[19] Then as later, the principal stimulus to original research sprang not from Washington's academic institutions but from the Smithsonian and the new scientific bureaus of the federal government.

Those sources were enough to put Washington into the front ranks of American science. In 1871, when anxiety about the decline of the American fisheries led Congress to establish a Fish Commission, Spencer Baird persuaded the legislators to provide for the appointment of a competent scientist to study the feeding habits of fish and when and where they spawned. Since the assignment carried no salary, Baird himself undertook the task, and, as it assumed the proportions of a careful

[18] *Bulletin of the Philosophical Society of Washington*, 1874; Ralph Gabriel, *The Course of American Democratic Thought*, p. 206. See also entries in *Dictionary of American Biography*.

[19] *Nation*, XVII, 126-28; *Star*, 24 May 1873; James C. Welling, *Brief Chronicles of the Columbian College*.

ecological study of ocean life, he enlisted the assistance of younger men eager to work under him even without pay. So G. Brown Goode, a gifted young ichthyologist, joined the Smithsonian staff in 1873 to begin a career scarcely less notable than that of Baird and Henry. The year 1871 also brought European-trained Cleveland Abbe to Washington to carry further the meteorological studies Joseph Henry had advocated and Colonel Myer of the Signal Corps had initiated. A wispy-looking young man, almost timid in his bearing, Abbe in the years ahead was destined to make the Weather Bureau a valuable government institution, its practical uses unquestioned, and its scientific findings respected throughout the world. Meanwhile Dr. Joseph J. Woodward, in the process of completing the first two volumes of the *Medical and Surgical History of the War of the Rebellion*, was turning the Army Medical Museum into a center of experimentation in methods and equipment for photomicrography; the techniques later applied by General George Sternberg to micro-organisms would enable Major Walter Reed and other army bacteriologists to defeat the dreaded killer, yellow fever. At the Naval Observatory the powerful 26-inch telescope installed in 1873 was increasing the range of astronomical research, and Simon Newcomb was gathering about him an exceptionally able staff. Government support, to be sure, could be fickle. When President Eliot invited Newcomb to become director of the Harvard Observatory, Secretary of the Navy Robeson urged the astronomer to accept, because "a scientific man here has no future before him." Newcomb, however, declined the offer, partly out of patriotism, but also for professional reasons: the Harvard Observatory, he wrote, "was poor in means, meagre in its instrumental outfit, and wanting in working assistants. . . . There seemed little prospect of doing much." Newcomb's wife, a granddaughter of Rudolph Hassler, strengthened his ties to Washington.[20]

In 1873, moreover, preparations were afoot to establish a new

[20] Dupree, *Science in the Federal Government*, pp. 184-87, 189, 236-37, 257; Simon Newcomb, *The Reminiscences of an Astronomer*, pp. 212, 214-23, 229-32.

government bureau to direct geological surveys. Army expeditions exploring to find the best railroad routes to the west coast were no longer necessary, but the Chief of Engineers had sent Clarence King, a brilliant young graduate of the Sheffield Scientific School, to conduct a survey in 1867 along the fortieth parallel from California to Colorado, and King's report whetted interest in the region; government funds during the next three years had supplied backing for three or four other scientific expeditions including John Wesley Powell's "Geographical and Topographical Survey of the Colorado River of the West." When Powell came to Washington in the autumn of 1873, his fame had preceded him. A red-headed giant who had lost an arm at Shiloh, the former major had traversed the length of the Colorado river by boat through the Grand Canyon in 1869 in one of the most daring exploits in nineteenth-century American history. In 1874 he became head of the newly established United States Geological Survey of the Rocky Mountain Region. His intense interest in American Indian civilization would in time make him also one of the country's first cultural anthropologists. In giving up his professorship at the Illinois State Normal University and moving to Washington before a permanent government post was assured him, Powell bore mute testimony to the importance of the federal government to the cause of science.[21] Indeed his move is an ironic indication, as one historian has noted, that despite all the chicanery and shallowness to be found in the capital of the early 1870's "Washington was beginning to be in fact the cultural and scientific center that the old Columbian Institute had hoped to create."[22]

Sculptors and painters were less certain about what the "new Washington" might open up, but the portents were not discouraging. In 1873 a first Civil War memorial, a statue of General John Rawlins, was placed on Pennsylvania Avenue at 9th Street. The next year Henry Kirk Brown's equestrian bronze of General Winfield Scott cast from cannon captured

[21] Dupree, *Science in the Federal Government*, pp. 195-201; W. C. Darrah, *Powell of the Colorado*, pp. 92-93, 205.

[22] Dupree, *Science in the Federal Government*, p. 201.

in the Mexican War was unveiled in Scott Circle, then virtually on the city's fringes at Massachusetts Avenue and 16th Street. No one would point out for another eighty-five years that the sculptor had endowed the General's beloved stallion with the characteristics of a mare. That the piece was not great art was beside the point; more significant were the multiplying commissions for other statues of national heroes. Having made a name for herself by executing a life-size statue of Abraham Lincoln, Vinnie Ream, now the wife of Engineer Lieutenant Hoxie, opened a studio facing the square where her bronze of Admiral Farragut would later stand. Visitors to the Corcoran Gallery of Art meanwhile looked at Hiram Powers' "Greek Slave" with curiosity, if not with critical judgment; some probably shared the sentiments of the managers of the Crystal Palace, who had installed a curtain to draw around the statue's marble nakedness whenever Queen Victoria attended the exhibition. The Corcoran trustees were not yet ready to allow aspiring young painters to set up their easels in the gallery in order to teach themselves by copying, but they could study carefully the masterpieces on view there. Inasmuch as the Smithsonian had deposited in the gallery on an indefinite loan most of the pictures that had escaped the fire at the National Museum in 1865, the Corcoran collection was now fairly extensive; the rest of the Smithsonian pictures went to the Library of Congress. In 1873 four hundred memorialists petitioned Congress to endow a national academy of art and erect a million-dollar building for it in Washington, for "such a school . . . would soon call forth the latent artistic talent of our country."[23]

Progress in enlarging the scope of the amenities was uneven at best. Under the weight of the country-wide depression, plans for a municipal opera house collapsed along with hopes for a national academy of art. While the *Star* consoled painters by pointing to the "many notably fine small private galleries here, a large number of lovers of art and many more than is generally

[23] S. J. Kauffmann, "Equestrian Statuary in Washington," CHS *Rec*, v, 124-28; Stanley Olmsted, "The Corcoran School of Art," Ms in possession of Corcoran Gallery; *Chronicle*, 20 Jan 1874; S Misc Doc 89, 42C, 3S, Ser 1546.

supposed who draw and paint well as amateurs," musicians felt the handicap of having no proper auditorium. Professional performers still had to depend upon the Willard Hotel ballroom, Carusi's Assembly Rooms, the newer Lincoln Hall, or one of the theatres, always provided that popular plays like Bret Harte's *Two Men of Sandy Bar* or that perennial favorite, *Rip Van Winkle* with "Joe" Jefferson in the lead, had not preempted the National Theatre or Wall's Opera House. The burgeoning choral societies generally gave their concerts in one of the churches. In architecture ponderousness and over-elaboration of detail replaced proportion. While a certain number of expensive, high-shouldered, red-brick Victorian mansions had gone up, the new samples of domestic architecture showed none of the grace of earlier houses, and the exterior of the one new public structure, the still unfinished State, War, and Navy building, would lead Henry Adams to call it "the architectural infant asylum next to the White House." Still Washingtonians had some reason to feel that the arts, like the sciences, were taking firmer root in the city than the local political furor had seemed likely to permit.[24]

Looking back at the immediate past, in the summer of 1874 the community by and large settled back to accept in an equable spirit whatever might come next. The prevailing attitude was that whatever difficulties the future might bring, they would be no worse than those Washingtonians had weathered during the preceding thirteen years. Now that the federal government was taking charge of local affairs, private citizens were free of worrisome political responsibility. The delights of the city would remain. Much of the engaging quality of the ante-bellum capital had somehow endured, a place where " 'twas the aim of all the residents to live on poker, punch and presidents."[25] And now the indications pointed to a Washington, adorned with splendid buildings and national monuments set in carefully landscaped, well-tended grounds, emerging as a true national city, an epitome of the best of American civilization.

[24] *Star*, 18 Feb 1875; Adams, *The Education of Henry Adams*, p. 253.
[25] Nicolay, *Sixty Years of the Literary Society*, p. 7.

CHAPTER XVI

THE EMERGENCE OF A NATIONAL CITY

WASHINGTONIANS after 1800 had thought of themselves as residents of a national city. Other Americans, including a majority of members of the first forty-four congresses, had not. At times senators and representatives had paid lip-service to the concept; and in authorizing new public buildings to replace those destroyed by the British during the War of 1812 they had revealed a readiness to give reality to the idea. Gradually, however, the idea had faded, recapturing a slight bloom in the late 1840's with the founding of the Smithsonian Institution, and then withering during the period antecedent to the irrepressible conflict, the war, and its aftermath. In that interval Washington had become a focus of northern antagonisms, more nearly an embodiment of the enemy than the city that represented national ideals and strength. The community again and again had endeavored to build up a vigorous economy able to survive without federal patronage, only each time to encounter frustration or disaster. For nearly three quarters of a century Washington had had neither recognized standing as an independent American municipality nor any whole-hearted acceptance as a capital for whose well-being the entire nation was concerned. Now that Congress was taking full control, the city, already visibly improved by Alexander Shepherd's work, might at last look forward to assuming the honored place her eighteenth-century founders had intended.

The contentment born of such hopeful, albeit still vague, notions unhappily was shaken by the deepening of the depression that had come in the wake of the panic of 1873. The federal payroll and an appropriation of $75,000 for the back wages of laborers whom the board of public works had not paid tempered distress in Washington during the last half of 1874, but a drastic reduction in the number of District jobs, followed by a cut in laborers' wages to a dollar a day, left hundreds of families in want by the summer of 1875. The Navy Yard had curtailed operations—there was talk of closing it altogether—and the Treasury had dismissed 400 employees. A brief flurry of strikes proved as useless as the series of clerks' advertisements offering a hundred dollars for a government post. The next year, after lengthening office hours from six to seven a day, the executive departments sliced the number of clerkships. The shutting down of the Bureau of Engraving brought 700 women to "the ragged edge of starvation," most of them too impoverished to journey home to their own states. Although the District commissioners pointed out that over 1,100 new buildings had gone up in Washington and Georgetown within the year and that crowds of visitors to the Centennial Exhibition in Philadelphia had stopped off in Washington to see the sights, people who had expected the federal government to make the capital as depression-proof as in 1837 and 1857 were discouraged.[1]

Worse lay ahead. During the next winter beggars and tramps swarmed into the District. The citizens' committee in charge of dispensing relief reported funds nearly exhausted in January and an average of 300 applications for help coming in daily. No one dared guess at the number of families who, unwilling to have their neighbors know of their poverty, were starving in quiet gentility. Necessities had always been notoriously high in Washington. Bread rose in price from six to seven cents a loaf. When spring appeared to bring an upturn in business to other sections of the country, it was "not very satisfactory to the people of non-commercial cities like Washington, as it simply amounts to a speculative rise in the price of provisions without supplying any additional occupation or increase in wages to enable the poor or unemployed to pay the increased price."[2] The District commissioners, their hands tied by a new law making it a penal offense to increase the District debt, eventually got permission to borrow from the United States Treasury in anticipation of taxes, but the lengthening relief rolls were alarm-

[1] *Star*, 7 May, 7 Jun, 10, 21 Jul, 1 Nov, 6 Dec 1875, 26 Feb, 20 Sep 1876; *Chronicle*, 3 Jan 1875, 1 Jul 1877; ptn, H43A-D1, 11 Jan 1875; Comrs Rpt, 1875, pp. 3, 15-16, Ser 1682.

[2] *Star*, 26 Aug 1875, 19 Apr 1876, 10 Jan, 19, 27, 30 Apr, 5 Sep 1877.

ing. While bank failures all but wiped out the funds of several charitable organizations, individuals who had long been mainstays of local philanthropy were themselves in financial straits. The closing of the Freedmen's Bank swept away the savings of hundreds of colored families. In speaking for a bill to provide $20,000 for the destitute, Representative Adlai Stevenson of Illinois testified to the "absolute starvation in this city," where suffering was acute "not only among the laboring classes, but among people who have never known penury until now." Congress voted the $20,000.[3]

The year 1877 was grim throughout the United States. Hungry men looking for work walked the city streets and the country lanes. That summer the most violent labor revolt the nation had ever known swept across the continent from the freight yards in Baltimore to San Francisco; and sympathetic strikes in a dozen industries followed upon the railroad strike. Washington had no industrial proletariat, but neither had her working classes reason to hope for prompt easing of pressures when industry and commerce elsewhere revived. The $20,000 from Congress constituted only a stopgap. Talk of developing the water power of the Potomac to bring factories to the area had stopped altogether, and plans for improving the harbor facilities to stimulate commerce dimmed to shadow.[4] During the tense weeks of the national railroad strike the lack of open violence in the District of Columbia appeared to be due not to better conditions here than elsewhere but to the despairing conviction of workingmen that action would not improve their lot.

In the upper brackets of society, however, where hunger was generally a word rather than a gnawing reality, faith in a make-work policy slowly strengthened. In the fall of 1877 a newly appointed District commissioner, Thomas B. Bryan, a Chicago

[3] 19 Stat. 211; ptns, H43A-B12, 25 Feb 1876, S44A-H8, 4 Aug 1876; Comrs Rpts 1876, pp. 21, 510-24, and 1877, pp. 54, 203-43, Sers 1751 and 1802; *Cong Record*, 44C, 2S, pp. 1059, 1088-92, 1186; Sayles J. Bowen to Comr William Dennison, 19, 24 Jan 1877, Bowen Mss.

[4] Ptn, S44A-H8, 25 May 1876; E. V. Ingram to S. J. Bowen, 17 Nov 1876, Bowen Mss; *Star*, 21 Jul 1877.

lawyer and real estate dealer, called a citizens' mass meeting to discuss ways and means of launching a Labor Exchange. His threefold proposal called, first, for shipping some of the unemployed out of the District to sections of the country that needed workmen, second, for opening a kind of public pawnshop where people could get an advance on their "jewelry" without paying interest, and, third, a public works program. Enthusiastic endorsers of his plan shut their eyes to the fact that labor surpluses apparently existed in every part of the United States; no one remarked on the resemblance of the loans on jewels to Marie Antoinette's nostrum; and optimists forgot that public works would need congressional approval. The *Star* cheerfully remarked that the first people the Exchange would send out of the area would be "the plantation hands who came here during the war . . . found employment to some extent while the extensive system of public works was going on, but who are now stranded here."[5] The scheme did not work that way. The committee in charge reported that the applicants for jobs were "noble fellows . . . and should be encouraged," but by the spring of 1878 a thousand of them were ready to accept wages of 50¢ a day in a city where only five years before the legal minimum had been set at $1.50. Fortunately Congress appropriated $15,000 for draining and filling the swampy land south of the Capitol along the line of the old canal, part of the stretch that in the 1950's would cause a three-year delay in erecting the third office building for the House of Representatives. The $15,000, together with $5,000 for medical care of the poor, $1,500 for a "Penny Lunch House," and the wages paid out by landlords who were able to undertake repairs while prices were low, sufficed to tide the community over the last year of the long depression.[6]

The three District commissioners from start to finish were more intent upon satisfying the President and Congress than

[5] *Star*, 9 Aug, 3, 6, 7, 15 Sep, 3 Oct 1877; *Chronicle*, 2, 16 Sep, 23 Dec 1877.

[6] *Star*, 5 Mar 1877, 15 Feb, 2 Apr 1878; *Cong Record*, 45C, 2S, pp. 1840, 2135, 3590, 3786, 4490; ptn, S45A-H4, 29 Mar 1878.

upon catering to local opinion. With the possible exception of Thomas Bryan, they were remote figures to all but a handful of Washingtonians. Strangers to the city, they approached their duties in much the spirit of eighteenth-century colonial governors. Warmth of feeling for the community apparently never entered into their decisions, and delegations of citizens did not seek out officials who looked upon them primarily as recipients of congressional justice. Former civic leaders dropped out of public view, and municipal administration became impersonal as never before. But because strict economy was clearly essential if the public finances were to regain stability, most citizens, other than those struck from the District payroll or faced with severe wage and salary cuts, accepted the commissioners' initial rulings without demur.[7]

School administration was among the first to receive an overhauling. Instead of perpetuating four separate school boards, one for Washington's white schools, a second for Georgetown's, a third for the colored schools of both cities, and a fourth for all public schools in the county, the commissioners established a single body made up of 11 trustees from Washington, 5 from the county, and 3 from Georgetown, 5 of the 19 members Negroes. The administrative simplification did not resolve the problem of educating nearly 19,000 children in 274 rooms with a staff of 262 teachers. The perennial shortage of funds necessitated additional half-day sessions, reduction of the school year from ten months to eight, and a continued disregard of truancy that left several thousand children without any schooling. Congressional largesse extended to giving the school system a public square in Washington and lending the trustees $75,000, but neither Congress, the commissioners, nor the school board considered the economies obtainable by combining the white and colored schools into a unitary system. Although radicals on the central Republican committee of the District of Columbia drafted a platform in 1876 which emphatically condemned

[7] Comrs Rpt, 1874, p. 13, Ser 1641; H Rpt 702, 44C, 1S, p. 21, Ser 1712; *Star*, 17 Jul 1874.

separate schools, by 1878 Negro leaders themselves had abandoned attempts to reopen that question.[8]

The two school superintendents made their annual reports as cheerful as truth would permit. James Ormand Wilson pointed out in 1877 that 78 teachers of the 209 in the white schools now had some normal school training; he did not mention that most of the rest had at best a grammar school education and some owed their $400 a year jobs purely to politically powerful friends. He bluntly stated, however, that the educational ladder was "not only too narrow but too short for its purpose. Both ends should be extended. The Kindergarten should be added below and the High School above." The lack of a high school was a specially sore point among parents. George F. Cook was equally troubled. The colored schools had accommodations for about 5,800 out of nearly 10,000 Negro children. His chief source of satisfaction lay in an arrangement concluded in 1877 whereby the trustees of the Miner Fund agreed to use the income for a colored normal school or a high school.[9]

The commissioners wisely left the board of health to its own devices for several years. "The first real impetus given to the question of sanitary reform and inviting physicians and scientists of all sections of the country to form cooperative associations for this purpose," boasted the *Chronicle* truthfully, "originated in this city, and was suggested by the success of our Board of Health." In 1875 representatives of the recently organized American Public Health Association and a delegation from Imperial Tokyo visited Washington to observe the methods in use here. Those still included the demolition of several hundred unsanitary dwellings and the painstaking assembly of vital

[8] *Chronicle*, 12 Sep 1875; Comrs Rpts, 1874, pp. 19, 105-107, 1875, pp. 16-18, 22, 317, 427; Rpt Trustees Public Schools, 1874-75; ptns, H44A-D1, B12, 22 Jan 1877, H45A-D1, B14, 18 Jan 1878; *Cong Record*, 45C, 2S, pp. 2923, 4418; Rpts Sec/Int, 1875, pp. xlv, 482, Ser 1681, 1876, pp. xxvii, xli, 439-40, Ser 1750, 1877, p. xxi, Ser 1801; enclosure to ltr, A. M. Green, President Republican Central Executive Committee, D.C., to S. J. Bowen, 19 Jan 1876, Bowen Mss.

[9] Rpts Board of Trustees of the Public Schools, 1876-77, pp. 119, 143, 261, and 1877-78, pp. 217, 221-22.

statistics. Reluctant public acquiescence in the continuing condemnation proceedings indeed probably sprang from the shock of learning that half the deaths in the District were among children under five years of age and that Negro mortality stood at 48.95 per thousand, considerably higher than the colored birth rate; the white death rate was 19.34 per thousand. Yet latent hostility and obstructive indifference to the health officers' program increased. Owners of slaughter houses fought the board's repeated recommendation that abattoirs be prohibited within the cities' limits, landlords of dilapidated tenements evaded compliance with the sanitary code, criticisms in Congress halted a year's appropriations for free medical treatment of the poor, and spreading resentment of regulation inspired the commissioners in 1877 to slice the public health budget.[10] Manifestly an efficient public health service would not be allowed to endure long.

The commissioners gave most of their attention to completing the unfinished jobs of the territorial board of public works. The police force came in for some censure when President Grant protested at the frequent "gross violations of law," although an examination of the misdemeanors that landed culprits in the workhouse suggested a severe, rigidly enforced legal code: in a single year 731 people committed for disorderly conduct, 309 for profanity, 33 for indecent exposure—understandable in a Washington summer—6 for "fast driving," 4 for obstructing sidewalks, 3 for cruelty to animals, and 1 for playing ball in the streets. That a large part of the offenders arrested were colored was evidently taken for granted.[11] Police routines seemed less important than laying the final stretches of unfinished sewer lines and replacing the rotting wooden pavements in various parts of the city, while accountants in the Treasury straightened out the fiscal tangle left by Alexander Shepherd

[10] *Chronicle*, 27 Jun, 18 Jul 1875; *Star*, 27 Aug 1876, 1, 2, 6 Aug, 5 Sep 1877, 27 Feb, 27 May 1878; S Rpt 456, 45C, 2S, Ser 1790; Rpts Board of Health, 1875-1877, Ser 1682, 1751, 1802.

[11] Comrs Rpts, 1874, pp. 110-11, 1875, pp. 18, 442-45; *Star*, 1 Feb, 7 Mar 1877.

and his underlings. Eighteen months after Lieutenant Richard Hoxie of the Army Engineer Corps had begun the thankless job of connecting sewer mains and macadamizing streets which had been paved only two years before, a storm broke out on the Hill. Congress learned that the street department had spent nearly a quarter million dollars on repairs in a single year and, under a system known as "extension of Board contracts," let to private firms of doubtful competence contracts totalling $4,236,-000. Over a million dollars of that sum was for work not authorized by law. No amount of explaining lessened congressional wrath. Outraged members of the House took tentative and ultimately useless steps to sue the commissioners and in the interim forbade the issue of additional 3.65 percent interest-bearing bonds which were to have paid the bills. According to one computation, the commissioners, so far from having reduced the District debt, had increased it by $5,200,000.[12]

Taxpayers were alarmed. By congressional mandate in 1873 the assessors had abandoned the custom recognized elsewhere of assessing at a half to a third the market value of property and now put full valuation upon it. But as real estate prices had dropped sharply after the panic, the comptroller declared assessments "greatly in excess of prices at which property is sold." As incomes shrank during the depression, tax delinquence rose.[13] Congress in wiping out local self-government had pledged that the federal Treasury would not only underwrite the 3.65 bonds but assume a "just proportion" of ordinary District expenses. Time had passed, and what represented a just proportion remained unsettled. "Taxpayers," wrote one observer, "certainly get rough treatment at the hands of Congress. That body assumes sole control over the District, and in the exercise of that

[12] *Chronicle*, 18 Aug 1874; *Star*, 3 Jul, 1 Nov, 16 Dec 1875, 16 Apr 1878; Comrs Rpts, 1874, pp. 160, 166-74, 212, 1875, pp. 4, 9, 15-16, 43-47, 185, 254, 316-419, 1876, pp. 7, 19, 42-43; A. M. Green to S. J. Bowen, 19 Jan 1876, Bowen Mss; *Cong Record*, 44C, 1S, pp. 595-98, 885-89, 1195-1201, 4858, 5432-34, 5676-77; H Misc Doc 103, 44C, 1S, Ser 1701; H Ex Doc 26, 44C, 2S, Ser 1755.

[13] *Cong Record*, 43C, 1S, pp. 5116-17; Comrs Rpt, 1874, p. 31, 1875, pp. 4, 6-8, 12-14, 26, 29.

control, and through officers of its own appointment, incurs an enormous indebtedness for District improvements. Then it turns around and repudiates the assumption of any portion of this indebtedness, and declares that the government shall pay no tax on the sixty-six millions of real and personal property . . . it owns in this District."[14] As people recognized the possibility that a future congress might refuse to pay the interest on bonds guaranteed by an earlier congress, taxpayers became obsessed with the urgency of persuading the federal government to act upon its financial responsibilities to the federal District.

In June 1874 the House Judiciary Committee, reiterating the thesis of the Southard report of 1835, had recommended that the federal Treasury pay 50 percent of the annual costs of running the District. The 44th Congress, like the 43rd, agreed that national funds should help maintain the national capital, but acceptance of that principle failed to create agreement about how to apply it. If federal money were to help pay the bills, federal officials must have control. What form of control and what share of the cost was a two-headed hydra. For the time being, each Congress voted some money for the District's yearly budget but on no exact predetermined basis. Plan after plan for a permanent scheme of local government took shape on paper, only one after the other to be shoved to one side without discussion or to be picked apart, amended, and then tabled. In 1876 when a joint House and Senate committee proposed that appointed commissioners take permanent charge of every municipal function from police and fire protection to health supervision and public education, with the federal government shouldering 40 percent of the cost, Senator George Spencer of Alabama filed a minority report against the "tyranny" that the arrangement would establish: "The people retire from legal consideration but not from legal responsibility. . . . The commissioners constitute the municipality less its obligations."[15]

[14] *Star*, 27 Jun 1876.

[15] H Rpt 627, 43C, 1S, Ser 1626; Comrs Rpt, 1877, pp. 17, 51; H Rpt 64, 44C, 2S, Ser 1769; S Rpt 572, 44C, 2S, Ser 1732.

But, as Augustus Woodward had foretold 75 years before, the mingling on the floor of Congress of "*great* and *small* concerns" meant disregard of the latter. The bill fell by the wayside amidst the furor over the disputed election of 1876.

New York newspaper correspondents described Washington in late November 1876 as "in a state of excitement unparalleled since Sumter was fired on in '61." The local press pooh-poohed the "false and exaggerated reports," but President Grant's ordering of 450 army regulars to the capital evidently persuaded some people that he was planning a "Man on Horseback" coup. Not until March 2, 1877, did the electoral commission's 8 to 7 decision ensure Rutherford Hayes' election. By then members of the expiring Congress had time only to join in hasty preparations for the inauguration or for immediate departure for home.[16]

Once "old 8 to 7," as Democrats dubbed President Hayes, had taken office, few informed Washingtonians expected a return of the local franchise to a community one-third Negro in make-up. For Hayes, while pledged to the protection of colored men, was also committed to the reconciliation of southern whites. Furthermore, the "Stalwarts," the rump of radical Republicanism that had formerly insisted upon Negro suffrage in the city, no longer controlled the party; despite the bungling mismanagement of which the commissioners had clearly been guilty, it seemed unlikely that the 45th Congress would be swayed by racial arguments into restoring "Home Rule." When at last in early 1878 debate opened in House and Senate on a bill to settle the question of local government, neither chamber considered conducting a referendum within the District, as Senator Oliver Morton had once urged. Members of both houses felt sure they knew what the community wanted or at least what it ought to want.

What District residents wanted varied from class to class and from individual to individual. In 1877 a Committee of One Hundred, the first of a long succession of such groups, organ-

[16] *Star*, 22 Nov 1876, 2, 5 Mar 1877; Ralph M. Goldman, "Party Chairmen and Party Faction, 1789-1900," pp. 409-50 (Dissertation, Univ. Chicago, 1951, Mcf. L.C.).

ized to beg first of all for an equal division of District expenses between the federal government and local taxpayers and, second, for commission rule with no elective offices. Bankers, brokers, doctors, lawyers, merchant-chiefs, if not the butchers, the bakers, or the candlestick-makers, endorsed the plea. Their desire to perpetuate disenfranchisement obviously stemmed from their fear lest a return of suffrage put them at the mercy of a property-less majority fortified by ignorant irresponsible Negroes.[17] While the *Star* contended that "the peaceable, law-abiding portion of our citizens" was surfeited with "the disgraceful scenes attending 'Elections' regulated by 'Murder Bay,'" John Forney declared in the *Chronicle* that the innuendoes directed at Negro voters were wholly unwarranted: "Whatever corruption the 'Feather Dusters' and 'Murder Bay slums' perpetrated . . . was not as much of their origination as the Executive-appointed power behind, and had the taxpayers been allowed a voice in its selection the territorial form of government might probably still be in existence." The experience with appointed commissioners, he argued, should prove to every taxpayer the cost of having no say about local administration.[18] Some leading Negroes and a great many white workingmen supported that view. In the end the factor that probably carried greatest weight among influential people and partly reconciled even dissidents to a permanent loss of home rule was the realization that Congress would never agree to share expenses unless it could also maintain direct supervision of the local government.[19]

The act that took effect in June 1878 compensated for "taxa-

[17] C. Vann Woodward, *Reunion and Reaction*, p. 24; ptn, Committee of 100, 9 Oct 1877, Folder, Bowen Mss.

[18] *Star*, 13 Apr 1876; *Chronicle*, 3 Feb 1878; ptns, S43A-H8, B85, 12 Dec 1874, 8 Feb 1875, S44A-H8, n.d., and 2 Oct 1876, H44A-D1, B12, 13 Nov 1876, and H45A-D1, B14, n.d.; *Sentinel*, 7 Apr 1877. From November 1874 until June 1878 the *Star*, the *Chronicle*, and the *Sentinel* repeatedly carried editorials, letters and articles on the suffrage question, the *Star* against, the other two papers generally for a return of the franchise.

[19] A. M. Green to S. J. Bowen, 19 Jan 1876, and enclosure, Addison Dent to Bowen, 19 Mar 1877, Bowen to George Holmes, Chrm Republican Central Committee, D.C., 20 Mar 1877, Robert Christy to Bowen, 16 Apr 1817 and enclosure, Bowen Mss. See also petitions listed in n. 18.

tion without representation" by pledging the United States government to meet half the District's annual budget, including interest on the 3.65 bonds. The 50 percent figure was based largely upon a recent appraisal that put the value of federal property at $95,000,000 and of privately owned real estate at $96,000,000. Congressman Hendee of Vermont explained that the financial provision and the denial of local suffrage amounted to a bargain struck: "When any appropriation is made on any tax levied, the citizens of the District have no voice in the matter; and so . . . it seems very proper that . . . the United States should come forward and agree . . . that it will pay its share of the expenses of this government and the interest upon this debt." The new law forbade an increase in the debt, fixed the tax rate at its existing level, required congressional approval of every entry in a detailed annual budget and express authorization from Congress of every contract of more than $1,000 for public works, and set up an elaborate system of checks and double-checks to safeguard against any repetition of the casual methods of handling public money that had prevailed under the board of public works and the commissioners who succeeded territorial officials. A section of the act limited the President's choice of two of the three commissioners to civilians who had had three years of continuous local residence, a provision that would prevent the community's being again saddled with strangers and inept defeated congressmen. The third commissioner was to be an officer of the Army Engineer Corps. Responsibility for the sinking fund was vested in the Treasurer of the United States. The judicial system remained as before, with the President appointing the justices of the District Supreme Court and the Chief Justice naming all lesser court officials. The commissioners might recommend needed changes in legislation and were to submit a full report annually to Congress.[20] Insofar as a statute could ensure honest, economical public administration, the new organic act of 1878 promised to supply it.

At the same time the new law gave three men autocratic

[20] 20 Stat. 102-108.

power over many phases of municipal life. Elimination of the Metropolitan Police Board and the board of health put the commissioners in direct control of police protection and public sanitation. Their authority to appoint police officials, like their continued right to select the nineteen nonsalaried members of the school board, aroused no opposition, but dispensing with the board of health had been fiercely contested. The seven-year-old system came under attack as costly and "inquisitorial": sanitary inspectors invaded the privacy of the home, and summary condemnations of unsanitary private property ignored the "due process" clause of the Constitution. Senator Windom of Minnesota silenced the talk of extravagance by comparing the results Washington's program had achieved at a fourth the cost with those of the less adequate services furnished in Baltimore, but his eloquent defense was unable to save the board.[21] Henceforward a single health officer, a physician to be appointed by the commissioners, was to carry on with a small staff and a sharply curtailed budget. In enforcing health regulations and collecting vital statistics, his every move was to be subject to the approval of the three nonmedical men in the commissioners' office.

If the new order thus created was disappointing in some particulars, articulate Washingtonians nevertheless appear to have judged it better than they had dared expect. During the preceding four years a good many residents, feeling helpless to affect the course of events, had resigned themselves to arbitrary rule. And people not desperately pinched financially found that life was none the less pleasant. Social affairs in fact were rather more agreeable than when parvenus, some of them now kept at home by business reverses, had overrun the capital; of those still on hand, a number took to the study of one of the multiplying books on Washington etiquette. Large receptions were still the standard vehicle of official hospitality, a scheme perhaps born of discovering it "the easiest way to give the greatest possible number of people the least possible pleasure"; but the "beau monde" divided the weekly calendar during the season so that

[21] *Cong Rec*, 45C, 2S, pp. 1926, 3789-90, 3818-24.

Cabinet wives received on Wednesdays, senators' wives on Thursdays, wives of Supreme Court justices on Fridays, the White House on Saturdays.

President Grant, never given to much formality, occasionally startled European diplomats by the casualness of the reception he accorded them. Like "Toujours Gai" making his first call upon Jefferson, the young Danish minister came in for a shock at the White House when, decked out in his dress uniform, complete with diamond-studded decorations, he had driven to the door, there to be greeted by a shirt-sleeved colored man who, while shrugging himself into a coat, affably invited the minister to "come right in, Sah." He had then cooled his heels for twenty minutes before he was ushered into a reception room to face a President fresh from a walk and dressed in a mud-spattered gray suit and Secretary of State Hamilton Fish scarcely more punctiliously attired. The flustered baron presented his credentials, listened to Secretary Fish read out a brief acknowledgment and remark on the nice weather, and then the astonished young man found himself in the hall again. Yet as time went on, Baron Hegermann-Lindencrone and his Boston-born wife came to enjoy Washington enormously. In 1877 the new First Lady, a pillar of the Women's Christian Temperance Union, quickly earned the name "Lemonade Lucy"; even at state dinners, Secretary of State William Evarts later remarked, "water flowed at the White House like champagne." Little by little the tarnishing gilded age yielded to a more cultivated, simpler era in which small teas, intimate dinner parties, and evenings of music, readings, or conversation formed the backbone of social intercourse between friends. The Washington that Henry James a quarter of a century later would call the "city of conversation" was emerging at the end of the 1870's.[22]

Symptomatic of this change was President Hayes' attendance as guest of honor at a dinner of the recently formed Yale Club

[22] Lillie Hegermann-Lindencrone, *The Sunny Side of Diplomatic Life*, p. 56; Poore, *Reminiscences*, II, 347; Marian Gouverneur, *As I Remember*, pp. 382-83; and numerous entries in the *Star*, 1876-78.

of Washington. Having announced in advance that he must leave at ten o'clock, the President so enjoyed the warm fellowship of the occasion that he stayed till two in the morning. For young people waltzing was still the profession, but the gay "Bachelors' Germans" held three or four times every winter were less showy affairs than the ostentatious balls of the late 1860's. Pretentiousness did not wholly disappear. When Lillie Greenough Hegermann-Lindencrone attended her first meeting of the Literary Society, the topic for the evening's discussion, she wrote her mother, was "The Metamorphosis of Negative Matter"; while Mrs. Dahlgren, "who as president sat in a comfortable chair with arms to it," called for comments, the baroness, impaled upon a cane-bottomed chair, thought agonizedly of the consequences for her blue velvet gown and felt the evening only partly redeemed by the introduction of positive matter in the form of scalloped oysters and chicken salad. No one, on the other hand, privileged to frequent the newly formed Cosmos Club found the talk there either trivial or boring. Organized in John Wesley Powell's parlor in 1878, the Cosmos Club brought together scientists, men of letters, and artists in a group as diverting and as distinguished as could be assembled anywhere in the United States.[23]

In 1874 George Bancroft, after twenty-five years' absence, returned to Washington to revise his six-volume *History of the United States*, to write his *History of the Formation of the Constitution* and his biography of Van Buren, and to grow American Beauty roses in the garden of his house on H Street facing Lafayette Square. Three years later Henry Adams abandoned Cambridge for the capital, partly to write history and, as it happened, novels, and partly because he decided that "as far as he had a function in life, it was as stable-companion to statesmen." At the Corcoran Gallery, where hesitant trustees had agreed to permit people to copy as well as look at the pictures, Eliphalet Andrews, a Washington artist of some local renown,

[23] Simon Newcomb, *Reminiscences of An Astronomer*, pp. 241-42; Hegermann-Lindencrone, *Sunny Side of Diplomatic Life*, pp. 16-17.

had begun to offer inexperienced painters suggestions during his frequent visits; from this voluntary association would come the Corcoran School of Art in the 1880's. Meanwhile a new Washington Art League engaged five or six professional painters to teach beginners.[24]

At the same time sculptors were attaining recognition. Some of it traced back to a congressional decision of 1864 to turn the one-time chamber of the House of Representatives at the Capitol into Statuary Hall in which each state of the Union might place the effigies of two of its famous native sons. In the 1840's when Clark Mills first came to Washington from South Carolina, the Italian stone-work at the Capitol, the shaft commemorating the naval heroes of the war with the Barbary pirates, and Horatio Greenough's ponderous marble of Washington were the only examples of sculpture to be seen outside of the congressional cemetery. Now seemingly every eminent figure in national life of the past must be commemorated in bronze or stone in the capital. In 1876 a second statue of Abraham Lincoln was unveiled; made possible by the voluntary subscriptions of freedmen, Thomas Ball's portrayal of the Great Emancipator, an unshackled slave at his feet, stirred the imagination of visitors to the beautifully planted new Lincoln Park at the then extremity of East Capitol Street. That same year saw the placing in McPherson Square of the equestrian statue of General James McPherson, Commander of the Army of the Tennessee, and the next year, in Stanton Square, Henry Kirk Brown's equestrian bronze of the Revolutionary General, Nathanael Greene.[25] Later generations came to look upon all this as a matter of course, some of it an exuberant expression of undiscriminating taste, but in the 1870's the tangible monuments to the great conveyed special meaning to the public.

Yet the city retained much of the small-town flavor of earlier years. Every summer well-to-do families packed up for a vaca-

[24] Adams, *Education of Henry Adams*, p. 317; Stanley Olmsted, "The Corcoran School of Art," Ms. Corcoran Gallery.

[25] S. J. Kauffmann, "Equestrian Statuary in Washington," CHS *Rec*, v, 124-28; *Star*, 14 Apr, 7, 20 Sep 1876.

tion at one of the popular resorts—Piney Branch on the lower Potomac, or Cape May, smart "Ocean Wave, Long Branch" patronized by General Grant, or perhaps Atlantic City or Monterey Springs, Pennsylvania—while householders unable to afford such expensive holidays substituted steamer excursions, sometimes by moonlight to Mount Vernon, to an amusement park farther downstream, or to picnic grounds nearer home. Fourth of July was still the great day of the year, now celebrated not by formal gatherings and two-hour orations but by outings under the aegis of Sunday schools and benevolent societies. In August came the Annual Schuetzenfest conducted by the Schuetzenverein and enthusiastically patronized by every constituent group in the new German American Union. Yearly P. T. Barnum's circus arrived; one year every purchaser of Barnum's *Autobiography* got a free ticket. It cost nothing to watch the annual yacht regatta on the river or the baseball games on the "White lot" below the White House whenever the Olympics played visiting nines. Come fall, boys went chestnutting in the woods along Rock Creek, while their elders hunted the geese and duck that still fed in the Potomac marshes on their flights south. Winter brought skating on the ponds in and about the city, church sociables, and singing sessions of choral societies.[26] Simple pleasures thus punctuated the daily routines of the workaday world. Slow though the pace of life was, the bulk of Washington's inhabitants had neither the time nor the intellectual training to philosophize about her place in the American scheme of things.

The city's intellectuals themselves, although undoubtedly aware of a new feel in the atmosphere, did not discuss Washington's prospects. If the decision of Congress in 1876 to undertake to complete the Washington Monument at national expense was a definite indication that politicians were ready to acknowledge the capital as a national city, still men of long memory may well have concluded that it was too early to believe in the imminent realization of Jefferson's dream: a capital rivalling in

[26] Scattered entries chiefly in the *Star*, 1874-1878.

beauty the great cities of Europe, a symbol of national ideals as evocative of patriotism as the flag. Yet as 1878 drew to a close, amid the material want and the enduring uncertainties, hopes rose that the goal of eighty-odd years was within sight.

What planning experts in mid-twentieth century would call "the image of the city," that is, a clearly etched mental picture of the ideal sought, was blurred at the end of the seventies. Changing taste had substituted Norman, Gothic, and ornate Renaissance forms for the classical style in public buildings and the chaste lines of domestic architecture of the federal era. Concepts of symmetry in the use of space prevailing when the "seat of empire" was founded had yielded first to enthusiasm for romantic landscaping and then to ideas of commercial utility, to which the railroad tracks crossing the Mall bore witness. Visions of the capital as the great "emporium of the continent" had long ago disintegrated, and determination to control the trade of even a relatively limited area of the South had weakened. Now, almost imperceptibly, a new image was taking shape. Shadowy as were its details, its broad outline was gaining clarity: an intellectually vigorous, physically comfortable city, touched perhaps by elements of grandeur but untroubled by unattainable political and industrial ambitions, a city in which free men could live in peace.

GLOSSARY OF ABBREVIATIONS

BIBLIOGRAPHICAL NOTE

GLOSSARY OF ABBREVIATIONS AND CITATIONS IN THE FOOTNOTES

ALL nonofficial manuscript materials cited are in the Manuscript Division of the Library of Congress unless other locations are specifically noted in the first mention in each chapter of papers elsewhere. Papers in the National Archives are identified where they first appear by the record group number. For petitions, the most frequently cited of the papers in the National Archives, the record group number is not repeated, since all petitions to the House of Representatives are in R.G. 233, all petitions to the Senate in R.G. 43.

L.C.	—	Library of Congress
N.A.	—	National Archives
R.G.	—	Record Group
Ptn	—	Petition, if to the Senate listed as S, if to the House of Representatives, listed as H, in each case followed by numerals and letters identifying the Congress and general topic and by the date.
F.B.	—	Files of the Bureau of Refugees, Freedmen and Abandoned Lands, in R.G. 105, N.A.
H Rpt __, __C, __S, Ser__		House of Representatives Report, followed by its number, the number and session of Congress and the serial number of the volume in which the report is bound.
H Ex Doc	—	House Executive Document
H Misc Doc	—	House Miscellaneous Document
S Rpt __, __C, __, Ser__		Senate Report, followed by its number, the number and session of Congress and the serial number.
S Ex Doc	—	Senate Executive Document
S Misc Doc	—	Senate Miscellaneous Document
ASP	—	*American State Papers*
Annals	—	*Annals of Congress*
Reg Deb	—	*Register of Debates in the Congress of the United States*
Cong Globe	—	*Congressional Globe*

ABBREVIATIONS

Cong Record	—	*Congressional Record*
—Stat.—,	—	*United States Statutes at Large*, with volume number preceding and page numbers following.
Comrs Rpt	—	*Report of the Commissioners of the District of Columbia*
Rpt Sec/Int	—	*Report of the Secretary of the Interior*
SHC	—	Southern Historical Collection, University of North Carolina Library
CHS *Rec*	—	Columbia Historical Society *Records*
N.I.	—	*National Intelligencer*, the *Daily* as soon as it began daily publication
Wshg Acts *Wshg Laws*	—	*Acts of the Corporation of the City of Washington* and the successor volumes listed as *Laws* beginning with 1817
Journal 61st Council		*Journal of the 61st Council of the City of Washington* and seriatim through the 67th Council.

BIBLIOGRAPHICAL NOTE

FOR the story of the founding of the national capital, the published writings of Washington, Jefferson, Madison, and Major L'Enfant, together with the manuscript volumes of papers of the Continental Congress and the proceedings and correspondence of the commissioners put in charge of building the federal city, constitute the principal sources. For Jefferson's part in the undertaking, I have used Samuel K. Padover's *Thomas Jefferson and the National Capital*, a selection of letters which adequately cover the relevant questions. L'Enfant's reports are published in the Columbia Historical Society *Records*, volume II, and some of his letters in Elizabeth S. Kite, *L'Enfant and Washington, 1791-1792*; apparently because of a faulty command of English, his language is often confusing, but his main ideas are generally clear. The Proceedings, the Letters Sent, and Letters Received by the Board of Commissioners for the District of Columbia, each of the three series arranged chronologically and indexed, are housed in the National Archives. Besides the congressional manuscript materials in the National Archives, the *Journals of the Continental Congress* and the *Annals of the Congress of the United States*, 1789-1824, are important, although generally the entries are extremely brief. Supplementing these are the *Documents relating to the First Fourteen Congresses*, cited in my text as the *Papers of the First Fourteen Congresses*. Assembled as completely as possible after the burning of the Capitol had destroyed the original collection, these House and Senate reports, many of them easily accessible in the volumes of *American State Papers*, are to be found in the Rare Book Division of the Library of Congress. Personal letters, diaries, memoirs, and travellers' descriptions written both before and after the arrival of Congress in the new capital add details. The two most useful of this type of source are Mrs. William Thornton's diary, reproduced for the year 1800 in volume X of the Columbia Historical Society *Records*, and the letters of Margaret Bayard Smith assembled by Gaillard Hunt and published under the title *The First Forty Years of Washington Society*. After 1800 the files of the local newspapers also become indispensable.

As in the case of the founding of the capital, the most essential and most voluminous source of reliable information about Washington's early economic and political life are official records. While they do not always reveal the reasons underlying action or inaction, the published reports submitted to Congress, the congressional debates, and the acts of the city councils provide the backbone of facts. When the congressional serial set begins with the 15th Congress, data become readily available. Special mention should be made of reports that summarize and clarify confusing problems, such as House Report 800, in Serial 295, dealing with District banking practices before 1836, the Southard report on fiscal relations, Senate Document 97, in Serial 268, a Senate Document entitled "Federal and Local Legislation relating to Canals and Steam Railways in the District of Columbia, 1802-1903," in Serial 4430, and several others identified in my bibliographical listing. Scarcely less important are newspaper articles and editorials, the opinions expressed in letters to the editors—unfortunately for the historian, almost always signed by pen names such as "Pro Bono Publico"—and, above all, the petitions and memorials collected in the National Archives. Petitions to the House of Representatives are unhappily no longer open to the public without written permission from the Clerk of the House, and the Senate petitions are being renumbered, so that my footnote citations made some time ago will soon be inexact. Yet the sheaves of petitions, tied by faded red tape into bundles addressed to each Congress in turn, contain keys to local wishes. They carry the memorialists' signatures and thus, once the city directories begin, enable the twentieth-century investigator to identify and group in a general way the persons who wanted or objected to particular measures. The first *Directory* did not appear until 1822; a second came out in 1830, a third in 1834, and thereafter at gradually diminishing intervals new directories until they became annuals in the late 1860's. The enumerators' original returns on Free Inhabitants for the federal census reports before 1850, schedules located in the National Archives, indicate only who was white, who black or mulatto, the ward in which he or she lived, the number of his children and the value of his real or personal property, if any. The returns for 1850, 1860, 1870, and 1880, on the other hand, contain figures on manufactures and social statistics which greatly enlarge the field of specific knowledge. Those schedules for the four sets of returns for the District of Columbia are at Duke University, but the Library of Congress Manuscript Division has microfilm copies. The published decennial census volumes supply less detailed but still valuable data, while the special census of

1867 for the District of Columbia published in 1870 as the "Special Report of the Commissioner of Education," in Serial 1427, includes statistical tabulations and historical sketches to be found nowhere else. The biennial *Register of Officers and Agents, Civil, Military and Naval, in the Service of the United States*, later entitled *Official Register of the United States*, begins in 1816; the volumes list the names, assignments, and salaries of every person employed by the government on September 30th of the preceding year or, very occasionally, of the year of publication.

Private papers, account books, and miscellaneous manuscripts touching on citizens' business and political interests have proved of minor importance for my study. A collection labelled District of Columbia Miscellany in the Library of Congress Manuscript Division has some helpful odds and ends, but all correspondence with Presidents of the United States has recently been removed to be filed with the presidential papers. Such of the letter press books of W. W. Corcoran as I thumbed through from among those open to examination in the Manuscript Division yielded little; the intensive work upon them begun in 1961 by Henry Cohen will undoubtedly produce more. Paul Gates' articles in the *Journal of Southern History*, v, and the *Political Science Quarterly*, LXVI, give the salient facts about Washington brokers and the General Land Office. Similarly, while the Library of Congress has a considerable collection of Chesapeake and Ohio Canal papers, Walter S. Sanderlin's published monograph, *The Great National Project*, served my every purpose. Indeed in pursuing every topic, I have used secondary sources whenever they were manifestly trustworthy and sufficiently detailed; the wastefulness of reworking the field seems obvious. B. B. French's letters, 1835-1870, in the Manuscript Division, contain sidelights on the career of a claims agent, comments on his political convictions and aims, and, as Lincoln's Commissioner of Public Buildings, his dealings with Mrs. Lincoln, but are chiefly useful for their portrayal of a householder's everyday routines in the 1840's and 1850's. I have omitted some of the standard Civil War diaries and journals, Gideon Welles', Edward Bates', and Louisa May Alcott's, for example, because they are not concerned with Washington as a community.

Of the newspapers the *National Intelligencer*, particularly after the *Daily* began, gives the best coverage of local politics and business aspirations before 1846 or 1847. Thereafter the Washington *News*, for a decade, and the *Evening Star* from the mid-

1850's onward are more useful. The *National Era*, 1847-1860, an abolitionist paper, pays special attention to the race issue. The *National Republican*, the *Sunday Morning Chronicle* and the *Daily Morning Chronicle* in the 1860's and early 1870's carry chiefly political news. The *Patriot*, 1870-1872, the *New National Era*, for a time called *New Era*, 1871-1875, Washington's first Negro newspaper, and, after 1873, the *Sentinel* cannot be neglected for the troubled days of the territorial government and its aftermath. Only *The Nation* among the contemporary periodicals contributed much of value. A body of ante-bellum pamphlet material assembled in more than 1,100 volumes entitled *Miscellaneous Pamphlets* form part of the collection in the Library of Congress Rare Book Division; the division's card catalogue lists under the heading "Washington, D.C.," some pertinent items for a study of the city. They are of unequal historical significance, but some of the pieces fill in areas largely neglected by the newspapers.

The development of municipal administration before 1871 emerges with reasonable clarity from the records of mayors and councils published first as *Acts*, then as *Laws of the Corporation* and, beginning in 1863, as the *Journals* of the councils. Letters to the press, local newspaper comment, petitions to Congress, congressional reports and, at intervals, debates in Congress on local affairs put some flesh on the bones of the brief entries in the city records. Twenty-five years after the demise of the municipality, the Columbia Historical Society began publishing articles on the city's mayors. The essays vary in quality but still supply some facts not to be found readily elsewhere. The biography of the most controversial figure of all, Mayor Sayles J. Bowen, is perhaps the least satisfactory, doubtless partly because it was written by the secretary of Bowen's great enemy, Alexander Shepherd. Fortunately some of Bowen's personal papers have survived and are in the possession of his wife's great-great nephew, Professor Charles Albro Barker of The Johns Hopkins University. The story of the growth of the school system has serious gaps. The Minutes of the Trustees for Public Schools, 1805-1818, originally called the Permanent Institution for the Education of Youth, are in the Manuscript Division of the Library of Congress, but after 1812 the record becomes sketchy and for part of its final six years covers only the "First District." From 1845 to 1871 the school trustees published under slightly varying titles annual reports, with the exception of 1867-1870 when one skimpy volume, omitting all controversial matters, encompassed four years. The special census of 1867 and the accompanying histories of the white and colored schools published in the *Special Report of the Commissioner of Education*, 1870, Serial 1427, offer some additional data. With the creation of the Department of the Interior in 1849, the Secretary's annual reports cover an ever-widening range of federal activities that related directly or indirectly to city affairs. Until 1874, when the District commissioners took over part of his responsibilities, his yearly summaries are enriched by subsidiary reports on the water supply, railroads and street railways, the Government Hospital for the Insane, the Columbia Institution for the Deaf, Dumb, and Blind, the colored schools, conditions at the jail, the penitentiary, the reform school, the troubles of the Metropolitan Police, and other matters. Indeed the variety of topics reveals the inseparability of federal and local concerns.

Administration and local legislation during the territorial regime are harder to follow. The published journals of the Governor's Council and the House of Delegates are diffuse and badly indexed. The reports of the board of public works, on the other hand, cover a year at a time and were published as House Executive Documents. The hearings of the congressional committees investigating "Affairs in the District of Columbia," 1872 and 1874, concentrate upon the sins and virtues of the board of public works. Pamphlets, again newspaper articles, and several items in the *Nation*, multiply the details. The Alexander Shepherd papers in the Manuscript Division of the Library of Congress add very little except a picture of Shepherd's personal magnetism. Between June 1874 and the end of 1878 the reports of the commissioners of the District of Columbia carry full, if dreary, accounts of every aspect of their jobs, and the annual reports of the United States Commissioner of Education, 1871 to 1878, supplement the local school board reports.

In addition to the discussion of poor relief in official municipal and federal records, an invaluable historical summary of the District's charities, private as well as public, appeared in 1898 in Senate Document 185 in Serial 3565. The Papers of the Lady Managers and Proceedings of the Washington Female Orphan Asylum, 1815-1878, in the archives of the Hillcrest Children's Center of Washington, the Minutes of the Trustees of the Washington Manual Labor School and Male Orphanage, 1835-1860, in the Library of Congress, and the published proceedings of a meeting in 1844 of the Female Union Benevolent Society are the only primary sources I located on private white charities, save for newspaper notices and an occasional allusion in Margaret Bayard Smith's letters.

In piecing together a picture of Washington's social life, personal letters, diaries, and memoirs become all-important. A number have been published in whole or in part, but those still in manuscript form add color, particularly the letters congressmen wrote to their families at home. Margaret Bayard Smith's letters in *The First Forty Years of Washington Society* are perhaps the single richest source for the years before 1835. Anne Hollingsworth Wharton quotes several other letter-writers in her *Social Life in the Early Republic* and *Salons Colonial and Republican*. Foreign travellers' accounts and especially their descriptions of the city's appearance tend to repeat each other. After 1800 those of Henry Fearon, Captain Basil Hall, and Harriet Martineau show the most insight. On the whole, local guide books, beginning with William Elliot's of 1822 and George Watterston's three prepared in the 1840's, give a better picture of the appearance of Washington. Of foreign diplomats' writings, the notes of Augustus John Foster written between 1805 and 1812, edited by Richard Beale Davis under the title *Jeffersonian America*, and the excerpts from the letters of the Abbé Correa, also edited by Davis, entitled *The Abbé Correa in America* are particularly rewarding. The petulant criticisms of the Marquis de Bacourt are relatively uninforming, while the communications dispatched to the British Foreign Office in 1871 by the British Minister, Sir Edward Thornton, contain only commentaries on congressional debates and official business. Conversely, the letters in *The Sunny Side of Diplomatic Life* written between 1874 and 1878 by Lillie Greenough Hegermann-Lindencrone, American-born wife of the Danish minister, are refreshingly frivolous. Besides the *Olivia Letters*, a newspaperwoman's portrayal of the Washington scene of the 1860's and 1870's, Madeleine Vinton Dahlgren's *Etiquette of Social Life in Washington*, first published in 1873, is revealing of a point of view. For an understanding of how people in the lower ranks of society spent such leisure as they had, the diversions listed in the daily press offer the best clue.

Sources bearing upon Washington's intellectual and artistic interests during the first half of the nineteenth century are somewhat elusive. George Brown Goode's *Genesis of the National Museum* in the *Annual Report of the U.S. National Museum* for 1891 gives the fullest account of the significance of the Columbian

Institute and its successor, the National Institute. The role of the Smithsonian Institution as such emerges from its annual reports. Passages from John Quincy Adams *Memoirs* and Margaret Bayard Smith's letters add sidelights, as do Samuel Flagg Bemis's, *John Quincy Adams and the Union*, Merle M. Odgers, *Alexander Dallas Bache: Scientist and Educator*, and Thomas Coulson, *Joseph Henry: His Life and Work*. For a later period Simon Newcomb's *Reminiscences of an Astronomer* and the brief *Bulletin of the Washington Philosophical Society for 1874* are important. The best synthesis of the work of the government's scientific bureaus is A. Hunter Dupree, *Science in the Federal Government*, a study based upon careful examination of both official and nonofficial materials. About the intellectual contributions of the colleges, information is meagre. James C. Welling's *Brief Chronicles of the Columbian College* discusses mostly the institution's physical growth. Moreover, specifics about the place of the arts and artists in Washington are singularly few. Charles E. Fairman's *Art and Artists of the Capitol* covers only the Capitol itself. From the notices in the *National Intelligencer* John Haskins put together a brief account of musical developments before 1812, and indeed newspapers supply most of the data about music, painting, sculpture, and the theatre throughout Washington's first seventy-eight years as capital. Benjamin Latrobe's *Journal*, the *Documentary History of the Construction and Development of the U.S. Capitol*, an article about the Patent Office by Louise Hall in the *Journal of the Society of Architectural Historians*, and an occasional descriptive passage and the photographs in Mary Smith Lockwood's *Historic Homes in Washington* eke out the extant visual evidence about architecture. Literature largely speaks for itself, assisted by Helen Nicolay's *Sixty Years of the Literary Society*, Thomas M. Spaulding's *The Literary Society in War and Peace*, and Paul Wilstach's "Literary Landmarks in the National Capital," in the July 1916 issue of the *Bookman*.

The materials on the ante-bellum Negro community are fragmentary. A main source of information to which every historian concerned with the subject has turned is the sketch written at the end of the 1860's and incorporated in the section on the colored schools in the *Special Report of the Commissioner of Education*, which grew out of the Census of 1867. If the author of that brief history appears at times uncritical, the facts he presented were never challenged. In Ellen M. O'Connor, *Myrtilla Miner, A Memoir*, and William B. Simmons, *Men of Mark*, a few supplementary facts appear. The *National Era*, 1847-1860, contains some illuminating observations, although those, like pieces in the other local newspapers, were usually directed at the slavery question and white attitudes toward free colored people. Michael Shiner's diary, 1813-1863, kept by a one-time slave and a Navy Yard employee, is on the whole disappointingly lacking in specifics about colored people. The enumerators' returns on Free Inhabitants for the second through the eighth federal census are more rewarding. The first two black codes were published in *Acts of the Corporation of Washington*, 1808 and 1812, and the three later amended codes were reproduced in James W. Sheehan, *Corporation Acts of the City of Washington*, in 1853.

On slavery and the slave trade in the District of Columbia the materials are abundant, if somewhat repetitive. The petitions on the subject alone are voluminous. Congressional debates and reports, books published between 1817 and 1860, newspaper pieces and occasional allusions in private letters tell much of the story. Curiously enough, the text of the first appeal of the Washington Society for the Abolition of Slavery in the District of Columbia appeared in Basil Hall, *Travels in North America during the Years 1827 and 1828*. The names of the men who signed the petition to Congress in 1828 appear in a House report of 1835. Walter C. Clephane, "Local Aspects of Slavery in the District of Columbia" in the Columbia Historical Society *Records* gives a helpful analysis of the legal problem. Frederic Bancroft's *Slave-Trading in the Old South*, based upon sources no longer available, has four or five pages on the trade in Washington. Carter Woodson, *A Century of Negro Migration*, Luther P. Jackson, *Free Negro Labor and Property-Holding in Virginia, 1830-1860*, and Jeffery R. Brackett's *The Negro in Maryland* furnish facts about the area surrounding the District.

For the Civil War era and the first years of reconstruction, again the petitions, the *Congressional Globe*, reports to Congress, particularly the reports of the trustees of the colored schools in the annual reports of the Secretary of the Interior, 1864-1870, the *Annual Reports of the National Freedmen's Relief Association*, the files of the Freedmen's Bureau in the National Archives, and the published journals of the Washington city councils, 1863-1870, constitute the principal primary sources. For the 1870's, however, besides such official data, the Negro newspaper, *New Era*, renamed

New National Era, 1871-1875, John Mercer Langston's *From the Virginia Plantation to the National Capital*, and some passages in Frederick Douglass' autobiography greatly enrich the available supply. Unhappily the extant files of the *New National Era* are incomplete after early 1873 and run out altogether in 1874. Two articles of Phineas Indritz, "Post Civil War Ordinances Prohibiting Racial Discrimination in the District of Columbia" and "Racial Ramparts in the Nation's Capital," in the *Georgetown Law Journal*, XL and XXXIX, respectively, discuss the civil rights legislation. The *Evening Star*, the *Chronicle*, and the *Sentinel* reflect the attitude of the white community toward colored Washington.

Category by category, the materials I have cited are listed below.

BIBLIOGRAPHY

I UNPUBLISHED SOURCES

OFFICIAL PAPERS

Domestic Letters of The Department of State, Record Group 59, National Archives.

Enumerators' returns for the District of Columbia for the second through the tenth United States Censuses, schedules of Free Inhabitants, second to eighth Census, and of Population, ninth and tenth censuses, National Archives; all other schedules for the seventh through the tenth Census at Duke University, with microfilm copies of schedules on Manufactures and Social Statistics, 1850-1870, in the Manuscript Division, Library of Congress.

Letters Received by the Board of Commissioners for the District of Columbia, 6 vols., 1791-1802, Record Group 42, National Archives.

Letters Sent by The Board of Commissioners for the District of Columbia, 6 vols., 1791-1802, Record Group 42, National Archives.

Minutes of the Board of Aldermen of the City of Georgetown, 1810-1822.

Minutes of the Trustees of Public Schools (originally Trustees of the Permanent Institution for the Education of Youth), 1805-1818.

Papers of the Continental Congress, 1774-1788, Record Group 11, National Archives.

Petitions to the House of Representatives, 1800-1878, Record Group 233, National Archives.

Petitions to the Senate, 1816-1878, Record Group 46, National Archives.

Proceedings of the Board of Commissioners for the District of Columbia, 3 vols., 1791-1802, Record Group 42, National Archives.

Records of the Bureau of Refugees, Freedmen and Abandoned Lands, 1865-1871, District of Columbia file, Record Group 105, National Archives.

Sir Edward Thornton, Letters to the British Foreign Office, 1871, Foreign Office correspondence, Public Record Office, photostatic copies in Library of Congress.

RECORDS OF CHURCHES AND SOCIAL AGENCIES

listed by location

Library of Congress Manuscript Division

Ethan Allen, Sketch of Washington Parish, 1794-1855, in District of Columbia Miscellany.

Minutes of the Trustees of the Washington Manual Labor School and Male Orphanage, 1836-1860.

Records of Proceedings of the Presbyterian Churches in the District of Columbia, October 5, 1841-May 2, 1842, relating to the Founding of the Fifteenth Street Presbyterian Church for Negroes, Carter Woodson Papers.

Hillcrest Children's Center, Washington
Papers of the Lady Managers and Proceedings of the Washington Female Orphan Asylum, 1815-1831, and of the Washington City Orphan Asylum, 1831-1878.

PERSONAL PAPERS, DIARIES, LETTERS AND JOURNALS

listed by location

Bancroft Library, University of California, Balch Papers, 1862-1865.
In possession of Professor Charles A. Barker of the Johns Hopkins University, Sayles J. Bowen Papers, 1846-1892, cited in the notes as Bowen Mss.
Columbia Historical Society Archives, James Topham & Co., Journal.
Library of Congress Manuscript Division
Anonymous, "A Canal Boat Journey, 1857."
Wilhelmus B. Bryan, Notes used in preparation of his two-volume *History of the National Capital.*
Chesapeake and Ohio Canal Stock Papers.
W. W. Corcoran, Letter Press Books, 1861.
Lewis Grant Davidson Papers.
District of Columbia Miscellany.
Benjamin Baker French Papers, 1835-1870.
Gales and Seaton Papers.
Louisa Kalisky Diary, 1822-1823, Lee Palfrey Papers.
James Madison Papers, 1815.
William Owner Diary, 1860-1867.
Eugenia Phillips, A Southern Woman's Story of her Imprisonment, 1861-1862.
John Pickett, Letterbook, 1866-1867.
William Plumer Papers.
John Sessford Annals, 1846-1860.
Alexander Shepherd Papers.
Michael Shiner Diary, 1813-1863.
Margaret Bayard Smith, Commonplace Book, Mrs. Samuel Harrison Smith Papers.
Benjamin Stoddert Papers, 1800-1805.
Alexander Stuart Papers.
Carter Woodson Papers.
Duke University Library
W. W. Corcoran Papers.
Richard Fendall Papers.
Harper Library, University of Chicago, John Robertson Papers.
Minnesota Historical Society
Thomas Newson Papers.
Alexander Ramsey Papers.
John M. Williams Papers.
University of North Carolina Library, Southern Historical Collection,
John Houston Bill Diary.
Kate S. Carney Diary, 1859.
John Chapron Papers.

William A. Graham Papers, 1834-1844.
Peter Hagner Family Papers, 1730-1940.
William Curry Harllee Papers, 1860.
Spencer Jarnagin Papers, 1844-1846.
William Lowndes Papers, 1815.
Benedict J. Semmes Papers, 1848-1857.
Sterling Memorial Library, Yale University, Griswold Papers.
George Washington University Library, Wright Collection.
Wisconsin Historical Society, Charles Billinghurst Papers.

MONOGRAPHS AND THESES

Dietz, Anthony G., "The Government Factory System and the Indian Trade," M.A. Thesis, the American University, 1953.

Goldman, Ralph M., "Party Chairmen and Party Faction, 1789-1900; a theory of Executive responsibility and conflict resolution," Ph.D. Dissertation, University of Chicago, 1951, microfilm, Library of Congress.

Lofton, Williston, "The Development of Public Education for Negroes in Washington, D.C., a Study of Separate but Equal Accommodations," Ph.D. Dissertation, the American University, 1944.

Mayo, Lida, "Japanese Fever," in possession of the author.

Olmsted, Stanley, "The Corcoran School of Art," in possession of Corcoran School of Art.

Piper, Ada, "Activities of Negroes in the Territorial Government of the District of Columbia, 1871-1874," M.A. Thesis, Howard University, 1943.

II PUBLISHED SOURCES

OFFICIAL RECORDS: FEDERAL

American State Papers, 38 vols.
Finance, 5 vols.
Military Affairs, 7 vols.
Miscellaneous, 2 vols.

Annals of the Congress of the United States, 1789-1824, 42 vols., Washington, 1834-1856.

Annual Reports of the Smithsonian Institution, 1847-, Washington, D.C.

Congressional Globe, 46 vols., Washington, 1834-1873.

Congressional Record, Washington, 1873-.

Congressional Serials, 1817-1878:
House of Representatives,
Documents
Executive Documents
Miscellaneous Documents
Reports

The Executive Documents ordinarily include the annual Reports of the Secretary of War, the Secretary of the Navy and the Secretary of the Interior, 1849-. Especially important:

"Memorial of inhabitants of the District of Columbia, praying for the gradual abolition of slavery in the District of Columbia," House Document 140, 23C, 2S, Serial 274.

"Banks in the District of Columbia," House Report 800, 24C, 1S, Serial 295.

"Alleged Hostile Organization Against the Government within the District of Columbia," House Report 79, 36C, 1S, Serial 1105.

"Special Report of the Commissioner of Education on the Condition and Improvement of Public Schools in the District of Columbia," House Executive Document 315, 41C, 2S, Serial 1427.

"Affairs in the District of Columbia," House Report 7, 42C, 3S, Serial 1576.

"Documentary History of the Construction and Development of the United States Capitol Building and Grounds," House Report 646, 58C, 2S, Serial 4585.

Senate,

Documents

Executive Documents

Miscellaneous Documents

Reports

The annual reports of the Secretary of the Interior appear also in Senate Executive Documents. Especially important:

"Southard Report," Senate Document 97, 23C, 2S, Serial 268.

"Report of the Joint Select Committee of Congress appointed to Inquire into the Affairs of the Government of the District of Columbia," Senate Report 453, 43C, 1S, Serials 1590, 1591, 1592.

"Investigation of Charities and Reformatory Institutions in the District of Columbia," Senate Document, 185, 55C, 1S, Serial 3565.

"Federal and Local Legislation relating to Canals and Steam Railways in the District of Columbia, 1802-1903," Senate Document 220, 57C, 2S, Serial 4430.

"History of the Washington Monument," Senate Document, 224, 57C, 2S, Serial 4436.

Journals of the Continental Congress, 1774-1788, from the Original Records in the Library of Congress, ed. Gaillard Hunt, 34 vols., Washington, 1904-1937.

Papers of the First Fourteen Congresses, in Library of Congress, Rare Book Division.

Register of Debates in Congress, 14 vols., Washington, 1824-1837.

Register of Officers and Agents, Civil, Military, and Naval, in the Service of the United States, 1817-1879, commonly called *Official Register.*

Reports and Addresses, Documents Relating to Freedmen, Howard University Library.

Smithsonian Miscellaneous Collections.

United States Census, Second through Ninth, 1800-1870.

United States Statutes at Large, 39 vols., Boston, 1875-1919.

BIBLIOGRAPHY

PAPERS OF THE PRESIDENTS

Abraham Lincoln, His Speeches and Writings, ed. Roy P. Basler, Cleveland and New York, 1947.

The Writings of James Madison, 9 vols., ed. Gaillard Hunt, New York, 1900-1910.

The Writings of George Washington, from the original manuscript sources, 1745-1799, 39 vols., ed. John C. Fitzpatrick, Washington, 1931-1941.

Thomas Jefferson and the National Capital, containing notes and correspondence between Jefferson, Washington, L'Enfant, Ellicott, Hallett, Thornton, Latrobe, the Commissioners, and others relating to the founding, surveying, planning, designing, constructing, and administering the city of Washington, 1783-1818, ed. Saul K. Padover, New York, 1946.

MUNICIPAL, STATE, AND TERRITORIAL RECORDS

listed by short titles only

Acts of the Corporation of the City of Washington, 11 vols., Washington, 1805-1816, continued as *Laws of the Corporation of the City of Washington*, 45 vols., Washington, 1817-1862.

Charter of the Town of Alexandria with the revised code of laws of the Corporation, comp. William Cranch, Alexandria, 1821.

The Code of the District of Columbia (to March 1929), Washington, 1930.

Debates and Other Proceedings of the Convention of Virginia . . . , June 1788, 3 vols., 2nd ed., Richmond, 1805.

Journals of the Council of The City of Washington, (61st through 67th Council), Washington, 1864-1871.

Journal of the Council of the District of Columbia, 5 vols., Washington, 1872-1874.

Journal of House of Delegates of the District of Columbia, 5 vols., Washington, 1871-1873.

Ordinances of the Corporation of Georgetown, with an appendix . . . , Georgetown, 1821, continued as *Ordinances and Resolutions of the Corporation of Georgetown*, Georgetown, 1838, and as *Ordinances of the Corporation of Georgetown*, Georgetown, 1840-1859.

Proceedings and Debates of the North Carolina Convention, . . . July, 1788, . . . Edenton, North Carolina, 1789.

Reports of the Commissioners of the District of Columbia, 1874-1878, in H. Ex. Docs. 1, 43C, 2S, 44C, 1S, 44C, 2S, 45C, 1S, 45C, 2S, Serials 1641, 1682, 1751, 1802, and 1852.

Reports of the Trustees of Public Schools of Washington, 1845-1874, under slightly varying titles, continued as *Annual Report of the Board of Trustees of Public Schools of the District of Columbia*, 1875-1879.

Rothwell, Andrew, *Laws of the Corporation of the City of Washington*, Washington, 1833.

Sheahan, James, *Corporation Laws of the City of Washington*, Washington, 1853.

The State Records of North Carolina, 26 vols., ed. Walter Clark, Goldsboro, North Carolina, 1886-1907.

Washington Board of Health *Nuisances*, Broadside, 1856.

Webb, William B., *The Laws of the Corporation of the City of Washington*, Washington, 1868.

AUTOBIOGRAPHIES, LETTERS, DIARIES, MEMOIRS

Where titles include long explanatory elaborations, only the short title is given.

Adams, Abigail, *Letters of Mrs. Adams, Wife of John Adams*, Boston, 1840.

Adams, Henry, *The Education of Henry Adams*, Modern Library ed., New York, 1931.

Autobiography of Amos Kendall, ed. William Stickney, New York, 1872.

Autobiography of Peggy Eaton, New York, 1932.

Briggs, Emily Edson, *The Olivia Letters*, Washington, 1906.

Corcoran, William Wilson, *A Grandfather's Legacy*, Washington, 1879.

Cutler, William Parker and Julia Perkins, *Life, Journals and Correspondence of the Reverend Manasseh Cutler, LL.D.*, 2 vols., Cincinnati, 1888.

De Bacourt, Adolphe Fourier, *Souvenirs of a Diplomat, Private Letters from America during the Administrations of Presidents Van Buren, Harrison, and Tyler*, New York, 1885.

Dodge, Mary A., *Gail Hamilton's Life in Letters*, ed. H. Augusta Dodge, 2 vols., Boston, 1901.

Douglass, Frederick, *Life and Times of Frederick Douglass*, New York, 1893.

Fremont, Jessie Benton, *Souvenir of My Time*, New York, 1887.

Gerry, Eldridge, Jr., *The Diary of Eldridge Gerry, Jr.*, New York, 1927.

Gobright, Lawrence A., *Recollection of Men and Things at Washington during the Third of a Century*, 2nd ed., Philadelphia, 1869.

Gouverneur, Marian, *As I Remember, Recollections of American Society during the Nineteenth Century*, New York, 1911.

Hines, Christian, *Early Recollections of Washington City*, Washington, 1866.

Jeffersonian America, Notes on the United States of America collected in the 1805-6-7- and 11-12, by Sir Augustus John Foster, Bart., ed., Richard Beale Davis, San Marino, California, 1954, cited in the notes, as Foster, *Jeffersonian America.*

King, Horatio, *Turning on the Light*, Philadelphia, 1895.

Langston, John Mercer, *From the Virginia Plantation to the National Capitol, or the First and Only Negro Representative in Congress from the Old Dominion*, Hartford, 1894.

Latrobe, Benjamin Henry, *The Journal of Latrobe, Being the Notes and Sketches of an Architect, Naturalist and Traveler in the United States from 1796 to 1820*, New York, 1905.

Lomax, Elizabeth Lindsay, *Leaves from an Old Washington Diary, 1854-1863*, ed. Lindsay Lomax Wood, New York, 1943.

Lundy, Benjamin, *The Life, Travels and Opinions of Benjamin Lundy*, Philadelphia, 1847.

Memoirs of the Administrations of Washington and John Adams, edited from Papers of Oliver Wolcott, Secretary of the Treasury, ed. George Gibbs, 2 vols., New York, 1846, cited in the notes as Gibbs, *Memoirs.*

Memoirs of John Quincy Adams, comprising portions of his diary from 1795 to 1847, ed. Charles Francis Adams, 12 vols., Philadelphia, 1874-1877.

Newcomb, Simon, *The Reminiscences of an Astronomer*, New York, 1903.

Poore, Benjamin Perley, *Perley's Reminiscences of Sixty Years in the National Metropolis*, 2 vols., Philadelphia, 1886.

Smith, John Cotton, *The Correspondence and Miscellanies of the Hon. John Cotton Smith*, New York, 1847.

Smith, Margaret Bayard, *The First Forty Years of Washington Society, portrayed by the family letters of Mrs. Samuel Harrison Smith*, ed. Gaillard Hunt, New York, 1906.

Eunice Tripler, Some Notes of her Personal Recollections, ed. Louis A. Arthur, New York, 1910.

DIRECTORIES AND GUIDE BOOKS

in chronological sequence

The Washington Directory, 1822, comp. Judah Delano.

Elliot, William, *The Washington Guide*, Washington, 1822 and 1837.

Elliot, Jonathan, *Historical Sketches of the Ten Miles Square Forming the District of Columbia*, Washington, 1830.

The Washington Directory, 1830, comp. S. A. Elliot.

A Full Directory for Washington City, Georgetown and Alexandria, 1834, comp. E. A. Cohen and Company.

Watterston, George, *A Picture of Washington*, Washington, 1840.

Watterston, George, *A New Guide to Washington*, Washington 1842.

The Washington Directory and Governmental Register for 1843, comp. Anthony Reintzel.

The Washington Directory and National Register for 1846, comp. Gaither and Addison.

Force, William Quereau, *Picture of the City of Washington and its Vicinity for 1845*, Washington, 1846 and 1848.

Watterston, George, *New Guide to Washington*, 1847-1848.

The Washington Directory and Congressional and Executive Register for 1850, comp. Edward Waite.

Washington and Georgetown Directory, 1853, comp. Alfred Hunter.

Washington and Georgetown Directory, 1855, 1858, 1860, 1862, 1863, 1867 and to date.

Richstein, William, *The Stranger's Guide to Washington City and Everybody's Pocket Handy-book*, Washington, 1864.

TRAVELERS' ACCOUNTS

Aristocracy in America, from the Sketchbook of a German Nobleman, ed. Francis J. Grund, 2 vols., London, 1839.

The Aristocratic Journey, Being the Outspoken Letters of Mrs. Basil Hall, Written during a Fourteen Months' Sojourn in America, 1827-1828, ed. Una Pope-Hennessy, New York, 1920.

Crowe, Eyre, *With Thackeray in America*, London, 1893.

De la Rochefoucauld-Liancourt, Duc Francois-Alexandre-Frédéric, *Voyage dans les Etats-Unis d'Amerique*, 8 vols., Paris, 1799.

Dicey, Edward, *Six Months in the Federal States*, London, 1863.

Dickens, Charles, *American Notes for General Circulation*, London, 1892.

Fearon, Henry B., *Sketches of America, A Narrative of a Journey of Five Thousand Miles through the Eastern and Western States of America*, 3rd ed., London, 1819.

Hall, Basil, *Travels in North America in the Years 1827 and 1828*, 3 vols., 3rd ed., Edinburgh, 1830.

[Ingeroll, Charles Jared], *Inchiquin, The Jesuit's Letters during a late Residence in the United States*, New York, 1810.

Janson, Charles, *The Stranger in America, 1793-1806*, reprinted from London edition 1807, ed. Carl S. Driver, New York, 1935.

Latham, Henry, *Black and White, a Journal of a Three-months' Tour in the United States*, London, 1867.

Lyell, Charles, *Travels in North America in the Years 1841-2, with Geological Observations on the United States, Canada and Nova Scotia*, 2 vols., London, 1845.

Macrae, David, *The Americans at Home, Pen-and-Ink Sketches of American Men, Manners and Institutions*, New York, 1952.

Marryat, Captain Frederick, *Diary in America, The Complete Account of his Trials, Wrangles and Tribulations in the United States and Canada, 1837-38*, ed. Jules Zanger, Indianapolis, 1960.

Martineau, Harriet, *Retrospect of Western Travels*, 3 vols., London, 1838.

Melish, John, *Travels Through the United States of America in the Years 1806 and 1807, and 1809, 1810 and 1811*, 2 vols., Philadelphia, 1815.

Olmsted, Frederick Law, *A Journey in the Seaboard Slave States in the Years 1853-1854*, 2 vols., New York, 1904.

Power, Tyrone, *Impressions of America during the Years 1833, 1834, and 1835*, 2 vols., London, 1836.

Stuart, James, *Three Years in North America*, 2 vols., Edinburgh, 1833.

Trollope, Frances, *Domestic Manners of the Americans*, ed. Donald Smalley, New York, 1949.

Warden, David B., *A Chorographical and Statistical Description of the District of Columbia, the Seat of the General Government to the United States*, Paris, 1816.

Weld, Isaac, *Travels through the United States of North America and the Provinces of Upper and Lower Canada, during the Years 1795, 1796 and 1797*, 2 vols., 4th ed., London, 1807.

OTHER PUBLISHED PRIMARY SOURCES

Adams, Francis A., *Our Little Monarchy; Who Runs it and What it Costs*, Washington, 1873.

Alexandria, Baltimore, Georgetown, New York, and Washington newspapers, 1791-1878.

American Baptist Magazine, IV and V, Boston, 1823 and 1825.

Andrews, Ethan Allen, *Slavery and the Domestic Slave Trade in the United States*, Boston, 1836.

Cunningham, A. F., *Oration delivered before the General Trades-union of The District of Columbia*, Washington, 1834.

Dahlgren, Madeleine Vinton, *Etiquette of Social Life in Washington*, 5th ed., Philadelphia, 1881.

Goodell, William, *Slavery and Anti-Slavery, A History of the Great Struggle in Both Hemispheres; with a view of the Slavery Question in the United States*, 3rd ed., New York, 1852.

Hamilton, Alexander, John Jay, and James Madison, *The Federalist*, ed., New York, 1902.

Johnson, Lorenzo D., *The Churches and Pastors of Washington, D.C., together with Five Hundred Topics of Sermons, Delivered in 1855 and 1856*, New York, 1857.

Medical Society of the District of Columbia, *Report on the Sanitary Conditions of the Cities of Washington and Georgetown, Presented to the Society, March 1864*, Washington, 1864.

Miscellaneous Pamphlets:

Address of the Association of Mechanics and Other Workingmen of Washington to the Operatives throughout the United States, 750:11.

Ceremonies and Oration at Laying the Cornerstone of the City Hall of the City of Washington, August 20, 1820, 277:4.

Report of the Proceedings at the Formation of the African Education Society: Instituted at Washington, December 28, 1829, with an Address to the Public by the Board of Managers, 411:20.

Report to Stockholders of the Bank of Columbia, 1826, 750:2.

The Nation, New York, 1865-.

Niles Weekly Register, Baltimore, 1811-37, 1839-1848.

Royal, Anne, *Sketches of History, Life and Manners in the United States*, New Haven, 1826.

Toner, Joseph, *Anniversary Oration delivered before the Medical Society of the District of Columbia, September 26, 1866*, Washington, 1869.

Torrey, Jesse, *A Portraiture of Domestic Slavery in the United States*, Philadelphia, 1817.

Transcripts of Manuscript Materials and Reprints in Periodicals and Other Serials

"The Diary of Mrs. William Thornton," transcript of the entries for the year 1800, Columbia Historical Society *Records*, X, and "The Capture of Washington," entries for 1814, *ibid.*, XIX.

"Doctor Mitchill's Letters from Washington, 1800-1813," reproduced in *Harpers New Monthly Magazine*, LVIII, April 1879.

"Extract from the Report of the Committee to Investigate Expenses and Accounts," reprint in Columbia Historical Society *Records*, IX.

"Home Letters of George W. Julian, 1850-1851," *Indiana Magazine of History*, XXIX, June 1933.

[Thomas Law] "Observations on the Intended Canal in Washington City," transcript in Columbia Historical Society *Records*, VIII.

"L'Enfant's Reports to President Washington, bearing dates of March 26, June 22, and August 19, 1791," transcript in Columbia Historical Society *Records*, II.

"Petition of Merchants of Alexandria," 1792, transcript in *The William and Mary Quarterly*, III, July 1923.

"Unwelcome Visitors to Early Washington," a reprint of Dr. James Ewell's "Capture of Washington," (originally published in an essay, "Bilious Fevers" in 3rd edition of *Planters and Mariners Medical Companion*), in Columbia Historical Society *Records*, I.

SECONDARY SOURCES

Adams, Henry, *History of the United States of America [during the Administrations of Jefferson and Madison.]* 9 vols., New York, 1889-91.

At Lee, Samuel Yorke, *History of the Public Schools of Washington City, D.C., from August, 1805, to August, 1875.* Washington, 1876.

Bancroft, Frederic, *Slave-Trading in the Old South.* New York, 1959.

Barton, Elmer Epenetus, *Historical and Commercial Sketches of Washington and Environs, Our Capital City, "The Paris of America."* Washington, D.C., 1884.

Belden, Thomas A. and Marva R., *So Fell the Angels.* Boston, 1956.

Bemis, Samuel Flagg, *John Quincy Adams and the Union.* New York, 1956.

Biographical Dictionary of the American Congress, 1774-1949. Washington, 1950.

Bond, Horace M., *The Education of the Negro in the American Social Order.* New York, 1934.

Brackett, Jeffrey R., *The Negro in Maryland: A Study of the Institution of Slavery*, in *Johns Hopkins Studies in Historical and Political Science*, VI, Baltimore, 1889.

Brant, Irving, *James Madison, The President, 1809-1812.* Indianapolis and New York, 1956.

———, *James Madison, Secretary of State.* Indianapolis and New York, 1951.

Brigham, Clarence S., *History and Bibliography of American Newspapers, 1690-1820*, 2 vols., Worcester, 1947.

Brooks, Noah, *Washington in Lincoln's Time.* New York, 1895.

Brown, Glenn, *History of the United States Capitol.* 2 vols., Washington, 1900-1903.

Bryan, Wilhelmus Bogart, *A History of the National Capital.* 2 vols., New York, 1914-16.

Cajori, Florian, *The Chequered Career of Ferdinand Rudolph Hassler.* Boston, 1929.

———, *The Early Mathematical Sciences in North and South America.* Boston, 1928.

Carman, Harry J., and Reinhard H. Luthin, *Lincoln and the Patronage.* New York, 1943.

Catterall, Ralph C. H., *The Second Bank of the United States.* Chicago, 1903.

Catton, Bruce, *A Stillness at Appomattox.* New York, 1953.

Clark, Allen Cullings. *Greenleaf and Law in the Federal City.* Washington, 1901.

Cowley, Malcolm, ed., *The Complete Poetry and Prose of Walt Whitman.* 2 vols. New York, 1948.

Coulson, Thomas, *Joseph Henry, His Life and Work.* Princeton, 1950.

Crane, Katherine E., *Blair House, Past and Present.* Washington, 1945.

Craven, Avery Odell, *Soil Exhaustion as a Factor in the Agricultural History of Virginia and Maryland, 1606-1860*, in *University of Illinois Studies in the Social Sciences*, XIII, Urbana, Ill., 1926.

Dangerfield, George, *The Era of Good Feelings.* New York, 1952.

Darrah, William C., *Powell of the Colorado.* Princeton, 1951.

Davis, Richard Beale, *The Abbé Correa in America, 1812-1820* in the American Philosophical Society *Transactions*, new series, XLV, Part II, 1955.

Dewey, Davis Rich, *State Banking Before the Civil War.* Washington, 1910.

Dictionary of American Biography. 22 vols. New York, 1928-1958.

Dupree, A. Hunter, *Science in the Federal Government, A History of Policies and Activities to 1940.* Cambridge, 1957.

Dyer, Frederick H., *A Compendium of the War of Rebellion.* Des Moines, Iowa, 1908.

Fairman, Charles Edwin, *Art and Artists of the Capitol of the United States of America.* Washington, 1927.

Gabriel, Ralph H., *The Course of American Democratic Thought.* New York, 1940.

Gonzaga College, An Historical Sketch From its Foundation in 1821 to the Solemn Celebration of its First Centenary in 1921. Washington, 1922.

Goode, George Brown, *The Genesis of the United States National Museum* in *Report of the U.S. National Museum*, 1891.

Gouge, William M., *A Short History of Paper Money and Banking in the United States.* Philadelphia, 1833.

Harrison, Fairfax, *Landmarks of Old Prince William.* 2 vols. Richmond, Virginia, 1924.

Hibben, Henry B., *Navy-Yard, Washington. History from Organization, 1799, to present date.* Washington, 1890.

Horan, James D., *Mathew Brady, Historian with a Camera.* New York, 1955.

Hungerford, Edward, *The Story of the Baltimore & Ohio Railroad, 1827-1927.* 2 vols., New York, 1928.

Hyman, Harold M., *Era of the Oath, Northern Loyalty Tests during the Civil War and Reconstruction.* Philadelphia, 1954.

Jackson, Luther P., *Free Negro Labor and Property Holding in Virginia, 1830-1860.* New York, 1942.

Jackson, Richard P., *The Chronicles of Georgetown, D.C. from 1751 to 1878.* Washington, 1878.

Kite, Elizabeth Sarah, *L'Enfant and Washington, 1791-1792.* Baltimore, 1929.

Larkin, Oliver W., *Samuel F. B. Morse and American Democratic Art.* Boston, 1954.

Leech, Margaret, *Reveille in Washington.* New York, 1941.

Lorant, Stefan, *The Presidency: A Pictorial History of Presidential Elections from Washington to Truman.* New York, 1951.

McMaster, John B., *A History of the People of the United States, from the Revolution to the Civil War.* 8 vols. New York, 1883-1913.

Meneely, Alexander Howard, *The War Department, 1861, A Study in Mobilization and Administration.* New York, 1928.

Miller, Harry E., *Banking Theories in the United States Before 1860.* Cambridge, Massachusetts, 1927.

Murray, Pauli, *Proud Shoes, The Story of an American Family.* New York, 1956.

Nichols, Roy Franklin, *The Disruption of American Democracy.* New York, 1948.

Nicolay, Helen, *Sixty Years of the Literary Society.* Washington, 1934.

Nicolay, John G. and John Hay, *Abraham Lincoln, A History.* 10 vols. New York, 1890.

O'Connor, Ellen M., *Myrtilla Miner. A Memoir.* New York, 1885.

Odgers, M. M., *Alexander Dallas Bache; Scientist and Educator, 1806-1867.* Philadelphia, 1947.

Pennell, E. R. and J., *The Life of James McNeill Whistler.* Philadelphia, 1911.

Phillips, Ulrich Bonnell, *The Life of Robert Toombs.* New York, 1913.

Porter, Sarah H., *The Life and Times of Anne Royall.* Cedar Rapids, Iowa, 1909.

Radcliffe, George L. P., *Governor Thomas H. Hicks of Maryland and the Civil War*, in *The Johns Hopkins University Studies in Historical and Political Science*, Series XIX, Nos. 11-12, Baltimore, 1901.

Sanderlin, Walter S., *The Great National Project: A History of the Chesapeake and Ohio Canal*, in *The Johns Hopkins University Studies in Historical and Political Science*, LXIV, No. I. Baltimore, 1946.

Sands, Francis P. B., *The Founders and Original Organizers of the Metropolitan Club, Washington, D.C.* Washington, 1909.

Schotter, Howard W., *The Growth and Development of the Pennsylvania Railroad Company.* Philadelphia, 1927.

Seaton, Josephine, *William Winston Seaton of the "National Intelligencer."* Boston, 1871.

Shanks, Henry T., *The Secession Movement in Virginia, 1847-1861.* Richmond, 1934.

Simmons, William J., *Men of Mark: Eminent, Progressive and Rising.* Cleveland, 1887.

Spaulding, Thomas M., *The Literary Society in Peace and War.* Washington, 1947.

Stampp, Kenneth M., *The Peculiar Institution: Slavery in the Ante-bellum South.* New York, 1956.

Sydnor, Charles S, *The Development of Southern Sectionalism, 1819-1848.* Baton Rouge, 1948.

Tucker, Glenn, *Poltroons and Patriots: A Popular Account of the War of 1812.* 2 vols. Indianapolis, 1954.

Tunnard, Christopher and Henry H. Reed, *American Skyline: The Growth and Form of our Cities and Towns.* Boston, 1955.

Washington Gas-Light Company, *Growing with Washington, the Story of our First Hundred Years.* Washington, 1948.

Welling, James C., *Brief Chronicles of the Columbian College from 1821 to 1873, and of the Columbian University from 1873 to 1889.* Washington, 1889.

Walsh, John J., *Early Banks in the District of Columbia, 1792-1818.* Washington, 1940.

Wharton, Anne H., *Salons Colonial and Republican.* Philadelphia and London, 1900.

———, *Social Life in the Early Republic.* Philadelphia and London, 1902.

White, Leonard D., *The Jeffersonians, A Study in Administrative History, 1801-1829.* New York, 1951.

Whyte, James, *The Uncivil War.* New York, 1958.

Willson, Beckles, *Friendly Relations: A Narrative of Britain's Ministers and Ambassadors to America, 1791-1930.* Boston, 1934.

Wilson, William B., *History of the Pennsylvania Railroad Company.* 2 vols. Philadelphia, 1899.

Wiltse, Charles M., *John C. Calhoun.* 3 vols. Indianapolis, 1944-1951.

Woodson, Carter, *A Century of Negro Migration.* Washington, 1918.

Woodward, C. Vann, *Reunion and Reaction: The Compromise of 1877 and the End of Reconstruction.* Boston, 1951.

PERIODICALS AND OTHER SERIALS

Bookman, CLIII.

Bowdoin Alumnus, June 1957.

Century Magazine, IV.

Columbia Historical Society *Records*, I-XLVII.

Georgetown Law Journal, XLI and XLII.

Journal of Negro History, XI.

Journal of Southern History, V.

Journal of the Society of Architectural Historians, XV.

The Key Reporter, XXV.

Magazine of American History, XIV.

Oneida Historical Society *Transactions*, IX.

Political Science Quarterly, LXVI.

Virginia Quarterly Review, XXXVI.

INDEX

WASHINGTON

VOLUME II

CAPITAL CITY

1879-1950

WASHINGTON

CAPITAL CITY

1879-1950

BY CONSTANCE MC LAUGHLIN GREEN

PRINCETON, NEW JERSEY
PRINCETON UNIVERSITY PRESS

Copyright © 1962 by Princeton University Press
ALL RIGHTS RESERVED
Published by Princeton University Press, Princeton, N.J.
In the United Kingdom: Princeton University Press, Guildford, Surrey
LCC 62-7402
ISBN 0-691-00585-0 (one-vol. paperback edn.)
ISBN 0-691-04572-0 (vol. 1, hardcover edn.)
ISBN 0-691-04573-9 (vol. 2, hardcover edn.)

First PRINCETON PAPERBACK Printing, 1976

Printed in the United States of America

IN MEMORY OF MY MOTHER AND FATHER

Lois Angell

AND

Andrew Cunningham McLaughlin

PUBLISHER'S NOTE

For some time before her unfortunate death in 1975, Constance McLaughlin Green had hoped to prepare a one-volume abridgment of her history of our nation's capital. Illness prevented her from completing her task, but her work is so valuable and the demand for it so great that Princeton University Press has reissued the history in its entirety. The cloth edition consists of the two volumes as originally published: Volume 1, *Washington: Village and Capital, 1800-1878*; Volume 2, *Washington: Capital City, 1879-1950*. For the paperback edition, the two volumes have been bound together, without change, and the resultant single volume has been given the title *Washington: A History of the Capital, 1800-1950*.

FOREWORD

STUDENTS of the American capital usually call Washington unique. Certainly nowhere else do national politics and execution of national policies loom so large day in and day out. Although the men directing those affairs have not always survived in history as major figures, there is probably no time when they did not command wider public attention than did Americans in other places. Accompanying that political prestige are the physical attributes of the capital of a wealthy and powerful nation: monumental government buildings, stretches of parks, foreign embassies, headquarters of national scientific institutions, learned societies, international labor unions, and a host of other non-profit or eleemosynary associations. As these institutions occupy great expanses of land, Washington is the only city in the United States in which more than half the real estate is tax-exempt. Other unique features, while clearly in evidence, are not an inevitable consequence of her national status.

In none of the old European capitals or newer twentieth-century creations such as Canberra and Brazilia is suffrage denied to local citizens. The twenty-third amendment to the Constitution, ratified in 1961, gives Washingtonians votes for President and Vice President but leaves them without representation in Congress, without a popularly elected city government, and, alone among American citizens, without any voice in the management of their own municipal affairs. A non-industrial, essentially non-commercial city, Washington is also set apart by the phenomenon of the indirect power exercised by a small group of businessmen, the Board of Trade. And the city expands less in years of country-wide economic prosperity than in periods of war and national crisis. Another characteristic has been the extraordinary cultivation and intellectual distinction of the upper-class colored community, which, though seldom fully recognized by white citizens, long made the city the undisputed center of American Negro civilization. Still another factor peculiar to Washington has been the number and social influence of high-ranking military men who chose upon retirement to live out their days here; the post-World War II era, in which big industrial corporations took to engaging the services of newly retired generals, admirals, and Navy captains, has diminished the role of elderly officers in the city's life, but until about 1948 that rootless, politically conservative group constituted an important element.

One of the most decisive features of Washington's history is the psychological impermanence of much of the upper strata of her population—"psychological" rather than "physical," because uncounted thousands of people who have lived here pleasurably for years have never labelled themselves Washingtonians, or they delayed so long in acknowledging their allegiance that the community lost much of the benefit of their participating presence. Thus vigorous young men who came in the 1930's to take jobs under the New Deal paid scant attention to the local community; they expected to leave within a year or two. Ten, twenty, or thirty years later, still in Washington, they would realize that their detachment had been costly to the city if not directly to themselves; at critical moments they had failed to support or oppose local projects about which they would later feel strongly. If most noticeable from World War I onward, the long-enduring unconcern of permanent temporary residents has handicapped the city for the past eighty-odd years.

In important respects, on the other hand, Washington is like other big American cities. Her aspirations and troubles duplicate theirs—the struggle to develop a sound public school system, to eliminate juvenile delinquency and reduce crime to a minimum, to provide humane, intelligently run welfare services, maintain an adequate water supply and sewage facilities, build highways capable of handling the evergrowing volume of traffic, and create and preserve beauty amidst the turmoil. Nor are the newer problems of mid-twentieth-century metropolitan areas pronouncedly different in the District-of-Columbia-Maryland-Virginia complex from those of other American metropolitan regions that cross state lines. The details vary, but the broad outline is the same.

One or two significant features of Washington's life, however, fall between the categories of the unique and the recognizable urban "norm." From 1880 down to World War I, the years of heaviest European immigration to the United States, the city attracted far fewer foreigners than did rapidly growing northern industrial centers. Like a number of southern cities, she escaped the social problems brought in the wake of the waves of non-English-speaking aliens, but at the same time she lost the enrichment of their varied cultural backgrounds. A large part of her in-migrants were Negroes from the agrarian South, an element that moved also into northern manufacturing cities during World War I and after. In the voteless District of Columbia one result early in the twentieth century was a curious local arrangement: colored people excluded from white neighborhood groups formed civic associations in endeavor to counterbalance the influence of white citizens' associations.

These strands of the unique, the distinctive, and the universal interweave to form the fabric of Washington's history. From it emerges a double pattern. Indeed this book might well borrow the title of a recent pamphlet published by the District League of Women Voters: *Washington D.C.: A Tale of Two Cities.* For the historian quickly discovers that alongside a pride-inspiring capital, a place captivating to residents and visitors, stands a city ridden by frustration and impotence. That duality, only faintly perceptible in the 1880's and not pronounced until World War I, sharpens with the sloughing off of federal responsibility for District finances in the 1920's and becomes thereafter the single most compelling factor in Washington's civic development.

Men and women, not abstract forces, brought about this and less dramatic elements of change over the years, but the further the story progresses in time and the larger the city grows, the less clear-cut the role of particular individuals. Hence my text takes on an impersonal quality, particularly after 1930, in spite of the colorful people who trod the stage of New Deal and wartime Washington. The submergence of the city as a community between 1940 and 1945 has led me merely to outline events that constitute part of world history and only to touch upon episodes that had special local impact. The postwar years opened up new vistas, but whither they would lead, or which of the series of alternatives would seem most desirable was uncertain at midcentury. My last chapter, therefore, attempts only to set the scene for acts that would be played out after 1950. As city becomes part of megalopolis and regional problems overreach political boundaries, city planners, sociologists, political scientists, and urban historians confront new themes that call for exhaustive study.

Not all readers will agree with my choice of emphasis. The course of race relations, for example, from the heartbreaking deterioration after the 1870's to about 1906, and the upward turns and the reversals thereafter, might be summarized at intervals merely by the phrase "more of same." And yet manifestly it was never exactly "same." Careful exploration of the painfully slow evolution has seemed to me essential. Why I pursue the half-century of conflict between the Board of Trade and other elements in the city may be less obvious. In Washington, the "power structure," a term beloved of sociologists and political scientists, rests on the Hill, in Congress; the President himself functions chiefly as interior decorator, and the community has been confined to strengthening or attacking the "influence structure." Hence the necessity, as I see it, of tracing the steps in that struggle. In examining the seamy side of the city's life, perhaps here and there I tend unwarrantably to exculpate Washingtonians themselves for their plight; if so, I can only defend that uncritical excess by pointing to the provocation: the sympathy evoked by observing the narrowness of the cleft stick in which they are caught. And if I spend more time in describing ineptness in city management than in discussing the growing dedication to music and painting and the pursuit of ideas, perhaps it is reasonable to point out that the emotion inspired by a Bach Invention, the appeal of a Rembrandt portrait, or growing awareness of the relationship of the fourth dimension to everyday life do not lend themselves to exact analysis, particularly as the responses of a half-million individuals are involved.

While the interpretations I have put upon my findings are my own, I am indebted to many people for assistance in locating data and for giving me the benefit of their experience in using them. Unlike my first volume on Washington, the second draws heavily upon interviews with participants in or observers of past events. In arriving at generalizations I cannot pretend to having employed a sampling technique on a large enough scale to rate as sociologically scientific. The last seven chapters, on the research and writing of which I worked single-handed, would especially have benefited from deploying a team of skilled interrogators to assemble an adequate cross-section of local opinion. As it is, a number of people with special information that nowhere else appears in print have discussed with me the questions under consideration, and several have read critically the chapters which deal with the problems they are peculiarly qualified to pass upon. Besides the staff of the Library of Congress and the Washingtoniana Room of the Public Library, the men and women of the recently organized Washington Center for Metropolitan Studies have given me invaluable help, most particularly my former assistant, Atlee Shidler.

Until the expiration in 1960 of the grant from the Rockefeller Foundation that inspired this study, an advisory committee of eminent scholars read every chapter as it appeared in draft. Dr. Waldo Leland, director-emeritus of the American Council of Learned Societies, Doctors Ernest Posner, Ralph Gabriel, and Arthur Ekirch of American University, Dr. Caroline Ware, recognized expert on community organization, and Dr. Oliver Wendell Holmes of the National Archives composed the active members of the committee; the ill-health of Dr. Solon J. Buck and the death of John Ihlder, authority on Washington housing problems, early denied me their invaluable help. Louis Brownlow has contributed more to this volume than any other one person with no official responsibility for it. A newspaperman when he first came to Washington in 1904, a District commissioner for five and a half critical years, and later the head of the Public Administration Clearing House, "Brownie" has supplied me with facts and insights I could have obtained in no other way, and, by his reading of most of the chapters covering the period of his years here, he has saved me more than once from drawing faulty conclusions. Dr. Rayford Logan of Howard University, Dr. John Hope Franklin of Brooklyn College, and Eugene Davidson, a leader in the fight for Negro civil rights, have between them scrutinized most of the text on colored Washington. Doctors Charles Wiltse and Louis Hunter have similarly gone over carefully the story I present from 1933 to 1950. In addition to many others on whose encouragement and help I depended, I wish to thank the trustees of the Chapelbrook Foundation for the two-year grant that enabled me to complete this study.

CONSTANCE MC LAUGHLIN GREEN

Washington, D.C.
November 1962

CONTENTS

ILLUSTRATIONS

Illustrations 1 through 16 following page 142

WASHINGTON

VOLUME II

CAPITAL CITY

1879-1950

CHAPTER I

THE INHERITANCE OF THE PAST

TO A LONG-LIVED MEMBER of the Oldest Inhabitants' Association, the Washington of 1879 undoubtedly looked very different from the village of the early years of the century. By the end of the 1870's the capital had acquired 140,000 permanent residents; another 9,000 lived beyond Rock Creek in Georgetown. The orchard that had covered the upper half of the President's Square in 1800 had become a park edged by the harmoniously proportioned St. John's Church and handsome houses looking out through elm and sycamore branches toward the equestrian statue of General Andrew Jackson. The Treasury erected in President Jackson's day and the new, ornate State Department building interrupted the sweep of Pennsylvania and New York Avenues to the east and the west of the White House; the tracks of the Baltimore and Potomac Railroad laid across the Mall between the foot of Capitol Hill and the red sandstone castle housing the Smithsonian Institution broke the stretch that L'Enfant had intended for a magnificent promenade reaching to the river; and the heavy Gothic stone railroad depot jutting out upon the Mall and North 6th Street underscored the recent changes in architectural taste more emphatically than did the red-brick mansard-roofed Department of Agriculture building placed to the west of the Smithsonian. Like a stubby thumb the unfinished Washington Monument cut the skyline above the tidal marshes along the Potomac and the ponds formed by draining and filling the old Washington Canal. Otherwise the main outlines of L'Enfant's original plan were still visible.

An unprepossessing huddle of sheds and small houses clustered along lower Pennsylvania Avenue above and below the new Centre Market, and, nearby, the National Hotel, once Washington's most famous hostelry, still offered competition to the more elegantly equipped Willard and the Ebbitt House. Office buildings interspersed with livery stables now flanked most of F Street from the Treasury to Judiciary Square, where the beautiful simple lines of the old City Hall caught the eye. Fashionable early and mid-Victorian dwellings along 6th Street still formed a select residential area as desirable as the newer section in the neighborhood of the British Legation on Connecticut Avenue below Dupont Circle. Tracks for the horse-drawn street-railway cars threaded a half-dozen thoroughfares out as far as Boundary Street and down to the Eastern Branch at the Navy Yard and the wharves below. At night yellow gas lights winked through the branches of the saplings planted in Boss Shepherd's heyday.

Yet, compared to the transformations in other cities, the physical changes in Washington were minor. New York, with more than a million inhabitants spread from the Battery nearly to 60th Street, had become one of the great commercial cities of the world—a city displaying all the elegance of wealth and all the squalor of poverty. Baltimore now contained solid lines of shops, warehouses, and dwellings for 332,000 people. Cincinnati had grown from a frontier settlement of 800 souls and a hundred-odd log houses to a river port and manufacturing center supporting a population of 255,000; Chicago, from an empty stretch of prairie on Lake Michigan's shore, had turned into a huge sprawling polyglot city fed by a network of railroads.

Washington's leading citizens nevertheless were gratified by what they saw about them. Largely because of that satisfaction they had acquiesced cheerfully in the new political order introduced in 1874, when bankruptcy had undermined the three-year-old territorial government. Congress, in enacting first a temporary law and then the Organic Act of June 1878, had stripped them of all local self-government but at the same time had guaranteed the solvency of the District of Columbia by underwriting its public debt and by pledging the United States to share equally with local taxpayers the annual expense of running the capital. To arch-southerners in Washington disenfranchisement represented a safeguard against a city government partly manned by Negroes, and many a big taxpayer, whatever his origins, had seen advantages in a regime free of pressures from non-propertied "riff-raff." Men who perceived dangers in rule by a three-man presidentially appointed commission with Congress in control of the purse-strings had the consolation of believing that this was only a temporary arrangement that they could bring to an end when the time was propitious. In the interim the seventy-year-old struggle to obtain federal funds for the public schools appeared to be a problem of the past. What optimists lost sight of was the depth of the conviction that had permeated Congress and would linger on for the next eighty years that Washingtonians were financially irresponsible, that if given another chance they would again plunge the District into heavy debt and again force the federal government to bail them out as it had twice since 1835. That distrust on the Hill would balk every effort of the next three generations to return to local citizens control of their own taxes and municipal expenditures seemed inconceivable to Washingtonians in 1879.

Intelligent colored men, however reluctant to lose the local voting rights they had enjoyed since 1867 as the political equals of whites, had not protested publicly against the new scheme of local government. Presumably the President, Congress, and the federal courts would protect Negroes' recently won civil rights; less than a decade earlier two municipal ordinances and subsequently an act of the territorial legislature had fortified those rights by prohibiting racial discrimination in public places. The tax-supported colored schools, opened in 1864, had so expanded that Negro illiteracy in Washington might well disappear within another generation. Howard University provided higher education and professional training for exceptionally able Negroes. Meanwhile, although white people tended to think of the colored community as one, it had become two—one group made up largely of black field hands who had migrated to the District of Columbia during and after the Civil War, and a second relatively small group of aristocratic old Washington families and newcomers with as much white as Negro blood who had been drawn to the capital by the exceptional opportunities open to them. While the black masses greatly predominated and at least half of them lived at a bare subsistence level, colored Washington included more upper-class Negroes than any other one place in the country. Perceptive and ambitious, these men expected to lead their people out of the wilderness. Hopes of rapidly reducing race prejudice had, to be sure, dwindled during the mid-seventies, but faith remained that its overt expression in discriminatory practices could be kept in check until experience taught white men that dark-skinned Americans were capable of responsible citizenship.

The social structure of the white community, in turn, had undergone changes since 1860. The very term "Federal City" had dropped out of use, as the enlargement of national power at the expense of the states enhanced Washington's political and social importance. What transpired in Richmond, Columbia, or Baton Rouge, or indeed in Albany, Topeka, or Sacramento, now mattered far less than what politicians decided on Capitol Hill; Americans must go to Washington to be in the swim. While the vulgarity of a new plutocracy had permeated much of official society during most of the postwar decade, after the panic of 1873 the social carpetbaggers had gradually ceased to exercise much influence. Old residents imbued with a strong sense of tradition, newcomers ready to share in community responsibilities, and a number of cultivated, highly trained men willing to risk the precariousness of government employment had succeeded in restoring dignity to social intercourse. Thus the upper brackets of Washington society felt able thenceforward to handle any new invasions of frivolous, wealthy, temporary residents. Four universities and the Library of Congress endowed the city with some scholarly standing.

The increasingly significant role of government scientists in itself enriched community life. Joseph Henry, eminent secretary of the Smithsonian Institution, had remarked in 1871 that no other city in the United States had "in proportion to the number of its inhabitants, so many men actively engaged in pursuits connected with science as in Washington."[1] Before the end of that decade residents knew that a city claiming a John Wesley Powell, a Simon Newcomb, a Cleveland Abbe, and a Lester Ward, let alone a Henry Adams, need no longer fear being branded a provincial village, a stage for tawdry display, or a nursery of bad taste.

At the end of the 1870's knowledgeable Washingtonians had come to see the city's future as forever tied to her status as national capital. Ambitions to use the Potomac waterway as a means of making her the chief "emporium" of the continent had evaporated in the 1850's; and determination to develop a commercial empire sustained by a complex of railroads had faded during the next two decades. The long lines of the unemployed drawn up at soup kitchens in America's big industrial centers and the violent railroad strike of 1877 that crippled and terrified commercial cities had deepened Washingtonians' gratitude for escaping the worst consequences of the country-wide panic and depression. Service to the United States government, to sight-seers in the capital, or to citizens who wanted to enjoy its pleasures during the "season" promised a more stable and satisfactory source of livelihood than could further costly attempts to develop manufactures and shipping. The community had emerged from the social revolution which the Civil War had launched and from the economic and political troubles of the 1870's into a stronger position than she had ever known before. Talk of moving the capital to the Middle West had ceased.

[1] Garrick Mallery, "Relations between Professor Baird and Participating Societies," *Annual Report of the Smithsonian Institution*, 1888, p. 719.

Washington still had nothing except national political news to sell in the markets of the rest of the country, but the seasonal crop of congressmen, lobbyists, and visitors ready to spend freely kept considerable money in circulation. The extravagances of senators who, if not commanding the $500,000 monthly income ascribed in 1878 to Senator Fair of Nevada, nevertheless had fabulous fortunes, inevitably benefited local business. The recently regained sense of permanence, coupled with the physical attractions of the modernized city, had brought her new residents and a certain amount of investment capital. Poverty was no less extreme in some parts of Washington than in big industrial cities, but here it was probably less widespread and certainly less evident to the casual observer. Although the gain in per capita wealth did not eradicate the miseries of the city's destitute, other residents could look upon it as proof of material progress and a hopeful portent. Rich or poor, white or black, people who had lived through the heartbreak of the Civil War and the harassing years that followed were not likely to believe in an untroubled future. Nevertheless, as 1878 drew to a close, an atmosphere of cautious confidence had begun to envelop Washington.

CHAPTER II

REAL ESTATE AND CIVIC ENTERPRISE, 1879-1901

THE economic history of Washington during the last years of the nineteenth century becomes a story of real estate. Convinced by the long depression of the folly of seeking to develop heavy industry and the far-flung commercial empire that had once seemed so desirable, after 1878 business leaders acquiesced in keeping Washington outside America's commercial and industrial orbit. Even the dismantling of the government's ordnance workshops at Arsenal Point occasioned little protest, and the halfhearted attempt to whip up fresh interest in exploiting the water power of the Great Falls quickly subsided before the greater attractions of investment in local residential property. The consensus ran that service to the federal government and to the host of yearly visitors offered the national city a sound basis for her economy; rooted in so fertile a soil, it needed nothing more to secure a sturdy growth. When the panic of 1893 checked real estate and building activities, a committee of businessmen spoke of the District's eligible factory sites and the unemployed workmen available as mill hands, but the committee insisted that the city must remain primarily a center of "learning and culture." Certainly only light industry of an "inoffensive" kind would be welcome; at most citizens should persuade the federal government to manufacture its supplies here.

Manufacturing, to be sure, expanded within a narrow range, but small shops without power-driven machinery still accounted for most of the local output except building materials, illuminating gas, flour, beer, and printing. (See Table I.) Two years after the Potomac Electric Power Company acquired land and water rights at the Great Falls in 1898, all manufacturing concerns together used less than 9,600 horse power, the equivalent potential of about seventy family automobiles of mid-twentieth century.[1] The production of consumer goods for a local public suited community leaders fearful of "the possible unrest . . . in the population whenever an unsatisfactory relation between labor and capital might arise." Although growth was more pronounced between 1880 and 1890 than in the next decade, the depression-ridden 1890's brought the District more establishments with more money invested, bigger payrolls, and a larger dollar value of product. Flour milling, on the decline since 1870, dropped off sharply after 1889 when a devastating flood so damaged the C & O Canal that for seven or eight years canal traffic ceased altogether. Brewing, on the other hand, grew in twenty years from a $275,000 to a $1,340,000 business, and the beer produced in Christian Heurich's imposing brick brewery near the mouth of Rock Creek commanded a wide market. Private book publishing and job printing gradually yielded in importance to newspaper and magazine publishing, but the tonnage of books and reports issuing from the Government Printing Office kept the balance about as before.

For stockholders probably the most profitable enterprise was the Washington Gas Light Company; its monopoly, unchallenged until electricity offered a glimmer of competition in the 1890's, permitted minimum dividend payments of 10 percent annually, although, compared to the 65 percent of the depression year of 1876, the return was small. A swelling population which included 350 bankers, about 9,000 well-to-do professional people, and a number of men listed in the city *Directory* merely as "capitalist" meant, as the Washington Board of Trade observed in 1899, an "unprecedented growth of demand on the part of consumers of every kind [which] has

[1] *Evening Star*, 22, 29 Mar, 19 Apr, 17 May 1879, 24 May 1884 (hereafter cited as *Star*); Andrew J. Rogers to Sayles J. Bowen, 8, 16 Jan 1878, and Memorial of Great Falls Manufacturing Co., 1882, Sayles J. Bowen Mss (in possession of Charles A. Barker of the Johns Hopkins University); *Annual Reports of the Washington Board of Trade*, 1894, pp. 6-7, 1896, pp. 6-7, 34-35, 1898, pp. 44-47, 1899, p. 52 (hereafter cited as *Rpt B/Tr*); *Twelfth U.S. Census*, 1900, *Manufactures*, Pt. II, p. 115.

taxed the facilities and ingenuity of merchants and manufacturers, absorbing their attention so completely as to leave little time or room for thoughts or theories of further expansion of industries."[2]

Shoppers were delighted when Isadore Saks opened his fine clothing store and S. Walter Woodward and Alvin Lothrop a department store modelled upon Wanamaker's of Philadelphia and Marshall Field's of Chicago. But despite advertisements of the latest Parisian pelisse, Washington, as one disappointed young woman noted, was not "a brag shopping place." Wholesaling firms were few. Well before the final collapse of the C & O Canal, the city focused her commercial aims upon becoming the convention center and show place of the country. As early as 1878 some three hundred businessmen obtained from Congress a charter for a National Fair Association. Although the thirty-year-old campaign again failed to win federal money for a large public auditorium, two or three exhibitions held at Ivy City near the Kendall Green school for the deaf were modest successes. In the late eighties Washingtonians proposed to stage a world's fair to celebrate Columbus' discovery of America, but, when Chicagoans outmaneuvered them, they found comfort in the steady rise of the tourist and convention trade,[3] and took pride in seeing the city turn into "a favorite place of residence for people of talent, culture and fortune."[4]

The ideal of making and keeping Washington "a favorite place of residence" was at once the cause and the result of widespread interest in local real estate. The purchase of city lots or suburban tracts became a fetish among people of small

[2] *Star*, 1 Jan 1890; Senate Miscellaneous Document 91, 53C, 2S, Ser 3167 (hereafter cited as S Mis Doc); Cleveland *Leader*, 19 Apr 1883; *Directory*, 1878 and 1900; *Rpt B/Tr*, 1899, p. 51.

[3] Virginia Grigsby to Hart Grigsby, Jul 1883, Gibson-Humphreys Mss (Southern Historical Collection, hereafter cited as SHC); *Star*, 22 Aug, 21, 23 Oct 1879, 8, 16 Oct 1880, 20 May, 18, 23 Nov 1882, 17 May 1883, 14 Jan 1885, 13 Sep 1887; *Sunday Chronicle*, 21 Aug 1881, 4 Jun 1882 (hereafter cited as *Sun Chronicle*); *Sentinel*, 12 Oct, 30 Nov 1889; Washington *Post*, 2, 4, 11 Oct 1889; *Rpt B/Tr*, 1891, p. 18.

[4] S Mis Doc 222, 52C, 1S, pp. 25-26, Ser 2907.

means as well as large: Washington real estate looked foolproof. Thus in 1883 Mrs. Susan Grigsby, an impoverished southern gentlewoman newly appointed to a $900-a-year clerkship in the government Land Office, wrote to her sister: "There are still big fortunes to be made in this city on very small real estate investments and I hope you and I will be amongst the fortunate ones." That Mrs. Grigsby's venture did not pay off in no way discouraged others. A building boom accompanied the snowballing speculation in land. While new office buildings and stores rose along F Street, houses multiplied in the rest of the city, some of them designed by expensive architects for individual clients, more of them contractor-built pseudo-Queen-Anne red brick rows.[5] Impressed by these signs of prosperity a young newspaper correspondent questioned a leading citizen about its source. "Washington," came the answer, "is more of a business town than most people think. Washingtonians have some wholesale groceries here which do a business up into millions." And, he added, "real estate values have been making regular jumps upward for the past two years . . . the day will come—I ought to say it has already come—when it will be as fashionable to have a winter house at Washington as it is to have a summer one at Newport or at Saratoga . . . Washington in the winter is the gayest of the gay."[6]

Washington, known since the 1840's for the gaiety of her season, had never enjoyed a comparable boom. Formerly most public officials and people who came for the winter's social whirl had rented houses or lived in hotels and boarding houses; now men holding important public office generally made a point of owning their houses, and scores of other temporary residents hastened to build or buy. For as industrial fortunes began to create a new American elite, men long preoccupied with entrenching themselves behind the power of money increasingly

[5] Susan Grigsby to Sarah G. Humphreys, 5 Aug 1883, 3 Aug, 5 Oct 1884, Gibson-Humphreys Mss; *Star*, 18 Jun 1881, 30 Sep 1882, 28 Apr 1883, 27 Mar 1884; *Sun Chronicle*, 21 Nov 1880, 24 Sep 1882.

[6] Cleveland *Leader*, 30 Sep 1883.

aspired to national political power and the more subtle power of social prestige. To achieve those aims a recognized position fortified by a fixed establishment in the national capital might be important, if only because it permitted frequent association with members of the *Corps Diplomatique*. For people already socially secure, a *pied à terre* in Washington also held the attraction of a place in which to entertain internationally known figures in agreeable surroundings. There was little to lose, since the federal government's commitment of 1878 to share District expenses kept taxes low. Assessments upon the rich were moderate: in 1893 the property of only 4,119 of the 31,700 District taxpayers was valued at over $10,000 and, despite frequent allusions to the city's large array of costly "mansions," only 1,300 holdings were assessed at more than $25,000.[7] The "opulent New Yorker," a merchant prince such as Levi Leiter of Chicago, or a Pittsburgher such as George Westinghouse, grown rich on his inventions, could build or buy his own residence in Washington, occupy it a few months of the year, and, when he wanted to dispose of it, count on making money on the transaction. What the very wealthy chose to do seemed desirable to people not so wealthy.

Permanent residents consequently began to build houses to sell or to furnish and rent. It was a very ill-equipped or badly located house that would not lease for the winter at a price high enough to bring the owner a handsome annual return. Rentals of furnished houses ranged in the mid-eighties from $75 to $3,733 a month; the average was $200. As land values rose, high-priced flats began to appear, a sign of urban growth both gratifying and slightly alarming to old residents. One businessman, marvelling at the changes he had witnessed since the war, noted that in 1865 Washington brokers never dealt exclusively in real estate but handled it along with claims, insurance, and stocks; fifteen years later the realtor

[7] *Rpt B/Tr*, 1893, p. 33; *Annual Report of the Commissioners of the District of Columbia*, 1893, p. 17 (hereafter cited as Comrs Rpt).

had come into being. Dozens of newcomers who had begun as government clerks turned into real estate dealers. So in 1863 fifteen-year-old Brainard Warner arrived from a small town in Pennsylvania, took a clerical job in the Judiciary Square Hospital and other clerkships in the next several years, and, after reading law with the famous Thaddeus Stevens and graduating from the Columbian Law School in 1869, founded a highly successful real estate business. George Truesdell, a New Yorker trained as a civil engineer, began his Washington career in 1872 as a clerk in the Treasury, only to open his own real estate office within a few years. And other ambitious young men followed the same path from government clerkships to heads of real estate companies. By 1885 there were a hundred-odd firms.[8] "The real estate men occupy the best offices, and along F street where they are mostly found, their carriages line the street curbs during business hours." More than 2,450 buildings went up in Washington in 1887 alone, and ground that had sold for 8¢ a square foot five years before sold for 48¢.[9]

Abetted by a new generation of astute young bankers, real estate syndicates embarked in the mid-1880's upon large-scale operations in the suburbs. One group bought Kalorama Heights, once part of Joel Barlow's estate lying between Boundary Street and Rock Creek; another acquired 240 acres along Massachusetts Avenue extended from the creek to the Tenleytown road, the Wisconsin Avenue of today; and in 1887 still a third purchased Chevy Chase, the old Joseph Bradley farm on the District's northwestern line, soon to be the site of Washington's first country club. The profits on these transactions were frequently quick and reportedly enormous. A house in one of these new sections virtually guaranteed the occupant

[8] Cleveland *Leader*, 5 Jan 1883, 17 Jun 1885; S. J. Bowen to Phebe Barker, 8 Nov 1881, Bowen Mss; *Star*, 10 Feb, 10 Mar 1883, 27 Oct 1888, 1 Jan 1890; John Hitz, "Homes for the People in the City of Washington," *Journal of Social Science*, xv, 145.

[9] Cleveland *Leader*, 1 Nov 1884; *Star*, 8 Oct 1887.

a place on the *Elite List*, a compilation of the names of socially acceptable Washingtonians. Less sophisticated residential areas beyond the city limits also rose sharply in value, although the appreciation was slower. Washington Heights, a section above Boundary Street near Columbia Road, increased in seventeen years from an assessed value of $112,000 to $1,137,400. Cleveland Heights, so named because the President's fifteen-room summer "cottage" was located on Woodley Road near the Tenleytown street railway, boomed in the late eighties; and a few years later, when the Naval Observatory rose on a hilltop in the vicinity, Cleveland Park came into existence.

As Washington became "a city for the rich," people of modest means found housing costs an acute problem. "It is strange," remarked John Forney's *Sunday Chronicle*, "that the capitalists and moneyed men of Washington seeking good opportunities for investment never think of building blocks of small houses within the reach of poor men and government clerks." Le Droit Park, a model cooperative apartment building venture of the 1870's, quickly became too expensive for many householders. Multiplying home loan and building associations helped the impecunious finance new homes, and some owners met the monthly payments on buying a house by occupying only a part and renting out the rest. Other families had to find quarters in localities beyond the reach of the street railways or in suburbs lacking piped water, such as Uniontown across the Anacostia or Mt. Pleasant to the north. Government clerks without children generally lived in Washington boarding houses; single women in fact had little choice.[10] Timid ladies whom the Civil War had impoverished and who were struggling to earn a living as federal employees were fearful of the remoteness of the suburbs and the expense of daily

[10] *Directory*, 1890; *Star*, 8 Nov 1879, 15 Mar 1882, 28 Jul 1883, 24 May 1884, 14 Feb, 27 May 1885, 7 May, 18 Jun, 9 Jul, 26 Nov, 3 Dec 1887, 7 Jan, 16 Jun 1888; *Post*, 27 Oct 1889; *Sentinel*, 16 Jul 1892; *Sun Chronicle*, 21 Aug 1881; Comrs Rpts, 1899, II, 131, 1900, I, 28-29; Joseph W. Moore, *Picturesque Washington*, pp. 244-45; Hitz, "Homes," pp. 135-45.

carfare.[11] The real estate boom, if sauce for the gander, was certainly not sauce for the goose.

What twentieth-century planners would call "suburban sprawl" had a twenty-year start before Congress took steps to ensure some order in the future outward thrust of the city. By 1888 a belt of "inharmonious subdivisions" where streets had no relation to those of the city ringed Washington's northern bounds. Recognizing for the first time a "metropolitan area" problem, Congress enacted a law requiring suburban developers to lay out their subdivisions in conformity with the street plan of the city. The act for a time checked the mushrooming of relatively inexpensive settlements on Washington's periphery but later simplified the extension of sewers, water mains, and street lights into the county. Even without those urban conveniences, real estate values in parts of the county increased nearly 500 per cent during the eighties. Until street railway lines ran over the Aqueduct Bridge into Virginia in the late nineties, Washington's suburbia included none of the area beyond the Potomac. But within the District the spectacular growth elicited rhapsodic comment: "In time the District will be one vast city, the most beautiful, uniform and attractive of any to be found, the centre of learning, thought, wealth and station, the pride of our Republican empire and the envy of the world."

The slowing of all business after 1893 retarded building operations in both city and suburbs, but recovery, beginning in 1898, was so rapid that the District building inspectors were swamped with work. While a group of civic-minded men intent on ending alley-dwelling in Washington organized the Sanitary Improvement Company and built a number of row houses suited to the purses of workingmen, extension of the trolley lines into the county beyond the Anacostia River hastened the peopling of that area "to the proportion of a

[11] Virginia to Hart Grigsby, Jul 1883, Gibson-Humphreys Mss.

city."[12] Carroll D. Wright, federal Commissioner of Labor, wrote in 1899: "These movements for the improvement of the city have given some wag the opportunity to say that the population of Washington is divided into two classes—real estate agents and those who are not—but the usual facetious remark about real estate agents is offset . . . by the fact that they have been instrumental in a very large degree in carrying on the improvements that make the present city."[13]

In 1882 a newspaper man estimated the personal fortunes of seventeen senators at over $600,000,000. Although rumors later circulated that a good many members of Congress acquired their wealth in shady local real estate deals and manipulation of public utility stocks, the money these men spilled about the city was a boon to business. The salaries paid by railroad magnates and powerful industrialists to lobbyists in the capital further swelled the sums spent on high living. Lengthening rosters of government clerks also increased the demand for commodities, services, and housing. Salaries, though very small, meant a regular monthly income worth fighting for. After as well as before the inauguration of competitive civil service examinations in 1883, every month about twenty newspaper advertisements read typically: "Will give $100 for a place as clerk or messenger in any of the departments: first class references." The 7,800 government employees of 1880 rose in number to 23,000 in 1890—more than Washington's entire population in 1840—and by 1901 the total ran to over 26,000. Moreover, as one promoter bragged, "We have at Washington, in all departments of

[12] Comrs Rpts, 1886, pp. 40-43, 1890, p. 43, 1896, p. 17, 1899, I, 12-14, 1900, I, 28; 25 *United States Statutes at Large*, 451; S Rpt 623, 53C, 2S, Ser 3192; petitions, Senate 51A-J1S, 22 Jul 1890, Record Group 46, National Archives, and House 53A-H6.1, 21 Feb 1895, Record Group 233 (hereafter cited as ptns, S or H); S Doc 234, 54C, 1S, Ser 3354; Washington *Bee*, 7 Jan 1893; *Chronicle*, 14 Sep 1890; *Rpts B/Tr*, 1896-1900; *Star*, 1 Jan 1898, 1 Jan 1900, and 1 Jan 1901. Beginning in 1890 the New Year's day issues of the *Star* carried summaries of developments of the year past; these are hereafter cited as *Star* summaries.

[13] Carroll D. Wright, "The Economic Development of the District of Columbia," *Proceedings of the Washington Academy of Sciences*, I, 180.

the Government, nearly a thousand experts . . . the whole body of them constituting the most important cluster of men of genius and rare attainments in the world."[14]

Federal public works, although less vitally important to the city than those of the 1850's, provided jobs for common laborers and skilled artisans—work digging the foundations, laying the brick, and emplacing the frieze of red and blue tile medallions of the National Museum on the Mall, completing the stone work of the Washington Monument, putting the finishing touches on the State, War, and Navy Building west of the White House, erecting on Pennsylvania Avenue the new granite city Post Office with its heavy Gothic clock tower, and building the Italian Renaissance Library of Congress on Capitol Hill. Redemption of the "Potomac Flats" gave day laborers several years' work when Congress in 1882 at long last appropriated funds for filling the tidal marsh that had stretched since the 1830's from 17th Street below the White House to the Long Bridge. Under the direction of the District engineer commissioner, the laying of water mains and sewers further increased employment during the 1880's. Although a few Washington contractors had earned the title of "eight-hour bosses," strikes aimed at an eight-hour day occurred in 1886, but the local unions, alarmed by the public hysteria over Chicago's Haymarket Riot on May Day, condemned any recourse to violence. When the building trades unions risked a fresh round of strikes four years later, they again failed to win any major concession. As wages were slightly higher here than elsewhere and working conditions no worse, labor organizations thereafter limited their activities to talk.

To Washington, secure in her own prosperity and seemingly walled off from the industrial strife that had shaken much of the country during the 1880's, the consequences of the worldwide depression of the early 1890's came as a shock. Private

[14] Cleveland *Leader*, 21 Dec 1882, 2 Jul 1883, 24 Mar 1884; *Official Register of the United States*, 1881 and 1901; *Bee*, 28 Aug 1886; S Rpt 825, 52C, 1S, Ser 2914.

building enterprise in the city declined before the end of 1893, and, except for brewers and bakers, wages dropped, but full realization of what had been happening in the rest of the country first struck the capital in the spring of 1894, when the "Army of the Unemployed," its initial contingent led by "General" Coxey of Ohio, began to roll in to ask the federal government for help. Washingtonians became increasingly apprehensive as the rag-tag bob-tail throng, arriving by tens and twenties, gradually swelled to several thousand men. There were no jobs for them in the District or nearby Maryland and Virginia, and the prospect of their settling down for an indefinite period in their makeshift camps was as alarming to the local labor unions as to other citizens. Few people, however great their sympathy for the unemployed, expected Congress to enact any measure of relief for men who appeared to be challenging the rights of capital to control labor. Yet the community was not prepared for the action taken in early May to halt a fifteen-minute "riot" on the Capitol grounds; billy clubs wielded by the Capitol guards drove back the men attempting to make their way to the building, mounted police trampled into the crowd, and General Coxey and his two principal lieutenants were arrested for walking on the grass. By June some of the "army" had drifted away, but several hundred men stayed on, hoping for something to turn up. For weeks the generous Frank Hume, Washington's biggest wholesale grocer, supplied them with food, and it was he who finally arranged with the District commissioners to pay for railroad tickets to take them home in mid-August.

American workingmen nevertheless concluded that Washington might well be a useful location for the headquarters of organized labor, such as it was. In 1895 the emasculated Knights of Labor, still headed by its founder, Terence Powderly, moved its central office from Philadelphia to a building "within the very shadow of the Capitol," while the American Federation of Labor, with some 2,000 new members and a newly organized labor bureau, found jobs for about 150 men. And as private building picked up at the end of the century, the building trades, always the mainstay of labor in Washington, regained some confidence.[15]

Congress, if unwilling to interfere with the workings of the American industrial order, displayed meanwhile a welcome interest in improving the capital. Reclamation of the Potomac Flats, a vital sanitary measure, was the most needed public project, but scarcely less important to the city were the founding of the zoo, the opening of Rock Creek Park, and the creation of Potomac Park, after the courts had vested in the United States title to the made land on the water front. Far-sighted citizens perceived that the skillful use of open space might ultimately contribute more to Washington's appearance and hence to her attractions for tourists than could a formless proliferation of individually handsome buildings. Prodded by the petitions of District residents and the occasional urgings of federal officials, Congress had talked since 1867 of acquiring the Rock Creek valley for a park, but not until 1889, when fears rose lest sewage from nearby dwellings irretrievably contaminate the creek, was money forthcoming. The District appropriation act for 1890 included $200,000 for the purchase of land for a National Zoological Park a mile north of the city limits. Eighteen months later additional funds permitted negotiation for a much larger stretch of the upper valley for Rock Creek Park, "a pleasuring ground for the benefit and enjoyment of the people of the United States."

The appropriation for the zoo came first because Samuel Langley, secretary of the Smithsonian Institution, convinced Congress of the need of a proper home for the live animals then kept on the Smithsonian grounds as models for the insti-

[15] Donald L. McMurry, *Coxey's Army, A Study of the Industrial Army Movement of 1894*, pp. 113-26, 256-58; *Star*, 4 Oct 1884, 14 Feb 1885, 24 Jun 1886, 3 Nov 1887, Summaries, 1890-1896; *Chronicle*, 12 Aug 1894; *Sentinel*, 24 Apr 1894, 29 Apr 1899.

tution's taxidermists. Besides "Dunk" and "Gracie," two magnificent elephants, the first denizens of the zoo included herds of deer and peccary, some rather moth-eaten buffalo, several cages of monkeys, and about two hundred other specimens of wild creatures. A former Barnum and Bailey man took charge as head keeper. Inasmuch as the law gave the regents of the Smithsonian direction of the zoo but put the entire cost of maintaining it upon local taxpayers, some angry complaints sounded at Congress for forcing the District to pay for national "monkey parks." Since, ran the argument, the zoo and Rock Creek Park were inaccessible for people without bicycles or horses and carriages, only speculators in the real estate adjoining the creek would benefit; the money might have been better spent on improving the Mall.

In actuality "the extremely economical ideas" of the House Committee on Appropriations dictated leaving the stretch of Rock Creek Park above the "Zoological Gardens" in its natural state; even at the end of the century only a few dirt roads wound through the woodlands. The new parks, however, formed a point of departure upon a course that would eventually restore salient features of L'Enfant's plan of the city. In response to pleas of Washington's Board of Trade and a committee in charge of the city's centennial celebration, in March 1901 Senator James McMillan proposed that the Senate appoint a commission to plan a complete park system linking the Capitol grounds, which had been landscaped by Frederick Law Olmsted in the seventies, the Mall, and Potomac Park with the zoo and Rock Creek Park. From that beginning would spring an elaborate plan for beautifying the city.[16]

The relations of Congress with the local community, while

[16] Comrs Rpts, 1886, p. 44; House Report 3820, 49C, 2S, Ser 2501 (hereafter cited as H Rpt); H Rpt 3866, 50C, 2S, Ser 2673; ptns, H50A-D1, 19 Feb 1889, H51A-D1, n.d.; H Mis Doc 72, 51C, 1S, Ser 2760; S Ex Doc 127, 51C, 1S, Ser 2688; S Rpt 1919, 56C, 2S, Ser 4064; *Star*, 2 Jan 1893; "The Parks and Proposed Parks of Washington City," *American Architect and Building News*, XLVII, 72; *Rpts B/Tr*, 1894, pp. 27-28, 1898, p. 55, 1899, pp. 65-66, 1901, pp. 20, 64-66.

now and again touched by controversy, eventually achieved a surface serenity that contrasted noticeably with the anger and frustration of the 1860's and 1870's. Not all congresses, it is true, gave the District much attention, and even those most inclined to constructive legislation shelved some bills important to Washingtonians. Congressmen frequently begrudged the time spent on District affairs. Whenever questions of property rights arose, one senator grumbled, "the Senate of the United States is converted . . . into a mere town council, and the wrangles that go on here resemble very much the interesting debates that occur in such bodies." Yet congressional impatience tended to yield to pride in the capital or, as some critics implied, to zeal for protecting congressmen's investments in local property. Whatever the reason, in the 1890's men on the Hill devoted a good deal of thought to the District and, in investigating problems such as the organization of charities, the public school system, or the tax structure, the District committees often revealed genuine interest in bettering matters. Despite some short-sighted obstructionism, frequently born of newcomers' objections to forcing their constituents to contribute to District expenses, congressional debates on local bills generally ended in accepting committee recommendations. Until 1893 appropriations went through yearly with at most minor deviations from the principle of equal sharing set forth in the Organic Act, and thereafter the chief exception was in meeting the costs of extending streets into the county. A bill to cancel the half-and-half arrangement in 1896 got very short shrift indeed after figures showed that the value of taxable property in the District came to about $191,418,000, whereas federal property, exclusive of the streets and alleys, was worth over $198,000,000.[17]

[17] Frederick L. Siddons, "Municipal Conditions of Washington," *Proceedings of the Second . . . and Third National Conference for Good City Government*, pp. 362-63; *Congressional Record*, 46C, 2S, p. 3063, 47C, 2S, pp. 890-93, 52C, 1S, pp. 1636-58, 54C, 1S, pp. 1178, 5599 (hereafter cited as *Rec*); H Rpt 1978, 54C, 1S, Ser 3464.

District taxpayers, for their part, understood the importance of the annual federal contribution. Although they resented having to carry the costs of the zoo, an explicitly national park under the direction of a federal agency, they knew that without federal money the park could not have come into being. Their anger rose at congressional refusal to apply the half-and-half principle to the county as well as the city when the time came to extend streets beyond Washington's and Georgetown's original limits; the law of 1878 had pledged the federal government to sharing the expenses of the entire District, not merely the part formerly under municipal jurisdiction. If charging half the cost of laying out suburban streets to abutting private property could be justified, only bad faith, local citizens believed, could account for putting the rest of the cost upon the District without any federal contribution at all. Still worse, after exercise of the right of eminent domain and assessment of half the expense upon abuttors' property, Congress again and again failed to vote the appropriation of District funds necessary to open up a street, thereby leaving adjacent land without the improvements for which its owners had already paid. In the House defenders of the scheme called it the means of saving their constituents and small local taxpayers from having to foot the bills of real estate speculators.

Summary dismissals of grievances periodically sharpened citizens' sense of helplessness. Disagreements among themselves admittedly often hampered congressional response to community appeals, but even when public opinion was virtually unanimous a mere whim on the Hill could block a measure. For example, in the face of city-wide uneasiness about the paucity of charitable institutions for colored children, House and Senate haggled over the terms on which they would accept the gift of a civic-minded Negro who offered his farm as a home for "the poor colored waifs of the city." Congressional inaction on codification of District law became so intolerable that private organizations finally paid a lawyer to draft a code;

Congress then adopted the first part of the two-part draft. Every new Congress presented a fresh hazard, since the men assigned to the District committees could impede badly wanted legislation or recast bills to suit their personal interests. Those assignments once thought undesirable were sought after in the 1890's because of "the chances open to that committee for promising speculation" in property in the politically impotent city.[18]

Rebellion against that impotence alternately waxed and waned during the 1880's. Ambivalence marked the thinking of most well-to-do people. While District representation in Congress looked desirable, could a non-voting delegate in the House be of any use and could the community obtain a voting voice in Congress without accepting a popularly elected local government? Reopening the questions settled by the Organic Act might result merely in scrapping the provision for federal appropriations without altering the District's non-voting status, or, more alarming to some Washingtonians, end federal financing but revive a city regime dominated by Negro and propertyless voters. Fear of prying the lid off a Pandora's box kept influential men silent except when provoked into speech by some flagrant congressional sin of omission or commission. Unlike wealthier citizens, the working classes were only incidentally concerned with perpetuation of the financial provisions of the Organic Act. Inasmuch as white workingmen obviously believed two whites could always outvote one Negro,

[18] *Memorial, . . . Joint Executive Committees of the Citizens' Associations of the District of Columbia Against the Repeal of the Fifty Percent Annual Congressional Appropriation Law*, Jan 1894; 27 *Stat.* 532; *Rec*, 52C, 1S, pp. 4570-82, 5665-74, 52C, 2S, pp. 1157, 2249; Comrs Rpts, 1899, II, i-v, 1900, I, 31, 1901, I, 84; *Rpts B/Tr*, 1897, p. 65, 1901, p. 29; *Star*, 5 Apr 1879, 1 Sep 1881, 5 Mar 1887, 18, 25 Feb, 3, 10 Mar 1888, 2 Jan 1899; *Capital*, 1 Jan 1888; *Sun Chronicle*, 23 Jan, 6 Feb 1881, 5 Mar 1882; *Chronicle*, 14 Sep 1890; ptns, H46A-D1, 8 Mar 1880, S50A-J12, 9 Jan 1888, H52A-D1, 30 Mar 1892; S Mis Doc 161, 53C, 2S, Ser 3171; S Rpt 1150, 55C, 2S, Ser 3625; Siddons, "Municipal Conditions," p. 365; Mary Noble Lee, "City Government of Washington," *Chautauquan*, XXII, 170.

labor groups from time to time repeated their earlier appeals for suffrage.

The local press generally opposed restoration of a popularly elected District government. Until 1888 the *Star* insisted that all the faults of the existing regime lay in the men appointed, not in the system. The *Post* and the *Sentinel*, a paper directed mainly to Washington's German population, at first held votes for municipal officials better than nothing but later veered away from that position. The *People's Advocate*, a short-lived Negro newspaper, declared: "Universal suffrage is wrong in policy of [sic] not in principle when applied to cities," and the *Bee*, a second Negro paper, switched back and forth but generally argued that colored people were better off under the protection of Congress than they would be under city officials elected by Negro riff-raff. Only the *Chronicle* and John Forney's *Sunday Chronicle* consistently took the line that a local electorate including colored men could do no worse for itself than did federal appointees.[19]

In 1888 Theodore Noyes, son of the editor of the *Star*, published a series of articles reviewing the eigthy-eight years of what he termed congressional neglect of Washington. Coming on the heels of a congressional session that had seen no action on important local bills, the analysis struck home with peculiar force. He rejected popularly elected municipal officers as useless. "Without representation," he argued, "suffrage is of no value; and, shut out from the bodies which make its laws and imposes taxes upon it," the District would gain nothing from seating a delegate in the House. The one measure that could give District citizens any power over their own destiny was a constitutional amendment enabling qualified voters to elect representatives to Congress and a corresponding

[19] Siddons, "Municipal Conditions," pp. 370-71; "A Study in City Government," *The Nation*, XXXVIII, 335; ptns, H51A-D1, 5 Dec 1890, H52A-D1, 30 Mar 1892, S55A-J18, 8 Dec 1897; frequent pieces in *Star*, 1879-1888, *Sentinel*, 1886-1894, *Post*, 1879, *Sun Chronicle*, 1881-1882, *Chronicle*, 1884-1895, *People's Advocate*, 1882, and *Bee*, 1883-1898.

number of members to the presidential electoral college. Later that year a Citizens' Committee of One Hundred examined Noyes' proposal. When a Washington notary had assembled letters expressing the ideas of well-known residents and had collected figures comparing the District's population, wealth, and contributions to the nation with those of a half-dozen states, the committee dispatched a memorial to the Hill. "They are unable to see," read the statement, "why they should be excluded from participation in the General Government any more than the people of State capitals should be excluded from participation in State governments." Several of the accompanying letters asked for an elected local government as well as national representation.[20]

Senator Henry W. Blair of New Hampshire presented the plea in the form of a resolution. In May 1890 the Senate committee to whom the matter was referred reported it back adversely. Incensed at the committee for holding no hearings on the measure, Blair spoke of the evil effects of civic irresponsibility upon young men growing up in Washington, where business monopolies exercised control through "combinations and rings and syndicates which derive their strength from unholy or indifferent relations to and with the representatives of national power." Because a constitutional amendment would take time to ratify, Congress must start the process at once in order to free the community from the prevailing "absolute political despotism, all the more alarming because so many are in love with it." Curiously enough, the newspapers did not pick up Blair's allusion to an unholy alliance between Congress and special interests in Washington, and substantiating comment was slow in coming into the open. Blair's speech began and ended the Senate discussion. Republicans ignored the issue.

[20] *Star*, 5 Mar, 15 Jun 1887, 18, 25 Feb, 3, 10 Mar 1888; *Rec*, 49C, 2S, p. 1172; S Mis Doc 126, 50C, 1S, Ser 2517; District of Columbia Citizens' Representative Committee of One Hundred, *Proposal to Improve the Present Form of Government of the District of Columbia*, 14 Feb 1888; S Mis Doc 237, 51C, 1S, Ser 2700; ptns, S51A-J15, 17 May 1890, H51A-D1, 19 Aug 1890.

TABLE I

MANUFACTURING AND ALLIED ENTERPRISES IN THE DISTRICT OF COLUMBIA, 1880-1900[a]

	1880	1890	1900
BUILDING MATERIALS AND CONSTRUCTION ENTERPRISES			
No. of Establishments	251	565	744
Persons Employed	1,718	7,321	7,322
Wages and Salaries	$ 596,042	$ 4,734,360	$ 4,186,013
Capital Investment	755,505	4,602,692	7,425,342
Value of Product	1,904,206	12,543,013	13,928,690
FOODS AND BEVERAGES			
No. of Establishments	82	99	119
Persons Employed	283	858	1,092
Wages and Salaries	$ 124,842	$ 518,995	$ 666,683
Capital Investment	559,040	2,192,020	3,510,117
Value of Product	2,053,843	3,827,437	4,010,971
CLOTHING			
No. of Establishments	37	140	208
Persons Employed	237	967	904
Wages and Salaries	$ 102,850	$ 512,318	$ 475,989
Capital Investment	115,550	601,173	648,813
Value of Product	386,415	1,170,353	1,526,326
PRINTING AND ENGRAVING[b]			
No. of Prvt Plants / Govt "	30	69	137 / 9
Persons Employed in Pvt Plants / " Gvt "	2,654	4,593	1,648 / 5,771
Wages & salaries in Ptv Plants / " Gvt "	$ 2,175,578	$ 3,733,469	$ 1,066,713 / 4,927,875
Capital Investment, Pvt / , Gvt	$ 2,118,800	$ 3,270,306	3,036,297 / 3,916,746
Value of Product, Pvt / , Gvt	$ 3,775,478	$ 6,121,703	2,687,369 / 6,566,663
OTHER[c]			
No. of Establishments	571	1,422	1,507
Persons Employed	2,254	9,665	10,039
Wages and Salaries	$ 935,300	$ 5,123,122	$ 5,123,878
Capital Investment	1,933,631	18,198,898	23,443,930
Value of Product	3,762,374	15,668,931	18,947,603
GRAND TOTALS			
No. of Establishments	971	2,295	2,754
Persons Employed	7,146	23,404	26,776
Wages and Salaries	$ 3,924,612	$14,622,264	$16,477,151
Capital Investment	5,552,526	28,865,089	41,981,245
Value of Product	11,882,316	39,331,437	47,667,622

[a] 10th U.S. Census, 1800, Vol. II, *Manufactures*, Pt. I, pp. 101-02; 11th U.S. Census, 1890, Vol. VI, *Manufactures*, Pt. II, pp. 598-605; 12th U.S. Census, 1900, Vol. VIII, *Manufactures*, Pt. II, pp. 118-21.

[b] Until 1900 the census made no differentiation between private and government printing and engraving.

[c] Mostly handicrafts.

The Democratic national party platform of 1892 included a District home rule plank; flimsy at best, it remained purely decorative until discarded.[21]

Thin hopes for success apparently lessened the petitioners' disappointment. If they were still, in Theodore Noyes' phrase, "political slaves," at least they had not become "bankrupt freemen" by loss of the federal sharing of District expenses. During the 1890's the suffrage question in one form or another cropped up occasionally but without arousing citizens to new efforts. In 1895 Frederick Siddons, a Washington lawyer whom Woodrow Wilson would make a District commissioner eighteen years later, prophesied at a national conference on good city government that growing dissatisfaction among the rank and file of Washingtonians would shortly invigorate the campaign for self-government, inasmuch as the existing system put them at the mercy of men uninformed about the needs of ordinary, socially obscure citizens. Siddons miscalculated. The suffering to be seen in other cities after the panic weakened the community's interest in political reorganization, since poverty and unemployment, bad enough in the District, could easily become worse. Furthermore, toward the end of the decade exceptionally generous appropriations made congressional rule relatively painless, and growing faith in citizens' associations and the new Washington Board of Trade persuaded taxpayers that, voteless though they were, they could make their wants known on the Hill and expect an eventual response.[22]

The citizens' associations were initially neighborhood groups each concerned with its own section of city or county. The East Washington Citizens' Association launched by property-owners on Capitol Hill in 1871 was the first, but others appeared

[21] *Rec*, 51C, 1S, pp. 10119-23; Lee, "City Government of Washington," 169; Robert Wickliffe Woolley, "The Plunderers of Washington," *Pearson's Magazine*, XXII, 623-36; Kirk Porter and Donald Bruce Johnson, *National Party Platforms, 1840-1956*, pp. 94-125.

[22] *Chronicle*, 7 Apr 1895; ptn, H52A-D1, 30 Mar 1892; Siddons, "Municipal Conditions," pp. 370-71; *Star*, 1 Jan 1900; *Sentinel*, 8 Jan 1901; Mary S. Logan, ed., *Thirty Years in Washington*, p. 524.

after 1874, and the number multiplied rapidly in the mid-eighties. Inasmuch as law forbade District borrowing and appropriations for public works were expressly tabbed for particular projects, each area had to compete with its neighbors to get the largest possible sum for itself. Every association ordinarily discussed only its own special needs. But now and again topics such as changes in the school system or methods of assessing property evoked city-wide interest, and the wish of all associations to have a voice in determining how taxes should be spent spurred efforts to set up a central body. In 1886 eight associations in Washington and the Mt. Pleasant association in the county proposed a presidentially appointed citizens' council empowered to prepare the District's annual budget for submission to Congress, but the failure of that petition, the dismissal of Noyes' plan for a constitutional amendment, and the frequently conflicting aims of the separate associations gradually undermined attempts at union.

The associations nevertheless were useful. While they had no purely social function, they bore some resemblance to the farmers' Grange and served the same purpose of clarifying and giving form to members' ideas. In the 1870's Colonel Henry Robert, later a District engineer commissioner, had drafted *Robert's Rules of Order* to help new associations conduct their meetings efficiently. "Difficult questions," remarked a detached observer, "are expounded with a fullness of detail and of technical precision that would never be dared before the usual political audience." The effort of Negroes excluded from White associations to form their own testified to the importance the community attached to these neighborhood pressure groups.[23]

Because it was more homogeneous, better organized, and possessed of wider vision of community needs, the Washington

[23] *Bee*, 14 May, 2 Jul, 12 Nov 1887, 28 Oct 1899; ptns, 51A-H4.2, 18 Apr 1890, H54A-H7.6, 30 Mar 1896; *Post*, 6, 12 Nov 1889; Louis Brownlow, *A Passion for Politics*, p. 63; C. Meriwether, "Washington City Government," *Political Science Quarterly*, XII, 418. From 1883 through 1888 the *Star* carried articles on citizens' associations at least once a month.

Board of Trade, founded in November 1889, immediately proved of greater value to the city as a whole than the avowedly parochial citizens' associations. Many a twentieth-century Washingtonian would come to look upon the Board of Trade as a body ruled by a handful of men for the sole benefit of real estate speculators and the bankers who financed them. Yet if, as the *Sentinel* contended, from its very beginning the board was a front for the street railway executives, bankers, insurance agents, and "sprinkling of real estate brokers, politicians and the like" who really governed the city, for some years they were of service to others than themselves. Although they showed little comprehension of workingmen's problems, in the main ignored the Negro third of the population, and took a complacent attitude toward the public schools, the committee reports from 1890 to 1901 in a dozen realms revealed painstaking investigation of civic wants and produced intelligent recommendations for meeting them.

Beriah Wilkins sent out the two hundred four-line letters of invitation to the meeting that gave birth to the Board of Trade. Having completed a third term in the House of Representatives as a member from Ohio, Wilkins had bought a controlling interest in the Washington *Post* and had chosen to settle permanently in a city he found at once congenial and challenging. He paved the way for the proposed Board of Trade in an editorial explaining that an organization of responsible businessmen could represent public opinion in the District more fully and would carry more weight with Congress and the commissioners than citizens' associations and individual petitions ever could.[24] The men who attended the meeting agreed.

Organization proceeded quickly. The charter members elected thirty-one directors; the next year the number was cut to thirty. The directors chose the president from their own

[24] *Sentinel*, 16 Jul 1892; *Rpts B/Tr*, 1890-1901; H. W. Crew, *Centennial History of the City of Washington*, pp. 460-61; *Post*, 12 Nov 1889. A copy of Wilkins' letter still hangs in the Board of Trade directors' room.

ranks, engaged the paid secretary, selected the treasurer, fixed the annual dues—$5 for an individual, $10 for a partnership or corporation—appointed the standing committees, and recommended or, as things worked out in practice, set policies. The entire board might vote upon the admission of new members and it annually reelected or replaced ten directors, but the bylaws enabled thirty men to run the organization. It soon came to exercise greater power in Washington than any body except Congress and the presidentially appointed District commissioners. Within two years the District committees of Congress and the commissioners were turning to the Board of Trade for advice, and by the end of the century it was an open secret that the commissioners themselves owed their office to the board's directors. Membership in the organization was much more inclusive in the 1890's than later. Neither religion nor color was a bar. Isadore Saks was a director during most of the nineties and Simon Wolf, a leader in Jewish welfare work, served on several committees. Interestingly enough in view of twentieth-century attitudes, James T. Wormley, son of the founder of the famous Wormley House, was a charter member, and three other Negroes were elected in the course of the next few years.[25]

While the board of directors never included all Washington's wealthiest men, the fifty-seven individuals who served before 1902 represented the city's economic dominants. Alongside such powerful persons as Charles Glover, president of the Riggs National Bank, S. W. Woodward, department store owner, and Brainard Warner, the city's foremost real estate broker, were nationally known lawyers, journalists and editors, doctors and engineers. The professional men were generally also directors of banks and other business enterprises, just as several of the bankers and real estate brokers held law degrees. Con-

[25] *Rpts B/Tr*, 1890, 1891, and *By Laws*, 1893, pp. 54-57; *Bee*, 2 Feb 1901; memo, 23 Apr 1900, McKinley Mss (L. C.); Siddons, "Municipal Conditions," pp. 366, 371.

trary to later popular belief, realtors as such were fewer than merchants and bankers, although the distinction between a real estate dealer and any other businessman was shadowy. Indeed a striking feature of the make-up of the Board of Trade directorate was the interlocking interests of its members.

Most of these men had come to Washington after the Civil War and in 1889 were still in their early forties. Several were completely self-made. Brainard Warner, an unknown country boy upon his arrival in Washington, had become head of the city's biggest real estate firm before he was thirty, the founder and first president of the Washington Loan and Trust Company at the age of forty-two in 1889, president of the Board of Trade in the nineties, and in the interim, while organizing a half-dozen other successful business enterprises, had built and moved into a red brick mansion in the millionaire section of Massachusetts Avenue beyond Dupont Circle. The dour-looking, witty Crosby Noyes, born in Maine, had walked into Washington on foot in 1848 and, by his literary skill, his insights, and his Yankee shrewdness, made his way up to a position of singular power not only as editor of the *Evening Star* but as a citizen passionately devoted to Washington's interests as he saw them. The suave Theodore Noyes, a native Washingtonian, inherited that devotion as well as the editorship of the *Star*.

Whether to the manor born or representing the rags to riches saga, the leaders of the Board of Trade all had some social finesse; over forty percent of them were listed in Washington's first *Social Register*. All played some part in guiding local charities and reform institutions. Beriah Wilkins acted for years as treasurer of the citizens' relief committee. The heavily built, round-faced, mustachioed Brainard Warner, outwardly the entrepreneur *par excellence*, repeatedly served on the school board and on the boards of the Industrial Home School and of the Central Free Dispensary and Emergency Hospital; he was president of the National Philharmonic Society, a vice president of the American National Red Cross, and a sponsor of the Washington Choral Society and Georgetown Orchestra. Another Board of Trade president, S. W. Woodward, identified himself closely with the YMCA; prim-looking behind his rimless eye-glasses and carefully pointed Vandyke beard, he held such firm religious convictions that he forbade the sale of playing cards in Woodward and Lothrop's department store, but he gave away thousands of dollars yearly and by his rectitude and gentleness won universal respect. That violent-tempered, blond giant, Charles Glover, threw his influence into getting public parks for the city and into launching the National Cathedral Foundation. Self interest, to be sure, usually went hand in hand with altruism but, according to their lights, the business leaders of this period were dedicated men. And Washingtonians by adoption were as eager as native sons to work for the city's well-being.

As the name "Board of Trade" implies, its first concern was to strengthen the city's economic position. The directors opposed local suffrage, but they saw that efficiently run charities, a sound public health program, and urban aesthetics were important assets to a residential city. Their aims, therefore, extended to reducing pauperism while providing for the helpless, to improving sanitation, and to realizing a plan for the "City Beautiful" which Congress through the Park and Fine Arts Commissions later largely adopted. Thus the board joined with the Associated Charities and the backers of a new Civic Center in organizing a company to build inexpensive model houses for workingmen. It was the board in collaboration with the District Bar Association that engaged Associate Justice Walter Cox of the District Supreme Court to codify District law, the board that campaigned successfully for a public library and led the fight to get the Pennsylvania Railroad tracks and the depot off the Mall. The organization was intrinsically undemocratic. When the membership committee in 1897 acknowledged that a tiny minority made all decisions, the remedies introduced still left an autocracy. Yet in light of the abuses of municipal governments elsewhere in America, Washingtonians who shrank from the mere idea of popularly elected city officials had reason to place faith in the Board of Trade. A political scientist writing for a learned journal indeed argued that this unofficial, self-appointed "city council" provided an ideal form of local government through a "representative aristocracy."[26]

[26] *Rpts B/Tr*, lists of officers and members, 1890-1901, and 1894, p. 50, 1895, pp. 47-48, 1896, p. 47, 1897, pp. 5, 39-40, 1898, pp. 22-24, 1899, pp. 21-22, 1900, pp. 37-43, 108-09; *Chronicle*, 12 Dec 1896; *Post*, 8, 9 Oct 1889; *Washington Social Register*, 1900; *A History of the City of Washington, Its Men and Institutions*, by the Washington *Post*, ed. Allen Slauson, pp. 69-70, 191-259, 341, 401-33 (hereafter cited as *Post History*); *Sentinel*, 18 Nov 1899; Meriwether, "Washington City Government," pp. 407-19.

CHAPTER III

MUNICIPAL HOUSEKEEPING, 1879-1901

THE long congressional debates which preceded the passage of the Organic Act of 1878 had convinced President and senators that they must put competent men, not party hacks, in charge of running a city which for seventy-one years had governed herself. With Congress enacting all local legislation and controlling all local public expenditures, the three commissioners must be men who commanded respect in the community, even though they were responsible to Congress and the President rather than to citizens of the District of Columbia.

Certainly the civilian commissioners between 1879 and 1901 were more conscientious than the politicians who had preceded them. *Bona fide* residents of Washington, they were familiar with the local scene, and the tacit understanding that one of the two appointees was to be a Republican and the other a Democrat minimized political partisanship in local administration. Except for John Ross, a former Georgetown University law professor who served from 1890 till his death in 1902, and the journalist Henry Macfarland, none of the commissioners possessed personal distinction. Lawyers, real estate dealers, and merchants with wide-ranging interests in the community, they represented Washington's top business stratum; all of them were members of the Board of Trade after its organization. Blind as they generally were to the problem of the little fellow, in their official acts they followed the line they thought Congress expected of them. A story published fifteen years after the rumored event told of a Grover Cleveland nominee who failed to win Senate confirmation because he had refused to promise to keep hands off certain powerful interests. But the charges of self-seeking or negligence which citizens occasionally levelled at one or another of the District commissioners rarely stuck. As public servants they ranked high in an era when municipal officials in America were by and large an unsavory lot.

By law, one of the three commissioners was always to be an officer of the Army Engineer Corps. Unlike his two civilian associates, he was usually a newcomer to Washington and consequently was ill-versed in the District's problems. Because his tour of duty was brief, he had little time to learn the job; in twenty years ten different officers held it. Washingtonians disliked what often seemed to be military highhandedness in the engineer's office. Since he had charge of all contracts for public works, he commanded considerable patronage and could exercise an arbitrary authority. Yet ordinarily the engineering work was efficiently executed, and much of it was planned with a vision that enabled two succeeding generations of Washingtonians to dismiss from mind a host of earlier problems.[1]

Past disasters had bred wariness in District residents. Although the Organic Act provided safeguards against irresponsible spending, taxpayers during most of the 1880's watched the commissioners' every move. In 1879 the financial tangle left by the territorial Board of Public Works was still a legacy of trouble. The new commissioners balked at imposing tax liens on property for assessments improperly levied or not paid because the improvements had never been made; adjustments cost the District about $2,000,000. But delinquency on all taxes continued. Citizens objected to the personal property tax and even more strongly to the haphazard methods of assessing real estate and handling appeals. Three-year intervals between appraisals piled up inequities of valuation in the rapidly growing community and fostered the rise of a single tax movement. The

[1] E.g., *Sentinel*, 20 Jul 1883, 27 Nov 1886, 2 Mar 1889, 16 Aug, 22 Nov 1890; *Bee*, 19, 26 Jul 1884; *Star*, 22 Sep 1887, 18 Feb, 28 Sep 1888, 9 Jan 1889; ptn, S50A-J12, 8 Oct 1888; S Rpt 2686, 50C, 2S, Ser 2620; *Chronicle*, 7 Sep 1890, 13, 20 Mar 1897; Henry Himber to S. J. Bowen, 14 Jun 1880, and Zalmon Richards to Bowen, 2 Jul 1881, Bowen Mss; Siddons, "Municipal Condition," *Third Ntl Conference for Good City Govt.*, pp. 365, 369; R. W. Woolley, "The Plunderers of Washington," *Pearson's Magazine*, XXII, 626; Louis Brownlow, *A Passion for Anonymity*, pp. 8-10.

commissioners themselves thought that taxes on improvements encouraged speculation in real estate and believed the personal property tax too easily evaded to be useful. In 1892, after scrutinizing the local tax laws, a congressional committee reported:

"[Since] land values are increasing at an enormous rate—on a conservative estimate to the amount of $40,000,000 annually . . . —the assessment of buildings and the under-assessment of land is operating to discourage greatly the growth and improvement of the capital . . . [On] a fair assessment of land alone it would be easy to obtain by a tax rate less than one-half of the present all the revenue required for the needs of the District."

The findings showed business property assessed frequently at less than 14 percent its true value and land held for speculation at less than 10 percent, while residential property "especially where the small homes are situated, is assessed at from 70 to 80 percent of its true value." Although reputable real estate dealers reluctantly admitted the validity of these data, at the last minute the committee shied away from any radical innovation. In 1894 a new law drafted largely by members of the Board of Trade merely required the assessors to conduct open hearings on complaints, to revise and equalize existing real estate valuations, and to systematize future assessments. The most glaring inequities disappeared thereafter. "Yet, as nearly every resident of the city of Washington is a single taxer," a congressman remarked at the end of the century, a tax on land alone would have better satisfied most of the local public.[2]

The $1,214,000 paid annually into the sinking fund, however, steadily pared down the District's long-term debt. As interest payments shrank and monies for reduction of the principal and for building up the fire and police department

[2] S Mis Doc 39, 46C, 2S, pp. 13, 90-97, Ser 1931; H Mis Doc 11, 46C, 3S, Ser 1981; Comrs Rpts, 1881, pp. 4-6, 1882, pp. 5, 176, 1887, p. 9; *Rec*, 47C, 1S, pp. 1317-24, 5352-54, 47C, 2S, pp. 3682, 3698; *Star*, 11 Dec 1879, 22 May 1880, 4 Aug 1888; *Sentinel*, 18 Dec 1886, 25 May 1889; ptns, H46A-D1, 8 Mar 1880 and dozens of similar petitions to every Congress during the 1880's.

pension funds dropped from 35.26 to 15.26 percent of the over-all budget, taxpayers felt easier. (See Table II.) They were dismayed at several congressional departures from the half-and-half principle, first in 1891 when the appropriation act charged the District with the full $3,000 cost of opening a public bathing beach, and then over the next six years by refusals to share some $357,000 of costs for street extension and minor items. But these exceptions were disturbing chiefly as warnings of restiveness in Congress over the 1878 commitment.[3]

Determined to forestall full repudiation of the financial arrangement, citizens generally swallowed their wrath. Although the murderous shooting of President Garfield in the summer of 1881 had called congressional attention to the need of a larger police force, for years the appropriation precluded engaging more patrolmen. (See Table II.) Two hundred men, only half of them on duty at any one time, were too few; ten years later, 365 were still too few for a city so geographically spread out. In actuality, in relation to population, neither violent crime nor less serious law-breaking was as frequent in the 1880's and 1890's as it had been in the 1850's and the Civil War era, but charges of police corruption, laxity, or brutality filled the newspapers until the replacement of venal officers and appointment of a new chief in 1886 restored some measure of public confidence. Gambling, vagrancy, and drunkenness were still the chief sources of trouble. In Washington, the *Star* suggested, "the general climate, the charitable disposition of the people who have means, the easy hours of work and the uncertain tenure of government employ, all contribute to help men downward." Every winter tramps and migrant seasonal laborers rolled in, and, as the commissioners reported gloomily, a national emergency like the war with Spain "brought many criminals and

[3] H Rpt 1469, 52C, 1S, pp. 1-4, 10, Ser 3046; S Bill 2046, 53C, 2S (mf, L.C.); *Star*, 1 Jan 1895; *Rec*, 56C, 2S, App, p. 181; S Doc 351, 57C, 1S, Ser 4245; *Rpt B/Tr*, 1897, pp. 62-63.

cranks to the city." New anti-gambling and anti-vagrancy laws failed to have much effect. The enlargement of the police force to 585 men and the addition of a bicycle squad at the end of the century helped far more.

As for years past, juvenile delinquency was a greater source of public anxiety than adult crime. Warfare between rival fire house gangs had ended when members of a paid fire department took up living quarters in the engine houses, but juvenile delinquents still roamed the streets. The Reform School for Boys and the school for incorrigible girls which opened in 1893 offered no cure, and the suggestion that lack of playgrounds encouraged mischief-making in a city where law forbade children's using the public reservations for ball grounds brought no response from Congress. As prohibition sentiment gained strength in the community, the newly organized Guardian League attempted to prove statistically the link between the growth of the liquor traffic and juvenile delinquency: between 1882 and 1887 there had been a 15-percent increase in population but a 40-percent rise in the number of licensed saloons and liquor wholesalers, a 90-percent increase in licensed billiard and pool halls, and countless places operating illegally. "Youths in consequence of these diabolical snares . . . abandon school and workshop and become tipplers, gamblers, harlots, vagabonds and paupers." Here juvenile arrests averaged 20 percent of all arrests, whereas in New York City the average was under 11, in Boston under 14, and in Chicago 15.5 percent. The *Star* disputed those findings; well-informed travellers were "ready to pronounce Washington the most orderly city of its size extant."[4]

Nevertheless, people throughout the United States petitioned Congress to institute in the capital reforms they frequently did not enjoy at home—freedom "from the curse of rum,"

[4] *Rec*, 47C, 1S, pp. 3801, 5232, 47C, 2S, pp. 188-89, 1452, 1526; Comrs Rpt, 1881, p. 101, 1887, pp. 14-16, 1890, pp. 66-67, 1898, pp. viii, xi, 1899, I, 12-15; *Star*, 17 Mar 1880; *Sentinel*, 3 Nov 1883, 20, 27 Nov, 4 Dec 1886; *Capitol*, 27 May 1883; S Mis Doc 24, 49C, 2S, Ser 2450.

TABLE II

District of Columbia Expenditures[a]

	1881	%	1891	%	1901	%	1911	%	1915	%	1917	%
TOTAL[b]	$3,737,049		$5,814,237		$9,437,829		$13,402,135		$14,845,469		$14,915,244	
General Administration & Miscellaneous	203,690	5.45	325,770	5.60	503,562	5.33	915,382	6.9	1,481,237	10.0	1,839,689	12.3
Debt Retirement[c] & Special Funds	1,346,915	35.3	1,294,855	22.3	1,459,776	15.5	1,650,091	12.3	1,843,963	12.4	973,205	6.5
Fire Protection	106,262	2.9	147,726	2.5	339,025	3.6	756,051	5.6	731,015	4.9	768,705	5.2
Law Enforcement Courts, Police & Reformatories	405,529	10.9	670,573	11.5	1,004,746	10.6	1,835,592	13.7	1,897,980	12.8	2,107,698	14.1
Health Services General; care of indigent D.C. patients at St. Elizabeths; other public hospitals[d]; subsidies to private hospitals; garbage removal	102,036	2.46	200,283	3.44	581,178	6.18	886,481	6.6	1,208,508	8.1	1,046,869	7.0
Welfare Washington Asylum[e]; poor relief; after 1900, Board of Charities, Board of Children's Guardians, other public charities[f]; subsidies to private charities[f]; playgrounds and bathing beaches	106,281	2.84	143,158	2.46	195,852	2.98	378,137	2.8	460,943	3.2	515,094	3.5

PUBLIC EDUCATION	527,311	14.3	940,495	16.2	1,524,373	16.2	3,193,513	23.8	3,164,464	21.3	3,420,107	22.9
Salaries	330,343		600,919		939,260		1,831,353		2,071,785		2,261,796	
New buildings	117,981		230,205		341,457		815,639		621,255		609,670	
PUBLIC WORKS (exclusive of school buildings)	919,426	24.8	2,090,371	36.0	3,957,596	40.6	3,787,039	28.3	4,047,260	27.3	4,236,580	28.4
Streets	623,513		1,584,865		2,389,849		1,693,305		1,888,000		2,036,315	
Sewers	121,648		221,965		1,411,051		469,039		584,247		567,375	

a Computed from figures in Comrs Rpts, 1881-1917.

b Including cash balances, water fund, police and firemens' funds, and, in 1917, repayment to the U.S. of $518,505 for a deficiency in District accounts pertaining to St. Elizabeths and court fines of the late 1870's.

c Including, in 1915, $586,000 for interest on the 3.65% bonds for the fiscal years 1877 and 1878.

d Freedmen's only till 1901, when $73,639 went for a site for a new municipal hospital. Till 1894 Congress appropriated for Freedmen's hospital in the Sundry Civil bill and the U.S. Treasury bore the entire expense. Expenditures for the Asylum Hospital were lumped with those for the almshouse and workhouse. Before 1902 St. Elizabeths was included in Welfare in the reports but in this table is added to Health. In 1915 $394,000 went for a new Columbia Hospital.

e Including workhouse, almshouse and hospital before 1911, and jails in 1911, 1915, and 1917.

f Approximately three-fifths for child care.

"Sunday Rest," anti-vivisection, juster divorce laws, or the forbidding of kinetoscope reproduction of prize fights. The country-wide concern to have the capital an ideal municipality at once gratified and irritated the local public. The WCTU campaign particularly irked German-born citizens who wished to drink their Sunday beer in peace. The commissioners, after exploring a plan for raising the liquor license fee from $100 to $500, chose instead to enforce Sunday closing, to increase fines for illegal selling, and to reduce the number of licenses granted, especially in the notorious "Division," the former Murder Bay area in the triangle southeast of the Treasury between Pennsylvania Avenue and the old Washington Canal bed.[5]

More important to most residents was the meagerness of the water supply. A Senate investigation showed that since 1863, when the receiving reservoir of the aqueduct opened, daily per capita consumption of water had risen to over 155 gallons, whereas the Chicagoan used only 119 gallons daily, the Bostonian 75, and the Philadelphian 58. Increases in water rental rates and house-to-house inspections to check on dripping faucets improved service but failed to resolve the basic problem: the insufficient head of water at the reservoir above Georgetown, leakages in the distributing system, and the inadequacy of a single three-foot distributing main to meet the needs of the rapidly growing population. Georgetown, being nearer the reservoir, was better off than most of Washington. Gravity feed ensured proper pressure in only part of the downtown capital; the eastern half of the city and sections supplied by pumping stations suffered from a water famine, while many of the suburbs had no piped water at all; St. Elizabeths Hospital pumped its supply from the turgid Eastern Branch.[6]

[5] S Mis Doc 114, 51C, 1S, Ser 2698; ptns, H46A-H7, n.d., H50A-H31.3, H51A-H7, n.d., S54A-J20, n.d., and hundreds more; *Sentinel*, 11 Dec 1886, 18 Oct 1890, 28 Mar 1891, 18 Jun 1892, 9 Jun 1894; *Star*, 12 Feb 1887; Comrs Rpts, 1890, p. 12, 1899, p. 18, 1901, p. 24.

[6] S Rpt 39, 46C, 2S, Ser 1893; *Star*, 10, 11, 17, 25 Jul, 4 Aug 1879, 15 Jan 1880, 1 Aug 1885; *Capitol*, 26 Jan 1879; *Sun Chronicle*, 9 Jan

The most economical answer, Congress finally concluded, was to increase the capacity of the Georgetown reservoir by raising the height of the Great Falls dam and running it to the Virginia shore and then to extend the aqueduct to a second reservoir to be located between the Soldiers' Home and Howard University. The dam was finished in 1886, but cave-ins due to faulty masonry halted work on the new "Lydecker tunnel," named for the Army engineer commissioner in charge of extending the aqueduct; only complete rebuilding at an ultimate cost of over $1,500,000 would make the tunnel usable. As lack of funds caused a thirteen-year delay in starting the job, the new reservoir would not be in use until 1907. In the interim a new main from the Georgetown reservoir relieved the worst of the water shortage on the Hill and somewhat bettered service in the rest of the city and the suburbs. But at the end of the century forty out of eighty-two schoolhouses still had no water closets, and in the big Wallach School east of the Capitol no water flowed through the urinals during the day time.[7]

An equally urgent need was an adequate sewage and drainage system. In 1879 the sewers in Georgetown and northwesternmost Washington emptied into Rock Creek, a thin trickle of a brook in summer; those in east and south Washington fed into the James Creek, which flowed through a crowded slum area into the Eastern Branch near the Arsenal grounds; the pipes from the central part of the city drained into the "B Street main," the old Washington Canal turned into a covered culvert debouching into the tidal marshes beyond the White House. During heavy rainstorms surface water pouring down from the hills into a single storm sewer threatened to flood the heart

---

1881; *Rec*, 47C, 1S, p. 4665, 49C, 1S, pp. 5844, 7519-22; *Sentinel*, 11 Dec 1886, 20 Aug 1887, 16 Nov 1889, 22 Feb 1890.

7 22 *Stat.* 168; 23 *Stat.* 132-33; 25 *Stat.* 573; "The Water Supply Problem in Washington," *Engineering Record*, XXXVII, 313; Capt. D. D. Gaillard, "Water Waste and Use in Washington," *Engineering Record*, XLII, 277-78; Comrs Rpts, 1883, p. 272, 1886, p. 25, 1887, pp. 18-19, 1889, pp. 292-93, 1890, pp. 11, 415-17, 1894, pp. 435-49.

of the city. During a freshet in 1877 the river had risen ten feet at 17th Street beyond the White House, and the next summer, when the Tiber arch broke, the lower part of the city had narrowly escaped "a horrible inundation." But the commissioners' proposed remedy required a $2,500,000 appropriation, and Senate objections to including a District sanitary measure in a general rivers and harbors bill delayed action until 1882. The undertaking then approved involved filling the marshes beyond the Monument grounds, building a tidal basin slightly downstream in order to control the flow of the tide, and dredging a deep channel that would skirt the shore from the Long Bridge to Arsenal Point.

As fill slowly reclaimed the swamps along the Potomac River front, Washingtonians began an ultimately successful campaign to have the new land turned into a permanent park. But hopes that elimination of the Potomac Flats would take care of sewage disposal were disappointed. In 1890 a special board of sanitary engineers reported the swamps at the source of the Anacostia and the tidal backwash into the James Creek canal still affecting the eastern part of the District, the flow of Rock Creek too sluggish to carry off the sewage of northwest Washington and Georgetown, and the pollution of the Potomac near the Monument grounds still a danger to the public. Thanks to correct estimates of Washington's future growth, Rudolph Henning, the foremost American sanitary engineer of the nineteenth century, helped the sanitary board draft a plan of such dimensions that it would serve the city adequately for the next sixty years; by extensions in the 1920's it would enable nearby Maryland communities also to feed sewage into the District's trunk lines; not until the late 1950's would sanitary experts find fault with a system that used the same mains for sewage and for the drainage of surface water.

The engineers of 1890 recommended construction of huge trunk sewers into which intercepting lines covering every thickly settled section of the District should flow; a pumping station at the foot of New Jersey Avenue would then force the sewage from the trunk lines into conduits laid under the Eastern Branch and extended three miles downstream to empty into deep water where the tides would not wash pollution back into Washington. Congress accepted the plan but refused to sanction a bond issue to pay for the work. A depleted federal Treasury during the mid-nineties shut off the other possible source of funds until the revival of the country's business in 1898 enabled the commissioners and the Board of Trade to prevail upon Congress to make yearly appropriations to meet the costs. By 1901, although sewage disposal was still "the most vital question" facing the city, an expenditure of over $2,000,000 saw the new system nearly half-finished.[8]

More than new sewer mains were needed to safeguard public health. In 1881 fewer than a third of the 30,474 houses in Washington and Georgetown had sewer connections. Hotels and boardinghouses rarely had more than one water closet to a floor. Many families pumped all their water from cisterns or carried it pailful by pailful from the wells in the public squares; where sanitation was primitive, seepage from the contaminated soil into wells spread typhoid and diarrheal diseases. Every year, to be sure, added to the number of dwellings equipped with plumbing, but in 1890 some 30,000 people, most of them Negroes, lived in squalid alley tenements which congressional views on the sanctity of private property prevented the District health officer from demolishing. Here tuberculosis flourished, annually the cause of one out of every four deaths. A forward step taken in 1892 was the enactment of a law prohibiting building of additional dwellings in alleys less than twenty

[8] S Mis Docs 13, 17, 19, and 25, 45C, 3S, Ser 1833; H Ex Doc 445, 51C, 1S, Ser 2752; ptns, H54A-H7.6, 14 Jan and 24 Feb 1897; Comrs Rpts, 1879, pp. 7-11, 1885, p. 184, 1887, pp. 20-21, 1889, p. 300, 1890, p. 535, 1900, I, 27, 1901, I, 30; *Star*, 16, 29 Jan, 4 Aug 1879, 1 Jan 1895; *Rec*, 47C, 1S, pp. 986, 2738-49, 3801, 5792, 5828-33; *Rpts B/Tr*, 1898, pp. 94-99, 1900, pp. 114-16; Staff Rpt, Joint Committee on Washington Metropolitan Problems, 86C, 2S, Dec 1958, *Water Supply and Sewage Disposal*, p. 13.

feet wide and not equipped with sewage and water mains and lights. Meanwhile periodic inspections of the public markets failed to stop the sale of spoiled foodstuffs. No dairy sold unadulterated milk.

The appearance of cholera in the United States in 1893 brought things to a head. A Sanitary League divided the city into districts and set up committees in each to report upon its sanitary condition. The health officer was then able to carry out his long-cherished plan of conducting a house-to-house sanitary inspection, and public opinion forced landlords and householders to renovate run-down property, replace defective drains, clean out yards and area-ways, and burn tons of rubbish and offal. The result was 350 fewer deaths than in the previous year. Infant mortality still accounted for one death in three, but by 1898 the over-all death rate in the city had declined to 19.32 per thousand; in the county a rate of 35.82 was partly due to the high incidence of malaria at St. Elizabeths Hospital. In the meantime a stricter building code prevented speculators from putting up more ramshackle houses without installing plumbing, and a law of 1897 decreed that all premises must be connected with sewers. Although the law was not wholly enforceable, the owners of 1,500 buildings promptly put in sewer connections.

At the same time the District health department closed a number of surface wells, placed dairies under surveillance, and with some success experimented with anti-toxin for diphtheria cases. When threatened smallpox epidemics emphasized the city's need of a contagious hospital, Congress voted to erect a suitable building on the site of the old jail and for the time being forced three existing hospitals to open isolation wards. Every new proposal, every innovating regulation, met with some opposition, and, as the health officer complained, small budgets constantly hampered the execution of useful laws. Nevertheless, the community became increasingly aware of the importance of his function, and, as interest in the "city beautiful" movement grew at the turn of the century, decent housing and clean well-kept streets began to command wider public support.[9]

Street paving, that never-ending chore in an expanding community, meanwhile continued to breed feuds. Rival citizens' associations resentfully saw the bulk of the funds spent in fashionable "Northwest" and in the suburbs beyond, where quick profits for speculators depended upon the early extension of paved streets and other urban conveniences. Taxpayers on Capitol Hill and in the Navy Yard section fumed over the sums poured into improvements along "Massachusetts Avenue extended" and Connecticut Avenue above Boundary Street until Northwest and its suburbs had twice as many miles of hard-surfaced streets as all the rest of the District. But when so powerful a politician as Senator John Sherman of Ohio insisted, for example, on giving priority to widening and grading 16th Street north of the city limits where he and some of his protégés owned land, property-owners elsewhere could only grumble futilely. That measure, followed by the extension of Massachusetts Avenue from Dupont Circle to Rock Creek, marked the first official recognition that Washington was outgrowing her old bounds. During 1888 the commissioners strove to evolve a rational scheme of naming a second and third tier of streets beyond the old "alphabet" streets, but not until 1905 was the present-day system adopted—two-syllable names of eminent Americans arranged in alphabetical order, followed by three-syllable names for the streets of "the third alphabet." In 1890 Boundary Street became Florida Avenue, in 1895 the name *Georgetown* officially disappeared by congressional mandate,

[9] Comrs Rpts, 1878, p. 48, 1880, pp. 294-303, 1881, pp. 365-66, 391-409, 1889, pp. 104, 394, 1890, p. 659, 1895, p. 13, 1897, p. 75, 1898, pp. xix-xx, 1899, I, 19-22; *Rec*, 46C, 2S, pp. 518, 2344-46, 2931; ptn, S51A-D1, n.d.; *Sentinel*, 20 Feb 1892; *Star*, 15 Mar 1882, 18 Dec 1888, and summaries, 1894-1896; H Mis Doc 188, 53C, 2S, Ser 3229; S Doc 385, 56C, 1S, Ser 3875; 25 *Stat.* 451; *Rpts B/Tr*, 1899, pp. 8, 11, 1900, pp. 10, 80, 1901, pp. 22-23; George M. Kober, *The History and Development of the Housing Movement in the City of Washington, D.C.*, pp. 6-9 (hereafter cited as Kober, *Housing Movement*); Lillian W. Betts, "The Every-day Washington," *The Outlook*, LXV, 868-73.

and in 1900 plans for bridging Rock Creek at both Massachusetts and Connecticut Avenues looked to the moment when Washington's streets would thread the entire area from the heights of the Potomac beyond Georgetown University to the upper reaches of the Anacostia.[10]

While the special interests of influential real estate owners undoubtedly affected the choice of areas to get first attention, the spread of the city into the county did not proceed in purely hit-or-miss fashion. On the contrary, a plan of orderly metropolitan expansion begun in 1888 acquired more precise form upon passage of a highway act in 1893 and the creation of the Park Commission in 1901. Those measures constitute the first conscious attempt to guide the suburban growth of an American community along lines that would ensure harmony between new developments and the parent city.

The act of 1888 merely required the platting of subdivisions of land in the county to conform to Washington's street plan; what represented acceptable conformity was uncertain. The highway act of 1893 carried planning very much further and provided the machinery to execute it. Instructed to engage a landscape architect to prepare a tentative layout of new streets and a system of parkways to ring Washington from Rock Creek to the Anacostia, the District commissioners were then to submit to a highway commission detailed maps of each suburban section; when the highway commission, consisting of the Secretary of War, the Secretary of the Interior, and the Chief of Engineers, had approved, the maps would represent the authorized plan of city enlargement. These "initiatory steps," taken before the opening of the Columbian World's Fair, indicate early stirrings of the "city beautiful" movement in America which the White City on Chicago's lake front brought to

[10] S Mis Doc 37, 45C, 3S, Ser 1833; *Star*, 8, 25, 28 Jan, 4 Feb 1879, 13 Aug 1883, 22, 23 Oct, 19 Nov 1886, 8 Oct 1887; *Sentinel*, 4 Jul 1885, 5 Mar 1887; *Sun Chronicle*, 1 Oct 1882; Comrs Rpts, 1882, pp. 135-36, 1885, p. 169, map p. 184, 1886, pp. 28-32, 1887, p. 21, 1889, pp. 260-62, 1900, II, 81; *Rec*, 47C, 1S, pp. 4619-32, 4663, 47C, 2S, p. 3159.

life. Frederick Olmstead, Jr., drafted the first layout of Washington's northwestern suburbs and, although the District commissioners had to modify it to meet the objections of property-owners in long established areas, by 1900 maps of the future "greater Washington," complete with reservations for parks and open spaces at avenue intersections, had been officially adopted. This headstart would enormously ease the problem of the advisory commission established in 1901.

A height of buildings act passed in 1899 further testified to a new readiness to put the orderly development of a beautiful city ahead of private property interests, an act inspired by public dismay at the conspicuousness of the recently built "Cairo," a fourteen-story yellow brick apartment house above Scott Circle. Unlike the short-lived decree of Thomas Jefferson and the federal commissioners in the 1790's forbidding the building of dwellings of less than three stories lest the new capital look mean in consequence, law a century later put an upper limit upon private buildings in order to prevent the rise of skyscrapers that would dwarf public edifices and darken the streets.[11]

Most of the streets were better kept than those in other American cities. "Carp," as Frank Carpenter signed his columns in the Cleveland *Leader*, observed in 1883: "Washington's streets . . . are kept clean by a patent twig brush run by horses. This sweeps them daily, and the thousands of fine carriages and hundreds of bicycles, which go spinning along them, are kept shining like black enamel and polished silver." Although the 65,000 carefully tended trees bordering the streets and avenues were little more than saplings, citizens took pride in them. When in 1882, ten years after the city first witnessed a demonstration of electric lighting, the commissioners contracted for the installation of a few arc lamps, public safety dictated a ruling that all wires must be laid underground, but

[11] 25 *Stat.* 451; 27 *Stat.* 532; 30 *Stat.* 922; Comrs Rpts, 1894, pp. 15-16, 1900, I, 31.

a by-product of the decision was the preservation of the trees. During an experimental display on Pennsylvania Avenue in the fall of 1881 a dynamo belted to an engine in an old sawmill nearby had fed power to lamps suspended from guy wires strung from housetop to housetop; at the click of a switch the sudden splutter of light from the Capitol to the Treasury had delighted the onlookers, but the danger of fire had been undeniable. While the cost of underground wires prevented the rapid replacement of gas lamps, before 1890 Washington boasted 181 arc lights and added seventy-five to a hundred yearly thereafter.

The battle for underground wires soon involved other utilities. Overhead telegraph lines had strung along Washington's streets since 1845, and that "selfish octupus," the Western Union, a particularly powerful corporation in a city where newspaper correspondents kept wires busy, continued to plant its "uncouth poles at will in front of any man's premises without his consent." After 1878 the new Chesapeake and Potomac Telephone Company also erected poles and wires, and in the 1890's, when street railway companies began to replace horse-drawn cars with trolleys, the traction interests entered the fight. The struggle intensified when Congress denied the commissioners authority to grant permits for new underground installations. Yet little by little public opinion won the day. By 1900 not only did Washington enjoy telegraph and expanding telephone service, electric street lighting, and electric street railways, but within the city limits more than half the wires ran underground. The principal exceptions were the lines running into private houses from poles placed in alleyways at the rear.[12]

[12] Cleveland *Leader*, 5 Jan 1883; *Patriot*, 22 May 1872; *Star*, 20 Oct 1881, 22 Jan 1883, and summaries, 1896, 1898; *Post*, 1 Mar 1887; Comrs Rpts, 1882, pp. 10, 140-41, 1885, p. 172, 1889, pp. 260-62, 296; Nevil Monroe Hopkins, "The United States Electric Lighting Company of Washington, D.C., and its New Equipment," *The Electrical Engineer*, XXVI, 425-33.

In scores of American cities of the 1880's and 1890's, utility and transit companies, their franchises secured to them by local political bosses, were exploiting the public mercilessly. In the capital, where Congress granted the franchises, the issue was not outright graft but the companies' disregard of local wishes. Indignant citizens believed the commissioners unduly subservient to these corporations. "Do the commissioners," inquired a newspaperman, "govern the District, or do the street railway companies govern the commissioners?" The sins of the "traction moguls" were everywhere evident: T-tracks projecting above the level of the pavements made the streets hazardous for horses and carriages; the space adjoining the rails was not kept clean, a particular affliction as long as the cars were horse-drawn; the cars were stuffy and cold in winter, dirty and overcrowded the year round; service was slow; tax evasion was frequent, and the fifteen separate companies operating in the city and suburbs produced confusion rather than wholesome competition. The commissioners themselves protested at these abuses. When the campaign against overhead trolley wires within the city limits met with sudden success in 1895 the commissioners were able to exact other reforms. Ground rails flush with the pavements supplanted the projecting T-rails, and express cars running at speeds up to ten miles an hour improved service.

Consolidation of competing lines provided the financing essential for these changes. When the Rock Creek Company bought out the Washington and Georgetown in 1895 to form the Capital Traction Company, $12,000,000 went into new equipment and a power house on 14th Street below the Avenue. In 1900 thirteen other independent lines merged to become the Washington Traction and Electric Company. The merger, effected with congressional blessing, several million dollars of new capital, and reportedly generous watering of stock, included the United States Electric Light and the Potomac Elec tric Companies. A congressman from Jersey City took charge.

No one at the time found it improper for a member of the House of Representatives to direct a huge public utility business in Washington while he served his term in Congress. The local public derived immediate advantages. Use of transfers whereever allowed cut costs for passengers, better heated and ventilated cars added to comfort, and more frequent runs reduced waits.[13]

The city's struggle with the Baltimore and Ohio and Pennsylvania Railroads followed a different and far less satisfactory course. Again public safety and urban aesthetics were the main points of argument, but the question of what to do and how to do it was complicated by sharp differences of opinion in Congress and by the awe in which public officials held the great railroad corporations. The safety campaign centered around the elimination of grade crossings within the city where the B & O tracks and those of the Pennsylvania's subsidiary, the Baltimore and Potomac, crossed the public ways at street level. Statistics assembled by the Board of Trade proved that fatal accidents or serious injuries to pedestrians at these crossings averaged about thirty a year. The most feasible of the proposed remedies called for sinking the rails into cuts below street level along part of the right of way and, along the remainder, elevating the tracks on embankments under which cross streets would tunnel. To obviate the hazards on the Long Bridge new construction would be necessary, for trains puffing over the narrow causeway and the railroad bridge set up vibrations in the shaky spans of the adjoining highway bridge, frightened horses, caused runaways, and made it generally unsafe for pedestrians and horse-drawn vehicles. Citizens declared, moreover, that

[13] Comrs Rpts, 1879, p. 7, 1886, p. 35, 1894, p. 40, 1898, p. xxii; *Star*, 28 Oct 1879, 16 Aug 1881, 3 May 1883, 13 Jan 1887, 1 Jan 1896; *Chronicle*, 10 Mar 1895, 10 Jul 1897; ptns, S49A-H14, 1886, H54A-H7.3 and S54-J21, 1894, and hundreds more; *Post History*, pp. 244-46; Nevil M. Hopkins, "The Displacement of the Cable by the Underground Trolley in Washington," *Electrical Engineer*, XXIV, 526-27; "The Open Conduit Electric System of the Capital Traction Company," *The Electrical World*, XXXII, 707-15.

the Baltimore and Potomac illegally used the streets in south Washington for freight yards and car sidings, while the B & O similarly exploited northeast Washington; as a result large areas of the city no longer had residential value. Finally, inasmuch as Boss Shepherd, while removing the Washington and Alexandria Railroad tracks at the foot of Capitol Hill, had not touched the B & P rails crossing the Mall to the Gothic stone station on the present site of the National Gallery of Art, the Pennsylvania Railroad dominated the public domain in the very heart of the national capital.

Seemingly more powerful than Congress itself, the railroad corporations expressed willingness to abolish grade crossings and build freight terminals provided the public pay most of the cost, but they fought every proposal to move the Baltimore and Potomac depot from its commanding position on the Mall or to erect a union station for all railroads entering Washington. For twenty years angry citizens watched the District commissioners yield to cavalier railroad officials and permit the collapse of every scheme for relocating tracks and terminals. The engineering problems were formidable at best. No plan found universal favor. Permanent residents opposed further railroad intrusions upon public property, but businessmen hesitated to support any scheme that would mean long wagon hauls from freight terminals on Washington's outskirts. Throughout the city taxpayers objected to shouldering the costs of safety measures that they believed the railroads could well afford to finance. Year after year Congress, in turn, reached no consensus. Bills were offered, debated, and shelved. Railroad officials stated that a bill of 1893 requiring the B & O to eliminate grade crossings would force the road into receivership. Congress dropped the idea. The B & O went into receivership anyway. Then, seven years later the Senate District Committee and all but two members of the House District Committee endorsed two astonishing proposals.

The first and the more obnoxious to Washingtonians offered to the Pennsylvania Railroad as inducement to change its grade crossings a gift of fourteen acres on the Mall and, for freight yards and sidings, twelve acres of Garfield Park southeast of the Capitol; the United States government and the District together would pay over some $1,644,500 to cover damages to private property and the cost of approaches to the right of way where streets would pass over or under the tracks; and appropriation of $568,000 for a highway bridge over the Potomac would leave the railroad in sole possession of the Long Bridge and causeway. The Pennsylvania was to build a huge new $1,500,000 station on the Mall, and public funds would create an imposing plaza opening out into B Street on the north. The train sheds would project southward into the Mall, and the tracks elevated on an embankment would slice diagonally across the park toward the Long Bridge. A new thoroughfare, "West Capitol Street," would pass under the embankment by means of a fifty-foot archway. Symbolically and bodily members of Congress would bow their heads to the railroad as they went to and from the Hill. Senator McMillan, whose name would later be associated with large plans for beautifying the capital, defended the scheme: "Indeed so far as sightliness is concerned, the proposed changes will add greatly to the beauty of that portion of the Mall."

The concessions tendered the B & O were less generous. Its freight yards and roundhouses were to be moved beyond the city limits, the Metropolitan branch and Washington-Baltimore branch lines were to be combined and rerouted within the city proper, and the company was to receive a free gift of the square north of the present Senate office building on which to erect a new passenger depot; tracks elevated on an embankment across lower land to the northeast would enter the new station at ground level. Thus one railroad would share the Hill with the Capitol; the second would occupy the central stretch of the park between Capitol and White House.

Congressmen William Cowherd of Missouri and Thetus Sims of Tennessee of the House District Committee had from the first labelled the entire scheme shortsighted and preposterously generous to the railroads. The Chief of Army Engineers and the federal Commissioner of Public Buildings and Grounds decried the folly of abandoning the very core of L'Enfant's original plan. One senator declared the two bills yoked together by "an interdependent mutuality of greed." Every citizens' association, the Washington Businessmen's Association, and the Single Tax Club voiced outrage, while the Board of Trade emphatically restated its ten-year opposition to any alienation of the city's public parks. Possibly the commissioners' unfortunate statement that the plan was the best the District could hope for encouraged illusions in Congress. Congressional leaders pronounced the bills satisfactory to "ninety-nine out of one hundred" Washingtonians, a misinterpretation of local sentiment which, Representative Cowherd remarked, showed the handicaps under which unrepresented citizens labored in trying to make their wishes understood. In February 1901 Senate and House passed both bills and President McKinley signed them.[14]

While the commissioners' deference to the railroad corporations offended citizens, they objected even more strongly to threats of interference with the school board. Admittedly the commissioners must appoint the board, but the vocal public felt that the trustees, once appointed, must have full authority over the school system. For, despite frequent squabbles about the disposition of funds and about appointments, particularly to teaching posts in the colored schools, the board generally functioned in keeping with citizens' wishes. The one insuperable problem was obtaining enough money to enable the schools to keep pace with the expanding population and with the de-

[14] S Rpt 1398, 56C, 1S, Ser 3895; *Rpt B/Tr*, 1898, p. 17; *Post History*, pp. 248-49; Comrs Rpt, 1885, pp. 9-10; H Rpts 2026 and 2036, 56C, 2S, Ser 4212; *Rec*, 56C, 2S, pp. 1801, 2104-06, 2180, and App. pp. 181-82.

mands created by temporary, non-taxpaying residents. Yearly, to taxpayers' wrath, the commissioners pared the figure the trustees estimated necessary, and yearly Congress, though appropriating more than the commissioners asked for, voted less than the trustees requested. Consequently a passionate outcry greeted the commissioners' announcement in December 1885 that they were taking over the duties of the school board because quarrels had destroyed its usefulness. At a mass meeting citizens asserted that the change would strip them of "the last that was left to them of popular government." Congress, besought to intercede, debated a school reorganization bill only to drop it. But the commissioners, obviously startled by the storm they had stirred up, quietly backtracked; the school board carried on, its membership later enlarged to include one white and one colored woman.[15]

Fortunately in 1885 the appointment of William Bramwell Powell as superintendent of the white schools suddenly pumped vitality into the system. The new superintendent inaugurated a whole series of innovations similar to the changes in educational approach later attributed chiefly to John Dewey. Brother of the famous head of the Geological Survey, Powell added to the curriculum courses in science and nature study, started manual training in the elementary grades, and dispensed with the rigid formality that had formerly ruled the classroom. Convinced that memorizing lessons was not good enough, he introduced field trips and demonstrations that, by relating book-learning to everyday life, awakened pupils' intellectual curiosity. In carrying out his program he fired ill-trained and uncooperative teachers, many of whom owed their jobs to members of Congress who considered the District's public schools part of their political

[15] *Star*, 13 Feb 1879, 10 Jan 1881, 12 Sep 1883, 23 Jan, 27 Mar 1886, 27 Dec 1887; *Rec*, 48C, 1S, p. 4225, 49C, 2S, pp. 121-30, 2516, 2546; *Sentinel*, 26 Jun, 11 Dec 1886; ptns, H50A-D1, n.d., and 2 Feb 1888; 27 *Stat.* 536; *Report of the Board of Trustees of Public Schools of the District of Columbia*, 1880, pp. 14-16, 151-52, 1886, pp. 6-7, 1892, pp. 36-81; Comrs Rpt, 1882, p. 7.

patronage. He thus won enmity on the Hill and, accused of sacrificing the three R's to frills, was dismissed in 1900. But despite the controversies he stirred up, in the intervening years he made Washington's school system one of the two or three best in the country.[16]

Yet much of the school story repeated earlier history—too little space, underpaid teachers, and always the school board quandary of choosing between expanding the primary schools and providing better for older, advanced pupils. In 1879 an arrangement with the trustees of the Myrtilla Miner Fund, a fund raised by private donors for Negro education, enabled the superintendent of the colored schools to open a colored high school, but until 1882 the nearest approach to a white high school was a scheme Powell's predecessor devised in 1881; he selected the best students in the eighth grades, put them into the third-floor rooms of one building and called the group a high school. The next year the white trustees insisted upon using the principal of the school fund that had been accumulating since 1826 to build a white high school. Unusually large appropriations for new schoolhouses lessened overcrowding in the lower grades during the late eighties, but scarcely was a new building opened than a new generation of school children overflowed it. Washington, observed the Board of Trade, was the only city in the country which allowed non-residents to attend her schools free of charge. By 1899, with enrollments 50 percent higher than in the mid-eighties, 68 white and 14 colored first grades held morning sessions only; second grades used the rooms in the afternoon. Night schools for children who worked during the day, a few summer "vacation schools," and kindergartens, first opened in 1898, put further pressure upon

[16] S Mis Doc 72, 49C, 1S, Ser 2343; William H. Darrah, *Powell of the Colorado*, pp. 325-26, 388; John W. Cook, "Memorial to William Bramwell Powell," National Education Association of the United States, *Addresses and Proceedings*, 43rd meeting, pp. 361-65 (hereafter cited as *NEA Addresses*); *Star*, 27 Jun 1900; Charles Zueblin, *American Municipal Progress*, 134-38.

limited budgets. And parental clamor mounted yearly for a high school course that would qualify graduates for college entrance. Yet the city yearly spent a million and a quarter dollars on public education.

Complaints from white and colored parents and teachers, principals, trustees, Superintendent Powell's political enemies, and sometimes complaints directed at the complainants, led the Senate to investigate. The outcome was an administrative reorganization spelled out in the appropriation act passed in 1900. It increased the school budget by a quarter-million dollars, left to the commissioners control of expenditures and the power to appoint a new seven-member Board of Education, and gave the board, instead of the superintendent, final say in hiring and firing teachers. A single superintendent was to have overall direction with two assistant superintendents under him, one for the white schools and a second for the colored schools. With Powell out of the picture, the Board of Education revised the curriculum "to make it more practical and to reduce the amount of home study." As the larger appropriation provided money for new schoolhouses, public agitation about the school system largely evaporated.[17]

Free public education ended in the two normal schools, although Washingtonians continued to hope for a national university. Howard University received a small federal appropriation annually, but Georgetown, Columbian, and the National Universities drew their support from private sources. A fifth institution came into being in 1889. One hundred years after John Carroll founded Georgetown Seminary, the Roman Catholic hierarchy celebrated its centennial in America with the opening of a theology school as a first unit of the new Catholic

[17] Comrs Rpts, 1887, pp. 5, 14, 1890, pp. 842-43, 1891, p. 8, 1895, p. 8, 1899, pp. 9-10, 1900, I, 9; *Sentinel*, 12 Mar 1892; S Rpt 825, 52C, 1S, Ser 2914; S Rpt 174, 54C, 1S, Ser 3362; S Doc 107, 54C, 1S, Ser 3350; *Rpts B/Tr*, 1898, p. 80, 1899, p. 89; S Rpt 711, 56C, 1S, Ser 3889; 31 *Stat.* 564.

University of America; schools of philosophy and science followed in the 1890's. Shortly afterward Methodists also took steps to establish a university. In 1891 Bishop John Hurst and a number of influential Washingtonians formed a board of trustees, raised $100,000, and purchased a beautiful stretch of wooded land above Georgetown. The energetic Bishop at once made overtures for a merger with the National University, hoping that the name *National*, reinforced by Methodism, might induce Congress to support an institution such as George Washington had willed his shares of Potomac Canal Company stock to found. The proposed merger fell through, Congress appropriated no money, and the Methodist trustees, choosing the name American University, erected Hurst Hall on the new campus in 1898. Building and campus stood unused for nineteen years. Meanwhile, the law school, the small medical school, and even smaller dental school that made up the National University set a pattern that later became standard in Washington: night classes enabling young men to get professional training while they earned a living in daytime government jobs. As none of the local universities had much scholarly prestige, Washington was richer in quantity than quality of higher education; but within the community the vision of the city as the future seat of American learning gained strength.

Interest in education, civic pride, and religious feeling apparently combined to inspire Charles Glover to propose to fellow Episcopalians that they establish a national cathedral foundation in Washington "for the promotion of religion and education and charity." Glover organized the campaign for funds and in 1893 obtained a charter from Congress, while Henry Satterlee, Bishop of Washington, selected Mt. St. Albans for the site on which the Cathedral of St. Peter and St. Paul should rise. There within the close the Phoebe Hearst School, later the National Cathedral School for Girls, opened in 1894. Four years later the Foundation completed the purchase of the entire hilltop with its commanding view of river and city.[18]

While the Cathedral Foundation, the universities, and other organizations lying outside the realm of the commissioners' and congressional responsibility contributed to Washington's distinction, Americans came to regard her local government as the best in the United States. Far from labelling the autocratic municipal administration a contradiction of republican principles, visitors and people who knew the city only from hearsay and from the pages of popular magazines joined with the chorus of prominent Washingtonians in praising the arrangement. In 1900 the *Atlantic Monthly* published a panegyric on Washington—on the honesty, efficiency, and economy of her administration, the courtesy of her police, her low taxes, model schools, splendid care of public health, and admirable protection of the indigent and sick; Alexander Shepherd, in redeeming the city's streets, "unconsciously rendered an even greater service to his beloved city and gave to his people an object lesson in the benefits to follow from a pure autocracy." At Washington's centennial celebration the address of Commissioner Henry Macfarland reflected that widely held view of the system: "Its greatest virtue is that it is distinctly a government by public opinion. The unusually high intelligence of the citizens of the District, and their remarkable interest and activity in the conduct of its affairs, make them its real rulers, under the constitutional authority of the President and Congress."[19]

[18] *Star*, 2 Jun 1879, 24 May 1888; *Post*, 13 Nov 1889; Federal Writers Project, *Washington, City and Capital*, pp. 466-67 (hereafter cited as *WPA Guide*); S Mis Doc 222, 52C, 1S, pp. 25-26, Ser 2907.

[19] A. Maurice Low, "Washington, City of Leisure," *Atlantic Monthly*, LXXXVI, 769; Henry B. F. Macfarland, *The Development of the District of Columbia*, p. 13.

CHAPTER IV

ONLY FOR THE WORTHY, 1879-1901

THE wave of humanitarianism that swept the western world in the second half of the nineteenth century reached Washington in the late 1870's. It was largely a secular movement. A dozen charities, it is true, sprang up under denominational aegis—Episcopal, Lutheran, Congregational, and Baptist; Washington's seven hundred Jewish families unobtrusively and efficiently cared for their own; and, as in the past, the Roman Catholic Church maintained an impressive array of eleemosynary institutions ranging from St. Ann's Infant Asylum to a home for the aged and the Providence Hospital. Yet the impelling spirit was not primarily religious; the sense of civic obligation seemingly transcended feelings of Christian and "guild" fellowship. Regardless of his church affiliation, the Washingtonian of recognized standing in the community expected as a matter of course to dedicate time, energy, and money to some charity, and usually to more than one. As enlightened self-interest heightened his sense of public duty, so duty forbade indiscriminate giving: only the "worthy poor" should receive help. Acceptance of that concept, rare in the ante-bellum city,[1] was linked in the last quarter of the century to a rising belief in the teachings of "social Darwinism," a conviction that selection of the fit must operate in the community.

Of the significant features of Washington's philanthropy the most immediately noticeable was the expansion of charitable institutions and relief agencies and the amount of money that was poured into them. During the 1880's prosperity enabled people in the upper brackets of society to give large sums of

[1] E.g., *Proceedings of the Sixth Annual Meeting of the Female Union Benevolent Society of Washington City and the Report of the Managers, 1844.*

money without great sacrifice, but in the hard times of the nineties contributions to charity shrank surprisingly little and far exceeded those recorded in the 1870's. For example, whereas a citizens' committee in the severe winter of 1878-1879 managed to raise $3,000 to supply fuel, food, and clothing to the poor, a similar committee in 1893-1894, another depression year, collected nearly $50,000. It is improbable that the later generation was intrinsically more generous; the difference in results doubtless sprang from the greater social pressures and better organized campaigning of the nineties. The contrast in effectiveness is nonetheless startling. A growing population explains some of the proliferation of charities, but, while population rose from about 175,000 to 277,000 souls between 1879 and 1901, the number of institutions doubled, and tax money spent for their support and for direct relief increased almost five-fold. Before 1879, Congress had resorted every winter to emergency appropriations for direct or "outdoor" relief, that is, for persons not in institutions; thereafter the District's annual budget included from $13,000 to $20,000 for outdoor relief. Public officials, like private citizens, accepted gradually broadening responsibilities toward the city's needy.[2]

Children were, above all, the beneficiaries. Just as the Washington City Orphan Asylum had been the first organized charity in the city, so orphanages and "child saving" institutions enlisted wider interest and stronger financial support than any other form of philanthropy; by 1899 they were receiving eight times as much money as in 1879. In the late nineties Washingtonians were maintaining eight non-sectarian homes for children in addition to three Roman Catholic orphanages and St. Rose's Industrial School for Girls. When the refusal of most of these institutions to accept any colored child over six created

[2] *Star*, 30 Jan 1879; Comrs Rpt, 1895, pp. 139-40, 153; S Doc 185, 55C, 1S, Joint Select Committee to Investigate the Charities and Reformatory Institutions in the District of Columbia, "Part I—Hearings," p. 157, Ser 3565 (hereafter cited as Ch Hrgs).

an acute problem, two more came into being—the Hart Farm School for destitute and delinquent Negro boys, and a temporary home for colored children sponsored by the Board of Children's Guardians.

The Board of Children's Guardians, itself, was an outgrowth of the mounting concern for child welfare. The board's predecessors, the Guardian Society of the early 1860's and a children's branch of the Washington Humane Society in the 1880's, had lacked both the authority and the resources to institutionalize neglected and abused children. In 1892 Congress accordingly created the Board of Children's Guardians, empowering it to place out or itself to support any child whom the courts committed to its care. Under the selfless and public-spirited leadership of William Redin Woodward, a Washington attorney, real estate broker, and title insurance company executive, the board staunchly advocated placing children in private homes instead of institutions, for, as Woodward pointed out, life in a private family would give a child its best chance to develop "a stalwart individual character." Woodward, a man of exceptionally keen mind and deep humanity, carefully studied the findings of the National Conference on Charities and Corrections in order to give Washington the benefit of the experience of other communities. He was able to report in 1901 that, of the 720 children permanently under the guardianship of the board, 534 were living in private homes where they were "bound out," boarding, or on probation. For white children the scheme was a pronounced success.[3]

Medical charities won only slightly less generous support. Private funds equipped and staffed a dozen new dispensaries, while most of the District budget for poor relief went into medicines, fees for the physicians to the poor, and free clinics. Hos-

[3] Comrs Rpts, 1879, pp. 55-56, 1892, pp. 194-97, 1895, pp. 139-40, 1900, I, 104, 290, 1901, 485, 500-01; S Rpt 700, 55C, 2S, Joint Select Committee on Charities and Reformatory Institutions, "Part II—Report," pp. 200-02, Ser 3565 (hereafter cited as Ch Rpt); Ch Hrgs, pp. 101, 146, 451, 455, Ser 3565.

pitals, no longer considered purely eleemosynary, had many more charity than paying patients, but the six institutions of 1880—the Washington Asylum, the Government Hospital for the Insane, Providence, Freedmen's, the Children's Hospital, and the Columbia Lying-in Asylum—grew to fifteen in the 1890's. Doubts arose about the wisdom of maintaining so many, but just as the Garfield Hospital chartered in 1882 as a memorial to the martyred President "made a stronger and more successful appeal to the charitable people of Washington than any other like institution has ever made," so citizens in advocating efficiency still believed medical charity should be "the last to be denied or . . . deferred." When a well-informed public official stated in 1897 that no other city in the United States could match Washington in provision for the sick and injured, he referred not only to the number of facilities but to the quality of service. At the Asylum Hospital, that catch-all for the helpless, conditions were appalling, the service "little above that of the primitive county poorhouse of an earlier day." But most of the public hospitals offered effective care, and two eminent physicians from the Johns Hopkins Hospital in Baltimore and Philadelphia's Pennsylvania Hospital pronounced the nursing and medical care at Freedmen's Hospital excellent, despite primitive sanitary facilities and a general aspect of "suffering and squalor."

For indigents stricken with contagious disease, alcoholics, drug addicts, the "mildly insane" and the chronically or incurably ill, on the other hand, provision was totally inadequate. Hospitals were unwilling to risk exposing patients to contagion and, until congressional threats in 1899 to cut off appropriations persuaded the staffs at Freedmen's, Garfield, and Providence to accept government subsidies and build isolation wards, all contagious cases had to be treated at home or in the smallpox hospital at the Asylum. A Home for Incurables founded in 1889 took a few patients, and a private hospital occasionally accepted one or two, but all medical institutions preferred to concentrate upon curable cases of a routine nature. Until 1900 and the opening of a small privately financed home, the indigent blind could go only to the almshouse. The aged or chronically ill, the "inebriate," the drug addict, and the mentally disturbed usually ended up at the Asylum Hospital, where the physician in charge had to make a place for them in the general wards. "It may be imagined," reported the Asylum commissioner, "the crowding, the bad air, and the consequent slow and poor progress towards recovery in many cases; when, besides, we take into consideration that all classes of patients, surgical cases before and after operation, chronic ulcers, syphilitic, acute and chronic diseases of all kinds, have to be treated in the same wards and in close proximity, it is a matter of surprise that the death rate is as low as it is."[4]

Help for women in distress, particularly those innocent of blame, was a third rapidly expanding charity. Although it rarely extended to colored women, it slowly reached out to include "fallen" white women despite public doubts about the wisdom of lowering the wages of sin. Before 1885 the Roman Catholic House of the Good Shepherd and the Episcopalian House of Mercy were accepting not only girls in need of "preservation" but also unmarried mothers, and in 1888 the Women's Christian Temperance Union set itself to join in salvaging girls "ruined" before they were nineteen years old. The WCTU Hope and Help Mission assisted them to become self-supporting while keeping their children with them, but the number of applicants soon outran capacity. In 1897 the mission came under the auspices of the National Board of Florence Crittenden Missions. Largely through the efforts of

[4] Comrs Rpts, 1880, p. 178, 1881, p. 146, 1882, pp. 267-68, 1890, p. 188, 1892, pp. 180, 662, 1894, pp. 102-07, 1896, pp. 113, 137, 160, 183-93, 227, 391, 1897, p. 266, 1899, I, 104, 297, 303-04, III, 20, 1901, I, 414, 500-01, 560-69; *Rpt B/Tr*, 1899, p. 40; Ch Hrgs, pp. 113-14, 208-13, 376, 380, and Ch Rpt, p. 56, Ser 3565; S Rpt 781, 55C, 2S, Joint Select Committee on Charities and Reformatory Institutions, "Part III—Historical Sketches," pp. 56, 57, 59-61, Ser 3565 (hereafter cited as Ch Hist).

various Protestant churches, homes for aged women also began to multiply, a badly needed service in a community which in the 1870's had only the almshouse, the Catholic Home for the Aged run by the Little Sisters of the Poor, and the Louise Home for a small carefully selected group of impoverished gentlewomen. Several organizations, furthermore, followed the example of the Women's Christian Association, which had opened a home in the 1870's and offered systematic assistance to transient women stranded in Washington without friends or work. Private subscriptions supplied the bulk of the funds for these women's institutions.[5]

While the tremendous growth of charities was the most dramatic feature of Washington's philanthropy, a second and equally significant characteristic was its lopsidedness. Besides the gaps in the program of medical charities, the community slighted services for needy men and for all Negroes. No agency, public or private, stood ready to assist the able-bodied unemployed male except during severe winters, and as soon as the weather moderated that help ceased. In an endeavor to save the city money by reducing the number of tramps who moved into the District in late fall and slept in the police station houses, in 1892 the commissioners opened a Municipal Lodging House and Wood Yard, where "professional vagabonds" could earn three days' keep by splitting fire wood for the schoolhouses. The establishment soon deteriorated into a variation of the workhouse. The aged male got scarcely more consideration than the unemployed. Although the Asylum housed some old men, and the Catholic Home for the Aged took a few, the aged male, like the unemployed, was expected to fend for himself. Public funds for all homes for the aged were virtually non-existent. Finally, the generous help given white women and children was conspicuously meagre for colored.

[5] Comrs Rpt, 1895, p. 102, 1897, pp. 467-68, 1898, pp. 277-79, 1899, I, 291-92, 1900, I, 474; Ch Hrgs, pp. 143, 290-96, 301-06, 387-91, 394, 398, 404; and Ch Hist, pp. 144-48, 150, Ser 3565.

The clinics and hospitals admitted Negroes to segregated wards and gave as good care to colored patients as to white, but usually only St. Ann's Infant Asylum and the National Colored Home accepted Negro children. The St. John's Parish Orphanage very occasionally took a Negro child, and in the early nineties the Newsboys' and Children's Aid Society accepted some colored boys but reversed its policy in 1898 when Congress refused to make a grant for a separate building for the colored. Catholics and Protestants shared the view of the Directress of St. Rose's Industrial School: "It would not be supposed we could mix them [Negro girls] with our young girls who are mostly orphans from good families." The difficulties of placing colored children in private homes led the Board of Children's Guardians in 1897 regretfully to request the courts to commit to it as few colored charges as possible, since it would have to crowd most of them into its temporary home. The restricted resources of the Home for Destitute Colored Women and Children, largely tax-supported, obliged the managers to limit the admission of children to those between the ages of three and ten. As "no householder will take into his family a colored child except as a servant and with the intention of getting a full equivalent for what he gives," Negro ten-year-olds, when turned out of the Home, usually wound up at the workhouse and the almshouse. "Because the world affords them no other place," said the commissioner of the Asylum, "at the end of their terms they constantly importune me to allow them to remain." A Home for Friendless Colored Girls founded in 1886 practically collapsed for want of support. Launched by a Negro woman when she discovered two little colored girls eating out of a garbage can, this was Washington's first Negro-sponsored charity. Yet the "band of worthy colored women" failed in their attempts to elicit funds from well-to-do Negroes, and the prominent white women whom Mrs. Grover Cleveland interested in the Home raised only $150 for it in two years of soliciting.

The story of help for colored women was much the same. A few found a refuge in the National Colored Home, and nearly fifty, thanks to the Little Sisters of the Poor, became inmates of the Catholic Home for the Aged. Otherwise before 1900 there was nothing but the Asylum and the Reform School for Girls, an institution more nearly penal than charitable. In 1900, greatly daring, the Hope and Help Mission, in collaboration with its "colored mission" in Alexandria, undertook to extend services to unmarried colored mothers. Triumphantly the director reported that "it has been proved that these colored girls can be cared for more easily and at less expense than the average white girl. As a rule, they are better trained for work, and more capable of earning their own living in a shorter time."

The Negro, as William Redin Woodward told a congressional committee in 1897, was "a race not yet recovered from the effects of slavery, practically without resources for the private support of necessary institutions for the protection of its own dependents, and for whose benefit wealthy citizens of the District of Columbia neither left large bequests nor contributed any considerable sums."[6] In most nineteenth-century cities, large gifts from wealthy individuals were a mainstay of charity. W. W. Corcoran, for forty years Washington's single most generous donor to good works, endowed the Corcoran Gallery and the Louise Home, gave large sums to Columbian University and the local orphanages, and on one occasion contributed $1,000 to St. Luke's Negro Episcopal Church, but upon his death in 1888 he left no bequest to any colored institution. Nor did other charitable Washingtonians. As whites tended to regard Negroes as an inferior breed of human being generally given over to indolence, the race

[6] S Mis Doc 93, 50C, 2S, Ser 2615; Comrs Rpts, 1882, p. 260, 1894, p. 101, 1896, pp. 347, 355, 1900, I, 290, 1901, I, 332; Ch Hrgs, pp. 100-01, 155, 197, 310-17, 396-97, 402, 554; Ch Rpt, p. 42, Ser 3565; Amos G. Warner, "The New Municipal Lodging House in Washington," *Charities Review*, II, 279-82.

suffered from the prevailing philosophy that stressed charity only for the "worthy." The question remains why that philosophy first took strong hold here in the eighties.

That it had little currency in the ante-bellum District was probably due to a widespread assumption that public obligation ended with caring for orphans and providing emergency relief for needy adults in winter. Before the war the derelicts produced by the industrial system and the commercial competitiveness of the North were a rarity in Washington, in spite of the yearly inflow of "transient paupers" seeking government aid. Indeed, these transients had ordinarily escaped the label "undeserving." Slaves were a responsibility of their masters, and free Negroes concealed their needs as best they could, lest the workings of the black code expel them from the District. Hence, because most of the visibly needy appeared to be worthy, charity for the rest did not loom large. The workhouse could take care of them. When the flood of contrabands swept in during the war, the Army and northern abolitionists bore much of the burden, and in the late 1860's Mayor Bowen's make-work scheme, which seemed to his political enemies to pander to deadbeats, sidetracked indignant taxpayers' attention from the basic problem of how far public duty should reach. Reexamination of that question was further delayed by the confusions of the territorial regime and then by the panic and depression. While migrant workers, attracted by the District's comparatively mild climate, continued to pour into the city every winter, the plight of the non-resident was a side-issue, primarily a problem for Congress.

It was apparently the enormous prosperity of the 1880's in the upper ranks of Washington society that brought into the open a philosophy of justification. Rooted perhaps in subconscious feelings of guilt and fed by the writings of Herbert Spencer, adapter of Darwinian theories to social evolution, the belief took hold among the city's intellectuals that discrimination in giving was essential to human progress, certainly to community progress. The spread of that point of view and the resulting determination to establish standards of worthiness was the third characteristic of the city's philanthropy.

The idea once well sprouted flowered quickly and lasted longer in Washington than in cities where industrial strife ploughed deep and unsettled men's earlier premises. Conscientious Washingtonians carried into the twentieth century the conviction that poverty sprang from the flaws in the character of the individual rather than from weaknesses in the social structure. As the moral regeneration of the poor must be the first aim of charity, public-spirited citizens, instead of giving in to sentimental sympathy for suffering, must bend every effort to teach the poor to develop habits of frugality, industry, temperance, cleanliness, and chastity. In 1882, a year after Washington followed the example of London and some sixteen American cities in organizing an Associated Charities, a set of formal "Suggestions to Friendly Visitors" included the following instructions to volunteers:

> 1. Give no money . . . because your chief object is to lift the idle, ignorant and dependent, out of pauperism, to make them self-supporting and self-respecting and to prevent their children becoming beggars.
>
> ....
>
> 2. Inform the idle and squalid of the sanitary laws of the District and show them that misery and suffering are the inevitable results of idleness, filth and vice. Make kindly suggestions concerning ventilation, clothing, digestion and household cleanliness.
>
> 3. Take a gift of a plant or picture or some other tasteful suggestive object of beauty, to each wretched home.
>
> 4. Write out a wholesome economical bill of fare, and show how a little saving and constant thrift will provide against illness and misfortune.

5. Ascertain what each member of a family can do . . . and see that every one over 12 years of age is engaged in some useful occupation looking toward permanent self-support.[7]

Whatever the reception accorded to the free advice and the gift of a "suggestive object of beauty," the volunteers assembled information about Washington's deserving poor which enabled the Associated Charities to establish a useful file of case histories. Otherwise the organization accomplished disappointingly little. It had envisaged itself as a clearing house which would eliminate duplication of services, halt indiscriminate charity, and introduce efficient methods to relieve distress. Before 1896 its volunteer part-time staff undertook to solicit funds and disburse them itself and, in so doing, added one more agency to the several already engaged in direct relief. Aware of the confusion over who was to do what and troubled by the lack of specific information about community needs, a group of citizens in the mid-nineties organized a Civic Center patterned upon Chicago's Civic Federation. The Center conducted a valuable fact-finding survey of alley dwellings but contributed little else to solutions of welfare problems. In these years of trial and error, competition between the Associated Charities and other organizations ran strong over who was to distribute the money raised yearly by an official citizens' relief committee. The committee, after years of using the police as its sole disbursing agents, in 1894 released part of its funds to the Associated Charities and in 1897 determined to drop the police and use the Associated Charities exclusively.[8]

Efficient and economical administration of philanthropy was a constant goal. Since the Associated Charities was unable to bring order out of the confusion, in 1890 Congress, acting upon the pleas of the District commissioners, created the office of Superintendent of Charities to supervise the work of all publicly

[7] *Star*, 8 Jun 1881, 12 Apr 1882.

[8] *Ibid.*, 12 Jan 1884; Comrs Rpts, 1892, p. 204, 1894, p. 107; Ch Hrgs, pp. 19-23; Ch Hist, p. 174, Ser 3565.

aided agencies in the city. By law a presidential appointee, the Superintendent was to be brought in from outside, obviously to ensure an unprejudiced view of the local picture. Amos G. Warner, former head of Baltimore's Charity Organization Society, was the first incumbent and the first professional social worker to hold office in Washington. His high national standing, heightened in 1894 by his textbook on social work, gave his words weight. His primary objective was to reverse the trend of the 1880's whereby private agencies obtained public money and used it as they saw fit. In 1892 medical charities drew 58 percent of their income from the public treasury, the Industrial Home School and reformatories nearly 90 percent, children's charities 65.5 percent, and temporary homes over 70 percent.

Warner, his two successors, and leading local citizens believed blanket subsidies to private institutions should cease and a central board should set the standards for admitting applicants to all institutions and allot any public money on a basis of a fixed sum per inmate. The system supposedly would limit institutional care to the deserving and, by applying similar rules to outdoor relief, end the waste of money and effort spent on impostors, paupers who drifted into the District from states which ought to support them, and people whose moral shortcomings left them beyond hope of redemption. At a time when well-to-do Virginians facetiously but with some truth called the District "Virginia's poorhouse," the argument for introducing rigid rules denying help to non-residents had considerable force.[9] (See Table II.)

Every penny saved by intelligent management naturally meant more money for desirable objectives, but it was not shortage of funds that inspired the campaigns for efficiency and economy. Year after year the citizens' relief committee

[9] Comrs Rpts, 1887, pp. 384, 393-94, 1892, p. 169, 1897, pp. 258, 279-82; Ch Hrgs, pp. 13, 21, 332, 459, Ser 3565; *Rpt B/Tr*, 1897, p. 27; Frank Bruno, *Trends in Social Work, 1874-1956*, p. 101.

limited the amount allotted to any one family to about two dollars and came out every spring with an unexpended surplus of funds, in some years as large as the total spent. More lavish spending, the committee felt, would simply encourage pauperism. The committee secretary, a man trained in the new profession of social work, asserted in 1897 that a large permanent relief fund would be dangerous once the poor, particularly indigent Negroes, got wind of its existence. "You go to the house and see absolute destitution. The money is there for relief purposes and has to be granted. By having such a fund you take all the backbone out of these people." When asked whether they would not starve if not given help, he replied they would then go to work.

Herbert Lewis, who became Superintendent of Charities in 1897, took a slightly different position. He opposed the subsidy system because it fostered sentimentality and permitted private agencies to devote themselves exclusively to "the hopeful, promising and pleasant, leaving without sufficient consideration the idiotic, defective and crippled for whose care it is increasingly difficult to procure sufficient funds." He put his finger on the crucial weakness of Washington's charities: the almost complete exclusion of colored children from institutions that provided excellent care for white children. While he was unable to alter that, he managed to substitute the so-called District supply system, namely payment in goods, for the old arrangement of turning over lump sums of public money to private charities. In 1900 after a long investigation, Congress dropped a half dozen sectarian institutions from the list of the publicly subsidized and created a Board of Charities to establish uniform rules for organizations receiving public money. By 1901, with centralized financial control thus ensured and with trained social workers in charge of the Associated Charities' ten branch offices, a new era of professionalism in welfare work was dawning in Washington.[10]

[10] *Star*, 19 Apr 1884; Comrs Rpts, 1896, p. 115, 1897, pp. 267, 277,

Throughout the 1880's and 1890's the theories of professionals and laymen coincided closely. But laymen found theory hard to put consistently into practice. Reginald Fendall, R. Ross Perry, and Simon Wolf of the citizens' relief committee reported defensively in 1884: "That some have been relieved who were not worthy of relief, in one sense, is probable. Abstractly considered, a man or woman who will not work ought to starve or freeze, but it will not do to enforce this abstract proposition. That such ought to be forced to work is evident, but until the law empowers us to enforce this work we must not let them starve or freeze. . . . The man who can comfortably eat a hearty dinner when he knows that another man is starving near him, and yet does nothing to relieve him, is at heart a murderer. Such men do not make good citizens, nor are they safe guides to follow. . . . But even should these chronic cases be left to their fate, what shall be done with their wives and children?. . . . We must help them. There is no other way out of it. By so doing we doubtless increase poverty, but by refusing to do so we hurt ourselves, our community, our nation." The quandary would be painfully familiar to Washingtonians of the 1960's.

Like the committee, rejecting the abstraction, the sanitary officer of the police force felt obliged to provide for non-residents who arrived in Washington sick, "without a penny in their pockets. . . . It would be inhuman to turn them away." In defiance of the tentative congressional stand that these people were no responsibility of the District, he hospitalized sick and helpless strangers along with local cases, all told 3,890 persons in 1896 alone. Private citizens responded similarly when confronted with human misery. Charles Glover, who repeatedly served on the citizens' relief committee and presumably subscribed to its doctrines, gave unhesitatingly

---

287, 1899, I, 285, 300, 513, 1900, I, 85; Ch Hrgs, pp. 1-2, 13, 21, 24-25, 332, 459; Ch Rpt, pp. 172-74, Ser 3565; *Rpts B/Tr*, 1897, p. 27, 1901, p. 46.

what the colored press described as "large sums" to his butler to distribute to the poor daily during a blizzard in 1899.[11]

The launching of the Sanitary Improvement Company in 1897 is the clearest evidence that intelligent citizens were beginning to understand that the moral weaknesses of the poor might not be solely responsible for the wretchedness and disease and crime that infested parts of Washington. Hard-headed business men sponsored the new scheme. Their primary purpose was to lower the city's disgracefully high death rate by providing the occupants of the noisome alleys with decent low-cost housing. The project was at once an investment in faith and a business proposition: stockholders were to receive 5 percent on their investment. By the autumn of 1898 the company had erected eight small double houses of four rooms each, equipped with a bath, gas, hot and cold water, a range, and a cellar, all renting from $9 to $12.50 a month. A month's rent was remitted to every tenant who kept his premises in good repair for a year. Three years later the company reported it had 162 dwellings occupied by workingmen's families, a large part of them Negro; tenants appeared to observe company rules, repairs were kept to a minimum, and company assets had risen to nearly $200,000. As a practical venture in instilling habits of cleanliness, thrift, and industry the enterprise could be labelled a success. The results, however, were less astonishing than they at first seemed, inasmuch as the original plan of transplanting alley-dwellers into the new houses had quickly given way to renting to "the better class of wage-earners," in the belief that "in work of this character it is always best to begin at the top."

"Character-building" organizations, as a later generation would call the YMCA and the Women's Christian Association,

[11] Comrs Rpt, 1884, p. 76; Ch Hrgs, pp. 231, 238, Ser 3565; *Bee*, 4 Mar 1899. For Wolf's philosophy see *Third Annual Report of the Charity Organization Society of the District of Columbia*, 1886, pp. 21-23.

were never regarded as full-fledged charities, although the WCA, in undertaking to help women adjust to life in a strange city, was sometimes accused of acting as a relief agency. During the 1880's both associations lost much of their one-time religious character. The YMCA gradually relegated Bible classes and prayer meetings to a secondary place and built up its membership by emphasizing sociability and the opportunity to use the gymnasium in the new building on New York Avenue. When the Young Women's Association appeared in 1884, the managers followed the same general course insofar as the lack of a gymnasium permitted.[12]

The charity organization movement, originated in London and Berlin, spread rapidly in the latter part of the nineteenth century. Orderly philanthropy might in fact be called a by-product of swift urbanization. While the capital was caught up by the challenge more slowly than bigger American cities, in the 1880's and after, humanitarianism ran strong in Washington. Despite the limitations earnest citizens imposed upon it, the vigor with which white people on the upper social levels threw themselves into reducing pauperism and want in the community was a distinctive feature of Washington's life of the day.

[12] *Rpts B/Tr*, 1897, pp. 28-29, 1898, pp. 42-43, 1899, p. 48, 1901, p. 44; Kober, *Housing Movement*, p. 31; *Post*, 11, 15 Nov 1889.

CHAPTER V

EVERYDAY LIFE IN THE WHITE COMMUNITY, 1879-1901

THE capital from the end of the 1870's to the turn of the century was more nearly a city of leisure than any other in America. "Compared with New York or Chicago," wrote an English visitor, "Washington, although it is full of commotion and energy, is a city of rest and peace. The inhabitants do not rush onward as though they were late for the train or the post, or as though the dinner hour being past they were anxious to appease an irritable wife." Another Englishman spoke of her air "of comfort, of leisure, of space to spare, of stateliness you hardly expected in America. It looks a sort of place where nobody has to work for his living, or, at any rate, not hard."[1]

By mid-twentieth-century standards, people did not work under high pressure. In reassuring her brother about her new job in the dead letter branch of the Post Office Department, Virginia Grigsby wrote in 1883: "We are fixed with every convenience, long desks, easy revolving chairs, footstools, plenty of servants and no specific amount of work to be done . . . There are all ladies in this room, and therefore they do as they choose, most of them bring dressing sacques and put them on to work in. Some even take off their corsets. You know Mama *never* wears any at home, perhaps she may be able to do all this in the Land Office." The "servants," that is government messengers, seldom hurried. Only common laborers, artisans, clerks in shops, and domestics worked long hours. Office workers breakfasted at eight or nine, at noon had a cup of coffee, a "dairy lunch" or a sandwich, and at four o'clock, when government offices closed, went home to hearty dinners or dined

[1] The Very Reverend S. Reynolds Hole, *A Little Tour of America*, pp. 309-10; G. W. Steevens, *The Land of the Dollar*, p. 92.

at a restaurant. "The lunch rooms of Washington are a characteristic of the city," wrote "Carp" in the early 1880's. "I know of no place in the world that has their like. They are found in every block and usually keep excellent coffee and delicious rolls." A dairy lunch room opposite the Treasury much frequented by government clerks served coffee in "pint shaving mugs"; customers helped themselves to sugar from two "holy water basins chained to the wall" and then relaxed in the wicker chairs about the room while they ate the sandwiches they had brought with them.

Save in the closing days of a congressional session, the pace of life was equally leisurely at the Capitol, "a little city in itself," peopled by "the busiest, wittiest and brainiest men" in the United States. In the House of the 1880's members talked and laughed, frequently with their feet propped on desks above the ever-present cuspidors, in an atmosphere as easy as that of a hotel barroom. Along the ground floor corridor leading from the House to the Senate, the chief street of the miniature city, stood small shops selling photographs, candy, and newspapers, a telegraph office ticking out messages, and at one end invariably a crowd of lobbyists, politicians, strangers, deadbeats, and bogus pension lawyers. The favor seeker knew that undue haste was self-defeating; his best opportunity might well come during an evening of billiards at one of the hotels, where congressmen played or watched "as though they were Monte Carlo gamblers." Early in the nineties the shops and stands were cleared out of the Capitol, and the House subjected itself to greater decorum, but representatives and senators, who always made a point of behaving with punctilio, took their time over their business and pleasures.

Some congressmen still lived in boardinghouses, but more of them, unable to afford to bring their families with them, patronized hotels and ate at restaurants, although "thirty-five or fifty cents is the least for which one can get a passable breakfast or dinner." The choice of places to dine was wide; some of the most famous were still popular in mid-twentieth century—the formal dining room opening off the Willard Hotel's Peacock Alley, the Ebbitt House, Harvey's Fish House, and Hall's near the river front, where a magnificent bar surmounted by a huge painting of a nude Venus added a special attraction. "Carp" informed his Cleveland readers "it would take the best part of a Congressman's salary [$5,000] to pay his board and whiskey bills, if he did not take a high room [above the second story] and leave his family at home. One New York congressman paid $600 a week for his rooms at one of the hotels." The pinch of hard times in the 1890's cut down that kind of extravagance.[2]

As "private board" at a minimum of $5 a week seemed high to most government employees, boardinghouses remained a Washington institution. At the end of the century, generals' and statesmen's widows ran many of the most select. Though these did not necessarily serve the best food, the seating arrangements followed rules of precedence as carefully as would the White House at a state dinner. Young men and women on their way up in the world occupied lowlier places than the eminent "has-been," and the lady in charge of the establishment exercised scrupulous judgment about who outranked whom in between top and bottom. Table mates, if frequently boring or slightly pompous, at least exposed the newcomer in Washington to a conic-sectioned view of the city's inhabitants ranging from salesmen to people "in office," as government clerks described their status.

The public market, patronized by society matrons as regularly as by boardinghouse keepers and economical housewives, was another Washington institution. On market day elegant ladies descended from carriages driven by stove-pipe-hatted

[2] Virginia Grigsby to Hart Grigsby, Jul 1883, Gibson-Humphreys Mss (SHC); Cleveland *Leader*, 22 Dec 1882, 5 Jan, 3 Apr, 29 Jun, 23, 30 Nov 1883; A. Maurice Low, "Washington, City of Leisure," *Atlantic Monthly*, LXXXVI, 759-71.

"darky" coachmen and, trailed by a retainer carrying a basket, made the rounds of the stalls at the Centre Market to select the fresh fruits and vegetables, the eggs and chickens, or the woodcock, wild duck, and other special delicacies of the season. There rich and poor rubbed elbows while chatting with the vendors and remarking on the weather to acquaintances. The true Washingtonian regarded marketing in person as much part of well-ordered living as making calls or serving hot chocolate to morning visitors.

For the government clerk with a family to raise, life was likely to be less eventful than for the temporary resident. "We rarely go to the theatre or to concerts," regretfully remarked a federal employee with a wife and three children to support on his $1,600 salary. With a monthly rental $30, the wood and coal bill $8, the gas bill $1.50, milk $2.30, groceries $15, perishables bought at the market $25, and the servant's wages $8 a month, he had little left over for entertaining guests or for expensive amusements. Thousands of families were in a worse position, since $1,600 was a handsome salary even in 1900 and placed a man well up in the ranks of government service. The man who earned $2,000 expected and was expected to give occasional formal dinner parties complete with soup, fish, game, roast, savory, and appropriate wines with each course. Although government pay rates remained at the levels set in the 1870's, any hardship caused by rising living costs was mitigated by the fact that everyone knew exactly what his neighbor earned and therefore what the proprieties demanded of him.[3]

As suburbs cut off city-dwellers from the fields and streams that had once made hunting, fishing, and picknicking universal pastimes, other diversions appeared. Bicycling on Washing-

[3] Louis Brownlow, *A Passion for Politics*, pp. 336-40; Mary S. Logan, ed., *Thirty Years in Washington*, p. 525; Moore, *Picturesque Washington*, p. 259; *Star*, 4 Dec 1884; *Official Register of the United States*, 1886; Carrie Angell Collier, Day Book, in possession of the author.

ton's smooth asphalt pavements had an early and long-lasting vogue. Bella Lockwood, the first woman lawyer to be admitted to practice before the Supreme Court and the only woman ever to be a party nominee for President, created a mild sensation when, with an unconcerned showing of her bright red stockings, she pedalled down Pennsylvania Avenue at ten miles an hour. More conservative ladies arrayed in elaborate cycling costumes soon took up the sport. When smaller wheels replaced the high front-wheeled models, a male dare-devil made sporting history by riding down the long flight of stone steps from the Capitol to the Mall. People of all ages played croquet, tried archery, and went boating on the "silvery Potomac." The Columbia Boat Club turned itself into the Athletic Club in 1887 and opened tennis courts, a running track and a lacrosse field on Analostan island. After 1891, thousands of people used the new public bathing beach on the river. Among the well-to-do, golf became fashionable when links opened at the country club in the late eighties. Amateur football, however, awakened more general enthusiasm. In professional sport interest divided almost equally between prize fights and baseball until the National League cut its teams to eight, and the Senators, who for years had ended the season at the bottom of the League, dropped out of sight.[4]

Custom, meanwhile, had not staled Washingtonians' pleasure in Saturday afternoon gatherings in the White House grounds: "Then the lawn is filled with a well-dressed crowd as cosmopolitan as you will find anywhere and the big Marine Band, one of the best in the world, clad in their flaming suits of red and gold, give forth the finest music. . . . Among the crowd you will find the best dressed and finest looking Negroes in the world; you may bump against a treasury clerk or a cabinet officer, and you may discuss the toilet of Frau Van

[4] *Star*, 30 May 1879, 18 May 1880, 1, 26 Jan 1889, Summaries, 1894, 1901, "Rambler," 27 Mar 1921; Comrs Rpts, 1899, p. 10, 1901, p. 494.

Nirgends, the chief lady of a foreign legation, or of pretty little peachy Miss Smith whose father is a messenger in the Treasury, and then the nature, the flowers, the trees and the long stretch of beautiful scenery away on the Potomac beyond the big white monument, make a combination of which any country may be proud."

National celebrations, moreover, periodically enlivened the everyday routine. Most memorable was the dedication of the Washington Monument on February 21, 1885, a day for which old inhabitants had waited thirty-six years. While children skated on Babcock Pond to the north of the Monument, shivering adults cheered Senator John Sherman's opening announcement that men might keep their hats on during the formal exercises; bitter weather reduced the prayer of the rector of Christ Church to a mere ten minutes. That night fireworks reflected by the snow covering the city made a magnificent spectacle. Every fourth year increasingly elaborate presidential inaugurations created a holiday mood. For President Garfield's inaugural parade grand stands for the first time lined the Avenue, and the newly finished National Museum, scene of the inaugural ball, resembled "a crystal palace," its rotunda and dome sparkling with "the whiteness of electric lights" while the rest of the building glowed with "the yellowness of the thousands of gas burners." In brilliant sunshine on March 4, 1885, nearly 100,000 people watched Grover Cleveland take the oath of office as the first Democratic President since James Buchanan. Men climbed to the roof of the Capitol and into the lap of Horatio Greenough's statue of Washington, and afterward, as a 25,000-man parade marched up the Avenue, "even the flags and streamers seemed to be affected by the general contagion which filled the air." Still larger crowds welcomed the next two Republican Presidents. A downpour of cold rain obliged President Harrison to stand under a dripping umbrella as he gave his address, but President McKinley in 1897 had the "Cleveland weather" that a snow storm had denied the Democrat at his second inaugural.[5]

Washingtonians on their own staged several impressive celebrations, notably an elaborate welcome for Alexander Shepherd when he returned on a visit in 1887. The demonstration had curious overtones; hundreds of people had been sharply critical of the Boss only fifteen years before. But it was good advertising for "the city which he plucked from the mire and set as a jewel in the sight of men," and most of his former enemies, their anger quenched by the prosperity of the immediate past, now greeted him as a symbol of "the new Washington." Fireworks on Pennsylvania Avenue brilliantly illuminated an hour-long evening parade. The entire District militia turned out, and in the wake of "mounted marshals with white sashes charging about" came some five hundred muddy-booted, overalled workingmen representing the street department. Behind them rode two hundred men on bicycles rigged with wire frames on which hung lighted Chinese lanterns. Every section of the procession carried "transparencies" with inscriptions such as "Population 1871, 80,000; 1887, 250,000," or "Washington suggested; Congress sanctioned; Shepherd made it."

Again at the end of the Spanish-American War when the District regiment of the National Guard returned from Cuba, flags and bunting draped from "windows, doors and sashes and even chimney tops" set the scene for a "reception that surpassed anything of a similar character ever before known in the history of the District of Columbia."

Two years later the city outdid herself in honor of her centennial. One innovation marked the parade from the White House to the Capitol: the Governor of Rhode Island and his staff rode in automobiles. Following the formal procession came "a number of real centennial-looking vehicles, manned by

[5] *Star*, 28 Feb, 5 Mar 1881, 4 Mar 1885, 9 Oct 1889, 4 Mar 1897; Cleveland *Leader*, 30 Sep 1883, 11 Apr, 5 Sep 1884, 4 Mar 1885.

the inevitable darky, with 'Express for Hire' scrawled in white chalk over the sides of the forlorn wagons, and in them the weary found repose for 'Only 10 cents, lady.'" At the Capitol, the "Avenue entrance to the [House] gallery was lighted by a suspended device, bearing the words, 'Capital Celebration, 1900,' in blazing incandescent lamps." Beneath this was a mammoth American flag in colored lights, mechanically contrived to pale and brighten to give Old Glory the appearance of waving. The celebration played up the theme of miraculous change: a city, for years a grubby village unworthy of the United States, now the embodiment of national greatness, a place of absorbing interest to every American.[6]

Although the lengthening roster of government officials gradually necessitated a stricter observance of the canons of rank, "official society" remained an elastic term. In the 1880's, according to a good-naturedly derisive journalist, it stretched to include "residents of Washington, strangers, and visitors." Any well-mannered white person, in short, who could afford servants and who meticulously followed the "cast iron" rules about making calls could be a part or hover on the fringes of Society. How far he and his wife got beyond the circumference was only partly a matter of rank. When Senator H. A. W. Tabor, the Vermont stonecutter who had struck it rich in Colorado silver mining, cast off a first wife and in a sumptuous wedding at the Willard Hotel married a glamorous little blonde, neither his senatorial office, his ostentatious spending, nor President Arthur's presence at the wedding enabled the groom and his bride to cut a swathe during his brief term in Washington. Distinguished family connections helped open doors, but distinction rested less upon ancient lineage than upon post Civil-War achievement. And a politician's social status, particularly after the Civil Service Act and repeal of the last sections of the Tenure of Office Act cut in upon his patronage,

[6] *Star*, 10, 22 Sep, 7 Oct 1887, 2 Jan 1899; *Sentinel*, 25 Feb 1888; *Bee*, 15 Oct 1898; *Post*, 11-13 Dec 1900.

might depend almost as much on his wife's social skills as upon his own place in the governmental hierarchy. "Society women," remarked the acidulous Emily Briggs, "have politicians for husbands, but not all politicians have society wives."[7]

If the character of politicians did not change, at least observant wives learned that a display of wealth was a poor substitute for rank, and rank without suave manners might be a bruised reed upon which to lean. Non-alcoholic state dinners disappeared after Mrs. Hayes left the White House, but the days of eighteen to twenty toasts at formal dinners did not return, and the quiet tastes of succeeding first ladies helped to emphasize elegance rather than lavishness in entertaining. The rich outsider intent on becoming an insider discovered the uses not only of the *Elite List* and the *U.S. Register* but also of Mrs. Dahlgren's *Etiquette of Social Life in Washington.* Madeleine Vinton Dahlgren, daughter of a congressman, widow of a distinguished admiral, and from the early 1880's till her death in 1898 the self-appointed doyenne of Washington society, doubtless saved many a parvenu from unforgivable blunders. "No dinner," she warned, "however superb in prandial show, can be agreeable if the *convives* are dullards. . . . No sordid computation of dollars can buy or measure the Promethean light of conversational effect." Even proper Bostonians or Philadelphia gentlemen welcomed reminders of how to address a Russian count or her Britannic Majesty's minister to the United States.[8]

Forty years later a cultivated American who knew European capitals well declared the Washington of President Arthur's time the most delightful city in the world. If visitors to the

[7] *Star*, 13 Jan 1879, 18 Nov 1881, 25 Feb, 15 Mar, 14 Nov 1882, 31 Dec 1884, 16 Mar 1885, 11 Dec 1888, 26 Jan 1889; Cleveland *Leader*, 5 Sep 1884; *Sentinel*, 6 Mar 1886, 29 Dec 1888; *Olivia Letters*, p. 413.

[8] Marian Gouverneur, *As I Remember*, pp. 371-72; Low, "Washington, City of Leisure," pp. 773-74; Madeleine Vinton Dahlgren, *Etiquette of Social Life in Washington*, 5th ed., 1881, p. 50; Rudolph Keim, *Society in Washington, Its Noted Men, Accomplished Women, Established Customs and Notable Events*, 1887.

President's private quarters were astonished to find his bedroom redecorated in pale pink with blue brocade hangings, all Washington was pleasantly surprised by the social graces of the affable host in the White House. When his successor brought a twenty-year-old bride to the capital in 1886, again Washingtonians found the warmth radiating from the White House singularly agreeable. The wife of Senator Foraker of Ohio indicated that that charm endured: "The opening nineties saw the old *regime*, Anglo-Saxon, conservative, making its last stand at the White House. The Harrisons gathered around them a fine best-families group; women who could give all their time to social perfections undistracted by suffrage, divorce, interior decoration or other extraneities . . . We still exchanged recipes, had not yet begun to discuss diet, except as a delight, changed our dresses exhaustingly-often during the day, and were, altogether, as conventional as a sideboard. It was a nice period."

By the standards of London or St. Petersburg or Vienna or Berlin, ceremony in Washington was thin, scarcely greater than in Grant's day when the President's casual attire and off-hand manner had scandalized the newly arrived Danish minister. But changes began in 1894 when Great Britain and France acknowledged the growing importance of the United States in world affairs by elevating their legations in Washington to the rank of embassies. In 1897 Italy followed that example, and at the end of the Spanish-American War the emergence of the United States as a prospective colonial power hastened the process that gradually turned the city into a sophisticated as well as an agreeable capital. Senators, conscious of the new prestige attaching to the men who ratified or rejected international treaties, abandoned the broad-brimmed felts and string ties of yesteryear and adopted high silk hats and frock coats as standard daytime attire. Foreign diplomats came to look upon a tour of duty in Washington as only a little less desirable than assignment to one of the five or six great courts of Europe, while wealthy Americans as never before wanted a taste of Washington society. Not every debutante could marry a Lord Curzon as had Levi Leiter's daughter, and the growing dearth of bachelors all but put an end to balls, but sipping tea, horseback riding and dining with titled foreigners added dazzle to the social round. New York's Four Hundred could rarely produce more eligible lords in a season than could Washington hostesses. Moreover, as improved printing techniques enabled magazines to publish photographs of silk-hatted big-wigs and everyday scenes in Washington, popular interest in the life of the capital heightened. It took on simultaneously a visible reality and a new romantic aura that encompassed not only political personages but everyone privileged to live in the city.[9]

The relationship between "resident" and "official" society often confused new arrivals, particularly if they recalled tales of local aristocrats' disdain of officialdom during and after the Civil War. Readers of Henry James' story *Pandora* saw in Mr. Bonnycastle, a character actually based on Henry Adams, a portrayal of the Washington blue-blood of the 1880's when he suggests to his wife that for once they ignore the social niceties in preparing their guest list: "Hang it . . . let us have some fun—let us invite the President." But even in the Grant era with all its bitter partisanship and vulgarity, the line separating families firmly rooted in the community from the temporary office-holders had not been drawn sharply, and in the course of the next decade it faded out almost entirely. Mrs. Dahlgren explained that "in real solidity of social importance, the resident society must . . . be classed as of the very elite." She added, "the old families of Washington have an

[9] Mrs. Reginald De Koven, *A Musician and His Wife*, pp. 51-82; Logan, *Thirty Years in Washington*, p. 519; Festus Summers, ed., *The Cabinet Diary of William L. Wilson*, pp. 9-10, 198; Mrs. Joseph Foraker, *I Would Live It Again*, pp. 185-200; Mrs. William Howard Taft, *Recollections of Full Years*, p. 27; Louis A. Coolidge, "On the Streets of the National Capital," *Cosmopolitan*, XXVIII, 365-76.

interest for us which none other in the land may claim, for their social life has gone hand in hand with that of the nation."

But how old was old? By the end of the century the distinction was blurred. Third-generation families who from the first had had the cultivation and money to move in upper-class circles were extremely few, and, in striking contrast to cities such as Philadelphia and Boston, Washington and Georgetown together could muster scarcely eighty well-established second-generation families. The prominent Washingtonian of the 1890's was as likely to be a native of a northern state as of the District of Columbia. Although by 1900 four out of every five native American whites in the District were born below the Mason-Dixon line, in the upper social brackets southern background had ceased to weigh heavily. (See Table III.) Washington's first *Social Register* contained the names of about 2,100 families in 1900. Some 820 were those of Army and Navy officers, high-ranking departmental officials, members of Congress, foreign diplomats and Americans listed in one of the five other *Social Registers* who chose to transfer to Washington for the season. Among the twelve-hundred-odd others named were people who had lived in the city at intervals for twenty to thirty years without identifying themselves as Washingtonians—Henry Adams, for example, and the diplomat John W. Foster, Secretary of State under Benjamin Harrison and grandfather of a later Secretary. Over four hundred of the fixed residents listed were widows or single women. Of all the permanent residents included, perhaps two-thirds had been relatively new to the capital when Mrs. Dahlgren wrote of "the very elite."

Yet the omissions from the *Register* of 1900 illustrate as well as the inclusions the uncertainty and flexibility of social status in Washington. The cultivated Ohio-born John Joy Edson, a Washingtonian from his Civil-War school days, head of a dozen civic enterprises, and president of the Board of Trade in 1900, was left out; Brainard Warner was admitted, although

TABLE III

POPULATION OF THE DISTRICT OF COLUMBIA, 1870-1950*

	1870	1880	1890	1900	1910	1920	1930	1940	1950
TOTAL	131,700	177,624	230,392	278,718	331,069	437,571	486,869	663,091	802,178
% increase in 10 years	75.4	34.9	29.7	21.0	18.8	32.2	11.3	36.2	21.0
WHITES	88,278	118,006	154,695	191,532	236,128	326,860	353,914	474,326	517,865
% increase in 10 years	40.1	33.7	31.1	23.8	23.3	38.4	8.3	34.0	9.2
Native	72,107	101,026	136,178	172,012	211,777	298,312	323,982	440,312	478,368
% native to D.C.	53.9	55.4	52.1	48.5	46.7	38.0	39.6	33.2	31.4
% native to all southern states	25.0	24.2	25.9	28.9	29.6	31.4	33.7	34.7	32.1
% native to South exclusive of Md. & Va.	1.7	2.9	4.1	5.4	5.7	9.4	10.1	14.6	15.6
% native to North and West	20.9	20.5	20.9	22.3	23.0	29.5	25.8	31.2	33.5
Foreign-born	16,171	16,980	18,517	19,520	24,351	28,548	29,932	34,014	39,497
% of total population	12.3	9.7	8.1	7.2	7.5	6.7	6.3	5.3	5.5
% of white population	18.3	14.3	11.9	10.2	10.3	8.7	8.5	7.2	7.6
NEGROES	43,404	59,596	75,572	86,702	94,446	109,966	132,068	187,266[a]	280,803[a]
% increase in 10 years	203.2	37.3	26.8	14.7	8.9	16.4	20.1	41.9	49.9
% of total population	32.9	33.6	32.8	31.1	28.5	25.1	27.1	28.2	35.0
% native to D.C.	31.0	41.6	41.9	41.9	42.8	42.4	39.8	39.4	40.4
% native to Md. & Va.	65.7	54.1	51.9	50.8	46.3	42.3	35.4	27.3	20.9
% native to South exclusive of Md. & Va.	1.9	2.4	3.4	5.2	7.3	11.3	20.2	28.9	32.1

[a] Negroes only; the nativity percentages are computed from subtotals which include all non-whites, but the number of non-whites other than Negroes was negligible.

* Compiled from *U.S. Census*, Ninth through Seventeenth.

his career in the capital was no longer or more notable and his bank account probably little larger than Edson's. Since the publication of the *New York Social Register* in 1884 and of later counterparts for Philadelphia, Boston, Baltimore, and Chicago, socially ambitious Americans had come to look upon a *Social Register* listing as a key to the pearly gates on earth; family position, fortified by money but untouched by scandalous notoriety, was at least theoretically a prerequisite. But inasmuch as expediency necessitated naming all high-ranking officials in the capital, including every senator irrespective of his forebears, the rules of selection in Washington lost some of their rigidity. The hope, however illusory, of exploiting that flexibility to squeak through the sacred portals drew to Washington people who knew they could not successfully storm the doors elsewhere.[10]

To newcomers Washington and Georgetown seemed one and the same, as officially they indeed were. But old Georgetowners, while sharing many of Washington's pleasures, felt themselves differentiated by their longer history and closer family ties. The sense of dignified antiquity which prevailed beyond the debris-strewn bank of Rock Creek was fortunately not a divisive factor in the larger community; residents of the city on one side of the creek admired the eighteenth-century houses of those on the far side without resenting their air of detached superiority. If Georgetowners preferred Sunday afternoon visiting with each other to mingling with the throng which promenaded along Connecticut Avenue to the accompaniment of a dozen different languages, Washingtonians enjoyed the cosmopolitan atmosphere of the capital nonetheless.

If few people considered Washington a center of creative

[10] Henry James, "Pandora," *Stories Revived*, I, 105; F. E. Mathiessen, ed., *Henry James' Notebook*; Low, "Washington, City of Leisure," p. 777; Dahlgren, *Etiquette*, pp. 33, 49. The figures on "old families" are based on a 20 percent sampling of the *Washington Social Register* of 1900 checked against the *City Directory* of 1846. See also Marietta Minnigerode Andrews, *My Studio Window*, pp. 101-02.

art, fewer still found her barren of opportunity. Nowhere else in the United States could sculpture be seen in such profusion—at the Capitol in the Hall of Statuary, in the Senate chamber adorned after 1886 with a growing array of busts of former Vice Presidents, in the Corcoran Gallery of Art, and in L'Enfant's spacious circles and squares, where equestrian bronze or stone generals and marble statesmen on imposing pedestals looked out over the city. Except for Vinnie Ream Hoxie's statue of Admiral Farragut in Farragut Square, none of the sculpture was the work of local artists. Most of it fell short of great art, but very little of it was patently inept, and when Henry Adams' memorial to his wife was unveiled in Rock Creek Cemetery in 1891, the beauty of St. Gaudens' simple tranquil figure, which Adams called "The Peace of God," led connoisseurs to declare it the finest sculpture in America. William Wetmore Story, the American expatriate whose statue of John Marshall stands on the Capitol grounds and who supposedly was Hawthorne's original for the sculptor in *The Marble Fawn*, remarked upon the rapid improvement in Americans' aesthetic taste when he lectured in Washington in the 1880's. The trustees of the Corcoran Gallery, impressed at the steadily increasing number of visitors, were themselves astonished in 1897 at the results of an experiment in opening the gallery on Sunday: a long queue of "wage-earners" formed at the entrance long before the doors opened, and few left before the closing bell sounded. The painting "Charlotte Corday" and Hiram Powers' "Greek Slave" commanded most attention.

Meanwhile the enthusiasm of the amateurs who flocked to the gallery to copy its pictures and to benefit from the free tutelage of Eliphalet Andrews led the trustees to offer a gold medal for the best piece of work and, in 1887, to pay Andrews a small salary to conduct classes such as he had taught as a volunteer for nearly a decade. The Corcoran School of Art came formally into being in 1888, for upon W. W. Corcoran's death in February a memorandum came to light among his papers setting aside $100,000 for an art school to be attached to the gallery. Plans for a new building on 17th Street therefore included spacious studios for classes. When the new white marble gallery opened in 1897, Andrews was able to persuade the artists who had been teaching paying students at the Art League to join him and his assistant at the Corcoran. By the end of the century the consolidation had secured the city an art school that would in time rank with Boston's and Chicago's.

Much of the local public preferred the ornate Renaissance style of the newly finished Library of Congress to the classical lines of the new Corcoran Gallery, while changes in taste rated Federal period domestic architecture below the heavy solidity of the Romanesque exemplified in the houses H. H. Richardson built on Lafayette Square for Henry Adams and John Hay. Formal schools of architecture were few in the United States. Young men learned the profession by serving virtual apprenticeships in the offices of established firms, just as a generation earlier young men read law in the offices of older men as preparation for the bar examinations. For aspiring young architects the buildings of the capital served as a kind of case book. If, like General Sheridan, they regretted that the red brick mass of the Pension Office was fireproof, awful examples of Washington's public architecture as well as her fine still served a useful purpose.[11]

In music Washington lagged behind other big American cities. A week or at most a fortnight of opera presented by companies on tour was her quota for the season. Occasionally a well-known instrumental soloist gave a concert, but professional performances were few. Like performing artists, composers were discouraged by the lack of a public concert hall.

[11] Teunis S. Hamlin, "Historic Houses of Washington," *Scribner's Magazine*, XIV, 475; Charles E. Fairman, *Art and Artists of the Capitol of the United States of America*, pp. 251 ff (hereafter cited as Fairman, *Art*); *Star*, 8 Jan 1879; Cleveland *Leader*, 23 Jan 1884; *Post*, 1 Mar 1897; Stanley Olmsted, "The Corcoran School of Art," Ms in possession of Corcoran Gallery.

The organist and later the pastor of the Congregational Church, however, composed a number of hymns, and John Philip Sousa, leader of the Marine Band, won local fame for his *Washington Post March.* He conducted the first performance in 1890 for a gathering of the Washington Amateur Authors' Association on the Smithsonian grounds. Later played at the Chicago World's Fair and at European courts, the gay *March* came to be known the world over. Unhappily for Sousa, before then he had sold the score for $35 to a Philadelphia publisher, and, unhappily for Washington, he left the Marines in 1892 to start his own band in New York.

Gifted amateurs could only partly fill the gap created by the absence of professional talent. The Georgetown Amateur Orchestra, starting in 1882 with thirty-one instruments, worked up to a hundred before 1901, and several churches, notably the Asbury and St. Luke's Negro Churches and the Congregational Church, had exceptionally well-trained choirs. For a number of years the German Saengerbund gave an annual *Lieder* concert, and the Washington Choral Society in the 1890's sang oratorios, including on one occasion the *Elijah a capella.* Beginning in 1886 a group of women with some leisure and a serious interest in music formed the Friday Morning Music Club, meeting at each others' houses to study and give private concerts. By the end of the century, the Club had begun to achieve professional stature. In 1897 some twenty talented Negro women organized the Treble Clef Club along similar lines. In an era when Edison phonographs and recordings were still an expensive innovation, most people had little chance to discover that listening engendered a taste for music. The city as a whole remained luke-warm to the art.[12]

[12] John Philip Sousa, *Marching Along*, pp. 115-17; *Post History*, pp. 339-40; *Post and Times Herald*, 3 Jul 1958; Frank Metcalf, "History of Sacred Music in the District of Columbia," Columbia Historical Society *Records*, XXVII, 175-202 (hereafter cited as CHS *Rec*); *Star*, 15 Dec 1879, 12 Apr 1882; Cleveland *Leader*, 2 May 1884; *Post*, 3 Nov 1889, 4 Mar 1897; *A Brief History of the Friday Morning Music Club of Washington, D.C.*, and programs filed under heading "Washington" in Music Div, L.C.

Literature, however, occupied an important place in Washington's life. The newspapers made much of the city's literary lights, perhaps partly because some of them were journalists who turned out an occasional novel or play in addition to their regular columns. Since dozens of independent newspapers had their own correspondents in the capital, numbers as well as talent kept reporters much in the public view. In 1889, having offended the Administration and thus somewhat weakened their own position, the leaders of the fraternity organized the Gridiron Club dedicated to giving an annual dinner for three or four specially invited, politically powerful guests. Yearly thereafter an anonymous skit, its authorship carefully concealed, neatly roasted the guest of honor, and members' secrecy about what went on was sufficiently well-kept to enable the victim to laugh with his tormentors. Public uncertainty about who wrote the "scorchers" for the Gridiron endowed all correspondents with a reputation for Rabelaisian wit.

While congressmen and retired generals penned memoirs and treatises on politics and the Civil War, a flood of verses, essays, short stories, and sketches of life in the capital poured out of Washington into the pages of popular magazines. Most of it left little permanent mark. Even Joaquin Miller, whose *Songs of the Sierras* and tales of the wild West seemed to ensure him lasting fame, might have dropped out of memory, had his log cabin on Meridian Hill not survived as a physical landmark long after he had departed. With a host of writers ready to participate, "literary evenings" became part of the social routine. The Shakespeare Club, the Circle des Precieuses Ridicules, the Unity Club, and a dozen others held readings, while the exercises conducted within the "enchanted circle of the Brain Club," as the Baroness Hegermann-Lindencrone had named the Literary Society in the 1870's, lost much of their former pretentiousness.[13]

[13] Theron C. Crawford, "The Special Correspondents at Washington," *Cosmopolitan*, XII, 351-60; Richard V. Oulahan, "Literary Bookland, the

By no means all of Washington's literary figures were dilettantes. Government scientists turned out enormously valuable studies, some of them rivalling in interest John Wesley Powell's descriptions of the Colorado River valley. In 1883 Lester Frank Ward published his epoch-making *Dynamic Sociology*, much of it written at his desk at the Geological Survey. The work of a distinguished, albeit still relatively obscure, paleobotanist and paleobiologist, Ward's presentation of the case for a planned society and his insistence that "ideas rule the world of men" struck with telling force; in the 1890's his *Psychic Factors in Civilization* and the *Outline of Sociology* further developed his social philosophy. Simon Newcomb, head of the Naval Observatory, produced not only lucid expositions of complex scientific problems but two books on political economy and, for good measure, a romance.

Historians made wide use of the archival materials in the Library of Congress, over which the bibliophile, author, and scholar Ainsworth Spofford presided until 1897. While the octogenarian George Bancroft completed his last book, from Henry Adams' study nearby at 1603 H Street came the anonymously published novel *Democracy*, a satirical commentary on Washington society, and in 1890 his history of Jefferson's and Madison's administrations. Next door Adams' intimate friend John Hay took time out from his collaboration with John Nicolay to write the *Breadwinners*, a novel attacking organized labor as he had seen it in Cleveland during the railroad strike of 1877. After Nicolay's and Hay's monumental ten-volume *Abraham Lincoln: A History* appeared, Hay confined his writing to letters and a few pieces of verse, and, while Adams wan-

---

Gridiron Club of Washington," *The Bookman*, XXIII, 146-52; *Star*, 8 Jan 30 Jun 1881, 6 Feb, 12 Apr, 1 Nov 1882, 9 Jan, 27 Feb 1883, 20 Jan, 25 Nov 1884; *Post*, 4 Nov 1889; "Literary works in progress," Cleveland *Leader*, 3 Mar 1884; Lillie Hegermann-Lindencrone, *The Sunny Side of Diplomatic Life*, pp. 16-18; Helen Nicolay, *Sixty Years of the Washington Literary Society*.

dered over the South Seas and Europe, the houses on H Street ceased to be a source of distinguished literature.[14]

The number of literary women in Washington frequently astonished visitors. "One of the lions of the capital" was the petite auburn-haired Frances Hodgson Burnett, who, in creating *Little Lord Fauntleroy*, imposed black velvet knee breeches and lace collars upon a whole generation of rebellious small boys. James G. Blaine's sister-in-law, the short, stout, rather homely Abigail Dodge, still using the pen name Gail Hamilton, in the 1880's was still producing widely read columns on politics and politicians. The sketches and stories of Mary Clemmer Ames, best known for her *Ten Years in Washington*, Emily Briggs' *Olivia Letters*, Kate Field's witty pieces appearing under the title "Kate Field's Washington," and the writings of half a dozen other newspaperwomen in turn commanded respect. Forty years of turning out saccharine tales had shrunk Mrs. Emma D. E. N. Southworth's literary standing, but in the nineties the works of newer women novelists in Washington had not yet obliterated the little Georgetown widow's books from memory. Her little frame cottage on the bluff above the Potomac remained a "literary landmark." Younger authors frequently followed Mrs. Dahlgren's example in drawing upon knowledge of Washington society for background. If Grace Denio Litchfield's poems and the plays and stories of Jennie Gould Lincoln, wife of an eminent Washington physician, sold the better for being the products of society matrons, the quality of what they wrote mattered less to the community than the recognition they won from the rest of the country.

Feminists, pointing to the successful professional careers of women in the capital, called Washington "a special center of women." In 1890 wives, mothers, daughters, and sisters who believed the "Dawn of Woman's Era" at hand organized the

[14] A. Hunter Dupree, *Science in the Federal Government: A History of Policies and Activities to 1940*, p. 205 (hereafter cited as Dupree, *Science*); Ralph H. Gabriel, *The Course of American Democratic Thought*, p. 207.

"Wimodaughsis," a society which hoped to open a building for meetings of the National Woman Suffrage Association, the WCTU, the Red Cross under Clara Barton, the Women's National Press Association, and the like. The project made scanty headway; attractive young government clerks preferred to spend their leisure in the company of the bachelors with whom their jobs or the "dairy lunches" brought them in contact, and older women, such as Virginia Grigsby's mother with or without her corsets at the Land Office, were generally too tired at the end of the day's work to care about elevation, while ladies established in the social world of the capital inclined to look askance at the "career woman." Yet women of all conditions and kinds could lead a fuller life in Washington than in almost any other American city of the time.[15]

Among men it was the scientists and scholars above all who found Washington congenial and who added most to the variety of the city's intellectual interests. While generals and bankers gravitated toward the Metropolitan Club, notables in a dozen fields of learning gathered at the Cosmos Club in the house where Dolly Madison spent her last years. Founded in 1878 largely by the men who had organized the Philosophical Society seven years before, the Cosmos Club was the rendezvous of some of the most interesting men in America; and, after the remodelling of the house in the mid-eighties, usually also the meeting place of the city's learned societies. Faculty members of the Columbian and National Universities made up part of the group, but scientists in government service were its backbone.

For in spite of some congressional opposition and even more from university scientists such as Alexander Agassis of Harvard who, imbued with laissez faire doctrines, objected pas-

[15] Cleveland *Leader*, 4 Aug 1883; Etta Ramsdell Goodwin, "The Literary Women of Washington," *Chatauquan*, XXVII, 579-86; *Wimodaughsis*, leaflet in Bowen Mss; Susan Grigsby to Sarah Humphreys, 4 Aug, 5 Oct 1884; Gibson-Humphreys Mss.

sionately to a wider government role in research, programs of the federal bureaus expanded steadily during the eighties. Under imaginative leadership, basic research not infrequently became the accepted accompaniment of the search for solutions to practical problems. The challenge of the work possible in the Washington bureaus attracted brilliant men: geologists and paleontologists at the Geological Survey; marine biologists pursuing oceanographic studies for the Fish Commission, geneticists, plant and animal pathologists, and chemists in the Department of Agriculture; mathematicians and astronomers at the Naval Observatory; meteorologists working at the Weather Bureau under "Old Prob" Cleveland Abbe, so nicknamed for his reliance on "probably"; and in the 1890's bacteriologists, Captain Walter Reed among them, brought together by Surgeon-General George Sternberg in his reorganization of the Army medical service. At the National Museum George Brown Goode carried on a many-faceted program that inspired the men he trained in research to call the era before his death in 1896 "a golden age of natural history." Partial reversal of congressional policies clipped the wings of some of these agencies in the last decade of the century, but new regulations and reduced budgets did not put an end to much of the work.

The intellectual vigor of these men permeated the community. Their versatility was in itself stimulating. John Wesley Powell, a bluff, daring, one-armed, red-haired giant, was not only the first white man to traverse the length of the dangerous Colorado canyon, an able geologist, and the author of the famous report on the arid lands of the West, but was also so well versed in Indian languages and tribal mores that in the 1890's, as head of the Smithsonian Bureau of American Ethnology, he laid the groundwork for an expanding science of cultural anthropology in America. Simon Newcomb, the most eminent American astronomer of his day, combined personal charm with scientific erudition; the initiator of a new system of computing the position of the stars and the mass and motion of the planets, he was also an inspiring lecturer and teacher. The gentle Spencer Baird, in the 1880's secretary of the Smithsonian, initiated and directed the Fish Commission's extraordinary program of marine research and was the mentor of a group of gifted younger naturalists known in Washington as "Bairdians." At his death, the secretaryship of the Smithsonian passed to Samuel Langley, whose measurements of the radiant heat of the sun were of major importance to astrophysicists and whose aeronautical experiments stirred the public imagination even while doubting Thomases ridiculed the idea of human flight. At the same time in the attic of the Department of Agriculture Building, a new field of science was emerging. From under the microscopes of a six-man staff came revolutionary discoveries about the nature and transmission of plant and animal diseases such as Texas cattle fever and wheat rust. There two twenty-year-olds, Walter Swingle and David Fairchild, began careers that made them in their early thirties the foremost "plant explorers" in the world.[16]

From these men and a half-hundred equally famous associates came the spark that brought into being six additional learned societies in Washington before 1894. Unlike the Philosophical Society, which aimed at investigation of "the positive facts and laws of the physical and moral universe," several of the newer societies were concerned primarily with popularizing science. Yet eminent members of the Philosophical Society and other academically trained men were not above joining the Anthropological or the National Geographic Society, which made no pretense of nurturing erudition. Indeed the enthusi-

[16] Dupree, *Science*, pp. 149-270; *Star*, 11 Feb 1879, 30 Jun 1881, 27 Feb 1883; "Scientific Research and the National Government," *The Dial*, XXII, 73-75; Simon Newcomb, *The Reminiscences of an Astronomer*, pp. 123-27, 216-23; Paul H. Oehser, *Sons of Science*, pp. 61-106; John W. Powell, "The Personal Characteristics of Spencer Fullerton Baird," *Anl Rpt Smithsonian*, 1888, pp. 746-52; David Fairchild, *The World Was My Garden*, pp. 18-27. See also *Dictionary of American Biography*.

astic participation of laymen in the affairs of the new societies bound much of upper-class Washington into an informal intellectual fellowship. Published transactions extended the influence of these societies into cities where no similar organizations existed. In order to pool resources for publication and public lectures, in 1888 a tentative federation evolved from which the Washington Academy of Sciences sprang ten years later. Significantly its first president was Gardiner Hubbard, a man of great cultivation and an exceptionally well-informed student of the physics of acoustics and aeronautics, but an amateur, not a professionally trained scientist. Hubbard, who was the financial genius behind the Bell Telephone Company, and his son-in-law, Alexander Graham Bell, in founding the National Geographic Society set out to promote scientific exploration and, through the pages of a non-technical, profusely illustrated magazine, to educate the American public about remote parts of the earth.

The swelling ranks of gifted and fascinating men thus gave life in Washington its peculiarly satisfying quality. The brilliance of the far-ranging conversation to be heard at dinner parties astonished newcomers prone to think politics the capital's only interest. Here was an urbane community appreciative of the arts, albeit with little creative artistic genius, a city in which hundreds of temporary residents on government assignments usually wanted to stay and often did. The slow pace of life left people time to enjoy it. "We live," remarked Dr. John Billings, "in a fortunate time and place—in the early manhood of a mighty nation, and in its capital city, which every year makes more beautiful, and richer in the treasure of science, literature and art."[17]

[17] *Bulletin of the Philosophical Society of Washington, 1874; Report of a Committee from the Geological Society on the history of the Joint Commission of the Scientific Societies of Washington; The Cabinet Diary of William L. Wilson*, pp. xix-xx, 180, 198, 215, 233; Dupree, *Science*, 230.

CHAPTER VI

COLORED WASHINGTON, 1879-1901

FOR Negroes the satisfactions of life in the capital diminished steadily after 1878. Between white and colored people such tolerant friendliness as had survived the seventies slowly disappeared. White citizens forgot that Negro leaders had formerly commanded respect and, by their behavior, had encouraged belief in the possibility of building an intelligent bi-racial community. In 1888 the Washington *Elite List* carried the names of five or six Negroes; by 1892 they had been dropped. The white press, increasingly critical of Negroes' "shiftlessness" and the high rate of crime among them, gradually reduced other news about colored people to an occasional facetious comment on a colored social gathering. Exasperation or disgust blotted out compassion for the great mass of blacks, while white people's interest in the careers of gifted Negroes became so condescending as to be insulting, the more so as the condescension was often unconscious. By the mid-nineties a reader of the white newspapers might have supposed Washington had no colored community, let alone three virtually separate Negro communities. White people, in short, in the course of the twenty-odd years resolved the problem of race relations by tacitly denying its existence.

Concurrent with the loss of recognition from whites was a progressive loss of cohesiveness within the three-tiered Negro community and a widening of the gulf between the upper-class group composed of people of predominantly white blood, the middle-class mulattoes, and the blacks. Except as seen in all Negroes' search for "*whiteness*—the ability to pass unnoticed in the crowd, the power to avoid humiliation and abuse,"[1] a community in the sense of a group of people united by common

[1] Pauli Murray, *Proud Shoes, The Story of An American Family*, p. 53.

aspirations and cultural identity had ceased to exist well before 1879. The biological accident of pigmentation, so far from supplying a basis for group accord, created growing resentments which colored people directed at each other more bitterly than at whites. By the end of the 1880's Negroes in the District were adhering to the social pattern common in the deep South: conflict within the caste and compliance with or carefully concealed hostility toward the white group outside.[2] Washington Negroes at the end of the Civil War had shown signs of escaping that mold of behavior. Intelligent colored men, without attempting to halt the swift growth of elaborate class differentiations, had striven to prevent a destructive divisiveness and to develop mutual helpfulness and respect within a single enlarged Negro community; for a time they had seemed to make headway. The tragedy of the last decades of the century was the withering of this earlier promise as the men who had worked to make Washington a center of American Negro civilization in its highest form, a city where all Negroes might live in dignity, abandoned the struggle.

The discouragements besetting the District's colored people undoubtedly contributed to the decline of their public spirit. Indeed the basic cause may have been the growing racism of whites. But cause and effect were intertwined. As time went on, the failure of the bulk of the city's black population to evince any sense of responsibility disillusioned whites who had once held high hopes for the race. That disillusionment fed racial hostility as surely as racial discrimination undermined Negroes' determination to help themselves. The result was a vicious spiral. Whites concluded that most Negroes would never make good citizens, and Negroes, feeling themselves steadily shoved further into a corner by prejudice, ceased to stand up for each other and let the fight degenerate into one of each man

[2] See John Dollard, *Caste and Class in a Southern Town*; Allison Davis and G. and M. Gardner, *Deep South*; and W. Lloyd Warner, "American Caste and Class," *American Journal of Sociology*, XLII, 234-371.

for himself. The exceptions were too few to alter the large picture. Gradually over the years any person known to be "tainted" by so much as a drop of Negro blood found himself stripped of incentives to self-improvement. The ensuing frustration, manifested in every aspect of Negro life in Washington, forms the central theme of Negro history of the period.

For upper-class Negroes civil rights were the key to progress. The nibbling away at those rights began early in the Hayes administration. Colored men here, though disturbed over the President's conciliation of southern Bourbons, still counted on the local anti-discrimination laws for protection: the municipal ordinances of 1869 and 1870 were still in force within Washington's city limits, the territorial civil rights acts still applied to Georgetown and county as well as to Washington, and a congressional act of 1875 was added insurance. After 1878 violations of these laws occurred with mounting frequency, but for a time they were apparently either too trivial or too skillfully cloaked to lead to court action. The *Peoples Advocate*, in 1879 Washington's only colored newspaper, urged Negroes to concentrate on fair play: instead of suing white proprietors for refusing them accommodation, first file complaints against Negro barbers who refused to serve other colored men. Two years later the editor was no longer sure of the wisdom of those tactics. "A respectable colored lady or gentleman, unless it happens to be a man like Frederick Douglass, John F. Cook, or Register Bruce [former United States Senator from Mississippi], is not readily accommodated, if at all, in the eating establishments, no matter how genteel he may be in appearance or in manners." The result was "more or less friction between the keepers of these saloons and a class of our citizens rapidly growing in wealth and intelligence." Still Washington Negroes relied upon patience to destroy prejudice.

In the summer of 1883 a Negro visitor from Connecticut sued a Washington restaurant owner under the criminal section of the federal Civil Rights Act. Newspapers throughout the country discussed the case, partly because it was only the second suit to be brought under the act of 1875, partly because the argument for the defense had an ominous logic: a government which sanctioned separate colored schools could not reasonably require a restaurant proprietor to seat boisterous unwelcome Negroes in a dining-room with whites; he had offered to serve the colored man in the pantry. The judge reviewed all earlier decisions in local civil rights cases, noted that several verdicts had been adverse to the plaintiffs, but in this case found against the defendant and fined him $500.

It was at best a Pyrrhic victory. It strengthened white animosities and inspired pronouncements that the judge's interpretation of the law would force restaurant owners either to accept an exclusively black clientele, or see their businesses ruined, or both. Negroes native to the District were ironically rewarded for their past forbearance by repeated statements citing their eight-year failure to sue under the federal law as proof that the color line was unobjectionable to them. Two months after the decision of August 1883, the United States Supreme Court declared the Civil Rights Act unconstitutional in the states, although still binding in the District of Columbia and all United States territories. Educated Negroes in Washington were angry, and the ignorant were badly frightened, expecting to see the whipping post brought back at any moment. The most optimistic view was that the Court would in time recant and in the meantime District laws would suffice. But no one favoring racial legal equality pretended that the decision was not a blow.[3]

[3] *Peoples Advocate*, 5 Jul, 15, 29 Nov 1879, 10 Jul 1880, 6 Aug 1881, 25 Aug 1883 (hereafter cited as *Advocate*); Washington *Bee*, 4 Aug, 8 Sep 1883 (inasmuch as the local colored press carried in practically every issue items discussing the topics dealt with in this chapter, specific citations of the *Advocate*, 1878-1884, and the *Bee*, 1882-1901, are hereafter confined to direct quotations and occasional fact or comment not found easily elsewhere); *Star*, 7, 13, 16, 18, 24 Aug, 17, 24 Oct 1883; *Chronicle*, 21 Oct 1883; *Sentinel*, 3 Nov 1883; Cleveland *Leader*, 23, 26 Oct, 26 Nov 1883.

During the next two decades local colored men filed a dozen or more suits; some were dismissed, others won, such as the case against a lunch room proprietor who had not posted a price list and had overcharged a Negro outrageously by demanding 50¢ for three eggs, some biscuits, and a cup of coffee. In the 1880's bar rooms generally served colored customers, but lunch rooms and ice cream parlors usually excluded them, a source of particular irritation to "genteel" Negroes. Yet the "genteel" clearly indicated their readiness to have vulgar blacks denied service. Petitions submitted to Congress in 1886 asked for stronger local laws extended to areas not covered in the municipal and territorial acts, but new laws seemed unlikely to improve white tempers. Congress dismissed all proposals for racial legislation, on the one hand bills forbidding miscegenation, and, on the other, those demanding a change in the District Medical Society's discriminatory rules. In the fall of 1900 a suit against the owner of the Opera House for refusing to let a colored man occupy the orchestra seat he had paid for netted the plaintiff damages of one cent.[4]

Nor were Negroes guiltless. A number of Negro-owned barber shops and some hotels and restaurants run by colored men would not accept Negro customers. A circular of 1888, for example, announced: "Preston's Pension Office barber shop, first class in every particular. Devoted *Strictly* to *White Trade.* The rumor that this shop has been serving any Colored Trade is false in every particular." The white press called attention to such incidents. "The refusal is based, of course," remarked the *Star*, "not on color prejudice, but on the business consideration that the best paying class of customers can be retained only by excluding those who for any reason are objectionable to their fastidious notions."[5] After the founding of the short-

[4] *Star*, 8, 22 Nov 1884, 4 Feb, 10 Dec 1887, 18 Feb 1888; *Rec*, 47C, 1S, pp. 1408-10, 1839; ptn, S49A-H12, 18 Jan 1886; *Bee*, 1884-1899, 24 Nov 1900; S Rpt 1050, 52C, 1S, Ser 2915.

[5] *Star*, 12 Dec 1887; *Bee*, 21 Jul 1888.

lived Afro-American League in 1890, a Washington branch sent delegates to its national conventions, but disunity, lack of a positive program to combat racism, and the magnitude of the problem stripped the organization of effectiveness. Its successor, the Afro-American Council, which came into being in 1898, was largely controlled by Booker T. Washington, whose seeming subservience to whites alienated Negro militants. As Jim Crow laws began to multiply in the southern states, Negroes in the District realized they were far better off than most of their race; but they saw that the local anti-discrimination laws had come to be more honored in the breach than in the observance.

Chance, moreover, played into the hands of segregationists. In 1901 Congress accepted the first part of a codification of District law but left "the second or municipal part" to be revised and adopted later. Although Congress specified that existing police regulations, unless expressly repealed, should continue in force—a stipulation that meant the civil rights laws were still valid—the fact that the published code contained no mention of the anti-discrimination ordinances probably encouraged white men to risk ignoring them.[6]

Washington's old, well-established colored families like the Cooks and the Wormleys had reason for a time to believe that they and distinguished newcomers such as Frederick Douglass, Blanche K. Bruce, and Dr. Augusta could enjoy some rights not specifically protected by law. Good manners, professional status, and money made them acceptable residents of any locality provided they did not obtrude themselves socially upon white people. But cultivated Negroes, even those

[6] *Colored American*, 9 Apr 1898; *Bee*, 16 Nov 1889, 27 Aug 1898; August Meier, "Booker T. Washington and the Negro Press," *Journal of Negro History*, XXXVIII, 85, n; *Rec*, 56C, 2S, pp. 3497, 3586, 3603; Walter S. Cox, "Attempts to Obtain a Law Code for the District of Columbia," CHS *Rec*, III, 127-32; Phineas Indritz, "Post Civil War Ordinances Prohibiting Racial Discrimination in the District of Columbia," *Georgetown Law Journal*, XLII, 196-201.

who looked almost white, discovered that each passing year made it harder for them to purchase or rent comfortable houses without paying exorbitant prices; by the 1890's, they could rarely buy at all in a conveniently located, orderly neighborhood. Mary Church Terrell's *A Colored Woman in a White World* tells of endless humiliations in the course of her house-hunt. Yet her husband was a *cum laude* graduate of Harvard, a respected lawyer, and after 1896 a member of the Board of Trade, and she herself was a graduate of Oberlin and one of two women before 1900 to be appointed to the school board.

Rising rentals hastened the exodus of Negro householders who in the seventies had lived along 16th Street a few blocks above Lafayette Square and out beyond Scott Circle. As the real estate boom in northwest Washington gained momentum, colored people moved farther from the center of the city. Whether sheer economics or, as rumor had it, combinations of real estate agents kept respectable Negroes from moving into desirable localities, the result was the same. It did not mean that clear-cut solid black belts arose outside of which Negroes could not find housing; some intersprinkling of white and Negro dwellings continued down into the 1930's. But by 1900 the barrier of caste, seemingly collapsing in the late 1860's, had become stronger than ever. The one notable exception lay in the Board of Trade: James T. Wormley was a charter member, and Dr. Charles Purvis, Washington's leading colored physician, George F. Cook, superintendent of the colored schools, and Robert Terrell were elected in the mid-1890's.[7]

Disregard of civil rights as a rule affected only upper-class Negroes. The workings of the criminal law, on the other hand,

[7] *Advocate*, 8 Sep 1883; *Star*, 4 Feb 1887; Edward Ingle, *The Negro in the District of Columbia*, in *Johns Hopkins University Studies in Historical and Political Science*, 11th Series, nos. III and IV, pp. 50-51, 90 (hereafter cited as Ingle, *The Negro in D.C.*); Coroner's maps in Comrs Rpts, 1882, p. 508, 1890, p. 826, 1900, p. 826; Joseph W. Moore, *Picturesque Washington*, p. 139; Mary Church Terrell, *A Colored Woman in a White World*, pp. 113-19; membership lists in *Rpts B/Tr*, 1897, 1899; *Colored American*, 26 Mar 1898; *Bee*, 1898-1901.

touched the lives of countless blacks living on a bare subsistence level. Of those some were undoubtedly vicious; and some, though vaguely well-intentioned, took to thieving, drunkenness, and disorderliness as the easiest way to blunder through a world that offered them at best very little. In a city where only one person in three was colored, the number of Negro arrests exceeded the number of white every year after 1889. People as ignorant of their rights as of their obligations were, to be sure, in some measure at the mercy of the police, and police brutality was all too common. The *Bee* asserted that policemen, particularly the Irishmen on the force, frequently clubbed Negroes savagely when arresting them, and the dark-skinned man was always the first suspect when a crime occurred. Officers "took delight in arresting every little colored boy they see on the street, who may be doing something not at all offensive, and allow the white boys to do what they please." The individual prejudice of police court justices was likely then to determine the severity of the sentences imposed. Perhaps the number of Negroes charged with misdemeanors and felonies was as much an index of white men's aversion to colored as a reflection of Negroes' criminal tendencies. Calvin Chase, editor of the *Bee*, as a boy having seen his father shot down in cold blood and his white assailant go unpunished, was vitriolic about Washington police methods. But more temperate men than he believed that racial equality before the law had largely disappeared by the end of the century.[8]

Despite the decline of Negroes' legal position, political preferment for colored men fell off surprisingly little. It is true that after 1880 a Negro rarely received a federal post of any importance, and after President Garfield and President Arthur failed them, colored men ceased to talk of appointments to the

[8] *Star*, 15 Mar 1882, 27 Oct 1887, 1 Jan 1897; *Chronicle*, 10 Mar 1895, 7 Jun 1896; *Sentinel*, 15 Oct 1892, 25 Nov 1893; *Bee*, 6 Aug 1887; Ingle, *The Negro in D.C.*, pp. 100-101; William J. Simmons, *Men of Mark, Eminent, Progressive and Rising*, pp. 118-19; Elizabeth M. Chapin, *American Court Gossip, or Life at the Nation's Capital*, pp. 36-40.

Cabinet. But before the depression of the 1890's Negroes held as many minor clerkships and custodial jobs as they had formerly. Frederick Douglass, though shorn of some of the one-time dignities of the Marshal of the District, kept that post through President Hayes' administration, while the lucrative position of District Recorder of Deeds continued to go to Negroes. President Garfield, moreover, appointed ex-Senator Bruce of Mississippi Register of the Treasury, a place that would be filled by a Negro for the next thirty-two years. Both before and after the introduction of competitive civil service examinations, colored men feared for their jobs when a new administration took over, but even the shake-up anticipated during Grover Cleveland's first term did not cut the number of Negroes on the federal payroll; on the contrary, scrupulous fairness in grading examinations enabled more Negroes than ever before to enter government service. In 1891 out of 23,144 federal employees in Washington, nearly 2,400 were colored; they held 337 of the 6,120 jobs in the Interior Department, and 127 ranked as copyists, "transcribers," and clerks. Once appointed, Negroes rarely encountered overt hostility from fellow white employees. Negroes got far less consideration from the District commissioners. In 1879 one appointment out of fifty to the police force was colored, none to the fire department. Later policy gave Negroes some of the jobs but never established a stable ratio of colored to white. Outside the colored school system, in 1891 Negroes held only 25 District positions above the rank of messenger and day laborer.

Cleveland's second administration, troubled as it was by country-wide unemployment, saw a drop in Negro preferment and the dismissal of "surplus" Negro clerks. Republican prosperity, launched with the election of William McKinley, failed to restore the earlier proportion of colored employees in spite of the liberal attitude of Secretary Lyman Gage and his assistants in the Treasury Department. The falling off in other departments, if less pronounced than white men expected, was at once a bitter disappointment to Negroes and a gloomily foreseen development in keeping with trends in other areas of American life.[9] Negro pride was badly hurt, moreover, when the new president of Howard University filled seven out of nine faculty vacancies with whites, and when General George Harries refused to enroll any of the all-Negro Washington Cadet Corps in the District regiment sent to Cuba in 1898.[10]

The collapse of earlier hopes for political and legal equality might have distressed Negroes less had their economic opportunities widened consistently. With the District's colored population growing from the 57,000 of 1880 to 90,000 twenty years later, Negroes trained in the professions seemingly should have found abundant openings. Besides several hundred colored teachers, Washington in the 1890's had about one hundred qualified physicians, somewhat fewer dentists, over ninety ministers, and scores of lawyers. Negro doctors, barred from the District Medical Society, formed the Medico-Chirurgical Society in 1884, the first Negro medical association in the United States. But except for the pastors, including those without much schooling, colored professional men faced hard sledding. About ten applicants for every teaching post in the school system created intense competition. Relatively few Negroes could afford to pay doctors', dentists', and lawyers' fees no matter how modest, and a discouragingly large proportion of the colored people of means preferred to deal with white men. The *Colored American*, in 1898 the *Bee*'s new competitor, observed that colored people in Washington went to a colored doctor "only when we wish to run a bill we do not intend to pay." Dozens of law-

[9] Laurence John Wesley Hayes, *The Negro Federal Government Worker, A Study of His Classification Status in the District of Columbia, 1883-1938*, pp. 22-25 (hereafter cited as Hayes, *Negro Govt Worker*); Cleveland *Leader*, 7 Nov 1884; *Nation*, xcvii, 114; *Sentinel*, 10 Apr 1880; *Advocate*, 3 Dec 1881; *Bee*, 1882-1901; *Star*, 9 May 1883, 2 Feb 1887; Ingle, *The Negro in D.C.*, pp. 48-49; Rpt Sec/Int, 1895, p. 724, Ser 3383; Summers, ed., *The Cabinet Diary of William L. Wilson*, p. 96.

[10] Capt. George W. Evans, "The Militia of the District of Columbia," CHS *Rec*, xxviii, 95-105; *Bee*, 3 Jul 1897, 13 Jan 1900.

yers, in a frantic scramble to find clients, hawked their services about the Police Court.

Colored business enterprises also suffered from Negroes' reluctance to patronize men of their own race. The failure of the Freedmen's Bank in 1874, although due primarily to white exploitation, had shattered confidence in their capacity to handle finances. A colored savings bank opened in 1888 increased the list of its depositors yearly, but for commercial purposes Negroes used white banks. As in other American cities, Negro merchants had enormous difficulty in competing with white for the colored trade and could rarely cater successfully to both races.[11] The career of John A. Gray, a restaurant owner, illustrates some of the hazards. "He kept one of the first houses in the city," reported the *Bee*. "He first opened it for white people and was having a success until the Negroes kept clamoring for a respectable place to go. He opened his house to the high-toned colored people and in less than a year they broke him up." Undeterred by the refusal of white merchants to employ Negro help, colored families persisted in trading at white shops. Perhaps credit was easier there or the selection of goods better, but a pettier motive, some Negroes believed, was more basic: in the city's colored business world the "great impediment has been jealousy and a dislike to see each other succeed."

Caterers were one of the few groups able to avoid the complications of seeking mixed or purely colored patronage, for the business, unique to Washington, depended solely upon a white clientele. Unlike the modern term, catering in the capital

[11] *Colored American*, 14 May 1898; W. Montague Cobb, "Washington, D.C.," in Dietrich C. Reitzes, *Negroes and Medicine*, pp. 193-94; Walter L. Fleming, *The Freedmen's Savings Bank*, pp. 53-99, 129-30; W. E. B. DuBois, ed., *The Negro in Business, The Report of the Fourth Conference for the Study of the Negro Problems, held at Atlanta University*, May 30-31, 1899, pp. 13, 28-29, 56-61 (hereafter the special studies and the reports of the proceedings of the conferences sponsored by Atlanta University every May from 1896 to 1900 are cited only by title, conference number, and date); *Advocate*, 30 Aug 1879; *Bee*, 31 Jul 1886; Ingle, *The Negro in D.C.*, pp. 91-92; John H. Harmon, Arnett G. Lindsay, and Carter G. Woodson, *The Negro as a Businessman*, pp. 34, 51-55.

of the 1880's and 1890's meant delivering hot meals twice a day to people living in rented rooms who wished to escape from the restaurant or dismal boardinghouse table by breakfasting and dining in their rooms. The best caterers charged from $25 to $30 a month per person. Those with fast teams of horses could deliver well-cooked dishes in the specially constructed double-racked tin containers before the food cooled. A skillful caterer with a hundred clients could clear a considerable sum in a year, despite the decline of his business in the months between congressional sessions. Since the enterprise, however profitable, smacked of menial service, white men rarely competed.

A few Negroes, it is true, made money in fields considered wholly dignified, notably real estate, building, and selling life insurance or shares in benefit and relief associations. James Wormley, owner of the famous Wormley House, left an estate of over $100,000; his sons, after nearly doubling their inheritance, so gossip said, by betting on President Harrison's election in 1888, put the family fortune into the construction business. Negroes who had owned local real estate before the war and had hung on to it through the disasters of the Board of Public Works era and the Freedmen's Bank failure might be very well off indeed, although the number whose holdings were ever extensive was certainly small. District Tax Collector John F. Cook, himself said to be the largest taxpayer of his race, reported in 1887 two local colored men worth $100,000, two worth $75,000, a flour merchant worth $50,000, and some forty men with property valued at a figure between $10,000 and $25,000.[12]

While the lack of racial solidarity hurt the Negro professions and business enterprises, the increasing hostility of white workingmen and the bars erected by labor organizations severely

[12] *Bee*, 22 Oct 1887, 17 Nov 1888, 12 Jan 1889, 12 Jul 1890; Cleveland *Leader*, 5 Jan, 7 Apr 1883; *Star*, 23 Oct 1884, 18 Apr 1926; Simmons, *Men of Mark*, pp. 249-50; Harmon et al., *Negro as Businessman*, p. 91.

handicapped the lower-class Negro. An analysis of 1881 attributed the troubles of Philadelphia's colored workmen to foreign immigrants: "Southern cities were built by colored mechanical labor. In this city twenty years before the late war, it was no unusual thing to find a majority of colored mechanics engaged in all the leading trades. . . . But Irish emigration was destined to strike a blow at the colored mechanic, from which it will take years for him to recover." Negroes in Washington looked upon Irishmen as enemies, but foreign immigrants in the capital were too few in the last decades of the century to be a determining factor in the local labor market.

In the early eighties the local carpenters' union drew no official color line, and one of the two mechanics' unions had mixed membership, but white mechanics made life for their colored fellows miserable in a dozen minor ways, and, by refusing to accept colored apprentices, the unions gradually excluded all Negroes. A colored lodge of the Knights of Labor, organized in 1884 as the Thad Stevens Assembly, fell apart even before the Haymarket tragedy in Chicago two years later undermined the national brotherhood. In 1886 a Negro waiters' union appeared, but within a decade colored men found that occupations "which by common consent were regarded as belonging to them, such as waiters and the like, are now being monopolized by the whites." Booker T. Washington's exhortations to Negroes to think less about political equality and more about acquiring competence as workers fell on sterile soil in the District; here economic independence appeared to be unattainable merely by hard work.[13]

To combat trade union discrimination, "the curse of which has more than any other, fettered the energies of the colored people," and to recapture civil rights, non-segregated schools seemed to some Negroes the first essential; only early association of the races would induce a "more generous spirit" in white

[13] *Advocate*, 21 Apr 1882; *Bee*, 1 Jan 1897, 8 Oct 1898; *Star*, 26 Jul 1885; Simmons, *Men of Mark*, pp. 270-72; *Sentinel*, 30 Mar 1889.

men. Unfortunately for the proponents of mixed schools, the opposition of other Negroes strengthened as the colored school system expanded and the number of teaching posts grew. The opening of a colored high school in 1878, two years before a white high school was established, weakened the integrationists' contention that the white schools invariably provided a quality of education superior to anything available in the colored schools. In actuality the Miner Fund, not tax money, supported the colored high school as well as the Negro normal school. The question of mixed schools came to the fore in 1881 and 1882 when the school trustees allowed two or three very light colored children to attend white schools. While Negro advocates of separate systems insisted that more money and Negro trustees less prone to toady to whites and less ready to show favoritism would correct every shortcoming in the colored schools, the *Star* declared school integration a "purely sentimental" notion:

"There is a small sprinkling of colored children in the white schools, but for the most part the colored people prefer to have their separate school organization with a superintendent and teachers of their own race; just as they prefer to maintain their own . . . benevolent and social associations. The colored schools get their full share of school moneys; and in proportion to numbers are supplied with better school accommodations than the whites. For various reasons the colored children get on better in schools of their own. One is that they are spared the disadvantageous competition with white children of their own age who have had greater opportunities at home and elsewhere for advancement in their studies. Again were the schools to be merged it would necessarily throw 165 colored teachers out of employment, as it could not be expected that the white school population of the District—outnumbering the colored about two to one—should give up their teachers to make room for colored teachers."

". . . Better let well enough alone."[14]

The comparative census figures on adults unable to write suggest the handicap under which the children of hundreds of Negro parents labored:

	1880	*1890*	*1900*
White	5.4	2.67	1.86
Colored	59.3	39.4	30.47

From the mid-1880's onward one group of colored people argued that vocational training was a wiser goal for the Negro schools than a more literary education; a curriculum like that of the white schools should wait until the economic level of the average colored family had risen enough to enable Negro children to benefit from academic courses. In the 1890's Booker T. Washington, by then head of Tuskegee Institute in Alabama, began to popularize that thesis among white people who saw in it a way to create a permanent, docile working class. In Washington dissidents, although believing the plan equivalent to giving up the fight for racial equality and accepting a position of inferiority for decades to come, gradually abandoned the campaign for integrated schools. After 1900 that issue dropped out of sight for forty years.

Meanwhile Negroes, anxious to develop an independent school system as good in every particular as the white, vigilantly watched the school board, particularly its colored members. Salaries were nearly 10 percent lower and teaching loads heavier in the colored than in the white schools. At an annual salary of $750 a colored high school teacher earned $74.54 less than his white counterpart, and the differential for grammar and primary grade teachers was as great or greater. In 1890, white classes averaged forty-one children to a teacher, the colored forty-seven. Otherwise the two systems ran generally

[14] *Advocate*, 25 Feb 1882; *Star*, 14 Sep 1881, 22 Feb 1882; *Bee*, 30 Dec 1882; *Rpt School Trustees*, pp. 29, 33, 67.

parallel. In spite of Negro complaints about favoritism in teaching appointments and incompetence on the part of George F. Cook, superintendent since 1870, the Negro schools made a good showing. Somewhat lower standards obtained in the colored grade schools than in the white, but in examinations given all high school students in 1899, the colored high school scored higher than either the Eastern or the Western High Schools. Still when Congress reorganized the entire system in 1900, most Negroes evidently concluded their schools would gain more in efficiency than they lost in prestige by having a white superintendent put above the colored assistant superintendent.[15]

Unhappily, relatively few Negro children stayed in school beyond the fourth grade, and of those who finished the eighth grade, still fewer, especially of the boys, went on. "There are inducements to keep white children in the white High School," remarked the *Bee*. "Our colored citizens should see to it that some effort be made to keep their boys in the schools." Quite apart from their poverty, the seeming futility of acquiring more than an acquaintance with the three R's deterred many Negro families from making the effort. They saw well-educated girls, barred from suitable occupations by an inflexible caste system, drift into the life of the *demi-monde* and Negro college graduates forced for want of something better to take jobs as waiters and hotel bell boys. It is not surprising that 325 of the 367 students at Howard University in 1898 were enrolled in its secondary school; as none of the 42 taking the college course

[15] Williston Lofton, "The Development of Public Education for Negroes in Washington, D.C., A Study of Separate but Equal Accommodations," pp. 164-87 (dissertation, American Univ, hereafter cited as Lofton, "Separate but Equal"); *Tenth U.S. Census*, 1880, *Population*, pp. 916-25; *Twelfth U.S. Census*, 1900, *Population*, II, Pt II, 22-23, 424-25, 434-35; *Bee*, 11 Feb 1888, 20 Aug 1897; ptns, S54A-J19, n.d., S56A-J14, 6 Apr 1900; *Rpts School Trustees*, 1890, 1892, pp. 153-202, 1899, pp. 273-97; S Rpt 711, 56C, 1S, pp. 1-4, 125-26, 195-96, 230-31, 296-97, and Supplemental Rpt, Pt 2, p. 14, Ser 3889; Booker T. Washington, *Up From Slavery*, p. 91; Ingle, *The Negro in D.C.*, pp. 34-37, 103.

were white men, the original ideal of a bi-racial institution vanished.[16]

Long before the Negro intelligentsia saw that public schooling in itself was unlikely to elevate greatly the general level of Negro society, Washington's colored aristocrats had begun to detach themselves from the Negro rank and file; for their own reassurance they must sharpen Negro class distinctions whether or not white people recognized them. Educated colored men in other cities also defended the thesis that the social equality of all Negroes was a concept destructive to racial progress. In 1880 a letter to the *Advocate* declared that Frederick Douglass, John F. Cook, and others to whom the community had once looked for leadership "have shown conclusively how little they care whether other colored men sink, as long as they swim." Calvin Chase of the *Bee*, not himself one of Washington's "first families" but occupying a place in the upper stratum of the rank just below, alternately defended the "exclusive set" and attacked it for a snobbery that he believed originated in the determination of the Lotus Club after 1863 to force contrabands to keep to themselves. Later societies heightened that snobbery. "The Monday Night Literary is a cast organization," wrote Chase. "There is more intelligence excluded than there is in the association . . . there are few holding clerkships who belong." Members had ceased to give New Year's Day receptions because they did not want to meet "objectionable upstarts."

The Negro press repeatedly insisted "There is more discrimination among the colored people than there is among the white against the colored." A petition complained to Congress in 1896 that only daughters of "the favored few" were admitted to the colored normal school. "The would-be leaders . . . John

[16] *Rpts School Trustees*, 1880, p. 152, 1886, p. 13, 1892, p. 17; *Rpt B of Education of the District of Columbia*, 1901, pp. 140-43 (hereafter cited as *Rpt B/Ed*); *Bee*, 14 May 1887; W. E. B. DuBois, ed., *The College-Bred Negro*, (Fifth Atlanta Conference, 1900), p. 16.

M. Langston excepted, have taken no interest in the general welfare of the masses of our people; political office by all means, after that, their wish is total exclusion from their race and to be white." Yet most of that small group composing the highest circle of Negro society were indeed nearly white, and many of them had personal distinction as scholars, office-holders, and professional men. They were certainly culturally closer to the white community than to the lower-class Negro. In displaying an ungenerous attitude toward their inferiors, they were behaving little differently from most self-made white men who reached positions of eminence in the face of enormous obstacles.[17]

The *Sentinel*, Washington's German-American newspaper edited by a former abolitionist, presented the tolerant white man's view of the Negro's position in 1883: "The colored people of Washington enjoy all the social and political rights that law can give them, without protest and without annoyance. The public conveyances are open to them, and the theatres, the jury box, the spoils of party power are theirs. Many of these men are wealthy. . . .

"But the color line is rigidly drawn in what is known as society. Wealth, learning, official place, give no colored family the right or privilege of entering the best or the commonest white society on terms of equality or endurance. In this respect the colored race lives as separate and exclusive a life as in the days of slavery, and as a drop of African blood was once held to make a man a negro, so now it taints him and makes an immutable barrier against social recognition.

"[Ex-Senator] Blanche K. Bruce, [formerly of Mississippi but now Washington's leading Negro,] lives in a handsome house that he owns on M Street. It is richly furnished . . . Mrs.

[17] *Advocate*, 4 Dec 1880; *Star*, 11 May 1880; *Bee*, 10 May 1884, 18 Sep 1886, 18 Sep 1887; ptn, H54A-H7.6, 2 Jun 1896; see cuts accompanying the articles on Washington Negroes in Simmons, *Men of Mark*; Richard Bardolph, "The Distinguished Negro in America, 1770-1936," *American Historical Review*, LX, 527-47.

Bruce is a handsome woman, with not a suggestion of her race in her face, and whose manners are regarded as the consummation of ease, grace and courtesy. She dresses as richly and handsomely as any woman in the city. In official circles Mr. Bruce is received in courtesy and as a political equal, but there the line is drawn."

Envious Negroes, averred the *Sentinel*, considered this exclusive set not good enough for whites and too good for its own race, but the next lower rank of Negro society was equally detached from the class below. Government clerks formed the basis of the second stratum. "They are well dressed, seem to prosper and are happy. For the great bulk of the colored population—the servants, laborers and the poor—they have sympathy, but have no more social relations than a white family would." Those at the base of the social pyramid "in the main are thriftless, living from hand to mouth; happy if they do nothing, happy if they get a job. Their social instincts are gratified by the organization and maintenance of societies of all sorts, benevolent, patriotic, social and economic. There are nearly one thousand of these organizations, supported almost entirely by the laboring colored people."[18]

That portrayal, if in any degree fitting the Washington of 1883, was too simple and too cheerful in tone to describe the Negro community a decade or more later. Before the end of the century the class structure resembled a pyramid less than a truncated cone capped by a needle. From the strata below, the Negroes who danced on the point of the needle appeared to be, not angels, but scarcely more accessible than heavenly creatures. Of the District's 700 octoroons and 1,100 quadroons, those who had, in addition to light color, the qualifications of antiquity of family, money, education, and honorable occupation belonged to the aristocracy; "honorable occupations" included the professions, political posts of more than trivial importance, banking, real estate brokerage, and businesses not

[18] *Sentinel*, 22 Dec 1883.

tinged with menial service. Washington's Negro "Four Hundred," as the *Bee* dubbed the aristocrats, probably numbered not more than sixty or seventy families.

The middle class in the 1890's apparently derived mainly from the District's 18,000 mulattoes. Only less fully than the Four Hundred with their very light skins and generally non-Negroid features were the mulattoes conscious of gradations of color: those of "doe-nut or ginger-cake color . . . said those blacker than themselves should be ignored." Yet the relative flexibility of the middle class permitted the occasional acceptance of exceptionally able, ambitious, full-blooded Negroes. Minor government employees still formed the core of this group, but even a government clerk, if a newcomer to the city, could not hope for immediate entree to upper-middle-class circles. Whether the barber, the caterer, the livery-stable man, the oyster-house owner, or the proprietor of any other small business was acknowledged as upper or lower middle class evidently depended upon the extent of his business success as well as his nativity and his complexion. Warnings frequently appeared in the *Bee* about unsuitable marriages between scions of established families and those of doubtful antecedents who wormed their way into the "social circle" by joining a "tony" church, by enrolling for a few weeks in one of Howard University's professional schools, or by making a specious show of great wealth. Differentiations among the "masses," that is, chiefly the city's thousands of full-blooded Negroes, were not a topic the press bothered to explore.[19]

From 1884 to 1898 Washington's Negro press was the *Bee*. It prided itself on its sting aimed at the shoddy and evil. Yet back-biting and destructive jealousy of one class and one Negro toward another became a striking feature of the paper. Let anyone get his head ever so little above his associates, and his

[19] *Bee*, 30 May 1885, 8 Jun 1889; W. E. B. DuBois, ed., *The Negro in Business* (Fourth Atlanta Conference, 1899), pp. 13, 19-20; *Eleventh U.S. Census*, 1890, *Population*, I, 397.

individual accomplishments and former services were forgotten in vitriolic attacks upon his real or imagined self-seeking. Instead of applauding a colored man who won recognition, especially from whites, his fellows at once set to work to belittle him and accuse him of sycophancy and putting on airs. The *New National Era* had eschewed that line, and the *Peoples Advocate*, which ceased publication in 1884, pursued it very little. The *Bee*, without wholly abandoning a crusading point of view, indulged in more sweeping condemnations of individual Negroes and organizations the longer it ran. Perhaps its publisher found it sold better when it concentrated upon scandal and malicious gossip. A comment on a problem affecting Washington as a whole was a rarity.

Booker T. Washington, after some months at the Baptist Wayland Seminary in 1878-1879, decided that Washington was no place for a Negro who wished to dedicate his life to helping his race; here false standards and selfishness predominated. Among immigrant minorities and among the Jews in the District, a sense of group solidarity produced mutual helpfulness. Not so among Negroes. The pressures of caste which kept the gifted colored man from going as far as his talents would otherwise permit split colored Washington into jealously competing fragments, with results damaging to every Negro. Congress, noted a Philadelphia journal, was naturally disinclined to do anything for Washington's colored people, because their squabbling made them ridiculous: rivals claimed "that this one's father was a horse thief, that one doesn't know who his father was, another is too black, another is too light and therefore does not represent the race, another does not belong to the best families and still another is an interloper." Bitterly the *Bee* asked in 1887: "Who of our so called colored representative men can point to a single thing of a public character beneficial to the colored people established and fostered by them? To their shame and to the humiliation of the race the record is a blank, and with all our boast about our wealthy . . . men the race is dependent upon the charity of whites." Yet if "you talk to our people about an excursion down the river in August, or a cake walk in December, they will listen to you and will no doubt purchase several tickets." And a large part of the funds of the mutual benefit societies, in which much of the social life of working-class Negroes centered, went for elaborate funerals rather than help for the living.[20]

The assertion that well-to-do Negroes never lifted finger for the needy was, of course, an exaggeration. John F. Cook, for years an active member of the citizens' relief committee, was also a trustee of the Home for Destitute Colored Women and Children, while a dozen public-spirited Negro women served on the board of manageresses. The woman who founded the Home for Friendless Girls also organized an Aid Society at the Berean Baptist Church. About the same time, two or three Negro women opened a free kindergarten and day nursery for the children of working mothers, and in the 1890's the newly organized Colored Women's League expanded the program. Although Alexander Crummel, rector of St. Luke's Episcopal Church, was more concerned with developing character in his people than with their material progress, he raised a large sum of money for the Episcopal Freedmen's Aid Society by sale of copies of one of his speeches. In 1887 the Colored Baptist Home Mission Society was "putting shoes on the feet of the poor, clothing on them, and giving immediate aid," but $95.72 represented the total sum collected in the course of several months from Washington's thirty-five colored Baptist churches and the members of the society.

During the worst of the depression of the nineties Negro volunteers worked with the Associated Charities, and the "Hill

[20] Jesse Lawson to Booker T. Washington, 6 May 1902, Booker T. Washington Mss (L.C.); Washington, *Up From Slavery*, pp. 88-90; *Congressional Globe*, 41C, 2S, p. 842; Ingle, *The Negro in D.C.*, p. 109; Philadelphia *Odd Fellows Journal* quoted in *Bee*, 23 Feb 1901; *Bee*, 15 Jan 1887, 12 Nov 1898.

Group" on 6th Street, moved by the suffering of the poor at the foot of the hill, distributed food and fuel in that neighborhood. Probably a good many relatively well-to-do individuals gave help without working through any organization, just as desperately poor Negro families often took care of the children of even poorer neighbors. From a mother-child center, opened in 1895, came the Southwest Social Settlement, and that year Miss Amanda Bowen, assisted by funds from the Metropolitan African Methodist Episcopal Church, launched the Sojourner Truth Home for Working Girls. Three years later the Colored Women's League undertook "Rescue Work" among young women. A study prepared for a conference on Negro problems held in Atlanta in 1898 listed thirty-eight Negro churches in Washington which spent $4,300 for charity, contributed to the support of eighty-three benevolent and missionary societies, and supplied twelve workers in the slums and the jail. The individual generosity of Professor William Hart of Howard University made possible the Hart Farm School for colored boys. And in 1900 a colored woman started the Stoddard Baptist Home for aged Negroes.

Yet when everything was added together, the record of Negro charities while not "blank" was distinctly thin, thinner than during the Civil War and Reconstruction, if accounts of that period be trustworthy. The impressively long list of welfare projects at the end of the century was deceptive, for most of the undertakings were small-scale and short-lived unless white people came to the rescue. And the uncooperativeness of well-to-do Negroes chilled the ardor of white philanthropists. "We all know," a white woman told a congressional committee, "that a good deal of what was good in the race has gone and they are now in a state of transition." What exasperated whites failed to take into account was that the social pressures that fostered philanthropy in the white community could not operate effectively among people who felt their precarious position in the city's over-all social structure progressively and inescapably weakening further. And white people probably attributed larger resources to prosperous Negroes than they actually had.[21]

Negro pastors and Negro churches, which in earlier years had not only provided spiritual leadership but taken an active part in lightening parishioners' material distress, apparently lost sight of both goals as congregations vied with each other in building big, costly edifices. Between the worldliness of the sophisticated churches and the excessive otherworldiness of those wedded to a somewhat primitive, highly emotional religion teaching that only heaven or hell in the hereafter mattered, the efforts of the handful of selfless civic-minded Negroes met with defeat. Proposals to turn over to the National Colored Home the proceeds of Emancipation Day celebrations fizzled because the money from ticket sales went into the pockets of "sharks" or for the rental and elaborate decoration of floats for the parades. Lack of funds threatened to close the Sojourner Truth Home three years after it opened. A small indebtedness, which modest gifts could have wiped out, shut down the colored YMCA. According to one critic of his people, when Negroes contributed to any good works their motive was notoriety, not Christian charity. Such behavior was characteristic of the *nouveaux riches* the world over, but the disturbing fact remained that the generosity that had once distinguished Washington's upper-class Negro society was rarely in evidence at the end of the century.[22]

[21] Katherine Hosmer, "What Women Have Done in Washington City Affairs," *Municipal Affairs*, II, 514; W. E. B. DuBois, ed., *Some Efforts of Negroes for Their Own Social Betterment* (3rd Atlanta Conference, 1897), pp. 14, 36-37, 57-59; *Bee*, 14 May 1887; Cleveland *Leader*, 29 Feb 1884; *Advocate*, 5 Feb, 20 Nov 1881; Ch Hrgs, p. 56, Ser 3565; *Anl Rpt of the Home for Destitute Colored Women and Children*, 1891; Inabel Lindsay, "Participation of Negroes in the Establishment of Welfare Services, 1865-1900, with special reference to the District of Columbia, Maryland and Virginia," pp. 124, 129-30, 137-55, 159, 164, 170-73 (dissertation, Univ. of Pittsburgh, hereafter cited as Lindsay, "Negro Welfare Services").

[22] Lindsay, "Negro Welfare Services," pp. 105-08, 112, 115-18, 133; *Advocate*, 5 Apr 1884; *Bee*, 1887-1901; Ingle, *The Negro in D.C.*, pp. 95-100, 107; Carter G. Woodson, *The History of the Negro Church*, pp. 224-30.

Negroes with means could scarcely plead ignorance of the want existing about them, for destitution was nearly as widespread as in post Civil War years. In the early nineties, amidst the enormous prosperity of much of the city, 16,000 persons, the great majority of them colored, were without visible means of support; in 1870 the number had been little greater. Until 1897 the police were responsible for reporting cases of destitution and illness and for distributing relief, but although Negro distrust of the police was an obstacle, the health department defended the system on the grounds that it hastened investigations of complaints and relieved the doctors of "the untidy class," presumably malingerers. The police found Negro families eking out existence by picking spoiled food from garbage cans and dumps. Households in the Negro slums were ridden with illness; a report of 1891 described a one-room shanty in which beside a dead infant lay five adults and six children stricken with influenza. Four-fifths of the patients at the Freedmen's Hospital were indigent Negroes; of the 17,048 persons to whom the District's seven public dispensaries ministered in 1891, over 12,000 were colored. The most conscientious physician could do little more than palliate momentarily the miseries he encountered daily.

In twenty years the colored death rate dropped to 28.12 per thousand from the 40.78 of 1876, but Negro mortality always greatly exceeded and in most years was double that of whites. Infant mortality, high for whites, ran in 1890 to 338.5 per thousand for Negroes and in 1900 to 317. The occasional charge that Negro "ignorance and indifference" was to blame was a part-truth. A larger cause, the health officer noted, was the foulness of the alley tenements in which thousands of Negroes lived.[23]

[23] *Star*, 15 Mar 1882; Comrs Rpts, 1887, pp. 16-17, 1889, p. 14, 1890, pp. 639, 756-57, 845-47, 1895, pp. 9-13; H Ex Doc 1, 51C, 1S, p. 94; *Chronicle*, 11 Sep 1899; *Eleventh U.S. Census*, 1890, *Population*, I, Pt. II, 20; *Twelfth Census*, 1900, *Population*, Pt. II, 22; W. E. B. DuBois, ed., *Mortality among Negroes in Cities* (1st Atlanta Conference, 1896), pp. 8, 18-19, 20-28.

Neither poverty nor illness, however, prevented Negroes from enjoying themselves at times. The gift of laughter, that capacity to create and delight in moments of gaiety in the midst of suffering and want, is a Negro characteristic that down to the present day confuses and baffles white people. As W. E. B. DuBois sardonically put it, "that we do submit to life as it is and yet laugh and dance and dream is but another proof that we are idiots." With a light-heartedness that sober-sided white Washingtonians called irresponsible, colored families not always able to feed themselves joined in church sociables and in club and fraternal society celebrations. The lower down the economic ladder, the more pleasure members of a society apparently took in giving it a high-sounding name, such as "Grand Ancient Order of the Sons and Daughters and Brothers and Sisters of Moses of the USA and the World at Large." A funeral, always an occasion, usually called for lavish spending on carriages and clothes. Noisy picnics complete with bands to furnish music took place on Sundays, in the 1880's frequently at the "Manor," once the John P. Van Ness house and grounds, where the National Red Cross Headquarters now stand; when a proprietor of the beer hall there closed the place in 1887, colored picnickers were allowed to use the Schuetzenverein park. Mutual benefit societies arranged excursions down the Potomac until the steamboat lines, adopting the pretext that every boat was already chartered, refused to sell Negroes tickets.

For lower-class Negroes the great event of the year was the annual District Emancipation Day parade on April 16th. Every colored organization in the District usually took part. Despite a downpour of rain, in 1883 the procession was a mile and a half long; among the scores of societies parading in dress array were the Chaldeans, the Knights of Moses, the Osceolas, the Galilean Fishermen, the Sons and Daughters of Samaris, the Solid Yantics, the Lively Eights, and the Celestial Golden Links. White onlookers, watching the elaborately decorated floats and the thousands of Negroes marching on foot to the accompaniment of twelve brass bands, were impressed, amused, or indignant at the money poured into the display. Sophisticated Negroes sensitive to white ridicule protested now and again that a church service would mark the day more fittingly. "The thought is already gaining ground," wrote Frederick Douglass in 1886, "that tinsel show, gaudy display and straggling processions, which empty the alleys and dark places of our city into the broad day-light of our thronged streets and avenues, thus thrusting upon the public view a vastly undue proportion of the most unfortunate, unimproved, and unprogressive class of the colored people, and thereby inviting public disgust and contempt, and repelling the more thrifty and self-respecting among us, is a positive hurt to the whole colored population of this city. These annual celebrations of ours . . . should bring into notice the very best elements of our colored population." But until the school board voted in 1899 not to dismiss the colored schools for the day, the parade on the 16th of April was more important to most of colored Washington than the 4th of July and Christmas and New Year's combined.[24]

Few middle-class Negroes were in a position to carp at the extravagances of their social inferiors, for display was an essential ingredient in most of their own pleasures. Below the thin top crust all Negro society was as intent upon keeping up with the Joneses as were ambitious, socially insecure whites. Booker T. Washington spoke with dismay of seeing "young colored men who were not earning more than four dollars a week spend two dollars or more for a buggy on Sunday to ride up and down Pennsylvania Avenue in, in order that they might try to convince the world that they were worth thousands." Plug-hatted "dudes" carrying canes swaggered about the streets

[24] W. E. B. DuBois, *Dusk of Dawn*, p. 147; Ingle, *The Negro in D.C.*, p. 106; Cleveland *Leader*, 19 Apr 1883, 28 Sep 1884; *Advocate*, 28 Apr 1882; *Bee*, 21 Apr 1883, 24 Mar 1888.

to impress their fellows. Clothes were all-important. At a club party "young gentlemen and ladies in and just leaving their teens, assembled, dressed in full reception style, the young gents in full dress suit, the ladies in every ornamentation art or fancy could give. One lady of family remarked, 'they are all plebians, too!'" Plebeians as well as aristocrats still attended the theatre occasionally, but, as time went on, evening parties at home or concerts at the churches became a more customary form of entertainment. Athletics had not yet begun to loom large, although Negro bicycle clubs appeared in the eighties, and in the nineties colored cyclists held races at the Park Cycle Track.

After the Lotus Club disappeared, for several years the Monday Night Literary Society embraced the most distinguished of the Negro intelligentsia. Later the Bethel Literary and Historical Society, founded in 1881 by Bishop Payne of the Metropolitan Methodist Episcopal Church, overshadowed the older clubs. The younger not only explored literature and philosophy but, more important, supplied the principal forum for enlightened discussion of race problems; the most notable colored men in America addressed the group. Business and professional men also valued membership in the Cosmas Club, organized in 1900. If the choral groups were less exclusive than the literary societies, the Treble Clef Club was as selective as the white Friday Morning Music Club and undertook equally ambitious programs.

The Negro newspapers gave a great deal of space to high-class weddings; the list of presents with the donors' name attached might fill over a column. The gowns, "a Worth dress of canary silk," or a "crimson velvet entrainee," were described in the same detail with which white society reporters wrote of the costumes at White House receptions. Even after discounting the braggadocio of the Negro press, the evidences of Negro wealth were startling—beautiful jewelry, handsome clothes, well-furnished houses tended by Negro servants, and expensive summer holidays. Every June the exodus began with "Saratoga trunks" packed for Newport, Harpers Ferry, and Cape May. In 1886 the *Bee* reported: "Mr. Richard S. Locke of Washington who spends his summers at Nonquitt Beach [Massachusetts] has sold his beautiful yacht; Mr. Locke is the only gentleman of color that ever owned a yacht at Nonquitt." By and large, the higher a Negro's social standing, the more exactly his diversions corresponded to those of white people of similar position.[25]

At the opening of the twentieth century Washington Negroes whose memory stretched back into the late 1860's had no cause for optimism. Since the days when colored men had shared in governing the city and the territory and the wall of caste had appeared to be crumbling, their bright prospects had darkened and then vanished in the shadows of a new and mounting racism. Frederick Douglass and his associates of the *New National Era* had marked 1870 as the high point for the Negro community and saw the shrinkage of its horizons as beginning with the creation of the territorial government. Witnessing the inexorable narrowing of their world after 1874, the wisest colored people doubtless knew that the splintering into mutually jealous groups had further reduced the elbow room for all contestants and had multiplied the difficulties of combatting white prejudice. Washington's revived racism was the harder to fight because the white community, increasingly oblivious to the existence of any other, recognized no opponent. "As long as the flat surface of color remained the lone dimension of a human being," from the standpoint of a white man a duel was impossible for lack of a human adversary. The few white Washingtonians who admitted that the city contained Negro citizens

[25] Cleveland *Leader*, 7 Apr 1884; Washington, *Up From Slavery*, pp. 88-89; *Advocate*, 1880-1884; *Bee*, Apr 1883 and 1884-1901; Francis Cardozo, Jr., to Booker T. Washington, 8 Aug 1902, Booker T. Washington Mss (L.C.); *New National Era*, 25 Jun 1874; Mrs. E. T. Williston, "History of the Treble Clef" appended to program, *Treble Clef Club*, 16 May 1923 (Music Div., L.C.); *Post*, 3 Aug 1902.

were prone to dismiss the possibility of any injustice by declaring the capital "the colored man's paradise."

The very light-colored Negro with three-fourths or seven-eighths white blood might find an answer for himself by contriving to pass permanently into the ranks of whites. Miscegenation, not unlawful in the District of Columbia and perhaps far more common than most people realized, eased the process for the stranger, but for a member of any well-known local family passing was difficult. In any case, it left the larger problem unsolved: how Negroes were to live with dignity in a white world. Frederick Douglass speaking in 1883 urged assimilation rather than isolation; he himself married a white woman a few months later, but presumably he was advocating the ideal of social rather than biological assimilation. Voluntary isolation might protect individuals from some humiliations but would scarcely ensure economic progress for the race. Preoccupation with these questions stripped colored Washington of interest in the well-being of the city as a whole.[26]

In 1901 for white Washingtonians the future stretched out in an ever-widening vista of prosperity and orderly living in a beautiful city whose national and world importance could only expand. The difference between that picture and what perceptive Negroes could envisage for their own people was heightened by the contrasts between their status then and that of a quarter century before. True, some families had made money in the interval, and others had achieved a modicum of financial security. Those who held government clerkships, while perpetually fearful for their tenure in office, usually enjoyed civil, if impersonal, treatment. Moreover, a careful unobtrusiveness permitted well-dressed Negroes to hover in the background at the reception celebrating Washington's centennial. But sensitive men and women found that concession a poor substitute

[26] *Advocate*, 5 Jun 1880; *Bee*, 18 Sep, 2 Oct 1886, 15 Dec 1900; *New National Era*, 20 Feb 1873; Murray, *Proud Shoes*, p. 88; *Star*, 17 Apr 1883.

for friendliness. Fortunately they could not foresee that events in the next fifteen years would force colored aristocrats and middle-class Negoes into a psychological ghetto along with irresponsible blacks.

While the most easily observed factor in the progressive disintegration of Washington's Negro world was the failure of economic opportunity to keep pace with the growth of the colored population and with the spread of education, that material loss was itself rather a manifestation than a cause of the change. The wealthy Negro knew all too well that financial security provided no safeguard against endless humiliations and frustration. The deterioration of Negro status sprang from a complex of causes, but the common denominator was the steady paring down of incentive. With the dwindling of the attainable external rewards for continuing the struggle, only the strongest individual able to draw upon deep inner resources could withstand the ceaseless battering of his self-respect. That the number of Negroes possessed of such spiritual fortitude would not increase rapidly in the bitter years ahead was a logical development.

CHAPTER VII

THE CITY BEAUTIFUL, 1901-1916

WHEN word reached Washington of President McKinley's assassination in Buffalo in September 1901, Secretary of State John Hay, shocked into immobility, shut himself into the study of his home on Lafayette Square and left his subordinates to notify foreign governments and arrange for the swearing in of Theodore Roosevelt. Yet, if here and there Americans counted the toll of three Presidents shot down in thirty-six years as evidence of national political instability, the vigorous "Teddy" quickly dispelled their fears. Within a matter of days Washington was turning to the future with greater enthusiasm and optimism than ever.

The city had reason to call herself blessed. She was known for her cultivated society. Alone among big American cities she had escaped and would continue to escape the social adjustments of assimilating thousands of non-English-speaking immigrants. The capital in 1901, and indeed in 1910, contained the largest Negro population of any city on earth, but the declining ratio of colored inhabitants to white was reassuring to the handful of whites who were faintly troubled about race relations. For most of white Washington, colored Washington existed but was of no real significance. The meagreness of industry in the city spared her the afflictions of more or less open warfare between labor and capital; her working classes were not subject to conditions such as Upton Sinclair would shortly portray in *The Jungle* describing Chicago's stockyards. While sensitive citizens realized that Washington's alleys were the local counterpart of the slums of New York and Chicago, the reform spirit that had stirred in the city since the late 1890's encouraged faith in the community's capacity to redeem those evils. President Roosevelt's extraordinary capacity to awaken idealism in young people strengthened Washingtonians' belief that they could make the capital in every respect the model for the rest of the country. In aiming at that goal, they assigned importance to beautification of the city.

When Senator James McMillan persuaded his colleagues to appoint an advisory Park Commission in 1901, the "city beautiful" movement in America was still in infancy. Born at the Columbian Exposition of 1893 in Chicago, where architects and artists had created the exquisite White City from a swamp on the Lake Michigan shore, the movement had a vigorous start. "Make no little plans," Daniel Burnham, chief architect of the Fair, had counselled, and city-dwellers throughout the country, excited over the miracle he and his associates had brought about, adopted the slogan. But the long depression of the 1890's had cooled the first ardor and delayed the appearance of a new profession of city planning. The return of prosperity had reawakened interest in recapturing for future generations neglected natural assets like lake and river fronts and in mapping out the form later city expansion should take. By the turn of the century Boston had purchased 5,000 acres of outlying lake- and wood-land for a vast urban recreation area, and Cleveland had given thought to a municipal lake-front development. But otherwise no big American city had drafted an over-all plan, let alone engaged experts to prepare it.

Upon this body of tentative ideas the proposals of the Park Commission for the national capital burst with powerful effect. It was intensified for Washingtonians by the realization that the plan, if accepted, would reverse the congressional decision of February 1901 to turn over a central piece of the Mall to the Pennsylvania Railroad. Popular magazines publicized the plan by publishing maps, artists' projections of what the national capital would look like, and photographs of the gardens, fountains, and the architectural splendors of European cities which Washington's beauties would one day surpass. The fame of the members appointed to the commission added weight to their recommendations; every American concerned with the "city beautiful" knew of the architects Daniel Burnham and Charles McKim, of the sculptor Augustus St. Gaudens, and of the son of Frederick Law Olmsted, the landscape architect who had laid out New York's Central Park and the grounds of the Capitol. The dimensions of the plan for the public domain in the national capital, moreover, stirred the most sluggish imagination. Americans who had never set foot in Washington or studied L'Enfant's original layout were suddenly eager to see it revived and elaborated. Thus, as the details became known, the project for Washington gave impetus to city planning throughout the country.[1]

When the Park Commission report appeared in January 1902, Washingtonians gratefully scrutinized it. The basic features of the grandiose plan were L'Enfant's with a few modifications and extensions into areas beyond the limits of the eighteenth-century city. Local citizens knew that they had prepared the way for the enlargement by prevailing upon Congress to impose restrictions upon suburban subdivisions, to purchase the land for the zoo and for Rock Creek Park, and to create the Highway Commission in 1893 empowered to supervise the orderly expansion of the city into the county. The publicists of the so-called McMillan plan were unfamiliar with its late nineteenth-century local antecedents; outside the District of Columbia people assumed that Washingtonians had contributed nothing and would merely reap the benefits of other men's aesthetic concepts. In fact magazine articles frequently contrasted the beautiful city that would emerge under Park Commission guidance with the dreary community in which the

[1] S Dis Comee, 58C, 1S, Hearings, "The Mall Parkway," pp. 23-24; Charles Zueblin, "Washington Old and New," *Chautaquan*, XXXIX, 156-67, and *A Decade of Civic Development*, pp. 60-62, 92-99; Frederick Law Olmsted, "Beautifying the City," and Carroll D. Wright, "The Embellishment of Washington," *Independent*, LIV, 1870-77, 2683-85; H. B. F. Macfarland, "The Rebuilding of the National Capital," *The American City*, I, 3; American Institute of Architects, *Of Plans and People*, p. 10; *Rpt B/Tr*, 1902, p. 11.

natives had supposedly been content to live until, in spite of themselves, Boss Shepherd in the 1870's had briefly shaken open their pocketbooks. Washingtonians themselves were unconcerned about who got the credit for the new project as long as it won congressional endorsement.

The members of the Park Commission declared their function to be the preparation of "a well-considered general plan covering the entire District of Columbia," so that when Congress provided for new buildings and parks, it would have a blue print to follow instead of resorting to the former "piecemeal, haphazard and unsatisfactory methods." Forty years later the phrase "general plan covering the entire District of Columbia" would baffle city planners who recognized the comprehensiveness of Burnham's ideas for Chicago, but could find nothing comparable in the scope of the proposals for the capital. Instead of including the business district and residential sections in the Washington plan, Burnham and his three associates viewed their mission as limited to a layout of parks in suitable relationship to public buildings.

For any city, consistency in sticking to a plan was more important, Frederick Olmsted insisted, than the adoption of any particular plan. The placing of the Treasury and the Library of Congress where they interrupted the sweep of Pennsylvania Avenue and the location of the State, War and Navy Building blocking off New York Avenue from the White House were departures from L'Enfant's original layout which the commission felt obliged to accept as irretrievable. It was also patently impossible to move the Washington Monument several hundred feet to the point where L'Enfant's east-west axis intersected the axis running south from the White House. And for unexplained reasons the commission recommended clustering all the executive office buildings about Lafayette Square. Otherwise the proposals were aimed at reviving the essentials of the original plan.

Museums and public galleries should line the Mall above

and below the Smithsonian. Edifices related to the legislative and judicial branches of the government should face upon the Capitol grounds. Restoration of the Bulfinch fence and gates at the foot of the Hill and a waterfall cascading from fountains on the western terrace into a lake at First Street would add to the grandeur of the Capitol itself. At the far end of the Mall a new memorial to Abraham Lincoln should rise, with a bridge across the Potomac beyond leading to Arlington Cemetery. A sunken garden, fountains, and a canal or reflecting pool should give dramatic emphasis to the drop in elevation from the base of the Washington Monument to the temple to Lincoln. Statues commemorating other national heroes should occupy some of the triangles formed by the radial avenues and the gridiron of streets. Fountains as magnificent as those at the Villa d'Este should refresh the eye in a dozen spots.

Remarking that the "dearth of the means of innocent enjoyment of one's leisure hours is remarkable in Washington, the one city in this country where people have the most leisure," the commission proposed to convert the area south of the Washington Monument into recreation grounds. Ball fields could be laid out on the long spit of made land forming one shore of the Washington Channel, while the Tidal Basin above, with its controlled flow of tidal water, "should have the most ample facilities for boating and for wading and swimming in summer, as well for skating in winter." Parks and boulevards like those already marked out on the Highway Commission's maps should encircle the city from Rock Creek to the Soldiers' Home and on to the Anacostia. The swamps bordering the Anacostia should be drained, the upper reaches of the stream made into a "water park" like Belle Isle in Detroit, and eventually the lower stretches treated like the quays of the Seine with a boulevard along the top and stone wharfage at the water's edge. Above Georgetown, drives and lookout points along the palisades of the Potomac up to and including the Great Falls would complete the ring of parks and boulevards.

Since the "government gardens" stretching from the Capitol to the Potomac were a vital element in L'Enfant's scheme, the park commissioners early realized that they must either abandon the Frenchman's plan or persuade the Pennsylvania Railroad to remove its tracks, train sheds, and the heavy-towered stone depot from the Mall. As the law passed in February 1901 had authorized the company to enlarge its holdings there and to erect a huge new station at 6th Street, the task of inducing the corporation to relinquish that valuable land promised to be difficult, if not impossible. In August 1901 Daniel Burnham, at the end of a Park Commission tour of European cities, sought out Alexander Cassatt, president of the railroad, in London. Unexpectedly Cassatt volunteered to withdraw from the Mall and to collaborate in building a Union Station, provided that compensation be made for the cost of the change and that proper approaches be ensured "worthy of the building the railroads propose to erect." That about-face made possible what Senator McMillan blandly called "a modification of the project of last year." The Union Station would "give a complete, adequate, and monumental treatment of the railroad terminals" and make it "in reality the great and impressive vestibule to Washington."[2]

Neither the Senate nor the local public greeted all the recommendations of the commission with undiluted enthusiasm. Some features of the over-all plan seemed visionary, and even with its execution spread out over decades the estimated cost ranging from $200,000,000 to $600,000,000 gave more than one official pause. Objections arose to moving the Botanical Garden from the foot of Capitol Hill, where the greenhouses had stood for sixty-odd years, and to locating new federal office buildings in Lafayette Square. When the commission placed on exhibit at the Corcoran Gallery plaster models of the

[2] S Rpt 166, 57C, 1S, pp. 3-50, 91-97, 105-16, Ser 4258; "The Embellishment of Washington," *Municipal Affairs*, v, 911-16; S Rpt 982, 57C, 1S, Ser 4261; S Doc 220, 57C, 2S, Ser 4430, a compilation of all canal and railroad legislation for the District, 1800-1903.

future city stretching westward from the Library of Congress, residents of east Washington feared they were again to be slighted. In spite of the recommendations for drives along the Potomac palisades and a reservation in the wooded valley of Foundry Run, the Glover-Archbold Park of today, Georgetown proper also received relatively scant attention. For her the most significant proposal lay in the plan to clear the banks of Rock Creek of the rubbish accumulated over the years and to lay a narrow ribbon of parkway along the creek to link Potomac and Rock Creek Parks.

The House as a body completely ignored the plan, for Senator McMillan had made the politically egregious error of not obtaining the concurrence of the lower chamber to the appointment of the commission. Touchy representatives consequently professed to think the work of the Senate's creature no concern of theirs. When "Uncle Joe" Cannon became Speaker in the autumn of 1903, his hostility, Charles McKim explained to the President, presented a major obstacle to obtaining congressional approval of any part of the plan. Furthermore, after Senator McMillan's death in the summer of 1902, none of his colleagues undertook to see that copies of the report received adequate distribution within the government. Inasmuch as the members of the commission had given, gratis, nearly a year of their time, the plan, McKim contended, should at least be considered on its merits. Interested as he was in the "Mall Park," President Roosevelt did not intervene. He appeared to be more anxious to see McKim complete the authorized additions to the White House than to prod Congress about action on the "city beautiful" as a whole. It was the founding of the American Civic Association in 1903 that kept the project alive after the first public excitement had worn thin.[3] Despite congressional delays in implementing the plan,

[3] *Rpts B/Tr*, 1902, pp. 52-53, 1905, pp. 7, 59-60, 1909, p. 30, 1916, p. 62; *Star*, 13 Mar 1903, 1 Jan 1908, 4 Aug, 30 Nov 1909; *Times*, 5 Dec 1906, 1, 2, 14 Nov 1907; *Post*, 30 Jan 1902, 5 Jan 1910; S Doc 89, 58C, 2S, Ser 4588; Frederick Law Olmsted to Daniel Burnham, 10 Aug

Glenn Brown of the American Institute of Architects later averred that it came to exercise "great moral force." When the time came to vote money for new buildings or new bridges or other public works, a majority of Congress accepted the principle if not the details of the Park Commission's recommendations.

Other than purchasing the land for the Union Station on Massachusetts Avenue and voting the railroads the compensation promised earlier for the elimination of grade crossings within the city, the first congressional measures relating to the commission plan authorized new government buildings rather than additional parks. As the railroad companies began to erect the elaborate new station and the tunnel under the Hill to carry the tracks underground across government property, work started on six new edifices: the long awaited District Building at 14th Street on the former site of the Capital Traction Company powerhouses, offices for the House of Representatives and the Senate on the Hill, a new building for the Department of Agriculture and a new National Museum flanking the Mall on the south and north respectively, and an imposing home on Arsenal Point for the recently organized Army War College. Except for the huge domed National Museum, all these buildings were finished and in use by 1908. They immediately added to the city's aura of dignity. It was heightened by the clearing of the Mall of the railroad tracks and depot in 1909 and the grading of the plaza in front of the new Union Station where Larado Taft's Columbus Memorial Fountain was unveiled three years later. On Mt. Vernon Place the District Public Library, built with money given by Andrew Carnegie, opened in 1903. The spring of 1910 saw the completion of Continental Hall erected by the Daughters of the American Revolution, and adjacent, on the site of David Burnes'

1903, to Charles Moore, 6 Oct 1903, and 14 Jun 1904, and Charles McKim to Theodore Roosevelt, 10 Feb 1904, copy, Charles Moore Mss.

farmhouse, the Hall of the American Republics, architecturally a skillful blend of Spanish and French Renaissance styles. As the "Marble Palace," headquarters of the American National Red Cross, began to rise nearby, lower 17th Street promised to present an unbroken phalanx of imposing structures.[4]

The return to neo-classical architecture for government buildings pleased a public tired of the vagaries of the preceding half-century—the romantic red sandstone Norman castle of the Smithsonian, the mansard-roofed Department of Agriculture building, the "architectural infant asylum," as Henry Adams had labelled the State Department building, the heavy square-towered Post Office on Pennsylvania Avenue, and the ornate Italian Renaissance Library of Congress. Uniformity of style and the use of marble and pale gray granite became the rule, with the exception of the red brick War College and the officers' quarters built on Arsenal Point. Stanford White's design for the War College and grounds illustrated the restoration of another late eighteenth-century canon of city planning, namely the creation of long vistas wherever possible. Thus White placed the building at the tip of Arsenal Point where the Anacostia would serve as backdrop and an unimpeded half-mile sweep of tree-bordered lawn stretching along the Washington Channel would provide a magnificent approach; he located the new Officers' Club and the line of officers' houses with their big white columns well to the right of the entrance gates in order to keep the War College the focal point of a unified design. The day he discovered that the War Department had refused to tear down the obstructing old arsenal buildings and the grim four-

[4] *Rec*, 57C, 1S, pp. 2648-61, 2730, 57C, 2S, p. 1350; Glenn Brown, *Memories: A Winning Crusade to Revive George Washington's Vision of a Capital City*, p. 270 (hereafter cited as Brown, *Memories*); Comrs Rpt, 1903, p. 11; *Rpts B/Tr*, as in n. 3 above, and 1912, p. 21; *Star*, 25 Mar 1903, 1 Jan 1915; *Times*, 11, 15 Feb 1914; International Bureau of the American Republics, *The Report of the Director to the Fourth Pan American Conference Held at Buenos Aires, Argentine Republic*, Jul 1910, pp. 46-51; *Annual Address, President James F. Oyster to Chamber of Commerce*, 14 Jan 1913, p. 13, Woodrow Wilson Mss (L.C.).

square red brick prison in which the conspirators involved in Lincoln's assassination had been hanged, the outraged architect turned on his heel and never again set foot in the grounds. Yet government officials generally strove to act upon the Park Commission thesis that landscaping of the areas adjoining new buildings and the approaches to bridges was as important as the architecture itself.

Unlike the purely utilitarian bridges of nineteenth-century Washington, those built after 1905 had harmonious proportions and decoration. An ugly but sturdy iron trestle "highway" bridge, to be sure, replaced the ricketty seventy-year-old Long Bridge across the Potomac, but in 1908 the magnificently engineered "Lion Bridge" spanning Rock Creek valley was adorned with placid stone creatures at the Connecticut Avenue approaches. Several other new bridges involved extraordinary feats of engineering, notably the skillful use of concrete to encase the old water mains that carried the Pennsylvania Avenue bridge over Rock Creek and the graceful strength of the arches of the Q Street bridge guarded by bronze buffaloes. The Park Commission plan included a memorial bridge as an extension of the Mall to Arlington Cemetery, but, although members of the Grand Army of the Republic laid a cornerstone for the bridge in May 1902, not until 1913 did Congress appoint a special commission to choose a site and a design. And work would not begin until the mid-1920's. A million-dollar appropriation meanwhile for a replacement of the old Aqueduct Bridge promised to improve the looks of the Potomac River front at Georgetown.[5]

As the conviction deepened that harmony must obtain between public buildings and space, Congress created a permanent Fine Arts Commission in 1910 to advise "upon subjects within the domain of the fine arts." The Park Commission, never recognized by the House of Representatives, ceased to

[5] *Rpts B/Tr*, 1902, p. 28, 1905, pp. 8, 19-20, 1907, pp. 15, 120, 1909, pp. 42-43, 1916, pp. 41-43; Comrs Rpts, 1909, p. 46, 1915, p. 45; Engineer's Office, D.C., *Washington's Bridges*, 1945.

exist after submitting its report in 1902. The new body, like its predecessor, had no authority. The architects, sculptors, painters, and landscape gardeners composing the new commission had no chance to oppose the rewriting of the Height of Buildings Act, by which Congress permitted fire-proof business blocks to rise twenty to fifty feet higher than the law of 1899 had allowed. Members of the commission objected in vain to the 18th Street location and characterless design of the Interior Department building erected in 1916, but, more often than not, Congress followed their advice. In the face of vigorously pressed counterproposals they chose the site and design for the Lincoln Memorial and selected the architect, Henry Bacon, and the sculptor, Daniel Chester French. Virtually the executors of the plan of 1901, they fought for simplicity of line in new buildings and particularly for heights and cornices that would correspond to those of adjacent structures. Before World War I the Fine Arts Commission had made itself the arbiter of public taste in the capital.

A serious conflict developed in 1916. Secretary of the Treasury William McAdoo insisted that economy dictated placing a new government power and heating plant at the head of the Washington Channel near the Bureau of Engraving, where, the Fine Arts Commission contended, four huge smoke stacks cutting the sky line would not only mar the view of the city when approached from the south but compete with the Washington Monument and the Capitol seen from any angle. While a citizens' committee joined in the protest, an unconvinced Congress let excavation begin. Glenn Brown of the American Institute of Architects then led the fight. When engineers sent up a balloon from the power plant foundations to mark the height to which the smoke stacks would rise, Brown hastily got a photographer to take pictures showing the balloon slicing across the shaft of the Monument and blotting out part of the Capitol dome. Prints sent to every member of Congress and published in the *National Geographic Magazine* failed to halt

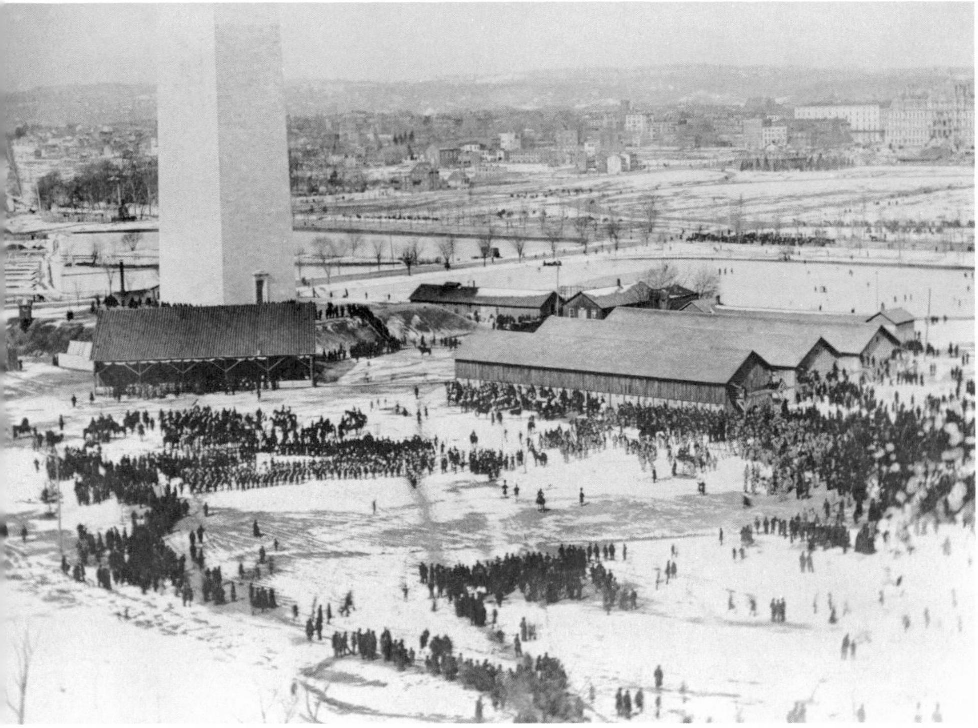

1. Dedication of the Washington Monument, February 21, 1885

2. Flood on Pennsylvania Avenue, 1889; the result of an inadequate storm sewer system

3. Tourists at the Capitol, 1880, from *Frank Leslie's Illustrated Newspaper*

4. Riggs National Bank on the right with the late W. W. Corcoran's office building on the left, ca. 1890. Newspapers and commercial firms rented part of each building

5. View of Virginia Avenue in 1894 showing in the foreground a race track and the John Van Ness house

6. View of Virginia Avenue in 1944 showing in the foreground the Munitions Building, the Hall of the American Republics, Continental Hall, and "New Interior"

7. Some of the "Army of the Unemployed" arriving by C & O Canal Boat, 1894

8. Members of Coxey's Army

9. The plant pathologists of the Department of Agriculture, ca. 1890

10. G. Browne Goode, ca. 1889

11. Samuel Langley and his "Aerodrome" with his mechanic on the left

12. School children visiting the Smithsonian Institution, 1899

13. School children visiting the Library of Congress, 1899

14. Three views of the Park Commission Plan of 1901: top, the Mall looking west toward the Potomac; center, the Mall looking east toward the Capitol; bottom, the "South-North Axis" from the river to the White House

15. Extension of the White House, 1903

16. Sailing on the Washington Channel. Beyond stands the line of officers' houses built by Stanford White on the grounds of the Army War College

the work. Brown then engaged a sign maker to paint sandwich boards, one board depicting the eighteenth-century plan of the city under the caption: "The Past—A Heritage from Washington," the other marked: "The Present—McAdoo's Smoke Stacks" portraying the city after the completion of the new power plant. Dressed in a long white robe, bare feet in sandals, and his face covered by a black mask, Brown wore the sandwich boards to a Beaux Arts ball given at the Willard Hotel to raise money for the children of French artists killed in the war against Germany. The only person with masked face, he walked back and forth, saying no word but letting everyone study the contrasting pictures. Overnight McAdoo became a laughing stock. Congress agreed to the Fine Arts plan of enlarging the existing power plant on low-lying land to the south of the Capitol, and the "Heritage from Washington" was saved.[6]

For thirty years before the appointment of the Fine Arts Commission statuary had been multiplying in the circles and triangles formed by the intersections of the avenues and streets. Once an organization had obtained permission from Congress to erect a memorial on the public domain, only the group commissioning the work or the sculptor executing it passed upon its suitability and artistic merit. Few people admired the towering Daniel Webster on his granite pedestal at Scott Circle, or the all too appropriately motionless equestrian figure of General McClellan at the head of Connecticut Avenue, or the already nearly forgotten Albert Pike, the Confederate general who had enlisted Indians in the fight against the Union and whose effigy now rose near the old City Hall. Public subscription had paid for the bronze of Boss Shepherd in front of the new District

[6] 36 *Stat.* 371; H Rpt 1294, 62C, 3S, Ser 6335; "The Proposed Lincoln National Memorial," *Harper's Weekly*, LVI, 21; *Post*, 19, 20 Jan 1913; *Rpts Fine Arts Commission*, 1913, pp. 15-18, 1914, 22-23, 35, 1915, pp. 5, 15-16, 27-28, 1916, pp. 12-14, 16, 19-22, 34-37, 52-53; Brown, *Memories*, pp. 301-03; *An Appeal to the Enlightened Sentiment of the People of the United States for the Safeguarding of the Future Development of the Nation*, March 1916.

Building, the one example in America of a politician portrayed with his hand behind him, but consensus labelled the memorial undistinguished.[7] Hence the community welcomed the new requirement that the Fine Arts Commission approve in advance the design and location of every new piece of sculpture proposed. Decisions as to who was to be commemorated in bronze or marble still lay with Congress, but that question would not trouble the public until mid-century.

Meanwhile the decorative planting of the public grounds and the voluntary elimination of billboards along the streets commanded public interest. Inasmuch as enforced removal of the unsightly billboards from scores of privately owned vacant lots meant interference with the sacred rights of the property owner, the campaign against hoardings proceeded slowly. But pleasure in seeing well-tended stretches of lawn and flowerbeds of pansies, tulips, and the traditional red cannas about the public buildings was an incentive to private property-owners to demolish eyesores. Washingtonians were especially caught up by excitement over the landscaping about the Tidal Basin when the plan took form in 1911 to ring the basin with Japanese cherry trees. David Fairchild, whose travels as a plant explorer justified his calling the world his garden, had brought back several flowering cherries in 1905 and successfully naturalized them in the woods about his home in Bethesda. The Department of Agriculture consequently could draw upon his experience when the mayor of Tokyo presented two thousand trees to Mrs. William Howard Taft, which she then gave to the city. She planted the first tree with her own hands. The discovery that several hundred trees were diseased necessitated burning the entire lot and replacing them with healthy stock, but by the spring of

[7] Macfarland, "The Rebuilding of the National Capital," *American City*, I, 8-9; Comrs Rpts, 1903, pp. 23-24, 1909, pp. 15-16, 1912, pp. 51-52, 1915, p. 46; *Rpts B/Tr*, 1909, p. 30, 1910, pp. 9-10, 61-62, 1913, 62-70, 1915, pp. 56-57, 62, 1916, pp. 59-62; "A National Monument to Columbus," *Harper's Weekly*, LVI, 17; *Post*, 3, 5 Mar 1913; *Times*, 19 Aug 1907, 21 Jan 1909, 16 Mar 1911; *Star*, 2 May 1909.

1915 the beauty of the delicately pink blossoms was breathtaking.[8] The "Speedway" along the river nearby and out on to Haines Point along the Washington Channel became the Washington equivalent of the Champs Elysée.

In the years ahead Washingtonians had occasion to wish that the Park Commission in 1901 had undertaken not only to emulate the surface beauties of St. James Park, the Champs Elysée, and the Bois de Bologne but also to adopt plans for a subway like the London "Underground" and the Paris "Métro." But horseless carriages were a novelty on the streets of the capital at the opening of the twentieth century. People walked to and from work, and fewer than 300,000 inhabitants in the entire District of Columbia made the growth of a metropolitan area of two million souls within a lifetime seem unthinkable. To spend money on placing a transit system underground appeared to be sheer folly in 1901. Furthermore, laws imposing any but sanitary restrictions on the use of privately owned land would have raised an outcry. The limit placed on the height of buildings was acceptable because Washingtonians were not yet ready to build higher than the law of 1910 allowed. But all Americans were wary of any measure smacking of "collectivism" or "socialism." Members of the Park Commission urged extensive purchase of land while it could still be bought relatively cheaply, but they confined their specific recommendations to the treatment of the public domain. Fifteen years before the first municipal zoning act in the United States went into effect in New York City, planned and controlled land-use affecting private as well as public property was an unpopular notion rarely discussed.

Today a careful examination of the plan of 1901 may induce a sense of disappointment that waterfalls tumbling from the west terrace of the Capitol to a pool at the foot of the Hill, a sunken garden below the Washington Monument, and boulevarded quays at the river's edge above and below the Navy Yard

[8] *Post*, 20 Jan 1913; Helen Taft Manning to the author, 4 Dec 1958; Fairchild, *The World Was My Garden*, pp. 254, 410-13.

have not come into being, and that bands of concrete highway and parking lots now occupy space designed for shady lawns and fountains. Still the concept of the "city beautiful" evolved at the turn of the century left its mark not only upon Washington but upon other American cities. In 1949 the American Institute of Architects labelled the proposals of 1901 "obsolete" at the time they were offered, a sign of an enduring "cultural colonialism" as disastrous for America as, in Louis Sullivan's opinion, the Chicago World's Fair had been in stifling all originality in native American art. Yet without a long-term plan and its partial execution before the first World War, skyrocketing real estate prices in Washington thereafter would almost certainly have stopped Congress from acquiring the land essential to any large-scale, orderly scheme, however faulty. City planning throughout the United States might well have suffered a setback, for the results visible in Washington at the end of 1916 kept alive the vision of the "city beautiful" in communities that had not yet taken constructive steps.[9]

[9] Montgomery Schuyler, "The New Washington," *Scribner's Magazine*, LI, 129-48; American Institute of Architects, *Of Plans and People*, pp. 10-12; "A List of American City Planning Reports," *American City*, XI, 1914, pp. 490-97.

CHAPTER VIII

THE REVERSE OF THE COIN: SOCIAL BETTERMENT, 1901-1916

AS MONEY poured into the adornment of the capital, a disturbing one-sidedness in the program troubled conscientious citizens. In 1901 the Associated Charities and the Central Relief Agency, speaking also for Washington's churches, begged the Park Commission "in formulating plans for the systematic beautification of our city to give especial consideration to its poorer neighborhoods." In the heart of Washington, behind the substantial houses that faced the streets bounding some 276 of her large squares, lay a warren of stables, shanties, and noisome tenements housing a few score of horses and thousands of human beings. The lack of playgrounds and the ramshackle condition of schoolhouses in poorer sections contrasted sharply with the landscaped grounds and architectural elegance of new federal buildings. Appropriations of $600,000 for new parks in northwest Washington and $275,000 for the bridge over Rock Creek at Q Street seemed out of all proportion to the $100,000 for reclamation of the malarial swamps near the mouth of the Anacostia and the $75,000 for making a playground out of the "notorious Willow Tree Alley" in the square later occupied by the federal Health, Education, and Welfare Building. At a national conference in 1910 speakers pointed out that city planners everywhere, captured by "a superficial quest for beauty," had paid too little attention to overcrowding in vital residential areas; consequently "from a social and hygienic standpoint" a community might continue to be undesirable "though outwardly it may be 'the city beautiful.' "[1] In Washington the bright face of the

[1] *Star*, 22 Aug 1901, 16 Jul, 2, 4 Aug 1909; *Times*, 5 Dec 1906, 18 Mar 1911; *Post*, 24 Jul 1904; *Rpts B/Tr*, 1904, p. 16, 1905, pp. 8-9; Max West, "Room for Improvement," *Outlook*, LXXIX, 625-26; George B. Ford, "Second National Conference on City Planning and Congestion,"

coin bore the clear imprint of the Park Commission plan; the reverse was blurred by shadowy indications of evils no one wanted to contemplate.

Indeed, a major difficulty in convincing Congress and the influential public of the existence of these evils within a stone's throw of the Capitol and within two blocks of millionaires' houses about Dupont Circle lay in the inadequacy of words to convey a vivid picture of Washington's inhabited alleys. No other city in America had their like. It meant little to say that "each 'alley' comprises a set of several streets which branch and turn about the center of the great city blocks"; that often six to twelve persons lived in a single room of an alley tenement with one water faucet to a floor of a dozen rooms; that leaky roofs and no gutters turned dwellings and the clay ground around them into foul morasses in wet weather; that lack of cross ventilation in summer made infernos of the closely packed houses and shanties; and that in winter newspaper wadded into cracks of the outer walls and about broken window panes kept in the bad air without warming it. Photographs taken among the shadows of those interior courts revealed a very small part of the misery and human degradation they enclosed. Neither words nor pictures reproduced the overpowering stench pouring out of doorless sheds lined with rows of uncovered wooden privies, rising from lidless barrels sunk in the ground, and pervading alley houses where each floor, occupied sometimes by as many as thirty families, was equipped with a single water closet in a windowless cubby hole.

From the street, a square containing a segment of the fetid, hidden slum world frequently appeared to be an ordinary respectable residential block. A diagram published in 1906 showed a typical layout: fifty-six brick and eight frame houses fronted on the four sides of the square and hid its interior; three

---

Survey, XXIV, 293-98; S Doc 247, 64C, 1S, "Fiscal Relations of the United States to the District of Columbia," pp. xlvi-xlviii, liii, lix, Ser 6915 (hereafter cited as *Fiscal Relations*).

openings led into an inner maze of courts formed by seventeen spacious stables and seventy narrow habitations and their accompanying outhouses. Bad as those physical features were, the secretary of the Associated Charities believed that the secret walled-off quality of alley life was its most destructive characteristic. A person who had never ventured down the alley openings could scarcely believe the tales of what he would find. The publicity social workers attempted to give to these conditions sounded like over-dramatized fiction to citizens who preferred to play ostrich rather than face such unpleasant facts.[2]

By 1907 the completion of the pumping station and sewage disposal plant, the water filtration system and enlargement of the District water supply relieved the District budget of the heaviest demands upon it and seemingly left funds available for playgrounds, roomy fire-proof school buildings, and a concentrated attack upon the great blight of the capital, the alley dwellings. But powerful members of Congress, having permitted the District to finance its costly public works by deficit spending, insisted that taxes must go first of all toward reducing the funded debt and next to repaying with interest the sums advanced from the United States Treasury for sewers and the water supply. The legislation of 1892 had prevented the building of additional shanties in narrow alleys but had not restored to District officials the authority exercised by the Board of Health under the territorial government to condemn and raze unsanitary tenements. Yet if Washington was to become the magnificent capital to which she aspired, the city must wipe out her slums.[3]

That task, as civic-minded people were coming to see, could not be achieved simply by the moral regeneration of alley

[2] Charles Weller, "Neglected Neighbors," *Charities*, xv, 762-67.

[3] *Times*, 17 Apr 1908; George S. Wilson, "Municipal Indebtedness, Washington, D.C.," *Annals American Academy of Social and Political Science*, xxv, 628-29, and Daniel E. Garges, "Washington, D.C.," *ibid.*, xxx, 157-60; S Rpt 943, 57C, 1S, Ser 4261; Comrs Rpt, 1906, p. 49; *Rpts B/Tr*, 1905, pp. 6, 9, 68, 1907, p. 127; *Star*, 24 Aug 1912.

dwellers. The reorganization of the Associated Charities in 1896 had started the process of changing Washingtonians' ideas about the battle against pauperism, and in the next dozen years the philosophy dominant in the 1880's and 1890's shifted considerably. Reduced to its simplest terms the change lay in a growing acceptance of the idea that environment might be as important as inherited character in making good citizens, and thus a good city. If "moral uplift" alone could not win the fight against the degradation of poverty, the campaign must be broadened to include provision for decent living conditions and wider economic opportunity for the city's poor. The "social betterment leaders," as the language of the day called them, continued to rely heavily upon education and persuasion to evoke cooperation, but they early realized that new legislation was also essential to the success of their enlarged program.

Among the leaders in this movement a half-dozen stand out as men of exceptional vision and tireless vigor. John Joy Edson is the best single example. His kindly, undistinguished face, partly hidden by untrimmed mustachios, showed little of the extraordinary force of his personality; he looked more like a small-town businessman than the powerful big city banker and the deeply religious, selfless social reformer that he was. He repeatedly refused appointment as a District commissioner, but for more than three decades he played a major part in every significant civic project, for twenty years shouldered the thankless task of heading the District Board of Charities, and blazed a new trail in penal reform. The contributions of Dr. George Kober of the Georgetown University medical faculty were equally valuable and, through his published articles, better known outside Washington than Edson's. Kober was at once a scientist, a gifted teacher, and a philanthropist initially concerned chiefly with sanitation and housing problems. Years of serving on the Board of Charities widened his interests; upon his seventieth birthday in 1920 grateful fellow citizens would acclaim him one of Washington's chief benefactors. Closely associated with him in the campaign against the alley slums was ex-Surgeon General George Sternberg, the distinguished bacteriologist who had reorganized the Army Medical Corps. Sternberg, with his military bearing and the prestige of his rank, carried enormous weight in the community and became the city's foremost authority on sanitary housing.

Washington also owed much to three successive secretaries of the Associated Charities. George Wilson more than any other man gave new direction to its work in the late 1890's, and his informed humane ideas continued to have great influence when he became the first secretary of the newly created public Board of Charities. Wilson's successor was Charles Weller. In 1900 still a man under thirty, he brought to Washington the experience he had acquired in five years' work with Chicago's Associated Charities. His insights and his youthful confidence that once Washingtonians fully comprehended the local problem they would find solutions gave him peculiar persuasiveness. In his eight years of directing the Associated Charities he trained hundreds of volunteers and taught them by example the meaning of constructive social service. Under his inspiration the Monday Evening Club, organized in 1898 by professional social workers anxious to learn about each other's work, became a vital force in the community. As the club expanded to include laymen, it turned into "an educational lyceum" on Washington's civic needs and gradually became virtually "a standing conference" on charities and corrections. Weller's cloak descended upon Walter Ufford in 1908. A Congregational minister before he took a Ph.D. degree in sociology at Columbia and undertook settlement work in New York, Ufford was a mild-looking man of forty-nine whose unimpressive appearance belied his gifts. Like Weller, he gave more than one well-intentioned Washingtonian a new concept of social work and philanthropy.

Scarcely less important were the contributions of several women, although, true to Victorian standards of lady-like behavior, they kept out of the limelight. The charming Elizabeth Brown Ufford, before her marriage herself an experienced social worker, supplied her innately conservative husband with his more forward-looking ideas. Older and outwardly more formidable, Mrs. Archibald Hopkins, who had grown up in Washington, had a warm feeling for Negroes and from the 1890's onward was a staunch behind-the-scenes campaigner for slum clearance. She incessantly prodded and encouraged the men who took charge. Similarly, Mrs. Whitman Cross, without ever letting her name appear, succeeded in launching reforms in a dozen seemingly hopeless areas. "When you wanted to get something constructive done in Washington," a contemporary later said, "you went to John Joy Edson or to Mrs. Cross."[4]

The attack upon alley dwelling, begun in the early 1890's, resumed with new earnestness after Charles Weller's arrival. Acting on his suggestion, in 1902 fifty prominent Washingtonians organized a Committee on the Improvement of Housing Conditions. Men of the stature of Sternberg, Kober, Episcopal Bishop Henry Y. Satterlee, and S. W. Woodward, president of the YMCA, headed the group. While the committee sponsored lectures, distributed circulars, and prepared notices for the press and for the local churches, Weller inaugurated the use of visual aids, a series of stereoptican slides, to show existing conditions to Washingtonians and members of Congress. The committee's invitation to Jacob Riis of New York to investigate Washington's alleys and describe what he found proved to be particularly effective. Riis, widely known for his

[4] "Anniversary Tribute to George Martin Kober . . . by his friends and Associates, March 28, 1920," *American Journal of Physical Anthropology*, III, 217-83; *American Biographical Directories: District of Columbia*, 1908-09; *Times*, 7 Jun 1911; Dupree, *Science*, pp. 253-57, 260, 263-67; Associated Charities, *Reports*, 1902, p. 5, 1905, pp. 10-11 (hereafter cited as A.C. *Rpts*); "How the Associated Charities has Recruited the Social Forces of the Capital," *Charities*, XV, 816-19; *Survey*, XXIV, 197-98.

book *How the Other Half Lives*, testified before a joint session of the House and Senate District committees that Negro alley dwellers in the capital lived under worse conditions and "one-room families" were more numerous than in the grimmest slums of New York City. President Roosevelt's message to Congress in 1904 pointed out that the death rate in one-room tenements averaged twice that in two-room, four times that in three-room, and eight times that in four-room tenements. The combined pressure of Riis' findings, the President's appeal, and the demands for remedial action pouring in upon Congress from constituents promised to produce the legislation for which Washingtonians had begged in vain for more than a decade.

With a new law in prospect empowering the District commissioners to demolish alley dwellings, in 1904 Dr. Sternberg and Dr. Kober launched a second housing company patterned on the then seven-year-old Sanitary Improvement Company, but with a 4 instead of a 5 percent limit on dividends, in order to have inexpensive housing available to the families that would be rooted out of the alley slums. In 1906 after several disheartening delays Congress created a board vested with authority to condemn unsanitary buildings. Within a year, 203 houses were razed and 53 more repaired, while the District commissioners ordered the opening up of twelve narrow alleys. Unhappily early in 1907 the Supreme Court ruled a key clause of the 1892 alley-opening act unconstitutional; assessing the costs upon property-owners would be legal only where a jury found the accruing benefits equal to the costs assessed. Thus all attempts to convert the alley ways into streets came to a halt, the Board of Condemnations had to limit its activities, and, in spite of the President's appointment of a Homes Commission, the campaign to wipe out alley-dwelling slackened. With only a 4 percent return and a sense of public service as bait, the Sanitary Housing Company attracted few investors. Unless public funds supplied money to build hundreds of cheap houses, the eviction of families from the alley shanties would mean doubling up in tenements on the streets. And Congress, particularly members from rural communities and primarily agricultural states, rejected the very idea of public housing.

While admitting the existence of the slum menace, a considerable body of white Washingtonians clung to belief that "alley evils are simply due to the racial traits of their principal inhabitants—the colored people." Move them out of the interior courts, and they would take their ignorance and shiftless habits with them to produce new slums in plain sight. How could a change of locale lessen the danger of Negro slum-dwellers' spreading disease to white households where hundreds of them worked as domestic servants by day? When Weller pointed out that "conditions in a typical white alley, inhabited by white people exclusively and nearly all of them native-born Americans," duplicated those in Negro-filled alleys, race prejudice again supplied an answer: Negroes set alley standards that then corrupted their white neighbors. Under such circumstances, President Roosevelt's Homes Commission perhaps deliberately chose to omit from its report specific comments on racial problems in housing.[5]

Although the report of the President's Homes Commission, published in 1908, produced no tangible results, it was not without significance. The commission's specific proposals stressed the futility of small-scale individual efforts, but its analysis of the causal relationship between low wages and alley dwellers' miseries helped to destroy lingering illusions that pauperism was due solely to the moral weaknesses of its victims and could be cured by moral uplift. Nor did the commission wholly subscribe to the Associated Charities' thesis that

[5] *Post*, 14 Apr 1902; *Rpt B/Tr*, 1902, p. 33, 1907, p. 3; A.C. *Rpts*, 1902, pp. 5, 9, 15, 1903, pp. 18, 32, 1905, p. 43; Jacob Riis, "Backing up the President," *Charities*, xv, 754; Charles F. Weller, "Neglected Neighbors," *ibid.*, pp. 764-777; Grace Vawter Bicknell, *The Inhabited Alleys of Washington, D.C.*, pp. 8-12; *Star*, 28 Dec 1903; H Rpt 2478, 58C, 2S, Ser 4583; 34 *Stat.* 157; Comrs Rpt, 1906, pp. 7, 29.

moving people out of the hidden alleys into the open light of the streets would effect a remedy. The recommendations indicated a new awareness that fundamental faults in the economic and social structure of the community contributed to the ills of which alley-dwelling was only a symptom.

The diverse backgrounds of the commission's fifteen members make their report the more remarkable. All served without compensation. No member was a trained social worker, and only General Sternberg and Dr. Kober qualified as professional housing experts. S. W. Woodward, philanthropist, tight-laced Puritan, and successful merchant, presumably looked at some problems from a different standpoint from that of the former cigar maker or the livery stable man on the commission; Attorney Frederick L. Siddons, confirmed single-taxer, doubtless differed at times with the Negro real estate broker; the ideas of George W. Cook, Negro dean of Howard University, perhaps troubled some of his associates; the two women members, Miss Mabel T. Boardman and Mrs. Thomas Gaff, both decidedly of the city's wealthy social elite, may have thought questions of wage rates beyond the competence of a Homes Commission or any non-employers, even those who had studied the Bureau of Labor *Bulletin*, which traced statistically the links between dependency and destitution in Washington and unemployment or annual wages of less than $600. Yet the commission's common concern to locate the "causing cause" and to suggest feasible remedies for the wretchedness of thousands of Washington families resulted in a penetrating and thought-provoking report.

Some of the proposals called for legislation—partial public financing for opening alleys and establishing playgrounds, government loans at low interest to enable "business philanthropy," like the Sanitary Housing Company, to build low-rental houses, an anti-usury law, a District Bureau of Labor, workmen's accident insurance, provision for more vocational training in the public schools, and better pay for government employees, which would include not only the unskilled but also the clerical force whose salary scale had remained unchanged since 1853. In an appeal to community conscience and enlightened self-interest, the commission also urged private employers to raise wages to ensure a minimum standard of living below which no family, irrespective of its morals or its wage-earner's skills, need exist. The one basic problem that the commission ignored was the effect of race prejudice upon the ability of nearly a third of the city's population to help itself.[6]

If Washingtonians were disappointed that the report failed to inspire action on the Hill, optimists persuaded themselves that past accomplishments were sufficient to meet the needs of the immediate future. Those accomplishments were in fact impressive. Congress yielding to community pressure had created a juvenile court, appointed a Prison Commission to study penal reform, passed a "non-support" act compelling fathers to contribute to the support of their children, enacted school attendance and child labor laws, established an Industrial Home School for Colored Children, replaced the almshouse with a new Home for the Aged and Infirm, opened a model tuberculosis hospital, and appropriated several small sums for public playgrounds. Groups of private citizens had raised money for additional playgrounds and summer outings for children; the Board of Trade had organized a free legal aid service; the Associated Charities staff had served as employment agents, and voluntary gifts had increased the charity fund fifteenfold within a few years. Perhaps still more noteworthy, though less well-known, Negroes had started an educational campaign against tuber-

[6] George M. Kober, "Report of Committee on Social Betterment," *Reports of the President's Homes Commission*, pp. 3-9; Weller, "Neglected Neighbors," pp. 761-94; *Times*, 3 Jan 1908; U. S. Department of Commerce and Labor, Bureau of Labor, *Conditions of Living Among the Poor*, 1906, pp. 593-698, and *Charity Relief and Wage Earnings* (prepared by Samuel E. Forman), 1908, pp. 876-922; ptn, U.S. and D.C. employees to the President, 19 Dec 1916, Wilson Mss.

culosis, organized an Alley Improvement Association, and founded a Children's Temporary Home.[7]

Unhappily the dedicated zeal that had made that record possible faded as citizens concluded they could no longer look for help from official Washington. A four-year lull set in when President Taft succeeded Theodore Roosevelt. As the White House ceased to provide initiative, new District commissioners settled into a do-nothing regime. The turnover in Congress occasioned by the elections in 1910, moreover, gave control of the District committees to men more concerned with attacking real estate speculators and the utility interests in Washington than with helping her poor. The one forward-looking local measure passed during an administration determined to check the spread of socialism in America was an act accepting most of the recommendations of the Penal Commission of 1908 and appropriating funds to carry them out.

The ensuing penal reform was primarily the fruit of the humane and courageous thinking of John Joy Edson, the commission chairman. Not content with spelling out the obvious need for a parole system, suspended sentences, and an expanded physical plant to relieve the shocking over-crowding at the workhouse and jail, Edson and his associates boldly advocated a totally new method of handling first offenders and minor misdemeanants: help them to rehabilitate themselves under watchful but unrestrictive supervision, instead of locking them up with hardened criminals in the penitentiary or with "the mass of derelicts" at the Asylum workhouse. Because the ladies of the Mt. Vernon Association objected to having a penal institu-

[7] *Times*, 16 Feb 1908; *Star*, 24 Nov 1909; A.C. *Rpt*, 1902, pp. 8-10, 1903, p. 23, 1905, pp. 5, 10-11, 26-28, 1909, pp. 8-9; William H. Baldwin, "Making the Deserter Pay the Piper, The District of Columbia Plan of Paying Prisoners' Wages to Their Deserted Wives," *Survey*, XXIII, 249-52; 31 *Stat.* 822; 33 *Stat.* 386; 34 *Stat.* 73, 86, 219, 482; 35 *Stat.* 303, 420; *Rpts B/Tr*, 1902, pp. 31-32, 1905, pp. 47-48, 1907, p. 64; Comrs Rpt, 1912, pp. 17-18; Henry S. Curtis, "The Playgrounds of Washington," *Charities*, XV, 830-31; Bicknell, *The Inhabited Alleys*, pp. 24-25.

tion adjacent to a national shrine, in 1912 Congress transferred to the War Department the site at Belvoir, Virginia, which had been purchased in 1910 for the reformatory for the "more hopeful" class of adult offenders. The change of location delayed the opening of the Lorton reformatory until November 1916; and legislation authorizing indeterminate sentences and parole had to wait till the 1920's. But the opening in 1911 of the new workhouse at Occoquan, Virginia, initiated a revolution in penal administration. Here was a large institution without bars, bolts, or other means of physical restraint, night or day. The inmates worked on the farm or at the brick kilns that by 1914 were supplying all the brick for the District government's building and repair work. Officials from every section of the United States and from Europe visited Occoquan to observe the astonishing success of a system that combined minimum custody with wholesome outdoor employment.[8]

While the pace of civic uplift slowed after 1908, interest in public health prevented its coming to a halt; the cleanliness of the city, like a lowered death rate, was as important to business promoters as to social workers. When a "clean-up week" sponsored chiefly by the *Evening Star* resulted in the collection of thirty-three wagon loads of rubbish from a single block, a "clean city" committee set itself to teach thoughtless citizens the principles of sanitation. By 1912 the Board for the Condemnation of Insanitary Buildings, though grumbling that "a school of good housekeeping" was the chief need of alley dwellers, had ordered the demolition of over 1,500 buildings. At the same time philanthropists, aroused to the plight of aged people, provided some seven new homes, chiefly under

[8] H Rpt 825, 61C, 2S, Ser 5592; S Doc 989, 62C, 3S, Ser 6364; *Times*, 9, 15 Jun 1907, 10 Apr 1908, 17 Jan 1909, 28 Feb 1913; Comrs Rpt, 1909, p. 28, 1915, p. 38; *Report of the Board of Charities of the District of Columbia*, 1917, pp. 9, 85 (hereafter cited as *Rpt B/Ch*); George Kober, "Charitable and Reformatory Institutions in the District of Columbia," S Doc 207, 69C, 2S, pp. 51-62, 69-73, Ser 8702. Kober's summary contains a history of penal administration and reform in D.C., 1865 to 1927.

denominational aegis, while private contributions continued to flow also into medical and children's charities. And, contrary to all logic, during these years of parsimonious appropriations for health and building inspection, for proper enforcement of the compulsory school attendance law, and for staff for the Board of Children's Guardians, Congress granted generous subsidies to private hospitals.[9]

Out of this curious situation grew a struggle that focused Washingtonians' attention for several years on administrative procedures. The fight lay between directors of private charities and the Board of Charities, that public body created to prevent overlapping services and to provide for needy people whom private institutions did not reach. The five-man Board of Charities felt strongly that public money should go only to public institutions; private resources could adequately support private philanthropies. But socially prominent Washingtonians resented that plan as belittling their own pet charities. Board arguments urging the economies of building a general municipal hospital financed by public funds and administered by public officials met with fierce resistance. The sanctity of custom and the prestige of its defenders defeated a recommendation of 1909 in which such influential men as John Joy Edson and Dr. George Kober proposed closing Emergency Hospital and denying the public Columbia Hospital $300,000 for a new building, since both institutions tended to spend their government monies on better care for pay patients instead of enlarging service to the poor for whose benefit the grants were intended.

The shortcomings of public institutions, it is true, were all too obvious. Meagre appropriations for the new almshouse, renamed the Home for the Aged and Infirm, forced economies in construction and a prison-like sparseness of furnishings and

[9] *Star*, 4 Apr, 27 Jun 1909, 8 Sep, 2 Oct 1912; Comrs Rpt, 1912, pp. 18, 47; Bicknell, *The Inhabited Alleys*, pp. 23-25; S Doc 422, 61C, 2S, Ser 5656; A.C. *Rpts*, 1903, pp. 18-19, 1913, pp. 12, 15; S Doc 207, 69C, 2S, pp. 22, 118, 131, 149-56, 167, Ser 8702.

facilities—neither screened porches, assembly rooms, chapel, diet kitchen, nor private rooms for the desperately ill or dying; the scanty funds allotted for running the home with its 130 inmates in need of 24-hour care kept the staff to 13 attendants. The provision for the education of colored children in the new Industrial Home School was equally thin; they received some training in domestic work, gardening, farming, and good habits, but no industrial or vocational schooling, and the physical plant was grossly inadequate. This public institution, which supplanted the Hart Farm School after 1906, was little improvement over that older subsidized private charity. On the other hand, the tuberculosis hospital opened in 1908 showed that a carefully planned, well-run public institution could perform services no private organization could equal.[10]

Apparently it was the presidential election campaign of 1912 that revitalized the city's interest in the substantive features of social betterment; for Woodrow Wilson's "New Freedom" promised far-reaching social as well as political changes. Moreover, Washingtonians realized that the admirable laws passed between 1905 and 1908 had become virtually dead letters for lack of appropriations with which to work; and the needs of a growing population in the interim had outrun what the earlier acts were designed to supply. Public charity was still sharply limited in scope; private philanthropy had widened its field very little; and urgent wants within the community still fell betwixt and between. Other than several old buildings at the Asylum, the District still had no place in which to care for the chronically ill or for drug addicts, alcoholics, and the "mildly insane." The program of the Board of Children's Guardians for placing

[10] *Post*, 5 Mar 1904; *Rpt B/Tr*, 1907, p. 87, 1912, Walter C. Clephane, "Public and Private Hospitals and Charities in the District of Columbia"; Comrs Rpts, 1902, p. 299, 1915, p. 39; *Rpts B/Ch*, 1907, p. 7, 1909, pp. 355-74, 1917, p. 231; George S. Wilson, *Supervision of Private Charities*, p. 4; *Star*, 1 Feb 1912; "Municipal Hospital for the Capital City," *Survey*, XXVII, 1924-25; S Doc 207, 69C, 2S, pp. 12, 15-16, 22, 109-117, 166-68, Ser 8702; *Times*, 22 Sep 1907; D.C. Village, *Fifty Years at Blue Plains, 1906-56*.

its wards with private families was imperilled by the smallness of the staff of inspectors assigned to visiting the widely scattered foster and boarding homes—only one inspector to 340 children, compared to 85 to 100 in most American cities. Over 700 feeble-minded children got no care at all. And the unwillingness of white people to give more than token sums for Washington's nearly 1,500 destitute colored children multiplied difficulties. No observant resident of the capital regarded Washington in 1912 as a model municipality.[11]

Yet when the new drive for social improvements began, it again centered on alley-dwelling. The most enlightened Washingtonians adopted the creed: good homes make a good community. Tacitly the creed implied that good housing might make responsible citizens out of Negroes. While members of the Monday Evening Club, the spearhead of the new campaign for legislation, prepared a directory of inhabited alleys, the Associated Charities, the Woman's Welfare Department of the National Civic Federation, the Men and Religion Forward Movement, and the Social Service Conference of the Episcopal Diocese of Washington studied the problem. A Central Housing Committee enlisted the cooperation of the press, church groups, and business associations in a united appeal to Congress for a federal housing commission with authority to act.

Help came from an unexpected quarter the following spring when Mrs. Woodrow Wilson began a tour of Washington's alleys and settlement houses. The daughter and granddaughter of slave-owners, Mrs. Wilson explained that her upbringing had taught her to accept work in behalf of Negroes as her Christian duty, a point of view Negroes themselves found objectionably condescending. During her first weeks in the White House she attended Associated Charities conferences and threw herself into the welfare work of the Civic Federation with such

[11] Comrs Rpt, 1915, p. 39; *Rpts B/Ch*, 1909, pp. 336, 360-61, 1917, p. 210; S Doc 207, 69C, 2S, p. 236, 327-31, Ser 8702; *Fiscal Relations*, p. lviii.

energy that, as one associate noted, "people flocked to our standard and everybody wanted to help in the alleys. It was laughingly said that no one could move in polite society in Washington who could not talk alleys." Debutantes formed a Neighborhood House Auxiliary to do kindergarten work in the settlements, and by May 1913 "Automobile tours of our best people, by way of 'studying the conditions' and 'helping' the poor, are now established as socially correct." While some of this activity was useless and essentially frivolous, citizens were aroused over alley-dwelling as they had not been since Charles Weller first showed his stereoptican views of Washington's slums.

By June 1913 women had raised $8,500 for the Sanitary Improvement Company, Senator Works of California had submitted a bill to establish a federal housing commission, bills in both House and Senate proposed the conversion of two of the worst alleys into parks, and a new citizens' committee had undertaken to draft a housing measure acceptable to businessmen and large taxpayers. At this point the Senate requested a tabulation of ownership of alley property. The forty-page list revealed more than a thousand different owners, most of whom had only a lot or two, many of whom were women, and a few of whom themselves lived in the alleys. Realty companies owned very little alley property. A disconcerting discovery was that title to six lots was vested in the Washington City Orphan Asylum. Hence the battle could not be fought against a mere handful of villains or a few unwitting exploiters.[12]

The plan that eventually emerged from the citizens' committee made no mention of public housing but called for conversion of alleys into minor streets or parks by drawing on the District's

[12] A.C. *Rpts*, 1911, p. 12, 1912, p. 15; Wilbur Vincent Mallalieu, "A Washington Alley," *Survey*, XXVIII, 69-71; Bicknell, *The Inhabited Alleys*, pp. 16-17, 20, 23-28; and "The Home Maker of the White House, Mrs. Woodrow Wilson's Social Work in Washington," *Survey*, XXXIII, 19-22; *Post*, 17 Apr, 20 May 1913; *Times*, 20-31 May, 1 Jun 1913; S Doc 120, 63C, 1S, Ser 6536.

general fund over a ten-year period. The proposal reached Congress early in 1914; by then popular excitement had died down and congressional opposition to spending federal money in the capital had grown. Nothing stirred on the Hill until mid-August. Then Congress learned that on the last morning of her life Mrs. Woodrow Wilson had told the President she would rest happier if she knew the alley bill had passed. Two months later what would soon prove to be a curiously unrealistic measure became law. It forbade after July 1, 1918, residence in any alley not converted to a minor street, but it provided no machinery and no funds and ignored the problem of where evicted families were to live. Shutting their eyes to the weakness of the new law, most Washingtonians elatedly assumed that the alley problem would now solve itself, inasmuch as a survey showed a decline in the alley population from the 19,076 of 1905 to 11,400 in 1912, and fewer than 8,500 still there in 1915. With the new Ellen Wilson Homes Association preparing plans for low-rental houses on the streets, concern about the families remaining in the alley slums dropped. No one foresaw in 1916 that within a year the demand for housing in the war-ridden capital would consign the alley act to limbo.[13]

Social betterment in other realms, notably child care, fortunately made more lasting progress. Infant mortality, on the decline since 1900, had dropped to one in ten by 1917. Thanks in considerable degree to a Children's Council formed in 1911, day nurseries, child welfare centers, public playgrounds, summer camps, and classes and clubs at the settlement houses multiplied in endeavor to check juvenile delinquency before it began. The Juvenile Court, to be sure, proved disappointingly ineffectual: it had only two probation officers, had to function as a criminal rather than a domestic relations court, and its

[13] *Times*, 22 Oct 1913, 27 Jan, 19 Feb, 25 Aug, 21 Sep, 1914; Bicknell, "The Home Maker of the White House," pp. 21-22; "Washington Alleys; A Half-way Measure," *Outlook*, CVIII, 240-41; 38 *Stat.* 716; *Rpt B/Tr*, 1916, pp. 104-05; H Dis Comee, 63C, 2S, Hrgs, "Certain Alleys in the District of Columbia," pp. 12, 22; Comrs Rpt, 1915, p. 189.

policy of making short-term or temporary commitments of children to the Board of Children's Guardians forced the Guardians to place an increasing number of their wards in institutions instead of private homes. Yet the Guardians succeeded in providing better care for colored children than was possible earlier, for, while the number placed with private families was pitifully small, the quality of the homes was higher. On the other hand, whereas good private homes had been available at the turn of the century for four out of every five of the white children, by 1916 the Board had to put more than half into institutions, since white families were reluctant to take temporary boarders, chances of adoption accordingly diminished, and after 1914 policy dictated abandoning all placement by indenture. The institutions were on the whole better run and more numerous than in the 1890's, but an institutional atmosphere hung over the best of them, even the new Episcopal Home with its spacious grounds beyond the Anacostia where the children were housed in groups of eight to ten on "the cottage system."[14]

More significant than the recurrent dissatisfaction with child placement was the growing realization that the most efficient handling of a social problem after it had developed was no substitute for prevention. In 1914 the president of the Board of Guardians, B. Pickman Mann, a Patent Office examiner and son of Horace Mann, studied the background of the board's 1,500 charges in an attempt to identify and find ways of eradicating the social forces that brought them into its custody. He concluded that two obstacles stood in the way of a constructive

[14] *Times*, 9, 11 Sep 1914, 8, 23 Jun, 15 Nov 1915, 17, 27 Oct 1916; *Rpts B/Ch*, 1912, pp. 358-59, 1914, pp. 352-65, 1915, pp. 312-15, 1916, pp. 239-45; A.C. *Rpt*, 1912, p. 14, 1913, pp. 10-15; Hastings Hart, *Child Welfare in the District of Columbia*, pp. 3-14, 72, 77, 117-123, 130-132 (hereafter cited as Hart, *Child Welfare*); Louis G. Weitzmann, *One Hundred Years of Catholic Charities in the District of Columbia*, pp. 120-25, 142-48; S Doc 207, 69C, 2S, pp. 234, 236, Ser 8702; Emma O. Lundberg and Mary E. Milburn, "Child Dependency in the District of Columbia," U. S. Department of Labor, Children's Bureau Publication No. 140, 1924, p. 67 (hereafter cited as Lundberg, *Child Dependency*).

attack upon delinquency and dependency in Washington, namely race prejudice and the lack of any means of keeping a family together when long illness, unemployment, or the desertion of the wage earner caused a domestic crisis. Mann had no panacea for racial antagonisms, but he believed extensive recourse to mothers' pensions, a plan the Associated Charities had followed as best it could since 1906, would cut the roots of many problems of child care. A law passed in 1914 limiting to eight hours the working day of women in mercantile and manufacturing establishments had had some beneficial effect, but in a non-industrial, generally non-commercial city, where jobs in factories and shops were few and virtually never open to colored women, the act did little to preserve family life, least of all among colored people, whose children yearly swelled the ranks of delinquents. Chiefly at Mann's instigation but with the co-operation of the judge of the Juvenile Court, the Children's Council, and other child welfare groups, in 1916 the Children's Protective Association came into being to carry on Mann's study of how to rectify the social maladjustments that underlay delinquency and dependency.[15]

An enlightened segment of the community began at the same time to take a new look at adult unemployment and its consequences. The fluctuations were confusing: the number of unemployed, homeless men who sought temporary refuge at the Municipal Lodging House rose from 6,800 in 1914 to 9,900 the next year and again dropped to 6,800 in 1916, when munitions plants in other parts of the country opened up jobs for the able-bodied. Although the Lodging House was designed for "tramps," the Monday Evening Club put a new, better-equipped Lodging House high on the list of civic needs. The ups and downs of employment for permanent residents troubled thought-

[15] *Rpt B/Ch*, 1909, pp. 322-23, 1913, pp. 424-38; Hart, *Child Welfare*, p. 124; "LaFollette-Peters Eight-hour Bill Enacted into Law," *Survey*, XXXI, 689; H Doc 1461, 62C, 3S, Ser 6460; *Times*, 15 Nov 1915; Consumers' League of D.C., *Third Anl Rpt*, 1915, pp. 4-5.

ful citizens even more. Because of the seasonal character of the building trades, unemployment rose alarmingly in severe winters, but its decline in a mild winter had long encouraged public reliance on stopgaps. Yet in the winter of 1914, if the superintendent of the Gospel Mission appeared to be making a moral judgment when he labelled most of Washington's 15,000 unemployed men "deserving," charitable citizens were too concerned with the basic facts of want to consider moral criteria. The Chamber of Commerce urged an immediate start on all public works for which there were appropriations; Walter Ufford wrote 3,000 letters to householders who might have jobs to offer, but he remarked: "What Washington really needs is an employment bureau under Government auspices, without the tinge of charity."[16]

Ufford went much further, for he advocated old age, sickness, accident, and unemployment insurance for all wage earners and minimum pay of $2.00 a day for common laborers. At the time, $1.50 to $1.75 was standard, despite findings that $720 a year was below a subsistence wage for a family of five. Ufford's thinking far outran that of most citizens and indeed would have little impact until the 1930's. Even the Consumers' League put its major emphasis on getting Congress to pass a women's minimum wage law. The Associated Charities felt obliged to continue to work on a finger-in-the-dyke basis that left little energy or time to plan far-reaching social reconstruction. In early 1916 Congressman Nolan of California, in response to a flood of petitions from government clerks, introduced a bill setting a minimum pay rate of $3 a day for all federal and District government employees. The proposal seemed unthinkably extravagant, particularly as seven hours constituted the normal day in government offices. Repeated pleas of government clerks for a pension system got even less attention. By and large, the

[16] *Times*, 21 Jan 1911, 13 Feb 1913, 22, 31 Dec 1914, 18 Nov, 15, 23 May, 7 Dec 1916; *Rpts B/Ch*, 1914, p. 393, 1915, p. 347, 1916, pp. 265-66; A.C. *Rpt*, 1915, pp. 4, 13, 1916, pp. 9-10.

American public at the height of the Progressive era still believed that laws of supply and demand, not federal legislation, must regulate wage rates and individual thrift and foresight must provide for "the rainy day."[17]

Theories of self-sufficiency notwithstanding, both philanthropy and public welfare services widened. Private gifts opened two new homes for the aged, one of them sponsored by colored people; and, under the leadership of Mrs. Archibald Hopkins, the Home for Incurables got more support. The long debated question of a municipal hospital, furthermore, appeared to be settled in 1914 by an appropriation voted for a building in northwest Washington. Bitter opposition from property owners who were unwilling to have a "pauper" hospital in their neighborhood caused a three-year delay, but a change of location back to the old Asylum grounds on the Anacostia disposed of those objections, and a politically adroit proposal of District Commissioner Brownlow won over reluctant members of Congress: the institution was to be named Gallinger Hospital in honor of the former chairman of the Senate District Committee.[18]

Sentiment, meanwhile, had been mounting to force the closing of the houses of ill fame in the triangle below Pennsylvania Avenue near the Treasury. Known as "Joe Hooker's Division" since Civil War days when General Hooker's determination to keep prostitution within bounds had led to a semi-official demarcation of a few squares along the Avenue, the red light district had spread until in 1913, according to investigating "suffragettes," it stretched from within two

[17] S Doc 422, 61C, 2S, Ser 5658; H Rpt 825, 61C, 2S, Ser 5592; A.C. *Rpts*, 1913, p. 7, 1916, pp. 7-9; Consumers' League, *Third Anl Rpt*, 1915, pp. 7-15; *Star*, 23 Mar 1916; H Dis Comee, 64C, 1S, Hrgs, "Resolution Authorizing the Department of Labor to Inquire into the Cost of Living in D.C."; *Rpts B/Ch*, 1902, pp. 207-08, 1916, p. 244; ptns and ltrs in D.C. file, Woodrow Wilson Mss; *Times*, 9 Apr 1911, 30 Apr 1913, 17 Jan 1914, 29 Jan, 22 Mar, 16 Apr, 25 Nov, 7 Dec 1916.

[18] *Bee*, 10 Apr 1915; *Rpt B/Ch*, 1916, pp. 225-27; *Fiscal Relations*, pp. lii-liii; Brownlow, *A Passion for Anonymity*, p. 101.

blocks of the White House to the edge of Capitol Hill. A tale indicative of the open acceptance of vice in the city told of a madame brought into court who, when asked whether she pled guilty, responded, "Your Honor, everybody knows I run the second-best house in the city." "Second best?" queried the judge. "Certainly," came the answer, "the Treasury runs the best." As the establishments advertised the city's vicious aspects to tourists, in 1914 Congress passed the so-called red light bill, but President Wilson refused to sign it until some provision was made to care for the prostitutes. The Florence Crittenden Mission thereupon undertook the task and the bill became law.

The new importance of women in the "civic uplift" movement, illustrated in the suffragettes' battle against vice, was also reflected in the non-political activities of the Women's Welfare Department of the National Civic League and in the anti-saloon campaign. Women made little headway in fighting the liquor traffic, particularly as the District Excise Board, established by law in 1909, did not relish their missionary zeal. If earnestness devoid of humor was a handicap, still they increasingly made their ideas count. In 1913 one writer said of the war against alley dwellings: "Never before have the women of the capital risen in a body"; the victory was theirs. Women's clubs were not the mainstay of volunteer social service as they were in other big cities. The National Professional Women's League, the Woman's Suffrage League, and the District Federation of Women's Clubs had in view either political objectives or professional advancement. Otherwise "club life" tended more to sociability than to public service. Ladies attended current events lectures at the Washington Club but carried on their civic activities through the churches and charity organizations.[19]

[19] Washington *Herald*, 21 May 1907; *Star*, 15 Feb 1912; "Washington's Red Light District Attacked," *Survey*, xxxi, 314; *Times*, 28, 31 Jan, 2 Jul 1914, 16 Feb 1916. S Rpt 391, 63C, 2S, Ser 6552; S Doc 981, 63C, 3S, Ser 6775. The story of the madame was told me by a former Secretary of State who heard it from a former judge.

In many parts of America women with leisure at their disposal first learned about community service when war work drew them into it. In Washington the sense of obligation came much earlier, doubtless partly through the skillful appeals of Charles Weller and later through the example set by women with the social prestige of a Mrs. Hopkins, a Mrs. Whitman Cross, a Mabel T. Boardman, and Mrs. Woodrow Wilson. While Dolly Madison and Frances Folsom Cleveland each had participated in her day, neither First Lady had played so direct a part in Washington's charities as Mrs. Wilson, and neither had occupied the White House in a period when social guilt ran strong in the upper ranks of American society. Mrs. Hopkins and Mrs. Cross indicated by precept and deed that for women the one justification for unearned wealth and leisure lay in good works. Miss Boardman, after serving on President Roosevelt's Homes Commission, began teaching Washington debutantes through the District chapter of the American Red Cross that their privileged place in the world put upon them a debt to society that they could best pay by personal service in worthy causes. Debutantes quickly learned that they could combine charitable activities with the gaieties of the social season and, after the founding of the Washington Junior League in 1914, a disciplined pursuit of the former was likely to enhance the latter, especially for young women of slightly insecure social background.[20]

City-dwellers the country over, spurred on by the muckrakers and preachers of the social gospel, were seeking solutions to urban problems as diligently as were Washingtonians. They rarely questioned their capacity to succeed. In 1916 District Commissioner Oliver Newman told the Monday Evening Club that Washingtonians had a wider interest in community affairs than he had seen in any of the other nine cities where

20 Edith Elmer Wood, "Four Washington Alleys," *Survey*, XXXI, 182; *Times*, 3 Nov, 17 Jul, 10 Sep 1914.

he had lived.[21] Perhaps nowhere was the optimism that characterized American reformers of the time so marked. If naïve and somewhat shallow, it nevertheless suffused the city with a golden warmth of hope.

[21] *Times*, 18 Jan 1916.

CHAPTER IX

THE BOARD OF TRADE AND PUBLIC AFFAIRS, 1901-1916

"OH, my sister cities of the land, harken to me . . . Young and strong, fair of body, clean of mind, I have kept our faith. I live and grow, in beauty and power, in the strength of the spirit that makes for good. . . .

"I am the Capital and blood kin to our Mecca of the East. Day by day, year by year, century by century, I will grow. . . . It shall be mine, by the example that I teach, to put order in thy houses, where disorder now reigns. It shall be mine to teach thee cleanliness of body and of mind, and honesty and the municipal faith. It shall be mine to teach thee the meaning and show thee the soul of the beauty that lies within and the beauty that shines without." So bragged the *Evening Star* in a eulogy of the capital in 1909.

In only less fulsome phrases presidents of the Board of Trade voiced similar complacency; occasional reminders that no one must rest on his oars scarcely interrupted the flow of self-congratulation over "the grandeur of our city." In addition to a "delightful climate," a magnificent physical layout, an ample supply of pure water, efficient local government, and moderate taxation, Washington offered "superb commercial and manufactural probabilities" and exceptional educational advantages through her universities and schools, art galleries and libraries.[1] "Is it any wonder," former District Commissioner Henry West asked rhetorically in 1913, "that during recent years there should have been attracted to Washington a most desirable class of residents—people . . . who are glad to live in a city which is attractive and well kept, where the society is cosmopolitan, where peace and order reign with freedom from polit-

[1] *Star*, 1 Jan 1909; *Rpts B/Tr*, 1905, p. 5, 1906, p. 37, 1910, pp. 13-14, 1912, pp. 5-6, 1913, pp. 33-44; S Doc 420, 63C, 2S, p. 11, Ser 6593.

ical disturbance, and where the constant march of progress is unchecked?"

Land prices mounted steadily. Row houses rose in the vicinity of Lincoln Park and in Mt. Pleasant, apartment houses adapted to families who could afford only one servant multiplied in more central areas, and the expanding "millionaire colony" about DuPont and Sheridan Circles was making the "City of Magnificent Distances" also the "Home of Palatial Mansions." Wall Street depressions had little effect upon banking or building operations in the District; real estate, on the contrary, attracted outside capital, and during the panic of 1907 one realtor boasted that Washington grew faster in two months than she had in twelve during the 1890's. As office buildings and stores took over the area immediately to the north and east of the Treasury, real estate brokers developed new residential sections along upper 16th Street, about Chevy Chase Circle, and, for people of very modest means, along the eastward extension of Rhode Island Avenue. Uneasiness about the attitude of the new administration in 1913 and then the outbreak of war in Europe lessened the volume of transactions; but, although over 4,700 houses stood vacant in early 1915, prices held up, and later that year the building of apartment houses again accelerated.

Built-up blocks interspersed with an ever diminishing number of vacant lots stretched for a mile or more north of Florida Avenue by 1907, making the formal city limits a limit only in name. Prophecies ran that within a decade Washington's suburbs would reach into nearby Maryland. By 1910 the area outside Washington contained a quarter of the District's total population. Trolley lines passing over the Aqueduct Bridge hastened the growth of Roslyn on the Virginia shore and inspired so many real estate ventures there that in 1909 a District commissioner argued that the federal government would soon have to negotiate for reannexation of the southern third of the original ten-mile square: Washington would need that area for factories and homes for her poor. The reannexation question never got beyond vague talk among Washington promoters, and by 1920 the creation of Arlington County would kill hopes that the Commonwealth of Virginia would relinquish so valuable a region.[2]

Building and loan associations financed most small householders' home-building, while the city's big national banks handled larger enterprises—entire suburban subdivisions, new office buildings, and the extension of utilities. Before the Wilson administration embarked on banking reform, the government itself treated the powerful Riggs National Bank with deference. For years the president of the bank, Charles Glover, kept a desk in the main Treasury, where he would be the first to hear of impending developments in official monetary policies. In 1915 when the Comptroller of the Currency, John Skelton Williams, invoked the authority of the new Federal Reserve Act to stop what he characterized as the improper practices of the Riggs Bank, its officers chose to defy the Treasury. Glover, by then denied his desk at the Treasury and incensed at charges which he labelled vindictive misrepresentations, hit Williams over the head with a walking stick when the two met by chance in Lafayette Square, and was summoned before Congress to make public apology. But once the courts had declared the bank's monetary transactions legal, Riggs' stature in American financial circles rose to new heights.[3]

In spite of virtually unbroken prosperity, the Chamber of Commerce, an offshoot of the Board of Trade started by small

[2] Because newspaper pieces on business progress, taxes, and District administration ran to thousands, I have limited specific citations to a mere sampling: *Post*, 6 Apr 1902, 13 Mar, 25 May 1913; *Rpts B/Tr*, 1903, p. 16, 1908, p. 23, 1910, pp. 13-14, 1912, p. 17; *Star*, Summaries, 1908-1916; *Times*, 9 Jun 1907, 28 Feb 1913, 18 Jun 1915; Comrs Rpt, 1906, p. 41, 1912, p. 57, 1915, p. 50, 1919, p. 575; *Rec*, 59C, 2S Index, p. 267; H. B. F. Macfarland, "The Rebuilding of the National Capital," *American City*, I, 11-12; S Doc 489, 64C, 1S, Ser 6954.

[3] Interview, Louis Brownlow; "The Riggs Bank Row," *Literary Digest*, L, 939-40; "The Riggs Bank Case," *Outlook*, CIX, 953-54; *Star*, 23 May 1916; *Post*, 25 Jan 1913; *Times*, 11 Oct 1915.

business interests in 1907, advocated a campaign to attract industry. Proponents argued that industry would reduce seasonal unemployment and give Washington her proper place in the American business world. The Board of Trade, on the other hand, as a body committed to developing the city as a show place and residential center, shied away from a proposal sure to antagonize Congress: "It is entirely unlikely," announced one representative, "that Congress could tolerate manufacturing districts here, with the massing industrial population, the danger of strikes, boycotts, lockouts, etc." And attempts to enter into industrial competition with other American cities, *Scribner's Magazine* contended, would cost "the spoiled child of the republic" the favors she enjoyed. The squeeze caused by rising prices in a community where fixed incomes were the rule led the president of the Board of Trade to suggest in 1915 that factories in the suburbs might furnish the District with badly needed revenue without proving offensive to residents of Washington. In fact a munitions plant opened on the far side of the Anacostia in 1914 operated without Washingtonians' discovering that it was there. But the difficulty of harnessing the Great Falls, the area's one major source of power, and reluctance to risk offending Congress combined to halt tentative anglings for industry.[4]

All businessmen talked about expanding Washington's commerce by means of improved railroad freight service, a shipping canal from the Anacostia to Chesapeake Bay to be built with federal subsidies, and the construction of a huge auditorium for conventions. None of these proposals, most of them bolstered by arguments familiar since the 1840's, produced

[4] *Rpt B/Tr*, 1902, pp. 39-46, 1905, p. 50, 1910, pp. 10-11, 1915, pp. 7-8; *Post*, 7 Jul 1906; *Herald*, 14 May 1907; *Times*, 29 Jun, 25 Aug, 10 Nov 1907, 23 Jan 1911, 9 Jan 1914; "Made in Washington," *Harper's Weekly*, LVI, 15 Jun 1912, p. 30; speech by Walter F. Fowler, D.C. Budget Officer, to Bankers' Association, Apr 1959, Ms in possession of Louis Brownlow; Montgomery Schuyler, "The New Washington," *Scribner's Magazine*, LI, 131-32; *Fiscal Relations*, p. 25, Ser 6915; *Star*, 6 May 1916.

results. Congress ignored the appeals for $250,000 of District tax money for a convention hall, and a National George Washington Memorial Association, which supposedly would raise $2,500,000 for it, failed to materialize. Not until the 1950's would plans for a "Washington Cultural Center" receive any encouragement. Yet yearly the flood of visitors ready to spend money in the capital rose. By 1908 Washingtonians were learning to recognize the arrival of spring less by the appearance of crocuses and daffodils than by the fleet of victorias and sightseeing wagonettes manned by megaphoned guides which lined up near the White House. By 1916, next to government business and real estate, the tourist trade ranked as Washington's chief financial asset.[5]

The Board of Trade meanwhile ceased to exercise the enlightened leadership that had originally distinguished it. In 1903 the president over-stated the case very little when he said that once a board committee, the directors, and the full membership endorsed any proposal, it immediately commanded "public attention, public respect and the support of all good citizens" as well as serious consideration in Congress. Thereafter a growing tendency to regard the welfare of the city as identical with that of the thin top layer of society gradually stripped the organization of its representative quality. Unlike the older, most of the younger generation of directors took little active interest in local philanthropies. Possibly the increasing professionalism of social welfare work accounted for part of that change, but it had the effect of divorcing board policy-makers from close associations with the social betterment leaders. The citizens' associations did not fill the gap, since they increasingly concentrated upon their own neighborhood problems to the exclusion of city-wide concerns. When

[5] *Star*, 2 Jan 1905, 2 May 1909, 28 Feb 1912; *Rpts B/Tr*, 1905, pp. 10-12, 51, 114, 1907, pp. 150-53, 1908, p. 40, 1910, pp. 13-14, 31, 92-98, 1912, p. 8; *Times*, 17 Jun 1908, 19 Mar 1911, 15 Sep 1915; George Fitch, "Seeing Washington through a Megaphone," *Ladies' Home Journal*, Aug 1907, p. 22; *Times*, 15 Sep 1915.

the Federation of Citizens' Associations was incorporated in 1911, it usually presented only the sum total of its members' complaints.

The *Times*, Washington's nearest approach to a left-wing paper, observed in 1911 that the Chamber of Commerce "represents the most advanced and most progressive thought of the community." From it came recommendations on questions the Board of Trade now bypassed—utility rates, milk inspection, and similar matters important to the rank and file of humble citizens. Unhappily, the Chamber carried less weight than its parent organization. After 1907 neither included any colored men. Never admitting that it no longer spoke for the city as a whole, the Board of Trade after 1910 devoted itself to city finances and the protection of the "half-and-half" principle from congressional inroads. The board of directors, men linked with the great real estate companies, the big banks, and the utilities, continued to have enormous influence, particularly as long as some members of Congress looked upon investment in Washington as a sure road to fortune. The comment of one congressman indicated that here and there that view still obtained in 1915; he assured Louis Brownlow in congratulating him on his appointment as District commissioner that a term in the District Building should net him at least $1,000,000.[6]

Irrespective of any incidental, albeit potentially sizable, financial benefits that might accrue to a commissioner, the post was sought after as an honor. But as an incumbent could affect the course of the city's development, the inner circle of the Board of Trade expected to name the civilians whom the President would appoint. President Roosevelt was not wholly amenable to that arrangement. He kept in office Henry Macfarland, whom one Washingtonian later described as "a nice

[6] *Reports of the President's Homes Commission*, p. 212; *Times*, 8 Jan, 26 May 1911, 17 Dec 1913; *Rpts B/Tr*, 1902-1906 inclusive, especially 1903, p. 6, and 1916, pp. 37, 94-96; *Star*, 2 Dec 1909.

piece of bric-a-brac," and, in the face of protest in 1902, appointed Henry West, another journalist. "It is not in human nature," Theodore Noyes wrote the President, "that the *Star* should view with any complacency the appointment to local municipal control of the employee and representative of a rival newspaper of democratic proclivities." Although bitter quarrels between West and Macfarland interfered with their functioning, both men served until late 1909. The retired general and the hardware merchant whom Taft appointed were more to the liking of the Board of Trade.

Board of Trade satisfaction turned to alarm in 1913 when Woodrow Wilson selected two former officers of the Monday Evening Club, Oliver Newman, an experienced newspaper correspondent, and Frederick L. Siddons of the District Bar.[7] Admittedly swayed by a judgment confided to him that the District government had been "controlled by men with connections in speculative real estate, a triangle of profit and power manned by a triumvirate," the President had made clear that he wanted no commissioner tied to the local real estate "ring."[8] In the eyes of powerful business interests both men named were tainted with radicalism. Resentment ran so strong among the old guard that one of the group brought a suit contesting the legality of Newman's appointment on the grounds that he was not a *bona fide* resident of the District; the plaintiff lost. Another blow awaited the former kingmakers in 1915. President Wilson elevated Siddons to the District Supreme Court, and chose as his successor thirty-five-year-old Louis Brownlow. In time to come "Brownie" would be recognized from coast to coast as an authority on public administration. In 1915 he was known in Washington as a competent reporter for a big news

[7] D. H. MacLedan to Albert Burleson, 3 Apr 1913, Wilson Mss; Henry Cabot Lodge to Theodore Roosevelt, 30 Jul 1902, Theodore W. Noyes to Roosevelt, 11 Aug, Crosby Noyes to Roosevelt, 15 Aug, and Mark Hanna to Roosevelt, 20 Aug 1902, Theodore Roosevelt Mss (L.C.).

[8] Quoted in Herbert Janvrin Browne, *Assessment and Taxation in the District of Columbia, and the Fiscal Relation to the Federal Government*, 1915, p. 64; *Post*, 7 Jan 1910, 28 Jan 1913.

syndicate, a friend of muckrakers such as Robert Wickliffe Woolley and, doubtless a source of special uneasiness to ultra-conservatives, a son-in-law of Congressman Thetus Sims, the old warrior of the House District Committee who for years had fought special privilege in the District.[9]

If Macfarland was smug, West easy-going, and Taft's appointees unimaginative and intellectually timid, those shortcomings were more than offset by the qualities of Siddons, Newman, and Brownlow. The engineer commissioners, moreover, one after the other set a high record of efficiency. All told, the successive boards of commissioners during the fifteen years preceding the United States' entry into the war achieved a standard of public service not again equalled in the District until the 1950's.

The commissioners' job was no sinecure. Ideally it meant maintaining and improving the appearance of the capital and simultaneously meeting the community's less immediately visible needs out of the funds Congress was willing to appropriate. It meant balancing the wants of one group of citizens against those of another and providing for intangibles, such as public health and police protection, without curtailing public works. And always it meant, after the administrators had mapped out what they considered the wisest allotment of money, a struggle to persuade the House Subcommittee on District Appropriations that the figure for each item was justified. The prohibition on borrowing in itself created a never-ending quandary even early in the century when Congress authorized Treasury advances at interest for enlargement of the water distribution system and construction of the sewage pumping station. The list of public works the commissioners

[9] *Star*, 13, 14, 18 Nov 1909; interview, Louis Brownlow; *Times*, 14 Nov 1909, 15 Jul, 22 Oct 1914, 31 Jan, 21 Jun 1915; memorandum for Edward C. Becherer, Mar-May 1913, and Elijah Knott to Woodrow Wilson, 19 May 1913, Wilson Mss; Brownlow, *A Passion for Anonymity*, pp. 1-12.

labelled urgent in 1909 and the estimated cost of each suggests the dimensions of the problem of meeting such needs out of current income:

Project	*Cost*
Reclamation of the Anacostia flats, a measure vital to the city's health	$2,552,320
Improvement of Rock Creek valley from its mouth to Massachusetts Avenue, most of the stretch still an unsightly and insanitary dumping ground	$4,750,000
Improvement of the harbor front	$2,880,000
Purchase of additional land for parks	$5,000,000
New buildings for the reformatory and workhouse	$1,000,000
Installation of a high-pressure fire protection system	$ 750,000
Extension of suburban trunk sewers, a project to be spread out over 12 years	$2,000,000
Extension of trunk water mains to the suburbs	$ 800,000
Enlargement of public hospital facilities	$ 150,000
Elimination of dangerous railroad grade crossings outside the city limits	$ 400,000

The total of some $20,282,000, even if spread over several years, would leave nothing over for new services, let alone the expansion of old, in a rapidly growing city whose local revenues had never reached $7,000,000. Then and later, some men on the Hill, like many Washingtonians, would have preferred less emphasis on physical embellishments and more on higher salaries for school teachers, additional school nurses and dentists, sanitary inspectors, larger staff for the Board of Children's Guardians, and a bigger, better paid police force. But critics on the floor of Congress rarely succeeded in redistributing funds in the District budget as it came from committee; at most they cut the over-all figure.[10]

Before 1910 the commissioners' programs got fuller support from Congress than did their successors'. Congressional constituents approved of expenditures for beautifying the capital, and the laws enacted to promote social betterment involved relatively little money. Furthermore, the financial interests of District Committee members pled Washington's cause. Stories, never denied, ran that Senator Arthur Gorman made $1,000,000 and Joseph Babcock, chairman of the House District Committee for some years after 1895, cleared $400,000 in Washington real estate and utility stocks simply by using their advance knowledge of which sections of the city were to get funds for improvements and what privileges were to be allowed the utility companies. And there were others. Congressional decisions to maintain high utility rates and occasional evasion of the 1878 commitment on sharing District expenses were annoying, but the friendliness of the "plunderers of Washington" brought some benefits to the entire community. The *entente cordiale* was undoubtedly more useful to the well-to-do few than to the impecunious many, but humble citizens were gratified that Congress heeded their pleas for a compulsory education law, the removal of an upper age limit for night school students, additions to the fire and police departments, and minor increases in the allowances for charities.[11]

But the honeymoon was over. Indications of growing ir-

[10] Comrs Rpt, 1909, pp. 57-58; Max West, "Room for Improvement," *Outlook*, LXXIX, 625-26; H. B. F. Macfarland, "The Needs of the National Capital," *Outlook*, LXXXIII, 518-21; *Star*, 6 Dec 1909, 15 Feb, 24 Aug 1912; *Times*, 29 Nov 1911; *Survey*, XXVII, 1591; S Doc 422, 61C, 2S, p. 19, Ser 5658; *Fiscal Relations*, p. liii, Ser 6915; *Rpts B/Tr*, 1906, p. 20, 1908, p. 28, 1909, p. 34.

[11] Robert Wickliffe Wolley, "The Plunderers of Washington," *Pearson's Magazine*, XXII, 631-35; *Times*, 30 Nov 1907, 18 Jan, 20 Mar, 9 Aug 1908, 9 Sep 1911; *Star*, 10 Jan 1903; *Rec*, 63C, 2S, p. 4536; Comrs Rpt, 1906, pp. 25-26; *Rpt B/Tr*, 1905, p. 80; Alonzo Tweedale, "The Budget for the District of Columbia," *Proceedings of the Cincinnati Conference for Good City Government*, 1909, pp. 273-83.

ritation in Congress over the half-and-half arrangement appeared in a law of 1909 which required the commissioners thenceforward to submit their annual budgets, not as in the past in the form of estimates of needs, but as statements of expected revenues from District taxes and matching federal funds. Although the innovation precluded long-term financing of major public works, the act at first looked innocuous, simply a way of tailoring the suit to fit the cloth. But new leaders in Congress were soon snipping away at the federal share of District expenses by reducing over-all appropriations. Thus when the commissioners estimated District tax revenues for 1913 at $6,477,000, Congress appropriated $10,531,000, of which less than $4,054,000 was federal money, more nearly a third than a half the total. While working on schemes to shift to the District the entire cost of street maintenance, the House dug into thirty-year-old records and exacted some $1,800,000 from local taxpayers for such items as interest on bonds of 1877 and 1878 and deficiencies in payments for services for which no bill had ever been rendered.[12]

Viewed from the perspective of half a century, three facts are clear about the fight that came out into the open in the early months of 1910: first, the congressmen who launched the attack believed they were engaged in a righteous battle with that monster, special privilege; second, they frequently used battering rams where fly swatters would have served; and, third, many of Washington's self-styled financial experts unwittingly undermined her defenses by shifting ground or by taking positions they could not fortify with incontrovertible figures. Promoters talked of the city's "moderate taxation" when they were trying to attract new business enterprise but insisted to Con-

[12] *Star*, 22 Sep 1909, 15 Jun 1912; *Fiscal Relations*, pp. 1628-39, Ser 6916; *Rec*, 60C, 1S, p, 1908, 60C, 2S, pp. 8, 818-19, 859-74; *Post*, 15 Jun 1910; Comrs Rpt, 1913, p. 97; Laurence Schmeckebier, *The District of Columbia, Its Government and Administration*, pp. 52-54; S Doc 403, 63C, 2S, Ser 6593; *Rpt B/Tr*, 1912, p. 14, and "Financial Relations of the District of Columbia and the Federal Government from 1871 to 1912."

gress that per capita taxes here were higher than in other like-sized cities and that any added burden would be ruinous. Confused thinking and much misinformation in Congress about District laws and practices complicated the struggle. Even members of long standing rarely understood the Treasury's accounting methods in handling District funds. Attendance during debates on District affairs was always slim. Congressmen periodically indulged in preposterous statements, asserting, for example, that the United States defrayed the entire cost of running the schools and paving the streets. Under these circumstances ill temper and a sense of outrage developed in both camps.[13]

The changed attitude of the congressional majority sprang partly from the increasing size of the commissioners' requested budgets: for fiscal year 1901 $7,657,773 was asked for, $7,532,519 voted; for 1910, the last year in which estimates of need determined the amount requested, $16,176,356 was asked for, $10,528,292 appropriated. If the city could manage on $7,500,000 in 1901, irate congressmen argued that more than twice that sum for 1910 was nonsense; they kept the appropriation below $12,880,000 for the next six years.

In the second place, when for unknown reasons the men in control of the House and Senate District committees ceased to invest heavily in Washington real estate and utility stock, they began to advocate economy and the cancellation of a fiscal arrangement that they felt enabled the city's millionaires to batten on the taxpayers of the rest of the country. Reformers from urban constituencies inclined to believe that only financially powerful exploiters of lesser citizens benefitted from the existing system. And senators and congressmen from agrarian districts were determined to hold the line against the march of

[13] *Fiscal Relations*, pp. 266, 296, 367-69, 930-69, Ser 6915, and 1742-44, Ser 6916; "A Square Deal for Washington," reprints from *Star* in Wilson Mss; *Times*, 14 Feb, 13, 27 May 1911, 14 Dec 1913; *Post*, 26 Jan 1913; *Rec*, 61C, 2S, pp. 200-01, 2923-24, 61C, 3S, p. 1597, 62C, 2S, p. 1226, 63C, 2S, p. 1014; *Rpt B/Tr*, 1911, p. 14.

"socialism," that insidious threat creeping out of teeming cities to engulf robust American individualism.[14] Fear of socialism took odd forms. A God-fearing, earnest representative from a farm district in Michigan fought tooth and nail against appropriations for public playgrounds in Washington because to him they represented a socialistic perversion of public obligation.

Conflict between rural and urban interests in Congress, sectional controversies, the admission of three western states between 1907 and 1912, the widening recourse to direct primaries, and after 1914 the popular election of senators, all affected the balance in both houses and bore upon attitudes toward the District of Columbia. Party politics and the constantly mounting pressure of legislative business for a nation grown to a world power pushed local affairs further and further into the background. The minority party usually opposed majority-sponsored District bills, and both parties postponed "District days" with increasing frequency. Compared to the spate of constructive local acts passed between 1902 and 1908, the measures enacted in the next decade were few and relatively insignificant. Badly needed social legislation sneaked through, if at all, only by the skills of its supporters in tying it to an appropriation bill.[15]

Still, by 1916 the community's fiscal condition was encouraging. The money borrowed from the Treasury in 1901 and after had been fully repaid and the funded debt reduced to $4,000,000. More equitable real estate assessments that

[14] *Letter from Secretary of Treasury Transmitting Estimates of Appropriations*, 1901-1917; "What the States Pay towards the District of Columbia's Municipal Expenses," *American City*, VIII, 119-20; *Rec*, 60C, 2S, p. 1832, 63C, 2S, p. 1162; H Rpt 937, 63C, 2S, Ser 6560; *Rpts B/Tr*, 1914, p. 9, 1915, pp. 10-12; *Times*, 13 May 1911, 17 Dec 1913.

[15] *Rec*, 60C, 1S, p. 4353, 4383-85; *Star*, 9 May 1909, 28 May 1911, 25, 26 Aug 1912; Louis Ottenberg, "Fatherless Children of the National Capital," *Survey*, XXXIV, 459-60; *Times*, 19 Dec 1913, 15 Jul, 6, 12 Dec 1914, 7 Jan, 18 Apr 1916; *Fiscal Relations*, pp. 963-66, Ser 6915; *Rpt B/Tr*, 1916, pp. 10, 13.

added $40,000,000 to over-all valuations cooled the heat of critics in Congress, and a law imposing a local tax on intangible personal property promised to catch up with "malfactors of great wealth." A newly created District Public Utilities Commission, made up of the three District commissioners, obtained authority to fix rates and control the sale and emission of utility stocks and securities. The difficulty of arriving at just valuations of the companies' property, the basis of the rates to be set, delayed final rulings until after the war, but the essential first steps in protecting consumers had already been taken. Still more important, the principle of some federal sharing of District expenses survived lengthy congressional hearings held late in 1915.[16]

The fiscal hearings revealed the intricacies of the problem and the strengths and weaknesses of both sides of the argument. Senator Gallinger pointed to complications arising from the long established custom whereby Congress authorized federal officials not responsible to the District commissioners to spend local funds voted "in the sundry civil and legislative appropriation acts, in deficiency acts," and others. Some of the data presented by both sides contained outdated figures and faulty comparisons with the taxes of other cities, but the testimony, if occasionally colored by passion, was illuminating to committee members who had never before examined the tangle of interrelated obligations. Several witnesses reverted to the arguments of the Southard report of 1835 setting forth the pledge implicit in the government's eighteenth-century agreement with the original proprietors of the land. Other men spoke of the paucity of manufacturing plants and great commercial houses such as supplied the bulk of taxes to other big cities and stressed the loss of revenue from the extensive tax-exempt federal holdings. Agreement that the national government should pay

[16] H Rpt 937, 63C, 2S, Ser 6560; *Rec*, 63C, 3S, pp. 1335-37; *Rpt B/Tr*, 1910, pp. 57-58, 1916, pp. 7-8; Brownlow, *A Passion for Anonymity*, pp. 90-91.

something left the main question of how much and by what method.

Local taxpayers opposed a sliding scale of federal payments on the grounds that it would mean constant uncertainty about how much money would be available in any given year. The two civilian commissioners favored a scheme by which the government would foot all the bills but would collect from District property-owners levies equal to, but not in excess of, those paid by residents of other like-sized cities. Louis Brownlow believed that plan sounder than the "legislative fiction" of half-and-half; he demonstrated the impossibility of separating the costs of services to the local public from those primarily benefitting the national government. In spite of Brownlow's convincing exposition, the committee, after decreeing half-and-half sharing no longer feasible or necessary, concluded that District taxes should be used solely for the District, and all local revenues be spent before drawing upon the United States Treasury. Congress took no action on the report, but it left the door open to future readjustments which, Senator Works remarked, should provide for the restoration of some authority to the community over its own expenditures and relieve Congress of some of its aldermanic responsibilities.[17]

Local self-government and "half-and-half" were so tied together by the Organic Act of 1878 that, quite apart from uneasiness over Negro suffrage, influential Washingtonians were still loath to contemplate an elective city government lest it kill all federal financial aid. Full voting representation in Congress, on the other hand, got increasingly wide support from 1909 onward. At a public dinner given for President Taft in May 1909 Chief Justice Stafford of the District Supreme Court made an eloquent plea: "Strip men of the ballot and you take away from society the most powerful inducement that

[17] *Rec*, 63C, 3S, pp. 143, 160-61, 1113-16, 1348, 4864-65; Bureau of the Census, *Statistics of Cities Having a Population of over 30,000*, 1907, pp. 330-33; *Fiscal Relations*, pp. i-lix, 43-44, 406-07, 963-80, Ser 6915, pp. 1639-40, 1742-57, Ser 6916.

can prompt selfish human nature to educate and elevate its helpless and its poor." In a scarcely veiled attack on white fears of Negro voting, he asked: "Shall we say we fear the suffrages of ignorance and vice . . . that could not last a generation if we did our duty by our fellow-men? . . . Never until the men of wealth and education have spent their last surplus dollar and exhausted the ingenuity of their brains in the effort to make their fellow-men worthy to be sharers in the government, never until then will they have a right to hide behind an excuse like that."[18]

The President derided Stafford's arguments, but a straw vote conducted the next year by the newly organized District Suffrage League polled 10,816 ballots favoring local suffrage to only 944 against. By 1915 the Board of Trade also decided the city had more to gain than to lose from a modification of the Organic Act. Residents felt little dissatisfaction with the administration of commissioners Newman, Siddons, and Brownlow, but the disadvantages of rule by congressional committee were emerging with unmistakable clarity. To much of the local public the surest remedy seemed to lie in having an elected District senator and representatives on the Hill, although some opposition to accompanying that change with an elected city government continued. Congressmen who discussed the matter at all inclined to think well of a watered-down home rule under congressional supervision, but they were more than doubtful about giving the District virtual statehood.[19] In short, what the community believed most beneficial was what Congress was least likely to grant. Yet at the end of 1916 confidence ran strong that city and Congress together could work out a mutually satisfactory solution.

[18] *Star*, 9 May, 23 Nov 1909; S Doc 684, 60C, 2S, Ser 5408; S Doc 1138, 62C, 3S, Ser 6365.

[19] *Star*, 15 May 1909, 1 Jan 1911; *Times*, 29 Apr, 8 Dec 1913, 14 Oct 1914, 26 Oct 1916; Archibald Butt, *Taft and Roosevelt*, pp. 29-31; *Post*, 16 Feb, 4 May 1913; *Rec*, 63C, 2S, p. 1161; *Rpt B/Tr*, 1916, pp. 13-16; S Dis Comee, 64C, 1S, Subcomee Hrgs on D.C., pp. 10, 21, 55-71.

CHAPTER X

THE CITY OF CONVERSATION, 1901-1916

IN Lafayette Square pigeons strutting, children playing Prisoners' Base while their governesses and nursemaids gossipped, men reading their newspapers in the warm sunshine and glancing across to the White House lawn to admire the reds of the tulips in the big round bed before the portico; open carriages drawn by well-groomed horses rolling along the Avenue; silk-hatted dignitaries and ladies in sweeping skirts and picture hats mounting the stone steps from the Mall to the Capitol terrace and nodding to the bandannaed colored women offering passers bunches of violets and daffodils; in the alleyways pickaninnies jostling for room for games of hopscotch or marbles under the clothes lines hung with rich people's wash,—spring-time in Theodore Roosevelt's Washington. In Rock Creek valley horse-back riders followed the paths through woods scarcely touched since Henry Adams found enchantment there in the 1860's; flat layers of white dogwood blossoms showed near the thickets of chestnut trees where, come fall, boys armed with sticks and pillowcases would be collecting the prickly bursting burrs. Frequently accompanied by the French ambassador or some other panting notable, the President, advocate of the strenuous life, often clambered about the ravines in Rock Creek Park and sometimes, after a vigorous walk, with a gusto equalling John Quincy Adams' eighty years before, stripped off his clothes for a swim in the Potomac. Delighted Washingtonians long talked of the day when J. J. Jusserand followed his example, only to have the President call back to him from midstream, "Look at your hands!"; the courtly ambassador had forgotten to take off his gloves.

Hot weather brought men, women, and children to the bathing beach on the Tidal Basin. When the basin froze, "the clerks and shopgirls of the city skated over the ice shoulder to shoulder with cabinet officers and their families and with important members of foreign embassies and legations."[1] And there was the zoo now accessible by trolley and now populated not only with buffaloes and elephants but also lions, tigers, and bears, exotic birds, fearsome looking reptiles, and, on pleasant days, thousands of the human species equipped with picnic baskets and bags of peanuts to share with the monkeys. The nineteen new municipal tennis courts were in constant use, while boys and young men played ball on the diamonds on the White lot, the Monument grounds and in Potomac Park. When the American League, organized in 1901, admitted the Nationals', Washington's baseball fever rose rapidly; the home games drew crowds seemingly untroubled at repeated defeats. When the Griffith Stadium opened in 1912, President Taft set the precedent of tossing out the first ball from the bunting-draped box in the grandstands. The first game of the season thenceforward became a state occasion lightened by a special camaraderie. During the summer of 1916 the excitement in much of Washington caused by the Nationals' standing for the first time within reach of the pennant largely blotted out concern over torpedoed shipping and the stalemate of trench warfare in Europe.[2]

"More and more," wrote a London newspaper correspondent, "Washington becomes the Mecca of the United States." Brides and grooms, now eschewing Niagara Falls, chose to honeymoon on the Potomac, high school students chaperoned by their history teachers came every spring by the trainload and, as automobiles ceased to be costly luxuries, entire families made the hegira by car. On spring and summer mornings, licensed guides, most of them Negroes, lay in wait for their prey in Lafayette Square. One man with a flair for the dramatic always

[1] *Times*, 4 Jun 1908; *Post*, 13 Jan 1910.

[2] Comrs Rpts, 1906, p. 35, 1909, p. 41, 1917, p. 19; *Times*, 17 Jul 1915; *Post*, 20 Jun 1904; *Star*, 26 Mar 1905, 28 Jun 1909; Souvenir Program, 1901-1951, *The Nationals of the American League*.

assembled his audience first at the bronze group commemorative of General Lafayette and, with a wave of the hand toward the sketchily draped figure kneeling at the hero's feet and extending a sword to him, announced: "Great General! He not look at naked woman. She say: 'General, you give me back mah clothes and ah give yo back yo s-ward.' " Commenting on "the vastness and variety" of Washington's floating population, an Englishman called her "at once the most and the least American city in America, the most American because there, if anywhere, one feels oneself assisting at the great composite panorama of American life."[3]

European visitors generally admired the public architecture and the layout of the capital which Charles Dickens sixty years before had ridiculed as "The City of Magnificent Intentions." The Honorable Maud Pauncefote, daughter of the British ambassador in 1903, thought "the red brick town" surrounding the white government buildings unprepossessingly ugly, but she considered Washington's cosmopolitanism and good manners a chief attraction, one not duplicated by the wealth of New York, or the blue-stocking atmosphere of Boston and Philadelphia. H. G. Wells, on the other hand, was not beguiled by Washington's easy-going amiability. In 1906 seeking to understand "the future of America," he found the capital an "anti-climax," a place not wholly "alive to present and future things."[4]

Henry James, by 1906 as British as he was American, wondered about "the 'real' sentiments of appointed foreign participants . . . before phenomena which, whatever they may be, differ more from the phenomena of other capitals and other societies than they resemble them." Struck by the "extraordinar-

[3] A. Maurice Low, "Washington, the American Mecca," *Harper's Weekly*, LVII, 11; Sydney Brooks, "Washington and the White House," *The Living Age*, CCLXXVII, 69-70.

[4] The Honorable Maud Pauncefote, "Washington, D.C.," *The Nineteenth Century and After*, CCCXII, 280-81; Montgomery Schuyler, "The New Washington," *Scribner's Magazine*, LI, 135; H. G. Wells, "The Future in America, Washington as Anticlimax," *Harper's Weekly*, L, 1420.

ily easy and pleasant" quality of life in Washington, he disagreed with Americans who thought politics always omnipresent; on the contrary, he noted a bewildering absence of "political permeation." In this capital, in contrast to the "social ubiquity . . . of the acceptable MP" in London, not more than "half a dozen members of the Lower House and not more than a dozen of the Upper" were part of the social scene. To him Washington presented two faces, "the public and official, . . . the Imperial part," and that of "a group of people engaged always in conversation." Her properest name was "City of Conversation." What did people talk about? Washington—almost nothing else. Unlike the rest of America, here men were "solidly, vividly present" as part of civilization outside "the market." Yet despite her differences, James thought the city the embodiment of the American spirit.

One anonymous "English Visitor" to the chief "legislative foundry" of the United States remarked upon what he labelled the very limited range of society. Besides the diplomatic corps, Cabinet members and the high-ranking military, the only people that counted were "distinguished scientists in government service," Supreme Court justices, a handful of senators and congressmen whose social position at home made them acceptable in Washington, a "few dozen old residential families," and a small selection of the recently arrived *nouveaux riches*. The fabric of society resembled a small piece of "exquisite embroidery overweighted by a fringe that is neither small nor exquisite. . . . The fringe in question is composed of Negroes, who form a third of the population, the shopkeepers and retail traders, the clerks in the government offices, about nine-tenths of the Senators, including their wives and daughters, and of course the entire army of trippers."[5]

The exclusion of most congressmen from the ranks of "soci-

[5] Henry James, "Washington," *North American Review*, CLXXXII, 662-68, 673-75, 905-07 (later published in *The American Scene*); "The Social Stride of Washington's Elite," *Harper's Weekly*, LV, 9.

ety" frequently distressed newly arrived congressional wives. Forgetting that the twentieth-century capital was no longer a small town in which a Dolly Madison would make them feel at home, and unaware that rich New Yorkers following "T.R." to Washington had endowed high society with a new sophistication, women from rural communities turned into "social tragedies." "While the ramparts are theirs to stroll around, the citadel itself is as securely barricaded against them as though it were the Austrian court." The Women's Congressional Club founded in 1908 probably lightened their loneliness and disappointment, but tea and committee meetings in the house on McPherson Square were a poor substitute for the "superb" dinners given within the "innermost stronghold." "When a young girl comes out," Maud Pauncefote noted with amusement, "she is called a Bud." But buds sprung from congressional stock were rare, and the cost of raising one in a Washington hothouse forbade families not to the manor born from attempting it.[6]

Yet touches of small-town simplicity remained. As the President had persuaded Congress to vote funds for a wing of executive offices at the White House, small Roosevelts and velocipedes took over the upper floors of the house while on Saturday mornings their father shook hands with visitors touring the mansion, his famous grin particularly warm for mothers trailed by a string of children. Almost any well-mannered white person could still wangle an invitation to a White House reception except during the weeks of preparation for the marriage of "Princess Alice" to Speaker of the House Nicholas Longworth. In fact, the character of official entertaining changed very little before 1913, although Mrs. Taft put footmen into livery at the White House, in order to spare visitors the discomfort

[6] Mrs. Henry T. Rainey, "The Women's Congressional Club," *New England Magazine*, n.s., XL, 265-71; Roberta V. Bradshaw, "The Congressional Club," *Good Housekeeping*, LVI, 27-30; *Times*, 13 Oct 1907; "What It Cost Me to be a Prominent Man," *American Magazine*, LXXI, 84-85; Pauncefote, "Washington," p. 281.

of mistaking a fellow guest for a servant. Sheer numbers of officials required such a tightening of the rules of precedence that one man mournfully found himself the dinner partner of the same woman thirty times over a single season. Public appetite for news about social doings was so keen that in 1910 a weekly magazine, *Washington Society*, began publication of every gleanable detail of who squired whom where, how Senator Henderson's wife, after getting 16th Street renamed "Avenue of the Presidents," served vegetarian fare to guests at "Henderson Castle," and who introduced the fashion of the large Sunday dinner parties that made the McKinley's hymn-singing Sunday evenings seem part of another age.

As a heavy sleet and snow storm during the night of March 3, 1909, held up trains filled with guests and made Washington's streets all but impassable, President Taft's inauguration lost much of its splendor, but that deprivation heightened the eagerness of citizens four years later to stage an elaborate inaugural celebration. To the consternation of local promoters, President-elect Wilson, having concluded that inaugurations were being commercialized, refused to allow an inaugural ball. Washingtonians and the 200,000 visitors had to content themselves with the formal ceremonies at the Capitol and a parade that disorderly suffragettes attempted to break up. "Society" received a further shock when the new President, professing lack of time for golf, declined membership in the Chevy Chase Club, which he obviously looked upon as a hotbed of unwholesome social standards nurtured by people with more money than good sense. Annoyance increased at his playing nine holes now and again at the unpretentious Congressional Country Club. For the first time since the founding of the Metropolitan Club in the 1870's, its officers extended no invitation to the President of the United States to join that select body.[7]

[7] Taft, *Recollections of Full Years*, pp. 27, 280-81, 372-73; "Spectator," *Outlook*, LXXXV, 305-06; A. Maurice Low, "Sundays at the Capital,"

To the group that prided itself on keeping "society and trade . . . divided by a gulf as broad as that which separates them on the other side of the water," the socialistic notions and puritanism of the erudite former professor in the White House were as offensive as a background of trade itself could have been. His disapproval of everything "undemocratic," according to a friend of the old regime, merely meant that instead of the former "well-ordered dignified affairs" held in private homes, now "state receptions and dinners were given in hotel parlors and dining rooms." Criticism of such lack of savoir faire found another outlet shortly after the death of old ex-Senator John Henderson; for his teetotaling widow smashed every bottle of his famous cellar so that the gutters of 16th Street below Henderson Castle ran red with vintage wines. The marriages of two of the President's daughters and in 1915 his own remarriage, one woman observed maliciously, at least "gave society plenty to talk about."[8]

The city's social structure, meanwhile, irrespective of political realignments, had undergone change. In 1905 Bishop Satterlee expressed an uneasiness shared by old families: "A new type of residents are [sic] gathering in Washington, who, while they bring wealth, magnificence and luxury to the capital of the country, are, as a rule, actuated by no sense of civic, moral or religious obligation regarding the welfare of the community, and it is a very serious question whether the material advantages that they bring are any compensation for the atmosphere of careless irresponsibility which they create." Self-protectively the descendants of the group Mrs. Dahlgren had called the "very elite" began to draw away from much of

---

Harper's Weekly, LVI, p. 9; *Post*, 7 Jan 1906, 30 Jan, 27 Nov 1910, 2, 27 Feb, 16 Mar 1913; Butt, *Taft and Roosevelt*, pp. 48, 189; *Star*, 7 Jan 1906; *Times*, 23 Feb, 9 Mar 1908, 3-5 Mar 1913; Mrs. John King Van Rensselaer, *The Social Ladder*, pp. 256-59; *Washington Society*, I-V, 1910-1915.

[8] Helen Nicolay, *Our Capital on the Potomac*, p. 454; Isabel Anderson, *Presidents and Pies, Life in Washington, 1897-1919*, pp. 167-68.

official society and its hangers-on. High-ranking government officials without independent means were themselves troubled at the growing elaborateness of the entertaining expected of them, but Washington and Georgetown bluebloods were seldom office-holders and in social matters thus had freedom of choice. That freedom gave birth to the "cave-dweller." The name was new; the phenomenon was not. Resentment of brash newly arrived politicians and their protégés had perhaps laid the groundwork for cave-dwelling as early as President Jackson's day. But neither that first breach nor that created by the distaste of dignified old families for the wealthy social carpetbaggers of the Reconstruction period had endured. The twentieth-century manifestation lived on into the 1950's.

Inasmuch as Washington society of the Roosevelt era had an undeniable brilliance, more than one observer believed that cave-dwelling arose from lack of money to keep pace. But some cave-dwellers had ample fortunes, and the non-intercourse policy apparently stemmed not only from rejection of the ostentatiously rich but also from dislike of the snobbery of rank. Furthermore, the constant turnover among officials discouraged attempts to winnow the chaff from the grain. Yet, in setting themselves apart, cave-dwellers wrapped themselves in an exclusiveness that socially ambitious outsiders longed to break in upon. Few people agreed at any given time about who was and who was not a cave-dweller. Some included New England-born-and-bred Henry Adams, and somewhat later the Leiters and McLeans, new to the capital in the 1890's, would claim to be part of the select group.[9]

Yet even had the voluntary withdrawal into their caves never occurred, the eminent old families of Washington and Georgetown must have played a progressively smaller part in the social life of the capital. As the international responsibilities

[9] *Star*, 26 Mar 1905; Henry Loomis Nelson, "The Capital of Our Democracy," *Century*, LIV, 39; Maria Columbia, "Washington: Its Cave-Dwellers and Its Social Secretaries," *Delineator*, LXV, 248-53.

of the United States multiplied and government functions widened, the new complexity of governmental operations began to create a compartmentalization that slowly affected social intercourse itself. The lengthening list of high-ranking federal officials also tended to shrink the importance of a local aristocracy dwindling in relative if not in absolute numbers. For forty-odd years sons had been leaving Washington to build careers wherever larger opportunities offered. Daughters stayed behind to marry or, by ill chance, to remain maiden ladies; but marriage itself took many young women away. A genealogical tracing of the native belles who married into the military services would, it is true, doubtless reveal a considerable group who departed but returned now and again and, upon their husbands' retirement, resumed permanent residence in Washington or Georgetown; nevertheless as Army and Navy wives they no longer represented the deeply rooted local tradition of their forebears. That steady drain upon the community's human resources had profound, albeit subtle, consequences, denying Washington, as time went on, a core of influential families conditioned by generations of devoted service and interest in local affairs.[10]

Experienced globe-trotters, captivated as they were by a pervasive charm that endured in spite of social climbing and occasional outright vulgarity, still observed in Washington a curious cultural provincialism. It contrasted sharply with the catholicity of taste and many-faceted artistic talents to be found in European capitals. Henry James implied that Washington's self-absorbed conversation at best touched very lightly on the creative arts. The anonymous "English Visitor" declared that the city had "no influence over the arts and letters of the American people. The day is infinitely distant and in all probability will never come at all when every American artist, author,

[10] Based on a sampling of the Washington *Social Register*, "Married Maidens," 1901-1916; Barry Bulkley, *Washington Old and New*, pp. 108-09; Schuyler, "New Washington," *Scribner's*, LI, 135.

dramatist, and musician will turn instinctively toward Washington."

Reporters covering the current American political and society news found Washington a happy hunting ground. The Gridiron Club dinners were still gala occasions for the men privileged to attend the "cannibal feast." But the novels, poetry, and essays turned out in Washington were fewer and of lesser quality than in the 1880's. No American poet worthy of the name deliberately chose to live in the capital. Symbolically as well as materially Joaquin Miller's log cabin stood empty on Meridian Hill until in 1912 the shell, minus poet, was moved to Rock Creek Park. Henry Adams, John Hay, Theodore Roosevelt, and Senator Henry Cabot Lodge formed a quartet of literary lights at the opening of the twentieth century, but John Hay soon left Washington for good, Adams was in Washington only intermittently thereafter, official duties increasingly dimmed the purely literary brilliance of the other three, and Hay died in 1905. Gaillard Hunt edited the letters of Margaret Bayard Smith and later wrote a charming social history, *Life in America One Hundred Years Ago*, while Thomas Nelson Page, before he became ambassador to Italy in 1913, turned out new tales of "Ole Virginia." Washington's literary colony, however, steadily dwindled; professional writers other than journalists, scientists, and a handful of historians bound to the capital by the demands of their work rarely lingered long in the city. J. J. Jusserand, the French Ambassador and British Ambassador James Bryce managed to write distinguished books while they were here, but Americans apparently found Washington distracting. Lord Bryce suggested that the federal system itself militated against having a single city at once the political, financial, and literary capital of the country.[11]

[11] "The Social Stride of Washington's Elite," p. 9; Richard V. Oulahan, "Literary Clubland, the Gridiron Club of Washington," *The Bookman*, XXIII, 151; Francis Weston Carruth, "Washington in Fiction," *ibid.*, XV, 451-63; Paul Wilsbach, "Literary Landmarks of the National Capital," *ibid.*, XLIII, 486-94; Anderson, *Presidents and Pies*, p. 26.

Popular plays at the National Theatre and the Lafayette Opera House, later renamed Belasco Theatre, generally drew fair audiences for matinees, but skimpy crowds for evening performances. Vaudeville flourished at theatres no longer able to support plays, and the three or four burlesque houses had a still larger clientele, of which Supreme Court Justice Oliver Wendell Holmes was probably the most notable individual. Movies, though not yet a recognized form of art, by 1910 were cutting in upon every other type of entertainment.[12]

In 1903 the public was still unaware that the Smithsonian Institution included a potential National Gallery of Art. When fire in 1865 destroyed the two hundred-odd Indian paintings of John Mix Stanley and William Bird King which had hung in the Smithsonian's art exhibition hall, the regents had loaned the remaining paintings and prints to the Corcoran Gallery and the Library of Congress. Reclaimed thirty years later but, for lack of a place, not put on display, the pictures had remained a secret nucleus of a national collection. In 1903 Harriet Lane Johnston, belle and hostess of the White House in her uncle James Buchanan's day, bequeathed her collection of old masters to a National Gallery when one should come into being. A friendly law suit followed which ended with a court decree that a National Art Gallery was already in existence. "Valuable as were the paintings," wrote an officer of the National Museum in 1909, "the real gain was in the stimulus given to art as a feature of the national collections, in the example set that the government might be trusted as a custodian of art for the people." The immediate result was an offer from Charles Freer of Detroit to give the National Gallery his paintings, largely canvasses by American artists, notably James McNeill Whistler, and a still uncompleted collection of oriental art, all to be housed in a special building; two years later William T. Evans of New York gave the gallery his collection of modern Amer-

[12] *Star*, 26 Mar 1905, *Times*, 28 Jul 1907.

ican paintings. When the new National Museum on the Mall opened in the spring of 1910, the central hall was hung with the nation's old and new art treasures.

In the interim local citizens organized the National Society of the Fine Arts and within a year or two affiliated with the country-wide American Society of the Fine Arts. While the Society's lectures and annual conventions held at the New Willard Hotel further quickened public interest, Washingtonians were disappointed in their hopes of seeing the city become not only "the foremost art center in the western world" but also the home of a distinguished school of American painters. Of sculpture the story was much the same. Daniel Chester French, Gutson Borglum, Lorado Taft, and other eminent sculptors commissioned to execute pieces for the government maintained their studios outside Washington.[13]

Fostered by the volume of building in the city and influenced by the taste emanating from the Octagon House, which the American Institute of Architects rescued from demolition in 1902 and made its own headquarters, architecture, at once a craft, an art, and a profession, supplied more native talent than appeared in other fields. While New York firms designed most of the new government buildings, a growing number of local architects commanded attention. The originality of a Frank Lloyd Wright, it is true, never materialized in the churches, office buildings, and expensive houses put up in these years, but construction was solid, proportions were usually well balanced, and the ornamentation was seldom offensive.

The beautiful and cultivated Mrs. Reginald De Koven rue-

[13] Richard Rathbun, *The National Gallery of Art*, Smithsonian Institution, U.S. National Museum *Bulletin*, No. 70, Reprint 1916, pp. 18-19; "National Gallery of Art," Rpt, Smithsonian Institution, 1910; the National Society of Fine Arts, *Articles of Incorporation, Constitution and Bylaws*, 1906; "Art in Washington," and "The Best Art in America," *Art and Progress*, III, 532, and IV, 1007-09; Leila Mechlin, *Works of Art in Washington*; *Star*, 2 Dec 1905, 1 Jan 1912; *Times*, 24 Nov 1913; Anderson, *Presidents and Pies*, pp. 2-3, 167; Marietta M. Andrews, *My Studio Window, Sketches of the Pageant of Washington Life*.

fully observed that Washingtonians cared less about symphonies than about tea. When Reginald De Koven and his wife moved to Washington, they believed that the city would support a professionally trained orchestra. His name was well known. His successful light opera *Robin Hood* had won him acclaim both abroad and at home, and his lyric "Oh Promise Me" became a standard addition to the Lohengrin and Mendelssohn marches at American weddings. Having persuaded several wealthy Washingtonians to underwrite the cost of six concerts, he assembled sixty qualified instrumentalists and launched a first concert in April 1902 with Paderewski as soloist. The *coup de grâce* was dealt the struggling new Washington Symphony Orchestra the next autumn, for scarcely had De Koven scheduled a series of Friday afternoon concerts for the 1902-1903 season than word came that the White House had chosen Friday afternoons for the official teas over which Mrs. Theodore Roosevelt would preside. Evening concerts were virtually out of the question because halls were not available at night, and society was dining out. After giving the six guaranteed performances, each well received by the critics, the orchestra disbanded.

That failure silenced the newspapers, which from time to time had talked of Washington's increasing dedication to music. In 1907 and again in 1910 and 1912 the Music Art Society of Washington vainly attempted to revive the local symphony. And yet in 1914 a Bostonian, who had expected to starve for lack of concerts in the capital, found "a veritable feast of music." Played chiefly by the Boston, New York Philharmonic, or the Philadelphia orchestras, afternoon performances confined audiences to people of leisure. Talented amateurs and professional musicians played for the Friday Morning Music Club, but the general public had a narrower musical choice: a limited selection of phonograph records, a week of opera every winter, church music, including the singing of the boys' choir at the open air services in the close of the National Cathedral, concerts given by the amateur choral societies or by the Marine Band, overtures before curtain-rising at the National and Belasco theatres, minstrel show rag-time and cakewalks at the vaudeville houses, and the pianos at local movies.

Colored people were usually refused admission to white concerts, but Negroes to whom good music in some form was all-important set high standards for their own choral societies. Negro church music excelled anything to be heard in white churches, and white people not infrequently edged their way into evening services of Negro congregations to hear the choirs. In 1904 a bi-racial audience considered the great musical event of the year the rendition of Samuel Coleridge-Taylor's *Hiawatha*, conducted in person by that gifted British Negro and sung by the Negro choral society named for him. The Marine Band supplied the orchestra.[14] Later the growing barrier between the races interfered with a repetition of that success.

As the government widened its fields of scientific investigation, every year brought more scientists into federal service. In spite of the continuing hold of William Graham Sumner's laissez-faire teachings upon industrial America, the scientific needs of industry itself led to new demands for answers which federal bureaus might supply. At the same time growing public concern over conservation of the nation's dwindling natural resources and over preservation of citizens' health put pressure upon government agencies to expand research. Thus between 1901 and 1905 alone, four new bureaus came into being in Washington—the National Bureau of Standards in 1901, the Bureau of Mines, and a separate Bureau of the

[14] De Koven, *A Musician and His Wife*, pp. 204-05; Washington Choral Society *Bulletin*, I, 55, V, 191; *Post*, 28, 29 Apr 1902; Sunday *Star*, 20 Nov 1932; *Times*, 27 Nov, 22 Dec 1915; *Program of the Eighth Concert of the Rubenstein Choral Club*, 1911-1912, Cuno Rudolph Mss (L.C.); miscellaneous programs and Notice of Samuel Coleridge-Taylor Choral Society (Music Div, L.C.); Elbert F. Baldwin, "An American Cathedral Close," *Outlook*, LXXX, 288.

Census in 1902, and in 1905 the Forestry Service. The century-old Marine Hospital Service, enlarged in 1902 and again in 1908, became the Public Health Service in 1912, and, in the meantime, units in other federal departments took on new scientific functions. The National Advisory Committee for Aeronautics, created in 1915, supplied the capstone of the impressive government structure.

Mounting stress upon applied rather than basic research, it is true, lost to government service brilliant men who preferred the disinterested, cloistered search for pure knowledge to the routine of seeking answers to practical problems. The universities took over most of the fundamental research which John Quincy Adams had believed the federal government should pursue. But if no Joseph Henry, no Simon Newcomb, and no George Brown Goode now represented the United States government in the ruling circles of science, and if "bureau builders," like the conservationists Gifford Pinchot and James R. Garfield, and Charles D. Walcott, Secretary of the Smithsonian, preached that scientific investigations "on the part of the Government should be limited nearly to utilitarian purposes evidently for the general welfare," the achievements as well as the broadened reach of federal scientific activities worked as a yeast in the community.

The successes in applying science to urgent public problems were stimulating. When Major Walter Reed and his associates in Cuba proved that the "Aedis Egyptae" mosquito was the carrier of the yellow fever bacillus, the work of the Army Medical School, which Major Reed directed from the dispensary at Arsenal Point until his premature death in November 1902, inspired fresh confidence in the value of government programs. Investigations begun in the 1890's under Harvey Wiley of the Department of Agriculture's Bureau of Chemistry not only informed the American housewife of the dangers of adulterated food stuffs and brought about passage of the Pure Food and Drugs Act of 1906, but also heightened interest in chemical research. Physicists at the Bureau of Standards were employing cathode-ray tubes and radio-active minerals before 1916, and the presence of the bureau's scientific staff generated a kind of electric current that linked Washingtonians to an exciting unknown universe. Forgetting the ridicule once heaped upon "Professor Langley's bird," during 1909 and 1910 citizens travelled by trolley across the river to Fort Myer to watch the performances of the Wright brothers' heavier-than-air plane. Even uninformed people expected great things from the National Advisory Committee for Aeronautics and its newly opened experimental laboratory.

Although the studies of Indian culture that John Wesley Powell had initiated in the Bureau of American Ethnology appeared to serve no immediately utilitarian purpose, the findings and the carefully ordered collections at the National Museum drew anthropologists to Washington. Data feeding in from the Geological Survey and the Department of Agriculture turned the National Museum of the Smithsonian Institution into a research center in anthropology, zoology, and botany, while the reports stemming from the oceanographic explorations of the Bureau of Fisheries' ship "Albatross" had perhaps as much significance for the student of evolution as for the American fishing industry.[15]

Nor was scientific work in twentieth-century Washington confined to the government. Andrew Carnegie's gift of $10,000,000, which launched the Carnegie Institution in 1902, restored to the city an important role in the realm of pure science. Of the Institution's eleven divisions, only the Department of Geophysics, the Department of Terrestrial Magnetism, and the Department of Historical Research carried on their programs in the capital, but the contributions of the

[15] Dupree, *Science*, pp. 182, 252, 268-97, 385; O. Edward Anderson, *The Health of a Nation; Post*, 20 Mar 1904; *Times*, 8 Aug 1911; *Proceedings of the U.S. National Museum*, XXXVIII; "Celebration of the One-Hundredth Anniversary of the Organization of the U.S. Coast and Geodetic Survey," *Journal of the Washington Academy of Sciences*, VI, 260-68.

"earth scientists" caught the attention of the entire world, and the work of the historical unit enabled American historians for the first time readily to locate essential archival materials. Explorations sponsored by the National Geographic Society, moreover, exposed Washingtonians vicariously to scientific adventure in remote parts of South America and Alaska. At the dinner celebrating the Society's twenty-fifth anniversary in 1913, seven hundred members and guests heard Professor Hiram Bingham tell of his expedition into the Inca country of the high Andes and then, crowning moment of the occasion that British Ambassador James Bryce declared had no parallel in all history, the distinguished audience watched Rear Admiral Robert Peary, "discoverer" of the North Pole, award the National Geographic Society gold medal to the Norwegian Captain Roald Amundsen for his feat in reaching the South Pole.

Social scientists and historical scholars were less in the public eye than the men working in the exact sciences, but the Cosmos Club provided a common meeting ground. There exchange of ideas might occur naturally between men of widely divergent intellectual interests—between, for example, the witty and dedicated pure food expert, Harvey Wiley, and the urbane and learned Herbert Putnam, Librarian of Congress; between the elderly economist and statistician Francis Walker and Walter Swingle, the plant explorer, or the young ichthyologist Austin Clark, whom the Swedish government would later decorate for his work on forms of marine life; General George Sternberg might talk easily with George Burgess of the Bureau of Standards or with J. Franklin Jameson of the Carnegie Institution and editor of the *American Historical Review.* Similarly the Library of Congress Round Table luncheons, which Herbert Putnam inaugurated and presided over, daily brought together eight or nine gifted men from many walks of life; Judge Wendell P. Stafford or Supreme Court Justice Oliver Wendell Holmes might lunch beside the engaging Gaillard Hunt, or Secretary Charles Walcott of the Smithsonian, or some still obscure young scholar engaged in research at the library. No university campus in America offered more varied intellectual nourishment than the "city of conversation."[16]

Conversation, after the German torpedoing of the "Lusitania" in May 1915, turned with mounting intensity to the question of American intervention in the war in Europe. For months "business as usual," meaning concentration upon domestic politics and the accompanying "social game," continued to be a widely accepted motto in Washington. The resignation of Secretary of State William J. Bryan in June and the appointment of Robert Lansing made a stir, but one cynic later argued that it arose not from hopes for a more aggressive foreign policy but from relief that the prohibitionist Bryan could no longer urge upon diplomats the virtues of grape juice. While State Department policy-makers both before and after that change spent anxious hours drafting notes to the Central Powers about the rights of neutrals, the League for the Enforcement of Peace won strong support, especially among older people in Washington. The German background of several influential families such as the Kauffmanns, chief owners of the *Evening Star*, had bearing upon attitudes. Clifford Berryman's cartoons in the spring of 1916 portrayed the mood of both the *Star* and the isolationist Washington *Post*: in March the figure of "D.C." stood rake in hand amid a litter of papers reading "Blockade Trouble," "Pursuit of Villa," "Armed Ships Question" and "Submarine Issue," while "D.C." said: "Can't let troubles stop my spring work"; in May, while the bloody campaign on the Meuse was under way, "D.C." armed with a fly swatter and a

[16] *Proceedings* and *Journals of the Washington Academy of Sciences*, 1901-1916; *Annual Reports of the Carnegie Institution of Washington*, 1910, 1916; Elizabeth Donnan and Leo F. Stock, eds., *An Historian's World, Selections from the Correspondence of John Franklin Jameson*, pp. 90-91; "Amundsen and Peary," *National Geographic Magazine*, XXIV, 113-30.

banner inscribed "Destroy the Fly" announced, "Forward March! Now's the time for a spring drive." But as war reached out into the mid-Atlantic, the younger generation of Washingtonians took the position that national dignity and morality demanded taking up arms in defense of American principles.

Shortly after the Beaux Arts ball held for the relief of French war orphans, a National Service School opened a "military encampment" at Chevy Chase to teach women to shoot rifles. Most of the six hundred trainees enrolled at the "Ladies Plattsburg" in April 1916 were ardent interventionists, although they reportedly explained that they liked "to get back to nature"; and, in spite of the rule forbidding jewelry, few of them saw any incongruity in "wearing heavy three-stone diamond earrings with a khaki suit that cost $10.50." When law authorized the tripling of the National Guard, the commanding general of the District militia emphasized the need of serious military preparedness. The District National Guard filled its quota. A "Preparedness Day" parade in June drew requests from scores of organizations to take part. For the first time in history, the President of the United States himself marched on foot the entire way. Preparedness, however, was not war, and, like countless other Americans, a great many Washingtonians apparently thought military training was designed chiefly to enable the United States to bring Mexican insurgents to heel. The reelection of President Wilson in November persuaded the capital that the even tenor of her ways would continue.[17]

Thoughtful people have often sought to explain the powerful attraction that Washington before the first world war held for almost every American who ever lived there. The knowledgeable Helen Nicolay, daughter of President Lincoln's secretary and biographer, described "a rambling, self-satisfied community with some of the characteristics of a watering place and

[17] Anon., *Mirrors of Washington*, pp. 214-16; *Star*, 13 Mar, 2, 5, 16, 18, 24 May, 21 Jun, 5 Oct 1916; *Rpt B/Tr*, 1916, pp. 76-78. The paucity of newspaper comment on possible American involvement in war is at least negative evidence of local attitudes.

some of a village, and more still of a thriving county seat. Precedents and prejudices and conventions hedged it about." Other cities were as friendly and less wedded to a rigid etiquette; the natural beauty of many places was more spectacular; creative art had wider scope in other communities, and the intellectual climate of the great universities was quite as kindly to scholarship and intensive research; the rewards of a business career were greater in American financial and industrial centers; the incessant jockeying for national political power in the capital was frequently disillusioning, and the perpetual shift in the city's *dramatis personae* could be disconcerting to the person who valued stability. Wherein, then, lay Washington's peculiar enchantment? As was true a hundred years earlier and in the late nineteenth century, the infinite variety of background and talent of the people living there or coming and going gave her social life unique fascination. "In Washington," wrote Mrs. Larz Anderson, "there is always something new under the sun."[18] Temporary residents left with regret, and uncounted men and women who called themselves temporary stayed on for twenty and thirty and forty years to see changes that heightened their affection for the relatively uncomplicated "city of conversation" they had known before the war.

[18] Nicolay, *Our Capital on the Potomac*, p. 512; Anderson, *Presidents and Pies*, p. 1; Nelson, "The Capital of Our Democracy," *Century*, LIV, 39.

CHAPTER XI

THE BEGINNINGS OF ORGANIZED NEGRO PROTEST, 1901-1916

THE optimism that warmed white Washington rarely penetrated the clouds hanging over the colored community. In the Deep South the exclusion of Negro voters from the polls in state after state had progressed inexorably, beginning with South Carolina in 1889 and, by 1901, extending to nine others. Determination to establish white supremacy on an immutable basis had multiplied Jim Crow laws and confined Negro education largely to the vocational and manual training deemed suited to a servile labor force. From Texas through the Gulf states and up into North Carolina, lynchings of Negroes had grown in frequency during the 1890's. Washington Negroes had not faced lynchings or overt intimidation. Here the black masses at the bottom of the heap were little worse off in 1901 than in the early eighties; in fact, with luck on jobs, consistent good health, and three or four years of schooling, hard workers might rise a peg into the ranks of the Negro lower middle class. It was the upper middle class and the aristocrats whose status and pride had suffered and from whom either courageous leadership or corrosive despair must emanate. During the preceding twenty years their role had become increasingly negative. Yet colored Americans throughout the country still looked to the privileged members of that group to act as standard bearers for them all.

Contrary to later, often quoted Republican claims, the position of Negroes continued to worsen during the Roosevelt and Taft administrations, although subtle changes rather than admitted shifts in official policy marked the decline. As President Cleveland's first Civil Service Commissioner, Theodore Roosevelt had exercised scrupulous fairness in putting the merit system into effect in government, but the Colonel of the Rough

Riders had deeply offended colored men by belittling the heroic services of the Black Cavalry at San Juan hill during the Spanish-American War. As President, the vigorous "Teddy" for a time seemed to colored Washington to be a staunch friend: one of his first acts was to invite Booker T. Washington to dine at the White House to discuss Negro appointments to office. Hopes built on that unusual gesture quickly shrivelled under the hot blast of arch-conservative Republican wrath. Within six months the Washington *Bee* was speaking of "the Negro political decapitation dinner."[1] The President stuck by his guns to the point of winning Senate concurrence in several Negro appointments, and he retained a number of colored men McKinley had put into office, but thereafter he made no further overtures. On the contrary, in 1906, when Negro troops in Brownsville, Texas, were involved in a brawl in which a white man was shot, presidential severity in approving the dishonorable discharge of the entire battalion for refusing to identify the guilty person alienated Roosevelt's colored supporters. His appointment of two Negroes to the Homes Commission in 1908 won him no applause since all members of the commission gave their services.

President Taft stirred up fewer animosities than his predecessor. Avowing belief in the Tuskegee philosophy of Negro economic advancement before enlargement of Negro political power, Taft declared himself unwilling to appoint colored men to posts in the South, where white resentment would create friction. But he selected colored men for several "offices of essential dignity at Washington," on the principle that it was better to give "large offices to well-equipped Negroes of the higher class" than to scatter "a lot of petty ones among the mass of their race." Rather apologetically he wrote to Robert

[1] E.g., Republican National Committee, *Republican Campaign Textbook, 1912*, p. 278; *Bee*, 15 Oct 1898, 19 Oct 1901, 8, 22 Feb 1902, 5 Aug 1905; Hayes, *Negro Govt Worker*, p. 22; Monroe N. Work, ed., *Negro Year Book, An Annual Encyclopedia of the Negro, 1912*, pp. 75-76.

Terrell: "I have not done all I ought to do or all I hope to do in the matter of the recognition of colored men, but positions are hard to find. Nobody resigns and nobody dies." However sound his reasons, Taft's policies offered the city's colored people meagre encouragement.[2]

Up to a point colored Washingtonians rejoiced at any Negro's receiving a responsible federal post, but they were dismayed at the President's consistently passing over well-qualified local Negroes even for the office of Recorder of Deeds for which local taxes paid half. The profound respect in which all colored Americans held Washington's upper-class colored community heightened the grievance. Upon Booker T. Washington's recommendation, President Roosevelt appointed Robert H. Terrell to a municipal judgeship, but colored Republicans from the states won the other six major federal assignments in the capital, namely the posts of Register and Deputy Register of the Treasury, Assistant District Attorney for the District of Columbia, Auditor of the Navy Department, the District Recorder of Deeds, and Chief Surgeon at the Freedmen's Hospital. President Taft added two more, the office of Collector of Customs at Georgetown and, still more gratifying, the position of Assistant Attorney General of the United States, a plum which fell to a prominent colored lawyer from Boston. At those nine, Negro preferment stood till 1913.

The significance all Negroes attached to those nine offices seems at first out of proportion to their number or their intrinsic importance. But between 1901 and 1913 they represented far more to colored people than sops to racial ambition. For, during the first dozen years of the twentieth century when no colored man sat in Congress, Negro civil service employees

[2] As in chapter VI, citations of the *Bee* are reduced in this chapter to a small sample, since relevant comments appear in almost every issue. *Bee*, 17, 24 Sep, 31 Dec 1904, 17 Mar, 21 Apr, 1, 8 Dec 1906, 4 May 1907; William F. Nowlin, *The Negro in American National Politics*, pp. 114-15; *Negro Year Book, 1912*, pp. 30-31; *Star*, 20 Jun 1909; President Taft to Judge Robert Terrell, 2 Mar 1910, Mary Church Terrell Mss (L.C.).

came to depend upon the President's Negro appointees to serve as their bulwark against injustice. In the 1880's and 1890's Negro congressmen had filled that role, or at least so colored departmental clerks believed. Now they must look elsewhere for help in getting merited assignments when civil service rules swayed precariously in the winds of a stiffening racism. In 1910 a Negro journalist jokingly called Taft's nine principal Negro appointees "the Black Cabinet." The name stuck, and with some reason: although their intervention was not always successful, it sometimes had the desired effect.[3]

Nevertheless the civil service held fewer opportunities for intelligent Negroes than in the 1880's and 1890's. The commission's rules had always allowed a department or division chief a choice among the three top candidates whose examinations qualified them for a vacancy, but after the turn of the century that latitude, Negroes believed, increasingly came to be a weapon of racial subjugation. Certainly promotions became fewer and fewer for Negroes; more often white associates of lesser education and experience and therefore presumably of lesser competence were pushed ahead of them. By 1908 not more than three or four colored men had advanced into supervisory positions and all colored federal employees in Washington had dwindled from the 1,537 of 1892 to 1,450, about 300 of them clerks, the rest messengers or common laborers. Until 1909 the State Department had no colored employee ranking above a messenger, and the lone Negro who then attained a clerk's rating achieved it, he later explained, because his personal friend, the incoming Secretary of State, insisted that the merit system recognize merit. While Republican campaign literature of 1912 claimed that the federal government then had more than 4,100 colored employees in Washington earning

[3] *Bee*, 19 Apr 1909, 23 Feb, 25 Mar, 11 Sep 1911, 29 Mar, 12 Apr 1913; William McKinley Clayton to Woodrow Wilson, 19 Mar 1915, Wilson Mss; *Negro Year Book, 1912*, pp. 70-71; Hayes, *Negro Govt Worker*, pp. 26-27, 32-35.

over $4,000,000 a year, those figures were manifestly exaggerated and in any case made little impression upon educated Negroes, who knew that the color of their skins would keep them in the bottom grades of government service.

In the District government civil service rules did not apply at all. The wishes of members of the House or Senate District committees might determine who was hired or promoted and, when congressional patronage did not interfere, the preferences of individual commissioners or their immediate subordinates were the deciding factor. The *Bee* insisted that the engineer commissioners never approved of Negroes in any but menial jobs, and of the civilian commissioners only Henry West displayed no "colorphobia." In 1908 out of a clerical force of 450 in the District Building, only 9 were Negroes; among 731 policemen and 498 firemen 39 and 9 respectively were colored; 79 clerks and 55 mail carriers were colored out of 881 city Post Office employees; 460 colored school teachers selected chiefly by the Assistant Superintendent completed the list of the District's Negro employees in white collar jobs. The pay scale put the yearly income of all but a very few at less than $1,000. Four years later a city containing some 94,000 colored inhabitants and 20,000 colored taxpayers had about 900 Negroes on the payroll, nearly half of them rated as unskilled laborers at wages of $500 or less a year.[4]

At the same time jobs open to Negroes in other fields, especially domestic service, shrank in number. Judge Terrell put the blame for householders' shift to white servants upon his own people; for too often, he said, they skimped their work

[4] Hayes, *Negro Govt Worker*, pp. 125-30; *Republican Campaign Textbook, 1912*, pp. 71-72; Osceola Madden, "A Color Phase of Washington," *The World Today*, XIV, 549-52; *Bee*, 22 Jul 1905, 11 May, 16 Nov 1907, 2 Oct 1909, 4 May 1912, 20 Feb 1915; Kathleen Dudley Long, "Woodrow Wilson and the Negro, 1912-1916," (M.A. Thesis, Bryn Mawr College, 1956), pp. 14-17; H Committee on Reform in the Civil Service, 63C, 2S, "Hearings on Segregation of Clerks and Employees in the Civil Service," pp. 4-5; Sherman's *Directory and Ready Reference of the Colored Population of the District of Columbia, 1913*, pp. 388-417.

while making unwarranted demands upon their employers. He viewed the refusal of Negroes to work for other Negroes as particularly serious in a city where he estimated a tenth to a fifth of the colored people were jobless; he told the National Negro Business League in New York of a colored woman who, having advertised for a washwoman, was informed by a colored applicant: "Lady, I can't work for you; I'm in society myself." The overcrowding of the professions in colored Washington, pronounced in the late nineteenth century, now intensified. In spite of the efforts of the local branch of the newly organized Negro Business League, and in spite of a few isolated examples of modest success—an insurance company, a shoe store, and several drug stores—Negro business enterprises made no progress. In 1903 Washington's one Negro Savings Bank failed; attempts to organize another came to nothing. While the *Bee* improved its appearance, gave better news coverage, and adopted a more dignified tone, the *Colored American*, which Booker T. Washington had largely financed, ceased publication in 1904 after a losing six-year struggle for existence. The *Bee*, in turn, ran into financial difficulties in 1908 when a rival, the Washington *American*, appeared. Calvin Chase's repeated attacks upon Mr. Washington's "Uncle Tomism" notwithstanding, the educator came to the *Bee*'s rescue, for he considered a vigorous Negro press an important weapon in the fight for advancement, and the national capital above all must have Negro newspapers.[5]

Accompanying the growing economic pinch was a gradual tightening of the cordon excluding Negroes from any slight share in a common social life in the city. The one exception was the children's annual Easter Monday egg-rolling contest on the White House lawn when for a few hours white and

[5] *Star*, 20 Aug 1905; *Bee*, 26 Aug, 25 Nov 1905, 27 Mar 1909, 15 Feb 1913; *Rpt B/Ed*, 1910, pp. 207-08; Booker T. Washington to Judge Robert Terrell, 19 Feb 1906, B. T. Washington Mss; *Negro Year Book, 1912*, pp. 170, 175; August Meier, "Booker T. Washington and the Negro Press," *Journal of Negro History*, XXXVIII, 68, 88-89.

colored children intermingled, "all beaten up as it were in a social omelette. Eggs of every color are rolled back and forth . . . and there are just as many shades, if not as many colors, of skin as of egg shell." The rest of the year race prejudice seeping down from parents poisoned the relations between white and colored youngsters. As Joe Gans, the Negro prize fighter, won fame in the ring, whenever a championship bout was scheduled, a boy of either race who ventured alone into Washington's streets beyond his own immediate neighborhood risked a beating up from a gang of the enemy intent upon upholding the honor of Gans or his white rival. One very light-colored, red-haired Negro boy faced double jeopardy, since colored contemporaries outside the Negro section of Foggy Bottom took him for a white, while white boys pounced on him as a Negro. Jack Johnson's victories over Jim Jeffries later made matters worse. Athletic prowess, which in post-World War II years would begin to bridge racial cleavages, merely widened the gulf.

The rapidity with which the breach developed in the first decade of the century is astonishing. In 1902 the Washington *Post*, with an unusual display of interest, devoted a half column to praise of the city's upper-class Negro society, "the Negro scholar in silk hat and frock coat," the well-to-do Negro lawyer, the half-dozen colored members of the Washington Board of Trade, the colored women graduates of Wellesley, Smith, Oberlin, and Russell Sage, the Treble Clef Club, "organized for the study of classical music," the Samuel Coleridge-Taylor Oratorio Society with its 225 voices, and the church choirs which "won golden opinions." Two years later the *Post* was deploring the unseemly ambition of Washington's colored leaders to get "the ballot, recognition, admission to theatres and restaurants, monopoly of the public parks and other like prerogatives," instead of pouring their efforts into establishing colored vocational and manual training schools as Negroes in the Deep South were doing. White residents overlooked the steady decline of illiteracy among Washington's adult Negroes; in 1910 it stood at less than 17 per cent. The *Star* suggested that white people should not draw the color line in giving Christmas charity; but otherwise, save for an occasional friendly notice in the Washington *Times*, after 1903 the city's white press confined its favorable comments on Negro activities to applauding Booker T. Washington's Tuskegee program with its implied acknowledgment of Negroes' inherent racial inferiority. By 1908 a dispassionate appraisal of race relations in the capital led a magazine writer to conclude that in Washington "the separation of the races is more nearly complete than in any other city of the Union. The better class of white and colored people know absolutely nothing of each other."

Intelligent Negroes were painfully aware of what was happening. An anonymous article entitled "What It Means to be Colored in the Capital of the United States" listed for readers of the *Independent* some of the new manifestations of racism: in January 1906 the Columbian Debating Society at George Washington University debated the question: "Resolved that a Jim Crow law should be adopted and enforced in the District of Columbia"; the affirmative won; a few months later a bill for Jim Crow street cars was introduced into Congress with a citizens' association endorsement; until 1900 the colored schools had had colored directors of music, art, cooking, sewing, manual training, and physical culture; now all were white. "For fifteen years," wrote the author, "I have resided in Washington, and while it was far from being a 'paradise for colored people' when I first touched these shores, it has been doing its level best ever since to make conditions for us intolerable."[6]

Mounting white antagonism had its effect: from 31 percent

[6] Mrs. R. Kent Beattie, "Easter Egg-Rolling," *Crisis*, XI, 313-14; *Bee*, 19 Feb 1916; *Post*, 3 Aug 1902, 9 Jan 1904; *Star*, 14 Dec 1903; Madden, "A Color Phase," p. 549; "What It Means to be Colored in the Capital of the United States," and "Our Washington Letter," *Independent*, LXII, 181-86, 1012.

of the total population in 1900, colored Washington dropped to 28½ percent in 1910 and would be only 25 percent by 1920. Knowing themselves unwelcome, the colored members of the Board of Trade resigned. At the request of the local chapter of the Women's Christian Temperance Union, Negro women withdrew in 1908 to form a Jim Crow unit. While the severity of sentences imposed on colored misdemeanants increased, white supremacists talked openly of reestablishing the whipping post to check Negro crime or of forcing all "niggers" out of the District. Even generously disposed northerners fell easily into the habit of using only the Christian name in speaking of or to a Negro, no matter how distinguished he might be. In her published *Recollections*, so kindly a person as Mrs. William Howard Taft alluded to her indebtedness to Arthur Brooks, a major in the colored unit of the District militia; but, perhaps because he was also a messenger in the War Department, she wrote of him as "Arthur," never "Major" or "Mr. Brooks"; every white person mentioned, except the Taft children and the uneducated Irish coachman, was dignified by his surname and title. Such minor slights were unimportant save as never-ending reminders to colored people that they had won scant respect from whites.

Probably a better gauge of the strengthening of the caste barrier lay in the attitude of white churchmen. At the Congregational Church, which had welcomed Negro members in the 1870's, a congressman from Maine received an ovation when he stated that colored men should never have been enfranchised *en masse*, but rather one by one as each proved himself ready. Episcopal Bishop Henry Satterlee went further. Giving Negroes equality through suffrage when they were not in fact equal, combined with the growth of the Negro population, he said, had promoted racial hostilities. Although he supported Christian missions for colored people, he thought Negroes "morally and intellectually a weaker race, and . . . even if they should become great landowners, men of wealth and of education, race antagonism would only become stronger and more sharply defined." Washington's Negro intelligentsia no doubt saw some truth in these pronouncements, but the Bishop's repudiation of education, wealth, and political power as means of closing the gap between the races and his statement that a solution must depend upon every Negro's winning for himself "a strong, robust Christ-like character" were profoundly discouraging. Seemingly, white men could remain devils, but colored must become saints. Told by white men year after year of the virtues of Booker T. Washington's subservient philosophy, Negro aristocrats listened without enthusiasm to the sage of Tuskegee when he informed them at the colored YMCA that the eyes of the world were upon them and they must set an example by ridding the city of loafers, drunkards, and gamblers.

Perhaps the most deadly blow the city's white churches dealt their dark-skinned Christian brethren came in 1910 with the assembling in Washington of the sixth World Sunday School Convention. The local committee on arrangements refused to seat local colored delegates or permit them to march in the parade because they were not members of the District Sunday School Association although they belonged to the World Association and had taken part in earlier conventions. The *Star* reported all "wrinkles . . . smoothed out" by a vote of the organization to make Booker T. Washington a life member, but as Mr. Washington represented "Uncle Tomism" to many local Negroes, the *Star*'s account smacked of belittling the issue.[7]

More alarming to colored Washingtonians were the multiplying instances of racial segregation in government offices. A "Jim Crow corner" first appeared in 1904 in the Bureau of

[7] *Rpt B/Ch*, 1901, p. 269; *Bee*, 11 Feb, 10 Dec 1905, 8 Feb 1908; *Post*, 18 Apr 1904, 7 Nov 1910; *Star*, 11 Jan 1905, 10 May, 20 Jun 1909, 20, 24 May 1910; Mrs. William Howard Taft, *Recollections*, pp. 279-80; *Times*, 14 Jul 1907; *Rpt B/Educ*, 1905, pp. 105-15.

Engraving and Printing. The *Bee* noted in 1905 " a systematic effort inaugurated to Jim Crow the Negro. The fever is spreading. . . . The Negro is afraid to complain." Race prejudice, having once gained a foothold under a Republican regime, quickly widened its reach. Before 1909 separate locker and washrooms and separate lunchroom accommodations had become the rule in several sections of the Treasury and the Department of the Interior, and, although the scheme did not spread far during the next four years, the administration made no move to check or forbid it.

What Republican officials saw fit to allow set the pattern for private concerns. In 1910, at the invitation of the Federation of Citizens' Association, ten recently organized Negro neighborhood groups attended a meeting, only to have their hosts then vote to exclude them from federation membership; the Negroes thereupon took the name Civic Associations and formed their own federation. The local civil rights acts still stood unrepealed, but restaurants, barber shops, and hotels now barred Negroes as a matter of course, theatres admitted them only to "nigger heavens," and railroads and buses carrying passengers into the District from Virginia and Maryland enforced Jim Crow seating. As a suit, if won in court, meant at most token damages for the plaintiff, Negroes ceased to invoke the law.[8] Indeed a good many of them obviously shrank from public complaint lest it feed fuel to the campaign to repeal the laws. White extremists might persuade Congress not only to destroy the last flimsy legal safeguards against racial discrimination in the District of Columbia but to make segregation mandatory.

From 1907 on, bills for Jim Crow cars in the District came up in the House of Representatives at intervals. While a new congressman from Georgia announced his determination to force all Negroes out of government service, agitation for a District anti-miscegenation law made headway. In February

[8] *Bee*, 3 Sep 1904, 11 Feb 1905, 7 May 1910, 4 May 1912.

1913 the House passed the bill in less than five minutes; only Senate inaction stopped it. When the Negro Register of the Treasury and a colored guest lunched in the House Office Building restaurant, five congressmen threatened a boycott that would close it down if such an affront to white manhood ever recurred; the manager assured them it would not. With lynch law rampant in the Deep South, Negroes in Washington had some reason to think the moment inopportune to protest the curtailment of their own civil rights. Possibly only a few men understood the seriousness of the trend in the capital; before the summer of 1913 perhaps the rank and file were not apprehensive for themselves. But over a ten-year span the evidence the *Bee* assembled and published periodically indicated clearly that Washington Negroes, although spared lynchings, were already subject to most of the discriminations imposed upon colored people elsewhere in America.

The city's upper-class Negroes, however, reacted with growing militance to the accelerating racism of white Washington. Booker T. Washington kept many close friends in the capital, but educated colored people who accepted his program of "racial solidarity, self-help and economic chauvinism" increasingly rejected his methods and his disregard of political action. His conciliatory policies, his anxiety to avoid friction with whites, and his stress upon patience led to a break between him and a group of Negro radicals in 1906 when some twenty-nine "rebels" headed by the brilliant, young W. E. B. DuBois of Atlanta University and William Monroe Trotter, editor of the Boston *Guardian*, launched the so-called "Niagara Movement" with a manifesto of Negro rights and aims. Four Washington Negroes took part in the first Niagara conference. Inspired by that example, leadership long dormant in colored Washington began to reassert itself.

Kelly Miller, professor of sociology and later dean at Howard University, George W. Cook, Treasurer of Howard, the Reverend Samuel Carruthers of the Galbraith AME Church, Francis J. Grimké of the 15th Street Presbyterian Church, three or four other local pastors, Mary Church Terrell, the first president of the National Association of Colored Women, Calvin Chase of the *Bee*, and a score of other men and women who commanded prestige now abandoned the tactics of suffering indignities in silence and began a campaign of outspoken protest against social injustice. Few of them openly criticized Booker T. Washington, and Mrs. Terrell, while serving on the Board of Education, rebuked a Negro newspaperman for objecting to the "Tuskegee idea" of Negro education, although she herself advocated giving the colored child in the District the same schooling as the white. But irrespective of their feelings about Mr. Washington, all of the group joined in publicizing the fact that colored people were not content to be hewers of wood and drawers of water and that whites were deluded if, like the New York *Times*, they thought "the Negroes of the United States are doing very well."[9]

Although Washington's Negro militants constantly gained adherents, the city was not initially in the front of the fight, perhaps because the District's voteless status gave political leadership to New York, Boston, and Chicago, perhaps also because colored people in the largest Negro city in the country, having escaped the excesses of "lily-white" agitation that the Deep South was experiencing, were wary about forcing an issue locally lest it boomerang violently. If, as one scholar avers, Booker T. Washington's greatest ascendency, which spanned the first decade of the century, "coincided with the period of greatest oppression Negroes have faced since the Civil War,"

[9] H Rpt 8072, 59C, 2S, Ser 5065; *Star*, 14 May 1909; *Herald*, 21 May 1907; *Post*, 11 Feb 1913; *Crisis*, v, 270-71; Hayes, *Negro Govt Worker*, p. 33; W. E. B. DuBois, *Dusk of Dawn*, pp. 88-89, 92-95; August Meier, "Booker T. Washington and the Negro Press," pp. 75, 79, 80-81; *Bee*, 25 Nov 1905, 25 Apr 1906, 26 Nov 1910, 29 Jul 1911; Mary Church Terrell to H. G. Pinkett, 9 Sep 1906, Terrell Mss; New York *Times*, 18 Apr 1913.

the birth of the National Association for the Advancement of Colored People in New York City in 1909 must be recognized as marking the beginning of the slow march upward. Started by a handful of earnest white people, the association from the first was intended to be bi-racial. But of its national officers and staff only W. E. B. DuBois was a Negro, and radicals such as William Trotter of Boston distrusted it too deeply to join or work with it. In Washington, caution and inertia apparently combined to delay until the spring of 1912 the organization of a local branch of the NAACP. Within a few months, it was one of the largest in the country and counted 143 dues-paying members, among them so distinguished a white man as Chief Justice Stafford. But, unlike the New York group, white members were few. Here the most able of the upper-class Negro community took charge, bending their first efforts to providing legal aid for Negro victims of discrimination.[10]

Grim as things looked for all American Negroes in 1912, gleams of hope were visible in Washington. They derived principally from the changing point of view of the city's professional social workers and the volunteers they trained as visitors in the slums. First-hand exposure to the conditions under which honest hard-working colored families had to live taught fair-minded investigators a good deal about the obstacles confronting the city's Negroes. The report of the President's Homes Commission and the United States Labor Department's eye-opening study had presented evidence that starvation wages and destitution were directly related. Businessmen occasionally talked as if lowering the Negro death rate was important only because high mortality interfered with favorable advertising for the city, but few men sounded as sure as once they had that Negro "shiftlessness" lay at the root of the problem.

[10] Meier, "Booker T. Washington," p. 88; *Negro Year Book, 1912*, p. 134; *Third Annual Report National Association for the Advancement of Colored People*, p. 23 (hereafter cited as *Anl Rpt NAACP*); Flint Kellogg, "Villard and the NAACP," *Nation*, CLVIII, 137-40; *Crisis*, VI, 190.

Furthermore, white assumptions that upper-class Negroes lacked civic-mindedness received a jolt when a compilation of scattered data revealed that Negroes had initiated and carried on several projects for their people, notably a day nursery for infants of working mothers. Of the $50,000 collected in Washington for a colored YMCA, colored people contributed $27,000. Conferences between Negro workers at the colored Southwest Settlement House and white philanthropists came to be "remarkably free from race consciousness, the one thought on both sides being the common welfare." Negroes thus brought into touch with whites active in Washington charities could feel the lightening of the atmosphere of censoriousness.[11]

Inasmuch as white men's respect, not their charity, was the goal of Negro leaders, any sign that a segment of white Washington was ready to work with them for the common good assumed importance. Reform was in the air throughout the United States as the presidential election of 1912 approached, and, noting the fervor with which white muckrakers and Progressives talked of the far-reaching social and political changes that must come, thoughtful colored men dared think reform might extend to race relations. None of the candidates made explicit promises, but while Republicans pointed to President Taft's record of Negro appointments and Theodore Roosevelt denounced "brutal" Democratic and "hypocritical" Republican racial policies, Woodrow Wilson preached the "New Freedom" with its guarantees of "fair and just treatment" for all. The *Bee*, wary of trusting any Democrat, urged its readers when the election was over to have faith in the assurances of Wilson's influential colored supporters that the incoming President would not countenance continued discrimination and segregation.[12]

[11] A C *Rpt, 1903*, p. 23; *Crisis*, III, 51; *Rpt B/Tr*, 1910, p. 8; *Times*, 5 May 1911; Sarah C. Fernandis, "In the Making," *Charities*, XVI, 703-05; *Bee*, 13 Apr 1907, 17, 24 May, 5 Jul 1913; Washington *Sun*, 12 Feb, 14 May 1915.

[12] Long, "Woodrow Wilson and the Negro," pp. 14-32; *Republican Campaign Text Book, 1912*, p. 238; Theodore Roosevelt, "The Progres-

Negroes in the capital waited eagerly for word of new appointments and measures that would wipe out the Jim Crow sections in government offices. March and most of April 1913 came and went. Confidence in the "New Freedom" gave way to uneasiness. Then piece by piece the world of colored Washington fell apart. Within the next few months the President dismissed all but two of the Negroes whom Taft had appointed "to offices of essential dignity at Washington" and replaced them with white men. He nominated a colored lawyer from Oklahoma for Register of the Treasury with the intention of making the Register's section an all-Negro unit, but when the nominee, intimidated by fierce opposition in the Senate, withdrew his name, Wilson appointed an American Indian. The District Recordship of Deeds, a colored preserve since 1881, went to a white man in 1916. By then the only Negro to hold an appointive position in Washington was Robert Terrell, confirmed in April 1914 for another term as a municipal judge. Disillusioning though these snubs were, they were pin-pricks compared to the segregationist policies officially sanctioned in government departments in the summer of 1913.

"Segregation," reported a white officer of the NAACP, "is no new thing in Washington, and the present administration cannot be said to have inaugurated it. The past few months of Democratic Party control, however, have given segregation impetus and have been marked by more than a beginning of systematic enforcement." As soon as the Virginia-born President was installed in the White House, a group of Negro baiters calling themselves the National Democratic Fair Play Association had undertaken to stir up trouble in order to get Negroes out of the civil service, to restrict them to menial jobs, or at the very least to keep white and colored workers separate. A Fair Play committee busily poking about in various offices

---

sives and the Colored Man," *Outlook*, CI, 909-12; *Journal of Negro History*, XXXII, 90; *Bee*, 12 Dec 1912.

had elicited complaints from "Democratic clerks and other white employees of the government who are inimical to the Negro," and had obtained the backing of office-seekers who declared it intolerable for white people to work in proximity to Negroes, let alone under their supervision.[13] The President, apparently convinced that racial friction was rife in the executive departments, was anxious to check it if only because it might imperil his legislative programs.

In view of the southern background of Postmaster General Albert Burleson, Secretary of the Treasury William McAdoo, and Secretary of the Navy Josephus Daniels, perhaps segregation would have become standard throughout their departments without the impetus supplied by outside agitation and the shocked disapproval of Mrs. Woodrow Wilson at seeing colored men and white women working in the same room in the Post Office Department. There the change, by whomever inspired, had gone into effect before the end of July 1913, and by autumn the Treasury, after cautiously watching public reaction, had consigned the colored employees of most divisions to separate rooms and forbidden all Negro employees to use the lunch tables and the toilet facilities that for years past they had shared with their white fellows. Similar rules applied in the Navy Department as well as in all federal offices where segregation had obtained under Republican rule.

"The effect is startling," the NAACP report noted. "Those segregated are regarded as a people apart, almost as lepers." White clerks, seemingly without personal convictions, now said they approved. To endorse the new arrangement had become "the thing to do." Yet ever since President Cleveland had quashed every proposal of segregation, the *Bee* pointed out,

[13] *Bee*, 29 Mar, 26 Jul, 25 Oct, 15 Nov, 6 Dec 1913; *Nation*, XCVII, 114; *Crisis*, VI, 9, 60-63, XII, 198; New York *Times*, 19 Feb, 25 Apr 1914; L. H. Pickford to Joseph Tumulty, 12 Jun 1916, Wilson Mss; *NAACP Report*, 13 Aug 1913, and "Segregation in Government Departments," *NAACP Report of an Investigation*, 1 Nov 1913, Wilson Mss (hereafter cited as *NAACP Rpt*, 1 Nov 1913); *Post*, 30 Apr 1913.

"Afro-American clerks" had worked side by side with white in "peace and harmony." In the summer of 1913 Booker T. Washington wrote a friend: "I have never seen the colored people [of Washington] so discouraged and so bitter as they are at the present time." Many of them refused at first to believe that the author of "The New Freedom" knew what was afoot, but in late October when a delegation led by William Monroe Trotter of Boston begged him to intervene, the President's evasive answer dissipated doubts: Jim Crowism in the federal government had his approval. A mass meeting to protest "the officializing of race prejudice" overflowed the Metropolitan AME Church, but for the moment Negroes in the government service dared go no further lest they precipitate a drastic change in the civil service law which would extend segregation into every federal department and be far harder to rescind then the word-of-mouth orders of departmental chiefs.[14]

Local leaders of the NAACP realized that "almost every man employed by the government and by the schools risks his position when he stands on our militant platform," but they believed that only a united front could stop the spread of racial discrimination. In November they organized a speakers' bureau to go from church to church, society to society, and lodge to lodge, "to arouse the colored people themselves to their danger, to make them feel it through and through, and at the same time to make them willing to make sacrifices for the cause." The response was "nothing short of a miracle." In a city notoriously rent by "all sorts of factions," Archibald Grimké, president of the Washington NAACP branch, almost disbelievingly saw "school teachers whom you would not believe cared for anything but pleasure, society women, young men," join in the

[14] *Post*, 2, 20 May 1913; Ralph Tyler to President Wilson, 12 May, Booker T. Washington to Oswald Garrison Villard, 10 Aug, enclosed in ltr, Villard to Wilson, 18 Aug 1913, and Villard to Wilson, 29 Sep 1913, Wilson Mss; *Bee*, 10, 17 May, 26 Jul, 6 Sep, 15 Nov 1913; Arthur Link, *The New Freedom*, pp. 245-54; *Crisis*, VI, 220, 289-99, VII, 89; *NAACP Report*, 1 Nov 1913.

campaign. At the M Street High School a group of exceptionally inspiring teachers passed on the torch to their students; for them W. E. B. DuBois became a symbol of liberty. By the early months of 1914 the Washington NAACP had over seven hundred dues-paying members and had sent nearly $4,000 to national headquarters.[15]

Personal letters from influential white men pleading with the President to alter his course and indignant articles in the liberal magazines and newspapers failed to persuade Mr. Wilson to reverse his position. On the contrary, his resistance stiffened. When a second Negro delegation, again led by William Monroe Trotter, reminded him of his earlier promise to see justice done, Wilson lost his temper and told the delegation he was not to be high-pressured. The remonstrances, however, were almost certainly instrumental in preventing the wholesale adoption of segregation throughout the government. In March 1914 when the House Committee on Civil Service Reform held hearings on two bills calling for mandatory racial separation of government employees, a Louisiana sponsor of the bills argued that to put a member of "this inferior race" in a position of authority over Caucasians was unrighteous. By the stamp of color the Lord had decreed a lowly place for Negroes. When Congressman Martin Madden of Illinois asked: "Who can say the Almighty decreed it?" the Louisianan replied: "History, experience, and first-hand knowledge." Northern representatives killed both bills in committee.[16]

In the meantime a Supreme Court ruling that the federal Civil Rights Act of 1875, which had long ago been declared

[15] *Crisis*, VII, 192-93, VIII, 32-33; Dr. Rayford Logan to the author, 9 Mar 1960.

[16] O. G. Villard, "The President and the Negro," *Nation*, XCVII, 114; Villard, "The President and the Segregation at Washington," *North American Review*, CXCVIII, 800-07; "Race Segregation at Washington," *Independent*, LXXX, p. 275; Washington *Herald*, 16 Nov 1914; *Times*, 13 Nov 1914; *Crisis*, IX, 119-27; *Negro Year Book, 1914-15*, pp. 34-36; H Comee on Reform in the Civil Service, 63C, 2S, *Segregation of Clerks and Employees in the Civil Service*, 6 Mar 1914, pp. 3, 7.

unconstitutional in the states, was invalid also in federal territory opened the door to new discriminatory laws in the District of Columbia. But fresh attempts to exclude Negroes from government service, District anti-miscegenation and Jim Crow street-car bills, and a segregated residential bill patterned on a Baltimore ordinance of 1913 all met with defeat. Pressures in fact eased slightly in 1915 when the Supreme Court in an unforeseen reversal of earlier opinions refused to allow nearby Maryland to write a "grandfather clause" into her constitution.

"More than seventy-five per cent of the present segregation," the *Bee* reminded its readers in 1915, "was transmitted to President Wilson by the Republicans," and the editor noted more Negro promotions in the civil service than in years past. But although the transit companies were not allowed to introduce Jim Crow cars, other District corporations and individual white citizens interpreted the administration policy to mean that short of open violence they could carry discrimination virtually as far as they chose. Informal agreements between sellers and buyers effectively strengthened the residential color line. In 1914 an eminent Boston lawyer persuaded the American Bar Association to rescind its recent ruling that no Negro could be elected to membership, but the substitute provision that applicants must state their race served the same purpose. While not all white Washingtonians shared the prevailing colorphobia and Chief Justice Wendell Stafford fought it in the District Supreme Court, most of the white community took it for granted that colored teachers should be excluded from a teachers' lecture series held in the Congregational Church and that Negro civic organizations should not be invited to join with the fifty-six white groups in planning better correlation of the city's recreational activities.[17]

[17] *Crisis*, VII, 117, 142, 169, 252-53; *Negro Year Book, 1914-15*, pp. 30, 34-35, 39; *Times*, 3 Dec 1914; *Bee*, 4 Oct 1914, 27 Feb, 5 Mar, 15 May 1915; *Sun*, 26 Mar, 30 Apr, 25 Jun 1915; H Rpt 1340, 63C, 3S, Ser 6766; H Dis Comee, 64C, 1S, Hrgs, "Intermarriage of Whites and

The attacks and the disheartening indifference of white people, however, had the effect of maintaining the new solidarity in the Negro world. In Washington's triple-tiered colored community a sense of cohesiveness, lacking for thirty years, had begun to emerge before 1911; it strengthened extraordinarily during the crisis of 1913 and 1914. Although, as the struggle against race prejudice dragged on, the failure to make headway might well have dissolved the new bonds, they endured. In northern cities also, upper-class Negroes, the "talented tenth" upon whom W. E. B. DuBois pinned hopes for the race, saw they could not remain detached from the lower-class black, no matter how superior they knew themselves to be and no matter how uncongenial they found his society. But the growth of "group-identification" among all classes of Washington Negroes had special significance, both because elaborate class distinctions were older here than in most of the United States and because all colored people recognized Washington as the center of Negro culture in America.

The new attitude of the *Bee* supplies an index to this change. Where the paper had once carried scathing accounts of Negro discrimination against Negro and had sneered at any colored man who achieved distinction, the editorials and news articles gradually took on a constructive character. The addition to the editoral staff of the wise, public-spirited George H. Richardson gave the *Bee* new dignity; his opinions carried weight. Calvin Chase, whose attacks on Booker T. Washington had stopped in 1908, lashed out periodically at W. E. B. DuBois, arch opponent of Mr. Washington's subservient teachings, but after the death of the Tuskegee leader in November 1915, those explosions ended. Chase and Richardson saw fit to needle colored men who sought their own advantage at the sacrifice of principle. Editorials called attention to the destructive selfish-

---

Negroes in the District of Columbia, and Separate Accommodations in Street Cars for White and Negroes in the District of Columbia."

ness of Negro candidates for office under the proscriptive Democratic regime. "Woody," one article declared, "believed his segregation policy was approved by the black gentry because so many of them were anxious to serve under him, segregation or no segregation." Sarcastically the *Bee* observed that no local colored men had had the courage to ask the President in person to define his position on race questions as William Monroe Trotter of Boston had twice obliged him to do, first in November 1913 and again a year later. Yet in taking cowards and the mean-minded to task, the *Bee* also accorded praise to colored men of firm convictions and larger vision. Scoldings at Negro short-comings became progressively fewer and turned instead into exhortations to push on with the noble work of establishing a self-respecting, self-sufficient Negro Washington within the larger community.[18]

Four other Negro publications were appearing regularly in Washington in 1914 and 1915—the short-lived *Sun*, put out by a talented but erratic protégé of Booker T. Washington, the *American*, the *Odd Fellows Journal*, and the *National Union*, organ of a Negro insurance company. In 1915 the *Journal of Negro History* began its long and useful career. The *American*, an uninspired, rather shabby sheet, and the ably edited *Sun* pursued the same line as the *Bee* in less bellicose language: buy colored, support colored charities and colored civic enterprises, take pride in Negro achievements, and don't be "Jim Crowed" by patronizing places where Negroes are segregated. The fourfold program, already familiar, put novel emphasis on Negro successes won by Negro cooperation. Gradually business firms and non-profit groups began to advertise what Negro solidarity had accomplished. They pointed out that the Howard Theatre, upon reverting to colored management after two or

[18] *Negro Year Book, 1914-15*, pp. 43-45; Arnold M. Rose, *The Negro's Morale, Group Identification and Protest*, pp. 57-95; *Bee*, 21 Nov 1914, 27 Feb, 5 Mar 1915; Colonel Campbell C. Johnson to the author, 9 Jun 1960.

three years of white, provided good entertainment—some plays, more minstrel shows, and musical hits like those of the "Black Patti Troubadours"—and by renting the premises for amateur performances now and again served as a kind of community cultural center; at the *Majestic* vaudeville theatre and two new Negro movie houses colored audiences never had to face Jim Crowism. Le Droit Park's 5,000 colored residents could enjoy a similar freedom by giving their custom to the Negro-owned grocery store.

The *Sun*, remarking that the local Negro Business League had gone "to sleep" in 1913, began in 1915 to carry a directory of reliable Negro business firms in the city. A colored department store in a building on 14th Street employed only colored help and met a long-felt want. U Street in northwest Washington was becoming the colored Connecticut Avenue. In southwest Washington the new Douglass Hotel offered colored tourists and conventions comfortable accommodations. The Negro press now insisted on use of the capital *N*, and after 1914 frequently capitalized "colored" also; doubtless in the interest of racial harmony, colored newspapers practically dropped the term "black." Despite the militance of the new propaganda, it was refreshingly free of the braggadocio that had formerly accompanied attempts to encourage Negro enterprise.

Indeed, there was more in which to take pride, as the social disorganization that had long characterized colored Washington began to yield to community effort. Progress, begun even before the disasters of the Wilson era added impetus, was particularly noticeable in the realm of charities and civic undertakings. By the spring of 1913 the recently opened colored YMCA, built brick by brick by Negro workmen, was able to meet its first year's operating costs of $8,200 and show a 56-cent balance. "The fraternal spirit existing between the Y and the local ministry is happily shown in the use by a number of the churches of the great swimming pool for baptismal purposes." As a true community center, the Y became the meeting place of the local branch of the NAACP, the Public School Athletic League, the Christian Endeavor Union, the Federation of Civic Associations, the Negro Medical Society, and other organizations. The colored YWCA expanded its program and paid off all but a small indebtedness during 1913. While public-spirited Negroes admitted that too few well-to-do families contributed to charity, a new determination to carry on without white philanthropy went far toward obliterating their earlier attitude: let the whites shoulder the burden, since they are responsible for the colored man's plight. Roscoe Conkling Bruce, Assistant Superintendent for the colored schools, reminded the audience at the annual meeting of the Colored Social Settlement in December 1913 that Dr. John R. Francis, Washington's leading colored physician, had launched the center "about which many and various efforts for social uplift are organized." In appealing for generous support of this primarily Negro-sponsored charity, Bruce pleaded also for teaching colored children about the great men of their own race; only thus would the younger generation escape being overwhelmed by white prestige and avoid impairment of colored initiative. In much the same vein the newly organized Oldest Inhabitants Association (Colored) of Washington announced its purpose to be the fostering of Negro civic pride.[19]

It would be untruthful to picture colored Washington in 1915 and 1916 as a unified community free of the old divisive jealousies and destructive backbiting, its individual members now single-mindedly working all for one and one for all. Leaders faltered, quarrels persisted—particularly over teaching appointments and promotions in the school system—and self-contempt, shown in the sheer meanness of Negro to Negro, continued to

[19] *Bee*, 17 May, 6 Dec 1913, 2 Oct 1915, 25 May 1916; *Sun*, 8 Jan, 12 Mar, 23 Apr 1915; *Crisis*, XI, 90-94; John H. Paynter, *A Souvenir of the Anniversary and Banquet of the Oldest Inhabitants Association (Colored) of the District of Columbia, April 16, 1914.*

interfere with the important task of raising the economic level of all classes. The *Sun* argued that the cost of racial disunity was as high for the light-colored Caucasian-featured person as for the black-skinned Negroid-looking, but few of the former were willing to discard class distinctions based largely upon degree of color. Moreover, the tightening of the net drawn by strengthened white hostility, while binding courageous colored people together in a common purpose, strangled the will of the weak and timid; circumstances that awakened a fighting spirit in some of the race stripped others of the capacity to hold up their heads at all. Nevertheless the energy with which Washington's Negro leaders fought lynching in the South and racial discrimination everywhere was impressive.[20]

W. E. B. DuBois later wrote of the early years of the Wilson administration: "Quite suddenly the program for the NAACP, which up to this time had been more or less indefinite, was made clear and intensive." The Washington branch forestalled adverse legislation, got a few Negroes reinstated in government jobs, and induced Congress to continue appropriations for Howard University and its 300 college students. Besides a vigorous separate University chapter, by 1916 the Washington branch of the NAACP, with 1,164 members, was the largest in the United States, and, according to national headquarters, constituted "really a national vigilance committee to watch legislation in Congress and lead the fight for Negro manhood rights at the capital of the nation."[21]

Differences of opinion inescapably arose over both long-term strategy and more immediate local tactics. For example, in which direction should Washington Negroes lean when the

[20] *Sun*, 12, 26 Feb 1915; M. C. Terrell to Robert Terrell, n.d., Terrell Mss. Practically every issue of the *Bee* carried some complaint about Negro school administrators' injustices.

[21] W. E. B. DuBois, *Dusk of Dawn*, pp. 235-36; *Sun*, 15 Jan, 12 Mar 1915; *Crisis*, IX, 217, XI, 35, 256, XII, 197; see also list of Washington members at the 1916 conference at Amenia, New York, *Programme*, Terrell Mss.

discussion of District Home Rule revived in 1916? At one time the colored press had argued that voting in municipal elections was essential to the progress of the city's Negro community. But as Henry West and Frederick Siddons had always treated Negroes with exemplary fairness and Oliver Newman and Louis Brownlow showed no racial prejudice, might not colored people be better off under the rule of commissioners like those than under officials chosen by a two-thirds white electorate? Most colored men side-stepped the question; if white citizens persuaded Congress to restore the franchise, then would be time enough for their colored neighbors to seek their share of local political power. Again, what was the wise course to pursue when "The Birth of a Nation" began its long run in Washington movie houses? Some men, seeing it as an incitement to race hatred, wanted to demand that the commissioners ban the picture, just as they had barred the prize fight film of Jack Johnson beating Jim Jeffries; other colored people believed that a petition for censorship would merely advertise the offensive D. W. Griffith film more widely.

While in the national arena Negro leaders examined alternatives as the presidential campaign of 1916 opened, in the voteless capital the question about working with whites for "national preparedness" caused uncertainty. In June 1916 the colored men who marched in a big preparedness parade were "Jim Crowed with a vengeance" and two days later were greeted with a formal segregation order from the War Department. At the request of a New Jersey congressman whose reelection hung in the balance, the order was later rescinded, but before the end of October the all-Negro battalion of the District National Guard was on the Mexican border. Six months later the United States' declaration of war upon the Central Powers would force upon all American Negroes a decision of whether to be Americans first and Negroes second or to let white Americans carry on without voluntary help from the people they treated as second-class citizens.[22]

Still, every Washingtonian daily rubbed elbows with or at least was aware of the presence of people not of his own race. Scores of Negroes were as acutely concerned with municipal taxation, civic betterment, and artistic growth as were their white-skinned neighbors. Whether they would or no, some give-and-take resulted. An experiment of 1913 in publishing a Negro city directory was not repeated. Colored Washington, largely separate and wholly unequal in status, was still part of the over-all community.

[22] *Bee*, 14 Nov 1908, 1 Apr 1916, 17, 19 Jun, 9 Sep, 21 Oct 1916; *Sun*, 9 Apr 1915; Rose, *The Negro's Morale*, pp. 38-39; *Seventh Anl Rpt NAACP*, 1917; *Crisis*, XII, 194, 268; W. E. B. DuBois to Woodrow Wilson, 10 Oct 1916, and Memorial, Boston Branch Negro Equal Political Rights League, 20 Apr 1917, Wilson Mss.

CHAPTER XII

THE GREAT CRUSADE AND ANTICLIMAX, 1917-1918

JANUARY and February 1917 came and went in Washington amid uncertainties about what President Wilson would consider sufficient provocation from Germany to force America into war. On January 22nd, the President spoke to the Senate of his hope of seeing "peace without victory" in Europe. Nine days later the Imperial German Government informed the United States that unrestricted submarine warfare, halted after the sinking of the "Lusitania" in 1915, would resume at once. On February 3rd the President broke off diplomatic relations by dismissing Ambassador von Bernstorff and recalling the American ambassador from Berlin. That done, the President appeared to be unwilling to go further than to obtain authority to arm American merchantmen. While the Central Committee of the American National Red Cross instructed its regional offices to prepare for war, the Council of National Defense, created by Congress in 1916, asked the recently organized National Research Council of the National Academy of Sciences to act as its scientific research unit. The "city of conversation," meanwhile, talked with more passion than urbanity.

The first week of March saw the mustering out of the District National Guard regiments returned from the Mexican border, the passage of a local prohibition act to take effect on November 1st, and President Wilson's second inauguration attended by a large, undemonstrative crowd. As the grandstands along Pennsylvania Avenue came down and visitors departed, the city returned to normal routines. Then on March 18th word of the torpedoing of three unarmed American merchantmen reached the capital. People who had watched unhappily the mounting anti-German feeling in Washington now agreed: "If the sinking of these ships is not war, it inevitably means war," but everyone reassured his neighbor and himself: "This will only be a war on paper or at most a war at sea."

During the next fortnight the capital burst into frenzied, if at times slightly ridiculous, activity. Bellhops at the New Willard drilled daily on the hotel roof. Two thousand boy scouts prepared to mobilize at thirty minutes' notice "for first aid work, police and detective duty." Superintendent Thurston introduced daily salutes to the flag in the public schools, and the Board of Trade met to condemn "German militarism," each member waving a flag to show that "there is no hyphen in the citizenship of Washington." While the War and Navy Departments increased the guard about government property, stationed infantrymen at bridge heads, and placed cavalry along the road to the reservoir, the District naval militia readied itself for a call to board "fighting ships" within twenty days, and recently mustered out national guardsmen prepared to return to active duty. Young men flocked to the enlistment stations opened in various parts of the city. The President requested Congress to convene in special session on April 2nd "to receive a communication concerning grave matters." As rumors spread about impending arrests of disloyal German-born citizens, the Chief of Police refused to permit a loyalty or a peace parade. But when David Starr Jordan, President of Leland Stanford University, and other pacifists hurried to Washington to plead with the President and Congress, serious disorders threatened; members of the District National Guard daubed yellow paint on the headquarters of the Emergency Peace Foundation and talked of "smashing the building." Throughout the city tensions rose.[1]

The weeks of soul-searching and waiting ended dramatically

[1] For a running account of events, see Mark Sullivan, "Over Here, 1914-1918," *Our Times*, v, 248-50, 256-66; Foster Rhea Dulles, *The American Red Cross, A History*, pp. 138-39; R. M. Yerkes, ed., *The New World of Science and Its Development During the War*, pp. 13-16 (hereafter cited as Yerkes, *New World of Science*); *Star*, 1, 11, 16, 19, 25-30 Mar, 1 Apr 1917; *Bee*, 17 Feb 1917.

on the evening of April 2nd. Over the city fell "a soft fragrant rain of early spring; the illuminated dome of the Capitol stood in solemn splendor against the dark wet of the sky," as the President, escorted by cavalry to save him possible annoyance from pacifists, drove to the Hill. The great chamber of the House of Representatives was crowded to the doors. "To every person present," wrote an eye-witness, "from members of the Cabinet and the Justices of the Supreme Court in the first row, to observers in the remote seats of the gallery, that evening was the most-to-be remembered of their lives." Among the diplomats seated behind the Cabinet expectancy reigned. "The present German submarine warfare," the President began, "is a warfare against mankind." Chief Justice Edward D. White nodded his head in assent. As the stirring words denounced the "war against all nations," eyes in the audience turned toward the Chief Justice. When the President declared the United States incapable of choosing the path of submission, White, "without waiting to hear the rest of the sentence, sprang to his feet, his action a cue for the entire Senate. His face worked almost convulsively. Great tears rolled down his cheeks. From that moment to the end he was vigorously applauding." Four days later Congress declared war upon Germany.

The declaration of war somewhat sobered the most loudly belligerent elements in the city, but it was the signal for a chorus of high-sounding, earnest pronouncements of the sort a cynical later generation would deride: "Our war is of the kind which God sanctions. . . . The call to arms in such a war hardens and strengthens the muscles, inspires the spirit and thrills the soul of every loyal American." Virtually overnight, Washingtonians long accustomed to the placidity of the prewar capital were caught up in turmoil. "Life seemed suddenly to acquire a vivid scarlet lining," wrote Helen Nicolay. "Old prejudices gave way to passionate new beliefs. Old precedents were wrecked in an endeavor to live up to the duty of the hour. The one invariable rule seemed to be that every individual was found doing something he or she had never dreamed of doing before. The rule worked even in those somnolent parts of Georgetown that seem under the spell of a Rip Van Winkle sleep."[2]

With decentralization of the government still a novel concept, the capital bore the brunt of the confusions attending the creation of a war machine, setting it in motion, and keeping it running. In the process the city lost most of her identity as a community and became a national war center. People eager to be useful poured into Washington during the first week of the war, and the flow did not lessen until after the Armistice in November 1918. Here were the headquarters not only for the armed services but also for the Liberty Loan drives conducted by the Treasury, for the Food Administration headed by Herbert Hoover, the War Trade, the War Industries, and the Shipping Boards, the Fuel Administration, the American National Red Cross, and, when the United States government took over the railroads in December, the railroad administration. At Fort Myer, across the Potomac, 1,200 student officers at a time were in training, and several hundred engineer trainees occupied the long-empty buildings of the American University; within a radius of 25 miles some 130,000 soldiers were stationed, most of whom spent their leaves in Washington. Foreign missions and uniformed representatives of all the allied nations came and went, for, as an Englishman remarked, "this newest and rawest of the capitals, which, yet in some sense in these straining times becomes the chief capital . . . is the fountain of capacity for war and victory." A city of some 350,000 inhabitants in April 1917 acquired about 40,000 new residents before autumn, and a year later estimates based upon street-car fares raised the total to over 526,000. These and the uncounted

[2] Sullivan, *Our Times*, v, 272-74; *Star*, 6 Apr 1917; Nicolay, *Our Capital on the Potomac*, pp. 512-13.

transients strained the facilities of the District to the bursting point.[3]

"Everyone," remarked Alice Roosevelt Longworth, looked for an "excuse" to come to Washington. Viewing the city not as a dedicated old resident like Miss Nicolay but as Society's "Princess Alice," she observed: "People . . . never seemed as solely occupied with 'war work' as they were in other places." Not unnaturally "it pleased the Washington that went to and gave dinners to feel that entertaining the representatives of the Allies had a recognized part in 'winning the war.' Anyway it was a far pleasanter form of war work than canteens, Red Cross classes and Liberty Loan drives!" Journalists made fun of the deprivations some of these "war-workers" complained of—for example, after prohibition went into effect in the District on November 1, 1917, the sacrifice of cocktails before dinner and only Pol Roget, 1904, to serve with every course. Young women imported to file mountains of War Department forms doubtless felt little kinship with women who "did their bit" by knitting diligently as their chauffeurs drove them along the Avenue in their Pierce Arrows. But a "war job" in Washington, whatever its nature, held a fascination for people in all walks of life and from every part of the country.[4]

Besides the thousands of obscure, relatively uninformed typists and clerks crowded into government offices, colorful personages of the American business and professional world thronged the city. In hot little cubicles in "emergency" buildings powerful industrialists such as Charles Schwab of the United States Steel Corporation and the one-time Wyoming cowboy, Alexander Legge of the International Harvester Com-

[3] Comrs Rpts, 1917, pp. 5-6, 1918, pp. 6, 26; Theodore Tiller, "Washington in War Time," *Review of Reviews*, LVI, 629-32; Richard Oulahan, "Washington of Today," *Country Life in America*, XXXIV, 36; *Star*, 1 Jul 1917; Henry Leach, "The Charm of Washington," *Living Age*, IX, 597.

[4] Alice Roosevelt Longworth, *Crowded Hours*, pp. 258-62; Jesse Lynch Williams, "Country Life in War Time," *Country Life in America*, XXXIV, 41-42.

pany, worked long hours as government "dollar-a-year men," while in other cubby-holes brilliant but impecunious college professors such as the economist Edwin Gay of Harvard and Walter Tower, economic geographer of Chicago, earned their modest salaries many times over in a single day. Not everyone stayed longer than was necessary to learn where and how he could most usefully serve, but the nerve center of the nation at war lay here. In the thick of frustrating delays, overlapping efforts, and exhausting hard work, the challenge of the job to be done endured, and the influx of talents and ideas left permanent marks upon the city: when the tide receded with the coming of peace, Washington would discover that these war-workers had endowed her with new goals, new institutions, and some gifted new residents.[5]

Generals and admirals, disturbed by the alarming shortages of conventional arms to equip a million or more fighting men, were equally alarmed at the gaps in military equipment for which no prototype had as yet been developed—listening gear to enable ships to locate submarines, aerial cameras to serve "as the eyes of the army," wireless communication systems for both aircraft and ground use, American-made optical glass to replace German imports, improved range finders for big guns, and a dozen more. In answer to the call of Robert A. Millikan of the University of Chicago, newly appointed executive of the National Research Council, physicists, chemists, and medical research men left their university classrooms and laboratories and, accompanied by a few men trained in industrial research, joined forces with scientists already in government employ or at the Carnegie Institution of Washington. Occasionally "finds" came from unlikely sources: in the spring of 1917, for example, an unknown electrician from Salem, Massachusetts, walked into an office at the Navy Yard with a package under his arm containing his design of an underwater mine; later produced

[5] Sullivan, *Our Times*, v, 380-88; Herbert Heaton, *A Scholar in Action, Edwin F. Gay*, pp. 98-138.

as the Mark VI, this almost casually tendered innovation proved the means of screening off from submarines the stretch of sea from northern Scotland to the Norwegian coast. But scientists enlisted by the National Research Council collaborating with the military and with industry planned the programs and conducted most of the work. As the Army and Navy took over the projects one by one and put civilian scientists into officers' uniforms, most of the actual research was transferred to new installations in other parts of the country, but Washington remained the clearing house for all scientific work underway.

Because fighting a world war required far more than military hardware, medical research reached out to devise new techniques of surgery and prevention of epidemic diseases in training camps and overseas, while psychologists developed intelligence and special aptitude tests for classification of draftees in a citizens' army. The government turned also to social scientists and historians. In the six months preceding the United States' entry into the war, several federal bureaus had benefitted from a few studies undertaken by political economists at a newly founded, privately financed Institute for Government Research, but the role of the inexact sciences widened in the spring of 1917. In April the British and French missions to Washington explained to the President that, if Germany were to be kept from overpowering western Europe, the United States would have to supply its hard-pressed allies with food, oil, and iron, as well as munitions and men. The undertaking would tax America's resources to the utmost and demanded, in the words of an eminent economist, "a new ordering of [national] life." The emergency boards and commissions that quickly proliferated in Washington contained a sprinkling of experienced government administrators but were manned chiefly by businessmen and college professors trained in assembling factual materials and interpreting their significance.[6]

[6] Yerkes, *New World of Science*, pp. 20-30, 291-350; Dupree, *Science*, pp. 308-23; Benedict Crowell and Robert E. Wilson, *The Armies of Industry*,

As federal census reports in the past had focused primarily on data needed to reapportion representation in Congress and to draft tariff legislation, the lack of precise information available in Washington about the character and extent of national resources posed an enormous problem, for, without accurate knowledge of the nature and quantity of national assets, planning could not proceed logically, and, without planning, the task of imposing restrictions upon the civilian economy was impossible. Hence the importance of the work undertaken by Edwin F. Gay and his "cabinet" of economists in the Shipping Board's Planning and Statistics Division. Similarly, since Americans would not accept interference with the sacred free enterprise system unless they understood the reasons, the Committee on Public Information drew upon scholars to educate the public about what was at stake and why drastic measures were necessary. The endeavors to effect "a new ordering" of national economic life ended with the cessation of fighting in Europe, but government officials and private citizens in the interim learned a good deal about the value of exact information and efficient procedures. Washington would feel the lasting effects of this hard-won wisdom.

"Scholars in the human sciences," Frederick Keppel of Columbia later noted, "did not dominate the situation as did scholars in the physical sciences," but the voluntary "mobilization of the history men" began in late April at a conference called by J. Franklin Jameson of the Carnegie Institution's Department of Historical Research. Eager to put "historical scholarship" to immediate use, a National Board of Historical Service enlisted lecturers, writers to prepare pamphlets on "war issues," and "Four-Minute-Men" to speak at Liberty Loan

---

I, 319; *Autobiography of Robert A. Millikan*, pp. 142-99; The Brookings Institution, *Institute for Government Research, An Account of Research Achievements*, pp. 4-18; Allyn A. Young, "National Statistics in War and Peace," *Quarterly Publications of the American Statistical Society*, March 1918, p. 2.

rallies. The board strove also to ensure the preservation of valuable wartime records and prepared background materials that might assist in the eventual negotiation of a just peace. Later sometimes accused of performing as propagandists rather than judicious scholars, historians in and out of Washington vigorously pressed the case for improving the quality of history teaching and textbooks in school systems throughout the country. Scholars' insistence on the importance of records was instrumental in creating historical branches in the State, War, and Navy Departments during the war and, a dozen years later, in persuading Congress to vote money for a public record repository—the National Archives. Out of the interest in better teaching came the American Council on Education in 1918, "an organization of organizations" in which school and college administrators joined with historians in an effort to raise the standards of American education. While undertaking to recruit 10,000 students for nurses' training, the council's directing heads in Washington soon realized that their chief tasks would lie in the postwar world. With a full-time director appointed after the Armistice, the council began its major work in 1920.[7]

Washingtonians occupied few important posts in the hastily established emergency agencies. A non-industrial city had no businessmen of the stature of Charles Schwab to take charge of shipbuilding, or of Henry Dennison of the Dennison Manufacturing Company, expert on business administration, or of Bernard Baruch whose spectacular lone-wolf career in the stock market made him a power to reckon with and a logical choice for head of the War Industries Board. Four or five professors of the "dismal science" at the local universities and a number of experienced men whose long service in Washington made them "permanent temporary" residents had responsible jobs with the federal wartime boards, and members of the Library

[7] American Historical Association, *Annual Report*, 1919, I, 131-89; *American Council on Education, Its History and Activities*, pp. 1-5.

of Congress staff and scholars attached to other federal offices volunteered assistance. But the civil service system of making appointments on a quota basis to citizens of the states kept local people out of war jobs until the housing shortage in Washington called attention to the desirability of employing qualified local talent.[8] Life acquired its vivid scarlet lining for most Washingtonians because they believed fervently in the "great crusade," and here where mighty events moved forward they felt themselves an intimate part of it. They served as the Marthas of the capital, the people who carried on the humdrum thankless chores of supplying as best they could the wants of the newcomers.

Yet the local community made distinct if little recognized contributions to the winning of the war. The foresight of District Commissioner Brownlow and several federal officials who believed some form of military conscription inevitable enabled the city to set an example to the rest of the country in drafting men for the armed services: the draft forms for the District were in print, and maps showing registration stations were ready for posting several days before the National Selective Service Act passed Congress on May 18, 1917; run by volunteers among the District government's employees, registration then moved so swiftly and smoothly that on September 4th the President himself underscored the achievement by leading a parade of the District's "citizens' army" up Pennsylvania Avenue. Although agitation about "rounding up slackers" went on for weeks thereafter, Washingtonians were proud of having 10,000 inductees and nearly 7,000 voluntary enlistments before the Armistice, in addition to the 2,000 men in service when war broke out.

Given a quota of $8,500,000 in the first Liberty Bond drive, the city raised more than twice that amount; in the second drive four months later she raised nearly $23,000,000 and oversub-

[8] H Dis Comee, 65C, 1S, Hrg, "Housing in D.C."; *Star*, 25 Oct 1918.

scribed her quotas in every later campaign. Some of the subscriptions came from temporary dollar-a-year men, but the local response was remarkable inasmuch as the spiraling costs of living in the overcrowded capital by 1918 had reduced by about 30 percent the purchasing power of federal and District employees, who even in 1916 were shockingly underpaid. Nor did householders escape acute privations: 5,000 families were without heat in sub-zero January weather when the city had less than a day's coal supply on hand even at strict ration levels. Volunteers appointed to a District Council of Defense cheerfully took charge of projects they "had never dreamed" of before; some five thousand war gardens produced over $1,000,000 in foodstuffs during 1918; a group cooperated with the Traveller's Aid in assisting newcomers to find places to live, and women made surgical dressings under Red Cross direction, organized camp entertainments, and manned canteens. As American troops began to move overseas, Washington, like every city and village on the continent, saw "tears and cheers; sudden marriages and sudden farewells. . . . And endlessly there was the suspense of waiting for the next war news."[9]

War, moreover, imposed unique problems on the District government, perhaps none more troublesome than keeping order in the war-swollen capital. In the spring of 1917 the national government had scanty machinery to provide for its own protection—a small Secret Service attached to the Treasury department to keep track of counterfeiting and three or four men assigned to the White House, a Capitol police force composed largely of political appointees, and the Federal Bureau of Investigation, which, established in Theodore Roosevelt's day to prevent fraudulent transactions in public land, had only two or three men located in Washington. In 1915 and 1916 Louis Brownlow, the District commissioner responsible for the police

[9] Brownlow, *A Passion for Anonymity*, pp. 44-82; Comrs Rpts, 1917, pp. 5-6, 1918, pp. 5-8, 1919, pp. 9, 557-67; *Star*, 15, 21 Jun, 12 Aug, 2, 28 Oct, 9 Dec 1917, 9, 28 May, 11, 17, 20 Oct 1918, 12 May 1919; *Rpt B/Tr*, 1917, p. 11.

department, and its newly appointed chief, Major Raymond Pullman, had taken the first steps to forestall German espionage. Not until the war was five months old did a new Emergency Division in the Department of Justice begin to handle all matters touching alien enemies, sabotage, and espionage; in the interim the local police carried much of the load. The force was always below authorized strength, partly because of Army enlistments, but even more because pay rates, set by Congress in 1916, stood at about half the figure offered by private employers. The *Bee* suggested the time ripe to add colored officers to the department, but either Negro candidates failed to qualify or Major Pullman was unwilling to risk antagonizing whites. At Brownlow's insistence, however, the department enlisted several policewomen, an innovation that initially scandalized conservatives.

One episode that assumed some international significance illustrates policing problems. As the first Allied missions began to arrive in Washington, militant women suffragists chose to picket the White House; their banners labelled the President and the administration more tyrannical than Kaiser Wilhelm or the Romanoff Czar. As infuriated clerks pouring out of the government buildings every afternoon tore down the offensive banners, street riots greeted the eyes of foreign emissaries. Commissioner Brownlow finally ordered the arrest of the leading pickets, all of them socially prominent women, and, upon their refusal to pay the court fines, sent them to the Occoquan workhouse. The President, unwilling to create martyrs, promptly issued pardons. The daily street riots resumed. Unfortunately, as enemy newspapers in Europe interpreted them as pro-German demonstrations, they hurt Allied solidarity. Without seeking presidential approval, which Wilson would probably not give, Brownlow then put some thirty of the most obstreperous women into a freshly painted, newly furnished, separate building of the District jail in cells without lockable doors. The new inmates at once went on a hunger strike. So the Commissioner had two stoves installed in the corridor and engaged three eight-hour shifts of cooks to fry ham night and day. The ham went to charitable institutions. Defeated by the fragrance of frying ham, the hunger strikers voluntarily left the jail, and the campaign of militant abusiveness collapsed.

While the police force, at times reduced to fewer than 700 men, struggled with a mounting volume of crime, President Wilson's passion for vaudeville added to troubles. Every week, in war as in peace, he attended Poli's Theatre on 15th Street, and crowds gathered nightly at the entrance in order to buy tickets for the performance that he chose. Lincoln's assassination at Ford's Theatre fifty-odd years before stood as a painful warning. The worried manager of Poli's fell in with Commissioner Brownlow's suggestion to reserve the entire balcony for reliably patriotic people whenever the President was to occupy his box. The manager cut a doorway through the theatre wall into the alley at the rear so that the White House limousine accompanied by a Secret Service man could deposit the President unobtrusively there whence a back stairway led to his box. But the President never decided when he would go until the morning of the day; then Brownlow would telephone the theatre to sell no balcony tickets for that night, and he himself issued free passes to people known to be trustworthy. President Wilson, unaware of these elaborate arrangements, later remarked cheerfully that the crowded balcony showed that at least Poli's profited from his patronage.

Other units of the local government also faced almost insoluble problems. Before the autumn of 1917 the experienced engineer commissioner, Major Kutz, and Commissioner Oliver Newman left for active Army service. An able but physically frail retired Brigadier General, John G. D. Knight, replaced the former, and W. Gwynne Gardiner, a Washington attorney, a little reluctantly succeeded the latter. For the next two and a half years, as Gardiner spent less and less time in his office, Louis Brownlow ran the District almost single-handedly. Short and slightly rotund, the sharp intelligence and humor in his snapping brown eyes partly concealed by gleaming pince-nez, Brownlow at the age of 37 looked more like an insurance salesman than an imaginative, widely read, forceful public servant. But neither experience nor energy could ensure adequate transportation on the overburdened, privately owned, street railway system, or, at the wage rates allowed, hire hands for vitally necessary public chores, or enlarge the public water supply.

The maximum safe capacity of the city reservoir and filtration plant was 65,000,000 gallons of water daily; by the summer of 1918 daily consumption at times exceeded 75,000,000 gallons. As private industry drew away the men operating the District sewage pumping station, where the pay scale ranged from $900 downward to $540 a year, only Brownlow's personal appeal to President Wilson obtained from the President's emergency fund the $8,000 needed to keep the sewage system in operation; the President filled out the forms and signed the requisitions in his own hand. When the contractor who collected the city garbage, after months of losing money, threw up the contract, Brownlow undertook to extract a deficiency appropriation from Congress to enable the District to make the collections and run the garbage reduction plant. When he presented a carefully figured cost estimate to the House subcommittee, the chairman immediately barked: "There is not one bit of use coming up here and asking us in time of war to start off the District government on a lot of socialistic experimentation." Fortunately, Congressman Vare, the Republican boss of Philadelphia who had made millions as that city's garbage and trash collector, persuaded his fellow committee members that the request was reasonable. The appropriation passed.[10]

Far worse troubles followed. Early in September 1918 the

[10] Interviews, Brownlow, and John Lord O'Brian, head of Emergency Div., Justice Dept, 1917-19; *Star*, 18 Aug 1917, 1 Jan, 8-10, 12 Jun, 8 Aug 1918; *Bee*, 17 Nov 1917; *Rpts B/Tr*, 1917, pp. 70-71, 1918, p. 81; Comr Rpts, 1917, p. 22, 1918, pp. 25-26, 1919, p. 26.

former District health officer who was now health commissioner of Boston, wired Brownlow to warn him that several cases of virulent disease called Spanish flu had occurred in Boston and to urge him to require Washington physicians to report any suspected cases. Prompt action on that advice failed to head off the plague; by September 21, it had hit the overcrowded capital with a force that broke down the reporting service and swamped doctors with desperately ill and dying patients. Both Commissioner Gardiner and General Knight were stricken. Brownlow and the new health officer, Dr. Fowler, closed the theatres, the movie houses, the churches, and most of the shops, persuaded the school board to close the schools, and, with the cooperation of the Visiting Nurses Association, the Red Cross, and a volunteer motor corps, opened nursing centers in four or five schoolhouses. But the epidemic spread. Physicians and nurses caught the disease. Every hospital bed in the city was filled. At one point George Washington Hospital, one of the largest, had every bed occupied and not a single nurse on duty. With half the trolley motormen on the sick list, street-car service was utterly disrupted. And as the death toll mounted, there were neither coffins nor gravediggers enough to meet the emergency.

In mid October, Brownlow later wrote, "it seemed that we had come to the end of our resources. There was a dreadful Saturday." That day he enlisted through the White House the help of every federal agency and arranged for a high-level meeting at the office of the War Industries Board on Sunday morning. A scrutiny of the records filed by war workers revealed people with nursing skills or medical experience. Judge Edwin B. Parker of the War Industries Board virtually commandeered a building just vacated by a division of the Army, and contractors and union representatives were told to ready the building for hospital use, while merchants assembled bedding. By eight o'clock Sunday night a seven-hundred-bed hospital was equipped, and a skeleton staff of doctors and nurses, brought together by Army and Navy medical officers, the Public Health Service, and Dr. Fowler, was ready to receive patients. Volunteer ambulance drivers worked through the night. By two o'clock in the morning every bed was filled. In the interval Secretary of the Navy Daniels ordered marines from Quantico, Virginia, to Washington to dig graves, and, on Judge Parker's instructions, two carloads of coffins in the Potomac railroad yards consigned to Pittsburgh were transferred to the city hospital, where Dr. Fowler took charge of distributing them at a fixed price. Thus the dead were buried, and the worst ravages of the plague halted. By November 4th the emergency was over. Official records showed 35,000 cases reported and 3,500 deaths in those six weeks, but no one could tally the unreported cases, and deaths resulting from later complications ran into hundreds. Only magnificent cooperation supported by unlimited authority rescued the capital from one of the worst disasters in its history.[11]

If the behavior of the local community during the crisis won it commendation, during most of the war outlanders held Washingtonians up to opprobrium as "rent sharks" and "profiteers." The commissioners' report of 1919 tells the essentials of the story:

"Not since the journeying of St. Ursula with her 11,000 virgins to their martyrdom at Cologne, some 1,500 years ago, has there been such a pilgrimage of young women as that which moved toward Washington after the beginning of the war in 1917.

"Many of the young women who were attracted by the relatively large salaries offered had never been away from home before, and in the nostalgic reaction . . . everything different from what it was at home was apt to seem objectionable. It had not occurred to these pilgrims that the expenses must also be figured on a new basis, and that the advantages of life at home

[11] Brownlow, *A Passion for Anonymity*, pp. 69-73.

in a small place could not be expected in a crowded city. This . . . led to a great many undeserved criticisms of Washington people who had never had outsiders in their homes before, but who were admitting them then from a patriotic desire to help share with them in this way the burden which war imposed." In most cases, said the report, rents were not raised exorbitantly, and congressional hearings indicated fairly clearly that sub-rentals accounted for the worst abuses; house-owners and real estate companies were relatively seldom party to them. But who bothered to read or weigh the facts presented in long official reports? The public image of the housing squeeze in Washington rested on magazine stories of extortionate charges, for example, the $30,000 a year rental paid by a dollar-a-year man.[12]

In the summer of 1917 square wooden boxes, called "tempos," began to rise on the Mall to provide temporary office space for war agencies that overflowed the business blocks the government commandeered. But not until January 1918 did federal authorities accept any responsibility for finding living quarters for incoming government clerks. A War Department grant then supplied money to furnish and open some unoccupied houses, but, as informed people acknowledged, without the intelligent planning and vigorous work of Mrs. Archibald Hopkins, head of the women's committee of the District Defense Council, that official scheme would have brought few results. In May 1918 alarming statements of the Civil Service Commission that half of its appointments were refused on the grounds that the pay was insufficient to meet the high cost of living in Washington led Congress to act. It passed a resolution aimed at preventing rent profiteering, appropriated several million dollars for building government dormitories, and, in order to avoid adding eight thousand alley dwellers to the

12 Comrs Rpt, 1919, I, 569-71, 576; Clara Savage, "On to Washington," *Good Housekeeping*, LXVI, 158; H Dis Comee, 65C, 2S, Hrg, "Housing in D.C."; Subcomee H Dis Comee, 66C, 1S, Hrgs, "The High Cost of Living in D.C.," pp. 807-17; *Star*, 8, 19 Mar, 9 Apr, 29 May 1918, 1 Jan 1919.

throng of homeless, waived the requirement of the Alley Dwelling Act of 1914 that called for evacuation of all alley houses by July 1, 1918. In September the Housing Corporation of the Department of Labor relieved the District Defense Council of the task of locating, inspecting, and listing available rooms, and commandeered a few private homes, but none of the government dormitories on the Union Station Plaza were ready before the Armistice. Consequently, the District commissioners observed, by and large "the problem of caring for incoming government employees was met by the citizens of Washington."[13]

Those citizens, aware of having stopped many gaps for the federal government, were indignant at hearing themselves excoriated as "profiteers." In spite of shortages of goods and higher tax assessments, business concerns almost without exception had made money, but so had business firms elsewhere. "That madman Ben Johnson," as Louis Brownlow forty years later dubbed the city's chief enemy on the Hill, led the attacks in Congress. Two weeks before the Armistice Theodore Noyes of the *Star* wrote angrily: "The last summer has been full of bitter days for the people of Washington; gloriously bitter in the cheerful endurance of necessary patriotic war sacrifices with other good Americans; humiliatingly bitter through discriminating, slurring, hurtful legislation, unnecessarily imposed or threatened, and through the slanderous vilification of Washingtonians which has accompanied it.

"Mr. Johnson denounces the property owners and landlords of Washington as the most unpatriotic people in the whole world. He poses as peculiarly the protector of the boys in the trenches and of the civilian war workers.

"Mr. Johnson's Washington constituency has sent more boys to the trenches to give their lives to win the war . . . has furnished more civilian war workers . . . [and] has put up more

[13] Comrs Rpt, 1918, p. 6, 1919, I, 576, 582-83; "Living in War-Swollen Washington is a Serious Problem," *Literary Digest*, LVII, 65; *Star*, 3, 6 Jan, 30 Mar, 25 May 1918.

money . . . in donations through the Red Cross and otherwise, in Liberty Loans and in war taxes, than his Kentucky constituency." When underpaid clerks who worked long hours of overtime protested at an increase in their hours without any increase in pay, some members of Congress condemned them as slackers.[14]

Unlike other American cities, Washington underwent crises not in periods of business depression but amid the booming activities of wartime. The War of 1812 had nearly extinguished the city; the Civil War and its aftermath had subjected her citizens to wholesale charges of disloyalty; the war against the Central Powers brought down upon her patriots the hostility of their countrymen. Yet as long as the world war continued, most Washingtonians were too absorbed in their war jobs, in the rush of business created by the swelling population, and in coping with the difficulties of running their households to be deeply disturbed by outlanders' complaints. Philosophical, longtime residents could recognize the harsh criticism as part of a hysteria born of overwork and anxieties they themselves shared. Conscious of doing their best, even at the sacrifice of local charities and other civic interests, they generally submerged their irritation at their detractors in belief that peace would restore sounder judgment to their critics. Unhappily, time would show that the attacks, coupled with the failure to forestall others, severely damaged community morale for a decade to come. Indeed Washington never fully regained her former faith in herself.

When the Armistice came, the capital celebrated less boisterously than cities whose responsibilities had been lighter. Since the commissioners requested postponement of a great victory parade until after the formal signing of a peace treaty, jubilation found expression chiefly in talk rather than, as in New York, in

[14] *Rpt B/Tr*, 1917, pp. 40, 42; Comrs Rpts, 1917, pp. 11-12, 1918, pp. 10-12; *Star*, 23 Sep, 8 Oct 1917, 7 Apr, 29 Oct 1918; H Rpt 288, 65C, 2S, pp. 3-4, Ser 7037.

flinging ticker tape from the windows of skyscrapers. At noon on November 11th the President rode down Pennsylvania Avenue through cheering crowds to deliver official confirmation of the thrilling news to Congress. That night forty-nine bonfires on the Ellipse lighted the sky from the Monument to the river. A day or two later, dollar-a-year men triumphantly began emptying their brief cases into office waste baskets, filling them with reports and regulations that need now be nothing but paper.

In the next weeks, however, the expected rapid exodus of the rank-and-file of war-workers did not occur; in fact, the demand for housing and the prices for all essentials continued to rise. While local business showed no signs of falling off, Washingtonians' zeal for good works waned rapidly. Only large contributions from government employees enabled the city that had met every earlier wartime challenge to raise her $800,000 quota for the "war chest" upon which the YMCA, the National Catholic War Council, the Jewish Welfare Board, the Salvation Army, and several other organizations depended in caring for servicemen. The drive for Red Cross members in December 1918 was close to a complete failure; Washington did about a third as well as the national average. Perhaps still more indicative of the community's spiritual exhaustion, the annual campaign to raise money for the Associated Charities fell $2,000 short of its modest $8,800 goal.[15]

The one project that appeared to evoke universal enthusiasm among Washingtonians was the drive for a constitutional amendment giving the District voting representation in Congress and the electoral college. In May and June 1917 resolutions offered in House and Senate and referred to the Judiciary committees had proposed a diluted version in the form of an amendment authorizing Congress whenever it saw fit to grant Washingtonians representation. The war relegated all District affairs to the background. Now with the fighting war over,

[15] Sullivan, *Our Times*, v, 520; *Star*, 14, 21 Nov, 16-17, 23-26 Dec 1918.

citizens with a singleness of purpose new in the District's political history set out to win the status which recent experience had convinced them was their surest safeguard against future injustice. Carefully laid plans included an educational campaign to enlighten congressional constituents throughout the United States about the handicaps under which residents of the capital suffered.

In January 1919 the undertaking got off to a good start. A citizens' committee had laid the groundwork in 1916 by visiting other cities to assemble data on their tax structure, so that a nucleus of organization was already in existence. The impressive feature of the new Citizens' Joint Committee on National Representation for the District of Columbia, headed by Theodore Noyes and John Joy Edson, was the all-inclusiveness of the white groups participating—the Chamber of Commerce, the Board of Trade, the Merchants' and Manufacturers' Association, the Central Labor Union, the Federation of Citizens' Associations, the Oldest Inhabitants Association, the Bar Association, the Monday Evening Club, the Real Estate Brokers Association, the 20th Century Club and a half dozen more—in short, every significant civic and business organization in white Washington. The local press carried long accounts of progress; out-of-town correspondents for metropolitan papers gave the program good notices. Local business firms attached to their out-of-town correspondence red stickers informing recipients that the District, with 400,000 inhabitants, paid taxes, obeyed federal laws, and went to war, but was voteless. The response was surprisingly quick and encouraging. Offers of support flowed in from many parts of the country where people expressed astonishment at learning that Washingtonians were disenfranchised or paid taxes in any form. Not a dissident note sounded for weeks. But neither did anything happen on the Hill.

Some opposition from Congress was to be expected, for, although the 1918 election had put Republicans in control of both houses, objections to a partly Negro electorate in the capital seemed likely, and hostility to the community still sounded on the Hill. "Washington," remarked one senator, "has more profiteers and grafters than any city in the United States." Give them representation and their demands for free gifts would allow Congress no time for anything else. But in early March the leader of the House reportedly said Congress was "making a mess of the job" of "long-distance" governing of the District, and when a conference of one hundred city mayors and state governors endorsed suffrage for Washington, prospects for early success looked rosy.[16]

While Congress, ostensibly waiting for completion of the peace negotiations at Versailles, delayed action on the District's appeal, the New York City press launched upon criticisms directed chiefly at Washington's modest tax rate and reliance on federal contributions. The New York *Post* declared that until the creation of the territory in 1871 "there had been no taxes in the District"; debts had accumulated only under territorial rule. Newspapers elsewhere picked up the theme of a greedy city. Unfortunately, local campaigners, for all their careful organization, had not devised a method of presenting an accurate picture of the incidence of taxes. Repeated statements that the District paid more in federal income and internal revenue taxes than did sixteen states did not provide fool-proof figures that would satisfy out-of-town inquiries about how the levies on Washington business firms compared with those of other cities. An exact, easily understandable comparison was, to be sure, impossible because of the intertwining of federal and District costs and services, but lengthy, involved explanations tended to raise as many doubts as they settled. Nor did the publicity drive home the basic difficulty of persuading Congress to sanction the use of District taxes for such acute needs as higher

[16] *Rpts B/Tr*, 1917, pp. 14-17, 1918, pp. 59-68; *Star*, Summaries, 1918, 1919, 17 Feb 1919; clippings and letters in J. D. Kaufman, Scrapbooks on Washington Home Rule, Jan-Mar 1919; *Times*, 4, 11 Mar 1919.

salaries for school teachers and new schoolhouses. Neither friend nor critic remarked on colored Washington's aloofness from the campaign.

By the time the 66th Congress convened in May 1919 and turned over new resolutions on a constitutional amendment to the Judiciary committees, Washingtonians' solid front was showing cracks. The Board of Trade advocated only representation in Congress and perpetuation of an appointed commission for local government. The Chamber of Commerce stood for securing a place in Congress before considering home rule. The labor unions, on the contrary, urged immediate substitution of elected local officials for the commissioners. Louis Brownlow had also reached the conclusion that home rule offered the only answer: "Because the membership of Congress was overwhelmingly rural in background, it was frequently impossible to get the necessary legislation or the required appropriations of funds to enable the District to keep up with the constantly increasing demands of American urban life." Even two District senators and two or more representatives in the House would not ensure parochial concerns attention from a body whose national and international responsibilities were mounting with every passing year. If aware of that probability in 1919, business leaders still preferred to take their chances on dealing with Congress to risking the rule of an electorate in which propertyless voters might predominate. Even had all Washington united in asking for full-scale enfranchisement, a favorable response was unlikely from a Congress still disgruntled about the city's supposed war record. But whatever chance of success the suffrage campaign had had early in 1919 vanished in July, when a flare-up of violence in the city's race relations chilled white ardor and obliterated Negro interest in political change.[17]

[17] New York *Post*, 29 Mar 1919, and other papers, Kaufman Scrapbooks; *Rec*, 66C, 1S, pp. 25, 1013; *Rpts B/Tr*, 1917, p. 15, 1918, p. 51, 1919, pp. 11, 128; *Times*, 9 Feb 1919; *Star*, 12 Feb, 9 Dec 1919; Brownlow, *Passion for Anonymity*, p. 100.

Civic lethargy enveloped most of the city for the next eighteen months. Postwar upheavals in other cities, Chicago's race riots, Seattle's general strike, Boston's police strike, and fear of worse to come in other places failed to arouse Washington from her apathy. Citizens' associations added members without producing constructive action. Local charities continued to limp along with little support. In October the campaign for representation in Congress resumed in tepid fashion when the Board of Trade issued a call to work for "that prized American privilege and power we so much desire and which the capital . . . so greatly needs." Out-of-town newspapers occasionally commented on war-workers' resentment of Washingtonians' touchiness and lack of cordiality, and an Arkansas paper urged cave-dwellers to take to their bosoms the congressmen's wives whose exclusion from "the local social set" engendered a bitterness that then infected their husbands. But neither self-exhortation nor advice from outsiders restored to Washingtonians their earlier enthusiasm and confidence.[18]

Several depressing aspects of life in postwar Washington contributed to a drying up of local pride. The resignation of nearly 150 of the most gifted white public school teachers who had taken better-paid jobs had stripped the school system of its chief asset; at the present salary scale the superintendent could not engage others. The very look of the city had changed for the worse. The Mall was a clutter of tempos; to the east of the Smithsonian a string of them stretched from B Street south to B Street north, another ugly cluster stood beyond the Monument, and near the center two great chimneys cut the skyline. From the Union Station to the Senate Office Building on the Hill starkly utilitarian barracks for government clerks occupied most of the Plaza. Residential sections also had altered in appearance. "Old Washington vanished never to return," wrote Helen Nicolay, "when its skyline changed from one of dormer

[18] *Rpts B/Tr*, 1919, p. 11, 1920, pp. 70-71, 131; *Star*, 1 Jan 1920; *Syracuse Journal*, 12 Feb 1920; *Little Rock Gazette*, 23 Oct 1919.

windows and aspiring chimneys to the great impersonal apartment houses of tile and light-colored brick, with their square outlines, and the private houses of French Renaissance or modified colonial types, also light in color, that have replaced the deep-red brick beloved of Mr. Corcoran and his contemporaries."

Even the character of the bookshops changed. Washingtonians no longer dropped in to browse and chat socially; "expensive knickknacks and cheap postcards by the acre" diluted the stock. Strangers were everywhere. "Most of the women wear fur coats and the latest cut of shoes, and the latest shade in face powder. It is a crowd such as could not have been in Washington ten years ago, or even five." Photographs of debutantes and hostesses never seen before the war filled the rotogravure sections of the newspapers. Washingtonians had trouble feeling at home in Washington.

The gates to the White House grounds, closed before the United States entered the war, remained shut, giving strange lifelessness to the very heart of the city. Old residents had looked forward to the moment when all would be as before. For a brief time after the Armistice prewar festivities had seemed about to resume, but early in January the *Star* regretfully reported: "As the New Year reception of the White House will never again be witnessed in its old form, the one day of the year when the representatives of kings and the humblest citizen might shake hands with the President and wish him good luck, so the cabinet day of old when the drawing rooms of cabinet homes were thronged with any who wished to call has gone the same way." For the first time since John and Abigail Adams had occupied the Executive Mansion, the American President was away from Washington for long periods—in Paris during the spring of 1919, in the autumn taking the League of Nations issue before the country. However much the old guard of Theodore Roosevelt's and Taft's day disliked the social attitudes of Woodrow Wilson, his absence in official society was rather like

Hamlet without Hamlet. Vice President Marshall had to review the parade of the First Division led by General Pershing. The President's illness upon his return to Washington had a further dampening effect in spite of the elaborate entertainment arranged for the visits of the King and Queen of Belgium and the Prince of Wales.

Above all, Washington's new impersonality troubled old residents. They could recognize it as the inevitable price of bigness and, indeed, could perceive the advantages of a country-wide awakening to "the possibilities of doing things on a national scale, of adapting the mechanism of national life to fit national ends."[19] But a sense of loss remained. As it became clear in the early months of 1920 that the intimacy of the leisurely old Washington was gone, a feeling of oppressive uncertainty engulfed the city.

[19] Comrs Rpt, 1919, IV, 11-13; Nicolay, *Capital*, pp. 515-20; *Star*, 17 Nov 1918, 5, 12 Jan, 14, 28 Sep, 12 Oct, 12 Dec 1919; Anderson, *Presidents and Pies*, pp. 237-38; Brownlow, *Passion for Anonymity*, pp. 86-88; Young, "National Statistics in War and Peace," p. 11.

CHAPTER XIII

THE AFTERMATH OF THE COLORED MAN'S WAR, 1917-1919

UNLIKE colored radicals in several northern cities in 1916, Washington Negroes had not seriously considered putting race before country. On the contrary, they early came to look upon the war as their opportunity to win recognition as loyal Americans and the inevitable postwar readjustments as a unique chance to establish themselves permanently in a sound economic position. The relative stability of the local colored population heightened the chances of success. Whereas industrial cities like Detroit and Chicago were inundated with southern Negroes who moved north to take jobs in war plants, Washington faced no comparable colored immigration. The intelligent local Negro community, consequently, was not submerged by a wave of ignorant blacks from the rural South. The Washington branch of the NAACP declared that patriotism did not require colored men to put up with injustice or to remain silent about lynchings in the South and unprovoked attacks such as those in East St. Louis, Illinois, but, from early 1917 till the return of colored troops of the AEF two years later, complaints about racial discrimination in Washington dwindled. The local Negro press underscored every instance of fair behavior from whites and exhorted colored people to make the most of the new openings which wholehearted cooperation would bring. However flimsy the foundations of that counsel of hope, colored Washington built on it.

Thus the District's colored candidates for officer training swallowed their dismay at being sent to an all-Negro camp at Des Moines, Iowa; there they at least might have a better chance to prove their worth than in a mixed camp. George Richardson of the *Bee* warned colored servicemen not to write home about every slight they endured; their record would plead their cause eloquently upon their return. Signs of white recognition seemed to be multiplying: Herbert Hoover appointed a Negro science teacher from the Dunbar High School to head the colored bureau of the Food Administration; Secretary of War Newton Baker made Emmett J. Scott an assistant in the War Department, and the local chapter of the Red Cross asked Scott to serve on the finance committee; the Labor Department assigned George Haynes to a responsible position, and Secretary of the Treasury McAdoo proposed to send fifty colored men across the country to explain national war aims to Negroes. Even the arch conservative Oldest Inhabitants' Association invited the Oldest Inhabitants' Association (Colored) to visit the white headquarters in the old firehouse at 19th and H Streets northwest.[1]

Yet proofs of lingering white antagonism were also numerous: new congressional proposals for residential segregation and other Jim Crow bills, which, though not passed, were a slap at the Negro war effort; the three-year sentence imposed by court martial on a Negro sentry for shooting a white man who disobeyed the command to halt; the failure of government offices to hire colored people qualified by civil service examinations and of the District police department to take on colored patrolmen; the refusal of the street railway companies to employ Negroes to fill some five hundred operator jobs; and Red Cross segregation of colored volunteers from white. District officials and Congress rejected a housing plan for alley-dwellers when Negro builders proposed a loan to enable them to put up low rental housing. When the president of Howard University retired, the trustees again elected a white man; and during the war for the first time Negroes heard themselves called "darkies" in a District courtroom.[2]

[1] *Crisis*, XIV, 4, 304, XVI, 217-19, XVII, 182-84, 194; *Bee*, 14, 21 Apr, 26 May, 2, 30 Jun, 28 Jul, 25 Aug, 1, 15 Dec 1917, 13 Apr, 4, 11, 18 May, 7 Sep 1918; *Star*, 21 Oct 1917, 1 Oct 1918.

[2] *Star*, 3 Sep, 25 Dec 1917, 3 Jan, 18 Jul 1918; *Bee*, 3, 10 Nov

Negro leaders knew that some white Washingtonians, like those who joined the local branch of the NAACP in 1918, deplored the continuing discriminatory practices and fully appreciated what Negroes were doing for their country. The best element in the colored community clung to hope that the perceptive element of the white community would insist upon racial justice in the postwar world. So the handsome Archibald Grimké, able head of the Washington NAACP and president of the American Negro Academy, told the academy in December 1918: "I am glad to say that associated with us . . . are a number of leading white men. We do not have to fight this battle alone." About the same time John R. Hawkins of Howard University presented to the Washington NAACP fourteen points, paralleling President Wilson's famous fourteen points for world democracy, which alone would give meaning to the word in the United States. While Mary White Ovington, one of the white founders of the National Association, wrote in the *Crisis* that "the last place to which the returning colored soldier can look for justice is Washington, the very foundation of the government he has so faithfully served," she added: "The power of numbers, but *organized* numbers, is the power that wins the battle. Every oppressed group . . . is engaged in a separate struggle to secure something of value for itself in the chaos that comes at the close of a great war. Now . . . while systems are fluid, before the structure of society becomes rigid again is the opportunity to win the reality of democracy."[3]

Colored Washingtonians won a first minor victory in January 1919 when Commissioner Brownlow established an all-Negro platoon in the fire department, an arrangement that

1917, 2, 9, 23 Feb, 9, 23, 30 Mar, 28 Sep 1918; *Crisis*, XIV, 139, XVII, 116; H Rpt 420, 65C, 2S, Ser 7304.

[3] Corcoran Thom to Mary Church Terrell, 25 Nov 1918, and Jane Ogle, to M. C. Terrell, 3 Dec 1917, Terrell Mss; *Star*, 26 Dec 1918; Mary White Ovington, "Reconstruction and the Negro," *Crisis*, XVII, 169-70, 172; *Bee*, 16 Nov 1918, 4, 18 Jan, 15 Feb, 21 Jun 1919.

ensured promotions for the department's four colored veterans of twenty years' service and gave new appointees a chance to prove their competence under men of their own race. Equally helpful to colored morale were several articles in the *Star* describing the valor of the District's "famous old 1st Separate Battalion" in action in France. Of the battalion's 480 Washingtonians, 25 had been awarded the Croix De Guerre, and the officers of the French regiment to which the battalion was attached had nothing but highest praise for the entire unit. The *Star* correspondent remarked that the city would surely want to stage a homecoming demonstration for these troops, for "every citizen of Washington—in fact of the United States—should feel proud of them." And the chief secretary of the national Salvation Army said he had "a pretty complete record" of the conduct of the colored soldiers and that "something ought to be done to show their courage and fidelity were appreciated." He had rented a building in the capital to house them when they returned late in March 1919.[4]

That was the last expression of general good will in Washington. The parade of returned white soldiers, led by President Wilson, took place before the 1st Separate Battalion reached home. As if alarmed by the praise already meted out to the colored heroes, after February 1919 Washington's white newspapers had nothing more to say of them or of Negroes' part on the home front. By late spring the *Crisis* reported that influential Americans were repeating comments supposedly originating with high-ranking officers of the AEF to the effect that "the Negro officer is a failure" and the behavior of colored troops in France had been cowardly in battle and improper in social contacts with French people. W. E. B. DuBois, after three months in Europe spent in collecting facts for a "History of the Black Man in the Great War," concluded that "no person in

[4] *Star*, 18 Jan, 14, 15, 17, 28 Feb 1919; *Bee*, 8, 22 Mar, 14 Jun, 19 Jul 1919.

an official position dare tell the truth" about the shabby treatment the American Army had accorded colored soldiers.[5]

While most of colored Washington was smarting with indignation over the seeming white conspiracy of silence about their war service, a group of colored parents launched a prolonged fight with the school board over its refusal to dismiss Assistant Superintendent Roscoe Conkling Bruce. The Parents' League, representing perhaps six or seven hundred colored parents, accused Bruce of favoritism in making teaching appointments and, worse, lack of vigilance in what came to be known as the "Moens affair." Armed with a recommendation from the Dutch embassy, which the president of the school board had forwarded without comment, Bruce had given a Dutch anthropologist by the name of Moens permission to photograph some of the city's colored school children for purposes of comparative anthropological data. Moens, so the stories ran, had then taken advantage of innocent children and indulged in indecent behavior with one of the colored teachers. White members of the school board and Mrs. Coralie Cook, a Negro member, upheld Bruce and inclined to regard the tales about Moens as gross, if unwitting, exaggerations or lies. But Negro women picketed the Franklin School week after week, whenever the school board met at its offices there. Only a small minority of the Negro community took stock in the lurid rumors about the Moens' affair or shared the view of the Parents' League that here was fresh evidence of white indifference to Negroes' good name, but lily whites insisted that the agitation proved all Negroes emotionally unstable and lacking in judgment.[6]

Still more important in increasing racial tensions in the first half of 1919 was the outbreak of a crime wave more serious than any since the 1850's and the Civil War. White newspaper

[5] *Crisis*, XVII, 111-12, XVIII, 9-11, 63-67; *Bee*, 14 Dec 1918, 15 Feb 1919.

[6] *Bee*, 29 Mar, 12, 26 Apr, 28 Jun 1919; *Star*, 10 Jun 1919, 1 Jan 1920.

accounts of street robberies and attacks upon women generally conveyed the impression that Negroes alone were responsible. At one point the *Post* accused the Negro press of "a plot" to stir up race hatred. By July a series of sex crimes, most of them, later evidence established, committed by a single colored man, had whipped the city into a fury of alarm and rage. While a Negro bishop assured whites that colored people would join in the manhunt, the *Bee*, aware that the temper of white Washington might lead to punishment of innocent colored people, insisted that the criminals were not local men and that an all-Negro precinct in the undermanned police department would be useful in bringing the assaults to an end. At the same time the local NAACP warned the city's white dailies that further "inflammatory headlines and sensational news articles" would encourage race riots. Hundreds of servicemen stationed in and about Washington roamed the streets during those hot July evenings and added to the pervasive sense of restlessness. In a situation already explosive their presence served as a fuse requiring only a minor episode to trigger violence. Military police had been withdrawn from Washington in June.

The "Red Scare," moreover, which was sweeping the entire country, had already assumed huge proportions in the capital. In June a bomb set in the house of the new attorney general convinced conservative citizens that "bolsheviks" were about to destroy the entire fabric of American society. "It is unsafe," announced the *Star*, "to wait for specific proof of individual criminality. It is dangerous to delay until jury-proof cases can be found." Although no one came out flatly with the accusation that colored Washington was one of the "red centers" in the United States, anxieties lest radicalism eat its way into Washington's working classes, at the bottom of which stood the city's black masses, undoubtedly increased racial animosities.[7]

[7] *Bee*, 16 Feb, 12 Jul 1919; *Crisis*, XVIII, 242. From mid-April to the end of July practically every issue of the *Star*, and, all during July, the

The first overt acts of race warfare occurred on a Saturday night, July 19th: "Men in Uniform Attack Negroes" announced the Sunday papers. "As a climax to the assaults on white women . . . a band of more than a hundred soldiers, sailors and marines last night invaded southwest and beat several colored persons before they were finally dispersed by a provost guard, a detachment of marines and reserves from three police stations." Worse followed. On Monday morning the Washington *Post*, after describing Sunday's fighting, carried an alarming article under a huge headline, *Scores are Injured in More Race Riots*:

"It was learned that the mobilization of every available service man stationed in or near Washington or on leave here has been ordered for tomorrow evening near the Knights of Columbus hut, on Pennsylvania Aveune between Seventh and Eighth streets.

"The hour of assembly is 9 o'clock and the purpose is a 'clean-up' that will cause the events of the last two evenings to pale into insignificance.

"Whether official cognizance of this assemblage and its intent will bring about its forestalling cannot be told."

If, as Commissioner Brownlow wrote later, "these white ex-service men were frauds, paid to provoke the trouble they began," and if the Washington *Post* deliberately fanned the fires, the wicked and malicious scheme succeeded. "That night, the race riot swept over Washington. If it had not been for the good work of police and soldiers who kept the large mobs from contact, the city would have been a shambles. During the week the race riots in Chicago and Knoxville followed and the month of July ended with a feeling of apprehension and disturbance."

In Washington colored people, convinced that the time for meekness had passed, fought back. Guns brought from Baltimore and distributed at 7th and T Streets provided weapons

---

Post, carried stories on Negro crime; equally frequent items on the bolshevik threat began in February 1919.

for men trained to their use by war service. Colored men then and later believed that it was the killing of whites by Negroes that brought the riot to an end within five days. Reinforcement of the police by some four hundred cavalrymen from Fort Myer and four hundred marines from Quantico unquestionably helped. But the restoration of outward order at the end of the week did not cool Negroes' anger, for, although every eyewitness of the opening fights testified that white men had been the aggressors, only eight or nine of the hundred-odd persons arrested were whites, and of those only one was convicted for carrying a concealed weapon. Soothing words in the white press to the effect that the "colored residents of Washington are law-abiding people, good citizens and dependable in all crises" came too late to allay bitterness.

Commissioner Brownlow felt sure that the riot had been a put-up job skillfully arranged by two or three outwardly respectable, unscrupulous men, who were determined to make trouble for the police and force him and Major Pullman to resign. The 1918 increases in tax assessments and Brownlow's refusal to exempt from the law persons who had long considered themselves entitled to special privileges had won the commissioner enemies, among them individuals not above employing any weapon, including a race riot, to undermine his authority and thus escape prosecution under the Mann Act. The inflammatory article of July 21st with its allusion to "official cognizance" of an "assemblage" that no one had heard of until the paper announced it lent some plausibility to the conspiracy theory. The *Survey* tentatively attributed the trouble to anti-prohibition forces which "welcomed and to some extent, planned a 'crime wave' in the nation's capital to illustrate the appalling consequences of the bone-dryness since July first."[8]

[8] *Post*, 21-23 Jul 1919; Brownlow, *Passion for Anonymity*, p. 84; Comrs Rpt, 1920, I, 223; Rayford W. Logan to the author, 9 Mar 1960; *Star*, 20-25, 27 Jul 1919; *Bee*, 26 Jul 1919; Edgar M. Gray, *The Washington Riot, Its Cause and Effect*, (mcf pamphlet, Arthur A. Schomburg

Colored leaders displayed extraordinary restraint. A week after the first night's outbreak Judge Terrell and Dr. Emmett J. Scott, former special assistant to the Secretary of War, issued a statement to Negro newspapers in the rest of the country pointing out that, whereas white servicemen were to blame for the Washington riots and Negro retaliation was natural, the most important fact was that "white and colored citizens freely counseling together in the interest of law and order" had successfully reestablished peace and that henceforward all efforts must be directed at preserving the "gains of mutual war-time sacrifices." James Weldon Johnson, the NAACP investigator sent down from New York, shared Brownlow's private opinion that the Washington *Post* had had a large part in fomenting the violence. His report in the *Crisis* contained humorous touches: the city editor of the *Post*, assuming that Johnson had come to tell Washington Negroes "to be good," had welcomed him cordially but had then suffered near-panic upon discovering that the NAACP might ask the Attorney General to bring action against Washington's white newspapers, the *Post* above all, for inciting to riot. Johnson averred that Negro courage had saved the day in Washington. By fighting "in defense of their lives and homes" instead of running, they had prevented Washington's being "another and worse East St. Louis." Indeed, he concluded, bad as things had been, white shame over the shocking events in Washington and Chicago "mark a turning point in the psychology of the whole nation regarding the Negro problem."

That note of encouragement, if overly optimistic in the long run, appeared justified in the months immediately following. Washington's white press, perhaps frightened by the consequences of its earlier propaganda, ceased to harp on Negro criminality. In December at a meeting called to raise money for

---

Negro Collection, New York Public Library); "The Darkest Cloud," *Survey*, XLII, 675.

a war memorial to colored heroes, white response was heartening. Secretary of War Newton D. Baker and Secretary of the Navy Josephus Daniels both spoke, and "the tabernacle quaked from the acclamation of approval" when Judge Stafford challenged the crowd: "Cite me a case of a Negro traitor"; "show me a Negro anarchist"; "let me see a Negro bolshevist"; "the only red rag the Negro ever carried was when his shirt was stained crimson by the sacrificial blood he gave for America."

The single most penetrating analysis of the Negro problem in Washington and in Chicago came from the pen of George E. Haynes, director of Negro Economics in the United States Department of Labor. His article entitled "Race Riots in Relation to Democracy" recognized the role of sensational journalism in contributing to racial hostility but pointed to three other, equally significant factors. First was the lack of mutual understanding that resulted from the loss of contact between the races: "The lack of contact has increased with the years. Older residents of Washington and Chicago tell you of the growing racial antagonism with the growth of separation. Only a few weeks before the riots in both cities, some leading people of Washington were discussing the fact that in former years the white and colored representatives of various philanthropic and community agencies were accustomed to meet more frequently than now for the exchange of views and plans on matters of community interest. The holding of such meetings has grown more difficult and less frequent." Second was the new Negro militance. Years of seeing the unequal enforcement of law had led the colored man to believe "his safety demands that he protect himself and his home," a conviction strengthened by a new conception of liberty which accompanied the higher standard of living that war had brought to thousands of colored families. Although well-to-do, well-dressed Negroes had been a familiar sight in Washington for forty years past, other observers than Haynes remarked upon white irritation at Negroes' improved economic status: "Everywhere one can hear expressions of disgust at the expensive clothes of successful Negroes, their owning automobiles, etc." The third factor was the realization by both white and colored Americans that the United States as a great world power was now "face to face with the problem of dealing with the darker peoples of Asia, Africa, Central and South America." Those peoples would judge the United States by the treatment white Americans accorded darker-skinned citizens within its borders. That an Abyssinian mission had been in the national capital during the riots was an uncomfortable reminder that race relations here had a wider bearing than a purely domestic local question.[9]

While much of the colored community benefitted from better paid jobs during and immediately after the war, school teachers and government clerks, who composed the backbone of the middle class, had suffered, like their white counterparts, from the pinch of rising living costs and minor or no salary increases. And even at the peak of employment the number of appointments to professional or clerical posts in Washington fell far short of the number of Negro candidates qualified either by graduation from the Miner Normal School or by civil service ratings. Assistant Superintendent Bruce, while fighting to get better salaries for colored teachers, implied in 1919 that those willing to leave Washington now had larger opportunities than formerly because of the prosperity the war had brought to Negroes in other cities. The opening of a colored Industrial Savings Bank on U Street and a new well-built, well-furnished Negro hotel indicated that, in spite of inflation, Negro business enterprises here also had enjoyed some success, and the wider support of charitable projects suggested that many Negro families had more financial leeway than ever before. But the

[9] *Star*, 27 Jul, 16 Dec 1919; *Crisis*, XVIII, 241-43; *Bee*, 2 Aug 1919; "The Darkest Cloud," and George E. Haynes, "Race Riots in Relation to Democracy," *Survey*, XLII, 675-76, 697-99.

NAACP and the *Bee* repeatedly reminded colored people that racial solidarity was essential to a continuing advance.[10]

In the autumn of 1919, while colored Washingtonians strove to believe they had gained more than they lost by the race riots, white business leaders betrayed brief uneasiness lest the outburst seriously injure the city's good name. On top of the accusations of wartime profiteering, a reputation for uncontrolled racial violence and for being a hotbed of Negro radicalism could do Washington infinite harm. But a large part of Washington soon ceased to think about the local riots at all. Senate ratification or rejection of the Versailles treaty, plans, quickly quashed, for a District policemen's union affiliated with the American Federation of Labor, wage strikes that threatened Washington's white building trades, and the intensifying conflict throughout the United States between capital and industrial labor preempted local attention. Although, like Americans everywhere, people here were frightened by the bogey of red infiltration into the ranks of organized labor, in a predominantly white-collar city fear of a red-infected local black proletariat had relatively little to feed upon.

In early October 1919 a National Industrial Conference, with Secretary of the Interior Franklin K. Lane in the chair and the level-headed Secretary of Labor William B. Wilson acting as special adviser, met in the Pan-American Union building to discuss workingmen's rights to collective bargaining and to find a formula for settling a nation-wide steel strike, by then at the stage of open warfare in the Midwest. Washingtonians, conservatives and liberals alike, awaited the outcome with interest but with considerable detachment. The A.F.ofL. repudiation of any connection with reds failed to win support for labor's cause; when Samuel Gompers walked out of the conference, workingmen silently acknowledged defeat. Neither

[10] Comrs Rpts, 1919, IV, 238, 1920, IV, 323-39; *Star*, 19 Mar 1920; *Crisis*, XIII, 168, 174-76, 280, XIV, 89, XVII, 116, XVIII, 154; *Bee*, 29 Mar, 26 Apr 1919.

the local business community nor federal officials linked Washington's race riots to labor radicalism. Although nine men had lost their lives in the street fights and more than thirty men later died from injuries, Congress saw no cause to investigate. Thus reassured, white Washingtonians determined to Americanize the foreign-born in their midst but banished from memory the uncomfortable events of July: they represented no more than an unfortunate episode best forgotten as quickly as possible.

Yet the wish to forget the unpleasantnesses of "the intense, restless, disturbed year," as a Board of Trade committee described 1919, had long-lasting consequences; it reinforced white prejudices, deepened the obliviousness of much of white Washington to the needs of a bi-racial city, and for nearly two decades defeated the attempts of an enlightened minority to seek closer cooperation with Negro citizens. The unyielding attitude of influential white people was an important factor in crippling endeavors to revive a vigorous community spirit. Just as country-wide reaction against the Red Scare in 1920 heightened Americans' longing for "normalcy," so Washingtonians' desire to return to a less troubled past undermined their will to examine its weaknesses and build better for the future.[11]

[11] *Rpt B/Tr*, 1919, p. 128; *Star*, 28 Nov 1918, 29 Jul, 29 Sep 1919, 1, 3 Jan 1920; Brownlow, *Passion for Anonymity*, pp. 84-89; Robert K. Murray, *Red Scare, A Study in National Hysteria, 1919-1920*, pp. 148-256; Gray, *The Washington Riot* (Schomburg Collection). Further evidence of local whites' unconcern about race relations derives from interviews with people living here in 1919 and from the disappearance of newspaper items about local Negro radicalism and all Negro ideas.

CHAPTER XIV

BUSINESS INTERESTS AND NATIONAL CITY PLANNING, 1920-1929

IF, as Senator Blair prophesied in the 1890's, long-enforced political irresponsibility bred in Washingtonians apathy about governing themselves, their indifference never extended to the outcome of a national election, for that was likely to affect every taxpayer, every wage-earner, and, by enlarging or shrinking the clover fields, every social butterfly in the District of Columbia. In 1920, irrespective of their convictions about the League of Nations and other national issues, adults in Washington first and foremost wanted an end of turmoil. With the collapse of the Red Scare in midsummer, that desire appeared to be more attainable than it had earlier. Wages in the building trades were still at wartime levels—as, unhappily, was the meagre pay-scale of permanent civil service employees—and, despite reductions in the federal payroll after the dismissal of some 16,000 temporary war-workers, business had not yet suffered. Still apprehensiveness endured.

The District commissioners managed to carry out essential services for a city approximately 25 percent more populous than the Washington of three years before and indeed effected several innovations. While Commissioner Gardiner practically withdrew from participation, Commissioner Brownlow and General Kutz, again made engineer commissioner in 1919, acted *ex officio* as a Public Utilities Commission and, after prolonged negotiations with corporation officers and lawyers and a fight in the courts, succeeded in establishing an acceptable cost basis for each utility company and then fixed rates. A more extraordinary feat—the two men drafted and won acceptance for a zoning ordinance. Thanks to frequent consultations with white citizens' and Negro civic associations while the maps were under preparation, the zoning ordinance satisfied everyone, even real estate firms from whom fierce opposition had initially seemed inescapable. Furthermore, although congressional hearings held in December 1919 limited the federal share of District appropriations to 40 percent instead of the theoretical former 50 percent, the new fiscal act provided for a sliding tax rate that permitted the commissioners later to lower the then rate of \$1.95 on every \$100 of assessed valuation.[1]

A controversy unhappily arose in the spring of 1920 over the refusal of the Board of Education to reappoint the well-meaning but ineffectual superintendent of schools and over the retention of Assistant Superintendent Roscoe Conkling Bruce in the face of demands from the Negro Parents' League for his ouster. The school fight involved the question of who was to succeed Gwynne Gardiner as District commissioner after his resignation at the end of 1919. In May the Senate refused to confirm President Wilson's nominee, Dr. John Van Schaick, a former president of the Monday Evening Club, suspect for its "radicalism," and president of the school board at the time of the Moens affair. Whatever the Senate's reasons in this case, Republican rejection of all President Wilson's nominees for all offices left the Board of Commissioners minus one man. A more serious loss befell in September: Louis Brownlow resigned to become city manager of Petersburg, Virginia, a city of 30,000, where he would receive double the \$5,000 salary allowed the administrative head of a city of 437,000 and the capital of the nation. One of his last acts as commissioner was to appoint an interracial committee of eminent citizens to explore

[1] Comrs Rpts, 1919, p. 5, 1920, I, 5-7, 11, 29, 226, 1921, p. 48; *Star*, Summaries, 1920, 1921; Brownlow, *Passion for Anonymity*, pp. 90-99; *Rec*, 66C, 2S, pp. 1444-54; *Rpts B/Tr*, 1920, pp. 73-74, 113-15, 183-86, 1921, p. 21; H Dis Comee, 66C, 2S, Hrgs, "Fiscal Relations between the U.S. and D.C.," pp. 3, 117-18, 134-51, 247-73; Paul H. Douglas, *Real Wages in the United States*, p. 376; Schmeckebier, *District of Columbia*, pp. 52-58.

ways of improving communication between white and colored Washington; the committee fell to pieces after his departure.

Since the Senate was not in session that autumn, two interim appointees, Miss Mabel Boardman and J. Thilman Hendrick, accepted office as commissioners. Miss Boardman, a rather overpowering-looking woman whose high pompadour added to her Victorian mien, in 1920 was best known as the chief organizer of the Women's Volunteer Services of the American Red Cross; Hendrick was a stockbroker scarcely known at all outside the city's financial circles. Under the two inexperienced new officials a stalemate obtained in District affairs. Meanwhile, in a bedroom at the White House an ailing President—how ill scarcely a dozen people knew—awaited with dreadful anxiety the decision of November 4th. "A feverish uncertainty, a reluctant looking for a something that every man and woman hoped might never come, has been the condition attendant upon the passing days of the year," wrote a Board of Trade official. "We are looking forward to the happy time, when, under new and settled conditions, the business and pleasures of our people, their thoughts, hopes and aspirations may once more be along normal lines; and unrest and I.W.W.-ism may become unknown in the universal endeavor to upbuild our industries and manhood, and curtail our all too large national debt."[2]

The election of Warren Gamaliel Harding snapped much of the tension in the capital. If knowledgeable Republicans had secret misgivings, no one voiced the opinion Mrs. Longworth later expressed: "Harding was not a bad man. He was just a slob." As the winter wore on, all classes of society, white and colored, appeared to relax visibly and, with the approach of the inauguration, an air of almost forgotten festivity settled over

[2] *Star*, frequent entries Feb-Jun 1920; *Bee*, 17 Jan, 13, 20 Mar 1920; S Dis Comee, 66C, 2S, Hrgs, "The Nomination of Dr. John Van Schaick, Jr., to be a Comr of the D of C," pp. 5-9, 56-59, 80, and *passim*; Comrs Rpt, 1920, p. 5; *Rpt B/Tr*, pp. 54, 131.

the city. It was dampened but not extinguished by an "economy howl in Congress," which persuaded the President-elect and the inaugural committee to cancel plans for an elaborate parade and an inaugural ball. The business slump and the consequent drop in employment that had struck most of the country had not yet affected the capital; gratitude for that reprieve—escape, the unwary called it—heightened Washington's enjoyment of the golden sunlight flooding the city on March 4, 1921.

Shock at sight of the wasted figure of Wilson seated beside the well-fed, handsome Harding when the presidential limousine rolled down Pennsylvania Avenue silenced the on-lookers momentarily, but pity and regret yielded quickly to interest in what lay ahead. The new President's inaugural address contained nothing startling unless it were his statement that "the Negroes of America . . . have earned the full measure of citizenship bestowed; that their sacrifice in blood on the battlefields of the Republic have entitled them to all freedom and opportunity, all sympathy and aid that the American spirit of fairness and justice demands." Negroes were elated; lily-whites were not disturbed. That night, while colored society celebrated at a large reception and a dance at "Convention Hall," two other non-official balls took place, one a benefit for the Child Welfare Society sponsored by the wife of newly deposed Vice President Thomas Marshall, the other a private dance given for some six hundred GOP merrymakers by "Ned" McLean, chairman of the inaugural committee. If on that occasion Mrs. McLean wore the famous Hope diamond, its reputed evil powers may have seemed to the superstitious to account for the ills that two years later overwhelmed several of her guests. Mrs. Harding herself, an arch believer in the clairvoyants she consulted periodically, apparently had no forebodings.

Springtime in Washington, along whose tree-lined streets in 1921 people still walked for pleasure, exercised peculiar charms that year. For the first time the war receded into the distant past. The very sight of the open gates of the White House grounds inviting the world to walk and drive in and out lightened the atmosphere; on Easter Monday children and Easter eggs again dotted the lawns. "Balloon men," wrote a senator's wife, "with their rainbow-colored balls floating lightly above them in great clusters, and vendors of flowers stand on every corner; the Japanese cherry blossoms, a mass of fragrant blooms, border the basin and speedway above the Potomac River; the starry dogwood scatters its petals in Rock Creek Park; and wisteria, drooping and feathery, hangs over doorways and porches, and clouds the rotunda at Arlington." Newly appointed federal officials took up their duties with leisurely zest, while with still greater enthusiasm wives new to Washington society set about mastering the mysteries of etiquette in the capital.

Nor did the pervasive gaiety entirely vanish when the countrywide business depression reached Washington in the early summer. "National Music Week" in June brought together on the Ellipse an assembly of school children such as the city had not seen since the homecoming welcome for the Army of the Potomac in May 1865. The chorus of more than 50,000 children's voices carrying the strains of the *Star-Spangled Banner* from the elm-bordered rim of the Ellipse to the flag-draped grandstand near the Monument moved everyone, from the dignitaries surrounding President and Mrs. Harding to the humblest parent on the outskirts of the audience. Week after week the baseball diamonds and tennis courts on the Ellipse and the Monument grounds and the nine-hole golf course in East Potomac Park were filled with light-hearted, light-skinned players; the dark-skinned, by order of the North Carolina-born commissioner of public grounds, were allowed to play only on Tuesday afternoons and were never permitted to use the equally popular bathing beach at the Tidal Basin. But few people, white or colored, were ready to plunge into the arduous task of remaking the city's social order. Official Washington, in delighted dedication to normalcy, embarked that autumn upon a whirl of parties abnormal even by standards of the Roosevelt and Taft eras. In fact in the upper echelons a pleasurable acceptance of things as they were survived the shock of the Teapot Dome scandals, President Harding's death in 1923, and every succeeding slight disruption before the autumn of 1929.[3]

The business slump, it is true, in mid-1921 halted building, brought unemployment, and, coupled with unexpectedly severe cuts in District appropriations recommended by the newly established federal Bureau of the Budget, caused anxiety to Harding's appointees to the District Board of Commissioners, but the depression ran a relatively short course. By the early autumn of 1922 a revival was in full swing, marked, as usual in Washington, by an expansion of private building—apartment houses, luxury hotels, office buildings, a high-shouldered auditorium in Foggy Bottom intended to attract the convention trade, and private houses built wholesale by contractors who bought entire blocks of lots and sprinkled them thick with undistinguished but salable dwellings. In 1925 alone, investment in building reached the unheard-of total of nearly $63,000,000. Two sides of Lafayette Square changed character completely. On Jackson Place the philanthropist Robert S. Brookings put up an office building to provide revenue for a recently founded center for economic research. Nearby on the site of the old W. W. Corcoran mansion rose the new headquarters of the United States Chamber of Commerce, constructed, the Board of Trade noted approvingly, under "the

[3] *Bee*, 5, 12 Mar 1921; Sullivan, *Our Times*, VI; Longworth, *Crowded Hours*, pp. 322-25; *Star*, 6, 9, 28 Mar, 4 Jun, 20 Nov 1921; Frances Parkinson Keyes, *Letters from a Senator's Wife*, pp. 191-259; Comrs Rpt, 1921, pp. 19-21; Washington *Tribune*, 16 Jul 1921.

American plan . . . on the basis of the open shop."[4] Next door the red-brick houses Richardson had built for Henry Adams and John Hay gave way to the stone Hay-Adams Hotel towering above Latrobe's "Church of the Presidents" across the way.

The Board of Trade took credit for much of this burgeoning growth. While the mounting demand for office space was probably due chiefly to Secretary of Commerce Herbert Hoover's far-ranging programs, which encouraged national trade associations to set up headquarters in the capital, Board of Trade advertisements of Washington's special advantages for investment offered counter-attractions to the New York stock market. A convention bureau reaped a first disconcerting harvest in the summer of 1925 when 25,000 hooded white-robed Ku Klux Klansmen gathered in Washington and staged a showy parade and a ceremony on the Monument grounds. A more satisfactory advertisement of the city was a pageant held in the spring of 1927 when the Japanese cherry trees around the Tidal Basin were in full bloom; the success of that first Cherry Blossom festival made it an annual event thereafter. Slum clearance and District representation in Congress dropped out of sight as younger and less civic-minded men replaced the older generation of board directors, but the organization's secretary proudly pointed "to the rapidly growing friendliness on the part of Congress toward the District of Columbia, especially when its needs are presented to them by representatives from the Board of Trade."

Indeed congressional hostility to the city largely evaporated after House and Senate fixed the federal contribution to annual District expenses at a flat $9,000,000. After that scheme went into effect in 1925, District taxes alone met over 70 percent

[4] Comrs Rpts, 1922, 47-48, 1925, p. 55; *Star*, 15 Aug 1925, 31 Dec 1927; 42 *Stat.* 1488; *Rpt B/Tr*, 1928, p. 64. Board of Trade reports, 1922-1929, deal exhaustively with the questions under discussion in this and the next three paragraphs and are therefore not cited in detail.

of the budget, but meanwhile a new ruling vested in the commissioners the authority to set the tax rate and thus to raise additional revenue by increasing the rate if they judged acute municipal needs warranted it. With the bonded indebtedness of 1878 paid off in 1921, with private property values rising, and with consumer purchasing power improved by a new federal pay scale that increased civil service salaries about 10 percent in the upper brackets and as much as 50 percent in lower, District finances were less crippled than taxpayers had expected. Loss of income from liquor licenses and the mounting cost of trying to stop bootlegging were annoyances, but the major difficulty was still the old one of persuading Congress to let the District government spend the city's taxes on the projects important to the community, albeit of no interest to congressional constituents.

Still, during the seven fat years of the 1920's, appropriations were big enough to enable successive engineer commissioners to reduce the backlog of badly needed public works that had accumulated during and after the war. As seen from the District Building everything ran smoothly. The Board of Trade expressed its wishes, Congress authorized larger expenditures of local taxpayers' money, and the commissioners acted. They increased the police force, in 1925 started a five-year school building program, enlarged the water supply by completing the Dalecarlia reservoir and a second conduit, gradually extended the sewage system not only into rapidly building-up sections of the city but also, by using money paid in by the Washington Suburban Sanitary Commission, into suburban Maryland. One commissioner, when asked thirty years later to name the District's chief problems during this era, replied: "There were no problems. Everyone was perfectly gentlemanly."[5]

Gentlemanly behavior, however, failed to dissipate traffic

[5] Comrs Rpts, 1924, pp. 26, 57-59, 1925, pp. 1-2, 61, 1926, pp. 20, 60, 1928, p. 28, 1929, p. 52; interview, Proctor L. Dougherty.

congestion. In 1921 and 1922 many people still walked to and from work, but, as population spread farther and farther, more people drove or rode. Gas fumes and the menace to life and limb from the rush of moving vehicles took most of the pleasure out of walking. In spite of a new regulation requiring applicants for driving permits to pass an examination, the installation of additional traffic lights, and somewhat stricter enforcement of the 22-miles-an-hour speed limit, "vehicular casualties" mounted. The nearly 9,400 accidents of 1925, to be sure, fell to 4,138 in 1928, but in the interval motor vehicle registrations rose and by 1930 topped 173,600, not counting commuters' or tourists' cars. Drivers unable to find legitimate parking spaces in the heart of the city left their cars all day on the Ellipse below the White House, on the Mall about the tempos, or in a fenced-off area of Potomac Park. "The entire Mall," protested the Fine Arts Commission, "has become an open-air garage; in the Department of Agriculture grounds automobiles are parked on the grass." The competing trolley and bus lines afforded inadequate service. In 1929, only 34.3 percent of the people who rode to work in downtown Washington used public conveyances; in Kansas City and Milwaukee, cities with the next smallest number, the figures stood at 45.5 and 50.3 percent, respectively. What the Board of Trade called the "best municipal government" in the United States was unable to provide an answer.[6]

Traffic itself was instrumental in persuading Congress to modify its postwar determination to reduce the national debt before investing money in expensive public works in the capital. While some citizens fumed about postponement of land purchases necessary to carry on the Park Commission's plan,

[6] Comrs Rpts, 1921, I, pp. 26-27, 212, 1925, pp. 28-30, 1928, pp. 7, 12, 31, 1931, p. 9; M. O. Eldridge, "Making the National Capital Safe for Motorists and Pedestrians," *American City Magazine*, XXXIII, 129-32; *Rpt Fine Arts Comm*, 1929, p. 31; *Civic Comment*, No. 15, 1 Sep 1927; Roderick McKenzie, *The Metropolitan Community*, p. 282; S Dis Comee, 66C, 3S, to 71C, 2S, "Hearings on Merger of Street Railways in the District of Columbia," (bound volume in S Dis Comee Room, S Office Bldg.).

members of the Fine Arts Commission announced in 1921 that they were not "concerned with the rate of progress; they are vitally concerned that the progress shall be always toward the goal set in 1792 and again in 1901." But they, too, recognized the dangers of delay. "All sorts of suggestions are being made for improvements and changes. Many of these new projects are based on the desire of individuals to exploit themselves. Others are due to ignorance of the existing plan and the progress of work being done in accordance with it." Three years after the Armistice the commission was first and foremost eager to see the execution of the plans for the long-talked-of bridge across the Potomac beyond the still unfinished Lincoln Memorial. "The Highway Bridge connects Potomac Park with a little race track, with marshes lately used as the city dump, and with Agriculture Department barns, so designed and constructed as to thrust their ugliness upon one's attention with all the insistence of a spoiled child at table. Through this variegated area a narrow, tortuous, dangerous road winds its uncertain way to Arlington National Cemetery. The bodies of the Nation's dead take this path to their last resting place." A traffic jam on Armistice Day in 1921 sharpened that picture.

Government officials had planned a solemn ceremony to mark the interment of the Unknown Soldier in Arlington Cemetery. From the Capitol, where the flag-draped casket lay in the Rotunda, a formal procession was to accompany the symbol of all American heroes to the great mausoleum across the Potomac. But at the approach to the river a traffic tie-up occurred, immobilizing for two hours and more the cars carrying important guests, among them foreign statesmen gathered in Washington for the opening of the Naval Disarmament Conference. A number of dignitaries did not reach the cemetery at all. Late that afternoon the Fine Arts Commission met to recommend immediate enactment of the legislation necessary to start work on the new bridge.

The formal dedication of the Lincoln Memorial on Decoration Day in 1922 intensified public interest. Where gulls had once swept over the marshy land bordering the Tidal Basin and the river front, the nation's personages now assembled before a marble temple from which the figure or statue of the Great Emancipator looked out over a pool reflecting the shaft of the Washington Monument. Impressive as was the setting, everyone present could see how much it would gain from bridging the Potomac at that point and landscaping the shore line. Congress voted a preliminary appropriation a fortnight later. As the bridge was an integral part of the Park Commission plan for the river end of the Mall, Washingtonians committed to the "city beautiful" ideal drew a deep breath when Congress accepted the designs submitted in 1924: a stone bridge of simple flowing lines placed slightly below the Lincoln Memorial, above it a water-gate for boats and a plaza with parkways radiating from it, and on the far shore a second bridge over the Virginia channel and the intervening Columbia island to an imposing entrance into the cemetery.[7]

Yet a magnificent approach from the Virginia side of the Potomac was not enough to make the capital a place of sheer beauty. Successful application of Washington's new zoning ordinance notwithstanding, private enterprisers were gobbling up land needed for parks and erecting buildings that threatened permanently to scar the looks of the city. As a first move to check architectural aberrations, in 1923 an advisory council of the American Institute of Architects collaborated with a Board of Trade committee and District officials to revise the District building code. Then, at the request of the commissioners, the council offered suggestions on design free of charge to appli-

[7] *Rpts Fine Arts Comm*, 1921, pp. 21-22, 37, 1925, pp. 45, 59; *Forty Years of Achievement Commemorating the 40th Anniversary of the Establishment of the National Commission of Fine Arts, 1910-1950*, p. 25 (hereafter cited as Fine Arts Comm, *Forty Years*); *Star*, 13 Nov 1921; Charles Moore, "The Transformation of Washington," *National Geographic*, XLIII, 583-666; S Doc 95, 68C, 1S, Ser 8240; *Rpt B/Tr*, 1923, p. 109.

cants for building permits. A few months later, from the recently formed Washington Committee of One Hundred on the Federal City came a revolutionary proposal: the creation of a board of trained architects empowered to regulate all private buildings in the District. Few members of Congress at that time would have dared suggest so "socialistic" a scheme, and in fact it was never adopted except for buildings adjacent to public edifices; but the committee, one of fifty organized in various parts of the country by the American Civic Association to promote the artistic and orderly development of the national capital, contained people eminent in public life. Weight attached to the recommendations of a body that included Secretary of State Charles Evans Hughes, Secretary of Commerce Herbert Hoover, William H. Holmes, director of the Smithsonian National Gallery of Art, several of the best-known artists and architects in Washington, District officials, and a score of well-to-do businessmen.

The preliminary report of the Washington committee pointed out that the Park Commission of 1901 had not provided for city planning as the term had since come to be understood. Urban planning in the 1920's must take transportation, recreation facilities, and over-all land use into consideration. In hammering away at the urgency of extending the District park system before construction companies obliterated the natural beauty of areas like Klingle Valley and sewage polluted every stream, the committee made itself heard. Six months after its preliminary report appeared, Congress established the National Capital Park Commission vested with authority to acquire land for parks, parkways, and playgrounds in the District of Columbia and in nearby Maryland and Virginia, subject only to the approval of the Fine Arts Commission on the sites selected. Half the purchase price was to come from the federal government, the other half from local taxpayers.

Here was progress, or so it seemed. Unhappily, authority to

buy did not provide cold cash. Because Congress voted less than a third of the expected appropriations, the new commission was all but helpless. Enlightened private citizens did what they could. One group bought land to hold until the Park Commission had money available; Charles Glover and Mrs. Anne Archbold gave outright a stretch of woodland along Foundry Run above Georgetown. But individual efforts could go only so far. Indignation stirred in the American Civic Association, already distressed at the ravages the steam shovel and the ax had wrought during the preceding five years. The District highway department had cut shade trees right and left in the process of widening downtown streets and building arterial thoroughfares. By 1925 devastation threatened every section of the District of Columbia.[8]

"Only a remnant of the Klingle stream was left," the *American Civic Annual* reported, "and the parkway connection [was] absolutely blocked by cutting, grading and building. The beautiful Broad Branch and Piney Branch valleys are now but pitiful stubs adjoining Rock Creek Park. Their waters are confined to underground sewers. Their wooded banks are laid desolate. Rectangular house lots take the place of shady slopes. Rows of shoddy, uninteresting houses perch precariously on the deep fills of yellow clay which flank the axial boulevard of 16th street. The stately Tiger Bridge, erected at great cost to span the stream, is now nothing but a street extension over a dry culvert. These tragedies . . . cannot be remedied. Nor can much be done about the acres of land which, since the war, have been plastered over with the wrong kind of houses set in the wrong kind of lots, served by the wrong kind of streets."[9]

[8] *Preliminary Report by the Washington Committee of One Hundred on the Federal City to the American Civic Association*, 3 Jan 1924, *passim*, especially pp. 2-5, 11-14, 27, 35-36; 43 *Stat.* 463; *Rpt B/Tr*, 1924, pp. 68-69; *Civic Comment*, 8 Jun 1924, p. 8; Comrs Rpts, 1924, p. 47, 1925, p. 52; *Herald*, 10 Apr 24; *Star*, 18 Mar 1926.

[9] Harlean James, ed., "The Federal City Committees of the American Civic Association," *American Civic Annual*, 1929, I, 66-68.

The one body with sufficient influence throughout the country to bring order out of laissez-faire anarchy appeared to be the American Civic Association. Founded in the heyday of the muckrakers, the association had set out to awaken a sense of public duty in citizens whose wealth, social standing, and artistic perceptions qualified them as leaders in their own communities, men and women willing to share in wresting control of municipal affairs from unscrupulous and ignorant political bosses and then ready to introduce efficient city government and a systematic program of civic improvements. Chicago had been one of the first places to feel the force of the planning mystique, but neither Chicago, where political reform had met with meagre success, nor any other city had as yet carried out more than a fraction of an over-all plan. Washington seemingly needed little political house-cleaning, but she obviously must have "external aid" if the plan of 1901 were to be expanded to cover the now very much larger city and if a modicum of public control over the use of privately owned land were to safeguard public interests.

The committees on the federal city from the first set their sights on the creation of an official body farsighted and strong enough to develop and carry out "a comprehensive, consistent and coordinated plan for the national Capital and its environs." It was an undertaking that ought to concern all, a Boston landscape architect averred, for if "our Federal City shall become an inspiring example of sustained interest and intelligent action in city planning, the benefits will spread in some measure to every city in the land." As the modest hopes pinned on the National Capital Park Commission proved vain, in the autumn of 1925 Frederic A. Delano, president of the American Civic Association and by then a resident of Washington, arranged a series of conferences between representatives of half a dozen national professional societies and federal and District officials anxious to evolve a planning bill with teeth in it. Forty years later, Washingtonians exposed to frequent pronouncements on the wrong-headedness or provincial backwardness reigning in the District of Columbia would marvel at the fervent interest other Americans displayed in perfecting the capital. In the mid-twenties zeal was both country-wide and, up to a point, effective. It brought into being the National Capital Park and Planning Commission.

The act establishing the new commission authorized the President to appoint for six-year terms four civilians to serve with the federal and District officials of the former commission and greatly enlarged the responsibilities of the new body; not only was the commission to prepare plans for orderly growth in the District but also, in cooperation with Maryland and Virginia authorities, to map out a scheme of harmonious development for Greater Washington that would forestall the pollution of the streams and preserve the region's natural beauties. But the law left the new commission with no more power than its predecessor to ensure acceptance of its recommendations. Its purchasing powers still depended upon uncertain congressional appropriations. State legislatures might or might not collaborate.[10]

Recognition of the regional aspects of planning nevertheless was a long step forward. Maryland set up a Maryland National Capital Planning Commission in 1927, and, although Virginia failed to take effective action, officials of Arlington county were ready to cooperate. In the opinion of Lieutenant Colonel U. S. Grant, III, grandson of President Grant and the federal commission's first secretary, the legal powerlessness of the planners was in fact a minor handicap; inasmuch as the federal executives and members of the Senate and House District committees who were in a position to reject or drastically amend every proposal were either themselves members of the commission or represented thereon, plans adopted in conference usually had an excel-

[10] *Ibid.*, p. 69; Arthur A. Shurtleff, "Guiding the Growth of the City of Washington," *American City Magazine*, XXXIII, 40; 44 *Stat.* 1330.

lent chance of receiving congressional blessing, if not large appropriations. The big stumbling blocks to action were the stipulation that prices paid for land never exceed its assessed valuation by more than 25 percent, the less than $4,000,000 available to the commission in its first four years, and its inability to borrow in order to buy land while it was relatively cheap. In the 1950's thoughtful people would sometimes regret that a Washington Metropolitan Regional Authority had not come into being before the depression of the 1930's cut off funds and chilled public interest in so drastic a political innovation. But in 1926 and 1927 responsible men believed they must first draft a detailed regional plan and only then seek the power to carry it out.[11]

The progress achieved before 1930 was due in considerable degree to Frederic A. Delano. An aristocrat imbued with a strong sense of civic obligation, an admirer of Daniel Burnham, and an active participant in launching the Chicago as well as the New York Regional plans, Delano, though a railroad executive and a financier rather than a landscape architect, had the background, the enthusiasm, and the persuasiveness to make him an invaluable member of the commission; in 1930 he became its chairman. He himself always denied that he contributed anything beyond a ready ear to other men's ideas, but his associates felt the force of his personality, visible in his commanding figure and the character in his strong patrician features. On every job he undertook, and they were many even when he was in his seventies, he gathered about him "top technical talent." His "modus operandi" consisted "of bringing men together—frequently at Cosmos Club luncheons—to pool their talents, even when their views and their interests

[11] Lt. Col. U.S. Grant, III, "Washington Looks Ahead," *American Civic Annual*, I, 69-74, and "Governmental Jurisdictions in the National Capital," *ibid.*, II, 90-91; Charles W. Eliot, II, "Planning Washington and Its Environs," *City Planning*, III, 177-93; *Rpts National Capital Park and Planning Commission*, 1928, p. 28, 1929, p. 29, 1930, p. 45 (hereafter cited as *Rpts NCPPC*).

were in opposition. Antagonisms faded out in his presence and never a tart rejoinder was spoken in his direction." His tact, his personal charm, and his social prestige were as great an asset to the planning cause as the authority represented by Army engineers and the special skills provided by the commission staff.

Still, without the insights and, on some measures, the initiating force of key members of the House and Senate, much of the program would have netted scant attention, and, without the unflagging support of constituents, the congressional majority might well have remained indifferent. In both houses the chairmen of the District committees, the Public Buildings committees, and the subcommittees on District appropriations were strong advocates of improvements for the capital, and a score of other men worked hard to get the necessary appropriations, while Congressmen Louis Cramton of Maryland and R. Walton Moore of Virginia pushed for federal and state legislation helpful to plans for Greater Washington. The Capper-Cramton Act passed in 1930 enabled Maryland to borrow from the federal Treasury for extension of the District park system into Montgomery and Prince George's Counties. When the planning commission presented its first formal "Progress Report" in January 1930, members of Congress, the Secretary of the Treasury, the governors of Maryland and Virginia, the legislature of Virginia, notables from the rest of the country, and Washingtonians nearly filled Constitution Hall. If, as Colonel Grant believed, the approaching bi-centennial of the birth of George Washington stimulated interest in the city whose original layout he had overseen lovingly, probably an even stronger impulse sprang from the growing awareness that sensible solutions to the manifold problems of expanding metropolitan areas must depend upon intelligent advance planning.[12] The capital was a logical place to begin.

[12] "Frederic A. Delano (1863-1953)," Vignette the Thirty-fourth, *Cosmos Club Bulletin*, VII, No. 2, pp. 2-5; Grant, "Washington Looks

Because the Planning Commission had to buy land piecemeal at constantly rising prices, developments dependent upon purchase moved more slowly than the beautifying of property already part of the public domain. While acquisition of the strip of land between Potomac and Rock Creek Parks permitted building and landscaping that parkway, several other major projects made no headway at all. Particularly disappointing to Delano and to humbler citizens in time to come was the gradual abandonment of an early plan for "a system of neighborhood centers," each designed to encompass a twenty-acre site containing a school, a library, a playground, and park facilities. Only three small playgrounds materialized. The parkways skirting both sides of the Potomac as far as Great Falls and the circumferential drive connecting sites of the twenty-four Civil War forts that ringed the District would still be under discussion in the late 1950's. The improvements taking form along the Mall, however, and the $50,000,000 federal building operations launched in 1926 lessened impatience at the relative slowness of park development.

The magnitude of the building program might well have proved self-defeating; scores of departmental executives, members of Congress, the Planning and the Fine Arts Commissions, and a host of architects, private citizens, and real estate firms had an immediate interest in it. It was able to move forward with astonishingly few hitches by reason of the federal Public Buildings Commission, which Congress had created in 1916 but which had had no opportunity to function during and after the war. The composition of the commission went far toward ensuring cooperation between the legislative and executive branches of the government; the minority as well as the majority

---

Ahead," *American Civic Annual*, I, 74, and Frederic A. Delano, "Progress Report," *ibid.*, II, 83; *Star*, 31 Dec 1926; Maj. Gen. U. S. Grant to the author, 16 Apr 1960; *Rpt B/Tr*, 1928, pp. 51-57; *Rpt NCPPC*, 1930, pp. 70-71; Eliot, "Planning Washington and Its Environs," p. 181; *Star*, 3 Apr 1927.

party in House and Senate was represented and shared in every decision; the commissioner of public buildings, the architect of the Capitol, and the supervising architect of the Treasury supplied administrative and technical knowledge and, through the Secretary of Treasury, access to the President. Even so, conflicts and costly delays seemed all too probable. Yet the record of the building commission in the late 1920's, in the words of one official, "affords an example of how coordination of action . . . can be and was achieved."

Buildings for the Bureau of Internal Revenue and the Commerce Department began to rise below Pennsylvania Avenue late in 1927, and government purchase of virtually the entire stretch of land from the Treasury to the foot of the Hill between the Mall and the Avenue foreshadowed the location of additional departmental offices in the "Federal Triangle." A Board of Trade housing expert warned against overcrowding the triangle with massive government structures, but the tentative plan published early in 1927 showing open park-like spaces between each building allayed anxiety on that score. Milton B. Medary, president of the American Institute of Architects, proposed the method adopted in developing the triangle: a board of experienced architects to draft a harmonious composition and each man to design one building of the group in order to avoid monotony in treatment. Since by law the supervising architect of the Treasury was responsible for the designs, the Medary proposal became feasible only because Secretary of the Treasury Andrew Mellon contrived the necessary legislative authority.[13]

The Fine Arts Commission pointed to other work afoot in mid-1929: the removal of the World War I dormitories from the Union Station Plaza and the landscaping of the terrain, plans for a new Municipal Center, the relocation of the Botanic

[13] S Doc 240, 69C, 2S, Report of the Public Buildings Commission, pp. 1-5, and plate facing p. 8, Ser 8707; Grant to the author, 16 Apr 1960; *Rpt B/Tr*, 1926, pp. 56-57, 1928, pp. 13, 54-57, 64-65; *Star*, 31 Dec 1927, 1 Jan 1930; Fine Arts Comm, *Forty Years*, pp. 25-26; Herbert Hoover, *Memoirs*, II, 250.

Garden and the beginning of the Arboretum, a new Department of Agriculture building adjoining the old, extension of tree-lined drives along the Mall, and the selection of a site for a Supreme Court building facing the Capitol. Not since the early years of the century had old residents seen so much permanent federal construction. If a few citizens would have preferred greater emphasis on land purchase as a safeguard against further despoliation, and if some hearts stood still at the felling of trees along B Street preparatory to making it a "great ceremonial avenue," Washingtonians by and large were elated at the new outward grandeur the city was attaining.[14] That they themselves had not produced most of it, that it was rather an expression of national pride in the capital, did not matter. Indeed by 1930 few people differentiated between a Washingtonian and any American temporarily living in the District of Columbia.

[14] H. G. Dwight, "The Horrors of Washington," *Harper's Magazine*, CLII, 64-72; Kenneth L. Roberts, "Nobody's Capital," *Sat Eve Post*, CIC, 20; Eliot, "Planning Washington and Its Environs," pp. 178-81; Louis C. Cramton, "Congress and the Federal City," *American Civic Annual*, I, 75-79; *Star*, 3 Jan 1930; *Rpt Fine Arts Comm*, 1929, pp. 4, 31.

CHAPTER XV

THE INTELLECTUAL AND SOCIAL CLIMATE, 1920-1929

A DECADE called in contemporary and later writings the "Age of the Golden Calf," the "Era of Wonderful Nonsense," the "Jazz Age," the "Hardboiled Era," and the "New Era" of science and technology was a period of contradictions that produced the distinctive literature of the "lost generation," a disillusioned rejection of everything serious, and at the same time a faith in the wonder-working powers of science that reached the point of "superstition in another guise."[1] No one in the capital produced a *Farewell to Arms*, or a *This Side of Paradise*, or a *Main Street*, and flag-pole sitting and dance marathons bypassed Washington, but most of the wonderful nonsense and the hard-boiled selfishness characteristic of the 1920's was in evidence here, and perhaps nowhere else in the country did dedication to research bite deeper.

Thoughtful Americans had realized before the Armistice that the United States could no longer draw upon Europe for the discovery of new basic scientific principles or for fresh approaches to the study of social phenomena. And the United States was ill-prepared to fill the gap. A coordinating body to direct and abet research on a nation-wide scale in both the natural and the humanistic sciences seemed the logical answer, an organization like the National Research Council of the National Academy of Sciences but not under government control or dependent on government money. The upshot was that shortly after the war Congress amended the Academy's charter authorizing a membership of three hundred and complete independence of the government. Private funds thenceforward sup-

[1] Henry F. May, "Shifting Perspectives on the 1920's," *Mississippi Valley Historical Review*, XLIII, 405-27; Frederick L. Allen, *Only Yesterday*; William F. Leuchtenberg, *The Perils of Prosperity*, p. 2.

ported the Academy and its operating agent, the Research Council. Consensus was general that Washington was the most suitable location for its headquarters. Financed by a gift of $5,000,000 from the Carnegie Corporation, a handsome new building rose on north B Street across from Potomac Park, where a permanent staff took charge. Through awards of fellowships and grants-in-aid in eleven fields, ranging from anthropology, psychology, and "Educational Relations" to geology, physics, and medicine, the National Research Council gradually supplanted the Smithsonian as the prime mover in American scientific research. For although the older institution still acted as a clearing house of scientific data and a series of popular books published from 1926 onward served to disseminate knowledge, an insufficient endowment and the growth of the National Museum had gradually transformed the institution's main function from exploration of new scientific frontiers into guardianship of the past.

Several of the federal bureaus also suffered in the postwar decade. Distaste for everything military cut War and Navy Department research. Although the Navy in 1923 got appropriations for a laboratory whence came radar in the late 1930's, and the Public Health Service under the aegis of the Surgeon General managed to carry on some investigations in the control of venereal disease and developed a vaccine for Rocky Mountain spotted fever, even the famous Army Medical Library fell upon hard times. Congress allowed funds for Weather Bureau research, and the Interior Department conducted some small-scale scientific programs, but only the Departments of Agriculture and Commerce succeeded in expanding their research. The achievements of the plant explorers who had introduced to the United States crops such as avocados, dates, and soy beans, and the progress made in the realm of plant and animal pathology and chemistry ensured continuation of that work; and the country-wide prestige of Secretary of Agriculture Henry Wallace, himself responsible for developing hybrid corn, enabled him to get congressional endorsement of a Department of Agriculture Graduate School. Opened in 1923 in a department building, the school offered evening courses in some twenty fields, by no means all limited to agriculture; anyone could enroll for a nominal fee. Secretary of Commerce Herbert Hoover, wedded as he was to private enterprise, also widened research in the bureaus under his control. In order to establish simplified labor-saving practices and commercial standardization in all American business, he instituted a cooperative program at the Bureau of Standards where representatives of private firms worked alongside government employees. He hoped to see industrial corporations contribute $20,000,000 to a national fund for basic research, but, while waiting vainly for that to materialize, he encouraged strictly utilitarian government projects. Scientists in government service thus played a lesser national role than they had in the 1870's and 1880's, but the value of their work in the 1920's was far from negligible.[2]

Research in the social sciences, intensified by the troubles of wartime agencies in assembling precise information, received further impetus after the war from dollar-a-year men who had seen the need of a clearer understanding within the federal government of the principles of political and business economy. Robert S. Brookings, a wealthy St. Louis manufacturer who had served on the War Industries Board, took the lead. In 1919 a slim, handsome, white-haired, trimly bearded man of 69 whose formal education had ended when he was 16 but whose intellectual interests had deepened as his fortune grew, Brookings virtually singlehanded raised the money to prevent the threatened demise of the privately supported Institute for Govern-

[2] Millikan, *Autobiography*, pp. 199-201; Dupree, *Science*, pp. 322-43; Frederick A. Ogg, *Research in the Humanistic and Social Sciences, Report of a Survey Conducted for the American Council of Learned Societies*, pp. 168-69; *Rpts Smithsonian Inst.*, 1923, pp. 6, 12-13, 23, 1924, pp. 2-3, 15-16, 1925, pp. 2-3, 16, 1927, pp. 2, 12, 1928, pp. 2, 5; *The Graduate School of the Department of Agriculture*, 1961.

mental Research. From the institute's dispassionate factual studies came the recommendations that Congress wrote into a law of 1921 creating an executive accounting system and the federal Bureau of the Budget. Under the direction of William F. Willoughby, formerly a Princeton University Professor, abetted by his twin, Wester W., an expert in international relations, the institute then moved on to prepare other useful monographs. The best known of these, an examination of the government's handling of Indian affairs, brought about the reorganization of the Indian Service.

Brookings meanwhile concluded that the economic problems facing the world—war debts, reparations, and labor questions—demanded the scrutiny of "trained scientists, avid of facts, suspicious of assumptions and detached alike from personal prejudice and from any obligation to score points in the name of Patriotism." So, with Carnegie Corporation funds and generous contributions from his own pocket, he founded the Institute of Economics in 1922 and persuaded Harold G. Moulton of the University of Chicago to head it. The outwardly domineering "manufacturer-turned-educator" promised Moulton that he and his staff would not be subject to interference, and the trustees, men of the calibre of the paleontologist John C. Merriam, president of the Carnegie Institution, and Frederic A. Delano, also pledged themselves to give free rein to every scholar participating in the institute's work. It was a commitment of more than ordinary importance to American intellectuals. For while the public, despite Tennessee's rejection of evolution at the Scopes trial, was ordinarily ready to accept the tenets of natural science, studies in the human sciences, especially of touchy economic questions, still seemed to most Americans to be matters of opinion. The independence given the men at the Institute of Economics heightened their responsibilities but also enormously strengthened the case for academic freedom throughout the United States.

Moulton, a round-faced, strong-jawed extrovert, an athlete who had once considered a career in professional baseball, was at the same time a scientist intent on getting at the truth and seeing it presented in lucid non-technical language. He gathered about him a distinguished group of men. Their findings laid the analytical foundation upon which the Dawes Plan for German reparations was built and so molded public opinion that a settlement of allied war debts to the United States became possible. The long postwar agricultural depression led to Edwin G. Nourse's thought-provoking studies, *The Legal Status of Agricultural Cooperation* and *The Cooperative Marketing of Livestock*, practical guides to new forms of economic organization. Whenever a new institute monograph appeared, Moulton invited congressmen, federal executives, and independent scholars to a formal dinner at the Brookings headquarters, where the author of the study outlined his central thesis and answered questions about it. As a result quotations from the book, duly accredited, not infrequently found their way into the *Congressional Record* and government reports.

Eager to ensure a constant flow of young scientific experts into government service, in 1924 Brookings raised money to open a graduate school where hand-picked students were to be exposed to the practical workings of the government as well as book-learning. But as most of the students, instead of apprenticing themselves for careers in civil service and statesmanship, prepared for teaching posts, a plan to consolidate the school with the Institute of Governmental Research and the Institute of Economics took form in 1927 which brought about the chartering of the Brookings Institution "devoted to public service through research and education in the social sciences." Perhaps the hard-headed economists and political scientists who carried out the research and writing and schooled younger scholars in their own exacting methods considered Brookings' dream overambitious when he envisaged the institution of the future as "a kind of cap-stone to the educational arch of the country." Nevertheless by 1929 the trustees and the staff believed the experiment had abundantly proved its value.[3]

The American Council on Education, meanwhile, periodically brought together in Washington leading figures in American higher education. The council worked on the principle Woodrow Wilson had once enunciated: "Find out what you want in a college graduate and let the ways of getting it work themselves out"—that is, through the initiative and efforts of local communities rather than by government fiat bolstered by federal subsidies. By means of *The Educational Record*, prepared by committees and the small headquarters staff in Washington, the council's influence reached into every university and college in the country. In serving the teaching profession, the government, industry, and occasionally foreign universities, the council undertook various tasks. For example, the *Record of Usage*, a study of the manifold duties of foreign service officers, indicated what instruction colleges should give men training for these careers; the factual basis of the study was the day-by-day notations kept, at President Coolidge's request, by some three hundred foreign service officers. Another analysis examined the teaching of foreign languages in American colleges and outlined methods of improving it.

The American Council of Learned Societies Devoted to the Humanistic Sciences in turn contributed to the city's scholarly standing and gave new vigor to the local universities. The primary purpose of this federation of fifteen independent societies was to lay the groundwork for interdisciplinary research in archeology, history, philosophy, modern European and Oriental languages, and other special fields of knowledge. Like the National Research Council, the Brookings Institution, and the

[3] The Brookings Institution, *A Consideration of the Application of Research in the Social Sciences to the Problems of Modern Civilization*, 1931, pp. 8-14, 16; Herman Hagedorn, *Robert C. Brookings, A Biography*, pp. 21-22, 252-69, 289; Dexter M. Keeger, "Making The Social Sciences Sociable," *Survey*, LV, 80-82.

Council on Education, the humanists drew upon foundations for financial support. Among the early projects of the ACLS was a series of conferences on "the gifted student," a topic that stirred a response from the general public only thirty years later. But full recognition of the council's services followed upon the publication in 1928 of the first volume of that invaluable scholarly tool, the *Dictionary of American Biography*. Another contribution lay in awakening American scholars to the importance of oriental civilization.[4]

Above all, the Library of Congress drew scholars in the humanities to Washington. For Herbert Putnam looked upon the collection in his charge as a national library rather than a legislative tool, although, in establishing the Legislative Reference Service in 1915, he provided an efficient system for furnishing Congress with exact information. Over the years he had won the complete confidence of Congress by the temperate character of his requests; when he asked for funds the House Appropriations Committee accepted his word for the need. He had built up the accessions by drawing upon his exceptional knowledge of books and manuscripts in many realms of learning and by exercising intuitive judgment about those he did not know; his decision was final. In the opinion of his subordinates he seldom made a mistake. Autocratic though his manner toward them was, his high standards of performance and his never-failing sense of justice robbed his rebukes of any sting. No library in America had so devoted a staff or such rich materials in so many fields.

The Chinese collections and the way the Library of Congress acquired them are a case in point. First credit goes to Walter T.

[4] David A. Robertson, Assistant Director American Council on Education, 1924-1930, to the author, 15 Apr 1960; *The Educational Record*, I, No. 1, pp. 33-36, No. 3, *passim*, and III, No. 10, *passim*; Ogg, *Research in the Humanistic . . . Sciences*, p. 161; *Bulletins of the American Council of Learned Societies*, I-X, 1920-1930, especially No. 4, Jun 1925, p. 25, No. 5, May 1926, pp. 43, 52, No. 7, Apr 1928, pp. 60-61, No. 9, Dec 1928, p. 29 (hereafter cited as *ACLS Bulletin*).

Swingle, plant pathologist and plant explorer of the Department of Agriculture, for, in the course of his travels to collect seeds and cuttings in remote lands of the East, he learned of rare books dealing with oriental agriculture, Chinese philosophy, and Chinese literature. From 1913 onward he wrote long, detailed descriptions of these finds to Putnam, and Putnam unhesitatingly acted upon Swingle's advice to buy them. Neither man could himself read any oriental language. Swingle accepted the judgments of learned Chinese friends; the librarian accepted Swingle's, even to the point of paying $1,000 for a unique 1590 edition of a Chinese herbary, huge volumes of ideograph that scarcely fifty men in the United States could read. A colored man, Armstrong Claytor, who unpacked the shipments of orientalia, taught himself enough Chinese to identify and catalogue the materials, while the courtly and persuasive Swingle induced the Department of Agriculture to employ a scholar to translate the books so that students of agriculture as well as historians could benefit. So distinguished had the Library's Chinese accessions become that in 1928 Putnam obtained appropriations to establish a division of Chinese literature headed by the gentle and learned sinologue Arthur Hummel. Japanese and Tibetan materials also multiplied, while the Freer Gallery, under the wing of the Smithsonian, furnished magnificent examples of oriental art. In that fashion Washington became the one place in the western world where the student of oriental civilization could find the resources he needed.

Indeed, the Library of Congress came to be virtually a national cultural center which private donations constantly enriched. In 1912 a bequest from Mrs. Gardiner Hubbard had created a fund for annual purchases of engravings and etchings, but not until 1925, after Mrs. Frederic Shurtleff Coolidge had offered an endowment that would build an auditorium and provide for chamber music concerts, did Congress create a Trust Fund Board to administer similar gifts and bequests. At the newly completed Coolidge Auditorium a chamber music festival first took place in October 1925. Mrs. Coolidge, herself a talented musician, had explained her wish that the concerts be considered "national and professional" events, and since "fashion is an enemy to art," guest lists omit "the fashionable element as such . . . if it has no musical qualifications." Abetted by the "Friends of Music in the Library of Congress," founded in 1928 and headed by Speaker of the House Nicholas Longworth, the annual festivals opened up to discriminating audiences musical opportunities rare in any city. Other gifts permitted the Library to establish "chairs" of American history, the fine arts, aeronautics, and, with funds from a new Hispanic Foundation, a chair in Spanish and Portuguese literature.[5]

Radio broadcasting and new concert series widened the city's interest in all music. In a single week of 1925, for example, Louise Homer sang at the Washington Auditorium, Marian Anderson, the already famous young Negro contralto, at the First Congregational Church, and Sophie Breslau at the National Theatre, the New York symphony played at Poli's, the American pianist Charles Cooper and the Davison Glee Club performed at the Masonic Auditorium, and the organist Henry Seibert at the Washington Auditorium. At morning musicals sponsored by Mrs. Lawrence Townsend, herself a composer of some note, leading artists made their Washington debuts. Although most of the symphony concerts were still day-time affairs, the Knights of Columbus opened an Evening School of Music, and societies such as the Arts Club and the United Art Society offered Sunday concerts.

In colored Washington music was a cultural cement. Negroes excluded from white concerts provided their own. Until the demise of the *Bee* in 1922, the paper regularly devoted a half-page to events "In The World of Music," and the *Tribune*, born

[5] *ACLS Bulletin*, No. 10, Apr 29, pp. 33-58; *Rpts, Librarian of Cong*, 1928, pp. 1-2, 6-7, 272, 287-316, 1946, "The Story Up to Now," pp. 202-14.

in 1921, for years followed much the same course. Here was a realm in which the Negro community knew it excelled. The Snowden Diamond Jazzologists, Duke Ellington's, and other bands made the city "known for its syncopation," even if as innovators they did not rank with New Orleans' musicians. In the 1950's Washington would proudly claim among her native sons jazz artists of the fame of Louis Armstrong. Nor did the colored community neglect classical and church music. Upper-class Negroes cultivated all music as an art and trained their children in its practice. Unknown to most white Washingtonians, least of all to the "smart set," the Mus-o-lit Society occupied a very special place in the life of what the *Crisis* came to call the "Secret City."[6]

While increasing enrollment in the Corcoran Art School and streams of visitors to the Freer and Corcoran galleries indicated a growing appreciation of the fine arts, informed Washingtonians realized that neglect was restricting the potentialities of the National Gallery. The pictures were crowded into a few rooms of the National Museum, where only part of the collection could be displayed and lack of space forbade accepting new accessions. "We are the only civilized nation that has not risen to a realization of the real value of art and of important functions of a National Gallery," wrote the Secretary of the Smithsonian in 1922. "No important art work has, for art's sake pure and simple, ever been purchased with the approval of the United States Government. The Nation has received as gifts and bequests, art works amounting to more than ten millions in money value, and has expended on their acquirement and care possibly one two-hundredth part of that amount." Unless Congress were to meet the cost of erecting a new building, only private sub-

[6] Programs, 1920-1929, Washington file (Music Div, L.C.); *Star*, 8 Nov 1925; *Bee*, 19 Feb, 12 Mar 1921; *Tribune*, 21 May 1921, 21 Jan 1922; *Crisis*, XXXIX, 185. Issues of the Sunday *Star* in October and November, when the concert season opened, carried yearly full notices of what was to come.

scription could give the national collection a suitable gallery and opportunity to expand, since the endowment of the Smithsonian was no longer adequate even for its scientific programs. Faced with that dilemma, several Washington business firms and the regents of the Smithsonian campaigned for a bigger endowment, while a committee of fifteen leading citizens arranged a special loan exhibition to promote interest in the gallery. By 1929 the Secretary could report: "The year has been gratifyingly and unexpectedly rich in progress. . . . The National Government and many friends of the Institution have added materially to its income—Mr. John Gellatly, of New York, has made the gift of his extensive collection comprising classic American and European paintings, outstanding specimens of jewellers' art, tapestries, furniture, and oriental art, valued altogether at several million dollars, . . . for eventual exhibition in the National Gallery."[7]

Meanwhile belief that "the sense of well-being and enriched capacity for living which art can give" should be "a privilege of the many as well as the technically trained and sensitive few," inspired Duncan Phillips, a discriminating private collector and art critic, to open to the public in 1920 what one admirer called an "Art Gallery for Delight." Housed in two rooms of the family residence, the paintings—an occasional sixteenth-century piece, some French impressionists, some Whistlers, and a few twentieth-century American artists—were regrouped periodically to illustrate particular ideas and themes. The Phillips Gallery came to be known to connoisseurs the world over. At intervals after the founding of the Washington Chamber Music Society in 1924, private concerts took place at the gallery.[8]

[7] *Star*, 3 Jul 1920; *Rpt Fine Arts Comm*, 1921; *Rpt Smithsonian*, 1921, p. 16, 1922, pp. 6, 49, 1923, pp. 6, 19, 1924, pp. 3-4, 1925, pp. 18-19, 1926, pp. 3-4, 7, 24, 1927, p. 25, 1929, p. 2; *Exhibition of Early American Paintings, Miniatures and Silver, Assembled by the Washington Loan Exhibition Committee, December 5, 1925-January 3, 1926*; Frederick P. Keppel and R. L. Duffus, *The Arts in American Life*, p. 67.

[8] Duncan Phillips, "Art and Understanding," *Art and Understanding*,

While science, scholarship, and a deepening interest in the arts thus took possession of much of Washington, an innovation aimed at strengthening the influence of religion brought the College of Preachers into being at the Cathedral of St. Peter and St. Paul. In a building erected in the Cathedral close in 1924, Episcopal rectors in groups of fifteen to twenty from parishes all over the country gathered for post-ordination "refresher" courses and discussions of how the church could widen its reach. Relatively few people knew anything about this college, but its very existence and growth during the Age of the Golden Calf pointed to a richness and variety in Washington's life that newcomers rarely expected.

If frequently startled to find such diversity, the discerning newcomer was invariably struck by Washington's persistent village-like quality. Its unexpectedness entranced most people. Here was a bucolic Cleopatra whose wiles seduced the good home-spun citizen. World capital though she was, "the chief official personages who people the scene are villagers with a villager's outlook and a villager's background." The sense of intimacy, which in 1920 Washingtonians had feared lost forever, again pervaded all strata of white society. When the Senators won the World Series in 1924, people of all sorts and kinds celebrated together at street dances in a dozen neighborhoods. Years later one man recalled a spring evening when, as he and his wife boarded a trolley, the long fringe of his wife's Venetian shawl caught on the conductor's sleeve button; instead of yanking it free the conductor followed her into the car and, slowly disengaging the strands, said very courteously: "Madam, you certainly have me on the string tonight." Even the critic who considered the city "rootless" and "without ambition," a place in which "material barrenness . . . [is] matched by its own cultural barrenness," admitted that a "dance is a

I, 1; "Art Gallery for Delight," *Weekly Review*, III, 611; programs Washington Chamber Music Society, 1924-1932 (Music Div, L.C.).

pleasanter place than a factory or a laboratory or a study; conforming travelers on the broad path are easier on their fellows' elbows than angular men of ideas and purposes."[9]

The picture of Washington that emerged from the popular press for the great American public was of a city given over entirely to dances, teas and dinner parties, incessant social climbing, and, as a way to the top, jockeying for political preferment. The canvas was narrow; the arts occupied little space, the world of learning even less. Political commentators, including radio broadcasters, talked of responses in Washington to national and international problems, but in the new Babylon, once the scandals of the Harding administration had blown over, politics as such generally netted less attention than Society with a capital S, although the farmer's son in the White House was not only "agin sin" but agin extravagance and disliked social functions. Month after month women's magazines carried descriptions of what the well-dressed senator's wife was wearing or what etiquette demanded in the capital; metropolitan dailies seized upon Washington gossip. The raw material lent itself admirably both to derisive and reverential treatment.[10] Bathtub gin and bootleg whiskey, sleek sports cars, backbiting and competition over precedence, short skirts and Zulu-like, bushy permanents on nine debutantes out of ten held the limelight.

The local newspapers, in adopting a worshipful tone toward high society, presented a one-sided view of the city's life. The *Times*, which ten years before had championed civic causes deserving public support, had changed hands and now swung far to the right. In the opinion of the crusading Oswald Garrison Villard of the *Nation*, the *Times* became a "noisy and insincere" paper, while the *Herald*, which had once promised substantial

[9] Robertson to the author, 15 Apr 1960; Edward G. Lowry, *Washington Close-Ups, Intimate Views of Some Public Figures*, pp. 7-9; John W. Owens, "A City Without a Main Street," *Nation*, CXX, 513-14.

[10] Nearly a quarter of the entries under the heading "Washington" in the *Reader's Guide to Periodical Literature* from 1920 to 1929 consists of articles about "high society."

fare, offered a bland diet only occasionally spiced with biting, politically loaded comments. Newspapermen despised the Washington *Post*, a "poison sheet" without moral integrity. The *News*, of which the courageous and gifted Lowell Mellett was the backbone, carried valuable items on its inside pages but spread trivia like the "Marble Championship" across its front page. The *Star*, one of the biggest moneymakers in the newspaper business, trod such a wary path lest an editorial or news item offend Congress or an important advertiser that every column appeared swathed in cotton wool. Readers naturally were happy to learn that Mrs. Herbert Hoover made history: for the first time "the wife of a President has operated a car while in the White House." Non-controversial items and homey "small-town gossip" were safer than opinions, even those well right of center, and kept for the *Star* a large local public. For, as Villard noted, there is "no such hide-bound conservative in all the world as your retired civil official or retired army or navy officer," and Washington was full of them. People who wanted to follow public affairs other than the "shifting social pageant" read the New York *Times*, the Baltimore *Sun*, or the *Christian Science Monitor*.[11]

Ridicule of the city's most publicized element came chiefly from outsiders. In this "most temporary Society in America," wrote a New Yorker, the native aristocracy often had a background of only two or three generations of residence. Hovering upon the borders of "that august group" was "a swarm of widows." The comment that, when a millionaire went to heaven, his wife took up residence in Washington, overlooked the scores of widows, wealthy and otherwise, who had originally come as wives of generals and admirals and stayed on because the rootlessness of military life made the capital the place where they

[11] Oswald Garrison Villard, "Washington: A Capital without a Thunderer," *Nation*, CXVII, 232-35, and *Some Newspapers and Newspapermen*, p. 175; *Star*, 4 Apr 1929; [Robert Allen], *Washington Merry-go-Round*, pp. 322-58.

felt most at home. Theoretically anyone "in trade" was anathema, but by 1923 the Chevy Chase Club had slipped so far as to lower the bars several times, leaving only the Grasslands Country Club and the fifty-member Alibi Club untainted. No Jew was allowed even as a guest in the country clubs. "A shrine for the non-political world of fashion" was the Massachusetts Avenue house of the three Patten sisters. Emphatically not cave-dwellers and with only one generation of moderate wealth behind them, they had set out before the war "to rule Washington by giving great tea parties at which one's presence was the sign manual of society. Their tireless energy in unearthing obscure facts raised gossip to the plane of research." In the popular phrase, the way to spread the news in the city was "telephone, telegraph, or tell-a-Patten." Their omniscience was simultaneously terrifying and fascinating. Social climbers, minor functionaries of the diplomatic corps, and gay young married couples yearned to be invited to Sunday afternoon teas that might furnish stories on which to dine out for the rest of the season.[12]

In colored society snobbery took slightly different form, since color itself entered into social gradations. But cave-dwelling had come to be as firmly established in Negro Washington as in white. A long line of Washington ancestors, non-Negroid features, and very light color were more decidedly marks of distinction in the 1920's than at the turn of the century. Colored ladies spent afternoons playing bridge and five hundred, their husbands took flyers in the stock market and bought expensive cars, and all the well-to-do gave select evening parties in their homes to which the cultivated Negro newcomer could not hope to be invited. Like whites, Negroes also made some obeisance to wealth. "When Washington Society 'Turns Out'" described that aspect of the colored city's life to readers of the *Tribune*: "There are two events in the District of Columbia which attract

[12] Mrs John King Van Rensselaer, *The Social Ladder*, pp. 248-72, 289; Dixon Wecter, *The Saga of American Society*, p. 418.

the undivided support of the 'well-known' and 'exclusive' Washington society. They are the Howard-Lincoln football game and the annual cadet corps drill. Just as the 'pretty school marms' exhibit their raccoons, chinchillas and sable skins at the gridiron classics, so the cadet drill occasions the display of the choicest most elaborate and scantiest spring frocks." When Washington's and Baltimore's "smart set" barred darker-skinned Negroes from the summer colony which Frederick Douglass had founded in the 1880's at Highland Beach, Maryland, the ensuing feud equalled in intensity the battles in white society.

At the end of the 1920's Langston Hughes, great-nephew of colored Washington's idol of the 1870's and 1880's, lashed out at the city's high yellow elite. Poems sketching the porter "climbing a great big mountain of Yes Sirs," the "Black Gal" crying "I hate them rinney yaller gals," and the "loud laughers in the hand of Fate" had won him some literary fame, but the disregard of his Washington neighbors angered him. They overlooked talent; they objected to Jean Toomer's *Cane* and Rudolph Fisher's *City of Refuge* because the main characters in both books were so "black." Many of the "best people" were newly rich, and many were not cultured at all. A true picture would reveal their "pseudo-culture, their slavish devotion to Nordic standards, their snobbishness, their detachment from the Negro masses and their vast sense of importance to themselves."[13]

As the Jazz Age was nearing its end, angry criticism of the shallowness of high white society also sounded. The anonymously published *Washington Merry-go-Round* described the bungling of the welcome prepared for the "Lone Eagle" as an illustration of the city's ineptness: the dinner in Charles Lindbergh's honor wound up with a recording of "They're Hanging Danny Deever in the Morning." In this "humdrum capital,"

[13] *Tribune*, 22 Apr 1927, 26 Oct 1929; Langston Hughes, *Fine Clothes for the Jew.*

where the diplomatic corps was "starched futility," "boiled bosoms" served as the brittle front for the emptiness of society leaders. "One of the most charming things about Washington is that it is almost never without a social, diplomatic or matrimonial war." Society was divided between "those who want to get their names into the papers and those who want to keep them out." And the heavy drinking of party-goers in a supposedly dry capital made them the more boring. Yet in being well supplied with bores and over supplied with bootleg liquor, Washington differed little from other American cities of the period.

Neither the adulatory nor the derogatory descriptions of Washington hinted at any complexity in the social structure, and over-simplification postulated a fixity in the white social order that did not obtain. The personable unattached male was still much in demand irrespective of his rank. If no agreeable young bachelor in a minor government post in the 1920's could successfully emulate James MacNeill Whistler's debonair scheme of pinning up his frock coat into tails and then sallying forth to captivate Washington hostesses, still seventy years later the presentable young man able to rent a dress suit might find himself invited to debutante balls. Rumor ran that, when asked what "book" he was listed in—the *Social Register*, the *Green Book*, successor to the *Elite List*, or *Who's Who in the National Capital*—one man replied: "The telephone book." While the label "cave-dweller" was increasingly sought after, some of that group had gone to seed and some kept to their caves as the only way of concealing the meagreness of their personal attainments. Georgetown, in particular, contained a number of odd characters, products of intermarriages within their own small circle, eccentrics whose status hinged upon aloofness from everyone without local antecedents going back into ante-bellum days. Yet the interpretation of Washington's social hierarchy as built upon "wealth and an imported aristocracy either directly or indirectly political" left out of account the variety of individual talent in the city and the ease with which doors barricaded against the social climber opened to genuinely gifted newcomers. The new arrival whose accomplishments and good manners qualified him for membership in the Cosmos Club received a cordial welcome that sometimes astonished him.

During an era in which business enterprise rode high in America, Washington's businessmen commanded curiously little social prestige, although the heads of several banks, fortified by years of controlling the credit of people ostensibly more powerful, were listed in the *Social Register*. While enjoying "Coolidge prosperity" Washingtonians, old and new, like thousands of other Americans, poked fun at the President's occasional gaucheries, just as they later delighted in grossly exaggerated apocryphal tales of the "elbowings" of Dolly Gann, the Vice President's stout, red-haired sister and hostess, in her successful efforts to see her brother officially outrank the Speaker of the House. But pontificaters on precedence and status-seekers alike tacitly admitted that they could not deny position to the city's intelelctuals.

President Hoover's "business administration" leaned heavily upon the scientists and social scientists in Washington. The President's zeal to put everything on a businesslike, scientifically efficient basis thus gave unexpected importance to men versed in research. He wanted no traditional folderol to interfere with scientific management, although neither did he want science that failed to produce the formulae he anticipated. He objected, for example, to some of the monographs prepared by the Brookings Institute of Economics which, he contended, had cost the economy of the United States a million dollars yearly.[14] Yet he

[14] *Washington Merry-go-Round*, pp. 10-33, 50, 85-87, 100-12, 262, 285; Longworth, *Crowded Hours*, pp. 313-17, 328-30, 336-37; interviews, especially Ralph W. M. Shoemaker of Georgetown, 1878-1961, and Edwin G. Nourse. See also Rowland Berthoff, "The American Social Order: A Conservative Hypothesis," *Am Hist Rev*, LXV, 499-514.

inaugurated during his first months in office the studies that culminated in the many-volumed *Recent Social Trends*, an invaluable detailed analysis of American resources and modes of life. In attempting to act upon his conviction that government was a task for specialists, he strengthened the position of the expert in Washington. Unwittingly he paved the way for the New Deal brain-trusters.

CHAPTER XVI

CIVIC CONSCIENCE, 1920-1929

A PHYSICALLY beautiful city in which some of the most interesting and many of the most talked-about people in the United States lived naturally had an aura of glamor. As the postwar depression lifted, well-to-do residents inclined to see little amiss in their surroundings. Life had its seamy side everywhere; that for several hundred Washington families there was no other side was an uncomfortable notion that only the sensitive conscience could entertain. And "the Hardboiled Era" did not encourage sensitivity. Philadelphia, Cleveland, Rochester, and several other cities, according to informed social workers, succeeded in maintaining a sense of community responsibility. But if a generations-old tradition of civic obligation enabled "Philadelphia gentlemen" to expand their philanthropies, and if the "quest for quality" similarly inspired Clevelanders and Rochesterians, in much of the United States the civic betterment movement of prewar days slowed or came to a halt. H. L. Mencken, once the high priest of the literary avant garde, struck a note congenial to many Americans disillusioned after the war: "If I am convinced of anything, it is that Doing Good is in bad taste."

Difficult as it was in other cities to enlist support for charities, let alone to arouse interest in the underlying causes of poverty and wretchedness, in Washington the problem was heightened by the steadily declining proportion of "old families," the group ordinarily readiest to acknowledge *noblesse oblige*. Householders who voted and paid taxes in other localities to which, often mistakenly, they expected to return were disinclined to concern themselves about Washington's well-being; that was a task for local citizens. Few of these, however, possessed large means; most of the fortunes in the city belonged to residents who considered themselves temporary. The constant turnover of intelligent people of widely varied experience, the very element that gave the capital much of its fascination, was a deterrent to the nurturing of civic spirit.

A more fundamental obstacle rested upon citizens' political impotence. A "city council" composed of outlanders who were rarely swayed by local wishes had to approve every measure involving public action or the spending of local taxes. As it happened, Congress during much of the 1920's was more responsive to District needs than at any time since 1906, but the necessity of begging for every constructive law and every appropriation still had a chilling effect upon the community. A life-time of participation in civic undertakings led one Washingtonian to aver in 1959 that from the moment Congress voted the first penny for a local project to the day when citizens could call its realization assured generally ran to five years.[1] But to get that first penny might take four or five years of patient persuasion, often took ten, and sometimes a full generation. The struggle for a municipal hospital and a home for feeble-minded children are cases in point. In other cities when local feeling ran strong about any needed service, elected municipal functionaries were prone to respond. Here when the nearly twenty-year-old campaign to rid the city of alley dwellings had reached fever-pitch in 1913, it took the death-bed plea of the President's wife to induce Congress to enact a law; and, because of the intervention of war, postwar exigencies, and the unacceptability of anything so radical as public housing, execution of the act of 1914 then had to wait another two decades. Small wonder that only the stoutest-hearted had the fortitude yearly to renew the welfare fight.

The sense of helplessness, moreover, blurred perceptions

[1] Minutes of the Board of Managers of the Associated Charities, 1921-1929, especially 11 Jun 1924, p. 4, 13 Oct 1925, p. 5, 13 Jan, 10 Mar, 12 May, 13 Oct 1926, *passim*, and 9 Mar 1927, pp. 1-3, typescript in possession of the Family and Child Services of Washington, D.C. (hereafter cited as Min As Ch); Mrs. Henry Grattan Doyle, statement at panel on Washington Problems held at the American University, April 1959.

about what welfare should encompass. Clevelanders, say, or Philadelphians could project an orderly scheme of community services, putting responsibility for matters of city-wide concern upon tax-supported agencies and leaving privately financed organizations to handle the rest. Washingtonians' inability to carry out a rational, comprehensive plan made its mere formulation an unrewarding exercise to be abandoned before seriously attempted. A clear over-all picture consequently did not emerge. Philanthropists, seeing only bits and pieces, focused their attention upon areas in which their efforts might count. Hence even while doubts mounted about the adequacy of private charity, the public-spirited tended still to look upon charity societies and church groups as the city's mainstay. Most Washington residents shrugged their shoulders.

Just as the Civil War destroyed long-established patterns of behavior and brought nearly two decades of confusion to the city, so World War I bequeathed to Washingtonians a nine-year legacy of bewilderment and apathy. The extent of community disorganization was not immediately evident. On the contrary, in 1920 several signs pointed to a strengthening of civic vitality. Intent upon keeping alive "the spirit of cooperation that characterized the communal life of Washington during the war period," a group of high-minded citizens first of all launched Community Services, Inc., with the purpose of opening neighborhood centers which, unlike the segregated units started in 1917 under school board aegis, whites and Negroes could enjoy together. Later in the year social workers in public and private agencies formed a bi-racial Council of Social Workers; it included employees of the police department, the Juvenile Court, the U.S. Public Health Service, the Visiting Nurse Association, the Associated Charities, the white and colored YMCA's, the NAACP, the Boy Scouts, Community Services, Inc., and half a dozen more. Members planned to exchange ideas and experiences over the lunch table and, in the process, improve race relations. As white restaurants would not serve Negroes, the first meeting took place at the Phyliss Wheatley colored YWCA. Shortly afterward, at the instigation of the energetic Mrs. Whitman Cross, laymen representing some twenty-five private charities, Protestant, Roman Catholic, Jewish, and non-sectarian, founded the Washington Council of Social Agencies to examine common problems, agree upon major objectives, and collaborate in achieving them. And in the last weeks of the Wilson administration, Vice President and Mrs. Thomas Marshall brought the secretary of the Boston Council of Social Agencies to Washington to draft a code of welfare laws for the District.[2] Each of these promising undertakings either collapsed completely within a matter of months or slid gradually into prolonged ineffectiveness.

The rift between the business community and do-gooders was partly responsible for that debacle. The split, first discernible about 1910, widened rapidly after the war. In 1920 businessmen who had been active participants in the civic betterment movement counted on seeing the prompt restoration of the old social order. Still smarting from accusations of war profiteering and indignant at the perpetuation of rent controls in the District, they wanted no further "socialistic" measures imposed upon the city. From conservatism a growing proportion of Board of Trade members soon swung into the ranks of reaction. With the Red Scare commanding newspaper headlines, Community Services, Inc., early became suspect. Despite the eminent respectability of its principal sponsors, it appeared to have the earmarks of a radical organization ready to back revolutionary changes. Since proponents of racially mixed recreational centers obviously must have left-wing leanings, a joint committee of the Board of Trade and the Chamber of

[2] *Rpt B/Tr*, 1920, pp. 199-210; Minutes, Council of Social Agencies, 14 Feb 1921, typescript in possession of Health and Welfare Council of the National Capital Area (hereafter cited as Min CSA); "The Hand of the Vice President," *Survey*, XLV, 621-23; Robert W. Kelso, "A Challenge," *ibid.*, XLVI, 151-53; *Bee*, 1 Jan 1921.

Commerce condemned the community center plan. Without the financial endorsement of businessmen the project could not survive, and after a flutter or two Community Services fell apart. When the Bostonian engaged by the Thomas Marshalls submitted his proposals for a District welfare code, the Board of Trades objected to his recommendations; a preoccupied Congress ignored them. Gauged by contributions to the Associated Charities, by 1925 the Board of Trade and the Chamber of Commerce had put themselves on record as having no interest in organized altruism; only 17 and 16 percent of their respective members subscribed to the charity fund, whereas 35 percent of Cosmos Club and Metropolitan Club members answered the appeal. The alienation of businessmen's sympathies was a severe blow to the cause of social welfare.

Faint uneasiness about the new professionalism of social workers for a time was a second, albeit minor, source of friction. Observable in other cities also, it was based upon belief that "social workers are . . . the worst sort of benevolent tyrant." The increasing emphasis upon case-work techniques and a psychiatric approach to social ills naturally bred in graduates of the new schools of social work a reluctance to use untrained help, and, as their assignments became more complex and time-consuming, their unwillingness to give the volunteer intensive training necessarily relegated the well-intentioned layman to a subsidiary role. Admirable and selfless though the aims of Washington's professionals were, in organizing the Council of Social Workers they set themselves apart from the volunteers whose support in the past had proved essential to the success of community undertakings. Here was a reversal of the course the Monday Evening Club had always followed. So far from strengthening cooperation, the new alignment threatened to erect fresh obstacles. The council, in actuality, early ceased to be a force of any kind, since a drifting away of white members within a year or two transformed the organization in essence into an ineffectual Negro body. Still, the feeling among lay members of charity boards that their services were unwanted except for money-raising weakened further an already thinning interest in civic and eleemosynary projects.

Certainly the decline of the Council of Social Agencies suggests a deepening sense of uselessness and defeatism among its directors. The monthly meetings during the first two years evoked some optimism: delegates examined the pros and cons of fund-raising through a community chest, drew up a list of the city's most pressing needs, and persuaded the District commissioners to borrow an expert from the Russell Sage Foundation to identify lacunae in services and assist a citizens' committee in drafting a public welfare code. But before the end of 1923 Newbold Noyes, son of Theodore and one of the few younger men to concern himself with civic matters, was voicing keen disappointment at the meagre attendance at council meetings. Colored delegates rarely came. Although the Associated Charities had two Negro districts, each headed by a trained colored worker, representatives of white philanthropies learned little about Negro needs, still less about Negro attempts to meet them. None of the twenty-eight objectives listed in 1921 and 1922 looked attainable without far more effort than the council's constituent organizations were supplying.[3]

The charity societies composing the Council of Social Agencies did not, it is true, embrace all volunteer groups intent on community service. The Washington Junior League and, under the guidance of Miss Mabel Boardman, the various corps of the American Red Cross Women's Volunteer Service undertook to direct Washington's yearly crop of debutantes into work helpful to the city. But the League, earnest as many of its officers were, had not yet fully evolved its training courses for "pro-

[3] *Rpt B/Tr*, 1921, pp. 50-51; Min As Ch, 8 Oct 1924, p. 6, 11 Mar 1925, p. 3; *Rpt B/Ch*, 1924, p. 2; *National Conference of Social Work*, 1929, p. 499; interview Col. Campbell C. Johnson; Min CSA, 1922-27, and Questionnaire of the Citizens' Chest Survey Committee, 1947, Appendix 5, "Résumé of Council Activities since 1923."

visional" members, and even thirty years later it would find itself unable wholly to escape the label of dilettantism attaching to any group in which membership hinged upon social position. The Red Cross corps, with their expensive uniforms and the faint air of aristocratic superiority with which Miss Boardman imbued them, fell even deeper into the category of very part-time ladies bountiful. For Miss Boardman, the quintessence of the Victorian lady, always immaculately and elegantly dressed, her hair coiffed in a Gibson-girl pompadour, looked upon professional social workers as a self-important, power-greedy lot most of whose duties intelligent society women could well handle as volunteers. Whether or not that thinly concealed hostility interposed difficulties, unquestionably the eighteen hours of service a year which the Volunteer Service stipulated was too little to have any perceptible effect upon Washington's welfare problems. Probably the chief value of both the Junior League and the Red Cross corps lay in preventing the total submergence of philanthropic impulses among young women caught up in the feverish gaieties of the Jazz Age.

Of more enduring importance was the work of the Voteless League of Women Voters of the District of Columbia. Made up initially of former campaigners for women suffrage, the Voteless League set itself to study legislation affecting the city. Because League committees made a point of sponsoring or opposing measures only after careful scrutiny, their recommendations were often slow to appear; but once they took form they represented an educated consensus. Members testified before congressional committees in behalf of stronger school attendance laws, mothers' pensions, minimum wages for women, and again and again for appropriations large enough to permit existing institutions to function efficiently. As members gained confidence with experience, they made League opinion count on every major issue.[4]

[4] Dulles, *American Red Cross*, pp. 238-41, 254-56; *A History of the League of Women Voters of the District of Columbia*, 1960.

Issues were all too numerous. A scathing article in the *Survey* entitled "Medieval Washington" described the primitive character of most of the city's services in 1923. A later study of the provisions for child welfare revealed that the facilities supported by private societies were by and large far less well managed than those in other cities. "The state of affairs in the public field," the specialist from the Russell Sage Foundation reported in 1924, "is illogical, wasteful, and intolerable, not only from the standpoint of the public which pays the bills but from the point-of-view of the neglected dependent clients whom this group of organically unrelated agencies and institutions attempts to serve." In the interim an open fight between the Board of Children's Guardians and the trustees of the Industrial Home School over placement of dependent children had brought on a congressional investigation. Although witnesses proved the Guardians guilty of highhandedness, testimony also showed that, in view of their limited funds and small staff, their record was surprisingly creditable. Nevertheless the hearings, the Russell Sage investigator's report, and the recommendations of the citizens' commission on a welfare code convinced Congress that a single board of public welfare should replace the three "organically unrelated" agencies, namely the Board of Charities, the Board of Children's Guardians, and the trustees of the Industrial Home School. The act went into effect in 1926.[5]

The centralization of responsibility for all public welfare and correctional institutions, except the National Training School for Boys, reduced the chances of friction with Congress and produced useful economies. The single, nine-man board appointed by the District commissioners and serving without com-

[5] Hart, *Child Welfare*, pp. 3-4, 22-23, 47-56, 102-03; Lundberg and Milburn, *Child Dependency*, p. 43; William Hodson, *Preliminary Report of the Commission on Public Welfare Legislation of the District of Columbia*; Mina C. Van Winkle, "Medieval Washington," *Survey*, L, 212-13; "They Guard the Past," *ibid.*, LI, 399-400, and *ibid.*, LII, 325; Jt Subcomee of S and H Dis Comees, 67C, 4S, Hrgs, "Investigation of the Bd of Children's Guardians," and 68C, 2S, Hrgs, "Establishment of a Board of Public Welfare in the D of C."

pensation included John Joy Edson, Mrs. Coralie Cook, and several others of recognized judgment and courage. The selection of George S. Wilson to head the staff was also a happy choice. With thirty years of experience, first with the Associated Charities and since 1900 as secretary of the Board of Charities, Wilson knew the city's problems intimately and how best to avoid administrative pitfalls. While he lacked breadth of imagination and seemed imperturbable in the face of miseries he could not end, he was far from indifferent to suffering. Hard-headed Scot that he was, he stood out against excessive cuts in the welfare budget. The District commissioners felt free, in their own phrase, to "leave it to George." In spite of closely trimmed appropriations, service to the needy and weak improved, and, in proportion as the welfare board did its job well, private charities were able to concentrate their efforts more narrowly. At the time no one objected to confining the public agency largely to the field of institutional care or foresaw that private philanthropy would stagger under an insupportable relief burden once depression struck.

Even in the flush 1920's serious gaps remained in the District's public welfare services. The Juvenile Court, still allowed only one judge at a salary a third smaller than that of other federal judges, needed expanded facilities and an administrative overhauling. Appropriations for the Board of Welfare were kept to a figure that meant an overworked staff paid at salaries below those offered in like-sized or smaller cities. Investigators for the Child Welfare division each carried at least 120 cases, twice the load recommended by professional organizations and considerably bigger than that customary elsewhere. The head of the division exhausted her energies in re-fighting the old battle against institutional care, instead of foster homes, for children. Public playground space, skimpy in 1920, fell far behind the growth in population, particularly in southwest Washington and in an area west of North Capital Street, already coming to be known as the "notorious second precinct." "Mildly" delinquent Negro boys were shoved into the overcrowded, shockingly ill-equipped Industrial Home School for Colored Children; delinquent small colored girls, if committed anywhere, had to go to the reform school intended for older Negro girls; no institution, public or private, would accept a Negro child under two years of age. Since Congress voted no money for inexpensive public housing, the Alley Dwelling Act of 1914 remained a dead letter; some 8,000 people, mostly Negro, continued to inhabit the alley slums.

Public health services taken for granted in most American cities were few in Washington and badly staffed before 1929. The tuberculosis hospital, twenty years earlier a source of community pride, was not only over-crowded but had a long waiting list and a woefully small corps of nurses and attendants. While the opening of a psychiatric ward in 1923 in the partly built Gallinger municipal hospital relieved some of the city's medical needs, until 1929 the old Asylum hospital had to suffice for general care, and only the generosity of Mrs. Anne Archbold provided the hospital with small, occupational therapy and social welfare departments. Fortunately the completion of Gallinger in 1930 gave the city a well-equipped, adequately staffed municipal hospital before the depression took its toll of public health.[6]

The basic weakness of the District's welfare system was its stress upon treatment rather than prevention. Like public administrators, the managers of the Associated Charities, the main source of direct relief to needy families, generally perceived the shortcomings of the finger-in-the-dike method of dealing with want. In 1928 a careful study showed that, of the $2,500,000 Washington raised for private charities, $1,269,000 was spent by hospitals for the cure of disease, $50,000 for pre-

[6] *Rpt B/Ch*, 1926, pp. xiv, 1-3, 91, 94; *Annual Report of the Board of Public Welfare*, 1929, pp. 3, 19, 1930, pp. 3, 88 (hereafter cited as *Rpt B/PW*); Lundberg and Milburn, *Child Dependency*, pp. 81-82.

vention, $270,000 for child welfare work, and $32,550 for handling juvenile delinquency. But to forestall poverty and despair born of periodic or chronic unemployment, of wages too small to support a family, of bodily illness, desertion, or death of the wage-earner—to name only the most frequent causes of destitution—demanded far-reaching social reforms that professional social workers could not initiate, conservative local citizens were loath to embrace, and more daring Washingtonians felt sure this bi-racial community would not support. In the earlier years of the century, when Washington was smaller and less heterogeneous, laymen such as John Joy Edson, S. W. Woodward, and B. Pickman Mann, together with professionals such as Charles Weller, Walter Ufford, and George Kober, had constantly sought ways of eradicating the underlying causes of social ills. Congressional inaction had blocked their programs. By the mid-twenties Weller had long been gone; Woodward and Mann were dead; Edson, Ufford, and Kober were old and tired. In the next decade women would gradually show initiative, but in the 1920's Mrs. Cross, the frail septuagenarian Mrs. Archibald Hopkins, and the other valiant fighters were handicapped by their sex, and the Voteless League of Women Voters supported but did not originate constructive proposals. Vigorous wide-ranging civic leadership had thus largely vanished.[7]

Whereas a considerable body of liberal local opinion before the war had urged social legislation upon unwilling congresses, in the 1920's successive congresses were ready to go further than was most of the articulate local public, especially the business community. As the decade wore on, the Monday Evening Club itself, once the advocate of measures so sweeping as to win it a reputation for dangerous radicalism, showed only lukewarm

[7] *Prelim Rpt Comee of 100 on the Federal City*, p. 60; *Survey*, LI, 387-88; *Rpt B/Ch*, 1923, pp. 6, 100, 1924; Min As Ch, 45th Anniversary Meeting, 22 Mar, and 12 Apr 1926, 14 May 1928; *Rpt B/PW*, 1927, pp. 6, 53-54, 56, 1929, pp. 19, 73; *Star*, 3 Mar 1926.

interest in new approaches to social problems. In 1920 Congress enacted a District minimum wage law for women, an act hailed by social workers throughout the country as a great forward step. The District Merchants' and Manufacturers' Association, which in 1917 and 1918 had endorsed the scheme, now protested at its application to mercantile establishments; and, ironically enough, it was a suit brought by the trustees of the Children's Hospital, Washington's most popular and widely supported private charity, that ended in the famous *Adkins* v. *Children's Hospital* decision declaring the minimum wage law unconstitutional. When Congress passed a District workmen's compensation act in 1928, the Board of Trade objected to its terms, although the obligations put upon employers were moderate compared to the provisions of some state laws.

In actuality the social legislation passed in the 1920's for the District of Columbia merely paralleled that already in force in many states: a new, more comprehensive child labor law and a strengthened compulsory education law, expansion of the school nursing corps and free dental and medical inspection clinics in connection with the public school system, and, perhaps most significant of all, a mother's pension act such as B. Pickman Mann had recommended in 1914. Furthermore, Congress voted appropriations for an institution for the feeble-minded and for a receiving home for children who were under Juvenile Court surveillance but not yet assigned to foster homes or institutions. If the larger proportion of representation for urbanized areas in House and Senate partly explained the changed temper of Congress, the social vision of the senators and representatives who held key positions on the District committees and appropriations subcommittee was more directly responsible. They were the same men who backed the National Capital Park and Planning Commission; they acted upon the principle Frederic A. Delano enunciated in 1924, that "in our desire to make the city *beautiful* we do not forget the multifarious needs of our population." The backsliding in popular local support presumably stemmed not only from the pervasive hedonism of the period and an accompanying disbelief in the reality of want in the midst of plenty, but also from large taxpayers' irritation at having Congress put new expenses upon them while it cut the federal share in District appropriations from 40 percent to 27 percent or less; if men on the Hill wanted to recast the District's social structure, let the Treasury help pay for it.[8]

The civic irresponsibility visible in Washington's affluent society troubled only a small group. Except where death had thinned its ranks, its nucleus was still the handful of men and women who from Charles Weller's day onward had led the fight to make the capital an ideal city. In the disorganized community of the 1920's public opinion was no longer a force in recruiting members of the younger generation. Chance brought Coleman Jennings into the struggle. A gay young bachelor about town, he had been oblivious to the city's problems until after his father's death, when Walter Ufford, a friend and admirer of the selfless older Jennings, gave the grief-stricken son a subscription to the *Survey* in his father's memory. Touched by that kindness, the young man began dipping into the journal. It opened his eyes to conditions he had not believed possible, led him to follow in his father's philanthropic footsteps, and brought him into close touch with the work of the Associated Charities. Together with a few contemporaries, notably Charles Carroll Glover, Newbold Noyes, and the somewhat older Edward Graham, Jennings threw himself into the task of awakening Washingtonians to the city's plight.

Although the 511 families on the Associated Charities' relief

[8] *Monday Evening Club Yearbook*, 1930; *Rpts B/Tr*, 1921, p. 62, 1926, p. 63, 1927; "District Minimum Wage Law," *Survey*, XLVI, 425, and XLVIII, 537; Florence Kelly, "Is the Minimum Wage Unconstitutional?" *ibid.*, L, 74; "The Fifteenth Compensation Law," *ibid.*, LX, 427; Elizabeth Brandeis, "Mercantile Wages in the District of Columbia," *Monthly Labor Review*, XV, 343-44; "Child Labor Law of the District of Columbia," *ibid.*, XXVII, 66-68; *Rpt B/PW*, 1927, p. 5, 1929, p. 3; Comrs Rpt, 1927, p. 2, 1928, p. 41; *Civic Comment*, No. 8, pp. 4-5.

rolls in 1927 represented only a small fraction of the District's 450,000 inhabitants, the fact remained that the help available to the destitute was always too little—generally half to a third less per capita than the sums spent in other cities. Furthermore, calls for direct financial aid were steadily mounting, in spite of Washington's outer mien of material abundance. While the Catholic Charities, organized in 1921, attempted to assist all Catholic applicants, and the Hebrew charities, as for years past, assumed responsibility for needy Jewish families, in a decade during which population increased about 30 percent and the cost of living about 18, Associated Charities' expenditures for direct relief more than tripled. The implications for the future were disturbing. But to persuade people secure in their own comfortable world to accept and ponder such unpleasant facts was hard at best and made immeasurably harder by the reluctance of white citizens to give any serious thought to colored Washington where want was concentrated. Unimaginative residents of white neighborhoods preferred not to hear anything about Negroes. And even the kindly disposed white who ventured into an impoverished solidly black area was likely to feel oppressed by its strange alien quality and shrink from taking any responsibility for improving it.[9]

In 1920 and early 1921 racial toleration had seemed to be regaining some of the headway lost after the Reconstruction era. Whether, as some colored men believed, Negroes' resistance to aggression at the time of the race riot of 1919 had won them grudging respect from whites and thus laid the basis of understanding, or whether the earnest endeavors of social workers before the war had at last begun to bear fruit, a new spirit of friendliness had appeared in the bi-racial Community Services and Council of Social Workers. Republican campaign promises

[9] Min CSA, 1921-29; Min As Ch, Joint Meeting with Citizens Relief Association, 12 May 1926, pp. 5-6, 13 Oct 1926, p. 3, 9 Mar 1927, pp. 1-3, 7, and 52nd Anniversary Meeting, 26 Feb 1934, pp. 2-4; interview Coleman Jennings; Douglas, *Real Wages*, p. 377.

and President Harding's inaugural speech had further encouraged hopes for a gradual revival of the attitudes of the early 1870's when, outside the schools and most of the churches, segregation had hardly existed at all. Those hopes were short-lived. By 1922 white acceptance of racial discrimination as a fact of life in the capital had become nearly universal. Some northerners doubtless deplored the consequences—the needless hurt to the pride of a distinguished colored man, the lack of care provided for the small Negro orphan, the persistent stifling of Negro ambition—but they, like native southerners, apparently thought the existing social order immutable.

If bootleggers and other elements of the underworld ignored color lines, the only places in the rest of the city where racial segregation did not obtain were on the trolleys and buses, at the Griffith Stadium, and in the reading rooms of the public library and the Library of Congress. When one of the "Senators" knocked out a home-run, white and black rooters in the stadium bleachers delightedly slapped each other on the back and together discussed the team's prospects. Although no colored player was allowed on the team, when Washington won the pennant in 1924, the *Daily American* wrote: "Long live King Baseball, the only monarch who recognizes no color line." In the libraries, Negroes might read and study in peace alongside whites, a circumstance, a Washington-born Negro scholar recalled, that alone had prevented his pursuing the path of a Richard Wright in his hatred of all white America.

Had the ratio of Negro to white inhabitants risen sharply during and after the war, the tightening of segregation in Washington might be easier to explain. Between 1910 and 1920 Chicago's and Detroit's colored populations had grown respectively nearly seven and six times as fast as their white, and the change had been only less pronounced in four or five other northern cities. All of them confronted an unfamiliar social and economic problem. For Washington a large Negro population was no novelty. Here, moreover, the proportion of Negroes to whites had dropped in a decade from the 28.5 percent of 1910 to 25.1, and, with the exception of 1920, the 27.1 percent of 1930 was below the figure shown in any census since the Civil War. White fears of being swamped in a black metropolis therefore had less validity than formerly. But Negroes' slightly improved economic position threatened to lessen the supply of cheap domestic and unskilled labor and, more important, by enlarging the Negro middle class, jeopardized the social status of lower class whites. Seemingly the best way for whites to minimize their discomfiture was to build an invisible wall about all colored Washington and then to forget about the inhabitants of that Secret City.[10]

Probably that walling off helped reduce overt white hostility to colored people. Certainly open friction tended to die down as Negro militance, weakened by frustration and fatigue, subsided. Negro crime and its obverse, police brutality, netted relatively scant space in the newspapers. The white press in 1922 allotted only two or three lines to the "silent parade" of 1,500 Negroes in wordless protest against southern lynchings, but the organization of a local Ku Klux Klan also failed to make a stir in the white city. While the showy parade of National Klansmen led by the Grand Kleagle and the exercises held on the Monument grounds in July 1925 caused the Negro community anxiety, white onlookers regarded the performance as merely a variation of the Shriners' convention held three years before. No white newspaper suggested any impropriety in permitting a formal gathering of the Klan in the capital. White Washington simply ignored Negroes as long as they did not get under foot.

Much of official Washington in November 1921 had watched Marshal Foch receive an honorary degree from Howard Uni-

[10] *Washington Daily American*, 9 Oct 1924, 13 Oct 1925; *Fifteenth Rpt NAACP*, 1924, pp. 21-23; Louise V. Kennedy, *The Negro Peasant Turns Cityward*, p. 34.

versity, "while scores of veterans of colored regiments who had served under the French military leader in the World War stood at attention." But the impressive ceremony had not inspired President Harding to appoint colored men to office. A year after his inauguration only three had received posts of any consequence; Negroes in civil service jobs were more fully segregated and all Negroes more rigidly excluded from the city's public recreational facilities than during the Wilson regime. Full realization of the situation came at the dedication of the Lincoln Memorial on Decoration Day in 1922. Dr. Robert Moten, president of Tuskegee Institute, had been invited to speak at the unveiling of the bronze of the Great Emancipator, but, instead of being placed on the speaker's platform, he was relegated along with other distinguished colored people to an all-Negro section separated by a road from the rest of the audience; and the language of the ill-tempered Marine who herded the "niggers" into their seats caused well-bred colored people as much indignation as the segregated seating itself. Chief Justice Taft's later explanation that the arrangement had not had official sanction failed to modify colored Washington's view: no Negro could hope to be treated as a full-fledged American citizen as long as the White House, Congress, and the overwhelming majority of the city's white residents looked upon him as a creature apart and inferior.[11]

That state of affairs underwent little change under the two succeeding Presidents. Only three colored men received desirable posts from Coolidge or Hoover, and one of those appointees, James Cobb, merely succeeded to the municipal judgeship that Robert Terrell held till his death. The federal commissioner of buildings and grounds who attempted to segregate the picnic places in Rock Creek Park and who sanctioned the Ku Klux Klan gathering on public property met with only one rebuke: when

[11] *Tribune*, 21 May, 25 Jun, 16 Jul 1921, 18 Feb, 27 May, 10, 13, 17 Jun 1922, 24 Jan, 14 Apr 1923; *Herald*, 9, 25 Jan, 16 Jul 1923; 4 Dec 1924; *Star*, 17 Nov 1921.

he barred Negroes from the public bathing beach at the Tidal Basin, Representative Martin Madden of Illinois, chairman of the House Committee on Appropriations, indignantly insisted that Congress cut off funds and close the beach altogether. At the end of 1926 the *Tribune*, by then Washington's principal colored newspaper, declared that segregation had "grown to the dimensions of a national policy." As a working arrangement it was in full force in the government departments, and "it remains only to observe that the Negroes themselves have about reached the stage of acquiescence in the practise." Colored civil service employees, fearful of losing their jobs, refused to lodge complaints, leaving NAACP officials without provable grounds for protest. The major gratification the colored intelligentsia had that year was the Howard University trustees' selection of a Negro president, Mordecai Johnson.

Uneasiness lest an organized Negro vote in the northern states put Al Smith into the White House led to a slight relaxation of departmental segregation rules in 1928, but civil service policies did not change. The Department of Labor published statistics contrasting the number of the government's Negro employees in 1928 and 1910: some 51,880 at salaries totalling nearly $64,484,000 compared to fewer than 23,000 paid less than $12,456,000. The *Crisis* promptly noted that laborers, charwomen, and messengers, earning on the average $1,243 a year, still made up the bulk of the list; well-paid jobs for Negroes were actually fewer than in 1910. When Oscar De Priest of Chicago was elected to the House of Representatives, colored morale rose a little; and it rose higher when Mrs. Hoover invited his wife to a White House reception with a small, carefully chosen group of other congressional wives. But otherwise the first Negro to be elected to Congress in twenty-five years could do little for the local community. In 1929 when at long last a published code of laws for the District of Columbia appeared, it did not mention the sixty-year-old ordinances and the territorial acts prohibiting racial discrimination, although those had never been repealed or declared unconstitutional. The NAACP's drive that stopped Senate confirmation of Judge Parker of North Carolina as an Associate Justice of the Supreme Court seemed to colored Washington a negative triumph, at best a block to new inroads upon civil rights.[12]

Outraged as were Washington's upper-class Negroes at segregated seating at concerts where Negro singers as famous as Roland Hayes performed, they regarded housing restrictions as peculiarly invidious. In 1926 the District Supreme Court upheld the legality of voluntary covenants among white property-owners aimed at preventing Negroes from purchasing or occupying houses in white neighborhoods. The battle against restrictive municipal ordinances had been won before the war; now voluntary compacts seemingly negated that victory and threatened to confine all Negroes to a true ghetto. As whites endorsing the covenants displayed as much passion as the Negroes who sought to halt them, ill-will between the races grew. Kelly Miller, professor of sociology at Howard University, contended that since white people were determined to prevent racial intermarriage, the "destiny of the Negro population in large cities is clearly foreshadowed. The Negro is to live and move and have his social being in areas apart from the whites." Yet, as Miller himself pointed out, tempting offers from colored men sometimes overcame white resistance: only a year after the Supreme Court verdict the "very block that was the subject of the test case in Washington is now occupied by negroes, in uncontested tenancy, although the court decision forbids persons of negro blood to buy or live in that block for a period of twenty-one years." Long afterward, Campbell C. Johnson, in the 1920's secretary of the colored YMCA, looked back upon

[12] *Tribune*, 2 Jul, 31 Dec 1926, 25 Jan, 14 Jun 1929; *Crisis*, xxxv, 337, 369-87, 418, 427, xxxvi, 298-99; Walter A. White, *A Man Called White*, pp. 110-11; Indritz, "Post Civil War Ordinances," *Georgetown Law Journal*, xlii, 201; William H. Jones, *Recreation and Amusements among Negroes in Washington*.

the fight against residential segregation as a constructive move, for the men who sued for their right to live wherever they could afford raised a banner around which other colored Washingtonians gathered; and when the court ruling made further litigation useless, their continued efforts to stop the spread of restrictive covenants contributed to reviving self-respect.[13]

If the housing controversy rekindled the sparks of racial pride, the embers had burned too low since 1921 to burst quickly into flame. Furthermore, as the covenants affected only well-to-do Negroes, the conflict did not reawaken in Washington's high yellow society its wartime zeal to "close ranks" with its social inferiors. On the contrary, civic-minded Negroes encountered among their educated fellows the same kind of indifference to the welfare of the black masses as public-spirited white people met with in high white society. By 1926 the Washington NAACP was no longer powerful. Some Negroes thought it too radical, others too conservative and too prone to appease; a good many gave it no thought at all. With a few rare exceptions, young men upon whom leadership might logically have fallen lacked the will or had lost faith in their capacity to win a respected place for their people. Negro real estate brokers and firms building Negro apartment houses made some money, and the National Life Insurance Company with three hundred employees in its home office on U Street paid a 10 percent dividend in 1928, but confidence in other Negro enterprises waned. When a Harvard graduate, after a distinguished but heart-breaking career in the AEF, became a convert to the necessity of never-ending Negro militance, he started the *Washington Daily American*, the second Negro daily in the United States; despite

[13] *Crisis*, XXVIII, 271-72, XXIX, 19, 27; *Tribune*, 1 Nov 1924, 9, 16 May 1925, 8 Jan 1926, 2, 9 Mar 1928, 18 Jan, 25 Oct 1929; Kelly Miller, "The Causes of Segregation," and Herbert J. Seligman, "The Negro Protest against Ghetto Conditions," *Current History*, XXV, 827-33; William H. Jones, *The Housing of Negroes in Washington, D.C.*; Bernard H. Nelson, *The Fourteenth Amendment and the Negro since 1920*, pp. 23, 31, 34; interview, Col. Johnson; "Housing of Negroes in Washington, D.C.," *Monthly Labor Review*, XXX, 972.

its excellence, the paper was unable to get enough advertising to survive. The *Tribune* absorbed it. Between the lines of newspaper exhortations to "buy Negro," give to Negro charities, and build up a self-sufficient community ran hints that calls for racial solidarity fell on deaf ears.

Upper-class families, tired of making common cause with needy blacks, washed their hands of every group but their own. Lightness of color was necessarily a bond, for where light-skinned people could move about in a white world with some freedom, the acceptance of a dark-skinned person into the group circumscribed the activities of all. It was a fact of life white people never had to face. Whites prone to think Negro social distinctions absurd lost sight of the obvious truth that the cultivated Negro had no more in common with the lower-class black than the white society leader with the white ditch-digger. The creed of the high yellow elite ran: let the uninformed masses applaud Marcus Garvey, "the Black Moses," or gather adoringly about "Papa Divine." Let the vulgar loaf on 7th Street, that "bastard of Prohibition and the War," where, sang Jean Toomer,

> Money burns the pocket, pocket hurts,
> Bootleggers in silken shirts,
> Ballooned, zooming Cadillacs,
> Whizzing, whizzing down the streetcar tracks.

All that need not touch the aristocracy. The very light-colored group, on the other hand, was frequently involved with "passing." Former associates of the person who chose to pass were at pains not to betray him; his success rarely provoked resentment: the joke after all was on the white folks. Morality was in no way involved. Tacit agreement among old friends decreed that each must decide what was right for himself. Passing was so common in the twenties that the National Theatre employed a black door man to spot and bounce intruders whose racial origins were undetectable by whites. And no Negro despised the door man for earning his living in that fashion; a job was a job.[14] Still, passing tended to disrupt the solidarity of the top level of Washington's colored world.

Washington during most of the 1920's was thus more nearly a geographic expression than a community. In addition to the rigorously maintained separateness of whites and Negroes in every lawful walk of life, seemingly unbridgeable gulfs yawned between class and class, between clique and clique, and between cave-dwellers and upstarts in both white and colored Washington. Self-styled Christians disliked association with Jews; Jews were wary of Gentiles. Some 70,000 white men, so the A.F.ofL. stated, were union members in good standing, but, in this non-industrial city, working men's problems had no reality for businessmen, politicians, and civil service employees. Here labor meant the building trades whose walking delegates dealt with contractors. The rumblings of trouble in the rest of the country over wage-earners' pay rates, hours, and the occasional timid proposals for unemployment insurance sounded faint in the District of Columbia. And, as always, a subtly divisive factor was the uncertainty about who was a Washingtonian and therefore responsible for developing community feeling, if indeed it were worth striving for. How so disorganized a city could achieve any sense of common purpose borders on a historical mystery. Yet in 1928 the miracle began to take form.

The awakening was primarily the cumulative result of the patient campaign conducted by the remnants of the old guard of the civic betterment movement and its few younger converts. Little by little they convinced some of their neighbors that the city's ills were not imaginary and that only a concerted attack upon them could provide a remedy. A slowly growing realiza-

[14] *Tribune*, 11 Apr 1925, 12 Aug, 30 Dec 1927, 18 Jan, 9, 30 Mar 1928, 1, 25 Nov 1929; *Crisis*, XXXI, 11-16, XXXIII, 186-87, XXXIV, 193, 212, 224; Eugene Davidson, *Black Boy on a Raft*; interview Eugene Davidson; Jean Toomer, *Cane*, p. 71; Caleb Johnson, "Crossing the Color Line," *Outlook*, CLVIII, 526-57.

tion that everyone, not merely the poverty-stricken, benefitted wherever a neighborhood spirit could be nursed into life also had some effect, as the community centers under school board direction came into wider use for amateur theatricals and other group pastimes. Possibly the sheer passage of time brought about a desire for unity among people living in geographical propinquity. Whatever the reason, a nascent revival of community consciousness began to emerge in 1928. Although overburdened professional social workers made no attempt to teach classes of volunteers, laymen set themselves to examining problems they had long ignored or never thought about. If they were useless as case-workers, they could at least raise money. The Board of Trade, determined to have business efficiency directing enthusiasm, engaged Elwood Street, an experienced fund-raiser from St. Louis, to organize a Community Chest in Washington.

The effect of Street's arrival and the announcement of his plan of action was electrical. To the dismay of lily-whites, he stated that this must be a united effort of the entire city, not of white Washington working apart from colored Washington; representatives of both races must meet and participate as equals. Accordingly at the initial organizing luncheon, for the first time in the memory of most people present, prominent white Washingtonians sat at the table alongside leading colored Washingtonians. No one protested then or later. That in itself gave the undertaking an element of drama. Frederic Delano accepted the presidency of the Chest, Kelly Miller the vice presidency. Equally valuable in creating a sense of common purpose as preparations moved forward was the exchange of information that went on week after week among organizations anxious to join the Chest. The benefits of that give-and-take, far in excess of anything the Council of Social Agencies had achieved, long outlasted the fund-raising campaign. In a fashion perhaps incomprehensible to cities where periodic political campaigns gave electorates a common albeit hydra-headed

17. President Wilson addressing Congress, April 2, 1917, to ask for a declaration of war

18. War workers' dormitories under construction in the Union Station Plaza, October 1918

19. Eminent Washingtonians: top (left to right) Gardiner Hubbard, John Joy Edson, Librarian of Congress Herbert Putnam; center, Commissio Louis Brownlow; bottom (to right) Archibald Grin Mary Church Terrell, fessor Kelly Miller

20. Bonus Army on the Capitol grounds, 1932

21. General Glassford inspecting Camp Marks

22. "Tiny Veterans" and posters at Camp Marks

23. Ku Klux Klan Parade, 1925

24. The Elder Lightfoot Michaux baptizing his sheep in water from the River Jordan, ca. 1938

25. Alley dwellings near the Capitol in Dingman Place, where four-room tenements with outdoor water taps and privies rented at about $15 a month each

26. Schott's Alley with the Senate Office Building in the background

27. Federal triangle, looking west along Constitution Avenue from 10th Street

28. At the zoo

29. National Symphony Orchestra Concert at the Watergate, 1938

30. Art show in Lafayette Square, ca. 1938

interest, Washington found herself for the first time in more than half a century absorbed by a single community objective. Temporary residents joined with natives in the fund-raising. Although the first drive did not quite go over the top, the heady discovery that the city could unite even briefly was exhilarating.

The change, to be sure, was neither so sudden nor so profound as ill-informed optimists believed. Years of work by a dedicated few had prepared the way. The Associated Charities and the Council of Social Agencies from 1921 onward had maintained a narrow, somewhat insubstantial bridge between white and colored Washington; individuals had tried to widen it. In December 1928 two hundred delegates representing some eighteen social service and interracial organizations throughout the country met in Washington under the sponsorship of the Social Science Research Council to discuss the statistical data assembled on race relations by Graham Taylor of Chicago and Charles S. Johnson of Fisk University, but the sessions had ended without producing any positive scheme of action. In 1929 the managers of the Associated Charities were still not ready to act upon the long-debated proposal to elect Negroes to the board. Although the Washington Federation of Churches in 1927 had commissioned William H. Jones, a young colored sociologist, to prepare a study of that most controversial problem, Negro housing, the federation rejected the arguments of Canon Anson Phelps Stokes of the National Cathedral, Richard W. Brooks, Negro pastor of the Lincoln Congregational Church, William Jernegin of the Fifteenth Street Colored Presbyterian Church, and some eleven other ministers of both races urging the admission of colored churches to membership. At the gala dinner held at the Mayflower Hotel to wind up the first Community Chest campaign, Elwood Street bowed to local mores: Kelly Miller did not dine with his white associates but, accompanied by Mrs. Street, came in afterward to make his report. The Community Chest scored its chief triumph in pricking the conscience of white people and arousing in colored people a deeper interest in Negro charities, but the immediate effect of the campaign on interracial collaboration was slight.[15]

Too many white people merely displayed condescension in new form, marvelling at their own broadmindedness in recognizing human attributes in the Negro. That he might respond to the question "What do colored people want?" with the blunt answer "Get out of our way" was an idea well-meaning whites could not yet grasp. Six months after the first Chest drive ended, Richard Brooks summarized Washington's situation as he saw it: economic conditions were uncertain, morals "blatantly corrupt," and race relations marked by more mutual ill-will than ever.[16] Yet thirty years later wise men, both white and colored, averred that the launching of the Community Chest was a turning point; from that moment the gulf between the races began to close, and the end of the 1950's would find Washington more nearly genuinely integrated than any big city in the country.

[15] Min CSA, 14 May 1928 to 11 Nov 1929; Min As Ch, 1928-30; "Street Accepts the Challenge," *Survey*, LX, 507; "Local and National," *ibid.*, LXI, 429; William H. Jones, *Housing of Negroes*, Preface; *Tribune*, 18 Oct, 1 Nov 1929; *American Journal of Sociology*, XXXV, 902.

[16] *Tribune*, 15 Nov 1929.

CHAPTER XVII

THE ROLE OF THE PUBLIC SCHOOLS, 1920-1941

ODDLY enough, amid the disintegrative forces at work in the city of the 1920's, interest in the public schools survived to provide a bond among Washington's disparate elements—"oddly," because the school system itself was dual, because citizens had no real control over it, and because the good private schools in the city might well have diverted the attention of well-to-do parents from public to private education. The depth and enlightened nature of concern, it is true, varied from time to time and from social class to social class, but the remarkable fact is that, sophisticated or naïve, wealthy or financially hard pressed, Washingtonians continued to keep a hawk-like watch over public school developments.[1] Although that watchfulness often produced scanty results, it probably prevented the further erosion of community feeling by perpetuating in one realm a sense of common purpose. It even transcended the color line, separate though the white schools were from the Negro. Consensus about how to reach the common goal was as rare as concepts were various about what constituted an ideal school, but unanimity endured for more than a decade about the over-all civic objective: to secure for Washington the best system of public education human wisdom could devise. That the intensity of interest waned in the mid-thirties may be attributed partly to premature belief in a victory already assured, but was probably also a consequence of a draining of community vitality as national affairs submerged local.

A good many American communities, the federal Commis-

[1] See the comments of the committee on schools in *Rpts B/Tr*, 1920-1930, and the lists of contributors to school projects in "School Achievements in Ten Years, July 1, 1920 to June 30, 1930," *Rpt B/Ed*, 1930, pp. 83-84 (hereafter cited as "School Achievements," 1930).

sioner of Education had implied in 1910, had come to take their public schools for granted. A statistical sampling he presented that year indicated that more than half the students enrolled in normal schools came from families in the middle and upper economic brackets of society and hence, inferentially, from home environments friendly to "that culture which should characterize the teacher." But, the commissioner warned, unless school boards raised teachers' salaries above the average of $57 a month and insisted upon better professional training, the standards of public education would sink below a level already "lamentable" in a number of towns and cities. Whether meagre pay and an accompanying loss of social standing did notably lessen the calibre of public school teaching in the course of the next generation is not susceptible of proof; that the public believed that a decline set in is clear from the chorus of dismay which arose with the discovery in the 1920's that gifted college graduates were no longer willing to embark upon school-teaching careers.[2] Some later comments suggested that the post-1910 proliferation of state requirements of courses in methodology preliminary to teacher certification, so far from raising standards, acted as a deterrent in the recruitment of able candidates. In most big cities, furthermore, as the impersonality of metropolitan life spread, tenuous evidence pointed to a loss of close collaboration between parents and teachers; the former tended to consider their responsibility ended where that of the latter began—at the school threshold. Wherever that change occurred, school questions took on meaning to the rank and file of citizens only when a crisis led them to conclude that they were paying a high price for an inferior brand of education for their children. In Washington that kind of inattention to the school system had not existed since the early 1870's.

From 1874 onward District citizens had had little say about school policies, and still less about expenditures. The Organic

[2] *Report*, *U.S. Commissioner of Education*, 1910, II, xxvi, 677; Bureau of Education, *Biennial Survey of Education*, 1920, p. 50.

Acts of 1874 and 1878 forbade bond issues; schoolhouse building, like all other public projects, stood on a pay-as-you-go basis; Congress fixed every detail of the budget. In 1900 the Board of Education won the right to choose the superintendent and the white and the colored assistant superintendents, and in 1906 a new law vested in the judges of the District's Supreme Court the appointment of the board's nine members, by custom, six white and three colored. But while the board thereafter set educational policies within budgetary limitations, its executive authority remained slight. Private citizens had no direct power at all. Yet their impassioned protests over any suspected neglect of the schools had had effect more than once. The reorganizations of 1900 and 1906 had grown out of popular demand for administrative changes. Over the years, despite the legal handicaps of the District's voteless residents, they had exerted enough influence to give some substance to their belief that the schools were their creation.

Although the city was the headquarters of the federal Office of Education, the National Education Association, and, after 1919, the American Council on Education, nothing suggests that Washingtonians as a whole were more knowledgeable than other Americans about curricula, teaching methods, physical plant and equipment, or the intangibles calculated to give every child a chance to develop his potentialities to the utmost. Nevertheless here parents, childless taxpayers, teachers, administrators, and clerks, all had opinions on these subjects. Perhaps financial impotence intensified interest, for as long as Congress decreed how much local tax money should go for any purpose, everyone could indulge in sensible or crack-pot suggestions without risking the consequence of having them put to the test. More probably criticisms of the school system in curious fashion served as an outlet for civic impulses that in other cities found expression in local politics.

Pride in what they had accomplished reinforced Washingtonians' proprietary attitude toward the public schools. Thanks to Superintendent William Bramwell Powell, at the opening of the twentieth century the capital's schools had attained an excellence that justified pride. Powell's three immediate successors had undertaken few significant changes except for emphasizing vocational training, a development that Congress had encouraged by appropriating money to build the white McKinley Technical High School and the colored Armstrong High School in 1902 and to enlarge the former in 1912. While fuming about congressional parsimony that severely limited new schoolhouse construction and necessitated half-day sessions in many elementary grades, parents and members of the Board of Education had on the whole continued to feel satisfied. Parents who would have preferred to forego private schooling for their small children sometimes had succumbed because of the doubling up in the public school primary grades, but in the higher grades patronage of private schools dropped rapidly. Teaching was reportedly unusually good at the long-established coeducational Sidwell Friends School, the much younger St. Alban's Episcopal School for boys, and the well-staffed expensive boarding- and day-schools such as the Convent of the Visitation, Miss Madeira's and the National Cathedral School for girls, but the number of local children enrolled in private schools had remained small.[3] In the 1950's old Washingtonians in looking back on the years before World War I would insist that "everybody went to the public schools in those days."

Colored people, to be sure, resented an arrangement whereby their children not infrequently were accommodated in somewhat dilapidated school-houses which, originally built for whites, were converted to Negro use when population shifts changed the racial character of neighborhoods. In fact, Washington Negroes looked upon the entire system as more separate than

[3] *Rpts B/Ed*, 1902-1914. Tables in the *Biennial Survey* show year after year that private school enrollments, including parochial schools, declined progressively above the primary grades.

equal, but that very fact heightened their gratification over the achievements of their own schools. They faced little competition from private or parochial schools. At the M Street High School, the principal, Dr. Winfield Scott Montgomery, a Phi Beta Kappa of the class of 1878 at Dartmouth, had gathered together an extraordinarily inspired and inspiring group of teachers; before 1916 scores of their students had gone on to Howard University or to good northern colleges and thence in some cases to pursue professional careers. No other single colored school in the country had turned out so many promising graduates. Ambitious Negro families occasionally had moved to Washington solely to enable their children to attend there. The Paul Dunbar High School, which replaced it in 1916, had also made its mark. While elementary schools had a less outstanding record, performance had at least equalled that in any other city that maintained a racially segregated system.[4] For two generations pride in the schools had gone further than any other social force in cementing colored Washington into a community. The prestige commanded by Negro public school teachers fortified the class structure but at the same time offered incentive to the gifted, industrious, lower-class Negro child to qualify for the honored position of teacher.

World War I had cost the white schools more than the colored. Both had suffered from inflation and from congressional disregard of local needs as long as there was a war to be won, but the relatively high-salaried war jobs that had stripped the white schools of a number of competent teachers had not siphoned off Negro teachers. Furthermore, although a considerable part of the war influx consisted of single women and men unaccompanied by their families, between 1917 and 1919 enrollment in the white schools, built to accommodate about 36,000 pupils, had jumped to over 44,300, whereas the colored schools had lost about 800. In casting about for ways of shoring

[4] *Crisis*, xxxv, 376; Dr. Rayford Logan to the author, 14 Jun 1960.

up the educational structure, Superintendent Thurston had encouraged the formation of parent-teacher associations, while the Board of Education, with the backing of the other civic organizations, had sponsored the use of school buildings and grounds as community recreation centers. The latter scheme, rather elaborately worked out with representatives of the citizens' associations in the neighborhoods involved, had served the transient adult population well, but had not lessened the difficulty of educating an increasing number of children in badly understaffed white schools, taught by discouraged, under-paid teachers. A parental rebellion probably explains why 1919 had found over 18 percent of Washington's school population entered in parochial and other private schools; a decade before the figure had stood below 10 percent. Thurston had tried to stem the tide by introducing junior high schools, an innovation that promised, in addition to other benefits, to reduce the congestion in the grammar grades and the four-year high schools. But the opening of one white and one colored junior high school in 1919 had slight immediate effect, and in the meantime "Americanization" classes for aliens started on a small scale that summer added another item of expense. By 1920 citizens were up in arms over the deterioration of the educational system.

An outraged public blamed Superintendent Thurston and Assistant Superintendent Bruce for most of the shortcomings in schools long starved for appropriations. Unjust though some of the criticism was, Thurston's timidity, coupled with charges that he lacked intellectual grasp, and Bruce's maladroit handling of human relations convinced the Board of Education that both men must go, the superintendent at once, his assistant somewhat later. Thurston's successor, Frank W. Ballou, former Assistant Superintendent of Schools in Boston, came with his eyes open. The Board of Education had warned him that he would inherit a large backlog of financial problems, would have to deal with congressional committees in solving them, might encounter some animosity from Thurston's friends, and in any case would have to establish a working relationship with an assistant superintendent of the colored schools and satisfy colored Washington. Gradually Ballou would prove himself able to clear every hurdle but the last. White people would look back upon his twenty-three year superintendency with gratitude; Negroes would merely state tersely that, among colored people, Ballou came to be the most hated man in the District of Columbia.

Short in stature, his slightly round face lengthened by a close-clipped black imperial, his rather protuberant eyes shadowed by heavy brows, Ballou looked like Mephistopheles in modern dress; but his outer mien gave little hint of his immovable determination to rebuild an antiquated school system into an effective educational machine. A Ph.D. in education from Harvard, years spent in responsible posts in the Cincinnati and Boston schools, and money inherited from a first wife had imbued him with a self-confidence that bordered on arrogance. He was as ready to contradict an ill-informed congressman at a school appropriation hearing as to rebuke an inept subordinate or to belittle the wisdom of a member of the Board of Education who disagreed with him. But his very imperviousness to criticism, his open disdain of stupidity, and his disregard of other people's feelings were assets to him in a tough job. His experience, particularly in the field of educational testing, was wide, his knowledge of educational theory extensive—and he charted his course on the basis of both. People who disliked him acutely as a person admitted that he was capable. And recognition of his competence revived their faith in the school system.[5] He waited till he had studied Washington's problems thoroughly before presenting his analysis of what was basically wrong. In 1922 he appended

[5] Comrs Rpts, 1917, I, 20, 1918, I, 19, 1919, I, 20-21; *Rpts B/Ed*, 1918, p. 11, 1919, p. 186, 1921, p. 101, 1922, pp. 36-39; *Rpt U.S. Comr Ed*, 1910, II, 670, 677, 703; *Biennial Survey*, 1920, pp. 50, 126, 144; Frank W. Ballou, "Junior High Schools in Washington," *NEA Addresses*, LXII, 416-17, 423.

TABLE IV

School Enrollments, 1920-1955*

	1920	1927	1931	1935	1937	1941	1944	1948	1950	1955
Total	77,355	80,882	92,706	106,876	107,723	109,345	103,780	109,198	112,810	124,754**
White										
Non-Cath. Private		2,258	1,907	1,565	1,549	2,287	2,448	2,508	2,682	
R. Catholic		7,713	9,599	11,224	11,822	13,410	12,971	14,088	13,851	
Pub Welfare						46	95	120	76	
Public	45,775	46,865	53,175	59,582	58,793	55,777	49,500	47,801	46,736	38,165**
Total		56,836	64,681	72,371	71,164	71,520	64,919	64,440	63,351	
% pub sch of all wh sch enrlmt	79.1	82.4	82.1	82.3	82.6	77.98	76.17	74.17	72.19	
Colored										
Non-Cath. Private		54	82	86	72	63	75	146	117	
R. Catholic		621	969	777	691	917	1,018	1,182	1,226	
Pub Welfare				144	171	179	188	172	136	
Public	19,523	23,371	26,974	33,498	34,625	36,666	37,768	43,264	47,980	68,877
Total		24,046	28,025	34,505	35,559	37,825	38,861	49,758	49,459	
Consolidation										
Non-Cath. Private	12,057	2,312	1,989	1,651	1,621	2,350	2,513	2,648	2,799	2,325
R. Catholic		8,334	10,568	12,001	12,513	14,327	13,989	15,193	15,083	14,241
Pub Welfare				144	177	225		292	212	543
Public	65,298	70,236	80,149	93,080	93,418	92,443	87,268	91,065	94,716	107,042**
% change in wh pub sch enrlmt		2.38	13.4	12.04	—1.32	—5.13	—11.2	—3.43	—2.22	—18.34

% colored of all pub sch enrlmt	29.89	33.4	33.6	35.9	37.	39.66	43.27	47.60	49.60	64.34
% non-Catholic prvt sch of pub sch enrlmt	18.45	3.29	2.48	1.77	1.73	2.54	2.89	2.90	2.95	2.77
% R. Catholic sch of pub sch enrlmt		11.8	13.1	12.89	13.39	15.49	16.02	16.68	15.92	13.30
% R. Catholic sch of all sch enrlmt		10.3	11.4	11.22	11.61	13.10	13.47	13.91	13.37	11.45

* The 1920 figures derive from the *Comrs Rpt*, 1920, I, 20 and from U.S. Comr of Ed, *Biennial Survey of Ed*, 1920, pp. 50, 126, 144, in which private school data are estimated. The rest of the tabulation is from the official records of the Statistics Dept. of the D.C. public schools. Roman Catholic includes parochial and private Catholic schools. In 1950 school records show 263 children in Hebrew and 96 in Seventh Day Adventist schools and in 1955, 317 in Hebrew, 88 in Seventh Day Adventist schools, who are shown here as entered in private schools. The Board of Public Welfare entry refers to schools at centers maintained by the board for children in its care.

** Exclusive of 603 white students in Americanization classes.

to the report of the school board a section entitled "Why Educational Progress in Washington is so Slow."

Any Washingtonian who had persuaded himself that all that was necessary to restore the public schools to their former high standing was to get larger appropriations and install a new superintendent must have felt shock upon reading that summary. It included the testimony of the United States Commissioner of Education before a congressional committee: "I could go on, as I started, about buildings and teachers' salaries, . . . because any tyro could see the many defects which exist," but even immediate big appropriations would not redeem the schools under the existing administrative system. Overhead organizations so fettered the superintendent that he was practically impotent. "I would not take the job," said the commissioner, "at two or three times the salary." The *Cyclopaedia of Education* noted: "The confusion existing is hardly credible. Authority and responsibility are hopelessly tied up with red tape" unfurled in the District commissioners' offices, the courts, and the United States Treasury. Congress in passing on appropriations could and did change basic policies. "Board of Education" was a misnomer for a board of school visitors. "Education conditions in Washington are among the worst to be found in any city in the Union" from an administrative standpoint. "Until Congress can be made to realize that it is incompetent properly to administer such an undertaking and will give the Board of Education the power and control which should belong to it there is little hope of a good, modern school system for the District of Columbia." Ballou's text spelled out the details.

A recent rigmarole over procuring pens for handwriting classes illustrated one kind of impediment to efficiency. By law, before the District purchasing officer could advertise for bids, the District general supply committee had to ascertain whether any government installation listed a surplus of the wanted item. As the Brooklyn Navy Yard reported an oversupply, the requisition had to go there while the penmanship teachers waited; when the consignment at last arrived, it contained only stub pens useless for instruction of children in the art of Spencerian script. Building repairs, whether requested as "urgent," "necessary," or merely "desirable," had to be approved by the District engineer commissioner, the District health officer, and the fire department before the men in the District repair shop could start; meanwhile roofs might continue to leak, furnaces blow coal gas into classrooms, and decrepit plumbing break down. Repairs to playground equipment, limited by decree of the District auditor to $45 a year for each of the seventy-eight school yards that had such luxuries as swings, seesaws, or backstops for ball games, had to receive the endorsement of the District recreation department. The issuance of work permits fell to the child labor office, the follow-up to the police department. Funds from the school budget paid the salaries for school doctors, nurses, and dentists, but the District health officer supervised their work. Such a minor matter as opening a corrective speech class required an act of Congress. Equally hampering was the authority vested in the Comptroller General, the General Auditing Office of the Treasury, and, by custom, the District auditor, which enabled two or three men to delay or prevent payment for a program already approved by Congress. They even exercised their power to decide which teachers were entitled to the "advanced standing" pay designed for those with special experience and training.

Frustration frequently drove members of the Board of Education to resign. Of the nine who were members when Ballou came in 1920, only three were still acting in 1922; the superintendent did not mention that one man had resigned because of congressional criticism of his connection with a local business firm that advertised its readiness to furnish children with school essays at stipulated prices. The turnover of officials at every level, in fact, interfered with planning and made a consistent educational policy impossible. The District had had seven different commissioners within two years. The Bureau of the Budget, only a year old in 1922, was shortly to get a new director. Three of the five members of the House Subcommittee on District Appropriations were new, and four of the nine members of the Senate District Committee.

Ballou climaxed his report with a recapitulation of the process of obtaining the school appropriation for the fiscal year beginning July 1, 1922. Fifteen months in advance, every principal had prepared a written list of his needs; the superintendents then held hearings to determine which items were indispensable and in July sent the Board of Education a detailed estimate; finding only essentials included, the board transmitted it to the District commissioners, who returned it with orders to cut it by 24 percent. The superintendents reworked the data, and the commissioners, without consulting the school board, sliced off an additional chunk before submitting the request to the Bureau of the Budget. There officials reduced the sum further, and, because the law expressly forbade publication of the figures before they reached Congress, until the House Subcommittee opened hearings on the school budget, private citizens had little inkling of what it contained or what had dropped out. By then time was too short to organize public opinion effectively, despite the strong feeling in the community that teachers' salaries must be raised and several million dollars spent for new buildings. The House pared 10 percent from the Budget Bureau's proposal and, after a compromise with the more generous Senate, voted approximately two-thirds the amount school officials had considered an absolute minimum.[6]

Without attempting to cast off completely the "legislative strait-jacket," as Ballou called the school act of 1906 with its manifold binding restrictions and procedural detail, the superintendent concentrated in 1922 on getting teacher salary in-

[6] *Rpt B/Ed*, 1922, pp. 136-37; *Star*, 1 Jan 1923.

creases, a fixed salary schedule instead of specified amounts in yearly appropriations acts, a revised promotion system, a new compulsory school attendance law with provisions for continual school censuses that would make it enforceable, and free high school text books. Cures for the ills of divided authority and classroom shortages he hoped would follow. Certainly the need for new buildings was obvious. A voluminous congressional report of 1908 had recommended immediate expenditure of $8,880,000 for school sites and buildings. Ten schoolhouses condemned at that time were still in use in 1922, although elementary grades had spilled over into 71 portables, 152 rooms were used in double sessions, classes of forty and fifty children were the rule, and, for lack of other space, pupils were jammed into basement rooms, converted offices, and storerooms in rented buildings. The $6,186,000 appropriated in driblets over the past fourteen years, so far from making up arrears, had not sufficed to keep pace with the growth in the school population; and, in the interim, building costs had risen from 17 cents to 50 cents a cubic foot. In short, school administrators, like the Red Queen, had to run faster and faster to stay where they were.

A good many men on the Hill distrusted local judgment, particularly when any federal money was involved, but fortunately a dozen members of both houses were as intent as school officials on raising Washington's educational standards. Hearings lasted for months. While waiting for Congress to act, PTA's and the District Public School Association, born in 1923, fostered patience, and the Teachers' Institutes, one for white and one for colored, supplied professional self-help through monthly discussions and seminar sessions. When Superintendent Ballou got permission in 1923 to establish a research department in both the white and the colored schools, educational testing and studies of ways to better instruction held out new hope for improvements. Still the legislative mill ground slowly. Not until June 1924 did a bill pass raising teachers' salaries, setting a uniform rate for elementary school teachers similar to that in the high schools, and so ending the cumbersome and wasteful system of the past, whereby a first-grade teacher could get higher pay only by assignment to a second grade, a second-grade teacher only by moving to a third grade, and so on. In contrast to the former top teaching salary of $2,250, the average after 1924 for principals, supervisors, and teachers was $2,350. That rate, together with later adjustments to retirement pay, boosted morale, enabled Ballou to recruit fresh talent, and opened the way to requiring more intensive professional training.

A few months later a rewriting of the school attendance law extended its application to all children between the ages of 6 and 16 and placed supervision of work permits, annual school censuses, and truancy under a school attendance department. And early in 1925 Congress authorized the long-wanted five-year building program that, at an estimated cost of $20,185,000, would supposedly wipe out by June 1930 the accumulated arrearages, ensure space for the yearly increase in enrollment without resorting to double shifts and half-day instruction, cancel dependence upon rented buildings, flimsy portables, and ill-lighted, ill-ventilated rooms, and safeguard against a pupil-teacher ratio of more than forty to one. Elation swept the community. As pride in the school system reached new heights, an overwhelming majority of "non-residents," that is, people who kept their state citizenship and paid taxes elsewhere, followed Washingtonians' example in sending their children to the public schools.[7]

The next five years saw several changes directed chiefly at introducing a moderate "progressivism." "Special" classes multiplied—atypical classes for mentally subnormal children, fresh

[7] Ballou, "Introducing Educational Research into Washington Public Schools," *NEA Addresses*, LXIII, 783-85; Subcomee H and S Dis Comees, 68C, 2S, Jt Hrgs, "Schools and Playgrounds in D.C."; Comrs Rpt, 1925, IV, 56-57, 66-67; *Rpt B/Tr*, 1925, p. 96; *Rpt B/Ed*, 1923, p. 25, 1926, p. 82, and "School Achievements," 1930, pp. 58-59.

air schools for tuberculars, ungraded classes for delinquents and truants, classes for the physically handicapped, night classes, vocational schools, and Americanization classes for adults. Unlike several cities where separate classes for unusually gifted children became a feature, Washington compromised. Standardized intelligence and achievement tests developed by the research department enabled principals to classify children according to capability and assign them to section X, Y, or Z, representing above average, average, and below average groups, respectively. Pupils behind in their work received coaching from "supplementary teachers." And when a research department study of teaching methods showed the wastefulness of repeated arithmetic drills, the Board of Education adopted exercise books that gave each child a chance to set his own pace. Here was an instance of a new flexibility that recognized the differing potentialities of every individual.

Neither Ballou nor the school board accepted the credo of the progressive extremists who twisted John Dewey's dictum, "freedom is achieved through the exercise of intelligence" into the opposite, "intelligence is achieved through the exercise of freedom," a freedom that rejected all discipline. The proof of the pudding was, of course, in the eating. Washington high school graduates who went on to college in the late 1920's found themselves far better prepared than students from most public school systems. Whether that gratifying record was due to superior pre-college teaching or to the richer cultural home background of Washington students did not come under scrutiny. The very fact that upper-class families in the capital sent their children to the public schools testified to a continuing confidence in their quality. Washington administrators believed that children whose education ended in high school or earlier also received as sound schooling as they could get anywhere. When Assistant Superintendent Garnett Wilkinson said that the District's colored schools were the best Negro schools in the United States, his statements stood unchallenged. The PTA's took credit for some of the achievements; others were due to experiments undertaken in Washington by national organizations, such as the National Research Council's Committee on Child Development.

Although Congress allowed the building program to lag and did nothing about physical education and medical care, some money was forthcoming for a few school libraries, and, when the "city council" authorized the conversion of the white and the colored normal schools to four-year teachers' colleges, the Board of Education made three, instead of two, years of professional training the prerequisite for a teaching post. Belief that "the progressive school of today cannot consider itself apart from the current of every-day affairs" inspired supervisors, principals, and teachers to direct instruction less at instilling facts into pupils and improving their skills than at encouraging initiative and independence of thought. The most noteworthy aspect of the decade of effort was the general feeling among school employees and citizens' organizations that they had all had a share in winning an important battle, that the single-minded strength of public opinion expressed repeatedly at congressional hearings had impelled Congress to act.[8]

Yet the most fundamental obstacles to further progress remained, namely divided authority and the iron grip Congress kept on the controls. Some citizens, among them taxpayers who disliked Ballou's methods, believed an elected Board of Education would remedy matters, but, as spokesmen for the Powell Junior High School PTA pointed out to a congressional com-

[8] *Biennial Survey*, 1928, p. 126; S Doc 58, 70C, 1S, pp. 4-17, 33, 43, 95-97, 126; *Rpt B/Tr*, 1929, p. 22; Boyd H. Bode, "The New Education Ten Years After," *New Republic*, LXIII, 63; Garnett C. Wilkinson, "Washington is Easily the Foremost Center of Negro Education in America," *School Life*, XI, 114; "Growing Children are Studied at the Washington Child Research Center," *ibid.*, XIV, 184-87, and Mrs. Giles Scott Rafter, "Social Hygiene Work of the Parent Teacher Associations," *ibid.*, pp. 15-18; Comrs Rpt, 1926, p. 20; *Rpts B/Ed*, 1922, p. 40, 1926, pp. 81-82, and "School Achievements," 1930, pp. 57-118.

mittee, the trouble lay not in the appointive character of the board but in its powerlessness to take needed action. Despite that reminder and the earlier warnings of the United States Commissioner of Education, Congress neither delegated any financial authority to the board nor cut the procedural red tape that enmeshed it.[9]

The first years of the depression threatened to destroy the American public school system. By late 1932 New York City had dismissed 11,000 teachers, Chicago had let a $28,000,000 arrearage in teachers' salaries accumulate, Alabama had closed 85 percent of her schools, and scores of cities had shortened the school year, cancelled building plans, and curtailed or dropped all special classes and services. At the same time adolescents unable to get work were pushing secondary school enrollments to a new peak. Angered at the neglect of education for which former supporters of American business ideals now blamed the "banker-power trust" and "the greedy manufacturer," the once conservative National Educational Association announced that only the public schools could save American civilization, and they must henceforward concentrate upon teaching social responsibility. In late 1933 and after, Public Works, Works Progress, and National Youth Administration funds helped revive school systems, and general economic recovery by 1938 resolved most of the difficulties caused by the financial crisis. But, contrary to expectations, the number of children entering high school continued to mount, and the percentage that graduated rose astonishingly: from the 16.7 percent of graduating age who finished in 1920 to 50.7 percent in 1940. Enforced attendance, the federal Office of Education noted, was not the sole reason; better teaching, courses of greater interest to students, and better transportation also contributed. While the long-run advantages to society of more schooling for young Americans appeared self-evident, sheer

[9] *Star*, 1 Jan 1930; Subcomee on Education, H Dis Comee, 71C, 2S, Hrgs, "Public School Ed in D.C.," pp. 10, 27-33, and 71C, 3S, pp. 5-6.

numbers of students inescapably complicated questions of how to recruit competent teachers and how to devise a scheme of education suitable for a political democracy in a world in which dictatorship was spreading and scientific discoveries were yearly widening the boundaries of knowledge.[10]

In Washington, reduced appropriations cut maintenance funds and salaries in 1933, but a capital outlay of about $4,490,000 in 1931-1932 had provided more new schoolhouses than in any one previous year in Washington's history; the sum, almost nine times that allowed in 1934, was twice the amount voted for any year thereafter until 1948. Moreover, unlike many cities, Washington, instead of losing, added teachers; the roster lengthened from the 2,764 of 1930 to 2,906 in 1935 and, with the restoration of pay cuts that year, the District's salaries ranked just below New York's and California's. By comparison with most of the United States, Washington was obviously well off. That reassuring knowledge, coupled with an easing of pressures on the schools, tended to induce a relaxation of vigilance in the community, for, while junior and senior high school enrollment continued to rise, the falling birth rate checked the yearly expansion of the elementary school population, and after 1937 the total number of pupils shrank.[11]

Meanwhile "character education" became a major topic of discussion. Apparently troubled by the disciplinary problems created by bored adolescents resentful of the school attendance law that kept them in school till they were sixteen, Superin-

[10] *Biennial Survey*, 1932, "State School Systems," p. 10, and 1940, II, "Statistical Survey," pp. 18-19; Doak S. Campbell, Frederick H. Baer and Oswald L. Harvey, *Educational Activities in the Works Progress Administration*, Staff Study No. 14; Merle Curti, *The Social Ideas of American Educators*, pp. 576-77; Robert E. Sherwood, *Roosevelt and Hopkins*, p. 57.

[11] *Rpts B/Ed*, 1932, p. 1, and 1940, "School Achievements, in Twenty Years, July 1, 1920 to June 30, 1940," pp. 16-17; Comrs Rpts, 1931, p. 26, 1933, pp. 35-37, 1934, pp. 56-65, 1935, pp. 26-35, 1936, pp. 32-41, 1937, pp. 30-39, 1938, pp. 32-41, 1939, pp. 52-62, 1940, pp. 50-60, 1941, pp. 52-63; *Biennial Survey*, 1940, II, "Statistical Summary," pp. 23-24.

tendent Ballou had appointed a teachers' committee in 1929 to prepare recommendations on curriculum changes and classroom techniques designed to develop in children cooperative attitudes and an eagerness to learn. In 1931 the committee reported that inasmuch as "the first aim of public school education should be training in character which will fit boys and girls for citizenship in a democracy," less emphasis must be placed upon academic subjects and more upon physical education and pupil participation in group activities. Parents, the community centers, playground directors, the churches, and social agencies should assist. While a citizens' advisory committee approved the proposal, until a Senate committee on racketeering and crime endorsed it, Congress hesitated. In 1934 an act appropriated money for a two-year experiment at one white and one colored school at every level from elementary through senior high school; a small corps of special teachers was to supervise the necessary changes in curriculum and teaching methods.

The scheme lapsed before it was well begun; in 1936, when a representative accused the staff of "teaching communism," Congress cut off funds. But the idea persisted that education must shift its focus. Superintendent Ballou appointed teachers' committees to plan a "Child Development" program for the public schools; the parochial schools under the leadership of Father John Ryan of Catholic University introduced social studies into their curricula; and before the end of the 1930's educators throughout the country endorsed the general concept that the function of the schools was to develop character which would then produce acceptable patterns of social behavior. Washington's avowed goal of ten years before, the nurturing of individual initiative and independence of thought in school children, was no longer all-important.[12]

The school board lay proud stress on the discarding of "sub-

[12] "Preliminary Report of the Committee on Character Education," *School Bulletin* 9, 1931; Curti, *Social Ideas of American Educators*, p. 578; "School Achievements," 1940, pp. 8-88; *Star*, 20 Oct 1935.

ject orientation" in favor of the new "child orientation" program. But in reviewing the achievements of the 1930's the board passed lightly over the abandoning of the X,Y,Z plan of grouping children according to their intelligence and achievement ratings. As parental objections grew, in 1932 the "three-track" system had given way to not very sharply differentiated X-Y and Y-Z units, corresponding generally to the A and B divisions within a classroom which were traditional in grade schools the country over. Since appropriations for the research department had always been so meagre that it had to entrust most of the administering and grading of the IQ and achievement tests to teachers who already had their hands full, not improbably the three-way placements had often been faulty. Financial pressures during the depression wiped out special classes for gifted children in every city school system except Cleveland's and Denver's, and before the end of the decade the informed American public, bristling over Nazi Germany's "Heldenschule," emphatically rejected the concept as contrary to democratic ideals. Not until the late 1950's would Washington's school administrators, recognizing the wisdom of paying more attention to bright students, introduce the "four track" system into the high schools.[13]

The Board of Education also took pride in the improvements in physical care achieved during the 1930's, the classes for adult illiterates, the units in vocational rehabilitation, the nursery schools, which opened with emergency relief funds in 1934 and disappeared in 1939, the cancellation of the so-called "Red Rider" to the appropriation act for 1936, which had denied salary to any teacher who "taught communism," and "the workshops and discussion groups democratically organized which were . . . broadening teachers' horizons." In keeping with the

[13] *News*, 23 Nov 1932; *Biennial Survey*, 1932, "The Education of Exceptional Children," pp. 9-11; George D. Strayer, *Report of a Survey of the Public Schools of the District of Columbia*, 1949, p. 428 (hereafter cited as *Strayer Report*); "School Achievements," 1940, pp. 1-123; "Demonstrating Child Welfare," *Community Service*, II, 5.

doctrine of equal opportunity for all regardless of ability, the widened reach of the junior and senior high schools, and, after the elevation of the vocational schools to the status of high schools, the granting of diplomas to graduates appeared to be further steps forward, since officials rejected any possible element of truth in the assertion of a mid-western high school teacher that "the gradual democratization of the American high school was lowering the scholastic standards of the secondary schools."

Within the Board of Education, however, faint apprehension was stirring before 1940 lest thoughtful parents lose faith in the public schools. The uneasiness arose not from the volume but from the source of the complaints, for they emanated from perceptive and discriminating citizens unlikely to carp at imagined grievances. Inasmuch as enlightened public opinion coupled with intense interest in the school system had always provided the Board of Education with such power as it had, withdrawal of that kind of support could undermine the schools for years to come. In the four years preceding Pearl Harbor school census figures supplied some statistical justification for that fear: white public school enrollments dropped by about 3,000, whereas parochial and other private schools added about 2,300.

Criticism of the quality of public education increased steadily from about 1937 onward. Emphasis on making children "happy," some parents felt, was leading teachers into an easygoing attitude toward home-work badly done or not done at all. Excessive attention to non-essentials, including high school athletics, left too little time for basic studies. A few people apparently thought teachers were no longer exerting themselves because financial security had robbed them of ambition. Parents were rarely aware of the new demands upon teachers who felt the superintendent's invitations to join in committee work amounted to "the Colonel requests." Time spent on drafting a new "Philosophy of Education" and evolving cirriculum changes to fit it could not be devoted to guiding the progress of individual pupils. In any case, performance proved something amiss, particularly in several schools where the socio-economic background of children was above average. Whereas high school graduates in the 1920's had entered reputable colleges without difficulty, in the late 1930's teachers now and again were informing parents that Johnny could not possibly hope for admission to, say, Harvard or Yale unless he had special tutoring. True, the fault might be Johnny's or parental failure to insist on home study, not a relaxing of teaching standards or an injudicious curriculum, but dissatisfaction continued to spread and in time to come would be a factor in the "flight to the suburbs."[14]

Logically, developments in the colored schools over the years should have paralleled those in white. Both systems were subject to the same rulings laid down by the bi-racial Board of Education; salary rates were the same for colored teachers as for white; and, from the early 1920's onward, in spite of pronounced inequities in congressional appropriations for athletic fields, classroom accommodations, and research staff, the dollar-and-cents equality of the separate systems was generally observed in budgeting for ordinary operating expenses: close to a third of the over-all revenues went to the Negro schools, which, until the late 1930's, embraced approximately 34 percent of the school population. Garnett Wilkinson, assistant superintendent for the colored schools, like the assistant superintendent of the white schools, came under the immediate supervision of Superintendent Ballou and received such briefing as Ballou thought necessary. Several times a year Ballou called white and colored supervisors and principals together to explain his plans, and

[14] Interviews, former teachers and Mrs. Henry Grattan Doyle, president of B/Ed 1935-1943; *Strayer Report*, pp. 406-07, 424-48, 497; Kathleen Brady, "The Depression and the Classroom Teacher," *Journal of the National Education Association*, xx, 263.

even in the 1920's he sometimes appointed one or two Negroes to teachers' committees. Yet the application of policies in the colored schools, or at least the results, diverged further and further from the white as time went on. The magnitude of the differences in some important respects would not be clearly revealed until racially integrated schools opened in Washington in the autumn of 1954. Wilkinson, a fine-looking, dignified, soft-spoken man, qualified for his post by an M.A. from the University of Pennsylvania, hewed strictly to the lines laid down by his superior, but in so doing, some of his own friends felt, he acted with a self-protectiveness costly to his people.

The separateness of the two systems in operation was so rigid that neither group of principals, supervisors, and teachers had first-hand knowledge of the programs and teaching methods employed in the other. For a white teacher to visit a colored classroom was virtually unthinkable, however unbiased he or she might be; such a step would have represented to the colored teacher an intolerable intrusion, an act of spying. Nor would a Negro visitor be welcomed in a white school. From the beginning of public schools for Negroes in the 1860's, the lack of communication had always obtained, but it became more costly to the colored schools once Superintendent Ballou launched research units to explore new ideas. At the suggestion of a representative of the Central Labor Union, in 1930 the Board of Education appointed a bi-racial citizens' advisory committee on vocational education, and thereafter white and colored teachers not infrequently sat on committees together. Still the joint discussions of particular problems failed to bridge the racial gulf.

If aware of the ten-year efforts of a white group that succeeded in 1938 in inaugurating vocational and educational counselling for white high school students, Negro teachers, cognizant of the racial restrictions on jobs, formulated no comparable plan for colored children. Negro principals, unlike white, apparently never dared introduce an innovation into the schools in their charge without first obtaining the explicit sanction of the assistant superintendent. Where white elementary school principals exercised a good deal of autonomy—perhaps an outgrowth of a widespread feeling that the elementary grades were "step-children" of the school system under Ballou—colored principals and their subordinates adhered to an autocratic chain of command. If that autocratic rule was frequently salutary, it nevertheless discouraged initiative in the lower ranks despite Negro teachers' curiosity about white teachers' experiments and achievements. The multitudinous voluntary associations that cropped up in the white schools—associations of high school principals and supervisors, of special teachers, of junior high school principals, and corresponding groups for the elementary grades—had few active counterparts in the colored schools. The staff of the latter saw no occasion to follow the lead of the former, even after bi-racial committees had begun to undercut the mutual isolation.

A second and ultimately more significant difference between the two systems lay in the tendency of the white schools to concentrate upon children of average or below average mentality and those with physical disabilities, leaving the unusually gifted to fend for themselves, whereas Negro school administrators believed their first obligation was to the upper strata of the colored school population measured in terms of learning capacity. To the distress of some members of the Board of Education, a good many colored principals and teachers appeared to take the position that truants, pupils who fell behind in their work or got into other trouble, the emotionally disturbed, and mentally retarded children were not entitled to special attention, for it would necessarily be at the expense of their more competent fellows. Since school resources were limited, and all Negro children faced discrimination in a predominantly white world, those able to make effective use of education must not be sacrificed to the less promising. While nothing in official reports openly acknowledged such a philosophy, it was a natural point-of-view in so class-conscious a community as colored Washington, where teachers, themselves occupying an enviable place in the social structure, would understandably want to preserve it intact.

Before World War II, only a very small unvociferous minority of Washington Negroes saw any advantage in school integration. On the contrary, a striking feature of colored school administration in the 1920's and 1930's was the jealousy with which it guarded its independence. Full recognition of its accomplishments and a larger, juster share of funds with which to better past records constituted the main goal. In 1933 when an official of the American Association of Teachers' Colleges gave Miner Teachers' College an "A" rating and declared that his survey had upset his settled conviction about the inferiority of Negro institutions, colored Washingtonians felt they had proved their ability to run their own show. Not improbably distrust of Superintendent Ballou, whom they considered tainted with racism, strengthened their determination to keep their schools free of white interference. The superintendent had approved the use of a white school building for a citizens' association meeting called in the 1920's to tighten restrictive housing covenants; he repeatedly, Negroes mistakenly believed, betrayed a dislike of colored people; and in 1939 when the school board was about to permit the famous colored contralto, Marian Anderson, to sing in the white Central High School auditorium, he had all but insisted that the permission be conditional on its not setting a precedent. Manifestly, observed the *Crisis*, if Washington's dual system were to be discarded, it would be at the insistence of economy-minded whites in the face of Negro opposition.[15]

[15] Robert Haycock, "The Capital's Unique School System," *School Life*, XVII, 102-03; *Tribune*, 25 Oct 1929, 5 Feb 1932; Lofton, "Separate but Equal," pp. 245-68; *Rpt B/Ed*, 1930, p. 36; *Crisis*, XXXIX, 39, XLVI, 170-71, and John Lowell, "Washington Fights," *ibid.*, 277.

The Negro intelligentsia, however, like the white, had begun to question the adequacy of the schools. "To some of us who got our schooling before the present-day reign of fads, futilities and 'activities' so-called," protested the *Tribune* in 1933, "it is no surprise to observe the shocking deficiency in the fundamentals—the three R's, if you please—of the present-day high school pupil." If school officials regarded wails about the "watered-down curriculum" and the lowering of teaching standards as merely the vaporings of fault-finders yearning for "the good old days," an investigation conducted by Dr. Howard Long of the colored school research unit eventually proved some of the fears justified. Starting with 1935, Long's meticulous study compared the Intelligence Quotient scores made by Washington's Negro school children year after year with the results of their achievement tests. His findings, first presented in 1943 to Assistant Superintendent Wilkinson, showed no loss in the IQ average but "a general downward trend in the achievement of pupils on all grade levels from the year 1935 to 1943," with the sharpest decline after 1937. While Long acknowledged that the large influx of Negro families from the deep South had bearing on the problem and explained that he "inclined to place a great deal of emphasis on the effects of cultural social-economic status of the pupils," he suggested that "ineffective instruction" was a contributing cause. His proposals of how to remedy the weaknesses failed to save him from bitter attack from colored Washington when mimeographed copies of his report reached the public in 1948.

Whether, as parental complaints implied, a comparable decline in achievement had begun in the white schools in the late 1930's is purely inferential. Not until outside experts submitted the Strayer Report to Congress in 1949 would a body of dispassionate evidence point to a lower record than the national norm in a number of Washington's white schools.[16] But before

[16] *Tribune*, 10 Mar 1933; Howard H. Long, "Intelligence and Achieve-

Pearl Harbor most of the local public was not alarmed. Washingtonians looking back over the preceding quarter century could see problems surmounted as well as some still unresolved. If school questions now occupied a lesser place in community thinking than in the 1920's, was that not a sign that successes in the interval had disposed of major troubles? Certainly in the autumn of 1941 Washingtonians by and large considered the school system among the least of their worries.

---

ment of Colored Pupils in the Public Schools of the District of Columbia," Parts II and III, mimeo, 1948; *Strayer Report*, pp. 417-18, 463-66, 552-53.

CHAPTER XVIII

BEFORE AND AFTER THE BONUS MARCH, 1930-1933

FEW Americans in 1930, Washingtonians perhaps least of all, thought of the depression that followed the stock market crash of October 1929 as the beginning of a country-wide economic collapse. Not until midsummer of 1931, when unemployment had reached unheard-of dimensions and was still increasing, did the business world realize that here was more than a sharp downward dip in the business cycle that would soon reverse itself. Even then the possibility that old residents of the capital would again see, as in 1894, an Army of the Unemployed encamped in their midst seemed remote.

In Washington, where government activity shielded citizens from the full force of the national catastrophe, cautiously optimistic prophecies filled the pages of the local press. During 1930 plans for new wings to the Smithsonian's Natural History Museum received congressional approval, and the vast building program for the Federal Triangle and the Department of Agriculture across the Mall kept a host of workers employed. Private building operations dropped by some $13,000,000 from the nearly $48,000,000 of 1929, a number of small businesses failed, and toward the end of the year the appeals from the Associated Charities for help for destitute families took on a note of desperation. But the Community Chest drive for the first time went over the top, and in February 1931 Congress authorized an immediate start on an eight-million-dollar District public works project of new buildings, street paving, sewer and bridge construction, and extension of water mains. Not only did the public school system thus acquire several long-needed new schoolhouses, but unemployment, which had begun to mount alarmingly, shrank as nine to ten thousand men got work. The nearly $5,000,000 spent by the National Capital Park and Planning Commission during fiscal years 1931 and 1932 also helped the city. And when private subscriptions brought the National Symphony Orchestra into being in the autumn of 1931, delighted Washingtonians dared hope it meant that the business slump was ending.[1] They later learned that the musicians frequently had to play for love, since Conductor Hans Kindler could not offer them salaries.

District Commissioners Luther H. Reichelderfer, a retired physician, Herbert B. Crosby, a retired general, and Major John C. Gotwals, appointed by President Hoover in 1930, betrayed no sense of anxiety in their first two annual reports. As in every city in the country, relief rolls lengthened while want and nameless fears turned tempers edgy, but here complaints about public welfare measures were relatively few. The police department was the principal sore spot. Its scandals and outright incompetence impelled Commissioner Crosby to look for a new superintendent. Chance provided the answer in the person of Pelham D. Glassford, who had been the youngest general officer in the AEF. In the summer of 1931 at the age of 47 he had retired in order to spend the years ahead ranching with his father and painting in Arizona. When his father's death upset those plans, he returned briefly to Washington to manage the Armistice Day celebration and then yielded to the persuasions of his one-time commanding officer, General Crosby, to accept the post of Major and Superintendent of the Metropolitan Police.

Glassford knew Washington well. During a tour of duty at the Army War College in 1924 and then another in the office of the Chief of Staff, he had taken a roomy, shabby old house in Georgetown, where he felt free to decorate the walls

[1] *Rpts Smithsonian*, 1930, p. 1, 1931, p. 1; Comrs Rpts, 1931, p. 58, 1932, p. 42, 1934, p. 46; *Rpts/NCPPC*, 1930, p. 45, 1931, p. 44, 1932, p. 29; Min As Ch, 12 Feb, 19, 21 Mar, 18 Jun 1930, 12 Jan, 11 Feb, 8 Apr 1931; *Star*, 1 Jan, 11 Dec 1930, 4, 11 Oct 1931; "Washington's Chest Expansion," *Survey*, LXVI, 99.

with his own murals. There he imposed upon his four children a regime combining Bohemia and discipline that led his friends to dub the household "the Borneo Embassy." Doubts assailed the public about the suitability of a man without police experience for so difficult a job as head of Washington's police force. Might not a military man prove to be the worst sort of martinet? Relatively few people at the time realized that Glassford represented the very best of Army tradition. Brought up as an "Army brat" in western posts, he had a deep devotion to duty, a dedication to the public interest. He lacked all political ambition.

Within a month of his appointment Glassford captured public respect by his handling of the "Hunger March." In December 1931 about a thousand jobless men arrived in the capital to stage as violent a demonstration as they dared contrive against the government. The new police chief instructed his men to be watchful but not to interfere with the soap-box orators as long as they fired only words. To the surprise and intense relief of the city, a week or so of listening to each other's bitter harangues without provoking any attack from constituted authority sufficed to discourage the Hunger Marchers; they faded away. A second group, encountering the same sort of treatment, similarly disintegrated. Glassford's unorthodox habit of riding about the city on a big blue motorcycle while he checked on police performance earned him the label of "screwball," but by the spring of 1932 he had won a reputation for friendly, unobtrusive competence.[2]

At that point the Board of Trade began speaking with renewed confidence. For the first time since its founding in 1889 the directors had omitted annual reports in 1930 and 1931, but the informal typescript prepared by the president in April 1932, though lacking the customary impressive format, presented a triumphant picture of the preceding twelve months.

[2] Fleta Campbell Springer, "Glassford and the Siege of Washington," *Harper's Magazine*, CLXV, 641-48.

"In drab surroundings," ran the summary, "at a time when every other organization that I know of is compelled to retrench and curtail their activities, the Board of Trade is ending the record year of its history." Five hundred new members, fewer resignations and fewer delinquent dues than every before, double the usual number of bills tendered to Congress and defended at hearings, and the bringing to Washington of sixty conventions, a hugely increased tourist trade, and $10,000,000 in new business were outstanding achievements. Besides holding the largest clam-bake ever attempted, the board had sponsored a dinner in honor of Post and Gatty, the "Round-the-World-Flyers." The Aviation Committee had prevented the placing of two-hundred-foot towers on the new Arlington Memorial Bridge, the Municipal Art Committee was preparing "the usual award for meritorious building," the Law and Order Committee had held several talks with the commissioners, the Finance Committee had fought off bills injurious to local business, and the American Ideals Committee, the committees on national representation, schools, alley-dwelling, public health, traffic, and a dozen other problems had all worked diligently. If the board president was deliberately pumping courage into his associates, the record supplied him with power. Prospects for a mounting number of visitors looked bright.[3]

In late May an unexpectedly heavy flood of visitors did roll in upon the capital with one object in mind: a vote in Congress for immediate payment of the bonus that World War I veterans would not otherwise receive until 1945. Starting from Oregon, the Bonus Expeditionary Force, as its members wryly called it, hitchhiked, rode freight trains, and gathered reinforcements along the way, as jobless men, some of them driving battered old cars, joined the march on Washington. Word of their coming ran before them. General Glassford, recognizing the grave possibilities of trouble, sought out congressional

[3] Rpt B/Tr, 1931-32, typescript in possession B/Tr.

leaders to beg quick action on the bonus bill, for, as long as it was tied up in committee, the Bonus Army would continue to expand. Only prompt defeat or passage of the bill would halt the march before it reached overwhelming proportions. When Congress disregarded his plea, he hurriedly prepared for the impending invasion by finding billets for the veterans. Neither then nor later did he doubt that most of them, for all their unmilitary appearance, were ex-servicemen, not the communist trouble-makers the administration would in time depict. He got permission to house the first contingent in a vacant department store, induced the Assistant Secretary of the Treasury to let others occupy empty buildings scheduled for early demolition on lower Pennsylvania Avenue, assigned some men to empty sheds and warehouses in southwest Washington, and, as he was unable to borrow tents from the Army or the District National Guard, he helped the main body of bonuseers establish a camp adjoining the dump on the mud flats across the Anacostia, where they set up ramshackle huts made from old packing cases, odd bits of lumber, scraps of canvas, and tin cans.

Before the middle of June over 20,000 bonus marchers had collected in the District of Columbia. Glassford issued orders to his subordinates not to harry them. He persuaded the National Guard to lend its rolling field kitchens and elicited money from rich friends to eke out the rations with which sympathizers in every part of the country were supplying the commissariat of this strange, bedraggled army. Thus abetted, Walter Waters, the elected commander of the Bonus Army, and his lieutenants succeeded in maintaining discipline within its ranks. On the Anacostia the heavily populated "Camp Marks," named for a former police chief, ran with a semblance of military order. Bugle calls sounded Reveille and Taps, K.P. details prepared mess, the men stood in chow lines, dug latrines they called "Hoover Villas," and organized baseball games.

Similar if less exacting discipline held among the men encamped within the city proper. Washingtonians, moved by curiosity or benevolence to visit the various encampments, marvelled to see white men and Negroes amicably sharing quarters. Gifts of bedding, odd bits of furniture, utensils, and food multiplied, as residents of the capital observed the needs and the orderliness prevailing among these ill-assorted lobbyists. "The arrival of the bonus army," remarked John Dos Passos, "seems to be the first event to give the inhabitants of Washington any inkling that something is happening in the world outside of their drowsy sun parlor."

The House of Representatives passed the bonus bill on June 15th. President Hoover said he would veto it as class legislation if it won in the Senate. Two days later, while Commander Waters vainly tried to see the President, the veterans collected on the Capitol grounds to await the Senate's decision. Thanks to Glassford, they were not arrested for walking on the grass, as "General" Coxey had been in 1894. They sat under the trees and on the Capitol steps or milled around restlessly. The afternoon dragged on and turned into twilight. Tension grew. At last the word came: the Senate had killed the bill. For a moment silence lay heavy, followed by some "boos" and a stirring of the crowd. Then Waters, prompted by a young woman reporter, called out: "Let us show them that we are patriotic Americans. I call on you to sing 'America.' " The song rang out. The men then quietly formed into platoons and walked back to their makeshift quarters on the Avenue, across the Mall, and on the mud flats of the Anacostia.

Neither the defeat of the bill nor the efforts of the administration to get the marchers out of the capital ended the story of the Bonus Army. While the Democratic convention in Chicago nosed it off the front page of the newspapers till after Franklin D. Roosevelt's nomination, the bonus marchers waited uncertainly. When the government offered them free rides home some of the men accepted; most stayed on, seeing nothing to be gained by returning jobless and penniless to homes that no longer existed. New arrivals, wives and children among them, swelled the army, for, until Congress adjourned in mid-July, hope for some constructive action lingered. An act passed cutting civil service salaries by 8⅓ percent and decreeing obligatory furloughs without pay for government employees, but such economy measures were of no help to unemployed veterans. While a band of fifty to a hundred avowed communists, ostracized by the rest of the bonus seekers, attempted to picket the White House, during the last days of the congressional session four hundred foot-weary "Death Marchers" shuffled back and forth in front of the Capitol for sixty hours to prove their determination to fight lawfully until they dropped; because the architect of the Capitol insisted that they not sleep on the grass and kept water sprinklers running night and day to discourage them, they napped occasionally on the lawn of the Library of Congress and, for relief of their necessities, used the library washrooms—indeed sometimes the ornately tiled hallways. The vigilant, kindly police chief saw to it that hot coffee lessened the rigors of the "Death March," and one night Mrs. Neddy McLean, divorced wife of the owner of the Washington *Post*, appeared at 2 a.m. with a thousand sandwiches. When an apprehensive Vice President called for a detachment of Marines to clear the approach to the Capitol, Glassford sent them back to their barracks with the statement that only the President could order out troops, and they were not needed. On the very last day of the session Congress voted a loan of $300,000,000 to be distributed to the states for unemployment relief. Gloomy veterans foresaw that it would take months to get into motion the massive machinery necessary to produce results.

Meanwhile General Glassford—"our friendly enemy," Waters called him—insisted that the men must go, since "the police department has not the means to continue much longer to provide for the thousands of veterans in the city." A solid core of the Bonus Army stood firm, reiterating its four-point rule: "Stay until the bonus is granted; no radical talk; no panhandling; no booze." Day after day smoke from the cooking fires in the city's parks and vacant lots drifted through the streets. The occupants of Camp Marks entrenched themselves doggedly, adding to the collection of pitiful huts they had put up earlier. Here and there tin cans planted with flowers appeared alongside, a reminder to visitors that this was becoming home to several hundred families. Half-buried garbage and summer heat bred flies and disease, and quarrels led with increasing frequency to fist fights that the omnipresent Glassford usually broke up with the admonition: "No fighting among veterans." With the flat decree that all must share alike, he quashed Commander Waters' plan to deny rations to the handful of communists who had collected about John Pace of Detroit. By their own count never more than a hundred in number, the communists found themselves thwarted in their every attempt to make the B.E.F. a tool of revolution, but they were a thorn in the gaunt flesh of the great body of men whose motto was: "Eyes front, not left."

Hunger had already become the major enemy. Foodstuffs and money had poured in from all over the United States, but by mid-July the Bonus Army's treasury was empty; the rations of mush, beans, and salt tripe on which the men had lived for days were running out. Glassford spent nearly $1,000 out of his own pocket to buy supplies; one $750 purchase furnished 1,000 pounds of coffee, 3,000 pounds of meat, 200 pounds of sugar, 200 pounds of salt, and some other staples. But when broadcasting companies stopped the radio appeals for food, voluntary contributions dwindled. To abide by the rule of no panhandling became increasingly difficult. The Board of Public Welfare was not in a position to draw for the benefit of non-residents upon the recently created emergency relief fund, and the over-burdened private charity societies could not feed 15,000 strangers, veterans or otherwise. If the families encamped on the Anacostia flats were to dig in permanently, who was to provide them with the necessities of life? At this juncture students of the past may have recalled the city's difficulties of the first decades of the nineteenth century when Congress year after year lifted never a finger to care for the throngs of "transient paupers" who collected in the capital.

President Hoover's refusal to see a delegation of the Bonus Army in June had disturbed a good many Americans, especially thoughtful Washingtonians who witnessed the direct effect. A month later, according to the recollections of a staunch local Republican, Hoover's "frozen-faced" dismissal of the wants of hungry American ex-soldiers baffled admirers of the "great humanitarian" who had taken charge of feeding starving Europe in 1918. B.E.F. Commander Waters contended initially that only non-veterans, derelicts who passed themselves off as part of the Bonus Army, resorted to panhandling, but it inevitably spread and sometimes took on a note of belligerence that timid householders found potentially ominous. In the heart of the business section from 7th Street to the Treasury, from Pennsylvania Avenue to G Street, idle, seedy-looking men stood about, not by and large soliciting openly, but by their mere presence creating vague apprehensions in passers-by. Businessmen came to feel they were under siege. At the same time grumblings began to be heard at the police for not enforcing the law requiring peddlers' licenses of the veterans who had set up soft drink stands and sold souvenirs on the streets. While the President and his advisers persisted in the view that the entire problem was purely a local affair, the District commissioners considered it a federal responsibility, the result of a national catastrophe; apparently the White House and the District Building concurred only in criticizing

Glassford for his "passivity." Temperate citizens, in spite of sympathy for the invaders, gradually reached the point of concluding that they must be persuaded to leave; the situation might soon become explosive.

Of the estimated 60,000 to 80,000 men who had joined the Bonus March at one time or another, not more than 10,000 were still in Washington by the last week in July. But official patience had run out. The Treasury demanded that the Pennsylvania Avenue buildings be vacated at once so that demolition could begin, and on July 21st the District commissioners instructed the police to have that area cleared of occupants within thirty-six hours, to have the squatters removed from all government property within the city proper by midnight of the 24th, and by August 4th to have everyone out of Camp Marks as well. Glassford, determined to avoid precipitating violence, promptly conferred with the commissioners; they rescinded the order, "pending the straightening out of certain legal matters." The police chief used the interlude first to extract from Waters and his lieutenants an assurance that the veterans would not resist eviction and, second, to hurry on an arrangement with Judge William Bartlett, who had tentatively agreed to let them set up a camp on his thirty-acre estate near Anacostia. During the next five days the ranks of the Bonus Army thinned perceptibly. The period of grace ended abruptly on July 28th.

That morning Glassford, acting on the commissioners' written orders, began the eviction of the veterans from the area near the tip of the Federal Triangle. As the police moved into the buildings, the men moved out, merely tossing a few mild curses at the "blues," while Waters and the police chief watched. Suddenly two new arrivals from Camp Marks tried to force their way into one building, and a brick hurled at a policeman set off a brick-heaving battle. It lasted for perhaps five minutes before Glassford and Waters, yelling the magic words "lunch" and "to Camp Bartlett," persuaded the combatants to halt the fight. With quiet restored, Glassford left to report to the commissioners. After the event, the commissioners declared he had then asked for federal help. This Glassford flatly denied; he had said the police could hold the section already cleared but warned that serious trouble would ensue if the commissioners insisted upon his moving further that afternoon. If force were to be employed, let federal troops, not the police, exercise it. He then returned to the "riot area." There everything was still quiet. Commissioners Reichelderfer and Crosby came to see for themselves and departed. A few moments later a scuffle originating no one knew quite how occurred in one of the buildings; a policeman drew his pistol and two veterans were shot and several men injured before Glassford got the trouble-makers under arrest and the situation again under control. Only then did the police chief learn from a reporter that the commissioners had already requested the President to call out federal troops. Glassford ordered the police lines back from the sidewalk so as to give the bonus seekers room to move. The veterans sat down along the curb to await developments.

Washingtonians, observing the final act of the Bonus Army drama, discovered that when men in power lose their heads, anything can happen. At three o'clock on that hot July afternoon word went out over the radio that troops called in from Fort Myer under General MacArthur's command were assembling at the Ellipse. Startled, incredulous spectators began to collect. A half-mile to the east the veterans sat patiently. They waited two hours. Then the march down the Avenue began—cavalry with sabres drawn, cavalry with sabres sheathed, infantry with bayonets fixed, tear bombs on belts, and an accompaniment of six Whippet tanks with hooded machine guns. In the lead rode General Douglas MacArthur, his medals shining on his immaculate uniform, his boots gleaming, his horse perfectly groomed. It was a magnificent sight. The bedraggled men sitting on the curb and the crowd gathered nearby watched with fascination. An order sounded, shattering the illusion of splendid make-believe. A screaming police siren scattered the on-lookers; the soldiers advanced; tear bombs drove the sitting men into a frantic scramble of retreat, and, while the cavalry couriers charged back and forth over the forty-yard stretch of "battleground," the squatters abandoned all attempts to salvage their meagre possessions. When every other encampment in the city had been similarly purged, the tanks, under command of Major Dwight D. Eisenhower, lumbered off to block the Anacostia Bridge, and about nine o'clock the infantry moved on to Camp Marks to drive its denizens out. The fires set to destroy their makeshift homes illuminated the riverfront; by 11 p.m. only embers, smoke, and rubble remained. Householders in Anacostia took in weeping, bewildered women and children and let the dazed remnants of the Bonus Army stretch out in their yards.[4]

Since the government "unsheathed the sword," wrote an indignant eye-witness, "the people . . . unsheathed the pen." Letters deluged the administration and the press. Most of the Washington newspapers avoided censoriousness, especially after official justifications began to appear from the Justice and War Departments. Attorney General Mitchell announced that the "extraordinary proportion of criminal, communist, and non-veteran elements among the marchers" had brought into the capital "the largest aggregation of criminals that had ever been assembled in this city at one time." General MacArthur assured the public that, had the President not summoned troops, "another week might have meant that the government was in

[4] Springer, "Glassford," pp. 645-55; Walter W. Waters, with W. C. White, *B.E.F.*, *The Whole Story of the Bonus Army*, pp. 56, 63-64, 149-98; *Post*, 1, 3, 5, 8-10, 12-17, 21-29 Jul 1932; John Dos Passos, "Washington and Chicago," *New Republic*, LXXI, 178, *Star*, 27-30 Jul 1932; *News*, 1-29 Jul 1932; "The Human Side of the Bonus Army," *Literary Digest*, CXIII, 25 Jun 1932, pp. 28-30; Roy Wilkins, "The Bonuseers Ban Jim Crow," *Crisis*, XXXIX, 316-17; Irving Bernstein, *The Lean Years*, pp. 437-55.

peril." Secretary of War Hurley—"the Cotillion Leader," as the *Washington Merry-go-Round* had named him—declared that his instructions to the Army had read: "Use all humanity consistent with the direct execution of this order." If, as Democratic journals contended, Republican leaders in this election year had chosen to campaign on the slogan "Hoover vs. Radicalism," the Washington *Post*'s comment on the use of troops was to be expected: "The roster of the opposition," notably Norman Thomas and Fiorello LaGuardia, "is enough to confirm the good judgment of the President." It was merely a pity that General MacArthur had let his sense of drama run away with him.

The *News*, on the other hand, noted that of the hundreds of letters received from Washingtonians, not one in ten expressed anything but anger and contempt for the ruthless handling of the Bonus Army eviction. Citizens who opposed the payment of the bonus and who had been troubled by the presence of the marchers condemned the "brutality" with which the military machine had rolled down upon defenseless men; it was sheer luck that casualties numbered fewer than seventy. Anacostia householders passionately denied that they had ever regarded the men at Camp Marks as a panhandling menace or felt anything but sympathy for them. Thirty years later a conservative Washington lawyer remarked sadly that the late summer of 1932 had "scarred" the community.

The scars were deepened by subsequent official acts. While Army sergeants searched the streetcars for B.E.F. left-overs and Justice Department agents rounded up two hundred supposed "reds," the commissioners ordered the police to deport from the District all "alleged radicals" and stop the ingress of newcomers whose purposes were dubious. General Glassford wrathfully pointed out that such measures were not only impractical but of doubtful legality. He challenged the Attorney General's statement about criminals and subversives:

police records showed that, of 362 Bonus Marchers arrested during more than two months, only twelve were charged with any crime; except for eight arrested for soliciting alms, the rest had been picked up for petty offenses such as trespass, drunkenness, or making speeches without a permit. In fact, the crime rate in August after the expulsion of the B.E.F. considerably exceeded that for June and July. Glassford did not last long thereafter. When the commissioners refused to let him fire unreliable subordinates, he resigned. He returned to Phoenix that winter to devote his energies to setting up camps for the bands of homeless boys who, like the swarms of starving children in postwar Russia, had begun to migrate across the country. With his departure, Washington lost more than a colorful, humane police chief; for, although a number of citizens thought he had been too casual in his methods, his going stripped the community of a subtle élan.[5]

The autumn of 1932 was a profoundly depressing period throughout the country. The Democratic victory in November raised hopes in some quarters without dispelling deep anxieties or filling empty bellies. For the first time Washington felt the full force of the national disaster, for, as one journalist put it, the depression hit the capital on July 1, 1932. The District's chief industry, government, had not collapsed, but the slicing of federal salaries, the obligatory furloughs without pay, and the reductions in force in every government department directly affected one family in every three, wiped out life-times' savings, and crippled business. Four banks went into receivership. President Hoover's plan to cut another $700,000,000 from the federal budget for fiscal year 1934 spelled doom to the federal building program, Washington's economic mainstay during the pre-

[5] Springer, "Glassford," p. 655; *News*, 30-31 Jul, 1, 2, 9, 18, 27 Aug, 22 Nov 1932; *Tribune*, 29 Jul, 5, 12 Aug 1932; *Star*, 1 Jan 1933; P. V. Anderson, "Tear-Gas, Bayonets and Votes," and "Republican Handsprings," *Nation*, CXXXV, 138-40, 188-89; *Post*, 30, 31 Jul, 1 Aug 1932; T. J. Joslin, *Hoover Off the Record*, pp. 263-72; *Literary Digest*, CXIV, 24 Sep 1932, p. 12; *New Republic*, LXXII, 139-41, 316, 326, 359.

ceding two years. In August the District commissioners had pared $10,000,000 from the requests for funds submitted by the District departments, and experience indicated that the budget, when passed, would be considerably below that estimated minimum. The 72nd Congress in actuality adjourned on March 3, 1933, without voting any District appropriation for 1934.

In April 1932 Coleman Jennings, president of the Associated Charities, had begged the House Subcommittee on District Appropriations to include in the welfare budget the $600,000 the President had recommended for local relief. Although Hoover let the Community Chest canvass government offices, the Chest's $185,000 deficit had forced member organizations to curtail their services; unless tax-supported agencies could assume a share of the load, the city would face untold suffering. The House assigned the $600,000 to preparing plans for the Municipal Center, a building project that, as it happened, would not materialize until 1937. Fortunately the District budget finally voted for the fiscal year 1933 did include $350,000 for unemployment relief. The Welfare Board at once assigned five of its members to a new emergency relief committee to administer the fund. Within two weeks of the August 1st opening of the committee office, 4,891 applicants for work had appeared. Every week thereafter added several hundred. Most of the relief fund went into hiring men to clear up the debris at Camp Marks and improve the grounds of Gallinger Hospital. By December the money was gone.

Estimates of the number of people out of work ran as high as 200,000. In that crisis the Community Chest turned over to its employment committee $100,000 to stop the gap till Congress should act. Just before New Year's Congress voted the Welfare Board a $625,000 deficiency appropriation, but the demands upon it were so great that the year's allowance for a destitute family had to be limited to $100. The emergency relief committee was forced to exclude from public assistance some five categories of needy: all single men, all families with less than eighteen months' residence in the District, families in which the unemployed wage-earner was over 60, families with part-time earnings too small to support them, and all cases where other social problems complicated unemployment.[6] When some 3,000 new "Hunger Marchers" arrived to demand that Congress enact national unemployment insurance, a dejected community, all passion spent, listlessly watched the police bait them. Major Brown, the new chief, made it clear that he would not be "soft" like General Glassford. No one paid much attention to the few die-hards of the defunct Bonus Army who, under the unfortunate name of "Khaki Shirts," had returned to campaign for federal unemployment relief for all jobless Americans. The Khaki Shirts nevertheless set a useful example of self-help by obtaining their headquarters rent-free in return for undertaking repairs and renovations to the building, one of the forms of barter to which men in other cities also were resorting.

In response to an appeal from the Council of Social Agencies, one real estate firm located several house-owners and landlords who were glad to reduce or forego rent in exchange for free renovations, but, the *Monthly Labor Review* noted: "little co-operation had been received from the real estate group as a whole." Elder Lightfoot Michaux, a recently arrived Negro evangelist, arranged the largest single transaction: he got the use, rent-free, of a big building at T and 7th Streets, which his followers at the "Church of God" repaired, and there he installed some forty Negro families evicted from their former quarters for non-payment of rent. The Council of Social Agencies also helped along two or three other self-help schemes: vegetable gardens in vacant lots during the summer, clothes

[6] *News*, 13 Aug, 22, 26 Nov, 6, 7, 10 Dec 1932; *Post*, 10 Jul 1932; Comrs Rpt, 1932, p. 25, 1933, pp. 82-83; *Anl Rpt Comptroller of the Currency*, 1932, pp. 19-20, 505-12; Min As Ch, 9 Mar, 15 Apr, 12 May, 14 Dec 1932; interview, Elwood Street, director of the Washington Community Chest, 1928-1934.

conservation by engaging unemployed women to collect, mend, and distribute over 18,000 garments to the desperately needy, and the "Old Woman in the Shoe" cobbling service, which rebuilt and issued to 20,000 applicants badly worn footwear donated by better-heeled persons. The Community Chest drive, however, fell nearly $500,000 short of its goal, and angry complaints multiplied about solicitors' high-pressure methods, particularly in government offices, where the average annual salary had dwindled to about $1,560. The $975,000 of public money appropriated to the Welfare Board was too little to prevent under-nourishment and concomitant illnesses from adding some 3,000 patients to the year's total in the already overcrowded Gallinger Hospital.[7]

From Reconstruction days onward Washington had always taken on much of the coloration of each successive administration. After twelve years of Republican rule, the top level of society awaited the impending change with trepidation. Bad as things were in the winter of 1932-1933, conservatives doubted that newcomers to office would do better. In shutting himself up behind locked gates at the White House during the Bonus March crisis, had President Hoover not at least discouraged further demonstrations, and, in opposing federal subsidies to the unemployed, was he not following a precedent as old as the Union? Even angry critics of his policies came to feel a touch of pity for the embittered, defeated man in the White House. After the convening of the lame duck Congress, high society carried on outwardly much as usual. If some of the elite were piqued at not being invited to the President's grand diplomatic reception, which traditionally opened the

[7] Slater Brown, "Red Day in Washington," and Malcolm Cowley, "King Mob and John Law," *New Republic*, LXXII, 153-55, 263; *Nation*, CXXXV, 652-53; *News*, 4, 28, 30 Nov, 3, 6, 24, 30 Dec 1932, 9 Mar 1933; Min As Ch, 10 Feb, 12 Oct, 10 Nov 1932, 31 Jan 1933; *Monthly Labor Review*, XXXV, 1038; "School Achievements," 1940, p. 89; Comrs Rpt, 1933, pp. 83-84, 87; *Pictorial Review of the Church of God*, pp. 26-27.

season, chagrin lessened when the word went out that political obligations to social nobodies from the Sticks had left Mr. Hoover no alternative. But gaiety at official functions that winter bore a resemblance to the false cheer that had offended Margaret Bayard Smith in the last days of John Quincy Adams' presidency.

Still, bright spots lessened the gloom. Brenda Putnam's marble Puck poised lightly over the fountain on the grounds of the new Folger Shakespeare Library reminded passers-by "what fools these mortals be," and in January 1933, thirty-one months after the laying of the cornerstone of the handsome building on East Capitol Street, the library's directors opened the reading room to the "limited use" of scholars while the staff hurried on the cataloguing of the priceless manuscripts and folios. At the DAR Constitution Hall the National Symphony Orchestra, unlike its short-lived predecessor in 1903 and 1904, played on Sunday afternoons so that the working public could attend, and the Philadelphia Orchestra scheduled a series of evening concerts. The chamber music concerts at the Phillips Gallery, formerly invitation affairs, were now open to everyone; the Library of Congress concerts continued; and a choral society at the Epiphany Church delighted participants and audiences equally. As amateurs showed their paintings, the Art League enlisted new members. Russian ballet dancers performed at the Central High School in November.

Indeed, hard times had a unifying effect upon the community. In July and August dancers and theatrical companies had staged weekly entertainments at the Sylvan Theatre on the Monument grounds, where seats cost only 25 cents, and spectators on the grassy slopes beyond could watch for nothing. The George Washington University Cue and Curtain Club drew enthusiastic audiences, and at the community centers neighbors shared in diversions ranging from classes in French or ceramics to bridge parties and amateur theatricals and pageants. During the fall crowds thronged to high school football games, which the local newspapers reported upon in flattering detail. The Board of Trade and the commission in charge of the bicentennial celebration of George Washington's birth sponsored a Hallowe'en parade and a street dance to orchestra and band music on the pavement of the newly christened Constitution Avenue. Colored Washington danced on a block of T Street.[8]

The "secret city," it is true, still stood apart from the white capital. In fact, intensifying competition for jobs strengthened sections of the barrier. Contractors for the new British Embassy on Massachusetts Avenue had to abandon plans to hire some colored builders and workmen because the A.F.ofL. raised a row about the use of non-union labor. White waiters supplanted Negro at the House of Representatives restaurant, and business firms that had customarily employed colored people for menial work took on whites instead. Even under General Glassford only forty of the thousand-man police force were Negroes. While white directors of charities deplored Negro unresponsiveness to appeals, Negro social workers, denied admission to local universities' schools of social work, were unable to acquire the professional training demanded for important posts in the welfare agencies. Victor Daly's *Not Only War*, a new novel by the colored Washington real estate dealer who thirty years later would hold a key position in the United States Employment Service, touched on the all-too-familiar theme of the effect of race prejudice on the careers of educated Negroes doomed to look in vain for "the elusive altruism which they imagined they had found in college."[9]

[8] *Star*, 4, 11 Oct 1931, 20 Nov 1932; *News*, 24 Aug, 1, 6, 22 Nov, 16 Dec 1932; programs and notices of musical events, 1930-33 (Music Div, L.C.).

[9] *Tribune*, 17 Jan, 28 Feb 1930, 8, 15 Jan, 5, 19, 26 Feb, 11, 25 Mar, 1 Apr, 10 Jun, 15 Jul, 30 Sep, 2, 9 Dec 1932; *Crisis*, XXXIX, 187, 234, 343-44, 362; Victor Daly, *Not Only War*.

Discrimination took all the old forms. Under the system of relief and mothers' pensions, the *Crisis* declared, white social workers set one standard for the budget of white families, another for colored. "The white visitors insisted on calling colored mothers by their first names, discouraged them in the education of their children, and suggested sleeping apartments in cellars." A Roman Catholic priest interrupted the prayers of a Negro woman kneeling in the white section of the Immaculate Conception Church and hustled her off to the gallery. A War Department regulation covering the pilgrimage of Gold Star mothers to Europe decreed segregated units, with the colored women assigned to converted cattle ships. With Congressman Madden safely in his grave, Colonel U. S. Grant, III, commissioner of public buildings and grounds, proposed in 1932 to revive segregation in picnic areas of Rock Creek Park. Congress and the school board earmarked 80.4 percent of the new building fund for white neighborhoods and part of the 19.6 percent for Negro schools for repairing the Business High School, a badly located building erected in the 1890's for white students. That only economy dictated this arrangement made it no less an affront to Negro dignity.

Yet the shock of the depression brought the Negro community a few positive gains, difficult though they were to perceive at the time. Carter Woodson, founder and director of the Association for the Study of Negro Life and History, spoke of the "blessings" of the economic disaster which was forcing every Negro to depend upon his own people and to "indulge in serious thinking." Some of that thinking found expression at a meeting called by Campbell C. Johnson, Secretary of the colored YMCA, at which Colonel West Hamilton, printer and publisher, J. A. G. LaValle, editor of the *Tribune*, Mary Church Terrell, and Lucy D. Slowe, dean of women at Howard University, and other leaders discussed Negro welfare services and methods of coordinating them. At the same time a newly formed Committee on Improving Industrial Conditions among Colored People in the District of Columbia undertook an educational campaign to combat the factors that interfered with Negroes' getting and keeping jobs: intractability, lack of skills, unreliability about reporting for work after Sunday and pay days, lack of cleanliness, and refusal or inability to work under Negro bosses. "Possibly for the first time in years," said a member of the new Associated Negro Press, "our local politicians, high-hatters, low-brows, schemers, and general hustlers found something that requires their attention to a greater degree that they have been faithfully and joyfully giving to their favorite pastime of trying to unload a President of Howard University or an assistant superintendent of the public school system." Common troubles were submerging the old divisiveness. The *Tribune*, to be sure, complained about the lack of a "representative militant organization": the PTAs had no drive, and "the civic associations are made up of pussy-footing government employees and scared school teachers." While the local branch of the NAACP was put to it to enroll 2,500 members, a delegation persuaded the Bureau of the Budget to transfer $315,000 from the white to the colored schools.

Breaches in the wall about the secret city, moreover, were beginning to appear. It was a matter of concern to some people that the first bi-racial dance to be held in Washington since President Grant's inauguration in 1873 was a party sponsored by the Young Communist League, but police officers noted nothing objectionable during the evening. Interracial social work conferences took place during 1931 and 1932, and the 19th Street Baptist Church was twice host to three white Baptist congregations at religious services. In 1932 the Associated Charities at last elected two Negroes to the board of directors, and at its fifty-first anniversary meeting Mordecai Johnson, president of Howard University, was the principal speaker. If Negro intellectuals who looked upon him as an untrustworthy self-seeker would have preferred to have some other Negro chosen, they concurred in his theme that, not free grocery slips, but jobs on public works with no racial strings attached would alone end the depression.

Colored Washington had observed with grim satisfaction that the 2,000 Negroes among the Bonus Marchers faced no Jim Crowism; white Washington had also noticed it. More astonishing in light of the hostility the police had often displayed toward colored people, there was no segregation at the annual metropolitan police Christmas party for Washington's needy. College alumni groups began occasionally to invite colored graduates to social gatherings. When the Supreme Court decreed a new trial for the seven Negro boys charged with rape in Scottsboro, Alabama, white people joined with Negro in a huge demonstration on the Capitol grounds to demand the freeing of the prisoners. The Scottsboro case promised to be as important in American history as the Sacco-Vanzetti; the outcome, many a Washingtonian prayed, would be different, although within the secret city perhaps only incurable optimists believed in that possibility. Still, the winds of public opinion in parts of the United States were obviously shifting slightly. National journals, particularly church publications and left-wing magazines, were giving race relations increasing attention and suggesting that white condescension was almost as destructive as overt racial antagonism. If the colored intelligentsia in the capital saw little basic change in the white city's point-of-view even when the National Theatre announced a "special" performance of *Green Pastures* on March 2, 1933, which would be "open to all," a white newcomer remarked upon an atmosphere so friendly to well-mannered

Negroes that the disappearance of racism in Washington seemed "just around the corner."[10]

[10] *Tribune*, 10 Jan, 14 Feb 1930, 5, 19 Feb, 1 Apr, 17 Jun, 23, 30 Dec 1932, 3 Mar 1933; *Crisis*, XXXIX, 187, 316-19; Min As Ch, 10 Dec 1930, pp. 4, 6, 50th Anniv Mtg, 12 Jan 1932, p. 7, 51st Anniv Mtg, 31 Jan 1933; *News*, 7 Nov 1932; *Negro Status and Race Relations in the United States, 1911-1946, The Thirty-five Year Report of the Phelps-Stokes Fund*, pp. 73-79. For typical exhortations about race relations, see *Christian Century*, XLVII and XLVIII, especially Hubert C. Herring, "An Adventure in Black and White," XLVII, 1526-29.

CHAPTER XIX

THE NEW DEAL CAPITAL IN WHITE AND BLACK, 1933-1940

A CHILL wind carrying a drizzle of rain swept across sullen skies above the Potomac on March 4, 1933. Anxiety rested heavy upon the crowd gathered on the Capitol grounds. Early that morning every bank in the United States had locked its doors, almost thirteen million Americans were out of work, and the means of relief seemed to have dried up in every city and hamlet across the continent. At noon, the President-elect, his son James at his elbow, walked out onto the East Portico. A cheer, then silence. Chief Justice Hughes administered the oath, and the new President began to speak. As the beautiful, resonant voice rolled out reassuring words, tension relaxed. Wild applause greeted his statement, "We have nothing to fear but fear itself." When he promised to act quickly to restore confidence to the nation, the crowd's ovation echoed across the plaza. As he concluded, the clouds lifted, and suddenly sunlight bathed the Capitol. Symbolically, the fulfillment of the promise had begun.

At the White House, Supreme Court Justice Benjamin Cardozo swore in the new Cabinet in the late afternoon. Twenty-four hours later, the radio announced that the President, exercising war powers granted President Wilson in 1917, was declaring a bank holiday and had summoned Congress into special session on March 9th. If fresh alarm struck here and there, a wonderful gaiety nevertheless took possession of Washington. That Sunday evening "Daisy" Harriman, National Democratic Party committeewoman, gave one of her famous supper parties. There General Douglas MacArthur shed benign charm on fellow guests who, like his hostess, had angrily criticized his treatment of the Bonus Marchers seven months before; Junius S. Morgan of Wall Street and several other die-hard Republicans cheerily talked of the future with ardent Roosevelt supporters. Other Washington households also celebrated that evening, while lights burned through the night at the Treasury, where officials began hammering out an emergency banking bill to present to Congress eighty hours later.

The new week brought sobering reminders that words and a beam of thin March sunlight would not alone put the world to rights, but a sense of adventure took hold as businessmen and housewives set about learning how to manage without money. While three shifts working round the clock at the Bureau of Engraving turned out two million $1,000 Federal Reserve notes to have in readiness for a new banking act, pseudo-promissory notes circulated as scrip. On Wednesday President Roosevelt met with the press to discuss his ideas on the banking crisis. When reporters, hopeful of learning the outcome of a presidential conference with congressional leaders, gathered on the White House grounds that evening, a downpour of cold rain impelled one of the Executive staff to invite the newsmen to stand in the shelter of the portico. "It was not long," reported the *News*, "before official members of the Roosevelt entourage accompanied by the correspondents were singing 'O Build Me a Home where the buffalo roam!' The White House cops stared and gaped, not realizing that serious business could be put to music without hurting either." Old Washingtonians, hardened to Herbert Hoover's curtness with the press, also gaped when they read of the incident.[1]

The emergency banking bill, presented to Congress shortly after noon on March 9th, became law before 9 o'clock that night. The act, which empowered the Secretary of the Treasury to release the newly printed Federal Reserve notes in exchange for

[1] Arthur M. Schlesinger, Jr., *The Coming of the New Deal*, pp. 1-21, 105, 182; *News*, 4, 6-9 Mar 1933. Throughout this and every succeeding chapter much of my most significant information derives from interviews.

currency and, under a system of licenses, to reopen the closed banks, brought gold and deposits flowing back into circulation. In the first of his "fireside chats" on the following Sunday evening the President talked to several million radio listeners about the act, making so complicated a subject as banking, Will Rogers said, understandable even to bankers. By March 14th, eight national banks, five trust companies, and seven savings banks in the District of Columbia were again transacting business. Over some protest, on March 20th Congress passed the Economy Act reducing veterans' pensions and cutting all government salaries 15 percent below the scale of nine months earlier. Before Congress adjourned in mid-June, it had enacted thirteen other major pieces of legislation and several of lesser importance.

While the speed of congressional action took Washington's breath away, the change in the social atmosphere was scarcely less astonishing. Days before the course of New Deal action became clear, the icy aloofness that had enveloped 1600 Pennsylvania Avenue gave way to a heart-warming friendliness. Herbert Hoover, tears sliding down his cheeks unobserved by the crowd at the Capitol, had left the city immediately after the inauguration. Grief and hopelessness seemed to vanish with him. A few hours, observed the head of the Secret Service, transformed the White House "into a gay place, full of people who oozed confidence." During that "renaissance spring," in Rexford Tugwell's phrase, the President "reigned in a splendid informality that shed its glow over all Washington." To the faint shock of society dowagers, Mrs. Roosevelt continued to write her newspaper column, "My Day," but she welcomed guests with a graciousness Dolly Madison herself could not have bettered. For, Alice Roosevelt Longworth explained to *Ladies' Home Journal* readers, her cousins Franklin and Eleanor "like people."[2]

[2] *News*, 13-15 Mar 1933; E. W. Starling, *Starling of the White House*, pp. 306-07; Alice Roosevelt Longworth, "Lion Hunting in the New Deal," *Ladies' Home Journal*, LI, 27.

"A good part of the national energy once bent on money-making animates the headquarters of the New Deal," wrote Anne O'Hare McCormick. College professors, lawyers, economists, social workers, some of them with "a passion for anonymity," some of them ridden by a cockiness congressmen and old Washingtonians found hard to stomach, the "brain-trusters" produced a ferment. Ideas were the currency of all the planners. And, as an old farm leader remarked rather sourly, like all uplifters they had "an unquenchable thirst for conversation. They were all chain talkers," from the brilliant economist, Rex Tugwell, and Secretary of the Interior Harold Ickes, the self-styled "Old Curmudgeon," to "Moley, Moley, Moley, Lord God Almighty," as the irreverent called political scientist Raymond Moley. Bright young men fresh from the universities and from offices without clients were soon pouring into Washington to man the new agencies created by congressional legislation. The first waves of New Dealers seldom doubted their capacity to establish a brave new world. "We were filled with a vast enthusiasm," one of them recalled, "although we didn't know exactly for what. And we didn't know what we were going to do. Most of us had to make work for ourselves."

The newcomers looked upon the city as theirs to use but not bother about and the aborigines as quaint at best, at worst a stuffy, negligible lot. The attitude was that of a sophisticated summer colony toward the natives. The natives' point of view also followed that pattern—irritation, touches of envy, thankfulness for material benefits, and anticipation of the day when the seasonal invaders would decamp, leaving the community to recapture its own. Yet within a year or two, the most supercilious of the New Dealers departed, and most of those who settled in learned little by little that not all the early settlers were dodos. And undeniably the new supply of red corpuscles enriched the bloodstream.[3]

[3] Thomas L. Stokes, *Chip Off My Shoulder*, pp. 362-63; Anne O'Hare McCormick, *The World at Home*, p. 231.

During most of 1933 immediate economic problems blotted out thoughts about the city's changed social climate. The "lurch into State socialism," almost universally welcomed during the "First Hundred Days," soon lost much of its appeal to Washington businessmen. As the Economy Act struck a blow at a city more dependent upon government payrolls than upon any form of private enterprise, the president of the Federation of Citizens' Associations foresaw a new low approaching on July 1st, when 17,000 Washington residents were to be "thrown off" the pension rolls. On top of the 15-percent cuts in federal salaries, a new ruling halved the already shrunken income of many a family, for, in effect, no one with a spouse in government employ could keep a government post; one to a family would spread the jobs. Places opening up in new federal agencies rarely fell to old-time civil service employees. Local bank deposits after rising slightly during the late spring shrank again during the summer. In October several of the District's savings banks were still in receivership, and depositors' prospects of reclaiming savings totalling some $12,500,000 were not bright.

A measure of the gloom was the listlessness with which baseball fans celebrated the Senators' winning of the American League pennant; nine years before, the capture of the World Series had people dancing in the streets. The day after the 1933 victory apparently no Washingtonian outside a small circle of scientists observed a brief newspaper notice telling of the discovery of heavy water. Householders feeling the economic pinch took little pleasure in hearing that the Turkish Ambassador, dean of the diplomatic corps, entertained 3,000 guests with champagne and caviar served by footmen in mulberry velvet on the very day the District tax assessor announced the impending sale of 28,000 pieces of real estate unless the $1,200,000 to $1,500,000 in back taxes were paid before Thanksgiving Day. As local building operations during the first year of the New

Deal dropped in value to less than half the $18,500,000 of the year before, financially hard-pressed residents tended to resent the accounts in metropolitan newspapers and magazines describing the exhilaration of living amidst the excitements of Washington.[4]

Yet by the end of 1934 journalists' picture of the capital was not over-painted insofar as it depicted the white business community. The Economy Act notwithstanding, the federal establishment in Washington grew steadily; the 63,000 government jobs of March 1933 expanded to about 93,000 before 1935, most of them filled by newcomers. Compared to salary reductions averaging 50 percent in other cities, the 15-percent federal pay cuts were slight, and 10 percent of the 15 was restored in July 1934, the rest the following spring. Months before the boarded-up shop windows along New York's Fifth Avenue ceased to be a commonplace, that index of business stagnation had disappeared in most of Washington. Mansions along Massachusetts Avenue, the Gold Coast of the 1920's, still stood empty, as former millionaires forewent the uncertain pleasures and the certain expense of spending the winter in the New Deal capital, but few smaller, unpretentious houses remained untenanted. The newspaper correspondents corps grew to five hundred, and, as the National Industrial Recovery Act demanded a framing of codes for every major industry, a stream of businessmen poured in month after month to sit around conference tables and later dilute their sorrows at hotel cocktail parties. Washington hotels that year, according to one report, took in $15,000,000. Concentrated campaigns of the Board of Trade enlarged the city's convention business; in 1934 the president estimated that the first formal Cherry Blossom Festival, with a beauty contest and the crowning of a queen, alone

[4] Oswald Garrison Villard, "Mr. Roosevelt's Two Months," *New Statesman and Nation* (new ser), v, 594; Comrs Rpts, 1933, pp. 37, 46, 49, 1934, p. 46; *Rpt Comptroller/Currency*, 31 Oct 1933, pp. 224, 229-30, 402, 590-92; *News*, 14 Apr, 22 Sep, 1, 2 Nov 1933; *Star*, 1 Oct 1933.

brought in over $500,000 of tourist money in a single week. While perhaps half the city's bankers, brokers, and real estate dealers joined the chorus which had begun to excoriate "that man" in the White House, the other half reminded them that as Washingtonians they had few valid grounds for complaint.

In describing Washington's business boom, Commissioner George E. Allen wrote that 40,000 people arrived daily at the Union Station in 1936. Though the city lacked heavy industry, he pointed to some $70,000,000 of "light manufactures," chiefly printing and bakery products, some of them doubtless far from light. The value of private building operations rose from the $7,000,000 of 1934 to about $24,000,000 within two years and within the next four reached $34,979,700. Still the nearly 1,800 new apartment houses, the more than 2,300 separate and row houses, and the 800 office buildings put up before 1940 fell short of demand. Every two weeks cash from the $8,500,000 in federal and the $1,000,000 in District government pay checks circulated in Washington shops and markets. "Effective buying income," asserted a magazine writer, averaged $3,782 in Washington, $2,000 in other American cities. It was easy to see why the *Star*'s advertising linage exceeded that of every other paper in the country. National unions, encouraged by New Deal friendliness to organized labor, began to set up permanent headquarters here. And, whereas the population of all other cities except Los Angeles declined during the decade, Washington's increased by 36 percent. Before midsummer of 1940, the federal payroll in the city swelled to about 166,000 employees.[5]

The public works program, briefly curtailed in 1933, soon expanded to embrace not only completion of the Federal Triangle, the massive Supreme Court, and the second House Office

[5] *Rpts B/Tr*, 1934-1936, *passim*, 1937, p. 10; *Star*, 21 Sep 1941; George E. Allen, "Washington, A Capital That Went Boom," *Nation's Business*, xxv, 32-33; Comrs Rpts, 1939, pp. 88-89, 1941, p. 78; Oliver McKee, Jr., "Washington As A Boom Town," *North American Review*, ccxxxix, 177-83; David L. Cohn, "Washington, The Blest," *Atlantic*, clxiii, 609-13.

Building but also construction of the Library of Congress Annex, new Department of Agriculture buildings to the south of the Mall, and beyond them a new central heating plant and a huge addition to the government warehouse alongside the railroad tracks. From the tip of the Triangle to the foot of the Hill, greensward and newly planted trees replaced the string of honky-tonk shops that had long been an eyesore along lower Pennsylvania Avenue. On the Constitution Avenue site of the old Baltimore and Potomac depot, the National Gallery of Art, gift of former Secretary of the Treasury Andrew Mellon, began to rise in 1937, while on Judiciary Square the Police Court building went up—the first unit of the long-talked-of Municipal Center. At the approach to the 14th Street Bridge, the new headquarters of the Bureau of Printing and Engraving looked out over the cherry trees encircling the Tidal Basin. "New Interior" facing the bulk of the "Old Interior" building across Rawlins Park and, beyond, a line of white marble edifices set in wide green lawns added dignity to the Potomac end of Constitution Avenue.

Although the neo-classical architecture for most of the new public buildings evoked occasional criticism, only the design and location of the memorial to Thomas Jefferson raised a storm of protest. When the specially appointed commission chose a site on the Tidal Basin and displayed John Russell Pope's model, one student of the eighteenth-century plan of the city insisted that a domed structure at that spot, by blocking the view from the White House southward over the Potomac River valley, would destroy a significant feature of L'Enfant's layout. Architects the country over denounced Pope's adaptation of Jefferson's design of the University of Virginia Rotunda, a "Roman Temple," singularly unsuited to a twentieth-century capital; they contended that the necessary cutting or transplanting of some of the Japanese cherry trees would further darken this "Twilight of the Gods." Not until the outcry of the 1960's over the projected "Stonehenge" in memory of Franklin Delano Roosevelt would popular indignation over architectural plans run so strong. The furor delayed construction of the Jefferson Memorial, and on the spring morning in 1939 when men and steam shovels arrived at the Tidal Basin to start digging the foundation, they found half-hysterical women chained to the cherry trees. Yet, when the building was at last completed in 1942, the columned, flat-domed temple, the bronze figure within, and the inscriptions from Jefferson's writings that ring the interior walls delighted the public.[6]

In guiding this huge public building program the Park and Planning Commission found itself playing a lesser role than formerly, first because instructions not to issue annual reports after 1932 meant dependence upon occasional newspaper articles to publicize proposals, and second because Congress omitted an appropriation until 1935 on the grounds that the $4,000,000 voted in 1930 and 1931 was to cover three years' expenditures. Fortunately Frederic Delano seized an unexpected chance to purchase a stretch of the Chesapeake and Ohio Canal; upon learning that the proprietors had applied to the Reconstruction Finance Corporation for a loan, he was able to buy at a bargain price the area from Rock Creek to the District line. The old tow path above the Aqueduct Bridge immediately became a favorite haunt of leisurely hikers, fishermen, and bird-watchers, and it encouraged the newly founded "Wander Birds" and the Capital Hiking Club to explore Potomac trails further. In 1935 when Congress again appropriated funds, it left the commission no discretion: the entire $800,000 was to go for the purchase of District playground sites. At the same time an organizational reshuffle enlarging the functions of the National Park Service diminished the

[6] Comrs Rpt, 1937, p. 68; Joseph Hudnut, "Twilight of the Gods," *Magazine of Art*, XXX, 480-81; Fred G. Vosburgh, "Wonders of the New Washington," *National Geographic Magazine*, LXVII, 457-88.

influence of the planning commission. While the Shipstead Act of 1930 required Fine Arts Commission approval of the architectural features of any new building or remodelling of old proposed on privately owned property adjoining or facing upon government buildings, and law broadened the Zoning Commission's powers to forestall construction that would intensify traffic, parking, or public health problems, the Park and Planning Commission largely turned into a land-purchasing agent for other government bodies.

Several of the planning commission's carefully thought-out proposals fell almost soundlessly into the void. Members and staff urged placing all buildings for the federal judiciary on the Hill in a cluster about a square east of the Supreme Court, which should be named in honor of the late Justice Oliver Wendell Holmes. Beyond the Folger Shakespeare Library on East Capitol Street a new building should go up to house the Surgeon General's Library. By extending federal construction eastward, the balance L'Enfant had intended would take form, and the beautifully planted, spacious Lincoln Park would assume the dignity designers had envisaged for the Hill 147 years before. After 1934, except for the Library of Congress Annex, no new government building would rise in that area until the mid-1950's. Fort Drive, projected in the 1920's as a scenic route encircling the city's Civil War forts, was shelved indefinitely.[7]

Meanwhile the creation of the Alley Dwelling Authority in 1934 promised the community more enduring benefits than new public buildings and parkways. Since 1917 the alley slums had worsened; now, under the direction of the able John Ihlder, eradication of those breeding spots of tuberculosis,

[7] Interview, Wm. McIntyre, Ntl Cap Planning Comm; *Star*, 2 Nov 1932, 18 Oct 1935, 15, 17 Apr, 1 May 1938, 5, 26 Jan, 13 Feb, 16 Nov 1939, 23 Mar, 19 Apr 1940; *Post*, 16 May 1941; *News*, 14 Aug 1935; David Cushman Coyle, "Frederic A. Delano: Catalyst," *Survey Graphic*, xxxv, 252-69; Coyle, "Washington Gets Broad Powers to Prevent Land Overcrowding," *American City*, LIII, 81.

juvenile delinquency, and crime within ten years looked possible. Unhappily the act came too late to be effective. Had it passed when drafted in 1930, Ihlder believed private builders would have cooperated in putting up inexpensive housing for the displaced "alley families," but by 1935 the building boom was in full swing, and projects on which profit would be narrow no longer interested contractors. They nevertheless opposed public housing. So the Alley Dwelling Authority had to spend most of its first two years fighting law suits aimed at stopping its acquisition of suitable sites. In that interval mounting prices limited the authority's purchasing power. The agency consequently sometimes cleared an area and sold the land instead of using it for new low-rental developments.

By 1937 some 9,000 houses were still lighted only by oil lamps, 7,000 multiple-family tenements were without inside water taps, and 11,000 families had no inside toilets. One of the worst slums stood within a hundred yards of the new air-conditioned office of the Federal Housing Administrator. Nor was the incredible squalor "behind the marble mask" of the capital confined to the alleys and Negro shanties. The tourist might drive along streets lined with what appeared to be respectable middle-class houses and never dream that behind the front doors fifteen to twenty families, white as well as colored, were packed into space designed for one. By 1940 construction of about 3,000 public housing units, including a 286-family Negro development on Benning Road, marked the total accomplishment of six years' work. Nine-tenths of the occupied alleys remained untouched.

Yet several forces combined after 1934 to shift population and ease housing for "the forgotten man" a notch above the bottom ranks of society. The Home Owners Loan Act, passed in the First Hundred Days, staved off mortgage foreclosures; the newer Federal Housing Authority guaranteed bank loans for private housing projects; and the Resettlement Administration, set up in 1935 under Rex Tugwell, undertook to open planned communities in the countryside beyond the congested areas of big cities. So Greenbelt, Maryland, a skillfully laid out town designed for about a thousand families in the middle-income bracket, began to rise within a half-hour's drive of downtown Washington; and in the spring of 1936 private enterprisers with some Housing Administration backing started in Clarendon, Virginia, a settlement of multiple-family dwellings, a pattern that spread as building and land prices in the area spiralled upward.[8] The outward push from Washington was hastened also by the business revival, the wish for play space for children, and the assumption that everyone above the pauper level would drive an automobile to work. Arlington, in 1920 set off from Alexandria under a county government, was one of the first suburbs to expand. Improved highways, the opening of the Memorial Bridge, the county's good public schools, and the comparatively modest cost of real estate in an agreeable semi-rural setting attracted scores of middle-class householders. The relatively well-to-do gravitated toward Chevy Chase in Maryland's Montgomery County, a much older, sophisticated region of roomy houses built on large lots in the vicinity of the country club. To the west the opening of two units of the National Institutes of Health encouraged a migration into Bethesda, while the overflow from the District pushed the growth of the small city of Silver Spring and began to affect Prince Georges County to the east.

The exodus from Washington was almost exclusively white. When the demolition of the curio shops along lower Pennsyl-

[8] *First Report of the Alley Dwelling Authority for the District of Columbia*, 15 Dec 1935; *News*, 15 Sep 1933; Rpt B/Tr, 1935, p. 11; John Ihlder, "Housing in Washington," *Council Bulletin*, I, Oct 1936, pp. 8-12; *Community Service*, I, Mar 1937, p. 9, May 1937, pp. 3, 6; "The United States and District of Columbia Housing," *ibid.*, Sep 1937, pp. 3-4; "We Can Get Rid of the Slums," *ibid.*, II, Feb 1938, p. 6, and "Alley People," *ibid.*, May 1938, p. 9; Comrs Rpt, 1938, pp. 173-74; NCPPC, *Washington Present and Future*, Monograph #1, 1950, p. 21; "Behind the Marble Mask," *Collier's*, CII, 3 Sep 1938, pp. 11-14; *Star*, 13 Oct 1935; Schlesinger, *New Deal*, pp. 370-71.

vania Avenue forced Chinatown to move, the colony of approximately one hundred Chinese families chose to locate on H Street on the fringe of the business district, but Negroes who would have preferred suburbia had no choice. Virginia and Maryland property-owners, real estate dealers, and builders stood fast against renting or selling to colored families irrespective of their financial resources; banks refused to make them loans. Hence a steady shrinkage in the percentage of nonwhites in the suburban population and a proportionate rise in the District of Columbia's followed. (See Table V.) And within Washington neighborhoods changed character.

TABLE V

Percent of Population Nonwhite in Suburban Jurisdictions of Metropolitan Washington and the District of Columbia 1930-1950

	1930*	1940	1950
Montgomery County, Md.	16.8	11	6
Prince Georges County, Md.	23.3	19	12
Arlington County, Va.	12.5	9	5
Fairfax County, Va.**	19.0	16	10
Alexandria, Va.	20.3	16	12
Falls Church, Va.	**	**	2
District of Columbia	27.1	28.2	35

* This was Negro only.
** Falls Church included in Fairfax County before 1950.

The most dramatic shift took place in Georgetown. Although a number of her beautiful eighteenth- and early nineteenth-century houses had been kept up over the years, a good many had fallen into disrepair before the turn of the century. In 1930 about half her inhabitants were poverty-stricken Negroes, most of them occupying substandard dwellings, some without running water or electricity. Yet the convenience of the location and the yeast of the abiding charm of the shabby little village had begun to work in the late 1920's. The remodelling started then had proceeded slowly during the depths of the depression but about 1934 suddenly gained momentum. Impecunious young New Dealers moved into the cramped restored little houses. Tiny fenced-off patches of ground at the rear, recently littered with rubbish, again turned into gardens and patios with lilac bushes and crepe myrtle nursed back to vigor by pruning and feeding. Every rejuvenated spot inspired the redemption of others, while real estate brokers hastily played down their decades-old argument that once a neighborhood had become part-Negro, it deteriorated with inexorable rapidity. The "decoloration" of Georgetown would not be complete before the 1950's, but it had gone far enough by 1940 to intensify Negroes' housing problems.

Colored families usually were unable to resist the prices white dealers offered for Georgetown property or else could not afford the higher rentals caused by improvements to adjoining property. Since the acceptance of a bi-racial mode of life beyond Rock Creek failed to permeate the rest of Washington, relocation was difficult. Black ghettos became more tightly packed, and the complexion of some erstwhile white neighborhoods darkened, for example, the area around the Morgan School above Florida Avenue. Rows of gerry-built little boxes in remote stretches of northeast Washington began to fill with up-rooted colored tenants. Kelly Miller of Howard University observed that, far from easing after the climax of the fight against housing covenants in 1926, strict residential segregation had increased. And from 1933 onward, Negro in-migrants from the Deep South poured in, undeterred by the fact that hundreds of colored people native to the District were out of work. Thus, whereas the nearly 120,000 white newcomers of the New Deal era were generally well-educated upper-class citizens qualifying for government posts, a large part of the 55,000 colored people added to the population stood at the bottom of the socio-economic pyramid. The colored school records later showed that the IQ's of children born in the southern states averaged five points below the 97.31 median of schoolchildren native to the city.[9]

Colored Washington had no share in the boom the white business world enjoyed. The depression killed traditional "Negro jobs," as white men asserted their superior claims to work they had formerly considered beneath them. After the upturn in white business, Negroes were seldom able to reclaim their places as waiters, bellhops, elevator operators, janitors, and barbers. The building trades unions kept Negroes out of skilled construction jobs, and colored men's brief hopes that the Capital Transit Company would hire Negro platform workers collapsed when the Transit Union threatened a walkout if a single "nigger" were employed. Although thirty-five new Negro-owned retail stores opened between 1929 and 1935, the volume of business was too small and payrolls were too thin to take up any of the slack in the Negro labor market. Advertising in the *Tribune* shrank month after month till finally the paper merged with the Baltimore *Afro-American.*

Convinced that the boycott was the one weapon available to the colored community to check discriminatory employment practices, in the fall of 1933 a small group of men formed the New Negro Alliance to organize Negro consumers in the struggle. Their first move was to picket a U Street hot-dog stand whose owner employed only white men. A week or two without Negro customers persuaded the proprietor to hire colored help. The prospect of a similar boycott proved effective when members of the Alliance sought out the proprietors of the scores of small Jewish-owned shops in the neighborhood. By 1934 the A & P chain had taken on a few Negro clerks in its branches in colored neighborhoods. For a time Howard University intellectuals, notably Ralph Bunche, objected that the movement represented an unwholesome racism certain to

[9] Census Tracts, D.C., 1930, Bureau of the Census; Eunice Grier, *Understanding Washington's Population*, pp. 10-13; see ch. XVII, n. 16.

boomerang, but Alliance leaders insisted that "buy where you work" merely meant using Negro purchasing power to give qualified Negroes an equal chance with whites. Criticism subsided as small successes multiplied: by 1936 nearly 300 jobs filled by Negroes in stores formerly manned only by whites. Fifteen months of picketing the two branches of the Peoples Drug Store located in solidly Negro neighborhoods clinched the argument, for although the company held out against hiring Negro clerks and sidestepped the "sit-down" challenge by removing the soda fountains where Negroes asked for service, the heavy financial losses of the chain convinced the community of the utility of the "consumer strike." That Mary McLeod Bethune, President Roosevelt's special advisor on minority affairs, joined the picket line probably gave special significance to that particular campaign.[10]

Until Mrs. Bethune's appointment in 1936, and indeed after, the New Deal did less for colored people than they had expected. They got more and better posts in the executive departments, it is true. The District Recorder of Deeds, a municipal court judge, and the Minister to Liberia were colored men; William Hastie received the federal judgeship for the Virgin Islands; some forty-odd minor administrative posts in Washington went to eminent Negroes; and in 1935 forty got places in a new analysis section of the Labor Department. But in 1938, of the 9,717 Negroes in the federal service in Washington, 90 percent held custodial jobs for which the top annual pay rate was $1,260; only 9.5 percent had clerical jobs, and only 47 men had subprofessional rank. In the matter of promotions, the merit system was as inoperative as in earlier years. When the Resettlement Administration proposed to relocate colored families in Negro Greenbelts, the *Tribune* blasted the plan as a sign of a deliberate policy of cutting Negro Americans

[10] *Tribune*, 13 Jul, 5 Oct, 23 Nov 1933, 3, 31 May 1934, 6 Dec 1935; *Afro-American*, 28 Jan 1939; *New Negro Opinion*, Oct 1933-Apr 1936; *New Negro Alliance Yearbook*, 1939.

off from the main body of American life. Similarly, the hypercritical wondered why the National Youth Administration should have a separate unit for Negro affairs instead of handling them as part of all youth problems.

Consensus, however, was general that Mary McLeod Bethune, former head of a colored girls' school in Florida, was the person to take charge of the NYA Negro division. Although nuances indicated a faint irritation among some of Washington's colored elite that she kept herself somewhat apart from the local community, they quickly realized that her breadth of knowledge, her perceptiveness, her political finesse, and her direct access to the President were invaluable to the Negro cause. In dealing with her white associates, as one young man recalled, her pronouncedly Negroid appearance in itself helped. With her deep-chocolate-colored skin, her heavy build, and rather prognathous jaw, she seemed like a product of darkest Africa—until she spoke. Then the exquisitely musical voice offering sagacious counsel in a perfect Oxford accent carried an impact that left no one in doubt that here was an extraordinary woman to whom any sensible person would listen with respectful attention.[11]

To some colored Washingtonians more important from the first than any political appointee or any New Deal agency was Elder Lightfoot Michaux and his "Church of God." Such confidence as they had in the President perhaps stemmed from the evangelist's assurance that Franklin D. Roosevelt was the Lord's chosen instrument. Not long after the Elder came to Washington in the depths of the depression, he managed, no one knew quite how, to get money for a daily radio program to tell listeners to lean on Jesus. Every morning at 7 o'clock the "Happy am I" preacher explained over station WSJV that W stood for willingly, J for Jesus, S for suffered, and V for

[11] Hayes, *Negro Govt Worker*, p. 104; John P. Davis, "A Black Inventory of the New Deal," and Abraham Epstein, "The Social Security Act," *Crisis*, XLII, 141-42, 334-38; *Crisis*, XLIII, 168, 204, XLVI, 271.

victory over the grave. His tub-thumping exhortations helped him quickly to collect a following as devoted as that of "Papa" Divine. Under the pastor's lead the little store-front Church of God on Georgia Avenue turned into a kind of institutional church that fed the hungry and housed the homeless. As a coast-to-coast network picked up the evangelist's broadcasts, one of his publications noted, "the people began to clamor for him to come out into the open and fight his War on the devil. Elder Michaux was himself eager to go directly to the front and boldly let the people eat right out of his hands the spiritual food they needed to keep the devil on the run." So the Elder organized the "Cross Choir" of 156 trained singers to stage elaborately executed programs of choruses and marches, usually at the Griffith Stadium.

The preacher won the ear of politically influential people. When the congregation of the Church of God elected five honorary deacons, District Commissioner George E. Allen, Dwight D. Eisenhower, "Steve" Early, personal secretary to the President, Clark Griffith, principal owner of Washington's baseball team, and Harry Butcher, vice president of the Columbia Broadcasting Company, all accepted the honor and a Bible each to seal the covenant. Upon hearing that a congressman, possessor of a race horse named "Not Worth Owning," was about to propose legalization of horse-racing in the District and revival of the old race track on Benning Road, the evangelist, pointing out that gambling was not pleasing to God, persuaded the congressman to drop his bill and sell Not Worth Owning. Having induced Honorary Deacon Allen to sell his horse also, Michaux then inveigled both men into helping him buy the race track at a bargain price. There in time to come he would put up Mayfair Mansions, a luxurious 596-unit Negro housing development. Until 1938 he engaged an excursion boat every summer to convey people awaiting baptism down the Potomac, but that year Honorary Deacon Clark

Griffith arranged to have a large canvas tank set up at the ball park, where the pastor, clad in a black robe, high rubber boots, and a black skull cap, baptized his sheep in water imported from the River Jordan. New Dealers prone to ignore all other local affairs and local citizens looked upon him as a personage, the one Washingtonian, white or colored, to excite their interest.

If nobody begrudged Elder Michaux his triumphs, neither were many colored Washingtonians willing to accept his brand of religious fervor or endorse his tactics. On the contrary. No doubt a number of white people were genuinely moved by his oratory and impressed by his good works, but the delighted amusement his methods provoked in much of white Washington contained the seeds of a derisiveness damaging to all colored people. The elements in American society that twenty years later would form the core of white citizens' councils naturally looked upon the Elder with favor as the epitome of the old-style camp-meeting Negro whose militance was directed at the devil, not in seeking equality with white men, a Negro to be patted on the back, helped when convenient, made use of, and ridiculed. Whether or not highly educated colored Washingtonians saw a potential threat in the racial image Elder Michaux presented, they looked for other paths than his to their goals.

The second half of the 1930's found much of the colored community groping. By 1936 the local chapter of the NAACP, unable to work with "the rowdy element," had faded out. The New Negro Alliance, however successful in opening up jobs, could not ensure fair wages, and colored Washingtonians were tired of waiting for whites to recognize Afro-Americans as more American than Afro. Hence when the brilliant and respected John Preston Davis, during NRA days executive secretary of the Joint Committee on National Recovery, issued a call to Negro organizations all over the country to evolve through a national Negro congress a national racial policy, the idea appealed strongly. But the conventions arrived at no plan of positive action, and in 1940 when Davis advocated the Communist party line, most of his followers repudiated him. The Congress fell apart. Meanwhile, in response to a proposal put forward by Assistant Superintendent of the Colored Schools Garnett Wilkinson, a handful of colored people turned to a new form of interracial conciliation by joining with a small group of earnest whites in founding the Washington Urban League. Chartered in December 1938, the league worked on the premise that persuasion was the only effective way to end racial prejudice and give Negroes economic opportunities. A gift from Canon Anson Phelps Stokes of the Cathedral provided funds for a first year, but the new organization made little headway. Ultra-conservative whites and, conversely, left-of-center Negro leaders considered the program of bi-racial conferences little more than talk and more talk. And talk opened no doors, not even to the movie theatres showing "Abraham Lincoln in Illinois" to which a colored man who had won a contest as the person looking most like Abe was refused admission.

Oddly enough, the most significant break in the color line to occur in Washington before 1939 occasioned little comment. Without any pressure, in 1937 the faculty of the graduate school of American University voted to admit Negro students. The unanimous decision came in answer to an application from an exceptionally well qualified candidate, a graduate of the Howard University Law School, who explained that she wanted to take a Ph.D. in political science; Howard neither offered sufficiently advanced courses nor conferred doctoral degrees. When the president and the most influential of the trustees endorsed the faculty vote, only one of the nearly 2,000 graduate students withdrew. Negro enrollment was not heavy. Some of the colored students found the standards of scholarship hard to meet, and professors were troubled now and again at having to give discouragingly low grades, but most of the candidates eventually completed the work for masters' degrees, and several won doctorates with distinction. Shortly after American University acted, Catholic University opened its school of social work to Negroes.

While this minor revolution went largely unnoticed, early in 1939 chance produced more dramatic results. The national limelight suddenly focused on racial discrimination in the capital when the DAR refused to allow the famous contralto Marian Anderson to sing in the DAR-owned Constitution Hall. When the Board of Education, after pondering the request for use of the white Central High School auditorium, hedged its permission about with a proviso that this was to be an exception, not a precedent, the furor aroused in the city and throughout the country exceeded any outburst of indignation within the memory of Washington's oldest inhabitants. Secretary of the Interior Harold Ickes immediately authorized the use of the Lincoln Memorial, and there on Easter Sunday afternoon the concert took place at the feet of the "Great Emancipator" before an audience of 75,000 people. No one present at that moving performance ever forgot it. It was the turning point, one man averred, in Washington Negroes' seventy-year-old fight against discrimination.

White people shed some of their condescension and more of their obliviousness, a revived NAACP chapter enlisted 2,500 members in a matter of months, and confidence in the future ran strong in colored Washington. Her 191 doctors, 72 dentists, 98 lawyers, and nearly 600 public school and university teachers upon whose "phenomenal culture" her name for distinction rested, in the opinion of the secretary of the new NAACP branch, in the past had sought white recognition too eagerly to heed their inferiors. Now a feeling of unity was emerging along with a belief that the New Deal was about to open the way for the "common man" of the Negro world, much as the age of Jackson had for white Americans a century before. In spite of the shortage of jobs, wrote Victor Daly, after six years of Roosevelt's administration colored people in Washington were better off "economically, socially and culturally" than anywhere else, and although custom perpetuated segregation in hotels, restaurants, and all places of entertainment, the concerted bi-racial movement fostered by the Marian Anderson episode promised to grow. The lessons of Nazi Germany's race doctrines were not wholly lost upon Washingtonians. Thus, before the American military build-up got under way in mid-1940, uninterrupted progress seemed assured.[12]

Social intercourse between the races was still rare. Distinguished colored musicians gave a few concerts at the White House; eminent Negroes occasionally attended official receptions or had tea with Mrs. Roosevelt; colored and white children shared the playgrounds in Georgetown parks; Negro graduate students met with white in university classrooms; and adults of both races periodically sat at conferences together. But during leisure hours the secret city of the 1930's was as remote from white Washington as in the 1920's. Cultivated colored people generally preferred it that way, just as they wanted separate, albeit truly equal, schools. Old families, though readier than in the 1920's to share in civic responsibilities, were, if possible, more than ever inclined to exclude the outlander from their social life. But neither were white cave-dwellers eager to take to their bosoms new arrivals brought to the capital by the government, institutions of learning, or business.

[12] *Church of God, A Pictorial Review*, pp. 6, 23, 26-27, 46, 51, 58, 60; Caroline Ware to the author, 21 May 1962; Address, Garnett Wilkinson at Twentieth Anniversary of the Founding of the Washington Urban League, 1958 (typesc in League files); *Tribune*, 22 Nov 1937; Victor Daly, "Washington's Minority Problem," and John Lovell, Jr., "Washington Fights," *Crisis*, XLVI, 170, 276-77; *Afro-American*, 7, 14, 21 Jan, 25 Feb 1939.

Formal white society itself underwent a considerable shakeup, for, apart from the diplomatic corps, official society, as Washington had known it from the 1880's onward, ceased to exist. It held little interest for New Dealers preoccupied with economic and social reforms; leading public figures now conversed on topics that ruled out the chitchat once heard at the dinner tables of sought-after hostesses or at the Misses Patten's teas. What newspaper correspondents regarded as news, furthermore, discouraged any attempt to restore the one-time glitter to "Society"; most of the columns from Washington in metropolitan dailies now dealt with such themes as the workings of the National Recovery Act, the new National Labor Relations Board, or the President's proposal to "pack" the Supreme Court. Only embassy parties retained touches of the old splendor, and those, too, lost some of their savor now that the press passed lightly over them. If sticklers for etiquette were aghast at hearing of a White House Cabinet dinner where the guests of honor were radio's "Amos and Andy"—in the flesh two personable young white men in white ties and tails—most Washingtonians merely wished they too could have been present. Perhaps a few *grande dames* of yesteryear deplored the disappearance of the formal afternoons at home, but the younger generation was glad to be rid of them. The great event of every winter became the annual Polio Foundation Ball. Otherwise, cocktail parties largely supplanted more elaborate entertaining. Even when Washington witnessed the largest crowd in her history on the occasion, in the commissioners' phrase, of the visit of the "King and Queen of Great Britain" in June 1939, the festivities in their honor lacked much of the pomp and circumstance that would once have attended them. Perhaps only the President and his royal guests at that moment were already hearing in imagination the rumble of tanks and the clump of army boots moving across Europe.[13]

[13] *Tribune*, 8 Feb 1934; *Afro-American*, 14 Jan 1939, 4 May 1940;

New attitudes born of the depression and a consequent reassessment of values were reflected also in larger church attendance, in an endeavor of the Washington Federation of Churches to widen its services, in the launching of the Roman Catholic Interracial Council, and possibly in the appearance in Washington of a small body of Black Muslims whose leader taught that white people were the source of all evil and only Mohammed's black followers would inherit the earth. But whereas heightened religious zeal was a foreseeable product of economic disaster, the tendency of the New Deal in its early stages to reject scientific research along with social frivolity and adulation of big business was an unexpected development. In 1933 and 1934 opprobrium attached to science as the source of over-production and, therefore, of the depression. Physicists and chemists, contended a writer in *Science*, had been travelling so fast that they had ceased to "heed or care what misapplications are made of their discoveries."

When the first New Deal Congress sliced the appropriations for military research, for the Bureau of Standards, and for the Census Bureau and the statistical branches of the Labor Department whose data were virtually essential to intelligent economic planning, alarm overtook the federal scientific bureaus. In 1933 a presidentially appointed Scientific Advisory Board headed by the physicist Karl Compton of the Massachusetts Institute of Technology drafted a blueprint for government cooperation in scientific work. But the President's closest advisers labelled the proposal extravagant, impractical, and overweighted in favor of the physical sciences. Secretary of Agriculture Wallace, on the other hand, unwaveringly advocated government funds for research, for, he argued, to charge it "with the responsibility for our failure to apportion produc-

---

Abell, George, and Evelyn Gordon, *Let Them Eat Caviar*, pp. 44-45, 191; Longworth, "Lion-Hunting," *Ladies' Home Journal*, LI, 27; Comrs Rpt, 1939, p. 121.

tion to need and to distribute the fruits of plenty equitably" was folly. Better controlled use of science and engineering would create more leisure and release more human energy "to enjoy the things which are non-material and non-economic, and I would include in this not only music, painting, literature and sport for sport's sake, but . . . the idle curiosity of the scientist himself."

Although appropriations for government research remained small throughout the decade, Wallace's view, with its stress on the social sciences and recognition of the value of basic research—"the idle curiosity of the scientist"—largely prevailed after 1935. At the President's request the National Resources Committee in 1937 undertook a comprehensive study of the "interrelation of government and the intellectual life of the nation," which put to rest any lingering fears lest the government withdraw altogether from scientific exploration. *Research —A National Resource* reviewed what had been done and what must be done under federal aegis not only in the physical and the social sciences but also in technology and education; the report stated unequivocally that problems confronting the federal government "ultimately compel the prosecution of fundamental, or pure, research." Nevertheless, while the National Research Council continued to sponsor scientific investigations and the Carnegie Institution, unimpeded by governmental doubts about its utility, carried on pure research in the fields of terrestrial magnetism and geophysics, during the 1930's Washington lost her dominant position as a center of research in the natural sciences.

Decentralization took to the suburbs the Department of Agriculture's research headquarters, set up in 1936 at an experimental farm in Beltsville, Maryland, and the National Cancer Institute, which the Public Health Service placed in Bethesda in 1938 as a second unit of the National Institutes of Health. Financial stringencies limited the work of the Smithsonian.

In the little building south of the red sandstone castle, Dr. Charles Abbot, secretary of the institution, pursued his studies in astrophysics assisted by Andrew Kramer, the instrument maker who had built Samuel Langley's aeronautical devices. There Abbott constructed solar-heat collectors that used the primal energy of the sun to run a small motor or to bake bread. "Who knows," he asked, "when he goes about an investigation to increase the bounds of knowledge, however remote his subject may be from the ordinary walks of life, what application the future may have in store for the results he gains?" Weekly nationwide broadcasts begun in 1936 presented "The World is Yours," dramatic non-technical accounts of what scientists through the centuries had learned about the universe, and the institution published some important monographs as well as an appendix to each annual report that constituted in essence a yearbook of contemporary science. But the big universities of the country conducted most of the fundamental research, and industrial laboratories, such as those of the American Telephone Company and DuPont, carried on much of the applied research.[14]

In the capital, research in the social sciences and the humanities, on the other hand, gradually took on fresh importance. Scholars made intensive use of the Folger Shakespeare Library, and many a jobless person spent hours in the Library of Congress learning while he could not earn. Foreigners accustomed to the red tape and rigid rules restricting the use of the great libraries of Europe were astonished at the ease with which anyone and everyone could draw upon the resources of this "storehouse of knowledge." In the general reading room, wrote James Truslow Adams, "which alone contains ten thousand volumes which may be read without even the asking, one sees

[14] Bureau of the Census, *Religious Bodies*, 1936, I, 395, 426-27; "Women's Department of the Washington Federation of Churches," *Miscellaneous Review*, LII, 546-48; Dupree, *Science*, pp. 344-68; Paul Oehser, *Sons of Science*, pp. 160-77; *Research—A National Resource*, I, 51, and *passim*.

the seats filled with silent readers, old and young, rich and poor, black and white, the executive and the laborer, the general and the private, the noted scholar and the schoolboy, all reading at their own library provided by their own democracy." The opening of the Annex in April 1939 added stack space for ten million books and made study rooms available both to American and foreign students engaged in research requiring constant use of the library's collections.

New gifts to the Trust Fund Board enabled Herbert Putnam to increase the number of library consultantships and chairs, while acquisition of the Joseph Pennell collection of Whistler drawings widened the resources of the Prints and Photographs Division. Still more gratifying to part of the local public was the enlargement of the concert program made possible by the Gertrude Clarke Whittall Foundation. In 1935 Mrs. Whittall, Nebraska-born widow of a prominent Massachusetts businessman, presented to the library her unique collection of Stradivari stringed instruments and Tourte bows and set up a fund to support additional chamber music concerts in the Coolidge auditorium, where the performers were to use the matchless instruments. When Mrs. Whittall offered to erect a "Putnam Pavilion" to house the instruments, the librarian gratefully accepted but told the donor: "You're a squandering squaw from Omaha! We'll call it the Whittall Pavilion." After 1938 the famous Budapest String Quartet became a resident orchestra and played regularly at the library.

Upon completing his 40th year as Librarian of Congress, Herbert Putnam retired in June 1939. President Roosevelt, acting chiefly on the advice of Supreme Court Justice Felix Frankfurter, chose a successor with characteristic speed and insistence. After unsuccessful preliminary negotiations with a reluctant Archibald MacLeish, the President summoned him to lunch at the White House. When the poet protested that he knew nothing about managing a great library, the President replied: "Nonsense! You can run the library between the time you wake up in the morning and the time you finish shaving. You'll have the rest of the day for your own writing." In October, a month after war broke out in Europe, MacLeish took up his duties with a high sense of mission, for, he believed, "time is running out, not like sand in a glass, but like the blood in an opened artery," and Americans must learn to value and preserve their inheritance lest "the nonculture, the obscurantism, the superstition, the brutality, the tyranny which is overrunning eastern and central and southern Europe" submerge the United States also. Faith that understanding of the accumulated wisdom of the past and awareness of the arts would save the nation from disaster guided his policies. In 1940 he brought to Washington the self-exiled French poet St. John Perse as a consultant in French literature. Urging high school students to use the library regularly, MacLeish strove constantly to make it a tool of popular education. His concept was a departure from Putnam's ideal of serving the world of learning, but the younger man's associates felt in working with him that his was "the brush of the comet."

Meanwhile, depression, New Deal, and the flight of scholars from the spreading despotism in Europe benefitted the local universities. As exceptionally able Washington high school graduates unable to meet the expense of going away to college entered local institutions, faculties expanded, curricula widened, and prospective competition for jobs after graduation produced a better quality of undergraduate work. Much the same sequence of cause and effect was observable in state universities, but in Washington the challenge was the more immediate because of the widening opportunities in the burgeoning government agencies. New federal bodies set up to handle problems unfamiliar to old-line civil servants wanted people trained to meet such novel responsibilities as assembling old age and survivors' insurance data in the newly organized Social Security

Administration; in that case a course given at American University by a German political scientist with first-hand knowledge of European practices resolved the dilemma. At the Department of Agriculture Graduate School experts taught evening classes in as many as fifty different subjects, and at the American University's downtown "campus" in the string of Victorian houses on F Street west of the White House, graduate students with daytime jobs sat at the feet of specialists willing to teach at night. Besides economics, sociology, public administration, education, and fields of history that had direct bearing on government needs, law attracted students to graduate work. The listings in *Who's Who* of the 1950's and early 1960's show how many men eminent in public life had received their training in the Georgetown, George Washington, National, or Howard University Law School of the 1930's. And mounting world tensions as the decade wore on enhanced the importance of the Georgetown University Foreign Service School, where Father Walsh, its director, impressed students by his penetrating analysis of Russian communism.

As growing numbers of distinguished foreign scholars for whom Europe had become intolerable or unsafe accepted teaching posts in the American capital, the air of provincialism that had long clung to all Washington's universities disappeared. The famous physicist George Gamow of Copenhagen and Edward Teller, known twenty years later as the "father of the hydrogen bomb," added to George Washington's academic stature, and notable German economists and historians similarly increased the scholarly standing of the other universities. In 1940 Mr. and Mrs. Robert Woods Bliss' gift of their collection of Near Eastern *objets d'art* and Dumbarton Oaks, their beautiful old Georgetown house, to Harvard University for a museum and center of Byzantine studies opened out prospects of still further achievements in the world of learning. The foreign legations and embassies for 140 years had lent official society a cosmopolitan touch, but the savants who came in the 1930's to make their homes in Washington endowed the entire community with a new perception of Old World civilization. And their appreciation of what they found here, sometimes admittedly unexpectedly, deepened Washingtonians' sense of their own American heritage; that men who had spent their lives surrounded by the works of art and the traditions of a great past now preferred to live in Washington was at once an accolade and a challenge. Approximately 4,100 recently acquired foreign-born residents, a number of them artisans and shop-keepers rather than teachers and highly educated people, could not entirely reshape the attitudes and tastes of a city of more than 620,000 inhabitants. Yet the variety of languages to be heard on the streets and trolley cars gave people the feeling of being part of a world community. Thus with all her prejudices and grievances Washington attained a mellowness that no one could have anticipated in 1932.[15]

One gauge of that mellowness was the place music and drama assumed. Movies, ball games at the stadium, and trips to the zoo were still major diversions, but the uses to which people put leisure widened. Twice a week during the summer of 1935 the National Symphony Orchestra played from a barge anchored in the river at the Ceremonial Watergate, a tier of steps rising from the Potomac to Riverside Drive above the Arlington Memorial Bridge. There the Marine and the Army bands and after 1936 an independent musicians' cooperative played to audiences of about 12,000 people, working men's families, government officials, and Washington bluebloods alike seated on the steps or stretched out on the lawns adjoining, with the river flowing by at their feet, while couples listened from canoes drifting in the shallows. The WPA Music Project helped organize orchestras, choruses, and bands in a number of government

[15] "The Story Up to Now," *Rpt Lib/Cong*, 1946, pp. 212-22; *Dept/Agriculture Graduate School*, 1961; Mrs. Whittall herself tells the story of the "Putnam Pavilion."

departments; the fifty-man chorus at the Government Printing Office, to name but one, early acquired an enviable reputation for its performances. Amateur drama groups flourished at the churches and community centers, while the WPA Federal Theatre Project, in addition to sponsoring several lesser productions, staged *Pins and Needles* before a racially mixed audience. All these do-it-yourself forms of entertainment gave the city of over a half million souls a pleasant, small-town flavor.

Partly through government encouragement, interest in painting also spread. In 1933 a grant to the Treasury started the Public Works of Art Project, which engaged artists—at craftsmen's wages, to be sure—to decorate the new public buildings with murals. From that beginning came a permanent section in the Treasury Department for paintings and sculpture. George Biddle's murals in the Department of Justice building depicting "The Sweatshop" and similar themes, and Henry Varnum Poor's series on "Entrance into Prison," "Release from Prison," "Surveyors at Work," and a half dozen more were among the most admired products of this federal patronage. Before the decade was gone, the Corcoran Art School had some five hundred students enrolled, and the enthusiasm of the amateurs whom the gifted Law Watkins taught in evening classes at the Phillips Gallery led him to start a small daytime school. While waiting eagerly for the completion of the Mellon Gallery, Washingtonians looked with fresh eyes at the pictures in the National Museum which for thirty years had constituted the National Gallery of Art and now received the name National Collection of Fine Arts.[16]

Books, pamphlets, and magazine articles pouring out of Washington throughout the New Deal years testified further to the city's intellectual vitality. Some of the output was ephemeral, some was trivial, and some suffered from the weakness

[16] WPA *Guide*, pp. 139-42; *Newsweek*, VI, 27 Jul 1935, p. 30; "General Information," Ntl Gallery of Art, *Bulletin*, I, Mar 1941; *American Magazine of Art*, XXVIII, 204.

Mark Twain described in rebuking his wife's attempts to cure him of swearing by repeating some of his phrases: "You've got the words right, Libby, but you haven't got the tune." Still no earlier period had evoked so much published material of enduring value. Besides the commentaries and reminiscences of brain-trusters and their opponents, journalists' news stories and accounts of the news behind the news frequently attained literary distinction. A book such as Thomas Stokes' *Chip Off My Shoulder* would be as moving in the 1960's as in the thirties. Dos Passos and writers in the *American Mercury*, to be sure, implied that much of what emanated from Washington had a sycophantic tone deriving from an awed subservience to the "Radio-Voice from the Blue Room." But Brookings Institution economists attacked New Deal agricultural policies and other experiments in fashion that left no doubt that independent thinking had not stopped. Poetry and fiction, except that purporting to be solid fact, rarely appeared, for, despite new-found pleasure in the arts, simple diversions, and casual, friendly social occasions, to the New Dealer life was real and life was earnest. His was the role of the missionary. Had he had the genius, the engrossing business of remaking American civilization left him no time to transpose that experience into an epic poem or the Great American Novel.

Outsiders generally assumed that these changes, good and bad, if not actually foisted upon the local community, had at least occurred without its help. Disparaging critiques of the local press strengthened that notion: the *Star* still served up pure eye-wash; the slightly more perceptive *News* shied away from real issues; the *Times* and the *Herald*, merged in 1939, were pro-Americanism, pro-Hearst, pro-Marian Davies, and anti everything else; while the *Post*, which ex-banker Eugene Meyer purchased in 1933 and talked of turning into a liberal sheet, was merely a banking organ with a fascist slant.[17]

[17] Dos Passos, "Washington: The Big Town," *New Republic*, LXXVIII, 120-33; Marguerite Young, "Ignoble Journalism in the Nation's Capital,"

Characteristically such appraisals passed over the quality of reporting on significant local matters. For newcomers the city as an entity in her own right apart from the federal government did not exist.

To a degree never equalled before or after, the New Deal era subjected Washingtonians to an unconscious patronage that assigned them to the position of non-contributing beneficiaries of the progress wrought by new arrivals. Those New Dealers who stayed would discover later that they too had become part of that once faintly despised, indefinable body known as Washingtonians. Yet as generous-minded long-time residents knew, the brain-trusters imbued America with a new social consciousness and fresh intellectual curiosity that left a lasting imprint in the capital. The constant belittlement that the community faced had the virtue of undermining any latent complacency. Conscientious citizens anxious to do better for the city resented New Deal high-handedness only as it ignored local reform movements.

---

and Eugene A. Kelly, "Distorting the News," *American Mercury*, XXXIV, 239-43, 307-18.

CHAPTER XX

RUNNING UNCLE SAM'S COMPANY TOWN, 1933-1941

SPECULATION about who would succeed Commissioners Reichelderfer and Crosby had begun in March 1933, but during the explosion of national legislation in the First Hundred Days Washingtonians reconciled themselves to waiting. Two days after the inauguration some indignation, reportedly shared by the President, had flared up at the metropolitan police for resorting to billy clubs, curses, and arrests in dispersing an unauthorized parade of some six hundred local unemployed—"mostly colored people under communist leadership," the commissioners explained airily—but, the politically wise realized, even new officials in the District Building would be unlikely to embark at once upon police reforms. In June a number of Hoover appointees were still holding various federal offices; obviously postponement of the exercise of the patronage left the President with a whip in hand. By midsummer, however, the local public was finding the delay "not only a mystery but also a source of some irritation." Then word circulated that the President was planning to reorganize the entire District government, substituting for the three-man commission a one-man rule like that of "Boss" Shepherd in the 1870's, minus a popularly elected legislature.

For several years past, national journals had been commenting on the ineffectualness of the District's government: it was an "Adventure in Autocracy" that subjected residents of the capital to indignities and endless inconveniences, including the ministrations of five separate bodies of police and a Public Utilities Commission that tolerated two mutually uncooperating transit systems and two gas companies in a city of fewer than 500,000 people. Let the city at least be under unified control;

the commissioners had become a "national laughing stock." Here was an about-face from the position publicists had taken in 1901 when they held up Washington's municipal government as a model. Within the city dissatisfaction had been growing as the depression deepened, but in the autumn of 1933 few people took much stock in the rumors of a basic reorganization. Still the Board of Trade, fearful of losing its influence in District affairs, was uneasy at reports that Roosevelt intended to put in charge for a ten-year term a city manager who was to be selected from the country at large rather than from the ranks of local citizens. The plan would strip the community, the board president contended, of its last vestige of local representation. No comment came from the White House. As October came and went, observers deduced that President Roosevelt had little interest in the capital city and had delegated decisions about the local government to one of his secretaries. Not until mid-November did the newspapers announce that Melvin D. Hazen and George E. Allen would be sworn in as commissioners on the 16th.[1]

Hazen, a spare, athletic-looking, gray-haired man of sixty, had been a District employee for forty years, city surveyor for thirty, and consequently was familiar with the routines of District business, but he had never had a hand in making policy or in drafting a District budget. He owed his appointment, gossip said, not to his experience in public affairs, but to his passion for horse-breeding and racing which had cemented a friendship with Admiral Cary T. Grayson, head of the Roosevelt inaugural committee and chairman of the American National Red Cross. For years Hazen had spent much of his time on his family estate in Virginia and avowed a preference for country over city living. To choose for District

[1] *News*, 9, 13 Mar, 26 Sep, 15 Nov 1933; *Star*, 7 Jun, 16 Jul, 3, 11 Sep 1933; Comrs Rpt, 1933, p. 72; *Post*, 22 Jun 1933; *Herald*, 13 Jul, 30 Aug, 26 Sep 1933; J. Frederick Essary, "An Adventure in Autocracy," *American Mercury*, xx, 290; Rpt B/Tr, 1934, p. 7.

commissioner a man without intense interest in urban problems seemed odd to some of his subordinates and distinctly unfortunate to citizens who believed the moment ripe for vigorous leadership in the local as well as the national government. Allen's appointment came as a still greater surprise. Nine Washingtonians out of ten had never heard of him. Roosevelt himself had never laid eyes on him. A Mississippian born and bred, he had lived in Washington since 1928 when he became manager of the Wardman Park Hotel and other local hotel properties. He himself later explained that he had angled for a public office for which he had no known qualifications purely because he decided, as the depression denuded the Wardman Park of its patrons one by one, that he could benefit from the publicity of having his name thrown into the pot of candidates. His golf and bridge crony, Senator Pat Harrison of Mississippi, with the backing of Postmaster General James Farley, had quickly arranged matters, and the stocky, slightly balding 36-year-old hotel man had soon found himself ensconced in the District Building. Major Gotwals, the engineer commissioner, stayed on until August 1934.

Whatever discomfiture the local public felt at having its government entrusted to "a Virginian, a Mississippian and an Army officer," as the *Herald* characterized the trio, no one voiced open criticism until Hazen enlisted the help of the Chamber of Commerce in preparing his first District budget, a step which subjected him to derision and accusations of catering to business interests. His announced satisfaction with the police department dismayed people exasperated with its inefficiencies and periodic displays of ruthlessness. He disliked the very idea of change unless it were to enhance the authority of the commissioners. A dignified, slow-paced hack, reappointed three times over, he died of a heart attack at his desk in July 1941. George Allen, on the other hand, presented a facade of casualness, using camaraderie and humor, forced or otherwise, as his weapons. In the opinion of the then secretary of the Board of Commissioners, Allen did more for the District of Columbia on the golf course than in his office. As he became increasingly the boon companion of senators and congressmen and, somewhat reluctantly, took on the role of "court jester" at the White House, he was in a position to accomplish a good deal for his fellow citizens. A self-confessed show-off, he nevertheless convinced the tough-minded Harry Hopkins, head of the Federal Emergency Relief Administration, that Commissioner Allen was the person to direct the District relief program in the bitter winter of 1933.

People who had hoped that the President would appoint a Louis Brownlow to office watched the performance in the District Building for the next four and a half years with incredulity, resigned indignation, or pure cynical amusement. Not long after he was sworn in, Allen undertook to discover at first hand how other cities were handling relief. Donning his shabbiest clothes and posing as an unemployed waiter, he set off by bus for Cleveland, Detroit, Chicago, and Milwaukee. Refused a job twenty times over, thrown out of respectable hotels, and insulted by social workers, upon his return to Washington he told Harry Hopkins that he better instruct his staff "not to act like God Almighty." But Allen in turn could be both arbitrary and cocky. Impatient with what he considered the moribund procedures of the Board of Public Welfare, he bypassed the board, engaged a member of Harry Hopkins' staff to manage District emergency relief, and set about persuading Congress to transfer full control of welfare to the commissioners—in short, to him. That particular struggle ended when George Wilson, after thirty-eight years' service to the city's private and public charities, resigned, and Elwood Street, director of the Community Chest, became the executive of the Welfare Board. But Allen continued to inject himself into the picture in an attempt, as the new director of the Community Chest saw it, to pull the strings without putting himself to any trouble about the puppets' performance.

A generation later the hassle over welfare administration would seem to have been rather silly, inconsequential feuding. In the mid-1930's it was the foremost community problem. Among public-spirited Washingtonians resentment of Allen's easy-going methods and flair for self-advertising spread. Newspapermen found him "good copy" and played him up accordingly, even while they poked fun at a white collar project he instituted for jobless reporters: tabulating the record of race-track favorites to see how often the most heavily bet-upon horses won. Yet, in the curious backhanded fashion of political maneuvering, the publicity the local press gave him and his rather slap-dash propositions probably benefitted the city.[2] For while one civilian commissioner strove to perpetuate the old order, his younger associate stirred up controversy and perhaps unintentionally drew attention to the weaknesses of the District's entire governmental system.

Allen's career as commissioner had chiefly symbolic importance. Certainly he was not the first person to hold District office merely because he had friends on the Hill. When he resigned in the summer of 1938 to return to the more congenial world of private business, the attitude of serious-minded Washingtonians was revealed in their reaction to the tales told of a farewell dinner given for him. The party was "off the record," but stories leaked out of how the fifty-odd people there, many of them closely linked to the White House, used the occasion to twit the "presidential joker" about his performance as a public servant. The speeches of congratulation upon his resignation carried a note of the sadistic verbal horseplay which, Allen observed, had always characterized President

[2] *Star*, 16, 17 Nov 1933; *News*, 16, 23 Nov 1933; *Herald*, 15 Dec 1937; George E. Allen, *Presidents Who Have Known Me*, pp. 46-48, 58-68, 71-72; Rpt Public Assistance Division B/PW, 1934; *Herald*, 25-30 Mar 1934.

Roosevelt's dealings with him. The resigning commissioner responded by remarking that, when he was sworn in, the death rate and the cases of destitution in the city had stood at relatively modest figures, but he had taken care of all that: the totals had risen steadily during the last four and a half years. The facetious statement was greeted with roars of laughter from the listeners. Earnest Washingtonians considered the episode not only undignified but a measure of the indifference with which, in their eyes, the President and his appointee looked upon the well-being of the capital. Allen later remarked that the odd jobs the President asked him to undertake had turned him into a species of White House errand boy and thus, he implied, interfered with his official duties.[3]

Citizens nevertheless came to believe that Roosevelt invariably displayed a readiness to dismiss Washington's problems in a cavalier fashion strangely at variance with the concern he showed for the rest of the country; only Mrs. Roosevelt's active interest in the city could partly redeem the record. His staunchest admirers were never able to account for his aloofness. The most obvious explanation, the overriding importance of national affairs which left no time for those of the capital, was not wholly satisfactory, inasmuch as well-informed people felt that ten minutes of listening and perhaps fifteen spent in expressing his convictions to congressional leaders would have sufficed to settle questions that instead were passed over until they became virtually insoluble. One old friend of the President privately assigned his indifference to a distaste for all urban affairs engendered in part by his struggles as Governor with Tammany in New York City and, in part, by his addiction to rural life as the Squire of Hyde Park knew it. Perhaps Roosevelt assumed that, unlike many a provincial city, Washington contained enough brains to resolve her own

[3] Allen, *Presidents*, pp. 73-85.

difficulties without his help, provided the community cared enough to make the effort.

The person who carried most weight in the District Building was Daniel J. Donovan, the District auditor. Possessed of a photographic memory, an intimate knowledge of the laws affecting the District, and strong convictions about what was important, the dynamic Irishman reared on the outskirts of Swampoodle had arrived at his position of behind-the-scenes power by sheer incisive intelligence, inexhaustible diligence, and the force of his personality. He had begun his career in the District government in 1900, became auditor at the end of World War I, and, when the federal Classification Act brought into being the District Personnel Board, became director of that also. When he bellowed "Great Jehovah and the Continental Congress," everyone within earshot sat up and took notice, and to be labelled by Donovan "an unmitigated nuisance" was enough to persuade his staff to withdraw or modify an offending proposal. Once he had made up his mind he was hard to budge from his chosen position. While he could not fix the size of the over-all budget, he could advise upon changes in the tax rate, and his recommendations about the distribution of the general fund were, a federal Bureau of the Budget officer later said, generally "99 percent effective" in shaping the budget that went to Congress. The auditor thus controlled District spending more completely than did the commissioners themselves. As a permanent fixture for twenty-five years Donovan largely determined the policies of his ostensible superiors who came and went. His long experience and his devotion to his native city probably saved Washington from falling completely under the domination of big, self-seeking business corporations that had some congressional backing.

Hazen and two successive engineer commissioners carried on without a third member of the board from the time of Allen's resignation in August 1938 till June 1939, when Allen accepted reappointment. He again resigned two months later. His successor, John Russell Young, had long been a staff member of the *Evening Star* and since 1920 head of the White House correspondents corps. Possibly the nomination of another prima donna without administrative background, and a conservative Republican to boot, would have aroused opposition had the appointment come earlier, but by mid-April 1940 the Nazi invasion of Norway and drive into the Low Countries was absorbing most of the attention of every informed person in the capital.

Long before then the self-defeating complexity of the District's governmental structure had impressed itself upon people in and out of the District Building. By 1928 law had surrounded the Board of Commissioners with some twenty-five independent or partly independent agencies, and the New Deal increased the number until the maze of channels through which officials must find their way obstructed the transaction of the most routine business. Fiscal relationships were so intricate that only Daniel J. Donovan understood them. When at the request of the Senate, an assistant director of the Bureau of the Budget, the District auditor, and the Associate Corporation Counsel undertook to analyze the organizational tangles and recommend simplifications, the report required nine volumes of text and enough charts to paper the walls of a room.

A rule that held for one agency had no validity for the next. Over the presidentially appointed Public Utilities Commission, for example, the commissioners had no control of any kind after 1926. They passed upon the budgets of the National Capital Park and Planning Commission and the National Guard but had no supervisory power over the expenditures of either. Over the District highway department, on the other hand, the commissioners' fiscal control was all-inclusive, even after a vigorous campaign conducted by the Board of Trade induced Congress to allot to the District a share of the federal appropriations voted to the states for road building. In some realms federal contracting services gave the District help on a cost-of-care or cost-of-commodity basis. After 1934 the federal Bureau of Public Assistance matched District funds, just as it did for the states, and a division of the local welfare board ran the program, but in vocational rehabilitation District taxes paid half the costs while the federal bureau took charge of the work; in 1937 a new national act excluded Washington from the benefits given the states. Inconsistencies were everywhere. Civil service procedures applied to some District departments, not to others.

In asking for a detailed study of this cumbersome machinery, the Senate's major concern was to get a workable plan of streamlining District administration in fashion that would relieve Congress of the time-consuming business of acting as city council. Apparently few men on the Hill considered the effect on the local community. The bulky mimeographed "Organization Report" was never published, but in 1934, as descriptions of its contents began to appear in the press, Washingtonians suddenly saw prospects of a local political New Deal, even though the recommendations aimed chiefly at greater efficiency rather than a new democratic basis for governing the city. The principal proposal was to substitute for the board of commissioners a presidentially appointed legislative council on which two or more members of Congress should also sit, vest in it all powers now scattered among the commissioners and the numerous special boards, authorize it to appoint a city manager as executive, and give it full control of the District budget once Congress had appropriated the over-all total. To safeguard national interests, Congress was to have a veto over all local legislative acts. Washington citizens were to have the right to elect a non-voting delegate to the House and select in primaries a slate of men from whom the President should appoint the members of the council. The desirability of placing greatly enlarged fiscal responsibility upon a local governmental body seemed self-evident to a great many people. Primaries for naming council members, moreover, promised the city's rank and file opportunity to express preferences.[4]

The feature of the plan that troubled many Washingtonians was that it denied the people who paid 90 percent of the costs of running the city a voice in congressional decisions or any check on acts of the council after its appointment. Senator Capper of Kansas and Representative Mary Norton, in 1934 chairman of the House District Committee, agreed that local voting rights should extend to more than primaries and electing a delegate to Congress. William King of Utah, chairman of the Senate District Committee, rejected that notion. Washingtonians, he asserted, "shy away from responsibilities and though they may talk about their interest in greater control of their affairs, they do not want too great a degree of autonomy when it comes to a showdown." He never attempted to provide the showdown. Ready as he was to concentrate power in the Board of Commissioners or in an appointed legislative council, he failed to attribute local objections to distaste for a plan that would merely heighten the authoritarian character of the District government.

The Organization Report commanded much more attention in the community than in House and Senate, quite possibly because Congress disliked the very idea of weakening its own control of the city's purse. Newcomers to the capital found the subject confusing and boring, and men and women ridden by anxiety about getting and keeping jobs gave the matter scant thought, but much of the rest of Washington examined every aspect of the questions involved. Articles in the *Herald* explored every possible solution of the basic problem of federal

[4] Schmeckebier, *District of Columbia*; "Organization Report," 1934, II-VIII (Washingtoniana Room, Pub Lib); H Dis Comee, 80C, 1S, Subcomee Hrgs, "Home Rule and Reorganization of the Govt of D.C.," pp. 13-27, and "Preliminary Rpt," pp. 5-6; Rpt. B/Tr, 1934, p. 7; *Star*, 20 May 1932, 7 Jun 1933, 18 Feb, 25 Mar, 15 May 1934; *Times*, 24 Mar 1932, 4 Jan 1934; *Herald*, 7 Oct 1932, 21-30 Mar 1934.

and municipal relationships, and over a period of weeks the *Star* carried statements by officers of citizens associations and leading businessmen. All of them favored some change in the system.

Several men put particular emphasis upon removing the existing financial inequities and confusions, first, by a divorce of the local from the federal budget, second, by a release of District tax-money held without interest in the United States Treasury because Congress had not authorized the expenditure of the accumulated surplus, third, by permitting District officials discretionary power to transfer money from one project to another, and, fourth, by a reversion to the old arrangement that had fixed the annual federal payment for the city's routine expenses at a percentage of the total budget instead of a flat sum, which had dropped since 1928 from nine to five million dollars. Other statements insisted that only the election of District senators and representatives with full voting rights in each house would guarantee respectful attention from Congress to Washington's needs. A surprising number of articles took up the cudgels for home rule, since, its proponents contended, elected municipal officials would respond far more promptly and fully to local mandates than Congress ever would.[5]

Fifteen years earlier, Washingtonians had largely bypassed the home rule issue in their vigorous postwar campaign for national representation. After the collapse of that drive, a few valiants had carried on the fight but with mounting discouragement. In 1922 the Senate Judiciary Committee had reported favorably upon a joint resolution calling for the needed constitutional amendment, at intervals thereafter

[5] *Times*, 24 Mar 1932, 16 Apr 1934; *News*, 12 Apr 1934; *Herald*, 21-30 Mar 1934, 3 Jun 1935; *Star*, 23-26, 30 Apr 6, 8 May, 15, 22 Jul, 5, 12 Aug, 30 Sep 1934, 9 Oct 1935; Comrs Rpts, 1929, pp. 2-4, 1935, p. 7. See the collection of clippings on Home Rule and reorganization plans of the 1930's in Washingtoniana Room, Public Library.

Senator Capper had introduced a similar joint resolution, and some hearings were held. There progress had ended. By the mid-1930's although the Board of Trade still officially backed Capper's stand, many a Washingtonian had lost faith in its feasibility and was ready to settle for the "half-loaf" of an elected municipal council with taxing and ordinance-making powers. And alongside the "whole-loafers" and the "half-loafers" were ranged people anxious for improvements in the governmental machinery but prone to think that a few simplified parts and grease on the wheels would suffice. Between 1934 and the spring of 1940 a dozen plans of reorganization cropped up, some originating in Congress, some in the community.

For a time a referendum proposal interested Washingtonians by offering them a chance to express approval or disapproval of impending administrative or legislative acts and thus provide a guide to Congress and District officials. But as such polls would be expensive and have no binding force, the idea fell into the discard. Commissioner Hazen believed that the commissioners themselves could bring order out of administrative chaos once the powers of the bodies like the public welfare and school boards were cancelled or sharply curtailed. One of a committee of private citizens he appointed to work out that kind of reorganization plan later said ruefully that no member of Congress ever looked at the recommendations; the only observable result of the study was the transfer of Gallinger, Freedmen's and the T.B. hospitals from welfare board supervision to the health department's. At President Roosevelt's request, George Allen, after his resignation as commissioner, also tried his hand at drafting a reorganization bill. Its provisions, like those of several other bills, consisted mostly of a reshuffling of District departments and their duties. Attorney General Homer Cummings jocosely wrote the author that the one intelligible clause in the entire ninety-page document read: "The term District means District of Columbia."[6]

The amount of time and effort which civic organizations, individual citizens, and a score of legislators devoted to the problems of District government was astonishing even in an era of political and social ferment. But as one proposal after another wound up in congressional committee pigeon-holes, frustrated advocates of far-reaching change began to shift tactics. The thirty-year-old District Suffrage League concluded that the very multiplicity of proposals and comment had created an image in Congress of a community that did not know what it wanted. In order to test the strength of public opinion upon the basic issues, in April 1938 a Citizens' Conference representing 271 local organizations undertook to finance and conduct a plebiscite on two questions: do you want to vote for President and for members of Congress from the District of Columbia, and do you want to vote for officials of your own city government in the District? For three weeks newspaper and radio publicity, posters, and speeches before church and civic organizations advertised the purpose of the poll and the rules laid down for it. Since it lacked official sponsorship and the election machinery to be found in every village in the United States, the Suffrage League obtained the school board's permission to set up voting places in thirty-eight public schools. On the evening of April 29th, men and women dressed as Paul Revere's contemporaries paraded through the streets to remind the onlookers that government only by the consent of the governed had been an American creed for 170 years.

[6] Rpts B/Tr, 1934, p. 7, 1935, p. 20, 1936, p. 17, 1937, p. 15; *Herald*, 23 Mar 1934; *Rec*, 75C, 1S, pp. 80, 6298, and App, p. 639; Arthur Capper, "Washington City and the Rights of the People," CHS *Rec*, XL-XLI, 63-77; *Star*, 15 Jan, 18 Dec 1935, 11 Mar 1936, 27 Feb, 1 May, 12 Jul 1937; S bill 2907, and H bill 8146, 75C, 1S; *Post*, 19 Jan 1935, 14 Sep 1936, 10, 13 Oct, 14, 15 Dec 1937; *Times*, 18 Aug 1937; Allen, *Presidents*, pp. 85-88; S bill 3425, 76C, 3S.

Reasoning that people who lived in the capital had an interest in it even if they voted and paid taxes elsewhere, the Suffrage League opened the polls to all adults irrespective of the state citizenship maintained by about half the city's residents. On April 30th, 95,538 people balloted. One Washingtonian reported that he had last exercised that privilege in 1874. Most of them had never voted before, and unfamiliarity with the procedures spoiled 804 ballots. When the judges of the District court who served as tellers announced the final tally, it showed a thirteen to one majority for seats in Congress, seven to one for home rule. Suffrage supporters were elated. In a city of some 627,000 souls, 95,500 represented less than 16 percent of the population, but according to political scientists that was an average turn-out for American municipal elections. Furthermore, careful calculation based on census estimates put the number of possible Washington voters, namely adults who did not exercise the elective franchise in any of the states, at 319,129 and thus raised the percentage taking part in the plebiscite to 30. Inasmuch as scarcely 56 percent of American voters had cast ballots in the 1936 presidential election, a suffrage leader pointed out, Washington's response to polling "on an abstract proposition with no candidates" was extraordinary. Here seemed to be the "showdown" that proved the error of Senator King's appraisal of Washingtonians' attitudes.[7] Only later would Suffrage Leaguers admit reluctantly that the evidence was anything but conclusive.

The House Judiciary Committee held hearings late in May on joint resolutions for national representation and a "Republican government" for the District, but the time allowed was short, much of the testimony was a rehash of familiar arguments,

[7] Clippings, Home Rule, 1938 (Washingtoniana Room); *Plebiscite News Sheet*; *Star*, 22 Apr, 6, 30 May 1938; *Post*, 1 May 1938; *Rec*, 76C, 1S, pp. 14864-65; *A History of the League of Women Voters of the District of Columbia*, pp. 76-77; S Judic Comee, 77C, 1S, Subcomee Hrgs on S J Resolution 35, "National Representation," pp. 226-30.

and committee members appeared preoccupied. Without explaining their reasons, they disapproved both resolutions. Lively hearings before the Senate committee had a similar ending. Yet the 74th Congress alone, one witness pointed out, had had to take time from national affairs to deal with 7 Senate and 3 House resolutions and 30 Senate and 138 House bills, 27 of which finally passed, all concerned solely with Washington. So far from killing discussion, the dismissal of the suffrage proposals inspired additional studies and a succession of new bills and resolutions. While the indefatigable Senator Capper again introduced his perennial resolution for a constitutional amendment authorizing District seats in Congress, and colleagues offered minor nostrums, two bills varying in details but fundamentally similar proposed an elective city council in which should reside all local taxing and ordinance-making powers, subject to congressional veto. The first bill was the more specific, but the second, prepared by the Suffrage League and submitted to the House in May 1939, had the twofold virtue of brevity and of furnishing a reminder to Congress that, if passed, the act would merely restore to the District its political status of 1871 without the superimposed appointed bodies that had wrecked the territorial government.

At this point William A. Roberts, the Washington lawyer who had written most of the Organization Report of 1934, spoke out sharply. The situation, he declared, had become critical. Washington was now the hub of a metropolitan area. Population growth had given new dimensions to civic problems, and the commissioners manifestly could not handle them. Theirs was "not a municipal government as such, but merely a jumbled and unassorted group of emergency departments." Six years of watching had convinced Roberts that a concentration of authority in any appointed body, be it legislative council or board of commissioners, would no longer answer. "Reorganization and suffrage," students of the question had come to agree, "go hand in hand and for practical purposes are inseparable." Washingtonians so far had not got the vote because they had been "too apathetic to fight for it." Of course "present District of Columbia officials have no real interest in suffrage, since it might affect the time of day they come to work or the horse races they like to attend." A *Handbook for District Suffrage* carried further the attack on the commissioners' "dismal failure" of the last ten years. "The commission government has swept problems under the bed till the rubbish caught fire and has done terrible damage to District health, welfare, education and municipal service." Let the disbeliever weigh Mrs. Roosevelt's evidence of the shocking conditions at the Home for the Aged and then judge for himself. The neglect of matters vital to the well-being of the community had reached a state where only a popularly elected city government could be expected to tackle the chore of clearing out the accumulated rubbish.[8]

Reasons for the mounting pressure for home rule are plain enough. The fear of losing the large federal payment toward District expenses, which for years had kept many Washingtonians out of the local suffrage ranks, no longer had bearing. Even when Congress boosted the $4,600,000 federal appropriation of 1934 to $6,000,000 for 1939, the higher figure amounted to scarcely 11 percent of the $44,000,000 District budget, every penny of which must be spent exactly as dictated on the Hill. The parsimony of the past decade underscored the need of an entirely new system. Furthermore, among the energetic newcomers whom the New Deal had brought to Washington were a number who considered her disenfranchised state preposterous; whether or not they stayed on in the capital, their indignation strengthened the self-government movement. And finally American horror at the spreading Nazi despotism in Europe gave new force to the contention that the

[8] H Judic Comee, 75C, 3S, Hrgs on H Resns, 232 and 564, "National Representation for D.C.," p. 63 and *passim*; H bills 6201 and 7095, 76C, 1S; S bills, 2776 and 3425, 76C, 3S; H bill 2984, 77C, 1S; Hrgs on SJ Res 35, pp. 52-53; *Star*, 5 Feb, 2 Aug 1940; *Post*, 12 Feb, 1939.

United States must uphold democratic processes throughout the nation, even in the capital.

The 76th Congress, troubled about the accelerating pace of the Nazi conquest and absorbed in the 1940 presidential election campaign, adjourned without acting on the District bills pending before it. But Washington's chances of achieving some political status improved that summer: after a bitter secret struggle, the platform committee of the Democratic Party inserted a plank pledging support for District suffrage. Probably because of that pledge the 77th Congress moved quickly to arrange hearings on a new three-part resolution calling for District representation in Congress, home rule, and a constitutional amendment granting District citizens the right to sue and be sued in the federal courts on an equal footing with citizens of the states. Opened in April 1941, the hearings before a subcommittee of the Senate Judiciary Committee commanded wider attention than those of three years before. At moments an air of solemnity filled the room. As a statute passed in 1940 seemed a sufficient guarantee of rights in the courts, the proposed amendment for that purpose dropped out of the discussion, leaving the floor to the representatives of some eighty local organizations and individuals eager to present their views on suffrage. Skillful though much of the argumentation was and useful as are the résumés of its historical bases, the chief interest of the volunteered statements lies in the sometimes deliberate, sometimes inadvertent, revelation of the sharpening conflict between the advocates of a new social order and the upholders of the old.

All power in Uncle Sam's company town rested ultimately in the company directorate—Congress. From the 1890's till the eve of World War I the most worldly of the directors had regarded a place on the House or Senate District Committee as a plum that, because of the advance information available there, offered a juicy bite of the returns on speculation in Washington real estate and utilities. After that era passed, the directors' "executive committee," while including some men genuinely interested in urban problems, contained also rural and small town representatives jealous of their prerogatives and wary of any group outside their own constituencies. As seats on the executive committee ceased to be sought after, any parochial-minded company director felt free to intervene in the management of company affairs. During the 1920's the struggle within the city to guide the hands pulling the strings had had to proceed, as never before, by elaborate indirection. Through a discreet word now and again at company headquarters and pointed suggestions to District commissioners impressed with the importance of big business, bankers, heads of large real estate firms, public utility executives, and the astute lawyers who furnished legal counsel to Washington's major business corporations had continued to exercise influence on the running of the town. But the depression with its accompanying distrust of all business introduced complications. Certainly the old methods would be unworkable in a community governed by popular elections where polls, not pocketbooks, would count and where the lean years had brought to the surface wants that would require large sums of money to satisfy—in short, higher taxes and probably bond issues.

Not every financially powerful Washingtonian shuddered at such a prospect, but the Board of Trade in the 1930's and after spoke for most of the city's big investors in opposing an elected city government. The local business boom evidently strengthened their determination to preserve the political status quo. Under the very nose of an administration intent upon bettering the lot of the "common man," they had tightened their hold upon the community's economic resources; at least the interlocking directorates among the biggest of the seventy-seven business corporations chartered in the District suggested a concentration of control in the hands of eighty to one hundred men. In 1941 their adroit technique before the Senate committee consisted of bypassing the topic of municipal self-government by focusing the discussion on seats for the District in Congress. No amount of maneuvering, however, could keep home rule from the center of the stage. The men and women who addressed themselves to that question represented a cross-section of the articulate community: lawyers, salesmen, newspaper men, women absorbed in welfare work, Parent-Teacher Association heads, and labor leaders. Despite an occasional dissident, by and large they took the line that entrusting the city's government to the rank and file was not only legal, just, and in accordance with American democratic principles, but would result in a better-run city. The committee room thus ceased to be the scene of pleadings for a common cause and turned into an arena in which the defenders of privilege fought off their critics.

The most forthright attacks on the existing regime came from men representing organized labor, an element rarely heard from at earlier inquiries. The head of Washington's Central Labor Union, with its 150 locals, bluntly characterized the commissioners and their appointed underlings as a "company union, organized and operated, and run by Congress." The secretary-treasurer of the Maryland-District of Columbia CIO informed the committee that, at the November 1940 convention of the Congress of Industrial Organization, delegates representing 4,000,000 American workers had unanimously endorsed suffrage for the District. "Local self-government is the real McCoy on this suffrage proposition." The only objection, he asserted, came from people "who are satisfied with their stranglehold on the status quo. It is obvious to the most superficial and casual observer that the policies and interest of certain powerful employer groups in the District of Columbia are the dominant voice in our District government." They relied upon "behind the scenes propaganda . . . accompanied by all kinds of bogies catering to popular fears." While the White House concerned itself with democracy in Europe, friends of the President apologetically admitted they had been unable to get "the President of the United States to concern himself with democracy in the District of Columbia."

Of the "bogies catering to popular fears" Negro suffrage had long been the most omnipresent and the least talked about. Colored Washington took no active part in the suffrage campaigns, as Negro proponents knew their public advocacy would damage rather than help. Although some Negroes had voted in the 1938 plebiscite, and at the subsequent hearings Senator King had asked how the bi-racial city would behave if enfranchised, few white people had been willing to discuss the racial question openly. To do so had seemed to them futile, even obscurely dangerous. "Behind the scenes propaganda" portrayed a city under an irresponsible electorate, run by a local Tammany that would use Negro "bloc voting" as its most potent weapon. By 1941 home rulers concluded they must expose the falseness of that picture. When the head of the United States Government Employees and National Negro Council argued at the hearings that continued congressional rule was safest for his people, and a teacher at the Armstrong High School declared federal aid to Negro education in the South a necessary preliminary to any change in Washington's status, dedicated white suffragists undertook to analyze and explain the insubstantial character of those and all other obstacles to their cause.

The complex class structure of colored Washington, they said, made it inconceivable that all Negroes would vote as a solid racial bloc on any issue. Although some of the recent in-migrants from the Deep South lacked education, colored illiteracy in the District of Columbia in 1930 had stood below the national average of whites and Negroes together, and Washington's public school system could be counted on to transform illiterate newcomers into responsible voters. Nor was there cause to worry lest national interests suffer from allowing locally elected officials to run the capital. Citizens here were Americans first, Washingtonians second. Anxiety about "double voting" was equally groundless. Let federal employees hailing from other places cast ballots in their own state and national elections but have the right to vote in municipal elections in the city they recognized as home. "The solid half of them," said the head of the Citizens' Committee on Suffrage, "are old-time Washingtonians." Their participation in local affairs would benefit the city without injuring the national government.

In the late spring of 1941 Congressman Sumners of Texas, a relatively new convert to home rule, remarked: "If either the Senate or the House are given the opportunity to vote on this legislation, it will pass." The opportunity was not offered.[9] Thirty months later, when a new Senate committee again delved into the question, Senator McCarran explained that the 1941 hearings had convinced him and his colleagues that national representation meant the equivalent of District statehood and therefore clearly ran counter to the intent of the signers of the Constitution; the eloquent pleas for home rule notwithstanding, doubts that most Washingtonians wanted it had persisted. Since 1934 thirty time-consuming congressional investigations of local problems had netted the community little but disappointment. In 1941 when a District official growling about the folly of seeking popular self-government asserted that Washingtonians got fuller hearings on their wants than could people anywhere else in the country, nobody bothered to make the obvious retort: hearings had rarely produced action.[10]

[9] H Judic Comee, 75C, 3S, Hrgs; Comrs Rpts, 1935, pp. 1-7, 1939, p. 7, 1940, pp. 8-9; Hrgs, SJ Res 35, pp. 69, 99, 140, 166-69, 212-15, 234-35, 250-51; Daly, "Washington's Minority Problem," *Crisis*, XLVI, 139. The data on corporation directorates derive from charts in the possession of Dr. Caroline Ware which were compiled by an American University graduate student from the 1940 listings for D.C. in *Poor's Register of Directors and Executives, United States and Canada.*

[10] S Dis Comee, 78C, 1S, Hrgs on S. 1420, "Reorganization of the D.C. Govt," p. 7.

CHAPTER XXI

"PURELY A LOCAL AFFAIR," 1933-1940

WHEN the New Dealers swept into the capital in 1933 to remake the national economic and social system, Americans looking to Washington for help thought of the city as the most enviable and exciting place in the country. Although that point of view underwent modification in the next two years, the picture of a singularly privileged community generally endured outside the District of Columbia. By overlooking the "rubbish" accumulating under the bed, a number of local residents also accepted that interpretation. Tourists had no occasion to lift the dust ruffles. The greenness of the parks and the avenues that still boasted trees and the sense of space conveyed by the city's layout struck visitors as vividly and agreeably in the 1930's as in the 1920's, and, more fully than ever before, her air of intellectual vitality was almost palpable. Hence to a good many ears complaints about the meagreness of community services sounded empty, at most the product of perfectionists' disappointment at the capital's falling short of the ideal.

It was clear to critics of District administration that budgetary strangulation accounted for the most acute troubles. It had existed in the flush times of the 1920's, crippling, for example, the Juvenile Court and, despite the five-year building program, the school system as well. When the depression struck Washington in 1932, exigent need brought new demands on a shrunken public purse. No community could meet all the demands the economic collapse put upon it. Washington's per capita wealth, though not tabulated during the most critical period, was probably no smaller than that of other American cities, and for two or three years she managed as well as they. Yet when industrial recovery began to ease pressures and encouraged an expansion of public services elsewhere, problems here intensified, and appropriations in relation to the city's enlarging resources became increasingly parsimonious.

In 1933, although several million dollars of District taxes collected in earlier years sat idle in the United States Treasury, the first New Deal Congress, instead of authorizing the spending of the "surplus," sliced the proposed District budget by a fourth. With tax delinquence mounting and property values declining, the commissioners reduced the tax rate about 10 percent; when business revived, they kept the lowered rate for several years and then raised it only to the modest level of $1.75 per $100 of assessed valuation. The 73rd and succeeding congresses approved some Public Works Administration loans to the District but still forbade bond issues that would spread over five to ten years the cost of urgently needed capital outlays. If installment buying was not yet a standard procedure for private householders, certainly the national capital was the only big city in the United States that had to pay for every service entirely out of current account. As drastic cuts in the federal share of over-all appropriations for running the capital left Washingtonians footing most of the bills, the detailed specifications on the Hill about how local taxes should be spent deepened resentment. While supporters of the Washington Taxpayers Association opposed a tax increase, a solid segment of the community looked upon that as preferable to the protracted penny-pinching that left essential wants unsatisfied. Indignation, stirring in 1934, grew as the decade wore on.

"Organized civic Washington," bitterly observed the *Star* in 1935, "is just about as cheerful over its budget going to the Federal Budget Bureau as it is to hear that the body of a dear friend is at the District morgue." People in other parts of the United States would assume that the slashes in District estimates saved the Treasury substantial sums, but "the dear public would never suspect that the funds saved did not belong to Uncle Sam at all." Indeed outside Washington misunderstanding was almost universal about the distinction between federal money and local tax money collected from District property-owners for local purposes and then by law deposited in the United States Treasury. President Roosevelt himself appeared to share that confusion, for in regretfully setting aside Dr. Harvey Cushing's plea for a new $2,000,000 building for the Surgeon General's Library, the President wrote that "out of Public Works funds we must keep the District of Columbia somewhere within a reasonable ratio of expenditure compared with the population"; a new government office building, a sewage treatment plant, "very much needed, as my nose on River trips testifies," a modern T.B. sanitarium, and a stack room to house important current documents would have to come first. Here in a single list were two purely federal projects and two primarily local for which the District would have to pay most of the bills. Some $4,000,000 from PWA enabled the District sanitary engineers to start construction of the sewage treatment plant in 1935, but $2,800,000 of that sum was a loan which had to be repaid with interest.[1] Admittedly whether or not the rest of the country was aware of whose taxes paid for what was not of major importance, but the general misapprehension was irritating. And the usual response of outsiders that all this was a "purely local affair" rubbed salt in the wounds of impotence.

A budget, a Director of the Budget observed, by definition cannot be merely "a shopping list" but must entail choices. Federal analysts assigned to the District budget in the 1930's believed the community prone to forget that truth. Having been denied any responsibility for making the choices for two generations, Washingtonians came by complaints readily. Since law reserved the special water and sewer fees for those

[1] Daniel Garges, "The Government of the District of Columbia," *American City*, XL, 107-08; *Star*, 20 Oct 1935; F. D. Roosevelt to Dr. Harvey Cushing, 1933, quoted in Dupree, *Science*, p. 348; figures on PWA loan assembled by Sanitary Engineer's office.

two services and the gasoline tax for highway maintenance, only the general fund was subject to argument. With Auditor Donovan as adviser on District spending, the federal Bureau of the Budget ordinarily made a judicious allocation among the competing demands. At the end of the 1930's the bureau occasionally yielded to the requests of citizens' organizations to send representatives to the hearings held yearly with District department heads, but shifts in the disposition of money rarely followed, and the scheme was then abandoned, probably because local importunities made a difficult job still harder. By 1940 real estate taxes in the country's "Number One Boom Town" brought in $21,196,400, tangible personal property and gross earnings taxes $3,712,144, and, because of collection difficulties, the newly imposed District income tax less than $3,100,000 of the $5,000,000 expected. Loans and small grants from federal agencies supplemented the amounts available, but the paper total, including a carry-over from earlier years of $4,265,000 that Congress had not authorized spending, was too little to provide adequate services for a city grown in a decade from 487,000 to 663,000 inhabitants.[2] A 20-percent bigger budget had to be stretched to meet the needs of a 36-percent larger population. Which needs were to receive priority was a decision on which the people most directly affected had no say.

Perhaps the single greatest handicap under which the bureau and the city suffered was the stipulation of the law that the expected revenues for each year must determine the size of the budget sent to the Hill. Only additional taxable property, upward revisions of assessed valuations, or a higher tax rate could enlarge the figure. And, experience indicated, bigger assessments and hence larger municipal income were likely merely to add to the surplus held in the Treasury. The law

[2] Comrs Rpts, 1933, p. 1, 1940, pp. 5, 8-11, 1941, p. 7; interviews, Daniel W. Bell, Director of the Bureau of the Budget, and Frederick Lawton, Assistant Director, 1934-39.

enacted in 1878 to safeguard against a repetition of the reckless spending of Boss Shepherd's day forbade borrowing; the act of 1909, ostensibly only further insurance against municipal extravagance, was more crippling because it meant that Congress was never confronted with a realistic summary of the city's needs. If the necessity of a sewage treatment plant thrust itself on congressional noses as well as the President's, the consequences of neglecting equally serious if less blatantly unsavory problems were rarely self-evident. Busy members of Congress seldom thought of the predictable results, for instance, of allowing no money to the Children's Division of the welfare board for a preventive program directed at checking juvenile delinquency before it got started. Thoughtful Washingtonians inclined to believe that if the budget, however staggering the total, were to reflect the true picture of conditions, Congress would not disregard it or would at least forego further cuts in figures already fixed below an amount essential to the orderly functioning of a great city.

In view of Washington's record of 135 traffic fatalities in 1934, 115 the next year, and, throughout the thirties, the rapid multiplication of motor vehicles on her streets, Congress logically enough gave particular attention to transportation and traffic control. As automobile registration fees and gasoline taxes yearly produced between two and three million dollars of income, and the District got a share of federal funds under the national road-building act of 1935, the highway department together with the Park and Planning Commission mapped out a huge network of through-way and bridge construction. Overpasses and underpasses, especially a tunnel under Thomas Circle on Massachusetts Avenue, additional stop lights, and complicated traffic arrows gradually reduced traffic hazards, but not until law required strict driving examinations and periodic inspections of motor vehicles did the accident rate drop sharply. While a merger at last brought the streetcar and bus companies into a single transit system, the Board of Trade persuaded the highway department to widen F Street in front of the old Patent Office by shearing off the steps from William Elliot's replica of the Parthenon. Moving traffic was more important than static aesthetics. As the Washington airport was nearing completion, the Board of Trade also initiated a study of the feasibility of a subway system, but at congressional hearings arguments that so costly a measure was quite needless buried it.

Meanwhile parking troubles constantly worsened. A long report of 1930 prepared at the instance of the Park and Planning Commission, the metropolitan police, and a half-dozen business organizations had proposed the use of the interior courtyards of the Federal Triangle and under- and above-ground tiers of parking space at the rear of other office buildings, but in 1941 the downtown section of the city had only two or three big garages. Installation of additional parking meters and prohibition of leaving cars standing along much-travelled stretches of streets during rush hours made no dent on the problem. As long as twice as many people as in other big American cities persisted in driving their own cars into the business district, the chances of arriving at a solution looked dim. Only wartime gasoline rationing would provide a reprieve.[3]

Pointing out that directing traffic at rush hours daily took a third of the policemen on duty, the superintendent of the metropolitan police invariably attributed the shortcomings in his department to undermanning of the force. Special details frequently had to be assigned to watch over the comings and goings at official or semi-official parties, to keeping order at

[3] *Rpts B/Tr*, 1936, pp. 5-15; *News*, 25 Nov, 1 Dec 1933; *Star*, 20 Oct 1935; *Rec*, 75C, 1S, p. 6298; H Dis Comee, 74C, 2S, "Traffic Investigation"; Comrs Rpts, 1934, pp. 29-30, 1935, pp. 90-91, 1937, pp. 113-15, 1940, pp. 128-29, 1941, pp. 9, 133; Miller McClintock, *Report on the Parking and Garage Problem of the Central Business District of Washington, D.C.*, 1930.

parades, and, with the newly organized tear-gas squad standing by, forestalling trouble at demonstrations like those attempted by the Hunger Marchers. Consequently men walking beats usually had to patrol from twenty to sixty blocks instead of the six to ten the chief considered the maximum for adequate protection. The report of the Woman's Bureau in 1935 squarely presented the case for larger appropriations: "The police have always the unhappy duty of trying to deal with all the failures of the community. Conditions which the community, except for a small group, tolerates year after year have been greatly intensified in the last two years. . . . The increase in volume [of work] without increase in staff spells decrease in ability to do a thorough-going job in the field allotted to us. . . . This Bureau was set up to deal with human beings as individuals, not as job lots, but beyond a certain point this has become a physical impossibility, and it takes all that we have and sometimes more not to lose sight of even the minimum standards of service." Although Congress thereupon authorized an increase to bring the force up to 1,471 officers and five years later approved the addition of another 50, burglaries, larceny, and assault kept Washington in the category of a city of violence. The depression itself provoked lawlessness, but two congressional investigations brought to light several other sources of trouble.

Superintendent Ernest Brown, who had joined the force in 1896 and worked his way up without benefit of special training, had little sympathy with new-fangled notions of police education. In nearly twenty years only one subordinate felt impelled to avail himself of the FBI courses opened in 1921. So far from following General Glassford's method of supervising his men by riding around town on a motorcycle, Major Brown sanctioned tactics described in 1941 as "Gestapo." If the wiretapping that went on within the Chicago police department was not one of the devices employed, still the metropolitan police made use of an internal spying system that, conscientious officers testified, undermined the morale of the entire force. Recruits had to pass civil service examination, but promotions proceeded by recommendation, and favoritism, especially congressional influence, could make or break a man's career. Just as sanitary inspectors learned never to issue an order to a congressman's household demanding obedience to regulations aimed at controlling rats in rodent-infested neighborhoods, so the police rookie quickly discovered the wisdom of adapting his law-enforcement zeal to fit the rank of the offender. Unequal application of the law created an atmosphere of subtle corruption and tried the souls of citizens unable to claim the tacitly recognized immunity of federal officialdom.

If the high proportion of big-wiggery in the city, the endless streams of tourists, and the succession of marches on Washington ever since the Bonus Army invasion all constituted unique complications in policing the capital, the rise in juvenile delinquency during the depression was a familiar problem in every American city. In the autumn of 1933 Frank Jelleff, a Washington merchant whose knowledge of the community was exceeded only by his generosity, pointed out that in the District of Columbia one boy in every fifteen between the ages of 10 and 15 landed in the Juvenile Court and, of the age group of 17- to 20-year-olds, one in five was arrested. He proposed to get $200,000 from the Public Works Administration for a building where youngsters could gather under friendly, unobtrusive police surveillance for games, boxing, wrestling, playing records or the radio—a clubhouse boys could think of as their own where they would agree to rules to ensure the rights of every member. As PWA bypassed the plan, Major Brown picked up the idea and instructed uniformed policemen to solicit funds from house to house to start the Metropolitan Police Boys' Club.

The response of the thousand white boys who immediately

made use of the first clubhouse in southeast Washington led to the opening of a second in the Kenilworth section, a third in 1935 in the slums of southwest Washington, and the next year a club for colored boys. Every year patrolmen rang doorbells on their beats to collect cash for the clubs. As membership rose to 16,500, the effects appeared in police and Juvenile Court records: although a change in categories of cases prevented exact comparisons, in five years the number of juvenile arrests dropped startlingly, a decline to which the chances opened to 17- and 18-year-olds to enroll at Civilian Conservation Corps camps and the work of the National Youth Administration undoubtedly contributed. Training courses and defense jobs made available in the autumn of 1940 lessened the importance of the boys' clubs, but men who had become interested in them regarded them as a vitally constructive force deserving public as well as private support.[4]

The ultimate cost to the community of cheese-paring appropriations, plain enough in the case of the understaffed police department and more so in the provision for penal and correctional institutions, was still heavier in the realm of public health and welfare. Needy people, as obscure as they were helpless, always tended to become statistics when tax expenditures were under discussion in the District commissioners' offices, at Budget Bureau conferences, and in committee rooms on the Hill. The overworked and underpaid medical and social workers of the District's public agencies never succeeded in portraying in compelling form the wretchedness they had to witness daily. Newspapermen trying to make the facts come alive merely earned the label "tear-jerker." Even comparative data made little impression. Testimony showed, for example, that other cities recognized an eight-hour day for hospital nurses;

[4] *News*, 8 Nov 1933; Comrs Rpts, 1933, pp. 71-74, 1934, pp. 89, 96, 1935, pp. 79, 84-85, 1936, p. 98, 1937, p. 105; H Dis Comm, 74C, 2S, "Investigation of Crime," *passim*, and 77C, 1S, "Investigation of the Metropolitan Police," pp. 2-7, 21-42, 66-88, 227-33, 382-405, 436-42.

at Gallinger they worked twelve. Built in 1929 to accommodate 300 patients, Washington's municipal hospital had a daily average of 691 in 1934 and 744 the next year. The cost of some social catastrophes could not be tallied statistically—the wasted potentialities of children, say, who got too little to eat and no care at home or who landed in run-down institutions and unsuitable foster families. While new concepts of social responsibility born of the depression brought fresh vigor to public welfare agencies in other cities, after 1935 Washington's had to mark time.

Why? Why above all in the capital, the nerve center of New Deal ideas and social experiment? The lag was certainly not due to the heartlessness of individual members of Congress or to the incompetence of the men and women in charge of the District programs. The principal reason is rather to be found in the remoteness of the men on the Hill, the decision-makers, from the problems of the city at their feet, and, besides the element of distance, the time dimension. Texans, Nebraskans, Indianians, and South Carolinians, however humane individually, could not be expected to feel and rarely showed profound concern for a community that was not their own; for them Washington's welfare was an abstraction when not an irritating chore foisted upon them at the cost of more rewarding assignments. Again and again months would slide by before preoccupied senators and representatives acted on an urgent local matter, and in the interim the situation changed, all too often for the worse. By the time Congress accepted a proposal originally put forward as an ounce of prevention, a pound of cure would no longer suffice. Members who served any length of time on the District committees generally came to understand the city's needs, but a single ill-informed or contrary member there or on the Appropriations Subcommittee or the Rules Committee might side-track a bill indefinitely. And southerners in Congress, loath to extend assistance to "niggers," let alone encourage Negro migration into the capital, were not above obstructionism. A second reason for delays and half-measures was the recurrent lack of community consensus about any particular remedy proposed. More than once well-intentioned citizens appeared at congressional hearings to fight against details of a plan carefully worked out by other well-intentioned people, with the result that everyone came away empty-handed, the entire project killed or indefinitely postponed. The history of Washington's health and welfare work thus became a constantly repeated record of too late and too little.

The District health officer optimistically ventured the opinion in 1940 that a recently-expanded public health program was at last redeeming the city's "adverse reputation." In 1934 her infant mortality rate of 66.1 per thousand was, with the exception of New Orleans, the highest of any big city in the country and a direct consequence, observers believed, of Washington's alley-slums; by 1939, new medical social services, the maternity and child care clinics made possible by grants from the U.S. Public Health Service and the federal Children's Bureau, and the demolition of some of the worst of the alley dwellings had reduced the rate to 48.1, lower than the national average. WPA help for several years kept the physical plant of Gallinger Hospital from irreparable deterioration, and in 1939 appropriations permitted the construction of several new buildings, but, as was the case also at Freedmen's and the T.B. hospital, too few nurses and doctors and a lack of equipment still made proper patient care an impossibility. In 1941 a reorganization and an enlarged professional staff held out hopes, unhappily ephemeral, that the institution henceforward could measure up to U.S. Public Health Service standards.[5]

The Board of Public Welfare functioned under still more

[5] Comrs Rpts, 1934, p. 134, 1935, pp. 128-29, 147, 1936, pp. 175-78, 1937, pp. 146-52, 1938, pp. 125-26, 149, 1939, pp. 143, 168-76, 194-208, 1940, pp. 139-42, 165-204, 1941, pp. 2, 5-16.

precarious circumstances. Until the summer of 1932, when the handling of the newly created $350,000 emergency relief fund fell to five of the nine laymen composing the board, its duties had been chiefly confined to periodic consultation with the executive director who supervised the District's public eleemosynary institutions. But, with the spread of unemployment and want, the unanticipated job of acting as almoner for tens of thousands of people became an overwhelming assignment. In every city and hamlet of America the foremost problem in 1933 was to get people back to work and in the meantime keep them from utter hopelessness and starvation. By midsummer 1933 Washington's emergency relief committee had spent $1,025,600 over and above the original $350,000 appropriation. During the next twelve months day after day despairing jobless men and women crowded the branch offices scattered through the city in old warehouses and shabby stores where a harried staff and flurried untrained clerical helpers tried to make pennies do the work of dollars. Some $10,658,000, four-fifths of it federal emergency funds, went into direct relief, wages paid through the short-lived Civil Works Administration, supplies, and social workers' salaries.

With such large-scale operations and such huge sums of money involved, inevitably confusions arose, and while George Allen fumed about inefficiencies, the administrative machinery geared to relatively simple tasks all but fell apart. The projects the emergency committee sponsored generally had long-term social value—community gardens, for one, for another the hot lunches for undernourished school children provided under school board aegis, and the nursery schools and adult classes frequently taught by women who had been dropped from the roster of regular teachers because they had close relatives on the federal payroll. Nevertheless cancellation of the federal Civil Works program in April 1934, when the number of families seeking help was still rising, called for a reorganization of the entire relief scheme. The emergency relief committee of laymen serving without compensation accordingly gave way to a professionally trained Public Assistance Division paid out of welfare funds.

When Elwood Street accepted the post of welfare director in June 1934, the highly qualified staff he put in charge of public assistance furnished only a partial answer. Here, as elsewhere, 1934 was a harder year than 1933. Eleven months after the National Industrial Recovery Act had started pump-priming, the Federal Emergency Relief Administration reported: "Industry is not absorbing the unemployed as rapidly as the number of those whose resources are exhausted is increasing." Washington's major industry had expanded in the interval, but as Secretary of the Interior Ickes kept a restraining hand on public works in the capital, and most of the people manning the new federal agencies came from other places, few new government jobs opened up for Washingtonians. The launching of the Works Progress Administration in the early summer of 1935, creating jobs as it did for white-collar and professional people as well as manual laborers, was all-important for a city of office-workers. Men and women with clerical training put school records in order and collected data for special census tracts, artists catalogued paintings, and the Federal Writers Project produced in 1937 the invaluable *WPA Guide to Washington.*

Still neither WPA, nor its subsidiary the National Youth Administration with its enlargement of the CCC program, nor the widening scope of newly formed "trade and barter" cooperatives disposed of Washington's relief problem. In 1935, after 134 years of shoulder-shrugging, the federal government undertook to care for the transients whom the Travellers' Aid could not help, and that summer Street reported that the number of families and unattached individuals on the relief rolls had dropped from the 23,423 of the preceding year to

18,298. But costs for 1934 had come to more than $10,600,000, and, Street warned, "in many areas of activity increasing expenditures will be necessary because of the growth of the city, the increasing complexity of urban life and the inadequacy of many citizens by experience and ability to adjust themselves to that complexity." In June, however, passage of the national Social Security Act, with its multiple provisions for unemployment compensation, old-age assistance, and pensions for the blind, moved the Board of Public Welfare to speak thankfully of its "sense of the vast and enduring significance" of measures that "represent the acceptance of the principle that government is responsible for at least a minimum of economic security for all its citizens."

For Washington's public welfare the year 1936 marks a watershed. Difficult though relief problems had been since 1932, federal help and fairly liberal appropriations of District funds had enabled the public agencies to manage the load. Enactment of the social legislation of 1935 seemingly promised to reduce greatly the future burden, although the first monthly government payments would not begin until 1942, and meantime the extent of help to the aged would depend on the size of the budget earmarked for that purpose. The change for the worse brought about at the end of 1935 apparently grew out of congressional conviction that the emergency was now over, that the WPA could handle any vestigial unemployment problems, and that the District's Welfare Board no longer needed large sums of money. In November all relief payments were stopped until every family had undergone reinvestigation, in December grants were reduced 25 percent, and the following spring a hard and fast rule cut off all financial help to any family that included an employable person.

The full meaning of that rule was hard to grasp. Everyone agreed that its basis was sound: jobs would replace the "dole" and leave only society's physical and mental incompetents to receive relief. But did the public know, asked the Washington Council of Social Agencies, that "a family is classified as employable even if the only potential wage earner is an adolescent boy or girl who not only has no job but has had no training or experience to equip him for qualifying for a job?" Did the community realize that in the 4,138 families dropped from the local relief rolls in April 1936, "the employable persons actually were either unemployed or employed at a wage far below that required to provide minimum needs for their families, and that many of these persons could not be absorbed in private industry or in WPA jobs?" Technically these people, if certified, were eligible for WPA, but, unlike most of the states, the District had no agency to make certifications for employables not already known to the Public Assistance Division. Month by month the division's task grew in difficulty. By mid-1937 social workers were carrying case loads of 140 families each, and constant criticism of performance made recruitment of additional case-workers impossible.

Other units of the welfare service suffered equally. Maryland refused to permit further foster home placements from the District until the Child Welfare Division reduced the number of children supervised by one social worker from 104 to 65. In 1937 the appropriation for aid to dependent children was so small that less than 19 percent of those eligible could receive help. A single demonstration unit begun in one neighborhood with Children's Bureau funds proved "the potentialities of preventive individualized casework treatment for children who present behavior problems but whose delinquency has not become so much that they need to be considered by the juvenile court," but lack of money forbade the extension of that kind of service to other parts of the city. At the Industrial Home School for colored children vocational training embraced only a third of the projected program. When Mrs. Roosevelt visited the Home for the Aged and Infirm she was scandalized at the overcrowding, the understaffing, and lack of equipment.[6]

While one source of Washington's troubles was congressional disbelief that problems could be mounting here in the midst of a business boom, another factor was the reluctance on the Hill to provide "a minimum of economic security" to Negroes. It was common knowledge that in a community less than a third Negro, two-thirds of the people on relief were colored. It was also obvious that as long as Negroes were "the last hired and the first fired," unemployment among them would always run higher than among whites. But arguments that denial now of help to the family of an able-bodied jobless Negro would extend the problem to the next generation were useless. Pleas for a change in the rules and for larger appropriations merely turned the Board of Public Welfare into the *bête noire* of the budget-makers. The chief analyst for the District at the Bureau of the Budget insisted that all social workers thought that money grew on trees and testily suggested that people who could not support themselves look to the churches for help. Officials' irritation at citizens' repeated begging for bigger appropriations hurt every phase of the welfare program.

Anger at that point of view flared out in 1937 after the head of the Washington Taxpayers Association asserted that, in view of the business revival, widespread unemployment no longer existed and that the "howl" for more welfare money came solely from relief workers fearful of losing their jobs. Speaking indignantly for the Family Service Association, the new name for the Associated Charities, Canon Anson Phelps Stokes, Coleman Jennings, Carroll Glover, and Dr. Frederic Perkins,

[6] *Ibid.*, 1933, pp. 81-84, 95, 1934, pp. 111-16, 1935, pp. 121-25, 135, 1936, pp. 166-74, 1937, pp. 160-70, 1938, pp. 183-97; *Herald*, 28, 29, 30 Mar 1934; *Rpt, Division of Emergency Relief, B/PW*, 1934, p. 24; "Private Agencies are Still Needed in the Relief Field," *Council Bulletin*, I, Nov 1936, pp. 1-2; Schlesinger, *Coming of the New Deal*, 293-96; "Demonstrating Child Welfare," *Community Service*, II, Jan 1938, p. 5, and CSA, 17th Anl Rpt, "Research," *ibid.*, Apr 1938, pp. 2-5.

none of them professional social workers and all of them men of property, testified that appeals for help in December 1936 had been more numerous and more urgent than in any month since 1933: "Indeed we consider the situation so serious that we would prefer to have our taxes increased if necessary, rather than to encourage the permanent human wastage which will almost inevitably result in hundreds of cases if promising material for human rehabilitation is allowed to go unaided this winter." While Jennings spelled out facts in letters to every member of Congress, a committee explained to the Bureau of the Budget that some of its data were faulty, especially on Negro chisellers. Since the Board of Trade research staff had reported $18,000,000 of public money spent that year on help for the unemployed, the Family Service Association undertook to prove that astronomical figure the result of charging a dozen public services to relief. At a mass meeting, 1,500 people asked for an additional $1,000,000 in welfare funds and revocation of the edict forbidding help for unemployed employables. Congress yielded to the extent of waiving the rule for a three-month period but then reinstated the restriction.

A special census early in 1938 showed forty-five out of every thousand Americans totally unemployed, sixty out of every thousand Washingtonians; fifteen out of every thousand Americans on emergency relief, sixteen Washingtonians. Here then was no imaginary crisis; "First City—Worst City" cried Community Chest officers. The Welfare Board recommended a general relief appropriation for 1939 of $3,247,750; the Budget Bureau itself proposed $705,000 for old-age assistance. The House, impervious to all urging, fixed upon $489,000 for the aged and an over-all welfare total of $900,000. While the bill was pending in the Senate, civic organizations, charity societies, and white labor unions mobilized in support of the original request; although the Board of Trade at first opposed it, a subcommittee later endorsed it. At a meeting of a newly formed Citizens' Committee on Unemployment and Relief, "interested organizations and large taxpayers gathered to protest their own right to pay for adequate relief to Washington residents who are in need." The House decision stood.

Later in the year as a result of congressionally authorized studies of District relief administration and child welfare agencies, the Children's Division netted an additional $30,120 for salaries and for extension of the "preventive individualized casework treatment" that the demonstration unit had found effective in forestalling child dependency and delinquency. In the meantime Elwood Street risked a direct appeal to Congressman Ross Collins of Mississippi, chairman of the House Subcommittee on District Appropriations. For several years past, 14-, 15-, and 16-year-old Negro girls, unaccompanied by their families, had been pouring into Washington from the South. Prepared only to live on the streets, many of them quickly landed in the colored unit of the National Training School for Girls. The school was overflowing; more space and more skilled supervisors were badly needed. Representative Collins, looking the social worker straight in the eye, said, "If I went along with your ideas, Mr. Street, I'd never keep my seat in Congress. My constituents wouldn't stand for spending all that money on niggers." Mississippi's racial views thus controlled correctional work in Washington. Shortly after that interview Street and his two most experienced assistants resigned.[7]

The efficacy of private charity inevitably depended in large measure upon the scope of the public agencies' work. Until

[7] *News*, 29 Mar 1933; Minutes of the Board of Managers of the Family Service Association, 13 Jan, 10 Feb, 10 Mar, 14 Apr, 12 May, 9 Jun 1937, 9 Feb, 9 Mar 1938 (hereafter cited as Min FSA); "Council Endorses Request for Deficiency Relief Appropriation," *Community Service*, I, Feb 1937, p. 6, and CSA, Anl Rpt, *ibid.*, Apr 1937, p. 20; "First City—Worst City," and "We Need Funds for Them," *ibid.*, Feb 1938, pp. 4-5, 11; "Everybody's Concern," *ibid.*, Mar 1938, p. 3; "Our Foremost Concern," *ibid.*, May 1938, p. 8; Comrs Rpts, 1938, p. 191, 1939, pp. 215-31, 1940, pp. 218-28.

1933 the Community Chest had carried almost the whole of the city's relief burden. Church charities, to be sure, lessened the load slightly. The Church of God, for example, ran a penny lunch room after the millionaire Bernarr McFadden, appalled by the pilferage from the establishment he had been financing, turned it over to Elder Michaux. The evangelist appealed to his radio audience for help, local people out of work gave their services and, when they got paying jobs, contributed money to the "Happy News Cafe," where thousands of hungry people were fed for a penny a meal. Still the city's organized charity societies, pledged to the Chest's single fund-raising campaign, could not adopt Michaux's method. Their "normal" functions of preventive work, rehabilitation, and health programs had to wait until the government recognized its obligation to provide food and shelter for the destitute. Seemingly that moment came with the expansion of the Welfare Board's duties and resources in 1934. That year the Associated Charities changed its name to the Family Service Association, appointed a successor to the elderly Walter Ufford, and joined with other social agencies in studying new approaches to community problems.

Thus, six neighborhood councils arose, each undertaking to abet and harmonize the activities of every organization concerned with dependency and delinquency in its area. Drawing upon sociologists at the local universities for surveys, the councils stressed that communities must pay in one of two ways "for the privilege of preparing the younger generation for future responsibilities. . . . The first way pays in both money and suffering through the delinquency and the crime which are the result of neglect. The second way pays by providing the suitable environment, including all kinds of opportunity for worthwhile activity, which remove the incentive and the occasion for abnormal conduct. Each community must decide how it prefers to pay." While an adult "Self Help Exchange" achieved some success, and the Voteless League of Women Voters worked for legislation, organizations such as the Legal Aid Bureau and the Washington Social Hygiene Society fought to cut the roots of particular social ills. Pioneering articles in the *Herald* were "the plow that broke the plains" in combatting public ignorance of the long-term consequence of 27,000 new cases of venereal disease every year. All the newspapers campaigned for funds for the summer camps sponsored by the Boy and Girl Scouts and a half-dozen child welfare societies. But in 1936, when Congress restricted public relief to families with no employable member, again the Council of Social Agencies had to man the breach at the cost of other services.[8]

Once past the fright of 1933 and 1934, affluent conservatives tended to revert to the view that public financing of welfare, whether through emergency relief, WPA, provisions of the Social Security Act, or public housing, ran counter to basic American principles. Granting that philanthropy was the logical alternative to tax-supported aid to the needy, much of the upper strata of society in the capital failed to act on that premise. As business recovered, gifts to the Community Chest shrank. Possibly former big contributors believed that tales of mounting want were fabricated by social workers. Perhaps some people considered generous help merely an invitation to irresponsible Negroes to milk soft-hearted whites. Whatever the reason, after 1935 the Community Chest fell short of its goal every year. "Defeat in our last campaign for financial support of private social work," stated the Chest's organ, *Community*

[8] Min As Ch, 10, 24 May, 14 Jun, 11 Oct 1933, 10 Jan, 26 Feb, 9 May, 13 Jun 1934; Min FSA, 11 Dec 1935, 8 Apr 1936; *Church of God, A Pictorial Review*, pp. 26-27; Herbert L. Willett, Jr., "Financing Washington's Welfare Work," and Thomas W. Gosling, "Neighborhood Councils," *Council Bulletin*, I, Oct 1936, pp. 2-5; "Skeleton of Relief," *Community Service*, II, Sep 1937, p. 5; "This Happened Here," *ibid.*, Oct 1937, p. 3; "Your Social Health," *ibid.*, Dec 1937, p. 3; Anne Geddes, *Trends in Relief Expenditures, 1910-1935*, Works Progress Administration, Monograph 10, pp. 91-93; *Forty Years of the Voteless League of Women Voters.*

Service, in 1938, "defeat in our battle for a more adequate relief appropriation from public funds, show that we have not yet succeeded in convincing the public of the value and necessity of our program." Catholic and Jewish organizations were free to canvass their own congregations, but Chest rules forbade non-sectarian societies to make independent appeals. Unable to find any other way to fill the gap in the relief program left by the public agencies, the Family Service Association repeatedly drew on the capital of its small endowment fund.

At this juncture the slow progress of slum clearance and public housing projects under the aegis of the Alley-Dwelling Authority and PWA inspired a new attempt to induce private builders to act. In an article in *The Nation's Business* entitled "A Philanthropy that Pays Dividends," a stockholder in the forty-year-old Washington Sanitary Improvement Company and the Sanitary Housing Company called attention to the fact that the former for many years had paid 6 percent dividends, the latter 5 percent, the original investments of $500,000 and $200,000, respectively, were now worth $1,120,000 and $340,000, and still the companies were able to maintain decent housing at rentals averaging $16.87 a month for tenants whose annual income was about $657. But even had the appeal convinced Washington building firms, an accelerated pace of demolition and rebuilding, one citizen observed sadly, would not in itself break "the dismal routine of slum living." The "individualized medical and social care required for the rehabilitation of slum dwellers," many of whom had occupied the same fetid shanties for more than a third of a century, would have to come both from public sources and private philanthropy.[9] Who or what was to awaken the government and Washingtonians collectively to the urgency of action?

[9] Min FSA, 15 Sep, 8 Dec 1937, 12 Jan 1938, 13 Dec 1939; "Do Your Part," *Community Service*, II, Oct 1937, p. 8; "Washington First and Last," *ibid.*, Nov 1937, pp. 8-9; "More and Better Publicity," *ibid.*, Mar 1938, p. 4; CSA, Anl Rpt, *ibid.*, Apr 1938, pp. 6-15; "Alley People," *ibid.*,

Contrary to congressional assumptions, 1939 brought more cases of need than had 1938, partly because the WPA ruled that no one could stay on its rolls for more than eighteen months, irrespective of whether he could find another source of livelihood. The rule applied in the states as well as in the District, but in the capital taxpayers' inability to increase the public welfare budget gave the edict particular harshness. Imposition of an arbitrary monthly maximum of $48 of public money for relief to any one family hastened the deterioration, the Family Service directors noted, "for which the community must ultimately pay." The summer camps for children had to cut their 1939 season from eight weeks to six. Despite the efforts of the minority, the community seemingly had decided to pay its obligations to the younger generation in the currency of neglect. As public and private agencies froze social workers' salaries below the sums paid in other cities, the turnover of experienced professionals, begun with Elwood Street's resignation in 1939, increased. Before the end of the New Deal era, the capital had the reputation within the social work profession of being the city where frustration and heartbreak would overtake the person of competence and vision more surely and quickly than in any other place in the country.[10]

Disappointing as was the accomplishment of seven years, "organized civic Washington" could see a few improvements in race relations. Certainly several white organizations had moved a considerable way toward recognizing colored Washington as an integral part of the community. Taken separately, the incidents that indicate a changing point of view are not impressive. The Associated Charities, after electing

---

May 1938, p. 9; Appleton Clark, Jr., "A Philanthropy that Pays Dividends," *Nation's Business*, XXVI, 21-22.

[10] Willett, "The Community Chest Buys Services from Its Member Hospitals," *Community Service*, I, May 1937, pp. 14-15; Min FSA, 30 Oct 1935, 14 Dec 1938, 8 Feb, 10 May, 13 Sep, 11 Oct 1939, 19 Jun 1940, 19 Feb 1941.

31. Inauguration of President Roosevelt, January 1945; the only inaugural ever conducted at the White House

32. "Press Conference," December 1941, drawing by Gluyas Williams for the *New Yorker*

33. World War II "tempos" and bridges over the Reflecting Pool on the Mall

34. The Jefferson Memorial

35. The National Gallery of Art with tempos in the foreground

36. Pentagon

37. Union Station, 1943

38. Queue at a shoe store just before a coupon was due to expire, 1944

39. Spectators at the Hancock statue waiting for the Civilian Defense Workers Recruitment Parade, 1943

49. Franklin D. Roosevelt's funeral procession on Constitution Avenue en route to the White House.

41. Georgetown houses built in the 1840's

42. Apartment house on Massachusetts Avenue, 1956

43. St. John's Church and the AFL-CIO Building

44. Southwest Redevelopment Plan of 1955, later modified

two Negroes to the board of managers in 1932, went further by adding Campbell Johnson of the colored YMCA and electing Dean Lucy Slowe of Howard University to the executive committee. After seven years of backing and filling, in 1935 the Washington Federation of Churches invited Negro churches to join, and, not without some hesitation, four Negro congregations accepted, doubtless chiefly because its new bi-racial committee on race relations seemed likely to reach further into strongholds of local prejudice than other organizations could. Although Negro quotas in Chest drives were minuscule—$9,500 in 1933, less than $5,000 in 1934—money to run the three Negro settlement houses, the Stoddard Baptist Old Folks Home, St. Ann's Home, the Phyllis Wheatley YWCA, and the colored YMCA, all came from Chest funds, and on the whole ungrudgingly. The *Star*, which for fifty years had rarely printed any but derogatory or facetious stories about colored people, in 1933 carried a long account of a meeting of the Association for the Study of Negro Life and History and at intervals thereafter the white press published news items that implied, as a home ruler put it, that "Negroes are people."

In some areas bi-racial cooperation sprang up spontaneously. A racially mixed group inaugurated a self-help cooperative in northeast Washington in 1934, white and colored people together raised the money to open the Northwest Settlement House on M Street, and, in response to a plea from the *Tribune*, an interracial committee conducted a drive to combat the excessively high tuberculosis death rate among Negroes. As careful studies drew attention to the fact that Negro mortality from all causes was 70 percent higher than white and stressed the direct relationship between the incidence of fatal disease and the occupance of alley slums, Director John Ihlder of the Alley-Dwelling Authority and some of his associates urged the placing of less emphasis upon housing developments for medium income families and more upon building for the poorest—namely

Negroes. Condescension, to be sure, persisted among most well-meaning whites, whether donors to the Church of God who nevertheless dubbed Elder Michaux's devil-fighting "corny," or board members of the Family Service Association who as late as 1937 took segregated seating for granted at the annual luncheons. But with every passing year patronizing behavior lessened and Negro touchiness declined. When Dean Slowe died, the entry in the board minutes of the Family Service Association was as genuine a tribute to a rare person as the obituary of that gentle old crusader, Mrs. Archibald Hopkins.[11]

White House policies, if somewhat noncommittal, helped, and Mrs. Roosevelt's warm interest in colored people as people was reassuring. Secretary of Labor Perkins and the "Old Curmudgeon" apparently were equally color blind. And yet had the administration completely ignored race relations, the change in attitude that had begun to emerge in Washington early in Hoover's presidency would probably have spread. That the admission of Negro graduate students to American and Catholic Universities made no stir in itself suggests that racial toleration was growing without political forcing. The chief outside stimulus to a reexamination of second-class citizenship was the shock of observing the application of race doctrines in Nazi Germany.

In 1933 not more than two or three American cities had well-organized, comprehensive public health and welfare systems. Private charity, Edith Abbott noted, was "accidental, spasmodic, sporadic, and almost unbelievably inadequate." By 1940, however, a number of municipalities with state help had

[11] Min As Ch, 14 Mar 1934; Min FSA, 8 May, 8 Dec 1937; *Tribune*, 17, 31 Mar, 23 Nov 1933, 19 Jul, 13 Oct, 17, 24 Nov 1934, 6, 27 Dec 1935, 22 Nov 1937; Washington Federation of Churches, *Yearbook*, 1936; *Council Bulletin*, I, Oct 1936, p. 13; Mrs. William Kittle, "Fiftieth Anniversary of the American Social Settlement Movement," *Community Service*, I, Feb 1937, pp. 2-3; Paul B. Cornely, "Health Problems of the Negro in Washington," *ibid.*, May 1937, p. 5; *Star*, 22 Oct 1933; *Afro-American*, 14, 21 Jan 1939.

developed extensive, intelligently administered, tax-supported welfare agencies generously supplemented by philanthropy. In Washington, on the contrary, private charity had shrunk, and public services, though reaching out into realms formerly left to private enterprise, had neither expanded enough to fill the hole temporarily nor attained a firm basis for future growth. Public funds had built some low-rental housing and a dozen monumental government buildings, and, in the process, provided employment. Congress had investigated traffic and crime, enlarged the police force, and approved a highway construction program. But the spending for engineering projects vastly outran that for the intangibles. For school counsellors, for branch public libraries, for books and librarians with the time and skill to interest children in reading them, for well-equipped playgrounds in over-crowded areas off the tourists' beaten track, for decent care of the aged, in short, for all the human elements that could make Washington an inspiring place for humble people as well as notables, money was lacking.

"Bad though Washington was," wrote an authority on American community organization a quarter-century later, "and worse than more responsible cities, its particular badness was an elaboration of widespread basic badness, and conditions were plenty worse in a number of congressional districts."[12] Yet less hypercritical citizens than those who coined the phrase "First City—Worst City" could admit it more descriptive than "First City—Best City." In the spring of 1940 consciences were beginning to feel the prick of the implicit challenge. No one foresaw that within a few months civic reform was destined to be engulfed for half a decade as Washington became the wartime capital of the free world.

[12] Edith Abbott, "The Crisis in Relief," *Nation*, CXXXVII, 400-02; Caroline Ware to the author, 21 May 1962.

CHAPTER XXII

CAPITAL OF THE FREE WORLD, 1940-1945

IN SEPTEMBER 1939 the Nazi invasion of Poland had carried a warning to Washington that the United States might soon have to abandon its concentration solely upon domestic affairs. The creation of a War Resources Board to plan American industrial mobilization, the President's declaration of a "limited national emergency," and the start made on recruiting the Army up to full statutory strength had created a stir. But after the partition of Poland and the beginning of the "phoney" war abroad, public alarm had subsided along the Potomac. As modification of the Neutrality Act permitted shipment of munitions to belligerents on a cash-and-carry basis, and orders placed by the Anglo-French Purchasing Board after January 1940 sharply reduced unemployment in American industrial centers, the struggle in Europe had receded further into the background. In April the Nazi drive into Denmark and Norway shocked Americans, but the WPA was still carrying thousands of people on its rolls, and farm problems were still commanding congressional attention in late May when the German armies swept through Belgium and the British evacuation from Dunkirk began. The swift movement of events in June, however, destroyed all hope that the United States could go its own way uninvolved in the upheavals in Europe—the Italian declaration of war on Great Britain and France, the Russian move into the Baltic countries, and, on the 22nd, the capitulation of France and the signing of an armistice with Germany. Like the dropping blade of the guillotine, the fall of France cut off the life of the New Deal.

By July 1940 the build-up of military strength was already superseding programs aimed at providing Americans with peace-time jobs, housing, education, beauty, and recreation. Despite the neutrality campaign of America-Firsters, Congress appropriated not millions but billions for defense. Two Republicans, Henry Stimson and Frank Knox, accepted the President's proffered posts of Secretary of War and Secretary of the Navy, and at the request of the Council of National Defense Vannevar Bush, president of the Carnegie Institution, set up the National Defense Research Council to focus scientific research upon weapons and means of transporting them.

One unmistakable sign that a rapid development of industrial and therefore military might now overrode in importance every other objective was the reappearance of American business leaders as government officials. For seven years they had formed the core of resistance to the policies mapped out by "college professors playing anagrams with alphabet soup." Now the captains of industry, whom General Hugh Johnson in early NRA days had called "Corporals of Disaster," were again honored in Washington as well as in Wall Street. To them fell the task of organizing government purchasing and industrial production amid a constant reshuffling of boards and labels and responsibilities. Before the end of the year the multiplication of offices filled by important businessmen proclaimed that the United States, unlike France, had chosen guns instead of butter. While the creation of offices of price stabilization and consumer protection indicated a serious attempt to preserve a balance, people who suggested that a preference for butter showed a preference for civilized living over the barbaric violence of shooting found their voices growing steadily weaker. As 1940 was a leap year, for the only time in history a congressional session lasted 367 days, from January 2, 1940, to noon of January 3, 1941.

National and international news crowded most District affairs out of the local newspapers during the summer and early autumn. People sat with ears glued to the radio, anxiously following the course of the Luftwaffe's intensive bombing of Britain. Although that frightening drama sped the passage through Congress of the Selective Service Act and the exchange of fifty over-age American destroyers for British military bases in the western hemisphere, relief at the RAF victory in the Battle of Britain was partly offset by Germany's announcement of a ten-year Axis alliance with Italy and Japan. While American defense appropriations rose to over 12 billion dollars, and the drawing of names for the draft began, a universal sense of strain endured. It prevailed up and down the eastern seaboard but inevitably appeared in most acute form in the capital whence decisions on national action must come. A return of confidence followed upon the President's "Arsenal of Democracy" speech in late December and his proposal to Congress to enact a lend-lease bill to support the "Four Freedoms," namely freedom from want, freedom from fear, freedom of speech, and freedom of religion. After months of hesitating, the United States appeared ready to assert its convictions.[1]

The multi-billion-dollar defense contracts went to industrial cities, but the influx of administrators and clerical workers into Washington during the fall of 1940 created a demand for housing and office space that seemed likely to transform real estate brokers and building contractors into petty czars, efforts of the Defense Housing Authority notwithstanding. The draft, meanwhile, made inroads upon the surplus labor force. At the colored Armstrong High School and the Phelps Vocational School regular classes met from 8 in the morning till early afternoon; night school courses ran from 3 till 11 p.m.; and from midnight until 8 a.m. special defense classes began the training of Negro youths in carpentry and metal work. Applicants on the register of the District Employment Center dropped from the 62,000 listed fourteen months before to

[1] For the chronology of events abroad, the steps in the formulation of American policy, the measures taken to implement it, and the men placed in charge, see "The War Production Board and Predecessor Agencies, August 1939 to November 1945," *Historical Reports on War Administration, Misc Publication No 1.* In describing local responses, I have drawn chiefly upon interviews.

27,000, of whom 11,000, chiefly white-collar and totally unskilled workers, were on the WPA rolls. By February 1941 all semi-skilled workmen in the city, the Family Service Association reported, had found jobs. For the next four and a half years unemployment ceased to be a problem for able-bodied, mentally competent adults, although the work they undertook was not always congenial or paid at rates commensurate with their abilities.

During 1941, the pattern of move and counter-move was frightening and sometimes exhilarating: the German invasion of Yugoslavia and Greece, the President's announcement of a state of "unlimited national emergency," the closing of the German and Italian consulates, the organization of the Office of Scientific Research and Development with almost unlimited funds and authority over military research, unbeknownst to all but a very few top-ranking American and British officials and nuclear physicists the starting of the Manhattan Project, the German attack on Russia, Japan's occupation of Indo-China, declaration of her Greater Asia policy, and suspension of shipping with the United States, congressional extension of the life of the Selective Service Act, and, after a conference at sea between Roosevelt and Winston Churchill, announcement of the Atlantic Charter. Dollar-a-year men began to arrive in Washington in November to take charge of new units of what everyone still called "the defense effort." Every week swelled the number of defense workers in the city. Washington as a community was lost in the shuffle.

In a matter of months the very look of the capital altered. In the spring of 1940 the Park and Planning Commission was attempting to clear the Mall of World War I tempos; by autumn the War Department was demanding more, not fewer. The highway department, in full agreement with the Los Angelan who declared that all city planning must revolve around the automobile, set about felling of trees right and left to widen streets, while exhaust fumes blanketed whole areas of the city at rush hours. The opening of the National Airport in the summer of 1941 merely heightened the volume of traffic. Despite the fact that Congress voted the planning commission $1,300,000 for land purchases for highway extension and city parks, and the planners finally persuaded the War Department that its projected headquarters might better stand on the Virginia shore in the shelter of Columbia Island rather than upstream at the end of the Arlington Memorial Bridge, where a large building would interrupt the vista from the Lincoln Memorial to the cemetery entrance, Frederic Delano resigned. The planning commission, he explained to the President, no longer performed any planning functions; the government agencies to which it had to turn over the land purchased for them usually failed to put it to suitable use; even the city playground sites were unimproved. The President himself was reportedly intent on building a dramatic five-sided windowless fortress for Army headquarters; he agreed to windows only because munitions experts convinced him that a bombing that would demolish solid masonry walls would merely blow the glass out of windows piercing them.

Looking at the double line of barracks-like wood and stucco tempos erected along the reflecting pool between the Washington Monument and the Lincoln Memorial, Secretary of the Interior Ickes remarked: "Army officers, by the mere fact of their constantly changing assignments, are not in a position to be fully cognizant of the importance of adhering to long range programs prepared by competent planning agencies." Urban aesthetics were no concern of the men responsible for recruiting, training, and equipping a 2,100,000-man Army, a two-ocean Navy, and, with the enactment of Lend Lease, supplying the British with matériel. Silence greeted a suggestion that the solidly built brick dwellings of the slums in southwest Washington be remodelled for offices and defense workers' living quarters.[2]

Changes in ordinary routines accompanied the physical changes. Military phrases began to crop up as part of the city's everyday language. "Government issue," shortened to G.I., was not yet a term applied to enlisted men, but employees in offices and shops became "personnel," a commodity like raw materials and machinery. With restrictions imposed on civilians' use of such items as silk and an order to the automobile industry to cut production of passenger cars by a fourth, "priorities" and "quotas" were words heard everywhere; citizens who had never set foot in an industrial plant adopted terms like "mock-up," "stockpile," and "tooling up." To the men dominating the Washington scene, by the autumn of 1941 "getting out production" had obviously come to mean something more vital than getting into Heaven ultimately or into the Army-Navy and Metropolitan clubs sooner. The simplicity that had characterized social affairs in New Deal days dropped away. "Protocol" replaced what Washington for a century had called "etiquette." Hostesses competed to catch the most important-sounding new arrivals in the city—a railroad executive turned government transportation expert, a New York corporation lawyer now in charge of new federal tax regulations, or a British scientist come for consultation with his opposite numbers in the Office of Scientific Research and Development. Army and Navy officers, though still in mufti, recaptured the social prestige denied them since 1919. In crowded drawing rooms and hotel cocktail lounges dignitaries arranged troublesome matters difficult to settle over office desks. Talk, however, no longer centered on schemes for putting a chicken into every

[2] *Afro-American*, 12 Oct 1940; Min FSA, 16 Oct 1940, 15 Jan, 19 Feb, 11 Jun 1941; Comrs Rpt, 1941, pp. 2, 133; *Star*, 20 Dec 1940, 23 Mar, 18 Apr, 22 May, 1 Aug, 18 Oct 1941; *Post*, 3 Aug, 19 Nov 1940, 9 Jan, 16 May, 18 Oct, 15 Nov 1941; Coyle, "Frederic A. Delano: Catalyst," *Survey Graphic*, xxxv, 252-70.

pot, but on aluminum and rubber supplies, aircraft engines, ships, and trucks.

Angry protests at conditions in Washington sounded from time to time in the press. "Murder Capital," cried *Newsweek*, in June 1941. "In proportion to population there are 250 percent more murders in Washington than in New York City, 40 percent more even than in Chicago. Those who commit felonies . . . have a two-to-one chance that no one will be arrested . . . fifteen-to-one that no jail sentence will be served." Inasmuch as the Mafia had never moved in upon the District and organized crime had no permanent foothold in the city, those figures were doubtless a somewhat hysterical response to a peculiarly grisly unsolved murder of a young woman of a good family, but the addition of fifty men to the metropolitan police force that summer failed to halt violence. While the government put up rows of small houses near the Pentagon at Fairlington chiefly for Army and Navy officers' families and helped finance Park Fairfax, another big development across the Potomac, the Defense Housing Coordinator considered constructing residence halls in Washington for unmarried government workers; still the housing shortage reached a point more acute than that of 1918. In the once elegant mansions that had lined Massachusetts and New Hampshire Avenues in the 1920's, as many as six strangers frequently had to share a bedroom designed originally as a library or a reception hall. Small wonder that inexperienced young women from country towns sometimes got into trouble.

In April 1941 a new District Council of Defense set up committees of volunteers to coordinate private and governmental efforts in providing recreation for servicemen in the city and nearby camps, compiling rosters of people with special skills, and establishing a housing register and a rent complaint unit, but the 19,000 volunteers who immediately made themselves available had no power to impose regulations; the

District commissioners appeared to be unable either to delegate responsibility or to exercise effective control themselves. Upon Melvin Hazen's death in July 1941, Guy Mason, a well-known attorney, took his place, and when Colonel McCoach was assigned to active Army duty, 71-year-old Brigadier General George Kutz for the third time became the engineer commissioner. Mason, highly competent though he was, lacked experience in the new job, Kutz was tired, and, according to local critics, Commissioner Young manifestly found the District Building less congenial than the drawing-rooms of the cocktail circuit where his talents for mimicking high-flown political oratory delighted fellow guests when he performed as head of the "John Russell Young School of Expression."[3]

During the "defense period" Congress and the White House showed no more concern for the local community than they had during the regime of the "presidential joker." Predictions in the fall of 1941 set the District budget for the next fiscal year at the unheard-of figure of $54,000,000, but with an estimated growth in population from the 663,000 of April 1940 to over 750,000, the commissioners' problem of sufficiently expanding municipal services looked insoluble. As the trend of well-to-do whites to enroll their children in private schools or move to the suburbs did not offset the overload on the colored schools caused by Negro in-migrants, the Board of Education had to choose between transferring white school buildings to colored use, finding money to erect new Negro school houses, or renting additional space. Law enforcement and public health became increasingly hard to ensure in a city to which every month added at least 5,000 new residents. Only Daniel Donovan's steady hand at the helm in the District Auditor's office kept confusion from turning into chaos. In early December a magazine article

[3] *American Speech*, XVI, 160; "Murder Capital," *Newsweek*, XVII, 24-25; Josephus Daniels, "A Native at Large," and "Confusion on the Potomac," *Nation*, CLIII, 35, 118; Comrs Rpt, 1941, pp. 2-3, 1942, pp. 2-3; Donald Wilhelm, "America's Biggest Boom Town," *Am. Mercury*, LIII, 338.

entitled "Washington: Blight on Democracy" repeated the tale of shockingly inadequate accommodations for incoming government employees, steadily rising living costs, and a salary scale that kept the earnings of half the people on the federal payroll to less than $1,500 a year. But the author directed his frontal attack on the District government: only elected municipal officials, he argued, could lessen the city's racial antagonisms. "Negroes who have lived in many parts of the country say that nowhere else in America is there such bitter mutual race hatred."

If white people were startled at that judgment, colored Washingtonians knew it was sound. The confidence they had felt in the months after the Marian Anderson concert at the Lincoln Memorial had received several rough jolts as soon as the Army expansion began in June 1940. The *Afro-American* had at first argued that, War Department orders to the contrary, the United States could not and would not allow color bars to continue in the armed services. With Hitler master of Europe, "Uncle Sam needs every citizen, not merely every white citizen to do his duty." A few months later the Army was putting only white officers into command of colored draftees, the Air Corps and the Marines refused to accept any Negro, and in the Navy colored men could hope for nothing better than menial assignments. Memories of the humiliations Negro officers and troops had suffered in World War I fanned the anger of colored Washingtonians; the promotion of Colonel Benjamin O. Davis to the rank of Brigadier General seemed to them the merest gesture. Within civilian offices discrimination, far from withering away, as optimists had expected in 1939, strengthened with the appearance of new defense agencies. Doubtless the handful of colored typists and file clerks in newly organized offices sometimes imagined slights; few of them admitted that their more limited background and education might deny them equality with their white associates. But white supervisors intent on getting the job done generally felt justified in placing Negro typists in separate rooms and separate stenographic pools assigned to the least exacting work. By the end of 1940 Negro militants in and out of the capital concluded the time ripe to dramatize their demands for non-discriminatory treatment.

Early in 1941 Eugene Davidson pointed out to A. Philip Randolph, head of the Brotherhood of Sleeping Car Porters, that the New Negro Alliance picket lines had opened up several hundred jobs in Washington shops to Negroes during the depression. Now that the government and American industry were desperately in need of competent workers, the two men and NAACP leaders agreed that similar action on a national scale should produce wider results. Randolph sent out a call for 50,000 Negroes to march on Washington in July to present to the President and Congress colored Americans' protests at job discrimination. By April, as colored men throughout the country pledged themselves to march, high ranking government officials began to ask: "What'll they think in Berlin?" Still, apparently unable to believe that a Negro army bigger than the Bonus Expeditionary Force and possibly far more belligerent might actually descend upon the capital, federal department heads took no positive action. Plans for the march went on. In early June with the militants' move impending in less than a month, Mayor La Guardia of New York arranged a meeting between Negro leaders, Mrs. Roosevelt, and government representatives. The white men urged patience. Mrs. Roosevelt suggested that in the long run the march would heighten the racism of southerners in Congress and provoke disastrous retaliation. Randolph replied that, as the mere prospect of the march had already proved useful to the Negro cause, colored Americans preferred to chance revenge rather than drop the mass protest in exchange for mere promises.

Ten days later a conference took place at the White House. There Randolph, Davidson, and Walter White, executive secretary of the NAACP, faced the President, Secretary of War Stimson, Secretary of the Navy Knox, William Knudsen and Sidney Hillman of the Office of Production Management, La Guardia, and Aubrey Williams of the National Youth Administration. The upshot was a commitment from the President to set up a group to study the situation and recommend the ruling with the "teeth in it" that Randolph declared essential. But a study was not action; the Negro leader refused to cancel the march. Not until a second White House meeting on June 25th did a solution evolve: that afternoon an Executive Order on Fair Employment Practices went out over the President's signature, laying down rules of non-discrimination for all plants with government defense contracts as well as for all federal offices and installations; a committee within the Labor Division of the Office of Production Management was to check the observation of the rules, and the President, if given proof of violations, guaranteed that he would cancel the contract of the offending firm. For the first time since the Emancipation Proclamation of 1863 a President of the United States had issued an official order protecting Negro rights.

Satisfaction in colored Washington was tempered by events in areas to which the Executive Order did not apply. It did not touch the labor unions or private employers without defense contracts. When the stage production of *Native Son*, directed by Orson Welles, was opening at the National Theatre, Richard Wright walked into a restaurant in the company of one of the white producers and a white woman, only to be told that the management would serve the distinguished author in a car at the curb. Seemingly the Marian Anderson triumph might never have occurred. As the American Red Cross began to enlarge its professional staff and volunteers thronged into the District chapter offices to offer their services, colored women were given to understand that, provided someone could be found to give them the necessary preliminary training, they might be used as Canteen or Home Service workers or as nurses aides in connection with colored units. In fact, so far from ending Negro resentments, the Executive Order appeared, as time went on, to increase Negro hostility to much of white Washington. With some logic, colored people reasoned that since the administration was ready to recognize them as first-class citizens, all white Americans should do so; because they did not, Negro belligerence tended to mount.[4]

Yet the official non-discrimination policy had considerable effect in Washington. A story describing an inspection tour the President and Harry Hopkins made of the nearly completed Pentagon told of their astonishment at finding four huge washrooms placed along each of the five axes that connect the outer ring to the inmost on each floor of the building; upon inquiring the reason for such prodigality of lavatory space, the President was informed that non-discrimination required as many rooms marked "Colored Men" and "Colored Women" as "White Men" and "White Women." The differentiating signs were never painted on the doors. More astonishing in view of southern sentiment in Congress and the history of segregation in Washington during the preceding quarter-century, a law passed in May 1942 creating the District Recreation Board contained no racial restrictions; one of the four private citizens appointed to it by Commissioner Mason was a soft-spoken colored woman whose persuasiveness, joined with that of the ex-officio government representatives, led the board to approve bi-racial use of all city playgrounds except those forming part of the white and colored school yards. The influx of northerners to take government posts, furthermore, strengthened opposition to racism. Gifted colored men, ranked

[4] Alden Stevens, "Washington: Blight on Democracy," and Earle Brown, "American Negroes and the War," *Harper's Magazine*, CLXXXIV, 50-51, 545-52; *Afro-American*, 8, 22 Jun, 12 Oct 1940.

as government messengers in 1941, would gradually move up in grade and a few would eventually win the coveted "P" or professional rating. Ralph Bunche, formerly a little known Howard University political scientist, would become head of a policy-making section in the State Department. In the Office of the Price Administration where morale was consistently high no color line of any kind ever existed.[5]

White or black, long-time resident or new arrival, volunteer or paid worker, everyone in Washington found occasional compensations for the discomforts and uncertainties surrounding him. In March 1941, three months after workmen put the finishing touches to the pale, rose-white marble building on the Mall opposite the tip of the Federal Triangle, the National Gallery formally opened its doors to the public. Besides the paintings and sculpture of Andrew Mellon's collection, the old masters given by Paul Kress lined the walls of the well-lighted rooms. While connoisseurs pointed to the gaps, notably the lack of representative works of the eighteenth- and nineteenth-century French schools, appreciative crowds looked at the pictures with delight and admiringly walked around the fountain in the black-marble-floored Rotunda ringed by massive, highly polished deep green marble columns. Still larger crowds found relaxation at the zoo and in the racially segregated movie houses and theatres. And few people were impervious to the feeling that by merely living in Washington they were touching the fringes of history in the making.

The sense of being in the center of things did not immediately induce people to open their purses to the Community Chest. Inasmuch as the government was manifestly attempting to arrange for the well-being of defense workers, why, new arrivals asked, should they contribute to local charities? In 1941 the

[5] *Second Annual Report of the Citizens Committee on Race Relations, Inc.*, 18 Sep 1945; National Committee on Segregation in the Nation's Capital, *Segregation in Washington*, pp. 68-70.

Chest had to cut the allotment to the Family Service Association to scarcely half the $84,000 the board of managers had requested. In early December the association's case workers were dealing with over 400 families who were ineligible for public assistance and whose resources were too meagre to make them self-sufficient. "It is economic defense for the community," the board concluded," to provide service to these families, and private agencies need to be maintained for this purpose." Organizations such as the Boy Scouts, the Police Boys' Clubs, the YMCA and YWCA were similarly indispensable in meeting needs outside the sphere of legalized public expenditure. Rather unexpectedly the problem of financing diminished after the declaration of war brought a War Chest into being. In return for running the campaigns, Washington's central organization got a percentage of the money raised for British War Relief, the "China Relief," and other special causes. The arrangement ended arguments about local versus national and international giving, and, after Arlington, Alexandria, and Montgomery County joined with the District in a single War Chest drive, Washington's charities netted more nearly adequate funds than ever before—in one year as much as $4,500,000.[6]

In mid-November 1941, when a special Japanese envoy arrived to discuss with the President possible ways of reducing tensions between the United States and the chief power in "Greater Asia," Washington had settled into a state of half-readiness for war without really expecting it to come in the immediate future. Seemingly everything might go on as it was indefinitely. Embassy parties were gay, private parties even gayer, despite the scarcity of domestic servants. People worked hard but with a sense of having matters in hand. Such anxieties as pervaded the upper echelons of the government

[6] "General Information," *Bulletin, National Gallery*, Mar 1941; *Newsweek*, XVII, 24 Mar 1941, pp. 58-60, XVIII, 14 Jul 1941, pp. 58-59; Min FSA, 12 Nov, 10 Dec 1941.

were well concealed. A Gallup poll of the city would probably have shown eight people out of ten preparing for a festive and relatively carefree Christmas.

On the afternoon of December 7th, Washington was relaxing over the Sunday radio programs and the newspaper stories of Saturday's Army-Navy football game when word of the attack on Pearl Harbor reached the White House. As the news spread, people talked of nothing but Japanese perfidy and the quick revenge the United States would mete out. Even a week later, after the formal declaration of war on Japan, the Japanese invasion of the Philippines, and, on December 11th, the German and Italian declaration of war on the United States, the emotional keynote in Washington was more nearly relief than fearfulness. "No one," wrote a careful observer, "showed much indignation. We are going into this war lightly, but I have a feeling that it will weigh heavily upon all of us before we are through." At least it should unite the country and put a stop to the anti-progressive, anti-labor agitation in Congress.[7] Confidence not unlike that shown in the city before the first battle of Bull Run endured for several weeks. Prime Minister Winston Churchill came and departed, men from every village and city in the United States applied in person or by letter for active military service, and, guided by the President with augmented powers, the creaking war machine moved into high gear.

For the next three and a half years Washington was like a city under siege. As the Japanese swept from victory to victory in the spring of 1942 and the German armies drove eastward upon Stalingrad and across North Africa into Tobruk, experienced and imaginative people in the American capital knew that life here was less precarious and that personal deprivations were far fewer than in the key spots of warring Europe and the Far East, but the realization that the fate of all depended upon

[7] *Star*, 7, 8, 29 Dec 1941; I. F. Stone, "War Comes to Washington," *Nation*, CLIII, 603.

decisions made and the speed of action taken in Washington imposed upon men in responsible posts here a burden that at times approached the unbearable. And they were not upheld, as in 1917, by belief that they were engaged in a holy crusade. The possibility of ultimate defeat was unthinkable, but with every passing month, as War and Navy Department telegrams beginning: "I regret to inform you that . . ." went out over the wires to American homes, the sombreness of spirit in high places in Washington deepened. It lightened in the early autumn of 1944, only to darken again during the Battle of the Bulge and the weeks that followed.

Washington's urbanity and vaunted southern charm shrank under the strain. In and out of government offices fatigue and fraying tempers found periodic release in snapping at anyone who commented on shortcomings in service: "Don'tcha know there's a war on?" While that phenomenon was by no means confined to the overworked, overcrowded, undersupplied capital, nowhere else on the continent, save perhaps in some of the mushrooming war production centers such as Willow Run, were living and working conditions more trying. Rent controls went into effect on January 1, 1942, without any protest from reputable real estate brokers who remembered World War I. But federal regulations that prevented monetary exploitation of newcomers did not provide them with housing, and many of them were aghast to discover that the legal rental of an "efficiency," a small room with bath and a kitchenette in a closet, ran as high as that of an entire house in their home towns. The residence halls put up for "white government girls" and Slowe and Carver Halls built for incoming Negro workers were soon overflowing. Tire and passenger car rationing, followed in the late summer of 1942 by gasoline rationing, brought hundreds of bicycles back onto the streets and so increased the difficulty of commuting that the suburbs lost most of their attraction. Thereafter, according to detective story writers, a tiny apartment in an old stable-turned-garage in a Georgetown alley became a pearl of price for which contenders might betray government secrets and involve themselves in murder cases. Office accommodations were equally meagre. Even a relatively high-ranking government functionary could feel lucky to have a desk in a pantry whence the butler had once dispensed champagne and fois-gras to the millionaire's family and guests.

Some war work was absorbing enough to blot out the day-by-day discomforts—for example research at the Bureau of Standards on target-seeking ammunition functioning by the so-called VT fuse, or the application of mathematics to the breaking of enemy codes, or the preparation of critical releases for the Office of War Information. Many assignments were deadly dull. While a government interdepartmental committee of personnel specialists arranged job transfers for the misfits and attempted to ease the personal difficulties of the homesick, the USO ran dances at the nearby Army posts with truckloads of delighted young women transported for the occasion from the blacked-out city. While a half-dozen national and local organizations clucked like mother hens over the young in government employ, according to magazine writers, most of the "government girls" were having the time of their lives. Even after the movement of troops to overseas stations accelerated, men outnumbered women in the capital, and the issue of marriage licenses reportedly went on at a rate to encourage any personable spinster under thirty-five. Still the turnover in government offices was huge, adding to municipal as well as federal problems.

Rationing, the blackout, the possibility of air raids, and the 48-hour or longer work-week curtailed the amenities. The National Symphony gave a few concerts, and the art galleries remained open, but the priceless collections of the Dumbarton Oaks museum were put into storage and the house turned over for the duration to the Office of Scientific Research and

Development. University enrollments dropped except for evening classes, and in those, some professors believed, standards of performance declined. Austerity marked affairs at the foreign embassies, and, with domestic servants unobtainable, food hard to buy, and fuel rationing so severe that well-to-do private householders shut off their drawing rooms to conserve heat during the winters, non-official dinner and cocktail parties became few and far between. Night clubs along G and H Streets flourished, and movie houses, USO lounges, and Red Cross canteens were crowded, but those resorts were frequented chiefly by transients, servicemen, and inexperienced newcomers unacquainted with the kind of dignified private entertaining that for sixty years had been a Washington hallmark. Indeed a cosmetic advertisement struck the dominant war-time note: in a black square the single phrase, "Beauty Can Wait."[8]

Local civic problems also had to wait except when they had direct bearing on national and international affairs. In June 1943 a race riot in Detroit sharpened memories of the summer of 1919 in Washington and brought into being a Citizens' Committee on Race Relations, headed by white ministers, lawyers, educators, laymen of the Catholic Interracial Council, and two or three prominent Negroes. Its purpose was to hold a watching brief and by factual publicity about sources of racial tensions reduce or eliminate them, whether springing from Negroes' anger at the segregation of Negro blood from white at Red Cross blood donor centers, from job and housing restrictions, or from white people's exasperation at Negroes' tendency to attribute their own inadequacies solely to white exploitation. The mere existence of the committee was useful, although it had to measure its wartime achievements in

[8] *First Report of the Rent Control Board of the District of Columbia*, Jun 1942, pp. 321-25; Charles Hurd, *Washington Cavalcade*, p. 282; Ernest K. Lindley, "Washington, Capital of the Allied World," *Newsweek*, xx, 7 Sep 1942, p. 40; "Social Doldrums," *ibid.*, 28 Sep 1942, p. 35; Helen H. Smith, "Uncle Sam's Seminary," *Collier's*, cx, 28 Nov 1942, pp. 18-19; and scores of other articles listed under "Washington" in the *Readers Guide*, 1942-1945.

terms of what didn't happen rather than what did. The Washington Housing Association, another volunteer organization, meanwhile hoped to make more and better living quarters available to colored families. Internal controversy over tactics proved an obstacle; one group advocated reliance on moral suasion to induce the Real Estate Board to abandon its transactions in "exclusive," that is, racially restricted, property, while another group wanted to stage an open fight both on that issue and over placing a Negro on the board of the National Capital Housing Authority, successor to the Alley-Dwelling Authority. One rabbi insisted that the association must take a strong stand against discrimination aimed at any minority, Negro, Jew, or other; a second rabbi passionately declared that to lump Hebrews with Negroes was to increase unwarrantably the handicaps under which Jews already suffered. Public housing for any but incoming federal workers made no progress at all. Elder Michaux, to the accompaniment of veiled charges that he was lining his own pocket, put up Mayfair Mansions into which nearly six hundred well-to-do Negro families moved in 1944, but of the 2,300 priorities allotted for low-rental Negro dwellings in 1943, private builders had undertaken only 30 by the end of the year and only 200 were finished in 1944. Obviously organizations without authority to force action could do little even if they had large memberships.[9]

That fact, together with the heavy demands the war put upon congressional time and the heightened confusions in the District Building after Auditor Donovan's death in 1943, apparently inspired the Senate Judiciary Committee that December to conduct hearings on a new bill for reorganization of the District government. Aware of the racial friction in the city, Senator McCarran opened the hearings with a plea for forthright discussion of Negro suffrage, a subject "which people often say you do not dare touch." One Negro witness deplored

[9] See n. 5; Dulles, *American Red Cross*, pp. 419-21.

"the injection of the race theme into the matter of local voting," but the inseparability of the two evoked outspoken objections to the bill from several people who regarded themselves as friends of both races. The gentle Clinton Howard, great-nephew of a founder of Howard University, argued that intensifying racial antagonisms in wartime Washington made the moment peculiarly unpropitious to talk of enfranchising "the under-privileged, illiterate, proletarian class who would at once possess the balance of power and, in the near future, a majority of the voting citizenry." In this, "the most southern city north of Richmond," where, he contended, the Negro population was permanent, the white largely temporary, "the law of fecundity" would rule. At his annual Christmas party in 1942 for all the children living in the square directly to the east of the Senate Office Building, there were no longer any white children in the houses adjoining his on northeast B Street, whereas in Schott's Alley at the rear were ninety-nine colored children, all of whom, scrubbed and well-behaved, came to his party. "Now that is Washington tomorrow. . . . The alley will dominate the avenue." By a touch of historical irony, within fifteen years the alley would have turned into a beautifully kept mews lined by small gardens and dwellings occupied chiefly by congressmen, while the marble mass of a new Senate Office Building and a parking lot would dominate the traffic-packed avenue.

Suffrage advocates during the hearings flared out angrily more than once at the worshippers of "The God of Things as They Are." The president of the Federation of Citizens' Associations asserted that the federal Treasury was now paying less than 10 percent of the cost of running the city, Congress was giving less time than ever to her problems, and, in defending the existing regime with its petty corruption in the water department, the tax collector's office, and at Gallinger Hospital, the Board of Trade spoke not for its several thousand members but merely for its small self-perpetuating board of directors. The well-intentioned Clinton Howard, a labor leader explained, simply didn't know what he was talking about when he forecast disaster for a self-governing Washington. The Senate committee, sympathetic to local voting though it appeared to be, shelved the bill as untimely. It had aroused meagre public interest; most people in the wartime capital saw no direct connection between local suffrage and defeating the Axis powers. Home rulers would have to wait till the war was over.[10]

By the early spring of 1945 military victories in every theatre of war brightened the prospects for peace. But April 12th brought news that stunned the nation: Franklin D. Roosevelt was dead. In the streets of Washington people wept. At the White House Harry S Truman took the oath of office, while preparations moved forward to bring the former Chief's body back from Warm Springs to the capital. The funeral procession along Pennsylvania Avenue two days later perhaps stirred in very old men memories of the muffled roll of the drums and the black-velvet-draped hearse of Abraham Lincoln's funeral cortege. Then the war had been practically over; in April 1945 fierce fighting still lay ahead in pockets of Germany and in the Pacific. On the 25th, the day the United Nations conference opened in San Francisco, the United States and Russian armies converged at the Elbe River. The lynching of Mussolini, Hitler's death in the subterranean bunkers of Berlin, and Germany's unconditional surrender followed in swift succession.

Celebration of V-E day was restrained in Washington. The pressure of work in government offices eased only momentarily. Japan was still undefeated. But the release of some Army supplies of canned goods, the lifting of purchasing restrictions on several other items, and War Production Board authorization of partial resumption of passenger car and domestic wash-

[10] S Judic Comee, 78C, 1S, Hrgs on "Reorganization of the Govt of D.C.," pp. 7, 9, 141, 149-55, 169-73, 227, 243-56, 287-304, and *passim*; clipping files on "Housing," Washingtoniana Room, Pub Lib.

ing machine manufacture encouraged public faith that the end was in sight. And with the completion of a United Nations charter and the United States Senate ratification of it in mid-July, hopes for a peaceful new world order rose. When the atomic bombs dropped on Hiroshima and Nagasaki in early August, and Secretary of War Stimson spelled out the story of how and why the United States had developed and used that devastating weapon, shock mingled with relief in Washington. Suspense hung over the city for nearly a week. While rumors of Japanese capitulation set off a frenzied victory demonstration in New York, the capital forced itself to wait. For three successive days quiet crowds began to collect at dawn in Lafayette Square and drifted in and out until disappointment dispersed them late in the evening. On August 14th they were rewarded. From the White House President Truman announced the Japanese acceptance of the allied terms of surrender.[11]

[11] *Star*, 13, 14 Apr, 7-11, 14 Aug 1945.

CHAPTER XXIII

POSTWAR DESIGNS FOR THE FUTURE, 1945-1950

V-J DAY made the steamy heat of a Washington August bearable. Bright lights streaming out over the capital at night revealed a beauty almost forgotten during the years of stress. Within a fortnight an official order cutting government employees' work week back to forty hours restored the luxury of free Saturdays. Everyone began to look forward to the return of the "boys" from overseas. Dollar-a-year men and high-ranking wartime officials were less precipitous than in 1918 about emptying their brief-cases into office wastebaskets and shaking the dust of Washington from their feet, but through September and October demobilization of the civilian work force proceeded, with the old, established government departments taking over the duties and some of the staff of the emergency agencies. Thanks to federal rent controls, rationing, and price stabilization, the city was emerging from the long strain without the spiritual scars World War I had inflicted; time and patient planning should erase the physical blights imposed by the military demands of the defense period and the war.

A lightheartedness unknown since 1940 enveloped the city during the fall. Householders who had taken in roomers as a public service reclaimed the privacy of their own homes, and the release of food stuffs long limited by rationing eased housekeeping. In the upper brackets of society mothers planned elaborate debuts for their daughters, and, as autumn moved into winter, the private dances and dinner parties hinted at a revival of that discard of 1932-1933, the Washington season. Gaiety born of the release from five years of tension permeated all social levels. Spring would allow the Cherry Blossom Festival to resume. Summer would revive the Watergate concerts, stopped by the wartime blackout, and open up to theatre groups the small outdoor stage in Meridian Park. In Rock Creek Park the Carter Barron outdoor theatre, given to the city several years before but unused during the war, would offer the pleasures of plays and ballet in a beautiful setting.

Yet uneasy thoughts of the more distant future stirred in the capital before the end of 1945. Demobilization officials prophesied that eight million Americans would be out of work in 1946. Even if industrial cities had to bear the initial brunt of that readjustment, a corresponding curtailment of governmental activities must eventually be costly to Washington. RIF's, that is, reductions in force, in the government had already cut deep. Scores of brilliant men attached to the Office of Scientific Research and Development had left the city by the end of the year, and drastic paring of government-sponsored research within a much discussed single Department of Defense might hamstring Washington as a scientific center. The talk of the dispersal of federal agencies into areas outside the District might soon turn into reality; it would save the city from further losses of taxable real estate but might cost her a number of more important assets.

Historical-minded residents could draw some comfort from thinking of the aftermath of other wars: a new federal city sprung up between 1815 and 1817; the years between 1866 and 1870 shadowed by fears about removal of the capital but succeeded by an era of extraordinary growth for the city; and after World War I, the transformation of uncertainty into fresh confidence and a multi-million-dollar burst of federal building. But now a new element was added: the competition of the suburbs. The resumption of passenger-car production and cancellation of tire and gasoline rationing opened the way to an exodus from the central city that could permanently undermine Washington's prosperity. She would unquestionably remain the nation's legislative center and keep the White House, the Supreme Court, the State Department, and the main units of the other executive departments; the foreign embassies were unlikely to move out of the District. All those, covering with other federal and District property about 46 percent of the land in Washington, were tax-exempt. What could the city draw on for funds if she neither had large tax-paying industries nor a long roll of residential property-owners subject to District taxation?[1] Washingtonians could only map out recommendations; the decisions would rest with Congress and the President.

Cleavages within the community had sharpened since 1943. The Board of Trade and the Real Estate Board, with its representatives from twenty-five banks, insurance and title companies, and building and loan associations, had defined their policy of tightening racial segregation and controlling the city's pattern of growth by every financial and political means at their command. Opposition to that formula had also mounted. In the ranks of its adversaries, ranged alongside all colored people, was a strangely assorted aggregation of whites—some wealthy individuals, a number of small businessmen, wage-earners, members of organizations such as the Urban League, the Catholic Interracial Council, and the recently formed Washington chapter of Americans for Democratic Action, most of the newspapermen reporting on city affairs, social workers, and a heavy sprinkling of the city's ministers and rabbis. Despite the disproportion of numbers on the left and on the right, the right-wingers had fended off change. The reluctance of officialdom to take any step to revamp the imbalance of power as long as the war was going on had strengthened their hands. In June 1945 the District Recreation Board had reversed its earlier non-segregation policy because the playground director had insisted that her staff could not handle mixed groups. A mass meeting

[1] "War Production Bd," *Historical Rpts . . . Misc Pub No. 1*; H & S Dis Comees, 80C, 1S and 2S, Jt Hrgs, "Home Rule and Dis Reorganization," p. 217 (hereafter cited as Home Rule Hrgs).

of protest held on V-J Day had failed to induce the board to rescind the order, but the defeat fanned resentment at perpetuation of oligarchic, discriminatory rule. In the autumn of 1945, with the peacetime future undetermined, Washingtonians in both camps prepared for a fight. On one side a compact body of powerful men set themselves to restore the old, solid-looking facade; on the other side stood people ready to demolish shibboleths and rebuild the city on broader social and economic foundations.

Still, the alignment of the opposing forces was not entirely clear cut. Some home rulers, the president of the Federation of Citizens' Associations for one, preferred to see segregation continue, and some believers in racial non-discrimination put little faith in an elected city government. People who vaguely disapproved of the local autocracy were frequently unwilling to campaign against it. The war had taken its toll of Washingtonians' energies; more than a few citizens felt the release from immediate anxiety too pleasant to sacrifice in a struggle in which the stand-patters had the backing of long-established custom. The unusually large number of high-ranking Army and Navy officers in postwar Washington also lent support to the extreme right, and their prestige had never stood higher. Although they avoided openly expressing opinions about District affairs, the arch conservatism of the armed forces, their unmistakable anti-Negro bias during the war, and the class tradition inbred at West Point and Annapolis tended to push them into the authoritarian fold. Many of the men who objected to basic change, moreover, were charming and cultivated individuals convinced that the city's economy would suffer from a fundamental social upheaval. Their friends disliked the idea of quarreling with them publicly. Wartime newcomers, who would later enter the lists with passionate fervor, in 1946 and 1947 rarely felt sufficiently informed about what was at stake to join in the battle. Because southerners as extreme as Theodore

Bilbo of Mississippi now controlled the District committees in Congress, an open fight involved the risk of skimpy federal appropriations for the District's schools, highways, and slum clearance. That threat, insubstantial though it proved to be, perhaps encouraged timid and lazy-minded citizens to stand on the side lines.[2] And probably not more than three people out of ten in Washington were aware of the conflict in the making. Congress was absorbed in federal reorganization.

Yet Congress had already showed interest in rescuing the capital from blight. A Redevelopment Act passed in May 1945 vested in the National Capital Park and Planning Commission authority to plan the rebuilding of all Washington's slum-ridden areas, to lay out a vast new highway system, to purchase land for additional parks and playgrounds, and to specify the sites for new public buildings. The program outlined by Lt. Gen. U. S. Grant, III, the commission chairman, awaited only detailed surveys and large appropriations. In the interim the demand for housing endured in spite of multiplying RIF's in government offices. While returning veterans and young couples with children looked for modest quarters in the suburbs, Washington real estate firms carried long lists of applicants for tenancy in the blocks of expensive efficiency apartments under construction. In order to rent anything more commodious, two years and more after the coming of peace would-be clients still had to grovel before lordly underlings in realtors' offices. Contrary to expectations, the sellers' market would last into the 1950's, and only the perpetuation of rent controls kept prices within bounds. Irrespective of rentals, houses or well-maintained apartments for new Negro families were all but unobtainable; they had to double up with relatives or acquaintances.

Amid all the discussion of redevelopment plans, a renewed

[2] Cit Comee on Race Relns, *2nd Anl Rpt*, pp. 8-9; National Committee on Segregation in the Nation's Capital, *Segregation in Washington*, pp. 82-84, and *passim* (hereafter cited as Ntl Comee on Seg, *Rpt*).

squeeze on Washington's colored residents had begun to gather force in the city. As if frightened by the slight inroads the New Deal and war years had made on the doctrine of white supremacy, avowed racists and, more numerous and more influential, men moved by an unemotional determination to keep Negroes to a servant class were busily perfecting schemes whereby all colored people would be housed in a geographical ghetto and their isolation reinforced by narrowed job restrictions. Now, while official redevelopment plans were going down on paper, was the time to fix the city's social pattern for generations to come. Washington's elected city councils had passed two non-discrimination ordinances during President Grant's administration; in 1947 his grandson announced that the National Capital Park and Planning Commission would see that "the colored population dispossessed by playgrounds, public buildings, parks and schools" was relocated in a remote section "in the rear of Anacostia." Segregation, explained a National Capital Housing Authority official, "is the accepted pattern of the community." Such statements staggered people who had dared think Washington's racial conflicts fading away. The challenge obliterated within the colored community the already weakened differentiations between light- and dark-skinned Negroes and the social distinctions linked to degree of color; the postwar threat, hitting every person with so much as a drop of Negro blood, closed the ranks.[3]

Inasmuch as a popularly elected municipal government would unquestionably induce changes in the leopard's spots, the question of local suffrage took on fresh importance. In 1945 the Washington *Post* had taken an informal poll of its readers; although responses were too few to represent city-wide opinion, 80 percent of the replies had favored District voting. A year later the Board of Trade organized a much-

[3] Ntl Comee on Seg, *Rpt*, pp. 35-47, 84-89; *Star*, 4 Sep 1946. As in Ch XXII, other data derive from a host of interviews and for the years after 1946 from personal observation and attentive reading of the daily press.

publicized plebiscite. The turnout was puzzlingly small; the results showed 70 percent of the adult participants supporting home rule—a more than 15-percent drop since 1938—and now nearly 60 percent of the white high school students, a scant 3 percent of the colored, against local self government. "Opposition to suffrage is on the increase," reported the *Times Herald*. The *Post*, commenting on the corrosive effect of deep-seated social ills, called Washington's disenfranchisement "a poisonous thing." Still a second poll conducted by the *Post* in February 1948 could count no more than 70 percent of the respondents anxious for change.[4]

Three developments of 1947 and 1948 nevertheless indicated that Washington was neither irretrievably sunk in political apathy nor committed to the racial containment program drafted by the real estate interests and endorsed by the head of the National Park and Planning Commission. First was the organization of the bi-racial Washington Home Rule Committee composed of well-informed, courageous residents. Taught by the mistakes of the now defunct District Suffrage Association, they limited their goal to the restoration of a popularly elected city government, prepared their every campaign with care, and for the next fifteen years refused to let repeated defeats sidetrack them; without ever winning acclaim, they came to represent the core of civic resistance to political impotence.[5] Second, and more immediately promising, were the joint House and Senate subcommittee hearings begun in July 1947 on District governmental reorganization. Third and ultimately most productive of results was the launching of a national committee of eminent Americans pledged to fight segregation in Washington. Their detailed report published in condensed form in November 1948 was probably the major force in the rout of aggressive racism in the capital.

[4] *Times Herald*, 6 Nov 1946; *Post*, 9 Nov 1946; Home Rule Hrgs, pp. 165-66, 392.

[5] Home Rule Hrgs, p. 271; files Washington Home Rule Comee.

The home rule bill of 1947 and 1948, named for its chief sponsor in the House, James Auchincloss of New Jersey, was in a sense the fruit of twenty-five years of congressional thinking, beginning in the early 1920's with Senator Capper's resolutions for District representation in Congress, moving on through the proposals of the 1930's for limited local voting, and followed by the home rule bills considered by the Senate Judiciary Committee in 1941 and 1943. But several circumstances, especially the fact that the Auchincloss bill reached the floor of the House, differentiated the postwar measure from the others. The hearings, opened at a time when the Real Estate Board was asserting its domination of the District's future, halted in July but resumed in February 1948 after an impasse had developed in the urban redevelopment program. The committee listened attentively to expressions of every shade of opinion, even to ideas on the management of the District dog pound. In content the home rule arguments were those of earlier years, but the tone revealed a conviction that a turning point had come. The protests at the "dual" voting provision that would give local suffrage to temporary non-tax-paying residents drew from the president of the Washington ADA the comment that, whereas once Americans had fought against taxation without representation, now the conflict appeared to be over representation without taxation.[6] Still most of the testimony concentrated on whether the community would benefit or suffer by regaining control of its purely local affairs.

From the first the joint committee's primary purpose was to design an act that would relieve Congress of the time-consuming chores of running the District; an efficient system responsive to local citizens' wishes was a secondary desideratum. Two years of intensive work on the part of an able committee staff produced a bill that met those specifications: Wash-

[6] Home Rule Hrgs, pp. 139, 146-47, 159-64, 195-99, 217.

ington residents, dual voters among them, were to elect a non-voting delegate to the House and a city council whose general legislation should come under the review of a joint Senate and House committee and be subject to presidential veto; the federal government was to pay the lesser of two amounts, either $15,000,000 or 14 percent of the city's yearly operating costs; all the special advisory boards were to be eliminated, leaving intact only the Public Utilities Commission, the Tax Appeal and Zoning Adjustment Boards, and the Redevelopment Land Agency of the National Capital Park and Planning Commission; otherwise all power was to be vested in the twelve-man council, four men chosen at large and two from each of the four geographical divisions of the city. The bill, approved by eight of the fourteen members of the House District Committee, reached the floor of the House in mid-May 1948.

For the first time in seventy years the lower house of Congress undertook to pass upon a revision of the Organic Act of 1878. The moment the debate opened, Representative Oren Harris of Arkansas, himself a member of the joint committee, demanded that the entire ninety-page document be read out word for word. So, hour after hour, the intoning voice of the clerk droned in the ears of representatives oppressed by the volume of legislation awaiting action before adjournment. At the end of two days the filibuster technique accomplished its purpose. An impatient majority shelved the bill. One perverse man, representing, Congressman Auchincloss estimated, the views of scarcely 50,000 citizens, had defeated the will of over 300,000 people.[7]

The blow to the hopes of the vast majority of Washingtonians intensified the determination of the National Committee on Segregation. Formed at the end of 1946 after the local com-

[7] *Ibid.*, p. 396, and App., pp. 429-30, 434-45; H Rpt 1876, 80C, 2S; Comee Recommendations on H 6227, 80C, 2S; interview George Galloway, comee staff director, 1946-1948.

mittee on race relations had dissolved, the national committee had opened headquarters in Chicago and engaged a competent research staff headed by an American University sociologist to pin down the facts of what Negroes in the capital were up against and to spell out the consequences for all America. Marshall Field, millionaire Chicago newspaper owner, Peter Odegard, president of Reed College in Oregon, Clarence Pickett, the Philadelphian who headed the American Civil Liberties Union, Hubert Humphrey, mayor of Minneapolis, Walter Reuther of the United Automobile Workers, Eleanor Roosevelt, and half a hundred other notables scattered from California to New York were not to be intimidated by a small, tight-knit, arch conservative group of men in Washington. Of the committee's ninety-odd members, only three of the thirteen who lived in Washington were Negroes. It was an impressive array of men and women without any personal ax to grind, intent only on reversing a trend that, left alone, they believed, would fasten a caste system upon the entire country. Over a period of eighteen months the staff collected a mass of irrefutable evidence. The findings condensed for publication by Kenesaw Mountain Landis, namesake of a former federal judge and czar of professional baseball, covered every phase of the pressures, old and new, which threatened to reduce Negroes in Washington to a servile status from which they could not escape without the help of energetic white people.[8]

Despite the impassioned language of the report and its overworked argumentation, a check on its sources forced the serious reader to conclude that here was an essentially truthful summary. Too painful, too shocking to become table talk, the report repeatedly emphasized that the pattern set in the capital would shape that of every community in the United States. The review of the steady degradation of Negroes from the 1870's on, if not news to thoughtful Washingtonians, worked

[8] Ntl Comee on Seg, *Rpt*, *passim.*

upon the consciousness and the conscience of people who would have preferred to forget. Although the report did not kill the anti-Negro movement in Washington, at least its force declined rapidly after November 1948. Within six years publicly authorized segregation would disappear, and the phrase "human relations" would begin to replace "race relations."

Contributing to that change was the publication early in 1949 of the Strayer Report on Washington's public schools undertaken at congressional request by George Strayer of Columbia University, a nationally recognized authority on public education. Assisted by a dozen other specialists, Strayer examined the strengths and weaknesses of the functioning of the Board of Education, the superintendent's and assistant superintendents' performance, and the quality of schooling provided at every level in both the white and the colored divisions. After analyzing the inadequacies in physical accommodations and the shortcomings in teacher recruitment and promotion, the experts discussed the work of the research departments and the areas in which pupils' achievements were above or below the national average. In general, the white high schools had a good record, in the junior high schools, a decade later labelled "the problem child of American education," pupils were a year behind the national norm in arithmetic but otherwise on a par, and the elementary schools varied from the excellent to those below the national standard. The colored schools, though as good as those in other cities with segregated systems, were definitely inferior to the white. Negro schoolrooms were more crowded, the pupil-teacher ratio disproportionately high, and equipment and teaching aids meagre. Although the investigators did not accept without qualification the interpretation that the head of the colored school research unit had put upon the IQ and achievement tests, the Strayer team observed the downward trend in colored children's achievements and attributed much of it to poor schooling in the regions from which Negro in-migrants came.

The matter-of-factness and lack of moralizing in the Strayer Report added to its impact. Praise as well as criticism dotted the 950-page text. But nobody studying it could fail to perceive the inequalities in the schooling offered the two races. The data verified a central thesis of the National Committee on Segregation, namely that the separate schools underlay the city's entire social structure. They formed the basis upon which the local universities built in maintaining racial bars. In 1948 only Catholic University had opened all its schools to Negroes. George Washington, Georgetown, the undergraduate college, though not the graduate school, of American University, the National University law and medical schools, all refused admission to colored students, and though Howard University did not exclude whites, only special circumstances occasionally led a white student to enroll there. Day by day association between young people of the two races thus never occurred.

If colored Washingtonians were glad to have outside authority validate their often repeated complaints, white people were dismayed at the new evidence of grave faults in the white schools, faults present in spite of the dropping enrollments that reduced the pupil-teacher ratio to a reasonable level. The flight of white families to the suburbs explained some of the decline in enrollments, but the increase in the entries in the city's private non-sectarian or church schools suggested a new parental rebellion at basic lacks in the public schools. (See Table IV.) "Wisely," the Strayer Report noted, the Board of Education had dispensed with the grouping of students according to ability. Counselling service, introduced in 1943, began with the 7th grade and was intended to give junior high school pupils guidance in their school work and help those with personality troubles, but the experts considered the number of counsellors too few and their consultations, therefore, too hurried to be of any real value. On the whole, teachers could feel they had come off well; criticisms were largely directed not at their individual frailties but at the system and the lack of the money with which to carry out teaching programs.

Educators who had followed closely the developments in American educational theory and practice of the preceding quarter-century could see that in several particulars Washington's public schools offered more than in the 1920's. But white parents, after skimming the report, tended to mourn gloomily for the good old days when the District's schools ranked among the three or four best in the country. Congress, on the other hand, took constructive action by voting larger appropriations for capital outlays in 1949 than in any year since 1931-1932.[9] Strong possibility exists, furthermore, that the survey laid the emotional groundwork on which a racially integrated system would rise five and a half years later, for, although not deliberately aimed at preachments on segregation, the findings revealed the monetary and social costs of the dual scheme. Certainly no other city where it had always obtained moved so quickly and effectively to discard it in 1954: four months after the Supreme Court ruling of May, all Washington's public schools opened on an integrated basis.

During the half-decade of postwar readjustment, national and international alarums and excursions distracted the city: the economic collapse of Europe, lightened but not fully dissipated by the launching of Marshall Plan aid, rumors of a far-flung Communist conspiracy within the government in Washington, Whittaker Chambers' testimony before the House Un-American Affairs Committee in August 1948 and the dramatic Hiss trial, the 1948 election, the outcome of which

[9] *Ibid.*, pp. 41, 46; Home Rule Hrgs, p. 191; *Strayer Rpt*, pp. 35-36, 414-16, 459-67, 497-98, 534, 550-52, 705-06, 940-41, 948, and *passim.*

startled everyone but journalist Louis Bean and Harry S Truman, and, slightly less than five years after V-J Day, war in Korea. In the interim, while retailers watched suburban shops cut in steadily upon business in the central city, the demand for down-town office space grew as the movement, begun with trade associations and learned societies of the 1920's and accelerated in the 1930's with the multiplication of headquarters of national planning groups in Washington, approached a crescendo that would make the political capital before the end of the 1950's the capital of all major American interests and aspirations. Throughout this confusing period of contraction and expansion, Washingtonians sought to reestablish a sense of community.

Stripped of the financial support of the War Chest, the Community Chest failed consistently to reach the quotas which would enable member agencies to maintain and extend their services, while the Public Welfare Department vainly endeavored to meet other needs of a city whose population, according to some estimates, had grown in seven years to over 900,000 souls, a third of them living at a bare subsistence level. If the term "population explosion" was not in common use before the 1950 census appeared, the dimensions of a future crisis were already visible in and about Washington. Private citizens ready to brave Roman Catholic opposition consequently organized Planned Parenthood to give advice and birth control information to clients wanting help. At the same time officials of the water department confronted the necessity of early construction of new reservoirs above the Great Falls to enlarge the city's water supply, a step that would involve vast expense and difficult negotiations with Maryland and Virginia. Simultaneously the ever-worsening pollution of the Potomac added to the troubles of the District sanitary engineers. Besides the rise in juvenile delinquency and new complaints about the dishonesty and inefficiency of law enforcement, the thickening traffic congestion harried the metropolitan police. At times Washingtonians felt caught in a tightening net, assailed by every quandary that could beset a geographically confined, racially divided, politically impotent area threatened by economic strangulation from the uncontrolled expansion of a surrounding megalopolis.[10]

The urban redevelopment program appeared to offer the best way out. Physical beauty unmarred by hidden slums and visible eyesores, convenience of access contrived by an improved highway system, and a new complex of cultural institutions and opportunities might give Washington a superiority over the outlying area that would ensure her domination of the entire metropolitan region. Few Washingtonians felt ready to define their ideas of urban beauty, convenience, and refreshment of the spirit, perhaps fewer still the relative emphasis each factor deserved. In 1946 and 1947 the Real Estate Board indicated that the first essential was a white metropolis with Negro servants' quarters in the rear. The District highway department, automobile salesmen, and doubtless householders living on the outer fringes of the District inclined to put chief stress on transportation. No one attempted to spell out the meaning of culture or how specifically to develop it for Washington's benefit. To the city's leading merchants and bankers the revitalizing of the downtown business center, however effected, was the foremost objective. Budget officers and big taxpayers never lost sight of the overriding importance of increasing District revenues. At every step congressmen, their constituents, and federal executives would probably have more say about developments than would Washingtonians.

Razing of the slums was by general consensus a necessary first move, particularly in the triangle of southwest Washington bounded by South Capitol Street, the Anacostia and the Wash-

[10] D.C. Welfare Dept, "Surveys of Income," 1947 and 1950 (mimeo); S Rpt 38, 86C, 1S, Final Report of the Joint Committee on Washington Metropolitan Problems, 1959, and Rpt Water Supply.

ington Channel, the main Department of Agriculture buildings and the Mall. The notorious "second precinct" adjoining North Capitol Street and Foggy Bottom beyond a new State Department building at 21st Street presumably should be the next. At that point agreement ended about use of the land when cleared. Instead of rebuilding with housing for the former occupants of the southwest area, General Grant implied that the National Capital Park and Planning Commission intended to turn most of it into parks and playgrounds, sites for public buildings, and highways to speed the traffic pouring in from and out to Virginia. If private contractors were disgruntled at the prospective loss of chances to erect expensive office and apartment buildings in the reclaimed space, Negroes were outraged upon hearing that the dispossessed were to be moved to remote sections of northeast or southeast Washington. In response to protests, in January 1948 the House Committee on Appropriations refused to grant the Redevelopment Land Agency the $3,400,000 needed to start operations; General Grant hastily declared that there had been a serious misunderstanding. Colored Washingtonians dared not count postponement as final victory but they believed white supremacists had at least received a rebuff. "Time," observed one wit, "wounds all heels."

The delay made Washington uneasy. While excavation of a Dupont Circle underpass destroyed old elms, slum clearance hung suspended. During the next two years every feature of official and private proposals for redevelopment underwent fresh scrutiny. Members of the American Institute of Architects issued diatribes against repetition of the "facadism" of the Federal Triangle, its "brutal stone masses" built in an eclectic style as boring as it was massive and unoriginal. Articles dealt with the ultimate cost of uprooting slum dwellers and relocating them in alien surroundings cut off from the life of the rest of the city. New York's experience in erecting huge apartment buildings to replace unsanitary old tenement houses pointed to the danger of substituting for the old a new and worse evil —impregnable and impersonal fortresses in which vice and crime and hopelessness extinguished every wholesome human impulse. Negro ghettos in the remotest section of the District might produce more ineradicable ills than those of the alleys. By 1950, moreover, some Washingtonians were beginning to wonder whether the projected many-laned highways were not likely to multiply instead of reduce traffic problems, to change pleasant, substantial residential sections into passage-ways for tourists' and commuters' cars, and to convert whole streets of small houses into blocks of apartment houses. And, irrespective of plans for the public domain, what of private development? Architecturally tasteless office buildings and residences could ruin the looks of much of the city, and exploitation of some sections for the benefit of others could reduce any over-all plan to meaninglessness.

Washington: Past and Future, the planning commission's first published report since 1932, set some fears to rest when it appeared in 1950, for it reflected a concern for the underdog and outlined a proposal that gave weight to human as well as financial values. Although work on a large scale would not start for another year, prospects brightened that the next decade would see a new Washington emerge embodying the best aspirations of an enlightened public. Demolition gangs and bull-dozers would wipe out every structure in southwest Washington except the government buildings flanking the Mall and at Fort McNair, two modern schoolhouses, two restaurants near the waterfront, and a beautifully proportioned brick row dating from about 1808 which lent itself to remodelling. In that wide expanse would rise some low-rental housing, a larger number of expensive apartments and town houses, a theatre, a shopping center, and an array of at least eight new government office buildings, all with extensive parking space. The architecture of the public buildings would abandon the neo-classical in favor of a modernized style using horizontal bands of windows interrupted by concrete grill-work to create an effect of screening, a style to be employed also for the brick apartment buildings; the lines of the town houses, flat-roofed and two-storied, would harmonize with both. Cutting across the area an elevated highway would run from a new bridge over the Washington Channel and Haines Point to a conjunction with an inner loop slicing through southeast Washington above the Navy Yard to Lincoln Park and thence northward.

Much of the elaborate plan seemed desirable, some of it disastrous—particularly the vague provision for families unable to afford even the lowest priced living quarters in rebuilt Southwest, not to mention the householders in Southeast who would be displaced by the demolition necessary to construction of the inner loop. The controversy encompassing changes undertaken in Foggy Bottom and elsewhere would continue into the 1960's. Thirty years had seen the District's share of the population of Greater Washington drop from the 72.2 percent of 1920 to 53.2 percent.[11] If no local Cassandra in 1950 was foretelling the further decline to 36.8 percent in the decade ahead, still the possibility remained that except for the public buildings the central city might become a series of concrete passage-ways lined by blocks of efficiencies, some expensive apartment houses, and warrens of cheap flats occupied, respectively, by single women and a few bachelors, well-to-do, elderly, childless couples, and Negroes.

Yet notwithstanding racial conflicts, political defeats, and wrangling over designs for the future, before midcentury Washington recaptured a charm as compelling as it is hard to explain. It was in fact more than a recaptured quality, for it had a com-

[11] Ntl Comee on Seg, *Rpt*, pp. 41, 46; Carl Feiss, "The Development of Washington," p. 15, *Washington Architecture, 1791-1957*, prepared by a Committee of the Washington Metropolitan Chapter, American Institute of Architects; NCPPC, *Washington: Past and Future*, 1950; editors of *Fortune*, ed., *The Exploding Metropolis*, pp. 106 ff.

prehensiveness that reached further than had that of the smaller, relatively uncomplicated community of the 1880's, or the sophisticated wealthy society of Theodore Roosevelt's and Taft's day, or the city of the New Deal era. The refusal of the Actors' Equity to play in a theatre that barred colored people forced the National, by then the only legitimate theatre left in the city, to close to stage productions in 1948. But other amenities widened in scope. Sociology and political theory did not enter into the pleasure householders of every complexion took in nursing their gardens and presenting trim lawns to the view of passers-by. While restoration of run-down houses in Georgetown moved forward rapidly, on Capitol Hill "Operation Bootstrap" began to take form, promoted by students at the Eastern High School who banded together as "Scrooch," Students' Committee for Redecoration of Old Capitol Hill. There residents, white and colored, set about sprucing up their neighborhoods with their own hands. If the amateur character of most of the performing arts and the naïveté of public appreciation of the visual arts denied the city a legitimate claim to being the "cultural center" of America, still a philistine spirit rarely marred Washingtonians' enjoyment of what was at hand.

In an old burlesque house opposite the Public Library the "Arena" opened, launched by a handful of Washingtonians interested in acting as an art and eager to try out a theatre-in-the-round. At Catholic University drama students presented plays ranging from *King Lear* to *Cyrano* with a finished skill that evoked the admiration of accomplished professional actors. Companies of dancers and vaudeville performers at the Carter Barron outdoor theatre added to the inexpensive diversions of summer evenings. Small private galleries opened displays of young painters' works, while accessions at the National Gallery put it into the front ranks of American collections. Nearly every evening offered a concert of an artistry that astonished

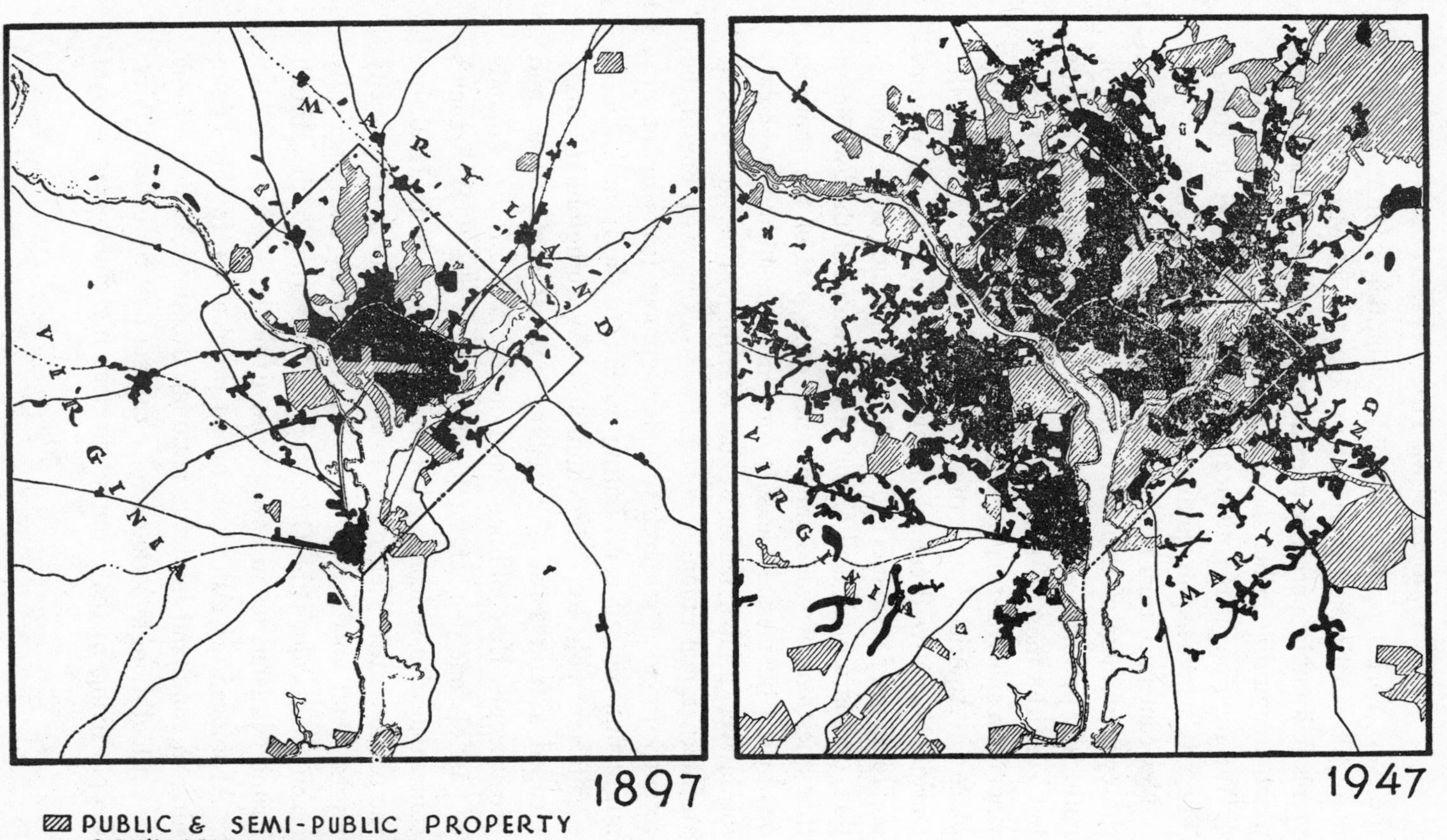
MARYLAND
VIRGINIA
1897
MARYLAND
VIRGINIA
1947
PUBLIC & SEMI-PUBLIC PROPERTY
BOUNDARY OF ORIGINAL CITY
URBAN DEVELOPMENT

the New Yorker prone to label Washington a cultural wasteland. The inclination of critics to poke fun at Margaret Truman's few public performances as a singer and at her father's piano strumming rather increased the secret pleasure of much of Washington in the musical interests of the White House. The city's home-spun quality was again in evidence.

Newcomers in turn felt the spell of Washington's magic. In the eyes of most of them it came solely from the streams of politically powerful and gifted personages who came and went; but even the most disdainful critics of the city's artistic provincialism spoke of this "fascinating city," the most "interesting place in America," and this "most beautiful capital in the world." No native dreamed of denying that her famous visitors and temporary residents endowed her with much of her fascination, or that a good deal of the rest grew out of the awareness that questions of world importance were part of the capital's day by day business. At least in roundabout fashion, the scholar, the lawyer, a labor leader at the Washington headquarters of an international union, or a scientist working with one of the recently founded research and development firms in the city might find himself contributing an iota to the formulation of significant policies. The humblest Washingtonian rarely escaped a faint sense of brushing against great events and great people. He could not stand on the White House grounds as part of "one democratic conglomerate," like B. B. French's contemporaries welcoming the Japanese mission in 1860, but the blackest little Negro boy in the mid-twentieth-century city might teeter on the curb as a parade went by and practically reach out to touch the Queen of the Netherlands, the British Prime Minister, or an envoy from Ethiopia.

At midcentury American urban problems were only beginning to command intensive national attention. Almost no one as yet had thought seriously of a cabinet post for urban affairs. People living in the countryside near big cities were not yet deeply alarmed by urban sprawl, and ideas of applying city planning to entire metropolitan regions were still novel. Washingtonians were frequently troubled by their own plight, but other Americans seldom saw it as it was, "A Tale of Two Cities." One of these, overwhelmed by financial difficulties, was a city of "slums, crumbling schools and hospitals, neighborhoods that are breeding places of preventable disease, unwanted children, juvenile delinquency, and a crescendo of crime on the streets," a community confronted by all the ills facing other metropolitan centers but, unlike them, powerless to check such miseries.[12] The other city was a beautiful capital of monuments and museums, green parks and tree-lined avenues, a place whose urbanity was heightened by its touches of provincialism. To dedicated Washingtonians the contrasts were ever-present: the distress and the frustration, and yet the delights. Far-sighted inhabitants of these two-cities-in-one perceived that the capital must enfold and redeem the lesser city if the Washington of the second half of the twentieth century were to become the symbol of American democracy at its best. In the early 1960's it was uncertain which pattern would prevail.

Yet the living testimony of two generations underscored the curious drawing power the dual city exercised. If the tendency in parts of the United States was to think of Washington merely as the center of an unwholesomely expanding bureaucracy that should be curbed, Americans who spent more than a brief time in the city rarely failed to experience an emotional response compounded of pride, pleasure, dismay, anger, and an intense interest in her future. Therein lay the hope for the years ahead.

[12] Washington League of Women Voters, *Washington, D.C.: A Tale of Two Cities*, p. 1.

GLOSSARY OF ABBREVIATIONS AND CITATIONS IN THE FOOTNOTES

All non-official manuscript materials cited are in the Manuscript Division of the Library of Congress unless other locations are specifically noted in the first mention in each chapter of papers elsewhere. Petitions, housed in the National Archives, are identified where they first appear by the record group number, but the number is not repeated, since all petitions to the House of Representatives are in R.G. 233, all petitions to the Senate in R.G. 46.

L.C.	—	Library of Congress
N.A.	—	National Archives
R.G.	—	Record Group
Ptn	—	Petition, if to the Senate listed as S, if to the House of Representatives, listed as H, in each case followed by numerals and letters identifying the Congress and general topic and by the date.
H Rpt __, __C, __S, Ser__	—	House of Representatives Report, followed by its number, the number and session of Congress, and the serial number of the volume in which the report is bound.
H Ex Doc	—	House Executive Document
H Misc Doc	—	House Miscellaneous Document
H __ Comee Hrgs	—	House Committee, identified by name and followed by the number and session of Congress, Hearings.
H Dis Comee	—	House Committee on the District of Columbia.
S Rpt __, __C, __, Ser __	—	Senate Report, followed by its number, the number and session of Congress and the serial number.
S Ex Doc	—	Senate Executive Document
S Misc Doc	—	Senate Miscellaneous Document
S __ Comee Hrgs	—	Senate Committee, identified by name, and followed by the number and session of Congress, Hearings.
S Dis Comee	—	Senate Committee on the District of Columbia

ABBREVIATIONS

Rec	—	*Congressional Record*
__ *Stat.* __,	—	*United States Statutes at Large*, with volume number preceding and page number following.
Comrs Rpt	—	*Report of the Commissioners of the District of Columbia* which, after 1935, is entitled, *Report of the Government of the District of Columbia.*
CHS *Rec*	—	Columbia Historical Society *Records*
AC *Rpt*	—	*Report of the Associated Charities*
Rpt B/Ch	—	*Report of the Board of Charities*
Rpt B/Tr	—	*Report of the Board of Trade*
Min As Ch	—	Minutes of the Board of Managers of the Associated Charities
Min CSA	—	Minutes of the Council of Social Agencies
Min FSA	—	Minutes of the Board of Managers of the Family Service Association

BIBLIOGRAPHICAL NOTE

Sources for Washington's political and economic history after 1878 are in the main published materials. Some information is contributed by petitions to the Senate and House of the 1880's and 1890's located in the National Archives, some letters in the Theodore Roosevelt, Woodrow Wilson, and two or three other collections of papers in the Manuscript Division of the Library of Congress, and the typescript summaries of Board of Trade activities between 1932 and 1935 prepared by its presidents and housed among its records, but otherwise manuscript data are of negligible value. The sheaves of petitions that served to measure local aspirations in earlier years cease to be revealing after 1910 when appeals to Congress about matters of wide local interest usually found their way into print. I have cited all petitions in the Archives by the numbers they bore when I used them, before a recataloguing began a year or two ago; those for the Senate are in Record Group 46, for the House in Record Group 233. Published official records, newspaper reprints, letters to the editors, editorials, reporters' columns, some magazine articles, and, from 1890 down to the 1930's, the published annual reports of the Board of Trade provide the backbone of fact and opinion on the community's business progress and political aims.

The official records, however, are embarrassingly abundant and, up to a point, informative not only about the whats but the whys. The detailed annual reports of the District commissioners, before 1921 sometimes running to two or three fat volumes for a single year, spell out the workings of every department of the local administration. Economy limited the reports to one volume for several years after 1921 and, from 1926 onward, to the slimness of a pamphlet omitting the accounting of each separate unit. Copies of the reports from 1926 to 1932, no longer included in the congressional series, are to be found only in the Washingtoniana Room of the District Public Library. From 1936 onward they appear under the title *Annual Report of the Government of the District of Columbia.* As District concerns slide into the category of the routine, the *Congressional Record* and House and Senate documents dealing with the city's affairs contain less of interest to the student of Washington's history than do the debates and reports of the preceding decades. Published committee hearings, on the other hand, not only multiply but after 1915 illuminate local and congressional views on specific questions more fully than do any of the earlier records. Thus the hearings on federal-local fiscal relations held in 1915 are a mine of information on that controversial topic. Most of the printed hearings are housed in the Library of Congress, but some are to be found only in the House or Senate libraries in the Capitol. Laurence Schmeckebier's *The District of Columbia, Its Government and Administration*, published in 1928, gives an informative picture of the workings of all the District's complicated governmental machinery down through 1927.

School board reports vary greatly in usefulness. Those for 1879, 1880, 1886, 1892, and 1899 furnish the best clues to superintendents' and trustees' educational philosophy in the period before 1920. The report for 1922, that of 1930 which contains a ten-year summary of "Achievements," and a similar twenty-year statement, 1920-1940, review the later aims of the Board of Education and administrators. In determining Washington's comparative standing in the realm of public education, the reports of the United States Commissioner of Education and the *Biennial Summaries* are helpful. The Strayer Report of 1949 provides a critical appraisal of outside experts for the 1940's.

For the theme of city planning and the "city beautiful" movement, articles in architectural journals and popular magazines constitute a source only less important than congressional documents and reports of the successive commissions—namely the Park, the Fine Arts, and the National Capital Park and Planning Commissions. Furthermore, several letters of Frederick Law Olmsted and Charles McKim among the Charles Moore papers in the Library of Congress Manuscript Division explain some of the difficulties created by the coolness of the House of Representatives to the Park Commission plan of 1901. The plan as presented to the Senate is published as Senate Report 166, 57C, 1S, Serial 4259. The publications of the American Civic Association, the organization that inspired Congress to establish the National Capital Park Commission and its successors, contain the salient facts for the early 1920's. The annual reports of the Fine Arts and the Planning Commissions from their beginnings down to 1932 are informing, but from then to 1950 the omission of formal reports leaves a serious gap, only partly filled by summaries of their programs and plans published in midcentury and in the interim by newspaper pieces and comments from the American Institute of Architects. The Washingtoniana Room of the District Public Library fortunately has files of clippings on the subject.

In pursuing the "Social Betterment" movement, manuscript materials, notably the minutes of the Monday Evening Club, the Associated Charities, renamed Family Service Association in 1934, and the Council of Social Agencies, born in 1920, provide detailed running accounts of local philanthropic endeavors to resolve welfare problems. In addition, a Senate report of 1897 on District charities and their history, the findings of President Theodore Roosevelt's Homes Commission of 1907, and the first report of the Alley Dwelling Authority in 1935 throw light on the social planning of their time. After 1903 *Charities*, later the *Survey*, includes several articles analyzing conditions in Washington before the mid-twenties. The annual reports of the Board of Public Welfare, after it came into being in 1926, are disappointingly general; those of the Public Assistance Division of the 1930's, though much more specific, are diffuse and hard to use in constructing a clear-cut picture of social progress or deterioration. Between 1936 and 1938 the official organ of the Community Chest, *Council Bulletin* renamed *Community Service*, discusses the major questions. Convinced that the facts and ideas contained in these sources covered the field, I made no attempt to examine the records of particular organizations such as the Washington Orphan Asylum or its successor by self-denying ordinance of the late 1940's, the Hillcrest Children's Center.

Foreign visitors' descriptions of Washington, rewarding for the pre-Civil War years, add little to an understanding of the city after 1890. Frank Carpenter's pieces written for the Cleveland *Leader* over the signature "Carp" in the early 1880's contain a number of effective vignettes of every day life; these appear also in somewhat different form in Frances Carpenter Huntington's *Carp's Washington.* Mrs. Reginald DeKoven's *A Musician and His Wife* adds touches to the picture of President Arthur's Washington. Thereafter the flood of periodical articles, many of them in the twentieth century illustrated with photographs, supplants the collection of personal letters that supplied invaluable insights into the first three-quarters of the nineteenth century. Doubtless diligent search might have turned up private letters that would supplement the published commentaries, but the variety of the latter appeared to justify foregoing the time-consuming hunt for less guarded personal comments. At the same time, the nearer my narrative comes to the present, biographies and autobiographies useful for my purpose diminish in number; relatively few discuss the local scene. Fortunately, Louis Brownlow's *A Passion for Anonymity* tells of his years as District Commissioner, 1915-1920, in far from anonymous terms and contains a wealth of specifics about the troubled World War I era.

The role of science in Washington down to 1940 is admirably summarized in A. Hunter Dupree's *Science in the Federal Government.* That study, the publications of learned and scientific societies, and the reports of the Librarian of Congress and of the Smithsonian Institution enable the student to piece together the growth of the city's intellectual life. The 1946 report of the Librarian of Congress is especially useful inasmuch as the long section entitled "The Story Up To Now" reviews the history of the library from its beginning but gives particular attention to the steps by which services widened to encompass the arts. Scattered newspaper and magazine articles and the descriptions in the WPA Federal Writers' Project, *Washington, City and Capital*, published in 1937, tell the tale of mounting preoccupation with music, painting, architecture and sculpture.

The story of colored Washington, like that of the white community, derives first from the local press. The newspaper files in the Library of Congress include most issues; those of the *Daily American*, short-lived sheet of the mid-1920's, and *New Negro Opinion*, the mouthpiece of the New Negro Alliance of the mid-1930's, are in the possession of Eugene Davidson, the editor of both. Also indispensable are occasional monographs, reports like those assembled by W. E. B. DuBois on the Atlanta Conferences, 1896-1901, articles in the NAACP organ, *Crisis*, after 1910, and pieces in a considerable range of journals during Woodrow Wilson's first administration and after the mid-1920's. All these clarify the relationship between Washington's situation and that of colored communities elsewhere. Above all, interviews with colored leaders and followers have added factual details and deepened my understanding of the minority problems.

Interviews, indeed, constitute the single most important source for my account of local attitudes from 1930 onward. By trying to seek out people likely to take widely differing positions, I have endeavored to present a balanced over-all interpretation. Many of the questions I posed are still highly controversial. Hence to save embarrassment for my informants and to avoid cumbersomely long explanations of the special qualifications of each person to speak, I have ordinarily omitted their names from the footnotes except where the validity of my presentation would suffer sharply from preserving the anonymity of a person willing to be quoted. This method involved the danger of assigning undue weight to the ideas of a small minority, but the problem is inherent, I believe, in the task of attempting to analyze the recent past. The incorporation of data that, seen in the light of longer perspective, may not hold up or that further intensive research may modify is an occupational hazard that I have welcomed, for it should provoke additional historical studies of significant questions confronting urban America.

A listing of the materials I have used, category by category, follows.

BIBLIOGRAPHY

I UNPUBLISHED SOURCES

OFFICIAL PAPERS

Library of Congress Manuscript Division
William McKinley Papers
Theodore Roosevelt Papers
Woodrow Wilson Papers
National Archives
Petitions to the House of Representatives, 1879-1909, Record Group 233
Petitions to the Senate, 1879-1922, Record Group 46

RECORDS OF SOCIAL AGENCIES AND BUSINESS ORGANIZATIONS

listed by location

Family and Child Services of Washington, D.C.
Minutes of the Board of Managers of the Associated Charities of the District of Columbia, 1921-1934, continued as Family Service Association, 1934-
Monday Evening Club Minutes, 1898-1929, and "Thirty Years Achievement," 1930
Questionnaire of the Citizens Chest Survey Committee, 1947
Health and Welfare Council of the National Capital Area
Minutes of the Board of Managers of the Washington Council of Social Agencies, 1921-1941
Washington Board of Trade, Reports of the presidents, 1932-1935
Washington Urban League, "The Founding of the Washington Urban League," statement of Garnett Wilkinson at Twenty-first Annual Meeting, April 1959

PERSONAL PAPERS AND LETTERS

In possession of Professor Charles A. Barker of the Johns Hopkins University, Sayles J. Bowen Papers, 1879-1892, cited in notes as Bowen Mss.
Library of Congress Manuscript Division
Charles Moore Papers, 1900-1932
Mary Church Terrell Papers, 1890-1940
Booker T. Washington Papers, 1870-1915
University of North Carolina Library, Southern Historical Collection
Gibson-Humphreys Papers, 1882-1886

MONOGRAPHS AND THESES

Lindsay, Inabel, "Participation of Negroes in the Establishment of Welfare Services, 1865-1900, with special reference to the District of Columbia, Maryland, and Virginia," Ph.D. Dissertation, University of Pittsburgh, 1959

Lofton, Williston, "The Development of Public Education for Negroes in Washington, D.C., a Study of Separate but Equal Accommodations," Ph.D. Dissertation, the American University, 1944

Long, Kathleen Dudley, "Woodrow Wilson and the Negro, 1912-1916," M.A. Thesis, Bryn Mawr College, 1956

Olmsted, Stanley, "The Corcoran School of Art," Corcoran School of Art, n.d.

II PUBLISHED SOURCES

OFFICIAL RECORDS

Annual Reports

Alley Dwelling Authority for the District of Columbia, 1935

Board of Charities of the District of Columbia, 1901-1925

Board of Children's Guardians of the District of Columbia, 1893-1925

Board of Education of the District of Columbia, 1901-1950

Board of Public Welfare of the District of Columbia, 1926-1932, 1934-1950

Board of Trustees of Public Schools of the District of Columbia, 1879-1899

Commissioners of the District of Columbia, 1879-1935, continued as *Government of the District of Columbia*, 1936-1950, cited in the notes as Comrs Rpts

Comptroller of the Currency, 1932-1935

Fine Arts Commission, 1911-1932

Home for Destitute Colored Women and Children, 1879-1892

Librarian of Congress, 1928 and 1946

National Capital Park and Planning Commission, 1927-1932

Proceedings of the U.S. National Museum, 1911, 1916

Public Assistance Division, Board of Public Welfare, 1934-1936

Smithsonian Institution, 1879-

Trustees of the Industrial Home School, 1879-1925

United States Commissioner of Education, 1900-

Campbell, Doak S., Frederick H. Baer, and Oswald L. Harvey, *Educational Activities of the Works Progress Administration*, Staff Study No. 14.

Code of Laws of the District of Columbia, 1929, 1951

Congressional Record, 1879-

Congressional Serials, Bills, and Hearings, 1879-

House of Representatives

Bills

Documents

Executive Documents

Hearings of committees, especially Committee on the District of Columbia, and on Reform in the Civil Service

Joint Hearings with Senate committees, especially House and Senate Committees on the District of Columbia, 80C, 1S and 2S, "Home Rule and Reorganization of the Government of the District of Columbia."
Miscellaneous Documents
Reports
Senate
Bills
Documents, especially Document 185, 55C, 1S, "Investigation of Charities and Reformatory Institutions in the District of Columbia," Serial 3565 and Document 247, 64C, 1S, "Fiscal Relations of the United States to the District of Columbia," Serials 6915 and 6916
Hearings of committees and select joint committees, especially: Subcommittee of the Senate Judiciary Committee, 77C, 1S, Hearings on Senate Joint Resolution 35, "National Representation," and Committee on the District of Columbia, 78C, 1S, Hearings on S1420, "Reorganization of the Government of the District of Columbia"
Index to Hearings in the Senate Library, 2 vols., 1907-1934 and 1935-1958
Index to Laws, Senate Reports, Documents and Committee Prints Relating to the District of Columbia, 1887-1903
Miscellaneous Documents
Reports, especially Report 700, 55C, 1S, "Charities and Reformatory Institutions" and Report 781, 55C, 2S, "Historical Sketches," Serial 3565
Report 711, 56C, 1S, "School Administration," Serial 3889
Report 1230, 85C, 2S, "Growth and Expansion of the District of Columbia and Its Metropolitan Area," 1958
Report 38, 86C, 1S, "Final Report of the Joint Committee on Washington Metropolitan Problems," 1959

Geddes, Anne, *Trends in Relief Expenditures, 1910-1935*, Works Progress Administration Monograph No. 10

Graduate School of the Department of Agriculture, 1961

International Bureau of the American Republics, *Report of the Director to the Fourth Pan American Conference held at Buenos Aires, Argentine Republic, 1910*

Letter from the Secretary of the Treasury transmitting Estimates of Appropriations, 1901-1917

National Capital Park and Planning Commission, *Washington, Past and Future*, 1950

National Gallery of Art, *Bulletin*, I, "General Information," 1941

National Resources Committee, *Research—A National Resource*, I, 1940

Official Register of the United States, 1879-1922

Reports of the President's Homes Commission, 1908

School Bulletin No 9, "Preliminary Report of the Committee on Character Education," 1931

Strayer, George Drayton, *Report of a Survey of the Public Schools of the District of Columbia, conducted under the auspices of the chairmen of the subcommittees on District of Columbia appropriations of the respective appropriations committees of the Senate and House*, Washington, 1949

United States Census, Tenth through Seventeenth, 1880-1950
Religious Bodies, 1916, 1926, 1936
Statistics of Cities Having a Population of over 30,000, 1907

United States Commissioner of Education, *Biennial Survey of Education*, 1918-1940

United States Department of Commerce and Labor, *Conditions of Living Among the Poor*, Bureau of Labor Bulletin, 64, 1906
Forman, Samuel E., *Charity, Relief and Wage Earnings*, 1908

United States Statutes at Large, 1879-1950, cited in notes as —*Stat.*—

War Production Board, *Historical Monograph No. 1*, 1946

RECORDS AND REPORTS OF SOCIAL AGENCIES AND BUSINESS EDUCATIONAL AND SCIENTIFIC ORGANIZATIONS

American Council on Education, Its History and Activities

American Council of Learned Societies, *Bulletin*, I-X, 1921-1930

American Historical Association, *Annual Report*, 1919, I

Associated Charities of Washington, *Annual Reports*, 1897-1920

Brookings Institution, *A Consideration of the Application of Research in the Social Sciences to the Problems of Modern Civilization*, 1931

———, *Institute for Government Research, An Account of Research Achievements*, 1922

Bulletin of the Philosophical Society of Washington, 1874

Carnegie Institution of Washington, *Annual Reports*, 1910, 1916

Charity Organization Society of the District of Columbia, *Third Annual Report*, 1886

Citizens' Committee on Race Relations, *Second Annual Report*, 1945

Conference for Good City Government, *Proceedings*. 3rd and 16th, 1895 and 1909, Philadelphia.

Consumer's League of Washington, D.C., *Third Annual Report*, 1915

District of Columbia Citizens' Representative Committee of One Hundred, *Proposal to Improve the Present Form of Government of the District of Columbia*, 1888

DuBois, William Edward Burghardt, ed., *Mortality Among Negroes in Cities, together with proceedings of the 1st conference for the study of Negro problems, Atlanta University, 1896*, Atlanta, 1896

———, ed., *Some Efforts of Negroes for Their Own Social Betterment, together with proceedings of the 3rd conference for the study of Negro problems, Atlanta University, 1898*, Atlanta, 1898

———, ed., *The Negro in Business, together with proceedings of the 4th conference for the study of Negro problems, Atlanta University, 1899*, Atlanta, 1899

———, ed., *The College-Bred Negro, together with proceedings of the 5th conference for the study of Negro problems, Atlanta University, 1900*, Atlanta, 1900

Dumbarton Oaks Research Library and Collection, Harvard University, *Bulletin Number One, 1940-1950.*

Forty Years of Achievement: Commemorating the Fortieth Anniversary of the Establishment of the National Commission of Fine Arts, 1910-1950.

Hodson, William, *Preliminary Report of the Commission on Public Welfare Legislation of the District of Columbia*, 1924

McClintock, Miller, *Report on the Parking and Garage Problem of the Central Business District of Washington, D.C.*, 1930

Memorial of the Joint Executive Committee of the Citizens' Associations of the District of Columbia against the Repeal of the Fifty Percent Annual Congressional Appropriation Law, 1894

Monday Evening Club Yearbook, 1930

National Association for the Advancement of Colored People, *Annual Reports*, 1911-

National Committee on Segregation in the Nation's Capital, *Segregation in Washington*, 1948

National Conference on Social Work, 1929

National Society of Fine Arts, *Articles of Incorporation, Constitution and Bylaws*, 1906

New Negro Alliance Yearbook, 1939

Preliminary Report by the Washington Committee of One Hundred on the Federal City to the American Civic Association, 1924

Proceedings of the Sixth Annual Meeting of the Female Union Benevolent Society of Washington City and Report of the Managers, 1844

Proceedings of the Washington Academy of Sciences, 1898-

Report of a Committee from the Geological Society on the History of the Joint Commission of the Scientific Societies of Washington

Washington Board of Trade, *Annual Reports*, 1890-1929, 1936-1938

Washington Federation of Churches, *Year Book*, 1936

AUTOBIOGRAPHIES, REMINISCENCES, LETTERS, AND DIARIES

Allen, George E., *Presidents Who Have Known Me*. New York, 1950.

Anderson, Isabel, *Presidents and Pies; Life in Washington, 1897-1919*. Boston and New York, 1920.

Andrews, Marietta Minnigerode, *My Studio Window*. New York, 1928.

Briggs, Emily Edson, *The Olivia Letters*. Washington, 1906.

Brown, Glenn, *Memories: A Winning Crusade to Revive George Washington's Vision of a Capital City*. Washington, 1931.

Brownlow, Louis, *A Passion for Politics*. Chicago, 1955.

———, *A Passion for Anonymity*. Chicago, 1958.

Butt, Archibald Willingham, *Taft and Roosevelt, The Intimate Letters of Archie Butt*. New York, 1930.

Columbia Historical Society, *Records*, 1894-.

Davidson, Eugene, *Black Boy on a Raft*. Washington, 1958.

DeKoven, Mrs. Reginald, *A Musician and His Wife*. New York and London, 1926.

Donnan, Elizabeth and Leo F. Stock, eds., *An Historian's World: Selections from the Correspondence of John Franklin Jameson*. Philadelphia, 1956.

DuBois, William Edward Burghardt, *Dusk of Dawn: An Essay Toward an Autobiography of a Race Concept*. New York, 1940.

Fairchild, David G., *The World Was My Garden*. New York, 1938.

Foraker, Mrs. Joseph, *I Would Live It Again: Memories of a Vivid Life*. New York and London, 1932.

Gouverneur, Marian, *As I Remember: Recollections of American Society During the Nineteenth Century*. New York, 1911.

Hegermann-Lindencrone, Lillie, *The Sunny Side of Diplomatic Life, 1875-1912*. New York and London, 1914.

Hole, The Very Reverend S. Reynolds, *A Little Tour in America*. London and New York, 1895.

Hoover, Herbert, *Memoirs*, II, *The Cabinet and the Presidency, 1920-1933*. New York, 1951.

Keyes, Francis Parkinson, *Letters From a Senator's Wife*. New York and London, 1924.

Logan, Mary Simmerson, ed., *Thirty Years in Washington*. Hartford, 1901.

Longworth, Alice Roosevelt, *Crowded Hours*. New York and London, 1933.

Millikan, Robert Andrews, *Autobiography of Robert A. Millikan*, New York, 1950.

Newcomb, Simon, *The Reminiscences of an Astronomer*. New York, 1903.

Sousa, John Philip, *Marching Along: Recollections of Men, Women, and Music*. Boston, 1928.

Starling, E. W., *Starling of the White House*. New York, 1946.

Stokes, Thomas L., *Chip Off My Shoulder*. Princeton, 1940.

Summers, Festus P., ed., *The Cabinet Diary of William L. Wilson, 1896-1897*. Chapel Hill, 1957.

Taft, Mrs. William Howard, *Recollections of Full Years*. New York, 1914.

Terrell, Mary Church, *A Colored Woman in a White World*. Washington, 1940.

Washington, Booker T., *Up From Slavery*. New York, 1909.

White, Walter Francis, *A Man Called White, the Autobiography of Walter White*. New York, 1948.

OTHER PUBLISHED PRIMARY SOURCES

American Biographical Directories: District of Columbia, 1908-09.

An Appeal to the Enlightened Sentiment of the People of the United States for the Safeguarding of the Future Development of the Nation, 1916.

Biographical Directory of the American Congress, 1774-1961.
Dahlgren, Madeline Vinton, *Etiquette of Social Life in Washington.* 5th ed., Philadelphia, 1881.
Elite List of Washington, 1888-1918.
Handbook for District Suffrage, 1938.
Oyster, James, *Annual Address to the Washington Chamber of Commerce, 1913.*
Paynter, John H., *A Souvenir of the Anniversary and Banquet of Oldest Inhabitants Association (Colored) of the District of Columbia, April 14, 1914.*
Programs and announcements of musical events in Washington file, Library of Congress, Music Division.
Sherman's Directory and Ready Reference of the Colored Population of the District of Columbia, 1913.
Social List of Washington, D.C., 1923-
Washington City Directory, 1879-
Washington Social Register, 1900-
Who's Who in the National Capital, 1921-1929, National Cyclopaedia of American Biography

III SECONDARY SOURCES

Abell, George, and Evelyn Gordon, *Let Them Eat Caviar*, New York, 1936.
Allen, Frederick Lewis, *Only Yesterday*. New York, 1957.
American Institute of Architects, *Of Plans and People*. Washington, 1949.
———, A Committee of the Washington Metropolitan Chapter, *Washington Architecture, 1791-1957*. Washington, 1957.
Anderson, Oscar Edward, *The Health of a Nation*. Chicago, 1959.
Anonymous, *The Mirrors of Washington*. New York and London, 1921.
Anonymous, [Robert S. Allen and Drew Pearson], *Washington Merry-go-Round*. New York, 1931.
Baker, Ray Stannard, *Following the Color Line*. New York, 1908.
Bernstein, Irving, *The Lean Years, A History of the American Worker, 1920-1933*. Boston, 1960.
Bicknell, Grace Vawter, *The Inhabited Alleys of Washington, D.C.* Washington, 1912.
Browne, Henry Janvris, *Assessment and Taxation in the District of Columbia and the Fiscal Relation to the Federal Government*. Washington, 1915.
Bruno, Frank John, *Trends in Social Work, 1874-1956; A History Based on the Proceedings of the National Conference of Social Work.* 2nd ed., New York, 1957.
Bulkley, Barry, *Washington, Old and New*. Washington, 1914.
Chapin, Elizabeth M., *American Court Gossip, or Life at the Nation's Capital*. Marshalltown, Ia., 1887.
Church of God, A Pictorial Review. Washington, 1944.

Clephane, Walter C., *Public and Private Hospitals in the District of Columbia.* (Report of Washington Board of Trade) Washington, 1912.

Crane, Katherine Elizabeth, *Mr. Carr of State.* New York, 1960.

Crew, H. W., *Centennial History of the City of Washington.* Washington, 1901.

Cronon, Edmund David, *Black Moses, The Story of Marcus Garvey and the Universal Negro Improvement Association.* Madison, Wis., 1955.

Crowell, Benedict, and Robert Forrest Wilson, *The Armies of Industry, Our Nation's Manufacture of Munitions for a World in Arms, 1917-18.* New Haven, 1921.

Curti, Merle, *The Social Ideas of American Educators.* Paterson, N.J., 1935.

Daly, Victor, *Not Only War, A Story of Two Great Conflicts.* Boston, 1932.

Darrah, William Culp, *Powell of the Colorado.* Princeton, 1951.

Davis, Allison, Burleigh B. Gardner, and Mary B. Gardner, directed by W. Lloyd Warner, *Deep South, A Social and Anthropological Study of Class and Caste.* Chicago, 1941.

D.C. Village, *Fifty Years at Blue Plains, 1906-1956.* Washington, 1957.

District of Columbia Engineer's Office, *Washington Bridges*, 1945.

Dollard, John, *Caste and Class in a Southern Town.* 2nd ed., New York, 1949.

Douglas, Paul H., *Real Wages in the United States, 1890-1926.* Boston and New York, 1930.

Dulles, Foster Rhea, *The American Red Cross, A History.* New York, 1950.

Dupree, A. Hunter, *Science in the Federal Government, A History of Policies and Activities to 1940.* Cambridge, 1957.

Editors of *Fortune*, ed., *Exploding Metropolis.* New York, 1954.

Fairman, Charles E., *Art and Artists of the Capitol of the United States of America.* Washington, 1927.

Federal Writer's Project, *Washington: City and Capital.* Washington, 1937.

Fleming, Walter Lynwood, *The Freedman's Savings Bank: A Chapter in the Economic History of the Negro Race.* Chapel Hill, 1937.

Gabriel, Ralph Henry, *The Course of American Democratic Thought.* New York, 1940.

Gray, Edgar M., *The Washington Race Riot, Its Cause and Effect.* New York, 1919 (Arthur M. Schomburg Negro Collection, New York Public Library).

Grier, Eunice, *Understanding Washington's Population.* Washington Center for Metropolitan Studies, 1961.

Hagedorn, Herman, *Robert Brookings: A Biography.* New York, 1936.

Harmon, John H., Jr., Arnett G. Lindsay, and Carter G. Woodson, *The Negro as a Businessman.* Washington, 1929.

Hart, Hastings Hornell, *Child Welfare in the District of Columbia.* New York, 1924.

Hayes, Laurence J. W., *The Negro Federal Government Worker: A Study of His Classification Status in the District of Columbia, 1883-1938.* Washington, 1941.

Heaton, Herbert, *A Scholar in Action, Edwin F. Gay.* Cambridge, 1952.

History of the League of Women Voters of the District of Columbia, 1960.

Hughes, Langston, *Fine Clothes for the Jew.* New York, 1927.

Hurd, Charles, *Washington Cavalcade.* New York, 1948.

Ingle, Edward, *The Negro in the District of Columbia,* in *The Johns Hopkins University Studies in History and Political Science,* 11th Series, Nos. III and IV.

James, Henry, "Pandora" in *Stories Revived.* London, 1895.

Johnson, Col. Campbell, *Fifty Years of Progress of the Armed Forces,* reprint from the *Pittsburgh Courier,* 1950.

Jones, William Henry, *Recreation and Amusement Among Negroes in Washington, D.C.: A Sociological Analysis of the Negro in An Urban Environment.* Washington, 1927.

———, *The Housing of Negroes in Washington, D.C.: A Study in Human Ecology.* Washington, 1929.

Joslin, Theodore G., *Hoover Off The Record.* Garden City, N.Y., 1934.

Keim, De Benneville Randolph, *Society in Washington, Its Noted Men, Accomplished Women, Established Customs, and Notable Events.* Harrisburg, Pa., 1887.

Kennedy, Louise Venable, *The Negro Peasant Turns Cityward.* New York, 1930.

Keppel, Frederick P. and R. L. Duffus, *The Arts in American Life.* New York and London, 1933.

Kober, George Martin, *The History and Development of the Housing Movement in the City of Washington, D.C.* 1st ed., Washington, 1907.

Leuchtenburg, William E., *The Perils of Prosperity, 1914-1932.* Chicago, 1958.

Link, Arthur S., *The New Freedom.* Princeton, 1947.

Lowry, Edward G., *Washington Close-Ups: Intimate Views of Some Public Figures.* Boston and New York, 1921.

Lundberg, Emma O. and Mary E. Milburn, *What Child Dependency Means in the District of Columbia And How It Can Be Prevented.* Washington, 1924.

Macfarland, Henry B. F., *The Development of the District of Columbia.* Washington, 1900.

McCormick, Anne O'Hare, *The World at Home.* New York, 1956.

McKenzie, Roderick Duncan, *The Metropolitan Community.* New York and London, 1933.

McMurry, Donald LeCrone, *Coxey's Army, A Study of the Industrial Army Movement of 1894*. Boston, 1929.

Matthiessen, F. O., *American Renaissance, Art and Expression in the Age of Emerson and Whitman*. New York and London, 1941.

———, and Kenneth B. Murdock, ed., *The Notebooks of Henry James*. New York, 1947.

Mechlin, Leila, *Works of Art in Washington*. Washington, 1914.

Moore, Joseph West, *Picturesque Washington*. 1st ed., Providence, 1884.

Murray, Pauli, *Proud Shoes, The Story of an American Family*. 1st ed., New York, 1956.

Murray, Robert K., *Red Scare: A Study in National Hysteria, 1919-20*. Minneapolis, Minn., 1955.

Nelson, Bernard H., *The Fourteenth Amendment and the Negro Since 1920*. Washington, 1946.

Nicolay, Helen, *Our Capital on the Potomac*. New York and London, 1924.

———, *Sixty Years of the Literary Society*. Washington, 1934 (Private printing).

Nowlin, William F., *The Negro in American National Politics*. Boston, 1931.

Oehser, Paul H., *Sons of Science, The Story of the Smithsonian Institution and Its Leaders*. New York, 1949.

Ogg, Frederick Austin, *Research in the Humanistic and Social Sciences: Report of a Survey Conducted for the American Council of Learned Societies*. New York and London, 1928.

Quillin, Frank U., *The Color Line in Ohio: A History of Race Prejudice in a Typical Northern State*. Ann Arbor, Mich., 1913.

Reitzes, Dietrich C., *Negroes and Medicine*. Cambridge, 1958.

Republican Campaign Textbook, 1912.

Rose, Arnold M., *The Negro's Morale: Group Identification and Protest*. Minneapolis, Minn., 1949.

Schlesinger, Arthur M., Jr., *The Crisis of the Old Order*. Cambridge, 1957.

———, *The Coming of the New Deal*. Cambridge, 1959.

———, *The Politics of Upheaval*. Cambridge, 1960.

Schmeckebier, Laurence, *The District of Columbia, Its Government and Administration*. Baltimore, 1928.

Sherwood, Robert E., *Roosevelt and Hopkins, An Intimate History*. New York, 1948.

Slauson, Allan B., ed., *A History of the City of Washington*, by the *Washington Post*. Washington, 1903.

Spaulding, Thomas M., *The Literary Society in Peace and War*. Washington, 1947.

Steevens, George Warrington, *The Land of the Dollar*. 2nd ed., Edinburgh and London, 1897.

Sullivan, Mark, *Over Here, 1914-18*. Vol. v of *Our Times*. 6 vol.: New York, 1926-35.

Toomer, Jean, *Cane*. New York, 1923.

Van Rensselaer, Mrs. John King, in collaboration with Frederic Van de Water, *The Social Ladder*. New York, 1924.

Villard, Oswald Garrison, *Some Newspapers and Newspapermen*. New York, 1926.

Washington League of Women Voters, *Washington, D.C.; A Tale of Two Cities*. Washington, 1962.

Waters, Walter T., as told to William C. White, *B.E.F.: The Whole Story of the Bonus Army*. New York, 1933.

Wecter, Dixon, *The Saga of American Society; A Record of Social Aspiration, 1607-1937*. New York, 1937.

Weitzman, Louis G., *One Hundred Years of Catholic Charities in the District of Columbia*. Washington, 1931.

White, William Allen, *A Puritan in Babylon, the Story of Calvin Coolidge*. New York, 1938.

Woodson, Carter G., *The History of the Negro Church*. Washington, 1945.

Woodward, C. Vann, *The Strange Career of Jim Crow*. New York, 1955.

Work, Monroe N., ed., *Negro Year Book, An Annual Encyclopedia of the Negro*. Tuskegee, Ala., 1912.

Wright, Carroll Davidson, *The Economic Development of the District of Columbia* in *Proceedings of the Washington Academy of Sciences*, I, Washington, 1899.

Yerkes, Robert M., ed., *The New World of Science; Its Development During the War*. New York, 1920.

Zueblin, Charles, *A Decade of Civic Development*. Chicago, 1905.

———, *American Municipal Progress*. New York, 1916.

INDEX